Introduction to Anthropology

SENIOR CONTRIBUTING AUTHORS
JENNIFER HASTY, UNIVERSITY OF PENNSYLVANIA
DAVID G. LEWIS, OREGON STATE UNIVERSITY
MARJORIE M. SNIPES, UNIVERSITY OF WEST GEORGIA

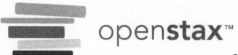

openstax™

978-1-711494-98-2

OpenStax
Rice University
6100 Main Street MS-375
Houston, Texas 77005

To learn more about OpenStax, visit https://openstax.org.
Individual print copies and bulk orders can be purchased through our website.

HARDCOVER BOOK ISBN-13	**978-1-711494-99-9**
B&W PAPERBACK BOOK ISBN-13	**978-1-711494-98-2**
DIGITAL VERSION ISBN-13	**978-1-951693-99-2**
ORIGINAL PUBLICATION YEAR	**2022**

1 2 3 4 5 6 7 8 9 10 RS 22

Printed by
XanEdu
17177 Laurel Park Drive, Suite 233
Livonia, MI 48152
800-562-2147
www.xanedu.com

OpenStax

OpenStax provides free, peer-reviewed, openly licensed textbooks for introductory college and Advanced Placement® courses and low-cost, personalized courseware that helps students learn. A nonprofit ed tech initiative based at Rice University, we're committed to helping students access the tools they need to complete their courses and meet their educational goals.

Rice University

OpenStax, OpenStax CNX, and OpenStax Tutor are initiatives of Rice University. As a leading research university with a distinctive commitment to undergraduate education, Rice University aspires to path-breaking research, unsurpassed teaching, and contributions to the betterment of our world. It seeks to fulfill this mission by cultivating a diverse community of learning and discovery that produces leaders across the spectrum of human endeavor.

Philanthropic Support

OpenStax is grateful for the generous philanthropic partners who advance our mission to improve educational access and learning for everyone. To see the impact of our supporter community and our most updated list of partners, please visit openstax.org/impact.

Arnold Ventures
Chan Zuckerberg Initiative
Chegg, Inc.
Arthur and Carlyse Ciocca Charitable Foundation
Digital Promise
Ann and John Doerr
Bill & Melinda Gates Foundation
Girard Foundation
Google Inc.
The William and Flora Hewlett Foundation
The Hewlett-Packard Company
Intel Inc.
Rusty and John Jaggers
The Calvin K. Kazanjian Economics Foundation
Charles Koch Foundation
Leon Lowenstein Foundation, Inc.
The Maxfield Foundation
Burt and Deedee McMurtry
Michelson 20MM Foundation
National Science Foundation
The Open Society Foundations
Jumee Yhu and David E. Park III
Brian D. Patterson USA-International Foundation
The Bill and Stephanie Sick Fund
Steven L. Smith & Diana T. Go
Stand Together
Robin and Sandy Stuart Foundation
The Stuart Family Foundation
Tammy and Guillermo Treviño
Valhalla Charitable Foundation
White Star Education Foundation
Schmidt Futures
William Marsh Rice University

Contents

PREFACE

About OpenStax

OpenStax is part of Rice University, which is a 501(c)(3) nonprofit charitable corporation. As an educational initiative, it's our mission to transform learning so that education works for every student. Through our partnerships with philanthropic foundations and our alliance with other educational resource companies, we're breaking down the most common barriers to learning. Because we believe that everyone should and can have access to knowledge.

About OpenStax Resources

Customization

Introduction to Anthropology is licensed under a Creative Commons Attribution 4.0 International (CC BY) license, which means that you can distribute, remix, and build upon the content, as long as you provide attribution to OpenStax and its content contributors.

Because our books are openly licensed, you are free to use the entire book or select only the sections that are most relevant to the needs of your course. Feel free to remix the content by assigning your students certain chapters and sections in your syllabus, in the order that you prefer. You can even provide a direct link in your syllabus to the sections in the web view of your book.

Instructors also have the option of creating a customized version of their OpenStax book. The custom version can be made available to students in low-cost print or digital form through their campus bookstore. Visit the Instructor Resources section of your book page on OpenStax.org for more information.

Art attribution

In *Introduction to Anthropology*, art contains attribution to its title, creator or rights holder, host platform, and license within the caption. Because the art is openly licensed, anyone may reuse the art as long as they provide the same attribution to its original source.

Errata

All OpenStax textbooks undergo a rigorous review process. However, like any professional-grade textbook, errors sometimes occur, and new perspectives highlight areas that require revision. Writing style guides and other contextual frameworks also change frequently. Since our books are web-based, we can make updates periodically when deemed pedagogically necessary. If you have a correction to suggest, submit it through the link on your book page on OpenStax.org. Subject matter experts review all errata suggestions. OpenStax is committed to remaining transparent about all updates, so you will also find a list of past errata changes on your book page on OpenStax.org.

Format

You can access this textbook for free in web view or PDF through OpenStax.org, and for a low cost in print.

About *Introduction to Anthropology*

Introduction to Anthropology is a four-field text, grounded in foundational content in cultural anthropology, archaeology, biological anthropology, and linguistic anthropology. This approach makes the text useful for both general and cultural introductory courses as well as for introductory courses in some of the anthropology subfields. Upon this strong foundation, two contemporary themes are highlighted: social inequality and the natural world. Ethnographies and examples throughout the text address the impacts of these two themes on human societies throughout history and around the globe.

Coverage and Scope

Introduction to Anthropology contains all of the foundational material necessary for introductory courses in anthropology. Methods and theories from all four fields are introduced in the first two chapters and woven throughout later discussions. The central concept of culture likewise is both explored in detail in its own chapter and referenced repeatedly in examples throughout the text. The evolution and diversification of the human species is centrally featured in two chapters, "Biological Evolution and Early Human Evidence" and "Physical and Cultural Evolution in the Genus *Homo*." The breadth of the discipline is apparent in the variety of examples and ethnographies as well as specific chapters dedicated to developing areas of anthropology, such as

"Medical Anthropology" and "Human-Animal Relationships." An engaging and inviting narrative will hold students' interest.

Addressing Societal Issues

The central themes of *Introduction to Anthropology*—social inequality and the natural world—connect the text's foundational material to two of the most pressing contemporary issues facing societies around the world.

- In addressing social inequality, the text drives readers to consider the rise and impact of social inequalities based on forms of identity and difference (such as gender, ethnicity, race, and class) as well as oppression and discrimination. The contributors to and dangers of socioeconomic inequality are fully addressed, and the role of inequality in social dysfunction, disruption, and change is noted. *Introduction to Anthropology* centers on the lived experiences of a wide range of people and provides ample opportunities for instructors and students to discuss and address preconceived notions, misconceptions, and potential solutions and outcomes.
- To illustrate the fundamental relationship between humans and their environments, the natural world is treated as both a setting for human existence and a key influence on human culture, economics, and politics. This focus makes the text uniquely suited to the contemporary era as climate change and environmental degradation play an increasing role in humanity's governance, intercultural relationships, and daily lives.

Illuminating an Evolving and Relevant Field

The text showcases the historical context of the discipline, with a strong focus on anthropology as a living and evolving field. A deep and reflective exploration of the origins of anthropology's methods and goals is featured in several chapters, including "Methods: Cultural and Archaeological Research Methods" and "Indigenous Anthropology." There is significant discussion of recent efforts to make the field more diverse—in its practitioners, in the questions it asks, and in the applications of anthropological research to address contemporary challenges. The authors who contributed to this text come from diverse backgrounds and geographic regions, providing balance and richness to the narrative, examples, and theoretical foundations of the text. The researchers highlighted in the Profiles in Anthropology sections, many still living and working, are likewise representative of the growing diversity of the field.

Unique chapters: Five of the text's 20 chapters introduce students to current and developing specializations within the discipline. These chapters offer an engaging and in-depth look at research fields rarely covered in introductory texts, fields that are particularly interdisciplinary in their aims and practices. They further stress that anthropology is an evolving and relevant field, offering insights into humanity's deepest questions and directions forward in addressing the toughest challenges. These chapters are:

- "Anthropology of Food," including material on food artifacts, ancient foodways and food reconstructions, food as cultural heritage, food prescriptions and proscriptions, and the globalization of food.
- "Anthropology of Media," addressing topics such as visual anthropology and ethnographic film, photography and representation, news media and the public sphere, the role of media in the development of national identity, and digital media.
- "Medical Anthropology," with material on the history of medical anthropology, the social construction of health, common medical anthropology methods and theoretical approaches, and applied medical anthropology.
- "Human-Animal Relationships," including discussions of multispecies ethnography, human-animal empathy, human-animal relationships among people practicing varying subsistence strategies, animal symbolism in oral tradition and religion, and pet keeping.
- "Indigenous Anthropology," which, through the lens of the experiences of the Indigenous peoples of North America, addresses the historical and contemporary challenges facing Indigenous people, including issues of agency, rights, and identity, as well as exploring Indigenous material cultures, perspectives, and worldviews.

Enriching and Engaging Features

Several feature boxes highlight the vibrant and applied nature of anthropology and give students practice using the methods discussed throughout the text.

- **Profiles in Anthropology.** Each chapter contains a profile of one or more anthropologists, many contemporary and some historical, who have made significant contributions to the discipline. These featured anthropologists represent a diversity of racial and ethnic backgrounds as well as a broad sampling of research interests and perspectives.

- **Ethnographic Sketches.** Ethnographic sketches taken from the authors' own fieldwork are spaced throughout the book. These engaging vignettes provide a window into the actual work of doing anthropology, providing readers with a sense of the pleasures and challenges of doing research in the field.
- **Mini-Fieldwork/Applied Activities.** Each chapter concludes with a simple fieldwork activity to give students practice thinking and researching like an anthropologist. These exercises provide them with hands-on experience applying the methods and theories discussed in the chapter to actual research conducted in their own communities.

Pedagogical Framework

An effective pedagogical framework helps students structure their learning and retain information.

- **Chapter Outlines.** Each chapter opens with an outline and introduction, familiarizing students with the material that will follow. Throughout the chapter, material is chunked into manageable sections of content within each of the larger main heads.
- **Learning Objectives.** Every main section begins with a set of clear and concise learning objectives. These objectives are designed to help the instructor decide what content to include or assign and to guide student expectations. After completing the section and relevant end-of-chapter exercises, students should be able to demonstrate mastery of the learning objectives.
- **Chapter Summaries.** Chapter summaries distill the information presented in each chapter to key, concise points.
- **Key Terms.** Key terms are bolded and followed by a definition within the text. Definitions of key terms are also listed in a glossary at the end of each chapter.
- **Critical Thinking Questions.** Each chapter ends with 8 to 10 critical thinking questions designed to help students assess their learning and apply it to their daily lives.
- **Suggested Readings.** This feature helps students further explore the chapter content by providing curated links to other information sources.

About the Authors

Senior Contributing Authors

Jennifer Hasty is an adjunct professor of African studies at the University of Pennsylvania. She studies media and politics in West Africa and the United States. Her book *The Press and Political Culture in Ghana* explores the cultural and historical forces shaping the practice of journalism in the recent period of democratization. In addition to working as a journalist for several Ghanaian media organizations, she has worked as a wedding videographer in the Philadelphia metro area and a community radio DJ in northern New Mexico. She is currently writing a book on corruption in Ghana. Chapters authored or coauthored in this text include the following:

Chapter 1: What Is Anthropology?

Chapter 2: Methods: Cultural and Archaeological

Chapter 3: Culture Concept Theory: Theories of Cultural Change

Chapter 6: Anthropological Thought

Chapter 7: Work, Life, and Value: Economic Anthropology

Chapter 8: Authority, Decisions, and Power: Political Anthropology

Chapter 12: Gender and Sexuality

David G. Lewis is a member of the Confederated Tribes of Grand Ronde of Oregon. He has a PhD from the University of Oregon (2009) and is an assistant professor of anthropology and ethnic studies at Oregon State University. David has conducted research on Oregon tribal history for some 25 years and has published numerous journal articles and book chapters. Additionally, he has researched and written over 470 essays for his blog, the *Quartux Journal* (https://openstax.org/r/QuartuxJournal), documenting tribal adjustments to colonization in the West. David conducts numerous presentations annually with community groups, at conferences, and at universities, educating about tribes in the region; consults with local governments and organizations on diversity, place naming, and land acknowledgments; and curates museum exhibits at local historical societies and museums. Chapters authored or coauthored in this text include the following:

Chapter 2: Methods: Cultural and Archaeological

Chapter 3: Culture Concept Theory: Theories of

Cultural Change

Chapter 19: Indigenous Anthropology

Dr. **Marjorie M. Snipes** earned a PhD in cultural anthropology from the University of Wisconsin–Madison (1996) and is currently a professor of anthropology at the University of West Georgia, where she teaches anthropological theory, ethnographic field methods, anthropology of religion, and animals and culture. Her doctoral fieldwork in the northwestern Andes of Argentina focused on religion and identity in an agropastoral society, in particular on understanding the relationships that herders forge with their animals and with each other. Among her recent publications are *Inside Anthropology* (2021, Kendall Hunt) and *The Intellectual Legacy of Victor and Edith Turner* (2018, Lexington). Chapters authored or coauthored in this text include the following:

Chapter 10: The Global Impact of Human Migration

Chapter 11: Forming Family through Kinship

Chapter 13: Religion and Culture

Chapter 14: Anthropology of Food

Chapter 18: Human-Animal Relationships

Chapter 20: Anthropology on the Ground

Contributing Authors

Dr. Todd A. Barnhardt, PhD

Dr. M. Anne Basham, Gateway Community College and Executive Director, Biodiversity Outreach Network

Sharon Gursky, Texas A&M University

Laura Jarvis-Seibert

Saira A. Mehmood

Dr. Sydney Yeager, Rollins College

Reviewers

Janet Altamirano, Texas A&M University–Kingsville

Dr. M. Anne Basham, Gateway Community College

Jack Bish, University of Wisconsin–Madison

Heidi Bludau, Monmouth University

Ryan Collins, Dartmouth College

Alejandra Dashe, Paradise Valley Community College

Bridget Fitzpatrick, Normandale Community College

Leslie Fitzpatrick, Mercyhurst University

Tony Fitzpatrick, University of Wyoming

Paul Hanson, Case Western Reserve University

David Hicks, Stony Brook University

Michael Hollis, St. Edward's University

Stewart Jobrack, The Ohio State University at Mansfield

Barry Kass, Orange County Community College

Phineas Kelly, University of Wyoming

Elizabeth Kickham, Idaho State University

Jonathan Marion, University of Arkansas

Annie Melzer, Northern Kentucky University

Kerith Miller, University of Arizona

Mackie O'Hara, The Ohio State University

Jenell Paris, Messiah University

Caroline Rivera, Florida Gulf Coast University

Megan Schmidt-Sane, Case Western Reserve University

Max Stein, Florida Gulf Coast University

Fay Stevens, University of Notre Dame

Antoaneta Tileva, American University

Kristen Verostick, Rowan University

Additional Resources

Student and Instructor Resources

We've compiled additional resources for both students and instructors, including an instructor's manual, test bank, and lecture slides. Instructor resources require a verified instructor account, which you can apply for when you log in or create your account on OpenStax.org. Take advantage of these resources to supplement your OpenStax book.

Comprehensive Instructor's Manual. Each component of the instructor's manual is designed to provide maximum guidance for delivering the content in an interesting and dynamic manner. The instructor's manual includes a chapter outline containing the learning outcomes for each section, section outlines, and section summaries. Chapter key terms are listed as well. Also included for each chapter are strategies for using the Mini-Fieldwork/Applied Activity and the Profiles in Anthropology. There are sample answers and strategies for using select critical thinking questions in the chapter. Each chapter also includes links to websites and organizations relevant to the content in the chapter as well as to content that extends examples in the chapter.

Test Bank. With nearly 1,100 multiple-choice, fill-in-the-blank, and short-answer questions in the test bank, instructors can customize tests to support a variety of course objectives. The test bank is available in Word format.

PowerPoint Lecture Slides. The comprehensive PowerPoint lecture slides provide a structure for course lectures. Chapter images, lesson learning outcomes, and bulleted content provide a starting place for instructors to build their lectures.

Community Hubs

OpenStax partners with the Institute for the Study of Knowledge Management in Education (ISKME) to offer Community Hubs on OER Commons—a platform for instructors to share community-created resources that support OpenStax books, free of charge. Through our Community Hubs, instructors can upload their own materials or download resources to use in their own courses, including additional ancillaries, teaching material, multimedia, and relevant course content. We encourage instructors to join the hubs for the subjects most relevant to your teaching and research as an opportunity both to enrich your courses and to engage with other faculty. To reach the Community Hubs, visit www.oercommons.org/hubs/openstax.

Technology Partners

As allies in making high-quality learning materials accessible, our technology partners offer optional low-cost tools that are integrated with OpenStax books. To access the technology options for your text, visit your book page on OpenStax.org.

CHAPTER 1
What Is Anthropology?

Figure 1.1 Artist's depiction of a woman hunting, created in 1565. Contrary to some long held beliefs, women have always played a role in hunting game. (credit: "Illustration of activities of Lapps and Finns: Men and women hunting with bows and arrows on snowshoes; "women hunt...as nimbly...or more than men" by Illustration of activities of Lapps and Finns/Library of Congress Prints and Photographs Division)

CHAPTER OUTLINE

INTRODUCTION Imagine a research project that contains these three members:

Randy Haas discovered the 9,000-year-old grave of a teenager buried with a hunting tool kit in the Andes mountains of Peru. Haas found that this hunter from long ago was a young woman. This discovery has upset the notion that hunting was the exclusive activity of men throughout human evolutionary history.

Daniel Miller is part of a global team researching how people use smartphones in various parts of the world, including Brazil, Cameroon, Chile, China, Ireland, Italy, Japan, East Jerusalem, and Uganda. The team is exploring how smartphones take on different functions in different cultural contexts. Focusing on Ireland,

Miller theorizes that smartphones become a kind of personal avatar, expressing and enacting the specific social identity of the user.

FIGURE 1.2 Red-tailed monkeys, the subject of anthropologist Michelle Brown's study, are primates that are found in Central and East Africa. This red-tailed monkey lives in Uganda. They are social animals and live in groups of 8-30 individuals. (credit: "Schmidt's Red-tailed Monkey" by Mehgan Murphy/Smithsonian's National Zoo, CC0 1.0)

Michelle Brown spends long days observing blue monkeys, red-tailed monkeys, and baboons in a conservation park in Uganda. She records the behavior of these primates as they find food, communicate, and fight with one another. She collects urine and feces to analyze hormone levels, intestinal parasites, and DNA. She wants to understand how primates compete as individuals and groups for access to various foods in their environment.

What kind of research project could encompass such a diversity of topics and methods? Since this is the first chapter of an anthropology textbook, you can probably guess. Though they conduct research on vastly different topics, all three are anthropologists. How could the work of these researchers be united in one academic discipline? The reason, as we will see, is that anthropology is vast.

Anthropology, the study of humanity, is guided by a central narrative and set of research commitments. Anthropology aims to overcome bias by examining cultures as complex, integrated products of specific environmental and historical conditions. Anthropologists use many different research strategies in their efforts to represent people from cultures very different from their own.

Anthropology explores controversial topics that may challenge individual assumptions and values. The goal is to understand the full experience of humanity, including elements that may seem unfamiliar or uncomfortable. Anthropology teaches a set of skills for setting aside personal perspectives and keeping an open mind while learning about the diversity of human practices and ideas. As discussed further at the end of this chapter, this does not mean abandoning individual personal values, but rather suspending judgment temporarily while learning to understand the perspectives of others.

1.1 The Study of Humanity, or "Anthropology Is Vast"

LEARNING OUTCOMES

By the end of this section, you will be able to:

- Define the study of anthropology in the broadest sense.
- Summarize the guiding narrative of anthropology.
- Restate and explain the central commitments of anthropology.

Anthropology is a vast field of study—so vast, in fact, that anthropology is interested in everything. Anthropology is unique in its enormous breadth and its distinctive focus. Consider other disciplines. In the arts and sciences, each discipline focuses on a discrete field of social life or physical phenomena. Economists study economics. Religious scholars study religion. Environmental scientists study the environment.

Biologists study living organisms. And so on.

Anthropologists study all of these things. Put simply, anthropology is the study of humanity across time and space. Anthropologists study every possible realm of human experience, thought, activity, and organization. Human as we are, we can only engage in social and natural worlds through our human minds and human bodies. Even engagement with nonhuman realms such as astronomy and botany is conditioned by our human senses and human cognition and thus varies across different societies and different time periods.

You may be thinking, If anthropology is the human aspect of absolutely everything, then does anthropology encompass the other social disciplines, such as political science, religious studies, and economics? This is not the case. Certainly, anthropologists are frequently multidisciplinary, meaning that while their research and teaching are focused within the discipline of anthropology, they also engage with other disciplines and work with researchers and teachers in other fields. But the way that scholars in the other social disciplines approach their subject matter is different from the way anthropologists approach those same subjects.

The distinctive approach of anthropology relies on a central narrative, or story, about humanity as well as a set of scholarly commitments. This central story and these common commitments hold the discipline together, enabling anthropologists to combine insights from diverse fields into one complex portrait of what it means to be human.

Anthropology is everything, but it's not just *anything*. Anthropology is the study of humanity guided by a distinctive narrative and set of commitments.

The Heart of Anthropology: Central Narrative and Commitments

Anthropologists are great storytellers. They tell many, many stories about all aspects of human life. At the heart of all of these stories is one fundamental story: the "story of humanity," a rich and complex narrative. A narrative is a story that describes a connected set of features and events. Narratives can be fictional or nonfictional. The narrative of anthropology is a true story, a factual narrative about the origins and development of humanity as well as our contemporary ways of life. The central narrative of anthropology can be summarized this way.

Human beings have developed flexible biological and social features that have worked together in a wide variety of environmental and historical conditions to produce a diversity of cultures.

Three features of this narrative are especially important to anthropologists. These features form three central commitments of anthropology. In academic study, a commitment is a common goal recognized by the scholars in a discipline.

Central Commitment #1: Exploring Sociocultural Diversity

As the narrative suggests, humans in a diversity of conditions create a diversity of cultures. Rather than trying to find out which way of life is better, morally superior, more efficient, or happier or to make any other sort of judgment call, anthropologists are committed to describing and understanding the diversity of human ways of life. Setting aside judgments, we can see that humans everywhere create culture to meet their needs. Anthropologists discover how different cultures devise different solutions to the challenges of human survival, social integration, and the search for meaning.

What are you wearing today? Perhaps a T-shirt and jeans with sneakers, or a tunic and leggings with flip-flops. What about your professor? Are they wearing a bathrobe and slippers, or perhaps a cocktail dress with stilettos? You can be (almost) certain that will never happen. But why not? You might assume that what Americans wear for class is completely normal, but this assumption ignores the question of what makes something "normal."

FIGURE 1.3 Ghanaian professionals wearing local fashions to promote the national textile industry. (credit: "Ghanaian Ladies" by Erik (HASH) Hersman/flickr, CC BY 2.0)

In many countries, for instance, university students typically wear dress shirts with slacks or skirts to class. Many Ghanaian students would not dream of wearing ripped jeans or tight leggings to class, considering such casual dress disrespectful. American students put much more emphasis on comfort than on presentation, an overall trend in American dress. Even in office settings, it is now acceptable for Americans to wear casual clothing on Fridays. In the West African country of Ghana, "casual Friday" never caught on, but office workers have developed their own distinctive Friday dress code. As the local textile industry became threatened by Chinese imports, Ghanaian office workers began wearing outfits sewn from locally manufactured cloth on Fridays, creating a practice of "National Friday Wear."

So which way is better, the American way or the Ghanaian way? Anthropologists understand that neither way is better and that each addresses a need within a particular culture. Casual Friday is great for Americans who crave comfy leisurewear, while National Friday Wear is great for Ghanaians who want to boost their local economy and show their cultural pride.

Anthropologists recognize not only diversity across different cultures but also the diverse experiences and perspectives within a culture. Do you ever buy used clothing at thrift shops, or do you know people who do? An old green men's trench coat bought at a vintage clothing store may be a favorite of a college student. The mother of that student may not feel the same way and offer to buy their child a new coat much to the distress of the owner of the coat! To people who have grown up in the 1930's and 1940's, used clothing was associated with the hard times of the Great Depression. For the newer generations, used clothing is a way to find unique, affordable clothing that can stretch the boundaries of mainstream style. Although people in a culture share a general set of rules, they interpret them differently according to their social roles and experiences, sometimes stretching the rules in ways that ultimately change them over time.

FIGURE 1.4 Ghanaian trader in her secondhand clothing shop (credit: "Market Woman - Kejetia Market - Kumasi - Ghana - 03" by Adam Jones/flickr, CC BY 2.0)

In Ghana, most used clothing is imported from the United States and Europe in large bales that local vendors purchase and sell in market stalls. A person from the United States or Europe is locally referred to as an *obruni*. Used clothing is called *obruni wawu*, or "a foreign person has died," reflecting the assumption that no living person would give away such wearable clothing. Many Ghanaians love to pick through the piles of *obruni wawu* in the market, thrilled to find recognizable brands and unusual styles. Some, however, associate *obruni wawu* with poverty. The stalls that sell *obruni wawu* are often called "bend-over boutiques," referring to the subservient posture adopted by customers rifling through the piles of clothing on the ground. *Obruni wawu* is suitable in some situations but certainly not in others. A particular Ghanaian movie included a scene where a man trying to woo a much younger woman. When the man gave his would be girlfriend a bag full of *obruni wawu* as a gift, it caused the audience to burst our laughing. The gift was humorous and inappropriate to the audience.

As with clothing, different cultures come up with different solutions to common challenges such as housing, food, family structure, the organization of work, and finding meaning in life. And people in every society discuss and argue about their own cultural norms. Anthropology seeks to document and understand the diverse range of solutions to common human challenges as well as the diversity of conflicting perspectives within each culture.

Central Commitment #2: Understanding How Societies Hold Together

Just as the various parts of our bodies all work together (the brain, the heart, the liver, the skeleton, and so forth), the various parts of a society all work together as well (the economy, the political system, religion, families, etc.). Frequently, anthropologists discover that changes in one realm of society are related to changes in another realm in unexpected ways. When farmers in Ghana began growing cocoa for export during the colonial period, the agricultural shift dramatically altered gender relations as men monopolized cash crops and women were relegated to vegetable farming for their families' consumption and local trade. As men benefited from the profits of the cocoa trade, relations between men and women became more unequal.

Anthropologists have a favorite word for the way that all elements of human life interrelate to form distinctive cultures: **holism**. Sometimes those parts reinforce one another, encouraging stability; sometimes they contradict one another, promoting change. Consider the caste system in India. Cultural anthropologist Susan Bayly describes how the beliefs and practices associated with caste in India have provided cultural integration and stability while also demonstrating a great deal of local variability and working as a force of social change (1999). Most Indians are familiar with two forms of belonging assigned by birth, the *jati* (birth group) and the *varna* (order, class, or kind). There are thousands of birth groups in the various regions of India, many specific to a single region. By contrast, there are four varnas known across India: Brahmins (associated with priests), Kshatriyas (associated with rulers and warriors), Vaishyas (associated with traders), and Shudras (associated with servile laborers). Another group, called "untouchables" or *dalits*, are outside the scheme of varnas.

As described in the Vedas, the four varnas are ordered in an interdependent hierarchy reminiscent of human anatomy. The *Rig Veda* describes how the gods sacrificed the first man, Purusa, dividing his body to create four groups of humanity:

> When they divided the Purusa, into how many parts did they arrange him? What was his mouth? What his two arms? What are his thighs [loins] and feet called? The *brahmin* was his mouth, his two arms were made the *rajanya* [*kshatriya*, king and warrior], his two thighs [loins] the *vaisya*, from his feet the *sudra* [servile class] was born. (Bayle, 1999)

Ancient texts envision caste as a means of social order as people in each caste perform different functions and occupations, all working together in harmony. Note, however, that such texts were written down by members of upper-caste groups, often Brahmin scholars. Anthropologists and historians who study the practices of caste argue that the caste system was never such a unitary and dominant force across the country but rather a flexible, regional, and constantly changing set of identities. In the colonial period, the British made the caste system more rigid and antagonistic, offering education and jobs to select caste groups. In the 20th century, many lower-caste groups have resisted their oppression by converting to Christianity or Islam and forming political parties to pressure the government for more opportunities for social advancement.

Anthropologists are curious about how different cultures create different categories of people and use those categories to organize the activities of social life. In many farming societies, for instance, men do certain kinds of agricultural work and women do others. In societies where land must be cleared in order to sow crops, men often chop down trees and clear the brush while women do the planting. In societies that utilize large-scale industrial farming, migrants or people of a specific ethnicity or assigned racial category are often recruited (or forced) to perform the manual labor required to grow and harvest crops. In industrial capitalist societies, one group of people owns the factories and another group works the machines that produce the industrial products. Relations between groups can be cooperative, competitive, or combative. Some cultures promote the equality of social groups, while many others reinforce inequality among groups. Holism is not the same as harmony. Anthropologists are interested in how society holds together but also in the conditions that can cause conflict, change, and disintegration.

You may have heard the word *polarized* used to describe the sense that two different groups in American society are moving farther and farther apart in their values, opinions, and desires. Some suggest that the contradictory perspectives of these two groups threaten to tear American society apart. Others suggest that Americans are united by deeper values such as freedom, equal opportunity, and democracy. Using holism to understand this issue, an anthropologist might consider how the perspectives of each group relate to that group's economic experiences, political convictions, and/or religious or moral values. A comprehensive use of holism would explore all of these aspects of society, looking at how they interact to produce the polarization we see today and suggesting what might be done to bring the two groups into productive dialogue.

Central Commitment #3: Examining the Interdependence of Humans and Nature

As our narrative suggests, anthropologists are interested in the natural environment, the way humans have related to the natural world over time, and how this relationship shapes various cultures. Anthropologists consider how people in different cultures understand and use the various elements of nature, including land, water, plants, animals, climate, and space. They show how people interact with these elements of nature in complex ways.

Archaeologists working in prehistoric sites all over the world have documented how prehistoric people understood celestial objects and used them to navigate their waterways, create calendars and clocks, regulate farming activities, schedule religious ceremonies, and inform political leaders. This area of study is called **archaeoastronomy**. In Chaco Canyon in the American Southwest, archaeologists have discovered that buildings in the major settlement areas were aligned so that certain windows would provide perfect vantage points to view the sun and moon at pivotal times of the year, such as solstice and equinox. The Sun Dagger, consisting of two whorl-shaped petroglyphs (stone etchings) on Fajada Butte, is precisely positioned under a rock crevice so as to indicate the solstices and equinoxes when the sun shines through the crevice. Unfortunately, tourist foot traffic at the site has altered the width and direction of the crevice so that the Sun Dagger no longer marks these celestial events accurately.

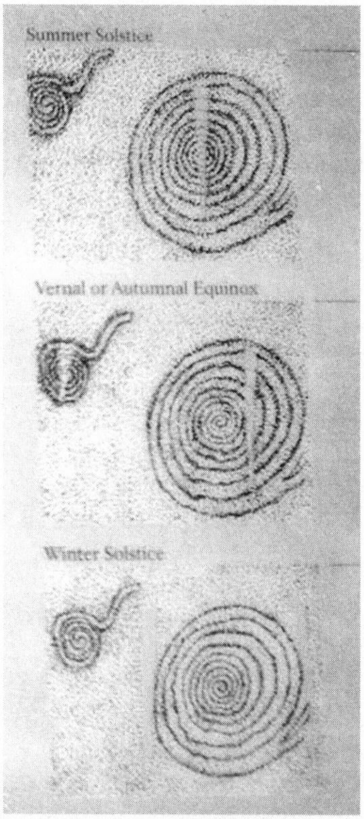

FIGURE 1.5 The Sun Dagger at Fajada Butte (credit: National Park Service/Wikimedia Commons, Public Domain)

The people of Chaco Canyon may have been particularly attuned to the features of their environment as they constructed their complex civilization in the challenging environment of the high desert. With scarce rainfall and brief growing seasons, their survival depended on accurate identification of opportune planting and harvesting times. With the onset of a 50-year drought, farming became more and more precarious. Eventually, the ancient peoples of Chaco were forced to abandon the area.

Some anthropologists study how people interact with the plants in their area. The field of **ethnobotany** examines how people in different cultures categorize and use plants for food, shelter, tools, transportation, art, and religion. Ethnobotanists also conduct research on plants used in healing to discover the relationship between cultural practices and the pharmaceutical properties of these plants. Some examine the cultural use of psychoactive plants such as mushrooms and peyote in religious ritual. For instance, anthropologist Jamon Halvaksz studied the controversial use of marijuana among youth in New Guinea (2006). Young people told Halvaksz that marijuana helped them work harder, overcome shame, and understand ancestral stories. Critics of the practice told Halvaksz that marijuana dried the blood of people who used it, making their offspring weak and feeble. Marijuana use has generated similar controversies in other countries, including the United States, with some arguing that the drug provides relaxation and pain relief while others claim it interferes with cognitive abilities and motivation.

Our relationship with nature is reciprocal. Nature shapes humanity, and humanity shapes nature. Exploring how nature shapes humanity, anthropologists speculate about how aspects of the environment have shaped the emergence and development of human biology, such as our ability to walk, the shape of our teeth, and the size of our brains. Dramatic climactic shifts over the past several million years have forced periods of rapid biological and cultural adaptation, resulting in new hominin species and new skill sets such as language and toolmaking. In more recent archaeological time periods, environmental characteristics have shaped religious beliefs, gender relations, food-getting strategies, and political systems. Environmental forces can trigger the beginning or the end of a society. Some archaeologists study how natural events such as volcanic eruptions and droughts have led to mass migrations and the collapse of empires.

Our reciprocal relationship with nature also works the other way around; that is, humans shape nature. Our environments are shaped by the food-getting methods of our societies as well as the way we acquire and trade resources such as oil, natural gas, diamonds, and gold. Many anthropologists explore how contemporary ways of life change the natural world at local, regional, and global levels. Farming dramatically impacts ecosystems with the clearing of prairies, wetlands, and forests. Fishing can deplete certain species, changing the whole ecosystem of rivers and coastal waters. Responding to population pressures, people construct dams to channel water to emergent cities. The redirection of water transforms regional ecosystems, turning wetlands into deserts and deserts into resource-hungry cities.

Scholars use the term **Anthropocene** to describe the contemporary period of increasing human impact on the ecosystems of our planet. Large-scale pollution, mining, deforestation, ranching, and agriculture are causing dramatic environmental disruptions such as climate change and mass extinction of plant and animal species. Many anthropologists are studying these problems, focusing on how people are working locally, regionally, and globally to promote more sustainable ways of living in our natural world.

1.2 The Four-Field Approach: Four Approaches within the Guiding Narrative

LEARNING OUTCOMES

By the end of this section, you will be able to:

- Identify and define the four fields of anthropology.
- Describe the work of professional anthropologists in each field.
- Provide an example of how the four fields work together to explore common issues.

Let's recall the central narrative of anthropology:

Human beings have developed flexible biological and social features that have worked together in a wide variety of environmental and historical conditions to produce a diversity of cultures.

Researching this argument is a vast endeavor requiring many complementary approaches and techniques. Anthropology comprises four main approaches, the four subfields of our discipline. Each subfield specializes in exploring a different aspect of the common narrative. Combining insights from the four fields gives us a rich and complex understanding of specific issues such as gender, inequality, race, and the environment. Let's take a look at each subfield and then examine how the subfields combine in the study of racial categories and relations.

Biological Anthropology

Biological anthropology focuses on the earliest processes in the biological and sociocultural development of human beings as well as the biological diversity of contemporary humans. In other words, biological anthropologists study the origins, evolution, and diversity of our species. Some biological anthropologists use genetic data to explore the global distribution of human traits such as blood type or the ability to digest dairy products. Some study fossils to learn how humans have evolved and migrated. Some study our closest animal relatives, the primates, in order to understand what biological and social traits humans share with primates and explore what makes humans unique in the animal world.

The Dutch primatologist Carel van Schaik spent six years observing orangutans in Sumatra, discovering that these reclusive animals are actually much more social than previously thought (2004). Moreover, van Schaik observed that orangutans use a wide variety of tools and pass down skills to their young. By studying these primates, van Schaik and other biological anthropologists gain insight into the origins of human intelligence, technology, and culture. These researchers also warn that habitat loss, illegal hunting, and the exotic pet trade threaten the survival of our fascinating primate cousins.

Biological anthropologists frequently combine research among primates with evidence from the human fossil record, genetics, neuroscience, and geography to answer questions about human evolution. Sometimes their insights are startling and unexpected. Anthropologist Lynne Isbell argues that snakes have played a key role in the evolution of human biology, particularly our keen sense of sight and our ability to communicate through language (Isabell, 2009). Isbell's "snake detection theory" posits that primates developed specialized visual perception as well as the ability to communicate what they were seeing in order to alert others to the threat of venomous snakes in their environment. She points to the near-universal fear of snakes shared by both humans and primates and has documented the prevalence of snake phobia in human myth and folklore. Isbell's research highlights how human-animal relations are central to humanity, shaping both biology and culture.

Not all biological anthropologists study primates. Many biological anthropologists study fossilized remains in order to chart the evolution of early **hominins**, the evolutionary ancestors of modern humans. In this field of study, anthropologists consider the emergence and migration of the various species in the hominin family tree as well as the conditions that promoted certain biological and cultural traits. Some biological anthropologists examine the genetic makeup of contemporary humans in order to learn how certain genes and traits are distributed in human populations across different environments. Others examine human genetics looking for clues about the relationships between early modern humans and other hominins, such as Neanderthals.

Forensic anthropology uses the techniques of biological anthropology to solve crimes. By analyzing human remains such as decomposed bodies or skeletons, or tissue samples such as skin or hair, forensic anthropologists discern what they can about the nature of a crime and the people involved. Key questions are who died, how they died, and how long ago they died. Often, forensic anthropologists can discover the age, sex, and other distinctive features of perpetrators and victims. Looking closely at forms of bodily trauma and patterns of blood or bullets, they piece together the story of the crime. They work on investigative teams with law enforcement officers and medical experts in ballistics, toxicology, and other specialties. Forensic anthropologists often present their findings as witnesses in murder trials.

Not all of these crimes are contemporary. Sometimes, forensic anthropology is used to understand historical events. Excavating the historic Jamestown colony of early English settlers in North America, archaeologist William Kelso found a human skull in the midst of food remains. Noticing strange cut marks on the skull, he called upon Douglas Owsley, a forensic anthropologist working for the Smithsonian Institution, to help him figure out what the markings meant. Owsley determined that the markings were evidence of intentional chopping to the skull with a sharp blade. He concluded that the skeleton belonged to a 14-year-old girl who had been cannibalized by other settlers after she died. This interpretation corroborates historical evidence of severe starvation in the colony during the harsh winter of 1609–1610.

Archaeology

Archaeologists use artifacts and fossils to explore how environmental and historical conditions have produced a diversity of human cultures – the study of **archaeology**. **Artifacts** are objects made by human beings, such as tools or pottery. **Fossils** are the remains of organisms preserved in the environment. Archaeologists have developed careful methods of **excavation**, or removing fossils and artifacts from the ground, in order to learn as much as possible about how people lived in times before and after the development of writing. They are interested in how people met basic needs such as clothing and shelter, as well how they organized their societies in family groups, trade networks, and systems of leadership. Many archaeologists seek to understand how humans lived in relation to the natural world around them, altering the environment at the same time that the environment was shaping their evolution and social development.

A group of archaeologists led by Tom Dillehay spent seven years excavating a set of sites in northern Peru, charting the development of human society in this area over a period of 14,000 years (2017). They traced the society from the early ways of life to the emergence of cities and early states, discovering how people there developed fishing, farming, and herding strategies that led to increased sociocultural complexity. The team collected data on the plants and animals of the area as well as the buildings, tools, cloth, and baskets made by the people. They concluded that the people who lived in this area placed a high value on cooperation and living in harmony with nature.

Some archaeologists focus on more specific topics in more recent time periods. Archaeologist Eric Tourigny examined the graves at pet cemeteries in the United Kingdom from 1881 to 1981(2020). Looking at the epitaphs on the gravestones of the pets, Tourigny noted a change from earlier Victorian ways of thinking of pets as friends to later, more modern ways of conceptualizing pets as members of the family. He noted, too, that epitaphs expressed an increasingly common belief that pet owners would be reunited with their pets in the afterlife.

Cultural Anthropology

Cultural anthropology is devoted to describing and understanding the wide variety of cultures referred to in anthropology's central narrative. Cultural anthropologists explore the everyday thoughts, feelings, and actions of people in different cultures as well as the cultural and historical events that they consider important. Examining social discourse and action, cultural anthropologists seek to understand unspoken norms and values as well as larger forces such as economic change and political domination. Cultural anthropologists also study how different societies are structured, including the roles and institutions that organize social life.

Cultural anthropologists often live for many months or years in the societies they study, adopting local ways of living, eating, dressing, and speaking as accurately as possible. This practice is called **fieldwork**. Anthropologists who undertake fieldwork might write an **ethnography**, an in-depth study of the culture they have been studying. Classic ethnographies of the early 20th century often portrayed the cultures of non-Western peoples as harmonious and unchanging over time. Bronislaw Malinowski, a pioneer of the long-term fieldwork method, spent nearly two years studying trade and magic among the Trobriand peoples living in what is now the Kiriwina island chain northeast of New Guinea. His ethnography, *Argonauts of the Western Pacific* (1922), describes how Trobrianders undertook canoe voyages from island to island for the ceremonial exchange of white shell bracelets and red shell necklaces among different island groups, an exchange system known as the kula ring. Curiously, these highly valued objects had no use whatsoever, as no one ever wore them. Rather, the exchange of bracelets and necklaces functioned as a means of enhancing social status (for the givers) and reinforcing trade relationships. Malinowski argues that this form of exchange took the place of warfare. Exploring the kula ring in great detail, Malinowski also learned about many other aspects of Trobriand culture, such as the making of tools and canoes, farming practices, gender roles, sexuality, and magical beliefs and practices.

Nowadays, cultural anthropologists tend to focus more on issues involving conflict and change, such as suicide bombing in Afghanistan (Edwards 2017), a creationist theme park in Kentucky (Bielo 2018), sperm donation in Denmark (Mohr 2018), and garbage pickers in Rio de Janeiro (Millar 2018). Often, anthropologists explore overlooked and marginalized perspectives on controversial issues, shedding light on the cultural complexities and power dynamics involved. Anthropologist Tracey Heatherington was interested in why some people were resisting the creation of a conservation park on the Italian island of Sardinia (2010). The central highlands of Sardinia are home to many endangered species and old growth forests, as well as local herding peoples who fiercely resisted the appropriation of their homeland. Heatherington's research identified three competing perspectives: those of global environmentalists, the national government of Italy, and the local people of Sardinia. The global environmentalists view the Sardinian highlands as a delicate ecosystem that should be protected and controlled by environmental experts. The Italian government sees in the same land an opportunity to develop ecotourism and demonstrate the Italian commitment to environmentalism. The local peoples of Sardinia treasure their homeland as the foundation of their way of life, an intimate landscape imbued with history and cultural value. As the controversy drew these three perspectives together, Western-led global environmentalism combined with national government to undermine the legitimacy of local knowledge and authority. Heatherington describes how stereotypes of Sardinians as ignorant and culturally backward were used to delegitimize their resistance to the conservation park, drawing our attention to forms of ecological racism that lurk in the global environmental movement.

Linguistic Anthropology

As you might guess, **linguistic anthropology** focuses on language. Linguistic anthropologists view language as a primary means by which humans create their diverse cultures. Language combines biological and social elements. Some linguistic anthropologists study the origins of language, asking how language emerged in our biological evolution and sociocultural development and what aspects of language might have given early hominins an evolutionary advantage. Other linguistic anthropologists are interested in how language shapes our thinking processes and our views of the world. In addition to its cognitive aspects, language is a powerful tool for getting things done. Linguistic anthropologists also study how people use language to form communities and identities, assert power, and resist authority.

Linguistic anthropologists frequently conduct the same kinds of long-term, immersive research that cultural anthropologists do. Christopher Ball spent a year living and traveling with the Wauja, an indigenous group in Brazil (2018). He describes the many routine and ritualized ways of speaking in this community and how each kind of talk generates specific types of social action. "Chief speech" is used by leaders, while "bringing the spirits" is used for healing the sick. Ceremonial language is used for giving people names and for conducting exchanges between different indigenous groups. Ball, like many linguistic anthropologists, also examined public speeches, such as the ones delivered by Wauja leaders to protest a dam on a nearby river. Ball also analyzed the forms of language used by state officials and development workers to marginalize and subordinate indigenous groups such as the Wauja.

Language is central to the way we conceptualize ourselves and our lives. Have you ever been asked to write an essay about yourself, perhaps as part of a school assignment or college application? If so, you might have used different phrases and concepts than if you'd been chatting with a new acquaintance. The purpose and intended audience of our language use shapes the way we represent ourselves and our actions.

Anthropologist Summerson Carr examined an addiction treatment program for homeless women in the midwestern United States, looking at the role of language in the therapeutic process (2011). After observing therapy sessions and self-help meetings, she describes how addiction counselors promote a certain kind of "healthy talk" that conveys deep cultural notions about personhood and responsibility. As patients master this "healthy talk," they learn to demonstrate progress by performing very scripted ways of speaking about themselves and their addiction.

How the Four Fields Work Together: The Example of Race

With their unique methods and emphases, the four fields of anthropology may seem like completely different disciplines. It's true that anthropologists from the four fields don't always agree on the best approach to sociocultural enquiry. Biological anthropologists often see themselves as "hard" scientists committed to studying humanity through the scientific method. Cultural anthropologists rely on the "softer" methods of observation, participation, and interviews. Someone who studies the genetic distribution of blood types and someone who studies an addiction treatment program may have a difficult time finding common ground.

Increasingly, however, urgent concerns such as inequality and climate change have highlighted the importance of an integrated approach to the study of humanity. The issue of racial inequality is an excellent example. Beginning with an approach from the cultural side of our discipline, many anthropologists explore what we think we know about the concept of race. How many racial categories do you think there are in the world? How can you tell a person's racial identity? What do you know about your own racial category?

Biological anthropologist Jada Benn Torres and cultural anthropologist Gabriel Torres Colón teamed up to explore how people use genetic ancestry testing to construct notions of collective history and racial belonging (2020). For instance, if you learn through genetic testing that your ancestors most likely came from Nigeria, you might begin to feel a certain identification with that country and with the continent of Africa as a whole. You might begin to feel that you have less in common with the people of your country of citizenship and more in common with the people of your country of ancestry, a racial connection perhaps felt as more fundamental than the sociocultural connection to your home culture. While concerned about the potential for spreading misconceptions about racial categories, Torres and Colon also note that racialized solidarity across national boundaries can foster transnational movements for social justice. Such research shows how we *actively construct* our concepts about race using biological information about ourselves, all the time believing that those concepts are embedded in nature.

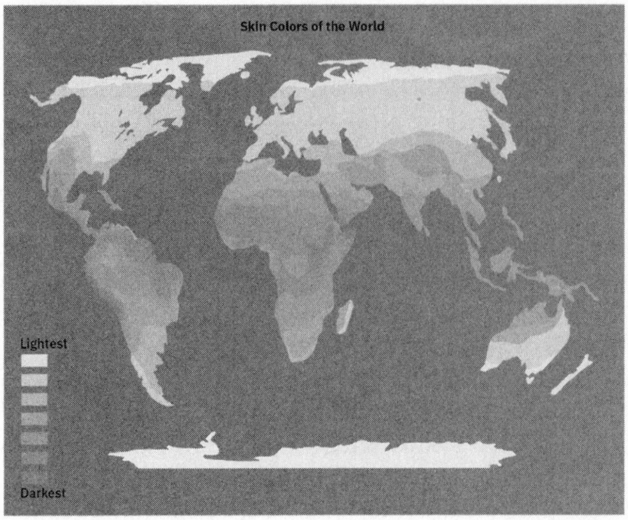

FIGURE 1.6 This map shows the predicted skin colors of people based on the levels of ultraviolet radiation in the areas where they live. (attribution: Copyright Rice University, OpenStax, under CC BY 4.0 license)

Importantly, biological anthropology demonstrates that our common notions of race are inaccurate. Biological anthropologists such as Agustín Fuentes (2012) and Nina Jablonski (2006) have looked carefully at the global distribution of human traits such as skin color, facial features, hair texture, and blood type, among other markers, in order to determine if humans are indeed grouped into discrete categories based on race. Short answer: biologically speaking, there are no real racial categories. Each human trait varies along a spectrum, and the various traits are mixed and matched among people in ways that make racial distinctions impossibly inaccurate. As an example, take the issue of skin color, which is the most common way people assign race. Jablonski demonstrates that skin color varies along a spectrum, from pinkish beige to dark brown, with people throughout the world having skin of every possible shade between those two. Originally, humans evolving on the African continent had dark skin to protect them from the direct ultraviolet light of the sun. As some early humans migrated north into environments with less direct sunlight, their skin lightened to allow the absorption of vitamin D from the much weaker sunlight.

Today, if we look at people with deep historical connections to particular geographical areas, we find that skin color shifts gradually with location. Imagine setting out on a road trip from Kinshasa, the capital of the Democratic Republic of the Congo, just a few degrees south of the equator in central Africa, and traveling all the way up to the city of Tromsø in Norway, north of the Arctic Circle. This 157-hour trip would take you through Nigeria, Niger, Algeria, Spain, France, Germany, Denmark, and Sweden. If you were paying attention to the skin color of the indigenous peoples in each location, you would notice a gradual shift from deep brown in Kinshasa to lighter brown in Algeria to dark beige in southern Spain to lighter beige in Sweden. You might also notice other changes, such as more green and blue eyes and more red and blond hair, as you head into northern Europe. At no point in your trip could you identify a boundary between groups. Rather, you would see a gradual spectrum of change.

Whether looking at visible characteristics such as skin color or invisible genetic markers such as blood type, biological anthropologists have demonstrated time and time again that there is no scientifically justifiable way to divide the human population into racial categories. Any way you draw the lines, there will be more variation within categories than between categories.

Does this mean that race does not exist? In terms of biology, that is exactly what it means. But in terms of social reality, unfortunately not. Race does not exist in nature, but race does exist in our minds, our practices, and our institutions. Archaeological excavations of the material lives of various groups in the United States, including people from China and Ireland as well as enslaved peoples from Africa, show how notions of race shaped their whole ways of life: the buildings in which they lived, the clothing they wore, the property they owned, and the structure of their families (Orser 2007; Singleton [1985] 2016). In contemporary societies, cultural anthropologists studying forms of racial inequality in societies all over the world—including the United States, the Dominican Republic, Brazil, Japan, Kenya, and Zimbabwe—have uncovered the different ways that each of these societies constructs racial categories and uses various criteria to assign (and often reassign) race to a particular person.

Moreover, in-depth ethnographies illuminate the severity of racism in the everyday lives of people of color in the United States and elsewhere. After three years of fieldwork on the West Side of Chicago, anthropologist Laurence Ralph documented the suffering of people in this Black neighborhood as they contend with discrimination, economic deprivation, gang violence, and political marginalization (2014). Ralph emphasizes that the people he observed dream of a better life for themselves and their children, in spite of these struggles, and describes how many turn to social and political activism in an attempt to make their neighborhood a better place for everyone who lives there.

Linguistic anthropologists are interested in how race is constructed and expressed through language. Marcyliena Morgan studied the underground hip-hop scene in Los Angeles, exploring how Black emcees and musicians craft linguistic codes that reference their experiences of police violence, urban unrest, gang activity, and gentrification (2009). Like Ralph, Morgan highlights the creativity and resilience of Black American communities in the face of enduring racism in American society.

Taken together, these various anthropological approaches to race provide more insight and understanding than any one approach ever could. Overturning the biological myth of race is essential to understanding the complex reality of human diversity, but it is not enough. It would be a mistake to pretend that racial categories do not matter just because the concept of race has no basis in biology. The combined work of archaeologists, cultural anthropologists, and linguistic anthropologists demonstrates how the mythic notion of race has been used to exploit and marginalize certain people throughout history and into the present. We also see how people respond to racial subjugation with creativity and resilience, inventing cultural forms of resistance and mobilizing their communities through social activism.

1.3 Overcoming Ethnocentrism

LEARNING OUTCOMES

By the end of this section, you will be able to:

- Define the concept of ethnocentrism and explain the ubiquity of ethnocentrism as a consequence of enculturation.
- Distinguish certain forms of ethnocentrism in terms of their historical relationship to forms of empire and domination.
- Identify primitivism in European and American representations of African peoples.
- Identify orientalism in European and American representations of Asian and Middle Eastern peoples.

Have you ever known somebody who seems to think the world revolves around them? The kind of friend who is always talking about themselves and never asks any questions about you and your life? The kind of person who thinks their own ideas are cool and special and their own way of doing things is absolutely the best? You may know the word used to describe that kind of person: egocentric. An egocentric person is entirely caught up in their own perspective and does not seem to care much about the perspectives of others. It is good to feel proud of your personal qualities and accomplishments, of course, but it is equally important to appreciate the personal qualities and accomplishments of others as well.

The same sort of "centric" complex operates at the level of culture. Some people in some cultures are convinced that their own ways of understanding the world and of doing things are absolutely the best and no other ways are worth consideration. They imagine that the world would be a much better place if the superior beliefs, values, and practices of their own culture were spread or imposed on everyone else in the world. This is what we call **ethnocentrism**.

Enculturation and Ethnocentrism

We are all brought up in a particular culture with particular norms and values and ways of doing things. Our parents or guardians teach us how to behave in social situations, how to take care of our bodies, how to lead a good life, and what we should value and think about. Our teachers, religious leaders, and bosses give us instruction about our roles, responsibilities, and relationships in life. By the time we are in our late teens or early twenties, we know a great deal about how our society works and our role in that society.

Anthropologists call this process of acquiring our particular culture **enculturation**. All humans go through this process. It is natural to value the particular knowledge gained through our own process of enculturation because we could not survive without it. It is natural to respect the instruction of our parents and teachers who want us to do well in life. It is good to be proud of who we are and where we came from. However, just as egocentrism is tiresome, it can be harmful for people to consider their own culture so superior that they cannot appreciate the unique qualities and accomplishments of other cultures. When people are so convinced that their own culture is more advanced, morally superior, efficient, or just plain better than any other culture, we call that ethnocentrism. When people are ethnocentric, they do not value the perspectives of people from other cultures, and they do not bother to learn about or consider other ways of doing things.

Beyond the sheer rudeness of ethnocentrism, the real problem emerges when the ethnocentrism of one group causes them to harm, exploit, and dominate other groups. Historically, the ethnocentrism of Europeans and Euro-Americans has been used to justify subjugation and violence against peoples from Africa, the Middle East, Asia, and the Americas. In the quest to colonize territories in these geographical areas, Europeans developed two main styles of ethnocentrism, styles that have dominated popular imagination over the past two centuries. These styles each identify a cultural "self" as European and a **cultural other** as a stereotypical member of a culture from a specific region of the world. Using both of these styles of ethnocentrism, Europeans strategically crafted their own coherent self-identity in contrast to these distorted images of other cultures.

Primitivism and Orientalism

Since the 18th century, views of Africans and Native Americans have been shaped by the obscuring lens of **primitivism**. Identifying themselves as enlightened and civilized, Europeans came to define Africans as ignorant savages, intellectually inferior and culturally backward. Nineteenth-century explorers such as Henry M. Stanley described Africa as "the dark continent," a place of wildness and depravity (Stanley 1878). Similarly, European missionaries viewed Africans as simple heathens, steeped in sin and needing Christian redemption. Elaborated in the writings of travelers and traders, primitivism depicts Africans and Native Americans as exotic, simple, highly sexual, potentially violent, and closer to nature. Though both African and Native American societies of the time were highly organized and well-structured, Europeans often viewed them as chaotic and violent. An alternative version of primitivism depicts Africans and Native Americans as "noble savages," innocent and simple, living in peaceful communities in harmony with nature. While less overtly insulting, the "noble savage" version of primitivism is still a racist stereotype, reinforcing the notion that non-Western peoples are ignorant, backward, and isolated.

Europeans developed a somewhat different style of ethnocentrism toward people from the Middle East and Asia, a style known as **orientalism**. As detailed by literary critic Edward Said (1979), orientalism portrays peoples of Asia and the Middle East as irrational, fanatical, and out of control. The "oriental" cultures of East Asia and Middle East are depicted as mystical and alluring. The emphasis here is less on biology and nature and more on sensual and emotional excess. Middle Eastern societies are viewed not as lawless but as tyrannical. Relations between men and women are deemed not just sexual but patriarchal and exploitative. Said argues that this view of Asian and Middle Eastern societies was strategically crafted to demonstrate the rationality, morality, and democracy of European societies by contrast.

In his critique of orientalism, Said points to the very common representation of Muslim and Middle Eastern peoples in mainstream American movies as irrational and violent. In the very first minute of the 1992 Disney film *Aladdin*, the theme song declares that Aladdin comes from "a faraway place / where the caravan camels roam / where they cut off your ear if they don't like your face / it's barbaric, but hey, it's home." Facing criticism by antidiscrimination groups, Disney was forced to change the lyrics for the home video release of the film (Nittle 2021). Many thrillers such as the 1994 film *True Lies*, starring Arnold Schwarzenegger, cast Arabs as America-hating villains scheming to plant bombs and take hostages. Arab women are frequently portrayed as sexualized belly dancers or silent, oppressed victims shrouded in veils. These forms of representation draw from and reproduce orientalist stereotypes.

Both primitivism and orientalism were developed when Europeans were colonizing these parts of the world. Primitivist views of Native Americans justified their subjugation and forced migration. In the next section, we'll explore how current versions of primitivism and orientalism persist in American culture, tracing the harmful effects of these misrepresentations and the efforts of anthropologists to dismantle them.

1.4 Western Bias in Our Assumptions about Humanity

LEARNING OUTCOMES

By the end of this section, you will be able to:

- Define and recognize cultural bias.
- Analyze forms of cultural bias in our own interactions and institutions.
- Describe how the four fields of anthropology can work together to expose and overturn the misconceptions of cultural bias.

Euro-American ethnocentrism is everywhere in American culture—in our movies, advertising, museums, amusement parks, and news media. Though the styles have shifted somewhat in the past century, both primitivism and orientalism still persist as two discernible styles of bias.

Primitivism and Orientalism in Popular Culture

Think for a minute about the last time you saw an image of an African person. Was it, perhaps, an image of wide-eyed girl in tattered clothing in an advertisement from a development agency requesting a charitable donation? Or maybe it was a news media photograph of a child soldier wielding an AK-47 in a conflict zone in the Democratic Republic of the Congo or another African country. Africa is still popularly represented as a dark place full of deprivation and crisis. Africans are frequently infantilized as simple children who need the support and tutelage of White Western helpers. But isn't it true, you may say, that poverty and violent conflicts are widespread in Africa? Isn't the representation accurate to some degree?

The most troubled places on the African continent are the places where European colonialism was most brutal and violent. In what is now the Democratic Republic of the Congo, the Belgian king Leopold II oversaw a reign of terror against the local peoples, encouraging their enslavement for the lucrative rubber trade. Elsewhere in Africa, European colonial governments stole land from local peoples and confined them to reservations, forcing them to work on European plantations in order to pay taxes to the colonial government. Colonial officials fomented conflict by privileging some ethnic groups and repressing others. Where you see violence and conflict in Africa today, the roots can often be traced to the colonial period. Is this painful history included in American representations of Africa?

Moreover, there are many bright spots in Africa, places such as Ghana and Botswana, with growing economies and stable democracies. Would it surprise you to learn that Ghana has a space program? That there are more mobile phones than people in Kenya? That several electric cars are manufactured in Africa?

Similar distortions are applied to Native Americans, frequently represented as victims of history, poor and helpless, in need of outside help. The primitivist gaze shapes the representation of Native Americans in museums, which often feature dioramas of humble people with stone tools, buckskin clothes, and tepees, either living a simple life close to nature or engaged in tribal warfare, their bodies painted with vibrant colors. Of course, Native Americans do not live this way now, but these are the images that come to mind in the popular imagination. It is of course important for non-Native Americans to learn about the cultures of Native peoples before and during their contact with European settlers, but it is equally important to understand the legacies of history in the contemporary living conditions and activities of Native communities. Rather than seeing Native peoples as passive victims, popular culture should also depict the dynamic and creative responses of Native Americans to the forms of cultural violence enacted against them.

FIGURE 1.7 One example of a healthy Native American dish is Navajo mutton stew with blue corn and dry bread. (credit: "Mutton Stew with Blue Corn and Dry Bread" by Neeta Lind/flickr, CC BY 2.0)

For instance, did you know that a Native food movement is surging across the United States, both on Native reservations and in American cities? Native food activists such as Karlos Baca and Sean Sherman are reviving and reinventing the balanced, healthy cuisines of their ancestors, featuring dishes such as braised elk leg and maple red corn pudding. Sherman and his partner, Dana Thompson, have founded the nonprofit group North American Traditional Indigenous Food Systems (NATIFS), devoted to preserving Native foodways. The group offers opportunities for tribes to set up Native cuisine restaurants, providing jobs and profits to communities with high unemployment. Watch this video (https://openstax.org/r/sheansherman) to learn more about Sean Sherman and the Native Food movement.

Like primitivism, orientalism has endured in American and European cultures. In the two decades following the al-Qaeda attacks on American targets on September 11, 2001, the most prominent example of orientalism in American culture has been the stereotype that *all* Islamic peoples are fanatical and violent. The indiscriminate application of this stereotype to Islamic peoples across the Middle East was a major contributor to the 2003 American invasion of Iraq, a country that had nothing at all to do with the September 11 attacks. To promote the invasion, politicians used the orientalist notion that Iraq was a violent and irrational country stockpiling weapons of mass destruction (which turned out to be false). As the war raged on, the Iraqi people came to be categorized as either "unlawful combatants" or helpless victims of a cruel dictator. American officials argued that Iraqis needed the help of American troops to save them from their subjugation and teach them democracy.

For many Europeans and Americans, these forms of ethnocentric bias distort views of peoples living in large geographical regions of the globe. Misunderstanding other cultures this way can result in policies and military actions that do not achieve desired results. Moreover, ethnocentric bias promotes and reinforces inequality among social groups within multicultural societies. When people with certain ethnic or racial identities are seen as helpless or violent, they face discrimination in their pursuit of education, employment, and justice.

The Bias of Backwardness

Common to both primitivism and orientalism is the notion that European and Euro-American cultures are more advanced and civilized than other cultures. Since at least the 19th century, Euro-American thinking has been dominated by the idea that the various cultures of the world can be evaluated on a scale of sociocultural sophistication from least advanced to most advanced. Typically, Native American and African cultures were considered the most primitive, while those of Asia and the Middle East were thought of as slightly more developed but certainly not as civilized as the societies of Europe, which were ranked at the top as the epitome of human progress.

Early anthropology played a role in promoting this ethnocentric way of thinking. Nineteenth-century anthropologists detailed various hypothetical schemes charting the developmental stages that each culture would go through in its pursuit of the European ideal of civilization. One very prominent scheme was proposed by the British anthropologist Edward Tylor. Tylor suggested that each culture progressed from "savagery" to "barbarism" to "civilization." Since the change from one stage to another could not be witnessed by the researcher, such "evolutionary" schemes were largely based on hypothetical conjecture, sometimes called "theorizing from the armchair."

While some anthropologists played a role in popularizing this way of thinking, others worked to expose it as misguided and inaccurate. The writings of American anthropologist Franz Boas highlighted the fact that no culture is isolated in its process of developmental change. Instead, each culture develops through interactions with other cultures, as new ideas and inventions diffuse from one culture to the next. Moreover, cultural change is not structured by an overall trajectory of progress as defined by the European example; rather, cultures change in many ways, sometimes adopting new ways of doing things and other times reviving and reclaiming older ways. Through these varied patterns of change, each culture forges its own unique history.

While the evolutionary schemes of 19th-century anthropology have been disproven, the underlying notion of sociocultural progress toward a Euro-American ideal is still a widespread form of ethnocentric bias outside of anthropology. Many people still refer to some countries as "developed" and "modern" and others as "undeveloped" and "backward." Think for a minute: Which countries are generally thought of as modern? Which ones are frequently referred to as undeveloped? What is really meant by these labels?

These labels are rooted in Euro-American values. Championing capitalism and technology, many Europeans and Americans view the generation of material wealth as the primary measure of the success of any society. The divide between the more and less "advanced" countries of the world is largely a distinction between the richer and poorer countries. European and American societies, which have become wealthy through the development of global trade and industrial capitalism, are considered the most successful. Societies that have not achieved the levels of wealth and technology associated with Euro-American industrial capitalism are sometimes labeled "undeveloped." Societies that have not industrialized at all are sometimes called "premodern" or simply "traditional."

As with older evolutionary schemes, this way of thinking relies on the notion that each society pursues economic development in isolation. The poorer countries of the world are told: if you work hard and apply the correct economic policies, then you too can become rich like the United States, the United Kingdom, and Germany. But how did those countries become rich in the first place? Certainly not in isolation. The Boasian emphasis on cultural interaction also applies to economic change. To a large degree, European and American societies became wealthy by dominating other societies and keeping them poor. European countries constructed a system of global capitalism designed to make them very rich by extracting raw materials and human labor from their colonies. In fact, that was the whole impetus for colonialism.

The cultural anthropologist Sidney Mintz is one of many who have studied how this happened. Mintz explored how European merchants designed a very lucrative system of production and consumption based on sugar (1985). As European consumers began developing a taste for sugar in the 17th century, European merchants developed sugar plantations in the New World using the labor of enslaved people transported from West Africa. Sugar produced on these plantations was exported to Europe and the rest of the world, earning a hefty profit for the European merchants who designed the system. Local people living in the places where sugar was produced did not benefit much from this trade, and enslaved people suffered and died for it. Similar systems were developed for the production of other global commodities such as cocoa, coffee, tea, and cotton. Some commodities required enslaved labor and others involved small farmers, but the basic structure of the trade was the same. The economies of many South Asian and African countries were designed entirely around the export of primary commodities, the production of which was controlled by European merchants who reaped the profits from this global trade. Many postcolonial countries still rely on the export of these primary commodities.

What do these historical processes mean for understanding the world today? European merchants and governments crafted strategic ways of thinking about the parts of the world they wanted to invade and colonize. To justify the development of the slave trade, the plantation system, and colonial rule, Europeans labeled many non-Europeans as backward peoples needing the civilizing influence of European domination. This form of bias persists in contemporary notions of backwardness applied to the poorer peoples and parts of the world.

In reality, the colonial system was a global mechanism for European merchants and governments to extract wealth from other parts of the world. European merchants took great care to maintain control over these forms of highly profitable trade, edging out local merchants and forbidding local competition. Even today, we see the remnants of this system in Euro-American domination of global trade. If the world seems divided between rich and poor, it is not because some countries work hard and others are "backward." It is because the global system was founded on forms of inequality that endure into the present.

PROFILES IN ANTHROPOLOGY

Franz Boas
1858–1942

FIGURE 1.8 Franz Boas (credit: "FranzBoas" by Canadian Museum of History/Wikimedia Commons, Public Domain)

Personal History: Franz Uri Boas was born in Germany to a middle-class Jewish family (Peregrine 2018). After completing a PhD in physics and mathematics, he worked as a geographer on an expedition to the Canadian Arctic, living and working with the Native Inuit peoples on Baffin Island. With his newfound passion for Native American culture, Boas returned to Germany to work at a museum and began conducting ethnographic and linguistic research among Native groups. In 1887, he came to the United States and established the first anthropology department at Clark University in Massachusetts. He spent most of his career as an anthropology professor at Columbia University and curator at the American Museum of Natural History in New York City.

Areas of Anthropology: Though he promoted a holistic approach integrating the four fields of anthropology, Boas was primarily a cultural anthropologist specializing in the Native peoples of the Northwest coast of North America. Between 1886 and 1900, he conducted 29 months of fieldwork in the region, focusing on the

Kwakiutl peoples of Vancouver Island. He recorded myths, songs, and folklore in Native languages and described cultural activities such as food collection and artistic styles. Focusing on the linguistic and psychological aspects of this rich ethnographic data, Boas sought to understand Native perspectives and values. As the leading anthropologist of his time, he established an American tradition of recording ethnographic observations in meticulous detail and promoted the goal of reaching for an insider's point of view.

Accomplishments in the Field: Boas profoundly disagreed with ethnocentric and racist theories circulating in the social sciences in the late 19th and early 20th centuries. Some anthropologists of the day identified some cultures as "primitive" or "savage," arguing that each culture developed in isolation along a common trajectory toward "civilization." Rejecting this model, Boas used his ethnographic data to show that cultures do not develop in isolation toward a common goal. Rather, each culture has its own unique historical trajectory, and cultures are constantly changing by sharing new ideas and practices.

Importance of His Work: Boas was horrified by the use of anthropological methods to support the theories and practices of White supremacy. In the 19th century, some American researchers measured the skulls of various ethnic groups, arguing that people who had immigrated to the United States from northern Europe had larger skulls and were therefore intellectually superior. In 1907, Boas conducted a survey for the U.S. Immigration Commission measuring the skulls of 17,821 American immigrants and their children. Comparing the head shapes of parents and children, Boas discovered that the children had larger skulls due to environmental factors in their new homeland, such as diet and medical care. His findings dealt a strong blow to race theory. Throughout his career, Boas spoke out against racism, arguing that biological differences have nothing to do with culture, language, or achievement.

1.5 Holism, Anthropology's Distinctive Approach

LEARNING OUTCOMES

By the end of this section, you will be able to:

- Define and give examples of holism.
- Analyze how different elements of society cohere with and reinforce one another.
- Identify how different elements of society can contradict one another, motivating social change.

In 2020, the COVID-19 pandemic swept across the globe. Nearly 210 million people had fallen sick with the coronavirus and more than 4 million had died as of August 2021. Medical researchers are still studying the long-term effects of this illness on the lungs and brains of people who have recovered. Some have discovered psychological effects as well, such as increased risks for depression, anxiety, and schizophrenia.

Beyond the medical realm, the effects of the pandemic reached into every aspect of our societies and our everyday lives. In societies all over the world, people were forced to remain at home, "sheltering in place" from the dangers of the disease. Businesses closed their doors to the public, and many shut down permanently, unable to pay their bills. By May 2020, nearly 50 million Americans had reported losing their jobs due to the pandemic. The epidemic of disease ballooned into an epidemic of grief as people mourned the loss of the those who had died and worried about those who had fallen sick. Stressed out by so many disruptions, some adults turned to alcohol and drugs, and addiction rates soared. Incidents of domestic violence escalated. Racial violence against Asian Americans increased as some Americans blamed China for the emergence and global spread of the disease. People everywhere reported feeling lonelier and more cut off from their friends and family members.

And yet there were also some positive consequences. Because people were not driving as much, air quality improved in many urban areas, giving relief to many people who suffer from asthma. Looking up into the night sky, some people were able to see stars for the very first time. Some people reported valuing their friends and family members even more now that they could not spend time with them in person. New social media technologies spread, such as Zoom, and many people learned to use existing technologies such as FaceTime and Skype. People also became aware of the valuable contributions made by "essential workers" in drugstores, hardware stores, and grocery stores as well as hospitals and nursing homes.

How did a virus cause so many changes? The various elements of society are entwined in a complex whole. Dramatic changes in one area, such as epidemic disease in the realm of public health, can trigger a chain of effects throughout other social realms, such as the family, the economy, religion, and the political system.

You'll recall the word *holism* from our earlier discussion about anthropology's commitment to understanding how the many parts of society work together. **Holism** is a distinctive method of analysis that foregrounds the ever-changing relationships among different realms of culture.

Society as an Integrated Whole

Throughout the 2010s, infant death rates in certain rural areas in Africa decreased dramatically. While thrilled with this positive trend, researchers did not initially know how to explain it. Were mothers and fathers doing something different to promote the health of their babies? Were African governments providing better health services for infants? Were aid agencies providing more resources? None of these things seemed to be true in any significant way.

The one thing that had changed in the areas with lower infant mortality was the spread of mobile phones. Could that have something to do with lower infant mortality? And if so, how? Researchers hypothesize that it wasn't just the possession or use of mobile phones that was making the difference—it was the capability to use mobile money transfers and other fintech. If a baby had a fever in the middle of the night, the mother could now immediately text members of her extended family to organize the necessary funds to take the baby to a hospital for treatment. Quicker treatment meant a better chance for recovery. Something that does not appear to be directly related to infant health may in fact have a great impact on it.

Recall from the beginning of this chapter our discussion of the very broad scope of anthropology. While other disciplines focus on one realm of society, such as medicine or technology, anthropology ranges across all realms of human thought and activity. Using the technique of holism, anthropologists ask how seemingly disparate elements of social life might be related in unexpected ways.

In American and European cultures, the most common form of marriage is a union of two people. In the United States, many marriages end in divorce and most people then remarry, resulting in a cycle of marriage-divorce-remarriage called *serial monogamy*. In other cultures, however, a man may have more than one wife. It might be tempting to think that the dominant form of marriage in a culture is related to morality or gender relations. It turns out, however, that one very significant influence on marriage patterns is the food-getting strategy of a particular culture. In small-scale farming cultures, the marriage of one man to two or more women provides an abundance of children to help out with the work of weeding, watering, fertilizing, and guarding the crops (Boserup [1970] 2007; Goody 1976). In cultures where children contribute to food production, the marriage of one man to multiple women is more prevalent. This isn't always the case, of course, as there are other factors that influence the form of marriage practiced in a culture, but the useful work of children does contribute to the popularity of this form of marriage.

In the contemporary United States, by contrast, most people work not on farms but in offices, shops, and factories. Children are not valued as sources of household labor, and they are not legally permitted to work for wages. In fact, children can be viewed as a drain on the household, each one requiring a massive investment of resources in the form of health care, childcare, special equipment, educational opportunities, and expensive toys. In this context, the increased fertility of multiple wives might impoverish the household. Moreover, our fast-paced, capitalist economy requires a flexible and highly mobile work force. American workers can lose their jobs, and they must be prepared to move and retrain in order to find further work. Many Americans experience periods of uncertainty and precarity in their work lives, conditions that affect the livelihood of their households as well as their relationships with their marriage partners and children. Such a context contributes to smaller family size and fragile marriage bonds. The cycles of stability and disruption in American work life are mirrored in the cycles of marriage and divorce involved in serial monogamy.

These are just two examples of why anthropologists are committed to taking such a broad view of the cultures they study. Often, the various realms of society are related in ways that are not at first apparent to the researcher. By specializing too narrowly on only one realm, the researcher might miss the wider forces that shape the object of study.

Sources of Contradiction, Conflict, and Change

Holistic analysis considers not only how the various features of culture hold together but also how change in one feature can generate cascading changes among others. Often, anthropologists begin their analysis by focusing on one significant change in the lives of a particular cultural group and then chart the ramifications of that change through various other realms of culture.

Attiya Ahmad conducted research among South Asian women who migrate to the Middle East for jobs as housekeepers (2017). She writes about how these women adapt to a new culture and living situation in Kuwait and the disruptions they face when they return to their families and home cultures. On the job in Kuwait, these domestic workers must learn to speak Arabic, operate household gadgets, prepare an entirely different cuisine, respect Islamic norms and practices, and perform their appropriate gender role as female members of a Kuwaiti household. They face the cultural requirement that women should be *naram*, or soft and malleable, as they develop emotionally charged relationships with the various members of the household. These requirements bring about profound personal transformations for these women as they deal with the contradictions of being both successful wage earners and subordinated cultural others.

The motivation to migrate is primarily financial: the need to pay for schooling, marriages, medical care, and other family expenses. While the women are working in Kuwait, their families become economically dependent on the money they send back home even as their emotional relationships with their family members become weaker and more difficult. When they return home, profoundly changed by their experiences in Kuwait, their natal families nonetheless expect them to behave exactly as they did before they left, observing the same gender and age-related norms that govern the household. This creates a sense of internal conflict for these women. Unable to truly reintegrate with their natal families, many either seek out new connections in their home communities or migrate back to Kuwait. Some begin learning more about Islam by attending special *da'wa* classes, where they meet other women in the same situation. Finding ethical inspiration in Islamic teachings, many do convert, against the objections of their natal families and their Kuwaiti employers.

All cultures are constantly changing, with small changes in one realm snowballing into larger and larger changes within and beyond that culture. The Me Too movement is another good example. What began in 2006 as a call by American activist Tarana Burke for solidarity and empathy with victims of sexual harassment has now spread into many sectors of American society and across the globe. Initially focused on high-profile celebrities and the movie industry, the Me Too movement has raised awareness of widespread sexual harassment and assault in the fashion industry, churches, the finance industry, sports, medicine, politics, and the military. Activists press for legal changes to protect workers, especially whistleblowers who come forward with allegations of inappropriate sexual behavior. Evaluations of patriarchal and chauvinistic behavior in these institutional realms have sparked scrutiny of the more informal cultural norms of American romance and dating. The Me Too movement challenges the way Americans think about the gender roles of men and women, appropriate speech and gestures, and the distinction between public life and private life.

The movement has prompted processes of dialogue and change in at least 28 other countries, including Afghanistan, China, Nigeria, and the Philippines. The global campaign has been interpreted differently in each of these cultural contexts as the transcultural intentions of American activists intersect with local norms of gender and sexuality. Indeed, some critique the Me Too movement as ethnocentric. Though the calls for reform resonated with French feminists, Me Too activism sparked a backlash among many other French people, with some men and even women arguing that French men should have the right to make sexually provocative comments and rub against women in public places.

While many anthropologists actively support the Me Too movement, our methods of cross-cultural comparison call on us to set aside our personal values (at least temporarily) in order to understand how people in various cultural contexts interpret and act on the cross-cultural campaign against gender-based harassment and assault. This method of suspending personal values is key to understanding how all the elements of a particular culture interact with one another, including pressures from the outside.

1.6 Cross-Cultural Comparison and Cultural Relativism

LEARNING OUTCOMES

By the end of this section, you will be able to:

- Define the concept of relativism and explain why this term is so important to the study of anthropology.
- Distinguish relativism from the "anything goes" approach to culture.
- Describe how relativism can enlighten our approach to social problems.

Recall our earlier discussion of cultural styles of clothing. American clothing style is *related to* American values. Ghanaian clothing style is *related to* Ghanaian values. We have seen how different realms of culture are interrelated, fitting together to form distinctive wholes. Anthropologists use the term **cultural relativism** to describe how every element of culture must be understood within the broader whole of that culture. Relativism highlights how each belief or practice is *related to* all of the other beliefs and practices in a culture. The anthropological commitment to relativism means that anthropologists do not judge the merits of particular beliefs and practices but rather seek to understand the wider contexts that produce and reinforce those elements of culture. Even when studying controversial topics such as piracy and guerilla warfare, anthropologists set aside their personal convictions in order to explore the complex web of cultural forces that determine why we do the things we do.

Relativism Is *Not* "Anything Goes"

Critics of the notion of relativism, believing so strongly in their own cultural norms that they cannot set them aside, even temporarily. They argue that relativism is amoral, a refusal to condemn aspects of culture considered to be wrong and harmful. For them, relativism means "anything goes."

For anthropologists, cultural relativism is a rigorous mode of holistic analysis requiring the temporary suspension of judgment for the purposes of exploration and analysis. Anthropologists do not think that violent or exploitative cultural practices are just fine, but they do think that the reasons for those practices are a lot more complex than we might imagine. And frequently, we find that the judgmental interventions of ethnocentric outsiders can do more harm than good.

Morality, Activism, and Cultural Relativism

A striking example of the application of cultural relativism in anthropology is the controversy surrounding female genital cutting (FGC), sometimes called female genital mutilation. FGC is a cultural practice in which an elder cuts a younger woman's genitalia, removing all or part of the clitoris and labia. The practice is common in parts of Africa and the Middle East. FGC is not only extremely painful; it can also lead to infection, urination problems, infertility, and complications in childbirth.

The World Health Organization and the United Nations condemn the practice as a form of violence against children, a danger to women's health, and a violation of basic human rights. These organizations view FGC as a form of discrimination against women, enforcing extreme inequality among the sexes. Efforts to ban FGC have focused on educating parents and children about the medical harms associated with the practice. Local governments are encouraged to enact laws banning FGC and impose criminal penalties against the elders who perform it.

FIGURE 1.9 Rendille Kenyan women attending a church dedication ceremony. (credit: "180818_TSCOKenya_EstherHavens_0997" by Ann/flickr, CC BY 2.0)

Despite decades of campaigning against FGC, however, the practice remains widespread. If condemning FGC has not been effective in reducing it, then what can be done? Anthropologist Bettina Shell-Duncan has taken a more relativist approach, attempting to understand the larger cultural norms and values that make FGC such an enduring practice. Setting aside her personal opinions, Shell-Duncan spent long periods in African communities where FGC is practiced, talking to people about why FGC is important to them. She learned that FGC has different functions in different sociocultural contexts. Among the Rendille people of northern Kenya, many people believe that men's and women's bodies are naturally androgynous, a mix of masculine and feminine parts. In order for a girl to become a woman, it is necessary to remove the parts of female genitalia that resemble a man's penis. Likewise, in order for a boy to become a man, the foreskin must be removed because it resembles the folds of female genitalia.

Other societies value FGC for different reasons. Some Muslim societies consider FGC a form of hygiene, making a girl clean so that she can pray to Allah. Some communities see FGC as a way of limiting premarital sex and discouraging extramarital affairs. In the colonial period, when FGC was banned by the colonial government, some Kenyan girls practiced FGC on themselves as a form of resistance to colonial authority. As FGC is promoted and carried out by senior women in most contexts, the practice becomes a way for senior women to solidify power and exert influence in the community.

People in communities practicing FGC are often aware of the efforts of outside groups to ban the practice. They know about medical complications such as the risk of infection. But the denunciations of outsiders often seem unconvincing to them, as those denunciations tend to ignore the cultural reasons for the endurance of FGC. People who practice FGC do not do it because they despise women or want to harm children. Shell-Duncan argues that parents weigh the risks and benefits of FGC, often deciding that the procedure is in the best interest of their child's future.

Personally, Shell-Duncan remains critical of FGC and works on a project with the Population Council designed to dramatically reduce the practice. Cultural relativism does not mean permanently abandoning our own value systems. Instead, it asks us to set aside the norms and values of our own culture for a while in order to fully understand controversial practices in other cultures. By suspending judgment, Shell-Duncan was able to learn two important things. First, while campaigns to eradicate FGC frequently target mothers, providing them with educational material about the medical risks involved, Shell-Duncan learned that the decision to go ahead with the procedure is not made by parents alone. A large network of relatives and friends may pressure a girl's parents to arrange for the cutting in order to ensure the girl's chastity, marriageability, and fertility. Secondly, Shell-Duncan learned that people who practice FGC do it because they want the best for their girls. They want their girls to be respected and admired, considered clean and beautiful, fit for marriage and childbearing.

Shell-Duncan argues that outside organizations should reconsider their efforts, focusing more on communities than on individual parents. Awareness campaigns will be more effective if they resonate with local norms and values rather than dismissively condemning them as part of the whole culture of FGC. Some researchers urge anti-FGC activists to connect with local feminists and women's groups in an effort to empower local women and localize the movement against FCG. Some alternative approaches press for more incremental forms of change, such as moving the practice to more sanitary conditions in clinics and hospitals and reducing the severity of the procedure to smaller cuts or more symbolic nicks.

As this example illustrates, cultural relativism is not an amoral "anything goes" approach but rather a strategy for forming cross-cultural relationships and gaining deeper understanding. Once this foundation has been established, anthropologists are often able to revise their activist goals and more effectively work together with people from another culture in pursuit of common interests.

1.7 Reaching for an Insider's Point of View

LEARNING OUTCOMES

By the end of this section, you will be able to:

- Define the notion of *insider's point of view*.
- Critique the notion of *insider's point of view*, explaining how it is never perfectly achievable.
- List and describe the distinctive methods anthropologists deploy in their attempts to represent an insider's point of view

Bettina Shell-Duncan's work on FGC demonstrates the importance of setting aside your own values and opinions in order to see an issue from the point of view of those directly involved. This often means working across contexts, whether studying another group or another culture. Anthropologists across the four fields apply this technique. Cultural anthropologists talk to people and participate in social activities in order to understand cultural life. Archaeologists rely on artifacts and fossils to reconstruct the sociocultural life of peoples in earlier times and different places. Through these different methods, anthropologists all aim for the same thing: they want to understand the perspectives of the people who practice a particular culture, sometimes called an **insider's point of view**.

The Challenge of Representing Others

The anthropological goal of representing an insider's point of view is controversial. Is it truly possible to step outside your own identity to really understand a different perspective? How can a researcher from a particular culture possibly understand exactly how it feels to be a member of another culture? Even anthropologists who study their own cultures may find themselves researching people from different classes, ethnicities, or gender categories. Is it possible to accurately represent the perspectives of people whose lives are so different from your own? Is it ethical? Is it valuable?

For decades, White European and American anthropologists conducted research and wrote ethnographies as if the challenge of representing cultures very different from their own was really no problem at all. Empowered by White privilege and ethnocentrism, many earlier anthropologists believed that long-term intensive fieldwork was enough to give them cross-cultural insight into the perspectives of the people they studied.

Too frequently, those anthropologists reduced the complexity of the non-Western cultures they studied to just one point of view, as if the people in that society all interpreted their cultural rules the same way and never disagreed or changed the rules over time. In her book about Japanese culture, *The Chrysanthemum and the Sword* (1946), anthropologist Ruth Benedict describes Japanese people in terms of common personality traits, such as reverence for the emperor and a moral sense guided by shame. Critics have argued that her conclusions are skewed by her overreliance on very few informants, all of them Japanese people confined to internment camps during World War II. As we have explored in this chapter, every culture comprises multiple perspectives that often contradict one another, generating sociocultural conflict and change. Recognizing this situation, contemporary anthropologists often conduct research among several different subgroups and geographical locations, integrating insights from these various arenas into a comprehensive and dynamic view of cultural complexity.

Then there is the question of deep-seated bias, often operating unconsciously among researchers and the people they study. Consider the situation above in which a White American anthropologist conducts research in an African country previously colonized by Europeans. European colonialism left behind a legacy of White privilege in postcolonial African countries. Earlier anthropologists did not often recognize how racialized power dynamics might shape their research and writing, distorting their representations of the peoples they studied. In the 1960s, anthropologists began to think more carefully about these issues, realizing that an insider's point of view is never perfectly achievable. As human beings, our own perspectives are conditioned by our own enculturation, our own ways of seeing and thinking about the world around us.

If an insider's point of view is never really possible, should we give up on this aspirational goal of the discipline? In such a scenario, researchers would only study and write about people from the same sociocultural categories as themselves. So, for example, Americans would only research and write about other Americans. But are all Americans really members of the same sociocultural category? Could an upper-class Asian American from Manhattan research and write about a poor Black community in the Deep South? Could a Latino man write about a group of Latinx/Latina/Latino people consisting of all genders? American culture is not unique in its complex array of identities. In all cultures, people have multiple identities as members of multiple sociocultural categories. While you may be an insider within your culture in some respect, you may be an outsider by some other measure. The ethical question of who can represent who is riddled with difficulties.

Moreover, resigning ourselves to studying "our own people," whoever they might be, is tantamount to giving up on cross-cultural research and the insight, empathy, dialogue, and transformation that frequently result from it. Anthropological insights have been key to rethinking American notions of sexuality, family, and race, among so many other pressing issues. We need the skills of cross-cultural research now more than ever. While perfect representations of different communities and cultures may be impossible, many anthropologists now deploy innovative methods designed to address the problems of history and power at the heart of the discipline. The aim is not to achieve perfect ethnography but to work ethically and collaboratively to produce what contemporary cultural anthropologist Nancy Scheper-Hughes has termed "good enough ethnography."

Collaborative Methods of Representation

Faced with the challenges of representation, many anthropologists practice methods of collaboration with the individuals and groups that they study. Collaborative ethnography has a very long history in cultural anthropology, traceable all the way back to early Euro-American ethnographies of Native Americans. Often, anthropologists began their research by employing a local person as a translator or field assistant, a role that usually evolved into something much more cooperative.

FIGURE 1.10 Francis La Flesche (credit: “Francis laflesche” by National Anthropological Archives, Smithsonian Institution/Wikimedia Commons, Public Domain)

Researching the Omaha peoples in the early 20th century, anthropologist Alice Cunningham Fletcher began working with a young Omaha man, Francis La Flesche. Through their collaboration, La Flesche became an ethnographer himself. While most anthropologists of the day merely acknowledged their local collaborators (if they did even that), La Flesche became a full coauthor of their joint ethnography, *The Omaha Tribe* (1911).

Today, anthropologists collaborate with the people they study in a number of ways. Some involve local people as readers and editors of their work, sometimes including community responses in the published ethnography. Some conduct focus groups to generate local feedback on particular chapters. Some anthropologists hold community meetings or forums to talk about the major themes and implications of their work. And some, like Fletcher, collaborate with members of the local community as equal coauthors on books and articles. Such methods strengthen ethnography by ensuring accuracy, promoting multiple perspectives, and striving to make anthropological work more relevant to the communities being studied.

Collaboration also draws attention to the personal side of ethnography. Instead of extracting ethnographic “facts” from the process of fieldwork, many contemporary anthropologists focus on describing particular people, insightful conversations, and cooperative practices encountered in their research. Through this kind of representation, culture is represented as a constellation of personal perspectives, each one shaped by the position of each person in that community. Anthropologists also now acknowledge that ethnography is shaped by the personal background and identity of the researcher as well as the motivations and intended audience of the research. Collaborative anthropologists frequently describe their research in the first person, openly acknowledging how their personal and cultural biases influence their research.

Anthropologist Luke E. Lassiter takes a collaborative approach in his study of the song and dance of contemporary Kiowa communities of southern Oklahoma (1998). Lassiter describes how he became interested in Kiowa song as a boy through his involvement in the Order of the Arrow, an affiliate of the Boy Scouts. Moving beyond the superficial representations of Native American culture in Boy Scout teachings, Lassiter went on to attend powwows, where he met singers and learned more about Kiowa culture. He developed a close friendship with renowned Kiowa singer Billy Evans Horse, who taught Lassiter how to sing Kiowa songs and encouraged him to pursue his interest in Kiowa culture in graduate school. Instead of foregrounding his own description of Kiowa song and dance, Lassiter highlights the individual experiences and opinions of his local collaborators as *they* describe how songs are created, passed down, and interpreted in the community.

Collaborative anthropology is not only more ethical and accurate; it is also more socially conscious and political. When anthropologists collaborate as equals, they often become socially involved and politically committed to the welfare of the communities they study. There are various terms for this, among them *engaged anthropology, public anthropology, anthropological advocacy,* and *applied anthropology.* When those communities face struggles over land, food security, medical care, or human rights abuses, many anthropologists support their interests in a number of ways. Anthropologists often speak out publicly, write sympathetic ethnographies, testify in court, participate in protests, and coordinate with organizations that can provide material aid. Anthropologist Stuart Kirsch was researching magic and sorcery in a Yonggom village in Papua New Guinea when he became concerned about pollution from local copper and gold mines nearby (2018). As the community he was studying mobilized to protect their environment, Kirsch became involved in their lawsuit against the Australian owners of the mine. He contributed to a social and environmental impact study and advised lawyers representing the affected communities. He spoke out to local media and scholarly publications, explaining the environmental problems caused by pollution from the mine.

Working across Cultures toward Common Goals

Stepping back for a moment, consider the problems facing us as humans on our shared planet. Climate change threatens the survival of humanity and the biodiversity of plants and animals. Forms of deeply entrenched inequality fuel racial, ethnic, and class conflicts within and between nations. These are global problems, transnational problems, cross-cultural problems. Human beings need to find a way to communicate and cooperate across the sociocultural boundaries that divide us, always recognizing the power dynamics involved in that process.

How can we do this? Anthropology teaches us that we may never understand exactly how it feels to be a member of a different culture or group within our own culture. But if we want to work together with people of different sociocultural backgrounds to solve these pressing global issues, we have to try. Long-term fieldwork and cross-cultural collaboration are not perfect solutions to the challenges of cross-cultural understanding, but these methods give us a place to begin. And anthropological methods and insights can be transformative, making possible the kinds of empathy and dialogue necessary to solve our global problems.

The goal of this anthropology textbook is to guide you in this process of transformation as you learn about the cultural lives of the various peoples with whom you share this planet.

MINI-FIELDWORK ACTIVITY

Representation and Otherness

List three characters from fictional movies or television shows who represent people from cultures different from your own. What adjectives would you use to describe these characters? How are they made to appear? How do they act? Are they central or marginal characters? What role does each play in the plot or theme? What might be the consequences of representing cultural groups in this way? Do you see evidence of ethnocentrism, primitivism, and/or orientalism as described in this chapter?

Suggested Readings

Engelke, Matthew. 2018. *How to Think Like an Anthropologist.* Princeton: Princeton University Press.

Hastrup, Kirsten, ed. 2014. *Anthropology and Nature.* Routledge Studies in Anthropology 14. New York: Routledge.

Otto, Ton, and Nils Bubandt, eds. 2010. *Experiments in Holism: Theory and Practice in Contemporary Anthropology.* Malden, MA: Wiley-Blackwell.

Key Terms

Anthropocene the contemporary period of increasing human impact on the ecosystems of our planet.

anthropology the study of humanity across time and space.

archaeoastronomy the study of how people in the past understood and used celestial objects for navigation, calendars, politics, and the timing of ritual events.

archaeology the field of anthropology that relies on the excavation of artifacts and fossils to explore how environmental and historical conditions have produced a diversity of human cultures.

artifacts objects made by humans, such as pottery or tools.

biological anthropology the field of anthropology that focuses on the earliest processes in the biological and sociocultural development of human beings as well as the biological diversity of contemporary humans. Biological anthropologists study the origins, evolution, and diversity of our species.

cultural anthropology the field of anthropology devoted to describing and understanding the wide variety of human cultures. Cultural anthropologists focus on such things as social thought, action, ritual, values, and institutions.

cultural other a stereotype of a person from a different culture, used to create a cultural distinction between "us" and "them."

cultural relativism understanding every element of culture within the broader whole of that culture. Cultural relativism highlights how each belief or practice is related to all of the other beliefs and practices in a culture.

enculturation the process of learning and acquiring a particular culture, often intensified in childhood.

ethnobotany the study of how people in different cultures categorize and use plants for food, shelter, tools, transportation, art, and religion.

ethnocentrism the notion that one's own culture is so superior that no other culture is worth consideration. Ethnocentric people often imagine that the world would be a much better place if the beliefs, values, and practices of their own culture were spread to or imposed on everyone else in the world.

ethnography a written book or article about a particular culture.

excavation the removal of fossils and artifacts from the ground in order to learn as much as possible about how people lived in times before and after the development of writing.

fieldwork a research method that requires cultural anthropologists to live for many months or years in the societies they study, adopting local ways of living, eating, dressing, and speaking as closely as possible.

forensic anthropology the application of the techniques of biological anthropology to solve crimes.

fossils the remains of organism preserved in the environment.

holism how the elements of human life are bound together to form distinctive cultures.

hominins the evolutionary ancestors of modern humans.

insider's point of view a goal of anthropological research, representing the perspectives of people who practice a particular culture.

linguistic anthropology the field of anthropology that explores the central role of language in human cultural life. Linguistic anthropologists study the origins of language, how language shapes thought, and how language operates as a tool of power.

orientalism the depiction of some cultural groups, particularly people from the Middle East and Asia, as exotic, irrational, fanatical, and sensuous.

primitivism the depiction of some cultural groups, particularly Africans and Native Americans, as exotic, simple, highly sexual, potentially violent, and closer to nature.

Summary

Anthropology is an incredibly broad discipline, covering the entire scope of human experience, but its enormity is controlled by a common narrative and set of three central commitments. The common narrative states that human beings have developed flexible biological and social features that have worked together in a wide variety of environmental and historical conditions to produce a diversity of cultures. The three central commitments are exploring sociocultural diversity, examining how societies hold together, and studying the interdependence of humans and nature.

Anthropologists have developed four main approaches to pursuing anthropology's common narrative, comprising the discipline's four fields: biological anthropology, archaeology, cultural anthropology, and linguistic anthropology. Each of these fields generates a particular type of knowledge about the human experience that can be integrated with knowledge from the other three fields into a deeper, richer understanding of humanity's central challenges, such as racial injustice and climate change.

Getting at that deeper understanding, anthropologists learn to recognize their own biases as forms of ethnocentrism such as primitivism and orientalism. Rather than categorizing societies according to levels of sophistication (as European scholars did in the 19th century), contemporary anthropologists use holistic techniques of examination and analysis, seeking to understand how the various elements within a culture fit together and how these elements can contradict one another, provoking change. Effective holistic analysis requires a commitment to the method of cultural relativism, which requires a researcher to set aside their own personal values in order to appreciate another culture on its own terms. An important contribution to a rich appreciation of another culture is the input and participation of cultural insiders. The ethical challenges of understanding and representing another culture have led anthropologists to develop collaborative ways of working with cultural insiders, aimed at addressing the power asymmetries of fieldwork and ethnography.

Critical Thinking Questions

1. Have you ever taken a course in one of the other social disciplines, such as economics, political science, history, or religion? How would anthropology study the same subject matter in a different way?
2. Which other social issues might benefit from a four-field approach? Propose one issue, and consider how each of the four fields might contribute to our understanding of that issue.
3. Have you ever thought or said something ethnocentric? What is an appropriate response if someone else says something ethnocentric in a conversation? How can people learn to recognize and rethink ethnocentric notions?
4. As mentioned in this chapter, one very dominant way of evaluating the sophistication of different societies is by measuring the amount of wealth generated by each one. Can you think of an alternative way of evaluating progress or development? Would that way reorder the global hierarchy? How might it change your way of thinking about your own society?
5. Identify a contemporary problem in your own society. How would you pursue a holistic analysis of that problem? What are the various realms of culture that directly or indirectly relate to that problem?
6. Is it really possible to set aside your own personal values when studying something you consider morally troubling or simply wrong? Identify a controversial topic in your own or another culture, ideally one that is personally meaningful to you. How would you practice cultural relativism when studying this topic? How would relativism change the way you interact with people in the course of your research? How would it change the kinds of questions you would ask in interviews?
7. Make a list of possible ways you could collaborate with someone from another social or cultural group in an effort to represent the perspectives of cultural insiders.

Bibliography

Ahmad, Attiya. 2017. *Everyday Conversions: Islam, Domestic Work, and South Asian Migrant Women in Kuwait.* Durham, NC: Duke University Press.

Ball, Christopher. 2018. *Exchanging Words: Language, Ritual, and Relationality in Brazil's Xingu Indigenous Park.* Albuquerque: University of New Mexico Press.

Bayly, Susan. 1999. *Caste, Society, and Politics in India from the Eighteenth Century to the Modern Age.* The New Cambridge History of India, vol. 4, no. 3. Cambridge: Cambridge University Press.

Bielo, James S. 2018. *Ark Encounter: The Making of a Creationist Theme Park.* New York: New York University Press.

Boserup, Esther. (1970) 2007. *Woman's Role in Economic Development.* London: Earthscan.

Carr, E. Summerson. 2011. *Scripting Addiction: The Politics of Therapeutic Talk and American Sobriety.* Princeton, NJ: Princeton University Press.

Dillehay, Tom D., ed. 2017. *Where the Land Meets the Sea: Fourteen Millennia of Human History at Huaca Prieta, Peru.* Austin: University of Texas Press.

Edwards, David B. 2017. *Caravan of Martyrs: Sacrifice and Suicide Bombing in Afghanistan.* Oakland: University of California Press.

Fredericks, Rosalind. 2018. *Garbage Citizenship: Vital Infrastructures of Labor in Dakar, Senegal.* Durham, NC: Duke University Press.

Fuentes, Agustín. 2012. *Race, Monogamy, and Other Lies They Told You: Busting Myths about Human Nature.* Berkeley: University of California Press.

Goody, Jack. 1976. *Production and Reproduction: A Comparative Study of the Domestic Domain.* Cambridge: Cambridge University Press.

Haas, Randall, James Watson, Tammy Buonasera, John Southon, Jennifer C. Chen, Sarah Noe, Kevin Smith, Carlos Viviano Llave, Jelmer Eerkens, and Glendon Parker. 2020. "Female Hunters of the Early Americas." *Science Advances* 6 (45): eabd0310. https://doi.org/10.1126/sciadv.abd0310.

Halvaksz, Jamon. 2006. "Drug Bodies: Relations with Substance in the Wau Bulolo Valley." *Oceania* 76 (3): 235–244.

Heatherington, Tracey. 2010. *Wild Sardinia: Indigeneity and the Global Dreamtimes of Environmentalism.* Seattle: University of Washington Press.

Isbell, Lynne A. 2009. *The Fruit, the Tree, and the Serpent: Why We See So Well.* Cambridge, MA: Harvard University Press.

Jablonski, Nina G. 2006. *Skin: A Natural History.* Berkeley: University of California Press.

Keim, Curtis, and Carolyn Somerville. 2018. *Mistaking Africa: Curiosities and Inventions of the American Mind.* 4th ed. New York: Routledge.

Kirsch, Stuart. 2018. *Engaged Anthropology: Politics beyond the Text.* Oakland: University of California Press.

Lassiter, Luke E. 1998. *The Power of Kiowa Song: A Collaborative Ethnography.* Tucson: University of Arizona Press.

Lassiter, Luke E. 2005. "Collaborative Ethnography and Public Anthropology." *Current Anthropology* 46 (1): 83–106.

Malinowski, Bronislaw. 1922. *Argonauts of the Western Pacific: An Account of Native Enterprise and Adventure in the Archipelagoes of Melanesian New Guinea.* London: Routledge.

Millar, Kathleen M. 2018. *Reclaiming the Discarded: Life and Labor on Rio's Garbage Dump.* Durham, NC: Duke University Press.

Miller, Daniel. 2019. "Smartphones: The Cultural, Individual and Technical Processes That Make Them Smart." The Conversation. January 8, 2019. https://theconversation.com/smartphones-the-cultural-individual-and-technical-processes-that-make-them-smart-106560.

Mintz, Sidney W. 1985. *Sweetness and Power: The Place of Sugar in Modern History.* New York: Viking.

Mohr, Sebastian. 2018. *Being a Sperm Donor: Masculinity, Sexuality, and Biosociality in Denmark.* New York: Berghahn Books.

Morgan, Marcyliena. 2009. *The Real Hiphop: Battling for Knowledge, Power, and Respect in the LA Underground.* Durham, NC: Duke University Press.

Nittle, Nadra Kareem. 2021. "Common Arab Stereotypes in TV and Film." ThoughtCo. March 18, 2021. https://www.thoughtco.com/tv-film-stereotypes-arabs-middle-easterners-2834648.

Orser, Charles E., Jr. 2007. *The Archaeology of Race and Racialization in Historic America*. Gainesville: University Press of Florida.

Peregrine, Peter Neal. 2018. "Boas, Franz (1858–1942)." In *The International Encyclopedia of Anthropology*, edited by Hilary Callan. Wiley Online Library. https://doi.org/10.1002/9781118924396.wbiea1299.

Ralph, Laurence. 2014. *Renegade Dreams: Living through Injury in Gangland Chicago*. Chicago: University of Chicago Press.

Said, Edward. 1979. *Orientalism*. New York: Vintage Books.

Schaik, Carel van. 2004. *Among Orangutans: Red Apes and the Rise of Human Culture*. Cambridge, MA: Belknap Press of Harvard University Press.

Singleton, Theresa A, ed. (1985) 2016. *The Archaeology of Slavery and Plantation Life*. New York: Routledge.

Stanley, Henry Morton. 1878. *Through the Dark Continent; or, The Sources of the Nile around the Great Lakes of Equatorial Africa and down the Livingstone River to the Atlantic Ocean*. London.

Torres, Jada Benn, and Gabriel A. Torres Colón. 2021. *Genetic Ancestry: Our Stories, Our Pasts*. New York: Routledge.

Tourigny, Eric. 2020. "Do All Dogs Go to Heaven? Tracking Human-Animal Relationships through the Archaeological Survey of Pet Cemeteries." *Antiquity* 94 (378): 1614–1629. https://doi.org/10.15184/aqy.2020.191.

CHAPTER 2
Methods: Cultural and Archaeological

Figure 2.1 These archaeologists are working to uncover a fresco on a building in Pompeii, Italy. Pompeii was famously covered in ash when nearby Mount Vesuvius erupted in 79 CE. The ash has preserved many structures and artifacts from the time. (credit: "Pompeii Restoration Work" by Justin Ennis/flickr, CC BY 2.0)

CHAPTER OUTLINE

INTRODUCTION Fieldwork is one of the most important practices of anthropology. While all of the subfields of anthropology conduct fieldwork in some form to gather information, each subfield may use different methods of conducting research. The concept of working in "the field" was traditionally based on the practice of traveling to distant regions to study other cultures within their native environmental contexts. In recent decades, "the field" has broadened to include diverse settings such as one's hometown (as in urban anthropology), the Internet (visual or virtual anthropology), or collections in university archives and museums (ethnohistory or museum anthropology).

2.1 Archaeological Research Methods

LEARNING OUTCOMES

By the end of this section, you will be able to:

- Describe archaeological techniques for uncovering artifacts.
- Explain the importance of context in making sense of artifacts and describe how researchers record content while working in the field.
- Describe the law of superposition as used in the field of archaeology.
- Describe the different types of relative dating methods used by archaeologists.
- Identify and briefly define four absolute or chronometric dating methods.

Many people have an inherent fascination with the human past. Perhaps this fascination stems from the fact that people recognize themselves in the objects left behind by those who have lived before. Relics of past civilizations, in the form of human-made cultural **artifacts**, temples, and burial remains, are the means by which we can begin to understand the thoughts and worldviews of ancient peoples. In the quest to understand these ancient societies, human curiosity has sometimes led to fantastical myths about races of giant humans, dragons, and even extraterrestrial beings. In the realm of archaeology, less speculative methods are used to study the human past. Scientific approaches and techniques are the foundation of archaeology today.

Archaeological Techniques

In archaeology, the first step in conducting field research is to do a survey of an area that has the potential to reveal surface artifacts or cultural debris. Surveys can be done by simply walking across a field, or they may involve using various technologies, such as drones or Google Earth, to search for unusual topography and potential structures that would be difficult to see from the ground. Cultural artifacts that are found may become the basis for an **archaeological excavation** of the site. A random sampling of excavation units or test pits can determine a site's potential based on the quantity of cultural materials found. GPS coordinates are often collected for each piece of cultural debris, along with notes on specific plants and animal found at the site, which can be indicators of potential natural resources. **Features** such as trails, roads, and house pits are documented and included in a full set of field notes. Government agencies have different protocols about what constitutes an archaeological site; the standard in many areas is six cultural objects found in close proximity to one another.

When preparing a site for excavation, archaeologists will divide the entire site into square sections using a grid system, which involves roping off measured squares over the surface of the site. This grid system enables archaeologists to document and map all artifacts and features as they are found in situ (in the original location). All objects and features uncovered are assigned catalog or accession numbers, which are written on labels and attached to the artifacts. These labels are especially important if artifacts are removed from the site.

Excavation is a slow process. Archaeologists work with trowels and even toothbrushes to carefully remove earth from around fragile bone and other artifacts. Soil samples may be collected to conduct pollen studies. **Ecofacts**—objects of natural origins, such as seeds, shells, or animal bones—found at a site may be examined by other specialists, such as **zooarchaeologists**, who study animal remains, or **archaeobotanists**, who specialize in the analysis of floral (plant) remains with an interest in the historical relationships between plants and people over time.

Every cultural and natural object and feature is fully documented in the field notes, with its exact placement and coordinates recorded on a map using the grid system as a guide. These coordinates represent an object's **primary context**. If uncovered objects are moved before documentation takes place, the archaeologist will lose the **archaeological context** of that object and its associated data. Archaeological context is the key foundation of archaeological principles and practice. In order to understand the significance and even age of artifacts, features, and ecofacts, one needs to know their context and association with other objects as they were found in situ. Objects that have been removed from their primary context are said to be in a **secondary context**.

Careful and proper documentation is vitally important. This information becomes part of the archaeological record and guides and contributes to future research and analysis.

FIGURE 2.2 This dig site in Vindolanda, England has yielded thousands of artifacts left behind by Roman occupiers in the years 85 – 370 CE. (credit: "Digging Archaeology 4" by Son of Groucho/flickr, CC BY 2.0)

Archaeological Dating Methods

Establishing the age of cultural objects is an important element of archaeological research. Determining the age of both a site and the artifacts found within is key to understanding how human cultures developed and changed over time. Other areas of science, such as paleontology and geology, also use dating techniques to understand animal and plant species in the ancient past and how the earth and animal species evolved over time.

Relative Dating

The earliest dating methods utilized the principles of **relative dating**, developed in geology. Observing exposed cliffsides in canyons, geologists noted layers of different types of stone that they called **strata** (**stratum** in the singular). They hypothesized that the strata at the bottom were older than the strata higher up; this became known as the **law of superposition**. According to the law of superposition, not just geological layers but also the objects found within them can be assigned relative ages based on the assumption that objects in deeper layers are older than objects in layers above. The application of the law of superposition to archaeological fieldwork is sometimes called **stratigraphic superposition**. This method assumes that any cultural or natural artifact that is found within a stratum, or that cuts across two or more strata in a **cross-cutting relationship**, is younger than the stratum itself, as each layer would have taken a long time to form and, unless disturbed, would have remained stable for a very long time. Examples of forces that might cause disturbances in strata include natural forces such as volcanos or floods and the intervention of humans, animals, or plants.

The law of superposition was first proposed in 1669 by the Danish scientist Nicolas Steno. Some of the first applications of this law by scholars provided ages for megafauna (large animals, most commonly mammals) and dinosaur bones based on their positions in the earth. It was determined that the mammalian megafauna and the dinosaur bones had been deposited tens of thousands of years apart, with the dinosaur remains being much older. These first indications of the true age of fossil remains suggested a revolutionary new understanding of the scale of geological time.

It was eventually determined that if a specific set and sequence of strata is noted in several sites and over a large enough area, it can be assumed that the ages will be the same for the same strata at different locations in the area. This insight enabled geologists and archaeologists to use the structures of soils and rocks to date phenomena noted throughout a region based on their relative positions. Archaeologists call this method *archaeological stratification*, and they look for stratified layers of artifacts to determine human cultural contexts. Stratigraphic layers found below cultural layers provide a basis for determining age, with layers above assumed to be more recent than those below.

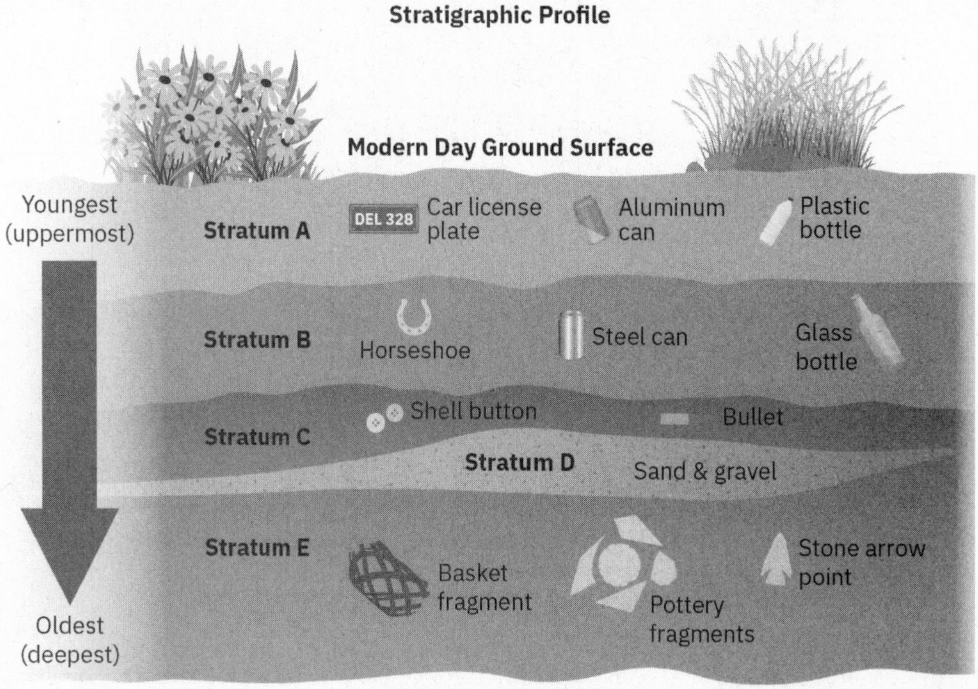

FIGURE 2.3 According to the principle of superposition objects found at deeper layers (called stratum) are older than those found above. In this illustration, the pottery fragments in Stratum E can be assumed to be older than the shell buttons found in Stratum C. The objects nearest the surface (aluminum can, plastic bottle) are obviously most recent. (attribution: Copyright Rice University, OpenStax, under CC BY 4.0 license)

Another method of dating utilized by archaeologists relies on **typological sequences**. This method compares created objects to other objects of similar appearance with the goal of determining how they are related. This method is employed by many subdisciplines of archaeology to understand the relationships between common objects. For example, typological sequencing is often conducted on spearpoints created by Indigenous peoples by comparing the types of points found at different locations and analyzing how they changed over time based on their relative positions in an archaeological site.

Another form of typological sequencing involves the process of **seriation**. Seriation is a relative dating method in which artifacts are placed in chronological order once they are determined to be of the same culture. English Egyptologist, Flinders Petrie introduced seriation in the 19th century. He developed the method to date burials he was uncovering that contained no evidence of their dates and could not be sequenced through **stratigraphy**. To address the problem, he developed a system of dating layers based on pottery (see Figure 2.4).

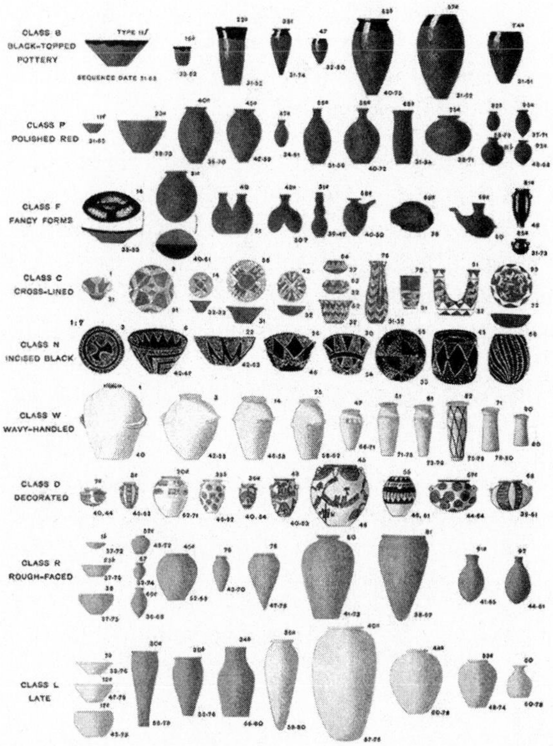

FIGURE 2.4 Petrie's Egyptian pottery seriation method is built upon the observation that styles change with time. Petrie arranged pottery artifacts into similar groups based on stylistic features and placed them along a relative timeline based on these features. (credit: "Evolution of Egyptian prehistoric pottery styles, from Naqada I to Naqada II and Naqada III" by W. M. Flinders Petrie and A. C. Mace/Wikimedia Commons, Public Domain)

Typological sequences of pottery, stone tools, and other objects that survive in archaeological sites are not only used to provide dating estimates. They can also reveal much about changes in culture, social structure, and worldviews over time. For example, there are significant changes in stratigraphy during the agricultural age, or Neolithic period, at around 12,000 BCE. These changes include the appearance of tended soils, pollens that indicate the cultivation of specific plants, evidence of more sedentary living patterns, and the increased use of pottery as the storage of food and grain became increasingly important. Archaeological evidence also shows a growing population and the development of a more complex cultural and economic system, which involved ownership of cattle and land and the beginning of trade. Trade activities can be determined when pottery types associated with one site appear in other nearby or distant locations. Recognizing the connections between objects used in trade can shed light on possible economic and political interrelationships between neighboring communities and settlements.

Chronometric Dating Methods

Chronometric dating methods, also known as **absolute dating methods**, are methods of dating that rely on chemical or physical analysis of the properties of archaeological objects. Using chronometric methods, archaeologists can date objects to a range that is more precise than can be achieved via relative dating methods. **Radiocarbon dating**, which uses the radioactive isotope carbon-14 (^{14}C), is the most common method used to date organic materials. Once a living organism dies, the carbon within it begins to decay at a known rate. The amount of the remaining residual carbon can be measured to determine, within a margin of error of 50 years, when the organism died. The method is only valid for samples of organic tissue between 300 and 50,000 years old. To ensure accuracy, objects collected for testing are promptly sealed in nonporous containers so that no atmospheric organic substances, such as dust, pollen, or bacteria, can impact the results.

Dating systems that measure the atomic decay of uranium or the decay of potassium into argon are used to date nonorganic materials such as rocks. The rates of decay of radioactive materials are known and can be measured. The radioactive decay clock begins when the elements are first created, and this decay can be measured to determine when the objects were created and/or used in the past. Volcanic materials are particularly useful for dating sites because volcanoes deposit lava and ash over wide areas, and all the material from an eruption will have a similar chemical signature. Once the ash is dated, cultural materials can also be dated based on their position relative to the ash deposit.

The technique of **dendrochronology** relies on measuring tree rings to determine the age of ancient structures or dwellings that are made of wood. Tree rings develop annually and vary in width depending on the quantity of nutrients and water available in a specific year. Cross dating is accomplished by matching patterns of wide and narrow rings between core samples taken from similar trees in different locations. This information can then be applied to date archaeological remains that contain wood, such as posts and beams. Dendrochronology has been used at the Pueblo Bonita archaeological site in Chaco Canyon, New Mexico, to help date house structures that were occupied by the Pueblo people between 800 and 1150 CE. The Laboratory of Tree-Ring Research, based in Tucson, is the world's oldest dendrochronology lab. Go on a tree-ring expedition! (https://openstax.org/r/tree-ring)

The most effective approach for dating archaeological objects is to apply a variety of dating techniques, which allows the archaeologist to triangulate or correlate data. Correlating multiple methods of dating provides strong evidence for the specific time period of an archaeological site.

Strategy	What It Is	How It Is Seen	How It Is Read	Assumptions
Dendrochronology	Tree ring width pattern	Growth in life, ring	Count rings and measure	1 ring = 1 year; no duplication or missed rings; regional comparability
^{14}C	Radioactive decay and atom counting	Decay after death	Count beta decay or ^{14}C per unit volume	Half-life of ^{14}C-^{12}C decay known; exchange with atmosphere and productions rates constant

TABLE 2.1 Chronometric Dating Techniques

2.2 Conservation and Naturalism

LEARNING OUTCOMES

By the end of this section, you will be able to:

- Describe conservation efforts undertaken in the United States in the 19th century.
- Define salvage anthropology and describe its origins and methods.
- Provide an example of an anthropologist who used their research to help the people they were studying.
- Explain why museums can be said to have created exhibits reflecting limited interpretations and describe efforts to correct this limitation.

Early Efforts

The conservation movement began in the 19th century as people in Europe and America began to realize that human settlement and the exploitation of the world's natural resources had led to the destruction or endangerment of numerous animals, plants, and significant environments. Efforts began in the 1860s to understand and protect the remaining natural landscapes and habitats. These efforts were partly motivated by concern for wildlife and natural areas. However, also significant were the concerns of sporting organizations and recreationists. The primary aim of early conservation efforts was to preserve significant natural ecosystems for parks or wilderness areas so that sportspeople and outdoor enthusiasts would have places to hunt, fish, and explore. Many areas preserved by these early efforts are still protected today, such as Yellowstone and Yosemite National Parks in the United States.

An element of this early period of conservation was the effort to collect specimens for display in natural history museums. This collection effort was part of a movement known as **naturalism**, which seeks to understand the world and the laws that govern it by direct observation of nature. The late 19th and early 20th centuries saw a marked growth in naturalist collections worldwide as many cities and nations sought to establish and fill their own natural history museums. These collections have been particularly useful to zooarchaeologists and archaeobotanists, who use specimen collections of mammals, birds, fish, and plants to identify natural objects and animal remains found at human burial sites. Many archaeology labs have collections of animal skeletons for comparative anatomy, analysis, and identification (see Figure 2.5).

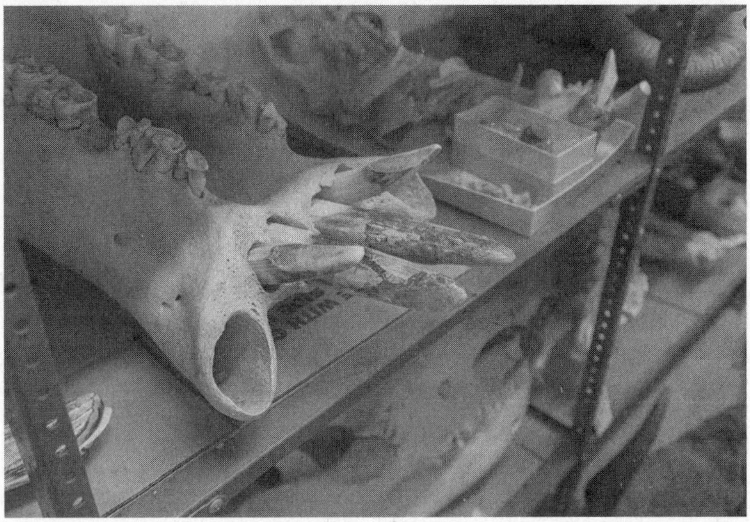

FIGURE 2.5 Collections of bones, such as this collection of specimens from various animal species housed at the Wildlife Forensics Lab in Ashland, Oregon, serve as a useful resource for zooarchaeologists. (credit: "Wildlife Forensics Lab" by US Fish and Wildlife Service Headquarters/flickr, Public Domain)

In addition to animal specimens, Native American baskets and other Indigenous art objects were collected and placed in natural history museums. When visiting the Auckland Museum in Auckland, New Zealand, visitors today encounter two large totem poles in the foyer. Northwest Coast totem poles are common in most older museums throughout the world. These totem poles were gathered from America's Northwest Coast in the late 19th and early 20th centuries as part of the worldwide conservation and naturalism movement. Most museums sought to purchase such artifacts, but in some cases, artifacts were stolen when Indigenous owners were unwilling to sell them. Many natural history museums also established dioramas depicting both Indigenous peoples and animals in their "natural" world. The practice of installing dioramas of Indigenous people is now heavily criticized because of the implication that Indigenous peoples are akin to animals and plants. Many museums have stopped this practice and have even dropped the phrase *natural history* from their names. However, the Smithsonian Institution's National Museum of Natural History in Washington, DC, and the American Museum of Natural History in New York both maintain the designation and still display dioramas of Indigenous peoples.

FIGURE 2.6 This diorama of Native Americans is on display in the Indiana State Museum in Indianapolis, Indiana. Such dioramas have come under criticism for the way that they depict Indigenous peoples and cultures. (credit: "Native Americans – Indiana State Museum – DSC00394" by Daderot/Wikimedia Commons, Public Domain)

Salvage Anthropology

Connected to the collecting of Indigenous artifacts is a practice known as **salvage anthropology**. Salvage anthropology was an effort to collect the material culture of Indigenous peoples in the United States and other parts of the world who were believed to be going extinct in the later 19th century. During this period, many anthropologists dedicated themselves to collecting material objects, stories, language lists, and ethnographies from tribal peoples worldwide. Many collections were made through legitimate means, such as purchasing objects or sitting down with collaborators (called *informants* in older anthropological vernacular) to record traditional stories, but some collecting involved the theft of tribal cultural items or purchases from intermediary traders.

Many of these anthropologists were hired by the Bureau of American Ethnology (BAE), a division of the Smithsonian Institution, and spent considerable time living with Native peoples on the reservations that were by then home to most Native Americans. Language was a special research focus for linguists and anthropologists, as many Native languages were rapidly going extinct. Through analysis of language, an anthropologist can understand the meaning of words and their context as well as gain a sense of a culture's philosophy and worldviews.

Anthropologists were not paid well to do this work for the BAE. Some began supplementing their income by buying cultural objects at a low cost from the people they studied and selling those objects at a much higher rate to museums. This practice is now acknowledged as unethical and exploitative. The anthropological research of this period has also been criticized for focusing solely on cultural knowledge while ignoring the hardships faced by the culture. For example, few anthropologists chose to help their subjects address the circumstances of living in poverty on the reservations.

Leonard J. Frachtenberg was an anthropologist working during the salvage anthropology period who did take action to help the people he was studying. Around the turn of the 20th century, Frachtenberg was conducting research to collect the languages of the people living on the Siletz Reservation, in Lincoln County, on Oregon's coast. He worked extensively with collaborators from the Coos, Coquille, Lower Umpqua, and Alsea tribes—some of whom were living at the Siletz Reservation and some who had returned to their native lands—and published a series of **oral histories** based on his research. He also helped the tribes locate lost unratified treaties from the 1850s and use those treaties to successfully sue the federal government. In the treaties, the government had promised to pay the Indigenous peoples of Oregon's coast for their ancestral land if they peacefully relocated to the Siletz Reservation. The people upheld their part of the bargain, but they never received any payment. Frachtenberg helped a Coquille man named George Wasson travel to Washington, DC, and locate copies of the treaties in the National Archives. In 1908, the tribes began the process of successfully suing the federal government for payment for their lands. This process took some 40 years to complete for many tribes, and not all tribes have been fairly paid to this day.

Museum Collections

Most of the materials collected by anthropologists during the period of salvage anthropology ended up in museums and university archives. Many natural history museums now display large dioramas featuring the material objects of numerous tribes. Museum research libraries house extensive collections of manuscripts and ethnographies. Archaeologists have contributed to these collections as well; many museums contain large collections of human remains. Indigenous peoples have criticized these collections, especially the gathering of human remains, which is seen as sacrilegious. Today, there are millions of sets of human remains (some full skeletons, but most single bones) in museum repositories that have never been studied and perhaps never will be.

Anthropologists spent so much of their time in the early period collecting that they had little time to study or analyze what they found. Many collections were put in storage after the anthropologists who had gathered them moved on to a new project or passed away. There are currently millions of material artifacts and ethnographic manuscripts that have never been fully studied. These archived materials offer research opportunities for anthropologists as well as for Indigenous peoples, who are making use of these collections to help recover parts of their cultures that were lost due to the assimilation policies of the past 200 years.

One person who has taken advantage of these archives is linguistic anthropologist Henry Zenk. Zenk has spent years studying the languages and cultures of the tribes of western Oregon, specifically the Chinook, Kalapuya, and Molalla tribes. He conducted research with the Grand Ronde tribe in the 1970s and 1980s and became a proficient speaker of Chinuk Wawa, a trade language spoken by tribes from southern Alaska to northern California and as far east as Montana. He has taught the language at the Grand Ronde Reservation for nearly 30 years. He is also one of the experts on the Kalapuya languages, spoken by the Kalapuya tribes of the Willamette and Umpqua Valleys, and in 2013, he began a project to translate the Melville Jacobs Kalapuya notebooks.

Melville Jacobs was an anthropologist from the University of Washington who studied the languages of the Northwest Coast from 1928 until his death in 1971. He filled more than 100 field notebooks with information on the languages of the peoples of western Oregon, with a special focus on Kalapuya. Jacobs published a book of Kalapuya oral histories in 1945, *Kalapuya Texts*. He also worked with Kalapuya speaker John Hudson to translate numerous texts prepared by earlier anthropologists Leonard Frachtenberg and Albert Gatschet. Jacobs and Hudson were able to translate several of these previously gathered texts, but many remained untranslated when Hudson died in 1953. Zenk, along with colleague Jedd Schrock, spent many years first learning Kalapuya and then translating a set of the Jacobs notebooks that recorded the knowledge and history of a Kalapuya man named Louis Kenoyer. In 2017, Zenk and Schrock published *My Life, by Louis Kenoyer: Reminiscences of a Grand Ronde Reservation Childhood*. Zenk and Schrock's work is a fine example of the research possibilities offered by the existing work of previous anthropologists.

Zenk worked closely with the Grand Ronde tribe on this project and endeavored to make sure that the translation of Kenoyer's story would benefit the people of the tribe to help them to better understand their own history. His research and work with members of the Grand Ronde tribe spanned 50 years, beginning with his PhD project, which involved extensive work with Grand Ronde members, who at the time were not a federally recognized tribe. In the 1990s, Zenk began working with the tribe to teach Chinuk Wawa to tribal members. The tribe today has an extensive language immersion project to teach the language to young people. Zenk has been a consistent influence, serving as advisor, teacher, master-apprentice instructor, and researcher. Zenk's work has helped the tribe recover parts of its culture and history that had been lost for many decades.

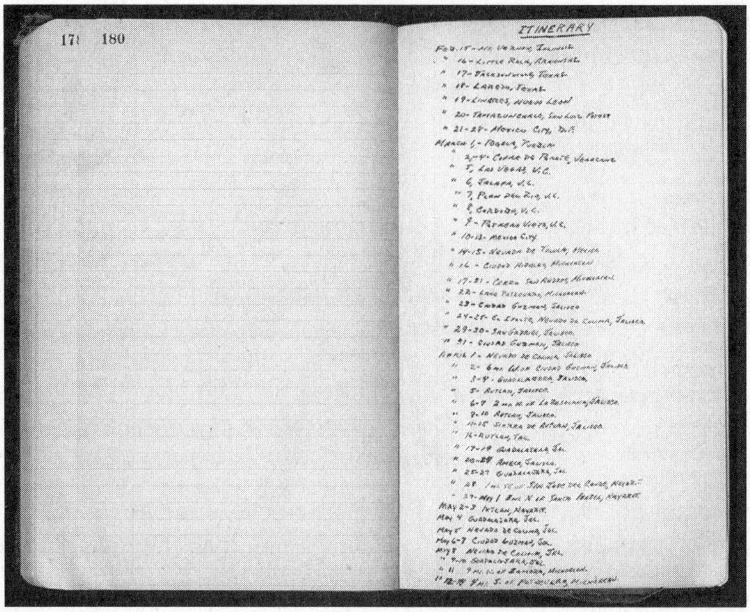

FIGURE 2.7 This page of an anthropologist's field notebook from 1949 contains a travel itinerary for several months. Contemporary anthropologists are likely to have such information in digital format. (credit: "Field Notes – Mexico, 1949 (Page 180) BHL46264382" by James Arthur Peters/Biodiversity Heritage Library/Wikimedia Commons)

PROFILES IN ANTHROPOLOGY

Albert Gatschet
1832–1907

FIGURE 2.8 Albert Gatschet was a Swiss-American ethnologist who pioneered the scientific study of Native

American languages. Here he is at age 61. (credit: "PSM V41 D306 Albert S Gatschet" by *Popular Science Monthly*/Wikimedia Commons, Public Domain)

Personal History: Albert Gatschet was a Swiss philologist and ethnologist who emigrated to the United States in 1868. He had a great interest in linguistics and Native American languages, and he gained attention in 1872 for his comparative analysis of 16 southeastern tribal vocabularies, which opened up new areas of research in linguistics. In 1877, he was hired to work on the Geographical and Geological Survey of the Rocky Mountain Region as an ethnologist. He also collected many notebooks of languages from Native peoples in California and Oregon. He is most noted for his studies of the languages of the southeastern tribes and his ethnography of the Klamath Tribes of Oregon.

Gatschet was fluent in numerous languages and published in English, French, and German in the United States and Europe during his career. He also became quite fluent in numerous Native languages. His first large work was *Orts-etymologische Forschungen aus der Schweiz* (Etymological research on place names from Switzerland, 1865–1867), a study of Swiss place names that is still the standard authority today.

Area of Anthropology: Philology, ethnology, linguistics

Accomplishments in the Field: One of Gatschet's most significant analyses was of the southeastern tribal languages, principally the Timucua language of northern Florida. Based on analysis of the notes of the Catholic priest Father Pareja, who had collected language texts from the Timucua people in 1612–1614, Gatschet determined that Timucua was a distinct language group that had gone extinct. Gatschet also examined the Catawba language of South Carolina, concluding that it was related to the Siouan languages of the western Great Plains. From 1881 to 1885, Gatschet worked in Louisiana, discovering two new languages and completing ethnographic descriptions of the southern tribes. In 1886, he found the last speakers of the Biloxi and Tunica languages and related them to the Siouan languages as well. He published his studies of the Gulf tribes in the two-volume work *A Migration Legend of the Creek Indians* (1884, 1888).

In 1877 and 1878, Gatschet spent time among the tribes of the Grand Ronde Reservation in Oregon. He collected some of the first professional field notes on the Kalapuya, Molala, and Shasta languages from some of the last speakers, and he published and made notes about the Kalapuya mounds. Upon leaving the reservation, he spent time researching the traditions of the Tualatin Kalapuya people in their traditional lands in the Tualatin Valley. He then went to the Klamath Reservation, where he collected field notes on the Klamath language. He worked his field notes into a two-part work, *The Klamath Indians of Southwestern Oregon* (1890), volume 2 of the US Department of the Interior's *Contributions to North American Ethnology*.

Gatschet was commissioned by the Bureau of American Ethnology (BAE) in 1891 to investigate the Algonquian people of the United States and Canada, a study he never fully completed. Illness forced him to retire, but near his death, he remained engaged in studies of Chinese languages.

After his death, his wife, Louise Horner Gatschet, sold his field notes to the BAE. She was also hired by the BAE to help translate much of his work. Gatschet's letters mention his wife being with him throughout his travels; she likely contributed in numerous ways to his field studies.

Importance of His Work : Gatschet was one of the first professional anthropologists to visit many tribes and was able to collect ethnographies and narratives from peoples who were gone within the next decade. He analyzed language families in the field and provided early frameworks of connected languages. Gatschet's work is fundamental to the study of the languages of western Oregon and the southeast Gulf area of the United States. His professional work, which applied rigorous methods to collect Native languages, predates much of the work of Franz Boas, who is credited with implementing scientific methods in the study of human societies.

Interpretation and Voice

There is increasing acknowledgement of the role of interpretation in the study of the human past. Although ideally grounded in well-conducted research and the best evidence available at the time, all conclusions about what might have been are based on the interpretations proposed by the authors of history. The backgrounds and viewpoints of those conducting research and publicizing findings play a significant role in the conclusions they reach and share with other scholars. Interpretation and perspective are affected by many factors, including racial category, nationality, religious beliefs, social status, political affiliation, ambitions, and education. For many years, anthropological studies were almost always conducted by White, male scholars who grew up in the Northern Hemisphere and were educated in the same system. These common backgrounds represent a significant interpretive bias.

After being accessioned into museums, many collections of cultural artifacts have not been altered in more than 100 years. When these material objects were initially placed on display, choices about their arrangement and the written descriptions that accompanied them were made by museum curators. Most of these curators did not reach out to the originators of the artifacts or their descendants for input, and many exhibits do not accurately depict or describe the objects on display. Museum exhibits have been found to contain inaccurate information about objects' material composition, makers, tribal cultures, collection sites, and proper use. Many other display objects are lacking this information altogether.

Several museums are now seeking the help of Native people to better understand and more accurately tell the story of their collections. These Native perspectives are correcting misconceptions about the meaning and context of cultural artifacts and providing correct information about basic things such as the materials and processes used in the objects' production. Native input is also guiding museums in making choices about how objects are arranged and displayed. This input has been invaluable in helping museums more accurately tell the stories and display the context of the peoples who originally created the objects on display.

2.3 Ethnography and Ethnology

LEARNING OUTCOMES

By the end of this chapter, you will be able to:

- Identify early anthropological practices pertaining to ethnography.
- Define ethnology and provide examples of how it is used in anthropology.
- Describe efforts to achieve multiple perspectives in anthropological research.
- Define feminist anthropology and describe its aims.

The Development of Ethnography and Ethnology

As discussed in What is Anthropology? ethnography is a method used by cultural anthropologists to create a description of a culture or society. Ethnographers gather and utilize information from many sources, such as fieldwork, museum collections, government records, and archaeological data. In the 19th century, a form of ethnography developed that was called **armchair anthropology**, in which theories about human societies and human behaviors were proposed solely based on secondhand information. Lewis Henry Morgan is a well-known practitioner of this type of research. The content of his most famous publication, *League of the Ho-dé-no-sau-nee, or Iroquois* (1851), was gathered primarily from other books he read. Morgan did meet with Native peoples at various times in his career, but he did not conduct ethnographic research among the Iroquois before writing *League of the Ho-dé-no-sau-nee, or Iroquois.*

In the later 19th century, numerous anthropologists and other scholars undertook research projects with hundreds of tribes throughout the Americas, many of them by then living solely on federal reservations. Many of these researchers were influenced by Columbia University professor Franz Boas, a German scientist who was originally trained as a physicist but became most famous as an anthropologist. Boas insisted that scholars obtain ethnographical information directly from the peoples they aimed to write about, rather than collecting information from other published sources. Boas quickly established himself as a leader in the field of anthropology and eventually took an associate role at the federal Bureau of American Ethnology.

FIGURE 2.9 Franz Boas is credited with establishing the standards of field research that became the foundation of contemporary anthropological practices. Here he is in 1915, 57 years old. (credit: “Franz Boas” by Canadian Museum of History/Wikimedia Commons, Public Domain)

Boas advocated for and published in all four fields of anthropology and asked many key questions in his scholarship. In his 1907 essay “Anthropology,” Boas identified two basic questions for anthropologists: “Why are the tribes and nations of the world different, and how have the present differences developed?” (Boas [1974] 1982, 269). Boas was responsible for hiring scholars and sending them out into the field to collect information about various Indigenous peoples. His standards of field research became the foundation of the contemporary science of anthropology.

One area of interest for early anthropologists was the similarities and differences between various Indigenous societies. This interest in comparison led to a branch of anthropology called **ethnology**, which is a cross-cultural comparison of different groups. In early anthropology, ethnology’s aim was to understand how various Indigenous societies were related to one another. This included the relations among language dialects, dress, and appearance and to what degree and in what direction various tribes had migrated from one location to another. Early anthropologists explored these questions with the hope of tracking changes in tribal cultures. Another leading concern was how Native peoples initially got to the Americas. Anthropologists have used the practices of ethnology to establish relationships and shared cultural elements that help illuminate migration patterns of peoples from the “old” to the “new” world. Ethnology is still a common practice in linguistics, archaeology, and biological anthropology.

Some additional uses of ethnology are fused with archaeological methods and analysis. Ethnoarchaeology is a form of archaeology in which, following methods largely created by American archaeologist Lewis Binford, archaeologists access ethnographic information about recent or existing human cultures to draw conclusions about human cultures in the archaeological past. In Binford’s 1978 study *Nunamiut Ethnoarchaeology*, he draws comparisons between the ways in which contemporary Indigenous peoples disposed of animal remains and the evidence observed in Nunamiut refuse sites. These comparisons inform a model that is used to understand more about how Indigenous peoples’ ancestors may have disposed of remains in the past. Such models are not perfect, but many Indigenous cultures have maintained aspects of their culture to the present day.

Perspective and Interpretation in Ethnography

Ethnography is still commonly used by cultural anthropologists. Practitioners today consult multiple informants during their research in order to gather a variety of perspectives on a culture or society. No one person has a full or authoritative view of their own culture; multiple viewpoints are essential to a full description. Many early anthropological studies only invited male perspectives, introducing a male bias into the resulting ethnographies. Now, anthropologists deliberately seek varied perspectives, consulting people of different genders and ages and who occupy different roles.

Anthropologists can introduce significant bias into an ethnography. The most challenging aspect of fieldwork in cultural anthropology is to observe and study another culture without bias. Having an **ethnocentric** or **etic perspective** means someone is judging a culture according to the standards of their own culture and belief system. To observe a culture from the perspective of the people being researched is to have an **emic perspective**. For anthropologists to be effective researchers, they must be able to observe and gather data from unbiased and emic perspectives. In addition, an anthropologist's **interpretation** of the information gathered can significantly alter their research findings. Earlier anthropologists were primarily male and White, so their findings were based on interpretations made through these lenses. **Feminist anthropology** attempts to address this male bias. Feminist anthropology is recognized as having begun as early as the 1850s, with attempts made (by male anthropologist) to include more information on women in their ethnographic research. In the 1920s, female anthropologists such as Zora Neale Hurston and Ruth Benedict began publishing in the field, but not until the 1928 publication of Margaret Mead's *Coming of Age in Samoa* did a female anthropologist gain prominence.

FIGURE 2.10 This U.S. postage stamp honors anthropologist Margaret Mead. Mead was one of the first female anthropologists to be acknowledged for her work and insights. (credit: "Margaret Mead Stamp" by John Curran/ flickr, CC BY 2.0)

Women's contributions and perspectives became much more pronounced in the later parts of the 20th century. Feminist anthropologists seek not only to claim a role for themselves in the field equal to that offered to men but also to expand the focal points of anthropological inquiry to include areas of life such as family, marriage, and child-rearing, as well as the economic and social roles played by women. The dominance of male anthropologists had biased analysis of human societies toward male-dominated roles and activities.

Many early archaeological research, for example, assigned no role to women in early societies or assumed that women's roles were limited to maintaining households and raising children. Evidence of women's subsistence and economic activities was either not looked for or ignored. It was also assumed that women in early societies had subservient roles to men, when in fact most early societies have now been found to be very egalitarian, with equal status accorded to women and men. Feminist anthropology has both expanded research to include women's roles and aimed to understand the gender roles in other societies on their own terms, rather than according to the gender roles of the researcher's own society.

Other perspectives emerged in anthropology in the 1970s as more members of minority groups began entering the field. One category of minority voices that has been a significant asset to anthropology is that of people with Indigenous ancestors. Practitioners with this type of background are part of a subfield called **Indigenous anthropology**. Indigenous anthropology is discussed in detail in Indigenous Anthropology.

2.4 Participant Observation and Interviewing

LEARNING OUTCOMES

By the end of this section, you will be able to:

- Define participant observation and identify best practices associated with it.
- Describe what makes a good informant for anthropological research.
- Describe best practices for conducting an interview from an unbiased and emic perspective.
- Explain the concept of ownership of cultural information.
- Identify the rights of study informants.
- List practices required by institutional review boards before research can begin.
- Describe the aim of long-term research projects in anthropology.

Participant Observation

Working in the field often places anthropologists in settings very different from what they are familiar with. Upon first arriving at an unfamiliar field location, it is common for anthropologists to feel out of place and uncomfortable as they adjust to a new culture and environment. Many anthropologists keep a daily log of their feeling and impressions in their new environment. Researchers studying other cultures practice a method called **participant observation**, which entails directly participating in the activities and events of a host culture and keeping records of observations about these activities.

Researchers may create various types of records of their interactions as participants and their observations about the host culture and environment. These might take the form of field notebooks, computer files, digital recordings, photographs, or film. Researchers working in the field may also collect objects that will remind them of the culture they are studying, often memorabilia such as maps, tourism brochures, books, or crafts made by the people they are observing.

Some researchers regularly record impressions of activities while they are occurring so that they do not forget to make note of important aspects of the culture. But many researchers will wait to take photos, draw images, or write in their notebooks until after an activity is over so that they do not disturb the culture through their efforts at documentation. In either case, it is important that researchers be respectful and responsible and always ask for permission from subjects before taking photos or recordings. Many researchers will have gathered signed permission from their subjects before beginning their research and will work with a documented plan that has been approved by their institution before going into the field.

Interviewing Informants

An important source of information about a culture is **interviews** with various people who grew up in that culture. Interviews can be uncomfortable for people, and it is important that researchers do all they can to help subjects feel at ease. Researchers will normally conduct an interview in a familiar space for the informant, such as the informant's home. They will help the subject ease into the interview by participating in introductory and hosting protocols followed in that culture when a visitor comes to someone's home. The researcher will start off the interview with the exchange of pleasant comments and will introduce themselves by explaining who they are, where they come from, and why they are doing this research. Then the interview may commence.

Interviews can be short or long, and there may be follow-up meetings and further interviews based on how knowledgeable the informant is. Many informants are chosen because they are deeply conscious of multiple aspects of their culture. This type of insider information is vitally important to an anthropological research project. In addition to interview questions, survey questions may also be asked during these meetings. The use of recording equipment, for both audio and video recordings, is common during interviews. However, such equipment may be considered intrusive by some, and their use is always at the discretion of the informant. Express permissions must always be obtained both to create a recording and to use a recording in future projects.

FIGURE 2.11 Ethnographic researchers engage with the cultures they are studying by spending time with their people. Here Josphat Mako, a Maasai man, greets Stuart Butler. Butler spent two months with Mako, walking between Maasai villages and visiting with residents to learn about both traditional customs and contemporary practices and challenges. (credit: "2015 06 24 Walking with the Maasai JPEG RESIZED 0025" by Make It Kenya Photo/Stuart Price/flickr, Public Domain)

Ethical Considerations

Contemporary sociocultural researchers and anthropologists must follow protocols established by an **institutional review board** (IRB) as well as any research protocols specific to the culture being researched. For social science research, IRBs are committees housed within a university that must review and approve research plans before any research begins. There may also be a parallel review process within the host culture. The proposed research is normally fully planned out before the review process can begin, with specific information about the type of research that will be conducted, including examples of questions to be asked, potential risk factors to subjects, plans for emotional support for subjects, means of protecting the identity of subjects, language used to fully disclose the intent of the project to subjects, and the final plan for archiving the research data. Many Indigenous nations have their own research protocols, and foreign countries will have their own research protocols and processes for securing permission to conduct research as well.

Researchers conducting sociocultural, medical, or clinical studies must gain written consent for all interviews from their informants, and they must be transparent as to why they are conducting research and how it will be used in the future. There are normally various levels of protocols pertaining to research, based on the potential to cause stress or harm to the subjects. At the highest level, full disclosure and signed permission as well as complete anonymity of the subjects involved in the project are required. A research plan should also specify whether recordings, notes, and data will be archived for future use or destroyed at the end of the project. Content gathered from research may make its way into articles or books or become part of a vast body of anonymous data available to other researchers. These possibilities should be discussed with collaborators. Collaborators are usually anonymous unless they choose to allow their names to be used. Many researchers now assign to their subject culture significant rights to review reports and edit and correct erroneous information and interpretations as well as ownership rights of the final product and the research data. Alternately, researchers may destroy research data once the project is over so that it cannot be used in ways other than what was originally intended.

Long-term research projects are becoming the norm for many professional researchers, who establish trusting relationships with collaborators over the length of their careers. During the early years of anthropology, it was almost unheard of for researchers to establish long-term relationships with the subjects of their research, but many scholars began to view short-term relationships as exploitative. Long-term relationships involve a regular return to the subject culture, on an annual or semiannual basis, to follow up on projects and programs. Researchers often include their subjects in the planning and administration of their projects and will at times seek a research objective based on the needs of their subjects. This type of research is more **open-ended** and often has an applied focus, seeking to solve problems and issues identified as significant by the collaborating culture. Those who engage in this type of research make it a primary aim to help the collaborating culture rather than to seek information pertinent to their personal projects.

This type of open-ended research has been developed in response to the criticisms of Indigenous scholars such as Vine Deloria Jr., who questioned whether early anthropologists did anything beneficial for the people they studied. A researcher working in this fashion will listen closely to the concerns expressed by those they are studying and aim to identify a project that will ultimately help the collaborating culture address issues identified as important, either by directly working toward a solution or by offering significant insights into the causes and subtleties of the issue. The researcher will include members of the culture in their team, and the results of the research will be given to the people for their use. Researchers working in this manner may still publish their findings, but the subject community will be part of the decision-making regarding what is important and what should and should not be published. The subject community will also have control over any projects that develop based on the findings. In some cases, the researcher is required to submit all manuscripts intended for publication to a committee formed by the collaborating culture for review, correction, and approval. Many Indigenous anthropologists who are tribal members are required to submit their publications to their tribal council for approval before they publish.

Contemporary anthropological researchers often assign ultimate ownership of the material they collect to the culture-bearers who provided the information. In fact, there are scholars today who, when publishing findings, assign authorship to the community they worked with and assign themselves the role of editor or compiler. An example is the text *Chinuk Wawa: Kakwa nsayka ulman-tilixam laska munk-kemteks nsayka / As Our Elders Teach Us to Speak It*, which is authored by the Chinuk Wawa Dictionary Project and published by the Confederated Tribes of the Grand Ronde Community of Oregon, with the scholar Henry Zenk acknowledged as the compiler of the information. Intellectual property protocols in many countries now assume that ownership of ethnographic content is assigned to the informants. Informants have rights, both legally and per IRB policies, to both participate and not participate in a study and to have their data removed from a study if they choose. Ethical researchers will listen to their informants, and if they are at all worried about the effect their findings will have on their informants or other people, they will either pull the data out of the study or find a way to make it completely anonymous. No researcher wants to have their informants adversely affected by their involvement in a research project. The IRB-informed consent paperwork, which must be signed by all informants, should address these concerns and allow the informants to freely choose their level of participation.

2.5 Quantitative and Qualitative Analysis

LEARNING OUTCOMES

By the end of this section, you will be able to:

- Identify differences between quantitative and qualitative information.
- Provide an example of how an anthropologist might model research findings.
- Describe the steps of the scientific method.

Differences between Quantitative and Qualitative Information

Quantitative information is measurable or countable data that can provide insight into research questions.

Quantitative information is one of the most direct ways to understand limited, specific questions, such as how often people in a culture perform a certain action or how many times an art form or motif appears in a cultural artifact. **Statistics** created from quantitative data help researchers understand trends and changes over time. Counts of cultural remains, such as the number and distribution of animal remains found at a campsite, can show how much the campsite was used and what type of animal was being hunted. Statistical comparisons may be made of several different sites that Indigenous peoples used to process food in order to determine the primary purpose of each site.

In cultural research, **qualitative data** allows anthropologists to understand culture based on more subjective analyses of language, behavior, ritual, symbolism, and interrelationships of people. Qualitative data has the potential for more in-depth responses via open-ended questions, which can be coded and categorized in order to better identify common themes. Qualitative analysis is less about frequency and the number of things and more about a researcher's subjective insights and understandings. Anthropology and other fields in the social sciences frequently integrate both types of data by using mixed methods. Through the triangulation of data, anthropologists can use both objective and frequency data (for example, survey results) and subjective data (such as observations) to provide a more holistic understanding.

Modeling

Many anthropologists create models to help others visualize and understand their research findings. Models help people understand the relationships between various points of data and can include qualitative elements as well. One very familiar model is a map. Maps are constructed from many thousands of data points projected onto a flat surface to help people understand distances and relationships. Maps are typically two-dimensional, but we are of course all familiar with the three-dimensional version of a world map known as a globe. Maps and globes are built on data points, but they also include qualitative information, such as the colors used to represent various features and the human-assigned names of various geographical features. Other familiar types of models include graphs, calendars, timelines, and charts. GPS is also a significant modeling tool today.

GPS, or the Global Position System, is increasingly used in archaeology. A model of a research site can be created using computer programs and a series of GPS coordinates. Any artifacts found or important features identified within the site can mapped to their exact locations within this model. This type of mapping is incredibly helpful if further work is warranted, making it possible for the researcher to return to the exact site where the original artifacts were found. These types of models also provide construction companies with an understanding of where the most sensitive cultural sites are located so that they may avoid destroying them. Government agencies and tribal governments are now constructing GPS maps of important cultural sites that include a variety of layers. Layering types of data within a landscape allows researchers to easily sort the available data and focus on what is most relevant to a particular question or task.

Wild food plants, water sources, roads and trails, and even individual trees can be documented and mapped with precision. Archaeologists can create complex layered maps of traditional Native landscapes, with original habitations, trails, and resource locations marked. GPS has significant applications in the re-creation of historic periods. By comparing the placements of buildings at various points in the past, GPS models can be created showing how neighborhoods or even whole cities have changed over time. In addition, layers can be created that contain cultural and historic information. These types of models are an important part of efforts to preserve remaining cultural and historic sites and features.

The Science of Anthropology

Anthropology is a science, and as such, anthropologists follow the **scientific method**. First, an anthropologist forms a **research question** based on some phenomenon they have encountered. They then construct a testable **hypothesis** based on their question. To test their hypothesis, they gather data and information. Information can come from one or many sources and can be either quantitative or qualitative in nature. Part of the evaluation might include statistical analyses of the data. The anthropologist then draws a conclusion. Conclusions are rarely 100 percent positive or 100 percent negative; generally, the results are somewhere on a continuum. Most conclusions to the positive will be stated as "likely" to be true. Scholars may also develop methods of testing and **retesting** their conclusions to make sure that what they think is true is proven true through various means. When a hypothesis is rigorously tested and the results conform with empirical observations of the world, then a **theory** is considered “likely to be accurate.” Hypotheses are always subject to being disproven or modified as more information is collected.

2.6 Collections

LEARNING OUTCOMES

By the end of this section, you will be able to:

- Identify and explain the issues and needs of archival collections.
- Identify and explain the issues and needs of three-dimensional collections.
- Describe current controversies regarding ownership of anthropological artifacts and human remains.
- Recall two pieces of legislature pertaining to questions of ownership.
- Define *provenance* and describe its importance in anthropology.

Not all anthropological research is done in the field. There is much to be learned from the collections of manuscripts and artifacts housed in universities and museums. These collections make it possible for anthropologists to study human cultures within the setting of special research laboratories that have been designed to preserve and organize materials collected and perhaps interpreted by scholars of the past.

Archives

Archival collections contain published, re-created, or original manuscripts that are deemed significant enough to be placed in conditions designed to preserve them against damage or loss. Such collections may contain correspondence, maps, drawings, original drafts of books, rare books, or other papers and media that need special care. Photographs are a major resource in many archives, and they need special handling. Preservation policies of archival collections include practices such as keeping resources out of direct sunlight and away from moisture.

While archives offer researchers a great range of valuable resources, they typically impose rather strict policies on those wishing to access these resources. Researchers typically must wear gloves when handling materials to prevent damage from the oils and acidity of human skin. Normally, archival collections do not circulate (i.e., cannot be removed from the host site), and researchers may have to apply for permission to enter the site or use any information. Archives may charge varying rates to make copies of material or to use images of the resources in their collection for publication. To access some archives, researchers must plan ahead by scheduling a time to visit and making previous arrangements to access specific collections. Some sites do not allow researchers to scan materials using flatbed scanners, instead stipulating the use of non-flash photography or overhead scanning. Some archives do not allow the patron to scan, photograph, or copy a manuscript in any way, with all arrangements for copies and reproductions having to go through the archive’s staff.

The first step in archival research is typically to review a list or similar finding aid that indexes and describes the resources available in a collection. These descriptive aids can help researchers determine whether a collection contains resources that fit their needs and can make a visit to a selected archive more efficient and worthwhile. Finding aids have become so well constructed that they may provide researchers with enough information to enable the researcher to request copies of specific materials and avoid the effort and expense of traveling to the archive in person. Most archives offer downloadable finding aids of their most important collections on their websites, and there may be additional printed finding aids available on request. Most archives will make requested copies for a moderate fee and will mail or email researchers a packet of the reproduced materials. The cost of procuring such copies is almost always much less than the cost of traveling to an archive site and paying for housing and meals. However, if a collection is potentially full of material important to a research project, it may be better to visit in person.

Three-Dimensional Collections

Three-dimensional collections of objects such as basketry and pottery are normally housed separately from manuscript collections. Such collections may host tens of thousands of individual cultural objects. These collections typically require much more care and management than manuscript materials. Extensive planning goes into determining the best way to contain and store each type of object in order to slow deterioration over time, with special attention paid to both the temperature and the moisture levels in storage areas. Handwoven baskets will be supported so that their fibers are not under stress, and all organic objects will have been previously frozen, perhaps several times, to destroy any insects that may live in the fibers. Collections of animal and human remains utilized by biological anthropologists or archaeologists must be properly stored and controlled against further degradation by reducing temperatures and maintaining moisture controls. Some very ancient organic collections may need to be chemically stabilized so they do not degrade. Objects made from organic materials—such as wooden canoes, basketry, reed sandals, or human remains—are particularly prone to degradation. Organic artifacts that have been sealed away from contact with the air for centuries, such as boats found on the bottom of a river or lake, will degrade fast once exposed to the air, so they may be kept permanently frozen or preserved with an ammonium glycol solution to stabilize decay.

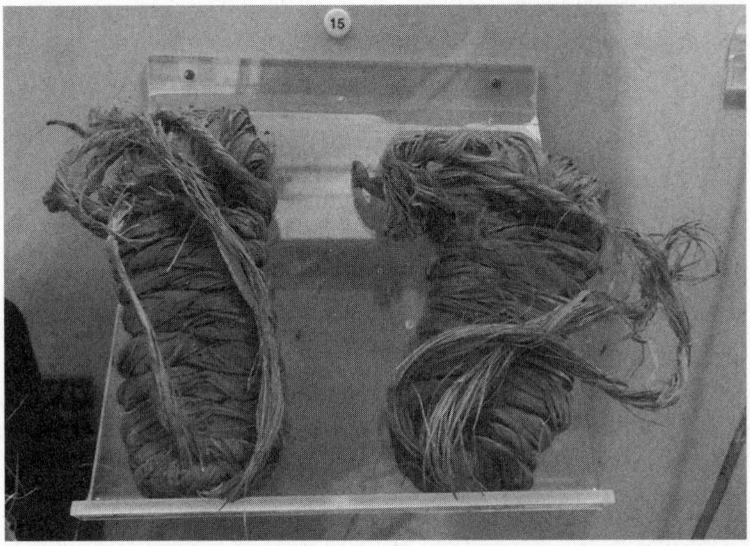

FIGURE 2.12 This pair of yucca sandals, collected in 1875, is an example of an organic artifact of the Southern Paiute people. Yucca is a perennial plant with large tough leaves that can be used for various purposes. (credit: "Sandals, Southern Paiute, yucca, collected in 1875 – Native American collection –Peabody Museum, Harvard University – DSC05570" by Daderot/Wikimedia Commons, CC0)

All objects in collections storage must be well organized to make them accessible for further research opportunities. Collection materials that have been used to make claims about human experience or evolution must remain accessible to future researchers in case there are challenges or additional questions about their findings. In addition, if an anthropologist who donated and is responsible for overseeing a collection at one institution should die or move to another research institute, there needs to be a plan for the period of retention for the collection, or the time that the collection will remain in the archive. Many biological and cultural collections have been preserved in repositories since the day they were collected, with no plans to ever remove them from an archive. There are collections in the Smithsonian Institution that have been there since the institution was built in the 1850s. These collections continue to grow at museums and universities around the world.

In the early 20th century, many museums adopted the practices of painting objects with lacquer and spraying organic collections with pesticides such as DDT to prevent insect damage. These solutions were proven to ultimately be harmful. Lacquer tends to alter the color and chemical structure of objects and is thus not a good preservation material, and DDT and other pesticides pose health threats to humans. Both museum staff and tribal members who receive repatriated objects and human remains are very concerned about the hazards these chemicals pose to humans—and to the environment, if they should be reburied. Efforts to clean many collections are underway.

Ownership

A question being asked by both anthropologists and subjects of research today is who owns the objects housed in material collections. In the past, anthropologists or their host institutions assumed ownership of anything they collected, along with the right to publish images of materials and sign over ownership of the objects to collections repositories. In recent decades, tribal peoples and other subjects of research have begun asking questions about whether such objects really should be considered the property of these repositories. Many of these artifacts were not even collected by scientists but rather donated or sold by collectors, some of whom removed the artifacts from burial sites. Artifact hunting is a common cultural practice in some countries, such as Peru, where many people dig in Inca sites to locate artifacts to sell.

Questions of ownership become particularly pressing when the objects in question are human remains. Until the 1960s, tribal peoples in the United States had little or no power to repatriate their ancestors. **Repatriation** is the process of restoring human remains and/or objects of religious or cultural importance to the peoples from whom they originated. In the United States, repatriation is executed under the Native American Graves Protection and Repatriation Act (**NAGPRA**), passed into law in 1990. Prior to 1990, Indigenous peoples in the United States had no legal means to claim return of any of the millions of human remains that had been collected and placed in museums and archaeological collections since the 19th century.

Another important piece of legislature is the National Historic Preservation Act (NHPA), passed in 1966. The act was passed to ensure that federal agencies would identify and take actions to protect and preserve the nation's historic sites and locations. It especially impacted Indigenous communities and their cultural and historical resources. Section 106 of the NHPA requires that federal agencies follow a formal review process before undertaking any type of development project (36 CFR 800). This process includes identifying what the actual undertaking is, such as the development of a road or other major capital project. Once this is established, the agency must make a good-faith effort to identify any historic resources (50+ years of age) in the area and determine if they are eligible for protection under the NHPA. After this identification measure is completed, the agency must initiate consultation with the state historic preservation officer (SHPO) or tribal historic preservation officer (THPO) and other interested groups and individuals. This step can include a variety of meetings or activities and a period of notification that a project is going to commence, during which feedback is requested by the lead federal agency. Public meetings might be held, with speakers selected to introduce and describe the project. During the consultation period, correspondence and feedback is welcomed from concerned tribes, institutions, or individuals. Tribes and other community groups with an interest in any cultural objects likely to be found on the site are required to be consulted. Successful consultation often takes place during the earliest planning stages of a project. Lack of early consultation can lead to a failure to identify historic resources of cultural and religious importance.

The process places the burden of determining the potential effects of the project on the federal agency, according to three established categories: no potential to effect, no adverse effect, and adverse effect. The agency must then seek concurrence from appropriate SHPOs and THPOs and potentially other consulting parties. If there is an adverse effect, the agency, the SHPO and/or THPO, and other consulting parties will negotiate mitigation terms and solidify them into a memorandum of agreement to ensure completion of the agreed-upon mitigation measures. In most cases, Native groups do not believe that archaeological excavations alone are an appropriate mitigation measure, but each community has its own interpretation of what is appropriate.

Generally, anytime a road is built or a building is constructed, there needs to be a section 106 review of the project because of the likelihood of encountering Native American cultural sites in almost all locations in the United States. Through the consultation process and cooperation between SHPOs and THPOs, decisions are made as to the status and disposition of any cultural objects recovered from cultural sites. Tribes typically advocate for the non-disturbance of human remains and the return of cultural objects to the concerned tribes. The NHPA is not perfect, as it does not completely halt construction that will destroy a cultural site and does not apply to collections placed in repositories before 1966.

In the early 20th century, the United States made it illegal for nonscientists to remove artifacts from archaeological sites on federal lands under a law called the American Antiquities Act (1906). More recently, NAGPRA made it possible for tribes to repatriate objects covered under the act, such as human remains and funerary objects. Under this law, more than 20,000 sets of remains had been repatriated as of 2010, but millions of artifacts and sets of additional remains are still in repositories. In addition, there are human remains and funerary objects of US origin in collections worldwide that are not subject to NAGPRA repatriation.

One problem surrounding repatriation is that many artifacts and remains lack clear **provenance**, or detailed information about where they were found. Lack of clear provenance also limits an object's usefulness to researchers. In many cases, wide regions are provided as the origin of an artifact, making it unclear which specific tribal culture it relates to. Objects that, for example, are labeled as coming from "New York" may have been created by members of dozens of tribes or bands of tribes. In general, the more specific a provenance is, the better. Narrowing an object down to Buffalo, New York, reduces its possible tribal sources to just a few. Objects that have too broad of a context are nearly impossible to repatriate because repatriation is supposed to return an object or human remains to the original tribe. In 2010, NAGPRA was expanded to allow for groups of tribes to repatriate objects of wide regional association back to a previously agreed-upon reburial or repatriation location. Under this expanded version of the law, a greater number of objects and human remains will be able to be returned to their communities.

Concerns about ownership have also been raised regarding the ethnological and ethnographic research collected in millions of documents in hundreds of research collections around the world. Some tribal peoples have raised concerns that this material represents their ancestral intellectual knowledge and that it was taken from them without full disclosure of how it would be used. Many anthropologists published books and/or made tenure at their universities based on such research. Meanwhile, little was done with the information to help the tribal peoples it described, who were struggling under political and legal pressures to assimilate. In some cases, tribal peoples have implemented research projects utilizing these manuscript collections that have the explicit goal of helping their people with cultural recovery efforts.

One example of Indigenous peoples utilizing archive materials to their advantage is offered by Oregon's Coquille Indian Tribe, which made use of archival documents to successfully restore their tribe to federal recognition in 1989 after the tribe was declared "terminated" by the federal government in 1954. Their restoration bid was made difficult by the fact that the records of their tribal culture were collected in faraway archives. Essential to the tribe's success was George Wasson Jr., son of the aforementioned George Wasson who was aided by Leonard Frachtenberg. Wasson Jr. designed and implemented an effort to collect copies of anthropological manuscripts pertinent to the Coquille tribe from the Smithsonian Institution.

In 1995, 1997, and 2006, the Southwest Oregon Research Project—a project initiated by the Coquille Indian Tribe, University of Oregon anthropologists, and students from western Oregon tribes—collected 150,000 pages of documents about the tribes of western Oregon from the Smithsonian Institution and the National Archives. These materials have since become a major collection at the University of Oregon's Knight Library Archives, special collections division, and additional copies have been given to 17 regional tribes.

These projects are examples of the repatriation of intellectual knowledge to the tribes that the information was collected from. Many libraries now have policies that allow concerned tribes to repatriate their intellectual knowledge in the form of copies of collection materials for little or no cost. Recordings of songs represent a particularly sensitive and special type of cultural artifact to many tribal people. Archives have historically not been very attentive to the concerns of tribes regarding their collections. For more information, consult the Protocols for Native American Archival Materials.

ETHNOGRAPHIC SKETCHES

Summers Collection and the Grand Ronde Tribe

by author David Lewis

The Summers Collection is a collection of more than 600 Native objects from the West Coast of the United States, collected by the Reverend Robert Summers, an Episcopalian minister. A large portion of the collection, some 300 objects, was collected from the Grand Ronde Indian Reservation, which is close to where Summers lived in McMinnville, Oregon. In the 1870s, Summers would regularly visit the people of Grand Ronde and purchase objects they had in their homes or were using. Most of these objects are woven baskets and trays made in a traditional manner, many predating the formation of the reservation in 1856. Sometime in the

1890s, Summers passed his collection on to his associate Reverend Freer, who donated the collection to the British Museum in 1900.

The collection has remained part of the British Museum collections since then. The value of this collection lies not only in the objects and their unusually good preservation but also in the care Summers took to document the people he purchased them from, their use, and their cultural background. It was unusual in early anthropology for a collector to be so comprehensive in documenting material collections. Summers was likely aided by his wife, who was a professional botanist and would have been meticulous in her work documenting botanical collections.

In the 1990s, the Grand Ronde tribe became aware of the Summers Collection at the British Museum. In 1999, representatives of the tribe visited the museum, viewed the collection, took photos of all objects related to the tribes, and copied all the notes they could. Since then, the tribe has worked through a series of museum curators to see if it would be possible to repatriate the collection to the Grand Ronde. The British Museum is one of the largest repositories in the world, holding sacred and cultural objects from numerous nations, many once part of Britain's extensive colonial empire. The British Museum rarely allows repatriations, fearful that allowing one to occur would set a precedent resulting in multiple other cultures submitting claims. Still, curators of the North American collections have suggested that something could be worked out if there were a book deal to help publicize their collections and significant enough publicity. In 2018, the Grand Ronde tribe was able to negotiate the loan of some 16 objects from the collection. The objects were placed on display in the new Chachalu Museum and Cultural Center in Grand Ronde. While there, the objects were studied by cultural experts who focused on understanding how they were made and how they might be able to replicate the techniques.

There are no protocols for international repatriation. The Grand Ronde tribe had to work diplomatically to form negotiated agreements and establish a beneficial relationship with the British Museum. After more than 100 years of assimilation, many traditional skills had been lost to the Grand Ronde people. The opportunity to regain some of this lost ancestral knowledge by studying these cultural goods is a rare gift.

MINI-FIELDWORK ACTIVITY

Participant Observation

When practicing participant observation, researchers immerse themselves in a cultural context and make observations and notes about what occurs. This activity is structured to take place in a few hours and can be accomplished in your community.

- Spend about an hour in a public place, such as a mall or store, coffeeshop, park, bus, train, or library, and observe what people around you are doing. Take notes about their actions, interactions, clothing, foods, mannerisms, and anything else that might seem interesting. Note characteristics and mannerisms pertaining to culture, language, ethnicity, masculine and feminine roles, and age-related roles.
- Try not to be conspicuous, and do not record conversations unless they are spoken quite loudly so as not to be intrusive. If anyone asks what you are doing, just explain that you have an assignment in a college course to make an anonymous report on local culture.
- Return home and write a two-page reflective report on your research. In the report, give specifics of what you witnessed, and analyze how you personally responded to different cultures or mannerisms. About two-thirds of the report should be ethnographic reporting, and one-third should be analysis.
- Try to eliminate your personal bias or admit when you have one, and identify when you are basing your analysis on personal opinions.
- Pay attention to the need to maintain the anonymity of your subjects as if this were an actual anthropology fieldwork assignment. Do not identify people by name; instead, use pseudonyms.

As a final step, give a five-minute presentation about your experience that summarizes the high points of your participant observation.

Suggested Readings

Boas, Franz. (1974) 1982. *A Franz Boas Reader: The Shaping of American Anthropology, 1883–1911.* Edited by George W. Stocking Jr. Chicago: University of Chicago Press.

Boyd, Robert T., Kenneth M. Ames, and Tony A. Johnson, eds. 2013. *Chinookan Peoples of the Lower Columbia.* Seattle: University of Washington Press.

Gross, Joan, ed. 2007. *Teaching Oregon Native Languages.* Corvallis: Oregon State University Press.

Kenoyer, Louis. 2017. *My Life, by Louis Kenoyer: Reminiscences of a Grand Ronde Reservation Childhood.* Translated by Jedd Schrock and Henry Zenk. Corvallis: Oregon State University Press.

Konopinski, Natalie, ed. 2014. *Doing Anthropological Research: A Practical Guide.* New York: Routledge.

Lewis, David G. 2009. "Termination of the Confederated Tribes of the Grand Ronde Community of Oregon: Politics, Community, Identity." PhD diss., University of Oregon. http://hdl.handle.net/1794/10067.

Lewis, David G. 2015. "Natives in the Nation's Archives: The Southwest Oregon Research Project." *Journal of Western Archives* 6 (1). https://doi.org/10.26077/e5e5-e0b1.

Sapir, Edward. (1949) 2021. *Selected Writings of Edward Sapir in Language, Culture, and Personality.* Edited by David G. Mandelbaum. Berkeley: University of California Press.

Spradley, James P. (1980) 2016. *Participant Observation.* Long Grove, IL: Waveland Press.

Thwaites, Reuben Gold, ed. (1905) 2003. *Original Journals of the Lewis and Clark Expedition, 1804–1806.* Vol. 7. Madison: Wisconsin Historical Society. https://content.wisconsinhistory.org/digital/collection/aj/id/16212/rec/7.

Key Terms

absolute dating methods (see also chronometric dating methods) dating methods that use physical and chemical properties of artifacts and structures modified by humans to establish their age without reference to other artifacts. For example, radiocarbon dating is used to date organic materials generally up to 50,000 years old.

archaeobotanist a specialist who studies plants and seeds appearing in an archaeology site.

archaeological context the place where an object was originally found, along with other associations, such as the stratum it was found in, specific features, and other objects associated with it.

archaeological excavation the scientific process of uncovering artifacts and other biological and cultural remains in the historic and prehistoric past of human-inhabited sites.

armchair anthropology a method of conducting anthropological research without doing fieldwork, relying instead on materials and documents previously collected by others.

artifacts objects that are portable and show evidence of human cultural activity; for example, bones that show evidence of drawings sketched on them, stone tools, pottery, etc.

chronometric dating methods dating methods used to analyze various physical or chemical characteristics of an artifact in order to assign a date or range of dates for its production.

cross-cutting relationship a principle in geology and archaeology that suggests that a geologic or cultural feature that cuts across another feature is the more recently deposited of the two.

dendrochronology an absolute dating technique that uses patterns of growth of tree rings and cross-dating to determine the approximate age of wood.

ecofacts natural objects found at an archaeological site, such as seeds, bone, shells, etc., that show no sign of human craftsmanship.

emic perspective viewing and attempting to evaluate other peoples and cultures according to the standards of those cultures; an "insider's" point of view.

ethnology the study of differences and relationships between various peoples, societies, and cultures.

etic (or ethnocentric) perspective viewing a culture from the perspective of an outsider looking in.

features cultural structures found at an archaeological site that are not movable or portable, such as parts of a temple, altars, tombs, etc.

feminist anthropology an approach to anthropology that seeks to transform research methods and findings by engaging with more diverse perspectives and using insights from feminist theory.

hypothesis a supposition that is subjected to research in order to be proven or disproven through data collection.

Indigenous anthropology the study of one's own culture or society using anthropological methods. The term has come to mean any application of Indigenous knowledge, perspectives, and scholarship in anthropology.

institutional review board a university research committee that reviews biomedical or social science research proposals to determine if they appropriately protect human participants, informants, and subjects.

interpretation the act of explaining the meaning of something.

interview a method of research in which the researcher asks questions of an informant to gain information about a person, society, or culture.

law of superposition the geological principle of stratigraphy that assumes that materials, normally rock layers, found beneath other materials are older that the materials on top.

NAGPRA the Native American Graves Protection and Repatriation Act (1990), a US law that protects human remains and cultural and ceremonial objects and artifacts from collection and requires the return of such items already collected to the originating tribes. NAGPRA also allows for the repatriation of the same materials from museums and other repositories.

naturalism an approach that seeks to understand the world and the laws that govern it by direct observation of nature.

open-ended in the context of anthropological research, describes a research method whereby the researcher allows informants to answer questions without a limit in time or subject.

oral histories histories of previous events, moral or ethical lessons, or stories of creation that are passed down by memorization. Many oral histories are also called mythologies, legends, texts, or folklore.

participant observation an anthropological

research method in which the researcher enters a cultural community and collects information through observation of and participation in the culture.

primary context the context of an artifact, feature, or site that has not been disturbed since its original deposition.

provenance the location of an artifact when it is first found. The provenance is normally recorded when the artifact is in situ, or before it has been removed.

qualitative data nonnumerical data, such as language, feelings, or impressions, that is normally collected when the researcher is at the research site.

radiocarbon dating a dating technique for organic substances that measures the decay of radioactive carbon in the sample; also called carbon-14 (^{14}C or C^{14}) dating. This is the most widely used technique for dating organic artifacts between 50 and 60,000 years old.

relative dating describes methods of determining the relative order of past events through comparisons of two or more artifacts without determining their absolute age; e.g., sample 1 is older than sample 2 because sample 1 was found beneath sample 2.

repatriation the process of returning human remains, associated funerary objects, and ceremonial items to the originating culture.

research question a question that can be proved or disproved through research and observation.

retesting the scientific practice of conducting experiments or research more than once in order to determine if the findings are accurate. Retesting helps eliminate human and other errors in testing and create a range of accuracy.

salvage anthropology a particular period in early anthropological practices (1870s–1930s) during which tribal cultures were subject to extreme collecting from researchers. The practice occurred because of fears that Native cultures would go extinct and there would be nothing further to study.

scientific method a method of expanding knowledge by asking questions, creating a hypothesis, collecting data, and presenting well-reasoned findings based on evidence.

secondary context the context of a cultural or natural objects that has been moved or disturbed from its original location and is thus no longer associated with its place of origin; for example, a burial that has been moved from its original location due to geological shifts or natural disaster.

seriation a relative dating method that places similar artifacts from the same area in a chronological sequence.

statistics the science of collecting and analyzing numerical data in large quantities and inferring proportions in a whole from those in a representative sample, or the numerical data collected and analyzed in this manner.

strata plural of *stratum*; in geology and archaeology, distinct layers of deposited natural or archaeological material.

stratigraphic superposition a relative dating method that assumes that any cultural or natural artifact that is found within a stratum, or that cuts across two or more strata in a cross-cutting relationship, is younger than the stratum itself.

stratigraphy the process of identifying the order and relative positions of strata.

stratum singular of *strata*; one specific layer of deposited natural or archaeological material.

theory a supposition or a system of ideas intended to explain something.

three-dimensional collection a collection of objects or artifacts.

typological sequence a set or group of objects ordered according to their types.

zooarchaeologist an archaeologist who specializes in the identification of animal remains at an archaeological site.

Summary

Chapter 2 discusses how anthropologists gather information. All of the subfields of anthropology conduct fieldwork in some form to gather information, each subfield may use different methods of conducting research. The concept of working in "the field" was traditionally based on the practice of traveling to distant regions to study other cultures within their native environmental contexts. In recent decades, "the field" has broadened to include diverse settings such as one's hometown (as in urban anthropology), the Internet (visual or virtual anthropology), or collections in university archives and museums (ethnohistory or museum anthropology). Research methods for cultural anthropology and archaeology are covered in detail. the chapter explores the issues that need to be considered when analyzing information gathered during research. This includes the biases of the anthropological researcher. Also covered is some of the history of the research methods used in anthropological study and how fieldwork and methods have changed over time.

Critical Thinking Questions

1. Explain how conservation, as practiced in the 19th and early 20th centuries, attempted to preserve animals, plants, and human cultures.
2. Describe salvage anthropology. Why was it practiced? What are some criticisms of this approach?
3. What is different about anthropology as practiced in the 19th century compared to the way it is practiced today?
4. Why is it important to have multiple perspectives when describing human culture? How do anthropologists gather these multiple perspectives?
5. What is a feminist anthropological approach to anthropological inquiry? What does this approach offer to the field?
6. What rights do tribal peoples have when research is conducted on them?
7. What are the ethical responsibilities of anthropologists when conducting research? What practices should anthropologists follow to be sure their research proceeds in a moral and ethical manner?
8. Name and describe the most important pieces of government legislation in the United States pertaining to the rights of Indigenous peoples to cultural artifacts and knowledge.

Bibliography

Adams, William Mark. 2004. *Against Extinction: The Story of Conservation.* London: Earthscan.

Boas, Franz. (1974) 1982. *A Franz Boas Reader: The Shaping of American Anthropology, 1883–1911.* Edited by George W. Stocking Jr. Chicago: University of Chicago Press.

Cole, Douglas. (1985) 1995. *Captured Heritage: The Scramble for Northwest Coast Artifacts.* Norman: University of Oklahoma Press.

Hale, Horatio. 1846. *Ethnography and Philology.* Vol. 6, *United States Exploring Expedition during the Years 1838, 1839, 1840, 1841, 1842, under the Command of Charles Wilkes, USN.* Philadelphia: C. Sherman, 1844–1874.

Hodgen, Margaret T. (1964) 1971. *Early Anthropology in the Sixteenth and Seventeenth Centuries.* Philadelphia: University of Pennsylvania Press.

Hymes, Dell. 1980. "What Is Ethnography?" In *Language in Education: Ethnolinguistic Essays*, 88–103. Washington, DC: Center for Applied Linguistics.

Morgan, Lewis Henry. 1851. *League of the Ho-dé-no-sau-nee, or Iroquois.* Rochester, NY: Sage & Brother. https://hdl.handle.net/2027/nyp.33433081750949.

Stocking, George W., Jr. 1966. "Franz Boas and the Culture Concept in Historical Perspective." *American Anthropologist* 68 (4): 867–882.

CHAPTER 3
Culture Concept Theory: Theories of Cultural Change

Figure 3.1 Now and in the past, people have called many different types of dwelling home. Top left, tent on K Street in Washington DC; top right, Puye cliff dwellings near Espanola, New Mexico; bottom left, a water village, Brunei, Indonesia; bottom right the International Space Station (credit: top left "K Street" by Daniel Lobo/flickr, Public Domain; top right "Puye Cliff Dwellings" by BFS Man/flickr, CC BY 2.0; bottom left "The water village. Burnei" by Bernard Spragg. NZ/flickr, Public Domain; bottom right "The International Space Station after arrival of ISS Roll Out Solar Arrays" by NASA/NASA.gov, Public Domain)

CHAPTER OUTLINE

3.1 The Homeyness of Culture
3.2 The Winkiness of Culture
3.3 The Elements of Culture
3.4 The Aggregates of Culture
3.5 Modes of Cultural Analysis
3.6 The Paradoxes of Culture

INTRODUCTION Though all humans have a set of basic needs, we meet those needs in very different ways in response to environmental conditions and social circumstances. For example, consider the basic human need for shelter. In places prone to flooding, people often build their houses on stilts, constructing patios and walkways to connect their houses together. In mountainous areas, people sometimes carve their houses into cliffsides. In societies with extreme inequality, some people live in luxury highrise apartments side-by-side with people who pitch their tents on the sidewalk. Humans have even constructed a complex dwelling adapted to the conditions of space, the International Space Center.

Similarly, humans have a wide range of solutions to human needs for clothing, food, family life, health, and social order. In each society, the various solutions combine in a complex totality called culture. In this chapter, we explore the concept of culture, what it is and how to study it. Taking the need for shelter as a central example, we will see how culture is created and how it changes. We will learn about how different elements of culture interact with one another. As culture is a central concept in anthropology, our understanding of culture will guide our exploration of human lifeways throughout this textbook.

3.1 The Homeyness of Culture

LEARNING OUTCOMES

By the end of this section, you will be able to:

- Explain the importance of culture to the concept of home.
- Identify the centrality of culture in the discipline of anthropology.
- Describe how each of the four fields deploys the concept of culture.
- Explain why culture feels familiar and "homey."

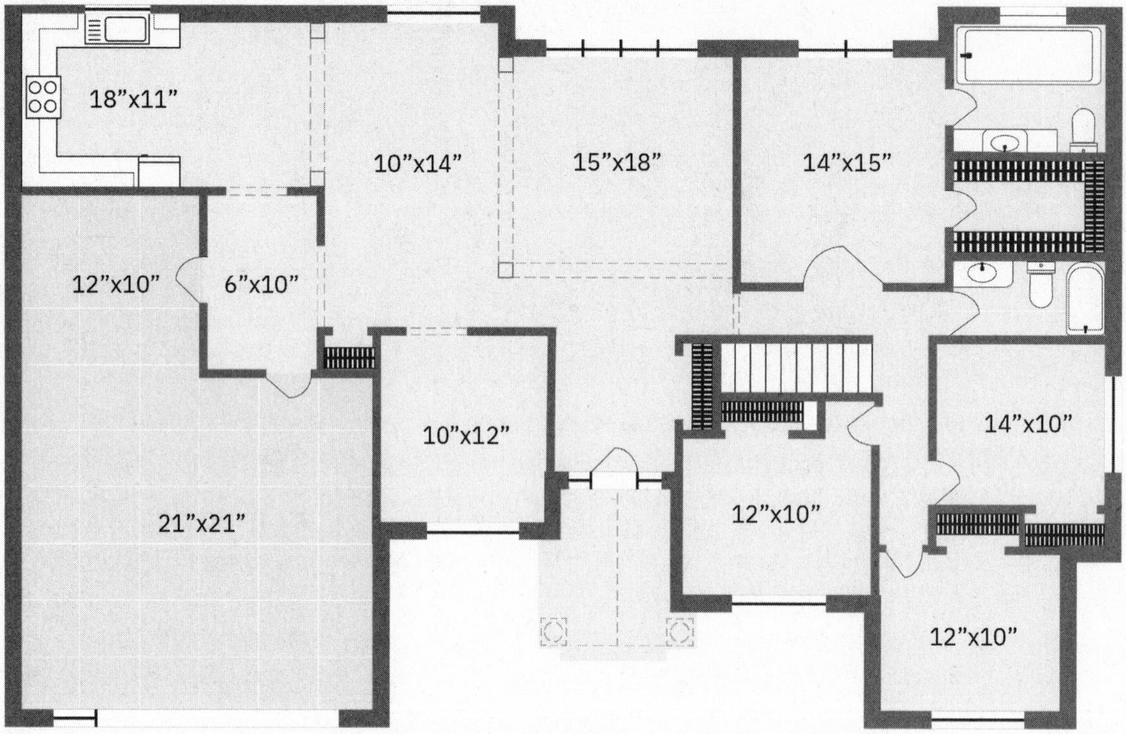

FIGURE 3.2 The floor plan of a typical 21st-century middle-class American house consists of many individual rooms, including three to four bedrooms, a large kitchen, a family room, and an attached garage. This floor plan depicts such a home. (attribution: Copyright Rice University, OpenStax, under CC BY 4.0 license)

What place do you call home? For some people, home is a large, angular structure made of wood or brick, fixed on a permanent foundation of concrete, and rigged with systems to provide running water, electricity, and temperature control. Such houses have separate rooms for distinct activities, such as sleeping, bathing, eating, and socializing. Often, one bedroom is larger than the others and connected to its own bathroom. This is the "primary bedroom," designed to accommodate a married couple while their children sleep in smaller bedrooms. The room for cooking (the kitchen) used to be separated from the room where people socialized (the living room or great room), as it was assumed that one person (the wife) would cook in the kitchen while another person (the husband) relaxed alone or with company in the living room. More recently, open-concept architecture has eliminated the wall separating the kitchen from the living room, as adults often cook together or socialize as one cooks and the other relaxes.

In the 1960s, French scholar Pierre Bourdieu (1970) analyzed a typical house of a Kabyle family in northern Algeria. Traditional Kabyle houses were rectangular buildings made of stone and clay with tiled roofs. Inside, a waist-high dividing wall marked off one-third of the house. This marked-off section, set lower than the rest of the house and paved with flagstones, was the stable, where animals were kept at night. A farming people, the Kabyle kept oxen, cows, donkeys, and mules. Above the stable was a loft where women and children often slept, though arrangements for sleeping and marital sex tended to vary.

FIGURE 3.3 These houses in Norther Algeria, built by the Kabyle people, are constructed of stone, and include open space for both animals and human inhabitants under a shared roof. (credit: PhR610/flickr, CC BY 2.0)

The floor of the larger section of the house was higher and paved with a layer of black clay and cow dung that women polished with a stone. This part was reserved for human use. In this larger, elevated section, a large weaving loom sat against the wall opposite the door. Facing east, this wall with the loom received the most light in the house. Guests and brides were seated here, as it was considered the nicest part of the house. Opposite the dividing wall in the larger section was the hearth, surrounded by cooking tools, lamps, and jars of edible grain. With the loom and the hearth, the main area of human activity in the house was associated with the work of women. Bourdieu explained that men were expected to remain outside the house from dawn to evening, working in the fields and associating with other men in public spaces. Women were supposed to remain in the home.

In Bourdieu's analysis, the Kabyle house was divided into two realms: a dark, low realm associated with animals and natural activities (sleeping, sex, childbirth, and death) and a lighter, higher realm associated with humans and cultural activities (weaving, cooking, brides, and guests).

Humans all over the world require a place to gather, work, socialize, and sleep. Some have Western-style houses, while others have compounds. Some live in tents made of wooden beams and covered with animal skins or cloth, in caves hollowed out of sandstone or volcanic rock, or in wooden structures built on stilts or in trees to avoid floods and predators. While these different forms of home are all designed to perform a common function as human living spaces, they are distinctively shaped by local environments and lifeways. Houses are most commonly built with locally available materials and designed to protect against local climatic conditions and predators. Over generations, people develop distinctive technologies to transform available materials into durable and functional homes. Different forms of family, different gender roles and relations, and different everyday activities determine the organization of space in these different homes. Dominant ideas about work, gender, marriage, parenting, hospitality, and status all shape the places we call home.

Home, then, involves a combination of materials, technologies, social relationships, everyday practices, deeply held values, and shared ideas. In every culture, these features are uniquely combined to produce distinctive versions of home. Other combinations of features produce distinctive versions of clothing, food, work, and health. Growing up in a particular social group, a person learns these ways of living, eating, working, and so on and comes to consider them normal and natural. Anthropologists have a word for such integrated combinations of social and environmental features, and that word is **culture**. The ways of your culture are familiar to you, often so deeply ingrained that they come naturally. Culture itself feels like home.

All four fields of anthropology are devoted to understanding human culture. Biological anthropologists are often interested in the emergence of culture in the course of human biological evolution. Archaeologists use material artifacts as keys to understanding the technologies, social practices, and ideas of ancient peoples. Cultural anthropologists often use participant observation to understand how the various features of culture fit together in contemporary societies. Linguistic anthropologists are interested in how language shapes and is shaped by other features in the constellation of culture.

This chapter explores culture as a central concept in anthropology. We examine what distinguishes culture from other aspects of human experience and activity. In an effort to organize the vast array of things included in culture, we divide culture into three levels and consider how those levels fit together holistically—and what happens when they don't. Finally, we identify a set of contradictions built into the concept of culture and see how those contradictions illuminate the nature of human social life.

3.2 The Winkiness of Culture

LEARNING OUTCOMES

By the end of this section, you will be able to:

- Provide E. B. Tylor's definition of culture.
- Distinguish natural behavior from cultural behavior.
- Describe deliberate and nondeliberate ways that people acquire culture.
- Explain how biological processes can be shaped by culture.

In the last section, we referred to culture as a combination of materials, technologies, social relationships, everyday practices, deeply held values, and shared ideas. Nineteenth-century British anthropologist Edward Burnett Tylor defined culture as "that complex whole which includes knowledge, belief, art, morals, law, custom, and any other capabilities and habits acquired by man as a member of society" (1873, 1:1). That's a lot to include in one concept! If all of that is culture, then what about human experience and activity is *not* culture?

Consider this scenario. A student comes to class one day, and the instructor says, "I've decided that you're all a bunch of failures and I'm flunking the entire class." Imagine then that the instructor simply stands there after that announcement, blinking calmly as the class erupts in protest.

Now imagine that same scenario with one very slight difference. The instructor announces, "I've decided that you're all a bunch of failures and I'm flunking the entire class." Then, as the class erupts in protest, the instructor calmly blinks *one* eye, leaving the other eye open.

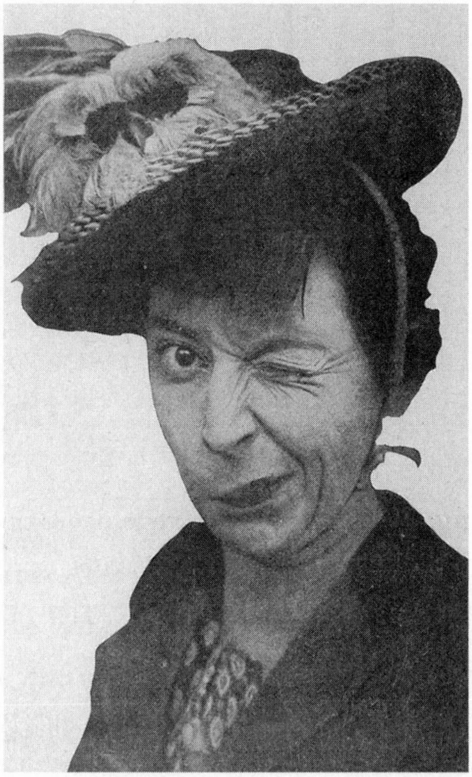

FIGURE 3.4 Would you take this woman seriously? In American culture, winking, related to the normal biological function of blinking, takes on special meaning in social interactions. (credit: Motion Picture News/Wikimedia Commons, Public Domain)

What just happened there? Blinking is a biological compulsion common to humans everywhere. Humans blink to keep eyes hydrated and clear of debris. Humans are born knowing how to blink; nobody has to teach us. On average, humans blink 15 to 20 times every minute. Without realizing it, people are necessarily blinking throughout every conversation, every social interaction, every activity during the day. The people we talk to and interact with are also blinking constantly, so often that everyone is accustomed to ignoring it. Blinking does not affect the perceived meaning of speech or actions.

But if someone deliberately blinks one eye, leaving the other one open, that's a completely different matter. In fact, leaving one eye open makes a blink a wink. Winking is not a biological necessity. Humans are not born knowing to how to wink, and it takes some practice to learn how to do it. Because it requires deliberate effort and people are not constantly doing it, winking can acquire special meaning in social interactions. In American culture (and many others), a wink often indicates that someone is joking around and that whatever they've just said or done should not be taken seriously. Of course, a wink can mean different things in different societies. Moreover, a wink can mean different things in the same society. If someone on a date takes their companion's hand and gives a cute little wink, the person may have reason to hope the winker is *not* just joking around.

American cultural anthropologist Clifford Geertz (1973) used the example of winking to illustrate two important aspects of culture. First, culture is learned. Innate human behaviors—that is, behaviors that people are born with—are biological, not cultural. Blinking is biological. Acquired human behaviors—that is, behaviors that people are taught—are cultural. Winking is cultural. This means that cultural behaviors are not genetically inherited from generation to generation but must be passed down from older members of a society to younger members. This process, as you'll recall from What is Anthropology? is called enculturation.

Some aspects of enculturation are deliberate and systematic, such as learning the rules of written punctuation in a language. At some point in an English speaker's childhood, someone explicitly told them the difference between a question mark and an exclamation point. Most likely, they learned this distinction in school, a fundamental institution of enculturation in many societies. Religious institutions are another common force of enculturation, providing explicit instruction in cultural rules of morality and social interaction. Extracurricular activities such as sports, dance, and music lessons also teach children cultural rules and norms.

While a great deal of very important cultural content is deliberately conveyed in these systematic contexts, the greater part of culture is acquired unconsciously by happenstance—that is, nobody planned to teach it, and no one made an effort to consciously try to learn it. By virtue of growing up in a culture, children learn what certain actions and objects mean, how their society operates, and what the rules are for appropriate behavior.

Going back to the cultural notion of home, did anyone ever explain to you why your childhood home was structured in a certain way? Did anyone ever point out the cultural assumptions about gender and family built into your house? Probably not. Now, imagine that you were taken away from your parents as a baby and adopted by a family far away, with a very different way of life situated in a very different environment. With your adoptive family, you might have been raised in a very different kind of home. Growing up, your everyday habits, activities, and expectations would have been shaped by the setup of that home. Living in that house, you would have wordlessly absorbed a set of assumptions about family, gender, work, leisure, hospitality, and property. And all of it would seem quite natural to you.

Many forms of culture are passed down through a combination of deliberate and unconscious processes. Perhaps when you were a child, someone told you what a wink was and showed you how to accomplish one; or perhaps you just witnessed a few winks, figured out what they meant from their contexts, and then learned how to accomplish one through trial and error. Geertz pointed out that there are two important aspects to winking: the meaning and the action. As both are learned, both are cultural. But perhaps more importantly, both the standardized action of winking and the assumed meaning of this action are commonly known among members of a group. That is, culture is shared.

Consider another aspect of human biology: dreaming. People in all societies dream, and no one has to teach them how to do it. Dreaming is biologically innate and spontaneously performed. Biological researchers hypothesize that dreaming helps the human brain process daily stimuli and convert recent experiences into long-term memories. As a biological necessity for brain health, dreaming is natural, not cultural.

But why do people dream in stories? And why are those stories so often confusing, even troubling? In many cultures, people are perplexed by their dreams, never really knowing what the objects and situations they dream about are meant to indicate—or if they have any meaning at all. In other cultures, however, dreams are recognized as arenas of spiritual communication with supernatural beings. In Ojibwa culture, young people are encouraged to fast for up to a week in order to bring on special visionary dreams (Hallowell 1992; Peters-Golden 2002, 188–189). In such dreams, a young person may be approached by a guardian spirit who imparts knowledge for successful hunting, warfare, or medicine. People are discouraged from discussing the meaning of these dreams, but young people are taught to expect and anticipate this kind of dream, and they know how to interpret the content of such dreams without discussion. The widely shared ability to dream such dreams and the shared knowledge to understand their content makes dreaming profoundly cultural among the Ojibwa.

Summing up, when an element of human experience or behavior is learned and shared, we know it is an aspect of culture. That delineates the concept of culture to some degree. However, the variety of things that are learned and shared by humans in groups is still quite enormous, as indicated by Tylor's rambling list (knowledge, belief, art, morals, law, custom, etc.). Instead of thinking of culture as one vast hodgepodge of things, it's helpful to break that hodgepodge into three basic elements. These basic elements of culture are understood to come together in larger combinations, or aggregates.

3.3 The Elements of Culture

LEARNING OUTCOMES

By the end of this section, you will be able to:

- Define the concept of material culture and provide examples of material culture.
- Provide a detailed example of cultural practices.
- Explain how cultural frames orient our experiences and actions.
- Describe how norms and values are threaded through culture.
- Explain how ideologies and worldviews shape our perception of the world around us.

The complex whole of culture can be broken down into three categories: what we make, what we do, and what we think. The boundaries separating these categories are somewhat artificial because so much of cultural life involves all of these things at once. However, it's useful to start with the basic building blocks of culture, then see how those blocks can be put together to produce more complex structures.

Culture Is What We Make

Museums are buildings where objects of historical, artistic, scientific, or cultural interest are displayed. The Smithsonian's National Museum of the American Indian has one of the world's largest collections of Native artifacts, including many two- and three-dimensional objects such as baskets, pottery, and preserved specimens representative of the lives of Native populations from all areas of the country.

FIGURE 3.5 This basket, woven by Kucadikadi (Mono Lake Paiute) artist Lucy Telles, is an excellent example of the art of basket weaving. Telles, whose work was done in the early part of the twentieth century, is widely admired for her use of color and innovative designs. (credit: "Mono Lake Paiute Basket" by Ernest Amoroso, National Museum of the American Indian/Wikimedia Commons, Public Domain)

People living in groups learn to craft the things they need in order to make a living in their environment. Early human ancestors learned how to make sharp blades useful for processing meat. They shared their knowledge of toolmaking in groups, passing those skills down to younger generations. Objects that are made and used by humans in group contexts are called **material culture**. All of the tools developed by early hominins (blades, arrows, axes, etc.) are examples of material culture. All of the artifacts discovered by archaeologists (buildings, pottery, beads, etc.) are examples of material culture. The specialized knowledge and skills used for making material culture are called **technology**. Today, the word *technology* is often used to refer to electronic devices such as smartphones and computers. For anthropologists, both smartphones and obsidian blades are forms of material culture produced through specialized technologies. That is, *technology* refers to the knowledge and skills required to make blades, phones, and other objects of material culture.

Material culture is not just found in museums, of course. Material culture is all around. All of the furniture, appliances, books, dishes, and pictures on the walls in a typical American home are elements of material culture, and they reveal a great deal about the whole way of life of a society.

Consider the toothbrush. It would be possible for people to clean their teeth with a found object such as a twig or leaf, or even with a finger. Ancient peoples often used a special chew stick, a twig with a frayed end. The bristled toothbrush was invented in 15th-century China and spread across Europe and into the United States, where it began to be mass produced in the late 19th century. Drugstores now feature many styles of toothbrush with an array of special features. Specialized teams design, manufacture, and market this wide variety of toothbrushes to consumers. Parents buy toothbrushes for their children and teach them the conventional techniques for brushing their teeth (little circles, two minutes, etc.). As adults, people often isolate themselves in a special room to brush their teeth in privacy. Even so, toothbrushing is a profoundly social act, relying on shared knowledge and observance of social norms for hygiene and health.

Trees, rocks, microbes, and planets are all material objects, but they are not material culture unless they are made and used by humans in group contexts. For instance, a tree growing in a natural forest is not an object of material culture. However, an apple tree can be material culture if it is planted by a farmer in an orchard designed to produce fruit for human consumption. A microbe can be material culture if it is manufactured to improve human digestion or genetically engineered to fight cancer.

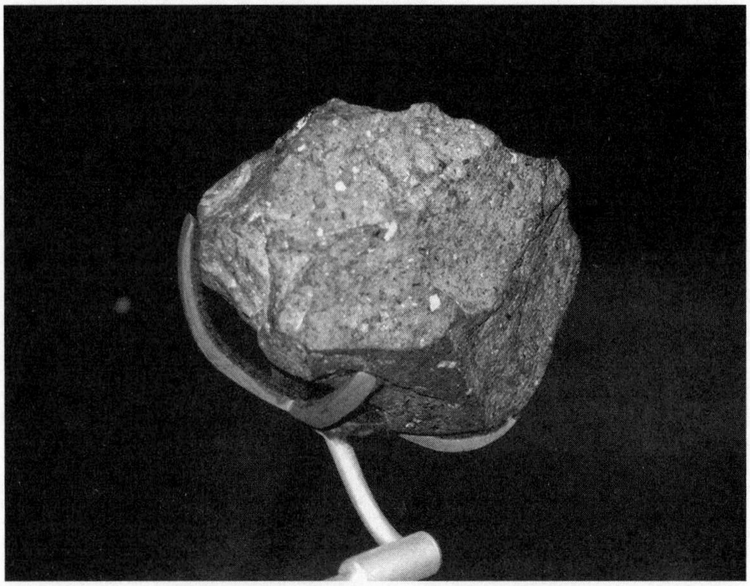

FIGURE 3.6 This rock is on display in the British Museum. While a rock is not in and of itself material culture, this rock, which carries special meaning for those who view it, is. (credit: Archaeomoonwalker/Wikimedia Commons, CC BY 3.0)

On display in the Cleveland Museum of Natural History is a gray rock. This rock was simply found by humans and never shaped for any particular use. Sitting there in the museum, it has no specific purpose other than to serve as an object of popular contemplation. Though it is a fairly unremarkable lump of basalt, thousands of people stop to gaze at this rock, reading the sign that describes how it was obtained, marveling at its presence there in the museum. Why? What's so interesting about a rock? This particular rock was collected by astronauts on the Apollo 12 mission to the moon. The rock serves as evidence of this magnificent feat of scientific engineering and a source of great pride to the culture that accomplished such a mission. We go to museums to view the items on display there, but clearly, the human activities surrounding those objects are what make them interesting to us. That is, culture is not just material objects—it's also what we do and what we think.

Culture Is What We Do

Ahmed is a carpet seller in the Istanbul Grand Bazaar. Every day, people from all over the world come into his stall to examine, and sometimes buy, the carpets in his inventory. Anthropologist Patricia Scalco (2019) met Ahmed while she was conducting research on market exchange in Istanbul. She carefully observed the set of sales strategies he had crafted to respond to customer desires and knowledge. When anyone pauses at the entrance, Ahmed greets the potential customer and ushers the person into his stall. Bringing out a silver platter, Ahmed offers the customer a cup of tea, a welcoming gesture. As the customer browses, Ahmed initiates a carefully constructed conversation designed to determine what sort of person this customer is, what they are looking for, and what they really know (and do not know) about carpets. He pulls out various carpets from the stacks, unfurling them as he describes their distinctive qualities. Ahmed identifies this interaction as a sort of game he must play with his customers. European tourists in this Turkish marketplace are often inspired by the desire for handmade traditional crafts made by local rural ethnic groups such as the Kurds. These days, however, most carpets sold in the Istanbul market are industrially produced in Pakistan, India, and China. However, in his many years of selling carpets, Ahmed has learned that he must play to Western orientalist fantasies, weaving a distinctive story around the origins and manufacture of a carpet, in order to win a sale. Like other merchants in this market, Ahmed has a family to support, and he cannot afford to openly contradict the knowledge and desires of his customers.

Centered on the material culture of carpets, Ahmed's work illustrates the importance of what people do and what they think in the making of cultural life. What people do and what they think are nonmaterial elements of culture. In his everyday interactions with customers, Ahmed has developed a set of habitual practices involving gesture and speech. Anthropologists use the term **cultural practices** to refer to this form of culture. Routine speech communicates meanings and values (such as the "authenticity" of a carpet), while routine action organizes social events (such as, hopefully, a sale). People from all walks of life develop similar combinations of habitual action and speech that constitute the everyday culture of people in those circumstances.

What do you do in the morning to get ready for the day? That is cultural practice. What do you do when someone comes over to your house? That is cultural practice. What do you do when you're hungry? That is cultural practice. Some cultural anthropologists focus on these everyday practices as keys to understanding culture, while others are more interested in special events such as ceremonies and festivals.

For instance, Carnival in Brazil is an annual festival of music and dance held every year to mark the beginning of the Catholic season of Lent. Parades of costumed dancers throng the streets of many cities, interacting with the audience and attracting crowds of followers. Cultural anthropologist Kenneth Williamson (2012) studied Carnival in Salvador, Bahia, in the north of Brazil. While Brazilian Carnival is framed as a national celebration, Williamson found that Carnival in the poorer and largely Black city of Salvador is distinctively animated by the politics of race. Local Carnival dance groups incorporate Black forms of movement such as capoeira, a combination of dance and martial art techniques created by Brazilian enslaved peoples. Forms of music and religion originating in Africa also contribute to the distinctiveness of Salvadoran Carnival. Carnival has become increasingly commercialized as a tourist attraction in Salvador, bringing in Black and White tourists alike. Black Brazilian activists complain that forms of Black culture are being appropriated and exploited as forms of cultural leisure with little understanding of their deep cultural meanings as expressions of resistance and survival. Meanwhile, most Black Salvadorans enjoy little benefit from the burgeoning tourist economy.

The practices of Turkish carpet merchants and Brazilian Carnival participants are both ways of doing culture, every day and on special occasions. As we see in both examples, the materials and actions of culture are infused with patterns of thought, some shared and some controversial. These ways of thinking constitute a third element of culture.

Culture Is What We Think

Imagine that you are walking down the street and you see a building. You notice a mailbox next to a driveway. You follow a little walkway lined with flowers to a front door. Below your feet, you find a mat that says, "Welcome!" Peering through a window, you see a central room where two people are sitting on a couch, eating chips, and watching television. Off to the side, there's a hallway. You can barely see the stockinged feet of a small person resting on a bed. A dog barks.

What kind of place is this? Are you sure? How do you know?

Now imagine you are walking down the street and see another building. There are neon lights in the front window and a large paved area to the side. As you enter the front door, a little bell jingles and young woman in a white blouse greets you from behind a long table. To one side of that table is a large black machine with buttons and numbers on it. The young woman carries a small leather folder in her hand and gives you an expectant smile. You look around to find a room full of people seated at tables of various sizes. Young people in white tops and black pants are scurrying here and there, some carrying giant platters. You hear music in the background. You smell something delicious.

What kind of place is this? How do you know?

In both scenarios, elements of material culture are combined with patterns of action and speech. In order to make sense of these two scenarios, we must use shared ways of thinking about them. What we know about the way of life in our society leads us to identify the first scenario as somebody's home. What we know about the circumstances of eating in public leads us to identify the second scenario as a restaurant.

These patterned, shared ways of making sense of situations are called **cultural frames**. Cultural frames tell people where they are, what role they they play in that context, and what forms of behavior and speech are expected and appropriate. There are cultural frames for places, times, events, and relationships. If a couple have been dating for over a year, they probably use a cultural frame for romantic relationships to structure their actions and expectations in that relationship. And if one of the romantic partners invites the other to spend a holiday with their family, the invited person will probably summon a cultural frame for that holiday to tell them what to expect and how to behave.

Cultural frames are complex cognitive models that incorporate various roles and actions patterned in space and time. A **cultural role** is a conventionalized position held by a person or persons in a particular context or situation. Sociocultural roles are associated with certain behaviors and actions. For example, "mother" is a sociocultural role in the cultural frame of "family." "Waiter" is a sociocultural role in the cultural frame of "restaurant." While these roles are found in many cultures, the actions and behaviors associated with them vary significantly across cultural contexts.

In cultures that celebrate Mother's Day, it is conventional to send one's mother a card along with flowers and/or a gift. Anyone who has ever been shopping for a Mother's Day card has been bombarded with images and text that convey the stereotypical behaviors and preferences associated with motherhood. Many Mother's Day cards feature pastel flower arrangements with birds, butterflies, and delicate calligraphy. The text lionizes the emotional and material work of motherhood, praising the constant care and sacrifice of the good mother. In return, the card promises eternal gratitude.

FIGURE 3.7 This American Mother's Day card from 1916 would still be considered appropriate today. The norm for a Mother's Day card in the United States has not changed much in over a century. (credit: Northern Pacific Railway/ Wikimedia Commons, Public Domain)

The behaviors and actions associated with a sociocultural role are collectively called a **norm**. Norms are not necessarily "normal" in the sense that they represent the most common features and behaviors exhibited by people in a certain role. Do all mothers prefer pastel flower motifs over, say, images of books or sports? Rather, norms tend to be idealized, a fantasy about how people in a role behave—or how they *should* behave. Why do we associate flowers, pastels, cursive, and self-sacrifice with motherhood?

The answer lies in another thinking element of culture: **values**. Cultural values are notions about what is good, true, correct, appropriate, or beautiful. A certain mainstream way of thinking about motherhood indicates that mothers should be delicate and feminine, concerned with beauty and decorum. Moreover, mothers should nurture and sustain growth. What better way of conveying these notions than through the imagery of pastel flower arrangements? Messages of gratitude describe the sort of behavior considered appropriate to mothers. A "good" mother is a mother who puts her children at the center of her life at all times, neglecting her own interests for the benefit of her family.

In any culture, norms indicate how people should behave, and values explain why they should behave that way. For example, the norm for women in the 1950s was to get married and work in the home rather than have a job in the public workforce. Not that all women did this, or even most. Many mothers, particularly women of color, were obliged to work outside the home just to make a living for their families. Nonetheless, normative depictions of women as housewives dominated media and public discourse in mid-20th-century America, establishing this idealistic norm. Why were mothers supposed to stay at home? A set of "family values" appointed fathers as the breadwinning heads of household, while mothers were relegated to serving men by keeping house and caring for children. Thus, the values that came to be associated with motherhood were subservience, self-sacrifice, gentleness, and nurture—the very values we see celebrated on Mother's Day cards.

Norms and values can combine in larger models that depict how various social realms operate, such as the family, the economy, the supernatural, and the political sphere. These models are known as **ideologies**. An ideology identifies the entities, roles, behaviors, relationships, and processes in a particular realm as well as the rationale behind the whole system. Take democracy, for instance. The political ideology of democracy envisions a society of equal individual citizens who each cast a vote on proposals for government action. The majority vote wins. The essential roles in this ideology are citizen voters and government. The essential actions are voting and government action. The rationale is that government should obey the wishes of the citizenry.

Is this how democracy really works, though? What about the influence of powerful organizations such as the media and large corporations? Moreover, in most democracies, people do not vote directly on government policies but rather elect representatives, who craft laws and then vote on those laws themselves. Those representatives are accountable to citizens through the process of voting, but they are also strongly influenced by lobbyists representing business interests and the campaign donations of wealthy individuals and groups. Obviously, this ideology is a simplification of the way any democratic system really works. Ideologies are always partial, foregrounding the perspectives of some people in society while obscuring the perspectives of others.

A **worldview** is a very broad ideology that shapes how the members of a culture generally view the world and their place in it. Worldviews tend to span several realms, including religion, economics, and politics. A worldview provides an overarching model for the purpose and process of social life, depicting "how the world works." Many West African cultures, for instance, are shaped by a worldview that identifies the rationale of society in the accumulation and distribution of material goods in extended families, communities, and the nation as a whole. People rise to leadership through their ability to accumulate wealth, but they are strongly obligated to distribute that wealth through their extended families and communities by funding the education and business ventures of family members and helping those in need. Beyond the family, the actions of political and business leaders are shaped by this worldview as well. A political leader is expected to support the generation of wealth while also making sure that the benefits are spread through the community. Moreover, leaders are expected to maintain relationships with departed ancestors who watch over their descendants. Through periodic rituals and offerings, leaders petition ancestors to bless their families and communities with prosperity and good fortune.

3.4 The Aggregates of Culture

LEARNING OUTCOMES

By the end of this section, you will be able to:

- Explain how elements of culture combine in aggregates.
- Give three detailed examples of cultural symbols.
- Explain how symbols are embedded in rituals.
- Describe how social structures organize important cultural processes.

An aggregate is a combination of elements. What we make, what we do, and what we think all combine in larger aggregates of culture. For instance, it's pretty clear that toothbrushes, moon rocks, restaurants, and Mother's Day cards must be understood as aggregates of material objects, practices, and ideas. In order to fully understand the toothbrush as a cultural object, we must examine not only its design and production but also *how* people use toothbrushes and *why* they use them. A set of routine practices surround our cultural objects (brushing), and those practices are supported by cultural ideas (hygiene).

Symbols

A **symbol** is an object, image, gesture, vocalization, or event conventionally associated with a particular meaning. anthropologist Jennifer Hasty was conducting fieldwork in Ghana during an election year, she noticed that the posters and pamphlets of one politician featured a broom. Confused, she asked a friend why a male politician would choose a humble domestic tool associated with women's work as his political motif. Making a sweeping motion with her hands, she explained, "Because he is promising to sweep away all the corruption." Turns out, he was the not the first to use this symbol. Over time, the broom has come to acquire political meaning as a symbolic anti-corruption tool in Ghana.

FIGURE 3.8 Featured in political posters and pamphlets, brooms like these have taken on special meaning in Ghanian politics, where they are understood as a symbol of a politician's intent to sweep away corruption. (credit: "Handmade Brooms at Granville Island Broom Co." by Ruth Hartnup/flickr, CC BY 2.0)

Colors, shapes, gestures, animals, plants—all of these commonly acquire specific cultural meaning. For a Hindu wedding, a bride typically wears a bright red sari, as red is an auspicious color associated with change, passion, and prosperity. White, on the other hand, is typically worn to Indian funerals.

Symbols are useful cultural aggregates because they provide a kind of shorthand for expressing complex ideas. Consider the American bumper sticker shown in Figure 3.9.

FIGURE 3.9 This popular American bumper sticker incorporates a variety of religious and social symbols. (credit: "Coexistence" by Rusty Clark/flickr, CC BY 2.0)

Combining symbols from Islam, Judaism, Taoism, Christianity, paganism, women, men, and the peace movement, this sticker aims to promote multicultural diversity. Rather than listing the various religions, identities, and ideologies and describing the conflicts among them, the message simply incorporates their symbols into a word urging mutual tolerance.

Although symbols have conventional meanings, they can mean different things in different contexts or to different people. Although the intended meaning of the above bumper sticker is diversity, some people interpret it as an emblem of radical atheism. In the wake of the 2016 presidential election, some Americans started wearing safety pins to show their solidarity with LGBTQIA+ people, people of color, and others who had become targets of post-election harassment. For some, however, the safety pin symbolized pretentiousness and hypocrisy.

Ritual

Combining objects, actions, and meanings, **ritual** is a special kind of repeated, patterned action conventionally associated with a particular meaning. Rituals incorporate symbols and roles along with routinized activities such as gestures, music, and movement. Many rituals are performed by specialists in group settings to accomplish specific group or individual goals. Rituals bring together symbols, practices, and worldviews.

Consider this popular American ritual. On the first Sunday in February, many Americans gather in each other's homes to watch the annual championship game of the National Football League (NFL) on television. So widespread is this practice that stores are nearly empty and many Christian churches cancel afternoon and evening activities. As a whole, the ritual consists of many roles and relationships as well as patterned actions and conventional meanings. At the heart of the action are the two teams competing against one another in a chaotic game featuring an oddly shaped ball carried forward in campaigns of full-frontal assault across a carefully marked field. The players are surrounded by referees, coaches, camera people, and cheerleaders, each group having a strategic role in the action. Surrounding the field are commentators who interpret and contextualize, giving meaning to the actions of the game. At home, some people watch the game closely, exclaiming with joy or disappointment and commenting on the comments of the commentators. Other people socialize with one another, watching the game intermittently. Vast amounts of food and drink are consumed by Americans on Super Bowl Sunday. Typical foods include potato chips, dips, barbecued chicken wings, and pizza. Beer is the beverage of choice for this occasion. An event celebrating competition, spectatorship, and consumption, Super Bowl Sunday is an effective ritual for reinforcing dominant values in a society structured by corporate capitalism. Notions of gender, race, and class are threaded through the various levels of play and consumption as well.

In the Akan communities of central and southern Ghana, in West Africa, leaders perform a ritual called *Adae* that uses important cultural symbols and reinforces cultural commitments to authority, ancestors, and shared prosperity. In the Akan society, people are given special wooden stools to mark certain stages in life, such as puberty and marriage. A person's stool is said to contain the personal power of the owner, symbolizing the life essence of that person.

FIGURE 3.10 This stool is more than just a place to sit down. In the Akan society which created it, it is understood to represent the personal power and life essence of the person it was given to. (credit: "Stool (Dwa)" by Museum Expedition 1922, Robert B. Woodward Memorial Fund/Wikimedia Commons, CC BY 3.0)

When an eminent person dies, that person's stool is enshrined in a special shed called a stool house, or *nkonuafieso*. Twice every 42 days (once on a Wednesday and once on a Sunday), a community leader makes a procession to the stool house of the ancestral leaders of the community. Entering the stool house, the leader must remove their sandals and lower the cloth worn draped around their shoulders, symbolizing their humility and respect for the ancestors. Then the leader greets the ancestral leaders one by one, making offerings of drink and food and asking for blessings and prosperity for the community.

Special rituals called **rites of passage** are used to mark the movement of a person from one social status to another. Naming ceremonies, puberty rites, weddings, and funerals are all common rites of passage. Anthropologist Arnold van Gennep (1960) identified three stages in rites of passage: separation, transition, and incorporation. In the first phase, separation, individuals, or groups are taken out of their everyday social context, leaving their original social status. In the second phase, transition, people exist in an in-between state outside of conventional norms of dress and action. In this phase, people are often dressed in special costume, made to engage in unusual behaviors, and taught special forms of secret knowledge. In the third phase, people are brought back into society in a formal ceremony and introduced as subjects in a new social category.

Initiation rituals are a common rite of passage in many societies. In many African societies that practice initiation, young people are gathered together in a group and taken to a special camp outside the town or village. This constitutes the separation phase. In the next phase, transition, members of the group are often dressed alike and made to follow a common set of rules and schedule of activities. They may be required to perform unusual feats, such as eating strange foods. Their bodies may be scarified or tattooed. Elders give them special knowledge essential to performing their future roles as women or men. For instance, girls may learn explicit lessons about conception and childbirth. Finally, when the transition is complete, initiates are returned to the town or village and presented as women or men. Often, the completion of initiation marks a young woman as formally eligible for courtship and marriage.

Social Structure

The way a society is formally organized is called **social structure**. Typically, a society organizes a set of routine activities and objects in space and time to accomplish a particular function, such as community decision-making, the production and circulation of goods, or religious observance. Social structure is the framework for those realms, designating when, where, how, and by whom these functions are accomplished. Social structures combine material culture (such as buildings) with practices (such as meetings) and ideas (such as the rules and procedures of those meetings).

Consider the social structure of community decision-making, or the political realm. In some societies, community decisions are routinely made under the authority of a person inhabiting an inherited political office, called a chief or king (such as the Akans, discussed in the last section). Chiefs often have a council of community elders, the heads of local extended families. A chief is expected to consult with this council in all community matters. Other groups in society may represent the interests of youth, women, farmers, or traders. Each group will have its own leader who communicates directly with the local chief. Regular procedures govern how issues are raised and discussed and how decisions are taken. Together, the groups, roles, relationships, and procedures all constitute the social structure of the political system.

Rather than seeing social structure as fixed and immobile, some anthropologists emphasize that people continually make and alter their social structures through everyday forms of interpretation, participation, and resistance. These processes mean that social structures are always subject to a variety of forces in a constant state of change.

3.5 Modes of Cultural Analysis

LEARNING OUTCOMES

By the end of this section, you will be able to:

- Explain how evolutionary theories have been applied to the study of human culture.
- Identify two critiques of evolutionary approaches.
- Describe how anthropologists have studied the functionality of culture.
- Distinguish Malinowski's functionalism from Radcliffe-Brown's structural functionalism.
- Explain how ontological anthropology defines the study of reality.

Anthropologists have a number of ways of studying the elements and aggregates of culture. Some approaches emphasize the development of a particular aspect of culture over time, while other approaches examine how the different parts of culture fit together.

Evolution, Adaptation, and Historical Particularism

Some anthropologists are interested in the origins of human cultural forms and how these forms have changed over long periods of time. Just as Charles Darwin applied the notion of evolution to explain how biological species change over time, many 19th-century anthropologists used evolution to explain how cultures changed over time. This approach is called **cultural evolutionism**. Like Darwin, these anthropologists believed that simple forms evolved into more complex forms. Comparing different cultures of the world, they assigned the ones they considered more rudimentary to earlier evolutionary stages, while the ones they considered more complex were assigned to the more advanced stages. For example, British anthropologist Edward Tylor argued that human culture evolved from savagery through barbarism to civilization. He identified savagery with people who used gathering and hunting to meet their basic needs. The domestication of animals and plants was associated with barbarism. Civilization resulted from more advanced forms of farming, trade, and manufacturing as well as the development of the alphabet. Not surprisingly, British scholars identified their own culture as highly civilized.

Elaborating on Tylor's scheme, American anthropologist Lewis Henry Morgan subdivided each of these three stages into an even more elaborate model and proposed a mechanism for moving from stage to stage. Morgan focused on technology as the primary driver of cultural evolution. New and better ways of making things, according to Morgan, resulted in new patterns of social practice and thought. Advanced technology was associated with advanced civilization.

But is technology the only measure of cultural accomplishment, or even the best one? Members of societies in which people gather and hunt for a living have vast stores of knowledge about their environments. Typically, they can name hundreds of plant species and tell when and where to find each of them. Many hunters can examine animal tracks to discern the species, sex, age, and condition of the animal as well as how long ago the tracks were laid. People in these societies also actively sustain and nurture diversity in their environments, careful to avoid depleting important resources. Is it really accurate to think of such cultures as simple? All cultures are complex, though in different ways. Technology is highly valued in American culture, while environmental knowledge and sustainability have historically been less valued. Is it any wonder that early American anthropologists ranked other cultures according to one of their own most cherished values? Perhaps people in more environmentally sustainable cultures might consider the United States to be an example of environmental savagery.

Both Tylor and Morgan, like most anthropologists of their day, thought that all cultures passed through this single set of stages in the march toward civilization. This kind of theory is called **unilineal evolution**. Disagreeing with this way of thinking, anthropologists such as Franz Boas argued that there is no single line of cultural evolution but that each culture changes according to its own unique historical trajectory. Moreover, cultures evolve not in isolation but in constant interaction with one another. Rather than focusing on technological changes within a culture, Boas highlighted the **diffusion** of material objects, practices, and ideas among cultures in complex relations of trade, migration, and conquest.

Though theories of unilineal cultural evolution have been largely abandoned, some anthropologists are still interested in discovering regular patterns that might govern how human cultures change over long periods of time. In the 1950s, American anthropologist Julian Steward developed an approach called **cultural ecology**, recognizing the importance of environmental factors by focusing on how humans adapt to various environments. Steward's approach showed how humans in each environmental zone develop a set of core cultural features that enable them to make a living. Central to each cultural core are ways of getting or making all the resources necessary for human survival—in particular, food, clothing, and shelter. Similarly, anthropologist Marvin Harris developed a theory called **cultural materialism**, arguing that technology and economic factors are fundamental to culture, molding other features such as family life, religion, and politics.

Though recognizing the importance of cultural change, many anthropologists reject the notion that all cultures change according to a general universal model, such as cultural materialism. Drawing from the Boasian notion that each culture follows its own historical path; many cultural anthropologists analyze change in terms of **historical particularism**. In this approach, contemporary processes are understood as products of the unique combination of internal and external forces unfolding over time in a particular culture.

Functionalism

Rejecting the comparative unilineal models that assigned each culture to an evolutionary stage, a number of cultural anthropologists developed a radically different approach that attempts to understand each contemporary culture in its own terms. **Functionalism** seeks to understand the purpose of the elements and aggregates of culture in the here and now.

Bronislaw Malinowski, an early proponent of this approach, argued that the function of culture is to meet human needs. All humans need to satisfy the need for food, clothing, and shelter. The fundamental purpose of culture is to provide a means of satisfying those needs. In the course of meeting those basic needs, humans in all cultures develop a set of derived needs—that is, needs derived from the basic ones. Derived needs include the need to organize work and distribute resources. Family structures and gender roles are examples of cultural elements addressing these derived needs. Finally, cultures also address a set of integrative needs, providing people with guiding values and purpose in life. Religion, law, and ideologies fulfill these integrative needs. Malinowski sought to understand both the biological and psychological functions of culture.

At first glance, this approach may not seem all that different from evolutionary approaches that identify the core set of cultural features devoted to human survival. What was so different in Malinowski's approach was his attempt to show that even so-called primitive societies had functionally complex cultural systems for meeting the full array of human needs. Malinowski's three-volume ethnography of the economics, religion, and kinship of the Trobriand people of Papua New Guinea demonstrated this fact in striking and elaborate detail.

A second version of functionalism, advocated by British anthropologist Alfred R. Radcliffe-Brown, identified the functions of various elements of culture in a slightly different way. Rather than looking for the way culture satisfies biological or psychological needs, **structural functionalism** focused more on how the various structures in society reinforce one another. Culture is not a random assortment of structural features but a set of structures that fit together into a coherent whole. Common norms and values are threaded through the family structure, the economy, the political system, and the religion of a culture. Structural functionalists conceptualized culture as a kind of machine with many small parts all working in tandem to keep the machine operating properly. While recognizing the value of this approach, contemporary anthropologists have complicated the mechanistic model of culture by pointing out that the various elements of culture come into conflict just as often as they reinforce one another. Although few anthropologists would now identify themselves as structural functionalists, the holistic approach to culture as an integrated system is derived from this important theoretical foundation.

Structuralism

In the previous paragraph, you learned about structural functionalism, an approach that marries functionalism with social structure. In a different sense, the term *structure* can refer to patterns of thought embedded in the culture of a people—that is, conceptual structure. French anthropologist Claude Lévi-Strauss pioneered this approach, sometimes called French **structuralism**. Lévi-Strauss considered culture to be a system of symbols that could be analyzed in the various realms of culture, including myths, religion, and kinship. In these realms of culture, objects and people are organized into symbolic systems of classification, often structured around binary oppositions. Binary oppositions are pairs of terms that are opposite in meaning, such as light/dark, female/male, and good/evil. For example, kinship systems are varied and complex, but they are fundamentally structured by oppositions such as male versus female, older versus younger, and relation by blood versus relation by marriage. Lévi-Strauss examined myths as well, showing how the characters and plots emphasize binary oppositions. Consider the many European folktales featuring an evil stepmother (Cinderella, Sleeping Beauty), a character that combines the opposition of good versus evil with the opposition of blood relation versus relation by marriage. Lévi-Strauss argued that myths operate as public arenas for conceptually pondering and processing the fundamental categories and relations of a culture.

Ontology

In recent decades, some cultural anthropologists have come to focus on the nature of reality, including but not limited to human perspectives and experiences. **Ontology** is the study of the true nature of existence. In some cultures, for instance, the social world consists not only of embodied persons but also of spirit beings, such as ancestors and witches, who interact with people in mysterious ways. And in some cultures, people are not just bodies but assemblages that include souls, spirits, characters, or fates. **Ontological anthropology** explores how culture constructs our social and natural realities, what we consider real, and how we act on those assumptions. Reaching beyond human realities, ontological anthropology also attempts to include nonhuman perspectives, relationships, and forms of communication.

For instance, in his provocative ethnography *How Forests Think* (2013), anthropologist Eduardo Kohn describes how the web of life in the Amazon rainforest consists of continual communication among plants, animals, and humans. He examines how Amazonian peoples engage with dogs, spirits, the dead, pumas, rivers, and even sounds. Humans and these nonhuman beings are both antagonistic and interdependent in this interactive web. Predators and prey read one another's behavior, interpreting intentions and motivations. Kohn's effort is to get beyond conventional modes of human thought and language to understand how humans are embedded in nonhuman ecological realities.

PROFILES IN ANTHROPOLOGY

Dame Mary Douglas
1921–2007

Dame Mary Douglas (https://www.openstax.org/r/wiki_Mary_Douglas).

Personal History: Mary Douglas was born in San Remo, Italy; her British parents had stopped off on their way home from Burma, where her father had been working as a colonial civil servant. As children, Mary and her younger sister lived with their mother's parents in England until they were old enough to be sent to Catholic boarding school—a fairly common practice for the children of colonial officers. After the death of her mother and her dearly loved maternal grandfather, young Mary found security in the order and routine of the convent school (Lyons 2011). This respect for rules and order combined with a reverence for the Catholic Church to shape her lifelong commitment to studying the sacred aspects of the social order.

Area of Anthropology: At Oxford, Douglas studied with the prominent structural functionalist E. E. Evans-Pritchard. From him, she learned that African belief systems such as witchcraft were structured by an underlying logic. In this approach, the goal of fieldwork is to examine oral forms of culture as well as ritual and social practice in order to discern the underlying logic that governs culture as a whole. Douglass went to the Kasai region of what was then the Belgian Congo, where she studied how the Lele people used animals in practical and symbolic ways. She was particularly interested in a strange animal called the pangolin. Though a mammal, the pangolin has scales and no teeth.

FIGURE 3.11 This pangolin is classified as a mammal but has scales like a reptile or fish. Pangolin were considered sacred to the Lele people, who did not classify them as a food animal. (credit: Official photographer of the U.S. Embassy in Ghana/Wikimedia Commons, Public Domain)

Douglas described how the Lele observed a fundamental distinction between edible and inedible animals. Animals who lived among humans, such as rats and domesticated chickens, were considered part of society and therefore inedible (most of the time). Only wild animals were considered food. Pangolins are wild animals, but the Lele did not eat them (usually). Why? Douglas argued that the weirdness of the pangolin made people single it out for special consideration. Pangolins have scales like fish, but they live on land and climb trees. They look vaguely reptilian, but they do not lay eggs, instead giving birth to live young. Rather than teeth, they have long snouts that they use to vacuum up small insects. Thus, the pangolin defied the conventional categories the Lele used for dividing up the animal world. This breach of categories made the pangolin both repellent and sacred to the Lele. Members of a special fertility cult engaged in rituals in which they ate pangolins to ingest the power of this anomalous animal.

As this examination of cultural categories and anomalies suggests, Douglas was also influenced by Claude Lévi-Strauss and the approach of French structuralism. Like Lévi-Strauss, Douglas viewed culture as a coherent system of categories that were expressed in oral culture and social practice.

Accomplishments in the Field: Following her work on the Lele people, Douglas went on to conduct a broadly comparative study of objects, practices, and people that were considered ritually dangerous, subject to rules of prohibition called taboos. She showed how the subjects of taboos are often "matter out of place" (Douglas 1966, 44), things that defy conventional categories for dividing up the social and natural world. In her most famous work, *Purity and Danger* (1966), Douglas examines a wide range of taboos, such as rules against eating certain foods or engaging in sex at certain times or with certain persons. She examines the set of social and dietary rules established by ancient Hebrews, detailed in the book of Leviticus in the Old Testament. According to these rules, the Jewish people were forbidden from eating pigs, shellfish, and certain wild animals. They were not allowed to wear garments made of cloth that combined different fibers—such as, for example, a linen-cotton blend. Men were prohibited from having sex with menstruating women. In fact, women were considered so unclean during menstruation that anyone or anything that touched a menstruating woman became contaminated for the rest of that day.

What do all of these prohibitions have in common? Douglas shows how each forbidden object or condition produced discomfort because it transgressed conventional categories. Shellfish, for instance, are sea animals, but they don't have fins or scales, and many of them do not swim. Menstruation is blood loss, but it does not indicate injury. Moreover, menstruation is hidden and connected to the dangerous states of pregnancy and childbirth. In Hebrew law, menstruation itself was considered a dangerous and contaminating exception to the purity of persons and objects.

In her later work, Douglas applied this style of analysis to a variety of other social phenomena, including humor and trickster figures. She argued that humor functions as a release for thoughts and actions that might threaten the social order. Whereas taboos regulate and prohibit interaction with dangerous objects, animals, and people, humor seeks to sap them of their dangerous power by making light of them.

Importance of Her Work: After more than 25 years of teaching at the University of London, Douglas moved to the United States, where she held positions at the Russell Sage Foundation and Northwestern University. She continued to publish widely on such topics as consumerism, environmental risk, and decision-making in bureaucracies. When she retired, she moved back to England. In 2006, she was made Dame Commander of the Order of the British Empire. She died in 2007 at the age of 86.

3.6 The Paradoxes of Culture

LEARNING OUTCOMES

By the end of this section, you will be able to:

- Identify four paradoxes in the concept of culture.
- Define four mechanisms of cultural change.
- Provide a detailed example of the mobility of culture.
- Describe culture as an arena of argument and contest.
- Explain how members of a culture can have different versions of their shared culture.

As European immigrants settled in the western frontier of the United States, they faced the challenge of reinventing the elements of culture familiar to them in very different environmental and social conditions. Used to living in houses made of wooden planks or logs, they found themselves on vast plains with very few trees. A common adaptation to this environmental limitation was to dig into a slope of earth to create a dugout home with turf walls and roof.

FIGURE 3.12 This Nebraska home, photographed with cow on its roof in 1870, was constructed in the side of the hill directly behind it. While such dugout homes were practical and functional, those who lived in them typically strove to replace them with wood-frame houses, as symbols of wealth and achievement. (credit: Solomon D. Butcher/Library of Congress, Public Domain)

While these homes were perfectly functional, many Euro-American settlers considered them dirty and backward. When their farming ventures became prosperous, they often undertook the great expense of importing wood from forested areas to build the kind of house familiar to them from life back east, either on the East Coast of the United States or in the European countries they originally came from.

While conducting fieldwork in Lesotho in the 1980s, cultural anthropologist Jim Ferguson observed that people who became prosperous often replaced their round homes made of mud and stone and thatched roofs with rectangular ones featuring cement floors and galvanized steel roofs. While the round buildings were functionally adapted to local conditions, made of local materials, cool on hot days, and warm in cool nights, the rectangular ones heated up like ovens under the hot sun and were noisy in the rain. The materials were imported and expensive. Talking to one man who was planning to replace his round house with a rectangular one made of cement and steel, Ferguson suggested that local building methods and materials might be superior to foreign ones.

> Looking me carefully in the eye, he asked, "What kind of house does your father have, there in America? ... Is it round?" No, I confessed; it was rectangular. "Does it have a grass roof?" No, it did not. "Does it have cattle dung for a floor?" No. And then: "How many rooms does your father's house have?" ... I mumbled, "About ten, I think." After pausing to let this sink in, he said only: "That is the direction we would like to move in." (Ferguson 2006, 18)

In both cases, for Euro-American settlers and Lesotho villagers, the idea of home is not a settled matter but subject to the forces of environmental adaptation, functionality, social status, and ideological debate. Both examples illustrate a set of tensions at the heart of the concept of culture. Originally, anthropologists studied culture as a fairly stable and consensual set of features commonly embraced by the people of a certain geographical area. In the course of the 20th century, however, anthropologists began to realize that this notion of culture was misleading and incomplete. In the early 20th century, American anthropologist Franz Boas argued that the elements of culture are highly mobile, diffusing through the cultural contacts of trade and migration. Since the 1960s, cultural anthropologists have come to emphasize the controversial aspects of culture: how people disagree and argue over the dominant values and practices of their societies. Much of this controversy stems from the unevenness of culture within a society—how people in different social categories and subgroups participate differently in their common culture, with different versions or perspectives on the same cultural norms and practices.

Despite these forces of change and controversy, there is something durable and shared about culture, some set of common elements that distinguishes the whole way of life of each society. Even as cultures change through innovation and contact, they often hold on to some of their distinctive features. In the 1980s, some scholars thought that increases in global trade, migration, and technology were transforming all the diverse societies of the world into one uniform global monoculture. In the 2020s, we see that the opposite has happened. In many parts of the world, we have seen a resurgence of cultural identities and explicit efforts to maintain, rehabilitate, and reinvent forms of cultural heritage.

So riddled with contradictions is the concept of culture that some anthropologists have suggested ditching the whole notion altogether and finding some other concept to bind together the four fields in their pursuit of knowledge about humanity. Perhaps such an integrated understanding of humanity isn't even possible.

Or maybe the contradictions of culture are the most illuminating aspects of the culture concept. Maybe those contradictions are anthropology's most important contribution to our understanding of humanity. This textbook takes the latter approach. Culture is the whole way of life of a people subject to a set of contradictory forces. These forces constitute four central paradoxes of culture.

Paradox 1: Culture Is Continuous, but It Changes

Cultural materials, practices, and ideas are handed down from older to younger members of a culture, giving some degree of continuity to culture over time. However, many factors can intervene in this process of cultural reproduction to subtly alter or dramatically change the elements and aggregates of culture. In some contexts, younger people either fail to precisely learn the culture of their elders or deliberately reject those cultural lessons. Through travel and trade, people learn about other ways of doing things, and they take these ideas back to their own cultures, trying them out to see how they might improve their own ways of life. Accidents and deliberate experimentation introduce new possibilities. People may simply get tired of doing things one way over and over and thrill at some refreshing style or craze.

We can identify four main mechanisms of cultural change. These four mechanisms overlap and interact as the history of a culture unfolds over time. Diffusion is the movement of an element of culture from one society to another, often through migration or trade. **Friction** occurs when two or more elements of culture come into conflict, resulting in alteration or replacement of those elements. **Innovation** is the slight alteration of an existing element of culture, such as a new style of dress or dance. **Invention** is the independent creation of a new element of culture, such as a new technology, religion, or political form.

In the examples at the beginning of this section, building techniques and ideals move along with human migration to new settings, where they must be altered to fit the materials and challenges of the new environment. In colonial and neocolonial contexts, dominant groups may introduce the techniques and ideals of their own homelands as "superior" even if they don't work very well in the environments of colonial conquest.

Some cultural inventions are so successful that they transform the whole way of life of a people. Consider the information technologies that have reshaped American life since the 1970s, such as computers, the Internet, and cell phones. These tools have changed the ways Americans communicate, work, learn, shop, navigate, and entertain themselves. Diffusing through trade, these inventions have transformed cultures all over the world in diverse ways. In many societies, modes of interacting through communication technologies come into conflict with norms for interacting face-to-face, creating friction between the two realms. Where the movements, behavior, and social relationships of young women are tightly controlled, for instance, mobile phones allow women to secretly make new friends, explore new topics of conversation, and engage in behavior their elders might not sanction.

Sometimes the forces of innovation and invention catch on, and sometimes they don't. In the 1970s, Ralph Hasty, a disc jockey from southwest Missouri, moved to Northern California, where he lived and worked for many years. There, he learned about a new technology for building houses in the form of geodesic domes, structures comprising intersecting polygons assembled from prefabricated kits. In late 1980s, he returned to live in southwest Missouri, bringing with him this enthusiasm for geodesic construction. He ordered a kit and built a geodesic dome house on a piece of rural land, intending to sell the house and use the profits to build more of these geodesic wonders. Well, things did not exactly go to plan. The locals apparently found the house far too weird to suit their notion of home. From the outside, the dome looked like some sort of futuristic greenhouse or zoo habitat. On the inside, conventional furniture did not fit in the oddly shaped rooms of the dome. Once finished, the geodesic home sat on the market for a number of months, and eventually, he had to sell it at a loss. It must be mentioned that Ralph Hasty, geodesic innovator, continued to live in a conventional rectangular house for the rest of his life.

FIGURE 3.13 Ralph Hasty stands in front of the geodesic dome he built. Although providing all of the needs of a secure and warm dwelling space, it was hard to find a buyer for this unconventional home. (credit: Jennifer Hasty, Public Domain)

Paradox 2: Culture Is Bounded but Mobile

Because many elements of culture are shaped by environmental forces, trading opportunities, and local histories of settlement, culture becomes associated with territory. But because of the mobility of people, objects, and ideas, culture rarely stays within the boundaries of any society; rather, it wanders restlessly along lines of travel, communication, conquest, and trade.

People move around a lot, and this is nothing new. On the popular British television series *Time Team*, archaeological excavations all over the United Kingdom uncover artifacts from ancient times that were produced in far-flung places such as Rome, Scandinavia, and the Middle East. In episode 4 of season 16 (2015), the team excavated a town in Wales that was constructed by Romans during the time of Roman conquest. There, archaeologists unearthed the foundations of Roman buildings along with a variety of Roman objects, including a third-century Roman coin, a Roman tool for removing earwax, a twisted-wire bracelet, and a knife handle decorated with gladiators. Other *Time Team* investigations have uncovered artifacts from travelers and pilgrims to sacred religious sites. These objects have diffused to British cultures through conquest, trade, and migration. As people move around, so do objects, technologies, practices, and ideas.

FIGURE 3.14 This fabric shop displays a number of colorful wax print patterns. Although wax print fabrics are now associated with Africa, the wax print technique actually originated in Indonesia. (credit: "National Colors" by Miranda Harple for Yenkassa.com/flickr, CC BY 2.0)

However, certain integrated sets of things, practices, and ideas do cluster in certain places. Take a look at the cloth in Figure 3.15. This kind of cloth is quintessentially African. It's called wax print, and indeed, clothing made of wax-print cloth is very popular in many parts of Africa. Wax-print cloth is industrially produced cotton cloth with intricate designs and bold colors. In most African countries, a vast selection of designs and brands of wax prints can be found in any market. Rather than buying ready-made clothes in clothing shops, people more often purchase cloth in the market and take it to a seamstress or tailor to be made into the garment of their own choosing.

Many wax-print designs are symbolic, serving as a means of nonverbal communication for the people who wear them. Some cloths are associated with proverbs, occasions, monuments, and famous people. In the West African country of Ghana, many cloth designs are named using the vivid proverbs of the large Akan cultural group. One popular design features a bird in flight, associated with the Akan proverb *Sika wo antaban*, meaning "money takes flight." Another elaborate motif is called *Akyekyde? Akyi*, or "the back of the tortoise," worn by wise people who move through life with slow intention. One design with long, corrugated stripes is called sugarcane, which is said to mean "I love you like sugar."

FIGURE 3.15 The various designs on these fabrics are understood to each have a special meaning. In the upper left, is an example of the *Sika wo antiban* design, meaning "money takes flight." (credit: Ninara/flickr, CC BY 2.0)

Though iconically associated with African dress, wax print actually originated in Indonesia, derived from local techniques for making batik cloth. Batik is made using wax to draw designs on plain cotton cloth that is then immersed in a dye bath. When the wax is melted off, the design remains against the background of color. When the Dutch colonized Indonesia in the 1700s, Dutch merchants were impressed with the beauty of local batik and sought to use their own methods of mass-produced block printing to imitate the vibrant colors and elaborate designs of Indonesian cloth.

In the 1880s, Dutch and British merchants introduced their own mass-produced wax prints to people in their African colonies, particularly along the west coast of Africa. Dutch wax cloth was enthusiastically embraced by Africans, who began to infuse certain patterns with social meanings. With independence in the mid-20th century, many African countries developed their own wax-print textile industries using designs developed by local artists.

Exemplifying the cultural paradox of locality and mobility, wax-print cloth is culturally embedded in African culture while carrying a complex history of global trade, appropriation, and colonial domination.

In the context of global power relations, the mobility of culture poses questions about who has the right to claim or use elements of culture diffused from elsewhere. As part of the process of cultural immersion and participant observation, many cultural anthropologists adopt the dress, diet, gestures, and language of the peoples they study while they are conducting fieldwork. Often, anthropologists bring their love of these cultural elements back to their home societies and continue to use and practice them to show their appreciation for the cultures they have studied. However, some people may find it unsettling to see a white Euro-American anthropologist wearing an African wax-print dress—or a silk sari from India, or an ornately woven lliclla cape from Peru. In your travels, have you ever purchased an item of clothing or jewelry worn by local peoples? Is it appropriate to wear such items in your home society?

If someone is using cultural items as a way of honoring that culture, many people would think it's perfectly fine. If someone is wearing items from another culture as a form of humorous costume, such as a sports mascot or Halloween costume, most people would find that offensive. An even more serious problem emerges when a person uses or claims cultural elements from another society in order to make a profit. What if, for instance, someone from the American fashion industry copied a wax print motif such as *Sika wo antaban*, using the design for American clothing, housewares, or art? The elements of culture, both material and nonmaterial, constitute the **intellectual property** of the people of that culture. Claiming or using the elements of another culture inappropriately is called **cultural appropriation**.

Paradox 3: Culture Is Consensual but Contested

In any society, people interact using a set of assumptions about the sorts of behavior and speech considered appropriate to certain people in certain situations. That is to say, culture is consensual; through their words and actions, people agree to a certain way of doing things. As discussed earlier in this chapter, culture includes conventionalized roles, behavioral norms, and shared ideas for framing situations.

For example, imagine that someone in the United States has just graduated from college and is looking for a job. What should that person do? In the United States, it is common to spend time crafting an impressive résumé, using a specific form of technical language that accentuates the quality of a person's skills and experiences while demonstrating their educational background. Instead of listing "worked as a camp counselor," someone might indicate that they "developed systems of cooperative leadership among youth in an environmental awareness program." A recent graduate would likely post this linguistic masterpiece to a job search website such as Indeed.com.

For many people in China, such a strategy would seem very rudimentary and even grossly inadequate. Seeking opportunities for education, employment, and business, people in China frequently rely on a cultural system known as *guanxi*. Informed by Confucianism, *guanxi* refers to gifts and favors exchanged among people in wide social networks based on mutual benefit. *Guanxi* is based on family ties but also includes relationships formed in schools, in workplaces, and even among strangers who meet at parties or through mutual friends (Yin 2017). While still in school, a student may be on the lookout for people who might be able provide access to employment opportunities in the future. Using the practices of *guanxi*, the student would seek to establish personalized links with such people in the hope that these links might prove advantageous in the future.

Say, for instance, a student hopes to get a job in solar technology after graduation. That student might seek out professors whose teaching and research suggest connections in that industry. To establish relations of *guanxi*, the student would not only take courses from that professor but also attempt to establish some sort of personal rapport. This is typically done through strategic gift giving. In a particularly brutal winter, a student might knit a sweater for the professor. An artistically inclined student might sketch a portrait of the professor and frame it as a gift. Importantly, the gift must go slightly beyond the bounds of their professional relationship as professor and student. Over time, the student might find ways to meet with the professor, further cementing the social bond. After carefully cultivating this personalized relationship over months or years, the student might then ask the professor to use industry connections to help them find a job.

What this means is that personal connections can be just as important as, if not more important than, the language or qualifications of a person's résumé. While Americans emphasize the importance of job-search techniques, personal connections also play a role in securing employment in the American context, particularly in highly paid, competitive industries such as software development and finance. In many societies, people prefer to work with people they trust. Rather than hiring a random stranger, many prefer to hire someone recommended by a trusted friend or business partner. In *guanxi* relationships, relations of trust are established through the exchange of gifts and favors over time.

But what if the people who are hired in competitive industries are the ones who deployed their strategic social connections and not necessarily the ones who are most skilled, talented, or otherwise best suited to the work? What if the companies who are hired to complete infrastructure projects such as roads and bridges are not necessarily the most competent or experienced ones but those who have given strategic gifts to government officials? What if people use their *guanxi* networks to obtain special privileges, such as government licenses or social services? Legal scholar Ling Li (2011) argues that some people use the cultural system of *guanxi* to facilitate and rationalize bribery and other acts of corruption.

In 2012, the Chinese government launched an ambitious campaign against corruption among government officials. More than 100,000 people have been investigated and charged with corruption, including many high-ranking government officials, military officers, and senior executives of state-owned companies. Investigations have revealed how powerful people use their extensive *guanxi* networks to secure deals, exert influence, and extract goods and services. The campaign against corruption in China raises questions about the morality and legality of *guanxi* practices.

Although *guanxi* is a widely accepted system for gaining access to goods, services, and opportunities, people who don't have elite connections may feel that this informal cultural system is unfair. For personal or ethical reasons, some people may challenge or resist the practices of *guanxi*. Chinese journalist Lijia Zhang (2013) describes how she was denied a promotion in her first job because she refused to give the expected *guanxi* gifts to her boss. Zhang reports that most Chinese people complain about the widespread practices of corruption but are forced to use their *guanxi* networks to get ahead in life.

Guanxi illustrates how culture can be generally taken for granted but also highly controversial. Many other cultural norms are also widely accepted but challenged and resisted by certain groups who are disadvantaged or limited by those norms. Gender roles are a good example, as are norms of sexuality and marriage.

Paradox 4: Culture Is Shared, but It Varies

The examples of *guanxi* and the geodesic dome both illustrate another paradox: how culture is widely yet unevenly shared among members of a group. Different members of and groups in a society have different perspectives on their shared culture—and different versions of that culture. Among elites, the use of Chinese *guanxi* (or American "networking") might seem to be a more personal and trustworthy process for making things happen. But for people who lack access to elite networks, these cultural norms may seem to be an exclusive and unfair tool of class oppression.

Returning to the notion of home, consider the many, many versions of home in your society. People in different subgroups and regions live in structures of different shapes and sizes that are made of different materials. And yet, the members of a culture do share a common set of assumptions about home. Home is where we live, where we sleep, and most often where our family lives as well. Even with such diversity, people in a society have a common image or ideal of home. On the West Coast of the United States, geodesic innovators sought to expand the notion of home with a new shape and a new way of building. But in southwest Missouri, that variation of home did not take root. Alas.

The four paradoxes all illustrate how culture operates as a force of stability in a society while also generating forms of constant alteration, adaptation, and change. As culture is mobile, controversial, and variable, some elements are always in the process of transformation even as other elements are maintained and reinforced. Over time, people reinterpret their cultural norms and practices and sometimes even reject them altogether in favor of some other way of thinking or doing things.

This paradoxical view of culture points to the dynamic tensions of people living in groups. Societies are collectivities of individuals, families, regional groups, ethnic groups, socioeconomic classes, political groups, and so on. Culture provides a way for people to live and work together while also allowing for the expression and performance of distinctive differences. Rather than breaking down, culture responds to pressures for change with adaptation to new conditions. The paradoxes that make culture seem impossible also make culture flexible and durable. In an era that combines increasing polarization with an urgent need for cooperative change, perhaps we need culture now more than ever.

MINI-FIELDWORK ACTIVITY

Romance over Time

Write down the answers to the following questions. What does a person in your culture do when they want to become romantically involved with a particular someone? Are there common practices for this? What rules guide this behavior, explicit or implied? What are the different roles involved? Are there symbols and rituals? Is there some amount of disagreement in your culture about any of these activities?

Now, find a person in your culture who is much older than you, perhaps a person over 70 years old. Ask that person to describe how people did the same things when they were your age. Ask the same set of questions, and write down the answers.

How have romantic relations changed over time? What forces have shaped this change? What aspects have remained the same? What explains the durability of some practices? Based on this trajectory of change, can you predict how romantic relations will change in the future?

Suggested Readings

"Anthropological Theories: A Guide Prepared by Students for Students." 2012. Department of Anthropology, University of Alabama College of Arts & Sciences. https://anthropology.ua.edu/anthropological-theories/.

Bachmann-Medick, Doris, Jens Kugele, and Ansgar Nünning, eds. 2020. *Futures of the Study of Culture: Interdisciplinary Perspectives, Global Challenges.* Boston: De Gruyter.

Geertz, Clifford. 1973. *The Interpretation of Cultures: Selected Essays.* New York: Basic Books.

Neumann, Birgit, and Ansgar Nünning, eds. 2012. *Travelling Concepts for the Study of Culture.* Boston: De Gruyter.

Key Terms

cultural appropriation claiming or using elements of another culture in an inappropriate way.

cultural ecology how humans develop culture as an adaptation to various environments.

cultural evolutionism the study of the origins of human cultural forms and how those forms have changed over long periods of time.

cultural frames patterned, shared ways of interpreting situations.

cultural materialism an evolutionary approach that identifies technology and economic factors as fundamental aspects of culture, molding other features of culture such as family life, religion, and politics.

cultural practices routine or habitual forms of behavior.

cultural role a conventionalized position in a particular context or situation.

culture the whole way of life of a society, combining material objects, technologies, social relationships, everyday practices, deeply held values, and shared ideas.

diffusion in an anthropological context, the spread of material objects, practices, and ideas among cultures in complex relations of trade, migration, and conquest.

friction occurs when two or more elements of culture come into conflict, resulting in alteration or replacement of those elements.

functionalism a form of analysis that focuses on the contemporary purposes of culture.

historical particularism an approach to cultural change that describes the combination of internal and external factors that shapes the unique historical trajectory of each culture.

ideology a model that depicts how a social realm operates or should operate. An ideology identifies the entities, roles, behaviors, relationships, and processes in a particular realm as well as the rationality behind the whole system.

innovation the slight alteration of an existing element of culture, such as a new style of dress or dance.

intellectual property material and nonmaterial products of an individual or group that are protected by national and international laws and cannot be used for profit by others without attribution or compensation.

invention the independent creation of a new element of culture, such as a new technology, religion, or political form.

material culture objects made or used by humans, such as buildings, tools, clothing, household items, and art.

norm the cultural expectations, including behaviors and attributes, that are associated with a cultural role.

ontological anthropology an approach that explores how culture constructs our social and natural realities, what we consider real, and how we act on those assumptions. Reaching beyond human realities, ontological anthropology also attempts to include nonhuman perspectives, relationships, and forms of communication.

ontology the study of the nature of existence.

rite of passage a ritual that moves a person or group of people from one social category to another, often more highly valued one. Examples of rites of passage include naming ceremonies, initiations, weddings, and funerals.

ritual repeated, patterned action conventionally associated with a particular meaning, often incorporating symbolic objects and actions.

social structure the organizational framework for a particular realm of culture, such as the family, the economy, or the political system. Social structures combine material culture with practices and ideas.

structural functionalism a form of analysis that describes how various aspects of culture fit together and contribute to the integrated whole of culture.

structuralism the study of culture as a system of symbolic categories embedded in the myths, religion, kinship, and other realms of a culture.

symbol an object, image, or gesture conventionally associated with a particular meaning.

technology specialized knowledge or skills required to produce objects of material culture.

unilineal evolution the idea that all cultures pass through a single set of developmental stages.

values cultural notions about what is good, true, correct, appropriate, or beautiful.

worldview a very broad ideology that shapes how the members of a culture generally view the world and their place in it. Worldviews tend to span several realms, including religion, economics, and politics.

Summary

The discipline of anthropology is centered on the concept of culture. What we make, what we do, and what we think constitute the basic elements of culture. These elements combine in aggregates such as symbols, rituals, and social structures. Since the 19th century, anthropologists have developed various modes of analysis for understanding culture, some examining change over time and others considering the functions of culture at one particular point in time. While it is an incredibly useful tool for understanding human social life, the concept of culture is riddled with paradox. Though durable and integrated, culture is subject to constant change, mobility, contest, and variability.

Critical Thinking Questions

1. Draw a floor plan for your ideal home. What rooms would you have, and why? How would those rooms be organized? How is the imagined structure of this home shaped by an imagined lifestyle? What form of family or social relations are embedded in your house plan? What forms of work? What notions about gender and age are assumed?
2. Describe your routine for getting ready in the morning. What aspects of this routine are governed by biology, and what aspects are cultural? Ask a friend to describe their morning routine. Are there differences? Commonalities? What norms and values shape these practices?
3. List the colors of the rainbow. With a friend, describe the symbolic meanings associated with each color. Do you agree on these meanings? Do some colors have multiple meanings in your culture? How do people use and interpret colors with multiple meanings?
4. List the social roles you inhabit in your culture. What are the ideal behaviors associated with those roles? Do you observe all of these norms, or do you choose to ignore or resist some of them? What happens when you publicly resist the norms of your culture?
5. What rituals mark the passage of children into adulthood in your culture? Identify symbolic objects and actions in those rituals. What norms and values are expressed?
6. Which sports are popular in your culture or region? Choose one. How might an anthropologist use an evolutionary perspective to analyze this sport? How might another anthropologist use a functionalist approach?
7. Do you believe in ghosts? Is this belief widely shared among the people you know? How might the belief in ghosts shape cultural ideas about life and death? Would ghost beliefs influence what people do after a person dies?
8. Under what circumstances is it appropriate for a person in one culture to adopt elements from another culture, such as dress, food, or speech? Is that cultural appropriation? Why or why not?

Bibliography

Bourdieu, Pierre. 1970. "The Berber House or the World Reversed." *Social Science Information* 9 (2): 151–170.

Douglas, Mary. 1966. *Purity and Danger: An Analysis of Concepts of Pollution and Taboo*. London: Routledge & Kegan Paul.

Ferguson, James. 2006. *Global Shadows: Africa in the Neoliberal World Order*. Durham, NC: Duke University Press.

Geertz, Clifford. 1973. *The Interpretation of Cultures: Selected Essays*. New York: Basic Books.

Gennep, Arnold van. 1960. *The Rites of Passage*. Translated by Monika B. Vizedom and Gabrielle L. Caffe. Chicago: University of Chicago Press.

Hallowell, A. Irving. 1992. *The Ojibwa of Berens River, Manitoba: Ethnography into History*. Edited by Jennifer S. H. Brown. Fort Worth, TX: Harcourt Brace Jovanovich.

Kohn, Eduardo. 2013. *How Forests Think: Toward an Anthropology beyond the Human*. Berkeley: University of California Press.

Li, Ling. 2011. "'Performing' Bribery in China: Guanxi-Practice, Corruption with a Human Face." *Journal of Contemporary China* 20 (68): 1–20. https://ssrn.com/abstract=1712390.

Lyons, Harriet D. 2011. “Dame Mary Douglas.” In *Fifty Key Anthropologists*, edited by Robert J. Gordon, Andrew P. Lyons, and Harriet D. Lyons, 46–51. New York: Routledge.

Peters-Golden, Holly. 2002. *Culture Sketches: Case Studies in Anthropology*. 3rd ed. Boston: McGraw-Hill.

Scalco, Patricia. 2019. “Weaving Value: Selling Carpets in the Liminal Space of Istanbul’s Grand Bazaar.” *Anthropology Today* 35 (5): 7–10.

Tylor, Edward Burnett. 1873. *Primitive Culture: Researches into the Development of Mythology, Philosophy, Religion, Language, Art, and Custom*. 2nd ed. 2 vols. London: John Murray.

Williamson, Kenneth. 2012. “Night Becomes Day: Carnival, Contested Spaces, and the Black Movement in Bahia.” *The Journal of Latin American and Caribbean Anthropology* 17 (2): 257–278.

Yin, Xiangru. 2017. “An Analysis of Corruption in China: The Guanxi Network of Chinese High Level Officials and Governors.” Master’s thesis, Clark University. International Development, Community, and Environment (IDCE) (140). https://commons.clarku.edu/idce_masters_papers/140.

Zhang, Lijia. 2013. “Author: In China, ‘Everyone Is Guilty of Corruption.’” CNN. October 24, 2013. http://edition.cnn.com/2013/10/23/opinion/china-corrution-lijia-zhang/.

CHAPTER 4

Biological Evolution and Early Human Evidence

Figure 4.1 The Grand Gallery of Evolution in the National Museum of Natural History in Paris, France displays 9,500 specimens of the estimated millions of species that currently live or once lived on the Earth in its collections. In addition to educating the public about the mechanisms of evolution, the exhibitions in the museum honor the scientists who helped contribute to our current understanding of the history of life on Earth. (credit: "Great Gallery of Evolution" by Mustang Joe/flickr, Public Domain)

CHAPTER OUTLINE

INTRODUCTION This chapter applies evolutionary concepts to the understanding of human origins and explains the biological variation seen in our ancestors across time. Chapters 4, Biological Evolution and Early Human Evidence and Chapter 5, The Genus *Homo* and the Emergence of Us, represent a field of study that is probably the most dynamic, controversial and highly debated subfield of anthropology. Perspectives and opinions vary not only within the mindset of the general public but also amongst scientists and anthropologists alike. As the human fossil puzzle begins to fill in with new discoveries, we find ourselves gaining valuable insights into what makes us human and the ways in which we are a part of, not separate from, the natural world. Despite our advances in the field, we also have to be prepared for the possibility we may end up with more questions than answers! It is these very reasons that explain why so many of us find this such a fascinating field and why so many of us take it so personally. It is after all a journey into the discovery of who we are and where we came from; and that should be of interest to all of us as members of the *Homo* genus.

4.1 What Is Biological Anthropology?

LEARNING OUTCOMES:

By the end of this section, you will be able to:

- Identify the five subfields of biological anthropology.
- Explain how each of the subfields contributes to our understanding of human origins and evolution.
- Understand the historical context of the field of biological anthropology.

Looking to the Deep Past

Biological anthropology, also referred to as physical anthropology or evolutionary anthropology, is one of the four major subfields of anthropology. While the other subfields focus on current and relatively recent human cultures, biological anthropology looks to the deeper past, asking questions about what it means to be human by exploring where humans came from as a species. Biological anthropology comprises numerous areas of study: human biological variation, paleoanthropology (human and primate evolution), primatology (the study of nonhuman primates), bioarchaeology (the study of bones found at archaeological sites), and genetic anthropology (the application of molecular science to archaeological, historical, and linguistic evidence to reveal the history of ancient human origins and migration). Each of these areas of study contributes something to anthropologists' understanding of current human physical characteristics and behaviors.

Exploring What It Means to Be Human

Studies of human biological variation evaluate the physical similarities and differences between human populations across both time and space. Differences in **morphology** include features such as height, jawline, eye sockets, and ear and nose shape and size. Biochemical differences account for variations in the sense of smell, mutations in the *CCR5* gene that offer resistance to HIV, and variations in skin pigmentation in response to levels of exposure to ultraviolet rays from the sun.

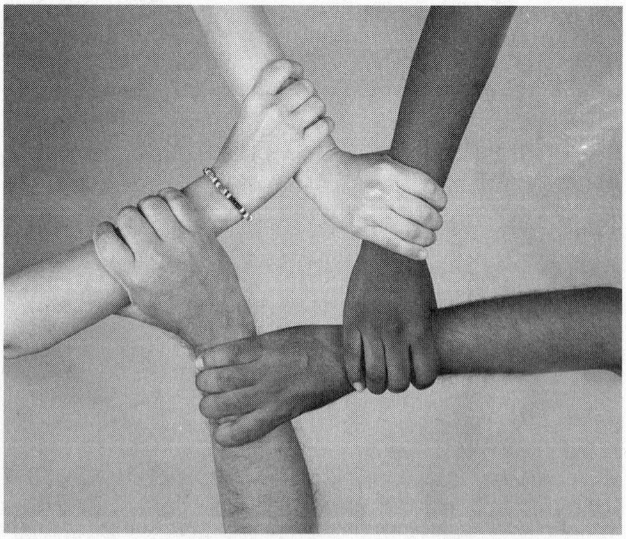

FIGURE 4.2 These variations in modern human skin pigmentation are the result of evolutionary adaptations to different levels of exposure to ultraviolet rays from the sun. (credit: "School Diversity Many Hands Held Together" by Wonder woman0731/flickr, CC BY 2.0)

The study of human biological variation is closely linked to the original conception of biological anthropology, which was formalized in 1930 with the establishment of the American Association of Physical Anthropologists, recently renamed the American Association of Biological Anthropologists. The change in name is an effort to move away from the term *physical anthropology*, which has come to be associated with views promoting scientific racism that no longer represent or align with views held by anthropologists today. In 1951, American anthropologist Sherwood Washburn introduced a "new physical anthropology," changing the focus from racial typology and classification to the study of human evolution and the evolutionary process. This new focus expanded anthropology as a field to include paleoanthropology and primatology

Paleoanthropology looks at the fossil evidence of humanity's ancestors along with ancient material culture such as tools and other human artifacts. The physical morphology (shape and size) of skulls and other postcranial material (skeletal remains other than the skull) allow paleoanthropologists to form hypotheses about important milestones in human evolution over time.

Primatology examines the behavioral and physical attributes of both living and fossil primates as well as their relationships with their environments. Humans are primates who share a common ancestry with nonhuman primates. By studying nonhuman primates, anthropologists can gain a better understanding of what it means to be a primate and what it means to be human.

Genetic anthropology is used within several areas of biological anthropology. In this specialized area, DNA testing is combined with archaeological, historical, and linguistic evidence to reveal the history of ancient human migration or to track human disease.

Forensic anthropology is a subfield of biological anthropology that applies scientific methods to the analysis of human remains for the purposes of identifying a victim and determining the possible cause of death. A major difference between forensic anthropology and other types of biological anthropology is that forensic anthropology is usually focused on crime scenes involving the death of an individual, whereas other types primarily focus on understanding patterns and features that may appear in a group or an entire population. Beginning in World War II, forensic anthropologists have been instrumental in helping identify victims of war and disasters. They have played critical roles in identifying victims of the Thailand tsunami in 2004 and the destruction of the World Trade Center on September 11, 2001. Today, most forensic anthropologists work in a medical examiner's office, assisting with autopsies and examinations of skeletal remains.

Bioarchaeology studies human remains in archaeological settings with a focus on what skeletal material can reveal about the culture, diet, and presence of disease in a population. Bioarchaeologists are also interested in the **socioecological system** of a population, which helps anthropologists better understand the roles of environmental and ecological pressures and influences in shaping cultural identity, social inequity, sustainability, and access to and use of resources. Based on the biological remains found at archaeological sites, bioarchaeologists explore questions pertaining to social and funerary behavior, diet and nutrition, health, and disease. Bioarchaeology offers a window into the connections among biology, society, and culture. An example of what a bioarchaeologist might study is skeletal evidence of infant cranial boarding, which was practiced by many cultures, including the ancient Maya, the Inca, and some Native North American groups. The process involved binding a child's head to a flat board in order to artificially deform the skull, possibly to meet an aesthetic ideal or to signify social status. Bioarcheologists have found that variations in how the board was attached to the skull provide important information about an individual's social identity.

FIGURE 4.3 This elongated skull is from a member of the Nazca culture, which flourished in what is now Peru in the years 100 BCE to 800 CE. It's long, oval shape is the result of infant cranial bonding, the practice of deliberately shaping the development of an infant's skull by bonding it to stiff boards. (credit: "Nasca Peru Deformed Skull" by VasenkaPhotography/flickr, CC BY 2.0)

PROFILES IN ANTHROPOLOGY

Ann Rosalie David
1946-

FIGURE 4.4 Professor Ann Rosalie David, Egyptologist and forensic and biological anthropologist at the University of Manchester, UK. (credit: Professor David, Public Domain)

Personal History: Professor Ann Rosalie David was born in Cardiff, UK and earned a bachelor of arts degree in ancient history from University College London in 1967 and a doctorate from the University of Liverpool in 1971. Her thesis was on ancient Egyptian temple rituals.

Area of Anthropology: The focus of Professor's David's work has been biological anthropology and Egyptology.

Accomplishments In the Field: Professor David is a Director of the KNH Centre for Biological and Forensic Studies in Egyptology at the University of Manchester. In this role, she established the Ancient Egyptian Mummy Tissue Bank, one of the only such tissue banks in the world. She served as the keeper of Egyptology at the Manchester Museum and has often worked in collaboration with Egypt's Ministry of Health and Population on public health projects. One such project involved the identification of antibodies against schistosomiasis, a parasite spread by freshwater snails, in Egyptian mummies.

David was made an Officer of the Order of the British Empire (OBE) in 2003 for her work in Egyptology. David has appeared in or consulted on several documentaries, including the television miniseries *Private Lives of the Pharaohs* (2000) and *Secrets of the Pharaohs* (2001) and the documentary short *Mummies: Secrets of the Pharaohs* (2007).

Importance of Her Work: Ann Rosalie David was the first woman in Britain to hold a professorship in Egyptology. She was a pioneer in biomedical research, conducting research on disease, diet, and lifestyles in ancient Egypt. In 2010, her work on ancient Egyptian mummies found evidence to suggest that cancer may be a human-created disease, attributable in part to modern pollution and changes in lifestyle and diet (David and Zimmerman 2010).

PODCAST

In this podcast (https://openstax.org/r/interview-mummies-withprof.annrosaliedavid), Professor Rosalie discusses her work with ancient Egyptian mummies.

4.2 What's in a Name? The Science of Taxonomy

LEARNING OUTCOMES:

By the end of this section, you will be able to:

- Describe the historical context of binomial nomenclature and scientific classification.
- Distinguish between the different categories of groups found in Linnaean classification.
- Explain the different definitions of species and how they are applied to different populations.

Defining the Science of Taxonomy

Taxonomy is defined as the classification and naming of things. Taxonomy organizes things into groups based on predefined criteria. The criteria can be as simple as color or height or as complex as the presence or absence of a trait, gene, or behavior. Taxonomy is a critical component of biological anthropology because it helps anthropologists organize humans and their evolutionary ancestors both spatially (by location) and temporally (through time).

Taxon refers to a specific subgroup, such as the genus. **Taxa** is the plural form of taxon, used to refer to all groups. The classification system used for organizing living organisms was originally developed in the 18th century by Swedish botanist Carolus Linnaeus. His system, which he called the *Systema Naturae*, uses a structure known as **binomial nomenclature**. Binomial nomenclature assigns two Latin names to each organism. The first is termed the genus name. The second is the specific or the trivial name, commonly called the species name. In print, genus and species names are italicized. The first letter of the genus is capitalized, while the species or trivial name is lowercase. For example, the scientific name for the house cat is *Felis catus*, and the name for modern human beings is *Homo sapiens*. Linnaeus's binomial nomenclature established a shared scientific language that would become universal across countries and cultures, avoiding the confusion caused by regional and colloquial names.

In addition to establishing a shared language, Linnaeus's naming system groups organisms that share common traits. For example, he grouped together animals with mammary glands into the category mammals. Mammals were further broken down according to other traits. For example, mammals that have opposable thumbs were grouped together as primates, and those without opposable thumbs were grouped as non-primates. This is a hierarchical classification scheme, meaning that organisms are grouped into successive levels from the broadest category of domain to the more specific level of species.

When Linnaeus first created his *Systema Naturae*, he built five hierarchical levels into his taxonomy: kingdom, class, order, genus, and species. Humans are in the kingdom Animalia, the class Mammalia, the order Primates, the genus *Homo*, and the species *sapiens*. Over time, many levels have been added to the Linnaean system of classification, including domain, phylum, subclass, superorder, family, and tribe. The addition of these taxon groups has enabled biological anthropologists to better understand the variations present in various groups of organisms. However, biological anthropologists spend the majority of their time trying to understand the species level.

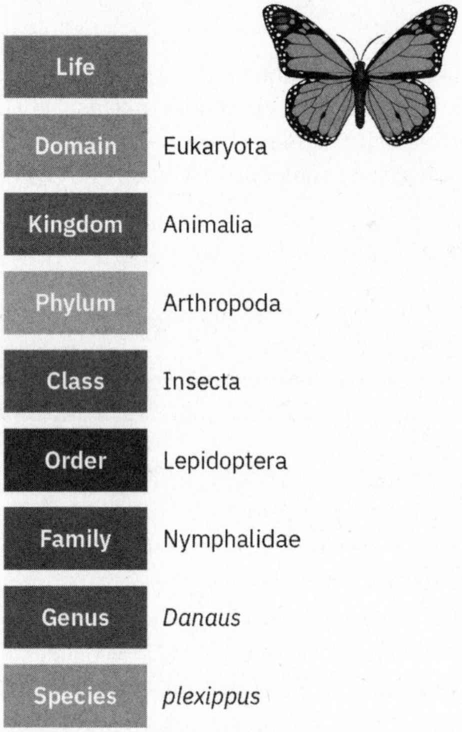

FIGURE 4.5 This chart details the Linnaean hierarchical classification for the monarch butterfly. The broadest category, "Life", appears at the top of the chart, with classifications of increasing specificity at each level that follows. "Species" is the most granular level. (attribution: Copyright Rice University/OpenStax, under CC By 4.0 license)

Defining a Species

While **species** is a word that most people are familiar with and comfortable using, just what determines a species is incredibly difficult to define. At the most basic level, a species comprises a group of organisms with shared characteristics that distinguish them from other groups. Most scientists distinguish a species based on behavior, genetics, and/or morphology. Species definitions are the basis for scientific names. The *common* name of a species, on the other hand, is usually based on general physical characteristics noted by a culture or local population. Common names are also referred to as folk taxonomy or **ethnotaxonomy** (classifications influenced by culture, etc.). There is a growing interest among anthropologists and the scientific community in preserving Indigenous classifications of the natural world and connecting them with scientific classifications.

Decisions related to classification often involve tremendous taxonomical controversy, especially within the field of biological anthropology. There are more than 20 distinct species definitions, or ways of categorizing or distinguishing one type of organism from another. Below are the four most common definitions of a species.

Biological Species

The **biological species definition** states that a species is a group of interbreeding organisms that are reproductively isolated from other groups of organisms. **Reproductive isolation** means that members of a species are not able to mate successfully with members outside their species. Gorillas, for example, cannot successfully breed with *Pan paniscus*, the bonobo. The biological species definition uses the ability to interbreed as its foundation because successful mating leads to gene flow, or the movement of genetic material from one population to another.

Ecological Species

The **ecological species definition** emphasizes the role of natural selection in maintaining species boundaries. This concept is based on the idea that gene flow is neither necessary nor sufficient to maintain species boundaries. Instead, natural selection plays an important role in maintaining the boundaries between species. In nature, species boundaries are often maintained even though there is a substantial amount of gene flow between species. Gene flow between species generally occurs at places called **hybrid zones**, areas of overlap where two species are known to successfully breed. A classic example of a hybrid zone occurs on the island of Sulawesi in Southeast Asia, where *Macaca maura* (the moor macaque) and *Macaca tonkeana* (the Tonkean macaque) are known to have successfully interbred for more than 150 years. Despite this, the integrity of the two distinct species has been maintained.

Phylogenetic Species

The biological species definition is based on breeding behavior, specifically whether species are capable of mating with one another. This foundation is problematic when trying to identify species over time. It is hard to know whether two fossil specimens were capable of interbreeding. It is also difficult in the fossil record to distinguish between **interspecific variation** (differences between members of two different species) and **intraspecific variation** (variation within a species). Imagine finding the bones of two individuals, one five feet tall and the other six feet four inches. Identifying whether these individuals were members of two different species (interspecific variation) or representative of the normal variation within a given species would be extremely challenging.

These problems are addressed by the **phylogenetic species definition**. The phylogenetic species definition states that a species can be determined by shared possession of one unique characteristic. For example, imagine you found a group of fossil leg bones. In order to decide if they were from the same species, you would need to determine if they had a trait in common that only these fossil leg bones possessed. If the bones all possessed trait A and this trait was not found in any other species already identified, then you would have a new species, and all of the fossil leg bones could be placed in that species.

Mate Recognition Species

The mate recognition species definition states that a species is a set of organisms that recognize one another as potential mates. A classic example of a group of species that can be distinguished using this definition is American crickets. Within a single habitat in the United States, there might be over 30 different species of crickets. Each species of cricket is known to produce a distinct song. Despite all these different species living side by side, the female cricket of each species will only mate with a male after hearing the male sing her species-specific song. The song, and the female recognition of it, constitutes a mate recognition system. This is analogous to the biological species definition in that the song acts as a reproductive isolating mechanism.

4.3 It's All in the Genes! The Foundation of Evolution

LEARNING OUTCOMES:

By the end of this section, you will be able to:

- Define alleles, genes, phenotypes, and genotypes.
- Distinguish the process of mitosis from the process of meiosis.
- Explain how Mendel's laws of heredity affect human variation.
- Explain how the multitude of evolutionary forces contribute to variation in the human condition.

The Units of Life

Cells are the basic units of life in all organisms. They are the smallest entities that are capable of self-reproduction. There are two main types of cells: prokaryotic and eukaryotic cells, named for the types of organisms in which they occur. Prokaryotes are single-celled organisms, such as bacteria and archaea. Eukaryotes are more complex, multicellular organisms, such as plants and animals (including humans). One of the most important components of eukaryotic cells is the enclosed nucleus at the center of the cell; prokaryotic cells do not have this nucleus. The nucleus of a eukaryotic cell houses all of the genetic material, or DNA (deoxyribonucleic acid), that controls cellular function. Normally, the DNA forms a long string within the nucleus.

There are two main types of eukaryotic cells: somatic cells and sex cells (also known as gametes). The somatic cells make up the structural components of a body, such as the tissues, muscles, and organs. The sex cells are specifically involved in reproduction. The function of the sex cells is to unite with a sex cell from another individual to form a fertilized egg, also known as a zygote. In animals, there are two types of sex cells: ova, or eggs, and sperm.

Cell division is the process that results in the production of new cells. However, sex and somatic cells divide differently. The cellular division of somatic cells is known as mitosis, while the cellular division of sex cells is known as meiosis. Mitosis of somatic cells is sometimes referred to as simple cell division because the parent cell divides once to produce two daughter cells that are genetically identical to each other and identical to the original parent cell. During mitosis, the DNA genetic material forms structures known as chromosomes. Each daughter cell inherits an exact copy of all 46 chromosomes found within the parent cell.

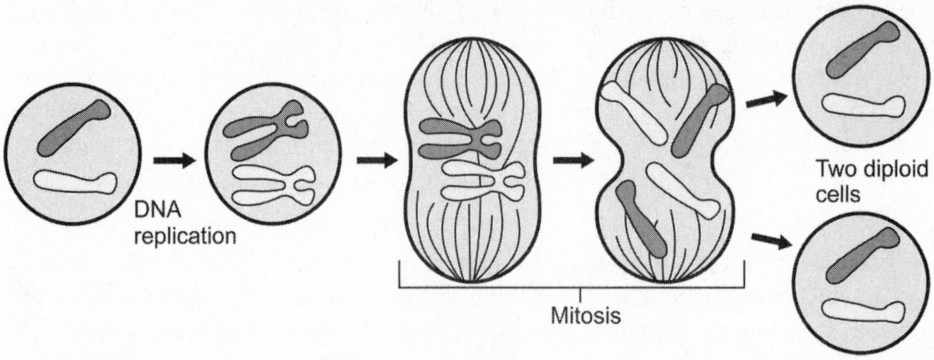

FIGURE 4.6 In somatic cell division, also known as mitosis, the parent cell divides to produce two daughter cells that are genetically identical to each other and to the parent cell. (credit: “Major events in mitosis”by Mysid/ Wikimedia Commons, Public Domain)

Meiosis, or sex cell division, is more complicated. This type of cellular division only occurs in the testes of males and the ovaries of females. Instead of just one division, meiosis results from two cellular divisions that produce four daughter cells. In meiosis, the four daughter cells each receive half of the original genetic material from the parental cell. Thus, each daughter cell only has 23 chromosomes.

It is on the chromosomes that genes are housed. Genes are the fundamental unit of heredity. They are best understood as the sequence or ordering of the DNA material that is housed in the nucleus. The **genotype** is the genetic material found within an organism's cells and it is the expression of these genes that will produce the **phenotype** or observable trait. Sometimes, the sequencing of the DNA material produces a variation of a gene, known as an **allele**. An allele is defined as a similar but slightly different form of the same gene that can activate the expression of a specific trait.

Gregor Mendel and the Laws of Heredity

The true nature of inheritance was not really understood until the beginning of the 20th century, when the 19th-century work of Gregor Mendel, a Catholic priest from Slovakia, was rediscovered. While in college, Gregor Mendel was introduced to cell theory, which states that all organisms are composed of cells and that cells are the fundamental unit of all living things. Cell theory raised many questions in Mendel's mind, including whether both parents contribute equally to the cells in their offspring. In 1854, Mendel began a series of experiments with pea plants to help resolve this question and better understand how traits are inherited from generation to generation.

FIGURE 4.7 Gregor Mendel was a Catholic priest whose experiments with selective breeding of pea plants established many of the rules of heredity. (credit: "Gregor Mendel Monk" by William Bateson, *Mendel's Principles of Heredity: A Defence*/Wikimedia Commons, Public Domain)

The first stage of Mendel's experiments was identifying plants that breed true, meaning that each parent only produces one kind of offspring when self-crossed. A self-cross is essentially a self-mating; some plants, such as peas, have both male and female parts and can self-fertilize. Not all self-crosses are the same as the parent plant, however. For example, self-crossed pea plants that have yellow pods sometimes produce offspring with yellow pods and sometimes produce offspring with green pods. Mendel continued to selectively breed only those pea plants that produced offspring that were the same as the parents. He called them purebreds and referred to them as the P1 generation. It took him more than two years to establish plants that always bred true.

Then Mendel selected seven traits of his pea plants that each had two distinct phenotypes, or observable expressions of the trait. For example, seed shape can be either round or wrinkled, while pod color can be either yellow or green. Over the next eight years, Mendel studied the mating and resulting traits of more than 28,000 plants. Mendel's first round of experiments used his purebred pea plants to create what is known as a monohybrid cross. A monohybrid cross is a mating between two purebred individuals who differ in a single characteristic. In Mendel's monohybrid crosses, the parent pea plants differed from one another in terms of whether the pods of the parental pea plants were yellow or green or whether the seeds of the parental pea plant were wrinkled or round.

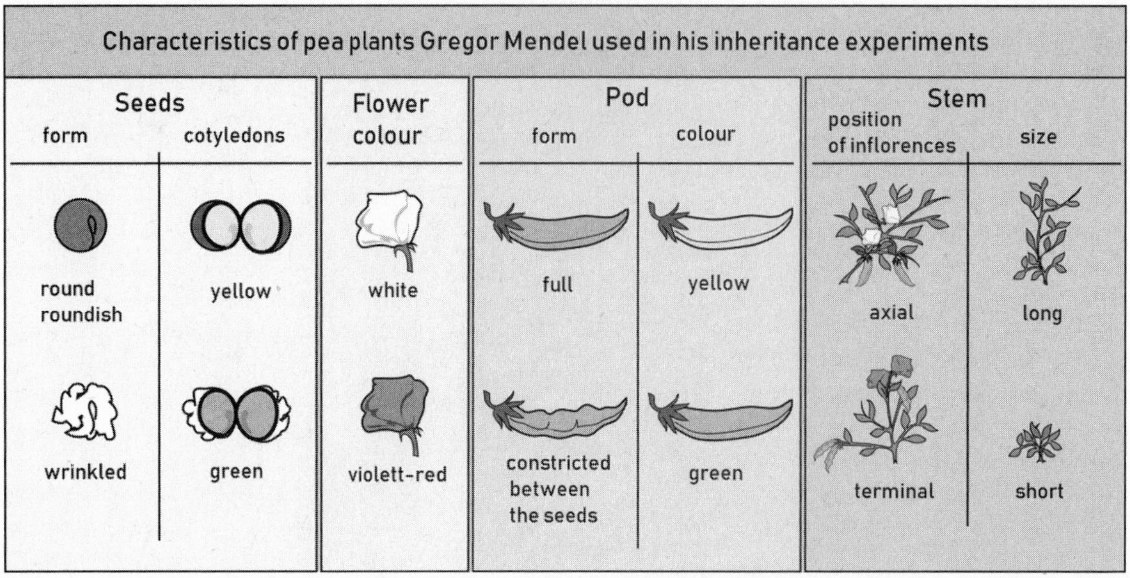

FIGURE 4.8 Mendel identified a number of distinct characteristics observable in the seeds, flowers, pods, and stems of pea plants. He used these observable traits as the basis for his breeding experiments, taking note of which traits were dominant and which unexpressed (or recessive) in offspring. (credit: "Mendel Genetics" by LadyofHats/ Wikimedia Commons, Public Domain)

In his first monohybrid crosses, Mendel mated a purebred yellow pea plant with a purebred green pea plant. He found that all the offspring resulting from this monohybrid cross were yellow, even though when the green peas self-crossed, all their offspring were green. In other words, all the *hybrid* offspring were yellow in color. A hybrid plant is one in whose parents differ in a term of a specific characteristic, such as pod color or seed shape. The trait that was expressed (yellow) Mendel referred to as dominant, and the trait that disappeared (green) he referred to as recessive. Mendel's next set of experiments involved mating two hybrid plants—in other words, those that resulted from the monohybrid cross. In these experiments, he found that the recessive traits reappeared in a ratio of three dominant to one recessive.

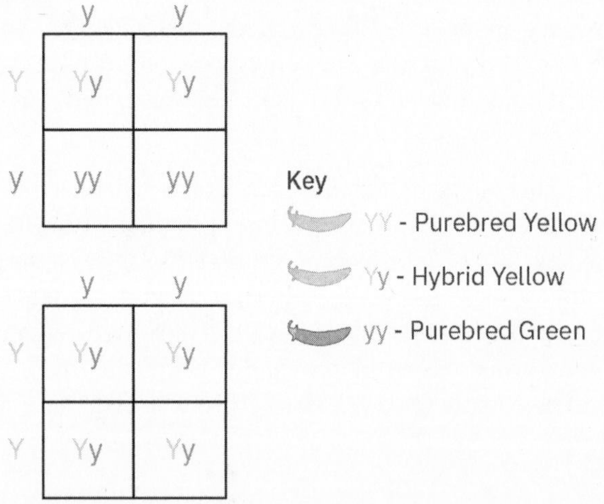

FIGURE 4.9 These diagrams are examples of Punnett squares, a simple method for predicting the observable results of breeding experiments. In the top square, a purebred green plant (yy) is crossed with a hybrid yellow plant (Yy). The four possibilities for offspring appear in the four interior squares of the diagram. In this case, half of the offspring will be hybrid yellow and half will be purebred green. The bottom diagram shows the results of a cross between a purebred green and a purebred yellow plant – in this case, all offspring are hybrid yellow. (credit: Copyright Rice University/OpenStax, under CC BY 4.0 license)

Mendel's experiments suggested two very important facts. First, Mendel noted that various expressions of a trait (such as pea color) were controlled by discrete units that occur in pairs and that offspring inherited one unit of each pair from each parent. This observation became Mendel's first law of inheritance, the **law of segregation**, which states that the two alleles for each trait segregate, or separate, during the formation of gametes (eggs and sperm) and that during the reproductive process, the alleles combine at random with other alleles. Today, we know that the process of meiosis—division of sex cells—explains Mendel's law of segregation. Each of the seven traits identified by Mendel is controlled by a pair of genes in the plant, one on each chromosome. During the reproductive cycle, the chromosomes separate from one another so that each gamete has only one allele for each trait. During fertilization, the alleles combine, and the two-gene state is restored.

After Mendel established his first law of inheritance, he extended his studies to more complex situations. He began performing experiments with two set of traits, using dihybrid crosses. A dihybrid cross is a cross between individuals who differ with respect to two gene pairs—for example, a cross between a plant with a round yellow pea and a plant with a wrinkled green pea. Because yellow and round are both dominant traits and wrinkled and green are both recessive, all the offspring resulting from the first-generation mating were 100% yellow and round. The green color and the wrinkled pea shape had disappeared. However, these recessive traits reappeared in a ratio of three dominant to one recessive when two round yellow individuals from the first-generation dihybrid cross were mated. The green color and the wrinkled pea shape had not truly disappeared. In the second generation of the dihybrid cross, Mendel found that 9/16 of the offspring were round and yellow, 3/16 were wrinkled and yellow, 3/16 were round and green, and 1/16 were wrinkled and green. The results of these dihybrid crosses indicate that the two characteristics—pea color and pea shape—segregate independently. The expression of one trait is not influenced by the expression of the other trait. This is known as the **law of independent assortment**, which is Mendel's second law of inheritance. There is nothing to dictate that round peas will be yellow or that wrinkled peas will be green. The alleles that code for different traits sort independently of one another during sex cell division (meiosis).

Mendelian Inheritance in Humans

Mendel's laws of inheritance also apply to humans. Indeed, the principles of segregation and independent assortment account for the transmission of certain human traits. Human blood type is one of the most familiar Mendelian traits. Blood type has three phenotypes—A, B, and O—based on three alleles of a single gene. If only the A allele or both the A and O alleles are present, the phenotype is A. If only the B allele or both the B and O alleles are present, the phenotype is B. If both A and B are present, the phenotype is AB. If neither A nor B is present, the phenotype is O. Note that O is recessive to both A and B, while A and B are codominant. Codominance means that instead of one allele masking the other, the products of both alleles are observed. Additional examples of Mendelian traits, or those controlled by a single gene, include Huntington's disease, widow's peak, cystic fibrosis, sickle cell anemia, Tay-Sachs disease, hemophilia, and red-green color blindness. OMIM, or Online Mendelian Inheritance in Man (https://openstax.org/r/onlinemendelian), hosts an online database of almost 5,000 Mendelian human traits.

It is important to note that the majority of human traits are not controlled by a single pair of genes. More often, a single gene can have multiple effects. Even more commonly, multiple genes are needed to produce a single effect. These are referred to as **polygenic traits**. Most human traits are polygenic, not Mendelian. A good way of determining if a trait is polygenic is to assess whether the trait can be measured. Traits that can be measured, such as height or weight, are polygenic. Also, traits that have a wide range or lots of variability and can be affected by environmental factors are probably polygenic. The survival of a species depends on genetic diversity and variation. If there is a reduction of a gene pool due to geographic isolation or other environmental factors than a species is at risk of extinction.

4.4 Evolution in Action: Past and Present

LEARNING OUTCOMES:

By the end of this section, you will be able to:

- Identify the major contributors to evolutionary theory and their specific theoretical contributions and historical context.
- Explain the theory of evolution and how it applies to the understanding of human origins.
- Identify the key differences between Linnaean classification and phylogenetics.
- Define key evolutionary processes such as genetic drift, allopatric speciation, etc.

Contemporary biological anthropologists utilize an evolutionary perspective. This means that the principles of evolution are used to understand how and why living organisms, including people, thrive in almost every environment on Earth. More specifically, natural selection is accepted as the guiding force that shapes why living things are the way they are. Out of all the possible variations of beings competing for the same resources on Earth, those that prospered were the ones better suited to their environments than all other competitors. The principles of evolution and natural selection will be discussed in some detail in the next few sections, but it is important to establish at this early point that this chapter relies on the foundational assumption that natural forces are the only forces directing the development of life on Earth.

Early Evolutionists and the Fixity of Species

Evolution is defined as change in the allele frequency within a gene pool that can lead to changes in an organism's morphology (form and structure) over time. Evolution involves the processes of mutation, natural selection, and speciation, which will be introduced in upcoming sections. Prior to the 19th century, the prevailing idea in Western thought was that nature was fixed and static; it was made by a supreme being in the form it currently appeared, and it did not change. Within this fixed natural system, living creatures were arranged within a set order that was considered to have been decreed by God, known as the **great chain of being**. This order featured God at the top, angels beneath God, and then humans. Below humans were various types of animals, followed by plants and minerals. This hierarchy was significant both because it placed some creatures above others and because it distinctly separated humans from the rest of the animal world.

During a period stretching from the 14th through the 18th centuries, some people began to question whether the natural world was as static as it was traditionally perceived to be. The British scientist and architect Robert Hooke is remembered as the first person in the Western world to claim not only that nature has changed over time but also that evidence of these changes remain. He hypothesized that fossils are the remains of actual plants and animals that were once alive. This conclusion was contrary to the previously accepted conclusion that fossils were nothing more than stone images. Hooke also noted that many marine fossils were located far away from any existing ocean, and he came to the then radical conclusion that Earth's geography and physical features had experienced dramatic changes.

The first person to propose a mechanism by which species could change was French naturalist Jean-Baptiste Lamarck, best known for having developed the first theory of macroevolution, a hypothesis about how the actual transformation from one species into another species could occur. Lamarck's theory relied on the now defunct idea of the **inheritance of acquired characteristics**.

Lamarck argued that the usefulness of a trait or organ could be ascertained based on its complexity or size. In particular, he believed that the usefulness of an organ could be judged by its size and the usefulness of a trait by its complexity. He speculated that organs and traits that help a creature to survive will become bigger and more complex over time, while those that are of little use will become smaller and simpler and eventually disappear. His classic example of this theory in action is the long neck of a giraffe. Lamarck speculated that as giraffes stretched their necks to reach the leaves at the tops of trees, their necks would grow longer, and furthermore, these longer necks would be inherited by the subsequent generations. This theory of the inheritance of acquired characteristics is also known as Lamarckian inheritance. One of the interesting things about Lamarck's theory is that he believed that wishes, desires, wills, and needs were all sufficient to motivate change. That is, wishing for or desiring a change in one's physical characteristics could make that change happen.

There are two primary problems with Lamarckian inheritance. First, desires, wishes, and needs do not change physical characteristics without a deliberate change in behavior. Someone may wish for blue hair, but their hair color will not change without dye. The second problem is that the inheritance of acquired traits is not possible. If someone dyed their hair blue, their children would not inherit blue hair. Traits that are acquired during a lifespan are not passed on to subsequent generations.

Just because Lamarck's theory of macroevolution is not correct does not mean that it is insignificant. Lamarck recognized the importance of interactions between organisms and their environments in the evolutionary process and was the first to propose a mechanism by which evolutionary change from one species into another could actually occur.

Georges Cuvier, another Frenchman and a leading scientist in the early 19th century, made numerous contributions to evolutionary thinking. He is best known for his theory of **catastrophism**, which he developed to explain the increasing number of fossils that were being found, some displaying impressions of creatures no longer found anywhere on Earth. Catastrophism proposes that floods, earthquakes, and other natural disasters—understood within the theory as acts of God—have been responsible for killing all the animals alive in certain places at certain times. According to Cuvier, either new animals have been created or the areas had been repopulated by animals from neighboring areas. To be consistent with emerging fossil evidence indicating that organisms had become more complex over time, Cuvier proposed that new organisms with a more modern appearance were the result of a more recent creation event. While scientists no longer adhere to catastrophism as a viable theory, Cuvier's idea of extinction continues to be an important component of evolutionary thinking today.

Another major contributor to evolutionary thinking was Scottish geologist Charles Lyell, known as the father of modern geology. He wrote a three-volume treatise, *Principles of Geology* (1830–1833), in which he argued that contemporary geological processes were the same as those that occurred in the past. These processes, such as wind and rain, produced the contemporary geological landscape. Mountains, lakes, and rivers were all created by these geological processes, many of them slow moving. This theory has come to be known as the principle of **uniformitarianism**. Lyell suggested that in order for such slow-acting forces to produce momentous change, Earth must be much older than previously suspected. Prior to Lyell's publication, the majority of natural historians believed that the earth was less than 6,000 years old, a number arrived at through calculations made based on the Old Testament. By altering the suspected age of the earth from several thousand years to millions of years, Lyell changed the framework within which scientists viewed the geological past.

Charles Darwin's Role in Changing Views of the Natural World

Charles Darwin introduced a new way of seeing the world that was both highly criticized and acclaimed in the scientific community of his time. In spite of resistance by various segments of society, his theories of natural selection became the foundation of biological science. New knowledge pertaining to genetics and molecular science has strengthened Darwin's theories rather than weakened them.

Darwin the Apprentice

When he was 17 years old, well before he gained a reputation as a naturalist, scholar, and scientist, Darwin was studying to be a medical doctor at the University of Edinburgh. Like many young people, he began to question his original choice of studies, and he decided to instead learn taxidermy under John Edmonstone. John Edmonstone was born enslaved and grew up on a plantation owned by a Scottish politician in what is now Guyana in South America. Charles Waterton, the son-in-law of the plantation owner and a renowned naturalist, would visit the plantation often. He started inviting Edmonstone to accompany him on his frequent travels into the rainforest. On his travels, Edmonstone gained considerable knowledge about the flora and fauna of South America along with impressive taxidermy skills.

After gaining his freedom in 1817, John Edmonstone taught taxidermy at the University of Edinburgh, where he served as a mentor to Darwin over a period of several months. It is believed that Darwin's relationship with Edmonstone may have influenced his abolitionist views, which were later strengthened by firsthand accounts of slavery while Darwin was on his infamous voyage to the Galápagos Islands off the coast of Ecuador.

FIGURE 4.10 At the University of Edenborough, John Edmonstone taught Darwin how to preserve birds. This is an example of *Embernagra platensis*, the great Pampa-finch, collected by Charles Darwin in Uruguay in May of 1833. (credit: "*Embernagra platensis platensis*, Great Pampa-finch, skin. Syntype. [B 19600]" by Michelle McFarlane/ Museums Victoria, CC BY 4.0)

Darwin the Explorer and Scholar

Charles Darwin left the University of Edinburgh and decided to pursue theology at Christ's College, Cambridge. His studies there led to his appointment in 1831 as a naturalist on the HMS *Beagle* for a five-year scientific expedition around the world. During this voyage, Darwin collected, dissected, and organized various specimens, especially in the Galápagos Islands, a chain of islands off the western coast of South America. His observations in the Galápagos marked a crucial point in his thinking on evolution. He noted that the fauna and flora of the western coast of South America were similar to those he observed in the Galápagos, but still distinct enough to be considered different species. More surprisingly, the animals of each of the various islands in the Galápagos chain differed slightly from one another. Darwin observed 13 different types of finches throughout 13 different small islands. The birds on each island differed in the structure of their beaks, their body form, and the color of their feathers. Each species was specifically adapted to the specific habitats on each of the islands. Darwin used the techniques that Edmonstone taught him to preserve the Galápagos finches, which became key pieces of evidence supporting Darwin's theory of natural selection.

FIGURE 4.11 Charles Darwin is acknowledged as the father of the theory of natural selection. His work built upon the ideas of many other thinkers. His great contribution was in synthesizing these ideas into a coherent theory explaining the diversity of life on earth and the great changes in life over geological time. (credit: A. C. Seward, Cambridge Philosophical Society, Cambridge University Press/Wikimedia Commons, Public Domain)

During his travels on the *Beagle*, Darwin had been thinking about **artificial selection**—the selective breeding of animals to produce traits that humans find useful, commonly associated with the process of domestication. Darwin understood that artificial selection provided important clues about the natural evolution of species.

While on board the HMS *Beagle*, Darwin read a book by English economist Thomas Robert Malthus titled *An Essay on the Principle of Population* (1798). Darwin obtained two important points from this book. The first was that human populations, if unrestrained, will grow exponentially. This means that they will double each generation. The second point was that food resources increase much more slowly than population does. Malthus noted that the growth of human populations is kept in check by a limit of food resources, which creates a struggle for existence. The struggle for existence is not just about getting enough food but also about survival. In other words, it is about an individual's ability to both find enough food and not become another organism's food. This simple concept, the struggle for existence, provided Darwin with a mechanism for how evolution could occur. Darwin realized that individuals with favorable characteristics for living in an environment are the ones that will survive to the age at which they reproduce, while those with less favorable variations will not. This mechanism for "selecting for" certain traits and features is known as the theory of **natural selection**.

Darwin concluded from his observations that when a group of animals of the same species are geologically separated, they develop into separate species. This evolutionary process is commonly referred to as **allopatric speciation** (or geographic speciation) and is based on the principles that related species share a common ancestor and that species change over time.

Darwin did not originate the idea of evolution. Many of the ideas used by Darwin in his theory of natural selection were developed by other thinkers. Darwin was also not the only person thinking about natural selection. Another British natural historian, Alfred Russel Wallace, developed the same idea at roughly the same time, entirely independently of Darwin. Whereas Darwin developed his ideas based on his travels to the Galápagos, Wallace's thinking was influenced by his own travels through the Malay Archipelago between

Indochina and Australia. Wallace outlined his theory of evolution by natural selection in a letter written to Darwin while he was in Malaysia. As Darwin had not yet published his own work, Wallace and Darwin jointly presented papers introducing the theory of natural selection. In 1859, Darwin finally published his book *On the Origin of Species*, some 20 years after his voyage on the HMS *Beagle*.

Understanding Darwin's Theory of Natural Selection

The theory of natural selection has five main components:

1. All organisms are capable of producing offspring faster than the food supply increases.
2. All organisms show variation.
3. There is a fierce struggle for existence, and those with the most suitable variations are most likely to survive and reproduce.
4. Variations, or traits, are passed on to offspring (inherited).
5. Small changes in every generation lead to major changes over long periods of time.

A popular but often-misunderstood concept related to natural selection is the term **survival of the fittest**. Survival of the fittest does not necessarily mean that the biggest and fastest survive; instead, it refers to those who are most *evolutionarily* fit. This means that an organism has traits that are sufficient for survival and will be passed on to future generations. The term *survival of the fittest* was not even introduced by Darwin; rather, it was first used by English philosopher, anthropologist, and sociologist Herbert Spencer, who promoted the now discredited ideology of social Darwinism. Social Darwinism applied the concept of Darwin's biological evolution to human societies, proposing that human culture was progressing toward the "perfect human." Spencer's writings became integrally related to the 19th-century rise of scientific racism and European colonialism.

FIGURE 4.12 This peppered moth is well camouflaged on the trunk of this tree. A darker colored moth would more easily be seen and eaten and would thus be less likely to pass on its genes to offspring. Natural selection relies upon the ability of natural variations to increase an individual's chances of reproduction. (credit: Ben Sale/Wikimedia Commons, CC BY 2.0)

Examples of Darwin's theory of natural selection can be found throughout the natural world. Perhaps one of the best known is the color change observed in peppered moths in England during the 19th century. Before the Industrial Revolution, peppered moths in England were a light grey color, well camouflaged on tree branches and less likely to be eaten by birds. Occasionally, through the process of mutation, black moths would appear in the population, but these were usually quickly eaten because they were more visible against light-colored bark. When soot from coal factories began to cover the bark of the trees, the black moths became better camouflaged and the white moths were now more visible. Consequently, the black moths were the ones to survive to reproduce, while the white ones were eaten. In a few decades, all the peppered moths in the cities were black. The process was termed **industrial melanism**. As coal usage decreased and the bark of the trees once again became lighter in color, white moths again dominated the urban areas.

Examples of natural selection in modern times are numerous. Pesticide resistance in insects is a classic example. Pesticide resistance refers to the decreasing susceptibility of a pest population to a pesticide that previously was effective at controlling it. Pest species evolve pesticide resistance via natural selection, with the most resistant individuals surviving to pass on their ability to resist the pesticide to their offspring. Another good example is the rise of "superbugs," bacteria that have become increasingly resistant to antibiotics.

The Processes of Evolution

Mutation is the creative force of evolution and represents the first stage of the evolutionary process. **Mutation** is defined as an alteration in a genetic sequence that results in a variant form. For a mutation to have evolutionary significance, it must occur in the sex cells (sperm and ova). This is because only genetic information that is in the sex cells is passed on from generation to generation. Mutations in non-sex chromosomes will not be passed on from one generation to the next. Whereas other evolutionary forces can modify existing genetic material, only mutation can produce new genetic material. One of the most interesting things about mutations is the fact that they are random. There is no way of predicting when a specific mutation will occur; all scientists can do is estimate the probability of a mutation occurring. Mutations do not necessarily appear when they are needed.

The conventional view is that mutations are harmful, but this is not always true. Some mutations are harmful, some are advantageous, and some are neutral. Advantageous mutations lead to changes that improve an individual's survival and/or chances of reproduction. The mutation that confers resistance to insecticide in mosquitos led to changes that improved their survival. Likewise, the mutation for black coloration in peppered moths led to increased survival during the Industrial Revolution. Neutral mutations have no effect on survival or reproduction. And some mutations are in fact quite harmful and do negatively affect certain individuals' survival and reproduction.

Mutations generally occur spontaneously in response to conditions in the body or in the environment. The exact cause of a mutation cannot usually be determined, and the rate of mutation is very difficult to determine. This is because mutations that are neutral or do not lead to obvious changes often go unnoticed. The probability of a mutation at any given gene is between 1 in 10,000 and 1 in 100,000. While the probability that a specific point in an individual's genetic material will have a mutation is clearly very low, the probability that the totality of an individual's genetic material will have at least one mutation is much higher. The point is that while rare, mutation is also common. For example, although many mosquitoes have adapted to insecticides through a mutation that confers some resistance to the chemicals, if the mutation had not already been present in the population, the mosquitoes would have died out. The need for a specific mutation had no effect on whether the mutation appeared or not.

There is currently a controversial pilot program in Florida aimed at dealing with mosquitoes against which insecticide sprays have increasingly become ineffective. The first genetically modified mosquitoes were released in the Florida Keys in May of 2021. The genetically altered mosquitoes produce female offspring that die in the larval stage, preventing them from growing to adulthood, in which they can then bite and spread disease. Genetic science currently has the power to use mutations to control or even wipe out an entire species. Genetic engineering has the potential to benefit humanity, but it will undoubtedly also raise ethical questions and controversy.

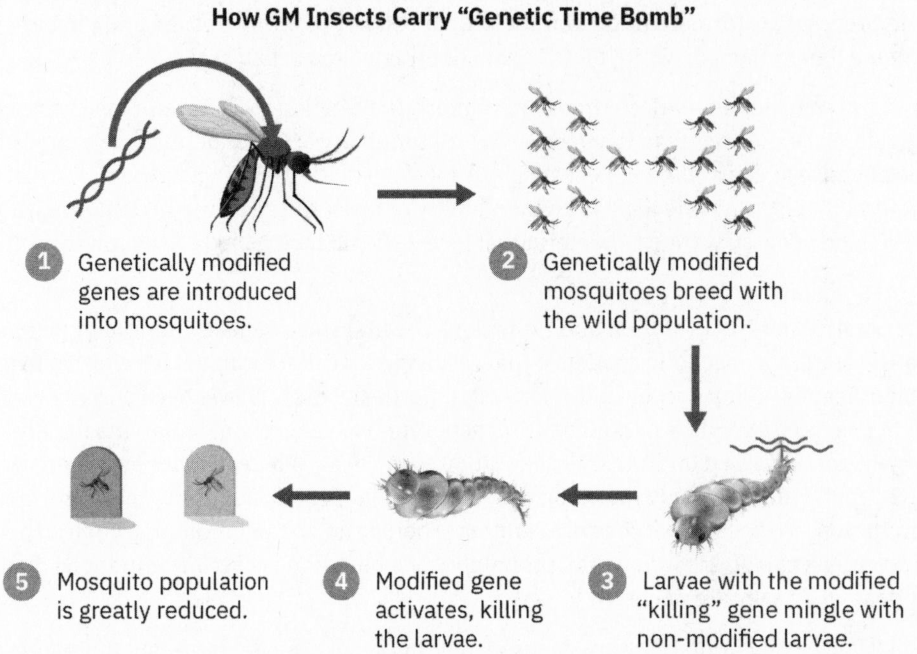
How GM Insects Carry "Genetic Time Bomb"
1 Genetically modified genes are introduced into mosquitoes.
2 Genetically modified mosquitoes breed with the wild population.
3 Larvae with the modified "killing" gene mingle with non-modified larvae.
4 Modified gene activates, killing the larvae.
5 Mosquito population is greatly reduced.

FIGURE 4.13 Genetically modified mosquitoes are currently being bred that will die in the larval stage, thus greatly reducing the mosquito population. (attribution: Rice University, OpenStax, under CC BY 4.0 license)

Genetic Drift

Genetic drift is defined as the effect of random chance on a population, notably the way in which it determines whether an individual survives and reproduces or dies. Imagine that you stick your hand into a bucket filled with Halloween candy. What is the probability you will withdraw a Snickers bar? The composition of Halloween candy in your bucket will be affected by the proportion of people handing out Snickers bars compared to other candy. If each bucket of Halloween candy were a population, then one could say that genetic drift—random chance—was affecting the composition of the candy in your Halloween bucket. An important point about genetic drift is that it is directly and inversely related to population size. The smaller the population, the larger the influence of genetic drift; the larger the population, the smaller the influence of genetic drift. In a large population, say 100,000, removing a couple of individuals will have a truly miniscule effect on the population. Note that in early human evolution, however, population sizes were small, so the effect of genetic drift may have been substantial.

Gene Flow

Gene flow is another important evolutionary force, involving the exchange of genetic material between populations and geographic regions. Without gene flow, there would be no diversity—and without diversity, a species is at higher risk of extinction. Gene flow can be seen in the process of pollination, in which bees or butterflies carry and transfer pollen from one area to another. Anytime a gene is introduced to a new population where it did not exist before, that is gene flow.

FIGURE 4.14 The process of pollination is a good example of gene flow. In this case, bees and butterflies transfer genetic material, in the form of pollen, from one flower to another. (credit: "Honey Bee on a Dandelion, Sandy, Bedfordshire" by Orangeaurochs/flickr, CC BY 2.0)

Speciation

Speciation is the rise of a new species in response to an environmental change or pressure. Allopatric speciation, mentioned previously, is the most common form of speciation event. During allopatric speciation, a species diverges when two populations become isolated from one another and continue to evolve. This isolation is created by geographic barriers such as mountains, rivers, or oceans. A good example of allopatric speciation is the different species of squirrel found on the two sides of the Grand Canyon. Descended from a common ancestor, the squirrels became reproductively isolated from one another by the Grand Canyon, eventually resulting in different species.

FIGURE 4.15 An example of allopatric speciation is the different species of squirrels that inhabit the Grand Canyon. The squirrel on the left is a Harris antelope squirrel and the one on the right is a white-tailed antelope squirrel. They look similar but are different species. (credit: left, "Harris Antelope Squirrel" by Saguaro National Park/flickr, CC BY 2.0; right, "White-Tailed Antelope Squirrel" by Renee Grayson/flickr, CC BY 2.0)

Sympatric speciation involves species that are descended from a common ancestor and remain in one location without a geographic barrier. A good example is the East African cichlid fish, which experience reproduction isolation due not to a physical barrier but to females' selection of mates with certain coloration. The amount of light that reaches different levels and depths of the lake impacts how colors in the males appear to the females. The East African cichlid fish are also a good example of adaptive radiation. Adaptive radiation is seen when one or more species give rise to many new species in a relatively short time. Research shows that an explosion of about 250 very diverse species of cichlids in Lake Tanganyika occurred in less than 10 million years (Takahashi and Koblmüller 2011). Other research suggests that the common ancestor was the result of a hybrid swarm from two different locations, as seen in Figure 4.16. (Meier et al. 2017).

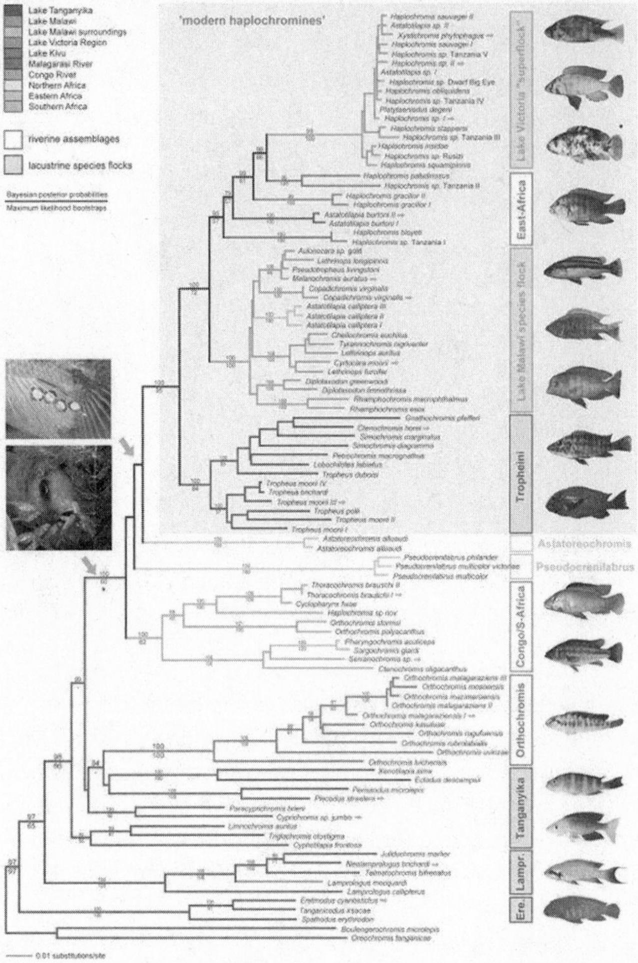

FIGURE 4.16 There are more than 250 different species of East African cichlid fish, all traceable to two common ancestors. The process through which a great number of species arises from a common ancestor within a relatively short period of time is known as adaptive radiation. (credit: "1471-2148-5-17-3" by Phylogeny Figures/flickr, CC BY 2.0)

In peripatric speciation, members of the same population are separated and over time evolve as separate species. Ring speciation is considered by some to be a type of peripatric speciation. Ring speciation occurs when several species coexist for a time in a region near one end of a geographic barrier. When part of the population migrates away from the original population (or gene pool) to the other side of the barrier, reproductive isolation results. Reproductive isolation is strongest for that part of the population that is farthest away from the original population. When too much variation has occurred between two groups, they will no longer interbreed, and as a result, speciation—the development of two separate species—can occur. While fairly rare, ring speciation is believed to explain the different species of the California salamander genus *Ensatina*.

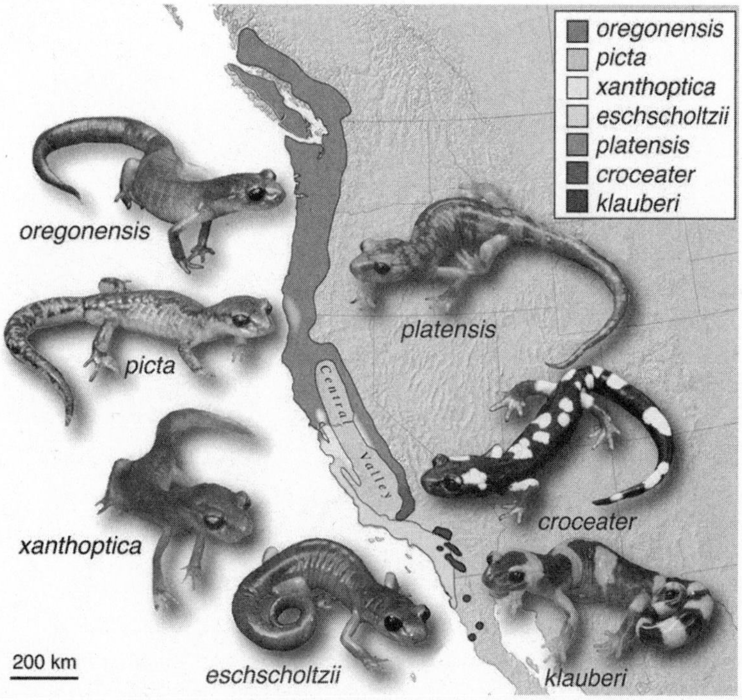

FIGURE 4.17 This map shows the range of different species of the California salamander genus *Ensatina*, believed to have developed through the process of ring speciation. In ring speciation, reproductive isolation leads to the development of new species from a common ancestor, due to separation caused by distance and/or a physical barrier. (credit: Thomas J. Devitt, Stuart J. E. Baird, and Craig Moritz/Wikimedia Commons, CC BY 2.0)

Gradualism vs. Punctuated Evolution

Biological anthropologists are interested not only in how a species is best defined but also in how often and by what means new species are developed. The traditional view of evolution assumes that morphological, behavioral, and genetic changes occur gradually and accumulate in a single unbroken and unbranching line; this view of evolution is known as **gradualism**. If this perspective is correct, scientists would expect to find numerous fossils exhibiting evidence that they are slowly and gradually transitioning into new and distinct species. However, while fossils are rare, fossils showing evidence of transitional forms are even rarer. While the dearth of transitional fossils is often attributed to the incompleteness of the fossil record, it has caused some biological anthropologists to question if evolution is truly gradual.

What can be observed in the fossil record are static populations that are interrupted by sudden bursts of change. This phenomenon of long periods of stasis, or no change, followed by quick periods of change is known as **punctuated equilibrium**. Instead of a gradual accumulation of small changes, punctuated equilibrium suggests that rapid changes due to a variety of environmental factors, including climate change, are characteristic of the formation of new species. The fossil data for a large number of organisms show just this—long periods of stasis followed by rapid and massive change. The scarcity of intermediary forms in the fossil record has led some to conclude that punctuated equilibrium is the dominant theory. However, the fact that intermediary forms do exist suggests that gradualism is also an important factor in the evolution process. One research study found that 30 to 35 percent of speciation events occurred as the result of a sudden event or change, while the remainder showed evidence of gradualism (Phillips 2006). In both the gradual and punctuated models, speciation takes the form of branches through time rather than a linear progression. Evolution is neither linear nor progressive, but rather a branching process—a tree of life containing both areas of divergence and points of a shared common ancestry.

The Tree of Life: Showing Evolutionary Relationships

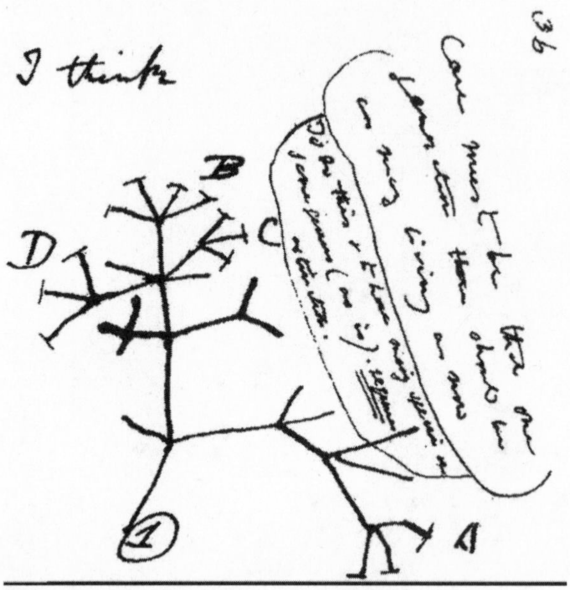

FIGURE 4.18 This sketch made by Charles Darwin illustrates his attempts to think through the branches of evolutionary relationships. (credit: Charles Darwin/Wikimedia Commons, Public Domain)

During Darwin's time, evolutionary relationships had to be determined largely by structural morphologies and physical characteristics. Molecular science had not yet been developed. The binomial nomenclature discussed earlier not only allowed distinction between species but also provided clues to evolutionary relationships. For example, which of the below species of butterfly would be the most distantly related?

- *Danaus gilippus*
- *Danaus genutia*
- *Limenitis archippus*
- *Danaus plexippus*
- *Danaus petilia*

The answer, of course, would be *Limenitis archippus*, the viceroy butterfly, which is a mimic of the monarch butterfly (*Danaus plexippus*). The first part of the viceroy's name, *Limenitis*, is the genus. The fact that it is different from the others shows that it is more distantly related.

FIGURE 4.19 Species can sometimes be difficult to identify by physical characteristics alone. The two butterflies in this image are examples of two different species, one a monarch and the other a viceroy butterfly. What differences can you see? (credit: left, **"Today's Mass Extinction and Holocene-Anthropocene Thermal Maximum"** by khteWisconsin/flickr, Public Domain; right, "A Viceroy Butterfly" by Benny Mazur/flickr, CC BY 2.0)

It is important to note that the Linnaean classification system has limits. Sometimes, species can be difficult to identify by physical characteristics alone. Species that exhibit mimicry and larval forms in different stages of development can take on the appearance of other organisms, resulting in errors in classification. Can you tell which of the butterflies in Figure 4.19 is the monarch? Close examination reveals that the markings on the wings are a bit different. The monarch is on the left, and the monarch mimic, the viceroy, is on the right. Likewise, in Figure 4.20, you can see how it might be difficult to correctly classify barnacles, crabs, and limpets based on physical appearances. One may be tempted to classify the barnacle and the limpet as being closely related due to the conical shells that they share, when in actuality, the barnacle is more closely related to the crab, as they are both crustaceans. The conical shells of the barnacle and the limpet are similar adaptations in response to similar environmental pressures, not evidence that they are closely related or share a common ancestor.

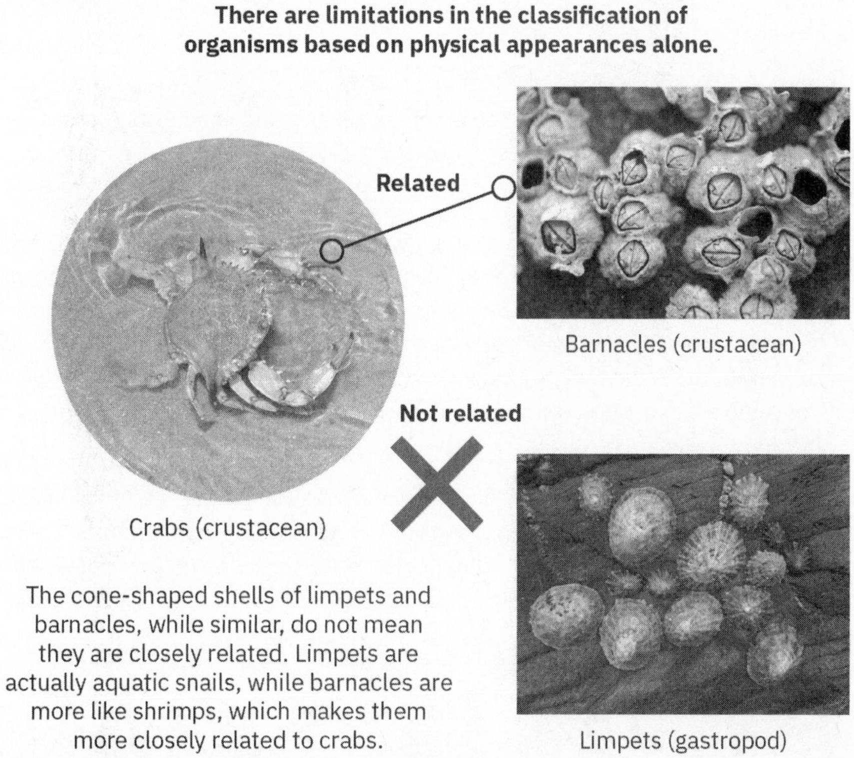

There are limitations in the classification of organisms based on physical appearances alone.
Related
Barnacles (crustacean)
Not related
Crabs (crustacean)
The cone-shaped shells of limpets and barnacles, while similar, do not mean they are closely related. Limpets are actually aquatic snails, while barnacles are more like shrimps, which makes them more closely related to crabs.
Limpets (gastropod)

FIGURE 4.20 Classifying species based on physical similarities alone can lead to false conclusions. Although barnacles and limpets look much more like one another than they do the crab on the left, barnacles are actually more closely related to the crab. (credit: left, "DSC_5206" by Sally Wyatt/flickr, CC BY 2.0; top right, "Barnacles" by Mo Riza/flickr, CC BY 2.0; bottom right, "Limpet Family at Sunny Cove" by Tim Green/flickr, CC BY 2.0)

Structural Morphologies as Evidence of Relationship

Structural similarities may be derived traits (**homologous structures**), inherited from a common ancestor, or they may have developed independently (**analogous structures**). An example of a homologous structure is the grasping hand found in both humans and chimpanzees, which suggests that humans and chimpanzees share a common ancestor that also had a grasping hand. Analogous structures are seen in the wing of a butterfly and the wing of a bat. While both wings serve a similar function, these two organisms likely developed their wings independently and do not necessarily share a common ancestor. Identifying homologies is essential for creating hierarchies of phylogenetic relationships because homology indicates that shared features are due to common descent. However, homologies can be difficult to identify in nature, and they are easy to confuse with analogous traits.

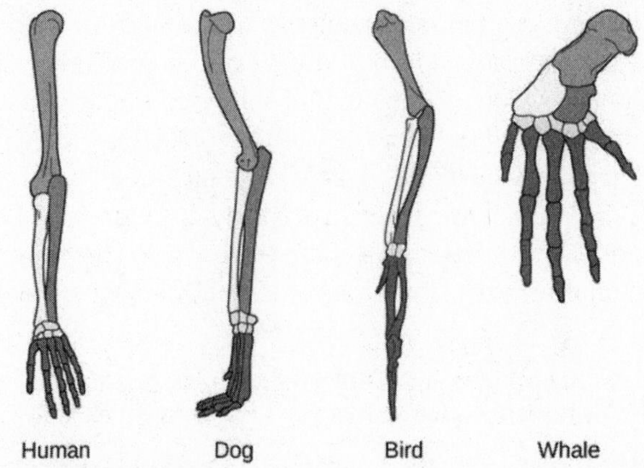

FIGURE 4.21 The structural similarities visible in these various species are homologous, meaning that the similarities are the result of these animals sharing a common ancestor. (attribution: Rice University, OpenStax, under CC BY 4.0 license)

Cladistics, or the use of cladograms, is a method of visually distinguishing between homologous *ancestral* and *derived* characteristics. **Ancestral characteristics** are found in the common ancestor of the species being classified, whereas **derived characteristics** are only found in the groups in question. An ancestral characteristic that humans share with common ancestors is opposable thumbs. In contrast, a derived trait that is only found in modern humans is the chin. By exclusively looking at derived characteristics, biological anthropologists can develop a clearer understanding of the relationships between the groups being studied.

The Molecular Tree of Life and Phylogenetics

The emergence of genetic and molecular science has provided additional tools and lines of evidence to verify evolutionary relationships. The phylogenetic tree is a model used by modern taxonomists to reveal the complexity and diversity of life and its many branches. Phylogenetic trees show how species and other taxon groups evolved from a series of common ancestors. They are based on both physical and genetic evidence.

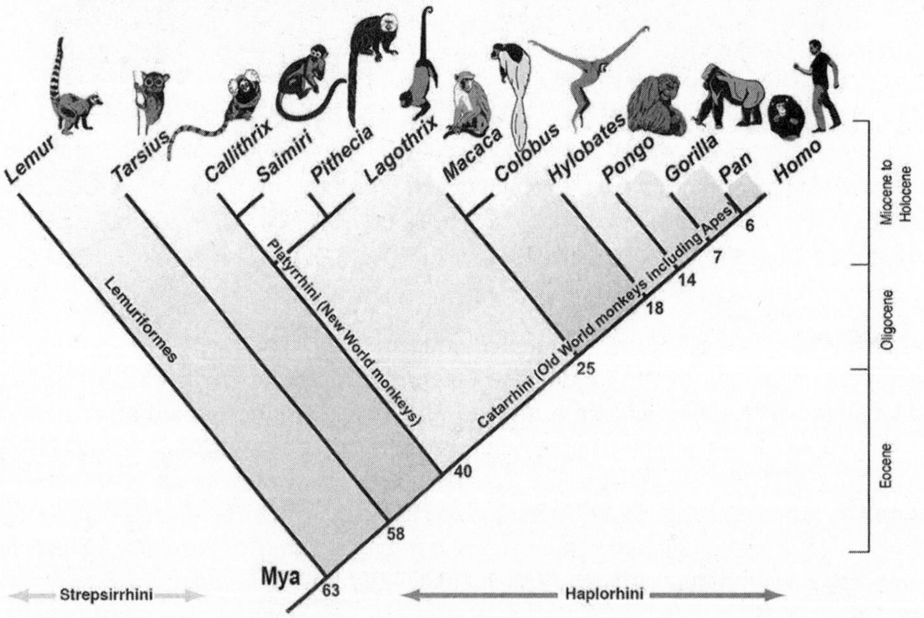

FIGURE 4.22 Phylogenetic trees illustrate how old species are believed to be and their degree of relatedness to one another. This particular tree pertains to primate species. (credit: Kosigrim/Wikimedia Commons, Public Domain)

4.5 What Is a Primate?

LEARNING OUTCOMES:

By the end of this section, you will be able to:

- Define primate.
- Describe the relationship between primate behavior and environment.
- Identify and classify the key taxonomic groups of primates.

What Is a Primate?

FIGURE 4.23 Orangutans, the only great ape from Asia, are one of many living primate species. Others include lemurs, monkeys, gibbons, and human beings. (credit: Dawn Armfield/Wikimedia Commons, Public Domain)

Primates—including human beings—are characterized by a number of distinct physical features that distinguish them from other mammals. These include

- opposable thumbs and (in nonhuman primates) opposable big toes;
- the presence of five digits (fingers or toes) on the appendages;
- flat nails instead of curved claws;
- pads at the tips of the fingers made up of deposits of fat and nerves;
- reduced reliance on sense of smell and a relatively small snout;
- depth perception;
- binocular vision (being able to see one image with both eyes);
- a relatively slow reproductive rate;
- relatively large brain size; and
- postorbital bars (bony rings that completely surround the eyes).

FIGURE 4.24 The hands of this bonobo, including its opposable thumbs, look very similar to human hands. Opposable thumbs or toes are a primate trait shared by no other group of mammals. (credit: "Bonobo Plankendaal" by Marie van Dieren/flickr, CC BY 2.0)

The first four traits enhance dexterity and enable primates to use their hands and feet differently from other mammals. Other traits on this list represent a shift in emphasis among the sense organs between primates and other mammals. Primates are characterized by a greater emphasis on vision and a reduced reliance on smell relative to other mammals.

Primate Behavioral Variation

Anthropologists regularly ask, "What makes us human?" Comparative studies of humans with nonhuman primates help answer this question. Comparing the behavior of nonhuman primates and the behavior of human beings helps anthropologists identify what culture is and develop operational definitions for it. Without the comparative perspective provided by primatology, anthropologists would be missing an important piece of the puzzle of what makes humans human. Without primatology, anthropologists would not be able to fully understand humankind.

Studying nonhuman primates in their environment is key to understanding variations in behavior and can shed light on humanity's ancient past. Primatologists are studying the chimpanzees at Gombe National Park in Tanzania, where they live in the rainforest. The behavior of chimpanzees that live in the tropical regions of Africa is quite different from the behavior of chimpanzees that live in the savanna at Fongoli in Senegal, in West Africa. Gombe chimps hunt red colobus monkeys without the use of tools, just catching them with their hands, while the Fongoli chimpanzees hunt galagos (also known as bush babies) using sticks that they adapt and used as spears (Pruetz, J.D, et al, 2015). The two environments also show differences in gender roles with both males and females in the Fongoli savannah group involved in hunting while only male chimpanzees hunt in the rainforests. Studying how these nonhuman primates both make and use tools is critical for understanding how humans' fossil ancestors may have used and constructed tools.

An important question that primatologists and biological anthropologists seek to answer is the question, do nonhuman primates have culture? Whenever we see an exchange of ideas where one individual is involved in teaching another and when that knowledge is passed on to others in a group is according to anthropologists, a form of culture. We see this happen in chimpanzee groups where older chimpanzees teach the young how to use sticks to termite-fish, the process of extracting termites from a termite mound using a stick.

FIGURE 4.25 This chimpanzee lives in the Gombe National Park in Tanzania. Chimps living in Gombe's rainforest environment have developed a very different set of hunting techniques and tool use from their relatives living in the grassy savannah. (credit: "Chimp Eden Sanctuary – Mimi" by Afrika Force/flickr, CC BY 2.0)

Explaining Primate Success

Why primates evolved as they did and how they filled and exploited the range of ecological niches they now fill are questions that have not yet been adequately addressed. Over the last century, various hypotheses have been raised to account for the evolution of primates and their unusual anatomical characteristics. These theories include the arboreal theory, the visual predation hypothesis, and the angiosperm theory.

The **arboreal theory** proposes that primates evolved the traits they did as an adaptation to life in the trees. Specifically, primates evolved thumbs and big toes that are perpendicular to the other digits to help them grasp onto branches.

Matt Cartmill, a professor of anthropology at Boston University who spent his career trying to understand why primates evolved the way they did, has complicated this theory. Cartmill recognized that forward-facing eyes are characteristic not only of primates but also of predators such as cats and owls that prey on small animals. Thus, forward-facing eyes, grasping hands and feet, and the presence of nails instead of claws may not have arisen as adaptations to an arboreal environment. Rather, they may be adaptations that helped early primates succeed as predators. According to the **visual predation hypothesis**, primate features are adaptations for hunting insects and other small prey in the shrubby forest undergrowth and the lowest tiers of the forest canopy.

The **angiosperm theory** states that the basic primate traits developed in coevolution with the rise of flowering plants, also known as angiosperms. Flowering plants provide numerous resources, including nectar, seeds, and fruits, and their appearance and diversification were accompanied by the appearance of ancestral forms of major groups of modern birds and mammals. Some argue that visual predation is not common among modern primates and that forward-facing eyes and grasping extremities may have arisen in response to the need for fine visual and tactile discrimination in order to feed on small food items, such as fruits, berries, and seeds, found among the branches and stems of flowering plants.

Primate Classification and Taxonomy

Scientists generally classify the order Primates into two suborders: **Strepsirrhini** (prosimians) and **Haplorrhini** (tarsiers and anthropoids).

The Strepsirrhini or Prosimians

The Strepsirrhini are considered to be primitive primates that evolved much earlier than other primates. This suborder includes lemurs and lorises. All the Strepsirrhini primates, or strepsirrhines, possess numerous anatomical traits that distinguish them from the Haplorrhini primates, or haplorrhines. These include a clawlike nail on the second toe, referred to as a grooming claw, and incisors in the lower jaw that are tightly packed together and protrude from the mouth, forming what is called a toothcomb. There are seven families of living strepsirrhines, and all of them are found in what anthropologists refer to as the Old World, which consists of the continents of Africa, Asia, and Europe. Five groups of living strepsirrhines are found only on the island of Madagascar off the coast of Africa. Two additional families are found in Africa and Asia.

FIGURE 4.26 The pygmy slow loris (*Nycticebus pygmaeus*) is an example of a Strepsirrhini primate. Pygmy slow lorises be found in Vietnam, Laos, and a province of China. (credit: Lionel Mauritson/Wikimedia Commons, Public Domain)

The Haplorrhini or Anthropoids

The Haplorrhini are broken down into two further infraorders, Simiiformes and Tarsiiformes, and the Simiiformes are further divided into Platyrrhini and Catarrhini. The **Platyrrhini**, or platyrrhines, are exclusively found in the New World (specifically Central and South America) and are colloquially referred to as New World monkeys. Their name is derived from the rounded shape of their external nostrils, which open off to the sides. New World monkeys are also distinguishable by their prehensile tails that serves as an extra limb for extra support when moving in the trees. The **Catarrhini**, or catarrhines, are found throughout Africa and Asia. They differ from the New World primates in that they possess narrow nostrils that face downward. The Catarrhini contain two superfamilies, **Cercopithecoidea** and **Hominoidea**, and are exclusively Old World. The Cercopithecoidea contain two main groups: cheek pouch monkeys (Cercopithecinae) and leaf-eating monkeys (Colobinae). The most distinctive feature of the cercopithecoid primates is their molars, which exhibit two parallel ridges. The most distinguishing feature of the hominoids is that they do not have tails and are largely terrestrial, or ground-dwelling. Examples of Hominoidea include gibbons, chimpanzees, gorillas, orangutans, and humans.

The Tarsier Puzzle

The tarsier, which belongs to the family Tarsiidae, has both prosimian and anthropoid characteristics, which has made it difficult for scientists to classify. Tarsiers are currently classified within their own classification under the haplorrhines. One of the characteristics that tarsiers share with other haplorrhines, (including humans) is the inability to manufacture their own Vitamin C. They are the smallest known primate and are nocturnal, with extremely large eyes that take up much of the space in their skull. Due to their size of the eyes, the tarsier cannot rotate them; instead, it can rotate its head 360 degrees like an owl. Tarsiers are also the only primate carnivore, eating largely flying insects and sometimes small animals like bats and lizards. Tarsiers do not do well in captivity. They are extremely sensitive to noise and can become easily stressed. In fact, they can become so stressed that they die by suicide by banging their heads against tree trunks.

FIGURE 4.27 The Philippine tarsier (*Carlito syrichta*) is found only in the southern portion of the Philippine islands. The tarsier has been challenging for scientists to classify, exhibiting both prosimian and anthropoid characteristics. (credit: "8thApril2007 – 'Tarsier' Monkey" by Jacky W./flickr, CC BY 2.0)

4.6 Origin of and Classification of Primates

LEARNING OUTCOMES:

By the end of this section, you will be able to:

- Explain the concept of deep time.
- Define fossils and explain some dating methods used on fossils.
- Identify some of the key characteristics of early primate fossils, including their respective time periods.

Understanding Concepts of Time

Geologists divide deep history into time periods known as eras. Eras are generally based on the fossil life forms observed. The oldest of the geological eras is the Eoarchean, which began approximately four billion years ago. The majority of the fossil evidence that we have for primate evolution comes from the Cenozoic era—the current geological era, dating from 65 million year ago (MYA) to the present. The Cenozoic era is divided into a series of epochs. Each epoch is associated with specific forms of primates that evolved during that time period.

Fossils and Dating Methods

Biological anthropologists primarily, although not exclusively, study fossil artifacts. A **fossil** is any remainder of a plant or animal that has been preserved in the earth. Upon the death of an organism, its body slowly decomposes until all that remains are the teeth and the bones or a mere impression of the organism's original form. Under most conditions, teeth and bones and impressions eventually deteriorate, too. However, occasionally conditions are favorable for preservation. Examples of favorable materials for fossil formation include volcanic ash, limestone, and mineralized groundwater. Scientists do not have fossils of everything that lived in the past, and in some cases, remains from only a few individuals of a species have been found. The fossil record is very incomplete. Robert Martin, a curator at the Field Museum of Natural History in Chicago, estimates that there have been more than 6,000 primate species, while the remains of only 3 percent have been found. Fossils are very rare, but they are extremely informative about human biological evolution.

Making Sense of Fossils

An important part of understanding fossils is determining how old they might be and putting them in chronological order. In order to use a primate fossil to reconstruct the evolutionary history of primates, anthropologists must first be able to estimate approximately how old that specific fossil is. For some time, relative dating methods were the only methods available for dating fossils. Relative dating calculates the approximate age of a fossil in comparison to other fossil specimens. The last half century has seen important advances in absolute dating, including techniques that have made possible the dating of the earliest phases of primate evolution. Absolute dating calculates the actual biological age of a fossil in years within a range of years.

Relative Dating Techniques

Stratigraphy is the best-known and most commonly used method of relative dating. Stratigraphy is based on the observation that soil is deposited in successive layers, or strata. The oldest layers of soil (and any artifacts or fossils within them) will appear beneath more recent layers of soil (and any artifacts or fossils within them). In addition to using the location of layers of soil to date fossils deposited within these layers, biological anthropologists also sometimes make use of other items consistently found in a specific layer of the soil. These items are referred to as indicator artifacts because they help indicate the relative age of fossils and other artifacts. The best indicator artifacts are those that have a wide geographic distribution, are presence for a short period of geological time, and/or are from a species that underwent rapid evolutionary change. Different indicator artifacts have been used to ascertain relative age in different areas of the world. In Africa, elephants, pigs, and horses have been used to establish relative dates of different geological strata. The stratigraphy at Olduvai Gorge in East Africa, for example, was established based on fossil pigs. The various species of pig in successive strata are different and distinct, allowing paleoanthropologists to distinguish the strata based on the pig species found within them. Once the stratigraphy of an area is established, the relative ages of two different fossils in different sites can be determined by the associated indicator artifacts.

If a site has been disturbed, stratigraphy will not be a satisfactory way to determine relative age. In such a situation, it may be possible to use absolute dating methods to estimate the age of fossils found together in a disturbed site.

Absolute Dating Techniques

Many absolute dating methods are based on the rate of decay of a radioactive isotope. A radioactive isotope is a chemical element that dissipates excess energy by spontaneously emitting radiation. These emissions happen at known and stable rates. Once the rate of decay of a radioactive isotope is established, the age of a specimen containing that isotope can be estimated within a range of possible error.

C-14

The best-known method for determining the absolute age of fossils is carbon-14 or ^{14}C (pronounced "C-14") dating. All plants and animals contain the isotope carbon-14 (^{14}C). Plants absorb ^{14}C from the air, and animals ingest plants containing the isotope. Because plants only absorb ^{14}C when they are alive and animals only consume plants when they are alive, scientists can determine how long ago an animal or plant died based on the amount of ^{14}C that remains in their cells. Carbon-14 has a known half-life of 5,730 years. This means that approximately half of the original ^{14}C in an organism will be eliminated in 5,730 years after its death. For example, if an organism had an original ^{14}C value of 100, then after 5,730 years, only 50 units of ^{14}C would be present.

Thermoluminescence

Another absolute dating technique that is frequently used by paleoanthropologists is thermoluminescence dating. Thermoluminescence dating requires that either the fossils to be dated or the sediments that the fossils are within have been exposed to a high-temperature event, such as a volcanic explosion. During such a high-temperature event, all the radioactive elements within the material are released. Consequently, the amount of radioactive elements that have accumulated in the artifact since the time of the high-temperature event can be used to calculate the artifact's age.

Primates of the Paleocene Epoch

The Paleocene epoch began approximately 65 MYA and ended about 54 MYA. It is the most poorly understood epoch of the Cenozoic era, as it is the time period with the fewest fossils to represent it. However, this epoch is considered important to primate evolution because it offers the first unequivocal record of the earliest primates. Evidence of the most primitive primate yet identified was found in the U.S. state of Montana, in a geological deposit that was dated to the earliest part of the Paleocene. This creature is known as ***Purgatorius***. *Purgatorius* is similar to extinct and living primates – and distinct from other mammals – in the presence of an elongated last lower molar and an enlarged upper central incisor (resulting in what one could think of as "Bugs Bunny teeth"). These two characteristics, which are shared by all living primates today, suggest that *Purgatorius* may be the common ancestor of later primates.

FIGURE 4.28 *Purgatorius unio* may be the common ancestor of all later primate. Remains of *Purgatorius unio* have been found in deposits dated to be about 63 million years old. (attribution: Rice University, OpenStax, under CC BY 4.0 license)

Primates of the Eocene Epoch

The Eocene epoch, which began approximately 54 MYA and ended about 34 MYA, is marked by the disappearance of *Purgatorius* and the first appearance of primates that more closely resemble modern-day primates, especially in the fact that they possess postorbital bars composed entirely of bone. A postorbital bar is a bony ring surrounding the entirety of the eye orbit. This contrasts with other mammals whose postorbital bars are part bone and part cartilage. Some fossil specimens also possess a toothcomb and/or a grooming claw, characteristics that are exclusively found in strepsirrhine primates today. Other anatomical characteristics that are significant would be the ankle bones which researchers believe played a key role in the evolutionary success of primates. The evolution of primates during the Eocene was tremendous. It has been hypothesized that there were four times as many strepsirrhine primates during the Eocene than there are living primates today. Fossil primates in Eocene deposits are common in North America and Europe and are becoming known in Asia and Africa. However, there are currently no known fossil primates from the Eocene in South America or Antarctica.

Primates of the Oligocene Epoch

The Oligocene epoch, which began approximately 34 MYA and ended about 22 MYA, marks the appearance of the first fossil monkeys. The earliest unambiguous haplorrhine fossils were found at the Fayum, an archaeological site about 60 miles from Cairo, Egypt, that today represents part of the Sahara. The Fayum primates are divided into two main groups: **Parapithecoidea** and **Propliopithecoidea**. Based on their teeth, these primates are believed to be the earliest New World and Old World monkeys, respectively. Teeth are generally described according to a dental formula that indicates the number of each type of teeth in each quadrant of the jaw. An organism with a 2.1.2.3 dental formula has two incisors, one canine, two premolars, and three molars in each quadrant of their upper and lower jaws. Based on the presence of a third premolar, a trait found in all New World monkeys, it is probable that Propliopithecus represents the earliest New World monkeys, even though they first evolved in Africa. Likewise, it is probable the propliopithecoids represent the earliest catarrhine primate, as they are the first fossil monkeys that possess a dental formula of 2.1.2.3 found in catarrhine primates.

Miocene Apes

The Miocene epoch contains fossil evidence of some of the earliest apes such as *Proconsul africanus* africanus which lived in Africa from 23 to 14 mya. The earliest Miocene ape, found in Africa, is ***Proconsul***. Unlike modern-day apes, the *Proconsul* lacked long, curved digits, suggesting that they were able to hang from branches but more often moved about on all four of their limbs. *Proconsul* also lacked a tail, which is why they are considered apes and not monkeys. Like all Old World monkeys and apes, including humans, their teeth show a pattern of 2.1.2.3. Another well-known ape from the Miocene is *Sivapithecus*. *Sivapithecus* fossils are very common throughout Asia, with a particularly large number having been found in Turkey. Like modern-day humans, they exhibit very thick dental enamel, suggesting that these apes regularly ate very hard foods. The most intriguing aspect of *Sivapithecus* morphology is that the skulls show a tremendous resemblance to the living orangutan in features such as its tall nasal openings and high eye sockets.

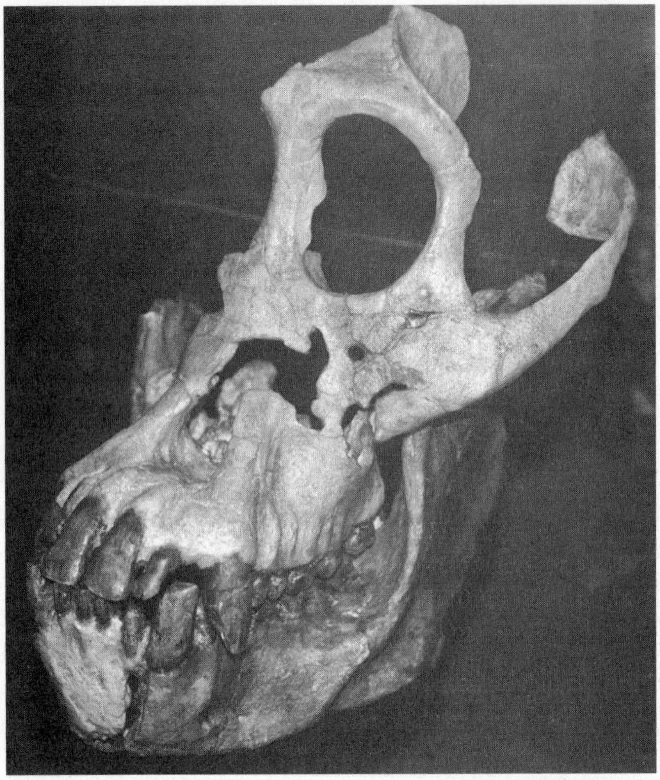

FIGURE 4.29 *Sivapithecus* is one the earliest known ape species. Fossil remains exhibit the tall nasal openings and high eye sockets currently visible in orangutans. (credit: "*Sivapithecus indicus* (Fossil Ape) (Dhok Pathan Formation, Upper Miocene; Potwar Plateau, Pakistan)" by James St. John/flickr, CC BY 2.0)

While it is known that orangutans probably evolved from a *Sivapithecus*-type ape, there are no clear candidates for the ancestors of modern African great apes. There have only been two fossils found that clearly and unequivocally belong to the ancestors of modern African apes. *Samburupithecus* is a large late Miocene ape found in northern Kenya. It is known to resemble modern African apes. It differs from other Miocene fossils in having molar teeth that are elongated in a direction from the front of the mouth toward the back, instead of from cheek to tongue. Another fossil from the late Miocene (9–10 MYA) that is sometimes identified as an ancestor of modern African apes is *Ouranopithecus*, found in Greece, which has facial morphology that links it to both African apes and humans.

4.7 Our Ancient Past: The Earliest Hominins

LEARNING OUTCOMES:

By the end of this section, you will be able to:

- Compare and contrast some early hominin species.
- Identify some key adaptations and characteristics found in early hominins.
- Identify key adaptations and derived traits that emerged in changing environments.

Walking on Two Feet

The term **hominin** refers to all species considered to be in direct lineage to humans, which include the genera *Homo, Australopithecus, Paranthropus,* and *Ardipithecus.* **Hominids** refers to all modern and extinct great apes, which include humans, gorillas, chimpanzees, and orangutans and their ancestors. These terms have been understood to represent different things over the years, but the definitions provided here are the most current. While all hominins may differ in varying ways from one another, they all share one anatomical behavioral complex: bipedal locomotion.

Scientists can hypothesize about how a creature moved by analyzing several aspects of its morphology. Brachiators, animals that move by swinging from branch to branch, generally have long arms, while leapers, animals that propel their bodies through the force of their lower limbs, have relatively long legs. Arboreal primates have arms and legs of equal length. In bipedal locomotion, one leg is called the stance leg, and the other is called the step leg. While the stance leg is on the ground, the step leg is off the ground and striding forward. During normal walking, both feet are on the ground only about 25 percent of the time. As speed of locomotion increases, the percentage of time that both feet are on the ground decreases. As a result, for most of the time that bipedal organisms are moving, their body is balanced on only one of their legs (the stance leg). To ensure that bipedal organisms do not fall over while balanced on their stance leg, they have undergone many anatomical changes since the earliest hominin ancestors.

One of the most important anatomical changes that facilitate successful bipedalism is the angling of the femur (upper leg bone) inward at what is referred to as a valgus angle, which positions the knees and feet under the center of the pelvis. Bipedal hominins have also evolved spinal curves that make it possible for the hips to balance the weight of the upper body. The evolution of the arch in the foot as well as the realignment of the big toe so that it is parallel to the other toes is also instrumental in transmitting weight during the step phase of bipedal locomotion.

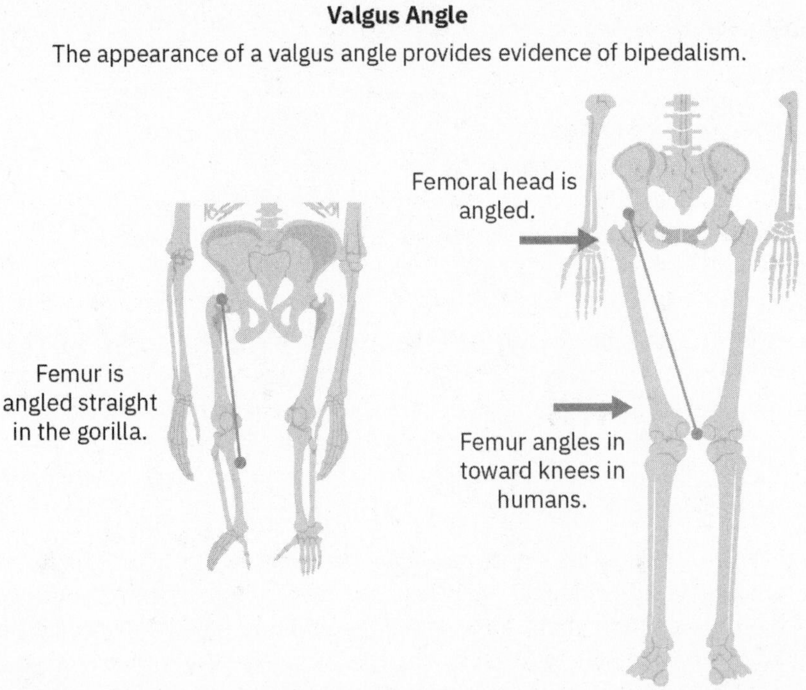

FIGURE 4.30 In humans, the femur bones angle inward. This adaptation, known as the valgus angle, makes bipedal locomotion (walking upright) more comfortable and more efficient. (attribution: Rice University, OpenStax, under CC BY 4.0 license)

The most important evidence of early hominin bipedalism is provided by the work of English paleoanthropologist Mary Leakey. In the 1980s, Mary Leakey discovered a 75-foot trail of footprints made by three bipedal individuals who had crossed a thick bed of wet volcanic ash about 3.5 MYA. These footprints were found in East Africa at the site of Laetoli. Based on the date and the location, it is probable that these footprints were made by *Australopithecus afarensis*. Analysis of the Laetoli footprints indicates a modern striding gait.

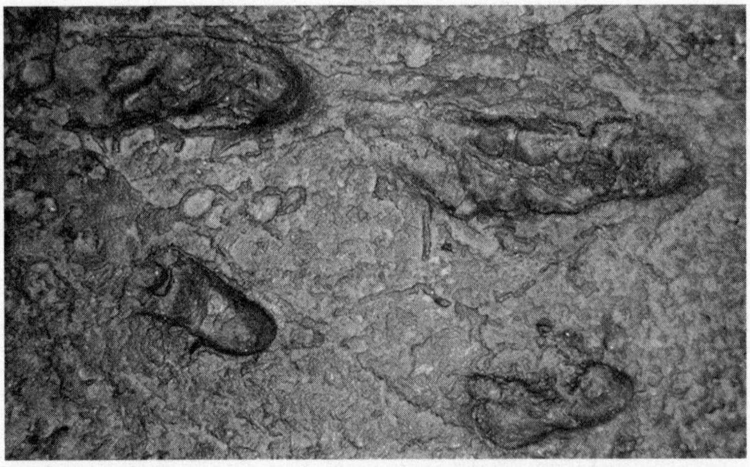

FIGURE 4.31 These replicas of the 3.6-million-year-old hominin footprints found in Tanzania by Mary Leakey are on display at the National Museum of Nature and Science in Tokyo, Japan. (credit: "*Australopithecus afarensis* Fossil Hominid Footprints (Pliocene, 3.6–3.7 Ma; Laetoli Area, Northern Tanzania, Eastern Africa)" by James St. John/ flickr, CC BY 2.0)

The evolution of hominin bipedalism required complex anatomical reorganization. For natural selection to produce such a tremendous amount of change, the benefits of these changes must have been great. There have been dozens of hypotheses for these changes, ranging from freeing hands to carry tools, food, or offspring to increasing energy efficiency or thermoregulation (the ability to maintain the body's temperature) by exposing more of the body's surface. None of the hypotheses are testable, making it truly challenging to understand why humanity's ancestors made such a huge behavioral shift. The next sections explore some of the key discoveries of early hominin fossils in which anthropologists see some of the earliest indications of the adaptation of bipedalism in the human story.

Miocene Hominids

The first hominid fossils appear in the late Miocene, 10 to 5 MYA. Sometime between 7 MYA and 4 MYA, hominids moved out of the trees and began to adapt more fully to a ground-based living niche. Unfortunately, the fossil evidence from this time period is extremely sparse, but new finds continue to be discovered.

A complete cranium of *Sahelanthropus tchadensis* was found in 2002 by French paleoanthropologist Michel Brunet and his team in Chad in West Africa. *Sahelanthropus* is a fossil ape that lived approximately 7 MYA and is claimed by some researchers to be the last common ancestor of humans and chimpanzees. Genetic studies indicate that humans and chimpanzees diverged from one another sometime between 5 MYA and 7 MYA, so this species lived right at the time of the divergence. The cranial capacity is a mere 350 cubic centimeters (cc), which is equivalent to a chimpanzee; the modern human cranial capacity is approximately 1,400 cc. *Sahelanthropus* also has a very large brow ridge (the large bone above the eyes), and the location of the **foramen magnum**, the opening at the base of the skull where the spinal column enters the skull, suggests that its head was not held over its spine and thus it was not bipedal.

Orrorin tugenensis was found in Kenya in 2001 by geologist Martin Pickford of the Collège de France and paleontologist Brigitte Senut of France's National Museum of Natural History. *Orrorin tugenensis* was dated to approximately 6 MYA. *Orrorin* was proposed to be a hominin due to anatomical traits that suggest bipedalism. For example, the femoral head (the big, rounded ball at the top of the leg bone that connects the leg to the hip) is much larger than in quadrupedal apes, suggesting the femur was being used to support the weight of the upper body. The muscles attached to the femur also suggest bipedal movement. Another feature that suggests that *Orrorin* is truly a hominin is the teeth, which exhibit thick dental enamel and small, square molars, much like modern humans.

Pliocene Hominins

The Pliocene epoch extended from 5 MYA to 1.8 MYA. Fossils from the Pliocene show evidence of the evolution of hominins that are clearly bipedal. They also show evidence of clear, albeit primitive, cultural behavior. Climatically, the Pliocene was colder than the preceding Miocene, which resulted in changing sea levels and an increase in ice at the poles, opening up some previously inaccessible areas. During this period, North and South America became connected through the Isthmus of Panama, and a land bridge across the Bering Strait appeared between Alaska and Siberia.

Ardipithecus ramidus

Ardipithecus ramidus was found in Ethiopia in 1992 by American paleoanthropologist Tim White and was dated to about 4.4 MYA. This is the first discovered hominin species to be dated to the Pliocene era. Based on the forward position of the foramen magnum, it can be concluded that *Ardipithecus* was bipedal. Also, the upper arm bones are very small, suggesting that the arms were not used to support weight during locomotion. *Ardipithecus* possesses numerous traits, such as thin dental enamel, evidence of a reduced canine, and an opposable big toe. As a result of the latter trait, many believe that *Ardipithecus* was bipedal on the ground and quadrupedal in the trees. This hypothesis is supported by the fact that the fossil bones were found in relatively heavily forested environments. The reduced canine is a derived trait appearing even earlier than *A. ramidus* and is not what we would typically see in African ape males who have large intimidating canines. Current hypotheses suggest that over time smaller canines became dominant when there became less need to show aggression along with a female preference for males with milder temperaments (Suwa, G., et al. 2021).

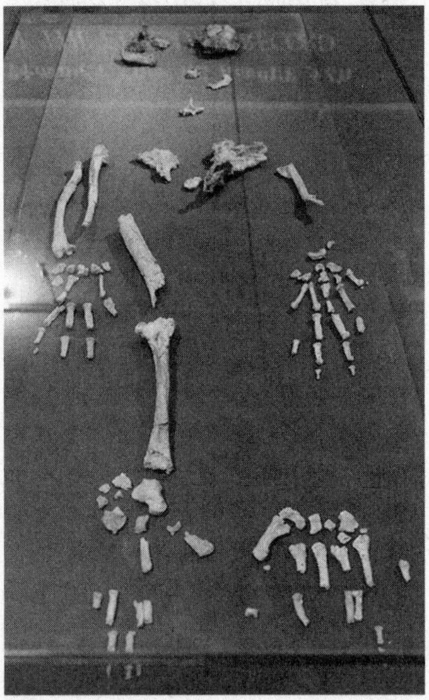

FIGURE 4.32 These skeletal remains have been identified as *Ardipithecus*, the first hominin species discovered that has been dated to the Pliocene Era. (credit: Sailko/Wikimedia Commons, CC BY 3.0)

The Robust and Gracile Australopithecines

The next few sections will examine various australopithecine species that had diverse physical characteristics related to morphology of the teeth and skull. Based on these characteristics, paleoanthropologists classified these species into *gracile* and *robust* forms, as illustrated in Figure 4.33. Gracile species had a more pronounced projection of the jaw (**prognathism**), less flared cheeks with no sagittal crest, and smaller teeth and jaws. The sagittal crest in the robust australopithecines accommodated large temporalis jaw muscles for chewing tough plant materials.

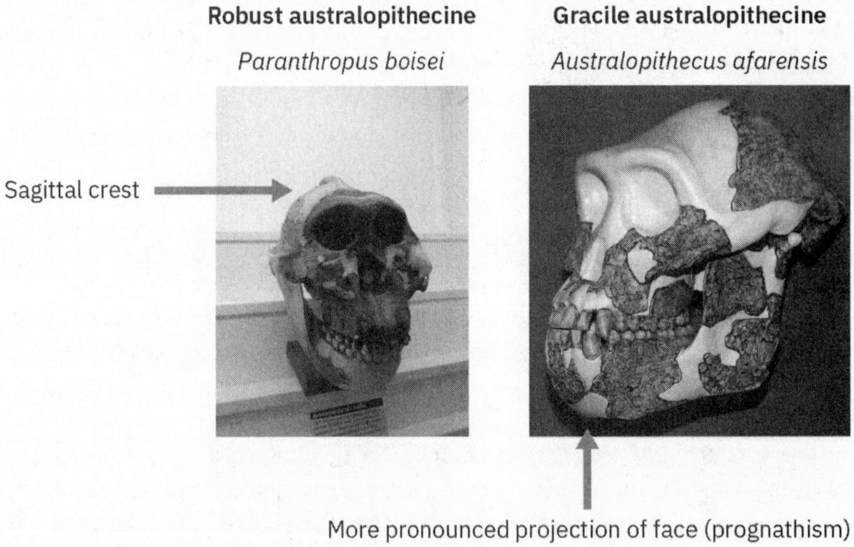

FIGURE 4.33 Australopithecine species are classified as either robust or gracile. A defining feature of the robust species is the sagittal crest visible on the *Paranthropus boisei* skull on the left. Gracile species, such as *A. afarensis*, on the right, display more pronounced projection of the face (prognathism). (credit: left, Rama/Wikimedia Commons, Public Domain; right, "*Australopithecus afarensis* Fossil Hominid (Pliocene, Eastern Africa) 1" by James St. John/flickr, CC BY 2.0)

Species considered to be the gracile include *Australopithecus anamensis, A. afarensis, A. africanus, A. garhi,* and *A. sediba*. The robust australopithecines (classified under the genus *Paranthropus*) include *Paranthropus robustus*, *P. boisei*, and *P. aethiopicus*. The gracile species emerged around 4 MYA and disappeared 2 MYA, while robust species continued to exist for another million years. The next sections will first take a look at some of the gracile forms of australopithecine, followed by the robust forms.

Australopithecus africanus

Australopithecus africanus was the first australopithecine discovered, in 1924, and was described by Australian anatomist and anthropologist Raymond Dart, who found the fossil in a box of fossils sent to him by lime quarry workers at a site called Taung in South Africa. The most notable specimen in the box was a skull from a child, which Dart had to chip away from the stone it was embedded in. It took Dart four years to separate the teeth. The skull is now known as the Taung skull or Taung child. Dart argued that the Taung child represents "an extinct race of apes intermediate between living anthropoids and man" (Wayman 2011). He noted that the skull was long and narrow, not rounded as in modern humans, and its brain averaged a mere 422 cc, equivalent to a chimpanzee. However, the Taung child did not possess brow ridges, had circular orbits, and had minimal prognathism as well as small canines and no **diastema** (space in the jaw for large canines to be positioned when the mouth closes). These latter traits are all analogous to modern humans. Most importantly, Dart noted that the forward position of the foramen magnum indicated that the skull was poised on top of the vertebral column, suggesting bipedalism and an upright posture.

FIGURE 4.34 This partial skull is from a specimen known as the Taung child. The species, *Australopithecus africanus*, displays traits that resemble modern humans in some ways but not others. (credit: Daderot/Wikimedia Commons, Public Domain)

Australopithecus afarensis

In 1973, a good portion of a skeleton (about 40 percent) was found in the Afar region of Ethiopia by American paleoanthropologist Donald Johanson. He called the skeleton Lucy, after a Beatles song. It was dated to around 3.75–2.8 MYA and was determined to be a member of the species *Australopithecus afarensis*. Like all fossils recently discovered, Lucy was given an identification or accession number, KNM-AL-288. The KNM acronym stands for the Kenya National Museum, where the fossil is housed, and AL stands for the Afar locality where the fossil was found. Since then, more specimens of this species have been found in Kenya, Tanzania, and Ethiopia, all in East Africa.

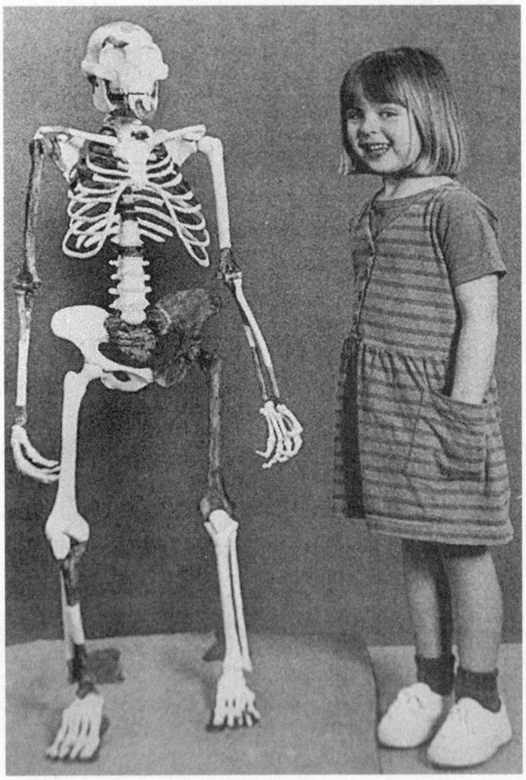

FIGURE 4.35 This child stands next to a recreated skeleton of *A. afarensis*. The long arms and long, curved fingers and toes of *A. afarensis* are apparent. (credit: "*Australopithecus afarensis* Fossil Hominid (Lucy Skeleton) (Hadar Formation, Pliocene, 3.2 Ma; Hadar Area, Afar Triangle, Northern Ethiopia, Eastern Africa) 2" by James St. John/ flickr, CC BY 2.0)

Australopithecus afarensis is dated from 3.9 to 2.9 MYA with an endocranial capacity of around 400 cc, which is approximately the same as a common chimpanzee. There are two morphological features that provide evidence that *A. afarenis* moved more like a great ape than a human. First, it had arms that were substantially longer than modern humans'. Long arms are generally found in animals that hang from branches, suggesting that *A. afarensis* also exhibited this behavior. Also, *A. afarensis* possesses finger and toe bones that are long and curved, another characteristic of animals that hang from branches. However, there is one important morphological feature of *A. afarensis* that suggests that this species may have moved somewhat like modern humans. The shape of *A. afarensis*'s pelvis (hip bones) looks substantially more like a modern human's than it does an ape's. Instead of the hip bones being long and narrow, they are short and wide. Most paleoanthropologists believe that this change in pelvic shape indicates that *A. afarensis* moved like modern humans do, on two legs. While *A. afarensis* may have locomoted bipedally, the morphological differences between *A. afarensis* and modern humans suggest they did not move in exactly the same way. Current consensus is that *A. afarensis* was both tree dwelling and bipedal. Other anatomical evidence of bipedalism includes a more anterior position of the foramen magnum and the angle of the femoral head and neck.

Australopithecus garhi

Also found in Ethiopia, *Australopithecus garhi* is dated to approximately 2.5 MYA. Its cranial capacity is slightly greater than *A. afarensis*, at 450 cc. *Australopithecus garhi* has incisors that are larger than those of any of the known australopithecines or *Homo*. The function of the large incisors is not yet known. The most exciting aspect of *A. garhi* is that it provides evidence of the earliest use of stone tools by a hominin. Specifically, *A. garhi* fossils were found with fossil bones of ruminants, such as antelopes, that displayed numerous cut marks. Cut marks are made on bones by the process of removing meat from the bones with stone or metal tools. Based on this finding, biological anthropologists have hypothesized that *A. garhi* used some type of stone tool for butchering.

Australopithecus sediba

In 2008, the clavicle bone of *Australopithecus sediba* was discovered by Matthew Berger, the nine-year-old son of American paleontologist Lee Berger, in Malapa, South Africa. Further excavation in a cave feature uncovered two partial skeletons, one of an adult female and the other a younger juvenile. *A. sediba* is considered an important species because it appears in the fossil record around the time of the first emergence of the genus *Homo* around 2 mya. The classification of *A. sediba* was initially difficult to determine, due to its complex overlapping features, which include humanlike spine, pelvis, hands, and teeth and a chimpanzee-like foot. This combination of traits suggests both tree climbing and bipedal adaptations. After studying the characteristics collectively, anthropologists classified *A. sediba* as a species of *Australopithecus*. It is considered a direct ancestor of *Homo erectus and Homo ergaster*, which are discussed in Chapter 5, The Genus *Homo* and the Emergence of Us . It is believed that *A. sediba* could be a descendent of *A. africanus*, which suggests the species may be a dead end within the lineage to humans. Its classification and relationship with the genus *Homo* will likely remain highly debated.

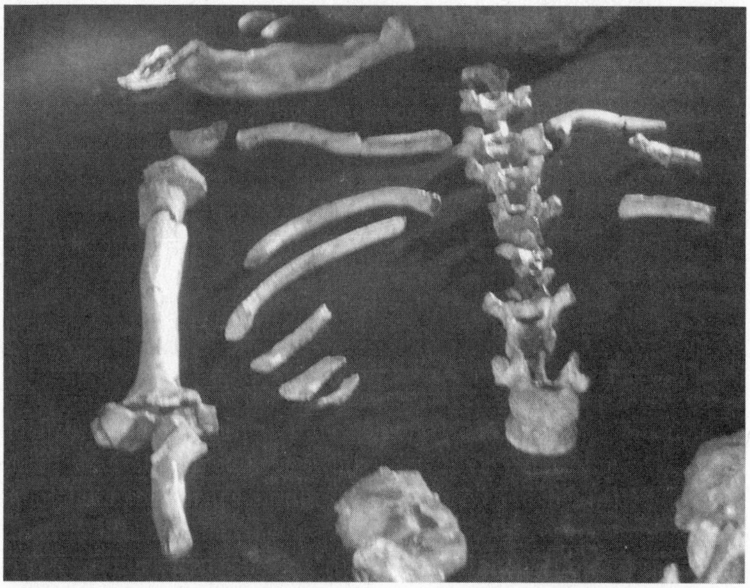

FIGURE 4.36 These bones are from *Australopithecus sediba*, which displays a humanlike spine and pelvis but a chimpanzee-like foot. (credit: Phiston/Wikimedia Commons, CC BY 3.0)

Paranthropus robustus

Thirteen years after Raymond Dart's discovery, South African paleontologist and medical doctor Robert Broom discovered *Paranthropus robustus* at a site called Kromdraai in South Africa**.** The most obvious difference between Dart's and Broom's respective fossils, *A. africanus* and *P. robustus*, is that the morphology of Broom's fossil is much larger. Its features include a sagittal crest and a flared zygomatic arch for the attachment of a large temporalis muscle for chewing a diet reliant on hard nuts and seeds. This interpretation was further supported by scanning electron microscopy (SEM), which was used to evaluate the markings etched into the teeth. As the teeth increased in size the incisors and canines shrank, giving *Paranthropus* a flatter face with less projection of the jaw. There are some who argue that depending on the environment and locale, some *Paranthropus* may have been omnivores, with varied diets similar to those of *H. ergaster*. (Lee-Thorp, Thackeray, and van der Merwe 2000).

Paranthropus boisei

Following in Broom's footsteps, other scientists began searching for fossils in East Africa. Beginning in 1931, Kenyan and British paleoanthropologist Louis Leakey and his wife, Mary Leakey, worked in what is known as the Eastern Rift Valley, which is a 1,200-mile trough extending through Ethiopia, Kenya, and Tanzania. They searched for almost 30 years before they found their first hominin fossil, *Paranthropus boisei* (OH-5)—originally classified as *Zinjanthropus boisei*—in 1959. It is often referred to as the hyper-robust hominin because of its mohawk of bone on the top of the skull. Other features include a low or absent forehead, a flat face, large jaws, and large attachment sites over the entire skull for chewing muscles.

Paranthropus aethiopicus

We have little knowledge about *Paranthropus aethiopicus* (shown in Figure 4.37), which has been dated to about 2.5 MYA and is referred to as the "black skull." It is believed that this species falls somewhere between the robust and gracile australopithecines, having characteristics of both. The species was discovered in Ethiopia in 1967 by a French expedition team headed by Camille Arambourg and Yves Coppens.

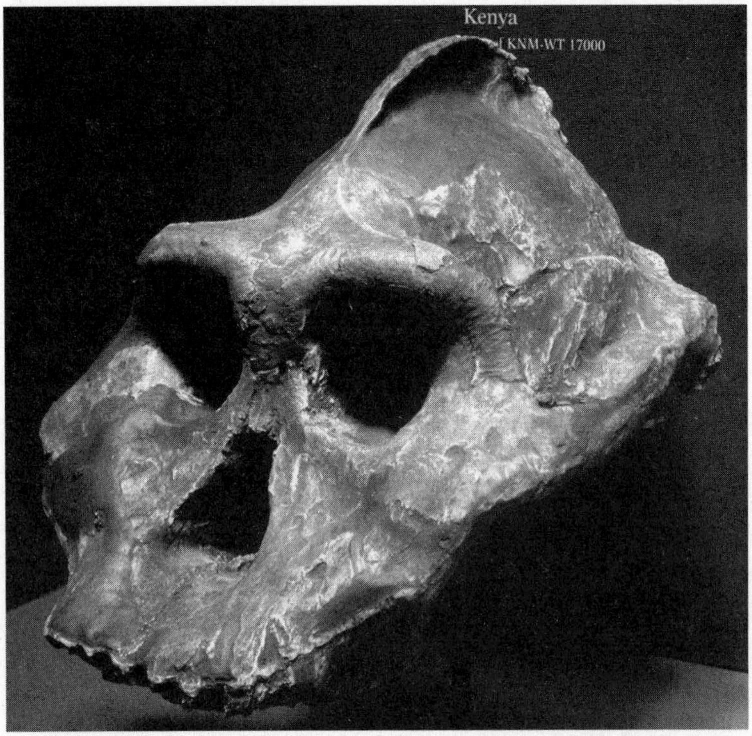

FIGURE 4.37 Much remains to be learned about *Paranthropus aethiopicus*, which has characteristics of both the robust and gracile australopithecines. (credit: "*Paranthropus aethiopicus* (Fossil Hominid) (Nachukui Formation, Upper Pliocene, 2.5 Ma; Lomekwi, Lake Turkana Area, Kenya) 3" by James St. John/flickr, CC BY 2.0)

Landmarks and Questions

While the fossils discovered up to this point have provided a small window into the story of humanity's past, they have also simultaneously raised numerous questions. Questions related to phylogenetic relationships and points of divergence are challenges for paleoanthropologists, who have only fragmentary fossil evidence to build hypotheses around. Nevertheless, the discoveries that have been made represent important landmarks in anthropologists' understanding, providing clues that will lead to the next steps in the human journey.

MINI-FIELDWORK ACTIVITY

Pedestrian Survey

Conduct a pedestrian survey to try to locate fossils near where you live (trilobites in New York, ammonites in Texas, shark teeth near riverbeds, arrowheads). Think about where you would most likely find a fossil and why. Try to extract one without destroying the environment around it, which provides important context. Try to figure out what kind of fossil it is by doing some Internet research. Why do you think that this fossil was preserved? What information would make the search for fossils easier?

Key Terms

allele an alternative form of a gene that arises by mutation and is found in the same place on a chromosome, directly impacting the expression of a genetic trait or phenotype.

allopatric speciation speciation that occurs when two populations of the same species become isolated from each other due to a change in the environment, such as geographic isolation.

analogous structures anatomical similarities between two species that suggest not a common ancestor but rather similar environmental adaptations.

ancestral characteristics homologous structures or traits that may also be found in the common ancestor of the species being classified.

angiosperm theory a hypothesis that suggests that primate origins and typical primate characteristics developed in response to the emergence of flowering plants.

arboreal theory a hypothesis that proposes that primates evolved the traits they did as an adaptation to life in the trees.

artificial selection the process of deliberately breeding certain specimens of plants or animals to encourage desired traits.

binomial nomenclature the scientific naming system developed by Carolus Linnaeus that represents two parts of a taxonomic name. The name is italicized, the genus is always capitalized, and the species is always lowercased. For example: *Homo sapiens.*

bioarchaeology the study of bones and other biological materials found in archaeological remains.

biological species definition a definition of species as members of populations that actually or potentially interbreed in nature.

Catarrhini a subcategory of the primate infraorder Simiiformes that includes any primate considered an Old World monkey, an ape, or in the lineage of humans. This classification features downward-facing nostrils and a 2.1.2.3 dental formula.

catastrophism the theory that changes in Earth's fauna and flora were caused by supernatural catastrophic forces rather than evolution.

Cercopithecoidea a superfamily of the primate infraorder Simiiformes, subcategory Catarrhini, that consists of Old World monkeys.

cladistics the classification of organisms based on branchings of descendent lineages from a common ancestor

derived characteristics physical traits that are present in related organisms but absent from their last common ancestor. They are often associated with a speciation event.

diastema a space or gap between the canines and the other teeth that allows for the upper and lower teeth to bite together.

ecological species definition a definition of species that explains differences in form and behavior as the result of adaptations to the environment and natural selection.

ethnotaxonomy the study of organism classifications and taxonomies developed and used largely by Indigenous peoples and other cultural groups.

evolution changes that appear in a species over time. Evolution is dependent on genetic variation and natural selection to pass on beneficial traits that will increase survival of the species.

foramen magnum the opening at the base of the skull where the spinal column and nerves enter to reach the brain. The position of the foramen magnum can be used to determine if a species was bipedal.

forensic anthropology a branch of biological anthropology in which scientific techniques are used to determine the sex, age, genetic population, or other relevant characteristics of skeletal or biological materials related to matters of civil or criminal law.

fossils any remains, impression, or traces of living things from a former geologic age.

gene flow alteration of the frequencies of alleles in a population that results from interbreeding with organisms from another population.

genetic anthropology a branch of biological anthropology that uses molecular science to explore questions concerning human origins, early human migrations, and the appearance of disease across time.

genetic drift random changes in the frequencies of alleles in a gene pool.

genotype a complete set of genetic material found in an organism.

gradualism the idea that species evolve slowly and continuously over long periods of time.

great chain of being a concept detailing a hierarchical structure of all matter and life.

Haplorrhini a suborder of primates that contains tarsiers, New World monkeys, Old World monkeys, apes, and humans.

hominid the group representing all modern and

extinct great apes, including humans, chimpanzees, gorillas, orangutans, and all their immediate ancestors.

hominin the group representing modern humans, extinct human species, and all of humanity's immediate ancestors, including the genera *Homo*, *Australopithecus*, *Paranthropus*, and *Ardipithecus*.

Hominoidea a superfamily of the primate infraorder Simiiformes, subcategory Catarrhini, that consists of gibbons, great apes, and humanlike primates, including *Homo* and related fossil forms.

homologous structures similar anatomical structures that appear in different species and suggest a common ancestor.

hybrid zones areas where two distinct species mate and produce offspring

industrial melanism the prevalence of dark-colored varieties of animals (for example, peppered moths) in industrial areas where they are better camouflaged against predators than paler forms.

inheritance of acquired characteristics the disproved idea that an organism can pass on to its offspring physical characteristics that it has acquired during its lifetime.

interspecific variation the genetic variation seen between two species.

intraspecific variation the genetic variation seen within a species.

law of independent assortment a law of inheritance stating that different genes and their alleles are inherited independently.

law of segregation a law of inheritance stating that when two alleles for a trait separate during the formation of new zygotes, these alleles will combine at random with other alleles.

morphology the physical shape and structural form of an organism or species.

mutation a change in the structure of a gene that results in a variant form that may be transmitted to subsequent generations.

natural selection the process by which a species that is able to adapt and to pass on beneficial traits to its offspring ensures survival of the species; first formally introduced by Charles Darwin.

paleoanthropology the study of the origins and predecessors of the present human species based fossils and other remains.

Parapithecoidea a superfamily of primates from the early Oligocene that is believed to represent the earliest New World monkeys, though they first evolved in Africa.

phenotype the set of observable characteristics or traits of an organism, such as color and structural morphology.

phylogenetic species definition a definition of species based on individuals all possessing specific derived traits.

Platyrrhini a subcategory of the primate infraorder Simiiformes that comprises New World monkeys

polygenic traits traits that are controlled by multiple genes instead of just one.

primatology the branch of biological anthropology dealing with the primates.

Proconsul a genus of ape from the early Miocene.

prognathism projection of the face, as seen in many nonhuman primates and early hominins.

Propliopithecoidea a superfamily of primates from the early Oligocene that is related to Old World monkeys and is believed to represent the earliest catarrhine primate.

punctuated equilibrium a hypothesis holding that the evolution of species proceeds in a characteristic pattern of relative stability for long periods of time interspersed with much shorter periods during which many species become extinct and new species emerge.

Purgatorius genus of the earliest primate or proto-primate.

reproductive isolation conditions that prevent potentially interbreeding populations from breeding.

socioecological system the interrelationship between the diversity of plants and animals, humans' environments, and the diversity of human culture and language.

species a class of individuals that have some common characteristics or qualities.

stratigraphy a branch of geology dealing with the classification, nomenclature, correlation, and interpretation of stratified rocks.

Strepsirrhini a suborder of primates that includes lemurs, lorises, and galagos (bush babies).

survival of the fittest the theory that the most evolutionarily fit members of a species will pass on their traits to later generations.

sympatric speciation speciation without a geographic barrier.

taxa the plural form of taxon, used to signify all taxonomic groups.

taxon a specific group or subgroup of organisms.

taxonomy the science or technique of naming and

classifying life.

uniformitarianism the concept that Earth's surface was shaped in the past by slow-moving geological processes.

visual predation hypothesis a hypothesis that explains the origins of unique primate traits as adaptations for preying on insects and small animals.

Summary

Biological anthropology strives to understand how humans interact and behave in the present, how humans evolved biologically, and how humanity's ancient ancestors lived in diverse climates and environments. The anthropological approach to exploring these questions is grounded in evolutionary theory. Charles Darwin was one of the first to propose a mechanism by which evolution occurred, which he called natural selection. Natural selection is based on the premise that those with more favorable characteristics survive and reproduce at greater rates than those without them. Natural selection depends on the evolutionary processes of mutation, speciation, gene flow, and genetic drift.

Darwin's theory did not address how these favorable characteristics could be inherited. Gregor Mendel's experiments on peas addressed this very question. Mendel's work resulted in two very important observations. He observed that the two alleles for each trait separate during the formation of the sex cells and that the probability of having one trait does not affect the probability that an individual will have another trait.

Carolus Linnaeus is best known for creating the classification system that taxonomists use today, which is based on physical similarities and differences. Phylogenetics is a hypothesis about how species are related to one another and to a common ancestor. Today, biological anthropologists apply taxonomies and phylogenies to the current nonhuman primate and hominin fossil record. It is in the Miocene that the first fossil apes, such as *Proconsul*, are seen. The first evidence of hominin-like fossils appears by the end of the Miocene. A large number of morphological changes observed in early hominins suggest considerable environmental and climatic change. During the Pliocene epoch, extending from 5 to 1.8 MYA, the evolution of hominins that were clearly bipedal is evident in the fossil record, as is evidence of cultures that used stone tools. The path is now ready for the next group in humanity's evolutionary history to enter the scene.

Critical Thinking Questions

1. How do anthropologists define being human?
2. What are some of the key differences between Linnaean classification and phylogenetics?
3. In what ways does the COVID-19 virus exhibit natural selection?
4. How do anthropologists define a primate?
5. What is the difference between absolute and relative dating methods? What methods are commonly used when working with hominin fossils?
6. What is the difference between a prosimian and an anthropoid?
7. What are some of the main differences between Old World and New World monkeys?
8. What are some of the key characteristics seen in early hominins, and what environmental forces may have contributed to those changes?

Bibliography

Aiello, Leslie C. 1986. "The Relationships of the Tarsiiformes: A Review of the Case for the Haplorhini." In *Major Topics in Primate and Human Evolution*, edited by Bernard Wood, Lawrence Martin, and Peter Andrews, 47–65. Cambridge: Cambridge University Press.

Blaxland, Beth. 2020. "Hominid and Hominin—What's the Difference?" Australian Museum. February 10, 2020. https://australian.museum/learn/science/human-evolution/hominid-and-hominin-whats-the-difference/.

Crompton, Robin. 1989. "Mechanisms for Speciation in *Galago* and *Tarsius*." *Human Evolution* 4 (2): 105–116.

Dasgupta, Shreya. 2019. "Super Variable California Salamander Is 'an Evolutionist's Dream.'" Mongabay. March 18, 2019. https://news.mongabay.com/2019/03/super-variable-california-salamander-is-an-evolutionists-dream/.

David, A. Rosalie, and Michael R. Zimmerman. 2010. "Cancer: An Old Disease, a New Disease or Something in Between?" *Nature Reviews Cancer* 10:728–733. https://doi.org/10.1038/nrc2914.

Dunbar, Robin I. M. 1988. *Primate Social Systems.* Ithaca, NY: Cornell University Press.

Fleagle, John G. 1999. *Primate Adaptation and Evolution.* 2nd ed. San Diego: Academic Press.

Fuentes, Agustín. 2019. *Biological Anthropology: Concepts and Connections.* 3rd ed. New York: McGraw-Hill Education.

Groves, Colin. 2001. *Primate Taxonomy.* Washington, DC: Smithsonian Institution Press.

Hill, W. C. Osman. 1955. *Primates: Comparative Anatomy and Taxonomy.* Vol. 2, *Haplorhini: Tarsioidea.* New York: Interscience.

Lee-Thorp, Julia, J. Francis Thackerary, and Nikolaas van der Merwe. 2000. "The Hunters and the Hunted Revisited." *Journal of Human Evolution* 39 (6): 565–576. https://doi.org/10.1006/jhev.2000.0436.

McKee, Jeffrey K., Frank E. Poirier, and W. Scott McGraw. 2005. *Understanding Human Evolution.* 5th ed. Upper Saddle River, NJ: Pearson Prentice Hall.

Meier, Joana I., David A. Marques, Salome Mwaiko, Catherine E. Wagner, Laurent Excoffier, and Ole Seehausen. 2017. "Ancient Hybridization Fuels Rapid Cichlid Fish Adaptive Radiations." *Nature Communications* 8. https://doi.org/10.1038/ncomms14363.

Phillips, Melissa Lee. 2006. "Genetic evidence for punctuated equilibrium." *The Scientist*, October 5, 2006. https://www.the-scientist.com/daily-news/genetic-evidence-for-punctuated-equilibrium-47144.

Pruetz, J.D., et. al, P. (2015). New evidence on the tool-assisted hunting exhibited by chimpanzees (Pan troglodytes verus) in a savannah habitat at Fongoli. *R. Soc.* open sci.2140507140507http://doi.org/10.1098/rsos.140507

Stringer, Chris, and Peter Andrews. 2011. *The Complete World of Human Evolution.* 2nd ed. London: Thames & Hudson.

Canine sexual dimorphism in Ardipithecus ramidus was nearly human-like. *Proceedings of the National Academy of Sciences*, 118 (49) e2116630118; DOI: 10.1073/pnas.2116630118

Takahashi, Tetsumi, and Stephan Koblmüller. 2011. "The Adaptive Radiation of Cichlid Fish in Lake Tanganyika: A Morphological Perspective." *International Journal of Evolutionary Biology* 2011. https://doi.org/10.4061/2011/620754.

Wayman, Erin. 2011. "How Africa Became the Cradle of Humankind." *Smithsonian*, October 17, 2011. https://www.smithsonianmag.com/science-nature/how-africa-became-the-cradle-of-humankind-108875040/.

CHAPTER 5
The Genus Homo and the Emergence of Us

Figure 5.1 Liang Bua Cave on the island of Flores in Indonesia. A potentially new species of the genus *Homo, Homo floresiensis* was discovered in this cave in 2003. (credit: "Flores: Ruteng to Bajawa" by Bryn Pinzgauer/flickr, CC BY 2.0) (credit: "Flores" by Ryan Somma/flickr, CC BY 2.0)

CHAPTER OUTLINE

INTRODUCTION Our human story continues with the rise of the genus *Homo* which at one time represented at least 8 different species in our human lineage – with only *H. sapiens* surviving. The genus *Homo* displays some of the most diverse and complex examples of both australopithecine and *Homo* characteristics, which has made the classification of species in this genus challenging. In this chapter we take a look at how paleoanthropologists have defined *Homo* and at attempts to answer the question, "What does a species of the genus *Homo* look like?"

5.1 Defining the Genus Homo

LEARNING OBJECTIVES

By the end of this section, you will be able to:

- Describe the time periods and geological context of the genus *Homo*.
- Identify some key differences between the genus *Homo* and *Australopithecus*.
- Define some of the limitations of and challenges in the classification of hominin species in the genus *Homo*.
- Explain the concept of encephalization as it relates to early hominin evolutionary development and as a tool for hominin classification.

Putting *Homo* into Context

Before learning about the hominin species that make up the category genus *Homo*, it will be helpful to become familiar with the key archaeological time periods with which *Homo* is associated. The species and cultural developments mentioned below will be explored in greater detail in the sections that follow.

- **Lower Paleolithic** (from roughly 3 million years ago to approximately 300,000 BCE): This period includes *H. habilis* and the Oldowan tool industry, followed by *H. ergaster* and the Acheulean tool industry.
- **Middle Paleolithic** (approximately 300,000–40,000 BCE): This period includes continued use of Acheulean tools by *H. heidelbergensis,* followed by *H. neanderthalensis* and the Mousterian tool industry.
- **Upper Paleolithic** (approximately 43,000–26,000 BCE): The Upper Paleolithic saw the emergence of cave art like that found in the famous Chauvet Cave in France (Figure 5.29), Venus figurines (Figure 5.28), and an increased use of bone and antler in tools and jewelry. The most recent ice age occurred during this time, with glaciers covering huge parts of the planet. The emergence of Paleoindians and the use of Clovis points, which were used to kill large game such as mastodons and mammoths, occurred near the end of this time period.
- **Neolithic (Agricultural Age)** (8,000–3,000 BCE): New innovations appear during the agricultural age, or "Neolithic revolution," as *H. sapiens* set up permanent settlements. Humans begin to transition from being hunters and gatherers to growing grow crops, owning land, and domesticating animals.

The Challenge of Defining the Genus *Homo*

The previous chapter introduced the australopithecines, who were diverse in their physical characteristics (gracile and robust), with large jaws and teeth and small brain size. A key characteristic shared by both the australopithecines and the genus *Homo* is bipedalism. The transition to bipedalism is linked with various anatomical changes, including longer legs, changes in spinal curvature, and the development of arches in the feet to conserve energy and increase balance when walking.

What criteria other than bipedalism might be used to classify a species under the genus *Homo*? Many anthropologists have attempted to establish specific criteria to use in determining a classification of *Homo*. Paleoanthropologists Mary Leakey, Louis Leakey, and John Napier, as well as primatologist Phillip Tobias, were among the first to extensively study the fossils of *Homo habilis*, considered to be one of the earliest species in the genus *Homo*. *H. habilis* had a brain size of around 661–700 cc, which was larger than the australopithecines', with hands that were capable of the dexterity needed for making tools, due to bone structure changes and a repositioning of the thumb, which allowed for better grip.

The type specimen OH 7 of *H. habilis* dated between 2 and 1.7 MYA and was found in 1960 at Olduvai Gorge by Jonathan and Mary Leakey. It was described by Louis Leakey in 1964. Type specimen refers to a specimen that serves as the standard for the taxon or classification group for that species. OH 7 is the identification or accession number of this specific specimen and stands for "Olduvai Hominid #7." The specimen consisted of a partial juvenile skull, hand, and foot bones. It possessed teeth that were much smaller than those of any australopithecine and was possibly in coexistence with the robust australopithecines (*Paranthropus*). Based on an **endocranial cast** (an imprint of the interior of the brain case), it was determined that *H. habilis* may have possessed what is called a Broca's area in the brain. **Broca's area**, which includes two Brodmann areas (referred to as 44 and 45), is located in the middle of the left cerebral cortex of the brain and is especially important for speech development (Figure 5.2). Some scientists have suggested that *H. habilis* started to develop the neural networks necessary for human speech, while others argue that *H. habilis* probably already had speech.

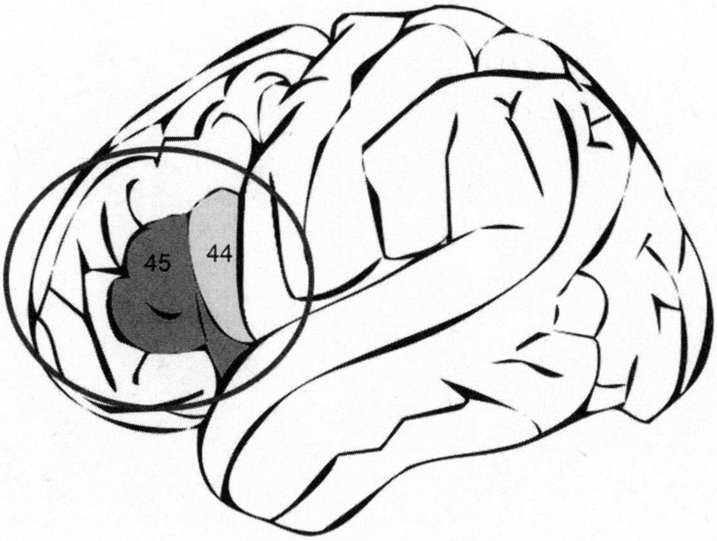

FIGURE 5.2 Position of the Broca's area in the brain, consisting of Brodmann areas 44 (yellow) and 45 (blue). Broca's area is associated with speech development and may have been present in the brain of *H. habilis.* (credit: Fatemeh Geranmayeh, Sonia L. E. Brownsett, Richard J. S. Wise/Wikimedia Commons, CC BY 3.0)

The **postcranial features** (skeletal structures in the body other than the skull) of *Homo habilis* are not as well established, as is the case for many other early hominin fossils. This can be problematic, as many hominin species coexisted with overlapping traits. Likewise, it can be problematic to have postcranial material and not the cranium or skull. The skull often serves as a diagnostic tool when postcranial materials do not provide enough evidence or provide confusing evidence.

Based on their research on *H. habilis*, Mary Leakey, Louis Leakey, and John Napier proposed the following criteria for classifying *Homo*: a brain size over 600 cc; a round, globular skull; tool use; reduced prognathism (protrusion of the jaw) and smaller jaws and mandibles; humanlike postcranial features; and feet that are fully adapted for walking (Leakey, Tobias, and Napier 1964). While this list established specific and fairly comprehensive guidance, the diversity of traits and the ways in which they overlapped didn't always line up with the criteria.

H. habilis has been at the center of several debates regarding their taxonomic position and relationship with other early archaic *Homo* species. For example, *H. habilis* was initially believed to have been a direct human ancestor through the lineage of *Homo erectus* and then modern humans. This viewpoint is now debated and has resulted in a scientific divide between those supporting *H. habilis* and those suggesting another *Homo* species, *H. rudolfensis*, as being the ancestor of *H. erectus. H. rudolfensis* is an archaic *Homo* dated to about 2 MYA, which coexisted with other *Homo* species during that time period. A cranium was discovered in 1972 along Lake Turkana in Kenya by Bernard Ngeneo, a local Kenyan. The specimen was later described by paleoanthropologist Richard Leakey. There is a lot that is not known about this species; scientists are missing postcranial materials, and as of yet no tools have been found. There are hypotheses that propose that *H. rudolfensis* might be a *H. habilis* male, exhibiting a larger cranium than that seen in a female *H. habilis*. Others suggest it is a completely different species. Another controversy centers on tool use. While *Homo habilis* was long regarded as the earliest hominin to use stone tools, it has been determined, based on evidence of cutmarks, that at least one australopithecine (*A. garhi*) used stone tools before *H. habilis*, at around 2.6 MYA (Semaw et al. 1997).

FIGURE 5.3 The specimen of *H. rudolfensis* on the left is noticeably different from that of *H. habilis* on the right. (credit: Conty/Wikimedia Commons, CC BY 3.0)

While there are still questions as to the phylogenetic relationship of *H. habilis* and *H. rudolfensis*, there is general agreement that *Homo* did evolve from *Australopithecus*. The timing and placement of the split between *Australopithecus* and *Homo*, however, is still debated. *H. habilis* was determined to not be an *Australopithecus* due to its smaller teeth, a humanlike foot, and hand bones that suggested an ability to manipulate objects with precision.

One of the main considerations in classifying *H. habilis* as a *Homo* and not an *Australopithecus* was its **cranial capacity**, which is a measurement that indicates brain size. With some exceptions, cranial capacity can serve as an indicator of where a hominin fossil might belong in the hominin phylogenetic tree. **Encephalization** refers to a progressive increase in brain size over time. In human evolution, we can observe encephalization beginning with *Homo habilis* and progressing more rapidly through *H. erectus*. Encephalization correlates with an increase in behavioral, cognitive, and cultural complexity. Cognitive developments correspond with our ability to construct and form ideas, including the ability think in and communicate via symbolic and abstract language, such as that used in storytelling, ritual, and art. There are always exceptions, however, such as the island-dwelling, small-brained *H. floresiensis*, who will be introduced later in this chapter. In spite of having a very small brain, *H. floresiensis* made and used tools and built fires. This discovery has challenged what we thought we knew about the correlation of brain size and cognitive development in human evolution.

The **encephalization quotient (EQ)** can serve as a good indicator (with some exceptions) of classification within the genus *Homo*. The encephalization quotient is a calculation arrived at by comparing the ratio between actual brain size (determined with either a mass or volume calculation) and expected brain size. Body size is a factor in these measurements as expected brain size reflects the relationship between brain and body size for a given taxonomic group (Jerison 1973). The larger the brain weight relative to the overall body weight, the more likely that the brain was used for more complex cognitive tasks. Harry J. Jerison (1973) was the first to develop EQ measurements. The formula he used for calculating EQ in birds and mammals is brain mass/ $0.12 \times (\text{body mass})^{0.66}$. Other formulas have also been proposed, such as EQ = brain mass (11.22 × body mass 0.76) (Martin 1981). While EQ is a strong tool for studying brain size in early hominins, there are always potential margins of error when dealing with fragmentary fossils, and increasingly alternative forms of measurements are being proposed. One study proposes that EQ should no longer be used as a tool in calculating brain size in primates and other vertebrate species, based on the premise that cognitive performance does not depend on body size and so body size should not be included in the formula (Schaik et al. 2021). Other theories consider the number of cortical neurons and neural connections as most important when considering cognitive ability (Roth and Dicke 2012). According to this approach, the density of the cortex is more associated with intelligence than is brain size. These alternate approaches would perhaps better explain those exceptions in the fossil records, such as *H. floresiensis*. Other interesting research is looking at potential levels of cognition and memory as it relates to levels of tool complexity (Read and van der Leeuw 2008).

In spite of these criticisms, many see EQ measurements as providing fairly consistent results. Modern humans (*Homo sapiens*) have an EQ of roughly 6.0–7.0 (meaning that their brain mass is six to seven times greater than what one would expect to find in a comparable mammal of the same body size). *H. erectus* has an EQ of 4.0, while for an australopithecine EQ is around 2.5 to 3.0 (Fuente 2012, 227). Figure 5.4 shows increases in average brain sizes for various species over time.

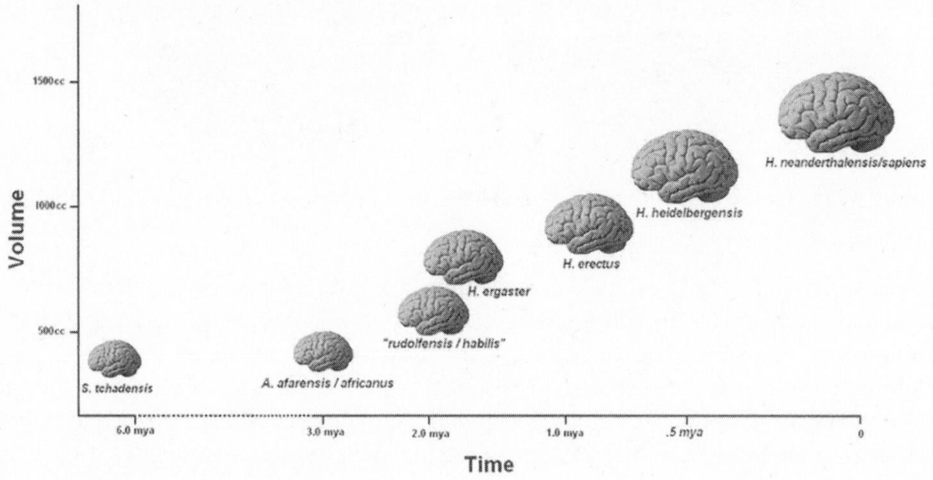

FIGURE 5.4 After remaining steady for millennia, average brain size increases noticeably in the last two million years. (Xiujie, Wu, and Norton 2007). (credit: Gisselle Garcia, artist (brain images), CC BY 4.0)

5.2 Tools and Brains: Homo habilis, Homo ergaster, and Homo erectus

LEARNING OBJECTIVES

By the end of this section, you will be able to:

- Compare and contrast the anatomy and material culture of *H. habilis, H. erectus*, and *H. ergaster.*
- Define the term "tool industry" and describe the tools typified by the Oldowan and Acheulean industries.
- Identify possible correlations between the environment, diet, new behaviors, and brain growth.

The Toolmakers

Archeologists use the word *industry* to describe a classification or assemblage of stone tools. The **Oldowan tool industry** is the oldest known stone tool industry. It dates from around 2.5 to 1.5 MYA. Because there were several hominins in Africa during this time, it is unclear whether these tools were created and used by *H. habilis* or by *Paranthropus boisei*, or by both (Susman 1991). Oldowan tools are fairly crude and primitive in appearance, which can make it difficult to find and identify them in the field.

FIGURE 5.5 An Oldowan tool. This chopper is made of quartzite and dated to the lower Paleolithic period. (credit: Locutus Borg/Wikimedia Commons, Public Domain)

Mary Leakey was the first to create a system to classify Oldowan assemblages, basing her classification on utility, or how the tools were used. Later efforts were made to classify tools based on how the tools were made. All Oldowan tools were created by using hard hammer percussion, in which flakes are chipped away from a stone, resulting in a "core". These cores served as basic tool that could have been used for killing game, cutting meat and plants, and possibly woodworking. Oldowan toolmaking is the earliest evidence of "flint knapping," a technique that became more complex over time, resulting in more sophisticated tools (Figure 5.6).

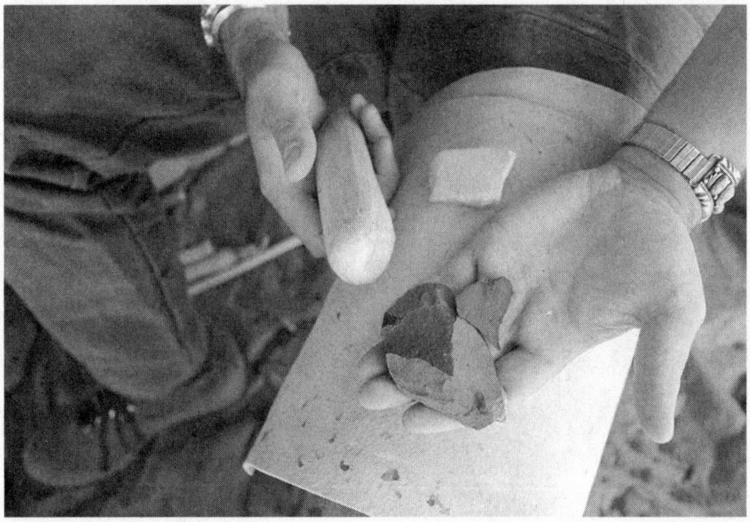

FIGURE 5.6 Demonstration of flint knapping, an ancient technique for shaping stones into useful tools. (credit: "Flint-knapping Demonstration" Tonto National Monument/NPS photo/flickr, CC BY 2.0)

Handedness, or brain lateralization (i.e., whether one is right-handed or left-handed), is a cognitive development that can be inferred through evidence of the use of a dominant hand in creating and using tools. The use of a dominant hand suggests a possible reorganization of the brain. It is believed that about 90 percent of humans are right-handed, which differs from apes, which are closer to 50 percent. David Frayer (2016), an anthropologist from the University of Kansas, has concluded that the brain lateralization of *Homo habilis* was more like that of modern human than that of apes. Frayer found striations on the teeth of a 1.8-million-year-old *Homo habilis* fossil that indicate right-handedness. He concluded that meat was pinched between the teeth and held in place with the left hand, while the right hand cut the meat with a tool. Brain lateralization, increasing brain size, and tool use are just some of the key developments we see in the genus *Homo.*

Homo ergaster

Homo ergaster is the first *Homo* that looks much like *H. sapiens.* A key difference between *H. ergaster* and earlier hominins is that *H. ergaster* exhibits substantially less **sexual dimorphism** in body size. *H. ergaster* males were only 20 percent larger than females. Likewise, modern human males are only 15 percent larger than females. This contrasts sharply with all other previous hominins, such as the australopithecines, in which males were 50 percent larger than females. It is well established that in mammals, significant dimorphism is associated with polygyny, and a lack of dimorphism is associated with a monogamous mating system. It has been suggested that the reduction in dimorphism seen in *H. ergaster* may indicate less male-male competition for access to females and perhaps a shift toward a monogamous mating system, with substantial parental investment in offspring.

Other similarities between *H. ergaster* and modern humans are seen in the teeth and postcranial features. The average cranial capacity of *H. ergaster* is 1,100 cc, which is just a bit smaller than that of modern humans, who average 1,400 cc. There is a very important specimen of *H. ergaster* that bears mentioning, the Nariokotome Boy. This specimen was discovered in 1984 by Kenyan paleontologist Kamoya Kimeu near Lake Turkana in Kenya. It is dated to approximately 1.6 MYA. The specimen is believed to represent a boy of about 12 years old, determined by various dental and cranial features. He was about 5 feet 4 inches tall, roughly the same height as a modern boy of the same age (Figure 5.7). It has been estimated that his adult height would be around 5 feet 10 inches, with an estimated cranial capacity of 900 cc. The Nariokotome Boy looks tremendously modern in appearance despite being 1.6 million years old.

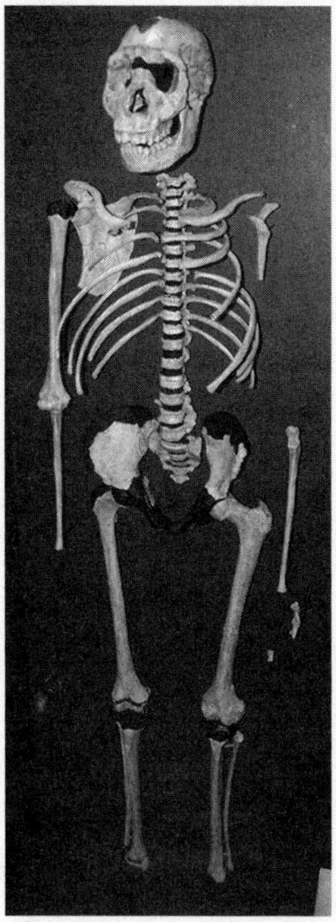

FIGURE 5.7 This specimen of *Homo ergaster* is known as the Nariokotome Boy. It is believed to be the remains of a boy who was about 12 years old at the time of death. (credit: "Homo ergaster (fossil hominid) (Lower Pleistocene, 1.5 to 1.6 Ma; Nariokotome, Lake Turkana area, Kenya) 4" by James St. John/flickr, CC BY 2.0)

Homo ergaster Technology

Homo ergaster continued to use Oldowan stone tools, but they also began to construct much more complex tools, referred to as the Acheulean industry (Figure 5.8). These tools have been found throughout Africa, Europe, and the Middle East and are first noted as appearing approximately 1.6 MYA to 200,000 years ago. These types of tools are rarely found in Asia. It is currently unclear whether this is because the Acheulean industry had not yet been developed when *H. erectus* migrated to Asia or because bamboo (a plant found in abundance in Asia) was found to be a more versatile resource than stone. As wood and bamboo are biodegradable, no remains of tools constructed from these materials would exist today.

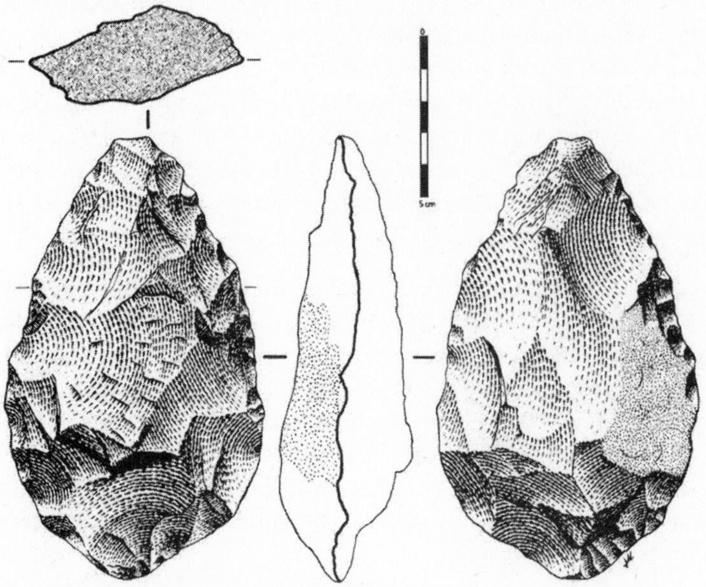

FIGURE 5.8 This hand axe, found in the Zamora province, Spain, displays the form and construction techniques typical of the Acheulean industry. (credit: Jose-Manuel Benito/Locutus Borg/Wikimedia Commons, Public Domain)

Unlike Oldowan tools, Acheulean tools actually look like tools. Acheulean tools are distinct from Oldowan tools in that they were modified on both sides, resulting in a symmetrical tool with two faces, also known as **biface**. One end of the tool was tapered, while the other end was rounded. The creation of symmetrical objects from stone materials is believed to represent an increase in cognitive ability as well as motor skills in the tool maker. These bifaces were struck from large flakes, which had themselves been struck from boulder cores. This required a more delicate technique than banging one rock into another. Acheulean tools were typically created used the soft hammer technique. In this technique, hard rock such as flint is chipped by striking it with a softer material such as bone or wood. The gentler blows detach small flakes that leave smooth, shallow scars, creating a straighter and more uniform cutting edge.

The main advantage of Acheulean technology is that it allowed hominins to get a better grip on their tools, as they were shaped to fit the hand. This tool type was used primarily as a hunter's knife but also for chopping, scraping, and even piercing. The most common type of biface tool is a hand axe. Note that even though these tools are called axes, they are held in the palm of the hand. Another type of Acheulean biface used by *Homo ergaster* is called a cleaver (Figure 5.9). The cleaver had a wide cutting edge across the end instead of a point and was best suited for hunting or hacking wood. Another Acheulean tool is the side scraper, used to scrape hides that could then be turned into simple clothing.

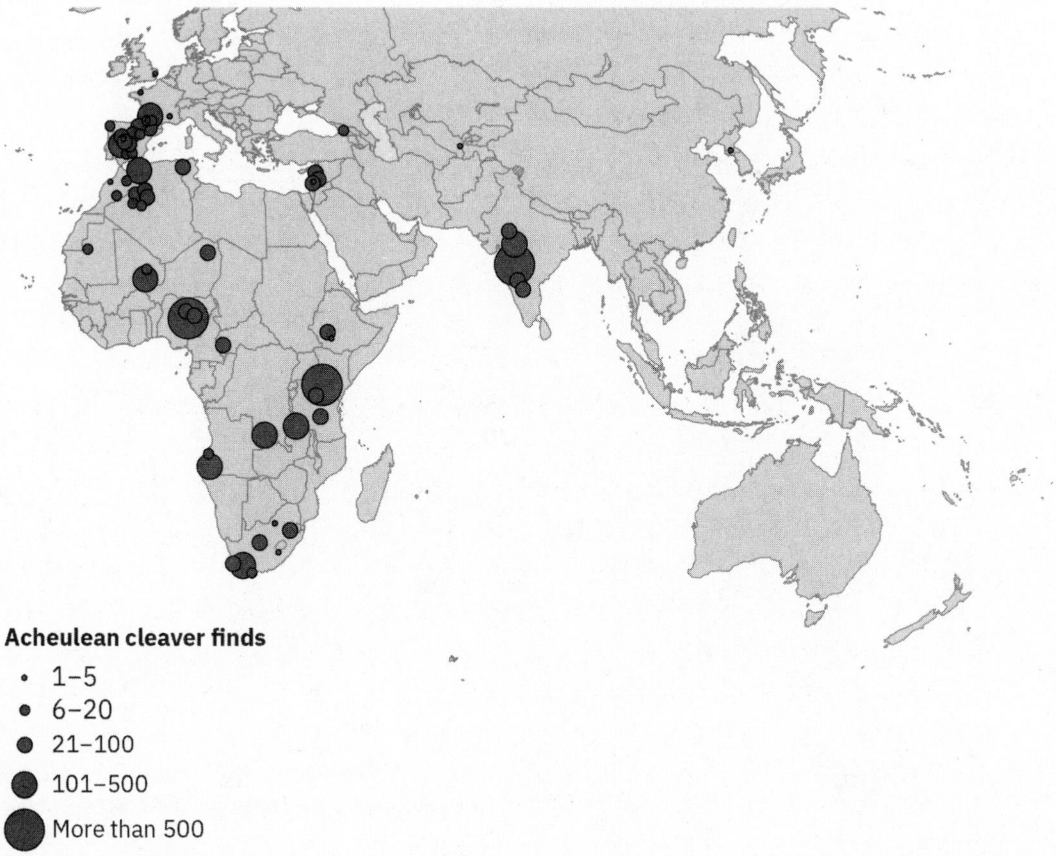

FIGURE 5.9 Map of Acheulean cleaver finds dated to the Lower Paleolithic (1.76–0.13 MYA). Note the concentration of artifacts found in certain areas of Africa and in Spain. (attribution: Copyright Rice University, OpenStax,under CC BY 4.0 license)

Evidence of an Increase in Meat Eating

In 1973, a specimen of *H. ergaster* known as KNM ER 1808 was found in Koobi Fora, Kenya. Dated to about 1.7 MYA, this is the most complete *H. ergaster* specimen ever found. Analysis of KNM ER 1808 suggests that *H. ergaster* may have been eating carnivore liver, which is high in Vitamin A. This may indicate a dietary shift toward increased meat eating by *H. ergaster*.

Homo erectus: A Success Story

Homo erectus is the longest-surviving species in the genus *Homo*. For almost two million years, *H. erectus* existed and evolved. Also known as the "Upright Man" or Java Man, *H. erectus* was first found in Indonesia in 1891 by Eugene Dubois, a professor of anatomy at the University of Amsterdam. At a site called Trinil, he found a skull cap and a femur. He named the specimen *Pithecanthropus erectus*. The most current dates for *Homo erectus* are 1.2–1.6 million years ago. *H. erectus* exhibits a cranial capacity averaging 900 cc and several distinguishing characteristics. These characteristics include a slightly projecting nasal spine, shovel-shaped incisors, a nuchal crest (a ridge in the back of the skull that supported strong neck muscles), very thick skull bones, and pronounced brow ridges. They also had longer legs, evidence that they were utilizing energy much more efficiently when walking and becoming effective hunters. We also see a diminishing of the protruding jaw (or prognathism) that was so prominent in the australopithecines.

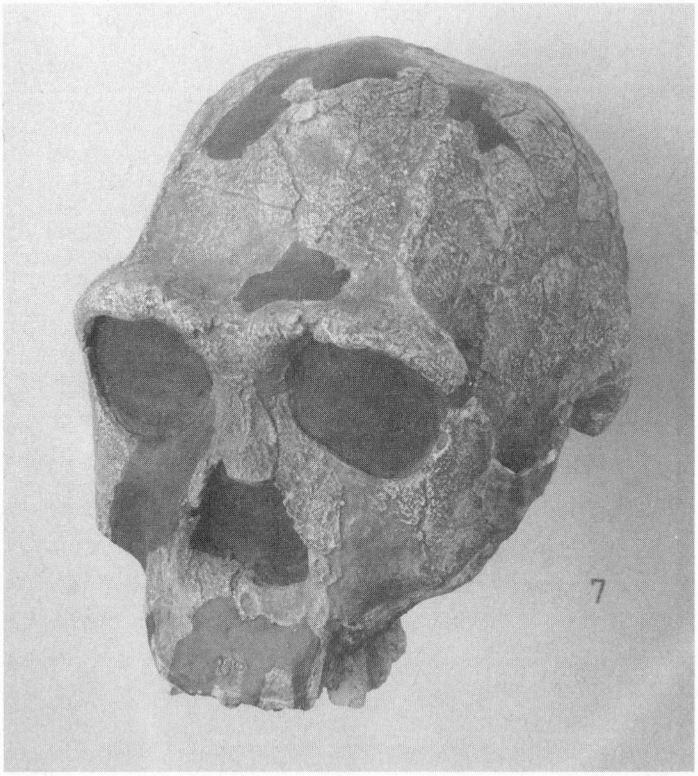

FIGURE 5.10 This *Homo erectus* cranium exhibits a number of defining features, including a projecting nasal spine, thick skull bones, and pronounced brow ridges. (credit: Daderot/Wikimedia Commons, Public Domain)

There is evidence that *H. erectus* was using fire around 1.7–2.0 MYA, which would make it the first or one of the first hominins to do so. Ancient hearths, charcoal, and charred animal bones have been found in Zhoukoudian, China. This evidence suggests that *H. erectus* was hunting, cooking, and eating meat. Also found at Zhoukoudian are a number of fossil skulls that were once thought to display evidence of cannibalism. However, recent research evidence suggests that the remains of these *H. erectus* were prey to animal scavengers such as hyenas (Boaz et al. 2004).

The Smithsonian Institution has created an interactive tool (https://openstax.org/r/human-evolution-interactive-timeline) that visually illustrates the interrelationships between an increasingly variable and colder climate, encephalization, bipedalism, and new technologies and tool use. These correlations align with fossil evidence indicating changes in diet and caloric requirements in response to a colder and changing climate, which ultimately fueled a growing brain. The "expensive tissue hypothesis" proposes that maintaining a brain is metabolically expensive and that, in order to meet the energy requirements of a larger brain, our digestive system became smaller and shorter, making it more suited for higher-quality, nutrient-dense food such as meat (Aiello and Wheeler 1995). The list below summarizes some of the key evolutionary changes seen in *H. erectus* from 2 MYA to possibly as recent as 50,000 years ago, which provide further support for these correlations (Dorey 2020).

1. There is a progressive increase in brain size in *H. erectus*, from about 550 cc to 1,250 cc.
2. There is evidence of increased use of fire and of eating cooked meat at *H. erectus* sites. *H. erectus* would have needed as much as 35 percent more calories than previous hominins (Fuentes 2012).
3. The eating of softer foods as a result of cooking meat and plants alleviated the need for large chewing teeth and jaws. Over time teeth became smaller, which resulted in thicker enamel.
4. There is a gradual decrease in prognathism, and as in *H. habilis*, skulls provide evidence of smaller teeth and jaws, which would have made room for larger brains.
5. *H. erectus* is taller than any other previous hominin, with longer legs that provided the ability to run great distances and chase prey. New research is shedding some additional light on the possible benefits of running in early hominins The fossil evidence suggests that endurance running is a derived adaptation of

the genus *Homo*, originating about two million years ago, and may have been instrumental in our evolution (Bramble and Lieberman 2004).

The *Homo ergaster* and *Homo erectus* Debate

There is great debate as to whether *Homo ergaster* and *Homo erectus* are one species or two. Some refer to *H. ergaster* as the "early" *H. erectus.* Their differences are largely geographical: *H. ergaster* is associated with Africa and *H. erectus* with Asia. Yet some researchers have concluded that *H. ergaster* and even *H. habilis* should be referred to as *H. erectus.* Whether to lump or split the diverse species in the genus *Homo* is an ongoing challenge in the scientific community. While there are some anatomical differences between *H. erectus* and *H. ergaster*, they are fairly minimal.

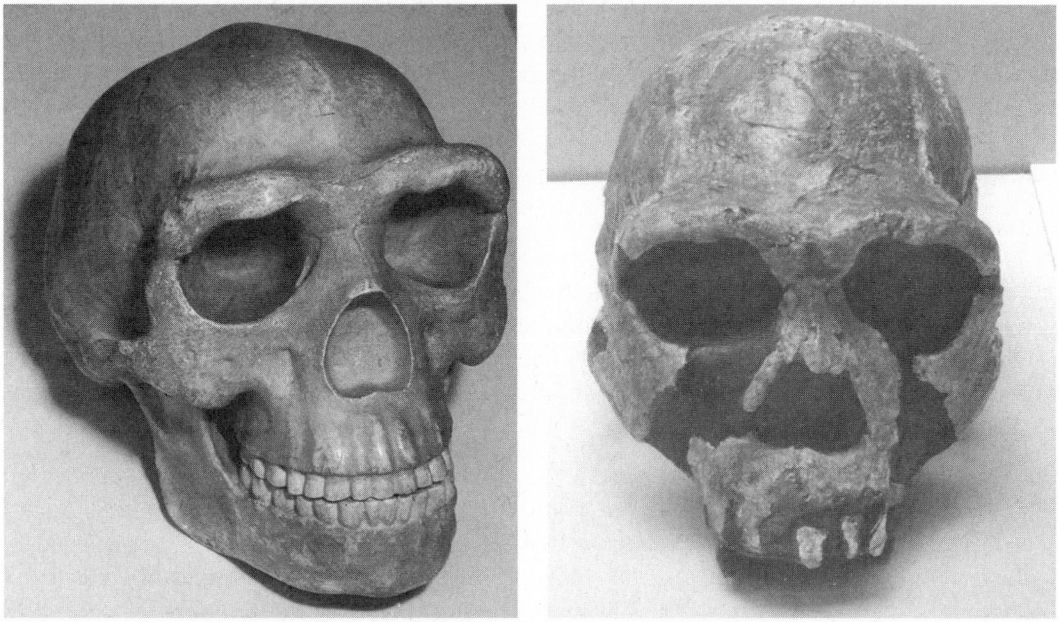

FIGURE 5.11 *Homo erectus* (left) has a sagittal keel (ridge on top of head), a shorter forehead, and a different-shaped skull than *Homo ergaster,* seen on the right. (credit: (left) kevinzim/Wikimedia Commons, CC BY 2.0; (right) Reptonix free Creative Commons licensed photos/Wikimedia Commons, CC BY 3.0)

The diversity and number of evolutionary changes seen in *H. erectus* indicate that *H. erectus* set the stage for the arrival of the archaic *Homo*, which we will cover in the next section.

5.3 The Emergence of Us: The Archaic Homo

LEARNING OBJECTIVES

By the end of this section, you will be able to:

- Describe the context, time frame, and key anatomical characteristics of archaic *Homo.*
- Explain the potential environmental conditions that led to evolutionary change in anatomy and material culture seen in archaic *Homo.*
- Compare and contrast the current hypotheses regarding the extinction of the Neanderthal.

Defining the Archaic *Homo*

There is no universal consensus on what is included within the term "archaic *Homo.*" The term is used as an umbrella category encompassing all the diverse *Homo* species after *H. erectus.* Hominin species classified as **archaic *Homo*** typically have a brain size averaging 1,200 to 1,400 cc, which overlaps with the range of modern humans. Archaic *Homo* are distinguished from anatomically modern humans by the characteristics of a thick skull, prominent supraorbital ridges (brow ridges), and lack of a prominent chin. Archaic *Homo* are viewed as transitional between *H. erectus* and *H. sapiens* and display many overlapping and varied traits. It has been proposed that archaic *Homo* may have been the first species to use language, based on the size of their brains and the fairly large social groups they lived in. Archaic *Homo* species as presented here will be divided into two groups: the Early Archaic (800–250 KYA) and the Late Archaic (300–30 KYA).

Early Archaic *Homo*

Homo antecessor

Homo antecessor has been found in Spain, France, and England and dates to around 1.2 MYA to 800 KYA. These specimens represent the oldest fossil evidence for the presence of the genus *Homo* in Europe. Some scientists have suggested that this species is the ancestor of *Homo heidelbergensis*, while others suggest that *H. antecessor* is the descendent of *H. ergaster*. *Homo antecessor* was first found at the Sima de los Huesos site of the Sierra de Atapuerca region in Spain. Within this site is a cave known as the Pit of Bones, where more than 1,600 fossils of 28 individuals have been found that date at or before 780,000 years ago. The site is an important one that stretches over a long period of time and displays the emergence and divergence of various *Homo* physical characteristics that later appear in the Neanderthal. Evidence from nuclear DNA suggests that early hominins at this site were related to the Neanderthal and not the Denisovans, indicating divergence earlier than 430,000 years ago (Meyer et al. 2016). The section on the Neanderthal will explore further the interbreeding and divergences of the Neanderthal, Denisovans, and modern *Homo sapiens*.

Homo antecessor was almost six feet tall and males weighed about 200 pounds, well within the range of variation for modern humans. Other anatomical features of this species include a protruding **occipital bun** (a bulge found in the occipital area of the skull), a low forehead, no strong chin, and a cranial capacity of about 1,000 cc. It has been suggested that the purpose of the occipital bun is to balance the weight of the anterior portion of the skull and face. One very modern trait exhibited by this species is the presence of a facial depression above the canine tooth called the **canine fossa**, which is also found in modern humans. The best-preserved fossil is a maxilla (upper jawbone) of a 10-year-old individual.

In addition to the fossil bones, 200 stone tools and 300 animal bones were also found at Gran Dolina, another location at the Atapuerca site, along with a carved stone knife. Stone tools at this site were predominantly Oldowan style and constructed from local raw materials. Tools included cutting flakes and hand-held cores. It has been suggested that the absence of retouched tools at this site indicates that these tools were created primarily for processing and eating meat. Cutmarks are present on the majority of animal remains. One of the most intriguing observations about this site is that there are numerous large animal carcasses (mostly deer) that are believed to have been transported to the site rather than consumed where they were killed. Some scientists have suggested that the practice of bringing food back to the site is evidence of social cooperation, suggesting both a division of labor and a custom of food sharing.

Many of the bones of *Homo antecessor* show the same evidence of cutmarks as the animal bones, indicating that flesh was removed from the bones with the goal of dismemberment. Some scientists have taken this to mean that *H. antecessor* practiced cannibalism. However, humans have also been known to remove the flesh from bones during funerary rites. Whether the cutmarks made by *H. antecessor* represent cannibalism, a funerary rite, or another yet unknown practice is still being debated.

Homo heidelbergensis

Homo heidelbergensis is an incredibly variable group. Many archaic *Homo* species are included in this group because they possess features that can best be described as a mosaic between *H. ergaster*, *H. erectus*, and anatomically modern humans (AMH). This section looks at just a few of the specimens that are regularly attributed to *Homo heidelbergensis*.

One of the most important *Homo heidelbergensis* specimens is known as Mauer. It was found in 1907 in Germany and is represented by a mandible (lower jaw) that is dated to approximately 600,000 years ago. It has a robust mandible and a receding chin like earlier *Homo ergaster* but has very small molars like anatomically modern *H. sapiens*. The jaw is so big and the teeth are so small that there is plenty of space for additional teeth to develop behind the wisdom teeth. Given that the third molar (the wisdom tooth) has already erupted, it has been suggested that this individual was between 20 and 30 years at death.

FIGURE 5.12 This jawbone from a *Homo heidelbergensis* specimen was found in Germany in 1907 and is dated to approximately 600,000 years ago. (credit: Gerbil/Wikimedia Commons, CC BY 3.0)

Another important specimen of *Homo heidelbergensis* is known as the Petralona cranium. It was found in 1960 in Greece. Dates are uncertain but believed to be in the range of 100,000 to 700,000 years. Animal fossils found with the specimen indicate Petralona is between 350,000 and 200,000 years old. It combines *Homo ergaster*–like traits, such as massive brow ridges and thick cranial bones, with a cranial capacity of 1,200 cc, which is similar to anatomically modern *H. sapiens*.

A third specimen of *Homo heidelbergensis* is known as Bodo. It is very possibly the oldest archaic human specimen from Africa and was found in Ethiopia in 1976. It is dated to approximately 600,000 years and has a relatively large cranial capacity of 1,250 cc, which is again within the range of variation for modern humans. It is a robust cranium with very thick bones and two separate brow ridges.

Homo heidelbergensis Technology and Culture

Bodo is associated with Acheulean bifacial hand axes. Some scientists have suggested that Bodo butchered animals because Acheulean hand axes have been found with animal bones. There are cutmarks on the Bodo cranium that resemble those made by cutting fresh bone with stone tools. It has been suggested that the Bodo cranium is the earliest evidence of the removal of flesh immediately after death using a stone tool. The cutmarks were made symmetrically and with specific patterns on the cranium, which is interpreted as strong evidence that the defleshing was done purposefully for funerary practices. Once again, others have suggested that the cutmarks indicate that Bodo may have been practicing cannibalism.

In addition to their use of stone tools from the Acheulean tool industry, *Homo heidelbergensis* is also believed to have used spears. The earliest known spears have been found in Schöningen, Germany, and are dated to about 400,000 years ago. The spears were made either from spruce or pine wood and are believed to have had a range of about 35 meters. Probably the most important technological achievement evident in these spears is the use of hafting technology. **Hafting** involves attaching stone points to a handle made of another substance, such as wood, metal, or bone. The spears found at Schöningen represent one of the first known instances in which hominins united separate elements into a single tool.

Hafting gives stone tools more utility, as they can now be thrown (as with a spear), shot (as with an arrow), or used with more leverage (like an axe). These hafted stone points are able to be used with increased force and effectiveness, allowing people to hunt and kill animals more efficiently. This increased efficiency in hunting and killing animals is believed to have created a situation in which *H. heidelbergensis* had regular access to meat and other high-quality foods. Some have suggested that the presence of spears represent evidence that *H. heidelbergensis* could hunt herd animals that can run faster than a human, and that they had sophisticated hunting strategies requiring cognitive skills like anticipatory planning.

Like *Homo ergaster* and *Homo erectus, Homo heidelbergensis* occupied both caves and open-air sites. However, they did not just use the sites as is, they modified them. One of the most interesting aspects of the cultural behavior of *Homo heidelbergensis* is that they are associated with clear archeological evidence for modified dwellings. For example, in the Czech Republic there is a modified dwelling that consists of a stone foundation that is approximately 700,000 years old. Most likely, this dwelling had a roof constructed of thick branches. Other modified dwellings have been found in Germany and France.

Evidence of controlled fire has been found at most reasonably preserved *Homo heidelbergensis* sites. The oldest established continuous fire site for *Homo heidelbergensis* is from Israel and is dated to around 780,000 years old.

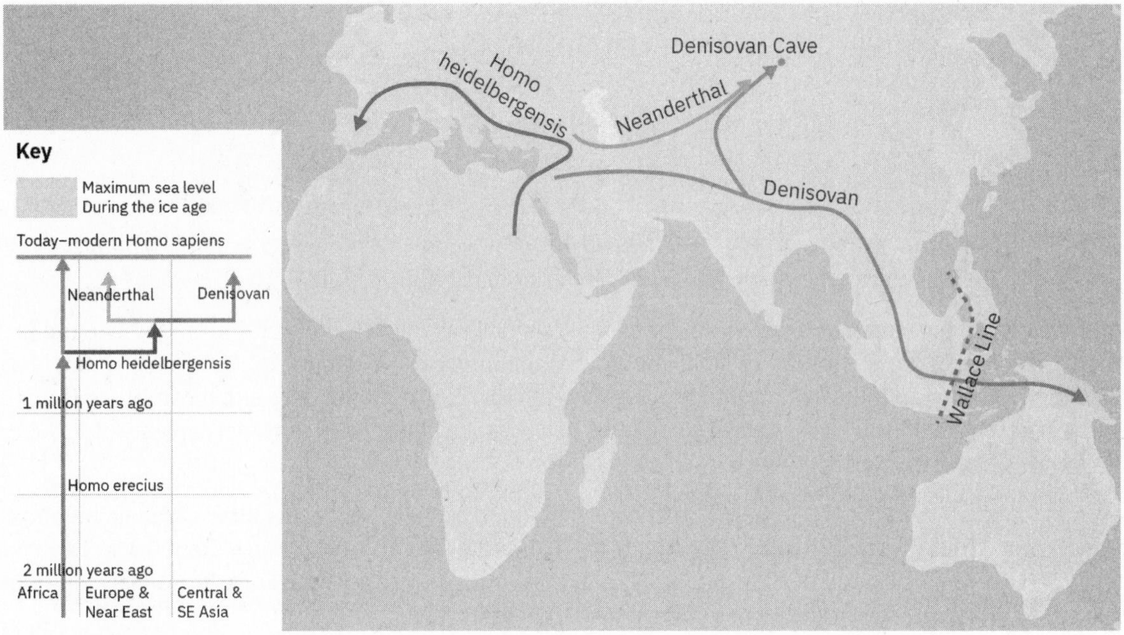

FIGURE 5.13 Phylogenetic tree and proposed migration routes of genus *Homo heidelbergensis* and later Denisovans and Neanderthals. (attribution: Copyright Rice University, OpenStax, under CC BY 4.0 license)

Late Archaic *Homo*

Homo naledi: A Rising Star

The most recently described archaic *Homo* is known as *Homo naledi.* They were found in the Rising Star cave system in South Africa in 2013 and 2014 (Figures 5.14–5.15) and are dated to approximately 235,000–335,000 years old. Over 1,500 bones from as many as 15 individuals were recovered from the cave, which is possibly the largest assemblage of a single hominin species yet discovered. Despite their relatively recent date, they have exceptionally small cranial capacities, comparable to the robust and gracile australopithecines, which are around 560 cc. The encephalization quotient of *H. naledi* is estimated at 4.5, which is the same as *H. floresiensis* but notably smaller than all other *Homo* (contemporary *Homo* are all above 6). The presence of this small-brained hominin at the same time that Neanderthals and *Homo heidelbergensis* were around is further evidence that multiple hominin lineages were coexisting and evolving at the same time. The classification of *H. naledi* proved to be a challenge, as the specimens presented a mosaic of traits and characteristics associated with an array of other hominin species.

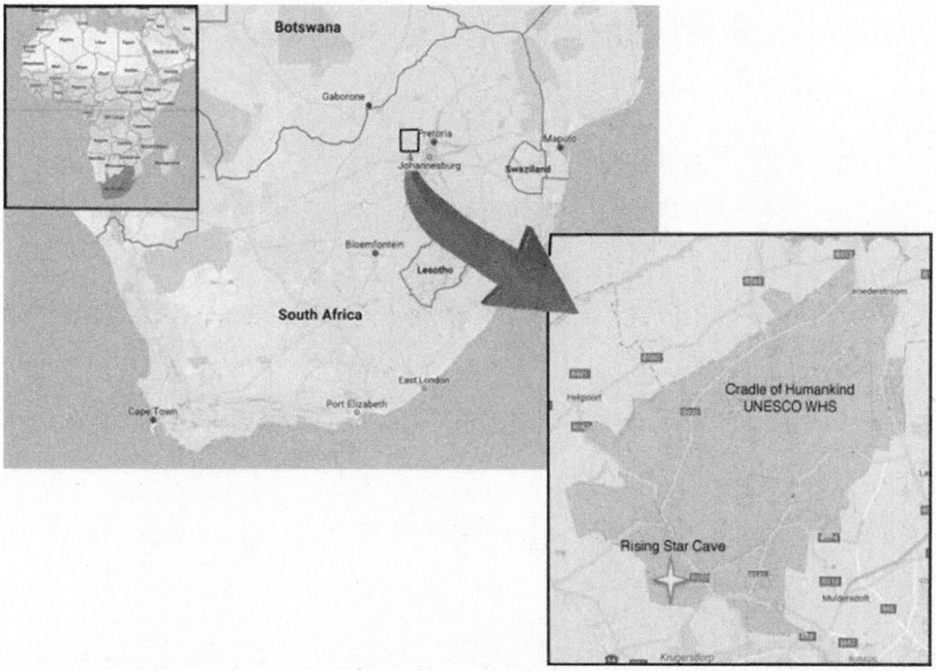

FIGURE 5.14 Maps showing the location of the Cradle of Humankind World Heritage Site in South Africa, where *Homo naledi* fossils were found in the Rising Star cave system. (credit: Hawks et al. (2017), *eLife*, CC BY 4.0)

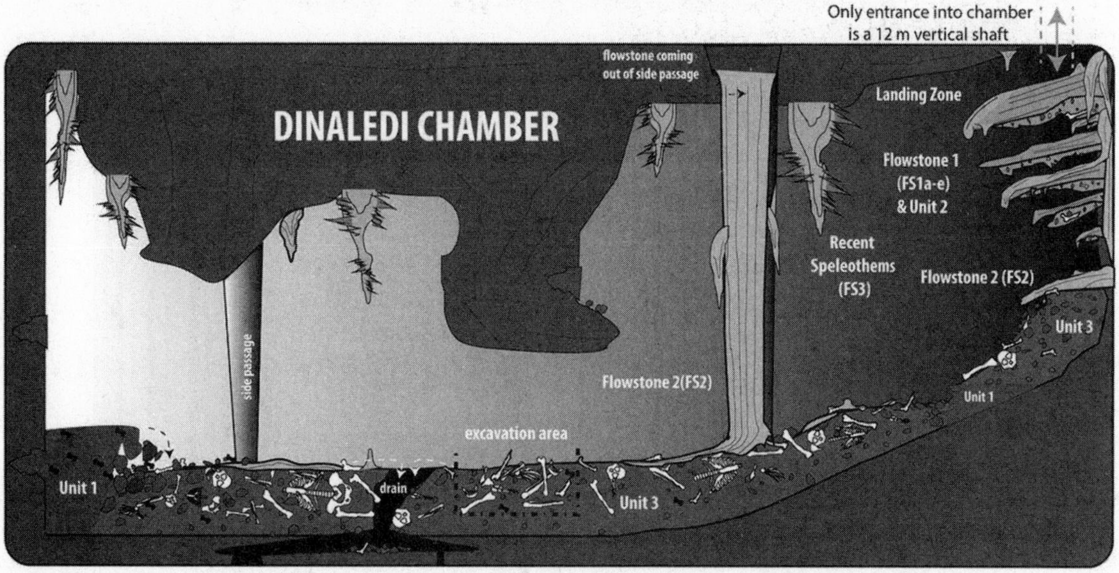

FIGURE 5.15 The Rising Star cave system, showing geological features and the location of the excavation area where numerous *Homo naledi* specimens have been found. (credit: Paul H. G. M. Dirks et al. (2015), *eLife*/Wikimedia Commons, CC BY 4.0)

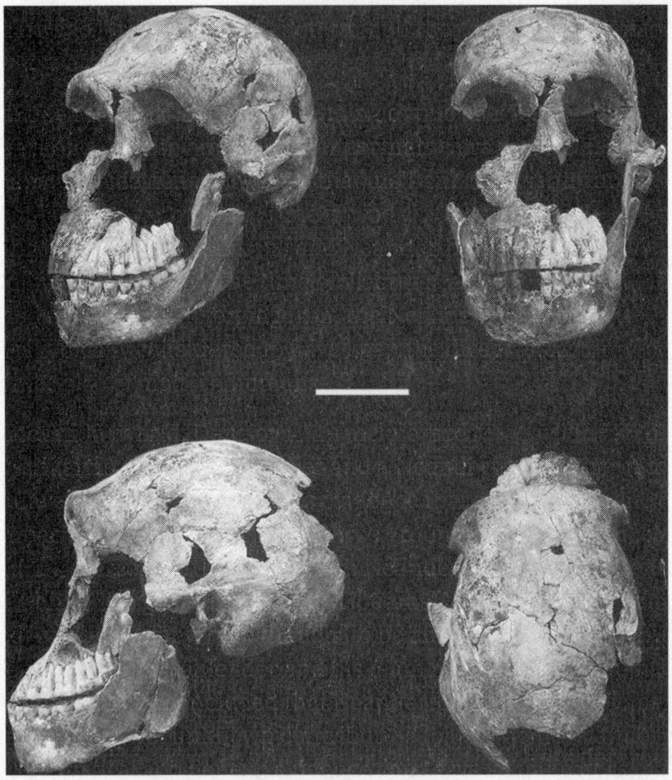

FIGURE 5.16 *H. naledi* skulls. It is apparent in these images that this species had rather pronounced prognathism (Credit: John Hawks, Marina Elliott, Peter Schmid et al. (2017), eLife/Wikimedia Commons, CC BY 4.0)

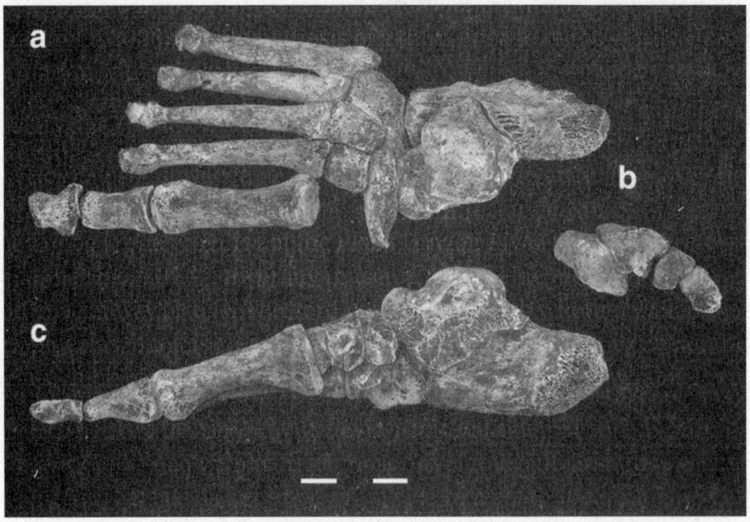

FIGURE 5.17 *H. naledi* feet were much like those of modern humans. (credit: W. E. H. Harcourt-Smith, Z. Throckmorton, K. A. Congdon, B. Zipfel, A. S. Deane, M. S. M. Drapeau, S. E. Churchill, L. R. Berger & J. M. DeSilva (2015)/Nature Communications/Wikimedia Commons, CC BY 4.0)

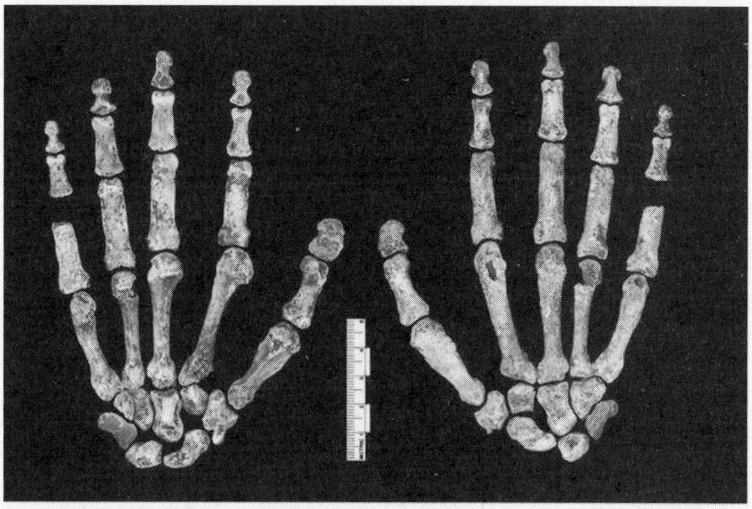

FIGURE 5.18 The hands of *H. naledi* display curved finger bones and large thumbs, indicating that it still had an adaptation for climbing trees. (credit: Lee R. Berger et al. (2015), eLife/Wikimedia Commons, CC BY 4.0)

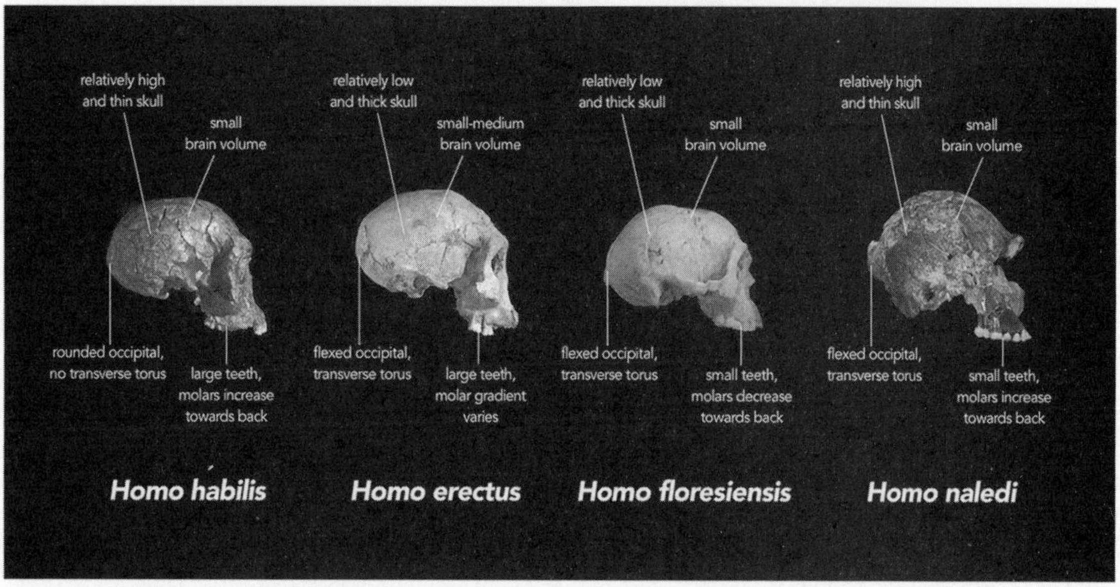

FIGURE 5.19 Comparison of some of the most commonly known *Homo* species (credit: Chris Stringer, Natural History Museum, United Kingdom (2015), eLife/Wikimedia Commons, CC BY 4.0)

Homo naledi: Did They Bury Their Dead?

Homo naledi has not yet been found in association with any stone tools. Despite a lack of established tool use, there is fairly convincing evidence that *H. naledi* may have used the cave system as a place to bury their dead. The hypothesis that *H. naledi* had a ritualistic mortuary practice is based on several observations, such as the bones appearing to lack evidence of gnawing marks from predators and the lack of evidence of layers of sediment that would suggest the bones were deposited by flooding (Dirks et al. 2015). In 2017 additional fossil remains were found in a second chamber in the Rising Star cave system (Hawks et al. 2017), but these remains don't as yet appear to offer additional evidence to support the hypothesis of an intentional burial.

Some scientists believe that there is insufficient evidence to conclude that *H. naledi* were involved in funerary ritual practices. They have noted that the preservation of *H. naledi* specimens are similar to that of cave-dwelling baboons that have died natural deaths. At Sima de los Huesos, remains of about 28 Neanderthal and *H. heidelbergensis* fossils were found in a cave dated to about 430,000 years ago. Researchers who examined the scattering patterns of the remains at both the Rising Star cave system in Africa and the Sima de los Huesos site in Spain (Egeland et al. 2018) concluded that the sites showed evidence of having been scavenged but that this doesn't disprove the possibility that they may also be deliberate burials. The verdict is still out on this. Lee

Berger and other scientists are conducting further investigations of the *H. naledi* skeletal deposits to further explore the possibility they might be evidence of something more deliberate than the actions of predators.

Rethinking the Neanderthal

Homo neanderthalensis

The word "Neanderthal" might conjure up stereotypical images of a brutish caveman-like creature holding a club in one hand and dragging supper with the other. No one said entertainment had to be scientifically accurate, but media can create false perceptions and stereotypes about the past. This section takes a closer look at who the Neanderthal people were and the role they played in the human story.

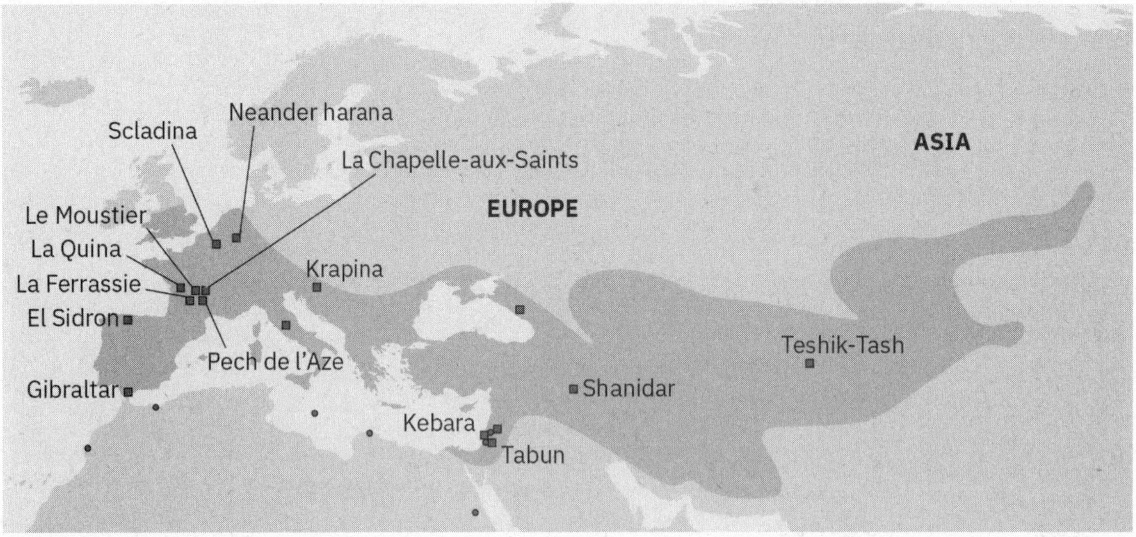

FIGURE 5.20 Distribution map of Neanderthal sites. The red squares mark locations of Neanderthal remains and the shaded area represents the supposed territory of Neanderthal people in Europe and Asia. (credit: modification of work **Neanderthal distribution** by Berria/Wikimedia Commons, CC BY-SA 4.0)

Neanderthals have been found only in regions of Europe and the Middle East and are dated to between about 400,000 and 40,000 years ago. The first fossils, which were found in the Neander Valley, were believed to be the remains of an extinct kind of human. The Germans called them the Neanderthals, the people of the Neander Valley.

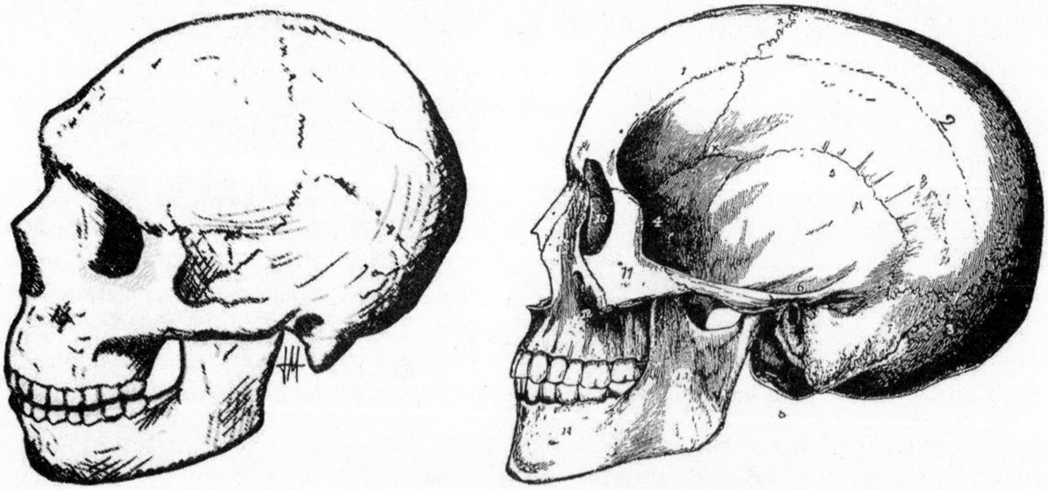

FIGURE 5.21 The Neanderthal skull on the left is noticeably different from the *H. sapiens* skull on the right. (credit: (left) Jose-Manuel Benito/Locutus Borg/Wikimedia Commons, Public Domain; (right) "Image from page 27 of "Human physiology" (1907)" by Furneaux, William S/Internet Archive Book Images/flickr, Public Domain)

Neanderthals possess several distinctive anatomical characteristics: the skull and brain is larger than that of humans, with an average size in Neanderthals of 1,520 cc compared to modern humans' 1200–1400 cc. Does the Neanderthal's larger brain size mean that it was more intelligent than modern humans? As mentioned earlier in this chapter, while there does seem to be a correlation between brain size and complex cognitive skills, the brain in some hominins may have been organized differently than that of modern humans, with different anatomical areas of the brain emphasized. It is believed that in the Neanderthal brain, the frontal region, which is the center of speech and language, was less developed, while the back of the brain, which deals with the senses, was more developed. This greater development in the back area of the brain could be a survival adaptation found in Neanderthals who had to hunt in often harsh and difficult conditions.

Philip Lieberman, a cognitive scientist at Brown University, argues that Neanderthals lacked the anatomy necessary for humanlike speech. He drew this conclusion based on a reconstruction of a Neanderthal throat, which indicated that the neck could not accommodate the vocal apparatus of modern humans (Lieberman,P. 2007). While there is evidence of a hyoid bone, a small horseshoe-shaped bone in the front of the neck, that would have been able to anchor the tongue muscles, other anatomical evidence suggests that the larynx in Neanderthals was placed high in the throat. A highly placed larynx limits an animal's ability to produce many sounds, such as vowels. In humans, the larynx is positioned further down into the throat. The Neanderthal has been determined to have possessed the gene FOXP2, which is linked to the ability to understand complex language, but the verdict is still out as to whether they were able to produce complex language. It is believed by some researchers that the ability to produce complex speech gave *H. sapiens* a significant edge over the Neanderthal.

Other skull characteristics of the Neanderthal include an occipital bun at the back of the skull (as also seen in *H. antecessor* and *H. erectus*), large brow ridges (which are not solid bone and create an air cavity), a large nasal cavity, and incisors that show a rounded pattern of wear, especially in older individuals. Their large front teeth typically show excessive wear. Chipping and pitting on the incisors are believed to have been caused by chewing on leather. The postcranial bones show that they had a broad scapula, which indicates that their rotator cuff muscles were well developed. They possessed a robust humerus with a massive head and the ability to rotate their arms, which suggests they were capable of throwing projectiles and using spears.

Some of the best-known Neanderthal specimens come from a place called Shanidar Cave in Iraq. Within this cave, various skeletal remains of eight individual Neanderthals were found. These remains are identified as Shanidar 1–9, which were discovered between 1957 and 1961, and Shanidar 10, which was discovered in 2006. Nearly all the skeletal remains show some evidence of trauma, suggesting that hunting was risky business. At various Neanderthal sites it has been observed that men and women exhibit similar cranial injuries, suggesting that women might have also engaged in hunting activities. However, the number of injuries in women were significantly fewer than those found in men (Beier et al. 2008). In a comparative study, it was established that during the Upper Paleolithic, modern *H. sapiens* sustained similar injuries as the Neanderthal, but interestingly, these injuries were less likely to result in death (Beier et al. 2008).

Shanidar 3 features a 40-to-50-year-old Neanderthal man who suffered a rib injury, potentially as the result of an encounter with an animal, and suggests healing as a result of care from others. Shanidar 1, called the "Old Man" (30–45 years old was old in Neanderthal terms), had multiple traumas to his body, one of which resulted in blindness in one eye. He was also missing the lower part of his right arm and hand, which suggests the earliest amputation on record. Although he did heal from this amputation, it may have left him paralyzed on the right side of his body. He also had no teeth. It is believed he was kept alive by taking food that had been chewed by others for him. There is evidence of many of these individuals healing from their injuries, which suggests that compassion and a sense of social responsibility for disabled members of the community existed.

FIGURE 5.22 This cave is the site of the Shanidar 4 Neanderthal flower burial site. Evidence found here and at other sites indicates that the Neanderthal practiced intentional burials of their dead. (credit: "Shanidar Cave, Iraqi Kurdistan" by Sammy Six/flickr, CC BY 2.0)

The Flower Burial Hypothesis

The remains found at Shanidar 4 in Iraq suggest that the Neanderthal practiced **intentional burials**, or deliberate placing of the dead in a ritualistic manner. At Shanidar 4, the individual is placed on his left side with his legs drawn up in a flexed position. Pollen analysis of the soil surrounding the corpse suggests that spring flowers had been placed in the grave, possibly indicating that the Neanderthal had a belief in an afterlife and established mortuary practices. However, there has been a lot of debate as to whether there is sufficient evidence to conclude that that the pollen found at some of the Neanderthal sites was a result of ritualistic placement of flowers. Opposing hypotheses propose that the pollen was brought into the cave and deposited by burrowing rodents (Sommer 1999). In spite of these counterclaims, the consensus supports the theory that the Neanderthal did practice intentional burials. This is largely based on evidence such as the careful placement of bodies in specially dug shallow pits. Recent research at both Shanidar Cave and other sites now support the claim that the Neanderthal did practice ritual and intentional burial.

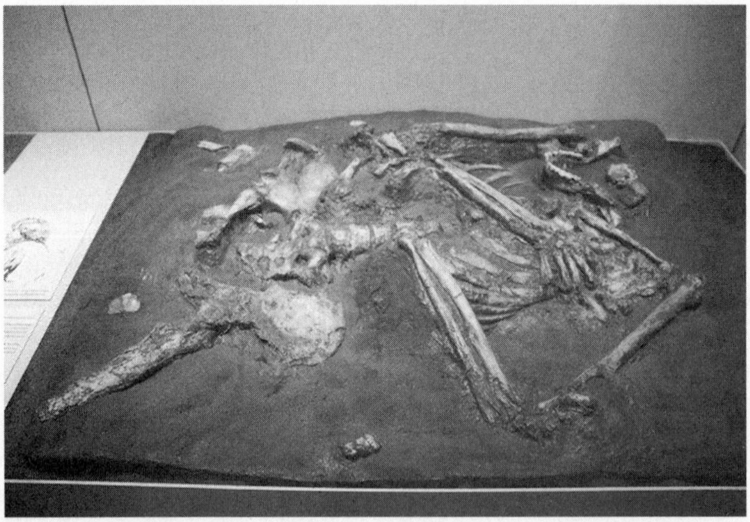

FIGURE 5.23 This reconstruction of a Neanderthal grave is housed in the Israel Museum in Jerusalem. (credit: "Neanderthal Burial, Cast" by Gary Todd/flickr, Public Domain)

Neanderthal Creativity and Material Culture

Neanderthals have been labeled, perhaps unjustly, as a species with a limited ability to communicate in symbolic or abstract forms. Until recently, the Neanderthal had been assumed to lack the cognitive skills associated with the practice of ritual and art. However, cave paintings discovered in Spain in 2012 by Alistair Pike, an archaeologist at the University of Southampton, UK, challenge that assumption. These paintings, which have been dated to around 65,000 years ago, before the arrival of *H. sapiens* in the region, have been determined to be the creative works of the Neanderthal and are currently considered the oldest cave art ever found. This discovery may change what people have previously thought about Neanderthal cognition and their ability to express symbolic thought. It should be acknowledged that the ability to depict the world evident in these paintings does not compare with that in the artwork from *H. sapiens* sites like Chauvet and Lascaux in France (to be discussed later in this chapter).

Neanderthals created more technologically advanced tools than those produced by *H. erectus* and seen in the Acheulian tool industry. The tool industry associated with the Neanderthal hominins is called the **Mousterian tool industry** or the Middle Paleolithic tool industry. Archeological sites that date to the Neanderthal period are dominated by flake tools. This means that the Neanderthal struck flakes from cores and then used the flakes as their tools instead of the core. This resulted in smaller and sharper tools with increased utility.

What Happened to the Neanderthal? What Gave Modern Humans the Edge?

The Neanderthal went extinct around 35,000 to 50,000 years ago. There have been various hypotheses as to what caused this, many connected to the fact that Neanderthal coexisted with *H. sapiens* in regions of Europe and Asia for an estimated 2,600–5,400 years. These hypotheses include an inability to adapt to a changing climate and colder temperatures, the spread of disease, competition for food with *H. sapiens*, and even aggressive takeover by the *H. sapiens*, who may have been better able to adapt to environmental changes due to more complex technology and language skills. Another theory points to evidence that the Neanderthal tended to live in small, scattered groups with limited genetic diversity and low birth rates, which potentially impacted the ability of the Neanderthal to be competitive. A low gene pool can result from reduced birth rates and low survival rates of young children. New genetic evidence shows that the Neanderthal were genetically less diverse and more isolated than *H. sapiens*. And then some argue that the Neanderthal didn't go extinct at all because some people still have Neanderthal genes in them.

Are You a Neanderthal?

Recent genetic evidence indicates that human-Neanderthal interbreeding (https://openstax.org/r/the-scientist) was happening as far back as 125,000 years ago. From one Neanderthal toe bone found in the Denisova cave in Siberia Russia, the Max Planck institute has been able to produce a whole genome which revealed evidence of inbreeding amongst the Neanderthal, along with interbreeding with their cousins the Denisovans (discussed further in next section), as well as a mystery yet to be identified species, as well as *Homo sapiens* (Pennisi, E., 2013). The genetic evidence is most prominent in people of East Asian descent, accounting for between 2.3 percent and 2.6 percent of their DNA. Various mutations and diseases are linked to this Neanderthal DNA, including diabetes, addictions, depression, allergies, and Crohn's disease. One study suggests that Neanderthal genes gave people some level of protection from getting a severe case of COVID-19 (Huber, J., 2018), although a later study (Zeberg and Pääbo 2020) proposes that Neanderthal genes may have increased the risk of respiratory failure as a result of the COVID-19 virus. Such differences may have to do with different genetic clusters in Neanderthal populations in different geographical regions (Mortazavi et al. 2021). Neanderthal genes are believed to have provided immunity to some viruses that *H. sapiens*, arriving from Africa, would not have had time to build up an immunity against. On the reverse side, *H. sapiens* may have brought diseases from Africa that the Neanderthal did not have resistance to, possibly playing a role in their extinction. As Janet Kelso, a computational biologist at the Max Plank Institute for Evolutionary Anthropology, states, "Viral challenges, bacterial challenges are among the strongest selective forces out there" (Akst, 2019).

The Denisovans

The Denisovans, like *Homo naledi*, are archaic *Homo*. There are not a lot of specimens—just one finger bone, three teeth, some long bone (https://openstax.org/r/Long_bone) fragments, a partial jawbone, and a parietal bone (https://openstax.org/r/Parietal_bone) skull fragment. Because of this lack of evidence, very little is known of their anatomical features. Some of the specimens come from Denisova Cave in Siberia, Russia, and are dated to between 500,000 and 30,000 years ago. These dates are arrived at based on the few fossils that exist, inferences made from genetic studies, and sediment analysis. More recently another specimen was found on the Tibetan plateau. In 1980 a jaw and two teeth were uncovered in the Baishiya Karst Cave by a monk, but it wasn't until 2010 that scientists were able to study the jaw. Dating placed the specimen at approximately 160,000 years ago. Protein analysis determined the jaw to be of Denisovan origin and from a member of a population who were most likely well adapted to living in high altitudes (Chen et al. 2019).

Because so few bones have been found, most understanding of this species comes from genetic analyses. According to nuclear DNA studies, Denisovans and Neanderthals were more closely related to each other than they were to modern humans. DNA evidence suggests that the Denisovans interbred with modern humans and with local Neanderthal populations over multiple time periods. Tracing the male Y chromosome, one study indicated that interbreeding between early humans and Neanderthals actually replaced the ancient Denisovan Y chromosome once found in Neanderthals. The time of divergence of the Denisovan is estimated to be around 700,000 years ago, with modern humans diverging from the Neanderthal around 370,000 years ago (Petr et al. 2020). *H. heidelbergensis* is typically considered to have been the direct ancestor of both Denisovans and Neanderthals, and sometimes also of modern humans.

One specimen is a first-generation hybrid, Denisova 11—nicknamed "Denny (https://openstax.org/r/Denny_hybrid_hominin)"—that had a Denisovan father and a Neanderthal mother (Slon et al. 2018). Denisova 11 was found in Denisova Cave in Russia and provides evidence that Late Pleistocene *Homo* species interbred when the groups met. Comparison of the DNA of these three groups suggest that most modern-day Europeans and Asians inherited about 1–4 percent of their DNA from Neanderthals, with no Denisovan ancestry in Europe and 0.1 percent in China. The genetics found in Tibetans, Melanesians, and Indigenous Australian are currently being challenged; originally, they were thought to be about 3–5 percent Denisovan and 2.74 percent Neanderthal. Statistical geneticist Ryan Bohlender and his team have investigated the percentages of extinct hominin DNA in modern humans. They concluded that Neanderthals and Denisovans are not the whole story and that there could be a third group yet unknown contributing to the Pacific Islander **genome** (Rogers, Bohlender, and Huff 2017). Statistical and genetic evidence can serve as indicators of the existence of a group for which no fossils have yet been found. These are referred to as **ghost populations**. For example, there are indications that 2–19 percent of the DNA of four West African populations may have come from an unknown archaic hominin that split from the ancestor of humans and Neanderthals between 360 KYA and 1.02 MYA (Durvasula and Sankararaman 2020). The hypothesis of a third lineage in the genus *Homo* appears to have received further confirmation with a discovery in China.

New *Homo* Genus Discovery *Homo longi*, or Dragon Man

Recently a new archaic *Homo* fossil surfaced in Harbin, China, dated to about 146,000 years ago (Ji et al. 2021). Given the name *H. longi*, it has also been called "Dragon man (https://openstax.org/r/dragonman)" as its origins were determined to be in the province of the Black Dragon River. The fossil (referred to as the Harbin cranium) was donated to the Hebei GEO University museum after being hidden away in a well in the 1930s during the construction of a railway bridge. The verdict is still out as to whether *H. longi* represents a lineage of the Denisovans or a new species, but it is clear it was robust and able to adapt to one of the coldest regions of China. It had a large brain, thick brow ridges, and fairly large teeth, similar to what is found in the Denisovans.

Regional Evolutionary Adaptations: *Homo floresiensis*

The Hobbit of Flores

Homo floresiensis, also known as "the Hobbit" or "Flores Man," was discovered on the island of Flores in Indonesia in 2003. The species has been dated to approximately 100,000–60,000 years ago. What was surprising about this species is its size. An adult individual stood about 3 feet 7 inches tall. Liang Bua, the cave where *H. floresiensis* was found, shows evidence of the use of fire for cooking and contains bones with cutmarks. Since the initial discovery, partial skeletons of nine individuals have been found.

H. floresiensis, like the earlier hominins, did not possess a chin, and its leg bones are thicker than those of modern humans. They had flat feet that were relatively long in comparison to the rest of their bodies. As a result of these anatomical differences, it is believed that their bipedalism was quite different from that of modern humans, with a high stepping gait and slower walking speed. *H. floresiensis* also had substantially more mobility in the elbow joint, which suggests that they were tree climbers.

Their small brain size is not believed to have affected their intelligence. This challenges the view that larger cranial capacity equals higher cognitive skills. Although *H. floresiensis* has a brain size of just 380 cc, equal to the size of an orange, evidence indicates that they made tools, used fire, and hunted very much like *H. erectus.* The brain of *H. floresiensis* does contain a Brodmann area, which is associated with cognitive abilities, that is the same size as that found in modern humans.

Some have suggested that *H. floresiensis* is a sister species of *Homo habilis* that branched off before or shortly after the evolution of *Homo habilis.* Other hypotheses suggest that they were the descendants of *H. erectus* who became stranded on the island after arriving via water, possibly on bamboo rafts.

Another *Homo* species similar in size to *H. floresiensis* was *H. luzonensis*, found on the island of Luzon in the Philippines and dated to at least 50,000–67,000 years ago. *H. luzonensis* displays a hybrid of australopithecine traits (including curved hands and feet) and *Homo* characteristics, yet lived alongside modern *H. sapiens.* Clearly the genus *Homo* is more diverse and complex than was originally thought, especially within the special evolutionary pressures of island environments.

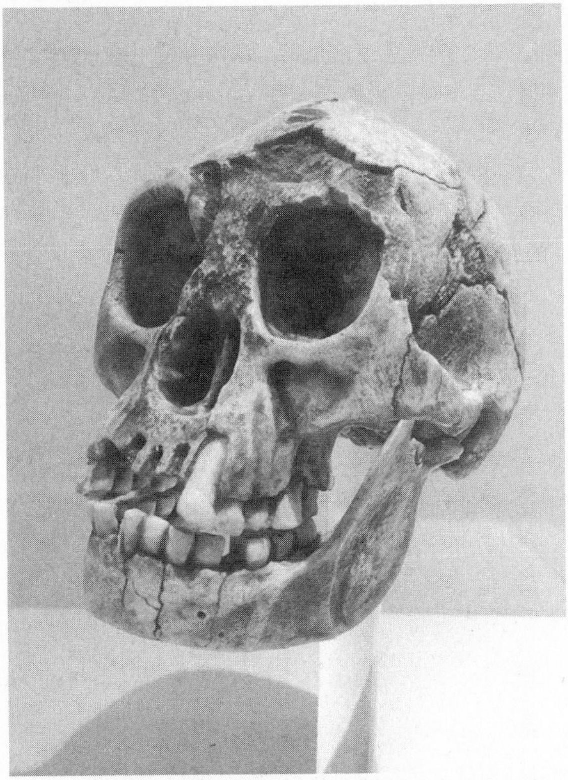

FIGURE 5.24 This *H. floresiensis* skull is on display at the Naturmuseum Senckenberg, a Natural History Museum in Germany. (credit: Daderot/Wikimedia Commons, Public Domain)

Island Dwarfism as an Evolutionary Explanation

Numerous hypotheses have been proposed to account for the small brain size found in both *H. floresiensis* and *H. luzonensis.* One initial theory was that *H. floresiensis* had microcephaly, which is a genetic condition creating an abnormally small head. This was discounted as an explanation once additional specimens were found exhibiting the same size. Perhaps the most convincing explanation is an evolutionary theory called **island dwarfism**, which notes that the evolutionary pressures on islands can be very different from those found on the mainland. Island dwarfism posits that mainland small animal species that colonize islands might evolve larger bodies if the island does not contain key predators. On the other hand, larger species may become smaller due to more limited resources in an island environment. According to the island dwarfism hypothesis, *H. erectus* made its way to Flores, where its descendants became isolated and grew progressively smaller to make the most of limited resources in the island environment. This theory is supported by the fact that there are unique sizes displayed by other animals found with *H. floresiensis*, including a dwarf species of primitive elephant called a *Stegodon.* As *H. floresiensis*'s body shrank, its brain may have undergone "neurological reorganization" to fit a smaller cranial space while maintaining its brain-to-body ratio. The only potential large predator that may have been a threat to *H. floresiensis* was the Komodo dragon, which ate most of the large mammals on the island. Nevertheless, predation pressures for the little people were likely quite low—that is, until *H. sapiens* arrived.

The Emergence of Us: *Homo sapiens*

Modern *H. sapiens* first appeared about 200,000 years ago in Africa. Anthropologists generally classify these people as "anatomically modern *H. sapiens*," which is a way of noting that while their bodies are the same as modern humans, they had not yet developed the cultural traditions, symbolic behaviors, and technologies that are seen among later *H. sapiens,* including people of today. Probably the most defining feature of anatomically modern *H. sapiens* is their chin. Modern *H. sapiens* is the first hominin to exhibit a projecting chin. One of the most common explanations for this anatomical feature is that the chin evolved in response to human speech and protects the jaw against stresses produced by the contraction of certain tongue muscles.

Sometime around 40,000 years ago there was an abrupt change in tool technology, subsistence patterns, and symbolic expression among *H. sapiens.* These changes seem to have occurred almost simultaneously in Africa, Asia, Europe, and Australia. While there is evidence of some creative artistic activity in earlier groups like the Neanderthal, they were not on the same scale as that seen during the Upper Paleolithic, which is also referred to as "the human revolution." The level of cultural changes associated with this period has been compared to the level of change that occurred during the Industrial Revolution of the 19th century.

Among these changes, *H. sapiens* began assembling a much more elaborate tool kit by constructing tools from a wider variety of materials including antler, ivory, and bone. During the Upper Paleolithic, humans shifted from the manufacture of round flakes to the manufacture of blade tools. This construction method is known as the blade tool industry. Blades are stone flakes that look like a modern knife blades—they are long, thin, and flat, and they have a sharp edge. They have a much longer cutting edge than flakes do and are thus more efficient than older technologies. The prepared-core technique of the Mousterian that provided pre-shaped flakes was refined and extended to create pre-shaped blades.

FIGURE 5.25 This Upper Paleolithic burin tool has a much longer cutting edge than anything that came before it and was much more efficient than previous technologies. (credit: "Large Knife Upper Paleolithic or later 35000-3900 BCE Africa" by Mary Harrsch/flickr, CC BY 2.0)

Over the 23,000 years of the Upper Paleolithic, there were many distinctive tool industries within the larger category of the blade tool industry, including the Aurignacian, Gravettian, Solutrean, and Magdalenian. The most significant tool during the Upper Paleolithic was the burin. The burin is a narrow-bladed flint capable of scraping narrow grooves in bone. Scraping two parallel grooves would allow a sliver of bone to be detached as stock for a needle, pin, or awl.

The Gravettian tool industry lasted from approximately 33,000 to 22,000 years ago. During this tool industry, there are many instances of animal remains being used for both decorative and traditional tool purposes. For example, the teeth of arctic foxes were used for decoration, while their arm bones were used as awls and barbs. Some animal bones such as mammoth tusks and bones were used to not only create tools, but also to make art, as seen in the Lion figurine in Figure 5.26. This figurine could be the earliest example of a figure having both human and animal characteristics, a form often associated with shamans or priests. Some have proposed that the "lion man" is actually a woman due to the lack of a lion mane.

FIGURE 5.26 An ancient figurine of a lion sculpted from a mammoth's tusk. This figure was discovered in a German cave in 1939 and dated to around 40,000 years ago, making it one of the oldest figurative sculptures yet discovered and the earliest example of an animal-shaped figurine. (credit: JDuckeck/Wikimedia Commons, Public Domain)

The Solutrean tool industry utilized tool-making techniques not seen before. It produced finely worked bifacial points made with lithic reduction percussion rather than flint knapping. **Lithic reduction** is the process of fashioning stones or rocks into tools or weapons by removing some parts. The lithic core, such as a partially formed tool or naturally formed rock, is held in one hand and struck with a hammer or percussor with the other hand. As flakes are detached, the original mass of stone or lithic core is reduced.

In addition to stone tool innovations, the Solutrean is characterized by the appearance of the atlatl (https://openstax.org/r/throwing-arrow), or spear thrower. An atlatl is a long stick used to propel a spear or dart. Functioning as an extension of the arm, this stick of wood or antler added kinetic energy, and therefore range, to a short spear tipped with flint or bone. The earliest archeological evidence for this tool innovation comes from France, where a 17,500-year-old atlatl was found constructed out of reindeer antler. It is believed that the atlatl was used by humans to hunt large fauna.

FIGURE 5.27 Contemporary man using an atlatl, a tool for launching a spear or a dart that is at least 17,500 years old. (credit: "Atlatl throwing demonstration" by Hannah Schwalbe/NPS/flickr, Public Domain)

By 17,000 years ago, the Solutrean tool industry was replaced by a new tool industry known as the Magdalenian tool industry. During this period, bone and ivory continue to be used, as well as stone. Unlike Mousterian tools, Solutrean tools are made not only from nearby rocks, but also from rocks that have been transported over relatively long distances. Keep in mind that this required not only transporting the selected rocks, but also finding and extracting them.

The Gravettian tool industry is best known for carved Venus figurines portraying a woman, typically made from ivory or limestone. Most figurines have small heads, wide hips, and large breasts. Most researchers believe that they served a ritual or symbolic function. Some have suggested that they represent an expression of health and fertility.

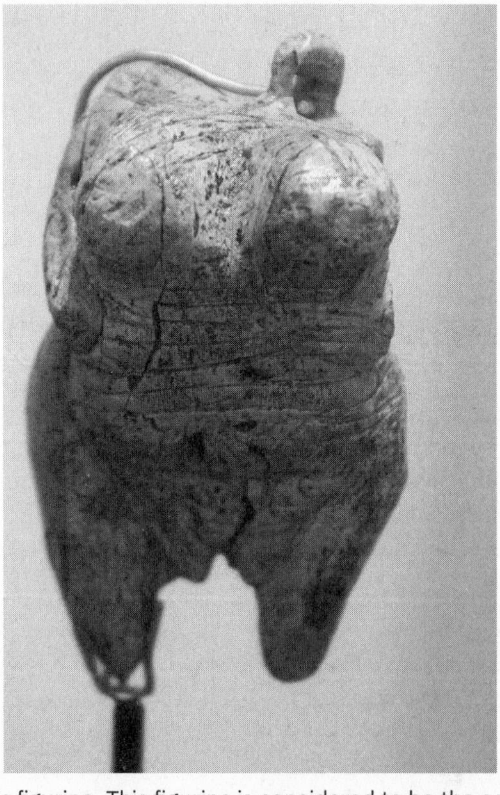

FIGURE 5.28 Venus of Hohle Fels figurine. This figurine is considered to be the earliest known depiction of a human being in prehistoric art. (credit: Anagoria/Wikimedia Commons, CC BY 3.0)

During the Upper Paleolithic, *H. sapiens* created a great deal of cave art. More than 350 cave painting sites have been discovered, the majority located in France and Spain. Cave art seems to have been created continually from 40,000 to 10,000 years ago and then disappeared around 10,000 years ago, likely due to climate change. As temperatures increased, underground shelters were gradually replaced by surface settlements. The most well-known cave sites in France are the Chauvet (https://openstax.org/r/chauvet-archeologie-culture) (32,400 years ago) (Figure 5.29) and Lascaux Caves (17,000 years ago). The art in both caves features common subjects, such as bison, horses, and deer, as well as tracings of human hands. Most of the animals depicted were commonly hunted but were not always found with associated deposits of bones. The cave art produced during the Upper Paleolithic show a level of sophistication and even sacredness not seen previously in human history.

FIGURE 5.29 These drawings of lions from the Chauvet Cave in France are dated to 32,400 years ago. (credit: HTO/Wikimedia Commons, Public Domain)

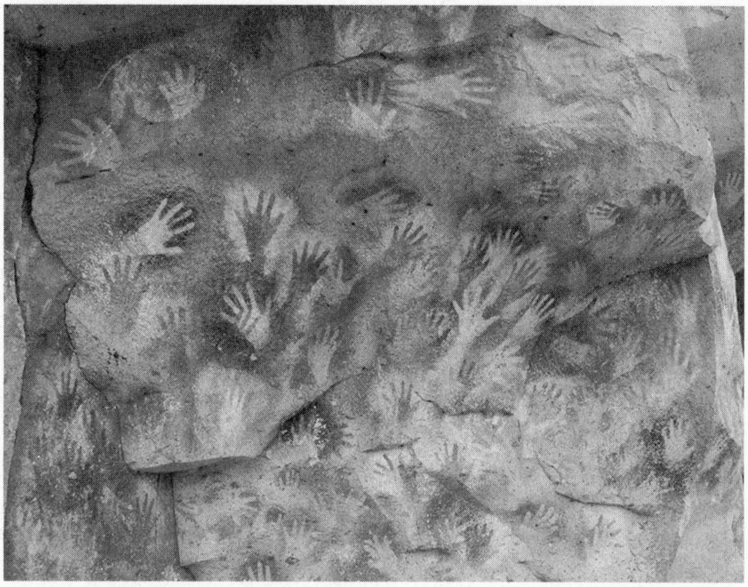

FIGURE 5.30 Handprints found in the Cuevas de las Manos upon Río Pinturas, near the town of Perito Argentina. Hand stencils on cave walls have been found in many locations around the world. (credit: "SantaCruz-CuevaManos-P2210651b" by Golan Levin/flickr, CC BY 2.0)

Cave paintings were made with natural pigments created by mixing ground-up elements, such as dirt, red ochre, hematite, manganese oxide, and animal blood, with animal fat and saliva. Paint was applied using twigs formed into brushes and blow pipes made from bird bones, through which paint was sprayed onto the cave wall. Hand stencils on cave walls can be found in many locations around the world including Africa, Argentina, Europe, and Australia. Anthropologist Dean Snow (2013) conducted research at eight cave sites in France and Spain to determine who the artists might be. Based on calculated measurements of the handprints, he concluded that 75 percent of the ochre stenciled handprints in the Paleolithic caves were made by women.

5.4 Tracking Genomes: Our Human Story Unfolds

LEARNING OBJECTIVES

By the end of this section, you will be able to:

- Describe how mtDNA sheds light on early human migrations and explain the Out of Africa model.
- Explain how studying the genomes and coevolution of lice can fill current gaps in the human fossil record.
- Describe the origin of human variation from an evolutionary perspective.

Mitochondrial Eve

Begun in 1990 and concluding in 2003, the Human Genome Project was an ambitious international effort that sequenced about 99 percent of the human **genome** with an accuracy of 99.99 percent. Genetics has thus far largely confirmed the **Out of Africa theory**, which proposes that early humans left Africa around 100,000 years ago and migrated to diverse areas of the world. When early humans left Africa and moved into Europe, they not only lived alongside but also interbred with non-African species such as the Neanderthal, who were already inhabiting the region.

Molecular anthropologists have an interest in determining when living human populations began diverging from one another. This has been difficult to do using nuclear DNA because it mutates much too slowly for measurable accumulations to occur in 200,000 years. Many of the genetic studies that have been conducted are thus based on genetic material carried in the **mitochondria (mtDNA)**, which are passed on maternally. There is no recombination in mtDNA, so unless the mitochondria carries a novel mutation, a child has exactly the same mitochondrial genes as its female genetic contributor (which may be its mother, egg donor, or someone in a similar genetic relationship). The mitochondria of every living person is a copy, modified only by rare mutations, of the mitochondria passed down via matrilineal descent from a population in our ancient past. This population is referred to as **Mitochondrial Eve or mtMRCA** (mitochondrial most recent common ancestor), believed to have lived in southern Africa 100,000–200,000 years ago.

As discussed in Chapter 4, the longer ago two populations share a common ancestor, the more time there is for mutations to occur and for adaptations and change to take place. Although genetic variation is small among the world's human populations, it is greatest in Africa. This indicates that the human populations in Africa have the longest established genetic lineage. While multiple hypotheses exist as to human origins and new evidence could change the current views, the consensus is an Out of Africa model traced back to the matrilineal descent of a population living in Africa about 200,000 years ago.

How the Genome of Lice Can Fill in the Gaps

While perhaps not a pleasant thought, lice have long been a part of human history. Studying the **coevolution** relationship between humans and lice has shed much light on human story. Dr. David Reed, the Curator of Mammals and Associate Director of Research and Collections at the University of Florida Museum, has been studying the coevolution of humans and lice, an area of research that has developed only within the last 20 years. Reed's groundbreaking research has the potential to fill in some big gaps in humans' rather sketchy fossil record and provides important data that might have applications in medicine and biology. Two questions that this research has already begun to ask are when did we become less hairy and when did we start wearing clothes.

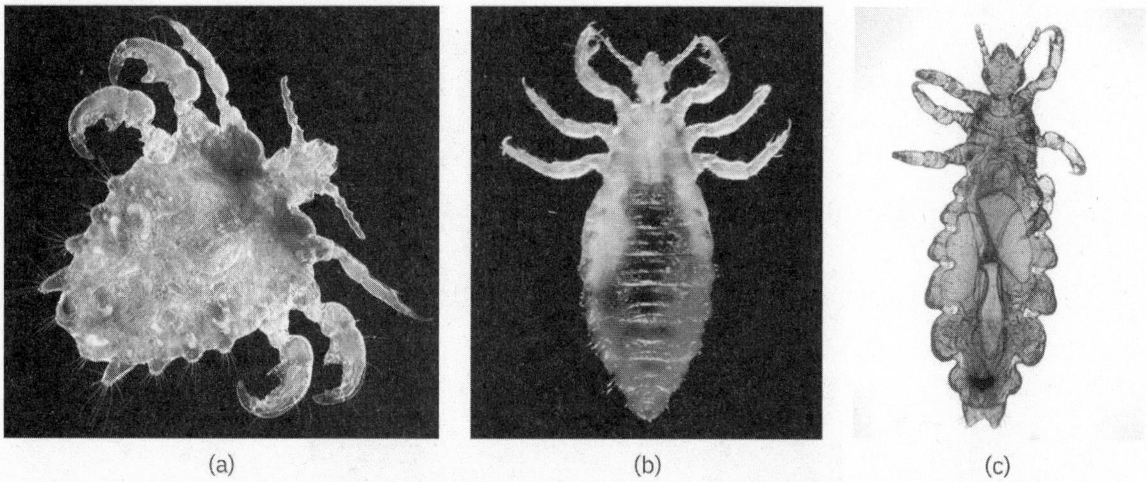

FIGURE 5.31 There are three types of lice associated with humans: (a) crab or pubic louse; (b) body louse; (c)) head louse. The coevolution of humans and lice is a developing area of research. (credit: (a) Noizyboy1961/ Wikimedia Commons, CC BY 4.0; (b) Janice Harney Carr, Centers for Disease Control and Prevention/Wikimedia Commons, Public Domain; (c) Dr. Dennis D. Juranek, Centers for Disease Control and Prevention/Wikimedia Commons, Public Domain)

Figure 5.31 shows three types of lice associated with humans: the head louse (*Pediculus humanus capitis*), the body louse (*Pediculus humanus corporis*), and the crab louse or pubic louse (*Pthirus pubis*). Body lice infest clothing and lay their eggs on fibers in the fabric. Head and pubic lice infest hair, laying their eggs at the base of hair fibers. The human head and body lice (genus *Pediculus*) share a common ancestor with chimpanzee lice, while crab lice (genus *Pthirus*) share a common ancestor with gorilla lice. By tracking louse variations, scientists have been able to determine when the head louse and pubic louse diverged, enabling estimates as to when we lost our extra hair and when we started to wear clothes. It is interesting to note that the divergence of the genus *Pediculus* (head and body lice) correlates with the divergence of the human lineage from chimpanzees about six million years ago. Research on lice also provides further support for the Out of Africa model of human migration. Reed has observed that the genome of African lice shows a higher degree of genetic diversity than that of lice found elsewhere in the world, supporting the hypothesis that both humans and lice existed in Africa first.

Many hypotheses about what may have triggered the loss of hair in humans point to **thermoregulation**, the need to control body temperature in extreme conditions. Living in the heat of the savanna, humans needed a cooling mechanism to enable them to be better hunters. Other evidence of adaptation to the heat includes the appearance of sweat glands, which are more numerous in humans than in other primates. Another theory about the cause of the loss of hair among humans suggests that it was an adaptation to control parasites on the body. Did people immediately throw on clothes after losing all of that extra body hair? Reed's research suggests that the wearing of clothes was not something that happened quickly. Humans lost body hair about a million years ago and didn't start wearing clothes until around 170,000 to 190,000 years ago. That's about 830,000 years living in their birthday suits! When humans began to wear clothes, the body louse adapted structures that enabled them to attach to clothes instead of hair.

FIGURE 5.32 Humans lost most of their body hair about a million years ago. (credit: “Neanderthal” by Eden, Janine and Jim/flickr, CC BY 2.0)

PROFILES IN ANTHROPOLOGY

Molly Selba

FIGURE 5.33 Molly Selba (holding skull) leading a study session. (credit: Molly Selba, Public Domain)

Personal History: From the time Molly was young, she knew she wanted to be an anthropologist.

She took an archaeology class at the local community college when she was a high school student and went to field school over the summer. In college, she completed a double major in archaeology and anthropology, with a minor in Museums and Society. She later gained experience working with different museum collections and held internships at the Baltimore City Medical Examiner’s Office and the Smithsonian Museum of Natural History. After completing her undergraduate degrees, she knew that she wanted to pursue anthropology as a full-time career and began working towards her master’s and doctorate in biological anthropology.

Area of Anthropology: For Molly the most interesting thing about biological anthropology is the information that bones can tell us. Initially she was interested in what the history of disease could tell us about the lives of people in the past, but as she worked with biological anthropologists, her focus shifted to understanding how evolution can impact the shape of different bones.

She received her undergraduate degree from Johns Hopkins University in Baltimore, Maryland, and her Master's degree from the University of Florida, where she is currently a PhD candidate. Her research interests include comparative anatomy, cranial morphology, and anatomical sciences education. She is most interested in how cranial morphology varies within and between species and how it is impacted by factors such as evolution and selective breeding practices. Her earlier research focused on the differences in cranial morphology in dogs created by artificial selection for facial reduction. Her dissertation research currently focuses on a comparative study of facial reduction across bats, primates, and dogs.

Accomplishments in the Field: For Molly her most important accomplishment in the field of anthropology has been in education and outreach. Throughout her time in graduate school, she was involved in school visits, working with teachers to facilitate the inclusion of human evolution into existing science curricula. She has specifically focused on helping educators find teaching materials that are culturally inclusive and responsive. She has led multiple professional development workshops for teachers on the same topic and has visited over two dozen classrooms and interacted with over 1,200 students in the last four years. Making science accessible to K-12 educators is an extremely important part of being a researcher, and she believes everyone in academia should strive to be effective science communicators.

"Studying biological anthropology helps us better understand our origin story as a species. It helps us recognize why our anatomy is the way that it is, how morphological changes over time can take place, and why we have such a diversity of life on earth. Just being able to recognize and identify our anatomy is only half the challenge—more important is our understanding why various traits are adaptive, how structure relates to function, or why leftover anatomical traits still persist in our body to this day."

Natural Selection and Human Variation: Are Humans Still Evolving?

Human variability is attributed to a combination of environmental and genetic factors, including social status, ethnicity, age, nutrition, quality of life, access to healthcare, work and occupation, etc. As mentioned in Chapter 1, anthropology contributes many insights into both the social construct of race and the impacts racial categories have on people's lives. The focus in this chapter is the role of natural selection in human variation.

A number of changes are associated with the Neolithic era and the rise of agriculture around 10,000 to 8,000 years ago. Many have noted that changes during this time period did not have positive effects on human and environmental health. The **evolutionary mismatch** hypothesis proposes that our bodies are best suited to the environments we have spent much of our evolutionary history in, which are very different from the environments we inhabit today (Li, van Vugt, and Colarelli 2018).

Humans evolved for one million years as hunter-gatherers. Today, human bodies are still trying to adapt to the largely grain-based diet brought about by agriculture, a diet characterized by less diversity and lower levels of nutrition than that of a typical hunter-gatherer. Incomplete adaptation to this change has made people susceptible to a number of diseases and nutritional deficiencies. Lactose intolerance is a prime example. The domestication of cattle and the drinking of cow's milk began during the agricultural age, not very long ago in evolutionary history. Currently 65 percent of humans are unable to digest cow's milk. Dental caries (cavities) are another problem linked to the change in diet associated with agriculture. The grain-based and high-sugar diets associated with agriculture are very different from the diet of hunter-gatherers. Neither our bodies nor the bacteria in our mouths have had time to fully adapt to this change.

Another adaptation that took place during the Neolithic era is related to variation in skin pigmentation. Humans who left Africa and settled in Europe about 40,000 years most likely had dark skin with high levels of **melanin**, which provides protection against ultraviolet radiation New data confirms that about 8,500 years ago, early hunter-gatherers in Spain, Luxembourg, and Hungary also had darker skin. Skin pigmentation is an adaptation to ultraviolet radiation, with different tones offering different advantages, depending on one's distance from the equator. As humans migrated to the Northern Hemisphere, they were exposed to less ultraviolet radiation, which also meant less absorption of the Vitamin D needed for strong bones and other important immune functions. In order to compensate for this loss and to allow for greater exposure to ultraviolet radiation, skin pigmentation became lighter.

Another example of human variation as a result of adaptation to the environment can be seen in Indigenous populations in the Andes, Tibet, and the Ethiopian highlands. Each of these three groups faces the same environmental challenge, living in a low-oxygen environment, and they have responded with unique adaptations. Tibetans compensate for low oxygen levels by taking more breaths per minute than people who live at sea level. Those living at high altitudes in the Andes have been found to have higher concentrations of hemoglobin in their blood than other people. Ethiopians living at altitudes of 9,800 to 11,580 feet have neither of these adaptations. The explanation as to how the Ethiopian highlanders thrive in their environment is still a mystery.

FIGURE 5.34 A valley in the Andes near Ollantaytambo, Peru. Indigenous peoples living at high altitudes in the Andes have been found to have higher concentrations of hemoglobin in their blood than other people. (credit: "Snows of the Andes" by David Stanley/flickr, CC BY 2.0)

This chapter has explored just some of the immense biological and cultural diversity of the genus *Homo*. This diversity has emerged in response to highly complex and variable environments connected to factors such as exposure to UV radiation, low oxygen levels at high altitude, changes in diet as a result of hunting or agricultural practices, geographic isolation in island populations, and climate variability and temperature. The genus *Homo* has proven to be resilient and adaptive in response to whatever environment or challenge it has faced. Variation is the key to survival. While scientists recognize that biological and cultural variation has greatly contributed to our human evolution, the human species is now facing a moment in which we must contemplate a difficult question: To what extent has our success as a species jeopardized the survival of other species and the health of the planet we all call home?

MINI-FIELDWORK ACTIVITY

Identify the Fossil

Imagine that you have just discovered a hominin fossil with some of the characteristics listed below. Write each of the characteristics on a card and shuffle them together. Then, working in a group, decide which characteristics belong in the *Homo* group and which belong in the *Australopithecus* group. What scientific name (genus/species) would you give it, and what criteria did you use? (Note: This is an actual hominin fossil!)

- Brain similar in shape and structure to modern human brains
- Hands suited for tool use
- Small jaws and teeth
- Third molar larger than other molars (found in australopithecines and some early *Homo* species)
- Skull shaped more like *H. erectus* or *H. habilis*
- A sagittal keel (as seen in *H. erectus*)—a small raised ridge on top of the skull
- Bipedal and walked with a human gait
- Humanlike feet with arches and ankles
- Flaring blades of the pelvis (primitive)
- Broad rib cage
- Lower part of pelvis like modern humans'
- Small braincase (EQ 4.5)
- Skull shows prognathism (protruding face)
- Primitive shoulder position suggests suitability for climbing and swinging
- Curved fingers (What would that suggest?)

Additional Resources

Visual timelines and maps

The Atlas of Human Evolution has put together a user friendly interactive map (https://openstax.org/r/atlasofhumanevolution) on the development of Homo sapiens.

The Smithsonian Institute's Human Evolution Interactive Timeline (https://openstax.org/r/human-evolution-interactive-timeline) provides an interactive overview of major milestones and species ranges.

Coevolution of lice and humans

David Reed, associate curator of mammals at the Florida Museum of Natural History, offers an explanation of his research (https://openstax.org/r/liceshowhumans) for a general audience.

The Smithsonian Magazine explores possible causes and benefits (https://openstax.org/r/smithsonianmag) of the human loss of hair.

Key Terms

Acheulean tool industry the production of more complex tools, including hand axes, by *H. erectus* from 1.6 million to 200,000 years ago.

archaic *Homo* the period of time that precedes the emergence of the earliest early modern humans (*Homo sapiens*) around 300,000 years ago.

biface tools a type of tool characteristic of the Acheulean tool industry, with both sides worked.

Broca's area a region in the frontal lobe of the brain (which includes two Brodmann areas) first found in *H. habilis* and connected with the production of speech.

canine fossa a facial depression above the canine tooth found in modern humans.

coevolution an interaction between different species that influences each species' evolution; the simplest case of this is predator-prey relationships.

cranial capacity the volume of the interior of the cranium or skull, providing an approximate size of the brain.

encephalization increased brain size over time.

encephalization quotient a measurement defined as the ratio between brain and body size.

endocranial cast an impression taken from the inside of the cranium (braincase), frequently used by paleoanthropologists to determine the shape and approximate size of the brain in hominids and other primates.

evolutionary mismatch a hypothesis that disease and nutritional deficiencies result when people's bodies are unable to adapt to an environment that they have not spent most of their evolutionary history in.

genome the complete set of genes or genetic material present in a cell or organism.

ghost population proposed group for which no fossil evidence has yet been found.

hafting the process of attaching stone points to a handle, which increases a tool's effectiveness for hunting.

handedness the use of a dominant hand, suggests lateralization of the brain and cognitive development.

intentional burials evidence of placing the dead in a specific manner, suggesting ritualistic practice.

island dwarfism mainland small animal species that colonize islands might evolve larger bodies if the island does not contain key predators. On the other hand, larger species may become smaller due to more limited resources in an island environment.

lithic reduction the process of fashioning stones or rocks into tools or weapons by removing some parts.

melanin substance that determines the color of skin pigmentation and protects people from ultraviolet radiation. Skin will have higher levels of melanin the closer to the equator one lives.

Mitochondrial Eve genes traced through mitochondrial DNA that represent the female genetic originator of all humans who lived 200,000 years ago in Africa.

Mousterian tool industry a complex stone tool technology largely associated with the Neanderthal.

mtDNA the DNA located in the mitochondria that can be passed down unchanged from female genetic contributor to child.

mtMRCA "mitochondrial most recent common ancestor," or Mitochondrial Eve, representing the common ancestor of *H. sapiens* around 200,000 years ago.

occipital bun an anatomical feature seen in the Neanderthal skull that appears in the rear of the skull.

Oldowan tool Industry the oldest and most primitive tool industry; production and use are largely in association with *H. habilis*.

Out of Africa theory theory that proposes that *Homo sapiens* developed first in Africa and then spread around the world between 100,000 and 200,000 years ago.

postcranial features skeletal material found in the body that is not related to the skull (cranial bones).

sexual dimorphism differences in physical characteristics other than reproductive organs that appear between males and females of the same species.

thermoregulation an adaptation that allows the body to control and regulate body temperature.

Summary

In this chapter we have explored our human journey as a member of the genus *Homo*, following a trail of adaptations and change that ultimately led to *us*. First on the scene were the australopithecines, who were already walking on two feet and paved the way for the evolutionary changes and cultural achievements that were to follow. A colder climate with drastic changes in climate were associated with an increased reliance on cooked meat, which may have contributed to a growing brain. A brain with highly developed cognitive skills gave humans the capacity to solve problems and create tools that enabled better hunting and survival skills. Adaptations provided *H. ergaster and H. erectus* the ability to walk and run longer distances, to more effectively track and follow game, and to explore nearby continents.

Genetic information provided by mtDNA indicates that all humans shared common ancestors who lived in Africa 200,000 years ago. Studies of genetics shows examples of coevolution and how even small organisms such as lice can shed light on the human story. The rise of agriculture created new challenges for humanity, with evolutionary mismatch still impacting people today. From the earliest toolmakers to the cave art of the Upper Paleolithic to the modern computer age, the predominant theme of human history has always been about change. The ability to adapt to this change is why humans are still here. Humans' evolutionary story, however, does not end with the emergence of the species. Today humans are faced with numerous challenges as they adapt to an increasingly changing environment as a result of climate change, loss of habitat, and decreasing biodiversity. In 2020, Darwin's theory of natural selection played out in real time as people began an arms race with a mutating and evolving COVID virus. Evolutionary change is not something that happened to people just in the past—it is very much still happening today, and it will continue to be part of the future.

Critical Thinking Questions

1. What are some of the key anatomical differences between *Australopithecus* and one of the species in the genus *Homo*?
2. What criteria would you use to define a species belonging to the genus *Homo*?
3. What are some of the limitations in using the currently known criteria for classifying a species under the genus *Homo*?
4. What are some of the explanations or hypotheses for the increasing brain size (encephalization) seen in the genus *Homo*?
5. Based on current evidence, form a hypothesis as to what you think caused the extinction of the Neanderthal. What gave modern humans the edge?
6. In what ways has genetic research enabled modern humans to track their story?
7. What are some similarities between *Homo naledi, Homo floresiensis,* and *Homo luzonensis,* and what makes them so unique?
8. In what way are humans still evolving today? Can you provide an example?

Bibliography

Ahern, Jim. 2015. "Archaic Homo." In *Basics in Human Evolution,* edited by Michael P. Muehlenbein, 163–76. Cambridge, MA: Academic Press. doi:10.1016/B978-0-12-802652-6.00012-8.

Aiello, L., and P. Wheeler. 1995. "The Expensive-Tissue Hypothesis: The Brain and the Digestive System in Human and Primate Evolution." *Current Anthropology 36* (2): 199–221. http://www.jstor.org/stable/2744104.

Akst, Jef. 2019. "Neanderthal DNA in Modern Human Genomes Is Not Silent." *The Scientist,* September 1, 2019. https://www.the-scientist.com/features/neanderthal-dna-in-modern-human-genomes-is-not-silent-66299.

Beier, J., N. Anthes, J. Wahl, and K. Harvati. 2018. "Similar Cranial Trauma Prevalence among Neanderthals and Upper Paleolithic Modern Humans." *Nature* 563:686–90. https://doi.org/10.1038/s41586-018-0696-8.

Boaz, Noel T., Russell L. Ciochon, Qinqi Xu, and Jinyi Liu. 2004. "Mapping and Taphonomic Analysis of the *Homo erectus* Loci at Locality 1 Zhoukoudian, China." *Journal of Human Evolution* 46 (5): 519–49. doi:10.1016/j.jhevol.2004.01.007.

Bramble, D., and D. Lieberman. 2004. "Endurance Running and the Evolution of *Homo*." *Nature* 432:345–52. https://doi.org/10.1038/nature03052.

Chen, F., F. Welker, C. C. Shen, S. E. Bailey, I. Bergmann, S. Davis, H. Xia et al. 2019. "A Late Middle Pleistocene

Denisovan Mandible from the Tibetan Plateau." *Nature* 569:409–12. https://doi.org/10.1038/s41586-019-1139-x.

Dirks, Paul HGM, Lee R. Berger, Eric M. Roberts, Jan D. Kramers, John Hawks, Patrick S. Randolph-Quinney, Marina Elliott et al. 2015. "Geological and Taphonomic Context for the New Hominin Species *Homo naledi* from the Dinaledi Chamber, South Africa." *eLife* 4:e09561. doi:10.7554/eLife.0956.

Dorey, Fran. 2020. "*Homo erectus*." Australian Museum. https://australian.museum/learn/science/human-evolution/homo-erectus/.

Dorey, Fran. 2019. "*Homo naledi*." Australian Museum. https://australian.museum/learn/science/human-evolution/homo-naledi/.

Dunsworth, Holly M. 2010. "Origin of the Genus *Homo*." *Evolution: Education and Outreach* 3:353–66. doi:10.1007/s12052-010-0247-8.

Durvasula, Arun, and Sriram Sankararaman. 2020. "Recovering Signals of Ghost Archaic Introgression in African Populations." *Science Advances* 6 (7): eaax5097. doi:10.1126/sciadv.aax5097.

Egeland, Charles P., Manuel Domingues-Rodrigo, Travis R. Pickering, Colin G. Menter, and Jason L. Heaton. 2018. "Hominin Skeletal Part Abundances and Claims of Deliberate Disposal of Corpses in the Middle Pleistocene." *PNAS* 115 (18): 4601–06. https://doi.org/10.1073/pnas.1718678115.

Fuentes, Agustin. 2019. *Biological Anthropology: Concepts and Connections*. 3rd edition. New York: McGraw-Hill Education.

Frayer, David & Clarke, Ronald & Fiore, Ivana & Blumenschine, Robert & Pérez-Pérez,FF Alejandro & Martínez Martínez, Laura & Estebaranz-Sánchez, Ferran & Holloway, Ralph & Bondioli, Luca. (2016). OH-65: The earliest evidence for right-handedness in the fossil record. *Journal of Human Evolution*. 100. 10.1016/j.jhevol.2016.07.002.

Hawks, John, Marina Elliott, Peter Schmid, Steven E. Churchill, Darryl J. de Ruiter, Eric M. Roberts, Hannah Hilbert-Wolf et al. 2017. "New Fossil Remains of *Homo naledi* from the Lesedi Chamber, South Africa." *eLife* 6:e24232. doi:10.7554/eLife.24232.

Holloway, Ralph L. 2018. *The International Encyclopedia of Biological Anthropology*. Hoboken, NJ: John Wiley and Sons.

Huber, J. 2018. "Inherited Neanderthal Genes Protect Us Against Viruses, Study Shows." *Scope*, October 5, 2018. https://scopeblog.stanford.edu/2018/10/05/inherited-neanderthal-genes-protect-us-against-viruses-study-shows.

Jerison, H. J. 1973. *Evolution of Brain and Intelligence*. New York: Academic Press.

Ji, Qiang, Wensheng Wu, Yannan Ji, Qiang Li, and Xijun Ni. 2021. "Late Middle Pleistocene Harbin Cranium Represents a New *Homo* Species." *The Innovation* 2 (3): 100132. https://www.cell.com/the-innovation/fulltext/S2666-6758(21)00057-6.

Leakey, L. S., P. V. Tobias, and J. R. Napier. 1964. "A New Species of the Genus *Homo* from Olduvai Gorge." Nature 202:7–9. doi:10.1038/202007a0.

Li, Norman P., Mark van Vugt, and Stephen M. Colarelli. 2018. "The Evolutionary Mismatch Hypothesis: Implications for Psychological Science." *Current Directions in Psychological Science* 27 (1): 38–44. https://doi.org/10.1177/0963721417731378.

Lieberman, P. 2007. "The Evolution of Human Speech: Its Anatomical and Neural Bases." *Current Anthropology*, 48 (1): 39-66. doi:10.1086/509092.

Meyer, Matthias, Juan-Luis Arsuaga, Cesare de Filippo, Sarah Nagel, Ayinuer Aximu-Petri, Birgit Nickel, Ignacio Martínez et al. 2016. "Nuclear DNA Sequences from the Middle Pleistocene Sima de los Huesos Hominins." *Nature* 531**:** 504–07. https://doi.org/10.1038/nature17405.

Monfils, A., J. Allen, B. W. Goodner, and D. Linton. 2020. "Louse and Human Coevolution." *Biodiversity Literacy in Undergraduate Education*, QUBES Educational Resources. doi:10.25334/JJBH-SG27.

Mortazavi, S., K. Kaveh-Ahangar, S. Mortazavi, D. Firoozi, and M. Haghani. 2021. "How Our Neanderthal Genes Affect the COVID-19 Mortality: Iran and Mongolia, Two Countries with the Same SARS-CoV-2 Mutation Cluster but Different Mortality Rates." *Journal of Biomedical Physics and Engineering* 11 (1): 109–14. https://doi.org/10.31661/jbpe.v0i0.2010-1218.

Nielsen, R., J. Akey, M. Jakobsson, J. Pritchard, S. Tishkoff, and E. Willersley. 2017. "Tracing the Peopling of the World through Genomics." *Nature* 541: 302–10. https://doi.org/10.1038/nature21347.

Petr, Martin, Mateja Hajdinjak, Qiaomei Fu, Elena Essel, Hélène Rougier, Isabelle Crevecoeur, Patrick Semal et al. 2020. "The Evolutionary History of Neanderthal and Denisovan Y Chromosomes." *Science* 369 (6511): 1653–56. doi: 10.1126/science.abb6460.

Pike, A. W. G., D. L. Hoffmann, M. García-Diez, P. B. Pettitt, J. Alcolea, R. De Balbín, C. González-Sainz, C. De Las Heras, J. A. Lasheras, R. Montes et al. (2012). "U-Series Dating of Paleolithic Art in 11 Caves in Spain." *Science* 336 (6087): 1409–13 doi:10.1126/science.1219957.

Schaik, Carel P. V., Triki, Zegni, Bshary, R. Heldstab, S.A., (2021) "Farewell to the Encephalization Quotient: A New Brain Size Measure for Comparative Primate Cognition" Brain Behav Evol 96:1–12 van Schaik/Triki/Bshary/Heldstab DOI: 10.1159/000517013

Toups, M.A. Kitchen, A., Light, J.E. Reed, D.L (2011). "Origin of clothing lice indicates early clothing use by anatomically modern humans in Africa" *Molecular Biology and Evolution*, Volume 28, Issue 1, January 2011, Pages 29–32, https://doi.org/10.1093/molbev/msq234

Read, Dwight, and Sander van der Leeuw. 2008. "Biology Is Only Part of the Story." *Philosophical Transactions of the Royal Society* 363 (1499): 1959–68. doi:10.1098/rstb.2008.0002.

Rogers, A. R., R. J. Bohlender, and C. D. Huff. 2017. "Early History of Neanderthals and Denisovans." *PNAS* 114 (37): 9859–63. doi:10.1073/pnas.1706426114.

Roth, G., and U. Dicke. 2012. "Evolution of the Brain and Intelligence in Primates." *Progress in Brain Research* 195:413–30. doi:10.1016/B978-0-444-53860-4.00020-9.

Semaw, S., P. Renne, J. W. K. Harris, C. S. Feibel, R. L. Bernor, N. Fesseha, and K. Mowbray. 1997. "2.5-Million-Year-Old Stone Tools from Gona, Ethiopia." *Nature* 385:333–6. https://doi.org/10.1038/385333a0.

Slon, Viviane, Fabrizio Mafessoni, Benjamin Vernot, Cesare de Filippo, Steffi Grote, Bence Viola, Mateja Hajdinjak et al. 2018. "The Genome of the Offspring of a Neanderthal Mother and a Denisovan Father. *Nature* 561:113–6. https://doi.org/10.1038/s41586-018-0455-x.

Snow, Dean. 2013. "Sexual Dimorphism in European Upper Paleolithic Cave Art." *American Antiquity* 78 (4): 746–61. doi:10.7183/0002-7316.78.4.746.

Sommer, J. D. 1999. "The Shanidar IV Flower Burial: A Re-evaluation of Neanderthal Burial Ritual." *Cambridge Archaeological Journal* 9 (1): 127–9. https://doi.org/10.1017/S0959774300015249.

"Study Finds Earliest Evidence in Fossil Record for Right-Handedness." 2016. University of Kansas. https://news.ku.edu/2016/07/21/study-finds-earliest-evidence-fossil-record-right-handedness.

Susman, R. 1991. "Who Made the Oldowan Tools? Fossil Evidence for Tool Behavior in Plio-Pleistocene Hominids." *Journal of Anthropological Research*, 47 (2), 129–51. http://www.jstor.org/stable/3630322

Xiujie, Wu, Liu Wu, and Christopher J. Norton. 2007. "Endocasts —The Direct Evidence and Recent Advances in the Study of Human Brain Evolution." *Progress in Natural Science* 17 (9).

Zeberg, H., and S. Pääbo. 2020. "The Major Genetic Risk Factor for Severe COVID-19 Is Inherited from Neanderthals." *Nature* 587:610–2. doi:10.1038/s41586-020-2818-3.

CHAPTER 6
Language and Communication

Figure 6.1 Family members gather at a sweet potato festival in Gushegu in northern Ghana. This highly social event brought together families, farmers, chiefs, and community members to celebrate the harvest of sweet potatoes. (credit: Official photographer of the US Embassy in Ghana/USAID in Ghana/Wikimedia Commons, Public Domain)

CHAPTER OUTLINE

INTRODUCTION Talk, talk, talk. As human beings, that is what we do all day (and sometimes all night). Even when we are alone, we might be listening to the radio, watching a video, reading, or texting—all activities that incorporate language. **Language** is often considered to be one of the quintessential elements of humanity, key to our social interactions and cultural development. No other animal does it the way we do. A few apes have been taught words in sign language, mainly using simple word combinations to ask for particular treats or desired activities. Is that anything compared to what we do with language?

Consider a situation from the author, Jennifer Hasty's own fieldwork.

> *While conducting research in Ghana, I once attended a large family gathering to honor the birth of a child, an event called an "outdooring." After everyone had arrived and socialized a bit, a middle-aged man stood up and took the microphone in his hand to pour libation. Libation is the ritual offering of*

drink to the ancestors, welcoming them to the ceremony and asking for their blessings. As he took the cup in his hand, he surveyed his audience, then stopped short, appearing extremely embarrassed. Looking down at his feet, he sputtered, "Oh! When the tongue is present, the teeth do not make noise."

Everyone laughed. It was a proverb I'd heard before, but I had no idea what it meant in this context. The speaker stepped aside as an even older man rose from a table at the edge of the gathering and slowly made his way to the microphone. The first speaker had assumed he was the eldest member of the family present at the gathering, but in fact, his older brother was there. By the rules of seniority, it was the older brother who should present the libation.

What did the proverb mean in that situation? In most cultures, people do not usually explain proverbs, so the listener has to piece together the meaning. In this case, the proverb was used metaphorically to compare the production of words in the mouth and the roles of the people involved in this particular performance of libation. The nimble tongue is central to human speech, while the teeth play a more fixed and supportive role, providing surfaces used by the tongue to make certain sounds. Alone, the teeth can only clash against each other meaninglessly. A tongue is needed to produce speech. Using the proverb, the first speaker was comparing his elder brother to the tongue—he was more central to the gathering and more proficient in the production of ceremonial speech such as libation. The younger man assigned himself the role of a tooth, only able to make noise rather than ceremonial speech.

In humans, language has developed into an extremely complex feature of sociocultural life. Just as the tongue is central to the production of human speech, language is central to the production of human culture. The subfield of linguistic anthropology examines the role of language in sociocultural life. Linguistic anthropologists are interested in how language affects our thinking and our experience of the world around us. Some explore the different categories of formal and informal speech that people have developed to organize rituals and ceremonies as well as everyday activities. Others listen carefully to various kinds of conversation, looking for patterns in the way people interpret and build on one another's speech acts.

The discipline linguistics is devoted to the study of language. Linguistics is the science of language, including subfields devoted to speech sounds, word forms, word arrangement, meanings, and practical language use. One subfield of linguistics, sociolinguistics, examines the social context of language use, such as how language varies according to age, gender, class, and race. While sociolinguistics and linguistic anthropology share an interest in the social side of language, linguistic anthropologists tend to focus on language as an aspect of larger cultural processes. Rather than looking at language as a sole object of study, linguistic anthropology studies language as one cultural element among many, all interwoven into the sociocultural life of a people.

6.1 The Emergence and Development of Language

LEARNING OUTCOMES

By the end of this section, you will be able to do the following:

- Describe the communicative abilities of wild animals such as birds and primates.
- Distinguish primate communication from human language.
- Identify the biological features of early hominins that were central to the emergence of language.
- Identify the archaeological evidence for the emergence of language.

There are some seven thousand languages spoken in the world today. Most people are proficient in at least one of them, possibly more. But people are biologically capable of mastering any of them, and have been since birth. Humans are born language ready. For a human baby, any language will do. With passive exposure to language (simply hearing it without any formal instruction), human toddlers learn the complex rules and vast vocabularies of the language spoken (or signed) around them. This astounding feat is made possible by specific biological features in the brains and bodies of human babies, features designed to help them understand and produce language. The learning of language then triggers further changes in our brains, making possible certain kinds of reasoning and thought as well as communication with others.

FIGURE 6.2 When teaching language to their children, some parents teach signs (such as those of American Sign Language) as well as spoken words for objects. The theory is that sign language and spoken language are processed in different parts of the brain. Teaching these two forms of language together may provide deeper cognitive reinforcement and greater chance of recall. This baby is making the sign for "bird." (credit: "Bri signs 'Bird'" by Bev Sykes/flickr, CC BY 2.0)

Drawing on biological and archaeological evidence, researchers seek to understand how, why, and when humans developed the biological features associated with language and, once language emerged, how the practice of language changed the way of life of early humans. Language became a building block for human culture of increasing complexity. Innovations such as stone tools, hunting, and using fire for heat and cooking were made possible by language. In turn, these new skills enhanced the survival of those who practiced them, increasing the likelihood that those people would live to pass on their genetic makeup to their offspring. This means that certain biological features were key to the invention of human culture and that human culture was key to the biological development of humans. We think of this as a reciprocal system of biocultural coevolution. Put another way, biology and culture developed in tandem, with language as the link between the two.

No one really knows when or how humans invented language. The problem is that language, whether spoken or gestural, leaves no direct trace in the archaeological record. Lacking direct evidence, researchers must be creative, combining various indirect forms of evidence to suggest theories about how language may have begun in humans. Based on such methods, researchers think that language may have emerged between 50,000 and 200,000 years ago. The largeness of this window of possibility is due to the indirect nature of the evidence and a great deal of controversy about which elements may have been most important in the process of language development. In this section, we look at these forms of indirect evidence, starting with communication in the animal kingdom.

Animal Communication

All animals communicate with each other and even with other species (Tallerman and Gibson 2011). Many use vocalizations like calls, growls, howls, and songs. Many also use gestures such as dances, postures, and facial expressions. Some change the color of their scales, skin, or fur. Some produce strong-smelling body fluids sprayed in their environment or rubbed on their own bodies. All of these activities are used to tell other animals about territory, food sources, predators, and mating opportunities.

FIGURE 6.3 Canada geese fly in a V formation to conserve energy and to keep track of all the birds in the formation. Coordination and communication are essential for the group. (credit: "Canada Geese" by Alex Galt, US Fish and Wildlife Service/flickr, CC BY 2.0)

Many people might be tempted to think that animals speak to each other just as we do, that their various forms of communication are roughly equivalent to language. Does your dog bark and jump excitedly whenever you pick up the leash? Isn't that a way of saying, "C'mon! Let's go for a walk!"

Some forms of animal communication are fairly simple, such as this canine leash mania. Others are far more complex, such as the way an octopus can change the color of and patterns on its skin for hunting, courtship, and camouflage. Fireflies use bioluminescence to attract mates and as a defense mechanism. Some fish generate electric fields to advertise their species and sex. Many animals use a vast lexicon of postures and gestures to communicate messages to one another and even to other species. When a bird issues a predator-alert call, squirrels respond as well. Many mammals pay attention to the predator warnings of birds.

Are these complex forms of communication equivalent to language? Take a closer look at one famous example of complex animal communication and compare it to human language.

A Waggle is Not a Word: The Complexity of Language

Consider the famous "waggle dance" of the honeybee. Upon finding a good source of nectar such as a grove of wildflowers, a worker bee returns to the hive and performs a special flight pattern consisting of a figure-eight waggle followed by a return loop alternating right and left. The direction and duration of the waggle communicate the direction and distance to the location of the desirable food source (Seeley 2010; Frisch 1993).

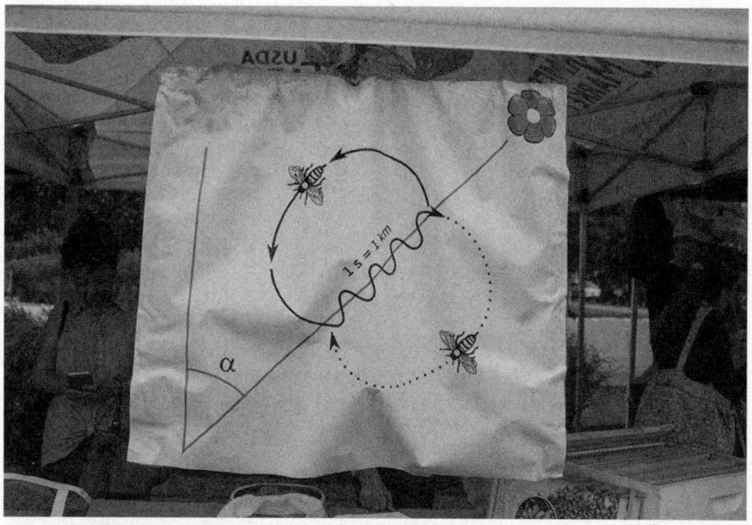

FIGURE 6.4 Diagram of the waggle dance of the honeybee. The movements performed by the bee during this dance communicate the direction of and distance to a food source to its fellow hive members. (credit: "20180622-FS-WashingtonDC-KTC-024" by Kelly Chang, US Forest Service/flickr, Public Domain)

The waggle dance is certainly a complex and effective form of communication, but does it qualify as language? **Communication** refers to the transfer of information from a sender to a receiver. Communication can be voluntary or involuntary, simple or complex. Language is a specific, complex, systematized form of communication involving the use of vocal or gestural units (words or signs) that can be combined and recombined in larger structures (sentences) that can convey an infinite array of complex meanings. Language is a form of communication. Not all communication is language.

Central to the infinite possibilities of language is a set of rules that govern just how sounds, signs, words, and phrases may be combined. These rules structure the order of words, dictating, for example, where to put subjects and actions in an utterance so that listeners will be able to find them. Rules also tell us whether words indicate a single thing or multiple things and whether actions occur in the past, present, or future. Complex forms of animal communication such as the waggle dance do contain some systematic rules governing the sequence, duration, and intensity of certain segments of the communication, but they are highly constrained to very limited contexts. For example, the waggle dance can be used to signal nectar sources near and far, but it cannot be used to discuss the weather or comment on the laziness of the queen. Unlike the relatively "closed" systems of communication common among animals, human language is open-ended. Our languages have the distinctive quality of allowing actors to combine units in an infinite number of ways to produce new meanings.

Simple Signs and Pant-Hoots: Language in Primates

Biological anthropologists posit that we share a common ancestor with the other great apes (gorillas, chimpanzees, bonobos, and orangutans) about five to eight million years ago. As nonhuman primates do not produce language in the wild, the biological and cultural features that promoted language must have emerged after that. However, studies aimed at teaching human language to nonhuman primates have revealed that individuals of these species are able to master basic vocabulary and use simple words and word combinations to obtain the things they want. So the great apes must have some biological features that enable them to learn human language in a partial and limited way.

You may have heard of Koko, the gorilla famous for learning to use sign language. Sign language is used in such studies because nonhuman primates lack the distinctive vocal tract required to make the sounds of human language. Researcher Penny Patterson taught Koko to use about a thousand signs, roughly the vocabulary of a three-year-old child (Patterson and Linden 1981). Patterson reported that Koko could comment on things that were not currently present in her environment, such as personal memories. According to Patterson, Koko could joke and lie and teach other gorillas to sign. She could even invent new signs. Many of these claims are disputed by other researchers. Some point out that the evidence is largely anecdotal and relies on the interpretation of Patterson herself, hardly an objective observer. Though controversial, Patterson's pathbreaking work with Koko provided a wealth of data and opened up new possibilities for understanding the language abilities of nonhuman primates.

FIGURE 6.5 Koko learning to play the guitar. Koko became famous for learning to communicate with humans using roughly 1,000 signs taught to her by researcher Penny Patterson. (credit: "ODCnewBegin9" by FolsomNatural/flickr, CC BY 2.0)

Human-reared chimps, gorillas, bonobos, and orangutans have all been taught to use gestures or tokens to refer to things in the world around them, often combining those signs in a rule-based way to make comments and requests. Even though many linguists are skeptical of these studies, the use of symbolic systems in cooperative interactions to achieve goals does seem to indicate that great apes have the basic capacity to generate some sort of protolanguage. **Protolanguage** refers to a very simple set of gestures or utterances that may have preceded the development of human language. But do apes display these abilities due to some innate capacity or because we have taught them symbolic systems? Perhaps learning a symbolic system has changed the brains of these individual animals in distinctive ways.

FIGURE 6.6 Chimpanzees use gestures and facial expressions as well as vocalizations to communicate with one another. (credit: "Chimpanzees" by foshie/flickr, CC BY 2.0)

Many primatologists conduct research on the vocal and gestural forms of communication used by primates in the wild, looking for those biological features that might underpin the human capacity for language. Wild chimpanzees, for instance, produce a wide range of calls, including hoots, pant-hoots, pant-grunts, pant-barks, rough-grunts, nest-grunts, alarm barks, waa-barks, wraas, screams, and soft panting play sounds (Acoustical Society of America 2018). Primatologists have listened closely to these calls. Some argue that chimp vocalizations are not much like human language, as calls are fairly fixed and limited in their meanings. Chimps may use a rough grunt to indicate a food source, but they do not seem to have specific grunts for specific food types. Monogamous pairs of gibbons, a smaller species of ape, are known to perform elaborate morning duets. Gibbons have an array of predator calls as well. Research comparing duets with predator calls suggests that gibbons compose their songs to convey specific information, each note carrying a certain meaning (Clark et al. 2006). While impressive, the ability to manipulate notes to convey a limited range of meanings is still a far cry from the infinite productivity of human language. The limitless recombination of signs that produces the flexible, open-ended quality of language is missing in the communication systems of wild primates.

Human Biology and the Emergence of Language

There must be something special about us to make possible the distinctively flexible and open-ended communication system of language. Research has focused on our throats, our brains, and our genes, looking for the biological features that allowed for the emergence of language.

The Vocal Tract

Humans have evolved a very unusual vocal tract with a descended larynx (otherwise known as the "voice box") and a large and rounded tongue positioned in the mouth to enable a remarkable array of sounds (Lim and Snyder 2015). Some researchers suggest that our throats may have evolved in response to walking upright or changes in diet or a combination of those two factors. Humans also have more deliberate control over breathing than nonhuman primates. In order to better understand when hominins developed this distinct vocal apparatus, researchers examine the hyoid bones of hominins to see if they resemble those of modern humans. The hyoid is a U-shaped bone in the human throat that helps us swallow and move our tongues. The few hyoids that have been found in the fossil record suggest that our distinctive vocal tract may have been developed around 500,000 years ago. This means that Neanderthals likely had the same vocal abilities as modern humans.

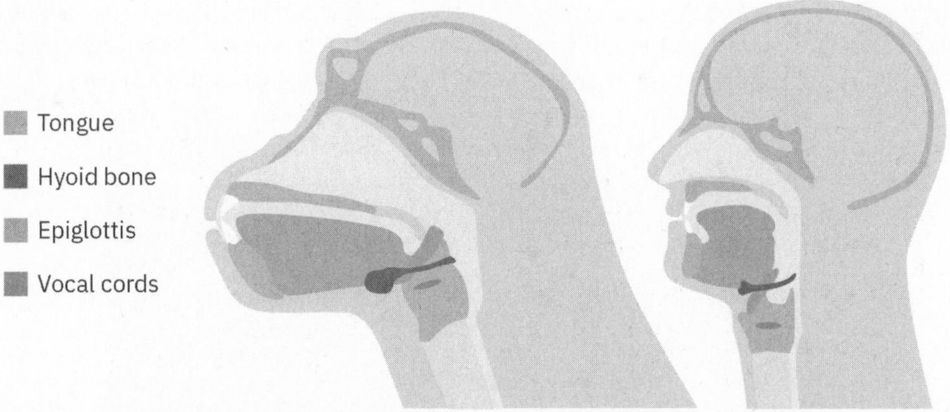

FIGURE 6.7 Evolutionary changes in the vocal tract enabled the development of spoken language in humans. The image on the left shows the vocal structures an early ancestor to humans. The image on the right shows the vocal tract of modern humans. The position of the vocal structures in the early ancestor allows for eating and breathing at the same time. The position of these structures in modern humans allows more sounds to be produced and more words to be spoken in sequence. (attribution: Copyright Rice University, OpenStax, under CC BY 4.0 license)

Brain Structure

Several features of the human brain are considered prerequisites to language, including the overall (large) size, the division into specialized hemispheres, and certain structures like Broca's and Wernicke's areas. Broca's area is a region of the brain associated with the production of speech. Wernicke's area is essential to the comprehension of language. Both are most often located in the left hemisphere of the human brain (for left-handed people, both *can* be located on the right side). How did we acquire these brain features so essential to language? A great deal of controversy surrounds this question, as researchers debate when and how these structures evolved.

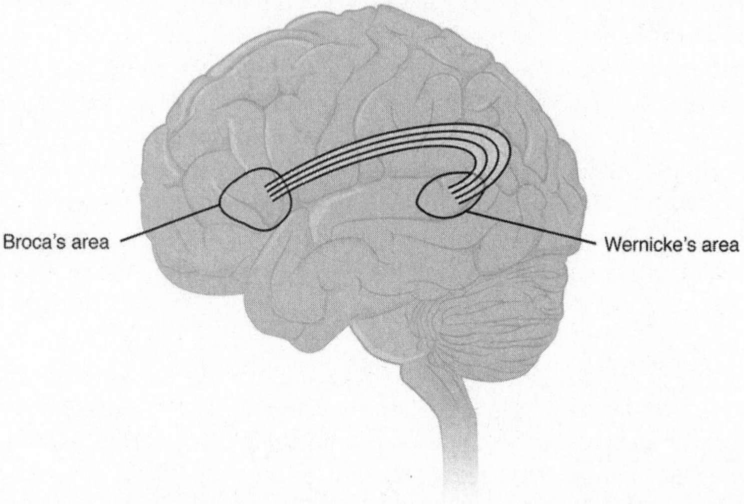

FIGURE 6.8 The locations of Broca's area and Wernicke's area in the human brain. Broca's area, responsible for the articulation of speech, is next to the motor area, where the movements of the body are controlled. Wernicke's area, associated with language comprehension, is situated beside the primary auditory area, where sounds are processed. (credit: "1605 Brocas and Wernickes Areas-02" by OpenStax College/Wikimedia Commons, CC BY 3.0)

Most recently, research has focused on "**mirror neurons**," special brain cells that seem to enable mimicry (Lim and Snyder 2015). Many researchers think that the ability to understand the actions of others and recreate those actions ourselves is a fundamental prerequisite for language. That is, in order to be able to talk to each other, early hominins must have been able to evaluate and interpret each other's actions and reproduce them in similar contexts. In primates like monkeys, scientists have discovered a system of specialized neurons called the "mirror neuron system" that enables primates to recognize and imitate actions. Monkeys and apes cannot talk, but they can recognize, interpret, and imitate actions performed by other primates. The neurological studies that revealed mirror neurons are too invasive to perform on humans, but neuroimaging studies suggest that a similar mirror neuron system does exist in humans.

FIGURE 6.9 Mirror neurons are most likely involved in the spread of contagious yawning. Mirror yawning happens between humans and can even happen across species. You can make your dog yawn! (credit: "Sleepy" by Toshimasa Ishibashi/flickr, CC BY 2.0)

Brain imaging studies on humans have located evidence for the mirror neuron system in a region of the brain close to Broca's area. So it is possible that the mirror neuron system inherited from primates provided a foundation for the later emergence of a brain structure devoted to language production in hominins. If imitation and language are in fact connected in this way, then a system of gestures may have paved the way for the development of language. Some researchers now hypothesize exactly this: that hominin language evolved from a system of gestures to a system of vocalizations.

The "Language Gene"

In the late 1980s, medical researchers became aware of a particular speech disorder common among members of one family in West London. Many members of this family could not pronounce words. Many stuttered. Many had very limited vocabularies. Geneticists traced the disorder to a genetic mutation on chromosome number 7 of the human genome. (See Biological Evolution and Early Human Evidence for more on chromosomes and genes.) The mutation was located on a gene named **FOXP2**, prompting some researchers to dub this "the language gene." Some hypothesize that FOXP2 may have played a role in the development of language in humans (Lim and Snyder 2015).

At first, researchers thought that only humans had the FOXP2 gene, but subsequently a form of this same gene has been identified in many vertebrates, including mice, bats, fish, and songbirds. In mice, the gene appears to be related to vocalizations. In birds, it seems to be linked to birdsong. All primates have FOXP2, but the human copy is slightly different than that of nonhuman primates. Some researchers think this mutation occurred around 260,000 years ago and may have enabled the development of spoken language in Neanderthals and *Homo sapiens*.

Other researchers are skeptical of the notion that one gene could be responsible for the emergence of spoken language (Tallerman and Gibson 2011). Many anatomical developments and cognitive processes—connected to different parts of the human genome—are involved in human language. These developments and changes would have required mutations in other parts of the genome of early Homo. While the mutation of FOXP2 in Homo may have played a role in language development, other mutations would have been important as well.

Hominin Material Culture

Evidence from the material culture of hominins such as *Homo habilis* and *Homo erectus* is also used to speculate about the emergence of human language. Early hominins developed stone tool technologies and created stunning works of art. The production and use of such tools and artwork must have required a complex set of social and cognitive abilities. Those same types of social and cognitive skills are important to human language. It is possible that language emerged as part of a whole complex of material culture.

Archaeological evidence and linguistic theory come together in a model suggesting that the invention of tools by early hominins was linked to the invention of language. Some linguistic theorists suggest that the evolutionary changes in brain structure that allowed for the development of tool use also support the emergence of language. Furthermore, the innovations of tools and language are entwined in a reciprocal relationship; evolutionary pressure to develop tools stimulated the development of language, and the development of language facilitated increasingly complex tool making and tool use.

There are two theories to explain the connections between advances in tool use and language. The first rests on the assumption that tool making requires a considerable degree of cognitive planning. You cannot make a useful tool by just picking up a rock and randomly chipping away at it. Hominins like *Homo habilis* and *Homo erectus* must have known just what kind of rocks would work as base and chipper and how to execute a set of precise chips in a certain sequence to achieve a sharp blade without breaking the core. The mental processes important to this sort of planning are hypothesized to have also enabled hominins to do the sort of quick planning involved in the production of complex speech (Tallerman and Gibson 2011).

A second theory linking tool use and language emphasizes the importance of imitation in passing along the complex set of skills involved in tool making. Neuroscientist Michael Arbib suggests that the ability to imitate may have generated the first gestural language among hominins (2011). And he has developed a model to describe how imitation and tool making may have evolved together over time. About 2.5 million years ago, *Homo habilis* began making basic stone choppers, cores with flakes removed, used for butchering carcasses. Such choppers are called Oldowan tools, named after the site in Olduvai Gorge in Tanzania where they were first found. Arbib has theorized that the production of Oldowan tools required the ability for hominins to imitate each other's actions. Simple imitation would make it possible for a learner to reproduce the actions of an accomplished tool maker through observation and mimicry. This ability to imitate is biologically rooted in the system of mirror neurons discussed earlier. As hominin brains acquired the ability of simple imitation involved in tool production, they might also become capable of the kind of gestural communication we see in apes today—not language, but a precursor to it. Investigate this diagram for more about the evolution of language (https://openstax.org/r/researchgate).

The array of action-oriented mirror neurons, tool innovation, and language all progressed together in hominin evolution. As tool technology developed, Homo erectus began making distinctive pear-shaped hand axes about 1.6 million years ago. A more intricate form of imitation would have been necessary to teach this sort of tool making to others, corresponding to the emergence of protolanguage. This protolanguage might have been a set of simple one-word utterances corresponding to concepts such as "yes," "no," "here," or "there."

We don't have any hominin brains to examine, but remember that in the human brain, the system of mirror neurons is assumed to be situated near Broca's area, which is associated with human speech. So very likely, protolanguage emerged in the same part of the brain as the ability to imitate. The explosion of innovations in tool making over the past 100,000 years is linked to the emergence of complex human language. While the development of mirror neurons and the ability to learn tool making required biological changes to the brain, Arbib argues that the last step, the emergence of language, was purely cultural.

6.2 Language and the Mind

LEARNING OUTCOMES

By the end of this section, you will be able to:

- Describe the role of language in categorizing items in the natural world.
- Explain the Sapir-Whorf hypothesis.
- Provide at least two examples of linguistic universals.
- Describe how metaphor shapes how we talk about abstract concepts.

As discussed in the previous section, certain cognitive abilities were crucial to the development of language in humans. And reciprocally, once language emerged, it shaped our thoughts and actions in ways that helped our species cooperate, invent, learn, and adapt to the environment. Language must have been a fundamental element in the creation of human culture (singular) and the eventual development into human cultures (plural) as different groups of humans moved into different geographical areas and began adapting to different conditions.

One key advantage of language is that it provides a way of encoding specific information about the environment and sharing that information with others so that it endures over time. If, say, there are snakes in an area, it would certainly be important to distinguish the venomous ones from the harmless ones, so probably there would be separate words for those two categories of snake or at least words for each specific snake so that people could alert each other to the presence of a dangerous one.

This means that early language must have been developed *relative* to environmental conditions. Linguistic anthropologists are interested in the way that language varies across cultures, reflecting different environmental, historical, and sociocultural conditions. This is called **linguistic relativity**.

On the other hand, languages are also constrained by human anatomy and cognitive abilities. Say there were two species of snake in an area, one poisonous and the other harmless, but you could not tell them apart by looking at them. (This is actually an adaptive strategy deployed by harmless animals called adaptive mimicry.) In this case, early humans probably would have had just one word for snake, indicating that sometimes a snake's bite made you sick and sometimes it didn't. As this example shows, the human visual apparatus shapes our understanding of the world, which, in turn, shapes our language.

Consider another example from the natural world—the beetle. There are over 300,000 types of beetles in the world. How many can you name? All of them? Ten of them? Two of them? Outside of written scientific taxonomy, there is no language in the world that contains separate terms for each kind of beetle. This is not only because there are only a few thousand of each type of beetle living in any one environment but also because of limits to the number of terms any person can learn and remember. Our vocabulary is constrained by the limits of human memory.

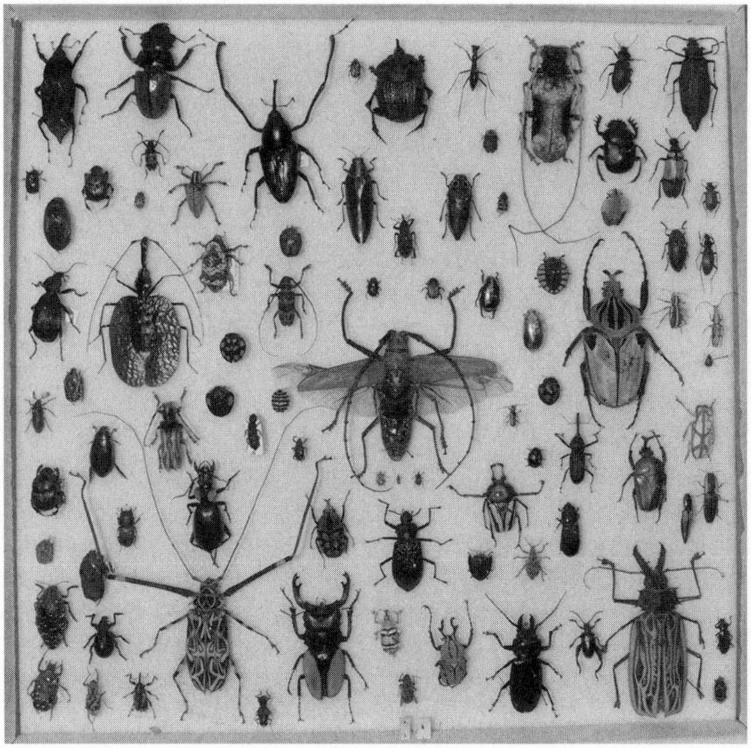

FIGURE 6.10 So many beetles. How many can you name? There are over 300,000 types of beetles in the world. Outside of written scientific taxonomy, no language in the world contains separate terms for each kind of beetle. (credit: "display drawer 3" by Joana Cristovao, Natural History Museum/flickr, CC BY 2.0)

So language is shaped not only by environmental conditions but also by how humans interact with their environments. Our common human anatomy influences our comprehension of the world, and that comprehension is expressed in language. This insight suggests that all languages must have some things in common by virtue of the fact that all humans have the same anatomy and cognitive abilities. Some linguistic anthropologists are interested in discovering these **linguistic universals**.

In the next section, we take a look at some intriguing research on both linguistic relativity and linguistic universals, seeking to better understand how language interacts with our human minds.

Linguistic Relativism and the Sapir-Whorf Hypothesis

As seen in previous chapters, it was lamentably common for scholars in the early 20th century to think of non-Western societies as backward and primitive, incapable of complex, abstract thought. Franz Boas worked hard to disprove these racist notions, seeking to demonstrate the equal sophistication of all peoples and cultures. Boas trained a student named Edward Sapir who was particularly interested in how non-Western languages conveyed forms of complex, abstract thought that were different from the Euro-American habits of thought. Sapir, in turn, trained a student named Benjamin Whorf who further elaborated on this theme in his own research (Ahearn 2017). The result is what we have come to call the "Sapir-Whorf" hypothesis.

The **Sapir-Whorf hypothesis** argues that the particular language you speak influences how you think about reality (Lucy 2001). Thus, different languages encourage different habits of thought. This is an essential tenet of linguistic relativity. Whorf based his argument on a comparison between the Native American language of Hopi and what he called "Standard Average European" (SAE), a broad category of European languages including English. Whorf was interested in how speakers of each language might think differently about time. In English vocabulary, time is divided into units that can be counted. English speakers talk about the number of seconds, minutes, or days before an event or consider the number of months or years since something occurred. In Hopi, according to Whorf, time is conceived as indivisible and enduring, a whole process unfolding. The Hopi talk about the flow of events in a completely different way, a processual way Whorf termed "eventing." Whorf argued that these linguistic features profoundly influenced sociocultural life in each of these two contexts. Holding with the understanding of time as process, Hopi culture emphasized preparation, endurance, and intensity. Coordinating with the SAE expression of time as countable units, Euro-American culture emphasized schedules, accounting, and record keeping. Many people use a calendar to keep track of meetings, appointments, and assignments. Whorf would argue that the English language encourages us to think of time and events in this way, as a spatialized set of boxes to be filled up with discrete objects.

In connection with the Sapir-Whorf hypothesis, it is sometimes said that the "Eskimos" have 400 words for snow. This notion is both problematic and untrue. The first problem is that "Eskimo" is considered a derogatory term by the Inuit and Aleutian peoples to whom it has been applied. And, secondly, the claim turns out to be wrong. Anthropologist Laura Martin (1986, also described in Ahearn 2017) has debunked the myth by documenting that Arctic peoples really have just two root words for talking about snow, one for snow that is falling and the other for snow that is on the ground. They use these roots much as English-speakers would, to talk about snowstorms, snowflakes, snow drifts, and snow melt. The Sapir-Whorf hypothesis is not typically applied to the vocabularies of different cultures anymore.

Recall the earlier example about snakes. We hypothesized that a culture might not distinguish between two species of snakes if those snakes looked identical. But if people gradually came to notice that the poisonous snakes were always found in trees while the harmless snakes were always found on the ground, it is likely that a different term would come to be used for the tree-dwelling kind of snake, the one with the harmful bite. That is to say, even if a culture previously had only one term for snake, the people in that culture could easily understand that there were, in fact, two kinds and would be able to change their language to mark that difference in their vocabulary for future reference. Their vocabulary would not limit their thinking to such a degree that they could not conceive of two different kinds of snake.

Rather than specific vocabulary words, researchers who study linguistic relativity have come to focus on larger abstract topics like space. In languages such as English, when people want to tell someone where a particular object is, they most frequently use language focused on their own bodies. English-speakers say, "You have a bit of arugula on the left side of your mouth" or "Grab the pink top hat on the shelf above you." This way of talking relies on the human body as a point of reference and therefore is relative to the bodies of the speaker and/or hearer. This creates confusion when the speaker is facing the person they are talking to, sometimes prompting someone to say, "No, *my* left, not *your* left!" Steven Levinson has conducted research on languages that do not use the human body to talk about direction at all (2003). Instead, they use the cardinal directions (north, south, east, west) and specific features of their environments (mountains, oceans) to talk about where things are. A speaker of the Australian indigenous language of Guugu Yimithirr might say, "Watch out for the snake just north of your foot!" This way of talking about space is absolute, not relative. Such speakers never have to say "No, *my* north, not *your* north," as there's only one absolute north. Research suggests that these different ways of reckoning give us different kinds of mental maps, such that a Guugu Yimithirr speaker might be better at absolute navigation than an English speaker, and perhaps more adept at finding her way back home if she lost her way.

Linguistic Universals and Folk Taxonomies

While linguistic relativists explore how different linguistic patterns shape different thought patterns (and vice versa), other linguists are interested in how all languages are constrained by our common human biology and in finding universal linguistic patterns. There are specific domains of language that lend themselves particularly well to this kind of inquiry. One of them is color. The reason for this is that color relies directly on our human visual system, invariant across cultures.

And yet there is enormous diversity in the ways that different cultures divide up the spectrum of possible color. Some cultures have hundreds of color terms, while others have only two or three. Researchers Brent Berlin and Paul Kay analyzed the color term systems of 98 languages and found that the diversity of color term systems is governed by one set of rules. All of these color term systems are comprised of a few basic colors with specific colors added to the scheme over time (Kay 2015, Berlin and Kay 1969). The color schemes of all cultures are based on the distinction between black and white (or light and dark). If a culture has only two terms, those two terms will always be black and white. The next most important color is red. If a culture has three color terms, those terms will be black, white, and red. Next comes green and yellow, then blue, then brown, then purple, pink, orange, and gray, always in that order. Berlin and Kay suggested that these rules form a pattern for the way all languages develop over long periods of time. Although the scheme proposed by Berlin and Kay has been revised a little in the past 50 years, the basic tenets have held up pretty well (Haynie and Bowern 2016).

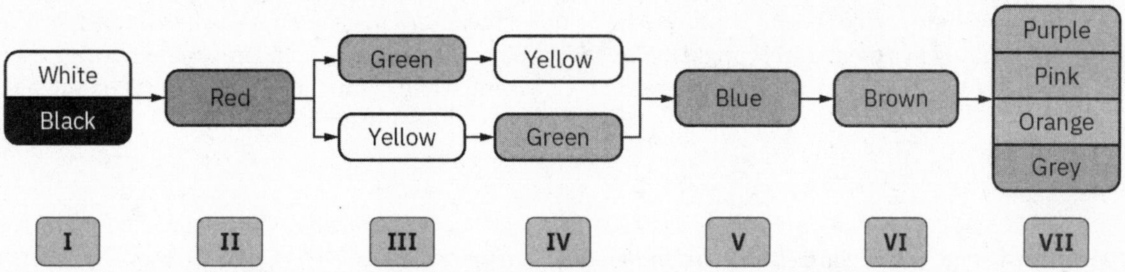

FIGURE 6.11 Berlin and Kay's developmental scheme for the elaboration of color terms. Some cultures only distinguish black from white. When another term emerges, that color is red. After that, green and yellow are added, either one first. Then blue and brown are added, in that order, and then one of these four: purple, pink, orange, or gray. (attribution: Copyright Rice University, OpenStax, under CC BY 4.0 license)

VIDEO

Vox: The Surprising Pattern behind Color Names around the World

Click to view content (https://openstax.org/r/surprisingpattern)

Oddly, though this finding lends very strong support to the notion of linguistic universals, the very same research has also been used to argue for linguistic relativity. Paul Kay later teamed up with another linguist, Willet Kempton, to consider how different color schemes might affect how people "see" color in the environment around them (1984). They presented people with color chips on the spectrum between true blue and true green. They asked subjects how they would group all the colors into two categories. People who spoke languages that had terms for both blue and green drew a more distinct boundary between the two colors than people who had just one word for both blue and green.

Clearly, relativity and universalism are both aspects of human language. Our common biology plays a role in how humans interact with the world, providing regularity to the way all languages categorize not only color but also plants, animals, weather, and other natural phenomena. Researchers who study the systems of categories people use to organize their knowledge of the world have a term for those cultural systems: **folk taxonomies**. The folk taxonomy for any area of human knowledge reflects both human biology and the surrounding environment and sociocultural practices. There are folk taxonomies for plants, animals, clouds, foods, and the cries of babies.

Folk taxonomies are not just vocabulary terms; they frequently structure any kind of distinction that is meaningful within a culture, even those that rely on simple qualifiers like "good" and "bad." One example is death, surely invariant across cultures. Societies all over the world distinguish between a "good" death and a "bad" death. These notions reflect cultural beliefs and values—such as the American notion that a good death is a painless one. Among the Akan peoples of Ghana, a good death is the death of someone who has led a very long life, achieving all of the culturally valued accomplishments in life, such as getting married, having children, accumulating property, and providing support to friends and family members (Adinkra 2020). Imagine a very old great-grandmother surrounded by her many descendants as she lies in her bed, heaving one final breath as she drifts away peacefully into death. That is a good death. A bad death is tragic and violent, the sudden death of a person who has not had the chance to really live a full life. Think of a young person drowning or dying in a traffic accident. That is a very bad death. If someone has had a good death, that person is eligible to become an ancestor if the correct rituals are performed. The body must be washed, publicly mourned, and buried in a beautiful casket in a public cemetery, often with grave goods like tools and money to help the person in the afterlife. Ancestors are important, as they watch over their living relatives, possibly helping them out if called upon through libation or other ritual means. If someone has had a bad death, however, they may become an angry ghost, haunting family members with bad luck. The funeral rites of bad deaths are rushed, minimal, and private in order to avoid commemorating or communicating with the agitated spirit.

Categorization is central to our perceptions, thoughts, actions, and speech. The way humans categorize objects and experiences is limited by the way our brains and bodies work, resulting in linguistic universals like the developmental scheme of color terms. However, the complex meanings associated with cultural categories vary widely, resulting in a great deal of linguistic relativity. Linguistic relativism and universalism are often described as opposite positions, but in fact, they are both essential and complementary features of human language.

Meaning and Metaphor

How are you feeling today? Are you feeling *up* or feeling *down*? If you're feeling *low*, try doing something fun to *lift your spirits*. Take care of yourself so you don't *fall into a depression*.

An old theory suggested that languages are primarily referential; that is, each language contains a set of vocabulary terms that correspond to elements in the natural world. According to this theory, language functions as a mirror of reality. We have seen in the last section, however, that different languages divide up the natural world in different ways, from the natural domains of color and plants to the human domains of life and death. Moreover, humans use language to talk about abstract issues like mood, social relationships, and communication itself. It is fairly easy to use our terms for spatial organization to talk about the location of concrete objects like arugula on somebody's face. But what about more abstract issues? How do we talk about becoming friends with someone? How do we discuss an argument we're making in a term paper? How do we talk about how we're feeling today?

Mood is like color insofar as the human physiology of mood structures a set of near-universal basic categories including happiness, sadness, anger, fear, disgust, and surprise. And yet, because mood occurs on a spectrum, it is divided up in different ways by different cultures. Consider "schadenfreude," a German word combining the roots for "damage" and "joy." Schadenfreude refers to taking pleasure in another's misfortune. There is no equivalent word in English.

We don't just use language to identify the emotions we're feeling. We also talk about the process of developing an emotion, how one mood leads to another, and how we can prevent ourselves from feeling a certain way. These are mysterious and abstract processes. How do we do this? We use metaphor. A **metaphor** is a linguistic idiom where use what we know about something *concrete* to think and talk about something *abstract*. Cognitive linguists George Lakoff and Mark Johnson argue that metaphor is the primary way we create complex meaning in language (1980). In terms of mood, we use our *concrete* language of direction to talk about our *abstract* experience of mood. A positive mood is understood as *up*, while a negative mood is considered *down*. If you're feeling really happy, you might say you're *on top of the world*. If you're really sad, you might say you're *down in the dumps*. In fact, the word for prolonged sadness, *depression*, literally refers to a sunken place or the act of lowering something.

Metaphor is one of those things that you don't notice until you start paying attention to it. And then you realize that it's everywhere: in the way you think about time, number, life, love, physical fitness, work, leisure, sleep, and thought itself, just to name a few highly metaphorical topics. Just about any abstract area of experience is structured by metaphorical thinking. Here are three common metaphors in English, with examples.

LIFE IS A JOURNEY

> He took the wrong *path* in life.
> As you *move ahead*, you should *follow* your dreams.
> When I left home, I came to a *crossroads* in life.
> If you work hard, you'll *arrive* at a sense of accomplishment later in life.

LOVE IS SWEET

> She's my *sweetheart*.

The newlyweds went on a *honeymoon.*
Sugar, would you pass the salt?
Our love was *sweet,* but then it went *sour.*

ARGUMENT IS COMBAT

The candidate launched a personal *attack* against her opponent.
His position on taxes is *indefensible.*
Armed with facts, she won the argument.
His criticism really *hit the mark.*

There are thousands and thousands of metaphors in English. Many abstract domains rely on a combination of various metaphors used to describe different aspects of the experience. You can think of love as sweet (as above) but also as a journey (as in "Will the couple *go forward* together, or will they go their *separate ways*?") or as combat (as in "He *slew me* with his come-hither glance").

Metaphor is found in all human languages. Some specific metaphors, like the directional metaphors used to describe mood, are found in many, many cultures. A study by Esther Afreh (2018) found that the king of Asante (in Ghana) frequently uses metaphorical language in his public speeches, including such familiar ones as "life is a journey," "life is a battle," "ideas are food," "knowing is seeing," and "death is sleep." Though the speeches were delivered in English, Afreh notes that these metaphors also exist in Akan, the local language of the Asante people. Alongside her analysis of the English-language speeches, she notes many proverbs and phrases in Akan that use the same metaphors.

As with our discussion of categorization in the last section, metaphor is both relative and universal. Lakoff and Johnson argue that our common human biology structures our experiences of things like emotion and life. When you're feeling really sad, you might literally feel like lying down, and when you're really happy, you might jump with joy. We may use the notion of a journey to structure our understanding of life, social relationships, and time in general because in our everyday life, we move forward in space to pursue objects and activities.

Sometimes the reasons for cross-cultural similarities are not so directly linked to human biology. English and Chinese have similar metaphorical systems for talking about moral issues. In both languages, the adjective meaning "high" is associated with things that are lofty, noble, or good, while the adjective "low" is used to describe things that are mean, contemptible, or evil (Yu 2016). Alternatively, it is also possible in both languages to describe moral behavior as "straight," while immoral behavior can be termed "crooked."

On the other hand (to deploy a useful metaphor), different cultures do rely on different metaphors to talk about some domains of experience, metaphors that emphasize certain aspects of those abstract topics. Consider the English notion that "time is money." This is a metaphor, pure and simple, but many English speakers believe it to be absolutely true. You can *spend* time, *waste* time, *save* time, and *invest* time. So time does seem like money in capitalist cultures. But time is *not literally* money. Nor is time a journey or a horizontal line in space, though these are common ways of thinking about time in the English language. Time is just time, an abstract idea. Certainly Whorf did not find the Hopi talking about time as money. English speakers think of time in terms of money because they live in a society in which time is *treated as* money, a society that tends to monetize nearly everything, from land and labor to advice, attention, and even body parts like human sperm.

6.3 Language, Community, and Culture

LEARNING OUTCOMES

By the end of this section, you will be able to:

- Explain the role of culture in the acquisition of language.
- Describe how language can form the foundation of sociocultural groups in speech communities.
- Describe how people code-switch among speech communities.

While language is critical to individual human thought, its basic function is to communicate messages in human communities. That is, language is fundamentally social. Through social interaction, humans learn the language of their community. And through language, humans express community identity and coordinate their activities.

Language Acquisition and Language Socialization

Imagine that someone handed you a babbling baby and said to you, "Teach this baby the basic rules and values of our culture." What would you do?

Likely, you'd start by teaching the baby your language. Without language, it's pretty hard to teach rules and values (unless you are a *really* good mime). Luckily, babies come into the world with special cognitive abilities that make them ready to learn language. Most babies undergo a rapid process of language learning between the ages of nine months and three years. Babies proceed through a set of stages that allow them to learn language just by being exposed to surrounding talk. Many scholars study the problem of **language acquisition**, examining precisely how humans manage to learn language in a diversity of sociocultural contexts.

So your babbling baby would probably learn language just by being exposed to it. But what if someone wanted to hasten the process or make sure their baby was particularly excellent with language?

An American would probably interact with the baby in a particular way, sitting the baby on their lap facing them, pointing to objects and asking basic questions in a quiz-like fashion. "See the cookie? Where did the cookie go? In my tummy!" The person might say these types of things while talking in a high-pitched, sing-song voice. Linguists call this type of talk "motherese." In many other cultures, caregivers do not interact with babies in this way. In some cultures, oversimplified "baby talk" is considered detrimental to language learning. The context of language learning might involve a whole host of characters beyond the baby and the caregiver, encompassing all household relatives, neighbors, visitors, and even strangers. Language is not always "taught" to babies, but is often witnessed and overheard. Rather than quizzing her baby American style, a mother in Kaluli society in Papua New Guinea is more likely to sit her baby on her lap facing outward, talking "for" the baby in conversations with siblings (Ochs and Schieffelin [1984] 2001). In West Africa, babies spend large parts of the day wrapped on the backs of their mothers where face-to-face interaction with her is impossible. But they overhear the talk around them all day long, and people frequently engage their attention in brief interactions. In the field of **language socialization**, researchers go beyond the various stages of language learning to focus on the social contexts in which language is acquired. As social contexts shape the way children learn language, language itself becomes a means of learning about sociocultural life.

Whether facing their caregivers or facing out to the social world around them, babies in all cultures learn to be proficient in their languages. And yet, in American culture, the notion persists that language proficiency relies on very precise forms of interaction between caregiver and baby, the American model of motherese. Every culture has specific ideas about language, how it is acquired, how it varies across social groups, how it changes over time, etc. These ideas are termed **language ideologies**. Some of these ideas, like the notion that babies have a special "window" of opportunity for learning language, are supported by linguistic research. Others, however, are challenged by ethnographic and cross-cultural research.

Speech Communities and Code Switching

A ten-year-old girl described one of her stuffed animals as "derpy." Here is a snippet of her conversation with her mother:

Thisbe: Look at his face. He's so derpy.
Jennifer: Derpy? I don't know that word. What does it mean?
Thisbe: Like, kind of stupid. Kind of dumb.
Jennifer: Oh, ok. Like Clover [our dog], when she fell off the couch. Was that derpy?
Thisbe: No, that's not derpy! It's like ... Mom, I just can't explain it to you. You just have to know.

All speakers of a particular language form a hypothetical community, sharing a common grammar and vocabulary, as well as a set of understandings about how language is used in different situations. Within this large group are smaller groups of speakers who use the common language in special ways unique to that group. Anthropologists use the term **speech community** to describe such a group (Muehlmann 2014). Speech communities often have distinctive vocabularies, grammatical forms, and intonation patterns. Using these features appropriately, members of the speech community demonstrate their membership in the group.

The concept of speech community was originally used to describe the distribution of dialects in a language. A **dialect** is a form of language specific to a particular region. For instance, in the Philadelphia metropolitan area, it's common for local people to pronounce the word "water" as "woohder," as if it nearly rhymes with the word "order." It's also common to use the phrase "yooz" for the second-person plural (as in, "Yooz better drink some woohder!"). Linguists William Labov, Sharon Ash, and Charles Boberg famously mapped out these dialectical differences in different regions of the United States (2006). Over time, a dialect can accumulate such unique linguistic features that it develops into a separate language. Indeed, the distinction between a well-developed dialect and a language is largely political. Nation-states may downplay regional differences as mere dialects in order to maintain linguistic unity, while separatist political movements may champion their way of speaking as an entirely different language in order to justify their demands for independence.

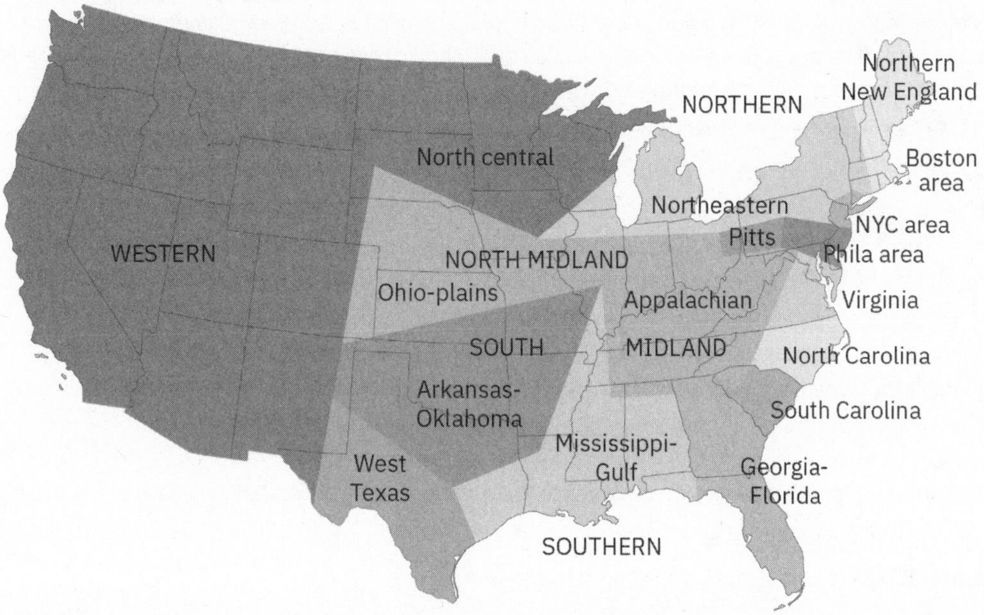

FIGURE 6.12 Map of American dialects. While English is the official language in all areas of the United States, the particular way it is spoken varies from region to region. (attribution: Copyright Rice University, OpenStax, under CC BY 4.0 license)

Other researchers have focused on the speech communities of ethnic groups and immigrants. Researchers use the term **vernacular** to describe dialects that are not necessarily regional but associated with specific social categories, such as groups based on ethnicity, age, or gender. Anthropological research on African American Vernacular English (AAE), Chicano English, and Native American English have all shown how these vernaculars shape distinctive forms of storytelling, arguing, and criticism (Chun and Lo 2015). Rather than seeing ethnic vernaculars as "incorrect" forms of English, researchers demonstrate how vernaculars like AAE are highly structured linguistic systems with regular grammatical patterns and innovative vocabularies (Labov 1972a). In formal settings like American classrooms and courtrooms, these alternative ways of using English are too often stigmatized as lazy, unintelligent, or just plain wrong. Believing their own English to be the "correct" form, authority figures often forbid the use of alternative vernaculars of English and refuse to engage in any effort to understand those forms.

More recent research on vernaculars has explored how speakers maneuver among the styles of language they encounter in their daily lives, engaging in various languages, dialects, vernaculars, and other elements of style. We all use a variety of linguistic styles, and many speak more than one language. Addressing different audiences, U.S. President Barack Obama used linguistic strategies to "Whiten," "Blacken," "Americanize," and "Christianize" his public identity, thus subverting racial stereotypes and indicating his membership in a diversity of communities (Alim and Smitherman 2012). In parts of the world that were previously colonized by Europeans, European languages have been maintained as the formal language of government and education even as most people speak local languages in their everyday interactions with kin, neighbors, merchants, and other community members. In these postcolonial contexts, people tack back and forth between various styles of their local languages as well as shifting between the local language and the European one. Such strategic maneuvering among linguistic styles, called **code-switching**, is done by people in many difference contexts.

For many people, the style of language spoken in elite settings such as schools and government institutions has the effect of disempowering and marginalizing them. Linguistic anthropologists examine how vernaculars associated with elite and professional groups become a means of in-group solidarity and out-group exclusion. Anthropologist and lawyer Elizabeth Mertz (2007) conducted participant observation in first-year classes at several American law schools, looking at how law students are taught to "think like a lawyer." Using a version of the Socratic method, law professors teach their students to set aside the moral and emotional elements of cases to view them purely as texts subject to abstract, professional analysis. The ability to master the linguistic maneuvering and arcane vocabulary of this form of analysis becomes a prerequisite for becoming a lawyer. The American justice system is thus dominated by people who are trained to set aside humanistic concerns in favor of textual authority and manipulation. Mertz's study shows how people are socialized by language throughout their lives, not just in childhood. And it alerts us to the way that language can be used to elevate the learned perspectives of elites, dismissing the moral and emotional perspectives of others.

6.4 Performativity and Ritual

LEARNING OUTCOMES

By the end of this section, you will be able to:

- Provide examples of the performative function of speech acts.
- Describe how ritual language can be performative.
- Identify the informal ways that people "talk back" to formal speech.

The Performativity of Language: Speaking as Action

Consider the following pairs of sentences. What are the differences between the two sentences in each case?

1. Boris and Natasha are married.
2. Boris and Natasha, I now pronounce you husband and wife.

1. Natasha: Boris lost his job.
2. Natasha: Boris, you're fired!

1. Boris: Natasha, I ate the last pickle.
2. Boris: Natasha, I apologize for eating the last pickle.

In all the above pairs, the first sentence is a report about an event. The second sentence makes an event happen. In the sentences about the pickle, the second sentence does not make the pickle disappear, but it does create an apology for that action, hopefully altering the consequences of the pickle-eating. In the previous section, we explored how we use language to think and reason about the world around us. This is an essential function of language, but it is not the only one. We also use language to *do* things—that is, to perform actions in the world.

Way back in the 1930s, Bronislaw Malinowski explored how people use language in culturally specific ways to play an active part in their societies (Duranti 2012). Malinowski described how the people of the Trobriand Islands used magical language to compel the growth of yams, bananas, taro, and palms in their carefully cultivated gardens. Magical spells, like all ritual language, aim at making something happen through the special manipulation of public speech. We see the same use of language in other ritual settings like marriages and naming ceremonies. The plot of many a Hollywood romantic comedy hinges on the moment the partners say "I do" and the officiant pronounces them married. In American marriage ceremonies, it is clear that ritual language is the tool that marries people—not the rings, or the pageantry, or the blessings of family and friends, or any other aspect of the ritual.

In his influential book *How to Do Things with Words* (1962), philosopher of language J.L. Austin coined a term for action-oriented language: performatives. The most obvious performatives use phrases like "I pronounce," "I order," "I promise," "I warn," or "I appoint." Sentences that begin with these phrases are explicitly uttered with the intention of doing something through the act of speaking. As he dug deeper into the performative function of language, however, Austin realized that performatives are not so much a separate category of utterances but an aspect of most of the things we say. Even when people are making a simple descriptive statement, they are saying it for a reason. The power of speech to make things happen is called **performativity**. Consider the following sentences:

The exam is next week.
The dog is pawing on the door.

The above sentences are statements about an event or situation. However, if a professor announces to the class, "The exam is next week," this is not merely an observation, but a warning—a cue to students to study in preparation for the upcoming exam. And if someone tells their roommate, "The dog is pawing on the door," they are essentially telling that person to let the dog out.

Like metaphor, performativity is one of those aspects of language that permeates everyday speech. Once you learn about it, you recognize performativity in just about everything you say. Spend a few hours paying attention to each utterance as you go about your activities. You'll find that you rarely use language to merely describe what's going on. You speak in order to generate a response or result, even when you just say "Hi."

The Performativity of Ritual Language

Just as Malinowski studied the special language used in garden magic among the Trobrianders, many contemporary linguistic anthropologists study the role of performative language in various ritual settings. In a recent article, Patience Epps and Danilo Paiva Ramos examine the performance of **incantations** among the Indigenous Hup community of the northwest Amazon (Epps and Ramos 2020). An incantation is a patterned set of phrases or sentences used to compel a magical result. Among the Hup, incantations are used by elders for protection, healing, and causing harm. While Epps and Ramos were conducting fieldwork in the area, Hup elders expressed concerns that the young men in the village were not learning the repertoire of important incantations properly, thus endangering the health and safety of the community. The elders invited Epps and Ramos to write down their incantations for healing and protection in order to preserve them for future generations. Epps and Ramos documented and analyzed these incantations in consultation with Hup elders.

In the article, Epps and Ramos analyze an incantation used by the Hup to protect travelers on paths through the rain forest. This incantation is recited by an elder before a group of Hup people embark on a journey. After providing the original text and its English translation, Epps and Ramos describe the incantation's structure and poetic features, including the use of metaphor and repetition of phrases. As a whole, the incantation lists various dangers and helpful entities and enacts certain magical practices through the speech itself. At the beginning of the incantation, the elder states that he is enclosing the entire path in a protective "canoe," much as a traveler on a river would ride in a canoe. This canoe is named after a particular snake, the mussurana snake (*Clelia clelia*), a constrictor snake that eats other snakes and is immune to their venom. Thus, the incantation is creating a metaphorical shield of protection around the travelers, making them safe from venomous snakebites. In the second section of the incantation, the elder lists all classes and subtypes of snakes that might be encountered in the rain forest, asserting a kind of taxonomic mastery over the snakes. Summoning the snakes one by one, he tells of lining them up, sitting them down, and feeding them sticky coca and tobacco. The snakes then sit quietly, their jaws stuck together by the sticky substance so that they are unable to bite anyone. The incantation goes on to deal with several other malevolent entities and engage with beneficial entities to help the travelers in their journey.

Informal Back-Talk: Teasing, Grumbling, and Gossip

Linguistic anthropologists most frequently rely on long periods of fieldwork, living in the communities they study and witnessing and even participating in ritual events where performative language is deployed. Such events include protection and healing magic, but also naming ceremonies, puberty rites, weddings, funerals, and other rituals that mark the passage of persons from one social status to another. Anthropologists term such rituals "rites of passage" (discussed in detail in Anthropology of Food). At such ritual events, elders or religious specialists are called upon to perform the ritual language necessary to publicly move persons from the previous category to the new one.

Naming ceremonies are a great example of the power of performative language in rites of passage. In many

West African societies, a baby is not considered a true person until they have been publicly named by an elder or religious official in a naming ceremony performed a certain number of days after the baby is born. Extended family and friends attend the ceremony as markers of their relationship to the baby. Guests bring gifts such as rice and cloth for the baby, and they are rewarded for their attendance with prepared food and kola nuts.

During his fieldwork in southeastern Senegal, linguistic anthropologist Nicholas Sweet witnessed the naming ceremony for a baby in a Pular-speaking village (2019). When the family were gathered in the compound of the baby's father, the imam rose, faced east, gave the blessings of the prophet, and then performed the naming of the baby girl (in Arabic, English translation below):

In the name of God, the gracious and the compassionate
O Allah, send blessings on our master Muhammad
O Allah, send blessings on our master Muhammad
O Allah, send blessings on our master Muhammad
The name of the child has come here, her mother and her father have named her Aissatou
The name of the child has come here, her mother and her father have named her Aissatou
This is what was written on the tablet of Allah
May God grant her blessings

While carefully recording the formal performative language so important to this naming ceremony, Sweet was also attuned to the more informal kinds of language that surrounded the main action. For instance, just before the imam's performance, some friends of the family were gathered around the baby, remarking on her beauty. As a way of showing their admiration, some of the men joked and teased one another about the prospect of marrying her someday. Other relatives teased the baby's parents with demands for kola nuts and other food. As dramatically performative as the official naming was, this informal language was also performative, providing a way for guests to socially configure their various relationships to the new person in their community.

Someone important had been left out of the ceremony—the great-aunt of the baby, also named Aissatou. As the baby was her namesake, Auntie Aissatou had been invited and should have been a featured guest at the ceremony. But when the time came to perform the ceremony, she had not arrived yet, and so they went on without her. Afterward, as guests were making their way home, they crossed paths with Auntie Aissatou, who was just then on her way to the event. Realizing that the naming had already been performed, she complained that she had been waiting for someone to fetch her and bring her to the ceremony. Auntie Aissatou was angry that she had missed the ceremony as well as the gifts distributed afterward.

Wrapping a scarf around her head in imitation of an imam, Auntie Aissatou continued on to the compound of the baby's father. Striding ceremoniously into the compound, she addressed a number of elders still gathered there. In a parody of the official naming performance, she faced east, delivered the blessings of the prophet, and then announced:

The name of the child has come here. It is Buubu Nooge (Trash Owl).

The audience of relatives erupted in laughter but also protest, interrupting Auntie Aissatou to correct her with the baby's true given name. But Auntie Aissatou persisted, saying over and over again that the baby's name had come and it was "Trash Owl."

Why Trash Owl? In this community, it is believed that witches turn themselves into owls when they fly through the night. "Trash" seemed to refer to the joke gifts of garbage (broken flip-flops, an old sock) in a small gourd that Auntie Aissatou presented in lieu of the usual baby gifts of food, cloth, and soap.

In the days following the naming ceremony, the teasing name for the baby became a running joke in the community, especially among people who had not been invited to the ceremony but felt that they should have been. In order to quash the teasing nickname, the baby's family was compelled to make a number of visits around the community with appeasing gifts of kola in an effort to get everyone to recognize the baby's proper name. Once Auntie Aissatou and the others had received their visits and kola, they abandoned the name Trash Owl, recognizing the baby as Aissatou, the namesake of Auntie Aissatou.

This incident illustrates the power of parody and gossip to steal performative power from the authoritative realm of formal speech, giving excluded and marginalized people a way to "talk back" to authority. There are many ways of doing this. Often, audiences to formal speech will deliberately misunderstand or creatively interpret the proclamations of authority figures.

6.5 Language and Power

LEARNING OUTCOMES

By the end of this section, you will be able to:

- Explain how language can operate as a gendered form of power.
- Identify how racial categories and bias are expressed through linguistic practices.
- Describe strategies used by communities to revive their dormant languages.

Gender and Language

In 2018, the word "mansplaining" was added to the Merriam-Webster dictionary. The word is defined as "what occurs when a man talks condescendingly to someone (especially a woman) about something he has incomplete knowledge of, with the mistaken assumption that he knows more about it than the person he's talking to does" ("Words We're Watching" 2018).

The word was inspired by an article written in 2008 by the feminist blogger Rebecca Solnit. In the article "Men Explain Things to Me," Solnit described an incident at a party in which she mentioned to a man that she had recently written a book about a particular photographer. Immediately, the man interrupted to inform her about a *very important* book that just came out about that same photographer, a book he had read about in *The New York Times*. After the man had described the book in great detail, Solnit's friend finally intervened to say that the book he was talking about was, in fact, written by Solnit. In the wake of Solnit's article, other women writers described similar experiences in their workplaces, schools, and relationships, and the whole phenomenon came to be called "mansplaining."

FIGURE 6.13 Rebecca Solnit, the author of the article "Men Explain Things to Me". The term "mansplaining" has become a well discussed topic in the years since she introduced the term. (credit: "Rebecca Solnit" by Charles Kremenak/Wikimedia Commons, CC BY 2.5)

Have you ever witnessed mansplaining? Have you ever mansplained to someone? Embedded in the very term is a notion about gender and language. The idea is that men and women have different styles of speech, styles that reflect and reinforce inequality between genders.

In recent years, many writers have pushed back against the term "mansplaining," arguing that *all* men do not *always* speak this way to *all* women. Some argue that many men are much more respectful and sensitive to the dynamics of power in their conversations with women. Some argue that privileged White women tend to speak in a mansplaining way to male waiters and salespersons or to people of color more generally. Others suggest that older people speak in a condescending way to younger people, or vice versa.

Have you ever become annoyed with a friend or relative who repeatedly interrupts you? Have you ever noticed how some people tend to end their sentences with rising intonation, making everything they say sound like a question? How about a person who ignores what you say but then rephrases your idea and takes credit for it? Many people associate these ways of speaking with gender, the way men speak or the way women speak. As noted in the discussion of language acquisition, every culture has ideas about how language operates, called language ideologies. The idea that American men and American women have distinctive styles of speech is a language ideology. Whether it is true or not is a question for linguistic research, but this idea has become a widespread way of thinking about gender, power, and language in American culture.

In the 1970s, linguists inspired by the women's movement turned their attention to the way gender shapes different patterns of speech. In her influential book *Language and Woman's Place* (1975), Robin Lakoff argues that women and men are socialized to speak in distinctive ways that empower men and subordinate women. Lakoff describes women's speech as uncertain, excessively polite, and full of hedges, emotional language, euphemism, and tag questions ("Don't you think?"). Other linguistic researchers have found that men tend to interrupt women far more than vice versa, even when the women speaking are doctors and the men are their patients (Zimmerman and West 1975, West 1998).

Building on this research, Deborah Tannen generalized beyond speech patterns to describe two entirely different communicative subcultures for American men and American women (1990). When men and women speak to one another, Tannen argues, they are speaking cross-culturally, deploying different motivations and expectations for talk. Men engage in conversation to assert their status in a social hierarchy, while women are more interested in building solidarity through social connection. Men authoritatively report information *to* their interlocutors, while women engage in conversational rapport *with* their interlocutors. In popular media, differences in the speech styles of men and women are frequently linked to purported differences in specific parts of male and female brains, such the corpus callosum, the amygdala, and the hippocampus. In this way, gendered patterns of speaking are naturalized as biological.

Like the pushback against the term "mansplaining," researchers have begun to challenge the view that women and men are embedded in different linguistic subcultures with different patterns of speech, motivation, and interpretation. Psychologist Janet Hyde conducted a meta-analysis of hundreds of quantitative studies to see if widespread notions about gender and language were actually borne out by linguistic data (2005). Along with notions of power, Hyde was interested in testing the idea that women are chattier and more deferential than men. Focusing on studies of children, Hyde found that boys and girls exhibited no differences at all in reading comprehension, verbal reasoning, and vocabulary. The tendency for boys to interrupt or speak assertively was only very slightly higher than for girls. The girls' tendency toward self-disclosure and cooperation with their conversation partners was only slightly higher than for boys. The only significant differences Hyde found were in smiling and correct spelling (girls did more of both).

How do we reconcile research demonstrating differences in the way men and women talk with data that suggests very little difference in the speech patterns of girls and boys? One could argue that children have not been entirely socialized into their assigned gender category. Perhaps the discrepancy suggests that gendered ways of speaking are cultural, not biological, and that, for children, the most intense period of socialization is yet to come in adolescence.

Moreover, ethnographic research by linguistic anthropologists shows that patterns of speech associated with men and women are culturally relative. Reversing the American stereotypes, anthropologists working in Madagascar and New Guinea have found that women are expected to speak in a more confrontational and argumentative style, while men are associated with more cooperative, euphemistic, and ceremonial speech (Keenan [Ochs] 1974, Kulick 1992, both cited in Ahearn 2017).

So both quantitative and ethnographic research overturn the notion that women and men are biologically engineered to use language in different ways. That leaves us with the conclusion that any differences in the ways men and women talk are entirely cultural. Literary scholar Judith Butler argues that gender identities are not biological but are performed through language and other cultural practices, particularly those centered on the body (1988). So when men and women speak in certain ways, they are socially performing their gender identities, whether consciously or unconsciously. Moreover, through their linguistic performances, people enact their own versions of gender in complicated ways that transcend the neat dichotomy of male and female. You probably have a language ideology that tells you how men and women speak in your culture, but do you *always* speak in the style associated with your assigned gender category? Nobody does. And some people rarely do. As these contradictory performances build up over time, the very notion of gender can change.

PROFILES IN ANTHROPOLOGY

Kira Hall
1962-

Area of Anthropology: Kira Hall's (https://openstax.org/r/colorado) work is situated at the intersection of sociolinguistics and linguistic anthropology. In graduate school, she studied with Robin Lakoff in the linguistics department at the University of California–Berkeley, earning her PhD there in 1995. For her dissertation, she examined the linguistic strategies of Hindi-speaking *hijras* in Banaras, India. Hijras are members of a third-gender group in many Indian communities. Most hijras were raised as boys and later adopted the intersex behaviors and language of the hijra identity. Hall analyzed how hijras navigated aspects of gender embedded in Hindi, such as certain verbs and adjectives that are marked as feminine or masculine. She showed how hijras alternate between these gendered forms, code-switching as a reflection of their own ambiguous identities. She explored how hijras use obscene forms of language to shame people into giving them money. She showed how they had developed their own secret language as a way of communicating with one another, signaling their identity to others, and excluding non-hijras from understanding their conversations.

Accomplishments in the Field: Reflecting her work at the boundaries of linguistics and anthropology, Hall has held academic positions in the anthropology department at Yale University and the linguistics department of Stanford University. Currently, she is professor of linguistics at the University of Colorado at Boulder, with a joint appointment in the anthropology department. She is also director of the Program in Culture, Language, and Social Practice at UC-Boulder. Since 2019, she has served as the president of the Society for Linguistic Anthropology of the American Anthropological Association.

Importance of Their Work: Hall's work highlights how language operates within hierarchies of gender, sexuality, and socioeconomic class. In addition to her work on hijras, she has published articles on language and sociality in autism, female mass hysteria in upstate New York, and Donald Trump's use of gesture and derisive humor in the 2016 Republican Party primaries.

Race and Ethnicity

On many government forms, people are asked to identify their "race." Forms in the United States often include five categories: Black, White, Asian, American Indian/Alaska Native, and Native Hawaiian/Other Pacific Islander. The category "Hispanic or Latino" is often listed as an ethnicity rather than a race. On the 2020 U.S. Census, people were presented with 14 racial categories to choose from: White, Black or African American, American Indian or Alaska Native, Chinese, Filipino, Asian Indian, Vietnamese, Korean, Japanese, Other Asian, Native Hawai'ian, Samoan, Chamorro, and Other Pacific Islander. Again, "Hispanic, Latino, or Spanish" was listed as a question of "origin." Even with so many options, many Americans still could not find a category that represented their racial or ethnic identity.

As you'll remember from earlier chapters in this text, race is not biological. There is no accurate way to divide up the gradual spectrum of human biological variation, meaning that biological categories of race are entirely imaginary. However, we also know that social categories of race are very powerful tools of discrimination, subordination, solidarity, and affirmative action. Earlier in this chapter, we studied how sets of categories, "folk taxonomies," are embedded in language. We saw how different cultures divide up the natural world differently.

Likewise, race and ethnicity are folk taxonomies, embedded in language and organizing the social world into a neat set of groups. These categories are real insofar as they have shaped the structure of our society, advantaging some groups and disadvantaging others. And they are real insofar as they shape our thoughts and actions and even our subconscious habits and tendencies.

Like gender, race and ethnicity are performed in language. We use language in conscious and unconscious ways to express racial and ethnic belonging as well as exclusion. Take the use of Spanish catchphrases by Americans who do not speak Spanish. Many Americans intend to be jokey and fun by using Spanish phrases such as "hasta la vista!" and "no problemo" as well as deliberately incorrect ones such as "buenos nachos" and "hasta la bye bye!" Anthropologist Jane Hill found that middle-class, college-educated White Americans were most likely (among other Americans) to use this "mock Spanish" (2008). People who use these phrases consider them harmless and even respectful, while Spanish speakers are often insulted by the association of Spanish with silliness. Hill argues that such phrases are only funny because they covertly draw from stereotypes of Spanish speakers as foolish, lazy, and inept.

Similar arguments about cultural appropriation and stereotyping can be made about the use of Black vernacular speech by White Americans. In the United States, a variety of English called African American English (AAE), or African American Vernacular English, is spoken by many people in predominantly Black communities. With the widespread popularity of Black culture, many White Americans have picked up phrases and grammatical features of AAE while knowing very little about the vernacular and the people who speak it as their primary language. To many Americans, AAE is just imperfect English (it is not, as we'll see in a moment). So what are White people signaling when they say things like "chillin'," "lit," "on fleek," "aa'ight" (for "alright"), "ima" (for "I'm going to") and "Yasss, Queen!" Does the use of this language convey respect for the communities associated with Black vernacular English? Or does it demean and subordinate Black Americans who speak AAE?

People who use mock Spanish and mock AAE typically do not mean to insult anyone. The problem is not one of intent, but of context. In American culture, most middle-class White people speak forms of English considered standard or mainstream (Lippi-Green 2012). In fact, Standard American English (SAE) is historically based on the language of Anglo American immigrants. The adoption of White Anglo-English has always been considered critical to successful assimilation by minority and immigrant groups. Success at complete assimilation is often measured by the ability to speak SAE without an accent. But SAE is not speaking "without an accent." SAE *is* an accent—the accent of White people whose ancestors emigrated from the British Isles.

SAE is the dominant language of American public spaces, including schools, workplaces, government, and media. People who speak SAE without effort or accent can speak freely in these spaces, knowing that their language will be understood and respected. Americans whose primary language is Spanish or AAE often struggle to be understood and taken seriously in American public life. Given this context, it can seem disrespectful for White Americans to appropriate Spanish and AAE as tools of humor while denigrating and marginalizing the actual speakers of these languages.

The issue is further complicated by the widespread and persistent notion among White Americans (and many Black Americans too) that AAE is not a language at all, but merely a hodgepodge of slang and bad grammar. This view is simply wrong, another language ideology that has no basis in fact. AAE is a rule-governed form of English with its own regular system of sounds, grammar, and vocabulary (Labov 1972b). For historical reasons, AAE shares many features with the English spoken by White southerners in the United States as well as working-class Cockney English from London (Ahearn 2017). Rooted in historical experiences of slavery and segregation, Black Americans have developed their own distinctive set of innovative linguistic features to supplement the more basic structure of American English. Consider the following three sentences:

He is angry.
He angry.
He be angry.

The first sentence is SAE, and the second and third are AAE alternatives. In SAE, this conjugation of the verb "to be" describes a situation happening in the present. But the SAE present tense of "to be" is a bit vague, as it can mean "right now, this very minute" or a more ongoing situation, perhaps describing a person who is frequently or enduringly angry. AAE helpfully distinguishes between these two possibilities. "He angry" means angry "right now," whereas "He be angry" indicates a more ongoing situation. In linguistic terminology, the second example is called "copula deletion" and the third is called "the habitual be." Both are used in regular ways to indicate the difference between momentary and enduring conditions.

AAE is governed by many more rules and features that provide its speakers with expressive possibilities not available to speakers of SAE. In other words, AAE is not only a rule-bound vernacular; it's a more developed and complex form of English. Linguists have been trying to convey this message to the American public since the 1970s (Labov 1972a). Read more about AAE at the Anti-Racism Daily website (https://openstax.org/r/Anti-Racism).

Rather than recognizing the innovative contributions of vernaculars like AAE, language policy in the United States stigmatizes non-SAE vernaculars as "bad English" spoken by uneducated and unintelligent people. Linguist John Baugh calls this "linguistic profiling" (2003). With colleagues Thomas Purnell and William Idsardi, Baugh (1999) compared the response of California landlords to apartment inquiries spoken in SAE, AAE, and Chicano-American English (CAE). In Woodside, California, landlords responded to SAE inquiries 70.1 percent of the time. Inquiries in AAE received responses only 21.8 percent of the time and CAE inquiries only 28.7 percent of the time. Research in American schools and courtrooms corroborates the discriminatory effects of linguistic profiling on access to housing, education, and justice.

The use of language to discriminate and marginalize is certainly not limited to American English. Elites in many cultures define their own way of speaking as "correct" and "official," using linguistic practices in public spaces to disempower other groups based on class, race, ethnicity, gender, and sexuality. How can people respond to these forms of linguistic marginalization? For many upwardly mobile speakers of "nonstandard" vernaculars and languages, the process of becoming successful has involved the abandonment of their primary way of speaking in favor of standard, elite forms of language privileged in public discourses. But there is another alternative. As speakers of nonstandard vernaculars and languages move into public discourses, they can hold on to their primary languages, code-switching from context to context. Some language activists celebrate the genius of their "home" languages and work to nurture and revive them, as we will see in the next section.

Can speakers of dominant languages contribute to the process of celebrating and revitalizing marginalized languages? Is it *always* insulting or racist for speakers of a dominant language to use phrases from another vernacular or language? Some people think so. Certainly it is harmful to use phrases that reference negative stereotypes (even indirectly). But what if your limited use of a few phrases can help you communicate with someone from a different background? What if SAE speakers started quoting Spanish or AAE in ways that highlight positive aspects of those speech communities? What if White people started learning AAE in order to publicize the genius and complexity of this American vernacular? What if you learn another language or vernacular in order to subvert the forces of cultural segregation in your own society? There are no easy answers to such questions.

Endangered Languages: Repression and Revival

In 1993, a Wampanoag (https://openstax.org/r/tribalpedia) woman living on a reservation in Cape Cod, Massachusetts, had a mysterious dream, recurring on three consecutive nights (Feldman 2001). In the dream, a circle of Wampanoag were singing in a language she did not understand. When she woke, words of the language stuck with her, and she longed to find out what they meant. Were these words of Wôpanâak, the language of her ancestors? Wôpanâak had died out in the mid-1800s.

The woman was Jessie Little Doe Baird, a social worker and mother of five. Haunted by those words, she began reading through documents from the 1600s written in Wôpanâak, including letters, deeds to property, and the earliest translation of the Bible printed in the Western hemisphere (Sukiennik 2001). Though frustrated in her efforts to find the meaning of her dream words, she developed a passion for the language of her ancestors and began working with local Wampanoag communities to reclaim their common language of Wôpanâak. Community response was enthusiastic. Committed to the project, Baird went to MIT to study linguistics, earning a master's degree. Based on her survey of Wôpanâak documents, she wrote a dictionary and began teaching Wampanoag students to speak the language (https://openstax.org/r/Women_of_the_Century).

By learning their ancestral language, Baird and her students found themselves reconnecting with Wampanoag culture in unexpected ways. The grammar of Wôpanâak, for instance, puts the speaker at the end of the sentence rather than the beginning. Whereas English speakers would say “I see you,” Wôpanâak speakers would say something like “You are seen by me.” Baird suggests that this word order highlights the value of the community over the individual, putting awareness of the other ahead of the self. Wôpanâak displays alternative logic in the formulation of nouns as well. For instance, in English, animal names reveal little or nothing at all about the animal. The words “cat,” “mouse,” and “ant” are based on arbitrary sounds that convey no information about their referents. In Wôpanâak, however, animal names frequently contain syllables that refer to the animal’s size, movement, and behavior. The word for “ant,” for instance, incorporates syllables communicating that the animal moves about, does not walk on two legs, and puts things away.

By now, you know that forms of cognition and culture are embedded in language. The languages of the world encode diverse experiences of time, space, life, death, color, emotions, and more. A language serves as a form of oral documentation of the surrounding environment, a survey of the flora, fauna, topography, and climate of an area. Forms of cultural wisdom are preserved in the stories and proverbs of a language. History is recorded in epic tales and legends. Language can be essential to maintaining cultural identity, affirming the common history and values of a people while providing them with a distinctive way of communicating with one another.

Among the seven thousand languages spoken in the world today, roughly 40 percent of them are in danger of dying out in the next hundred years. A language is considered dead when it is no longer spoken by any living person. Wôpanâak was once considered a dead language. Some linguists argue that no language should ever really be considered “dead,” however, and prefer the terms “dormant” or “sleeping.” So long as there are written or audio records of a language, it can come to life again, a process called **language revitalization**. Returning to a language that has become dormant or endangered, community members can develop strategic programs to spread, nurture, and modernize the language, ensuring it has a future for generations to come.

Languages generally become endangered or dormant through processes of colonialism and imperialism. In North America, as Native Americans were forcibly removed from their lands and confined to reservations in the 1800s, they were compelled to send their children to boarding schools where they were forbidden to speak their Native languages or practice their Native cultures. As foreign settlers seized lands in Australia, New Zealand, and Hawaii, they established similar schools, aimed at assimilating Indigenous children by stamping out their language and culture. Elsewhere, more gradual processes of endangerment can occur when a new language offers opportunities for employment and trade only available to speakers of that language. Parents may encourage their children to learn the new language in order to take advantage of these opportunities, and children may come to reject their own language as a backward language of old people.

Many, many languages have risen from dead or comatose states, among them Cornish, Hawaiian, Hebrew, Scots-Gaelic, the Ainu language of Japan, the Indigenous Australian language of Barngarla, the Indigenous New Zealand language of the Māori people, and the Native American languages of the Navaho and Blackfoot peoples. Often, as with Wôpanâak, the impetus for language revival comes from energetic community members who feel the loss of their language as a threat to their cultural survival. These concerned people create programs to document the language and teach it to children and adults. They establish contexts where the language is spoken routinely and exclusively. Sometimes they work with linguists to develop these programs.

The most successful of these revitalization strategies are immersion schools and master-apprentice programs. In the early 1980s, Māori language activists developed full-immersion preschools, called *Te Kōhanga Reo*, or “language nests” (King 2018). In these nests, very young children are taught language and culture by Māori elders—grandmothers and grandfathers in the community. Native Hawaiians have developed a similar program of language nests, called *Pūnana Leo*. Early on, some parents worried that children in immersion schools would not learn the dominant national language well enough to be successful in later life, but research has shown that such children do just as well or better in later classroom performance and standardized testing. Many language revitalization projects combine early immersion with later bilingual education (Hinton 2011, 2018). The Navaho Immersion School in Arizona provides immersion education for the first three years of schooling and then introduces English as the medium of instruction through grade seven. From grades eight to twelve, children are taught in Navaho half the time and English the other half.

FIGURE 6.14 Sign in front of a full-immersion school in Seatoun, New Zealand. All classes are held in the Māori language. (credit: "Te Kura Kaupapa Maori O Nga Mokopuna" by Tom Law/flickr, CC BY 2.0)

One of the challenges of school-based revitalization programs is finding enough adults sufficiently proficient in the language to teach it to children. Among the strategies of language revitalization that target adult learners is the master-apprentice approach. The original Master-Apprentice Language Learning Program was founded in California by the Advocates for Indigenous California Language Survival (Hinton 2018). The strategy has since spread all over the world. In these programs, a proficient speaker and a motivated learner spend 20 hours a week together, using the target language plus gestures and other nonverbal communication to engage in various activities.

When successful, language revitalization can empower individuals and energize communities. Learning their heritage language, people come to understand the distinctive genius and complexity of their culture while preserving a crucial means of transmitting that culture across generations.

MINI-FIELDWORK ACTIVITY

Dispute Analysis

Choose a friend, relative, or acquaintance with whom you might disagree on a particular issue. Suggested issues might include musical taste, what makes a good restaurant, how to behave on a date, the best form of physical exercise, or anything else you feel comfortable talking about but might disagree on. Ask the person if they would consent to being recorded for an anonymous fieldwork exercise. If so, record a 5-to-10-minute conversation with that person in which you discuss the issue. Then, review the conversation. What seem to be the goals of the two interlocutors? What is the pattern of turn taking? What truth or knowledge claims are made by each speaker, and what are the bases of those claims? How is authority constructed and challenged? How does each one respond to the assertions of the other? How does the conversation turn out in the end?

Suggested Readings

Ahearn, Laura. 2017. *Living Language: An Introduction to Linguistic Anthropology.* 2nd ed. Chichester, West Sussex, UK; Malden, MA: Wiley-Blackwell.

Duranti, Alessandro. 1997. *Linguistic Anthropology.* Cambridge, UK: Cambridge University Press.

Key Terms

code-switching the practice of tacking back and forth between various linguistic styles depending on contexts and interlocutors.

communication the transfer of information from a sender to a receiver; can be voluntary or involuntary, simple or complex.

dialect a form of language specific to a particular region.

folk taxonomies systems of categories that people use to organize their knowledge of the world.

FOXP2 a gene on chromosome number seven that is found in many vertebrates; sometimes called "the language gene" because the human mutation seems to be associated with language.

incantation a patterned set of phrases or sentences used to compel a magical result.

language a complex, systematized form of communication involving the use of vocal or gestural units (words or signs) that can be combined and recombined in larger structures (sentences) that can convey an infinite array of complex meanings.

language acquisition the process of learning a language.

language ideologies specific ideas about language that are widespread in a culture, including how language is acquired, how it varies across social groups, how it changes over time, etc.

language revitalization the process of reviving an endangered or dormant language using strategies such as immersion schools and master-apprentice programs.

language socialization the social contexts in which language is learned as well as the role of language in social learning.

linguistic relativity the way that language varies across cultures, reflecting different environmental, historical, and sociocultural conditions.

linguistic universals common elements found in all human languages, attributable to human anatomy, perception, and cognition.

metaphor a linguistic idiom using something *concrete* to think and talk about something more *abstract*.

mirror neurons special brain cells that seem to enable mimicry.

naming ceremony a public ritual that officially grants personhood by bestowing a name.

performativity the functional power of language to make things happen.

protolanguage a very simple set of gestures or utterances that may have preceded the development of human language.

Sapir-Whorf hypothesis the theory that the particular language you speak influences how you think about reality.

speech community a community of speakers sharing a common grammar and vocabulary, as well as a set of understandings about how language is used in different situations.

vernacular dialects that are not necessarily regional but associated with specific social categories such as groups based on ethnicity, age, or gender.

Summary

Language and culture are closely entwined in the evolutionary development and contemporary diversity of human societies. Human language differs from animal communication in its complexity and flexibility, aspects of human communication made possible by unique human biological and genetic features. The complexity of language makes it a powerful tool in shaping human thought, providing categories and metaphors for organizing our information about the world. Though language shapes thought and action in universal ways, many aspects of language vary widely relative to local cultures. The social aspects of language are particularly relative, influencing how children learn languages in various sociocultural contexts as well as how people use language to create speech communities. In ritual contexts, language is used performatively to accomplish social action as well as challenging those actions. As a tool of power, language structures gender, race, and ethnic dynamics. Recognizing the fundamental importance of language to the preservation of culture, many Indigenous communities have developed strategies to revive their heritage languages using immersion schools and master-apprentice programs.

Critical Thinking Questions

1. What might humanity be like if humans had never developed language? What social and

cultural forms would not be possible without language? How would we survive? Would we be capable of creating tools or art? Would our social relationships be different? Would our social groups be different?
2. Describe a romantic relationship, one you have experienced or observed. How did it begin, develop, endure, or end? Now, make note of how many times in your description you relied on various metaphors. Is it possible to fully describe romance without the use of metaphor? Do these metaphors shape the way we think about romance?
3. List the speech communities to which you belong. Do all members of a speech community share exactly the same vocabulary and practices? Do speech communities overlap?
4. Aside from weddings, list rituals in your culture that rely on the performance of language. How do people use forms of commentary and back talk to reshape those performances?
5. How does language operate as a form of power in schools and universities? Consider the gendered norms of language as well as racial and ethnic dynamics.

Bibliography

Acoustical Society of America. 2018. "Can Chimpanzee Vocalizations Reveal the Origins of Human Language? While Closely Related to Humans, Researchers Discover that Chimpanzees' Vocalizations Resemble Human Language Less than You'd Expect." *ScienceDaily.* May 8, 2018. www.sciencedaily.com/releases/2018/05/180508081505.htm.

Afreh, Esther Serwaah. 2018. "Metaphors Otumfo? Lives By: A Cognitive Linguistic Study of Metaphors in Some Addresses by Otumfo? Osei Tutu II, Asantehene." *Cognitive Semantics* 4 (1): 76–103.

Ahearn, Laura. 2017. *Living Language: An Introduction to Linguistic Anthropology.* 2nd ed. Chichester, West Sussex, UK; Malden, MA: Wiley-Blackwell.

Alim, H. Samy, and Geneva Smitherman. 2012. *Articulate While Black: Barack Obama, Language, and Race in the U.S.* New York: Oxford University Press.

Arbib, Michael. 2011. "From Mirror Neurons to Complex Imitation in the Evolution of Language and Tool Use." *Annual Review of Anthropology* 40:257–73.

Austin, J. L. 1962. *How to Do Things with Words: The William James Lectures Delivered at Harvard University in 1955.* London: Oxford University Press.

Baugh, John. 2003. "Linguistic Profiling." In *Black Linguistics: Language, Society and Politics in Africa and the Americas*, edited by S. Makoni, G. Smitherman, A. F. Ball, and A. K. Spears, 155–68. New York: Routledge.

Berlin, Brent, and Paul Kay. 1969. *Basic Color Terms: Their Universality and Evolution.* Berkeley, CA: University of California Press.

Butler, Judith. 1988. "Performative Acts and Gender Constitution: An Essay in Phenomenology and Feminist Theory." *Theatre Journal* 40 (4): 519–31.

Chun, Elaine W., and Adrienne Lo. 2015. "Language and Racialization." In *The Routledge Handbook of Linguistic Anthropology*, edited by Nancy Bonvillain. Abingdon, UK: Routledge.

Clarke, Esther, Ulrich H. Reichard, and Klaus Zuberbühler. 2006. "The Syntax and Meaning of Wild Gibbon Songs." PLoS ONE 1 (1): e73. https://doi.org/10.1371/journal.pone.0000073.

Duranti, Alessandro. 1997. *Linguistic Anthropology.* Cambridge, UK: Cambridge University Press.

Epps, Patience, and Danilo Paiva Ramos. 2020. "Enactive Esthetics: The Poetics of Hup Incantation." *Journal of Linguistic Anthropology* 30 (2): 233–257.

Feldman, Orna. 2001. "Inspired by a Dream: Jessie 'Little Doe' Fermino, a Mashpee Indian, Is Working to Revive the Wampanoag Language." *Spectrum.* http://spectrum.mit.edu/spring-2001/inspired-by-a-dream/

Frisch, Karl von. 1993. *The Dance Language and Orientation of Bees.* Cambridge, MA: Harvard University Press.

Gibson, Kathleen, and Maggie Tallerman. 2011. "Introduction." In *The Oxford Handbook of Language Evolution*, edited by Kathleen Gibson and Maggie Tallerman. Oxford, UK: Oxford University Press.

Hall, Kira. 1995. "Hijra/hijrin: Language and Gender Identity." PhD diss. University of California, Berkeley. ProQuest Dissertations Publishing.

Haynie, Hannah, and Claire Bowern. 2016. "Phylogenetic Approach to the Evolution of Color Term Systems." *Proceedings of the National Academy of Sciences* 113 (48): 13666–71.

Herrick, J. W. 1995. *Iroquois Medical Botany.* Syracuse, NY: Syracuse University Press.

Hill, Jane H. 2008. *The Everyday Language of White Racism.* Malden, MA: Wiley-Blackwell.

Hinton, Leanne. 2011. "Revitalization of Endangered Languages." In *The Cambridge Handbook of Endangered Languages*, edited by P. K. Austin and J. Sallabank, 291–311. Cambridge, UK: Cambridge University Press.

Hinton, Leanne. 2018. "Approaches to and Strategies for Language Revitalization." In *The Oxford Handbook of Endangered Languages*, edited by Kenneth L. Rehg and Lyle Campbell. New York: Oxford University Press.

Hyde, Janet. 2005. "The Gender Similarities Hypothesis." *American Psychologist* 60 (6): 581–92.

Kay, Paul, and Willett Kempton. 1984. "What Is the Sapir-Whorf Hypothesis?" *American Anthropologist,* 86 (1): 65–79.

Kay, Paul. 2015. "Linguistics of Color Terms." In *International Encyclopedia of the Social & Behavioral Sciences*, edited by James D. Wright, 231–4. Amsterdam, NY: Elsevier.

Keenan [Ochs], Elinor. 1974. "Norm-Makers, Norm-Breakers: Uses of Speech by Men and Women in a Malagasy Community." In *Ethnography of Communication*, edited by R. Bauman and J. Sherzer, 125–43. Cambridge, UK: Cambridge University Press.

King, Jeanette. 2018. "Māori: Revitalization of an Endangered Language." In *The Oxford Handbook of Endangered Languages*, edited by Kenneth L. Rehg and Lyle Campbell. New York: Oxford University Press.

Kulick, Don. 1992. *Language Shift and Cultural Reproduction: Socialization, Self, and Syncretism in a Papua New Guinean Village.* Cambridge, UK: Cambridge University Press.

Labov, William. 1972a. "Academic Ignorance and Black Intelligence." June 1972. https://www.ling.upenn.edu/courses/ling001/Labov1972.pdf.

Labov, William. 1972b. "The Logic of Nonstandard English." In *Language in the Inner City: Studies in the Black English Vernacular*, 201–40. Philadelphia, PA: University of Pennsylvania Press.

Labov, William, Ash, Sharon, Boberg, Charles. 2006. *Atlas of American English: Phonetics, Phonology and Sound Change.* New York. Mouton de Gruyter.

Lakoff, George, and Mark Johnson. 1980. *Metaphors We Live By.* Chicago: University of Chicago Press.

Lakoff, Robin. 1975. *Language and Woman's Place.* New York: Harper and Row.

Levinson, Steven. 2003. *Space in Language and Cognition: Explorations in Cognitive Diversity.* Cambridge, UK: Cambridge University Press.

Lim, Yen Ying, and Peter Snyder. 2015. "Human Language: Evolutionary Precursors." In *International Encyclopedia of the Social & Behavioral Sciences*, edited by James D. Wright, 329–34. Amsterdam, NY: Elsevier.

Lippi-Green, Rosina. 2012. *English with an Accent: Language, Ideology, and Discrimination in the United States.* London and New York: Routledge.

Lucy, John. 2015. "Sapir-Whorf Hypothesis." In *International Encyclopedia of the Social & Behavioral Sciences*, edited by James D. Wright, 903–6. Amsterdam, NY: Elsevier.

Martin, Laura. 1986. "'Eskimo Words for Snow': A Case Study in the Genesis and Decay of an Anthropological

Example." *American Anthropologist*, 88 (2): 418–23.

Massachusetts Institute of Technology. "Did Humans Speak through Cave Art? Ancient Drawings and Language's Origins." *ScienceDaily.* February 21, 2018. https://www.sciencedaily.com/releases/2018/02/180221122923.htm.

Mensah, Adinkrah. 2020. "'If You Die a Bad Death, We Give You a Bad Burial': Mortuary Practices and 'Bad Death' among the Akan in Ghana." *Death Studies*. doi: 10.1080/07481187.2020.1762264.

Mertz, Elizabeth. 2007. *The Language of Law School: Learning to "Think Like a Lawyer."* Oxford, UK: Oxford University Press.

Miyagawa, Shigeru, Cora Lesure, and Vitor A. Nóbrega. 2018. "Cross-Modality Information Transfer: A Hypothesis about the Relationship among Prehistoric Cave Paintings, Symbolic Thinking, and the Emergence of Language." *Frontiers in Psychology.* February 20, 2018 https://doi.org/10.3389/fpsyg.2018.00115.

Muehlmann, S. 2014. "The Speech Community and Beyond: Language and the Nature of the Social Aggregate." In *The Cambridge Handbook of Linguistic Anthropology*, edited by N. Enfield, P. Kockelman, and J. Sidnell, 577–98. Cambridge, UK: Cambridge University Press.

Ochs, Elinor, and Schieffelin, Bambi. (1984) 2001. "Language Acquisition and Socialization: Three Developmental Stories and Their Implications." In *Linguistic Anthropology: A Reader*, edited by A. Duranti, 263–301. Oxford, UK: Blackwell.

Patterson, Francine, and Eugene Linden. 1981. *The Education of Koko*. New York: Holt, Rinehart, and Winston.

Purnell, Thomas, William Idsardi, and John Baugh. 1999. "Perceptual and Phonetic Experiments on American English Dialect Identification." *Journal of Language and Social Psychology* 18 (1): 10–30.

Seeley, Thomas D. 2010. *Honeybee Democracy.* Princeton, NJ: Princeton University Press.

Shatwell, Justin. 2012. "The Long-Dead Native Language Wopânâak Is Revived." *Yankee Magazine.* October 9, 2012. https://newengland.com/yankee-magazine/living/profiles/wampanoag-language.

Solnit, Rebecca. 2008. "Men Explain Things to Me; Facts Didn't Get in Their Way." *Common Dreams.* April 13, 2008. https://www.commondreams.org/views/2008/04/13/men-explain-things-me-facts-didnt-get-their-way.

Sukiennik, Greg. 2001. "Woman Brings Tribe's Dead Language Back to Life." *Los Angeles Times.* March 24, 2001. https://www.latimes.com/archives/la-xpm-2001-mar-24-mn-42039-story.html

Sweet, Nicholas. 2019. "Ritual Contingency: Teasing and the Politics of Participation." *Journal of Linguistic Anthropology* 30 (1): 86–102.

Tannen, Deborah. 1990. *You Just Don't Understand: Women and Men in Conversation.* New York: Ballantine Books.

West, C. 1998. "When the Doctor Is a Lady: Power, Status, and Gender in Physician-Patient Encounters." In *Language and Gender: A Reader*, edited by J. Coates, 396–412. Oxford, UK: Blackwell.

"Words We're Watching: Mansplaining." 2018. *Merriam-Webster.com Dictionary.* Merriam-Webster. https://www.merriam-webster.com/words-at-play/mansplaining-definition-history.

Yu, Ning. 2016. "Spatial Metaphors for Morality: A Perspective from Chinese." *Metaphor and Symbol* 31 (2): 108–25.

Zimmerman, D., and C. West. 1975. "Sex-Roles, Interruptions, and Silences in Conversation." In *Language, Gender and Society*, edited by B. Thorne, C. Kramarae, and N. Henley, 89–101. Rowley, MA: Newbury House.

CHAPTER 7
Work, Life, and Value: Economic Anthropology

Figure 7.1 Four entertainment professionals indicate their job satisfaction (credit: "De los Carnavales de Valdemoro" by manuel m. v./flickr, CC BY 2.0)

CHAPTER OUTLINE

INTRODUCTION If you are in college, someone has probably asked you the question, "So, what you want to do after you graduate?" Are they asking about the hobbies you would like to pursue? Are they asking about the vacation spots you would like to visit, the sporting events you would like to attend? No, of course not. When people ask about your plans postgraduation, they are asking about work. After you graduate, you will be faced with a similar question: "What do you do in life?" or "What do you do for a living?" It is one of the first things people ask when they meet someone new.

What do people mean when they ask what someone does for a living? Certainly, they are wondering what kind of work that person does in order to meet basic needs for food, clothing, and shelter. But they are wondering more than just that. If someone answers, "I'm a circus clown," or "I'm a tax accountant," what does that reveal? Only where their paycheck comes from? Or does it also give some idea about where they live, what they eat, how they spend their days? Does it hint at what is important to that person? Of course, it can be misleading to generalize. But the way a person makes a living does often say something about that person's way of life.

In some cases, the question of what a person does for a living is not just an individual matter but one for the whole society. In some societies, most people meet their basic needs by doing roughly the same thing. And even in societies where different people play different roles, there is a fundamental process for making and distributing things that people need and want. Economists and anthropologists agree that this is the most basic definition of an economy: the central way in which societies meet basic material needs and wants. More specifically, an economy is a system for making, circulating, and using things, including material goods, services, and information. Economic systems are shaped by ideas about the meaning and value of objects, actions, and people. In many economic systems, some groups gain control over the work and leisure of others, structuring relations of inequality that operate through techniques of discipline (in the realm of work) and persuasion (in the realm of consumption).

Like nosy strangers at a cocktail party, anthropologists always want to know what people do for a living. Archaeologists are curious about how people in the past developed strategies for making a living in response to different environmental conditions and sociocultural pressures. Physical anthropologists are interested in how human biology evolved alongside ways of using the environment to meet basic needs. Cultural anthropologists study the social and cultural implications of different ways of making a living. And linguistic anthropologists focus on the roles of language, classification, and metaphor in shaping different strategies for making a living.

This chapter takes a close look at the primary ways in which humans interact and have interacted with the environment to meet their basic needs, in the past and in the present day. This area of study is called economic anthropology.

7.1 Economies: Two Ways to Study Them

LEARNING OUTCOMES

By the end of this section, you will be able to:

- Distinguish between economic anthropology and the discipline of economics.
- Describe the universalist and normative approaches to studying economic issues.
- Understand the importance of diversity, holism, environmentalism, and cultural relativism to economic anthropology.
- Explain how economic anthropology foregrounds social groups and power relations.

Maybe you've had a course on economics or read a book by an economist. There are many good ones. A favorite of the author of this chapter, Jennifer Hasty, is *Capital in the Twenty-First Century*, by the French economist Thomas Piketty. It is an unusual book for a contemporary economist to have written. In fact, it's almost anthropological.

Most economics research is not very anthropological. Recall the three commitments of anthropology—in short, diversity, holism, and environmentalism. Across the four fields, anthropologists also value cultural relativism and reaching for an insider's point of view. When an anthropologist considers how societies, groups, and individuals make a living, they incorporate these commitments and values. Take a look at a few of the articles featured in the January 2021 issue of *Economic Anthropology*:

- "Religious Networks and Small Businesses in Senegal"
- "Honesty and Economy on a Highway: Entanglements of Gifts, Money, and Affection in the Narratives of Ukrainian Sex Workers"
- "Gendering Human Capital Development in Western Alaska"
- "'No trabajaré pa' ellos': Entrepreneurship as a Form of State Resistance in Havana, Cuba"

Note the diversity of cultural contexts (the West African country of Senegal, the eastern European country of Ukraine, the North American state of Alaska, and the Central American island country of Cuba). Other articles in this same issue focus on economic issues in Kentucky, Spain, Italy, China, and Colombia. The titles also demonstrate an interest in linking ways of making a living to other aspects of society, such as religion, gender, and political resistance. All are based on long-term fieldwork aimed at understanding the multiple perspectives of local peoples and groups. Note also terms such as *gendering* and *resistance*, indicating an anthropological interest in social groups and power relations.

Perhaps most importantly, the point of these articles is not to evaluate economic practices as better or worse compared to an ideal. Rather, economic anthropologists analyze the cultural and historical features that shape economic practices in different cultural contexts. As for environmentalism, this issue also features a discussion by five anthropologists on the topic of what economic anthropology contributes to the understanding of climate change. In this one issue, all of the central elements of anthropology are on full display.

How is this approach different from the one taken by the discipline of economics? Compare *Economic Anthropology* with a premier economics journal, the *American Economic Review* (AER). The January 2021 issue of AER features such articles as the following:

- "Going Negative at the Zero Lower Bound: The Effects of Negative Nominal Interest Rates"
- "The Distributional Consequences of Public School Choice"
- "Politically Feasible Reforms of Nonlinear Tax Systems"
- "Lack of Selection and Limits to Delegation: Firm Dynamics in Developing Countries"
- "Job Seekers' Perceptions and Employment Prospects: Heterogeneity, Duration Dependence, and Bias"

The first thing you might notice in this list is the lack of any cultural context, with the one exception being the vague reference to "developing countries." School choice where? Whose tax systems? Which job seekers? Although some of these articles do specify the context in the article text, that detail is not considered a sufficiently important part of the analysis to warrant inclusion in the title. This suggests that mainstream economic analysis assumes that history and culture do not play a very strong role in economic issues such as school choice, tax systems, and job seeking.

Economists tend toward **universalism**, which assumes that economic processes operate in much the same way all over the world. In fact, a central concern of economics is to discover the universal principles that govern economies anywhere and everywhere. Implicit in most economic analysis is the idea that most realms of society work like markets, responding to universal forces of supply and demand. Moreover, economists view people as self-interested, rational actors situated within the various market-driven realms of society. Economists use statistics rather than fieldwork to evaluate these market-driven activities, sometimes searching for best policies to encourage economic growth or discourage inequality. Most of the articles in the January 2021 issue of the AER focus squarely on the economic realm, tracing relationships between factors *within* this realm rather than reaching *beyond* it, as anthropologists tend to do.

And finally, in the January 2021 issue of the AER, there is no mention of environmental issues.

This comparison is not intended to denigrate the discipline of economics but rather to show the difference in how anthropology frames economic issues. Anthropologists take a human-centered approach to economic issues, describing what people think and do as they make a living and how their practices change over time. Economists take a market-centered approach, describing how market mechanisms shape different areas of human life and how those processes change over time.

7.2 Modes of Subsistence

LEARNING OUTCOMES

By the end of this section, you will be able to:

- Define modes of subsistence.
- Describe the general elements of all modes of subsistence.
- List the four main modes of subsistence humans have used to make a living.
- Understand how each society has a predominant mode of subsistence but may also practice strategies from other modes.

Anthropologists have a term for the way that people interact with their environments in order to make a living: **mode of subsistence**. There are four main modes of subsistence that have been used throughout human history: gathering-hunting, pastoralism, plant cultivation, and industrialism/post-industrialism. Each of these modes incorporates distinctive strategies for producing, exchanging, and consuming the things that people need to survive. At the most fundamental level are the basic necessities of food, clothing, shelter, and health. Modes of subsistence provide solutions to meet these needs by generating materials from the environment and developing techniques of labor and forms of technology to process those materials. Beyond these very important functions, modes of subsistence also organize society to get the necessary work done. Societies develop roles, groups, and institutions to divide up the workload of producing things. Modes of subsistence also entail specific ways of trading and circulating things within and beyond local groups. And finally, modes of subsistence emphasize certain ideals and values.

This chapter will examine the four basic modes of subsistence one by one, including their development and a detailed ethnographic example of each. While each mode of subsistence is explored separately, it is important to recognize that most societies have a predominant mode of subsistence that incorporates various practices from other modes. The chapter also discusses the contemporary predicaments faced by many peoples practicing the first three strategies and why one might want to protect and support those economic lifeways.

7.3 Gathering and Hunting

LEARNING OUTCOMES

By the end of this section, you will be able to:

- Define the subsistence strategy of hunting and gathering, also known as gathering-hunting.
- Identify and distinguish gathering-hunting groups in prehistory and contemporary societies.
- Articulate how gathering-hunting promotes certain other cultural forms.
- Overturn assumptions about the supposed "hard life" of gathering-hunting groups.
- Recognize the challenges facing most gathering-hunting groups today.

Imagine that you were stripped of all possessions and transported to a grassland environment along with 30 or so other people. How would you begin to make a living? How would you find food and shelter? How would you keep your body comfortable and healthy? Throughout the millions of years of hominin evolution, those living in such environments practiced a strategy known as **gathering-hunting**. Some peoples still practice this flexible and congenial way of life. In gathering and hunting societies, people rely on the natural resources readily available in their environment. They gather fruits, nuts, berries, and roots and collect honey from wild bees. They hunt and trap wild animals, and they fish in rivers and lakes. Many gathering-hunting groups also engage in limited ways in other modes of subsistence, which will be examined later in the chapter, but their main way of making a living is through gathering and hunting.

You might be surprised to see the word *gathering* appear before *hunting* in describing this subsistence strategy. The word order reflects a key debate about this subsistence strategy. Some researchers object to *hunting and gathering* because it privileges hunting as the most important activity of such groups. Early interest in these groups focused on the hunting activities of men as the most prestigious and valuable subsistence practices. In fact, gathering—done by both women and men—provides the vast majority of calories in the diets of such groups. This chapter will refer to this subsistence strategy as *gathering-hunting* and the people who practice it as *gatherer-hunters*.

The Hadza: Gathering-Hunting as a Subsistence Strategy

The Hadza of northern Tanzania are a resilient example of the way of life of gathering-hunting peoples as well as the contemporary challenges facing such groups. Like most gathering-hunting peoples, the Hadza traditionally lived in **seminomadic** groups of 20 to 30 people, called **bands**. About one-third of contemporary Hadza still practice this way of life. Hadza bands settle temporarily to gather and hunt the resources of a particular area, then move on to other areas in seasonal migrations. Sometimes, groups agglomerate into camps of several hundred to take advantage of seasonal foods such as berries.

On most days, both men and women venture out into the savanna to gather food. Men seek out meat, honey, and baobab fruit, while women gather tubers, berries, and greens. When work is assigned based on a person's sex, anthropologists call this a **sexual division of labor**. In Hadza society, men and women do specialize in obtaining different foods, but the division is not hard and fast; sometimes men pick berries, and sometimes women gather honey.

FIGURE 7.2 Women of the Hazda cooking and socializing. The Hazda practice a traditional gathering-hunting lifestyle. (credit: "Day 5 - Time with the Hadza tribe" by sueomstead/flickr, CC BY 2.0)

Women go out gathering in small groups, picking fruits by hand and using digging sticks to bring up edible roots. They carry foods in grass baskets and leather pouches. People feed themselves throughout the day and bring home foods to share with the whole band in the evenings.

Hadza men often hunt in pairs at dawn and dusk, using bows and arrows coupled with expert tracking skills. They use animal ligaments for bowstrings and craft their arrows from wood and guinea fowl feathers. They use the sap of the desert rose plant to poison their arrow tips. Back when the area was teeming with large animals, hunters brought down zebras, giraffes, and buffalo. As the big game have diminished, they more often target antelope, monkeys, and warthogs.

The Hadza have forged a mutually beneficial human-animal relationship to obtain honey, a highly valued food that contributes 10 to 20 percent of the calories they consume. Hadza men whistle or strike trees to summon a honeyguide, a gray-brown bird that eats beeswax. Hearing this summons, the bird calls back to the honey hunter in a chattering response. Using this call-and-response, the honeyguide leads the hunter to a beehive. Hunters use smoke to calm the bees while they cut into the hive to harvest the honeycomb. After eating some of the honey on the spot, hunters then leave wax for the birds. Some honey is also brought back to camp to share with other members of the band.

FIGURE 7.3 Hadza men have forged a mutually beneficial relationship with this bird, known as a honeyguide. The bird helps the men locate beehives and, after harvesting the honey from the hives, the men leave wax from the honeycomb for the bird. (credit: "Lesser Honeyguide, Indicator minor, at Pilanesberg National Park, South Africa" by Derek Keats/flickr, CC BY 2.0)

Like most gathering-hunting peoples, the Hadza are highly **egalitarian**, meaning that all people are considered equal and all resources are shared equally. Gathered foods brought back to the camp, including meat, are shared among all members of the band. Gathering-hunting groups deplore stinginess as the worst human fault, and people who refuse to share are met with gossip, ridicule, and even ostracism. Decisions are made through public discussions leading to group consensus. No person has any sort of leadership role. Rather, people with experience in certain areas of social knowledge provide their expertise as needed. In-group fighting is not common, but it does occur, sometimes leading to personal violence and even a split in the band if the conflict cannot be resolved. Violent conflict between groups is very rare among gatherer-hunters.

The Sociocultural Complex of Gathering and Hunting

Anthropologists have identified features of Hadza society as distinctive to gathering-hunting groups found all over the world. Groups such as the Martu and Pintupi in Australia, the Cuiva and Pumé in South America, the Paliyan and Kattunayakan in Asia, and the Inuit and Shoshone in North America have all constructed similar lifeways based on gathering and hunting (Lee 2018). The social features of this way of life include mobility, sexual division of labor, egalitarianism, and vast knowledge of their environments.

The most common feature of gatherer-hunters is mobility. Such groups typically move in seasonal cycles over broad territories, regularly meeting up with other groups at specific spots such as water sources and patches of ripe vegetation. Bands tend to confine their subsistence activities to their own territories, but if faced with a scarcity of resources, they will commonly ask other groups for permission to gather and hunt in neighboring territories. These requests are facilitated by cross-band friendships and marriages that develop when bands camp together at certain times of the year. As a result, such requests are nearly always approved.

The second feature common to gatherer-hunter societies is the sexual division of labor. Often, men do most or all of the hunting, though recent archaeological evidence suggests that some women also hunted in the past. Both women and men gather, but they often gather different things, and women bring home the majority of gathered foods. The relative equality of women in gatherer-hunter societies is linked to their primary role in supplying calories to the gatherer-hunter diet. Hunting is a prestige activity, however, giving prominence to men who are particularly successful hunters.

FIGURE 7.4 A Hadza man returns from a successful hunt. Like other gatherer-hunter societies, the Hadza utilize a sexual division of labor, with women doing the bulk of the gathering and men doing most of the hunting. (credit: "Success" by Anja Pietsch/flickr, CC BY 2.0)

The third feature of gatherer-hunters is a strong tendency toward egalitarianism. As they are so often on the move, gatherer-hunters do not typically own many material possessions, and those they have are circulated through the band on the basis of need. All gathered and hunted foods are shared among all members of the band. Generosity is praised and admired. People are considered equal and are actively discouraged from valuing themselves above others. Greed and excessive pride are stigmatized and punished with gossip and criticism. People who fight or refuse to share can be ostracized from the band.

These are broad generalities. The gatherer-hunter mode of subsistence commonly coordinates with these sociocultural features, but some groups do provide exceptions. In particularly productive environments, gatherer-hunters can settle down in one place for periods of time. The year-round availability of fish allows gatherer-hunter groups in coastal or riverine areas to form permanent or semipermanent settlements. Diet and labor patterns also vary. Closer to the equator, gatherer-hunter groups rely more on gathering because plants are plentiful year-round. Farther from the equator, in cooler climates, vegetation is scarce in winter, and gatherer-hunters rely more on hunting. Degrees of inequality and conflict also vary somewhat, often in association with the availability of resources. Situations of scarcity often generate social conflict. While one can describe a general mode of subsistence, it is important to acknowledge the diversity of strategies and features within this mode.

All gatherer-hunters, however, absolutely must possess deep knowledge of the plants, animals, and sources of water in their environments. Many gatherer-hunters can identify over a hundred sources of plant and animal foods in their environments, along with detailed information about where and when they can find each type. Often, they rely on a few staple foods that are readily available year-round. When the Dobe Ju/'hoansi of the Kalahari Desert cannot find other foods, they count on mongongo nuts, a highly nutritious, drought-resistant food. Eating 300 mongongo nuts (a hefty serving) supplies 1,200 calories and 56 grams of protein. At certain times of the year, mongongo nuts constitute nearly half of the diet of the Dobe Ju/'hoansi.

Contemporary Challenges to Gathering and Hunting Societies

Originally, all Hadza lived as foragers. In the early 20th century, the British colonial government attempted to convert them to farming and Christianity, but the Hadza successfully resisted. Since the 1950s, however, farmers and herders have claimed their territory, making the Hadza squatters on land they have occupied for millennia. The plants they rely on for food have been clear-cut to make way for the onion and sweet potato crops planted by farming groups. Hadza watering holes have been appropriated for irrigation. The Tanzanian government has responded with yet another attempt to settle the Hadza, building villages on their lands and attempting to convert them to farming. About two-thirds of all Hadza people now live part-time in these villages, where they receive donations of food from the government. They live in poverty on the land stolen from them by their farming and herding neighbors, who discriminate against them as troublesome primitives. Many Hadza now farm for part of the year and then leave their villages to engage in gathering-hunting for several months.

Over the past few years, however, the Hadza have won several victories in their struggle to regain control over their lands. In 2007, the local government leased 6,500 square kilometers of Hadza land to the royal family of the United Arab Emirates for use as a "personal safari playground." Removed from the land and confined to a government reservation, the Hadza protested, and some resisters were imprisoned. Their campaign against the deal was supported by a coalition of local and international groups. The controversy garnered attention in the global news media, and the government eventually rescinded the deal. In 2011, the Hadza asserted a claim to 57,000 hectares of land, and the Tanzanian government consented, granting them title to this land. It was the first time the Tanzanian government had ever recognized the land rights of gathering-hunting peoples.

Like the Hadza, all contemporary gathering and hunting groups face economic and political pressures that threaten their way of life. Herders and farmers encroach on their territories, leasing or purchasing their lands and then forcibly evicting the original inhabitants. Local and national governments attempt to settle such groups in permanent villages in order to establish their own rule of law, collect taxes, provide education and medical care, and assimilate them as citizens. Often, gathering-hunting groups agree to settle and then, after a while, abandon the villages established for them and escape to their lands to resume a gathering-hunting lifestyle. Many Hadza say they love living close to nature, making their own material culture, and working and resting at will, always on the move.

The Original Affluent Society: Comparing Ancient and Contemporary Foragers

In agricultural and industrial societies, people often assume that gathering-hunting peoples must live a hard life, oppressed by the struggle to find enough food and plagued by malnutrition and poor health. Archaeologists and cultural anthropologists who have studied gathering and hunting groups have found otherwise. Researchers have discovered that gatherer-hunters have stronger bones, lower blood pressure, and less heart disease than neighboring farmers, likely due to the amount of walking they do and the abundance of fruits, nuts, and vegetables in their diets (American Heart Association 2012; University of Cambridge 2014). In his ethnographic work among the Dobe Ju/'hoansi, anthropologist Richard Lee found that they worked on average three to four days a week obtaining food and spent the rest of their time socializing and enjoying life. He described the Dobe Ju/'hoansi as fit, healthy, and free of nutritional deficits (1993). Indeed, some Hadza have remarked that the notion of famine is unknown to their culture. While Harvard economist John Kenneth Galbraith has referred to the wealthy industrial economy of the United States as "the affluent society," anthropologist Marshall Sahlins describes the gathering and hunting lifestyle as "the original affluent society."

For some 95 percent of evolutionary history, humans and human ancestors relied on gathering and hunting to make a living. In evolutionary terms, it is only very recently that humans have established other modes of subsistence. Farming was invented around 12,000 years ago, far too recently to have shaped humans' biological evolution very much. By contrast, hominins were practicing gathering and hunting for more than two million years. If humans have evolved to practice any lifestyle, it would be gathering-hunting. This suggests that humans' brains and bodies might be best suited to the lifestyle described by ethnographers who study gathering-hunting groups: long walks in nature; a diet of mostly fruits, nuts, and vegetables; and plenty of leisure time to relax and talk. Maybe humanity's ancestors were as robust and happy in their way of life as many contemporary foragers. Maybe.

The problem with this sort of thinking is that people today really don't know what life was like for humanity's gathering-hunting ancestors. The archaeological record of fossils and artifacts can reveal much about the diet and diseases of early hominins, but they tell very little about early social structures and cultural values. Some anthropologists have looked to contemporary gathering and hunting groups to understand the way of life of humanity's ancestors. Maybe they, like contemporary gatherer-hunter peoples, lived in egalitarian bands with group decision-making and a flexible division of labor based on gender, valuing sharing and deploring stinginess. Certainly, they must have had impressive knowledge of the resources and dangers in their environments.

And yet it is a mistake to view the way of life of contemporary gathering-hunting societies as examples of the way of life of humans' evolutionary ancestors. Groups such as the Hadza are not frozen in time, practicing a static lifeway of the deep past, but rather constantly changing and innovating, blending new ideas and practices with older ones just as farmers, herders, and industrialists do. Most contemporary gathering-hunting groups have lived side by side with farming and herding groups for centuries, often trading with those groups and even experimenting with their subsistence methods from time to time. Most gatherer-hunters have been forced to relocate to less advantageous lands due to the encroachment of these herders and farmers. The culture of many gatherer-hunter groups has been shaped by their incorporation as marginalized minorities in larger nation-states such as Tanzania. As the way of life of contemporary gatherer-hunters has changed so dramatically just in the past century, it's difficult to draw firm conclusions about human evolutionary history based on their example.

7.4 Pastoralism

LEARNING OUTCOMES

By the end of this section, you will be able to:

- Describe the process of animal domestication.
- List the array of practices associated with the subsistence strategy of pastoralism.
- Identify the cultural features associated with the herding way of life.
- Provide a detailed example of a pastoralist society.
- Discuss the challenges facing contemporary pastoralist societies.

In many gathering and hunting societies, bands follow herds of wild game as they move in seasonal migrations. Researchers speculate that such hunting practices may have led to the development of a new subsistence pattern around 10,000 to 12,000 years ago. Relying on their expert knowledge of the behavior and biology of game animals, hunters might have begun to control the movement of wild herds, steering the animals to territories that might be especially rich in grazing resources or conducive to certain hunting strategies. These new practices may have been a response to the diminishing of key game species due to overhunting, prompting hunters to devise strategies to enhance the animals' diet and reproduction.

This human-animal relationship may have deepened over time as people discovered the nutritional resources available from live animals, such as milk and blood. Rather than killing an animal for meat, early herders figured out how to benefit from live animals and guide their reproduction to enlarge the herds. They began to selectively breed the healthiest and heartiest animals in their herds. They learned how to process animal products such as milk, hides, and hooves for use as food, textiles, and tools, and some used dung to fuel their fires. This process is called **animal domestication**. Humans in different environments domesticated a wide range of prey animals, including sheep, goats, cattle, water buffalo, yaks, pigs, reindeer, llamas, and alpacas.

Pastoralism is the mode of subsistence associated with the care and use of domesticated herd animals. Pastoralism shares many features with gathering-hunting, in particular the practice of ranging over a broad territory in seasonal cycles. Indeed, as they move with their herds to optimal grazing lands, many pastoral peoples gather fruits and nuts or occasionally hunt small game. Unlike gathering and hunting, however, herding promotes a sense of ownership over resources, as families develop close relationships with specific herds. Rather than sharing resources as foragers do, pastoralists consider their herds to be family property. Herds associated with a family are passed down to subsequent generations, most frequently from fathers to sons.

Archaeologists believe that pastoralism was developed around the same time as farming. In many regions, the two subsistence strategies are practiced by neighboring groups in symbiotic relations of trade. Often, a group will combine pastoralism with farming. Where rain is plentiful and soils are rich for cultivation, farming is used to take advantage of these resources. Pastoralism is utilized in areas with more marginal soils or unpredictable rainfall, conditions not optimal for farming but able to support herd animals if they are moved regularly to newly grown pastures and freshwater sources. Pastoralists who don't farm usually trade meat, milk, and other animal products for the grains and vegetables grown by neighboring farmers. Most contemporary pastoralists find it necessary to supplement their diet of animal products with the vitamins and carbohydrates in cultivated plant foods and are able to do so through small farming and trade.

The Bedouin: Flexible Pastoralism

Across the dry grasslands of Arabia and northern Africa live about three million Arab peoples collectively known as the Bedouin. Before the 20th century, Bedouin peoples made their living primarily by herding camels, sheep, goats, and cattle. Many still do, although they often cultivate crops or work as wage laborers as well. Among those Bedouin still devoted to herding, most specialize in one or two herd animals particularly suited to the climate and available pastures in their environment. In areas around Jordan, Syria, and Iraq, sheep and goats are preferred, while cattle are kept by Bedouin groups in southern Arabia and Sudan. In very dry regions such as the Sahara and the Arabian Deserts, Bedouin groups herd camels, hardy animals with scant need for water. Camels are valued as transport but also for their high-quality milk and tasty meat. Camel herding, though a prized tradition, is becoming increasingly rare among Bedouin. Bedouin supplement their camels' diet with feed, and many have been forced to sell off their camels as the price of feed rises. Since the 1960s, trucks and cars have replaced camels as a means of transportation for the Bedouin, sometimes used to bring food and water to herds in arid regions.

FIGURE 7.5 A herd of goats relaxes at a Bedouin camp near Jericho, in what is now the West Bank. Bedouin peoples rely on herding animals – such as camels, sheep, cattle, and goats – for meat, milk, and fiber. (credit: "Bedouin Goats 1557" by James Emery/flickr, CC BY 2.0)

Bedouin pastoralists have traditionally lived in small camps that are moved as frequently as needed to find fresh pastures for their herds, sometimes as often as every few days. This form of herding is called **nomadism**. Each camp consists of several tents, each one housing an extended family. Typically, a tent might house a married couple with their children and one or two siblings of the husband. Within the camp, several tents might house people who are related to each other, as sons marry and establish their own tents. For instance, a camp could comprise 70 to 100 people, including the families of several brothers, each tent housing the family of a brother, a son, or an elder. Often, the families of the camp move together during the summer months, then converge with other groups in larger camps during the winter months. Camps usually consist of 3 to 15 tents.

FIGURE 7.6 A Bedouin tent in Jordan. Tents can be quickly constructed and easily transported, making them the perfect home for those practicing a lifestyle that requires frequent movement. (credit: "Bedouin Camp" by young shanahan/flickr, CC BY 2.0)

Instead of ranging freely, other Bedouin have traditionally moved their herds between two permanent settlements, one for the summer months and the other for winter. This pattern of pastoralism is known as **transhumance**. In societies that practice this form of subsistence today, young children and the elderly often remain in permanent camps year-round, benefiting from government health care and schools. Some Bedouin use transhumance to combine herding with small farming. For instance, some Egyptian Bedouin plant barley in the fall and then move with their herds into the desert, leaving behind a few people to tend to the crops. In the summer, the mobile group returns to harvest the crops, and the entire group spends the summer together.

Stone houses have replaced tents in many permanent camps. Both tents and houses are rectangular, divided into two or three rooms. One area is for women, with a kitchen and storeroom. One area is primarily for men, where guests and relatives are entertained. Sometimes, a third area is devoted to the care of sick or young animals.

Like gatherer-hunters, pastoralists divide work according to a sexual division of labor. For the Bedouin, that division is determined by the types of animals herded by the group. When both large and small animals are kept, men take responsibility for larger animals, such as camels and cattle. Women herd, feed, and milk smaller animals, such as goats and sheep. But when only small animals are herded by a group, men usually do the herding, while women do the feeding and milking. Where sheep are kept, women spin the wool into yarn, then weave it into strips used to make tents.

FIGURE 7.7 A Bedouin woman working at a loom. Spinning and weaving are tasks typically assigned to women in

Bedouin societies. (credit: “Weaving Demonstration” by Alan Kotok/flickr, CC BY 2.0)

Unlike foragers, pastoralists strongly value private property, primarily in the form of their herds. The wealth of a family is judged by the size of their herds. Bedouin sons and daughters both inherit herd animals from their fathers, though sons receive more than daughters. Because women are barred from caring for large animals, if a woman inherits camels, she usually entrusts them to a brother or cousin. All property is shared among members of the family.

Bedouin who live in desert regions have extensive knowledge of their challenging environment. They have a large vocabulary for describing different kinds of sand and analyzing dune shapes and other changes in their surroundings (Eastep). Men often go on long drives through the desert, scouting out good grazing spots or looking for rabbits to hunt. Arabian Bedouin are expert trackers, able to judge the age and physical condition of a camel from its tracks as well as when the track was laid and the weight of the animal’s burden.

The Sociocultural Complex of Pastoralism

As with gathering-hunting, the subsistence mode of pastoralism is coordinated with particular sociocultural features. First and foremost, these are cultures that revolve around herd animals. All aspects of culture are shaped by a preoccupation with herds. The size of a family’s herds is a measure of wealth and social status. Animals are used for meat, milk, blood, cloth, and leather. Animals are gifted to cement social relationships such as marriage and slaughtered to commemorate special occasions or the visit of an honored guest. Animals are passed down from fathers to children, establishing the social position and durability of families. Many pastoralist societies have vibrant traditions of music and oral poetry celebrating their animals and their herding lifestyle.

A second feature of pastoral societies is mobility. When herding is the primary livelihood, the group must constantly be on the move. Many agricultural societies also keep domestic animals, but in these cases, the people and their animals stay put on the farm, as crops are the fundamental means of survival. Therefore, farmers tend to have many fewer animals than herders. With larger herds feeding from what are often marginal lands, pastoralists must drive their animals to fresh pastures on a regular basis, often in seasonal cycles over large rangelands. The mobile life of herding groups is structured by various strategies of nomadism and transhumance, as with Bedouin groups. Mobility discourages the accumulation of private property other than herd animals, further enhancing the value of animals to herding groups.

Third, pastoralists rely on a division of labor based on gender and age. And the workload is heavy. Those living in pastoralist societies must herd animals to good pasture, provide them with water, search for new pastures, protect animals from predators, care for sick and weak animals, process animal products such as meat and milk, and produce or obtain all the other elements of material culture necessary for daily life (Bollig 2018). Day-to-day herding is often carried out by boys, while older men take on more complex tasks such as providing water from hard-to-access wells and hunting down predators (Homewood 2018). Older men also manage herds, buying and selling animals to optimize ratios of male to female, old to young. And men settle arguments and make family decisions about resources and security. Women are frequently responsible for milking animals, processing milk products such as cheese and yogurt, and selling those products in local markets. Women and girls make tents and mats, set up and break down camps, gather firewood and wild foods, and do the cooking. Women also care for sick animals and people, maintaining the store of knowledge about available plant medicines.

The fourth feature of herding societies is a vast store of knowledge about animals and the environment. Pastoralists have developed an intimate understanding of the vegetation and water sources necessary for their herds as well as medicinal and edible plants available in different zones of their rangelands. They have deep insight into the anatomy and behavior of their herd animals. They know the qualities associated with different species and how to mix species by gender and age to maintain the availability of animal products such as milk, meat, and wool. Previously, scholars thought that pastoralism was destructive to the environment because of overgrazing. In recent decades, however, studies have demonstrated that herding groups strategically rotate their herds across their rangelands to control the impact on the environment, creating a sustainable way of life.

Contemporary Challenges to Pastoralism

Like many pastoralists, the Bedouin require large tracts of land to continually provide fresh grazing for their herds. Families are associated with defined territories and rarely go beyond them. The nation-states that encompass Bedouin territories do not recognize their right to ownership, however, and consider those lands state-owned. Eager to control this land, governments have asserted various policies to settle the Bedouin, providing schools and health clinics in order to lure them away from their nomadic pastoral lifestyle.

In Egypt, for instance, the government has seized desirable coastal areas from Bedouin groups and sold the land to investors who want to build hotels for the tourism industry. In 1999, the Egyptian army bulldozed a tourist campground run by local Bedouin in order to clear the way for a hotel. The Tourism Development Authority claimed that the Bedouin had only recently lived on the coastal lands and so did not have any right to remain there. In Israel, the government often destroys Bedouin camps and villages in order to make way for settlements and military zones. In November 2020, Israeli soldiers demolished Bedouin structures in the occupied West Bank. Tens of thousands of Bedouin have been displaced by such demolitions and banished from their grazing territories.

Pressured by government regulations and military interventions, many Bedouin now live settled lives in villages and cities across North Africa and the Middle East. Many combine sedentary herding with small farming. Some work as taxi drivers or managers of cafés or campgrounds. Some have become wealthy by investing in the tourist economy and other ventures. Many speak nostalgically of their nomadic way of life and sometimes venture out into the desert again to pasture their herds.

FIGURE 7.8 A Bedouin Palestinian woman in front of the remains of her home, which was destroyed by Israeli law enforcement. Tens of thousands of Bedouin have been displaced by the nation-states that now encompass Bedouin territory. (credit: Eman/Wikimedia Commons, Public Domain)

The predicament of the Bedouin is shared by many contemporary pastoralists. Climate change has made rainfall increasingly unpredictable, threatening the sustainability of grazing herds on marginal lands. Governments and global investors are eager to gain control over land in order to cultivate crops or create tourist attractions and conservation zones (Homewood 2018). Some governments have sought to formalize land ownership among pastoralist groups, creating a competition among groups and individuals to gain title to collective rangelands (Galaty 2015). In some places, such as Botswana, elite groups of herders have seized control over land, making life difficult for small herders.

Some nomadic pastoral groups, such as the Wodaabe of West Africa, have cultivated their distinctive cultural practices as forms of heritage to be protected by human rights organizations or otherwise marketed to tourists. Welcoming researchers and filmmakers to study their unique dances, the Wodaabe have been the subject of over 17 documentary films. Spectacular images of the elaborate dress, costume, and face paint of Wodaabe dancers have been featured on the cover of *National Geographic*, *Elle* magazine, a World Bank brochure, and several CD and album covers (Kratz 2018). Some Wodaabe groups perform their ceremonies for audiences of European tourists. In their *geerewol* and *yaake* dances, groups of young men compete to be selected as the most beautiful dancers by the young women judges. While such involvement in tourism can provide income to impoverished pastoral groups, many anthropologists worry about the commodification of culture and the exploitation of marginal groups for privileged Western audiences.

Some question the future viability of pastoralism as a way of life, suggesting that it might give way to more sedentary forms of ranching. But the transition to ranching would require huge investments of labor and money in necessities such as fencing, feed supplements, veterinary care, permanent wells, trucks, mobile phones, and even airplanes. If herding is practiced in harmony with the environment without these costly inputs, pastoralism may continue to provide a sustainable way of life.

7.5 Plant Cultivation: Horticulture and Agriculture

LEARNING OUTCOMES

By the end of this section, you will be able to:

- Identify and distinguish horticulture and agriculture as distinct subsistence strategies of plant cultivation.
- Describe the cultural forms associated with horticulture and agriculture.
- Trace the connection between the development of agriculture and the development of villages, towns, and cities.

Many thousands of years ago, one of humanity's ancestors might have spied a sprout emerging from a refuse pile of pits, nuts, and seeds. Perhaps it was a lightbulb moment: "Hmm, I wonder if I could do that on purpose...." Or maybe it was somebody who dug up a plant and moved it closer to camp: "Genius! Now I don't have to walk so far!" Somehow, people discovered that they need not rely on the whims of nature to provide them with plants; rather, they could grow the plants they wanted in places more convenient to them. This basic manipulation of nature is called **cultivation**, and gather-hunters were experimenting with it for thousands of years before the development of farming.

The real revolution happened when people began to design their whole way of life around the sowing, tending, and harvesting of plant crops, depending primarily on those crops as sources of food. By planting the seeds of the most desirable plants, humans began to alter the features of those plants over generations of sowing and harvesting. This process of **plant domestication** first took hold around 10,000 to 12,000 years ago, possibly spurred by the warming climate after the last ice age. As plants became bigger, tastier, more nutritious, and easier to grow, larger groups of people could be supported by permanent gardens with no need to migrate. Eventually, some people didn't have to farm at all and could specialize in crafts such as pottery, metalwork, basketry, and textiles. Markets emerged as farmers, herders, and craftspeople became entwined in symbiotic relations of trade. Villages grew into towns and cities and, eventually, regional empires. This might all seems like a great leap forward in human development, and indeed it was a big transformation, but farming came with its share of drawbacks as well.

Archaeologists used to believe that agriculture was separately invented in three primary regions of the world: the Fertile Crescent of the Middle East (11,000 years ago), northern China (9,000 years ago), and Mesoamerica (8,000 years ago). Each of these regions featured the domestication of grains as carbohydrate sources. These grains were combined with lentils and beans as sources of protein, along with meat obtained through trade with neighboring pastoral groups. In the Middle East, wheat, barley, peas, and lentils were cultivated. In China, millet, rice, and beans were grown. It is now known that farming was independently invented in many other regions as well (Bellwood 2019). In addition to the three already mentioned, plants were domesticated in sub-Saharan Africa, India, New Guinea, South America, and the eastern woodlands of North America.

Two Methods of Cultivation: Extensive Horticulture and Intensive Agriculture

The first form of farming that humans developed is known as **extensive horticulture**. Before a plot of land can be cultivated for the first time, the trees and vegetation must be cleared away, an arduous task usually done by men. Sometimes, a strategy called **slash and burn** is used, which involves cutting down the trees and shrubs and burning the rest to the ground, then tilling the ash into the soil as fertilizer. Using digging sticks and hoes, horticultural farmers cultivate the top layer of soil before they sow. As seedlings sprout, they water them and feed them with natural fertilizers such as animal dung, and they weed the gardens regularly.

Horticultural societies plant not just one crop but many. They have learned that certain plants are "friends"—that is, they enhance one another's growth—and so they plant these crops side by side. This is practice is known as **intercropping**. For instance, in Mesoamerica, squash, corn, and beans were planted closely together in flat-topped mounds, a combination known as the "three sisters." Several corn plants were planted first, in the center of the mound. Once the corn seedlings were well established, squash and beans were planted at their base. As they grew, the corn plants provided stalks for the vining bean plants to climb. The bean plants contributed nitrogen to the soil, fertilizing the other two plants. The squash plants spread across the ground, blocking weeds and protecting the root systems of all three. Typically, societies practicing extensive horticulture have vast knowledge of such sustainable farming methods. These techniques are natural ways to optimize the health and yield of each plant while providing a variable and balanced diet throughout the year.

FIGURE 7.9 In a "three sisters" plot, corn, squash and beans are grown together. Each plant benefits the other. (credit: "Three Sisters" by GreenHouse17/flickr, CC BY 2.0)

Incorporating organic methods of fertilization and pest control, horticulture is a sustainable form of farming. Over time, however, this method does deplete the nutrients in the top layer of soil. After a certain number of seasons growing crops on a particular plot, it becomes necessary to let that plot lie **fallow**. When horticultural farmers let a plot lie fallow, they stop cultivating it and let the grasses and brush grow in naturally, which promotes the accumulation of fresh nutrients in the soil. Plots can be left to lie fallow for as little as one season or as many as 20. While one plot regenerates, the farmer moves on to clear, till, and sow another plot for cultivation. Horticulturalists often have several plots of land in various stages of fallow and cultivation. This method of rotating crops over various plots of land is called **extensive** or **shifting cultivation**, as it involves multiple plots over large areas. Horticulture farmers usually have a variety of plots with distinctive soils and climate features, and they tailor specific farming strategies, including crop species, fertilizers, watering methods, and farming-fallow cycles, for each one.

Often in horticultural societies, land is not owned as private property but held in trust by family heads or village leaders who allocate plots of land to individuals. People have the right to use the land assigned to them but not to own or sell it, a practice known as **usufruct rights**. These rights to use certain plots are passed down through families, via either the father or the mother. When newcomers move into an area, they may approach the leader to ask for plots of land to farm. In many African societies, it is also common for people to loan out their plots to one another in gestures of friendship and mutual aid.

Extensive horticulture typically provides enough resources to support extended-family households, perhaps with a bit left over to sell in local markets. This amount left over after the needs of the family are met is called **surplus**. The modest surplus of horticulturalists is sometimes accumulated by families or village leaders in silos or other structures, held in safekeeping for community use in the lean months before the next crops can be harvested. Horticulture does not usually generate enough surplus to support groups of people who do not farm. Craftspeople, religious specialists, and group leaders must all carry on farming alongside these other important activities.

Extensive horticulture provides a good way to cultivate crops on land that is not particularly rich with nutrients. Tropical climates tend to have such soils due to the lack of winter dormancy. In temperate zones (23 to 66 degrees latitude), vegetation dies off in the autumn, depositing dead matter into the soil, which then decomposes into a rich substance called **humus** (hyoo-mus). Humus is essentially built-in fertilizer, feeding new plants as they grow in spring and summer. Because vegetation does not ever die off in tropical areas, tropical soils do not accumulate humus to the extent that temperate soils do. With less humus, it is more advantageous to use a plot of land a few times, then let the natural vegetation grow back. Slashing and burning regrowth is a way for tropical farmers to mimic the natural die-off of vegetation in temperate climates.

In climates with warm and cold seasons, the layer of humus-rich soil is much denser and thicker than in tropical regions. In these areas, it is advantageous to dig deeper to prepare soils for sowing, distributing the layer of humus into a thicker layer of soil to serve as a reservoir of nutrients for the new plants.

The seasonal deposit of nutrients in the soil also happens in areas surrounding large rivers that flood and recede in a yearly cycle. Along the Nile in North Africa and between the Tigris and Euphrates in the Middle East, ancient farmers were able to use the same soils over and over again as the rivers helpfully dumped organic matter onto their farmlands every year. Riverine farmers learned to control flows of water, creating systems of irrigation to continually water their crops. Sumerian farmers in the Mesopotamian crescent between the Tigris and Euphrates were the first to use the plow, using oxen to pull large blades through their garden plots. Plowing makes the soil even richer for planting.

FIGURE 7.10 A Sumerian plow. Sumerian farmers were the first to use the plow, making possible greater yields. (credit: "John Deere Plow" by Public.Resource.Org/flickr, CC BY 2.0)

The use of a plow, the development of irrigation systems, and the continuous cultivation of the same plots are part of a way of farming called **intensive agriculture**. A good way to remember the difference between extensive and intensive cultivation is to think about how extensive farming involves farming multiple plots over *extensive* territory, while intensive farming involves applying *intensive* methods to the same plots over and over again. Intensive agriculture generates much greater yields than horticulture, supporting far larger populations. Greater yields mean greater surplus, which means that societies practicing intensive agriculture generate groups of people who don't need to farm, such as specialists in craft production, trade, religion, and government.

Farmers who practice intensive agriculture focus on a small number of crops, frequently grains or legumes. They use the surplus generated from intensive methods to trade for other foods, tools, and material goods to meet the needs of their households.

Most people use the word *agriculture* to mean plant cultivation of any kind. For anthropologists, however, agriculture is just one form of plant cultivation—the kind involving intensive methods such as plows, draft animals, irrigation systems, and repeated use of plots. This chapter uses the term *plant cultivation* to refer to both extensive horticulture and intensive agriculture. References to specific types of cultivation use the terms *extensive horticulture* and *intensive agriculture*.

The Kayapó: Flexible Horticulture

In the eastern Amazonian rainforest, beside the Xingu River, live a group of people known by their neighbors as the Kayapó. Mixing slash-and-burn horticulture with gathering and hunting and some animal domestication, the Kayapó have created an ingenious and flexible way of life that carefully cultivates the resources of the rainforest, savanna, and intermediate zones (Posey 2002).

Like most farming societies, the Kayapó rely on a small set of staple carbohydrate crops, including sweet potato, manioc, maize, and taro. Every three to five years, they clear new plots for their gardens, leaving the old plots fallow. Rather than passively letting the old plots regenerate, however, the Kayapó plant fruit trees, medicinal plants, and other desirable vegetation that keep the plots productive throughout the fallow period. They also transplant edible and medicinal plants alongside the paths that serve as transit routes throughout their territory. The Kayapó venture out on these paths in gathering-and-hunting expeditions that supplement their farming endeavors during part of the year. Women gather fruits, nuts, and berries, and men hunt armadillos, deer, anteaters, and wild pigs. Like the Hadza, the Kayapó regularly harvest honey, the sweet treat of the forest. Another delicacy is the tortoise, slaughtered in large numbers for special festivals. The Kayapó also fish with bows and arrows as well as nets and plant-based poison. Sometimes, women stay in the village while men go hunting or fishing.

Because they farm, the Kayapó live in villages for most of the year. Extended-family houses are situated in a circle surrounding a central public space with a men's house in the center. Social activities are coordinated by groups based on gender, age, and extended family. Most villages have two men's societies, each one associated with a women's society. When a boy becomes a man, he chooses which society he wants to join, usually that of his intended father-in-law. After he marries, his wife joins the women's society associated with her husband's group. Each society has its own leader and meeting place.

FIGURE 7.11 A multiethnic celebration attended by the Kayapo and eight other ethnic groups. The celebration promotes the interaction of indigenous groups with each other and the public. (credit: "VI Aldeia Multiétnica no XV Meeting of Encontro de Culturas Tradicionais da Chapada dos Veadeiros" by Oliver Kornblihtt/Secretaria Especial da

Cultura do Ministério da Cidadania/flickr, CC BY 2.0)

Kayapó life is organized according to seasons. Planting is done in the “low water” season, and farming continues until harvest. After this, wild fruits ripen, attracting game for the hunting season, the “high water” time. This is followed by a period of leisure, family activities, and increased fishing. Then, a new year begins. Kayapó culture marks these seasons with a calendar of ceremonies. Festivals celebrate the farming and hunting seasons, and specific rituals are performed to promote the success of these subsistence methods.

The Kayapó are deeply knowledgeable about their environment and work diligently to cultivate the diversity of flora and fauna in the various ecological zones of their territory. In addition to an impressive store of general knowledge, each village has individuals with expertise in soils, plants, animals, and medicines. The Kayapó identify many different micro-zones within the continuum between forest and savanna, associating each zone with a distinct set of interrelated plants, animals, and soil types. They attract certain species of game for hunting by sowing specific plants in specific areas. For farming, they use ground cover such as plants, logs, leaves, straw, and bark to adjust the moisture, shade, and temperature of soils. They fertilize certain crops with the ash of specific plants, making use of the vegetation cleared and weeded in farming. They meticulously design their gardens in concentric circles to provide optimal light and water to each species of plant, and they practice complex forms of intercropping of plants that benefit one another. For instance, several plants are considered “banana neighbors,” good to plant next to bananas. Among these is a plant called “child-want-not,” a plant used by Kayapó women to regulate fertility.

In open areas, the Kayapó create small areas of special diversity called *apêtê*, or “forest islands.” To create an *apêtê*, they first spread a layer of organic matter, such as termite nests, then sow seeds and transplants of useful trees and plants in the mound of nutrient-rich soil. As the plants grow, the Kayapó cut down the highest trees in the center to provide more light throughout the *apêtê*. The result is a store of medicinal and edible plants as well as a nice, shady place to rest in the middle of an open field. Sometimes, *apêtê* include vines that produce potable water, providing a sort of drinking fountain for people as they travel about the territory.

The nurturing of plant biodiversity is important to the practice of medicine among the Kayapó. They identify and cultivate hundreds of plants used to treat specific ailments such as diarrhea, scorpion stings, and snakebites. They organize their knowledge of both illnesses and plants in complex classificatory schemes. The Kayapó identify 50 separate types of diarrhea and treat each one with a specific plant medicine.

The Kayapó are also masters of zoology. They study the anatomy and behavior of the animals in their environment and use that knowledge for hunting and farming. For instance, when a garden is infested with leaf-cutting ants, Kayapó farmers deliberately plant nests of smelly ants around the plot. The pheromones of the smelly ants scare away the destructive leaf-cutting ants. Smelly ants can also be crushed and inhaled as a medicine to clear the sinuses.

The Kayapó keep many pets, including birds, snakes, spiders, and various mammals. One survey found more than 60 species of animal kept as pets in one village alone! Children are encouraged to observe the behavior of their pets to learn as much as possible.

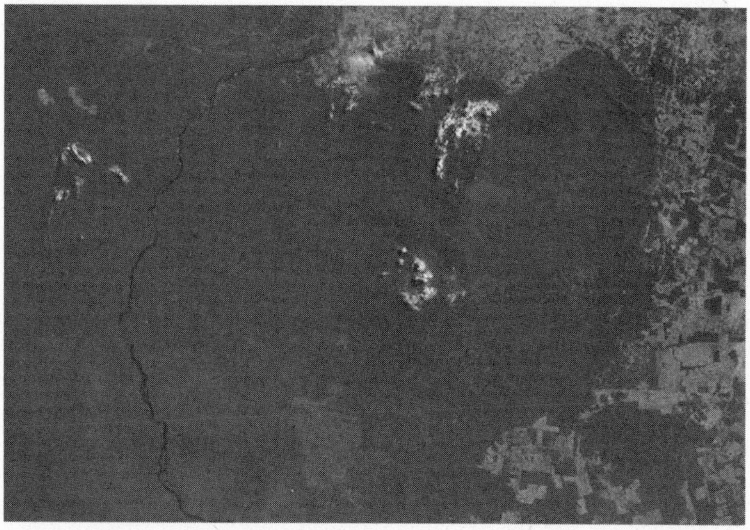

FIGURE 7.12 An arial view of the land of the Kayapó. The Kayapo are deeply knowledgeable about the ecology of their environment and have developed a number of horticultural practices designed to preserve and enhance the natural abundance around them. (credit: NASA/Wikimedia Commons, Public Domain)

The Kayapó have developed a vast store of knowledge about their surroundings, and they use that knowledge to promote plant and animal biodiversity and nurture their environment. Some anthropologists suggest that industrialized societies could learn much about environmental management and ecological sustainability from horticultural groups such as the Kayapó.

The Sociocultural Complex of Plant Cultivation

As with the Kayapó, horticulture is often combined with gathering and hunting and even pastoralism to form a flexible, sustainable, and highly successful subsistence strategy. Many societies practicing intensive agriculture also forage and keep animals on the side, although they spend much less time gathering and hunting. As they come to rely more and more on their crops, farming peoples settle down to form permanent villages. Frequently, as with the Kayapó, those villages consist of extended-family houses with a central area for public meetings. Most villages consist of several extended families, each with its own family leader or set of elders. As agricultural methods intensify, it becomes necessary for families to cooperate in the development of irrigation schemes, trade networks, and the allocation and protection of land. Forms of community leadership and group decision-making emerge to organize these activities. Those political forms will be discussed in the next chapter.

Plant cultivation requires a *lot* of work, substantially more than gathering-hunting. Clearing small trees and brush for new garden plots is backbreaking work, followed by the physical challenges of tilling, sowing, watering, weeding, controlling pests, and (hopefully) harvesting. Throughout the year, crops must be either processed for market or household meals or made into something useful. Tools such as hoes, scythes, and plows must be bought or made and constantly maintained. Where used, plows and draft animals require daily care. In order to get all of this work done, agricultural societies rely on the labor of extended families, with chores divvied up by gender and age.

Often, men are responsible for clearing land, while women do the sowing as well as the daily work of weeding and watering. Children help with garden chores, often charged with carrying water or scaring away the birds and small mammals that scavenge crops. Men make and maintain tools and also tend to draft animals, while women process materials for home consumption, such as food and craft items. Women make pottery, baskets, clothing, and shoes (until this work is taken over by craftspeople). Girls are put to work as babysitters, taking care of younger children while their parents work at other tasks. Typically, men assume positions of power in the public realm as leaders of extended families and villages, but women often represent their interests in their own groups with their own leadership, as in Kayapó society.

The gendered arrangement of work and power is highly variable. In some societies, men take charge of marketing crops, while in others, women take on this role. Frequently, as cultivation intensifies with the growing of large cash crops such as wheat and rice, men market the cash crops while women sell the vegetables from their gardens.

The work of plant cultivation is structured by the yearly cycle of the changing seasons. Frequently, the social life of plant-cultivating societies is organized into a similar annual calendar, with festivals, ceremonies, and rituals marking various stages in the process of cultivation. For instance, "garden magic," such as the recitation of spells, is often an integral part of preparing garden plots for the growing season. Magical spells and blessings provide a means of encouraging good weather and healthy plants and help manage the anxieties of communities that are heavily dependent on the success of their crops. Harvest time is frequently marked by a large festival, with feasting, the performance of special songs and dances, and the commemoration of gods and ancestors.

Successful plant cultivation requires a great deal of knowledge about plant and animal biology, soil composition, geology, and weather patterns (see Edington 2017 for a wonderful overview). Many cultivators have a deep understanding of the relationship between soil and seed. Sukuma farmers in Tanzania identify six types of soil, five good for planting a specific crop—rice, corn, sorghum, two kinds of groundnut—and a sixth soil type only good for grazing cattle. Peruvian potato farmers have knowledge of 35 different potato varieties and are able to match each one to the soil type and environmental conditions most conducive to a healthy harvest. Cultivators rely on environmental indicators to let them know optimal times for planting and harvesting. They watch for the flowering and fruiting of wild plants, migratory movements of birds, and changing patterns of stars in the night sky. Many farmers in India look for the blossoming of yellow flowers on the laburnum trees to indicate the imminent arrival of the monsoons. Others rely on the pied crested cuckoo, which arrives just ahead of the monsoon rains.

Farming societies have various techniques for managing weeds and garden pests. Some weeds are welcome as sources of food and materials for crafts such as baskets. Animals attracted to growing crops are frequently hunted as supplementary sources of protein. Grasshoppers and locusts can be fried into crispy treats, and larger animals such as rodents can be trapped and eaten as meat. Many cultivators use specific plants to repel weeds and pests. Traditional Chinese farmers used the root bark of the thunder god vine to keep caterpillars and aphids away from their crops. Other plants, such as neem and mint, are used to protect harvested produce from being eaten by insects.

This vast knowledge of the natural world is undergirded by a value system that emphasizes environmental conservation and protection. Often, environmental knowledge is entwined with supernatural beliefs and cultural values and preserved in songs, stories, legends, and ritual practices. Ancient religious texts often function as records of environmental knowledge and values as well as supernatural beliefs and practices. In ancient India, for example, Hindu texts such as the Vedas commanded that humans should live in harmony with nature rather than exploiting it (Jain 2019). Certain trees and plants with particular value to humans were revered and associated with supernatural beings. The Vedas called for the protection of those trees and plants and assigned penalties for cutting them down. Typically, the cultures of plant cultivators promote reverence for nature and compel people to practice sustainable forms of farming that protect the soil and preserve biodiversity.

As mentioned earlier, intensive agriculture produces a much larger surplus than horticultural methods. As agricultural surpluses and human populations both grew, villages expanded into towns, which evolved into cities. Emerging about 7,000 ago, the city of Uruk, located in what is now Iraq, was the first large urban center in Mesopotamia and possibly the world (Nardo 2007; Wallenfels and Sasson 2000). At its peak population, it housed 50,000 to 80,000 people, with more living in the surrounding metropolitan area. Surrounding peoples practiced agriculture and herding and traded their surplus in the city markets. Within the city, a class of craftspeople supported themselves without doing any farming, prominent among them cloth makers and metalworkers. Uruk peoples traded widely with groups throughout Mesopotamia and what is now western Iran. The accumulation of wealth in the city supported the building of great temples and city walls by a class of construction workers (Pittman 2019). Such public buildings are called **monumental architecture**. Cuneiform writing was invented as a method of accounting, used to keep track of trade and inventory. Coordinating this complex economy was a centralized government headed by a king.

Like Uruk in Mesopotamia, the early cities of Abydos in Egypt, Harappa in the Indus Valley, and Anyang in China all emerged close to waterways, locations where intensive agriculture stimulated increases in population (Rizvi 2007). Cities provided sites for craft specialization, the organization of regional trade, the building of monumental architecture, the development of writing, and the centralization of power. With its large stone plaza, pyramids, and ball courts, the Zapotec city of Monte Albán emerged as an administrative capital in Mesoamerica around 4,000 years ago. With its own plaza and pyramids, the site of Caral in present-day Peru developed into a city around the same time as Monte Albán. Built on a base of agricultural surplus, all of these cities demonstrate urban planning, heterogeneous populations, regional trade, and monumental architecture.

Contemporary Challenges of Farming Societies

Communities relying primarily on extensive horticulture or intensive agriculture are generally able to meet their own subsistence needs. However, with the development of cities into regional empires, many cultivators became incorporated into larger structures of trade and government. Under pressure from these structures, farmers past and present were and are obliged to sell their surplus for cash in order to pay taxes and purchase agricultural inputs such as seed and fertilizer. As cities and states grow, they exert pressure on cultivators to produce ever higher yields to support greater populations and more elaborate state projects. As cultivators become incorporated into demanding states, they become a class of **peasants**. A peasant is a farmer with a small plot of land incorporated into a larger regional economy. Nearly all contemporary cultivators are part of a peasant class in their nation-states (Sillitoe 2018). Peasants are often marginalized and disadvantaged, reliant on economic and political structures they cannot control, and exploited by urban elites. Many farmers now make up a rural underclass.

Extensive horticulturalists such as the Kayapó require large areas of land in order to allow their fallow plots to regenerate before reusing them. Over the past 30 years, cattle ranchers, loggers, and miners have moved into Kayapó territory. Unlike the Kayapó, ranchers and loggers practice ecologically damaging methods, leaving large areas of barren wasteland in their wake. Early on, some Kayapó communities accommodated iron and gold mining operations, signing contracts that granted mining companies permission to operate in exchange for a small percentage of profits. However, mining practices polluted the rivers that the Kayapó rely on for drinking, bathing, and fishing. With the emergence of gold rush towns and the flood of foreigners into the area, the Kayapó began to see unwelcome changes in their communities, such as increases in disease and problematic alcohol use. Many Kayapó turned against outsiders, attacking loggers and miners to force them off of Kayapó land. As a further problem, the Brazilian government has proposed a series of large hydroelectric dams on Kayapó rivers to generate power in the Amazonian hinterlands. These dams would flood Kayapó territory, displacing more than 20,000 people. Recognizing these projects as threats to their culture and way of life, the Kayapó have joined with other Amazonian Indigenous groups in dramatic protests attracting global attention and support (Turner and Fajans-Turner 2006). The rock star Sting attended one such protest and later founded the Rainforest Foundation Fund to support the efforts of the Kayapó to protect their land.

FIGURE 7.13 Kayapo representatives are shown a map of mining concessions within their lands. Mining is just one of the threats to the Kayapo way of life and to the ecological health of their territory that has emerged in the recent decades. (credit: Beto Ricardo/Instituto Socio-Ambiental/Wikimedia Commons, Public Domain)

You may have heard this story before—the story of Indigenous peoples who come to be surrounded and dominated by extractive capitalists and state officials. In their relations with Indigenous peoples practicing gathering-hunting, pastoralism, and horticulture, states often argue that such people are resisting inevitable progress. Indeed, American world history textbooks often represent the emergence of cities, the expansion of trade, and the creation of bureaucratic states as steps in the triumphal march of progress, key achievements in the development of civilization.

But progress for whom? The more that is learned about life in nonindustrial, noncapitalist societies, the more questions are raised about these notions of progress.

7.6 Exchange, Value, and Consumption

LEARNING OUTCOMES

By the end of this section, you will be able to:

- Outline four types of exchange.
- Define the concept of reciprocity.
- Define the concepts of money and market exchange.
- Describe how money expresses conflicted notions of morality.

Before moving ahead to discuss the last of the four major subsistence methods, it's worth reviewing the ways in which goods circulate in societies in accordance with each mode of subsistence. The four subsistence strategies are defined primarily by their techniques of production—that is, the way people use materials from their environments to make the things they need, such as food, clothing, shelter, and medicines. Previous sections have described how each production strategy entails its own distinctive methods of allocating those needful things to individuals and groups within the community. This section details the various methods of circulating things through social groups.

Most societies rely on one primary strategy for making a living, though they very often combine it with one or more others in flexible ways over time. If key foods become impossible to find, gatherer-hunters may take up farming for a few seasons. Many herding groups regularly hunt and sometimes plant crops along their nomadic routes, returning the next season to harvest the crops. Many farmers also keep domesticated animals. So it is with modes of exchange. Most societies practice not just one strategy but a combination of many, dominated by the form of exchange that dovetails with the main subsistence strategy.

Forms of Exchange

Recall the importance of egalitarian sharing in gatherer-hunter societies. When hunters return to camp bearing large game, they divide it equally among members of the band. When gatherers bring back loads of nuts or fruit, they hand them out freely to anyone who is hungry. Everyone is expected and required to share with everyone else. **Generalized reciprocity** is the anthropological term to describe how people share things with no regard for their value or interest in compensation. This form of exchange doesn't look like exchange at all; it looks much more like altruism. But when rigorously practiced by a group, with social sanctions used to punish laziness and stinginess, the result of generalized reciprocity over time is more or less the equal exchange of goods among all members of the group.

Outside of gathering-hunting societies, generalized reciprocity is also common in many close relationships, such as family relationships and friendships. When you're staying in your parents' house, does it occur to you to pay them when you grab a soft drink from the fridge? If a friend wants to borrow a pair of boots, do you charge them a rental fee? Probably not. However, the logic of exchange changes as the intensity of the relationship decreases and value of the object increases. Your parents might give you a car if you needed one, but you would not expect a friend to do so without some sort of compensation.

In gathering-hunting and horticultural societies, another form of reciprocal exchange is common among individuals. Among the Dobe Ju/'hoansi and other San groups in southern Africa, people develop relationships with one another based on a gift-giving practice called ***hxaro*** (Barnard 2018). The relationship begins when one person asks another person, often someone in another band, to give them a particular item, such as a digging stick or a cooking pot. This request may be rejected or accepted. If accepted, the two enter into an ongoing relationship of exchange, which may last forever or be broken off at some future point. After an unspecified period of time, the receiver makes a return gift, often of somewhat of equal or slightly greater value. The value of the items is never discussed; nor is the time between episodes of gift giving. All is made to seem natural and spontaneous. This form of exchange is known as **balanced reciprocity**. These relationships come with many advantages—for instance, the right to hunt and gather in the band of your *hxaro* partner. For this reason, many people maintain as many as 10 to 12 ongoing *hxaro* relationships. The main point of balanced reciprocity is not to gain resources and opportunities. Rather, the whole point of these serial exchanges of things is to establish and affirm relationships among people. Some degree of unspoken calculation is involved in choosing gifts that affirm and intensify the relationship over time, with givers slowly raising the value of gifts to deepen the relationship. These special relationships based on reciprocal gift giving are found in many other horticultural and agricultural societies as well.

While such gift-giving relationships seem to be governed by a sense of mutual goodwill, a more fierce and competitive form of balanced reciprocity developed among the Indigenous peoples of the Pacific Northwest coast of Canada and the United States (High 2018). Among groups such as the Haida, Kwakiutl, and Tlingit, chiefs sponsored great feasts called potlatches to commemorate births, weddings, deaths, and other important events. At these **potlatch** feasts, the chief of the host community would present an abundance of gifts to the chief of an invited community. Such gifts included blankets, animal skins, copper plaques, and preserved food. Sometimes, these items were deliberately burned in spectacles of extravagant waste. By foisting this abundance of gifts upon a guest chief, the host chief demonstrated their wealth and power and levied a challenge to the guest chief to counter with an even more lavish feast and greater trove of gifts. Power among neighboring communities was established and reinforced through this competitive feasting, not by acquiring wealth but by giving it away. More recent interpretations of potlatch suggest that such ceremonies not only operated as forms of reciprocity but also helped distribute specific goods found in one community to surrounding areas where those goods might be impossible to find.

FIGURE 7.14 A potlatch in British Columbia in the 1890s. In potlach ceremonies, the power and wealth of a group was demonstrated not by what they acquired but by what they gave away. (credit: Edward S. Curtis/Wikimedia Commons, Public Domain)

The role of extended-family leaders in the practice of potlatch is an example of the tendency for leaders to gain control of community wealth and use it for distribution as well as prestige. This practice is particularly pronounced in agricultural societies that have chiefs, such as the peoples of the Hawaiian Islands in the precolonial era. Before contact with Europeans, the Hawaiian Islands were ruled by a multilevel system of chiefs who controlled land, natural resources, and trade. Commoners were required to pay tribute to their chiefs in the form of labor, food, and other products. For farmers, this meant that a portion of their agricultural surplus was relayed to local chiefs. These local chiefs then relayed a portion of the tribute they received to regional chiefs, and so on up the pyramid to the great chief. This tribute supported government at each level, including royal courts, political advisers, priests, military strategists, guards, and entertainers. In this way, political leaders became centers of the concentration of wealth, which was then used to provide communities with the benefits of government, such as social order, conflict resolution, military protection, trade coordination, and the construction of public works such as fishponds, water channels, and temples. In this hierarchical system, tribute flowed up to elites, while government goods and services flowed down to commoners. This two-way flow is called **redistribution**, and it's a very common feature of chiefdoms, as will be discussed in the next chapter. Tribute was used by leaders to finance monument building, warfare, trade, and ceremonial feasting as well as the chief's own lavish regalia and large retinue of assistants, bureaucrats, and servants.

Redistribution is practiced in all state societies. Consider the roads in your neighborhood, the postal service, the public schools, the libraries, government-funded scientific research, the courts, the prisons, the police—all are paid for by taxation, the form of redistribution conducted by states. While some see taxation as a predatory fee extracted by unproductive elites, taxation makes possible the social order, the economy, and the well-being of state citizens. It's important to recognize that redistribution is not a way for individuals to purchase goods and services from the state but rather a system of allocating resources for the well-being of society as a whole.

Read this first-hand experience of the author of this chapter, Jennifer Hasty,

> *Imagine that you go to take a shower and discover that you're out of soap. How can you solve this problem? Gift exchange? A government program? Surely not. In contemporary Western society, forms of reciprocity and redistribution have become increasingly sidelined by the other main form of economic exchange:* ***markets****. A market is an institution that makes it possible for buyers and sellers of goods to meet for the purposes of exchange. In the most concrete sense, a market is an actual place. If you need a bar of soap (or shampoo, or a towel, or a bathtub), you go the market and buy one. In fact, I never pack soap when I travel to Ghana, as one of the first thing I do when I get there is head for the nearest market.*

West African markets are noisy, vibrant places full of shrewd women traders with their neat stacks and haphazard heaps of colorful goods. At big markets such as Makola and Kaneshie, you can find almost anything you might want, from large appliances to clothes, school supplies, fresh spices, and produce. The air is infused with the shifting aromas of fried plantain, "stinky" fish, and freshly baked bofrot, a kind of Ghanaian doughnut. Music blasts from radios posted at kiosks here and there. Mobile vendors ply the crowded paths, their goods carefully draped on their bodies or stacked on their heads. Customers from all walks of life browse the rows upon rows of seated vendors, everyone chatting and socializing, buyers and sellers haggling the price of goods. Early on, I learned that the value of a product is not fixed but contingent on many factors, such as time of day, amount of stock, and the perceived identity of the buyer. Just buying a few bars of soap can be a complex social interaction combined with a rich sensory experience.

FIGURE 7.15 Makola Market in downtown Accra, Ghana. West African markets are noisy, vibrant places, very different from Western grocery stores. (credit: "Clothes Market" by Francisco Anzola/flickr, CC BY 2.0)

More recently, Western-style grocery stores have opened up in Ghana. In contrast to the intense sensory experience of markets, these stores are quiet and, to me, a bit underwhelming. A small number of shoppers silently push their carts up and down the aisles, avoiding eye contact with one another. At checkout, a bored clerk rings up your items and informs you of the total. It does not matter who you are—rich or poor, the total is the same. This is a routinized, predictable experience. In the United States, automatic checkout is becoming increasingly common in stores, eliminating the off chance that you might have any sort of meaningful human contact in the course of your market transaction. With online purchasing, the market is no longer a place at all but a virtual site on a computer screen that absolutely precludes any possibility of direct human interaction. Consumers have responded to the desocialization of online market relations by embracing the highly expressive and interactive realm of consumer reviews. And even in the brick-and-mortar shops, people resist the boring antisocial regimen of modern shopping by talking on their cell phones, enjoying food samples, and looking for romantic partners.

All of these forms of exchange can be found in contemporary capitalist societies. Generalized reciprocity is practiced among family members and very, very close friends. Balanced reciprocity is the unspoken logic guiding most exchanges among friends and acquaintances. If you ask your neighbor to collect your mail while you're out of town, you might expect your neighbor to ask you for a similar favor in the future. Recently, while I was out of town for a week, I asked the parents of my daughter's school friend if they could take her to and from school. They kindly obliged. A month later, I had to leave town again for a week. In that intervening month, I had been unable to reciprocate for the favor of shuttling my child around, so I hesitated to ask those same parents to do it again. Instead, I hired someone, the friend of a friend but a stranger to me.

Among strangers, market exchange is the most common form of transaction. In capitalist societies, market exchange is the default setting; if all else fails, pay for it. Market transactions are quick and easy, and the participants walk away relatively unencumbered by future obligation. If this is the advantage of market exchange, it can also be a big disadvantage. Without the relations of mutuality and trust established by forms of reciprocity, the participants in market exchange are motivated by the desire to get more than they give. A society dominated by market exchange is therefore dominated by the logic of self-interest and greed rather than cooperation and social well-being.

Money

In the midst of the COVID-19 pandemic, many shops witnessed a scarcity of hard currency, prompting them to put up signs requesting people to use credit or debit cards or mobile payment apps to make purchases. This episode is part of a larger shift over the past several decades away from coins and bills and toward more abstract forms of payment such as chip cards and "fintech," the mobile debit apps accessed through smartphones. And even more abstractly, now there are even virtual currencies such as bitcoin and other cryptocurrencies. Bitcoin is a currency generated by a computer dedicated to solving complex mathematical problems. How is that even money?

What is **money**? In the formulation of classical philosophy, money is defined by three functions: it serves as a medium of exchange, a unit of account, and a store of value. Imagine that two friends from neighboring groups, one a pastoralist group and the other a horticultural group, meet in town. The pastoralist has a freshly slaughtered goat slung over their shoulder. The horticulturalist is carrying a small sack of vegetables. They decide they'd like to trade. The farmer wants all of the meat, but the herder wants only a small portion of the vegetables. Each person wants the trade to be equal; that is, they both want to give and receive the same value. How can they conduct this transaction? How do they know the value of the things they want to trade?

It seems natural to imagine these two trader friends attempting to negotiate some sort of barter. The swapping of goods on the spot, however, was never a dominant form of exchange in any culture in the past. Instead, many anthropologists argue that precapitalist peoples relied more on gift exchange, redistribution, and debt to circulate goods through society. So it's more likely that the pastoralist would make a good-faith gift of the whole goat to their gardening friend, knowing that both would remember the gardener's obligation to return the favor with more vegetables (or something else of fairly equal value) in the future. If this seems complicated, it probably was. Individuals would have been involved in many such relationships simultaneously – whole communities of people all mutually entwined in relations of credit and debt.

The other possible solution is money. If these two traders live in a society that uses some arbitrary other thing to enumerate value, they would know that all of the meat has the value of 50 units (or shekels, cowrie shells, tally sticks, bones, animal skins, brass rods, gold coins, bank notes, or any one of the myriad other objects used as money in the past). A small portion of vegetables might have the value of only 10 units. If these two have come with their wallets, they can use money to make two separate transactions for items of different value rather than trying to negotiate one swap. They can make the exchanges and walk away without entanglement.

FIGURE 7.16 Examples of local currencies. Local currencies are designed to be used only within designated

geographic areas, with the goal of enhancing the economy of the community. (credit: Mune/Wikimedia Commons, Public Domain)

There are two kinds of money, general purpose and special purpose. The transaction described above is an example of **general-purpose money**—that is, money that can be exchanged for a wide variety of goods and services. Dollars, euros, pesos, yen, and bitcoin are all forms of general-purpose money. General-purpose money is portable, divisible, and easily available. **Special-purpose money** is currency that is used to purchase one particular kind of thing. In some pastoral societies of West African, cattle have been used as forms of bridewealth, or the payment made by a groom to the family of his prospective bride. The Tinputz people of Papua New Guinea had two forms of special-purpose money, strings of flying fox teeth and strings of shell disks. These were used for marriages and other socially important occasions. Special-purpose money is generally more difficult to obtain, transport, and/or measure precisely. In American society, many grocery stores now offer special-use "points" for loyal shoppers that can be used to buy gas at particular gas stations. Credit card companies, airlines, and other businesses offer similar forms of special-purpose points. Such special-use currency illustrates the arbitrary nature of money.

7.7 Industrialism and Postmodernity

LEARNING OUTCOMES

By the end of this section, you will be able to:

- Define industrialism and describe how it developed.
- Articulate the cultural forms associated with industrialism.
- Describe how the development of industrialism instigated the establishment of colonial empires and the global economic system.
- Evaluate the long-term effects of colonial subjugation on postcolonial economies and societies.
- Define the concepts of modernity and alternative modernity.

All of the modes of subsistence previously discussed rely on human labor applied directly to environmental resources to produce relatively small batches of food, tools, and other goods. In the past 10,000 years, gathering-hunting, pastoralism, and agriculture all existed side by side, and most groups dabbled in more than one of these modes.

In these systems, most work is conducted by extended-family groups in the context of the household, whether settled or mobile. These family groups regulate their own work cycles and determine how goods are produced and distributed based on their own needs and strategies. In the 1700s in Britain, a new way of producing goods began to develop, slowly at first and then growing exponentially to sweep the globe. That mode of subsistence is **industrialism**: the use of wage labor, machines, and chemical processes to mass-produce commodities. Taking hold first in Europe, this mode of subsistence drew sets of people away from their households into factories where they performed repetitive forms of labor in return for regular wages. In the factory setting, workers have very little control over their own work cycles and no claim whatsoever on the goods they produce.

As a mode of subsistence, industrialism drew from and transformed other modes of production, such as pastoralism and agriculture. Industrialism did not supersede other modes but rather used them as sources of raw materials and labor. Gatherer-hunters, with no surplus to supply industry, are deemed useless to industrialism. Gatherer-hunter groups are thus marginalized by contemporary states, often being confined to reservations where their way of life is difficult or impossible to practice.

Cloth, Factories, and Slavery: The Rise of Industrialism

In the early 1700s, small-scale sheepherders were producing raw wool throughout the British countryside. As large-scale cloth manufacturing was limited in England at the time, traders exported much of that raw wool to European countries such as the Netherlands, where it was processed into cloth. A general rule in economics is that selling raw materials is not nearly as profitable as processing them into commodities to sell to consumers. Envious of European textile processing, British manufacturers sought to greatly expand local processing of British wool into cloth for export. As British manufacturers bought more and more wool, the price of wool skyrocketed. Large British landholders began to evict small-scale peasants from their land so that they could expand their own sheep herds to take advantage of the rising price of wool.

FIGURE 7.17 Industrial weaving was often done by young women. Working long hours in a textile factory was a very difference experience from the weaving that these women's mothers and grandmothers may have done at home. (credit: "The Bobbin Girl" by National Park Service/Wikimedia Commons, Public Domain)

Landless people flooded into British cities looking for work around the same time that manufacturers were looking for a cheap source of wage labor to process wool into cloth in the new factories. The drive to increase productivity while lowering production costs prompted several key technological innovations, such as the large-scale use of water mills and, later, the steam engine to power these factories. Moreover, new techniques for managing the labor force emerged, such as the clock-regulated workday and sets of work rules known as shop-floor discipline. The twin forces of technological innovation and labor management (some would call it exploitation) stimulated similar shifts toward mass production of cotton cloth, pottery, and metals.

By the mid-1800s, the entire economy of England was completely transformed, now dominated by the mass production of commodities in factories for export all over the world. This model of industrial manufacturing of mass commodities spread across western Europe, reshaping urban national economies in the Netherlands, Germany, France, and beyond.

Soon, these burgeoning industries had outgrown local supplies of raw materials for their factories and started looking for additional sources of cotton, sugar, tea, tobacco, and other materials that could be processed into commodities. One solution was found in the expansion of the African slave trade in the 1700s and the use of enslaved persons on plantations in the New World to produce raw materials to supply the factories in England.

That is a lot of history, and this is an anthropology textbook, but it is important to know why European societies shifted to industrial production in the 1700s. It was not because it provided a better way of life for the majority of people but because it generated stupendous profits for classes of large landowners, factory owners, and transnational traders. For peasants kicked off their land and forced to live in squalor in urban slums, working 14-hour days under the harsh discipline of the shop steward, this was not progress. For enslaved persons abducted from their homes and shipped to a foreign land, worked to death under threat of the lash, this was not progress. For a class of European consumers eager for fancy new clothes and tasty new foods, perhaps it seemed like progress.

In fact, the modern industry of advertising was invented during this time to tell people that it *was* progress. Advertising was necessary to stimulate the consumption of all the mass-produced commodities created by European manufacturers. From a holistic perspective, the notions of progress and development that emerged in 19th-century Europe went hand in hand with the demands of the industrial economy, providing rationales for the new forms of conflict and domination.

Colonialism and Global Capitalism

A second reason for providing the brief history lesson in the last section is to show how the development of the industrial economy in Europe generated the global system of capitalism that exists today. After the European slave trade was abolished in the early 19th century, Europeans expanded their control over African, Asian, and New World territories, cultivating new sources of such raw materials as peanuts, cocoa, and palm oil to develop even more lucrative European industries. This expansion of control took the form of **colonialism**, the political domination of another country in the interest of economic exploitation.

From the 1500s to the 1900s, European countries strove to dominate much of Africa, Asia, and the Middle East as well as North, Central and South America. Different techniques of rule were practiced at different times and places, but all colonialism involved a set of key features, including violent rule by a European government, the extraction of raw materials, forced labor, taxation, the spread of Christian missions, the denigration of local cultures, the introduction of diseases, and increased local conflict. While their motivations were primarily economic, European colonizers claimed to be inspired by a "civilizing mission"—the idea that European domination was necessary to bring the benefits of progress, such as hospitals and schools. For colonized peoples, the hardships and injustices of colonial rule far outweighed the meager benefits offered to some groups.

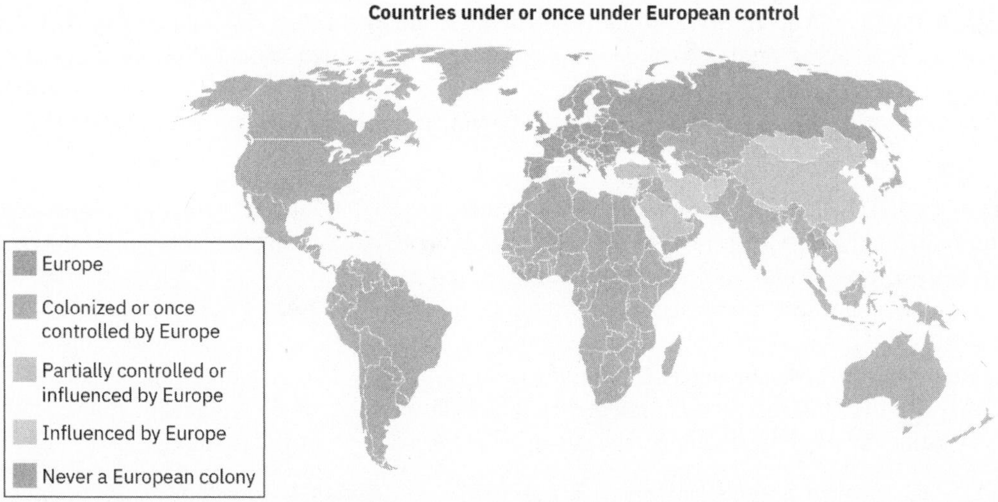

FIGURE 7.18 Postcolonial countries of the world. Note the pervasive influence that European nations have had around the globe, with just a few isolated areas that have remained free of European influence or control. (attribution: Copyright Rice University, OpenStax, CC BY 4.0 license)

Economically, the whole purpose of colonialism was to design a system for extracting raw materials to support the industrial economies of Europe. Therefore, European countries such as Britain, France, and Germany sought out sources of valuable minerals for the mining industry as well as good land for growing crops that European manufacturers could process into commodities. In Africa, many fertile regions were seized and sold to White settlers to establish plantations for growing tea, cotton, and other cash crops. The African peoples who lived there were relocated to less fertile lands and forced to work on the White plantations in order to survive. In places where White people found it hard to live (e.g., places with widespread tropical diseases such as malaria), colonial governments recruited African farmers to grow cash crops such as coffee and cocoa. Colonial subjects were taxed by colonial governments in order to force them to work in mines and on plantations or grow cash crops for export. African businesspeople were edged out of international trade, and industrial development was curtailed in the colonies to protect European industry.

Most colonized countries became independent in the mid-20th century. Economically speaking, however, colonial domination never quite ended for the vast majority of postcolonial countries. The economies of most African countries are still dominated by a few mining and cash crop exports. As the global prices of such raw materials fluctuate widely from year to year, postcolonial governments find it hard to budget and plan ahead. Moreover, the actual value of raw material exports erodes over time, forcing countries to export more and more just to maintain their economies, making real economic growth and development almost impossible.

In response to this dilemma, many postcolonial countries, including India, have adopted ambitious schemes to industrialize their economies in order to get out of the colonial economic trap. Currently, the government of Ghana is pursuing a renewed effort at industrialization, hoping to add value to cash crops such as pineapples and groundnuts and provide jobs to Ghanaians by manufacturing commodities of higher value for local use and export. The One District, One Factory initiative aims to establish a new factory in each of Ghana's 216 government districts.

Modernity, the Sociocultural Complex of Industrial Societies

What happens when a country industrializes? Anthropologists have been interested in how processes of industrialism have unfolded in non-European contexts such as India, China, Brazil, and Mexico. Wherever this transformation occurs, certain other sociocultural conditions tend to follow. Social scientists refer to the complex of features that accompanies industrialization as **modernity**.

While anchored by a set of commonalities, modernity takes different forms in different contexts. There is no one modernity but rather a whole spectrum of modernities that develop as societies industrialize in different ways. Some, such as China and Mexico, focus on strategic industrial zones. Some, such as Ghana, seek to establish factories evenly throughout the country. Moreover, societies accommodate the changes of industrialism using their own cultural institutions, practices, and belief systems, informed by their own historical experiences. Some versions of modernity emphasize individualism and allow for vast amounts of inequality among people in different social categories. Other versions of modernity emphasize community well-being and equality. Some scholars use the term **alternative modernity** to describe versions of modernity that have developed outside of Europe.

Nevertheless, industrialism does entail a set of sociocultural forces that interact with local cultural features to produce these distinctive versions of modernity. The first of these forces is urbanization. As with the evicted peasants in 18th-century Britain, people are pushed or pulled into urban centers to find jobs when factories are established. Rural farmers must rely on unpredictable factors such as weather and volatile market prices for their goods. And those who grow cash crops usually find they have to sell more and more just to maintain their standard of living. These challenges have made farming unattractive to many young people, prompting them to seek better lives in urban areas. As societies industrialize, the pull toward urban areas becomes greater, and trading towns grow into industrial cities, which grow into metropolitan regions.

The second notable feature of industrial society is regimented wage labor. In the other modes of subsistence, people are obligated to work to survive, but they maintain control over the conditions of their work, such as when they start and end their workday, when they take breaks, what tasks they perform that day, how they perform those tasks, and how much they produce in a given day. In the factory setting, the nature of work changes profoundly.

FIGURE 7.19 Punching the time clock. Regimented wage labor is a defining feature of industrial societies. (credit: “Detroit, Michigan (Vicinity). Chrysler Corporation Dodge Truck Plant. War Workers ‘Punching In’ for Their Job of Helping to ‘Punch’ the Axis” by Arthur S. Siegel/Library of Congress)

Factory workers are required to begin work at a certain time and continue until the official end of the workday. Many are made to “clock in” and “clock out” by inserting a card into a machine that records their starting and ending times. The work performed in factories often involves repetitive motions and procedures rather than the varied work of other subsistence modes. Regimented labor is supervised by managers, who determine work conditions and procedures and enforce predetermined levels of productivity. If a worker does not conform to these expectations, they can be fired. Even as many industrialized societies have shifted to services as the basis of their economies, they have retained the fundamental structure of regimented wage labor for the vast majority of shop and office workers. It is remarkable that societies purporting to value personal “freedom” require most people to work under such authoritarian conditions.

A third feature of industrialism is the grouping of people into social classes. In other modes of subsistence, society is structured primarily by family groups, gender groups, age sets, and regional associations. In industrial societies, extended-family systems tend to be increasingly challenged and sometimes replaced by much more mobile nuclear families. Social identity is increasingly reckoned according to occupation. In non-Western contexts, class often combines with ethnic and religious identities to create complex cultural forms of inequality and conflict. Inequality among social classes is discussed in Social Inequalities.

A fourth feature of industrial societies is an increase in commodity consumption. People of all classes in industrial societies buy, consume, and own an extraordinary amount of stuff. This is necessary, of course, because industrialized capitalist economies produce so much stuff. Food retailers throw away more than 45 billion tons of unsold food products every year. Many clothing companies shred or burn the clothes they cannot sell. Marketing and advertising have evolved to stimulate increased consumption by attaching specific meanings to commodities. Often, ads portray commodities such as perfumes or cars as powerful objects that possess the ability to transform their users. This association of commodities with magical powers is called **commodity fetishism**. People are encouraged to think that owning or consuming certain commodities makes them beautiful or enviable or gives them membership in a more powerful social class.

In fact, commodities do not really have the power to transform people. Commodities are inert. Rather, it is people who have power—the power to transform materials into commodities. Moreover, there is a difference between consuming the same things that powerful people consume and actually being a powerful person. Nevertheless, people in industrial and postindustrial societies often experience a sense of power and control through shopping, perhaps because those experiences are denied to them in the workplace. Rather than thinking about the consequences of industrialism, such as work discipline, inequality, and environmental damage, people in societies dominated by consumerism are invited to view the world as an endless array of exotic and empowering commodities on offer to the modern citizen.

Finally, as suggested by their patterns of commodity consumption, people in industrial societies often place a high value on individualism. Increasingly in industrial and postindustrial societies, people develop identities based on their personal tastes, attributes, experiences, and goals rather than those of their surrounding families or other social groups to which they belong. Rather than living with family, many people in US society live alone for years or even decades. On the one hand, this development provides people with opportunities to choose their own paths in life, to explore new identities and ways of living. On the other hand, individuals are increasingly expected to rely on themselves rather than cultivating relations of mutuality and reciprocity with others. In societies that emphasize self-reliance, people often face material and emotional hardship alone. Feeling isolated and cut off from social relationships, many experience a sense of alienation.

Postindustrialism and Postmodernity

In the 1970s, the economies of the United States, Japan, and many western European countries began to shift from a base of manufacturing to a base of services and information. Seeking to maximize profits, large manufacturers moved their factories to poorer countries with cheaper labor, weaker environmental regulations, and lower overall operation costs. Therefore, industrialization increased in places such as China and Brazil just as the United States and other countries became postindustrial. As production is moved to other parts of the globe, consumption also becomes increasingly global, with large companies seeking to sell their goods to ever larger markets. Increasingly global processes of production and consumption are referred to by the term **globalization**, a key feature of national economies since the late 1970s.

Social theorists such as David Harvey and Frederic Jameson have suggested that this economic shift has generated a cultural shift from modernity to **postmodernity**. The essential structures of work, consumption, leisure, and social life are not radically reshaped but rather intensified in the shift from industrial to postindustrial society. Work discipline becomes more rigorous, trade becomes more global, and technology becomes more pervasive and intrusive.

In postindustrial societies, professional, educated elites work in the services and information industries, such as health care, data processing, finance, and technology. These are typically secure jobs with benefits such as health insurance, paid sick leave, and retirement funds—but the market for such jobs is increasingly competitive, making them increasingly demanding. Easier to find are working-class jobs in retail, transportation, customer service, and other lower-paying service industries. The class of workers previously employed in manufacturing now competes for these less attractive jobs, which offer few or no benefits. Many turn to the "gig economy," working as drivers, house cleaners, and handypeople—jobs that provide freedom from regimented work discipline in exchange for unstable compensation and no benefits. Inequality increases between those with secure, elite jobs and the vast majority of workers with more insecure employment. Theorists of postmodernity argue that these changes in the conditions of work create a pervasive sense of anxiety and **precarity** among all classes of postindustrial workers. Precarity is physical and psychological harm caused by lack of secure income. Increasing precarity and inequality are linked to rising sociocultural polarization and the resurgence of ethnic, religious, and nationalist identities.

In both work and leisure, technologies penetrate deeper into the everyday lives of people living in postmodern societies. New media forms shape their social identities and relationships. Through these new forms of technology and media, people in postmodern societies are constantly bombarded with new information, new products, and new demands, giving people the sense of time speeding up. Moreover, flows of information, goods, and people across the globe create a sense of a shrinking world. David Harvey refers to these changes in our sense of time and space as **time-space compression**.

PROFILES IN ANTHROPOLOGY

David Graeber
1961–2020

FIGURE 7.20 David Graeber (credit: Guido van Nispen/Wikimedia Commons, CC BY 2.0)

Personal History: David Rolfe Graeber was born in New York and grew up in a working-class family steeped in radical politics. While in junior high school, he became fascinated by Mayan hieroglyphics and translated many glyphs that had only partially been translated before (Cain 2020). He sent his translations to a Mayan scholar, who was so impressed that he helped Graeber get a scholarship to a prestigious prep school in Massachusetts.

Area of Anthropology: Graeber studied anthropology as an undergraduate at SUNY Purchase and then earned his PhD in anthropology at the University of Chicago. For his dissertation fieldwork, he lived in Betafo, a rural community in Madagascar. He observed that people in Betafo lived beyond the reach of official government, without police or taxation. They had developed their own methods of governing themselves through community consensus. This experience profoundly shaped Graeber's sense of political possibility. Throughout his life, he advocated for direct democracy as the most fair and logical way to organize society.

In 1998, Graeber became an anthropology professor at Yale University and began engaging in political activism, which included protesting the World Economic Forum and the International Monetary Fund. Despite his impressive academic accomplishments, Yale decided not to renew Graeber's contract in 2005. He believed the decision was largely due to his radical politics. He subsequently landed a job at Goldsmiths' College, University of London, and then at the London School of Economics.

Accomplishments in the Field: In his widely acclaimed book *Debt: the First 5,000 Years*, Graeber (2014) describes debt as a central mechanism for creating and maintaining inequality in ancient and modern societies. Examining the first recorded debt systems, in the Sumerian civilization of 3500 BCE, he found that large numbers of farmers became indebted, forcing them to pawn their children to work off their debt. The increasing enslavement of people in this system led to widespread social unrest. Sumerian kings responded by periodically canceling all debts. Also practiced in ancient Israel, this periodic cancellation of debt came to be called the Law of Jubilee.

Widespread indebtedness in American society has also led to increasing precarity and social unrest, resulting in protest movements such as Occupy Wall Street. Graeber called for the reintroduction of the Jubilee, in particular a cancellation of student loan debt and predatory mortgages.

Examining the world of modern work, Graeber argued that most white-collar jobs are pointless and meaningless, calling them "bullshit jobs." In his book *Bullshit Jobs: A Theory*, published in 2018, he describes how technological advances and increased bureaucracy have led people to work longer hours in pursuit of greater productivity in order to generate profits for shareholders. Much of what white-collar workers produce, however, is useless, bureaucratic make-work that makes the lives of other people more difficult. Such workers include telemarketers, insurance analysts, corporate lawyers, lobbyists, and investment CEOs. Knowing their work to be unnecessary, even damaging, people in these jobs suffer moral and spiritual damage from the regimented futility of their daily lives.

Importance of His Work: David Graeber was one of the most innovative economic thinkers of modern times. He forged new ways of thinking about the basic elements of modern economic life, such as work, bureaucracy, debt, and exchange. As a political activist, he participated in social movements working for greater equality, better working conditions, and environmental sustainability. He was a founding member of Occupy Wall Street, the 2011 protest movement against economic inequality.

While on holiday in Venice with his new wife, David Graeber died suddenly (Hart 2020). He was 59.

Environmental Impacts of Industrial and Postindustrial Societies

Industrialism has taken a heavy toll on the environments where it has become a primary mode of subsistence. The burning of fossil fuels to power factories causes air pollution, particularly the buildup of carbon dioxide and other greenhouse gases in the atmosphere. This has triggered global climate change. Where factories are built next to water sources, local water supplies can become contaminated with dangerous chemicals. Toxic chemicals such as lead can leach into soils, contaminating crops. The clearing of land for mining, logging, ranching, and cash crops leads to habitat loss, causing dramatic reductions in plant and animal biodiversity. Much of this environmental degradation occurs in poorer countries and poor regions of postindustri al countries.

As discussed in this chapter, anthropologists in all of the four fields are interested in how people make a living by engaging with their environments, creating systems of production and exchange. Anthropologists also study how such systems create forms of meaning and value as people study, classify, and experiment with the plants, animals, soils, and climate features of their surroundings. With its deep-seated interest in the interdependence of humans and nature, anthropology has been quick to respond to the environmental threats generated by unsustainable modes of subsistence, such as fossil-fuel-driven industrialism and postindustrial hyperconsumption.

Practicing "climate ethnography," many cultural anthropologists have described how previous modes of subsistence have become impossible due to climate change, particularly in "climate sensitive" parts of the world such as deserts and areas at or near sea level (Crate 2011). Contributions to a 2016 book, *Anthropology and Climate Change*, detail the profound sociocultural effects of climate change in places such as Siberia, Bangladesh, Ethiopia, Papua New Guinea, the Amazon, Peru, Australia, and Alaska (Crate and Nuttall 2016). Anthropologist Jerry Jacka (2016) reports how extreme climate fluctuations are causing droughts, floods, and frosts that threaten local subsistence strategies in Papua New Guinea. In heavily affected areas, horticulture becomes impossible, and people are forced to migrate, sometimes leaving the sick and the elderly behind to die. In areas where people continue to farm, invasive weeds and insects have taken over, destroying crops and firewood. Unpredictable rainfall and flooding cause frequent food shortages when crops fail. Local peoples have responded with a set of strategies to mitigate these changes, such as switching crop species, but horticulture remains a threatened way of life in New Guinea. Similarly, anthropologist Susan Crate's (2016) work in Siberia shows how cattle keeping is becoming increasingly difficult due to flooded rangelands, unpredictable rainfall, and other unstable climate factors. More and more Siberian young people are abandoning their parents' way of life and moving to cities in search of wage work.

In this chapter, we have surveyed the four main ways of making a living that people have used throughout human history. These four modes of subsistence did not occur in a neat evolutionary sequence, each new one outmoding and replacing the one before. Rather, new strategies were adopted as primary modes of subsistence by some groups and supplementary methods by others. Many groups have experimented with different modes of subsistence, combining them in various ways over time. People change their subsistence strategies in response to population pressures, forced migrations, the spread of new technologies, trade opportunities, and, most recently, global climate change.

There is a notable difference between the first three strategies discussed in this chapter and the very last one. Industrialism and postindustrialism are strategies that encompass the world, drawing all other modes of subsistence into the pressures and opportunities of the global capitalist market. As states and corporations seek to gain control over land and natural resources, the modes of subsistence that rely on these resources are threatened. Many people are forced to abandon gathering-hunting, pastoralism, and plant cultivation and the whole ways of life associated with those ways of making a living.

There is one more important difference between all previous modes of subsistence and the mode of industrialism/postindustrialism. Gathering-hunting, pastoralism, and plant cultivation are very often (though not always) practiced in ways that sustain and protect the environment. Despite efforts at environmental reform, industrialism and postindustrialism are still practiced in ways that harm and deplete the environment. Perhaps people who practice ecologically smart ways of making a living have lessons to teach those who don't. Losing these smart ways of making a living would be a cultural tragedy as well as an environmental disaster.

MINI-FIELDWORK ACTIVITY

Unstructured Interview

Unstructured interviews are a qualitative research method used for research in social sciences and sometimes for interviews for jobs and college entrance. Unstructured interviews are free flowing and are more spontaneous than a planned interview. The goal of this less structured type of interview is to have the interviewee relate information in a more open and neutral environment. Use an unstructured interview method to interview a person about their job. While the interview will be unstructured some light preparation should be done. Think about these questions as you plan your interview.

How did the person acquire that job? By choice, convenience, or necessity? Is the job temporary or permanent, and why? What are the challenges of the job? Are there risks or dangers? What are the rewarding features? Does the person get bored? How would the person describe the people they work among? How would they describe their relations with the boss? Are there aspects of unfairness or inequality in the workplace? Does the job allow the person to express creativity? Is the job personally satisfying? Does the person feel free or unfree on the job? What might your interview indicate about work in your society?

Reflect on the interview. Was the conversation more relaxed? Did you feel you were able to get sufficient information from your subject? What differences were there in this style of interview from a more formal interview process? How might the information you got be different?

Key Terms

alternative modernity versions of modernity shaped by local social and cultural forms.
animal domestication the processing of animal products for use as food, textiles, and tools.
balanced reciprocity the practice building social relationships through the exchange of gifts of roughly equal value.
band a form of social organization associated with gatherer-hunter societies. Bands are relatively small, often around 50 people, ideal for a nomadic or seminomadic lifestyle.
colonialism the political domination of another country in the interest of economic exploitation.
commodity fetishism the association of commodities with magical powers of personal transformation.
cultivation basic manipulation of nature, such as the intentional growing of plants.
egalitarian emphasizing equality and sharing.
extensive horticulture a form of plant cultivation in which new plots are regularly cleared, prepared with digging sticks or hoes, and fertilized with animal dung, ash, or other natural products.
extensive or shifting cultivation a horticultural practice in which plots of land are farmed for a period of time, then left to lie fallow as farmers move on to cultivate other plots.
fallow describes a plot of land that is not cultivated for a period of time so that wild vegetation may grow in naturally.
gathering-hunting the mode of subsistence in which people rely on resources readily available in their environment. Gathering-hunting peoples collect fruits, nuts, berries, and roots and harvest honey. They also hunt and trap wild animals.
general-purpose money money that can be exchanged for a wide variety of goods and services.
generalized reciprocity the practice of sharing without regard for the value of objects or interest in compensation.
globalization the dramatic increase in global processes of production and consumption since the 1970s.
humus organic matter in soil formed by the decomposition of plants.
hxaro a friendship developed through gift exchange, practiced among the Dobe Ju/'hoansi and other San groups of the Kalahari.
industrialism the mode of subsistence that uses wage labor, machines, and chemical processes to mass-produce commodities.
intensive agriculture a form of plant cultivation in which one plot is farmed over and over again using labor-intensive methods such as plowing, terracing, and irrigation.
intercropping planting certain species of plants side by side to enhance their health and growth.
markets institutions that allow for buyers and sellers to meet for the purposes of economic exchange.
mode of subsistence a way in which people interact with the environment to meet their needs. Each mode of subsistence involves its own forms of knowledge, techniques, technologies, and social organization.
modernity the complex of sociocultural features associated with industrial society.
money a medium of exchange, unit of account, and store of value.
monumental architecture large structures built for public viewing or use, such as pyramids, temples, sports arenas, and coliseums.
nomadism the practice of moving frequently in search of resources.
pastoralism the mode of subsistence associated with the care and use of herd animals.
peasants small-plot farmers incorporated into larger regional economies, often states.
plant domestication the process of adapting wild plants for human use.
postmodernity the cultural shift associated with postindustrialism.
potlatch a feast in which a trove of gifts is presented by the host chief to the guest chief in order to demonstrate wealth and gain prestige.
precarity physical and psychological harm caused by lack of secure and stable income.
redistribution a system whereby goods are collected and stored by a leader and later given out or used for public benefit.
seminomadic the practice of settling in one place for a period of time, usually a few weeks, then moving to a new site to find fresh resources.
sexual division of labor the assignment of work based on a person's sex.
slash and burn the technique of preparing a new plot by cutting down the trees and shrubs, burning the vegetation to the ground, then tilling the ash into the soil as fertilizer.
special-purpose money money that is exchanged for specific items or services.
surplus amount of harvest left over after supplying

the needs of the household.

time-space compression the postmodern feeling that time is speeding up and global space is shrinking.

transhumance a technique practiced by many pastoralist groups that combines a settled lifestyle with routine movement. Societies that practice transhumance may move between two permanent settlements in an annual cycle. Another transhumance strategy involves most people residing in a settlement and sending a smaller group out to pasture the animals at certain times of the year.

universalism the belief that social systems have operated roughly the same way all over the world at all times past and present.

usufruct rights rights to use a resource but not to own or sell it.

Summary

Anthropologists take a human-centered approach to studying economic issues, examining how social and cultural features relate to economic production, markets, and consumption. Humans use four main modes of subsistence to meet their needs: gathering-hunting, pastoralism, plant cultivation, and industrialism. Gathering-hunting societies such as the Hadza are highly mobile and egalitarian. Pastoral societies such as the Bedouin are also mobile but allow for the accumulation of wealth in the form of herd animals. Plant cultivators are settled peoples who practice either extensive horticulture or intensive agriculture. Cities and craft specialization are developed from the surplus generated by intensive agriculture.

In the first three modes of subsistence, forms of reciprocity structure the circulation of goods in society. In intensive agriculture and industrialism, the market economy based on money forms the dominant mode of exchange.

Industrialism was first developed in Europe and motivated the colonization of many other parts of the world. Industrial societies are associated with wage labor, work discipline, social classes, commodity consumption, and high degrees of inequality. Some industrialized societies have become postindustrial by shifting production to poorer parts of the world with cheaper labor costs. In postindustrial societies, more people work in the service industries than in manufacturing. The intensive extraction, pollution, and waste associated with industrial and postindustrial societies are increasingly harmful to the environment.

Critical Thinking Questions

1. If you could choose to practice a mode of subsistence for just one year, which one would it be? What would be the advantages and disadvantages of your choice?
2. Why is egalitarianism so prominent in one form of subsistence and less prominent in others? How could egalitarian behavior be encouraged in industrial and postindustrial societies?
3. Programs that attempt to change the lifeways of gatherer-hunters, pastoralists, and horticulturalists are often called "development" programs. Do you think the target groups of such programs see them as development? What are the advantages and disadvantages of such programs? Do you view them as development?
4. Have you or someone you know experienced precarity? What might be the solution to this widespread problem in contemporary societies?
5. How can industrial and postindustrial societies learn the lessons of environmental sustainability from peoples who practice other, more environmentally friendly modes of subsistence? What needs to be done to promote the knowledge, values, and practices of environmentalism?

Bibliography

Akcigit, Ufuk, Harun Alp, and Michael Peters. 2021. "Lack of Selection and Limits to Delegation: Firm Dynamics in Developing Countries." *American Economic Review* 111 (1): 231–275. https://doi.org/10.1257/aer.20180555.

American Heart Association. 2012. "Hunter-Gatherers and Horticulturalist Lifestyle Linked to Lower Blood Pressure Increases, Atherosclerosis Risks." ScienceDaily. May 21, 2012. https://www.sciencedaily.com/releases/2012/05/120521163621.htm.

Avery, Christopher, and Parag A. Pathak. 2021. "The Distributional Consequences of Public School Choice." *American Economic Review* 111 (1): 129–152. https://doi.org/10.1257/aer.20151147.

Barnard, Alan. 2018. "Hxaro." In *The International Encyclopedia of Anthropology*, edited by Hilary Callan. Hoboken, NJ: John Wiley & Sons. https://doi.org/10.1002/9781118924396.wbiea1320.

Bellwood, Peter. 2019. "Agricultural Origins." In *The International Encyclopedia of Anthropology*, edited by Hilary Callan. Hoboken, NJ: John Wiley & Sons. https://doi.org/10.1002/9781118924396.wbiea2385.

Bierbrauer, Felix J., Pierre C. Boyer, and Andreas Peichl. 2021. "Politically Feasible Reforms of Nonlinear Tax Systems." *American Economic Review* 111 (1): 153–191.

Bird-David, Nurit. 2015. "Hunting and Gathering Societies: Anthropology." In *International Encyclopedia of the Social and Behavioral Sciences*, edited by James D. Wright, 2nd ed., 428–431. New York: Elsevier. https://doi.org/10.1016/B978-0-08-097086-8.12090-2.

Bollig, Michael. 2018. "Pastoralists." In *The International Encyclopedia of Anthropology*, edited by Hilary Callan. Hoboken, NJ: John Wiley & Sons. https://doi.org/10.1002/9781118924396.wbiea1930.

Cain, Sian. 2020. "David Graeber, Anthropologist and Author of Bullshit Jobs, Dies Aged 59." *Guardian*, September 3, 2020. https://www.theguardian.com/books/2020/sep/03/david-graeber-anthropologist-and-author-of-bullshit-jobs-dies-aged-59.

Cochrane, Laura. L. 2021. "Religious Networks and Small Businesses in Senegal." *Economic Anthropology* 8 (1): 22–33. https://doi.org/10.1002/sea2.12185.

Cohn, Bernard S. 1996. *Colonialism and Its Forms of Knowledge: The British in India*. Princeton, NJ: Princeton University Press.

Crate, Susan A. 2011. "A Political Ecology of 'Water in Mind': Attributing Perceptions in the Era of Global Climate Change." *Weather, Climate, and Society* 3 (3): 148–164. https://doi.org/10.1175/WCAS-D-10-05006.1.

Crate, Susan A. 2016. "Gone with Cows and Kin? Climate, Globalization, and Youth Alienation in Siberia." In *Anthropology and Climate Change: From Actions to Transformations*, edited by Susan A. Crate and Mark Nuttall, 2nd ed., 139–161. New York: Routledge.

Crate, Susan A., and Mark Nuttall, eds. 2016. *Anthropology and Climate Change: From Actions to Transformations*. 2nd ed. New York: Routledge.

Edington, John. 2017. *Indigenous Environmental Knowledge: Reappraisal*. Cham: Springer.

Eastep, Wayne. 2018. *Bedouin*. Philadelphia: University of Pennsylvania Press.

Galaty, John G. 2018. "Transhumance." In *The International Encyclopedia of Anthropology*, edited by Hilary Callan. Hoboken, NJ: John Wiley & Sons. https://doi.org/10.1002/9781118924396.wbiea1403.

Graeber, David. 2014. "Finance Is Just Another Word for Other People's Debts: An Interview with David Graeber." By Hannah Chadeayne Appel. *Radical History Review* 118:159–173.

Hart, Keith. 2020. "David Graeber (1961–2020)." David Rolfe Graeber. https://davidgraeber.org/memorials/obituary-keith-hart/.

High, Holly. 2018. "Potlatch." In *The International Encyclopedia of Anthropology*, edited by Hilary Callan. Hoboken, NJ: John Wiley & Sons. https://doi.org/10.1002/9781118924396.wbiea1960.

Homewood, Katherine. 2018. "Pastoralism." In *The International Encyclopedia of Anthropology*, edited by Hilary Callan. Hoboken, NJ: John Wiley & Sons. https://doi.org/10.1002/9781118924396.wbiea1559.

Jacka, Jerry K. 2016. "Correlating Local Knowledge with Climatic Data: Porgeran Experiences of Climate Change in Papua New Guinea." In *Anthropology and Climate Change: From Actions to Transformations*, edited by Susan A. Crate and Mark Nuttall, 2nd ed., 186–199. New York: Routledge.

Jain, Pankaj. 2019. "Modern Hindu Dharma and Environmentalism." In *The Oxford History of Hinduism: Modern Hinduism*, edited by Torkel Brekke. Oxford: Oxford University Press. https://doi.org/10.1093/oso/9780198790839.003.0015.

Junker, Laura L. 2015. "Chiefdoms, Archaeology Of." In *International Encyclopedia of the Social and Behavioral Sciences*, edited by James D. Wright, 2nd ed., 376–382. New York: Elsevier.

Kratz, Corinne A. 2018. "The Case of the Recurring Wodaabe: Visual Obsessions in Globalizing Markets." *African Arts* 51 (1): 24–45. https://doi.org/10.1162/AFAR_a_00390.

Lee, Richard B. 1993. *The Dobe Ju/'hoansi.* 2nd ed. Fort Worth, TX: Harcourt Brace College Publishers.

Lee, Richard B. 2018. "Hunter-Gatherers and Human Evolution: New Light on Old Debates." *Annual Review of Anthropology* 47:513–531.

Lowe, Marie E., and Suzanne Sharp. 2021. "Gendering Human Capital Development in Western Alaska." *Economic Anthropology* 8 (1): 46–60. https://doi.org/10.1002/sea2.12184.

Marlowe, Frank W. 2010. *The Hadza: Hunter-Gatherers of Tanzania.* Berkeley: University of California Press.

Mueller, Andreas I., Johannes Spinnewijn, and Giorgio Topa. 2021. "Job Seekers' Perceptions and Employment Prospects: Heterogeneity, Duration Dependence, and Bias." *American Economic Review* 111 (1): 324–363. https://doi.org/10.1257/aer.20190808.

Nardo, Don. 2007. *Ancient Mesopotamia.* Farmington Hills, MI: Greenhaven Press.

Northeast Editing, ed. 2017. "Kayapos." In *Worldmark Encyclopedia of Cultures and Daily Life*, 3rd ed. Vol. 2, *Americas*, 384–389. Farmington Hills, MI: Gale.

Pittman, Holly. 2019. "The First Cities." In *Journey to the City: A Companion to the Middle East Galleries at the Penn Museum*, edited by Steve Tinney and Karen Sonik, 45–74. Philadelphia: University of Pennsylvania Museum of Archaeology and Anthropology.

Posey, Darrell A. 2002. *Kayapó Ethnoecology and Culture.* Edited by Kristina Plenderleith. New York: Routledge.

Rachok, Dafna. 2021. "Honesty and Economy on a Highway: Entanglements of Gift, Money, and Affection in the Narratives of Ukrainian Sex Workers." *Economic Anthropology* 8 (1): 34–45. https://doi.org/10.1002/sea2.12187.

Rizvi, Uzma Z. 2007. "City, History Of." *Encyclopedia of Anthropology*, edited by H. James Birx, vol. 1, 509–511. Thousand Oaks, CA: Sage Publications.

Rogall, Thorsten. 2021. "Mobilizing the Masses for Genocide." *American Economic Review* 111 (1): 41–72. https://doi.org/10.1257/aer.20160999.

Rössler, Martin. 2018. "Redistribution." In *The International Encyclopedia of Anthropology*, edited by Hillary Callan. Hoboken, NJ: John Wiley & Sons. https://doi.org/10.1002/9781118924396.wbiea1595.

Sillitoe, Paul. 2018. "Subsistence." In *The International Encyclopedia of Anthropology*, edited by Hilary Callan. Hoboken, NJ: John Wiley & Sons. https://doi.org/10.1002/9781118924396.wbiea1406.

Turner, Terence, and Vanessa Fajans-Turner. 2006. "Political Innovation and Inter-ethnic Alliance: Kayapo Resistance to the Developmentalist State." *Anthropology Today* 22 (5): 3–10. https://doi.org/10.1111/j.1467-8322.2006.00458.x.

Vertovec, John. 2021. "'No trabajaré pa' ellos': Entrepreneurship as a Form of State Resistance in Havana, Cuba." *Economic Anthropology* 8 (1): 148–160. https://doi.org/10.1002/sea2.12191.

Wallenfels, Ronald, and Jack M. Sasson, eds. 2000. "Uruk." In *The Ancient Near East: An Encyclopedia for Students*, vol. 4, 141–143. New York: Charles Scribner's Sons.

Wood, Brian M., Herman Pontzer, David A. Raichlen, and Frank W. Marlowe. 2014. "Mutualism and

Manipulation in Hadza–Honeyguide Interactions." *Evolution and Human Behavior* 35 (6): 540–546. https://doi.org/10.1016/j.evolhumbehav.2014.07.007.

Ulate, Mauricio. 2021. "Going Negative at the Zero Lower Bound: The Effects of Negative Nominal Interest Rates." *American Economic Review* 111 (1): 1–40. https://doi.org/10.1257/aer.20190848.

University of Cambridge. 2014. "Hunter-Gatherer Past Shows Our Fragile Bones Result from Inactivity since Invention Of Farming." ScienceDaily. December 22, 2014. https://www.sciencedaily.com/releases/2014/12/141222165033.htm.

CHAPTER 8
Authority, Decisions, and Power: Political Anthropology

Figure 8.1 For people all over the world, newspapers provide daily information about political actors and events. (credit, clockwise from top left: “Tourist Couple” by Pedro Ribeiro Simões/flickr, CC BY 2.0; “Intensely Reading the Newspaper in Addis Ababa” by Terje Skjerdal/flickr, CC BY 2.0; “Reading the Newspaper” by kuhnmi/flickr, CC BY 2.0; “Reading Is Fundamental” by Ernie/flickr, CC BY 2.0)

CHAPTER OUTLINE

INTRODUCTION What’s going on in the world? In your country? In your community? Visit any news site or pick up any newspaper, and look at the top stories. The most prominent news of the day usually involves one or more of the following: the actions of leaders, social decision-making, legal issues, social protest, and forms of social violence. These are all elements of the sociocultural dynamics of power—more commonly referred to as **politics**.

The actors in this global drama are most often nation-states, or more specifically, the people and groups representing nation-states. Britain is leaving the European Union. Russia is wracked with protests again Putin. Myanmar has been taken over by a military coup. When people think about what’s going on in the world, they often think about actions of or within nation-states. Our very notion of the world is primarily structured by the nation-state form. Just look at any globe.

Because of this state-centric focus, it is tempting to think that politics essentially refers to the internal and external dynamics of nation-states. Anthropologists, with their attention to human history and sociocultural diversity, recognize that the nation-state is one system among many used by humans to make collective decisions and maintain social order. Over the past 200,000 years, modern humans have developed a wide variety of political systems for managing power in coordination with the other elements of society. The nation-state is a relative newcomer among political forms, dating back only a few hundred years. Much more common in human history are decision-making systems based on extended families and positions of formal leadership associated with those family systems.

The field of political anthropology was originally established with the goal of categorizing the diversity of political systems found all over the world. Initially, anthropologists identified one fundamental difference among political systems—whether or not they have a centralized leader or leaders. Building on this distinction, anthropologists have explored how certain subsistence patterns coordinate with specific political systems.

Anthropologists studying colonialism have described the global spread of the nation-state form as it dominated, incorporated, and sometimes eliminated other political systems. Though the nation-state political form now governs most societies, alternative forms of leadership and decision-making still exert a great deal of influence, either directly or indirectly. In some places, these alternative forms continue to exist, although they are marginalized by the power of the state. In other places, the alternative political structures have been destroyed, but the values associated with them persevere in the hearts and minds of contemporary peoples.

8.1 Colonialism and the Categorization of Political Systems

LEARNING OUTCOMES

By the end of this section, you will be able to:

- Trace the colonial origins of political anthropology.
- Identify European misconceptions about non-Western political organization.
- Discuss the importance of the book *African Political Systems.*
- Distinguish between acephalous and centralized political organization.
- Describe the association between modes of subsistence and political organization.
- Identify and briefly define Max Weber's three types of authority.

As discussed in Work, Life, Value: Economic Anthropology, many European countries began developing formal colonial rule over other parts of the world in the late 1800s. Their main motivation was to secure the raw materials they needed to fuel their own growing industrial economies. As they began to establish their own governments in colonized societies, European administrators were highly influenced by ethnocentric stereotypes of non-Western peoples. Typically, they assumed that non-Western societies either were ruled by overbearing tyrants or were chaotic anarchies with no political organization whatsoever.

The establishment of colonial rule provided the administrative context for anthropologists to study non-Western societies in countries under European domination. As cultural anthropologists conducted research in African colonies during the early part of the 20th century, they made the surprising discovery that European assumptions about African political organization were completely misguided. In 1940, British anthropologists Meyer Fortes and E. E. Evans-Pritchard published a particularly important collection of essays written by a variety of anthropologists with ethnographic experience in societies all over Africa. This book, *African Political Systems*, completely invalidated the idea that Indigenous African politics were either oppressive or chaotic. The eight chapters all demonstrated that African societies were meticulously organized systems with well-defined institutions for political representation and collaborative decision-making.

In their overview of the chapters, Fortes and Evans-Pritchard make a primary distinction between centralized political systems, which feature rulers such as chiefs, and acephalous (meaning "headless") societies, where power is exerted through families or village meetings rather than formal political office. Africa featured a broad array of both centralized and acephalous forms of political organization, each one an effective means of maintaining social order. In an effort to demonstrate the cohesion and stability of precolonial political forms, Fortes and Evans-Pritchard applied a structural-functionalist perspective to show how the various elements of each society fit together in a durable whole, reproduced through social action over time.

With the resurgence of evolutionary social theory in the 1960s and 1970s, anthropologist Elman Service drew from previous typologies to propose four main forms of social organization, each with its own political system. His four main categories of social organization are band, tribe, chiefdom, and state, and they are linked to the subsistence patterns discussed in Work, Life, Value: Economic Anthropology (Service 1962). Gathering and hunting is associated with bands. Horticulture gives rise to tribal societies. Chiefdoms are developed on the basis of agricultural surplus. And states rely on multiple modes of subsistence as well as military conquest and extensive regional trade, leading to the development of multiethnic territories. Critical of the timeless representations of structural functionalism, neo-evolutionists such as Service were interested in understanding how societies moved from one category to the next in an evolutionary sequence.

Contemporary political anthropologists are much more interested in history than evolution; that is, they emphasize the importance of the past while rejecting the notion that all societies can be classified according to stages in an evolutionary scheme of development from simple to complex. Anthropologists are similarly critical of the structural-functional approach that represents non-Western societies as timeless and unchanging. More often, political anthropologists explore the particular histories of political practices and institutions in the societies they study, emphasizing the equivalent political sophistication and unique historical trajectory of each society.

While based on fieldwork, political anthropology is also informed by models of political structure devised by sociologists. Sociologist Max Weber defined politics as the exercise of power (or at least the attempt to exercise power). **Power** is the ability to influence people and/or shape social processes and social structures. In many acephalous societies, power is spread widely among members of a society, while in **centralized societies**, power is concentrated in one or more sociocultural roles. These roles are called positions of **authority**. Weber defined three types of authority: traditional, charismatic, and rational-legal (Weber 1946). Priests and family elders exercise traditional authority, based on religious expertise or position in family structures. Charismatic authority is power exercised through personal qualities such as skilled oratory, extraordinary abilities, or social charm. Such power is persuasive, meaning it is based on the ability to convince others rather than force them to obey. Rational-legal authority is power that is defined by a legal role in society, such as prime minister or president. Once elected or assigned to a rational-legal position, a person exercises the authority vested in that position. Such power is coercive—that is, based on the legal ability to force people to obey.

In the next two sections, we'll take a look at the four main types of social organization described by Service, along with the political forms associated with each. The first two, bands and tribes, correspond with the category of acephalous societies noted by Fortes and Evans-Pritchard. The last two, chiefdoms and states, are forms of social organization featuring centralized leadership. Throughout this chapter, we will consider the features of each idealized category, mindful that the diversity of political organization in the world is more of a spectrum than a set of discrete categories. At one end of the spectrum, power is more widely shared among all members of a community, while at the other end, power is more centralized and formalized in bureaucratic institutions. Moreover, while each society is fundamentally structured by a particular model of political organization, most societies feature a variety of forms of authority, representation, and decision-making that intersect and interact with the dominant form—and sometimes contradict and undermine it. While archaeologists often consider how one form of sociopolitical order might develop into another, cultural anthropologists are typically careful to avoid simplistic typologies of cultural evolution.

In this chapter, we'll take a modified approach between those two positions by detailing the categories of political organization and discussing common paths of social change from one system to another. However, it's important to emphasize that societies develop not along one single evolutionary path but through complex and often unpredictable processes of historical change.

8.2 Acephalous Societies: Bands and Tribes

LEARNING OUTCOMES

By the end of this section, you will be able to:

- Define the category of acephalous societies.
- Identify three types of acephalous political organization.
- Describe leadership in band societies.
- Outline the organization of lineage orders.
- Explain why many anthropologists avoid the use of the word *tribe*.
- Define the roles of leopard-skin chiefs and big men.
- Explain how age-grade systems complement lineage organization.
- Describe the village democracy of precolonial Igbo society.

Any group without an official leader is acephalous. When you go out with a group of friends, how do you make decisions about where to go, how to get there, and who will pay for what? Probably someone makes a suggestion, people chime in with their own ideas, and you discuss things as a group and reach an informal consensus. This is what many small groups do.

Until the early 20th century, many Europeans believed that all humans were essentially selfish and would relentlessly pursue their own personal interests without the moralizing forces of civilization to force them to be more cooperative. They assumed that any non-Western society without formal leadership and codified laws would necessarily be a chaotic free-for-all of greed, coercion, and violence. Anthropologists discovered otherwise. Just as you and your friends easily make decisions without electing a leader or writing down rules, people who live in small communities do just fine without formal leadership and law.

In such communities, power is not concentrated in any formal position of leadership but rather diffused throughout society. Elders or people with experience in certain areas may give valuable advice, but they do not have the power to enforce their judgments. Their authority is based on **persuasive power**—that is, their ability to convince others and build group consensus. Certainly in any group there will be some people who want to exert power or force their own ideas on others, but without a formal mechanism allowing such people to enforce their will, others can generally ignore or evade them. The result is a mostly cooperative social order rather than chaos and strife.

Fortes and Evans-Pritchard described three types of **acephalous societies**. The first corresponds to what we have called **band societies**, or gatherer-hunters living in small groups of 20 to 30 people. As we learned when we discussed the Hadza in Chapter 7, Work. Life, Value: Economic Anthropology, such groups are strongly egalitarian, stressing equality, cooperation, and sharing. People make decisions through discussion and consensus. Those with knowledge and experience in particular areas may exert influence in those areas, but there are no formal positions of leadership.

Social groups often face decisions regarding their mode of subsistence. As just one example, nomadic gatherer-hunter groups must decide where to camp and how long to stay there before moving on. Frank Marlowe, an anthropologist who studies the Hadza, describes how men sometimes suggest that it's time to move on, but the group won't move "until the women are good and ready" (Marlowe 2010, 40). As the primary gatherers, women are best able to gauge whether food resources have been depleted in the area. When they have to walk too far to gather food, they agree that it's time to move camp. On a daily basis, women going out in gathering groups must decide where to go and which resources to target, making such decisions through a quick conversation.

Most people known someone in their family or group of friends who likes to tell others the best way to do things, and perhaps even wants to get their own way all of the time. This is the case in many small groups. Among the Hadza, if someone tries to tell other people what to do, the others just ignore that person. If the problem persists, people might just move to another camp to get away from the bossy person. Government officials and missionaries who try to tell the Hadza what to do are often met with the same general tendency to ignore or avoid potential authority figures.

While band societies have no political structure whatsoever, a second type of acephalous society relies on extended family structures and/or councils to organize leadership, decision-making, and conflict resolution. Elman Service (1962) referred to these as **tribal societies**. Service's "tribal" form of social organization is associated with modes of subsistence such as pastoralism and horticulture, in which extended families control certain resources such as animals or land. Such communities are typically larger than bands, living in groups ranging from a few hundred to several thousand people.

A cautionary note about the words **tribe** and tribal. Too often, the *adjective tribal* is used to describe seemingly irrational group loyalties and conflicts, particularly in non-Western societies. Western journalists sometimes attempt to explain civil wars and guerrilla resistance in non-Western parts of the world in terms of "ancient tribal hatred" among various groups. The word *tribe* carries connotations of primitive lifeways and collective groupthink. In fact, many contemporary conflicts that are attributed to "tribal" animosity occur between groups that got along just fine before the colonial period of European domination. In Rwanda, for instance, the horticultural Hutu and pastoral Tutsi were engaged in cooperative relations and symbiotic forms of trade in precolonial times. Under a divide-and-rule strategy of colonial domination, the Belgians privileged the Tutsi with educational opportunities and jobs in colonial administration, which created resentment among the mostly agrarian Hutu. In this competitive context, group identities became fixed and rigid. The 1994 genocide in Rwanda is largely a result of these colonial processes fostering division, bias, and competition among these two groups.

Because the word has been so often misused, some anthropologists have replaced the term *tribe* with the term *ethnic group* to describe large collectivities based on a sense of common ancestry and shared culture. Many anthropology texts do continue to use the term *tribal* to refer to a specific form of sociopolitical organization based on extended family groups. Many Indigenous groups also use the term to refer to their social groups. It's one thing for people in a group to use the term *tribe* to refer to their own social group and quite another to use the word to describe a whole category of social organization. Service's term *tribal* was never a unified category anyway, as it refers to communities with a great diversity of forms of political organization. Some rely primarily on extended family structures to provide authority and processes of decision-making, while others rely on special groups or councils and still others use both.

As you will learn in Chapter 11, Forming Family through Kinship, a lineage is a group of people related by a common ancestor through either the maternal or the paternal line. In **lineage orders**, communities consist of two or more lineage groups, each one with an elder or group of elders that plays a prominent role in establishing consensus and settling disputes within the lineage. Such leaders do not occupy formal positions of leadership, but rather exercise informal authority through their accumulated knowledge and their ability to persuade members of the lineage to follow their instructions. Like band societies, lineage orders tend to be fairly egalitarian.

Some lineage societies, such as the Nuer of South Sudan, are **segmentary lineages**. These consist of family units called minimal lineages, which are encompassed by larger groups called maximal lineages, which are subsumed by even larger groups called **clans**. Minimal lineages are groups that trace descent from a common great-grandfather. In disputes between minimal lineages, people can recruit allies from the larger groups of kin, though there are no leaders in these larger groups. In this way, the Nuer mobilize their interlocking kin networks to maintain group cohesion and settle conflicts.

In his ethnographic work, E. E. Evans-Pritchard (1940) describes the Nuer as both fiercely independent and strongly egalitarian. Rather than accumulating wealth, people shared with others in their kin groups. However, fighting was very common. Since there were no formal methods of settling conflicts, people responded to offenses and disputes by fighting with clubs or spears. When someone was killed (which was not uncommon), the perpetrator would seek out the assistance of a special mediator called a **leopard-skin chief**, so named because they wore leopard skins to indicate their role. These mediators were not really chiefs at all, as their positions were informal and they had no power to coerce anyone or enforce their judgments. Leopard-skin chiefs were outside the lineages of the disputing parties and therefore respected as neutral parties. Their role was to negotiate a settlement between the perpetrator and the victim's family in order to avoid retaliation and an escalation of violence. Typically, compensation took the form of cattle paid out to the victim's family over a period of several years.

FIGURE 8.2 Nuer people in 1906. Nuer culture has been described as both fiercely independent and strongly egalitarian. When conflicts grew intense, people consulted a "leopard-skin chief" to mediate between fighting parties. (credit: "Nuer People, 1906" by National Geographic/Wikimedia Commons, Public Domain)

Another informal position of leadership, common to lineage-order societies in Melanesia and New Guinea, is the role of the **big man**. Although lineage orders are generally egalitarian, a man can distinguish himself through the accumulation of wealth, public acts of generosity, and the performance of verbal skills. Like leopard-skin chiefs, big men do not hold formal office and have no official power to enforce their will. Their power is persuasive, not coercive. By sponsoring feasts and helping young men pay bride wealth, big men attract loyal followers who respect their authority and follow their commands. Big men settle disputes within communities and represent local peoples in their dealings with outsiders. Though the accumulation of wealth and prestige is necessary to become a big man, far more important is the equitable distribution of wealth and service to the community. Greed and selfishness are abhorred. Anthropologist Leopold Pospisil (1963) described an incident among the Kapauku of New Guinea in which a man who refused to share resources with the less fortunate in his community was punished by death.

In some acephalous societies, communities are fundamentally organized through a system of age-related groups called **age sets**. An age set is a group of similarly aged people in a community who share a common social status with permitted roles, activities, and responsibilities. An array of age sets may be organized into a hierarchical age grade system, dividing members of the community into children, youths, adults, and elders (the term age *set* refers to the group, while the term age *grade* refers to the level in the hierarchy). Most often, age sets are gendered, with female and male versions of the same grade. In adolescence, males and females of similar ages are summoned at different times for initiation into the age set of their teenage years, either young men or young women. Strong lifelong bonds are formed through age sets, creating solidarities that cross lineage and clan boundaries in a community.

The Shavante (or Xavante) of central Brazil have eight age sets, spaced approximately five years apart (Flowers 1994; Maybury-Lewis 1967). Children are not formally in an age set but constitute an undifferentiated group of socially immature beings. Boys between the ages of 7 and 12 leave their family household and go to live in a bachelor's hut. After about five years, the set of boys is initiated into the age set of young warriors through a complex set of rituals that takes about a year to complete. In the lower age sets, senior men teach young men the important skills of hunting, singing, and performing public ceremonies. Initiated men of all age sets attend councils every evening where community matters are discussed and debated. Girls have their own age sets and initiation rituals. When a woman has her first child, for instance, she is awarded her formal adult name in a public ceremony and thereby enters the adult women's age set.

In addition to bands and lineage orders, a third and more atypical form of acephalous political organization is **village democracy**. Western students are often taught that democracy was invented in the ancient Greek city-state of Athens. Considering themselves heirs to the classical political tradition, Europeans who established colonial rule over African territories typically thought that they were bringing more enlightened ways of governing to African societies. But the Igbo of eastern Nigeria were already practicing a highly effective form of homegrown democracy before the arrival of the British. Indeed, many anthropologists reject the notion that democracy was invented by the Greeks. Lacking formal rulers, most acephalous societies practice forms of discussion and consensus-building that resemble democratic systems. In fact, the egalitarian and highly participatory form of democracy in such societies might be considered far more democratic than the form of representational democracy in large, Western societies, dominated by wealthy campaign donors and powerful lobbyists.

In precolonial Igbo villages, an array of social groups provided arenas for public discussion and the representation of different interests and perspectives (Isichei 1978, 71–75). Each group met frequently for discussion of current issues. A nuclear family formed a group headed by the father, and each lineage formed a larger group headed by a lineage elder. Women and men each had their own groups, and people were further divided into gendered age grades of people of roughly the same age. In some villages, there was even a group of very old women who inspected the town to maintain sanitation. At the highest level was a group of town elders comprising the leaders of other groups. After consulting on a particular issue, the elders would summon a general town meeting attended by everyone in the community. At this meeting, anyone could stand up and voice their opinion. Good contributions were cheered and applauded, while frivolous ones were jeered and dismissed by the audience of townspeople. The goal of group discussion at all levels was to reach consensus. With no formal positions, leaders had no coercive power. The role of group leaders was to chair discussion and facilitate the process of reaching consensus.

Anthropologists have described similar systems of decision-making through public councils in many societies all over the world, even in communities within chiefdoms or states. Anthropologists Audrey Richards and Adam Kuper formed a research group to compare and contrast forms of decision-making in councils, resulting in their book *Councils in Action* (1971). While in acephalous societies, councils are the main arena of public decision-making, councils play a more advisory role in societies with centralized authority.

8.3 Centralized Societies: Chiefdoms and States

LEARNING OUTCOMES

By the end of this section, you will be able to:

- Describe how lineage orders may develop into chiefdoms.
- Evaluate the economic, religious, and militaristic aspects of chiefdoms.
- Identify practices of popular representation in chiefdoms.
- Provide two detailed examples of chiefdoms.
- Explain integrative and conflict pressures of state formation.
- Enumerate the features of state societies.
- Describe social inequality in state societies.
- Define ideology and hegemony and explain their importance in state societies.

As mentioned in the last section, lineage orders are commonly associated with horticultural and pastoral societies, as well as societies that practice some combination of the two. Recall from Work, Life, Value: Economic Anthropology that such societies produce little beyond what they consume locally; they don't produce substantial surplus. If conditions are favorable, some such societies may intensify their farming methods with the development of irrigation systems, terracing, or use of the plow. The organization of labor and resources necessary to develop terracing and systems of irrigation fosters stronger forms of community authority. These intensive methods generate agricultural surplus, which allows some members of the community to specialize in craft production as well as in forms of religious and political leadership. Agricultural surplus can also be traded with other communities in regional networks. These factors promote the local accumulation of wealth.

The process of agricultural intensification often results in the centralization of power. Big men or lineage elders acquire the authority to command the labor of others and control the storage and distribution of agricultural surplus. They take on the role of organizing regional trade. They oversee the construction of infrastructure such as roads and irrigation systems. They organize groups of local young people to protect the community. They perform important community rituals to ensure agricultural productivity and community prosperity. Over time, such leaders may seek to hand down their leadership roles to their own kin in subsequent generations. As leadership becomes inherited, one lineage in a community may emerge as a royal lineage.

Chiefdoms

Anthropologists refer to those with formal, inherited positions of community leadership as **chiefs**. Over time, a chief can expand their dominion to incorporate several towns and villages into a small **chiefdom**. Chiefs may form political alliances with other regional chiefs in large pyramidal systems consisting of various levels of village chiefs and regional chiefs, with one very powerful chief at the top. When a chiefdom expands to encompass multiple ethnic groups in a regional empire, the leader is referred to as a **king**.

Chiefdoms are a very common form of political organization, found in historical and contemporary societies all over the world. Archaeologists and cultural anthropologists have discovered chiefdoms in Africa, Oceania, the Middle East, Europe, East and Southeast Asia, and North, Central, and South America. While there is considerable diversity in the way these various systems of chieftaincy operate, anthropologists have identified a set of elements common to many of them. The fusing of multiple forms of power is the defining feature of chiefdoms, common to all of them. Economic, political, religious, and military power are all concentrated in the position of the chief.

In Mesopotamia, the cities of Sumer were initially ruled by religious priests who represented local gods and oversaw work on common lands. Over time, priests began to share their power with secular governors who maintained law and order, managed the economy, and led military campaigns. Eventually, religious and civil power became fused in the office of the *lugal*. As *lugals* solidified their power, they began passing down their office to their sons, establishing dynasties.

Central to the power of a chief is control over economic resources such as land, agricultural surplus, and trade. Chiefs often hold land in public trust, determining who may farm where and also allocating farmland to newcomers. They have their own farming plots, commanding regular public labor to work on them. Farmers are obliged to channel a portion of their surplus to the chief, who holds it in storage facilities for public feasts or distribution to those in need. Chiefs regulate local trade and negotiate regional trade networks to benefit their own communities. They control the production and distribution of certain prestige goods, such as royal textiles and ornaments made of jade, gold, copper, or shell.

Imperial Chiefdoms: Hawaii and Asante

FIGURE 8.3 Statue of Chief Kamehameha, the founder and first ruler of the Kingdom of Hawaii, in Emancipation Hall in the U.S. Capitol Building. Hawaiian chiefs used the wealth they accumulated to build public works and military fortifications. (credit: Tyfferz Y/flickr, CC BY 2.0)

Chiefdoms developed throughout the Polynesian Pacific, including the peoples of Hawaii, Tahiti, Samoa, and Tonga and the Maori of New Zealand. In Hawaii, chieftaincy developed from the intensive cultivation of taro using systems of irrigation and terracing (Earle 2011). Hawaiian chiefs controlled the distribution of land, giving out subsistence plots in return for labor in their own gardens. They used accumulated wealth and communal labor to build roads, garden terraces, fish ponds, and military fortifications. Their power was reinforced by a belief system that identified chiefs as god figures responsible for agricultural prosperity and social welfare. Chiefs conducted important annual religious rituals to ensure the success of crops. They commanded public labor to build and refurbish shrines for the worship of local gods, personal gods, and high gods such as Lono. Military forces were recruited and commanded by chiefs who used them to defend their chiefdoms and expand their territories.

Militarism is another common feature of chiefdoms throughout the world. While the power of leaders in acephalous societies depends on their ability to persuade others to do what they say, chiefs have **coercive power** to force people to carry out their commands. The powerful West African chiefdom of Asante was originally founded in 1700 as a military confederation of chiefs who united to defeat the neighboring Denkyira. Under the Asantehene (the king), the top chiefs commanded different divisions of the military, including the scouts, the advance guard, the main body, the right and left wings, and the rear guard. As commander in chief, the Asantehene coordinated these divisions into a highly effective military machine that conquered a region larger than present-day Ghana. Subduing neighboring groups enabled the Asantehene to collect tribute in the form of agricultural surplus, trade goods, and slaves.

Also common to many chiefdoms is the promotion of moral and religious ideology that supports the legitimacy of their rule. Like Hawaiian chiefs, Asante chiefs were considered to be embodied links to the realm of the supernatural, and they conducted rituals and ceremonies for the benefit of the community. Every 40 days, Asante chiefs led processions to present ritual gifts of food and drink to the ancestors and ask for their blessings to ensure the fertility of the land and the well-being of the people. Although they wielded great power,

Asante chiefs were bound by a morality that compelled them to use resources such as land and gold for the good of the people rather than for private benefit.

FIGURE 8.4 Otumfuo Nana Osei Tutu II, the current Asantehene, the title for the monarch of the Asante people. The Asantehene traditionally held the role of commander in chief of the Asante military. (credit: "Asantehene Otumfuo Nana Osei Tutu II, Kumasi, Ghana" by Alfred Weidinger/flickr, CC BY 2.0)

Europeans who colonized African societies often assumed that African chiefs were cruel despots who used violence and exploitation to enrich themselves and oppress their subjects. On the contrary, research by historians and anthropologists has revealed that many African chiefdoms were highly moralized political systems that incorporated checks and balances on the rule of the chief.

Among the Akans (the larger cultural group that includes the Asante), there were several avenues for popular representation and critique as well as a procedure for getting rid of inept and corrupt chiefs. At the advisory level, the chief was guided by a council of elders as well as the queen mother, often his aunt, mother, or sister. The young men of the community formed a group called ***asafo*** that had as one of its many purposes the responsibility to represent popular opinion to the chief and his advisors. If the people wished to depose their chief, they could communicate their wishes to the young men, who then conveyed the message to the queen mother, who would then advise the chief to mend his ways. If he didn't, the young men could seize him, touch his feet to the ground (thus ritually defiling him), shoot off a gun, and declare him deposed. At that point, the queen mother would meet with the elders to nominate a new chief. In Akan societies, it was far easier to depose a bad chief than it is to impeach a bad president in the US political system.

States

Starting around 5,000 years ago, a new form of political organization emerged independently in many parts of the world, including Mesopotamia, China, Egypt, India, Mesoamerica, and South America. As some societies in these areas became more populous and hierarchical, their leaders developed modes of governance that combined forms of economic extraction such as taxation and tribute with mechanisms of social control such as law and policing. These governments used public revenues to build infrastructure and monuments. They developed extensive bureaucracies to interpret and enforce laws and maintain social order. Large military forces defended and expanded control over territory, resulting in multiethnic empires. The government asserted a monopoly on the use of violence, meaning that only the government was allowed to use extreme forms of violence to control or punish anyone. Societies with this form of political organization are called **state societies** (Brumfiel 2001).

Many of the features of states mentioned above are common to the political organization of chiefdoms, and indeed states have generally emerged from the increasing centralization of political power in large chiefdoms. This concentration of power happens gradually over time, stimulated by a variety of pressures, some very general and universal and others more particular to the context of specific societies. Population growth and increasing **social stratification** are among the more general pressures, while the militaristic threats of specific neighboring societies and the particular opportunities of regional trade affect societies in different ways. Attempting to explain the rise of the state, theorists emphasize two sets of forces that propel the process: integrative pressures and conflict pressures.

Integrative pressures arise from the need for greater coordination in order to satisfy the needs of a growing population. As the population increases, agricultural production must also be increased to meet subsistence needs and for trade. Leaders are compelled to organize more complex irrigation systems and forms of landscape management, such as terracing and raised fields. These complex systems are built and maintained using public resources and labor. Increasing trade also exerts an integrative force, as leaders strive to maximize the wealth of their societies by stimulating production of agricultural and craft goods and establishing local markets and regional trade opportunities. As agriculture and trade become more complex, power becomes more centralized in order to manage the necessary conditions and infrastructure for economic growth.

Conflict pressures arise from the need to manage both internal and external threats to the power of leaders and the integrity of their societies. Some theorists argue that political power becomes increasingly centralized as a leader builds a large military force and wages long-term warfare to defend and expand territory. Conquering neighboring societies allows leaders to command regular tribute. In addition to conquest, military forces provide leaders with large cadres of loyal, well-armed supporters. Other theorists argue that internal tensions are just as pivotal to the centralization of power. State societies are built upon a system of social stratification; that is, they feature class and caste systems with unequal access to wealth and power. With the emergence of a class of privileged elites governing over urban craft workers and rural peasantry, leaders face new forms of inequality and potential conflict. Systems of law and ideology are developed to command the cooperation of disadvantaged groups.

Archaic States: The Aztecs

In the 14th century, the Aztec state of Mesoamerica arose from a combination of integrative and conflict pressures. Migrants to the area, the Mexica (as they called themselves) first worked as mercenaries for other regional powers, then established their own city of Tenochtitlan on an island in the middle of Lake Texcoco (Peters-Golden 2002). As newcomers, the Mexica were keen to build up the military might necessary to defend their new settlement. They joined forces with two neighboring states to defeat the regional superpower and establish a "Triple Alliance" of three city-states, which they came to dominate. To strengthen their position, they also sought to generate wealth through agricultural surplus, craft manufacture, and trade. At the height of its power in the 15th century, the Aztec state comprised some 50 individual city-states, each with its own ruler who served the Aztec king. The Aztec empire spanned most of present-day central and southern Mexico.

FIGURE 8.5 A rendering of Tenochtitlan, the capital of the Aztec empire, by artist Diego Rivera. Tenochtitlan was a complex and professionally planned city, constructed on an island, and housing temples, pyramids, and palaces. (credit: "Diego Rivera Mural of Mexican History: Ceremonial Center at Tenochtitlan" by Gary Todd/flickr, Public Domain)

The Aztec state was constructed on a foundation of intensive agriculture, particularly the cultivation of maize. Beans, squash, chiles, cotton, cacao, and other produce also contributed to subsistence and trade. Farmers used a variety of cultivation methods, the most intensive being chinampas agriculture. **Chinampas** are rectangular plots constructed out of layers of mud and vegetation piled up in a shallow part of a lake and secured with anchoring poles. Using this cultivation method, farmers produced a hefty surplus, which was heavily taxed by the state. This surplus fed urban classes of craftspeople, warriors, bureaucrats, and nobles. Farmers formed the class of commoners who lived outside the urban centers of government and trade. They lived in mud houses roofed with thatch and wore simple clothes with cloaks that were required by law to end above the knee.

The agricultural base was diversified by urban classes of craft manufacturers, including weavers, sculptors, goldsmiths, and feather workers. Many of these products were not for general use but reserved for rulers and nobles, giving these craftspeople a class distinction above agricultural commoners. These craftspeople were organized into guilds and lived in exclusive neighborhoods near the nobles they served. Also included in the urban classes were merchants who traveled throughout central Mexico, trading Aztec goods within and beyond the empire.

The Aztecs were a highly militant society, valuing perpetual warfare as a political and religious necessity. All young men were expected to serve in the military, waging wars of conquest to collect tribute and captives. A class of warrior elites enjoyed high social status, living among other elite classes in major urban centers. This class was divided into two groups, the Eagle and Jaguar cults.

At the top level of this highly stratified society were nobles who could trace their ancestry back to the first Aztec rulers. Only nobles could live in two-story stone houses and wear headbands, gold armbands, and jewels in their lips, ears, and noses. Nobles owned land and monopolized positions in government and religion. Each city-state was governed by a noble ruler, considered a representative of the gods, who collected tribute from commoners, organized military campaigns, sponsored public feasts, and settled disputes. Government consisted of the city-state ruler and their advisors, a bureaucracy for collecting tribute, a justice system of high and lesser courts, and the lesser rulers of provinces and towns.

At the very bottom of the class system were serfs and enslaved people, who were commoners who had gotten into debt and/or been sold into slavery. People who fell on hard times economically could sell themselves or their kin into servitude.

Through the coordinated labor of these classes, the Aztecs built a sprawling empire of tributary provinces all channeling wealth to the core of three city-states, headed by Tenochtitlan. The largest city in the Americas at the time, Tenochtitlan was a professionally planned symmetrical city with well-maintained roads, canals, gardens, and markets. The center of the city was dominated by around 45 large stone buildings, including temples, pyramids, and palaces. The ruler's palace had 100 rooms, each with its own bathroom. The city had a zoo, an aquarium, and botanical gardens. Life was congenial and luxurious for nobles who lived in such a beautiful and culturally stimulating environment.

Life was not so great for the vast majority of commoners, serfs, and slaves who toiled long hours on the land, struggling to pay the tribute and taxes that supported the very luxuries that were denied to them. Why did they do it?

Every state has a set of institutions for maintaining social order, such as law, courts, police, and military forces. The Aztecs had a complex legal system that banned drunkenness, adultery, and homicide, among other crimes. Even more important for the cohesion of social classes were laws that banned any behavior above one's own social class. Commoners who wore elite forms of dress, built elaborate houses, or tried to obtain private property could be punished by death. Under these conditions, people tended to accept the social class they were born into rather than struggle to change their class status or the hierarchical system of classes as a whole.

Even more powerful than state law was a set of ideas and practices threaded throughout the daily lives of Aztec peoples at all levels of society. The official religion of the Aztecs emphasized the importance of continual sacrifice in order to keep the world functioning. In the Aztec origin myth, the gods sacrificed themselves to generate the world, offering up their own blood to put the sun in motion. This act of sacrifice put humans forever in debt to the gods, with continual rituals of human sacrifice required to appease them. Without blood sacrifice, the world would end. Priests conducted ritual sacrifices of men, women, and children throughout the year. Many victims were warriors captured in constant battles with neighboring states. Conquered provinces were required to provide a continuous supply of victims to fuel the ritual calendar.

Ideology and Hegemony

People are often shocked to learn about the prevalence of human sacrifice in Aztec society. We might wonder, how could people go along with such routine public violence conducted by representatives of the state? How did they not protest?

Every society develops a set of dominant ideas that frame the existing social order as the way things should be. These ideas form a narrative about the way the world works and the roles of different groups in promoting social harmony and collective prosperity. Typically, a society has many competing ideas about the way the world works, each one reflecting the perspectives and experiences of a particular group. The worldview of a particular group or class in society is called an **ideology**. Literary theorist Terry Eagleton (1991) describes ideology as an intertwined set of ideas, values, and symbols that can be either conscious or unconscious. When an ideology transcends one group to become the dominant way nearly all people in a society think about social reality, it becomes **hegemony**. Hegemony is a strategic set of "common sense" ideas that support the social order.

As a form of sociopolitical organization, the state requires the vast majority of citizens to lead lives of hard labor and sacrifice in order to support classes of artisans and nobles who live in great cities full of bustling trade, luxurious goods, and monumental architecture. Tearing the heart from a victim on a public altar may seem shocking, but the logic of sacrifice serves as a metaphor for the bodily sacrifice of commoners required to endure lives of hardship to support the well-being of the state. To manage the inequality of classes and ensure the cooperation of all groups, the Aztecs came to embrace the hegemonic notion that sacrifice was necessary to ensure the very existence of the world.

The wealth of all state societies, past and present, rests on the hardship of manual laborers at the bottom of the social hierarchy. The dominant ideas of any state are ways of justifying the inequality inherent to all states. These ideas are highly variable. Some societies emphasize religious ideologies of self-sacrifice or the dangers of eternal damnation. Others celebrate economic ideologies of economic growth and consumerism. In American society, for instance, some believe it is necessary to keep the minimum wage of workers very low in order to protect economic growth, an idea not so far removed from notions of bodily sacrifice. In recent decades, the American system has offset these low wages by supplying working-class people with a vast array of cheap consumer goods. The relentless stream of advertising pervading social life continuously reiterates the consumerist mantras of affordability and satisfaction. Ironically, however, those goods are cheap because American manufacturers have relocated their factories to parts of the world where they can pay workers even less than they would pay Americans. The dominant ideology of consumerism draws attention away from the conditions of work and production and toward the ideals of choice and leisure.

As both Aztec and American societies demonstrate, the economic and political systems of state societies are deeply entwined, and this relationship is often reflected in the dominant ideas of a society. **Political economy** is the study of the way political and economic realms frequently reinforce and sometimes contradict one another over time.

8.4 Modern Nation-States

LEARNING OUTCOMES

By the end of this section, you will be able to:

- Distinguish nation from state and describe how the two are linked in modern nation-states.
- Define the concept of imagined communities.
- Identify the importance of colonialism in shaping postcolonial nation-states.
- Describe the field of postcolonial studies.
- Explain the fragility of postcolonial states.
- Provide two examples of the consequences of globalization for national identities and politics.

Before 1400 or so, the world was a variegated array of empires, kingdoms, and chiefdoms with their tributary societies, loosely linked by trade with acephalous societies at the peripheries. The contemporary globe is an economically integrated order fundamentally organized into nation-states. How did this happen?

The **nation-state** is a hyphenated concept joining two entities, the state and the nation. As discussed earlier, the state is an institution exercising centralized rule over a territory. States have bureaucracies that make, interpret, and enforce law. States collect taxes and use them to build infrastructure and public works. States organize and regulate the economy. States maintain monopoly on the use of force through the military and the police. Because states tend to be militant and expansionist, they also tend to form multiethnic empires, dominated by one ruling group. Ancient empires did not attempt to absorb their tributary societies into one common ethnicity or peoplehood. Ancient states were defined by territory and bureaucracy alone, with no effort to achieve cultural uniformity.

The nation is a much more idealistic and cultural notion. A **nation** is a sense of cultural belonging or "peoplehood." A cousin of the word *native*, the term *nation* refers to the original inhabitants of a territory, those who were born there. Nations often claim a common language as a sign of group membership. Nations tell a common origin story about where they came from, and they ritually commemorate that story in a ritual calendar of feasts and holidays. Nations claim a common destiny, a special future or sacred duty assigned to them by God. And finally, nations promote certain social norms and values, evaluating individuals and groups according to those ideals. The concept of nation is close to the old-fashioned notion of culture as communal and unchanging. A nation-state is a state with a common culture, in some cases a dominant ethnicity.

Political scientist Benedict Anderson (1983) argues that all modern states deliberately cultivate this sense of peoplehood for those living in the state. They draw from a large repertoire of methods to summon the loyalty of their citizens and reinforce the legitimacy of the state system. Through practices both within and beyond the government, state societies encourage their citizens to imagine themselves as part of a larger community of like-minded people in a harmonious society bound by a common history and common destiny. Government promotes national identity through practices such as elections, censuses, taxes, schools, and the dramas of law making, interpretation, and enforcement. Modern states rely on meaningful public rituals and symbols, such as flags, anthems, pledges of allegiance, national holidays, historical monuments, and national museums. Outside of government, the mass news media highlights the importance of the daily actions of the state, providing continual coverage that fixes the attention of citizens on the state as the central power in society.

As a citizen of a nation-state, you will never know all of the members of your national community. Such communities are far too large to generate organic social groups based on face-to-face interaction. Without all of the practices and rituals listed above, you might not even consider yourself a member of the larger political community at all. Because of this, Benedict Anderson refers to nations as **imagined communities**. By *imagined*, Anderson is not arguing that such communities are simply *imaginary* or not real, but rather that national identity is a powerful sense of unity that is strategically constructed by the state and mass media.

The nation-states of western Europe grew out of an assemblage of kingdoms and territories, some of them once incorporated into the Holy Roman Empire. From the 15th to the 19th century, the states of Europe slowly emerged, one by one, as the various European powers entered into peace agreements that established international borders and sovereignty over territories. In general, the wars and treaties of political elites meant very little to the common farmers and traders living in these territories. Among English commoners, for instance, their sense of community was not much affected by the continually changing map of territories that constituted the state of England. What did make a difference for European commoners was the development of the printing press around 1440.

The printing press targeted a growing population of literate commoners. Driven by the capitalist profit motive, printers sought to reach the widest possible audience. Thus, they printed their books, pamphlets, and newspapers in local languages rather than in Latin, which was the pan-European language of elites and the Catholic Church. For each emerging nation-state, mass media helped standardize a diversity of dialects into one common language that could be used to spread common messages and carry out common practices such as schooling, law, political campaigns, and government bureaucracy.

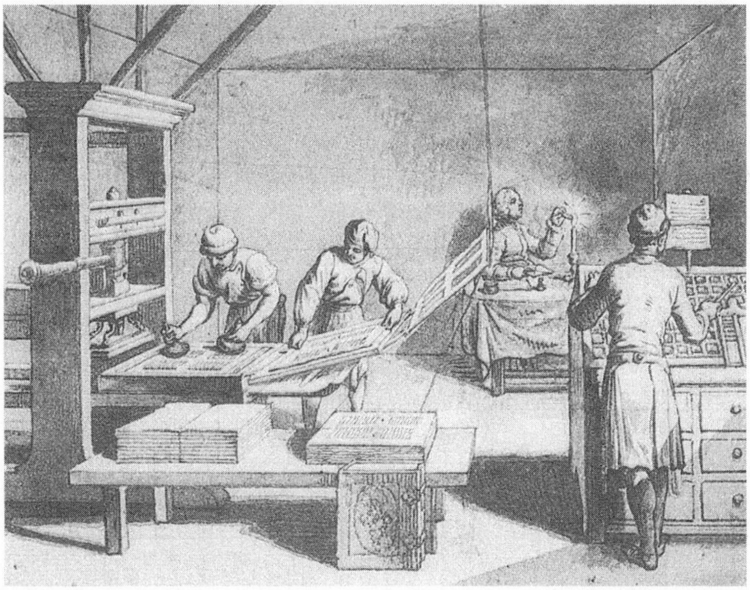

FIGURE 8.6 Depiction of the printing process using an early press. The printing press made available ideas and news to common people in their own language, helping to cement nation-state identities. (credit: Daniel Nikolaus Chodowiecki/Wikimedia Commons, Public Domain)

Of course, the printing press did not singlehandedly create the modern nation-states of Europe. Around the same time that the press began churning out mass discourse, a rising class of capitalist merchants was gaining economic power, hoping to displace forms of political leadership associated with the church and the feudal monarchies. The felicitous coincidence of class motivation and printing technology combined to propel the development of European nation-states.

For Max Weber, the nation-state is associated with the complete formalization of rational-bureaucratic power—that is, power concentrated in bureaucratic institutions with legal authorities. The legal and political systems of nation-state bureaucracies often purport to be based on rules and procedures rather than social status or identities. For instance, in the American system, the ability to vote is based on legal citizenship, not social class, gender, or ethnic identity. However, legal and political bureaucracies reserve the power to determine who *is* and who *is not* a citizen as well as procedures for voter registration and voting in elections. Through these procedures, certain categories of people can be barred or discouraged from voting, resulting in racial or ethnic bias. If people of color are less likely to have state-sponsored photo identification (such as a driver's license), then laws requiring such ID to vote may constitute forms of racial discrimination.

French philosopher Michel Foucault (1978, 2007) describes such power to define and control populations of citizens as biopower. A special form of power exercised in modern states, biopower includes ways of regulating the bodies of citizens, such as practices associated with birth, death, sexuality, wellness, illness, work, and leisure. The ability to count and categorize the inhabitants of a state is a form of biopower. The ability to confine people who have certain illnesses or bodily conditions or have engaged in certain behaviors is a form of biopower. When you walk through a body scanner in an airport security station, you are experiencing a form of biopower. While Weber focused on specific institutions in which power is concentrated, Foucault describes biopower as a diffuse form of social control, widely practiced by citizens both within and outside state bureaucracies. In American society, people routinely carry state-sponsored identification on their bodies (in a pocket or purse) wherever they go. The information on this identity card links to bureaucratic files associated with a person's citizenship status, criminal history, voter registration, and many other data sets. Bureaucratic power is thereby melded to bodies of modern citizens.

Colonial and Postcolonial States

Outside of Europe, a similar array of kingdoms, chiefdoms, lineage orders, and village democracies patterned much of the rest of the world. Recall that ancient state societies had emerged at various times in Mesopotamia, Egypt, China, India, and Central and South America. Kingdoms were prevalent forms of centralized rule on most continents as well. All around these highly centralized societies were smaller chiefdoms and acephalous communities.

The continent of Africa, for instance, featured large, centralized states and kingdoms such as Egypt in the north; Aksum, Zimbabwe, and Swahili in the east; Luba and Kongo in central Africa; and a multitude of kingdoms across West Africa, including the great trade-based empires of Ghana, Mali, and Songhai (Monroe 2013). As noted in the discussion of acephalous societies, communities outside of these great kingdoms and states were politically organized, with forms of leadership, decision-making, and dispute settlement that maintained social order.

British historian Basil Davidson (1992) has argued that African societies such as the Asante and Zulu were **proto-states**, or states in formation, at the time of European colonization. Between 1400 and 1900—the time frame during which European nation-states were emerging—many African societies were undergoing similar developments as militant kingdoms consolidated large territories of empire. Based on intensive agriculture and extensive trade networks across the continent (and beyond), such highly centralized societies had state bureaucracies, multiethnic populations, systems of law, and monumental architecture. They also had dominant ideologies that emphasized the accumulation and appropriate distribution of wealth. In other words, many African societies were state societies well on their way to becoming modern nation-states.

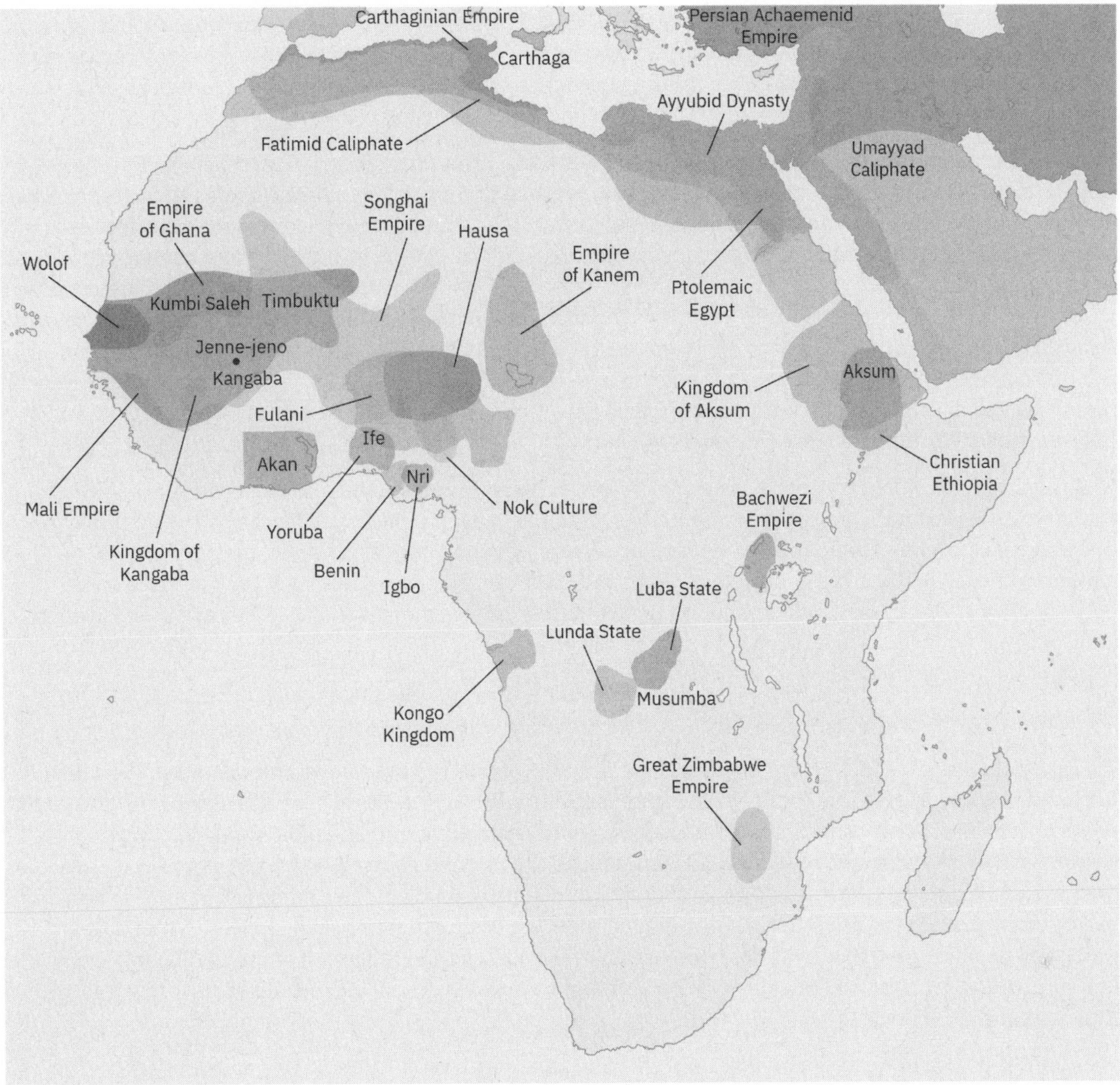

FIGURE 8.7 Precolonial states and empires in Africa. Note how different these are from the way Africa is divided into nations today. (credit: "African civilizations map pre-colonial," by Jeff Israel/Wikimedia Commons, GNU Free Documentation License)

Instead, colonialism happened. As we learned in Work, Life, Value: Economic Anthropology, the growth of industrial capitalism prompted the major European powers to seek access to raw materials and markets for their finished goods. Many set their sights on the mineral wealth and agricultural potential of Africa. European representatives met in Berlin in 1884–1885 to negotiate their territorial interests on the African continent. Laying out a map of the continent, they drew boundaries around the areas they hoped to control, though they knew very little about the land or peoples in much of those areas. They agreed that they could maintain exclusive claim on those areas only if they established government administrations to rule over the people who lived there.

By the early 20th century, Europeans had established colonial government over nearly all societies in Africa, subordinating local African political systems under European rule. As the whole point of colonialism was to secure resources to fuel European colonies, the **colonial states** established by Europeans were authoritarian, militaristic, and extractive. They invaded African territories and slaughtered Africans who would not submit to European rule. They forced Africans to work on colonial projects such as mines and roads. They made Africans pay taxes to fund the colonial enterprise. And they designed and controlled African economies to channel profits to European merchants and manufacturers. Oddly, as European nation-states pulled away from direct control over their own economies, European colonial states exerted complete control over colonial economies. Moreover, as European nation-states became increasingly participatory and democratic, European colonial states were managed in ways that were repressive, authoritarian, and openly violent.

Because of colonial rule, the two forces that contributed to the rise of the modern nation-state in Europe—a wealthy capitalist class and the printing press—were prevented from playing the same role in African societies. Africans were deliberately sidelined from the import-export trade and were not allowed to start factories, preventing a class of wealthy capitalists from developing under colonial rule. Instead, colonial rule established a two-tiered system of governance in the colonies consisting of a militant authoritarian state apparatus governing over local African political systems, including proto-states, chiefdoms, lineage orders, and a few scattered band societies. In places where there were chiefs, colonial officials used those chiefs to carry out colonial policies, often against the wishes and interests of the chiefs' own people. In places where there were no chiefs, colonial authorities often forced Africans to pick one to perform those duties. In some colonies, African political institutions were banned altogether.

Anthropologists working on political issues in previously colonized states (such as most African ones) often combine historical and contemporary research to understand the intersection of local and foreign influences that make up this complex picture. In one form or another, colonial processes shaped the development of political systems in Africa, the Middle East, South and Southeast Asia, the Caribbean, the Americas, and eastern Europe. The interdisciplinary field of **postcolonial studies** emerged in the 1970s, combining history, anthropology, political science, and area studies in an effort to understand the diversity, complexity, and legacy of colonialism throughout the world.

"Fragile" States and "Failed" States: The Legacies of Colonialism

The study of African politics provides an excellent example of the weaving of local culture and colonial history in the making of contemporary postcolonial societies. Journalists and political scientists frequently lament the political instability of African states and their susceptibility to popular unrest, ethnic conflicts, coups, and corrupt leadership. Some refer to African states as fragile states or failed states. A **fragile state** is a government that cannot *adequately* perform the essential functions of a state, such as maintaining law and order, building basic infrastructure such as roads and bridges, guaranteeing basic amenities such as electricity and clean water, and defending its citizens against violence. Such a state is fragile because it is susceptible to popular uprising, coups, civil war, and foreign invasion. A **failed state** is a state that can no longer perform any state functions *at all.*

Many anthropologists are critical of this simplistic and ahistorical way of stigmatizing non-Western governments. Rather than viewing the world as a set of discrete states in isolation, anthropologists pay attention to historical processes of interaction among states that have shaped global patterns of inequality. Examining the notions of state fragility and state failure through a critical lens, anthropologist note how some states have become more powerful while others have struggled to meet the needs of their peoples.

At various times over the past 30 years, many African states have qualified as fragile or failed, including Somalia, Liberia, Sierra Leone, Côte d'Ivoire, Mali, Zimbabwe, and the Democratic Republic of the Congo. Since 2005, the Fragile States Index has ranked all states in the United Nations according to a set of key political, economic, and social indicators. Among the top 50 "most fragile" states in the 2020 index, all but two have experienced some form of colonial rule, and 35 of the top 50 most fragile states are African states. For more information on fragile states see Fragile States Index (https://openstax.org/r/fragilestatesindex).

Why do so many African states face such deep-seated problems? How did colonialism contribute to the current fragility of postcolonial states?

As an example, take the postcolonial West African state of Ghana. What can an anthropological approach tell us about contemporary politics in Ghana? Most African countries won independence in the middle of the 20th century. Once free from colonial domination, new classes of African political elites won control over the colonial apparatus of the state, including its colonial institutions and boundaries and its bureaucratic rule over African chiefdoms and acephalous societies. In other words, at independence, the structure of the state as it had existed under colonialism remained essentially unchanged. The new leaders of these African states faced the near-impossible challenge of politically and economically restructuring their states while holding together the diverse groups existing within colonial boundaries, groups frequently pitted against one another under colonial rule. As an additional stress, finances were limited and unpredictable.

Leaders such as Kwame Nkrumah, the first prime minister and, later, the first president of Ghana, sought to reform the state to make it serve the interests of Africans. He started schools and hospitals and built roads, bridges, and dams in an effort to do all the things a state should do to command the loyalty of its citizens. He used symbols of chiefdom to promote his own political power, even though he was not a chief or even from a royal lineage. His administration reduced the regional power of chiefs in an effort to enhance the centralized power of the state. Nkrumah was wildly popular at first, but over time, economic and regional factors challenged his rule. Some cocoa farmers felt they were being exploited to fund grand projects benefiting urban elites. Facing widespread criticism, Nkrumah became increasingly autocratic, throwing political opponents in prison.

FIGURE 8.8 Dr. Kwame Nkrumah, the first prime minister and later the first president of Ghana, is shown on the right in traditional kente cloth clothing. On the left, he is seated (center in the front row) with the Gold Coast Cabinet. Nkrumah's leadership was characterized by successful reform efforts at first, but he eventually developed autocratic tendencies and was overthrown by a military coup. (credit: (L) "CO 1069-43-65" by The National Archives UK/flickr, Public Domain; (R) "f9577" by Tullio Saba/flickr)

In 1966, nine years after declaring Ghanaian independence from the British, Kwame Nkrumah was overthrown by a military coup that accused him of corruption and political repression. Over the next 15 years, Ghana endured four more military coups and two (brief) elected governments, an exceptionally long string of political instability. Each military coup justified its takeover by claiming the previous regime had been massively corrupt—and each one eventually became the target of the same accusations of corruption.

Political instability, popular unrest, military coups, corruption—a similar narrative describes the political development of many other African states. The commonality of political crisis in Africa has prompted many journalists and policy experts to wonder what is wrong with African states. What is the underlying problem? Postcolonial studies suggest that we must think both culturally and historically to understand how postcolonial societies function. Postcolonial states are very often fragile states not because they are doing something wrong but largely because of the legacies of colonialism.

In many African societies, colonialism tainted precolonial political systems while also constructing a repressive, authoritarian state. Recall our earlier discussion of checks and balances in the system of chieftaincy practiced by the Akans. Akan chiefs were expected to act in the interests of their people or else face the consequences. If a community became unhappy with their chief, the *asafo* could eventually depose the chief by force. Though *asafo* had many civic duties, the term itself literally means "war people," referring to their role in defense and in deposing bad chiefs.

British colonial rule put Akan chiefs in a contradictory position. Forced to act as agents of colonial rule, chiefs were ordered to collect colonial taxes, supply teams of forced labor, and enforce unpopular colonial laws. At the same time, chiefs were presented with new economic opportunities in the colonial system—such as selling off land and pocketing the money—that further undermined their commitment to the welfare of their own people. As their positions became increasingly conflicted, some chiefs succumbed to the temptations of embezzlement, extortion, and authoritarianism.

Fed up with these corrupt chiefs, many *asafo* groups took action. In the 1920s, a spate of *asafo* uprisings deposed unpopular chiefs throughout the southern part of the colony. Fearing the consequences of African popular protest, British colonial officials quickly suppressed the *asafo* uprisings and forbid the *asafo* from any further action against their chiefs. So, to be clear, British colonialism corrupted the institution of African chieftaincy and then forbade the exercise of African protest against that corruption.

Now jump ahead to that long period of political instability in Ghana in the latter half of the 20th century. Ghanaian anthropologist Maxwell Owusu (1989) argues that this colonial history of corruption and protest has shaped postcolonial politics in Ghana. Just as the pressures of colonialism undermined and tainted the Akan chieftaincy, the near-impossible mission of the postcolonial state undermined and tainted the Ghanaian presidency. Just as *asafo* groups were motivated by allegations of corruption to rise up and depose their chiefs, the Ghanaian military rose up time and time again to depose Ghanaian leaders accused of corruption.

Nation-States and Globalization

In the latter part of the 20th century, increasing global flows of trade, people, technologies, communication, and ideas all coalesced in a strong but uneven wave of globalization rippling across the globe. To be clear, the world has always been integrated by such flows, but advanced technologies combined with the profit drive of corporate capitalism forced a sudden acceleration of these processes roughly from the late 1970s into the 2000s.

As people, objects, and messages began to travel across national boundaries with increasing frequency and speed, many scholars argued that nation-states would lose their relevance as structures of economic and political order for their populations. Some scholars thought that globalization would result in the erasure of cultural and national differences, replacing global diversity with a uniform culture based on American corporate capitalism and consumerism. Would globalization result in the "McDonaldization" of the world?

As global researchers with a powerful toolkit of cross-cultural methods, anthropologists were uniquely poised to address this question. In short, the answer was an emphatic "No!" Rather than diminishing the importance of local structures and identities, globalization has transformed and enhanced them. Consider the increasing popularity of global travel. Why would anyone go anywhere if things were the same wherever you went? Many nation-states invest heavily in their distinctive cultures, monuments, and environmental features in order to attract global travelers keen to experience something new and different.

Consider another strong force of globalization, the increasing tendency for large corporate manufacturers based in the United States to relocate their factories to poorer countries where labor is cheaper and environmental regulation may be weaker. Initially, this technique undermined the power of nation-states and local communities to challenge corporate practices. Over time, however, the resulting loss of well-paid working-class jobs in the United States has generated a great deal of political controversy. This loss of working-class jobs has resulted in rising levels of inequality in American society. Some politicians call for the American government to create incentives and regulations to keep American jobs within American borders. Ironically, then, globalization may provoke citizens to enhance the power of their nation-states.

In poorer countries, globalization has resulted in increased environmental damage as globalized industries take advantage of looser regulations. Industrial pollution and the dumping of hazardous waste by global corporations pose serious threats to the health of local communities in many non-Western countries. Responding to these threats, local peoples turn to their governments to enact environmental protections. Moreover, the forces of globalization have created a strong network of transnational resistance to environmentally destructive practices with organizations such as the Global Alliance on Health and Pollution

(GAHP) and the United Nations Environment Program (UNEP).

In the wake of Benedict Anderson's (1983) formulation of nation-states as imagined communities, many anthropologists have considered how globalization creates transnational forms of imagined community alongside the nation. Cultural anthropologist Arjun Appadurai (1996) argues that globalization freed popular imagination from the constraints of the nation, creating multiple realms of imagined community cross-cutting national borders. Appadurai postulates five dimensions of global flows, constructing realms of activity and imagination: ethnicity, technology, finance, media, and ideology. The global environmental movement, for instance, constitutes a transnational imagined community based on ideas of environmental sustainability. Through media and communication technologies, people all over the world join in the discussions and activities of this imagined community.

Appadurai has also pointed to the darker consequences of globalization for national and transnational politics. While globalization might seem to be associated with free flows and flexibility, the forces of transnationalism have also resulted in a proliferation of forms of political violence, especially violence against ethnic, racial, and religious minority groups (2006). With increasing global flows, many communities are subject to increased cultural mixing and pressures for change. With rising immigration, for instance, national communities may be forced to reformulate notions of common language, practices, and values. While some citizens of a national community may embrace a more cosmopolitan and multicultural identity, others may experience a sense of insecurity and threat to their way of life. This insecurity is particularly keen among those working-class and poor groups that suffer from the increased inequality brought about by globalization. Appadurai describes how cultural and economic insecurity can provoke majority ethnic and racial groups to acts of violence against minority groups in their national communities. Seeking an elusive and imaginary national "purity," dominant groups seek to reassert their power over political, economic, and cultural institutions. Anti-immigrant politics in the United States and anti-American politics in some non-Western countries are both dangerous and sometimes violent responses to the common forces of globalization.

PROFILES IN ANTHROPOLOGY

Laura Nader
1930-

FIGURE 8.9 Laura Nader (right) engaged in conversation. (credit: "Moët Hennessy • Financial Times Club Dinner" by Financial Times/flickr, CC BY 2.0)

"What was proven in the last election is that the United States is not an electoral democracy, by which I mean the two parties' stranglehold on power has made it impossible for other voices to be heard." —Laura Nader (in Nkrumah 2005)

Personal History: Born and raised in Winsted, Connecticut, Laura Nader grew up in a family with strong commitments to community and public service. Her mother, Rose, was a politically minded schoolteacher who frequently wrote letters to the editor of the local newspaper. Her father, Nathra, owned a restaurant where local people met to talk about community and political issues. Laura's parents challenged her and her siblings to debate political issues and develop their own opinions.

Area of Anthropology: Nader earned a BA in Latin American studies from Wells College (Aurora, New York) and then went on to study anthropology at Harvard, earning a PhD from Radcliffe College in 1961. Nader's areas of interest include politics and law, in particular how the legal-political system operates as a form of social control.

Accomplishments in the Field: For her dissertation, Nader studied local courts in the Zapotec village of Talea in southwestern Mexico (1990). She discovered that the legal system in Talea was shaped by a strong emphasis on harmony rather than conviction and punishment. When conflicts arose, the courts brought people together face to face to engage in discussions aimed at reaching reconciliation and balanced solutions. Rather than focusing on blame and criminality, the legal process sought to restore community solidarity and consensus in the wake of the rift. Nader traced this "harmony ideology" to the context of colonial conquest by the Spanish, showing how missionaries and colonial administrators emphasized the moral value of harmony in order to dominate and pacify Indigenous peoples. She argued that local peoples in villages such as Talea have appropriated harmony ideology to their own ends, adopting methods of conflict resolution in order to prevent outside authorities from interfering in their affairs.

Bringing the lessons of her research back home to the American legal system, Nader argued that harmony ideology operates as a strong force against Americans seeking justice against large corporations. Though the American system is focused much more on blame and conviction, large corporations are able to evade the consequences of wrongful actions by using sophisticated legal procedures and forcing monetary settlements. Many such settlements include stipulations preventing people from publicly talking about the controversy, essentially purchasing the silence of complainants. Though governed by harmony ideology, the goal of such legal processes is not the restoration of good relations among community members but rather the forcing of capitulation and silence on complainants. Nader's comparative work on the law in Talea and the United States is vividly portrayed in the ethnographic film *Little Injustices* (1981).

Importance of Their Work: In 1960, Nader was the first woman hired for a tenure-track anthropology position at the University of California, Berkeley. From 1984 to 2010, she taught an innovative and popular course called Controlling Processes, exploring dominant ideologies and techniques of power in complex industrialized societies such as the United States (the author of this chapter took this course at Berkeley in 1990). Nader's own research identifies controlling processes that shape law and justice in many societies, exploring how citizens participate and challenge these hegemonic legal processes. Throughout her career, she has worked to make legal anthropology a force for justice reaching beyond the scholarly arena into public life. She has been a visiting professor in law schools at Yale, Stanford, and Harvard.

8.5 Resistance, Revolution, and Social Movements

LEARNING OUTCOMES

By the end of this section, you will be able to:

- Define the concept of social movement.
- Distinguish between political parties and social movements.
- Identify the goals of the Arab Spring.
- Describe how democratic institutions may fail to represent majority and minority groups.
- Give an example of how anthropologists study social movements.
- Explain how Indigenous groups have formed social movements to protect Native lands and cultures.

Politics includes all activities associated with governing a society. Thus far, we've focused on the institutions and practices of government. But politics happens both inside and outside the realm of government. In fact, what happens outside of government may be even more important to understanding how a society is ruled. Outside of government, people respond to social and political conditions with commentary, critique, and social action. They form groups to express their views and demand social change. These groups are called **social movements**.

FIGURE 8.10 Arab Spring protest in Tunisia. This widespread social movement spread throughout the Arab world in the early 2010s, voicing popular demands for greater participation in government and a more equitable distribution of wealth. (credit: "Tunisian Revolution -Jan20 DSC_5305" by Chris Belsten/flickr, CC BY 2.0)

In the early 2010s, a series of protests spread across the Arab world from Tunisia to Libya, Egypt, Yemen, Syria, Iraq, and many other countries (Blakemore 2019). Through marches, demonstrations, and armed rebellions, people called for an end to oppressive governments and poor living conditions in their countries. Fueled by the expansion of social media, this large and diverse pro-democracy social movement came to be called the **Arab Spring**. At the heart of the movement were demands for more participation in government (a political demand) and a more equitable distribution of wealth (an economic demand).

There are many different kinds of social movements. Some social movements express **resistance** to current social conditions. When groups gather to protest the outcome of an election or the passing of a law, they show their disagreement with government actions without necessarily suggesting specific action or redress. Other social movements campaign for specific **reforms**. In response to police shootings, for instance, protesters might call for changes in the training and routine practices of police in their communities. More ambitious still are social movements calling for revolution. A **revolution** occurs when a social movement successfully changes the structure of the political system—whether through peaceful actions or violence.

Many social movements are rooted in political economy; that is, they work to change political and economic conditions and the relationship between those two realms. In democratic societies, political parties are social movements that have transformed into formalized political institutions. Political parties play a routine, conventional role in democratic societies. For instance, in American society, the Democratic Party consistently argues that the government should play a role in organizing and regulating the economy, while the Republican Party consistently argues that government should avoid economic interference. Political parties are fully integrated into the political system of democratic societies, structuring elections, lawmaking, government policy, and even the judicial process.

Political parties may fail to represent the views of some groups—or even majority opinion. In the U.S. Congress, the views of a very wealthy minority of Americans exert a strong influence over the laws that are passed. Political scientist Martin Gilens (2012) conducted public opinion research among groups of poor, middle-class, and wealthy Americans and then compared the views of these three groups to the policy actions of government. Gilens found that when poor people and rich people disagree on an issue, government policy nearly always supports the views of the wealthy. This effect is largely due to the role of money in American politics, with the wealthy actively seeking to influence government policy through lobbying and campaign contributions.

So what can people do when the formal mechanisms of democracy fail to represent their views? The vast majority of social movements are less like political parties and more like the Arab Spring; that is, most social movements are informal groups engaging in activities outside of the formal realm of political activity. Social movements often originate in a particular incident or string of incidents, such as mass shootings, sexual assaults, police violence, or environmental disasters. When people feel that the truth of such incidents is hidden, obscured, or misrepresented by government officials and media, they may find dramatic ways to publicize the truth and demand remediating action. French philosopher Michel Foucault (2001) used the term **parrhesia** to describe how people are morally inspired to engage in risky public speech in order to speak truth to power.

In the wake of the global financial crisis of 2008–2009, many Americans became worried about the role of the financial sector in creating economic inequality and instability. In September 2011, a group of protesters met in Zuccotti Park in Manhattan to protest rising inequality and corporate influence over American politics. Over time, this movement, known as Occupy Wall Street, spread to cities throughout the United States and then the world, and members of the movement articulated a platform of sociopolitical goals that included a more balanced distribution of wealth, better jobs and working conditions, regulation of banks, bankruptcy protection for student loan debt, and a freeze on home foreclosures. Protesters set up a participatory community in the park, organizing a form of self-governance through working groups and democratic consensus. Some protesters camped on-site in tents, while others visited the park each day. In November 2011, police in riot gear forcibly removed protesters from Zuccotti Park, arresting some 200 people in a single day.

In many countries, extractive industries such as mining and logging produce forms of environmental damage that threaten the health and livelihoods of local peoples. When governments fail to intervene, farmers often join with urban activists to form coalitions aimed at environmental reform. Anthropologist Fabiana Li (2015) has explored the emergence of protest against multinational mining corporations in Peru. In 2004, 10,000 peasants gathered to protest a mining operation that would have leveled the mountain of Cerro Quilish. While company officials viewed the mountain as an obstacle to the extraction of minerals, urban activists and peasant leaders described it in sentient and supernatural terms, as a sacred place of spirits. Li also studies the response of mining officials to popular demands for accountability. When local people protest against the degradation and pollution of their lands, corporations often respond with technical fixes that are presented as fair solutions. For instance, when blood tests revealed high levels of lead in children living near a Peruvian mining operation, the mining company responded with a program to bus those children to a distant kindergarten, thus reducing the number of hours of daily exposure to mining pollution.

Many Indigenous peoples encompassed by contemporary nation-states engage in social movements to gain formal political recognition and to protect their lands and cultures. Work, Life, Value: Economic Anthropology discussed efforts by the Hadza, the Bedouin, and the Kayapo to protect their lifeways by forming coalitions with global allies and engaging in sustained public protest. As discussed in Chapter 6, Language and Communication, Indigenous groups such as the Wampanoag and the Maori have formed social movements around the revitalization of language and culture. In 2016, a group of Standing Rock Sioux and other Native Americans began campaigning to protect Native lands and cultures from the damaging effects of a proposed oil pipeline, the Dakota Access Pipeline. Running under waterways and across Native territories, the pipeline threatened the water supply of Native peoples as well as many sites, archaeological and otherwise, considered sacred by Native groups. Thousands of Native Americans and environmentalists gathered in multiple camps to protest the building of the pipeline over several months. Despite the protests, the Trump administration allowed the construction of the pipeline to begin in 2017. In January 2021, however, a US Appeals court vacated the Army Corps of Engineers' construction permit and called for extensive environmental review of the project.

FIGURE 8.11 A coalition of Native American groups protesting the Dakota Access Pipeline. Thousands of Native Americans, joined by environmentalists, spent months protesting the pipeline's construction, many living in makeshift camps near the proposed construction site. (credit: "Rally against the Dakota Access Pipeline" by Fibonacci Blue/flickr, CC BY 2.0)

As the examples above illustrate, most social movements combine protests against specific conditions with more general agendas involving justice, equality, democracy, and political economy. When the power of money overwhelms the formal political institutions of a democratic society, social movements provide an alternative means of political expression and potential influence.

MINI-FIELDWORK ACTIVITY

Courtroom Observation

Visit your local county courthouse to observe the legal process in action. Sketch a map of the courtroom, indicating various areas of activity. Note how the structure of the room shapes and guides the activities. What categories of persons (roles) are assigned/confined to certain areas? How does the organization of the room indicate the relationships of these categories of people to one another? What are the main roles in the court proceedings? What bodily postures and behaviors are associated with each role? What forms of voice? How is authority enacted? How do other participants respond to these forms of authority? Pay close attention to the proceedings. How might your knowledge of linguistic anthropology inform your understanding of the pronouncements and conversational exchanges in this setting? Do you see notions of race and ethnicity played out in the courtroom?

Key Terms

acephalous societies communities with no formal positions of leadership.

age sets gendered groups of people of roughly the same age who play a distinctive role in society with important social obligations and abilities. Age-grade systems tend to be associated with acephalous societies.

Arab Spring a series of protests that spread throughout the Arab world in the early 2010s, demanding an end to oppressive government and poor living conditions.

asafo in Akan societies, the group of young men charged with protecting the town, performing public works, and representing public opinion. *Asafo* could depose corrupt and unpopular chiefs.

authority the exercise of power based on expertise, charisma, or roles of leadership.

band societies communities of gatherer-hunters in which leadership is temporary, situational, and informal.

big man an informal leader who has gained power by accumulating wealth, sponsoring feasts, and helping young men pay bride wealth.

centralized societies communities in which power is concentrated in formal positions of authority, such as chiefs or kings.

chief the inherited office of leadership in a chiefdom, combining coercive forms of economic, political, judicial, military, and religious authority.

chiefdoms societies in which political leadership is regionally organized through an affiliation or hierarchy of chiefs. Chiefdoms are associated with intensive agriculture, militarism, and religious ideologies.

chinampas agricultural plots created from layers of mud and vegetation in the shallow part of a lake.

clans large kin groups that trace their descent from a common ancestor who is either not remembered or possibly mythological.

coercive power the ability to enforce judgments and commands using socially sanctioned violence.

colonial states state governments imposed by foreigners to rule over local peoples.

failed state a state that cannot perform any of the essential functions of a state.

fragile state a state government that cannot adequately perform the essential functions of a state, such as maintaining law and order, building basic infrastructure, guaranteeing basic amenities, and defending its citizens against violence.

hegemony a powerful ideology that has become generally accepted by most groups in society as common sense. Hegemony emphasizes the norms and values that support the existing social order.

ideology an organized set of ideas associated with a particular group or class in society. Ideologies are used to explain how various realms of nature and society work, including such realms as economics, politics, religion, kinship, gender, and sexuality.

imagined communities citizens of a nation-state joined together by rituals and practices that give them a collective, imagined sense of community.

king hereditary ruler of a multiethnic empire based on a chiefdom.

leopard-skin chief an informal mediator in Nuer society who negotiated settlement in the case of homicide.

lineage orders societies in which extended family groups provide the primary means of social integration. Leadership in these societies is provided by elders and other temporary or situational figures.

nation a sense of cultural belonging or peoplehood based on a common language, common origin story, common destiny, and common norms and values. National identities are actively constructed by states.

nation-state a political institution joining the apparatus of the state with the notion of cultural belonging or peoplehood.

parrhesia courageous public speech inspired by a moral desire to reveal the truth and demand social change.

persuasive power the ability to influence others without any formal means of enforcement.

political economy study of the ways in which political and economic realms continually reinforce and sometimes contradict one another over time.

politics all elements of the sociocultural dynamics of power

postcolonial studies an interdisciplinary field that combines history, anthropology, political science, and area studies in an effort to understand the diversity, complexity, and legacy of colonialism throughout the world.

power the ability to influence people and/or shape social processes and social structures.

proto-states societies that exhibit some but not all of the features of state societies.
reform the call for systemic changes to address social problems.
resistance the expression of disagreement or dissatisfaction with the social order; may be explicit or implicit.
revolution the replacement of one social order with a different one, often to create enhanced justice, equality, stability, or freedom.
segmentary lineage a kind of lineage order in which family units called minimal lineages are encompassed by larger groups called maximal lineages, which are subsumed by even larger groups called clans.
social movement an organized set of actions by a group outside of government aiming at achieving social change.
social stratification the division of society into groups that are ranked according to wealth, power, or prestige.
state societies large, stratified, multiethnic societies with highly centralized leadership, bureaucracies, systems of social control, and military forces exerting exclusive control over a defined territory.
tribal societies an older term used by anthropologists to refer to pastoralist and horticulturalist societies in which extended family structures provide the primary means of social integration.
tribe an old-fashioned term used to describe ethnic groups or groups organized by lineage. Avoided by many anthropologists now because of connotations of primitivism and groupthink.
village democracies acephalous societies in which an array of social groups provide arenas for discussion and consensus.

Summary

All societies have ways of exercising authority, making decisions, and settling disputes. In the 1940s, anthropologists distinguished between those societies with informal means of accomplishing these functions and those with formal roles and systems for doing so. In acephalous societies such as bands and lineage orders, leadership is situational and temporary, and people make decisions using discussion and consensus. Leaders in such societies have persuasive power but no formal means of enforcing their will. In centralized societies such as chiefdoms and states, various forms of power are condensed in the formal hereditary role of the leader. As military leaders, chiefs and kings have coercive power to collect taxes and tribute, enforce their commands, settle conflicts, and wage war to enlarge their territories. As societies become more centralized, they also become more stratified, with social groups ranked according to wealth and power. With social stratification and centralized rule, systems of ideology and hegemony develop to support the social order. Modern nation-states combine the state apparatus with a strategically cultivated sense of peoplehood based on common culture. European colonialism imposed an authoritarian state form to rule over local forms of political organization such as chiefdoms and lineage orders, often malforming those original political forms. The structural and social problems of many postcolonial states are rooted in the destructive processes of colonialism. Outside of the formal realm of government, people seek to influence social and political conditions through social movements. Some social movements provide a means of expressing dissatisfaction, while others press for specific forms of social change or complete reorganization of the political order.

Critical Thinking Questions

1. Of Weber's three forms of authority, which ones can you identify in your own society? How do these forms of authority interact?
2. What are the limitations of informal leadership in acephalous societies? Are there some forms of community action that might be impossible or time-consuming? What kinds of activity become possible with formal positions of leadership?
3. In your own culture, are there age-related groups that provide structure and organization to society? How do these groups promote social norms and values?
4. What are the advantages and disadvantages of living in a state society? Which groups benefit most? Which groups benefit least? What can those groups do to improve their situation?
5. In what ways is your own nation-state an "imagined community"? What rituals and institutions construct this community? What is the common "origin story," and how is it told in

ritual and monuments?

6. If many postcolonial states are fragile due to the damaging effects of colonialism, what might be done to repair the damage and enhance their functionality?
7. What social movements can you identify in your own society? Have you participated in any of them? If so, describe your experiences. What thoughts and feelings are associated with participation in social movements?
8. How do social movements achieve social change? What methods do they use? Which ones seem to be most effective?

Bibliography

Anderson, Benedict. 1983. *Imagined Communities: Reflections on the Origin and Spread of Nationalism*. London: Verso.

Appadurai, Arjun. 1996. *Modernity at Large: Cultural Dimensions of Globalization*. Minneapolis: University of Minnesota Press.

Appadurai, Arjun. 2006. *Fear of Small Numbers: An Essay on the Geography of Anger*. Durham, NC: Duke University Press.

Blakemore, Erin. 2019. "What Was the Arab Spring and How Did It Spread?" *National Geographic*, March 29, 2019. https://www.nationalgeographic.com/culture/article/arab-spring-cause.

Brumfiel, E. M. 2001. "States and Civilizations, Archaeology Of." In *International Encyclopedia of the Social and Behavioral Sciences*, edited by James D. Wright, 2nd ed., 371–375. https://dx.doi.org/10.1016/B978-0-08-097086-8.13012-0.

Davidson, Basil. 1992. *The Black Man's Burden: Africa and the Curse of the Nation-State*. New York: Times Books.

Eagleton, Terry. 1991. *Ideology: An Introduction*. London: Verso.

Earle, Timothy. 2011. "Chiefs, Chieftaincies, Chiefdoms, and Chiefly Confederacies: Power in the Evolution of Political Systems." *Social Evolution & History* 10 (1): 27–54.

Evans-Pritchard, E. E. 1940. *The Nuer: A Description of the Modes of Livelihood and Political Institutions of a Nilotic People*. Oxford: Clarendon Press.

Flowers, Nancy M. 1994. "Shavante." In *South America*, edited by Johannes Wilbert, 300–302. Vol. 7 of *Encyclopedia of World Cultures*, edited by David Levinson. New York: G. K. Hall.

Fortes, Meyer, and E. E. Evans-Pritchard, eds. 1940. *African Political Systems*. London: Oxford University Press.

Foucault, Michel. 1978. *The History of Sexuality*. Vol. 1, *An Introduction*, translated by Robert Hurley. New York: Pantheon Books.

Foucault, Michel. 2001. *Fearless Speech*. Edited by Joseph Pearson. Los Angeles: Semiotext(e).

Foucault, Michel. 2007. *Security, Territory, Population: Lectures at the Collège de France, 1977–78*. Edited by Michel Senellart. Translated by Graham Burchell. New York: Palgrave Macmillan.

Gilens, Martin. 2012. *Affluence and Influence: Economic Inequality and Political Power in America*. Princeton, NJ: Princeton University Press.

Heim, Joe. 2016. "Showdown over Oil Pipeline Becomes a National Movement for Native Americans." *Washington Post*, September 7, 2016. https://www.washingtonpost.com/national/showdown-over-oil-pipeline-becomes-a-national-movement-for-native-americans/2016/09/06/ea0cb042-7167-11e6-8533-6b0b0ded0253_story.html.

Isichei, Elizabeth, comp. 1978. *Igbo Worlds: An Anthology of Oral Histories and Historical Descriptions*. Philadelphia: Institute for the Study of Human Issues.

Junker, Laura L. 2015. "Chiefdoms, Archaeology Of." In *International Encyclopedia of the Social and Behavioral*

Sciences, edited by James D. Wright, 2nd ed., 376–382. https://dx.doi.org/10.1016/B978-0-08-097086-8.13025-9.

"Laura Nader." 2001. *Gale Literature: Contemporary Authors*, Gale Literature Resource Center. Updated April 23, 2001. https://link.gale.com/apps/doc/H1000071872/LitRC?u=mlin_oweb&sid=bookmark-LitRC&xid=784e09d7.

Li, Fabiana. 2015. *Unearthing Conflict: Corporate Mining, Activism, and Expertise in Peru*. Durham, NC: Duke University Press.

Marlowe, Frank W. 2010. *The Hadza: Hunter-Gatherers of Tanzania*. Berkeley: University of California Press.

Maybury-Lewis, David. 1967. *Akwe-Shavante Society*. Oxford: Clarendon Press.

Monroe, J. Cameron. 2013. "Power and Agency in Precolonial African States." *Annual Review of Anthropology* 42:17–35.

Nader, Laura. 1990. *Harmony Ideology: Justice and Control in a Zapotec Mountain Village*. Stanford, CA: Stanford University Press.

Nkrumah, Gamal. 2005. "Laura Nader: Speaking Out." *Al-Ahram Weekly On-line*, January 20–26, 2005. https://web.archive.org/web/20071011182529/http://weekly.ahram.org.eg/2005/726/profile.htm.

Owusu, Maxwell. 1989. "Rebellion, Revolution, and Tradition: Reinterpreting Coups in Ghana." *Comparative Studies in Society and History* 31 (2): 372–397.

Peters-Golden, Holly. 2002. *Culture Sketches: Case Studies in Anthropology*. 3rd ed. Boston: McGraw-Hill.

Pospisil, Leopold. (1963) 1972. *Kapauku Papuan Economy*. New Haven, CT: Human Relations Area Files Press.

Richards, Audrey, and Adam Kuper, eds. 1971. *Councils in Action*. Cambridge Papers in Social Anthropology 6. Cambridge: Cambridge University Press.

Service, Elman. 1962. *Primitive Social Organization: An Evolutionary Perspective*. New York: Random House.

Weber, Max. 1946. "Politics as a Vocation." In *From Max Weber: Essays in Sociology*, edited and translated by H. H. Gerth and C. Wright Mills, 77–128. New York: Oxford University Press.

CHAPTER 9
Social Inequalities

Figure 9.1 These images illustrate some examples of national and international movements against social inequalities. There have been movements in response to inequalities of race, class, and gender, among other characteristics. This chapter will discuss important concepts for the critical examination of inequalities. (credit: top left, "Million Women Rise 2019 - 04" by Garry Knight/flickr, Public Domain; top right, "March4Women 2018 - 08" by Garry Knight/flickr, Public Domain; bottom left, "Los Angeles March for Immigrant Rights" by Molly Adams/flickr, CC BY 2.0; bottom right, "Black Lives Matter Protest in South Minneapolis" by Fibonacci Blue/flickr, CC BY 2.0)

CHAPTER OUTLINE

INTRODUCTION As a student, have you ever experienced social inequalities, whether based around your race, gender, sexuality, class, or abilities? In this chapter you'll see definitions and examples of the ways social inequalities affect individuals and societies. Over the history of anthropology, the ways we identify and define social inequalities has constantly evolved. The ways social inequalities are experienced has also evolved. This chapter will provide an overview of the important concepts and levels of social inequalities, and then an examination of the experiences of individuals within groups and societies. From this, you can develop a framework for understanding the inequality in your own communities.

9.1 Theories of Inequity and Inequality

LEARNING OUTCOMES

By the end of this section, you will be able to:

- Differentiate between systematic and systemic inequities.
- Discuss theories of social inequality and anthropology's past of upholding social inequalities.
- Describe the connections between power, agency, and resistance.

Social Stratification

Division of labor, in and of itself, is not hierarchical, but when different values are assigned to different types of labor and some positions or people have power over others, this creates a hierarchy. A **hierarchy** is a type of social organization in which certain people or roles are given more power and prestige than others. As discussed in Economic Anthropology, there are various possible divisions of labor depending on a group's mode of production. Many gatherer-hunter groups experience a social structure described as **egalitarian**, in which the diverse roles in a system of production are all given the same decision-making power and accorded the same respect among the group. In such societies, power is usually afforded by age grades, with the elders holding the most power.

Conversely, when there are differences in status or power between various roles, social stratification results. **Social stratification** is the hierarchical organization of different groups of people, whether based on racial category, socioeconomic status, kinship, religion, birth order, or gender. In horticultural societies, this stratification can be linked to charismatic leaders or leaders whose power is culturally imbued at birth. State societies, and specifically market economies, are considered the most stratified, meaning they have the highest resource inequities. Whether in the Inca Empire of the 1300s or the contemporary United States, a complex system of social hierarchy and social inequality accompanies state-level societies.

Levels of Inequality

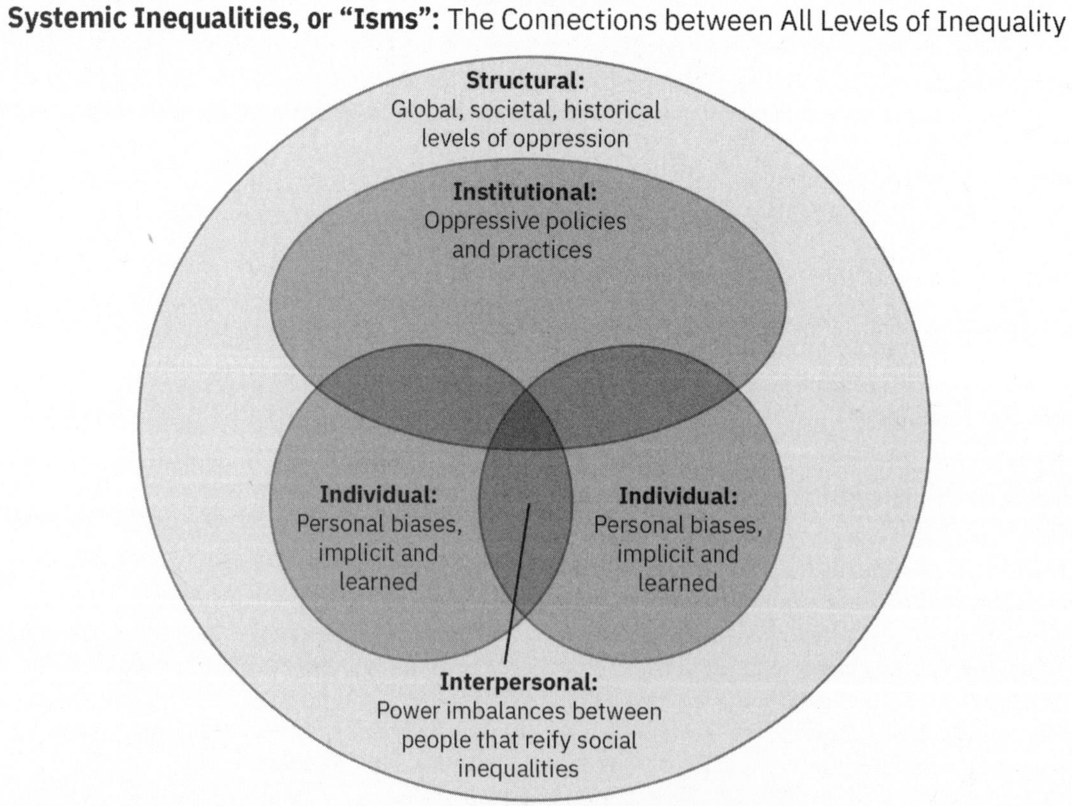

FIGURE 9.2 This graphic depicts various levels of social inequalities. Social inequalities are often seen as separate phenomena, but they are frequently interconnected, existing in many different interactions between people and

institutions. (attribution: Copyright Rice University, OpenStax, under CC BY 4.0 license)

Although it is important to understand the ways in which societies control resource accumulation, it is also important to study the phenomena and experiences of inequality in one's own culture. This section will examine how individuals experience different levels of social inequalities. In contemporary societies, experiences of social inequalities often have roots in systems of capitalism, colonialism, racism, and sexism, which all include a perceived superiority of one group over another.

Interpersonal inequalities, which are power imbalances that are rooted in personal biases, occur every day, reifying and naturalizing inequalities that exist at institutional and systemic levels. **Institutional inequalities** stem from the policies and practices of organizations (educational institutions, government, companies) that perpetuate oppression. Institutional inequalities exist outside of the day-to-day interactions that people experience, are often unseen, and feel like the status quo. **Structural inequalities** exist at a level above personal interactions and institutions because they are based on the accumulated effects of institutional decisions across society and history. This type of inequality is pervasive, global, and especially difficult to disrupt. Structural inequalities can reaffirm individual biases, creating a self-reinforcing cycle. Finally, **systemic inequalities** are the confluence of interpersonal, institutional, and structural inequalities; these are often portrayed by "isms" such as racism, classism, and sexism.

Inequality refers to the unequal distribution of resources. Most people learn about inequality at a young age when they are exposed to people from different socioeconomic classes in places such as schools, places of worship, or social organizations. They recognize that some people have more resources at their disposal, whether through inborn talents or social connections. Such people may wear more expensive clothing, drive more expensive cars, and even have more opportunities than others. Social inequalities are based on individual people's backgrounds and how their opportunities in life have been affected by racism, sexism, classism, and other forms of **oppression**. In this context, oppression is defined as unjust exercises of power that may be overt or covert and are often used to control or inflict harm on entire groups of people. **Inequity**, on the other hand, refers to the unequal distribution of resources due to an unjust power imbalance. It is a type of inequality caused by this unequal distribution, often as a result of injustices against historically excluded groups of people. In the United States, inequity is seen today in areas such as the banking industry, access to voting, and the housing market, where minority groups continue to face challenges related to fairness and equitable distribution of resources. Social inequalities lead to inequity when the groups in charge of distribution allocate resources in ways that further oppress marginalized groups.

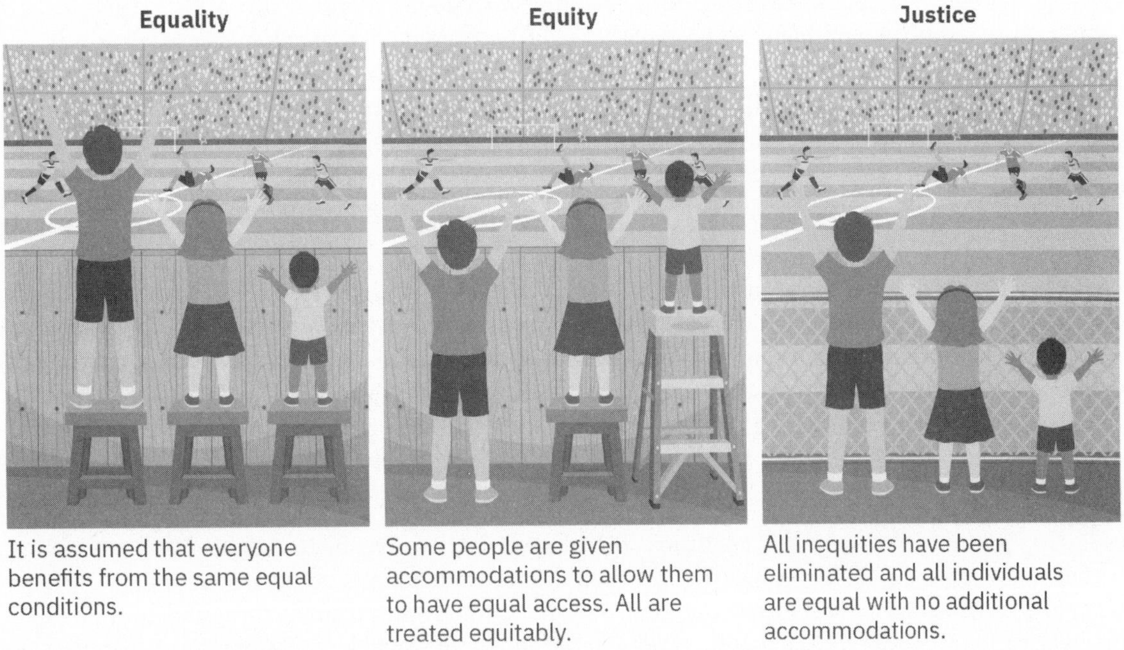

Equality
Equity
Justice
It is assumed that everyone benefits from the same equal conditions.
Some people are given accommodations to allow them to have equal access. All are treated equitably.
All inequities have been eliminated and all individuals are equal with no additional accommodations.

FIGURE 9.3 This visual representation shows the difference between equality, or providing the same resources to

everyone even when needs differ, and equity, or providing resources according to people's needs. In a truly just society (the third panel), all individuals can be treated equally with no additional accommodations. (attribution: Copyright Rice University, OpenStax, under CC BY 4.0 license)

You may have seen images on social media trying to explain the difference between inequality and inequity—or, on the flip side, equality and equity. One problem with such images, as Sarah Willen, Colleen Walsh, and Abigail Fisher Williamson (2021) point out, is that because they depict individuals, audiences may interpret these images as calling for localized or individual solutions rather than systemic changes. Oppression and inequity most often are not interpersonal but exist on a structural level of economics, politics, and socialization that normalizes their presence.

In order to understand the differences between inequality and inequity, systematic oppression and systemic oppression, it is important to know that the word *system* has two different definitions. A system can refer to a formula for methodically attaining a goal, such as a system someone creates to study vocabulary before a foreign language exam. The term **systematic oppression** derives from this meaning; it is the intentional mistreatment of certain groups. On the other hand, the term *system* can also mean a combination of parts to form a complex whole, such as the organs in an organism. This definition is the root of the term **systemic oppression**, which describes how political, economic, and social inequalities are normalized and perpetuated. Many scholars have determined that systemic oppression is permanently ingrained in US laws, government, and society, with the result that it is both unseen and subconsciously upheld daily.

When discussing inequality and inequity, it is also important to understand **power**, which, in its simplest sense, is the ability to exert control, authority, or influence over others. Individuals with more power have more **agency**, or capability to act and make decisions. Agency should not be confused with free will because an individual's agency is often heavily shaped by social characteristics such as race, gender, and class. Along with social inequalities, this chapter will discuss power, agency, and how the two are conceptualized by anthropologists through various perspectives and theoretical frameworks.

Classic Theories of Social Inequality

The remainder of this chapter will examine social inequalities in detail. It will cover racism, classism, and sexism along with some common paradigms and theoretical frameworks that explain systems of inequality and power.

According to philosopher Thomas Kuhn, **paradigms** are worldviews that often define a scientific discipline during a specific time period. In *The Structure of Scientific Revolutions* (1962), Kuhn argues that paradigms can shift when a dominant paradigm cannot explain newly discovered phenomena under which normal science operates. Each of the theories that follow was based on a paradigm shift in the social sciences of its time period. The frameworks that anthropologists use to understand power imbalances have been built on the critiques of many of the initial anthropological explanations for power imbalances and social inequalities.

Social Darwinism and Unilinear Cultural Evolution

Social Darwinism played an important role in the colonialist attitudes of the 19th and 20th centuries. Charles Darwin's theory of evolution, discussed in detail in Biological Evolution and Early Human Evidence, speaks of how traits beneficial to the procreation of a species are passed down, creating changes over time that lead to the evolution of species on Earth. In his *Principles of Biology* (1864–1867), social scientist Herbert Spencer applies the principles of evolution to human societies, combining his concept of the "survival of the fittest" with French naturalist Jean-Baptiste Lamarck's views that acquired characteristics can be passed down. Spencer argues that characteristics such as a tendency to work hard and achieve success are passed down from generation to generation, as are traits such as weaknesses and laziness, thus attributing ongoing social inequalities to biological differences.

Social Darwinists of the 19th and 20th centuries utilized Spencer's survival theory (under Darwin's name) to argue that competition for resources meant that "weak" human individuals should die out so that "stronger" traits could be passed down to the next generation. Social Darwinists claimed that any group that conquered another was better fit to survive and that those who were conquered would benefit from the civilizing influence of more powerful nations.

Although popular among certain social scientists, *social Darwinism* was not a term often used in anthropology. Anthropologists instead turned to the theory of unilinear cultural evolution (UCE), made famous by anthropologists E. B. Tylor and Lewis H. Morgan in the 19th century. UCE, which was based on comparing and contrasting different cultures, theorized that societies progressed in a linear fashion, from the lowest level of savagery through barbarism to civilization. Social Darwinism and UCE upheld social inequalities because these theories argued that the defining features of civilization were social hierarchy and inequality. They were the basis for White Europeans' claims that their culture held more power, had more value, and allowed them to exert military power over lands that were not their own.

Functionalism

Functionalism is a theory attributed to French sociologist Emile Durkheim in the early 20th century. In anthropology, the best-known of the functionalists are Bronislaw Malinowski and A. R. Radcliffe Brown, who examined the purpose that certain cultural characteristics serve in the order of society. For functionalists, egalitarian societies have certain rituals or beliefs that maintain equality, while in stratified societies, the hierarchy of roles maintains order when conflict arises. The function of social stratification, then, is to give power to those who are most equipped to lead, or to motivate those with talents to achieve positions of power and create wealth for the larger society. A functionalist view understands social inequalities as a reflection of people's varying levels of benefit to the group.

Later theorists criticized functionalism for its use of research that was **ahistorical**, meaning that it did not acknowledge the specific historical experiences of a group and thus attempted to understand societies without taking into consideration their connections to other cultures. For instance, functionalists largely ignored the impacts of colonialism on small, seemingly isolated populations, arguing instead that social stratification—and, consequently, global political inequalities—was an unyielding and inevitable part of the process of becoming a "complex society."

Conflict Theory

Conflict theory, created by the late 19th-century political philosopher Karl Marx, offers a more pessimistic view. Marx argued that hierarchy is not a means of keeping society balanced but rather the main source of conflict among humans. He and Friedrich Engels originally conceptualized two classes of capitalism in terms of ownership. The **bourgeoisie**, descended from powerful families, were the owners of the means of production, while the **proletariat** were those who sold their labor and lived off a wage. The powerless majority, the proletariat, were far removed from the decision makers and power holders, who had separated the proletariat from their own skills through industrialization and mechanization. In this view, the conflict between those with wealth and the means of production and those without is the basis of all social conflict.

As more social scientists grappled with differences in class and wage, they began to critique conflict theory more. W. E. B. Du Bois ([1940] 1984), an American sociologist working in the early 20th century, added wage and race theories to the classic examination of class conflict. He questioned whether there was a relationship between one's knowledge in a trade and one's wages and subsequently concluded that the worth of labor was determined solely by capitalists (the bourgeoisie). Du Bois further observed that class distinctions were forming among Black groups in Philadelphia, mostly unnoticed by White people, who continued to generalize them as one monolithic group. His critique was that conflict theory did not take race into account as both an area wherein class differences occur and another area that can cause conflict (and detract from issues of class and wage). Du Bois's pioneering ethnographic studies at the turn of the 20th century were among the earliest scientific research on Black Americans' lived experience of race and racism in the United States. His influence on and relationship with anthropologist Franz Boas were significant factors in Boas's own disavowal of race as a determinant of the value and worth of diverse cultures. Du Bois's work remains relevant in the present day as anthropology continues to address its own historical roots in colonialism.

FIGURE 9.4 W. E. B. Du Bois's pioneering ethnographic research was among the earliest scientific studies of race and racism in the United States. (credit: "W. E. B. (William Edward Burghardt) Du Bois, 1868–1963" by Cornelius Marion Battey/Library of Congress, Prints & Photographs Division, Public Domain)

Critical Race Theory

Critical race theory (CRT), developed by legal scholars in the 1980s, asserts that much of the inequity experienced by oppressed people in the United States can be understood through the critical lens of race. CRT states that racism is endemic, or regularly found in the laws, policies, and institutions of the United States. Thus, people who are socialized in American institutions often do not see the ways in which racism plays out in their daily lives. Notions of color blindness and meritocracy uphold the idea that racism either does not exist or is actually related to class, socioeconomics, or other factors. **Color blindness** is the idea that people "don't see color," meaning that they are unaware of the ways in which someone may experience the world because of the color of their skin. A **meritocracy** is a system in which people succeed entirely through their own hard work; thus, someone who believes in the notion of meritocracy overlooks any structural or racial inequities that may keep individuals from accessing the resources necessary for success (Delgado and Stefancic 2013). In the United States, these two concepts are often used together to blame poor (especially poor Black) individuals and families for their own misfortunes instead of looking to structural causes of poverty and income inequality. The term *welfare queen* is often used by politicians and the media to refer to a specific (Black or minority) demographic, even though statistically, White women are the most common recipients of government benefits. One way to challenge everyday endemic racism is to utilize counter-storytelling. These stories counteract the socialized assumptions that keep people of color marginalized. For instance, counter-stories are important in challenging the power of stereotypes such as the "welfare queen."

Critical race theory has become a hotly debated topic among politicians in the United States. CRT is often misunderstood by critics, who see it as a one-sided examination of (particularly American) history and society because CRT examines society through the lens of power and oppression. It often focuses on which groups benefit from cultural changes, including such things as civil rights legislation, essential to a democracy's guarantee of equal opportunity and protection under the law. In anthropology, CRT is an important tool for examining both modern institutions and the experiences of individuals in the United States, especially in regard to social inequalities. As just one example, CRT can shed light on the decisions made by those in power when redrawing the boundaries of voting districts. These decisions are often made with the goal of cementing a majority for a particular political party while diluting the voting power of citizens who don't typically belong that party, a practice known as gerrymandering. It is important for social scientists to consider the potential role of race and racism in making these decisions. If race and/or racism were found to be a factor, then these political decisions would be considered an example of systemic oppression.

Power

More contemporary frameworks of social inequalities include an understanding of power. This section dives into the concepts and frameworks used in studying power. To recap, **power** is the ability to exert control, authority, or influence over others; **agency**, which comes from power, is the capability to act and make decisions. Power can be conceptualized as both subtle and coercive; in some contexts, it's obvious who has power and how it's utilized, but in other contexts, there are power imbalances that are allowed in everyday life. The point of this section is to contemplate why people allow certain power imbalances to exist while challenging others. Often, people allow power imbalances that they benefit from and resist imbalances that they do not benefit from. To better understand this, it is useful to discuss various concepts related to power, including hegemony, the state apparatus, biopolitics, and necropolitics.

Hegemony

Antonio Gramsci, famous for his writings on philosophy, political theory, sociology, linguistics, and history, came up with the concept of hegemony while imprisoned by the Fascist Italian government. A founding member of the Communist Party of Italy, he was arrested by Benito Mussolini's Fascist regime for provoking class hatred and civil war and was sentenced to 20 years of imprisonment. In *The Prison Notebooks*, composed of 33 notebooks written during his imprisonment, Gramsci writes about power using the notion of hegemony. **Hegemony** describes how people with power keep their power through the subtle dissemination of certain values and beliefs. Hegemony relies on the maintenance of a "groups'' authority and various mechanisms through which those in marginalized groups accept the leadership of another group's authority. These mechanisms include cultural institutions such as education, religion, family, and common practices of everyday life. When a paradigm is so dominant that no one questions it, it becomes hegemonic. For instance, the idea that the United States is a democracy, even though many Americans are disenfranchised from voting and several presidential candidates have won the popular vote but lost the election, could be considered a hegemonic paradigm.

The State Apparatus

French Marxist philosopher Louis Pierre Althusser is known for his writings about ideologies of exploitation. Asking how those who are exploited continue to remain exploited, Althusser developed the concept of the **state apparatus**. The state apparatus consists of two intertwined but distinct sets of institutions, the repressive state apparatus and the ideological state apparatus, which function together to maintain state order and control. **Repressive state apparatuses** include institutions through which the ruling class enforces its control, such as the government, administrators, the army, the police, the courts, and prisons. These institutions are repressive because they function by violence or force. Althusser argues that the state also consists of **ideological state apparatuses**, which include distinct and specialized institutions such as religious institutions, public and private education systems, legal systems, political parties, communication systems (radio, newspapers, television), family, and culture (literature, arts, and sports). Ideological state apparatuses, although they include different institutions that are dominated by ruling class ideologies, are also sites where the ideologies of exploited classes can grow. Therefore, ideological state apparatuses can be places of class struggle and social change.

Biopolitics

French philosopher Michel Foucault conceptualized power through **biopolitics**, which refers to the ways populations are divided and categorized as a means of control, often by the state. This categorization and division—in terms of race, religion, or citizenship status, for instance—seeks to further marginalize certain groups and increase the power of the state. Biopolitics can be understood as the use of power to control a population through surveillance, which Foucault refers to as *biopower* in his book *The History of Sexuality* ([1978] 1990). An example of biopower in action is government control of immigrants, especially undocumented migrants. In his ethnography *Pathogenic Policing: Immigration Enforcement and Health in the*

US South (2019), me dical and legal anthropologist Nolan Kline describes immigrant policing as a form of biopower that attempts to control and govern immigrants through tactics based on fear, making undocumented immigrants fearful as they go about the normal activities of their daily lives, with many afraid to even seek health services when necessary.

Necropolitics

Cameroonian philosopher and political theorist Joseph-Achille Mbembe, known as Achille Mbembe, writes about power through the idea of necropolitics (the power of death). **Necropolitics**, an extension of Foucault's biopolitics, explores the government's power to decide how certain categories of people live and whose deaths are more acceptable. Mbembe describes this as a power to decide "who matters and who does not, who is disposable and who is not" (2003, 27). The p ower to determine a life's worth resides within both political systems and the decisions that policy makers are tasked with. It has, quite literally, life-or-death consequences, from who has access to life-saving medical technology to who is most policed and most likely to end up in jail.

The Black Lives Matter social justice movement is a response to an understanding that modern necropolitics in the United States treats Black people as disposable. The Black Lives Matter movement has grown beyond the United States in response to other nations' state policies that are seen as treating people of color as not worthy of protection or care.

Agency

Agency, or the ability to act and make decisions, has become an important concept in anthropology because it helps make sense of how powerful institutions interact with individuals.

With the theory of agency and structuration, British sociologist Anthony Giddens paved the way for the growth of theories on how humans interact with systems. **Systems** are the powerful, overarching beliefs through which the world is organized, which influence the ways in which individuals interact with their world. Although they most often go unnoticed and unquestioned, systems influence the decisions humans make. In terms of social inequality, in systems with unequal access to resources, the ability to decide or the options that one can choose between differ depending on diverse variables. The more power people have, the more choices they may be presented with, and the more they can mold and shape the systems in which they live through their decisions.

French sociologist Pierre Bourdieu attempted to explain how societal structures are upheld *and* changed by processes generated by individuals. The idea of **habitus**, or the ingrained habits and dispositions that are socialized into people from birth depending on their status in society, is used to explain how individuals uphold cultural systems such as capitalism, class, racism, or patriarchal values. Habitus is understood both to imbue people with certain skill sets and perspectives according to their life experiences and to make possible social change because it understands systems as generative instead of static. For instance, the modern capitalist system has not always existed as know it is today. Many smaller decisions, practices, and consequences have formed and reformed capitalism, reflecting diverse interests over time.

Resistance

In their attempts to better understand power and agency, Marxist and feminist anthropologists in the 1980s and 1990s wrote a number of ethnographies about the relationship between resistance and the systems that create social inequalities and oppression. **Resistance**, at the basic level, refers to the act of challenging power and domination. Power is nearly always resisted in both overt and subtle ways, but the difference is often reflected in how much agency individuals have in resisting systems of domination and oppression. This section uses the example of Palestine to explore ways in which Palestinians are resisting power.

The creation of the state of Israel in 1948 dispossessed the Palestinians who were indigenous to the land. Between 400 and 600 Palestinian villages were destroyed, and between 700,000 and 750,000 Palestinians were exiled from the portion of Palestine that became Israel.

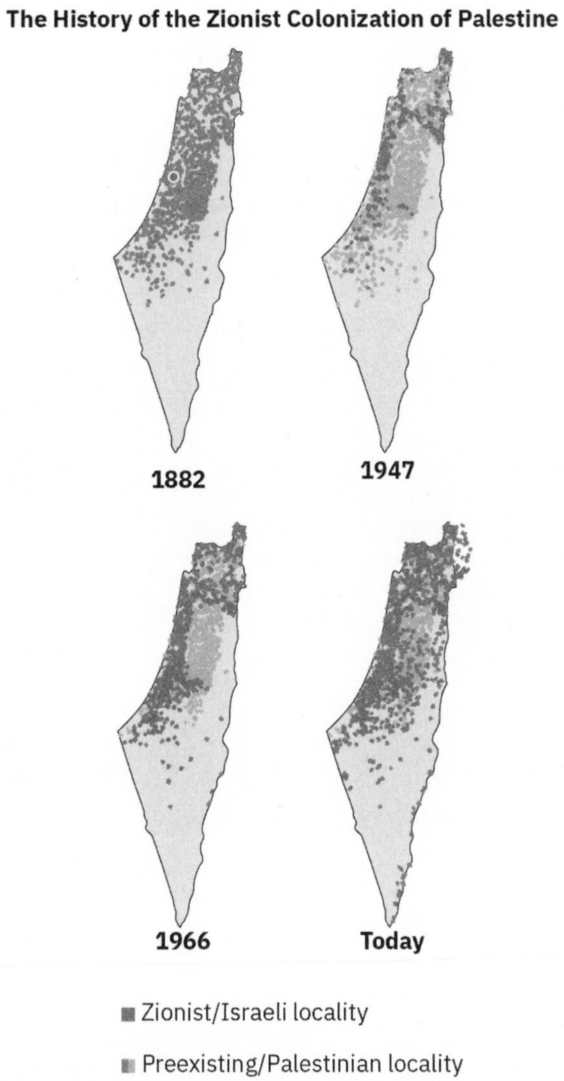

FIGURE 9.5 Zionist colonization and the erasure of Palestinian land and people (attribution: Copyright Rice University, OpenStax, under CC BY 4.0 license)

While Israelis celebrate achieving independence in 1948, Palestinians refer to this period of displacement of hundreds of thousands from their homes as the **Nakba**, which translates from Arabic as "disaster" or "catastrophe." The Nakba is ongoing in the Occupied Palestinian Territory (OPT), which includes the West Bank, East Jerusalem, and Gaza, where the occupation by Israel is illegal according to international laws. The Nakba is also ongoing for members of the Palestinian **diaspora** (the dispersion of a people from their original home) around the world who do not have the right to return.

Palestinians living in the West Bank and East Jerusalem live under a system of checkpoints, military occupation, and segregation from Jewish settlers. Palestinians in Gaza are living in an open-air prison with extremely limited access to clean water, inconsistent electricity, and no freedom of movement (Erakat and Azzeh 2016). Despite this level of oppression, Palestinians in different parts of the OPT and the Palestinian diaspora still have agency, and they use this agency in different ways to resist Israeli oppression and the devaluation of the Palestinian experience. While political and social movements are critically important for combating injustice and oppression, there are also Palestinians and Israelis working together to create cultural bridges between the communities. One example of this is the West-Eastern Divan Orchestra.

Founded in 1999 by pianist and conductor Daniel Barenboim, who was born in Argentina and moved to Israel as a child, and Palestinian scholar and activist Edward Said, the West-Eastern Divan Orchestra (https://openstax.org/r/west-eastern-divan) is a group of Israeli, Arab, and Palestinian musicians who work to promote equality and understanding across sociopolitical divides. The orchestra travels and performs internationally as an "orchestra against ignorance," founded on the idea that when musicians come together to create music, they must work in harmony and respect each other. Not only intended to forge strong bonds among the musicians, the orchestra also serves to highlight the importance of respecting cultural differences and of recognizing a common humanity within the Middle East as a whole. Barenboim states emphatically (https://openstax.org/r/classical-musicandopera) that the orchestra's purpose is not to make peace but to create the *conditions* for peace. Ethnocentrism underlies oppression, and model initiatives such as the West-Eastern Divan Orchestra serve as reminders of the importance of tolerance and respect as deterrents against oppression.

FIGURE 9.6 The West-Eastern Divan Orchestra brings together musicians from throughout the Middle East with the goal of promoting understanding across cultural divides. (credit: "Barenboim WEDO Salzburg 2013" by WolfD59/Wikimedia Commons, Public Domain)

9.2 Systems of Inequality

LEARNING OUTCOMES

By the end of this section, you will be able to:

- Explain the meanings of the terms racism, Whiteness, and White supremacy.
- Differentiate between economic, social, and cultural capital in relation to class or social mobility.
- Explain the relationship between capitalism and social inequalities.
- Describe gender relations, patriarchy, and oppression.

Many introductory anthropological texts will examine how types of social stratification align with modes of production. This text has something of a different focus, critically considering what it means for some lives to matter more or less than others. This section looks at how modern modes of production create systems of social inequalities such as racism, classism, and sexism.

Race and Racism

Racism is best understood as power intertwined with racial prejudice. Racism can be perpetuated through interpersonal, institutional, and systemic practices. Anthropologists Alan Goodman, Yolanda Moses, and Joseph Jones define racism in *Race: Are We So Different?* (2020) as the use of race to establish and justify a social hierarchy and system of power that privileges and advances certain individuals or groups of people, usually at the expense of others. Many individuals understand interpersonal examples of racism, but what are institutional or systemic forms of racism? To explore this question, this section will discuss the history of race and its social construction.

What Is Anthropology? discussed the fact that race is a social construct. Where did the social construct of race originate? Johann Blumenbach, a German physician and anthropologist, was influential in establishing existing racial categories. Working in the field of craniometry, a now debunked pseudoscience that studied human head shape and brain size, Blumenbach proposed five racial categories to divide humans in the late 1700s: "Caucasian" for White people, "Mongolian" for Asians, "Malayan" for Brown people, "Ethiopian" for Black people, and "American" for Indigenous people of the Americas (Goodman, Moses, and Jones 2020, 30).

Blumenbach intentionally made these categories hierarchical and put White people at the top of this hierarchy. In many ways, the remnants of this hierarchy still exist today. For instance, have you ever seen the term *Caucasian* on a form asking about race? Why does this term still exist? Many other labels from the classifications Blumenbach created have been challenged, but Caucasian is still used in both scientific and popular usage. Anthropologist Carol Mukhopadhyay (2008) argues that this term's continued usage conveys a false scientific authority of Whiteness.

Black anthropologists, including Williams S. Willis Jr. (1972) and others, have pointed out many racist undertones throughout anthropology's history of studying the "other." Anthropology began as the practice of White anthropologists studying the non-White other, which was rooted in an inherently unequal perspective. The White anthropologists' beliefs were considered the "norm," and people they studied were considered outside of the norm. In contrast, many of the first Black anthropologists trained in the United States were involved in activism, advocacy, public service, and social justice. These Black pioneers in anthropology were committed to fighting racism and instigating social change, focuses that were reflected in their scholarship and how they approached anthropology (Harrison and Harrison 1999). In "Reflections on Anthropology and the Black Experience," St. Clair Drake, discussing why some Black scholars became anthropologists, said, "A few of us chose careers in anthropology forty to forty-five years ago because we believed the discipline had relevance to the liberation of black people from the devastating consequences of over four centuries of white racism" (1978, 86).

In 1941, anthropologists Allison Davis, Burleigh Gardner, and Mary Gardner argued that the United States had a racial caste system. **Caste** is a system of social inequality based on an individual's circumstances of birth, wherein people are not allowed to move out of the social group into which they are born. Davis, Gardner, and Gardner observe that racism is a powerful force in American society that produces inequitable social relations that seem permanent but vary regionally and are subject to change over time. They argue that political, social, and economic structures all maintain that caste system, often in violent and coercive ways (Davis, Gardner, and Gardner 1941).

A number of scholars have also examined White racial identity; these "Whiteness studies" show that the racial category of White has been defined in different ways throughout US history. For instance, certain ethnicities in American history were not originally considered White but became included in the White identity over time. **Whiteness** is usually based on the maintenance or pursuit of power and proximity to power. Historian Nell Irvin Painter's book *The History of White People* (2010) provides a detailed history of European civilization, race, and the frequent worshipping of Whiteness and explains that the concept of one White race is a recent invention.

White privilege is conceptualized as the ways in which White people have been given advantages at the expense of other populations. In Peggy McIntosh's classic article "White Privilege: Unpacking the Invisible Knapsack" (1989), she compares White privilege to an invisible weightless knapsack that comes with special provisions or advantages. According to McIntosh (who identifies as White), these advantages—or even just lack of obstacles—include not having to think about one's race all the time, knowing that one will probably be represented wherever they go, and not worrying about having to speak for all the people of one's racial group, among many other examples. Thus, White privilege is the experience of one's Whiteness as the standard.

White privilege is often linked to the cultural concept of **White supremacy**, which is the idea that White people are a superior race and should dominate society at the expense of other, historically oppressed groups. People often think of White supremacy as extremist behavior, but White supremacy can actually be seen in many examples of systemic social inequalities. Ideologies of the Ku Klux Klan and neo-Nazis are examples of overt White supremacy that many people acknowledge as being racist. However, there are many covert examples of White supremacy that are problematic and racist but are overlooked.

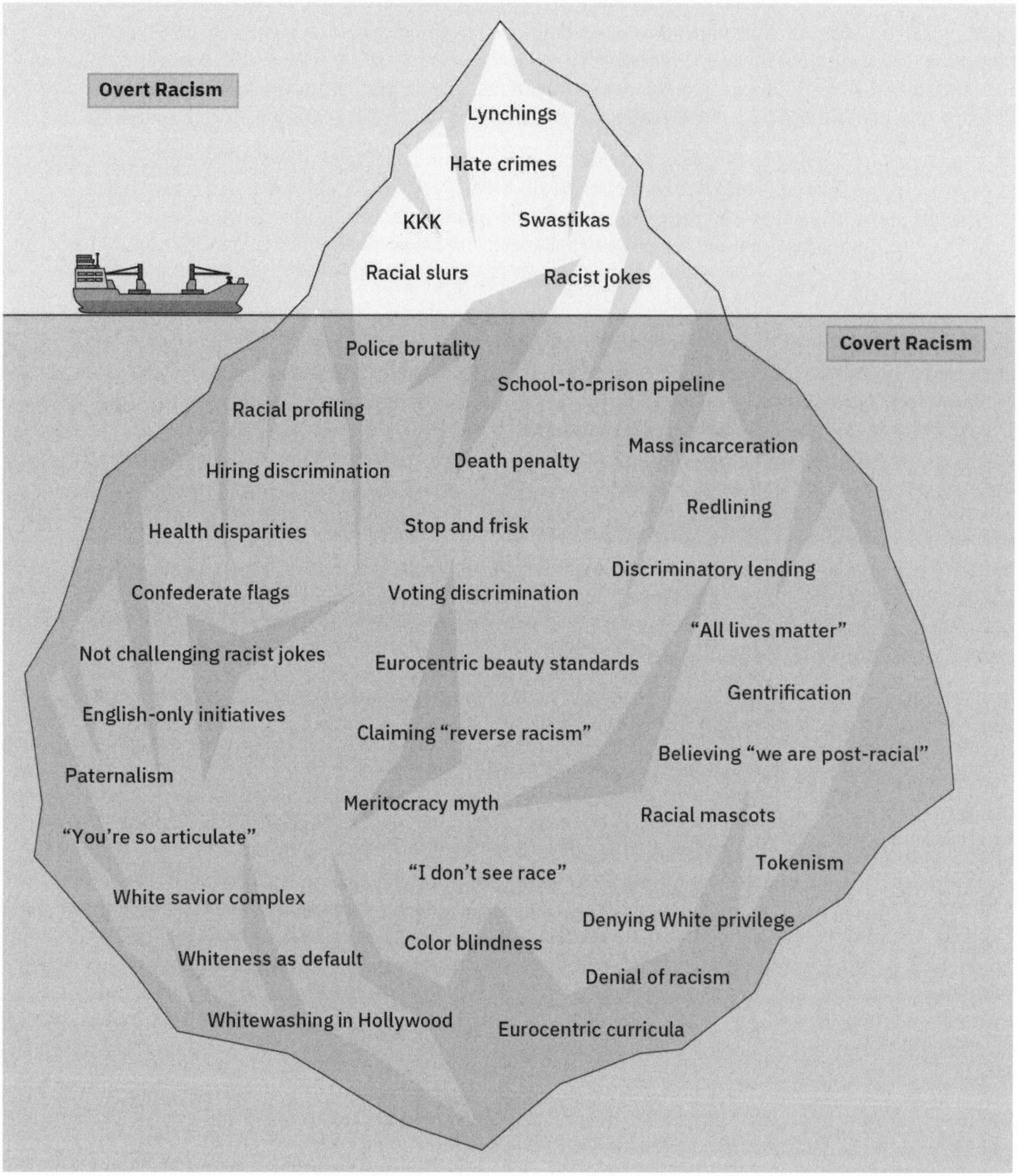

FIGURE 9.7 The "White supremacy iceberg" lists examples of overt, and covert racism. (attribution: Copyright Rice University, OpenStax, under CC BY 4.0 license)

The concept of White supremacy is a contentious one in modern media and politics. You may have come across an image like the one in Figure 9.7 explaining different types of White supremacy. Although the examples in the diagram labeled "Overt" can be agreed on as socially unacceptable by most people in American society, the examples in the "Covert" section are often explained on an individual level instead of as a symptom of racism. For instance, the school-to-prison pipeline can often be explained as the consequence of individuals who do not obey the rules instead of a consequence of underfunded schools and racist policies.

The avoidance of talking about race, or **racial refusal**, can be understood as a silent form of racism. Anthropologist Dána-Ain Davis, in her ethnography *Reproductive Injustice: Racism, Pregnancy, and Premature*

Birth (2019), writes that not acknowledging race in certain contexts can perpetuate inequalities. For her study of Black women who give birth to premature infants, Davis interviewed Black mothers and their partners; NICU (neonatal intensive care unit) staff, including nurses and doctors; birth workers; and March of Dimes administrators. In her research, Davis found that many doctors refused to discuss race and consequently ignored how racism is connected to disparities in health, premature birth, and medical treatment. Instead, discussions of premature birth disparities centered on class, despite the fact that Davis interviewed professional Black women who were college educated. Davis argues that racial disparities and medical racism perpetuated by systemic and structural racism cannot be addressed in healthcare settings if healthcare workers do not discuss race. This racial refusal has a historical precedence in the United States, where history and how that history has affected people's lives is routinely omitted (Davis 2019, 88).

Finally, **microaggressions** are everyday instances of racism, homophobia, sexism, ableism, and other isms that are observed in the world as thinly veiled insults directed toward individuals from historically excluded groups. People who commit microaggressions might not even be aware they are committing them. Microaggressions include verbal and nonverbal snubs and insults that communicate hostile, derogatory, or negative messages to individuals based solely on their identification with a marginalized group. For example, one of the coauthors of this chapter, Saira Mehmood, identifies as a Muslim woman of South Asian descent, born in New Orleans. Saira is often asked, "Where are you from?" When she answers, "New Orleans," the next question is often "Where are you *really* from?" This type of microaggression denies Saira's agency as an American.

Class

Class refers to a group of people with the same socioeconomic status and proximity to power. In a class-based system, status stems from wealth and one's proximity to the power that wealth builds. Economically, class systems are most often associated with the capitalist mode of production. People in the United States often think of the term middle class when considering class systems.

Capitalism—the economic mode of production based around markets, ownership of land and resources, and wage labor—has produced classes that are grounded in the acceptance of the idea that *earned* wealth or status is the basis for social hierarchy within a nation. In capitalist nations, a person's status in society directly relates to the amount of money they have acquired or the position they have achieved in their career. Class-based systems often emphasize social inequalities because of the hegemonic idea that relation to capital determines a person's value in society. For instance, Bill Gates is looked up to for his status as a billionaire, while those who work in fast food are often seen as not deserving of a living wage. This system of inequality, especially in the United States, is tied to the idea of meritocracy, with those at the top of the class system assumed to have worked hardest or to be most deserving of high-level positions and those at the bottom assumed to be personally at fault for their lack of wealth.

Capitalism includes the concept of **social mobility**, or the ability of an individual to move up into higher and thus more powerful classes merely by working hard. Social mobility is the basis for the "American Dream," the idea that poor Americans can attain a higher class. On the other hand, anthropologist Katherine S. Newman has done decades of research on **downward social mobility**, or the ongoing loss of capital and ensuing loss of social status. Newman (1999) found that in the last decades of the 20th century, divorce, emigration, company downsizing, and technological advancement left many middle-class individuals struggling to maintain their class (also see Gans 2009). Furthermore, the 2008 recession and the economic crash experienced due to the COVID-19 pandemic led to downward social mobility for millions.

In addition to class, the United States also uses the concept of "collar." *White-collar* jobs are assumed to require higher education, involve less manual labor, and pay more, while *blue-collar* jobs are considered less skilled, more manual, and lower paying. However, *Forbes* magazine found that there are many "blue collar" jobs (e.g., plumbers and electricians) that have higher earnings than many "white collar" jobs (such as entry- or mid-level finance), yet they carry lower status within US social hierarchy. What distinguishes white-collar from blue-collar jobs if it isn't just about how much money they make? German social scientist Max Weber argued that there were considerably more than two classes that determined the social inequalities and conflicts among people in capitalist societies. In his seminal essay "The Distribution of Power with the Community:

Classes, Stände, Parties" (2010), originally published in German in 1921, Weber argues that there are multiple, overlapping systems from which to gain power and links social stratification to three components: socioeconomic status, prestige, and political party connections.

Power, in capitalist and class societies, often stems from capital, which is wealth in the form of money or other assets. **Economic capital** is monetary but is not the only form of capital. French sociologist Pierre Bourdieu distinguished between various forms of capital: economic, social, cultural, and symbolic. Bourdieu defined **social capital** as the nonmonetary resources people use to gain social status, such as mutual acquaintances, shared cultural knowledge, or shared experiences. Social capital can also determine one's power. **Cultural capital** refers to the competencies, skills, and qualifications that people acquire that create cultural authority; in an institutionalized form, this takes the form of educational attainment. **Symbolic capital**, or the resources available to an individual because of honor, prestige, or recognition, is tied to economic, social, and cultural capital. For instance, successful athletes often have symbolic capital, and this type of capital can increase their social capital and economic capital with endorsements from corporations and other opportunities. However, athletes can also lose their symbolic capital when a scandal or controversy involving them is uncovered, resulting in them losing their endorsements and contracts, which in turn affects their economic and social capital.

A good example of how individuals utilize social capital in the United States is the networking that exists in top-tier schools. In *Pedigree: How Elite Students Get Elite Jobs* (2016), sociologist Lauren Rivera utilizes participant observation to show how top-tier investment banks, consulting firms, and law firms decide who gets hired and who doesn't, drawing on analysis of social and cultural capital in the American class system. Often, interviewers from elite firms use the phrase "not a good fit" when deciding not to hire someone in order to skirt around potential accusations of discriminatory intent. Riviera concludes that if a candidate is not from a top-tier school, the only way for them to get hired by such a firm is to have some other social capital connection vouch for their abilities.

When those with symbolic capital use their power against those with less power in order to change their actions, they are exercising symbolic violence. **Symbolic violence** is a type of nonphysical violence manifested in power differentials between social groups (e.g., upper class and lower class). For Bourdieu, symbolic violence reinforces ideologies that legitimize and naturalize the status quo. In many instances, symbolic violence reinforces social inequalities. This is perhaps most evident in the language used when referring to other groups. During the long history of migrations toward the US-Mexico border, symbolic violence has been used linguistically by English speakers to refer to migrants in terms that alienate them and set them outside of a common human identity. Labels such as "illegals," "illegal aliens," and "undocumented workers" are applied across cultures, defining families and individuals by a single dimension. Linguistic slurs are especially associated with symbolic violence. When human beings are represented in such simple and stark terms, it can become more socially acceptable to oppress them and see them as undeserving of empathy and respect.

Capitalism and class systems can also be analyzed in terms of race. Initially popularized by political science and Black studies scholar Cedric J. Robinson in *Black Marxism: The Making of the Black Radical Tradition* (1983), **racial capitalism** is the process through which the key aspects of capitalism (credit/debit, production/surplus, capitalist/worker, developed/underdeveloped, etc.) become articulated through existing relations of racial inequalities. In Robinson's framework, capitalism is racial not because of some conspiracy to divide workers or to justify slavery but because racialism had already spread through Western feudal society when capitalism developed. Racial capitalism can clearly be seen in the slave trade and colonialism. Scholar Saidiya Hartman states that slavery still "persists as an issue in the political life of black America . . . because black lives are still imperiled and devalued by a racial calculus and a political arithmetic that were entrenched centuries ago." Hartman describes this as "the afterlife of slavery—skewed life chances, limited access to health and education, premature death, incarceration, and impoverishment" (2007, 6). Slavery was a racialized system of capitalism, one that continues to exploit others to the present day.

Class systems emphasize social inequalities because for some people to have money and power, those individuals must exploit and oppress other groups. Capitalism and class societies are often supported by the ideas that those with power earned that power and those without it have individual moral failings instead of acknowledging that the structure of capitalism, which necessitates a working class, generates inequalities.

Gender and Patriarchy

Although there is a detailed exploration of gender, patriarchy, and power in Gender and Sexuality, this chapter will discuss how gender is tied to social inequalities. Anthropologists have studied how gender relations play a big part in experiences of inequality. Gender relations can interact with various other powerful cultural institutions to further oppress individuals.

An important concept to grasp when seeking to understand gender and power is **patriarchy**, a system of social inequality based on gender in which power is assumed to be in the hands of men and characteristics associated with femininity are less valued. Patriarchy is related to male lineages and contexts in which men hold more political, social, and economic power or prestige. Recently, the claim that patriarchy remains a powerful force has been challenged by some social commentators, who argue that this system of oppression does not exist in modern society and that women and men experience equal opportunities in terms of employment, rights, and salary. Many anthropologists and other social scientists challenge this claim, pointing out ways in which patriarchy still impacts women's lives.

Many anthropologists have made connections between gender and patriarchy, poverty, and race. In her fieldwork in the poor, mostly Black midwestern suburb of "Meadow View," sociologist Sharon Hicks-Bartlett (2000) observed a particular type of oppression experienced by local women. Women living in poverty were relied upon and expected to keep their families together. Hicks-Bartlett described women tasked with managing low-wage, part-time work in a place where public systems of care and assistance, or even buses, were largely unavailable.

The interpersonal and even internalized forces of patriarchy and power can also make women "compete to lose," meaning they will deliberately not succeed at some things in order to gain social capital among their peers. For instance, anthropologist Signithia Fordham, (2013) who spent two years studying the interactions of Black teenage girls in a predominantly White high school (which she aptly named "Underground Railroad High School"), found that the girls in this middle-class high school downplayed their achievements in order to fit in with peer groups and friends. Academic success was sometimes experienced as a social hindrance for those whose goals were family and children.

PROFILES IN ANTHROPOLOGY

Dr. William S. Willis Jr.
1921–1983

Personal History: Dr. William S. Willis Jr. (https://openstax.org/r/william-shedrick-willis) was a Black intellectual, anthropologist, historian, and anti-racist scholar of the 20th century. He was born in Waco, Texas, but his family moved to Dallas because of threats from the Waco Ku Klux Klan. After graduating from Howard University as a history major, Willis volunteered for service with the US Coast Guard. Eventually, he began his graduate studies in anthropology at Columbia University, drawn to the program by the scientific anti-racism of the Boasian tradition.

Area of Anthropology: As a graduate student, Willis wanted to study Black culture and Black relations at home and abroad, but he was not able to do so because of the dominance of the study of Native Americans in American anthropology at the time. Nevertheless, Willis remained convinced of the importance of the historical approach in anthropology and of studying cultural change through time, considerations that were largely ignored by other theoretical frameworks popular in anthropology at the time.

Importance of His Work: Willis became the first Black faculty member at Southern Methodist University (SMU). While he was popular as a professor in the Department of Sociology and Anthropology at SMU, he faced numerous hurdles. He received the least pay and has said that he felt like he was the "workhorse of the department" (quoted in Harrison and Harrison 1999, 253), teaching the greatest number of new courses. Despite being promoted to associate professor with tenure, Willis resigned from SMU in 1972, citing the covert and overt racism he experienced in the anthropology department.

His 1972 article "Skeletons in the Anthropological Closet," published in *Reinventing Anthropology*, declared that anthropology's claim of being the "science of man" was delusional and asserted that anthropology's virtual silence on the domination and exploitation of people of color at home and abroad, living outside the boundaries of White societies, was not consistent with the field's tradition of scientific anti-racism. Willis argued that anthropology was organized around the needs of White people and that most White anthropologists did not see people of color as real human beings.

9.3 Intersections of Inequality

LEARNING OUTCOMES

By the end of this section, you will be able to:

- Explain and give examples of intersectionality.
- Discuss how accumulated wealth creates systems of social inequality.
- Give examples of the ways that governing bodies can negatively impact the lived experiences of individuals.
- Explain caste systems as a type of intersection of political, economic, and racial inequalities.
- Explain implicit mentalities around poverty, wealth, and equity disparities.

Intersectionality

When thinking about social inequalities, it is useful to conceptualize race alongside other characteristics. **Intersectionality** is the observation that one's class, race, sexuality, age, and ability can all define and complicate experiences. The concept of intersectionality can be traced back to pre–Civil War America, when Sojourner Truth made her "Ain't I a Woman" speech in 1851 at the Ohio Women's Convention in Akron, Ohio, addressing the exclusion of Black women from the fight for women's rights. However, the term *intersectionality* was officially coined by critical race theorist and legal scholar Kimberlé Crenshaw (1989) in the context of discussing Black feminism. Crenshaw argued that the experience of being a Black woman could not be understood in independent terms of either being Black or being a woman; instead, it needed to include interactions between the identities, which often reinforce one another. Intersectionality discredits the notion that one single aspect of identity—race, for example—can capture the multidimensional nature of people's experiences of oppression. In other words, intersectionality emphasizes the ways in which identities pertaining to features such as race, gender, and class interact to impact people's lives.

Anthropologist Faye Harrison, coeditor of *African-American Pioneers in Anthropology* (1999), has done extensive work on intersectionality. She argues that "race is always lived in class- and gender-specific ways" (Harrison 1995, 63). For instance, the lived experience of a woman of color will be different from that of a White woman. Even though they both experience oppression from patriarchal systems, a woman of color has the added intersection of race, impacted by her identity as a woman.

Much of the work on intersectionality has come out of a critique of the original feminist movement, which sometimes generalized women's experiences as monolithic (Hill Collins 2000; A. Y. Davis 1981; McCall 2005; Sacks 1989). Feminist and women's studies scholar Chandra Mohanty (1984) criticized the White-middle-class-based approach of previous feminist authors, arguing not only that women of color don't need White women to save them but that their experiences are vastly different. By incorporating race with gender and class, feminist scholars have illustrated how experiences of race are dynamic.

In the collection of studies of race, class, and gender that occurred around the turn of the 21st century, anthropologist Leith Mullings (2002) developed the concept of the **Sojourner syndrome** to capture the interlocking ways in which race, class, gender, and resistance to oppression shape Black women's bodies and biology. The Sojourner syndrome emphasizes that race, class, and gender are not necessarily multiplied to mean more oppression, but they change the ways people experience oppression. In the Harlem Birthright Project, funded by the Centers for Disease Control and Prevention (CDC) to study racial disparities in health, Mullings uses the Sojourner syndrome to argue that Black women, because of intersecting structural inequalities, are forced to do more work than either their White female or Black male counterparts, which increases their stress levels and negatively impacts their health.

Another way intersectional identities can compound oppression is captured by the term *misogynoir*. **Misogyny** is the socialized prejudice against women and feminine characteristics. **Misogynoir**, a term coined by queer Black feminist Moya Bailey, describes the anti-Black racist misogyny that Black women specifically experience. Misogynoir is the intersection of the systems of sexism and racism experienced by Black women. More recently, Bailey has written about Black women's digital resistance to misogynoir on YouTube, Facebook, and other online platforms (2021).

In addition to creating challenges to the status quo, intersectionality can also inspire creative opportunities for new perspectives and new role models. On January 20, 2021, former senator Kamala Harris was inaugurated as the 49th vice president of the United States. Not only is she the first female vice president and the highest-ranking female official in US history, but her ethnic and racial background makes her the first Black American and the first Asian American person to hold this office. When she broke these "glass ceilings" (barriers to promotion that often affect women and members of minority groups), she was celebrated as a role model for many. There is even an unofficial Twitter fan group that calls itself "The #Khive Movement (https://openstax.org/r/khive-kamala-haris)" as well as other pro-Harris groups inspired by her example (e.g., Mamas for Momala). Her supporters frequently cite her background as an inspiring triumph that allows for new voices representing diverse groups in our society.

Overall, the Biden administration has pledged to have "the most diverse cabinet in American history" (see the "Biden Diversity Tracker (https://openstax.org/r/biden-diversity-tracker)"). On October 28, 2021, President Joe Biden appointed **Sara Minkara** (https://openstax.org/r/get-to-know-sara) as the US special advisor on international disability rights. In this foreign policy role, Minkara, who lost her eyesight at the age of seven, will promote and protect the rights of people with disabilities, again representing diverse voices of historically underrepresented groups.

FIGURE 9.8 Kamala Harris participates in a meeting on voting rights with Black women leaders on July 16, 2021. Harris is the first woman to hold the position of vice president of the United States as well as the first Black American and the first Asian American to hold this office. (credit: "V20210716LJ-0291-2-1" by Lawrence Jackson/ The White House/flickr, Public Domain)

PROFILES IN ANTHROPOLOGY

Dr. Yolanda T. Moses
1946–

FIGURE 9.9 Yolanda T. Moses (credit: "HBCUs as Sites of Global Citizenship" by Olivia Crum/Bart Everson/flickr, CC BY 2.0)

Personal History: Yolanda Moses was born in Washington, DC, but spent most of her childhood in Southern California. An active participant in the civil rights movement in the 1960s, she was inspired to pursue a doctoral program in anthropology after meeting Margaret Mead.

Area of Anthropology: Dr. Moses is currently professor of anthropology and associate vice chancellor for diversity, excellence, and equity at the University of California, Riverside. Her research focuses on the origins of social inequalities, relying on both comparative ethnographic and survey methods. She has examined gender and class disparities in the Caribbean, East Africa, and the United States. Dr. Moses's most recent research has focused on issues of diversity and change in universities and colleges in the United States, India, Europe, and South Africa.

Accomplishments in the Field: Dr. Moses has served as president of the American Anthropological Association (1995–1997), the City University of New York's City College of New York (1993–1999), and the American Association for Higher Education (2000–2003). She received the Donna Shavlik Award for leadership and mentoring of women from the American Council on Education in 2007 and the Franz Boas Award for Exemplary Service to Anthropology from the American Anthropological Association in 2015.

Importance of Her Work: Dr. Moses has received numerous grants from the Ford Foundation, the National Science Foundation, and the National Endowment of the Humanities. These grants have been awarded for projects examining the experiences of faculty who are women of color, questions of leadership and diversity in higher education, and, more broadly, race and human variation. She is a coauthor of *Race: Are We So Different?* and was influential in the RACE Project, a national public education project on race and human variation sponsored by the American Anthropological Association.

Global Inequalities

Anthropologists, along with other social scientists, recognize that all social systems and structures have developed through a multitude of decisions made by people with social, political, and economic power as well as through the daily interactions and imaginations of individuals. The current world system is the result of an amalgamation of events and historical forces that led humanity, step by step, to the world as it is today. Social systems and social structures are constructed and governed by the people who live within them; they are not ahistorical, and they are not unchanging. Capitalism is an economic system, but it is also the result of the ways in which people and groups interact with each other and with the natural world. Presidents elected by slim margins, compromises that benefited one political party over the other, and responses to natural disasters and other events, some of which may have seemed inconsequential at the time, all played a role in creating the current reality. Structures exist and order the world, but they do not exist outside of it.

When talking about the effect of capitalism, it is important to recognize the ways in which these systems of inequality can intersect to both benefit the powerful and exploit the poor. Wealth inequalities and capital accumulation have deeply impacted and continued to impact cultures around the world, leaving almost none untouched. There are two broad forces that shape this movement of economic capital. One of those forces, which encourages further and further accumulation of wealth within a single family, is **intergenerational wealth**. Intergenerational wealth is wealth that is passed down through generations, accumulating interest over many years. This money is typically invested to increase its value rather than circulated in the economy, further impacting wealth inequalities. The other force that has affected global wealth inequalities is colonialism. Colonialism is a system through which European (and eventually American) countries exerted power over areas of the world in order to exploit their natural and human resources. Capitalism relies on the extraction of resources, laborers to process those resources, and consumers to purchase the finished products. Colonialism provided all three in the form of a global proletariat (worker) class: a group of people whose labor is the foundational resource for production. Contemporary scholars recognize colonialism as one of the most important forces in the current global system of inequality.

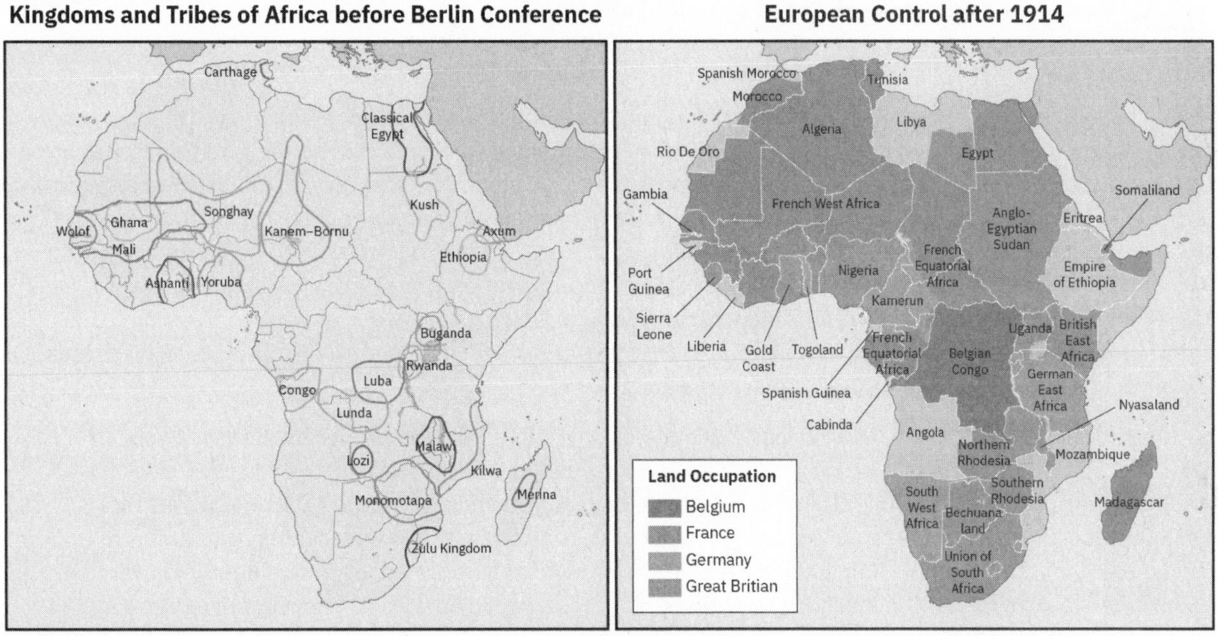

FIGURE 9.10 Map of Africa before and after the Berlin Conference. These maps show the diversity of African cultures before colonization and the arbitrary colonial borders established by European nations. (attribution: Copyright Rice University, OpenStax, under CC BY 4.0 license)

In the middle of the 20th century, many previously colonized countries gained independence. Due to worldwide economic downturns and ongoing colonial relationships with powerful Western countries, most did not have the means to develop their infrastructure, political organization, or economic sectors. These countries were also at a disadvantage as a result of decisions made by European powers at the Berlin Conference, which split Africa according to the wants of Western colonial powers rather than established Indigenous territories and spheres of political influence. Part of the ongoing turmoil within Africa stems from the fact that national boundaries were created with resources in mind, instead of the people who lived there.

What exactly does this have to do with social inequalities, poverty, or wealth? And how do international trade and development policies affect people without power at local levels? In the simplest terms, international structures of power affect every part of daily life for those living in poverty, especially people of color, women, and people living with disabilities. The intersections of political, economic, and social institutions reduce the number of resources available, leading to profound levels of inequity. Recognizing the long-standing effects of colonialism is vital to understanding the continuing inequities and poverty that are characteristic of so many territories that were once colonized.

To understand international structures of poverty and wealth, it is useful to also examine neocolonialism. **Neocolonialism** refers to the indirect ways in which modern capitalist interests continue to put pressure on poor nations through economic, political, or military means in order to further exploit wealth for multinational corporations and their allies. Rosemary Hollis, professor of Middle Eastern studies, once argued that Britain "went out the door and came back in through the window" (H.C. Foreign Affairs Committee 2013, Ev 20), meaning that it gave up its colonial holdings only to influence these nations through other means.

The main way in which neocolonialism plays out is through economic relief programs. The Global North, a term that represents powerful nations along with corporations and intergovernmental groups run by individuals from these countries, exerts power through targeted economic relief. The best-known agencies for economic relief are the World Bank Group and the International Monetary Fund (IMF). These groups, which have a lot of money, loan that money to Global South nations, which are exploited and "underdeveloped" countries that are experiencing economic or political crises. However, these loans come with many stipulations, most of which are called *austerity practices*. Austerity practices force governments to reduce public funding for health and education sectors, thus privatizing health care and education. For countries whose citizens are poor, introducing private health and education sectors results in a severe lack of access because many individuals cannot pay for these services.

Structural Violence

Privatization is also part of global neoliberal economics. **Neoliberalism** is an economic model that prioritizes privatization of public services in order to decrease government spending, based on the idea that free markets and supply and demand will lead to economic progress and development. Neoliberal policies have historically led to power structures that increase inequity for those who are already marginalized: the poor, women, and people of color. When individuals cannot fulfill their basic needs, they experience ongoing harm. Norwegian sociologist Johan Galtung calls this experience of intersecting, overlapping structures of discrimination (racism, sexism, classism, ageism, etc.) **structural violence**. Structural violence occurs when social institutions or practices reinforce inequalities, preventing certain social groups from obtaining basic needs. This can be an intentional or unintentional consequence.

Anthropologist and physician Paul Farmer's (2003) work in Haiti addresses the connections between neoliberal practices and structural violence. Farmer notes that the intersection of gender, race, class, and health disparities in Haiti result in specific health challenges for which the political, economic, and social systems take little responsibility. In the township of Cange, Haiti, where residents were predominantly farmers, a dam funded by the IMF flooded a fertile valley and displaced residents from their fields, forcing them to move to the less fertile hillsides or to cities. They were provided with no subsequent public support networks, such as schools or hospitals. The amalgamation of these factors—loss of economic resources from farming, forced wage labor in the cities, and privatized education and health—resulted in what Farmer described as an inherently oppressive way of life. Many of the villagers who moved to Port-au-Prince, the capital of Haiti, were forced to rely on wage labor, with some resorting to the sex tourism industry to survive. In the 1980s, some of these villagers became infected with HIV. For these Haitians, the displacement from their villages, caused by the dam funded by the IMF, was the root cause of their later inability to fulfill basic needs and their experience of further suffering. This is a prime example of structural violence.

By understanding how class systems, poverty, wealth, and economic inequities intersect around the world, anthropologists can hope to change international programs that are based on presupposed hierarchies between the "first world" and "third world" and between the powerful and exploited classes. Anthropologist William S. Willis Jr. firmly states that "anthropologists must give no credence to the vicious theory that poor people are responsible for their poverty" (1972, 149). Theories of inequity show that poverty and success are most often the result not of individual actions but of the identities that individuals have, the diverse obstacles they have experienced, and, in large part, the lottery of their birth. Anthropological examinations of inequity must take careful consideration of institutional and structural inequalities while still upholding the ability of the individual to be an instigator of broader change. According to Willis, anthropology's goal is to end the "poverty and powerlessness" (1972, 149) experienced globally by people of color.

9.4 Studying In: Addressing Inequities within Anthropology

LEARNING OUTCOMES

By the end of this section, you will be able to:

- Examine the effects of White supremacy in anthropology.
- Give examples of how anthropologists in other subfields are working against White supremacy and colonialism.
- Explain what decolonizing anthropology entails.

This section explores how anthropologists have looked within their own discipline to address ways in which they may be reproducing inequities through their practices and approach. Anthropologist Laura Nader uses the phrase "studying up" (1972) to call for more research on people and institutions with power. Following anthropologist Pamela Runestad (2017), this chapter uses the phrase "studying in" to address how anthropologists have looked at their own practices, training, methodologies, and assumptions and how anthropology as a discipline may in fact be contributing to inequities for students, practitioners, and the communities with which anthropologists engage.

Even though the construct of race has roots in anthropology, anthropologist Leith Mullings (2005) argues that critical studies of race and racism did not originally develop in anthropology. Mullings attributes this to the fact that anthropologists still do not agree about the role of race and racism within the discipline or how the categories of race have emerged and persisted in society. In addition, Mullings argues that many cultural anthropologists have focused on ethnicity, becoming "race avoidant" by not even mentioning race in ethnographies. Mullings warns that "race avoidant" anthropologists consequently ignore racism (Mullings 2005, 670).

In recent years, anthropologists have looked at the ways in which knowledge production and anthropological methods are rooted in White supremacy. Within the subfield of archaeology, anthropologists Maria Franklin and colleagues discuss how "archaeology has been used to justify imperialism, the displacement of Native Americans and Indigenous peoples from their lands, scientific racism, ethnocentrism, and xenophobic nationalism" throughout the world (Franklin et al. 2020, 754). However, archaeology does not exist in a vacuum, and these anthropologists also discuss ways to reimagine archaeology to do anti-racism work, especially in light of the Black Lives Matter movement. These efforts include encouraging growing numbers of members of minority groups as academic colleagues and seeking research sites that represent the lived experiences of minority populations. In 2020, Meredith Poole, a researcher for the Colonial Williamsburg Foundation in Williamsburg, Virginia, began a project (https://openstax.org/r/williamsburgs-black-archaeologists) identifying previously unrecognized Black archaeologists and excavators who had worked for Colonial Williamsburg in the 1930s. Additionally, Colonial Williamsburg archaeologists are currently working to excavate the First Baptist Church (https://openstax.org/r/first-baptist-church), one of the earliest Black churches in the United States. Projects such as these are critically important to the academic search for truth. Not only does this knowledge correct inaccuracies in the historical record, but it also serves to correct the course of future academic work.

FIGURE 9.11 In recent years, Colonial Williamsburg has undertaken various projects aimed at highlighting the contributions of Black archeologists and the lived experiences of people of color in the American colonial period. Additionally, they have added interpreters representing the lives of both free and enslaved Black individuals. (credit: "Colonial Williamsburg Virginia Duke of Gloucester St." by C Watts/flickr, CC BY 2.0)

Archaeologists Kylie Quave and colleagues (2020) have written about the ways in which introductory archaeology classes taught in the United States have often been problematic and how those teaching these courses are currently using anti-colonial and decolonial theories to revise curricula to promote equity within the discipline. Quave and her colleagues found that students taking revised curricula developed more complex understandings of the benefits and harms of archeological knowledge production and were better able to articulate the inequities in the discipline.

In April 2021, the Association of Black Anthropologists (ABA), the Society of Black Archaeologists (SBA), and the Black in Bioanthropology Collective (BiBA) released a collective statement regarding the possession and unethical use of the remains of the children of MOVE and the Africa family. In May 1985, the city of Philadelphia dropped two bombs onto the MOVE compound, home of "a revolutionary group of Black people opposed to capitalist growth and committed to environmental justice and interspecies harmony" (ABA, SBA, and BiBA 2021). The bombs killed 11 MOVE members inside the compound, including five children, and destroyed the neighborhood, incinerating at least 61 homes. Two forensic anthropologists, Alan Mann and Janet Monge, were hired by Philadelphia officials to identify the remains. In April 2021, various news outlets revealed that either Mann or Monge kept the remains two child victims, Tree Africa and Delisha Africa, in their personal possession after the investigation, moving them between the University of Pennsylvania and Princeton University. In addition, the family of the deceased were never notified of the remains, nor were the remains returned to the family. In response, the ABA, SBA, and BiBA supported and republished the demands of Mike Africa Jr., who was six years old when the Philadelphia police dropped the bomb on MOVE. The collective statement acknowledged the long history of White supremacy and anti-Blackness within the discipline and called on White anthropologists to actively work to undo the violence committed against non-White communities.

In *Decolonizing Anthropology: Moving Further toward an Anthropology for Liberation* (2010), edited by anthropologist Faye V. Harrison, the term **decolonizing anthropology** is used to emphasize the responsibility of anthropologists to work for the enhancement and empowerment of those most alienated and dispossessed. While decolonization refers to different ideas in different disciplines, the principal goal of the *Decolonizing Anthropology* volume is "to encourage more anthropologists to accept the challenge of working to free the study of humankind from the prevailing forces of global inequality and dehumanization and to locate it firmly in the complex struggle for genuine transformation" (Harrison 2010, 10). This work to decolonize, transform, and liberate anthropology is still happening, and the discipline still has a long way to go in decolonizing each of the subfields of anthropology and decolonizing methods and pedagogy to make classroom spaces more equitable.

Suggested Resources

Documentaries:

Adelman, Larry, prod. 2003. *Race: The Power of an Illusion.* https://www.racepowerofanillusion.org/.

Davidson, Kief, and Pedro Kos, dirs. 2017. *Bending the Arc.* https://bendingthearcfilm.com/.

Books/Articles:

Cargle, Rachel Elizabeth. 2018. "When Feminism Is White Supremacy in Heels." *Harper's Bazaar*, August 16, 2018. https://www.harpersbazaar.com/culture/politics/a22717725/what-is-toxic-white-feminism/.

Crenshaw, Kimberlé, Neil Gotanda, Gary Peller, and Kendall Thomas, eds. 1995. *Critical Race Theory: The Key Writings That Formed the Movement.* New York: New Press.

Jenkins, Destin, and Justin Leroy, eds. 2021. *Histories of Racial Capitalism.* New York: Columbia University Press.

Williams, Bianca C., Dian D. Squire, and Frank A. Tuitt, eds. 2021. *Plantation Politics and Campus Rebellions: Power, Diversity, and the Emancipatory Struggle in Higher Education.* Albany: State University of New York Press.

Websites/Podcasts:

James, Alyssa A. L., and Brendane A. Tynes. 2020–. *Zora's Daughters.* Podcast. https://zorasdaughters.com/.

Smithsonian Institution. 2020. "Talking about Race." National Museum of African American History and Culture. Last updated June 2, 2020. https://nmaahc.si.edu/learn/talking-about-race.

MINI-FIELDWORK ACTIVITY

American Census Archive Research

Browse through the US Census Bureau website (data.census.gov (https://openstax.org/r/data-census-gov)). Look at the categories from 1790, when the first US census was taken. Compare them to the 2020 census. How are these categories different? Who is being counted and how? Who is excluded?

Go one step further and search through two different zip codes. Look at the demographic makeup of each area. Can you see differences in household income? Education attainment? What if you go to Google Maps? Can you correlate this information with other causes of inequities? Are there grocery stores in these areas? Bus and subway stops? What is the population density of the area? Do you know anything of the history of the zip code?

Construct a visual that best explains the differences between the historical and contemporary censuses. Then, do the same with the two zip codes. Draw conclusions about social inequalities throughout history and in contemporary times.

Key Terms

agency the capability to act and make decisions.

ahistorical not acknowledging the specific historical experiences of a group, and thus attempting to understand societies without taking into consideration their connections to other cultures.

biopolitics the ways in which populations are divided and categorized as a means of control, often by the state.

bourgeoisie the class of people who own the means of production. Historically, the bourgeoisie were descendants of powerful feudal families.

capitalism an economic mode of production based around markets, ownership of land and resources, and wage labor. Capitalism has produced classes that are grounded in acceptance of the idea that earned wealth or status is the basis for social hierarchy within a nation.

caste a system of social inequality based on an individual's circumstances of birth, wherein people are not allowed to move out of their social group.

class a group of people with the same socioeconomic status and proximity to power.

colonialism a system through which European (and eventually American) countries exerted power over areas of the world in order to exploit their natural and human resources.

color blindness the idea that people "don't see color," meaning that they are unaware of the ways in which someone may experience the world because of the color of their skin.

cultural capital competencies, skills, and qualifications people acquire that allow them cultural authority. An institutionalized form of cultural capital is educational attainment.

decolonizing anthropology an approach to anthropology that emphasizes the responsibility of anthropologists to work for the enhancement and empowerment of those most alienated and dispossessed.

diaspora the dispersion of a people from their original home.

downward social mobility an ongoing loss of capital and the ensuing loss of social status.

economic capital monetary assets, including material assets that can be converted to money.

egalitarian describes a society or other group in which diverse roles are all given the same decision-making power and accorded the same respect among the group.

habitus the ingrained habits and dispositions that are socialized into people from birth depending on their status in society; used to explain how individuals uphold cultural systems.

hegemony the ways in which people with power keep their power through the subtle dissemination of certain values and beliefs.

hierarchy a type of social organization in which certain people or roles are given more power and prestige than others.

ideological state apparatuses distinct and specialized institutions such as religious institutions, public and private education systems, legal systems, political parties, communication systems (radio, newspapers, television), family, and culture (literature, arts, and sports).

inequality the unequal distribution of resources.

inequity the unequal distribution of resources due to an unjust power imbalance.

institutional inequalities power imbalances that stem from the policies and practices of organizations (education, government, companies, etc.) that perpetuate oppression.

intergenerational wealth wealth that is passed down through generations of descendants, accumulating interest over many years.

interpersonal inequalities power imbalances that are rooted in personal biases and occur every day, reifying and naturalizing inequalities that exist at institutional and systemic levels.

intersectionality the notion that characteristics such as class, race, gender sexuality, age, and ability can all define and complicate one's experiences, and a single aspect of identity—race, for example—is insufficient to capture the multidimensional nature of people's experiences of oppression.

meritocracy a system in which people succeed entirely through hard work and natural abilities. Someone who believes that they live in a meritocracy consequently overlooks any structural or racial inequities that may keep individuals from accessing the resources necessary for success.

microaggressions everyday instances of racism, homophobia, sexism, etc. that are observed in the world as thinly veiled insults directed toward historically excluded groups.

misogynoir the anti-Black racist misogyny that Black women experience.

misogyny the socialized prejudice against women

and feminine characteristics.

Nakba the 1948 displacement of hundreds of thousands of Palestinians from their homes; translates from Arabic as "disaster" or "catastrophe."

necropolitics an extension of Foucault's biopolitics that explores the government's power to decide how certain categories of people live and whose deaths are more acceptable.

neocolonialism the indirect ways in which modern capitalist interests continue to put pressure on poor nations through economic, political, or military means in order to further exploit wealth for multinational corporations and their allies.

neoliberalism an economic model that prioritizes privatization of public services in order to decrease government spending.

oppression the unjust exercise of power, either overt or covert, that is often used to control or inflict harm on entire groups of people.

paradigms worldviews that often define a scientific discipline during a specific time period.

patriarchy a system of social inequality based on gender, in which power is assumed to be in the hands of men and characteristics associated with femininity are less valued.

power the ability to exert control, authority, or influence over others.

proletariat the class of people who sell their labor and live off a wage, a.k.a. the powerless majority.

racial capitalism the accumulation of capital through existing relations of racial inequality.

racial refusal the refusal to mention or talk about race. Racial refusal is a silent form of racism.

racism power intertwined with racial prejudice.

repressive state apparatuses institutions through which the ruling class enforces its control, including the government, administrators, the army, the police, courts, and prisons.

resistance the act of challenging power and domination.

social capital the nonmonetary resources that people use to gain social status, such as mutual acquaintances, shared cultural knowledge, or shared experiences.

social mobility the ability of an individual to move up into higher and thus more powerful classes merely by working hard.

social stratification the hierarchical organization of different groups of people, whether based on racial category, socioeconomic status, kinship, religion, birth order, or gender.

Sojourner syndrome the interlocking ways in which race, class, gender, and resistance to oppression shape Black women's bodies and biology. The Sojourner syndrome emphasizes that race, class, and gender are not necessarily multiplied to mean more oppression, but they change the ways people experience oppression.

state apparatus a system consisting of two intertwined but distinct sets of institutions, the repressive state apparatus and the ideological state apparatus, which function together to maintain state order and control.

structural inequalities power imbalances that exist at a level above personal interactions and institutions and are based on the accumulated effects of institutional decisions across society and history.

structural violence the experience of intersecting, overlapping structures of discrimination (racism, sexism, classism, ageism, etc.).

symbolic capital the resources available to an individual because of honor, prestige, or recognition.

symbolic violence a type of nonphysical violence that is manifested in the power differential between social groups and reinforces ideologies that legitimize and naturalize the status quo.

systematic oppression the intentional mistreatment of certain groups.

systemic inequalities power imbalances created by the confluence of interpersonal, institutional, and structural inequalities.

systemic oppression the ways in which political, economic, and social inequalities are normalized and perpetuated.

systems the powerful, overarching beliefs according to which the world is organized that influence the ways in which individuals interact with their world.

White privilege the ways in which White people receive advantages at the expense of other populations.

White supremacy the idea that White people are a superior race and should dominate society at the expense of other, historically excluded groups.

Whiteness an identity based on the maintenance or pursuit of power and proximity to power.

Critical Thinking Questions

1. Name two situations impacted by social inequality that you have personally experienced.

In each of these situations, did you consider yourself to be in the position of more or less power?
2. The "American Dream" is a pervasive ideology in the United States. What is the role of social mobility in this ideology? To what extend do you think that systems of inequality restrict people's ability to achieve the American Dream?
3. Did you ever take a standardized test for admission to a school, undergraduate program, or graduate program? What kinds of inequities might these types of tests reinforce?
4. What social class do you think your family occupies? What are three ways you would describe that social class? Are they economic, social, racial, gendered?
5. Have you ever filled out a form that asks you what your race or ethnicity is, perhaps for a college application or at the doctor's office? What categories do you recall? Do you ever question these categories? Are you ever conflicted about these categories?
6. What are some examples of necropolitics that you can see in your everyday life experiences?
7. How does accumulated wealth create systems of social inequality?
8. What are some examples of hegemony that you can think of in your culture?
9. Have you seen diversity, equity, and inclusion practices gain popularity at your institution? Discuss the reasons a campus might need these practices, as well as who benefits from them.

Bibliography

Abu-Lughod, Lila. 1986. *Veiled Sentiments: Honor and Poetry in a Bedouin Society.* Oakland: University of California Press.

Alper, Loretta, and Jeremy Earp, dirs. 2016. *The Occupation of the American Mind: Israel's Public Relations War in the United States.* Northampton, MA: Media Education Foundation. DVD.

Association of Black Anthropologists, Society of Black Archaeologists, and Black in Bioanthropology Collective. 2021. "Collective Statement Concerning the Possession and Unethical Use of Remains." Association of Black Anthropologists. April 28, 2021. https://aba.americananthro.org/collective-statement-concerning-the-possession-and-unethical-use-of-remains/.

Bailey, Moya. 2021. *Misogynoir Transformed: Black Women's Digital Resistance.* New York: New York University Press.

Bonilla-Silva, Eduardo. 2017. *Racism without Racists: Color-Blind Racism and the Persistence of Racial Inequality in America.* 5th ed. Lanham, MD: Rowman & Littlefield.

Crenshaw, Kimberlé. 1989. "Demarginalizing the Intersection of Race and Sex: A Black Feminist Critique of Antidiscrimination Doctrine, Feminist Theory and Antiracist Politics." *University of Chicago Legal Forum* 1989 (1): 139–167. https://chicagounbound.uchicago.edu/uclf/vol1989/iss1/8/.

Davis, Allison, Burleigh B. Gardner, and Mary R. Gardner. 1941. *Deep South: A Social Anthropological Study of Caste and Class.* Chicago: University of Chicago Press.

Davis, Angela Y. 1981. *Women, Race, and Class.* New York: Random House.

Davis, Angela Y. 2016. *Freedom Is a Constant Struggle: Ferguson, Palestine, and the Foundations of a Movement.* Edited by Frank Barat. Chicago: Haymarket Books.

Davis, Dána-Ain. 2019. *Reproductive Injustice: Racism, Pregnancy, and Premature Birth.* New York: New York University Press.

Davis, Uri. 2003. *Apartheid Israel: Possibilities for the Struggle Within.* London: Zed Books.

Delgado, Richard, and Jean Stefancic, eds. 2013. *Critical Race Theory: The Cutting Edge.* 3rd ed. Philadelphia: Temple University Press.

Drake, St. Clair. 1978. "Reflections on Anthropology and the Black Experience." *Anthropology & Educational Quarterly* 9 (2): 85–109. https://www.jstor.org/stable/3216192.

Du Bois, W. E. B. (1940) 1984. *Dusk of Dawn: An Essay toward an Autobiography of a Race Concept.* New

Brunswick, NJ: Transaction Books.

Erakat, Noura. 2019. *Justice for Some: Law and the Question of Palestine*. Stanford, CA: Stanford University Press.

Erakat, Noura, and Dia' Azzeh, dirs. 2016. *Gaza in Context*. Washington, DC: Quilting Point Productions. Video, 20:24. https://www.youtube.com/watch?v=bmRPkfAN2EU.

Farmer, Paul. 2003. *Pathologies of Power: Health, Human Rights, and the New War on the Poor*. Berkeley: University of California Press.

Fordham, Signithia. 2013. "Competing to Lose? (Black) Female School Success as Pyrrhic Victory." In *The Social Life of Achievement*, edited by Nicholas J. Long and Henrietta L. Moore, 206–228. New York: Berghahn Books.

Franklin, Maria, Justin P. Dunnavant, Ayana Omilade Flewellen, and Alicia Odewale. 2020. "The Future Is Now: Archaeology and the Eradication of Anti-Blackness." *International Journal of Historical Archaeology* 24:753–766. https://doi.org/10.1007/s10761-020-00577-1.

Foucault, Michel. (1978) 1990. *The History of Sexuality*. Translated by Robert Hurley. Vol. 1, *An Introduction*. New York: Vintage Books.

Gans, Herbert J. 2009. "First Generation Decline: Downward Mobility among Refugees and Immigrants." *Ethnic and Racial Studies* 32 (9): 1658–1670. https://doi.org/10.1080/01419870903204625.

Goodman, Alan H., Yolanda T. Moses, and Joseph L. Jones. 2020. *Race: Are We So Different?* 2nd ed. Hoboken, NJ: Wiley-Blackwell.

Green, Dan S., and Earl Smith. 1983. "W. E. B. DuBois and the Concepts of Race and Class." *Phylon* 44 (4): 262–272. https://www.jstor.org/stable/274576.

Harrison, Faye V. 1995. "The Persistent Power of 'Race' in the Cultural and Political Economy of Racism." *Annual Review of Anthropology* 24:47–74. https://doi.org/10.1146/annurev.an.24.100195.000403.

Harrison, Faye V., ed. 2010. *Decolonizing Anthropology: Moving Further toward an Anthropology for Liberation*. 3rd ed. Arlington, VA: American Anthropological Association.

Harrison, Ira E., and Faye V. Harrison, eds. 1999. *African-American Pioneers in Anthropology*. Urbana: University of Illinois Press.

Hartman, Saidiya. 2007. *Lose Your Mother: A Journey along the Atlantic Slave Route*. New York: Farrar, Straus and Giroux.

Hicks-Bartlett, Sharon. 2000. "Between a Rock and a Hard Place: The Labyrinth of Working and Parenting in a Poor Community." In *Coping with Poverty: The Social Contexts of Neighborhood, Work, and Family in the African American Community*, edited by Sheldon Danziger and Ann Chih Lin, 27–53. Ann Arbor: University of Michigan Press.

Hill Collins, Patricia. 2000. *Black Feminist Thought: Knowledge, Consciousness, and the Politics of Empowerment*. Rev. 10th anniversary ed. New York: Routledge.

House of Commons Foreign Affairs Committee. 2013. *The UK's Relations with Saudi Arabia and Bahrain*. Vol. 1, *Report, Together with Formal Minutes, Oral and Written Evidence*. 5th Report of Session 2013–14. London: Stationery Office Limited. https://publications.parliament.uk/pa/cm201314/cmselect/cmfaff/88/88.pdf.

Isacowitz, Roy. 2015. "Apartheid Policies Put Israel on Path to Becoming Failed State." *Haaretz*, September 3, 2015. https://www.haaretz.com/opinion/.premium-apartheid-policies-put-israel-on-path-to-failed-state-1.5394664.

Kline, Nolan. 2019. *Pathogenic Policing: Immigration Enforcement and Health in the US South*. New Brunswick, NJ: Rutgers University Press.

Kuhn, Thomas. 1962. *The Structure of Scientific Revolutions*. Chicago: University of Chicago Press.

Mbembe, Achille. 2003. "Necropolitics." Translated by Libby Meintjes. *Public Culture* 15 (1): 11–40. https://doi.org/10.1215/08992363-15-1-11.

McCall, Leslie. 2005. "The Complexity of Intersectionality." *Signs* 30 (3): 1771–1800. https://doi.org/10.1086/426800.

McIntosh, Peggy. 1989. "White Privilege: Unpacking the Invisible Knapsack." *Peace and Freedom*, July/August 1989, 10–12.

Mohanty, Chandra Talpade. 1984. "Under Western Eyes: Feminist Scholarship and Colonial Discourses." *boundary 2* 12 (3): 333–358. https://www.jstor.org/stable/302821.

Mukhopadhyay, Carol C. 2008. "Getting Rid of the Word 'Caucasian.'" In *Everyday Antiracism: Getting Real about Race in School*, edited by Mica Pollock, 12–16. New York: New Press.

Mullings, Leith. 2002. "The Sojourner Syndrome: Race, Class, and Gender in Health and Illness." *Voices* 6 (1): 32–36. https://doi.org/10.1525/vo.2002.6.1.32.

Mullings, Leith. 2005. "Interrogating Racism: Toward an Antiracist Anthropology." *Annual Review of Anthropology* 34:667–693. https://doi.org/10.1146/annurev.anthro.32.061002.093435.

Nader, Laura. 1972. "Up the Anthropologist—Perspectives Gained from Studying Up." In *Reinventing Anthropology*, edited by Dell Hymes, 284–311. New York: Pantheon Books.

Nairn, Charlie, dir. (1974) 2003. *Ongka's Big Moka: The Kawelka of Papua New Guinea*. Newton, NJ: Shanachie Entertainment. DVD.

Newman, Katherine S. 1999. *Falling from Grace: Downward Mobility in the Age of Affluence*. Berkeley: University of California Press.

Ortner, Sherry B. 1974. "Is Female to Male as Nature Is to Culture?" In *Woman, Culture, and Society*, edited by Michelle Zimablist Rosaldo and Louise Lamphere, 67–88. Stanford, CA: Stanford University Press.

Painter, Nell Irvin. 2010. *The History of White People*. New York: W. W. Norton.

Pappé, Ilan, ed. 2015. *Israel and South Africa: The Many Faces of Apartheid*. London: Zed Books.

Quave, Kylie E., Shannon M. Fie, AmySue Qing Qing Greiff, and Drew Alis Agnew. 2020. "Centering the Margins: Knowledge Production in the Introductory Archaeology Course." *Advances in Archaeological Practice* 9 (2): 87–100. https://doi.org/10.1017/aap.2020.43.

Rivera, Lauren A. 2015. *Pedigree: How Elite Students Get Elite Jobs*. Princeton, NJ: Princeton University Press.

Robinson, Cedric J. 1983. *Black Marxism: The Making of the Black Radical Tradition*. London: Zed Press.

Rosaldo, Michelle Zimbalist, and Louise Lamphere, eds. 1974. *Woman, Culture, and Society*. Stanford, CA: Stanford University Press.

Runestad, Pamela. 2017. "Time to 'Study In.'" *Anthropology News* 58 (1): e299–e302. https://doi.org/10.1111/AN.319.

Sacks, Karen Brodkin. 1989. "Toward a Unified Theory of Class, Race, and Gender." *American Ethnologist* 16 (3): 534–550. https://www.jstor.org/stable/645273.

Spencer, Herbert. 1864–1867. *The Principles of Biology*. 2 vols. London: William and Norgate.

Weber, Max. 2010. "The Distribution of Power within the Community: Classes, Stände, Parties." Translated by Dagmar Waters, Tony Waters, Elisabeth Hahnke, Maren Lippke, Eva Ludwig-Glück, Daniel Mai, Nina Ritzi-Messner, Christina Veldhoen, and Lucas Fassnacht. *Journal of Classical Sociology* 10 (2): 137–152. https://doi.org/10.1177/1468795X10361546.

Willen, Sarah S., Colleen C. Walsh, and Abigail Fisher Williamson. 2021. "Visualizing Health Equity: Qualitative Perspectives on the Value and Limits of Equity Images." *Health Education & Behavior* 48 (5): 595–603. https://doi.org/10.1177/1090198121994520

Willis, William S., Jr. 1972. "Skeletons in the Anthropological Closet." In *Reinventing Anthropology*, edited by Dell Hymes, 121–152. New York: Pantheon Books.

CHAPTER 10
The Global Impact of Human Migration

Figure 10.1 Refugees are people who have been forced out of their homelands for various reasons. This is a camp in Haiti that arose after the 2010 earthquake. An estimated 1.5 million people were displaced after this catastrophic event. (credit: "Military Relief Efforts in Haiti After Devastating" by Fred W. Baker III/Wikimedia Commons, Public Domain)

CHAPTER OUTLINE

INTRODUCTION The word *migration* is likely to bring to mind a stereotype familiar to American culture: people voluntarily coming into another country in search of work and other opportunities. Yet this is only one aspect of the meaning of migration as understood by anthropologists. **Migration**, put simply, is movement from one place to another that reestablishes a household, either permanently or temporarily. Examples of migration include seasonal movements in search of work, temporary movements due to a crisis or local challenges, transnational movements from one nation to another, and even occasional moves from one household to another over a lifetime (sometimes referred to as *internal* versus *external migration*). **Migrants**, by extension, are simply people who move. Other than those relatively few people who are living in the same house they were born into, we are all migrants of one sort or another. Within this larger category of migrants, **immigrants** are individuals who move permanently from one country (where they are referred to as *emigrants*) to another country (where they are called *immigrants*).

The human species, along with our ancestors, has practiced migration from our earliest origins. It is part of who we are. Most living species migrate in some way, but humans move more widely than other species and modify the landscape the most through their movements. Human migration impacts the world in innumerable ways.

10.1 Peopling of the World

LEARNING OUTCOMES

By the end of this section, you will be able to:

- Describe the early migration patterns of the genus *Homo*.
- Distinguish the primary controversies in the peopling of America theories.
- Identify major pre-Clovis sites in the United States.

Early Hominin Migrations

Human species were migratory from the beginning, moving as small populations of gatherers and hunters within eastern and southern Africa. By following game and the availability of seasonal vegetation from place to place, these small groups of nomads learned about their landscape, interacted with each other, and met their subsistence needs. Their daily needs came through interaction with a changing environment. With the emergence of *Homo erectus* around 1.89 million years BP (before the present), hominins expanded their territories and began to exhibit increasing control over their environment and an ability to adapt, evidenced by the development of new subsistence systems, including cultivation, pastoralism, and agriculture, and an upsurge in migration within Africa and, eventually, into Asia and Europe. This expansion into new geographical regions was a hallmark of the later human species.

There are several theories on possible migratory sequences within and beyond the African continent. One possibility is that by 1.75 million years ago, *Homo ergaster* had begun migrating out of Africa, moving northward into Eurasia. Another theory argues that an earlier hominin species, either australopithecine or an early as-yet-unknown species of the genus *Homo*, migrated out of Africa around 2 million years ago, eventually evolving into the population of Dmanisi hominins who were settled in eastern Europe by 1.85 million years ago, possibly representing another link between *H. erectus* and *H. ergaster*. Although settlement dates are currently being retested and reexamined for precision (Matsu'ura et al. 2020), it is known that between 1.3 and 1.6 million years ago, *H. erectus* settled on Java, an island that is now part of Indonesia. They likely traveled there by a land route, as seas were lower during the Pleistocene Ice Age (approximately 2.588 million–11,700 years ago), allowing for more passage through interior coastal routes. (For more on early human migrations, see The Genus Homo *Homo* and the Emergence of Us.)

Regardless of the specific time frame and migration pattern, it is well established that there was gene flow between various hominin populations, which indicates that there were migration and exchange. With the migration of these early hominin populations, cultural practices and improvements in toolmaking spread as well. Wherever humans traveled, they carried with them their traditions, intermingling and reproducing both physically and culturally.

Controversies Surrounding the Peopling of the Americas

Current evidence points to the emergence of the genus *Homo* in Africa. From these beginnings, human populations began moving toward the global north, east, and south in migratory waves. Motivations for these migrations included animal movements, overcrowding and resource scarcity, and, likely, curiosity and adventure. The movement into the Western Hemisphere, into North and South America, occurred significantly later than migrations into Europe and Asia; how much later is a question of enormous controversy today. How did the first peoples make their way to the Americas? When did they first arrive, and how did they migrate within these vast continents? The available evidence is inconclusive, leaving us with one of the biggest enigmas in human evolution. While there is some debate on whether earlier human species migrated into the Americas, the evidence we have today points to members of the species *Homo sapiens* being the earliest humans to do so. At this point, there is no evidence of any earlier hominin species in either North or South America. The Western Hemisphere was wholly settled by migrants coming from other continents.

There are many theories regarding the first human migration into the Western Hemisphere. Because of changing global climate conditions and the retreat of glaciers toward the end of the Pleistocene epoch, new lands opened to migrating animals and the humans who were likely hunting them (Wooller et al. 2018). As always, because of limited and ambiguous artifact and fossil findings, the primary pieces of evidence are open to multiple interpretations. Upon examining the range of theories, two primary arguments are apparent. Both of these arguments are backed by supporting evidence, and both rely on migratory patterns of *H. sapiens* in the Americas that have been definitively established. While both migration theories are valid, the question that remains open to argument is which came first, coastal or interior migration?

- The *interior route*, also called the Bering Strait theory, is the best-known and most accepted theory for the first human migration into the Americas. The foundation of this theory is the Beringia "land bridge," which connected northeast Siberia and what is now Alaska when sea levels were lower due to glacial ice formation on the continents. This theory proposes that the earliest human habitants of the Americas crossed this marshy land on foot, most likely beginning around 15,000 years ago based on artifacts and dating sequences. The Beringia land bridge was alternately exposed and submerged multiple times over the earth's history. According to the interior route theory, the earliest humans crossed this marshy land in pursuit of migratory herds of mammals and then proceeded to filter southward, splitting into multiple groups, some of which penetrated into the interior of North America as they continued to move east and south.

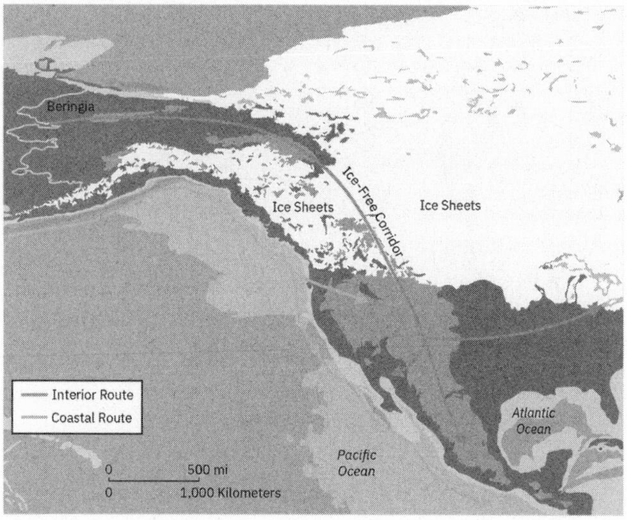

FIGURE 10.2 The interior route theory argues that a northeastern Siberian population of hunters first entered the Americas on foot from Beringia following migrating herds, while the coastal route theory argues that the earliest migrants followed fish and sea animals by boat along the Pacific coast of the Western Hemisphere. Although the precise date for the earliest migrations is debated, it is estimated to be between 15,000 and 18,000 years ago. (credit: Copyright Rice University, OpenStax, under CC BY 4.0 license)

- The *coastal route* is also based on the migration of a northeastern Siberian population into the Western Hemisphere, but by boat rather than on foot. This theory, sometimes called the kelp highway hypothesis, proposes that the earliest migratory populations followed the continental coastline southward, subsisting on kelp, fish, shellfish, birds, and sea mammals. Research by archaeologist Jon Erlandson (Erlandson et al. 2007; Ocean Wise 2017) suggests that migrants may have followed these food sources all along the continental shelf, a shallow sea area near the shore. Some believe that they eventually reached as far south as Chile, in South America, before breaking into groups and penetrating the interior lands.

Each theory presents its own probabilities and problems in relation to dating sequences and artifacts, and there were possibly multiple early routes for the peopling the Americas. Scientific research does agree on some known facts, however. Genetic sequencing shows continuity between the earliest Americans and populations in northeastern Siberia that indicates the earliest inhabitants of the Americas arrived no more than 25,000 years ago, making the Americas the most recent continental habitation (outside of Antarctica). Humans were already inhabiting Australia by the time other humans first arrived in the Americas.

Archaeological sites in the Americas present fascinating evidence of early human migrations, with the dating sequences continually being retested and revised. Based on some of the early archaeological evidence, scientists had believed that the first American inhabitants were part of what is known as the Clovis culture, identified with a leaf-shaped projectile point used in hunting. As excavations have continued, though, there is growing indication of an extensive pre-Clovis culture, evidenced by a pre-Clovis technology based on gathering, hunting, and fishing, with dates extending back further than 13,200 years before present. Pre-Clovis projectile points are smaller, less standardized, and less worked (flaked), indicating a less advanced tool production. Many pre-Clovis sites are located below the Clovis period occupation. As archaeologists have continued excavations, the dates for earliest occupation continue to be pushed backward.

FIGURE 10.3 Clovis points from the Virginia Aquarium and Marine Science Center. Clovis points are long, leaf-shaped points that are bifacial, or flaked on both sides. (credit: "Virginia Aquarium & Marine Science Center Arrowheads Clovis Point Stone Tools" by C Watts/flickr, CC BY 2.0)

Why so much debate about the settling of the Americas? There are various reasons for the difficulties in establishing settlement dates. The Bering land bridge was periodically exposed and submerged under water during periods of glacial growth and retreat. Using core samples obtained by drilling down into the shallow sea floor, archaeologists have found evidence of large mammals and even fluted points (hunting tools) in and around the Aleutian Islands, through which the land bridge would have crossed. Establishing and cross-checking dates, though, has been difficult because most evidence is now submerged. This is a challenge also for the coastal route theory, as coastlines have receded since the end of the Pleistocene, and encampments would have likely been small, possibly temporary sites. Many sites are likely now submerged offshore (Gruhn 2020).

Among the best-known pre-Clovis sites are the following:

- *Monte Verde Site*, Chile. This is one of the most studied pre-Clovis sites. An extensive array of artifacts has been found at Monte Verde, including hearths, wooden and stone tools, animal bones, and even human footprints. The dates assigned to these artifacts, as early as 16,000 BP, put this site within the range of pre-Clovis dates seen in North America.
- *Debra L. Friedkin Site*, Texas. This pre-Clovis site has a dating sequence of 13,500 to 15,500 BP. A wide range of pre-Clovis tools have been found here, including partially flaked tools, blades, and scrapers.
- *Cactus Hill Site*, Virginia. A well-document Clovis site has been identified at Cactus Hill, but below this level of artifacts, there is evidence of pre-Clovis projectile points. Although controversial, these points have possible dating sequences of 18,000–22,000 BP.

FIGURE 10.4 A pre-Clovis archaeological site in Sussex County, Virginia, in the United States (credit: "Nottoway Archaeological Site Entrance" by Nyttend/Wikimedia Commons, Public Domain)

Based on this new evidence, scientists now agree that the Americas were first settled by a pre-Clovis population. How they arrived, when they arrived, what movements they made, and in what order they made them are major archaeological questions today. What we can conclude is that human populations continued to migrate after peopling the Americas.

10.2 Early Global Movements and Cultural Hybridity

LEARNING OUTCOMES

By the end of this section, you will be able to:

- Explain the ways that globalization connects local populations through the phenomena of flows.
- Describe the roles that colonialism played in shifting populations between colonizing and colonized nations.
- Distinguish between diaspora, transnationalism, and cultural hybridity.
- Explain the contemporary forces of postcolonialism and forced migration.

Colonialism and Migration as Global Forces

The global movement that characterizes our current period in history is not preordained. The volatile and powerful nature of multinational cultural change and economic exploitation associated with this global movement is connected with specific historical forces. One of the most consequential early global forces was *colonialism*, an exploitative relationship between state societies in which one has political dominance over the other, primarily for economic advantage. Colonialism did not only affect the countries enmeshed in colonial relationships; it also established world alliances and enduring social, political, and economic changes.

Some scholars date the earliest emergence of colonialism to the city-states of Mesopotamia in western Asia, an area occupied today by parts of Iran, Iraq, Turkey, Kuwait, and Syria. Evidence indicates that by around 3500 BCE, the northern and southern regions were connected by exploitative trade relationships and intense and prolonged warfare. US archaeologists Guillermo Algaze and Clemens Reichel (Algaze 2013; Wilford 2007), in excavations at Uruk in ancient Mesopotamia, have unearthed trade goods that indicate a vast exchange network involving items such as pottery, jewelry, metalwork, and even wine. There is also a pattern of destruction and warfare at Uruk and, more recently, at Tell Hamoukar in modern-day Syria, which indicates the movement of populations as well as trade goods. Tell Hamoukar was a major site of obsidian tool and blade manufacture as early as 4500 BCE, with raw materials coming from as far away as modern-day Turkey, some 100 miles to the north. At Tell Hamoukar, collapsed walls and a large number of penetrating clay bullets, likely delivered by slingshots, are some of the oldest known artifacts of organized warfare. The archaeological sites indicate that there was armed conflict and that groups of people were moving between locations. The patterns of destruction across these various sites suggest that populations were most likely vying for control over resources and production sites, similar to conflicts associated with more modern colonialism, which also were primarily characterized by a drive for political control based on access to raw materials and resources.

After these early beginnings, colonialism spread, including the development of European and Mediterranean settlements in northern Africa. The Phoenicians, from what is now modern-day Lebanon, established the city of Carthage in what is now Tunisia to facilitate and control trade throughout the Mediterranean area. Carthage remained an important hub for trade from its founding in the 9th century BCE until it was destroyed by the Roman Empire in 146 BCE. In what is now modern-day Egypt, the Macedonian king Alexander the Great founded the city of Alexandria in 331 BCE. Alexandria rapidly grew in economic and political influence because of its control over Mediterranean trade routes; in the Greek confederation of city-states, only Rome was more powerful. As colonizing nations consolidated their political and economic influence, they increasingly sought to expand their access to the natural resources and human labor of other societies. Colonial occupations were repeatedly marked by violence.

By the end of the 15th century, when Christopher Columbus began the first of what would be four voyages (1492–1504) to the New World, many of the nations of Europe were aggressively seeking new territories, establishing what is now called the Age of Discovery (1500s–1700s). During this period, Spain, Portugal, the Netherlands, Belgium, France, Germany, and Great Britain all funded sea and land voyages to seek out new territories in order to expand their global influence. The modern-day European world order of developed and developing nations emerged from the colonialism begun during of the Age of Discovery.

Across the globe, generations of Indigenous peoples contested European colonizers. Often fighting with less effective weaponry; having little or no immunity to Old World diseases such as smallpox, measles, typhus, and cholera, which decimated their populations; and balancing efforts to defend their homelands and families with the desperate need to maintain agricultural production to fend off famines, Indigenous people frequently migrated from one area to another, leaving behind land and crops. In the Andean area, *forasteros*, a group of Indigenous peoples, became nomadic to flee oppression. Declaring ownership and control over lands and people who had few effective means to challenge them, European nations quickly established colonies throughout North and South America, the Caribbean, Africa, and Asia. Politically, most colonies were beset with conflict and periodic uprisings, such as the Great Rebellion of Tupac Amaru II from 1780 to 1783 in Cuzco, Peru, during which Andean peoples came very close to toppling the Spanish government after almost 250 years of oppression. During this period, there also emerged new sociocultural institutions and rituals blending colonizing and Indigenous cultures as aspects such as food and religious beliefs became entangled (Carballo 2020). This blending is referred to as *creolization*. Culturally, the dismantling of Indigenous languages, religions, and other institutions continues to be devastating.

Late European colonialism of the 18th to the 20th century, sometimes called *classic colonialism*, was a period in which the institutions of control and extraction were standardized, especially in Africa. This period of colonialism is characterized by very specific goals, policies, and attitudes. The colonial relationship was symbolically depicted as one of benevolence between the "mother country" and the colony, with people such as missionaries, colonial advisors, settlers, businesspeople, and teachers all working together to promote economic development and Europeanization in the colony. The official justification for these practices was that European Christians had a "White man's burden" to spread their civilization worldwide. Beneath this rhetoric, however, the goals were power and control. Colonialism was an extractive and exploitative economic venture with a social structure designed to dehumanize Indigenous peoples. Raw materials were extracted from the colonies using low-paid Indigenous labor and sent to European nations, where they were transformed into goods that were then sold back to the colony and its Indigenous peoples at an enormous profit for the Europeans. Indigenous cultures were severely damaged or destroyed. Frequently, Indigenous peoples were removed from their homelands and settled on reservations or within territories that were of less use to the Europeans, freeing up large swaths of land for European immigrants. Many young Indigenous people, handpicked for their skills and aptitude, were sent to European countries to be educated and acculturated as future leaders in the colonies. The intention of this preparatory system was to disrupt the influence of Indigenous cultures and create enduring pro-European institutions within the colonies. It also served to divide the Indigenous populations, further weakening them. In other cases, Indigenous peoples were bought, sold, and traded as commodities, moving them away from their languages, cultures, and families. From the 16th to the 19th century, it is estimated that between 10 and 12 million Africans were enslaved and transported from

Africa to the Americas in the transatlantic slave trade. The massive scale of this forced migration changed the world ethnically, culturally, linguistically, and economically. Untold millions of Africans died in the enslavement process, fracturing families, communities, and societies. While the movement and mixing of so many different peoples resulted in expansive cultural innovation in areas such as languages, foods, religions, and rituals, the cost of this massive displacement in human lives and human potential was incalculably high, leaving scars and challenges that continue today.

These policies, of removing peoples from their homelands and of sending young people far from home for schooling and enculturation, are just two examples of the ways in which colonialism forced people onto new lands and into new cultures. As colonies grew into empires, with many different nations under the control of a single European nation—such as Great Britain, which had colonies in places as far apart as Kenya, Australia, and Canada—there was a global movement of people and cultures across continents.

Colonization also affected those living in European countries, influencing contemporary identities in many ways. The area of modern-day Poland was partitioned several times by neighboring nation-states and was colonized by both Germany and Russia during World War II and its aftermath. In this eastern European nation, the impacts of migration and change continue to affect the way Poland sees itself today. The various movements of peoples and cultures have left Poland uneasy with its own history and national identity. In her research on culture-focused museums in Poland, sociocultural anthropologist and curator Erica Lehrer (2020) studies the contested narratives within the legacies of collecting, categorizing, and displaying objects in postcolonial countries where prior migrations have changed the nature of national identity.

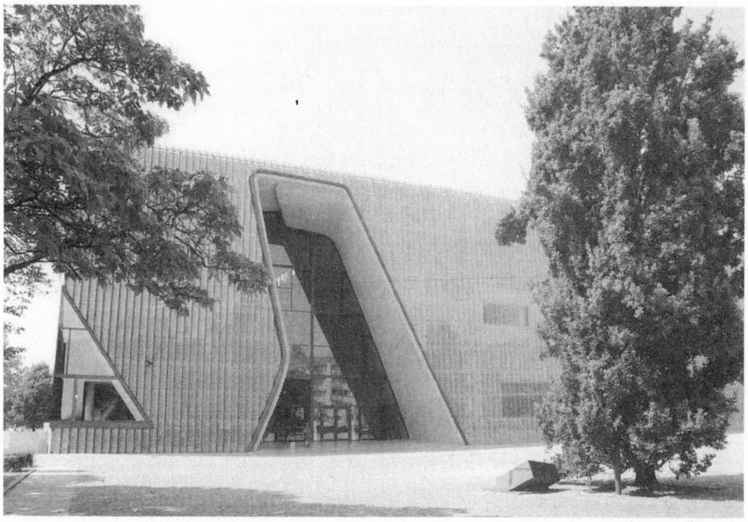

FIGURE 10.5 The Museum of the History of Polish Jews opened in Warsaw, Poland, in 2005. It focuses on Jewish history in Poland, with a mission of promoting openness, tolerance, and truth. (credit: "Warszawa - Muzeum Historii Żydów Polskich POLIN" by Fred Romero/flickr, CC BY 2.0)

In its history, Poland has been both the colonizing nation (in regard to neighboring states in eastern Europe) and the colonized (in regard to its long history as a colony of Russia and its later occupation during World War II). Depleted by wars, out-migration, territorial shifts, and genocide, Poland's contemporary population is far more homogeneous by race, class, and religion than it was prior to World War II. Museum depictions of Poland's culture and national identity have created a host of what Lehrer calls "awkward objects" (2020, 290) that hark back to earlier, and sometimes darker, historical periods. These include museums objects made by non-Jewish Poles representing their memory and imagination of Jews in the pre–World War II era, some depicting ambiguous racial stereotypes, as well as hybrid objects that could have been artifacts of either Jewish or Catholic communities but are depicted by object origin and associated with only one of those communities. One example is a collection of children's noisemakers, which were depicted in the museum as artifacts from a Catholic Polish community without noting that Jewish Polish children would have played with similar toys at that time. And how should a Polish cultural museum handle darker awkward artifacts, such as carvings of a gas chamber at Auschwitz? The roles and responsibilities that contemporary societies have in telling these parts of their history are relevant to museums and cultural institutions around the globe.

Museums often house artifacts of colonialism. Think about cultural and historical museums that you have visited. How did they tell the story of the darker parts of history? Are certain historical periods overlooked or underdeveloped?

Lehrer calls for *pluralist contextualization*, meaning that museums should not just include the cultural origins of the object but also indicate how they were obtained and how they connect with other cultural communities. Citing a need for ethical curatorial principles, she says:

> Strategic curatorial approaches can frame objects to function as a source of ethical inspiration and empathy, spurring people to acknowledge and address those histories that are *un*chosen by national or communal authorities. . . . Decolonising the museum here is not about restitution. These "awkward objects" are most valuable to us curated in ongoing, caring conversation wherever historical injuries still resonate, reminding us that we are tied together by our wounds. (307, 311)

Postcolonialism, Indigenous Identities, and Forced Migration

Although colonialism as a direct politico-economic policy is usually associated with earlier historical periods, it continues to have effects on the world today. The enduring politico-economic relationships established by colonialism have left behind concentrations of capital and technology, wealth and privilege in the former colonizing countries, mainly in Europe, as well as inequality, racism, and violence in the relationships between these nations and their colonies. These aftereffects of colonial relationships are referred to as **postcolonialism**. As independence movements began to take hold in the early 20th century, former colonies found themselves depleted of resources and competing against European countries whose growth came from their own demise. Today, postcolonialism is a significant topic for anthropologists whose research focuses on the effects of colonialism, marginalization, and intersectionality, where race, gender, and class identities come together.

One of the most prominent consequences of colonialism is the inequality between the so-called developed countries and the developing or underdeveloped ones. Following World War II and the rise of a new world order, many political and economic theories began to distinguish between "first world" countries, which had the highest GDPs (gross domestic products) based on the total value of all goods and services produced in a country, and those with the lowest GDPs, referred to as "third world" countries. The "second world" tier was typically reserved for those countries with a socialist or communist government. In this tiered and hierarchical system, the former colonizers were always within the top tier and their former colonies in the lowest ranks. Much of this inequality was due to the exploitation of resources and the brain drain migration of Indigenous peoples, in which the wealthiest and most educated members of Indigenous societies relocated to the former colonizing nation for education and employment, many leaving their homelands permanently. This out-migration devastated many Indigenous families and enhanced the productive capacities of richer nations. Many former colonizing countries thus continued to exert influence over their former dependencies even after independence. This relationship of unequal influence is referred to as *neocolonialism*.

Many Indigenous societies are involved in neocolonial relationships (meaning relationships that are structured to make one country dependent on another) with the nation-states in which they live, a situation sometimes referred to as *second colonialism* (Gandhi 2001). Indigenous groups continue to be uprooted, and sometimes forcibly removed, from their homelands and moved onto reservations, into "model villages," or simply into urban areas. This type of **forced migration**, an involuntary or coerced removal from a people's homeland, can result in poverty, alienation, and loss of cultural identity. Native peoples in the United States have been subjected to repeated waves of forced migration since the arrival of Europeans. Many societies were forced to move multiple times as White settlers pushed them onto more western and less fertile lands. All of this forced dislocation has had significant cultural and economic consequences. As Native Americans Richard Meyers (Oglala Lakota) and Ernest Weston Jr. (Oglala Sioux) write:

> Tragedies of many kinds are often all too common for many people who reside on our reservation. Endemic poverty creates endless problems for community members, from violent dog packs to pervasive alcoholism and diabetes. Dismal statistics paint our reservation as the "Third World" right here in the United States. The numbers are hard to pin down but always dreary: Unemployment is sometimes listed as being as high as 85–95 percent, and more than 90 percent of the population lives

below the federal poverty line. (Meyers and Weston 2020)

While many Indigenous peoples in Western nations face unique problems of Western historical paralysis, in which the nation-state extols the virtues of Indigenous people at a specific time in its history with little or no regard for contemporary Indigenous identities, some Indigenous peoples are adapting their cultural traditions to urban areas where they have been forced to migrate. In her study of Indigenous Manchineri youth in the Brazilian state of Acre, Finnish anthropologist Pirjo Virtanen (2006) found a cultural revival of traditional puberty rituals for young Manchineri adults. The Manchineri are a lowland Amazonian people who traditionally practiced slash-and-burn cultivation. Over the past century, their access to farmland has become increasingly limited, leaving them unable to make a living in the forest. Many young Manchineri have migrated from their traditional homelands to live in urban areas among other lowland Amazonian Indigenous peoples. These Manchineri sought to strengthen their cultural identity by reviving and adapting certain traditional rituals, such as the ayahuasca ceremony, in which pubescent boys ingest a hallucinogenic substance as a spiritual experience, and a menstruation ceremony in which girls are instructed by their elders on their new status as adults. Few Manchineri remain on their ancestral homelands, and many of these cultural traditions were in danger of dying out.

In Acre, the urban Manchineri found that being an “Indigenous person” had social value with Westerners who appreciated traditional Indigenous cultures. Much of this growth in appreciation came as a result of the rapid decline of Indigenous cultures and populations and the increasing urbanization and alienation of people from rural environments. The younger generation of Manchineri began to appreciate their traditional cultural roots and see the value of maintaining their specific cultural identity, rather than being “lumped” into a broad category of Indigenous persons, while living in an urban environment. By marking themselves as Manchineri, they were able to leverage a higher social standing. This process of using identity as a way to gain status is an example of symbolic capital, or the use of nonmonetary resources to gain social prestige.

Maintaining a specific Indigenous identity within Western nation-states is challenging, as the numbers of Indigenous peoples continue to decline and migration into urban areas creates a mixture of cultures that frequently results in the loss of traditional identities. Indigenous identity is complex and not monolithic, as specific cultural groups have distinct identities; no single spokesperson can realistically represent all Indigenous people. Recently, pan-Indigenous activist movements have developed worldwide to increase the visibility and strengthen the voices of Indigenous peoples. These global movements of people and ideas make it possible for Indigenous people to form alliances for change.

Globalization in Motion

As the connections and interactions between communities, states, countries, and continents have intensified, a global network of linked forces and institutions known as globalization has emerged. Unlike earlier worldwide movements, globalization tends to be decentered, meaning it is not controlled by any particular nation-state or cultural group. Emerging from earlier worldwide historical movements pertaining to exploration, colonialism, and capitalism, globalization has exceeded them with its reach and has created a worldwide interdependence far more intense and transformative on a global scale than anything ever before seen in human history. It involves all aspects of our lives (e.g., political, economic, social, and religious), and it has no center or origin point. Changes and interactions occur within a dynamic and seemingly arbitrary field of connections among people, ideas, countries, and technologies.

Globalization causes the movement of people, resources, and ideas in various ways. Not only do people migrate for work and travel, but they also share ideas and technology, resulting in cultures and populations that are no longer restricted and contained by geographical boundaries. These globalized cultures and networks have changed the way that anthropologists think about culture. Culture is no longer solely attached to a local place and community; rather, it is diffuse and possibly widespread, due to the complicating forces of globalization.

One of the early scholars of globalization is Indian American anthropologist Arjun Appadurai. His research is grounded in the idea of a new global *cultural* economy that traffics in multiple simultaneous flows of material goods, ideas, images, and people, reminding us that global movements and transformations affect every one, whether or not we actually change the nation or community in which we live. Within globalization, local and global communities are deeply intertwined in fluid and dynamic relationships of mutual influence. These interconnections sometimes lead to unpredictable outcomes. Appadurai (1990) identifies five different global cultural flows, tagging each with the suffix *-scapes* to call attention to the fluidity and multiple ways of viewing these flows:

- *Ethnoscapes*: the flow of new ideas and new ways of living created by the ongoing migration of people—whether tourists, immigrants, refugees, exiles, guest workers, or other groups—across cultures and borders. As just one example, the descendants of the Zainichi Koreans who immigrated to Japan following World War II have established Korean schools and a Korean university in Japan.
- *Technoscapes*: the worldwide movement of technology, both equipment and information, as well as the multinational origins and manufacturing process of technology along a global assembly line. One example is an iPhone, which has component parts and a manufacturing process that involves many different places.
- *Financescapes*: the movement of money and capital through currency markets, national stock exchanges, and commodity speculations. The funds of even the most local investors are intermingled and invested on the global market.
- *Mediascapes*: the various types of media representations that influence the way we experience our world. These are "image-centered, narrative-based . . . strips of reality" (Appadurai 1990, 299) diffused through digital media, magazines, television, and film, introducing characters and plots across cultural settings and meanings.
- *Ideoscapes*: the flow and interaction of ideas and ideologies. Appadurai describes ideoscapes as "terminological kaleidoscopes" (1990, 301) in which words and ideas carrying political and ideological meanings are trafficked across cultures. In this process, their meanings become increasingly amorphous and obscured. One example is the political change that resulted from a reawakening of democratic movements in the Middle East in the 2010s, inspiring the Arab Spring, a series of anti-government protests and rebellions. Anti-government protests in Tunisia spilled over into Egypt, Libya, Yemen, Syria, and Bahrain, toppling government leaders and triggering social violence.

Appadurai speaks of these -scapes as primary agencies and intersections within the global cultural economy; in other words, each of these -scapes creates change through interactions with others. In this fluid exchange of ideas, material goods, and persons, the -scapes interact, overlap, and contradict one another as cultures themselves come to be commodities produced and consumed by the global community.

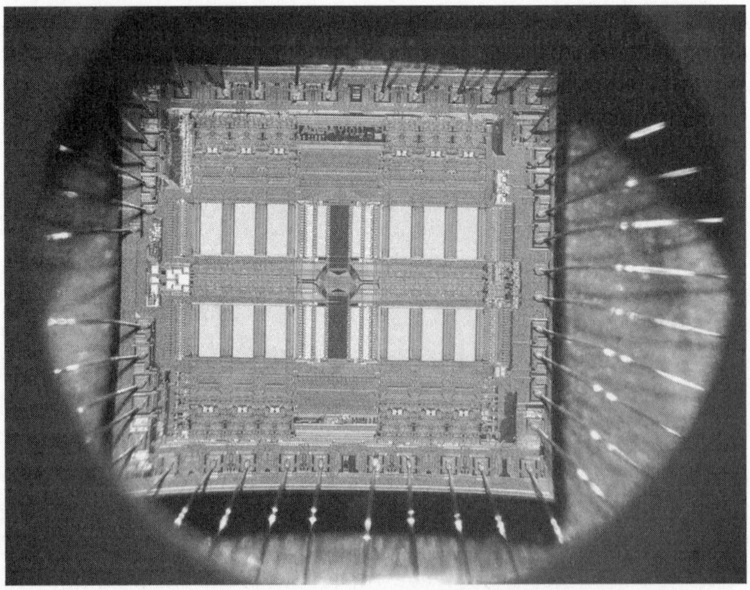

FIGURE 10.6 Semiconductor chips are currently made in only a few countries. The United States imports these chips for use in automobiles, medical technology, and computers. In 2021, facing a worldwide shortage of computer chips, President Joe Biden pledged funding to support the creation of chip manufacturers in the United States. (credit: "EPROM-EPLD ALTERA EP910" by yellowcloud/flickr, CC BY 2.0)

There are multiple perspectives for understanding globalization. It can be interpreted as an imperial force in which certain countries and cultures have dominance over others, with their images, capital, and ideas predominating in the global marketplace. Indian anthropologist Sekh Mondal aptly says, "The people earlier had been the creators and creatures of culture, but today the corporate bodies and media have emerged as the creators and carriers of cultural attributes" (2007, 94). Globalization can also be viewed as an open-access community in which governments and corporations have lost the ability to control and isolate populations, ultimately allowing for more cultural diversity and equality. Globalization today transforms virtually everything about anthropology—its subject matter, the locales for research, its understanding of the concept of culture, and the goals that anthropologists bring to their work. Within this context of great change, anthropology is uniquely capable of making sense of this new global community and its rapidly shifting beliefs and behaviors.

Diaspora, Transnationalism, and Cultural Hybridity

Migration impacts individuals and cultures in diverse ways. It prompts the dissemination and diffusion of cultural ideas and artifacts from one cultural context to another, the development of new cultural forms and practices, and hybridity, in which cultures intermingle in unpredictable ways. **Cultural hybridity** refers to the exchange and innovation of ideas and artifacts between cultures as a product of migration and globalization. It is a commingling of different cultural elements resulting from the interactions of people and their ideas. While individuals and small groups convey their cultures as they migrate, the movement and dispersal of large ethnic groups can bring about far more rapid structural changes. This large-scale movement, which might be caused by warfare, institutionalized violence, or opportunities (most commonly education and employment), is called **diaspora**. Related to diaspora is **transnationalism**, the construction of social, economic, and political networks that originate in one country and then cross or transcend nation-state boundaries. While diaspora and transnationalism can both be related to large-scale migration, transnationalism also refers to the cultural and political projects of a nation-state as it spreads globally (Kearney 1995). One example of this is transnational corporations, which are anchored in one country with satellites and subsidiaries in others.

Diasporic communities typically have a sense of identity that has been shaped or transformed by the migration experience. They are characterized by cultural hybridity and often take these new cultural forms with them into their new homelands, generating cultural revival. The African diaspora resulting from the transatlantic slave trade brought a wide array of cultural elements to the United States, including new foods (such as okra and yams), new instruments and musical forms (such as the drums, the banjo, and the development of African slave spirituals), and new language (words such as *jazz*, *gumbo*, and *tilapia*). Besides the common experience of being formed through migration, diasporic communities share other characteristics. These include a collective memory about the ancestral homeland; a social connection to the country of origin, typically through family still living there; a strong identity as a distinct group; and fictive kinship with diasporic members in other countries ("Migration Data Relevant" 2021). Diasporic communities are inherently political (Werbner 2001), as their movements connect nation-states in a variety of ways—economically, socially, religiously, and politically. Some of the best-known diasporas are the African diaspora that was driven by the transatlantic slave trade from the 15th to the 19th century, the Irish diaspora during Ireland's Great Famine of the mid-1800s, and the Jewish diaspora, which began under the Roman Empire and continued through the establishment of Israel as a Jewish homeland in 1948. Today, India is the source of the largest diaspora in history, with some 18 million Indians living outside of their country of origin. These mass movements, which are becoming more common as a result of globalization, affect cultures worldwide.

FIGURE 10.7 An immigrant solidarity rally in Minneapolis, Minnesota, in 2017. About 3,000 people gathered to protest against President Trump's immigration ban and the increasing militarization of the U.S-Mexico border. (credit: "Solidarity March with Immigrants & Refugees" by Fibonacci Blue/Wikimedia Commons, CC BY 2.0)

American anthropologist and South Asian scholar Ritty Lukose has done fieldwork in India and in U.S. immigrant communities exploring diaspora and postcolonial identities. In her research with Indian diasporic communities in the United States (2007), she focused on ways in which education could better connect with immigrant families, thus strengthening both. The percentage of children in the United States population who are immigrant children, defined as those who have at least one foreign-born parent, increased by 51 percent between 1994 and 2017 (Child Trends 2018). Immigrant families constitute a significant portion of the population within American schools today. Based on her research, Lukose argues that there needs to be a realignment in American education that better acknowledges immigrant identities. As an example of the urgency of this need, she cites the 2005–2006 California textbook controversy, in which the Hindu American Foundation (HAF) sued the California State Board of Education for using sixth-grade social studies textbooks that contained what the HAF and many Indian parents deemed to be biased and discriminatory views of Hinduism. Lukose advises that instead of presenting the migrant experience as fractured between voluntary and involuntary immigrants or focusing on conflict between immigrants and other minorities (such as racial minorities), American educational pedagogy, curricula, and practices should present identity formation itself as one of the richest experiences of being a citizen. An educational approach that emphasizes immigrant identity, not as a hybrid of pieces and parts, but as a legitimate and practical way of functioning within a globalized world could better prepare all students in the United States for a future in which we focus on what links us together rather than what divides us.

10.3 Peasantry and Urbanization

LEARNING OUTCOMES

By the end of this section, you will be able to:

- Explain how industrialization and internal migration are connected to the creation of a peasant class.
- Articulate the characteristics of peasantry from an anthropological perspective.
- Describe cultural changes associated with internal migration.

Peasantry in Anthropology

Peasants, a rural, subsistence-based agricultural class with limited landholdings, are the product of both urban development and rural–urban migration. Prior to the emergence of capitalism and the industrial state, agriculturalists were the most populous class within state societies. The development of the industrial economy prompted an ongoing process of **internal migration**, the domestic movement of people from rural to urban areas for economic opportunities, education, and employment. For many peasants, internal migration was used to meet immediate family needs, whether taking agricultural goods to urban markets—which may be weekly, monthly, or seasonal—or temporarily moving to work for cash at agricultural tasks for larger farms and companies. The coffee, sugar, and fruit industries, for example, absorbed many small, rural agriculturalists whose families needed money.

Cultural anthropologist Robert Redfield (1956) was one of the first anthropologists to identify peasants as a distinct social group, referring to their local identity and culture as a "little tradition" (70), meaning a culture that is less unified and involves a changing mixture of customs based on oral traditions. He identified the primary characteristics of peasant cultures as attachment to the land from which they make a living, dependence on urban areas that control the value of their small surplus, and traditionalism in regard to social practices. Later studies built on these earlier ideas about peasantry. Eric Wolf (1966) referred to peasant groups as "closed corporate communities" (86), meaning communities that are more detached from urban centers and less prone to cultural changes as a result of migration. He also saw them as distinct from farmers in that they produce a more limited surplus and are involved in more asymmetrical (i.e., exploitative) market transactions.

Instead of being simple subsistence farmers, peasants are aware of the wider capital markets and are directly affected by the fluctuating value of their products, even though they have no power over these forces or control over the profit they earn. Sometimes, frustration over this sense of powerlessness leads to attempts to affect political change. In 1994, on the same day that the North American Free Trade Agreement, or NAFTA, came into effect between the United States, Mexico, and Canada, the Zapatista rebellion broke out in Chiapas, Mexico. This movement was led by Indigenous peasants who implicitly understood that the treaty, which made it possible for agricultural products to move among the United States, Mexico, and Canada without tariffs, meant that they could no longer sell their small agricultural surpluses for a living wage. Now, they would be competing with giant corporations that were able to flood local markets with cheaper products.

As the reach of globalization continues to expand, connecting local communities ever more tightly with global forces, some scholars now speak of a post-peasant class. This term is used to refer to rural cultivators who migrate to urban areas but retain many of the cultural attributes of their ancestral traditions. These might include a patriarchal family structure, a tendency to favor local traditions over global innovations, or a more conservative political outlook (see Buzalka 2008).

Internal Migration: Rural-Urban Continuum

Indian anthropologist Tame Ramya (2017) studied the push and pull factors—a phrase used to describe circumstances and forces that push migrants away from their homeland and pull them toward a new location—affecting the internal migration of different hill tribes of Kurung Kumey, a district in the state of Arunachal Pradesh, India, to the foothills region of the neighboring district of Papum Pare. Although there were several ethnic groups involved in this study, the majority of migrants to Papum Pare are ethnically Nyishi. The Nyishi, the largest ethnic group in their district, are rural cultivators who raise paddy rice, supplemented with cucumbers and maize. Traditionally, they practiced polygyny and had large families with many children. Ramya's study shows that the primary motivation for voluntary internal migration in this region is to access new economic opportunities, prompting people to move from more peripheral geographical areas to urban centers. Although the motivation for migration is primarily economic, these relocations result in a series of cultural changes.

On tribal lands in the hill country of Kurung Kumey, the most common form of subsistence is *jhum*. This is a form of slash-and-burn cultivation that requires families to practice a semi-sedentary settlement pattern, moving occasionally when land resources are depleted. Ramya argues that this experience with periodic movement makes voluntary migration somewhat less disruptive to their lives. These are people who are accustomed to occasional relocations. Recent internal migration to the urban area of Papum Pare is motivated by various factors. A rise in local political instability, increasing intra-ethnic conflicts, and a lack of employment opportunities for those seeking hard cash "push" many people, particularly young people, to migrate to the nearby urban area of Papum Pare. People are also "pulled" by a range of employment opportunities in urban industries that are unavailable in Kurung Kumey, by relatives who have already migrated, and by increased access to educational and health facilities in the city.

FIGURE 10.8 A Nyishi man in Arunachal Pradesh, India. The Nyishi are one of many people whose society has been deeply affected by migration from rural areas into urban centers. (credit: "Nishi Tribal Man Arunachal Pradesh – India" by Diganta Talukdar/flickr, CC BY 2.0)

As with any form of migration, culture change and adaptation have been a part of the migrant experience of the people of Kurung Kumey. Among the migrants, Ramya found a set of specific cultural shifts that are common in rural–urban migration across cultures. One is an imbalance of generations, with older family members remaining in the rural hills while younger family members migrate to the city. Also evident is a change in family structure. Migrants establish urban households consisting of just the nuclear family instead of the larger extended family common in rural households, as larger families are now considered too costly to house and feed. Also typical of urban–rural migration are myriad changes in regard to food, dress, language, and alcohol consumption. Traditional curry is cooked in bamboo tubes in the hills region, but migrants in the city no longer use bamboo and do not consume as much boiled food as their rural relatives. Instead, the urban diet is marked by fast food and the use of larger quantities of cooking oil. In addition, Ramya found higher alcohol consumption and addiction among the migrants. Migrants have also begun to abandon the traditional dress that marks them as a tribal and non-urban people and to use their own tribal languages less frequently, preferring the more commonly spoken Hindi and official language of English. All of these changes are typical as individuals and groups move from rural to urban areas. Internal migration is the primary cause of the diminishment of cultural and linguistic diversity worldwide.

10.4 Inequality along the Margins

LEARNING OUTCOMES

By the end of this section, you will be able to:

- Identify contemporary types of migration.
- Describe the major migrant routes and some of the risks migrants face.
- Identify and give an example of circular migration.
- Describe the global impact of refugees.
- Give an example of a pandemic.

Contemporary Types of Migration

Because of emerging global forces of all kinds—social, economic, environmental, and political—there has been a recent rise in migration within geographical regions and across countries. Four of the most common types of contemporary migration are listed below. Each derives from different causes and is associated with different push and pull factors (Woldeab 2019). In some situations, these types of migration may overlap, such as in the aftermath of a natural disaster.

- **Labor migration** is the movement of people for the purpose of employment and/or economic stability. It may be an internal migration from one town to another within the same country of origin, or it may involve travel across countries in search of opportunities. In 2017, the United Nations International Labour Organization estimated that there were 164 million labor migrants worldwide (Global Migration Data Analysis Centre 2021).
- **Forced migration** or **displacement**, also called *involuntary migration*, is migration due to persecution, conflict, or violence and involves refugees and those seeking asylum. The UN Refugee Agency (UNHCR) estimated that as of the end of 2019, there were some 79.5 million forced migrants or displaced persons worldwide. More than two-thirds (68 percent) of those displaced persons came from just five countries: Syria, Venezuela, Afghanistan, South Sudan, and Myanmar (UNHCR 2020). One out of every 108 people was displaced in 2018 (UNHCR 2019).
- **Forced labor**, **human trafficking**, and **modern slavery** are a set of linked terms defined as the recruitment, transportation, transfer, and/or harboring of persons by means of threat or use of force or coercion for the purpose of exploitation (UN 2020). This includes sexual slavery and forced labor. As of 2016, some 25 million people were involved in forced labor and some 40.3 million in modern slavery worldwide, while an estimated 15.4 million were in forced marriages (https://www.ilo.org/global/topics/forced-labour/lang--en/index.htm). While a large proportion of the victims are women, human trafficking involves men and children as well. The Counter Trafficking Data Collaborative (https://www.ctdatacollaborative.org/) estimates that nearly 80 percent of international human trafficking journeys pass through airports and other official border control points.
- **Environmental migration** is displacement caused by natural disasters, such as earthquakes, hurricanes, or droughts. It can be permanent or temporary and is a rapidly growing area of migration due to global climate change. In 2018, 17.2 million people were displaced due to environmental conditions; by 2019, the number had risen to 24.9 million (https://www.internal-displacement.org/global-report/grid2019/).

Anthropologists who study migration are often involved in multi-sited ethnographic research, exploring not only migrant populations but their communities of origin as well. Understanding the social and cultural attributes of communities of origin helps researchers gauge the level and types of adaptation caused by migration. Also, communities of origin typically remain part of migrants' wider social networks and are vital to their well-being and success. It is not uncommon for relatives and other members of the migrants' home communities to follow them to their new settlements and reestablish a sense of community and a set of self-help networks there. This process of serial migration from the same community of origin is known as **chain migration**.

Labor Migration and Migrant Routes

While migration, in its widest sense, is any movement that reestablishes a household, many migratory patterns are specifically associated with socioeconomic need, mainly shifting employment opportunities. Labor migration can be permanent or circular. **Circular migration** is a repeated pattern of movement between locations, usually mapped to the availability of work. One type of circular migration is seasonal migration, which is migratory movement that coincides with seasonal labor needs, such as planting, harvesting, service, and construction work. Some seasonal workers migrate, with or without their families, for temporary, often low-paid work. Other seasonal workers have long-term relationships with their employers and legal work permits (also called Employment Authorization Documents, or EADs, in the United States) and will return to the same work sites year after year, sometimes maintaining a joint household with other families at the work site. These individuals will often maintain a family household in their country of origin and send home **remittances**, or transfers of money from workers to their home countries, usually for their families. Today, one in nine people worldwide depends on remittances from migrants (Global Migration Data Analysis Centre

2021).

Many people migrate in search of work and a better life without legal permits or assurance of employment. The migration journey made in search of opportunities can be filled with dangers, hardships, and even death. Some regions of the world have well-established migrant trails, which are the routes of most worldwide migration. The most congested migration routes are:

- the eastern Mediterranean route, with a flow of migrants from the Middle East and North Africa to Europe, crossing through Turkey;
- the Mediterranean Sea route, with migration from the Middle East and North Africa to Europe, across the Mediterranean Sea;
- the Southeast Asian route, with migrants primarily moving southward from the Asian mainland into Indonesia and Malaysia; and
- the Central American route, which brings migrants from South and Central America into North America.

These migrant trails have a huge impact on the social, political, and economic life of all of the countries that are a part of the route, bringing both benefits and challenges. Those in the United States are most familiar with the Central American route, which begins as far south as South America and extends as far north as Canada. The most contested part of the "trail," however, is the portion along the Rio Grande, the river that separates Mexico and the United States.

In his remarkable four-field study of undocumented migrants entering the United States across the border with Mexico, *The Land of Open Graves* (2015), Chicano anthropologist Jason De León reveals a less visible side of undocumented migration. He describes a type of cat-and-mouse game between migrants and those attempting to stop them, resulting in widespread suffering and high human and financial costs. De León conducted a multi-sited ethnography, doing research in various locations in both Mexico and the United States and consulting various groups along the migration route, including illegal migrants and border patrol agents as well as smuggling groups and drug traffickers.

PROFILES IN ANTHROPOLOGY

Jason De León
1977-

FIGURE 10.9 Anthropologist Dr. Jason De León (credit: Michael Wells, Undocumented Migration Project)

Personal History: Jason De León is a U.S. anthropologist and Mexican-Filipino American who grew up in several cities in the United States, including McAllen, Texas, near the U.S.-Mexico border; and Long Beach, California, where he graduated from Wilson High School. He earned his bachelor's degree in anthropology from the University of California, Los Angeles and his master's and doctoral degrees from Pennsylvania State University. His doctoral work focused on ancient tool production and trade in the Valley of Mexico.

Area of Anthropology: Although De León's training includes a specialization in archaeology, his holistic research approach is four-field, combining archaeology with ethnographic research, physical anthropology analyses, and linguistic anthropology. His work is multi-disciplinary in nature and multi-sited, involving not just Mexico and the United States but also numerous other countries of migrant origin. His interests include undocumented migration, photo-ethnography, and human smuggling. He seeks out the stories not only of people, such as migrants and their families, smugglers, and border guards, but also of their material artifacts—the items they bring, wear, and use to survive their dangerous journeys.

Accomplishments in the Field: De León is the executive director of the Undocumented Migration Project (UMP), a nonprofit organization founded in 2009 that focuses on the long-term anthropological study of clandestine movements between Latin America and the United States. UMP sponsors an educational exhibit called *Hostile Terrain 94* (HT94), a pop-up participatory art project that displays the handwritten toe tags of some 3,200 migrants who have died while trying to cross the Sonoran Desert in the southwestern United States since the mid-1990s, showing the locations where each of the individuals died along their journey. It is a poignant reminder of the many dangers of migration, both human and environmental.

De León received the prestigious five-year MacArthur Foundation Fellowship (2017–2022) for his work on undocumented migrants. This award, given for talent, creativity, contribution to one's field, and potential, allows scholars to focus on future research in an area of great importance. In addition, De León's 2015 book, *The Land of the Open Graves: Living and Dying on the Migrant Trail*, has received various awards and commendations.

FIGURE 10.10 Art on the Mexican side of the wall that divides the city of Heroica Nogales in Mexico from the United States. (credit: "Wall Art in Nogales" by Jonathan McIntosh/flickr, CC BY 2.0)

Importance of Their Work: Anthropologists often work in specific places and more geographically bounded settings. The research of Jason De León expands our understanding of the lives of those who migrate and the various ways that movement ties together people, places, and cultures.

In his article "On Not Looking Away," digital and multimedia advisor Arran Skinner (2019) reports on the tragic deaths of Mexican migrants Óscar Martínez Ramírez and Angie Valeria, his 23-month-old daughter, both of whom drowned and washed up on the shores of the Rio Grande. "We are choosing to ignore this evidence [of atrocity], to actively look away," Skinner writes. But De León is not looking away. Through his research, he is bringing to light the stories of those who migrate in search of hope and better lives. As global movements become more common because of political, economic, and environmental challenges, studies such as De León's illustrate the growing importance of migration for our species.

Since 1994, the US Border Patrol has had a policy of "prevention through deterrence" that attempts to prevent undocumented migrants from reaching the U.S. border. Legal international entryways in cities such as Tucson, Arizona, and El Paso, Texas, were heavily fortified with fencing and additional patrol agents to make undocumented crossing exceptionally difficult. As a result, migrant entry points shifted away from urban areas and into more hostile terrain, such as the Sonoran Desert region of Arizona. While this has not significantly lowered the frequency of these crossings, it has made the journey much more dangerous and far less visible to residential populations and humanitarian groups. In addition to the threat of harsh and rugged landscapes, there are the dangers of extreme weather, dehydration, bandits, and even wild animals. De León concludes, "The Border Patrol has intentionally set the stage so that other actants [agents of deterrence] can do most of the brutal work" (61).

During his study, De León and his team located the body of Maricela Zhagüi Puyas, a woman originally from Cuenca, Ecuador. She had left her family, including her children, in Ecuador in order to seek employment in the United States, hoping to send money home to them. She was in debt for more than $10,000, most of it to the trail guide (called a *coyote*) who was supposed to guide her on her journey. Such trail guides often extort large sums of money from vulnerable migrants and then leave them to make their way alone. Maricela had made a journey of more than 5,000 miles from Cuenca, Ecuador, all the way to the Sonoran Desert in Arizona, when she died of exhaustion and exposure, technically having reached the United States. In the 14-year period between 2000 and 2014, 2,721 migrants were found dead in Arizona's Sonoran Desert, approximately 800 of whom remain unidentified today. In 2020, there were an estimated 227 migrant deaths in the Sonoran graveyard, making it the deadliest year on record for that corridor trail (Snow 2021). De León's work continues today through a series of pop-up exhibitions and workshops entitled *Hostile Terrain 94*.

FIGURE 10.11 Migrant routes: (left) the U.S.-Mexico border wall at Nogales, Arizona, in February 2019; and (right) an immigrant camp of asylum seekers in Matamoros, Mexico, near Brownsville, Texas, in January 2020. (credit: (left) "Nogales Border Wall and Concertina Wire" by US Customs and Border Protection/Wikimedia Commons, Public Domain; (right) "Congressional Hispanic Caucus Visit to Matamoros, Mexico 05" by Jimmy Panetta/Wikimedia Commons, Public Domain)

This humanitarian crisis is far from being resolved. In 2020, 400,651 undocumented migrants were apprehended and expelled by the U.S. Border Patrol (U.S. Customs and Border Protection 2020). Immigrants, both documented and undocumented, make up a majority of the farmworkers and meatpacking workforce in the United States today. Once employed, these immigrants, who are frequently separated from their families, face hazardous working conditions, language barriers, long hours, low pay, and substandard housing. Because of their legal status, many also struggle with inadequate access to health care and rising discrimination.

Biocultural anthropologist Shedra Snipes and her team (Snipes et al. 2007) conducted focus group interviews among 69 male and female Mexican immigrant farmworkers in the Yakima Valley of Washington State. They were particularly interested in the ways the farmworkers defined and experienced stress. Their interviewees distinguished between physical and mental stressors and cited the most common causes of stress as work, personal illness, lack of work, family illness, and family stress. Snipes et al. noted that many stressors were linked by a common theme of inconsistent work and the *injusticia* (injustice and unfairness) of low pay and poor working conditions. One farmworker noted, "Sometimes there are many people wanting to work in the field. You complain about something like not having water, or the bathrooms being dirty, [and] they tell you right away, 'If you don't like it go find a job somewhere else'" (366). Another common theme was the stress of living in a different culture. Several farmworkers commented that cultural differences, such as language barriers, communication from schools regarding their children, or complaints from neighbors when they had rowdy family get-togethers, contributed to their experience of stress. As this example shows, at the intersection of culture and migration, many factors affect an individual's ability to adapt to new living conditions.

Refugees Beyond the Nation-State

Refugees are persons who are forced to cross international boundaries to seek residence. Pushed out of their countries, most commonly because of war, famine, or persecution, they typically arrive under extreme circumstances with little food, clothing, or material possessions. They are frequently separated from their relatives and have little chance of finding employment or reestablishing their household. Because of their status as stateless persons (persons forced to leave their countries) and their inability to procure proper travel documentation, refugees are protected under the 1951 United Nations Refugee Convention, which derives from Article 14 of the Universal Declaration of Human Rights, passed in1948. The Universal Declaration of Human Rights establishes an international legal right for people to seek **asylum**, which is legal protection extended by one country to citizens of another. The United Nations High Commissioner for Refugees heads the UN Refugee Agency, a global organization that directs troops and aid workers to set up refugee camps and organizes international efforts to ease the suffering of refugees.

FIGURE 10.12 (left) An aerial view of the Za'atari refugee camp in Jordan, a camp settlement for Syrian refugees, in 2013; (right) a Syrian refugee family waiting for asylum. (credit: (left) "An Aerial View of the Za'atri Refugee Camp" by US Department of State/Wikimedia Commons, Public Domain; (right) "Idlib Bekaa Refugees" by Russell Watkins/ Department for International Development/Wikimedia Commons, CC BY 2.0)

In her ethnographic study of Congolese refugees in the Ugandan capital city of Kampala, cultural anthropologist Georgina Ramsay (2016) focuses on the ways in which refugees protect themselves, both physically and psychologically, by what they call "avoiding poison." In 2012, there were approximately 50,000 refugees living in Kampala as a result of ongoing political instability, warfare, and corruption in the Democratic Republic of the Congo. Housed initially in a refugee settlement away from urban areas, the group of refugees interviewed by Ramsay opted to move to Kampala for greater opportunities and more security, as the refugee settlements were troubled by crime and violence. As one informant told Ramsay, "There are bad people everywhere in the camp" (115). The government of the Democratic Republic of the Congo allowed resettlement in Kampala if the refugees procured a legal permit and a way to make a living independent of government funding or humanitarian aid. Given their displacement from their own ethnic communities and social networks, refugees faced unreliable social communities, in which their relationships were recently formed, as well as fear and the looming threat of having to return to the settlements if they lost their jobs or housing arrangements. Many either relied on or supplemented their wages with remittances from relatives living elsewhere in an effort to create greater security in the urban environment.

The "poison" feared by this group of refugees is a symbolic agent administered by "unknown assailants" (113), most often sprinkled into the food they prepare, and capable of making them sick both physically and psychologically. The administering of this poison is not always intended as a personal attack; rather, the refugees believe that their day-to-day life outside of their cultural homelands makes them vulnerable. They believe that they are most vulnerable during cooking and eating. In their home communities, cooking and eating were normally times of social interaction and sharing, but cooking and eating are now highly privatized acts for them. Families eat only with each other, within their own homes, and do not accept any shared food, even when they are hungry. The result is an intentional physical distancing from each other and a strengthening of family-only social bonds. While this approach clearly weakens the refugees' ability to build a large and sustainable self-help community in Kampala, it does afford them a sense of positive control (agency) over their day-to-day lives. This sense of social agency over the threat of "poison," giving the refugees an ability to control some aspects of their day-to-day lives, is an example of the adaptive nature of culture under very challenging circumstances.

Pandemic as a Global Migration

People and goods are not the only things that migrate. Along with human migration, there is a host of secondary movements that can affect the human population globally. Diseases are a prime example. Diseases that may have once been contained in a single region can move, along with their human and animal hosts, into new geographic areas, where they can become even more virulent. When diseases spread more than expected among a given group of people, they are referred to as **epidemics**. An outbreak of a disease over a very broad area, typically crossing international boundaries, is called a **pandemic**. Some early pandemics in Europe were the plague of Athens in 430 BCE (possibly typhus or typhoid fever or Ebola), the Antonine plague from 165 to 180 CE (possibly smallpox), and the Black Death from 1347 to 1351 (caused by a bacterium carried by fleas and infected rodents). In the Americas, Mexico and Central America suffered from various documented pandemics, starting with the arrival of the Spanish in Mexico in 1519, which set off a widespread smallpox outbreak that extended into South America. There have been other pandemics, including the cocoliztli epidemic from 1545 to 1548, likely a form of enteric fever, and the so-called Spanish flu, first detected in the United States in 1918 (Alchon 2003; Vågene et al. 2018). The most serious recent pandemic in the United Stated had been the swine flu pandemic of 2009–2010 ... until 2019–2020.

In the last few months of 2019, the viral coronavirus SARS-CoV-2, known as COVID-19, began a global migration from Wuhan, Hubei Province, China, to every continent of the world. Carried between geographically distant locations by human hosts traveling for all sorts of reasons—including work, study, tourism, visitation, and displacement—as well as within towns and communities by people shopping, attending religious services and schools, or even visiting friends and families, COVID-19 quickly became a global emergency. First reported to the World Health Organization (WHO) on December 31, 2019, COVID-19 was officially declared a global pandemic on March 11, 2020. Throughout 2020, the disease continued to spread rapidly, overwhelming medical facilities, ravaging countries' economies, and forcing people to alter the structures of most social institutions, including schools, churches, weddings, and even funerals. By October 2021, some 248 million people had been infected, including several world leaders, and more than 5 million people had died from the disease.

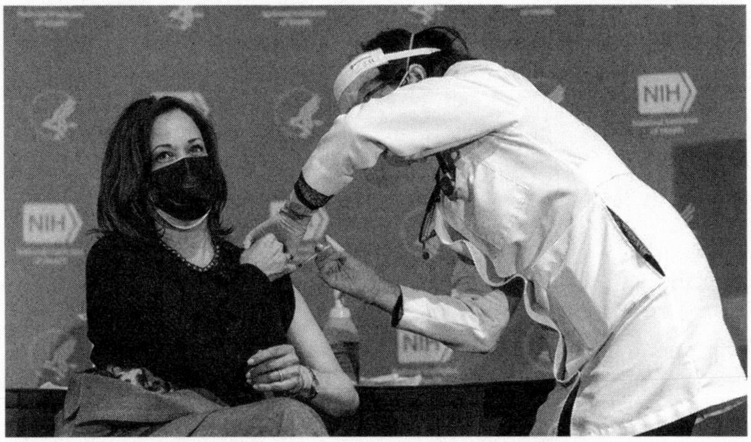

FIGURE 10.13 United States vice president Kamala Harris receives a COVID-19 vaccine in January 2021. (credit: "Kamala Harris Getting Her Second COVID-19 Vaccination" by Lawrence Jackson/Wikimedia Commons, Public Domain)

The COVID-19 virus spreads through airborne transmission when someone inhales droplets expelled by an infected person coughing, sneezing, or even exhaling. As with measles and tuberculosis, the only fully effective form of containment outside of a vaccine and the development of antibodies is quarantine. When the WHO declared COVID-19 a global pandemic, the most important advice was to limit all unnecessary movements and gatherings, wear masks, and practice physical distancing. But given the global nature of our lives today, it was very difficult to halt either the movement of people or the spread of the disease. On January 20, 2020, the first reported case in the United States was diagnosed in Washington State, in a man in his thirties who had just returned from Wuhan. By that point, the virus had already spread to Taiwan, Japan, Thailand, and South Korea. On January 24, the first European cases were reported in France. The disease continued to quickly spread all over the world, including on international transport, such as cruise and cargo ships. In December 2020, there were several cases reported in Antarctica. Only 14 countries reported no COVID-19 cases as of April 2021, all except two of them island nations or territories in the Pacific and Atlantic Oceans with strict travel policies: Tuvalu, Tonga, Tokelau, St. Helena, the Pitcairn Islands, Palau, Niue, Nauru, Kiribati, the Federated States of Micronesia, the Cook Islands, and American Samoa. (The two non-island nations, North Korea and Turkmenistan, are believed to have unreliable data.) As a result of migration, the disease transformed peoples' lives everywhere.

But migration can also bring relief from pandemics. The same conveyances that led to the initial spread of the disease have also brought relief workers, food, medical supplies, and life-saving vaccines to communities worldwide. In addition, scientists and researchers worked tirelessly in multinational efforts to sequence the

COVID-19 genome so that vaccine development could proceed rapidly. Globally, several countries developed lifesaving vaccines and began working together to disperse them to communities in need. As our world becomes increasingly interdependent, it is critical that we understand the important role of migration in so many aspects of our survival.

ETHNOGRAPHIC SKETCHES

Migration in El Angosto

Experience of Marjorie Snipes, chapter author

We often think of rural communities as being separate from global forces, but this is not always true. In El Angosto, a small Indigenous community in the northwestern Andes of Argentina, diverse forms of migration, dependent on internal and external factors, are part of people's day-to-day lives.

I conducted fieldwork in El Angosto, Argentina, during the 1990s and early 2000s (Snipes 1996). This small highland community is located at about 11,000 feet above sea level and nestled in a rugged river valley along the Río Grande de San Juan, the international boundary between Argentina and Bolivia. At that time, the community had a population of about 200 people, most practicing agropastoralism, with each family raising corn, wheat, alfalfa, and broad beans and tending herds of goats and sheep. In order to provide ample pastureland and keep animals away from their gardens, they were transhumant, moving their herds to higher altitudes during the spring and summer seasons, away from the primary households with their gardens and accompanied by seasonal shepherds. After the herds moved from their winter corrals, families cleaned them out and used the manure to fertilize the gardens. Through transhumance, families benefit from this dual subsistence system, producing most of their daily food needs.

Although not dependent on money for their daily food, Angosteños participate in the global economy in various ways. Historically, the community is part of a vast Andean trade network that connects small highland communities of northern Argentina and southern Bolivia through itinerant trade. Extensive long-distance trade networks have been an integral part of Andean life for centuries (see Alberti and Mayer 1974; Murra 1975). Annually, traders come through El Angosto from the *altiplano* of Bolivia, a high plains region at an average altitude of 12,000 feet above sea level. Because of the harsh climate at that altitude, the Bolivian communities rely almost exclusively on herding camelids (llamas and alpacas), having little to no ability to raise needed crops. In the springtime each year, Bolivian traders pass through El Angosto with pack animals (usually llamas) loaded with wool ropes, bags, and dried camelid meat that they produce during the winter months, seeking fresh vegetables for trade.

Although traders negotiate each transaction based on their particular family's needs, all parties are well aware of the current market value of their animal and vegetable products, as families listen daily to radio broadcasts on trade. I tried my hand at negotiating with Gumercindo, a young trader from San Antonio de Lipes, Bolivia, for a small, handwoven rope. When I asked him the cost of the rope, he looked at me with kind amusement and asked me what I offered to exchange. "Pesos!" I said (Bolivian money). He told me the rope was worth 10 pesos (approximately $10 at that time) but that he needed corn and wheat and that one *arroba* (approximately 25 pounds) of grain was worth around $12. In other words, I would have to pay the higher cost because he would need to take the money and try to buy an *arroba* of grain. Most highlanders are more aware of current trade values than even those living in cities.

Other forms of migration affect life in El Angosto. In order to earn cash for manufactured items, many highland families periodically send a family member to work away from the community. The *zafra*, the annual lowland sugarcane harvest, can usually temporarily absorb anyone willing to work, and young people occasionally seek out urban employment opportunities, such as domestic service in private households. Migration is an enduring part of the fabric of Andean life, binding communities to each other and, ultimately, to each of us.

MINI-FIELDWORK ACTIVITY

Migration Interviews

For this fieldwork activity, you will compile three ethnographic accounts of migration. Choose three diverse research participants/key informants to interview about their personal histories of moving, as a child and/or an adult, from one home location to another. Some may have moved from one country to another, from one city to another, or even from one house or family to another. Log each of their movements separately, giving the years and duration of the period spent living there, why they moved, how things shifted in their lives as a result of the migration, and their feelings and/or emotions about moving. You may choose to add your own account to this study as well. Once you compile each of the accounts, summarize your findings and compare the accounts to each other, making conclusions about the impact of migration on your participants' lives.

Key Terms

asylum legal protection extended by one country to citizens of another.

chain migration the process of sequential migration from the same community of origin.

circular migration repeated pattern of movement between locations, usually associated with work.

cultural hybridity the exchange and innovation within cultures that is a product of migration and globalization.

diaspora the movement and dispersal of large ethnic groups from their homelands because of warfare, institutionalized violence, or opportunity (usually education or employment).

displacement migration due to persecution, conflict, or violence; involves refugees and those seeking asylum.

environmental migration displacement caused by natural disasters, such as earthquakes, hurricanes, or droughts.

epidemic a disease that spreads more than expected among a given group of people.

forced labor the recruitment, transportation, transfer, and/or harboring of persons by means of threat or use of force or coercion for the purpose of financial exploitation.

forced migration migration due to persecution, conflict, or violence; involves refugees and those seeking asylum.

human trafficking the recruitment, transportation, transfer, and/or harboring of persons by means of threat or use of force or coercion for the purpose of exploitation. A form of modern slavery.

immigrant an individual who moves permanently from one country to another.

internal migration the domestic movement of people from rural to urban areas.

labor migration the movement of people for the purpose of employment and/or economic stability.

migrant a person who moves from their place of origin to reestablish a household.

migration movement from one place to another that reestablishes a household, whether temporarily or permanently.

modern slavery the recruitment, transportation, transfer, and/or harboring of persons by means of threat or use of force or coercion for the purpose of exploitation.

pandemic an outbreak of a disease over a broad area.

peasants a rural, subsistence-based agricultural class with limited landholdings.

postcolonialism enduring politico-economic relationships between former colonizers and their former colonies that continue to have negative effects on the former colonies after independence.

remittances transfers of money from workers back to their home countries, usually for their families.

transnationalism the construction of social, economic, and political networks that originate in one country and then cross or transcend nation-state boundaries.

Summary

Migration is an important characteristic of human behavior. People migrate for all sorts of reasons, moving from place to place in search of economic opportunities, refuge from political or social oppression, educational opportunities, health resources, fulfillment of family needs, or simply the pleasure of travel itself. From our earliest ancestral beginnings, humans have moved from place to place, sometimes on a seasonal basis and sometimes permanently.

The earliest hominins migrated within and out of Africa, settling parts of Europe, Asia, and eventually Australia, adapting to their new environments and diversifying biologically as a species. The last major continental settlement was North and South America. Archaeological evidence shows early human occupations in the Americas as early as 20,000 years before present. These humans may have arrived by several possible routes, including across the Bering land bridge and along the Pacific coastline of North and South America.

Historically, global forces have also contributed to migration, including seafaring explorations, colonialism, and the transatlantic slave trade that led to a diaspora (dispersal) of millions of African peoples into the Western Hemisphere. Today, many of these historical forces continue to impact our lives as migrants seek opportunities and better, safer lives. Finance, media, and ideologies increasingly entangle the global world today.

Anthropological research has shown the reach of globalization into small communities where peasants and Indigenous peoples, once mistakenly thought to be simple rural farmers or subsistence producers, negotiate the market value of their labor and products, sometimes against large countries or corporations and often facing unfairness and injustice. This disparity typically leads to internal migration from rural areas into urban zones. As with any form of migration, culture change and adaptation have always been a part of the migrant experience.

Because of emerging global forces of all kinds, there has been a rise in voluntary and involuntary migration within geographical regions and across countries, leading to inequality along the margins. Contemporary migrations include labor migration, forced migration or displacement, forced labor, human trafficking or modern slavery, and environmental migration, typically caused by global climate change. There are numerous well-trod migrant routes worldwide connecting countries in both formal and informal ways. One of the most violent routes is the Central American route, which connects South America, Central America, and Mexico to the United States. Refugees are among those in greatest need of humanitarian aid today.

People and goods are not the only things that migrate. Along with human migration, there are secondary movements that can affect the human population globally. Diseases move along with people. Historically, there have been many epidemics within populations and pandemics across regions and countries. In 2019, COVID-19 began migrating globally, eventually affecting every country and causing deaths, chronic illnesses, and economic devastation. As our world becomes increasingly interdependent, it is critical that we understand the important role of migration in so many aspects of our survival.

Critical Thinking Questions

1. What is the role of migration in human evolution?
2. What do the theories about the peopling of the Americas reveal about early human migration?
3. Why is there so much debate about the peopling of the Americas?
4. Using Arjun Appadurai's concept of -scapes, explain the ways in which global movements connect local populations.
5. How did colonialism function as a global movement?
6. What examples of evidence of postcolonial identities are in your communities?
7. What is forced migration, and what impacts might it have on a cultural group?
8. In what ways do peasants contribute to the global economy, and how might it affect them?
9. Refugees are a unique kind of migrant. Describe the ways in which refugees participate in migration.
10. How did global migration contribute to the spread of COVID-19?

Bibliography

Alberti, Giorgio, and Enrique Mayer, eds. 1974. *Reciprocidad e intercambio en los Andes peruanos*. Lima: Instituto de Estudios Peruanos.

Alchon, Suzanne Austin. 2003. *A Pest in the Land: New World Epidemics in a Global Perspective*. Albuquerque: University of New Mexico Press.

Algaze, Guillermo. 2005. *The Uruk World System: The Dynamics of Expansion of Early Mesopotamian Civilization*. 2nd ed. Chicago: University of Chicago Press.

Algaze, Guillermo. 2013. "The End of Prehistory and the Uruk Period." In *The Sumerian World*, edited by Harriet Crawford, 68–94. New York: Routledge.

Appadurai, Arjun. 1990. "Disjuncture and Difference in the Global Cultural Economy." *Theory, Culture, and Society* 7 (2–3): 295–310.

Balachandran, Manu. 2016. "Which Country Has the Largest Diaspora?" World Economic Forum. January 15, 2016. https://www.weforum.org/agenda/2016/01/which-country-has-the-largest-diaspora/.

Blaxland, Beth, and Fran Dorey. 2020. "The First Migrations out of Africa." Australian Museum. April 3, 2020. https://australian.museum/learn/science/human-evolution/the-first-migrations-out-of-africa/.

Buzalka, Juraj. 2008. “Europeanisation and Post-Peasant Populism in Eastern Europe.” *Europe-Asia Studies* 60 (5): 757–771.

Carballo, David M. 2020. *Collision of Worlds: A Deep History of the Fall of Aztec Mexico and the Forging of New Spain.* New York: Oxford University Press.

Chappell, Bill. 2019. “A Father and Daughter Who Drowned at the Border Put Attention on Immigration.” NPR. June 26, 2019. https://www.npr.org/2019/06/26/736177694/a-father-and-daughter-drowned-at-the-border-put-attention-on-immigration.

Child Trends. 2018. “Immigrant Children.” December 28, 2018. https://www.childtrends.org/indicators/immigrant-children.

Conant, Eve, and Matthew W. Chwastyk. 2015. “The World’s Congested Human Migration Routes in 5 Maps.” *National Geographic*, September 19, 2015. https://www.nationalgeographic.com/news/2015/09/150919-data-points-refugees-migrants-maps-human-migrations-syria-world/.

De León, Jason. 2015. *The Land of Open Graves: Living and Dying on the Migrant Trail.* Oakland: University of California Press.

Echavarri, Fernanda. 2020. “2020 Was the Deadliest Year on Record for Migrants Crossing the Arizona Desert.” *Mother Jones*, December 22, 2020. https://www.motherjones.com/politics/2020/12/record-deaths-migrants-arizona-.desert/.

Erlandson, Jon M., Michael H. Graham, Bruce J. Bourque, Debra Corbett, James A. Estes, and Robert S. Steneck. 2007. “The Kelp Highway Hypothesis: Marine Ecology, the Coastal Migration Theory, and the Peopling of the Americas.” *Journal of Island and Coastal Archaeology* 2 (2): 161–174.

Gandhi, Ajay. 2001. “Indigenous Resistance to New Colonialism.” *Cultural Survival*, September 2001. https://www.culturalsurvival.org/publications/cultural-survival-quarterly/indigenous-resistance-new-colonialism.

Global Migration Data Analysis Centre. 2021. “Migration Data Relevant for the COVID-19 Pandemic.” Migration Data Portal. March 10, 2021. https://migrationdataportal.org/themes/migration-data-relevant-covid-19-pandemic.

Gruhn, Ruth. 2020. “Evidence Grows That Peopling of the Americas Began More Than 20,000 Years Ago.” *Nature*, July 22, 2020. https://www.nature.com/articles/d41586-020-02137-3.

Jarus, Owen. 2020. “20 of the Worst Epidemics and Pandemics in History.” Live Science, March 20, 2020. https://www.livescience.com/worst-epidemics-and-pandemics-in-history.html.

Kearney, Michael. 1995. “The Local and the Global: The Anthropology of Globalization and Transnationalism.” *Annual Review of Anthropology* 24:547–565.

Lehrer, Erica. 2020. “Material Kin: ‘Communities of Implication’ in Post-Colonial, Post-Holocaust Polish Ethnographic Collections.” In *Across Anthropology: Troubling Colonial Legacies, Museums, and the Curatorial*, edited by Margareta von Oswald and Jonas Tinius, 289–322. Leuven, Belgium: Leuven University Press.

Lukose, Ritty A. 2007. “The Difference That Diaspora Makes: Thinking through the Anthropology of Immigrant Education in the United States.” *Anthropology & Education Quarterly* 38 (4): 405–418.

Matsu’ura, Shuji, Megumi Kondo, Tohru Danhara, Shuhei Sakata, Hideki Iwano, Takafumi Hirata, Iwan Kurniawan, Erick Setiyabudi, Yoshihiro Takeshita, Masayuki Hyodo, Ikuko Kitaba, Masafumi Sudo, Yugo Danhara, and Fachroel Aziz. 2020. “Age Control of the First Appearance Datum for Javanese *Homo erectus* in the Sangiran Area.” *Science* 367 (6474): 210–214. https://doi.org/10.1126/science.aau8556.

Meyers, Richard, and Ernest Weston Jr. 2020. “What Rez Dogs Mean to the Lakota.” *Sapiens*, December 2, 2020. https://www.sapiens.org/culture/rez-dogs.

Mondal, Sekh Rahim. 2007. “Globalization and Anthropology.” *Indian Anthropologist* 37 (2): 93–98.

Murra, John V. 1975. *Formaciones económicas y políticas del mundo andino.* Lima: Instituto de Estudios Peruanos.

Ocean Wise. 2017. "Riding the Kelp Highway." November 10, 2017. https://ocean.org/articles/riding-kelp-highway/.

Orlove, Benjamin. 2007. "Editorial: Current Approaches to Hybridity." *Current Anthropology* 48 (5): 631–632.

Ramsay, Georgina. 2016. "Avoiding Poison: Congolese Refugees Seeking Cosmological Continuity in Urban Asylum." *Social Analysis* 60 (3): 112–128.

Ramya, Tame. 2017. "From Hills to Foothills: An Anthropological Perspective on Internal Migration of Tribals in Arunachal Pradesh." *Indian Journal of Research in Anthropology* 3 (1): 21–27.

Redfield, Robert. 1956. *Peasant Society and Culture: An Anthropological Approach to Civilization.* Chicago: University of Chicago Press.

Skinner, Arran. 2019. "On Not Looking Away." *Nation*, July 16, 2019. https://www.thenation.com/article/archive/oscar-alberto-martinez-photograph/.

Snipes, Marjorie M. 1996. "When the Other Speaks: Animals and Place as Social Space in the Argentine Andes." PhD diss., University of Wisconsin–Madison. ProQuest (AAT 9636601).

Snipes, Shedra A., Beti Thompson, Kathleen O'Connor, Ruby Godina, and Genoveva Ibarra. 2007. "Anthropological and Psychological Merge: Design of a Stress Measure for Mexican Farmworkers." *Culture, Medicine, and Psychiatry* 31 (3): 359–388.

Snow, Anita. 2021. "Arizona Border Deaths Hit 10-Year High after Record Heat." AP News. January 6, 2021. https://apnews.com/article/arizona-phoenix-mexico-immigration-tucson-50b462c927f2824e2cb10bc53f3f08af.

Tarlach, Gemma. 2018. "The Peopling of the Americas: Evidence for Multiple Models." *Discover*, August 8, 2018. https://www.discovermagazine.com/planet-earth/the-peopling-of-the-americas-evidence-for-multiple-models.

Taylor, Derrick Bryson. 2021. "A Timeline of the Coronavirus Pandemic." *New York Times*, January 10, 2021. https://www.nytimes.com/article/coronavirus-timeline.html.

US Customs and Border Protection. 2020. "Southwest Border Migration FY 2020." November 19, 2020. https://www.cbp.gov/newsroom/stats/sw-border-migration-fy2020.

UNHCR. 2019. "UNHCR Global Trends: Forced Displacement in 2018." ReliefWeb. June 19, 2019. https://reliefweb.int/report/world/unhcr-global-trends-forced-displacement-2018-0.

UNHCR. 2020. "Global Trends: Forced Displacement in 2019." June 2020. https://www.unhcr.org/flagship-reports/globaltrends/globaltrends2019/.

Vågene, Åshild J., Alexander Herbig, Michael G. Campana, Nelly M. Robles García, Christina Warinner, Susanna Sabin, Maria A. Spyrou, Aida Andrades Valtueña, Daniel Huson, Noreen Tuross, Kirsten I. Bos, and Johannes Krause. 2018. "*Salmonella enterica* Genomes from Victims of a Major Sixteenth-Century Epidemic in Mexico." *Nature Ecology and Evolution* 2 (3): 520–528.

Virtanen, Pirjo Kristiina. 2006. "The Urban Manchinery Youth and Social Capital in Western Amazonian Contemporary Rituals." *Anthropos* 101 (1): 159–167.

Werbner, Pnina. 2001. "The Limits of Cultural Hybridity: On Ritual Monsters, Poetic Licence and Contested Postcolonial Purifications." *Journal of the Royal Anthropological Institute* 7 (1): 133–152.

Wilford, John Noble. 2007. "Ruins in Northern Syria Bear the Scars of a City's Final Battle." *New York Times*, January 16, 2007. https://www.nytimes.com/2007/01/16/science/16batt.html.

Woldeab, Rafael. 2019. "Why Do People Migrate? The 4 Most Common Types of Migration." *PopEd Blog*, Population Education. October 30, 2019. https://populationeducation.org/why-do-people-migrate-the-4-most-common-types-of-migration/.

Wolf, Eric. 1966. *Peasants*. Englewood Cliffs, NJ: Prentice-Hall.

Wooller Matthew J., Émilie Saulnier-Talbot, Ben A. Potter, Soumaya Belmecheri, Nancy Bigelow, Kyungcheol Choy, Les C. Cwynar, Kimberley Davies, Russell W. Graham, Joshua Kurek, Peter Langdon, Andrew Medeiros, Ruth Rawcliffe, Yue Wang, and Williams John W. 2018. “A New Terrestrial Palaeoenvironmental Record from the Bering Land Bridge and Context for Human Dispersal.” *Royal Society Open Science* 5 (6). https://doi.org/10.1098/rsos.180145.

CHAPTER 11
Forming Family through Kinship

Figure 11.1 Anthropologists study kinship to understand the various ways that societies are structured. Here, Ben Schmidt poses with his family in Cordell, Oklahoma. (credit: "Ben Schmidt family, Cordell, Oklahoma" by Mennonite Church USA Archives/flickr, Public Domain)

CHAPTER OUTLINE

INTRODUCTION Whom do you consider part of your family? How many mothers do you have? Could you or would you marry your cousin? Each of these questions asks us to consider how our societies structure kinship. Families reflect the social and cultural contexts in which they are formed. Through the study of kinship within our own and other societies, we better understand such things as the connections that individuals have across generations; how a cultural group manages procreation and childcare; the ways that material assets, power, and influence are inherited; and the choices an individual has for marriage.

11.1 What Is Kinship?

LEARNING OUTCOMES

By the end of this section, you will be able to:

- Identify kinship and explain how it is a sociocultural construction.
- Identify the importance of kinship in anthropology.
- Restate the important early works in the anthropological study of kinship.
- Distinguish between terms of reference and terms of address.

Social scientists commonly refer to social norms and behaviors—for example, as explored in Chapter 1, the ways that individuals are assigned to racial categories and what these categories mean about an individual's place within that society—as **sociocultural constructions**. Such norms and behaviors create categories and rules according to social criteria (not biological truths) and thus vary across cultures. **Kinship** is also a sociocultural construction, one that creates a network of social and biological relationships between individuals. Through kinship systems, humans create meaning by interpreting social and biological relationships. Although kinship, like gender and age, is a universal concept in human societies (meaning that all societies have some means of defining kinship), the specific "rules" about who is related, and how closely, vary widely. Depending on the way kinship is determined, two individuals who would call each other cousins in one cultural group may not even consider themselves to be related in another group.

The common assumptions that kinship is static and created by biological relationships reveal the strength of sociocultural constructs in our lives. It is culture—not biology—that defines for us whom our closest relatives are. Biology relies on genetics, but kinship is determined by culture. One interesting and very familiar example of the sociocultural dimension of kinship is the practice of adoption, through which those who have no necessary genetic relationship to one another are considered both legally and culturally to be family. Biological relatedness is determined at the genetic level. This form of knowledge is detected through specialized DNA testing and typically has little meaning in our day-to-day lives except within legal and economic contexts where paternity or maternity may be in question. Otherwise, across history and cultures, including within our own society today, family are those we live with, rely on, and love. These individuals, whether or not they have a specific genetic relationship to us, are those we refer to using family terms of reference—my mother, my son, my aunt.

The study of kinship is central to anthropology. It provides deep insights into human relationships and alliances, including those who can and cannot marry, mechanisms that are used to create families, and even the ways social and economic resources are dispersed within a group. One of the earliest studies of kinship was completed by Lewis Henry Morgan (1818–1881), an amateur American anthropologist, in the mid-nineteenth century. Intrigued by the cultural diversity of the Haudenosaunee living in upstate New York, Morgan began to document differences in kinship terminology between cultural groups, based on historical accounts and surveys from missionaries working in other geographic locations. In *Systems of Consanguinity and Affinity of the Human Family* (1871), he defined three of the primary kinship systems that we still recognize today, identifying each with either descriptive kinship terms, such as "mother's sister's son," or classificatory terms, which group diverse relationships under a single term, such as "cousin." Although Morgan used different names, today we know these three systems as lineal kinship, bifurcate merging kinship, and generational kinship. The publication of his book marked the beginning of kinship studies in anthropology.

FIGURE 11.2 (left) Lewis Henry Morgan described the diversity of kinship structures and terms across cultures. (right) Bronislaw Malinowski researched the ways that kinship functions as a social institution. (credit: (left) “Lewis Henry Morgan” by Kelson/Rochester Historical Society/Wikimedia Commons, CC-PD-Mark (right) credit: “Bronislaw Malinowski” by Library of the London School of Economics and Political Science/Wikimedia Commons, Public Domain)

After Morgan’s research, anthropologists began a more methodical examination of kinship. W.H.R. Rivers (1864–1922) introduced the *genealogical method* in fieldwork in a 1910 article, “The Genealogical Method in Anthropological Query.” Using a series of basic questions about parents, grandparents, and siblings, Rivers approached the study of kinship as a systematic inquiry into the social structure of societies, seeking to understand how different cultures define family and family roles. Although he focused on small-scale societies, he argued that investigating kinship was a good way of establishing rapport with people and opening them up to sharing more detailed information about their lives regardless of the size of the society. Today, ethnographers continue to use a form of the genealogical method, through either face-to-face interviews or surveys, especially when doing fieldwork in small-scale societies. In this way, the ethnographer seeks to understand the sociocultural relationships in society and the ways that family affects those relationships.

In the 1920s, British anthropologists Bronislaw Malinowski (1884–1942) and A.R. Radcliffe-Brown (1881–1955) expanded the understanding of kinship as a social institution by studying the ways that kinship intersected with other institutions in society, such as inheritance, education, politics, and subsistence. Malinowski did fieldwork in the Trobriand Islands of Papua New Guinea, a matrilineal society where descent and inheritance were traced solely through mothers and grandmothers. In his work *Argonauts of the Western Pacific* (1922), he examined the functional role of kinship in Trobriand society, exploring how it works with other social institutions to address basic needs. Expanding kinship exploration beyond its early beginnings as a study of linguistic terminology only, Malinowski (1930, 19-20) says, “Kinship terminologies . . . are the most active and the most effective expressions of human relationship, expressions which start in early childhood, which accompany human intercourse throughout life, which embody all the most personal, passionate, and intimate sentiments of a man or woman.” He saw kinship as a driving force connecting individuals to each other by means of enduring bonds. A. R. Radcliffe-Brown also focused on kinship as a social institution in his study *The Andaman Islanders* (1922), but instead of looking at the function of kinship, Radcliffe-Brown examined the roles and statuses created for an individual by the practice of kinship.

Through these early studies in kinship, anthropologists began to better understand the diverse ways that cultural groups think about things like family and community. Kinship relationships determine both rights and obligations to other people. These connections contribute to the way a society functions and resolve problems associated with everyday life. In small-scale societies with low population density, kinship identity plays a significant role in most of the life choices an individual will have, while in larger-scale societies, kinship plays a smaller and more limited role. In all societies, however, kinship provides guidelines on how to interact with certain other individuals and the expectations that are associated with these relationships.

Cultures call attention to kinship relationships through the way people speak to and refer to one another. Anthropologists sort this kinship terminology into two categories: **terms of reference** and **terms of address**. Terms of reference are the words that are used to describe the relationship between individuals, such as "mother," "grandfather," or "father's brother." Terms of address are the terms people use to speak directly to their kin, such as "Mom," "Uncle," and "Grandpa." Sometimes the same word is used as reference and address: "This is my father" and "Hello, Father." These terms are important because they designate relationships between individuals that carry responsibilities and privileges that structure human societies.

11.2 Defining Family and Household

LEARNING OUTCOMES

By the end of this section, you will be able to:

- Define and contrast family and household.
- Describe how families differ across cultures.
- Differentiate between consanguineal and affinal ties.
- Distinguish between different family types.
- Understand the roles of fictive kin.

A **family** can be defined as two or more people in an adaptable social and economic alliance that involves kinship, whether perceived through blood, marriage, or other permanent or semipermanent arrangement. It frequently, but not always, involves reproduction and the care of offspring and coresidence within the same locale. Families vary greatly across cultures and also adapt to changing social and economic needs. Sometimes families aggregate into larger units for short periods to meet challenging needs, such as eldercare, illness, job loss, transition between college and career, etc. A **household** is a group of individuals who live within the same residence and share socioeconomic needs associated with production and consumption. A family and a household may be the same unit, but they do not have to be. Sometimes families live within larger households, where there may be two or more families residing; at other times a family may be physically separated as family members migrate to work or study temporarily in other locations.

Like the concept of kinship, family is a sociocultural construct. Family is defined and recognized differently across cultures according to differing social norms. Some cultures consider families to be only those people believed to be related to each other, living together, and sharing similar goals, while other cultures define family as a disperse set of individuals with an ancestral history. The definition of family that a cultural group endorses reflects such things as kinship and the social interpretation of biology, cultural traditions and norms, and socioemotional ties. It is commonly scaled from the intimate unit in which children are raised to a larger, more amorphous web of relatives.

Many Western societies perceive family to be a *nuclear family* of parents and their immediate offspring living together in a household. The extended family, on the other hand, is a loose collection of relatives with varying degrees of perceived kinship, from those referred to as blood relatives (*consanguine*) to those who have married into the family (*affine*). Among the Mundurucú in the lowland Amazonia of Brazil, the resident family includes only the mother and her preadolescent offspring, while the father resides in the tribal men's house. Among the Mosuo of China (also called the Na), women form sexual alliances with men from outside of their families to produce offspring, and then remain with their brothers in their own households to raise their children. The children are considered to be part of the women's lineage unit and family.

FIGURE 11.3 The Mosuo of China do not formally recognize a separate fatherhood role. Mosuo girls (left) and Mosuo boys (right) remain with their mother and her extended family, and fathers have no social or economic obligations for their biological offspring, though they often have significant responsibility for their nieces and nephews. (credit: "P8310032" and "P8310036" by Sherry Zhang/flickr, CC BY 2.0)

Reading and Using Kinship Charts

Anthropologists graphically illustrate relationships between family members with kinship charts (also called kinship diagrams). Anyone who has ever used an online genealogy program like Ancestry.com is already familiar with the ways that family relationships can be depicted. Anthropological charts use **EGO** as their starting point. The term EGO identifies the person whose chart is depicted. EGO marks the starting point for the kinship chart, and relationships are read as alignments between EGO and other individuals. The sum of kinship relationships identified through EGO is referred to as EGO's **kindred**. Serving as a map and model, the kinship chart can be "read" like a text, with its own syntax and grammar identifying each individual within a society by means of their relatedness to each other.

Kinship charts depict two types of relationships, consanguineal and affinal. A **consanguineal tie** between individuals indicates a perceived biological connection (a connection "by blood") and is indicated by a single line, regardless of whether it is drawn vertically or horizontally. A consanguineal tie is most often considered to be permanent. An **affinal tie** depicts a contractual relationship by marriage or mutual agreement and is drawn as a double line. Such ties usually can be broken, and if they are, a forward slash will be struck though the double line. There is also a hashed line (----) used for relationships that do not conform completely to type (e.g., to indicate adoption or an honorary family member). Hashed double lines are used to distinguish between a formal marriage and a relationship of cohabitation. The following is the most basic legend of the kinship chart:

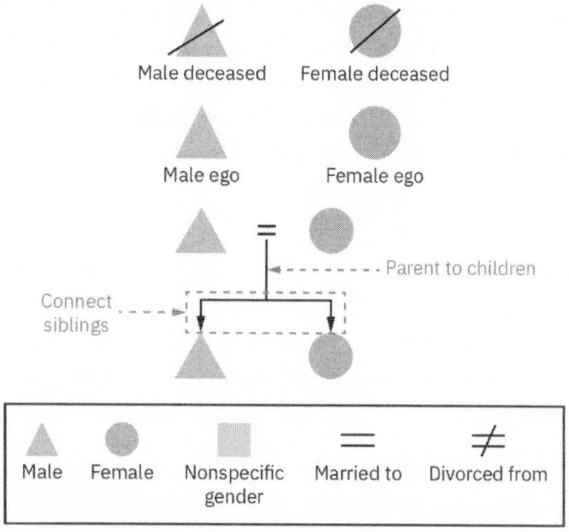

FIGURE 11.4 An anthropological kinship legend. The iconography of kinship denotes such things as gender, relationships of marriage and descent, and individual terms of reference. (attribution: Copyright Rice University, OpenStax, under CC BY 4.0 license)

Kinship charts can be read both vertically and horizontally. Individuals who share the same horizontal line are considered to be in the same cohort or generation, and individuals above and below EGO are in relationships of **descent**, meaning they are believed to be connected by blood or enduring kinship bond across generations. Anthropologists use common abbreviations to depict kinship relations across cultures, allowing us to compare families: father (FA), mother (MO), brother (BR), sister (SI or Z), aunt (AU), uncle (UN), son (SO), daughter (DA), and then compound terms, such as mother's or father's brother (MoBr, FaBr) or mother's or father's sister (MoSi, FaSi). Grandparents are usually designated as GrFa and GrMo.

Figure 11.5 depicts a kinship chart utilizing standard icons and abbreviations. Within this chart, EGO is depicted as a part of two different families: the **family of orientation**, which is the nuclear family unit in which EGO was reared and nurtured as a child and adolescent, and the **family of procreation**, which is the family that EGO creates, usually as a result of marriage. Test yourself and see if you can read it.

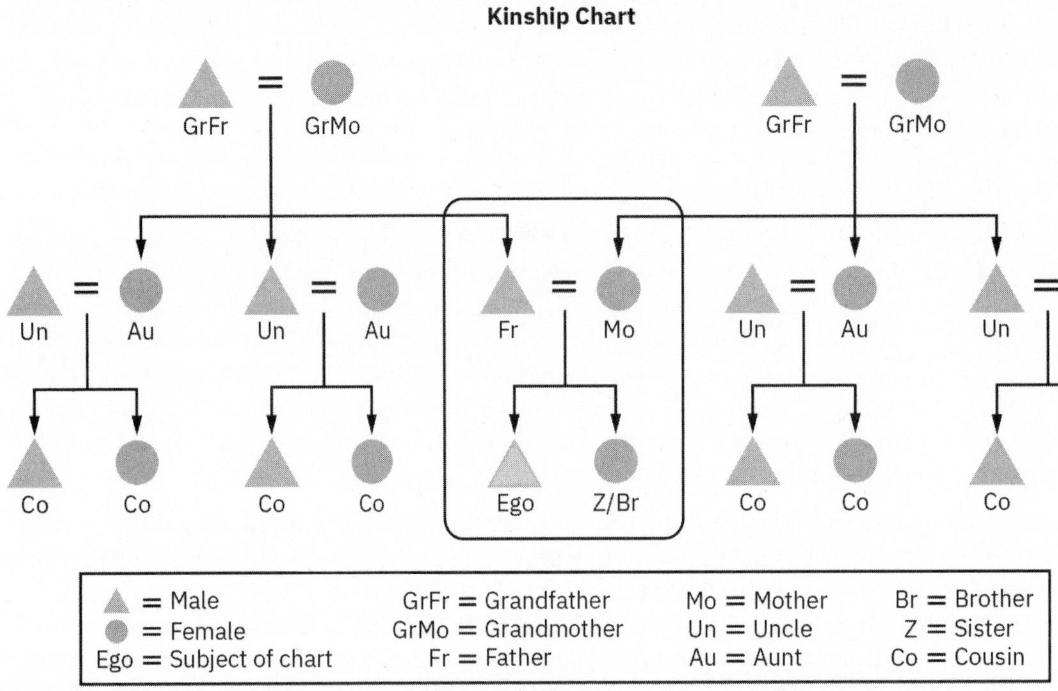

FIGURE 11.5 This generic kinship chart shows three generations, with a family of orientation. (credit: "Eskimo Kinship Chart" by Fred the Oyster/Wikimedia Commons, CC0)

As you can see in Figure 11.5, EGO has multiple ties and embeddedness within the kinship network, leading to a complex web of rights and obligations. These concurrent ties with more than one family involve descent rules (how an individual traces relatedness across generations), residence rules (where an individual will live following marriage), and in some societies, even remarriage rules (how marriage will be reinstated following the death of a spouse). Each of these will be discussed later in the chapter.

Family Types across Cultures

Although family is difficult to categorize because of its diversity, anthropologists have defined four basic family types that are duplicated across cultures with minor variations. Each of these types is adapted to the social and economic needs of the family unit and is normally associated with particular subsistence strategies. Some families change to address immediate needs, such as when elderly parents can no longer live on their own independently. Regardless of its type, the family unit is a remarkably adaptive cultural mechanism.

Nuclear families: Also known as a single-couple family, a **nuclear family** is composed of one or two parents and their immediate offspring. It is the smallest family structure and is often found in societies where geographic mobility is valued. The nuclear family is common in small-scale foraging societies (bands) and industrial/postindustrial and market societies (states), both settings in which subsistence activities require families to relocate with some regularity. Although the model of the American nuclear family consisting of a two-parent household with one or more children has become less typical over the last several generations, it continues to be a norm. As of the 2016 census, 69 percent of US children under the age of 18 were living in a two-parent household, a decrease from 88 percent in 1960.

There are, however, other kinds of nuclear families. In the 2016 US census, 23 percent of children under 18 were living in a female single-headed household (mother), almost triple the number living in female single households in 1960 (8 percent). There was also an increase in children under 18 living in male single households (father), from 1 percent in 1960 to 4 percent in 2016 (United States Census Bureau 2016; Kramer 2019). Another growing nuclear family type is same-sex families. These may or may not include children. In the 2020 census, 14.7 percent of the 1.1 million same-sex couples in the United States had at least one child under 18 in their household (United States Census Bureau 2020 (https://openstax.org/r/censusgovprograms)). In cases where the alliance between adults is temporary or informal, these families may be *nonconjugal nuclear families* or *cohabitation families*. (Note: The above terminology related to sex, gender, and family relationships is consistent with US Census data collection and reporting terminology, and may not reflect the terminology used by readers.)

Extended families: The **extended family** can be very complex. It includes two or more family units functioning as a single integrated family. It may involve three or more generations (e.g., grandparents, parents, and children), polygamous families with multiple spouses and their offspring, or married siblings living together with their children, a type of extended family known as *joint families*. The extended family can be an effective social and economic unit because it involves multiple adults able to contribute to the household. Extended families have been most commonly associated with agricultural societies, where a high value is typically placed on labor and self-subsistence. In the United States today, we commonly see the emergence of the extended family during times of transition, such as when family members are changing jobs, returning to school, or recovering from economic hardship. Worldwide, the extended family is the most common type of family.

FIGURE 11.6 An extended family in Pretoria, South Africa, including several generations. A family functions as a combined socioeconomic unit, where family members cooperate and support each other within the same household. (credit: Henry M. Trotter/Wikimedia Commons, Public Domain)

Blended families: **Blended families** are families in which there is more than one origin point for the members. This typically occurs when one or more divorced and/or widowed adults with children remarry, combining two formerly independent units into a new blended family. Blended families are common in the United States and in societies in which we find serial monogamy. Although the US census does not collect data specifically on stepfamilies, in 2009 Pew Research estimated that 16 percent of all American children lived in blended families.

Fictive Kinship

Some families also include **fictive kin**, a kinship tie in which individuals are defined as family regardless of biology. Fictive kinship is based on intentional relationships such as godparenthood or other close social ties.

One form of voluntary fictional kinship is a type of godparent relationship called **compadrazgo**. Originally developed as a social institution within the Catholic Church, the godparents of a Catholic child are named during the ritual of baptism when the child is an infant. These godparents are selected by the child's parents as role models to encourage their child in religious instruction and living a "godly" life. Godparents are most frequently chosen from among the child's relatives, thus *reinforcing kinship ties*. Although godparenthood is not formally practiced in every society, families in all societies do cultivate non-blood relationships and close friendships.

The Spanish and Portuguese empires introduced godparenthood into Latin America following the 16th-century conquest. The institution was adapted to meet the particular needs of populations suffering from disease, warfare, and mass casualties. These social disruptions often left children without parents who were able to adequately take care of them. In such a setting, children's godparents shifted from being chosen from among relatives to being selected from friends and acquaintances. This use of fictive kin relationships served as an extension of family for a child and *created new kinship ties* between families not previously related. It created a contract (Foster 1961) between the godparents (who referred to the child as *ahijado/a*), the child (who referred to their godparents as *padrino* and *madrina*), and the parents (who, along with the godparents, referred to each other as *compadre* and *comadre*), which provided an ever-widening social network.

FIGURE 11.7 Godparenthood (called compadrazgo in Spanish-speaking societies) is a formal designation and acknowledgement of fictive kin. It is commonly associated with Catholic Church rituals such as baptism. Here, an infant is photographed with baptismal godparents. (credit: "Godparents and Chris" by Brian Smith/flickr, CC BY 2.0)

Over time, the practice of compadrazgo adapted to the specific needs of this new cultural setting. A symmetrical form developed in which parents choose friends and coworkers of their same socioeconomic status to serve as godparents for their children. An asymmetrical form also developed, in which parents contract with individuals or couples who are in a higher class or status group to provide opportunities for their child. This form functions very similarly to a social security system. Many members of the upper classes see it as their Christian duty to sponsor a large number of godchildren within their communities or workplaces.

In addition, compadrazgo extends beyond religious rituals into secular society, including the practice of naming compadres for such things as a child's first haircut or the purchase of a new house. In smaller communities, compadrazgo is even practiced as the ritual sponsorship of community buildings or initiatives. In 1980 in Ica, Peru, the installation of a new water tower included the designation of compadres.

Those serving as compadres enjoy an enhancement of social status in Latin America. Over a lifetime, individuals typically have a series of new and expanding compadrazgo relationships. People gain new compadres through life changes such as marriage, the birth of children, and sometimes even the acquisition of expensive material items. While these relationships may change over time—for example, when a child has become an adult, the birth compadres may no longer send gifts or offer advice—the relationships themselves endure as (fictive) family connections. The respect and acknowledgement of these relationships remains important to all the individuals involved in the compadrazgo family.

Adoption

Adoption of children is widespread across cultures, sometimes constituted legally, but more often through informal structures of support and sponsorship. There were an estimated 1.5 million adopted children under 18 in the United States in 2019, about 1 out of every 50 children, and adoption is increasing, especially among same-sex couples. In 2019, 43.3 percent of children of same-sex couples were adopted or stepchildren.

Across cultures, informal adoption and foster care have long been practiced to strengthen families and provide opportunities for young people. Anthropological studies in West Africa, Oceania, Latin America, and in minority communities in North America document the prevalence of these practices, as well as their benefits and risks. In general, cultures that see social relationships as open and fluid are able to provide a greater range of opportunities to children. One common form of informal adoption relocates children from rural birth families to relatives living in urban areas, where they have more opportunities for education, employment, and career training. Sometimes informal fostering helps to provide caretaking for shorter periods of time. A family may send an older child to temporarily live with a relative or even a friend who has a new infant or is facing a family crisis. These relationships may be mutually beneficial, allowing older children to meet new people and develop a wider network of friends and relatives. Historically, adoptive ties have played a major role in family security and in creating stronger social ties between families, some of which may provide future educational, work, and career opportunities.

11.3 Reckoning Kinship across Cultures

LEARNING OUTCOMES

By the end of this section, you will be able to:

- Describe the importance of kinship in social structure.
- Distinguish between different kinship systems.
- Illustrate three forms of kinship.

By defining relationships between individuals, cultural understandings of kinship create kinship systems or structures within society. This is the institutional aspect of kinship, and it is bigger than the family itself. In smaller societies with lower populations, kinship plays a major role in all social institutions. In larger societies with higher populations, kinship places the local and familiar in opposition to a wider, more amorphous society, where relationships have less and less significance. In effect, kinship frames the way the individual and family are viewed in relation to the larger society and embodies social values.

Types of Kinship Systems

In his early research, Lewis Henry Morgan distinguished three basic forms of kinship structure commonly found across cultures. Today, we refer to these kinship forms as lineal, bifurcate merging, and generational kinship. Each one defines family and relatives a bit differently and so highlights different roles, rights, and responsibilities for these individuals. This means that depending on the kinship structure used by a society, EGO will refer to a different set of individuals as kindred and will have a different relationship with those individuals.

Lineal kinship: **Lineal kinship** (initially referred to as *Eskimo kinship*) is a form of kinship *reckoning* (a way of mapping EGO to other individuals) that highlights the nuclear family. While kindred in a lineal system is traced through both EGO's mother and father (a practice called bilateral descent), the kinship terminology clearly shows that the rights and responsibilities of the nuclear family far exceed those of other kindred. In effect, lineal kinship, associated frequently with North American and European societies, suggests a very small and nominal family with little power and influence across other social institutions.

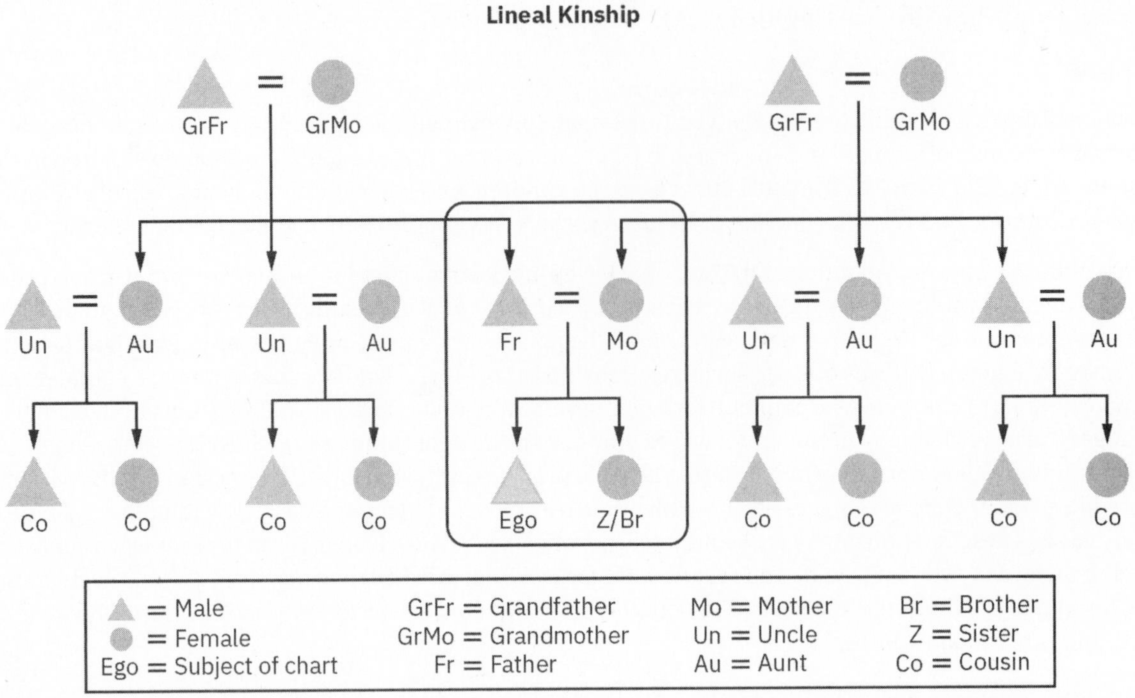

FIGURE 11.8 A lineal kinship diagram. Note the distinction of the nuclear family. (credit: "Eskimo Kinship Chart" by Fred the Oyster/Wikimedia Commons, CC0)

On the lineal diagram (Figure 11.8), note the following: each of the members of the nuclear family have specific kinship terms, but bilateral kin (through both EGO's mother and father) and **collateral kin** (EGO's siblings and their offspring) are lumped together with similar terms. These relationships are not highlighted by individualized terms because there are minimal rights and responsibilities between EGO and kin outside of the nuclear family of orientation and procreation.

Bifurcate merging kinship: **Bifurcate merging kinship** (initially referred to as *Iroquois kinship*) highlights a larger family of orientation for EGO by merging EGO's parents' same-sex siblings and their offspring into the immediate family (creating parallel cousins) and bifurcating, or cutting off, EGO's parents' opposite-sex siblings and their offspring (creating cross cousins). Figure 11.9 depicts bifurcate merging kinship with unilineal descent (either patrilineal or matrilineal). This means that once descent is introduced into the diagram, EGO's relationships, with associated rights and responsibilities, will shift toward either the mother's or father's side. This form of kinship reckoning, quite common to tribal societies, is found extensively, and it creates a distinction between the family of orientation, which is merged together from various lines, and other relatives, who are bifurcated, or cut away.

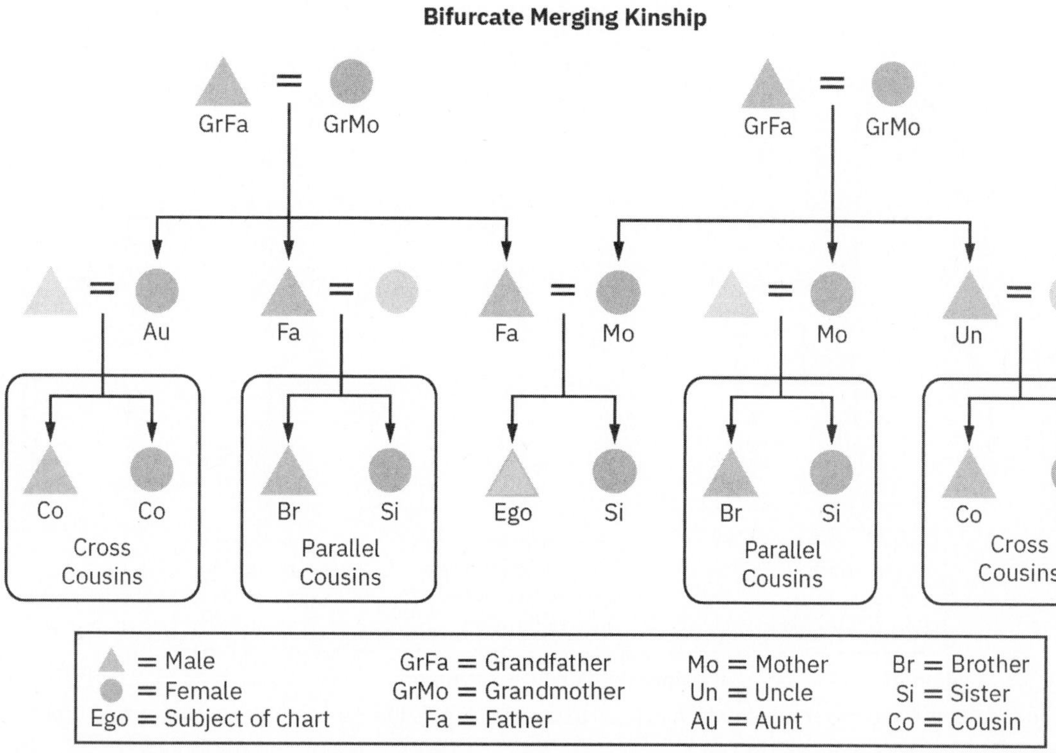

FIGURE 11.9 A bifurcate merging kinship diagram. Note the distinction between parallel and cross cousins. (credit: "Iroquois Kinship Chart" by Fred the Oyster/Wikimedia Commons, CC0)

On the bifurcate merging diagram (Figure 11.9), note that the members of the family of orientation share kinship terms that indicate a close intimacy with EGO. As an example, while EGO knows who his biological mother is (the woman who gave birth to him), his relationship with his biological mother has the same rights and responsibilities as his relationship with his mother's sister(s), etc. Notice also that the category of individuals lumped together as "cousins" under the lineal diagram are here distinguished depending on EGO's relationship with their parent. EGO's mother's sisters are called "mother" and his father's brothers are called "father," which means that any of their offspring would be EGO's brothers or sisters. Notice, though, that the mothers and fathers highlighted outside of EGO's biological parents are married to non-kin members; EGO does not refer to his mother's sister's husband as father—he is referred to as "mother's husband." Mother's brothers and father's sisters produce offspring who are bifurcated and lumped as "cousin." Anthropologists distinguish between **parallel cousins** (EGO's brothers and sisters through his parents' same-sex siblings) and **cross cousins** (EGO's cousins through his parents' opposite-sex siblings). In many tribal societies, EGO would choose his (or her) marriage partner from among his (or her) cross cousins, thereby merging their children back into a primary kinship line. In this way, the family unit (the kindred) maintains a stable and significant presence across generations.

Generational kinship: **Generational kinship** (initially referred to as *Hawaiian kinship*) presents a very different case. Widespread in Polynesia, especially during the times of chiefdom societies, generational kinship provides a distinction in kinship terms only along gender and generational lines. Generational kinship has the least complicated kinship terminology of all kinship systems, but the impact of creating a family of orientation this large and powerful is immediately apparent. In reading this chart, it is obvious that the intimate family was as large as could be configured and it would have significant sociopolitical impact within the society.

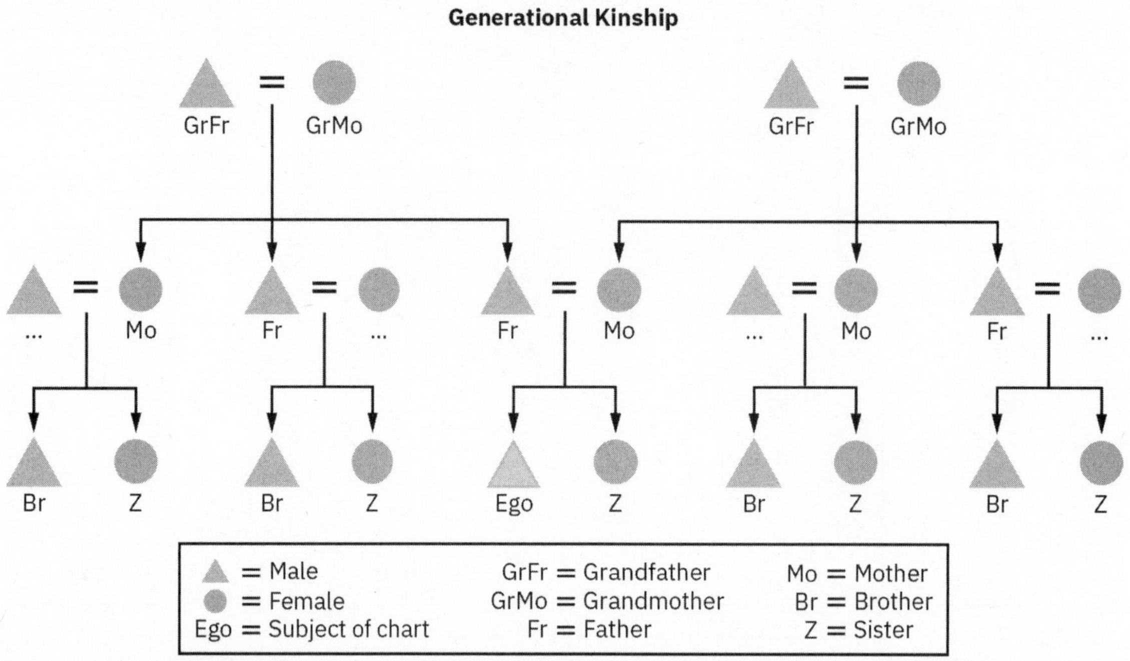

FIGURE 11.10 A generational kinship chart. Note the family of orientation, which is now at its maximal size. This graphically indicates the important role family has in all aspects of EGO's life. (credit: "Hawaiian Kinship Chart" by Fred the Oyster/Wikimedia Commons, CC0)

Descent

Kinship structure is highly diverse, and there are many different ways to think about it. Descent is the way that families trace their kinship connections and social obligations to each other between generations of ancestors and generations to come. It is a primary factor in the delineation of kinship structures. Through descent, the individual highlights certain particular relationships with kindred and drops or leaves off other possible relationships. Descent ultimately determines such things as inheritance, alliance, and marriage rules. There are two common ways that a cultural group can trace descent across generations:

Unilineal descent: **Unilineal descent** traces an individual's kinship through a single gendered line, either male or female, as a collective social rule for all families within a society. The patrilineal or matrilineal relatives that connect to and from EGO form EGO's **lineage**. This lineage is believed to be a continuous line of descent from an original ancestor. Lineages believed to be close in relationship are gathered into **clans**, a tribal social division denoting a group of lineages that have a presumed and symbolic kinship, and eventually into **moieties** (the social division of a tribe into two halves).

- In **patrilineal (or agnatic) descent**, the descent of both males and females is traced solely through male ancestors. Females hold the patrilineal descent of their fathers, and males pass on the descent through their children.

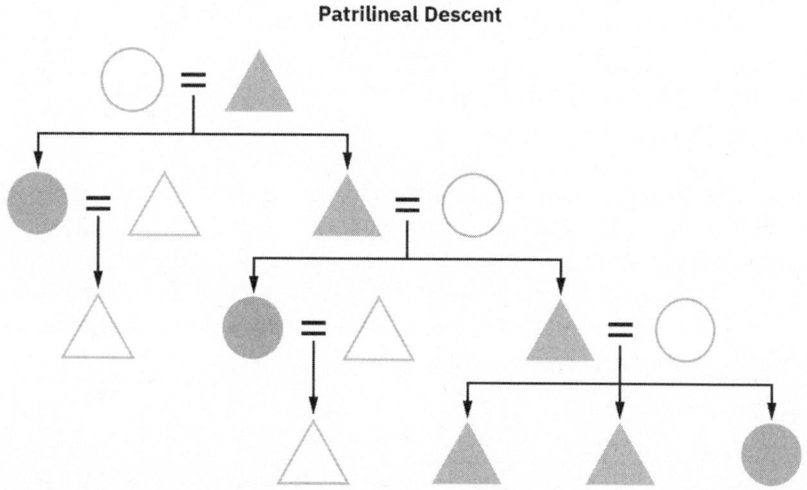

FIGURE 11.11 A chart illustrating patrilineal descent across several generations. Note that all offspring individuals marked in blue are part of their father's descent, but descent only passes through males. (attribution: Copyright Rice University, OpenStax, under CC BY 4.0 license)

In **matrilineal (or uterine) descent**, the descent of both males and females is traced solely through female ancestors. Males hold the matrilineal descent of their mothers, and females pass on the descent through their children.

Cognatic descent: **Cognatic descent** is a kinship structure that follows descent through both men and women, although it may vary by family.

- In **ambilineal descent**, an individual's kinship is traced through a single gendered line, with each family choosing *either* the mother's or the father's descent line; in societies practicing this type of cognatic descent, some families will trace descent through the mother and others through the father. Usually families will choose their descent type at marriage based on the different opportunities presented by either the mother's or father's family, and they will use this for each of their children. While societies practicing ambilineal descent might initially look like those of unilineal descent, they are different. Within these societies, families are diverse and do not follow a single type of descent reckoning.
- In **bilateral descent** (also referred to as bilineal descent), an individual's kinship is traced through *both* mother's and father's lines. This is the most common form of descent practiced in the United States today.

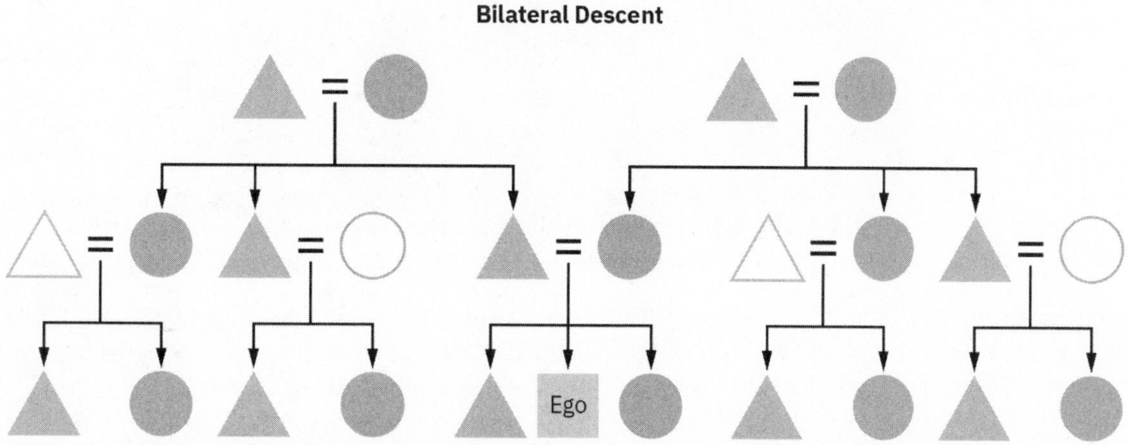

FIGURE 11.12 A chart illustrating bilateral descent across several generations. Note that all offspring trace their lineage through both mother and father. (attribution: Copyright Rice University, OpenStax, under CC BY 4.0 license)

Why does descent matter? It structures the way the family will be formed (who counts most in decision-making). It determines the choices individuals have in forming their own families. And it directs how material and symbolic resources (such as power and influence) will be dispersed across a group of people. As the example in the next section shows, descent affects the whole structure of society.

A Matrilineal Society in the United States

The Navajo are among the most populous of the Indigenous peoples in the United States, exceeding 325,000 members. Roughly half live in the Navajo Nation. Covering some 27,000 square miles, the Navajo Nation is an autonomous jurisdiction that crosses New Mexico, Arizona, and Utah. Traditionally a matrilineal society, the Navajo trace descent and inheritance through their mothers and grandmothers. Such a descent pattern would normally lead to the establishment of matrilocal households, with daughters bringing their husbands to live with or near their matrilineal kin following marriage.

In his study of the contemporary Shonto Navajo, however, William Yewdale Adams (1983), an anthropologist who spent part of his childhood living on the Navajo reservation, found that this wasn't always the case. While matrilocal residence remained the ideal for Navajo families, it was not followed any more frequently than patrilocal residence (living with or near the groom's father). Neolocal residence (a separate, independent household) was also practiced across the Navajo Nation. While the ideal Navajo family type endured as part of their identity, the actual everyday practices of families depended on their particular circumstances and might change over the course of their lives. When job opportunities and economic choices necessitated that families live in different areas, they adapted. When families became large and less manageable as a socioeconomic unit, they might splinter into smaller units, some into nuclear families living alone. However, during major life events, such as marriage and childbirth, it is the matrilineal family that will most support the couple by providing resources and any needed labor and help. Matrilineal descent also elevates the role of women in society, not by excluding men, but by recognizing the vital roles that women play in the establishment of both family and society.

FIGURE 11.13 A contemporary Navajo family (credit: "IMG_1123" by Neeta Lind/flickr, CC BY 2.0)

Traditionally, the Navajo constructed houses (called hogans) of timber or stone frames covered with earth (Haile 1942). There are multiple types of hogans, including a male hogan, which is conically shaped and used for more private rituals, and a female hogan, which is circular and large enough to accommodate the whole family. Although today most Navajo live in Western-style homes with electricity and running water, many families still construct one or more hogans for ritual and ceremony. For families that continue traditional Navajo ceremonies, the most common hogan form today is the female hogan. As Adams aptly argues, the Navajo are very much like other societies in regard to kinship—while it defines an ideal within Navajo society, its primary function is to provide "possibilities and boundaries" around which individuals will construct kinship (1983, 412). It adapts to the changing environment and the needs of family.

PROFILES IN ANTHROPOLOGY

Louise Lamphere
1940-

Personal History: Louise Lamphere (https://openstax.org/r/Louise) is a professor emerita of the University of New Mexico, where she held the honorary post of Distinguished Professor of Anthropology. Her scholarly career in anthropology began with bachelor's and master's degrees from Stanford University and a PhD in anthropology from Harvard University.

Area of Anthropology: Lamphere's research in cultural anthropology extends over many areas of the discipline, including gender and feminist anthropology, kinship, social inequality, and medical practices and reform in the United States and across cultures. She has worked extensively with indigenous peoples, including the Navajo, and in urban contexts. She seeks to understand the intersections between sociocultural institutions and individuals. A recent focus is social and economic changes emerging from the deindustrialization of nation-states. Her work has had wide-ranging impact on generations of anthropology students and scholars.

Accomplishments in the Field: Lamphere's research contributions are extensive (and continue). She served as the president of the American Anthropological Association from 1999 to 2001, leading the organization toward public support of policies focused on current themes such as poverty and welfare reform in the United States (see this letter from Lamphere (https://openstax.org/r/americananthro)). She has received numerous awards and commendations for her research and service. In 2013 she was awarded the Franz Boas Award for Exemplary Service to Anthropology from the American Anthropological Association. This award, which is presented annually, recognizes extraordinary achievements that have served the anthropological profession and the greater community by applying anthropological knowledge to improve lives. In 2017 Lamphere was awarded the Bronislaw Malinowski Award by the Society for Applied Anthropology in recognition of her use of social science to solve the problems of human communities today.

Lamphere's research interests have been important in addressing current needs of human societies, including gender inequalities, socioeconomic challenges, and issues of migration and adaptation. She has also worked to address inequalities and discrimination in her own life. In 1968 she was hired as an assistant professor at Brown University, where she was the only woman on the anthropology faculty. She was denied tenure in 1974, with the university claiming that her scholarship was "weak." Together with other two other female faculty, Lamphere put forth a case accusing the university of widespread sexual discrimination. In September 1977, then Brown University president Howard Swearer entered into a historic consent decree to ensure that women were more fully represented at the institution and agreed to an affirmative action monitoring committee. This was a landmark settlement for female anthropologists everywhere. For more on the case, see "Louise Lamphere v. Brown University (https://openstax.org/r/brown)." On May 24, 2015, Brown University awarded Dr. Louise Lamphere an honorary doctorate for her courage in standing up for equity and fairness for all.

11.4 Marriage and Families across Cultures

LEARNING OUTCOMES

By the end of this section, you will be able to:

- State the anthropological definition of marriage.
- Provide examples of different forms of marriage across cultures.
- Summarize economic and symbolic dimensions of marriage (marriage compensations).
- Describe how marriage intersects with residence rules.
- Explain the social importance of remarriage obligations.

Anthropological Definition of Marriage

FIGURE 11.14 Customers peruse goods in a market in downtown Lima, Peru. Some Indigenous people in Peru begin marriage with a practice known as *servinakuy*. In *servinakuy* , a couple establish an independent household and live together until the birth of their first child, after which they are formally considered to be a fully married couple. (credit: "Lima, Peru" by YoTuT/flickr, CC BY 2.0)

Marriage is the formation of a socially recognized union. Depending on the society, it may be a union between a man and a woman, between any two adults (regardless of their gender), or between multiple spouses in polygamous societies. Marriages are most commonly established to provide a formal structure in which to raise and nurture offspring (whether biological or adopted/fostered), but not all marriages involve reproduction, and marriage can serve multiple functions. One function is to create alliances between individuals, families, and sometimes larger social networks. These alliances may provide political and economic advantages. While there are variations of marriage, the institution itself, with a few notable exceptions, is universal across cultures.

Marriage is an effective means of addressing several common challenges within families. It provides a structure in which to produce, raise, and nurture offspring. It reduces competition among and between males and females. And it creates a stable, long-term socioeconomic household in which the family unit can more adequately subsist with shared labor and resources. All societies practice rules of marriage that determine what groups an individual should marry into (called *endogamy rules*) and which groups are considered off limits and not appropriate for marriage partners (called *exogamy rules*). These rules are behavioral norms in a society. For example, in the United States, individuals tend to marry within the same generation (endogamy) and usually the same linguistic group, but they marry outside of very close kin (exogamy). Those considered to be too closely related to marry are prohibited by rules of *incest*, a relationship defined as too close for sexual relations.

Across all cultures, there is an **incest taboo**, a cultural norm that prohibits sexual relations between parents and their offspring. This taboo sometimes extends to other relations considered too close for sexual relationship. In some societies, this taboo may extend to first cousins. In the United States, first-cousin marriage laws (https://openstax.org/r/Cousin_marriage_law) vary across states (see "Cousin Marriage Law in the United States" for current state laws). French anthropologist Claude Lévi-Strauss argued that incest is the original social structure because it naturally separates groups of people into two types—those with whom an individual has family ties (so-called *biological ties*) and those with whom an individual can have sexual relations and establish ties.

Defining marriage can be complex. In the southern Andes of Peru and Bolivia, Indigenous people begin marriage with a practice known as *servinakuy* (with spelling variations). In *servinakuy*, a man and woman establish their own independent household with very little formal social acknowledgement and live together until the birth of their first child, after which they are formally considered to be a fully married couple. Not a trial marriage and not considered informal cohabitation, *servinakuy* is, instead, a prolonged marriage process during which family is created over time. Andean legal scholars argue that these unions should carry with them the legal rights and protections associated with a formal marriage from the time the couple begins living together (Ingar 2015).

Like all social institutions, ideas about marriage can adapt and change. Within urban Western societies, the concept of marriage is undergoing a great deal of change as socioeconomic opportunities shift and new opportunities open up for women. In Iceland, in 2016, almost 70 percent of children were born outside of a marriage, usually to committed unmarried couples (Peng 2018). This trend is supported by national social policies that provide generous parental leave for both married individuals and those within a consensual union, but the change is also due to the more fluid nature of family today. As norms change in Iceland across generations, it will be interesting to see if the practiced form of consensual union we see today eventually comes to be considered a sanctioned form of marriage.

Forms of Marriage

Anthropologists group marriage customs into two primary types: a union of two spouses only (*monogamy*) or a union involving more than two spouses (*polygamy*). **Monogamy** is the socially sanctioned union of two adults. In some societies this union is restricted to a man and a woman, and in other societies it can be two adults of any gender. Monogamy, because it produces an overall smaller family unit, is especially well adapted to postindustrial societies and cultures where family units are highly mobile (such as nomadic foragers). Monogamy also includes same-sex marriage. In June 2015, in *Obergefell v. Hodges*, the US Supreme Court legalized same-sex marriage in the United States, following earlier legal recognitions in many other Western countries. Today, same-sex marriage is legal in 30 countries. While the movement to legalize same-sex marriage has been long and tumultuous in many of these countries, same-sex marriages and unions have historically played significant roles in both Indigenous and Western societies.

Serial monogamy: **Serial monogamy** is a form of monogamy in which adults have a series of two-person monogamous marriages over a lifetime. It is increasingly common in Western societies, but it is also practiced in some small-scale societies, such as bands. In serial monogamy, divorce and remarriage are common.

Polygamy: **Polygamy** is the socially sanctioned union of more than two adults at the same time. In polygamous societies, families usually begin with a two-person marriage between a man and a woman. In some cases, the marriage will remain as a single couple for a long period of time or for the duration of their lives because of lack of resources or availability of partners. Adding partners is frequently a sign of status and is considered an ideal for families in polygamous societies. In some cases, too, polygamy is practiced to address extreme social stress due to things such as warfare or skewed population distributions caused by famine and high mortality rates. In her cross-cultural study of polygamy, cultural anthropologist Miriam Zeitzen (2008) noted a great deal of diversity within polygamy, from de jure unions that are formal, legal contracts (such as is found in Gambia) to de facto polygamy, which may be just as enduring, stable, and acceptable within a society (such as is found in Ivory Coast).

FIGURE 11.15 In a polygynous marriage, there is one husband and more than one wife. This is the cast of *Sister Wives*, a television series about a polygamous household in the United States. (credit: "Sister Wives Cast on Valder Beebe" by Valder Beebe Show/Wikimedia Commons, CC BY 3.0)

There are two principle kinds of polygamy, depending on the partners involved, as multiple men and multiple women in a single marriage (called *group marriage*) is not common. **Polygyny**, which is the more common form of polygamy, is the marriage of one man to more than one woman. There is often marked age asymmetry in these relationships, with husbands much older than their wives. In polygynous households, each wife commonly lives in her own house with her own biological children, but the family unit cooperates together to share resources and provide childcare. The husband usually "visits" his wives in succession and lives in each of their homes at various times (or lives apart in his own). It is common, also, for there to be a hierarchy of wives based on seniority. Polygyny is found worldwide and offers many benefits. It maximizes the family labor force and the shared resources and opportunities available for family members and creates wide kinship connections within society. Commonly in polygynous societies, larger families are afforded higher social status and they have stronger political and economic alliances.

Polygyny is prevalent in Thailand today, with as many as one in four Thai men between the ages of 30 and 50 having a second wife, called a *mia noi* (minor wife). In her research in Thailand, cultural anthropologist Jiemin Bao (2008) studied polygyny among a group of *lukchin* Thai (Thai of Chinese descent). She found that the *lukchin* practiced polygynous marriages as a joint husband-and-wives economic enterprise, many times sending remittances back to family members still living in China. Bao found that husbands frequently seek their wives' consent before adding another wife and that the family overall considers polygyny to create greater economic opportunities for all family members because multiple wives create a pool of stable laborers with individual skill sets. Even so, Bao observed turmoil and conflict even within economically successful polygynous families and observed that many marriages were conducted as if they were "cutting a business deal" (151). Gender politics of polygynous marriage among the *lukchin* often left women with few choices except to work for her husband's family. Economic success for the family was culturally attributed to the male head of household and not his wives.

A second form of polygamy is polyandry. In **polyandry**, which is comparatively rare, there is one wife and more than one husband. Polyandrous marriages minimize population growth and may occur in societies where there is a temporary surfeit of males and scarcity of females or scarcity of resources. In **fraternal polyandry**, brothers marry a single wife. This is the most common in Nepal, where it is practiced by a minority of mainly rural families. Fraternal polyandry offers several benefits for societies like Nepal with scarce resources and dense population. Where there is extreme scarcity of land acreage, it allows brothers to share an inheritance of land instead of dividing it up. It reduces inequality within the household, as the family can thus collectively subsist on the land as a family unit. Also, in areas where land is scattered over large distances, it allows brothers to take turns living away from home to tend herds of animals or fields and then spending time at home with their shared wife. It also minimizes reproduction and population growth in a society where there is a very dense population (Goldstein 1987), as the wife can carry only one pregnancy at a time.

Postmarital Residence Rules

Following marriage, a couple begins a new family and establishes a shared residence, whether as a separate family unit or as part of an already established family group. The social rules that determine where a newly married couple will reside are called **postmarital residence rules** and are directly related to the descent rules that operate in the society. These rules may be adapted due to extenuating circumstances such as economic need or lack of housing. In the United States today, for example, it is increasingly common for newly married couples to postpone the establishment of a separate household when work, schooling, or children create a need for familial support.

There are five postmarital residence patterns:

- Under **neolocal residence**, a newly married couple establishes an independent household not connected to either spouse's family. This pattern of residence is mostly associated with bilateral descent. While this is a norm in our own society, during times of economic stress or familial need, couples in the United States do occasionally live in the household of one spouse's parents.
- More common worldwide is **patrilocal residence**, associated with societies practicing patrilineal descent. In patrilocal residence, the newly married couple establishes their new household with or near the groom's father or the groom's father's relatives. What this means is that at marriage the groom remains within his household and/or family group, while the bride leaves her parents. Their future children will belong to the groom's lineage.
- **Matrilocal residence** is associated with societies practicing matrilineal descent. In matrilocal residence, the newly married couple establishes their new household with or near the bride's mother or the bride's mother's relatives. At marriage the bride remains within her household and/or family group, while the groom leaves his parents. Their future children will belong to the bride's lineage.
- Less frequent but also associated with matrilineal descent is **avunculocal residence**, in which the newly married couple resides with or near the groom's mother's brother. In societies that practice avunculocal residence, the groom has commonly had a long-term relationship with his maternal uncle, who is part of his own mother's matriline. By joining with household of the groom's maternal uncle, the couple is able to benefit from both the husband's and the wife's matrilines.
- Under **ambilocal residence**, the couple decides which spouse's family to live with or near. Ambilocal residence is associated with ambilineal descent. In ambilocal residence, the newly married couple will usually have made their decision about which spouse's family to join with prior to their marriage. Their future children will then trace descent through that particular line.

Marriage Compensation

In all cultures, marriage is a consequential matter not only to the adults immediately involved, but also to their families and to the broader community. In societies that practice unilineal descent, the newly married couple moves away from one family and toward another. This creates a disadvantage for the family that has "lost" a son or daughter. For example, in a patrilineal society, while the wife will remain a member of her birth lineage (that of her father), her children and her labor will now be invested mostly in her husband's lineage. As a result, in societies practicing unilineal descent, there is a **marriage compensation** from one family to the other for this perceived loss. Marriage compensation is the transfer of some form of wealth (in money, material goods, or labor) from one family to another to legitimize the marriage as a creation of a new social and economic household. It is not seen as payment for a spouse, but as recognition that the marriage and future children are part of one lineage rather than another (Stone 1998, 77). There are several forms of marriage compensation, each symbolically marked by specific cultural practices.

Bride wealth: **Bride wealth** (also called bride price) is the transfer of material and symbolic value from the groom's to the bride's family. Depending on the cultural group, this may involve transfer of money, cattle, house goods, jewelry, or even symbolic ritual artifacts. Bride wealth is the most common form of marriage compensation across cultures. In her study of the Thadou Kukis of northeast India, Burma, and Bangladesh, Indian sociologist Hoineilhing Sitlhou (2018) explores how bride wealth has changed over time. Historically, the items exchanged included cows, copper gongs, silver earrings, and ceremonial clothing for the bride's parents. Today, more contemporary items are offered, such as gold jewelry, cars, furniture, appliances, and land. One practice that has not changed is paying a portion of the bride wealth prior to the marriage ceremony and the remainder at some later point so that the groom remains in respectful debt to the bride's family. In other societies, bride wealth must be paid in full before the marriage is considered legitimate. If marriages conducted using bride wealth end in divorce, normally the bride wealth (or equivalent value) is returned to the groom's family to signify the dissolution of the contract.

Bride service: Similar to bride wealth, **bride service** involves a transfer of something of value from the groom's to the bride's family, but in this case the arrangement involves the contracted labor of the groom, whether before or after the marriage. Future grooms may work for months or years for the bride's family (usually her father's household) prior to the marriage, or husbands may work for months or years with the bride's family after the marriage. In the first case, the groom completes his service prior to the marriage and then moves with the bride back to his family after the marriage. In the second case, the newly married couple remains in residence with the bride's family until the service is concluded. The advantage of the second type of service is that frequently the wife is living with her mother when her first child (or children) is born. While her children are aligned with her husband's family as far as descent (and inheritance), her parents are able to support the couple and their first child or children for a period of time.

The contractual obligations of bride wealth and bride service are not without conflict. In many unilineal societies, these obligations create a great deal of strife and conflict that can go on for years. What if the marriage is temperamentally difficult? What if the wife is barren or a child dies? What if the husband's family suffers economic challenges that create a disparity between what he can offer their family of procreation and what the wife's lineage could offer the children? Each of these situations creates conflict. Sometimes these conflicts between lineages (because marriage is seen as a contract with the larger family) spill over into the larger society and create larger social divisions.

Dowry: **Dowry**, a third form of marriage compensation, functions differently than bride wealth and bride price. Dowry is a form of material value, such as money, jewelry, house goods, or family heirlooms, that the bride brings into her own marriage to provide her with wealth within her husband's lineage. In some societies women turn their dowry over to their husbands, but in other societies they retain rights to this wealth as married women. Among Nepalese Brahmans, sons inherit land and property equally at the death of the father, while women receive a dowry of clothing, jewelry, and household utensils from their own patriline at marriage (Stone 1998). They will use this wealth for status within the marriage. In other societies, women create a dual inheritance for their own daughters from their dowry, passing their dowry down through their daughters. Regardless of how the wealth is used, a woman's most stable route to higher status within a patrilineal society is through the birth of her sons. It is sons within the patriline who will bring wives into their father's household and increase the size and prominence of the patriline through the birth of their children. In patrilineal societies, women with many sons typically carry a higher social status.

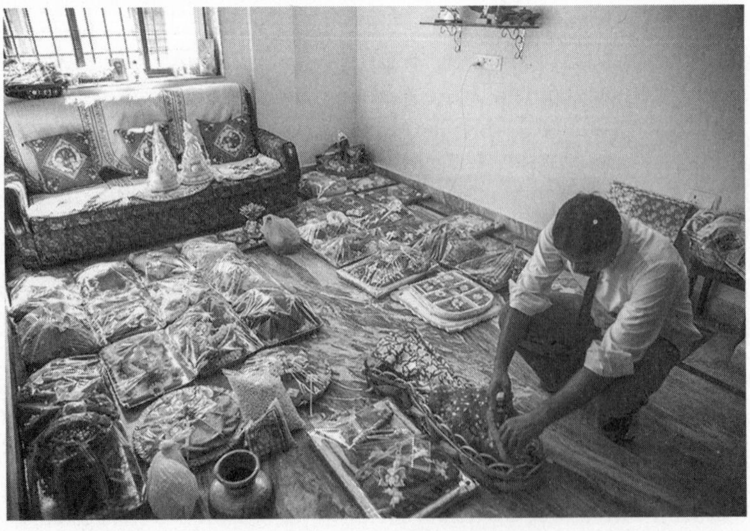

FIGURE 11.16 A display of a woman's dowry in Turkmenistan, in Central Asia. These goods have been laid in

preparation for the woman's marriage. (credit: "wedding gifts 2" Salvatore D'Alia/flickr, CC BY 2.0)

While marriage compensation is most commonly associated with patrilineal societies, it is important to note that almost all marriages represent shared investments of one kind or another. Since marriage is the creation of a new family, spouses most often bring with them into their marriage their skills, traditions, and social networks, all of which carry symbolic weight within societies.

Remarriage Obligations

The many rules and corresponding obligations specific to marriage in unilineal societies (such as residence rules and marriage compensation) are evidence that families and communities invest a great deal in marriages and the formation of new families. So what happens if a young and newly married spouse dies? What about the marriage compensation and the new household? In many unilineal societies (most especially in patrilineal societies), **remarriage obligations** ensure that in these cases the marriage contract endures. Remarriage obligations require the widowed spouse to remarry someone from the same lineage in order to maintain the stability of the family unit.

There are numerous issues that affect when and how remarriage obligations are enacted. The factors that most affect remarriage obligations are the ages of the spouses and amount of time that has passed since the marriage occurred, the ages of the offspring and whether there are young children within the family unit, and the particular marriage contract and value of the marriage compensation. Cultures (and families) determine how best to enact these rules within their own value systems and based on current need. But the primary underlying purpose of remarriage obligations is to maintain the alliance that was made between the two lineages at the time of the marriage. These are intended to be enduring ties that benefit all members of each lineage.

If the husband dies and there is a surviving wife (now widow), under the **levirate** remarriage rule she will marry one of her husband's surviving brothers. While levirate will not be invoked in every case, it is quite common when there are young children remaining within the immediate family unit. Because levirate is usually practiced in societies with polygynous families, a married brother taking an additional wife will not disrupt his existing family, and the *new* wife and her children will remain within the lineage where the children were born.

The **sororate** applies to situations in which the wife dies and there is a surviving widower. Under this remarriage rule, the deceased wife's lineage must provide a replacement female, preferably the former wife's sister. If her sisters are already married or there are no sisters available, another female from the same lineage can be sent as a replacement. Sororate allows young children from the first marriage to remain with their father in his lineage and also maintain a symbolic and emotional bond with their biological mother's kindred.

Finally, there is also the highly variable practice of **ghost marriage**, where a marriage is performed between one or two deceased individuals in order to create an alliance between lineages. Among the Dinka and Nuer of South Sudan, a ghost marriage is similar to the levirate, with the deceased husband's brother standing in for him in a ghost marriage. Unlike the levirate itself, any children from this second (ghost) marriage will be attributed to the deceased husband and not to the brother or the wider lineage itself. Among Chinese immigrants to Singapore, there are ghost marriage claims in which both spouses may be deceased (Schwartze 2010), continuing a tradition that began generations earlier (Topley 1955).

Arranged Marriages

While all marriages are planned, some are arranged, whether between the spouses involved and/or their families or through a third party. Today, an interesting adaptation of arranged marriages has developed involving online websites and hired marriage brokers to help individuals living in different countries find a suitable spouse from their birth culture. As transnational corporations spread worldwide and individuals become more highly mobile (even nomadic) for work, finding a spouse who shares the same cultural values can be difficult. Although there are marriage brokers for many different cultural groups, there is a proliferation of matchmakers for individuals of Indian nationality or descent. While not all of these sites are reputable, the explosion of marriage brokering businesses reminds us that marriage is, first and foremost, a cultural institution.

Kinship is an adaptive mechanism across cultures. While kinship systems vary, they each address critical elements for a social group. Through families of orientation and procreation and within kinship networks, households are created, offspring are produced, and alliances are established.

MINI-FIELDWORK ACTIVITY

Kinship Interview

Do a kinship interview with a friend or peer. Collect information about their immediate family and relatives, including information about marriage and descent, being sure to note deceased relatives and any prior marriages. Draw a kinship chart that graphically depicts the information that you collected through the interview. Ask your participant informer to critique your chart, and then make any needed adjustments. Present the results of your project along with a reflection on the highlights of this work. What most challenged you, and how did this work help you better understand your friend/peer? What interesting things did you learn about their life?

Key Terms

affinal tie a contractual relationship by marriage or mutual agreement that is depicted as a double line on the kinship chart.

ambilineal descent tracing an individual's kinship through a single gendered line, with each family choosing either the mother's or father's descent line.

ambilocal residence a postmarital residence pattern in which the couple chooses one lineage for their offspring, either the mother's or the father's; associated with ambilineal descent.

avunculocal residence a postmarital residence pattern where a newly married couple resides with the groom's mother's brother; associated with patrilineal descent.

bifurcate merging kinship a broader chart of EGO family relation that connects kinships by merging EGO's parents' same-sex siblings and their offspring into the immediate family (creating parallel cousins) and bifurcating, or cutting off, EGO's parents' opposite-sex siblings and their offspring (creating cross cousins); also called *Iroquois kinship*.

bilateral descent tracing an individual's kinship through both the mother's and father's lines.

blended families a family in which there is more than one origin family for the members.

bride service a transfer of wealth from the groom's to the bride's family through labor, usually the contracted labor of the groom, either before or after the marriage.

bride wealth the transfer of material and symbolic value from the groom's to the bride's family in order to legitimize the marriage contract.

clans a tribal social division in which a group of lineages have a presumed and symbolic kinship.

cognatic descent a kinship structure that follows descent through both men and women, although it may vary by family.

collateral kin EGO's siblings and their offspring.

compadrazgo a form of godparent relationship introduced originally as a social institution within the Catholic Church and later adapted as popular Catholicism in Latin America in which godparents are named for a Catholic child or young person during rituals such as baptism, confirmation, and marriage.

consanguineal tie a biological (bloodline) connection between individuals that is indicated by a single line on a kinship chart; it is considered to be a permanent tie that cannot be broken.

cross cousin EGO's cousins through their parents' opposite-sex siblings.

descent individuals who are believed to be connected by blood or who have an enduring kindship bond across generations.

dowry material value carried by the bride into her own marriage to provide her with symbolic leverage within her husband's lineage.

EGO the starting point for the kinship chart; used to read relationships as alignments between EGO and other individuals.

extended family two or more family units functioning as a single integrated family; may involve two or more generations.

family two or more people in an adaptable social and economic alliance that involves kinship, whether perceived through blood, marriage, or other permanent or semipermanent arrangement.

family of orientation the family unit in which EGO was raised and nurtured as a child and adolescent.

family of procreation the family that EGO produces, usually as a result of marriage.

fictive kin a kinship tie that is socially interpreted to be by blood or marriage and that is based on intentional relationships, such as adoption, godparenthood, or intimate personal ties.

fraternal polyandry a form of marriage in which biological brothers marry a single wife.

generational kinship a kinship system in which the terms of reference are for gender and generation only, creating large units of immediate family; also called *Hawaiian kinship*.

ghost marriage a marriage between one or two deceased individuals in order to create an alliance between lineages.

household a group of individuals who live within the same residence and share socioeconomic needs associated with production and consumption.

incest taboo a prohibition against sexual relations that is universal between parents and their offspring and sometimes extends to other relations considered too close for sexual relationships.

kindred the sum of kinship relationships that is defined through EGO.

kinship a web of relationships in which people consider themselves related to each other in a social and biological way.

levirate a remarriage obligation in which the surviving widow (wife) must marry her deceased husband's brother; the levirate occurred within polygynous societies.

lineage a continuous line of descent from an original ancestor.

lineal kinship a form of kinship reckoning that highlights the creation of a nuclear family; also called *Eskimo kinship*.

marriage the formation of a new, socially sanctioned family as it is defined across cultures and societies.

marriage compensation the transfer of some form of wealth from one family to another to legitimize the marriage as a creation of a new social and economic household.

matrilineal (uterine) descent the descent of both males and females traced solely through the female ancestors.

matrilocal residence a postmarital residence pattern in which the newly married couple establishes their new household with or near the bride's mother or the bride's mother's relatives; also called *uxorilocal residence*.

moieties the social division of a tribe into two halves.

monogamy the formally sanctioned union of two adults.

neolocal residence a postmarital residence pattern in which the newly married couple establishes an independent household not connected to either spouse's family.

nuclear family a family composed of two parents and their immediate offspring.

parallel cousin EGO's brothers and sisters through their parents' same-sex siblings.

patrilineal (agnatic) descent the descent of both males and females traced solely through male ancestors.

patrilocal residence a postmarital residence pattern in which a newly married couple establishes their new household with or near the groom's father or the groom's father's relatives; also called *virilocal residence*.

polyandry is the marriage of one wife and more than one husband.

polygamy the formally sanctioned union of more than two adults at the same time.

polygyny the marriage of one man to more than one woman.

postmarital residence rules the social rules that determine where a newly married couple will reside following marriage.

remarriage obligations responsibilities to replace a deceased spouse with a new spouse from the same lineage in order to maintain the stability of the family unit.

serial monogamy a form of monogamy in which two adults have a series of marriages over a lifetime.

sociocultural construction a concept that is defined according to social criteria (not biological) and varies across cultures.

sororate a remarriage obligation in which the surviving widower (husband) must marry his deceased wife's sister or another female relative from her family.

terms of address the terms (words) we use to speak directly to our kin.

terms of reference the terms (words) that are used to refer to our kin.

unilineal descent tracing an individual's kinship through a single gendered line, either male or female, as a collective social rule for all families within a society.

Summary

Kinship is an adaptive mechanism. As a sociocultural construction, it is defined differently across cultures to adapt to the specific needs of a society. While most of us think of kinship as a biological relationship, it is, in fact, a relationship defined by culture. Historically, anthropology approached the study of kinship as a collection of terms and relationships. Lewis Henry Morgan did early research on the diversity of kinship across societies. Bronislaw Malinowski and A. R. Radcliffe-Brown revealed kinship's institutional nature and how it connects to other aspects of social life, such as politics, economics, and subsistence. Today, anthropologists view kinship as one of the foundational social structures and institutions within a society. It defines the way an individual (EGO) fits within a larger kindred (depicted by terms of reference) and the rights and obligations that EGO has to these individuals (depicted by terms of address).

Embedded within the larger kinship structure is the family, those believed to be related to each other and who have distinct rights and responsibilities to the family unit. Some families live together with mutual goals while others are disperse, claiming ancestral kinship ties. Families also include individuals who share ties of descent (consanguineal ties) and ties of marriage (affinal ties). A household is a group of individuals who live within the same residence and share socioeconomic needs. This may or may not include more than one family. There are various types of families across cultures, including the nuclear family, extended family, and blended family. Many families also include fictive kin, individuals who are included within the intimate family and perceived to have relationships as close as those of blood or marriage. Godparenthood, called *compadrazgo* in Latin American, is an example of fictive kin.

Kinship is graphically depicted by means of a kinship chart, which shows the kindred connected by consanguineal and affinal ties. All kinship charts use a point of reference referred to as EGO, the individual whose relationships are traced on the chart. There are three major types of kinship structure: lineal kinship, which highlights the nuclear family; bifurcate merging kinship, which distinguishes between parallel and cross cousins; and generational kinship, which greatly expands the family of orientation to include all kindred within the same generation. Ties of descent, whether unilineal, ambilineal, or bilateral, drive connections within a kinship chart. In some families, descent (and inheritance) is traced through only one of EGO's parents (unilineal or ambilineal), and in others descent is traced through both parental lines (bilateral).

EGO's family of orientation is ideally created through a marriage (affinal tie), but what constitutes marriage varies greatly across cultures. In short, marriage is best defined as the formation of a new, socially sanctioned family. Some societies practice monogamy, the marriage of only two adults at a time. Where individuals can and do change partners during their lifetimes, they may practice serial monogamy. In other societies, polygamy is the marriage ideal. While polygamous unions usually begin as two adults, polygamy sanctions a marriage of more than two adults. When there is an ideal of one man with multiple wives, it is known as polygyny, and where there is one woman with more than one husband, it is called polyandry. How and who one marries is also regulated by rules of postmarital residence, including neolocal, patrilocal, matrilocal, avunculocal, and ambilocal types. Each of these is adapted to the descent rule utilized by the society in reckoning kinship.

Unilineal descent, with the creation of lineages distinguishing the husband from the wife, also involves marriage compensations, such as bride wealth, bride service, and dowry. Marriage compensation formalizes the alliance between the two lineages involved in the marriage and compensates one lineage for the loss of a young person and their offspring (as residence rules will require them to live with the lineage of their spouse). Remarriage obligations are also common in unilineal societies where the marriage is structured to endure even beyond death.

Critical Thinking Questions

1. What is kinship, and how does it affect the way society functions?
2. How do terms of reference and address affect relationships within the family?
3. Draw your own kinship chart using lineal kinship terminology. Then, redraw the chart in the bifurcate merging and generational forms. How does your family change as a result of changing the way you define family?
4. How does kinship affect your life? Give three examples of kinship relationships in which you have rights and/or responsibilities. You may choose to include an example of fictive kinship.
5. Describe the different types of marriage with which you are familiar in your own community. How are they alike and different?
6. What is the role of individuals' families in your community before and after marriage?
7. Marriage compensation occurs in many different cultures. What are the potential advantages and disadvantages of each of these forms of compensation? Consider the importance of each of these forms over the course of an individual's lifetime.

Bibliography

Adams, William Y. 1983. "Once More to the Fray: Further Reflections on Navajo Kinship and Residence." *Journal of Anthropological Research* 39 (4): 393–414.

Adoption Network. "US Adoption Statistics." https://adoptionnetwork.com/adoption-statistics#:~:text=There%20are%20about%201.5%20million,one%20out%20of%2050%20children.

Bao, Jiemin. 2008. "Denaturalizing Polygyny in Bangkok, Thailand." *Ethnology* 47 (2/3): 145–61.

Bao, Jiemin. 2003. "The Gendered Biopolitics of Marriage and Immigration: A Study of Pre-1949 Chinese Immigrants in Thailand." *Journal of Southeast Asian Studies* 34 (1): 127–51.

Child Welfare League of America. 2019. "The Nation's Children 2019." March 2019. https://www.cwla.org/wp-content/uploads/2019/04/National-2019.pdf.

Ember, Carol R., Melvin Ember, and Peter Peregrine. 2014. *Anthropology*. 14th ed. New York: Pearson.

Foster, George. 1953. "Cofradía and Compadrazgo in Spain and Spanish America." *Southwestern Journal of Anthropology* 9:1–28.

Foster, George. 1963. "The Dyadic Contract in Tzintzuntzan: A Patron-Client Relationship." *American Anthropologist* 65 (6): 1280–94.

Fox, Robin. 1977. *Kinship and Marriage: An Anthropological Perspective*. London: Penguin.

Goldstein, Melvyn C. 1987. "When Brothers Share a Wife." *Natural History* 96 (3): 38–49.

Haile, Berard. 1942. "Why the Navajo Hogan?" *Primitive Man* 15 (3–4): 39–56.

Hua, Cai. 2008. *A Society without Fathers or Husbands: The Na of China*. Translated by Asti Hustvedt. New York: Zone Books.

Ingar, Carmen Mez. 2015. "Necesidad de desarrollar el derecho consuetudinario." *Revista Jurídica "Docentia et Investigatio"* 17 (1): 21–30.

Jacobi, Jeffrey S. 2006. "Two Spirits, Two Eras, Same Sex: For a Traditionalist Perspective on Native American Tribal Same-Sex Marriage Policy." *University of Michigan Journal of Law Reform* 39 (4): 823–50.

Keesing, Felix. 1958. *Cultural Anthropology*. New York: Holt, Rinehart and Winston, Inc.

Kramer, Stephanie. 2019. "U.S. Has World's Highest Rate of Children Living in Single-Parent Households." Pew Research Center. December 12, 2019. https://www.pewresearch.org/fact-tank/2019/12/12/u-s-children-more-likely-than-children-in-other-countries-to-live-with-just-one-parent/.

Lamphere, Louise. 2005. "Replacing Heteronormative Views of Kinship and Marriage." *American Ethnologist* 32 (1): 34–36.

Leinaweaver, Jessaca. 2014. "Informal Kinship-Based Fostering Around the World: Anthropological Findings." *Child Development Perspectives* 8 (3): 131–35.

Malinowski, Bronislaw. 1922. *Argonauts of the Western Pacific*. London: Routledge & Kegan Paul Ltd.

Malinowski, Bronislaw. 1930. "Kinship." *Man*, 30:19–20.

Mintz, Sidney W., and Eric R. Wolf. 1950. "An Analysis of Ritual Co-Parenthood (Compadrazgo)." *Southwestern Journal of Anthropology* 6 (4): 341–68.

Mattison, Siobhán M. "Paternal Investment and the Positive Effects of Fathers among the Matrilineal Mosuo of Southwest China." *American Anthropologist*. 116 (3): 591–610.

Morgan, Lewis Henry. 1871. *Systems of Consanguinity and Affinity of the Human Family*. Washington, DC: Smithsonian Institution.

Murphy, Yolanda, and Robert Murphy. 1985. *Women of the Forest*. 2nd ed. New York: Columbia University Press.

Peng, Jessica. 2018. "To Marry or Not to Marry? Consensual Union Is Popular in Iceland." Reykjavik Grapevine. June 4, 2018. https://grapevine.is/mag/articles/2018/06/04/to-marry-or-not-to-marry-consensual-union-is-popular-in-iceland/.

Radcliffe-Brown, A. R. 1922. *The Andaman Islanders*. Cambridge, UK: Cambridge University Press.

Radcliffe-Brown, A. R. 1952. *Structure and Function in Primitive Society.* London: Cohen and West Ltd.

Rivers, W. H. R. 1910. "The Genealogical Method of Anthropological Inquiry." *The Sociological Review* 3 (1): 1–12.

Schulte, Ernest L. 1965. *Manual for Kinship Analysis.* New York: Holt, Rinehart and Winston, Inc.

Shapiro, Warren. 2015. "Not 'From the Natives' Point of View': Why the New Kinship Studies Need the Old Kinship Terminologies." *Anthropos* 110 (1): 1–13.

Sitlhou, Hoineilhing. 2018. "Symbolism of Bride Wealth and Gift-Giving in Marriage System of the Kukis." *Indian Anthropologist* 48 (1): 31–46.

Stone, Linda. 1998. *Kinship and Gender: An Introduction.* Boulder, CO: Westview Press.

Schwartze, Lucas J. 2010. "Grave Vows: A Cross-Cultural Examination of the Varying Forms of Ghost Marriage among Five Societies." *Nebraska Anthropologist* 25:82–95.

Topley, Marjorie. 1955. "Ghost Marriage among the Singapore Chinese." *Man* 55:29–30.

United States Census Bureau. 2016. "The Majority of Children Live with Two Parents, Census Bureau Reports." November 17, 2016. https://www.census.gov/newsroom/press-releases/2016/cb16-192.html.

Van Vleet, Krista E. 2008. *Performing Kinship: Narrative, Gender, and the Intimacies of Power in the Andes.* Austin: University of Texas Press.

Zeitzen, Miriam Koktvedgaard. 2008. *Polygamy: A Cross-Cultural Analysis.* Oxford, UK: Berg.

CHAPTER 12
Gender and Sexuality

Figure 12.1 "It's a _____!": When someone announces the birth of a new baby, a first question is often whether the infant is a boy or girl. (credit: "It's a Boy!" by George Ruiz/flickr, CC BY 2.0)

CHAPTER OUTLINE

INTRODUCTION A friend announces, "My sister just had a baby last night!" Many people will immediately ask, "Is it a boy or a girl?" Gender is central to the way people think about and interact with others. Anthropologists are curious about the many ways in which gender shapes impressions and assumptions about people and why gender is such a primary concern. Gender influences how people think about their own identities, how they present themselves to others, and how they plan to lead their lives. People's sexual identities and desires are shaped by gendered notions of themselves and others.

Since the beginning of the discipline, anthropologists have described how cultures construct gender roles and sexual practices in many different cultural contexts. This chapter will explore the origins of gender and consider various forms of biological evidence for gender differences. And it will consider how power operates in cultural constructions of gender and sexuality. Anthropologists have discovered great diversity in human systems of gender and expressions of sexuality.

12.1 Sex, Gender, and Sexuality in Anthropology

LEARNING OUTCOMES

By the end of this section, you will be able to:

- Define the concepts of sex and gender and explain the difference between the two concepts.
- Describe various cultural expressions of sexuality.
- Identify the difficulties in applying primate research to human gender and sexuality.
- Critique the "man the hunter" thesis of human evolution.

For many people, *male* and *female* refer to natural categories that neatly divide up the human population. Often, people associate these two categories with different abilities and personality traits. Setting aside these ideas and assumptions, anthropologists explore aspects of human biology and culture to understand where notions of gender come from while documenting the diversity of gender and sexuality in cultures all over the world, past and present.

The Terms: Sex, Gender, and Sexuality

In the social sciences, the term **sex** refers to the biological categories of male and female (and potentially other categories, as discussed later in this chapter). The sex of a person is determined by an examination of biological and anatomical features, including (but not limited to): visible genitalia (e.g., penis, testes, vagina), internal sex organs (e.g., ovaries, uterus), secondary sex characteristics (e.g., breasts, facial hair), chromosomes (XX for females, XY for males, and other possibilities), reproductive capabilities (including menstruation), and the activities of growth hormones, particularly testosterone and estrogen. It may seem as though nature divides humans neatly into females and males, but such a long list of distinguishing factors results in a great deal of ambiguity and diversity within categories. For instance, hormonal influences can produce results different from the ways that people typically develop. Hormonal influences shape the development of sex organs over time and can stimulate the emergence of secondary sex characteristics associated with the other sex. Clothes on or clothes off, people can have body features associated with one sex category and chromosomes associated with another.

While sex is based on biology, the term ***gender*** was developed by social scientists to refer to cultural roles based on these biological categories. The cultural roles of gender assign certain behaviors, relationships, responsibilities, and rights differently to people of different genders. As elements of culture, gender categories are learned rather than inherited or inborn, making childhood an important time for gender enculturation. As opposed to the seeming universality of sex categories, the specific content of gender categories is highly variable across cultures and subject to change over time.

The two terms, biological sex and cultural gender, are often distinguished from one another to clarify the differences embedded in "nature" versus the differences constructed by "culture." But are biological sex categories based on an objective appraisal of nature? Are sex categories universal and durable? Some scholars question the biological objectivity of sex and its opposition to the more flexible notion of gender.

FIGURE 12.2 Transgender activist Aurora Claire Borin at a women's march in Calgary, Canada. (credit: "Women's March in Calgary" by JMacPherson/flickr, CC BY 2.0)

Associated with sex and gender, the concept of **sexuality** refers to erotic thoughts, desires, and practices and the sociocultural identities associated with them. The complex ways in which people experience their own bodies and perceive their own gender contribute to the physical behaviors they engage in to achieve pleasure, intimacy, and/or reproduction. This complex of thoughts, desires, and behaviors constitutes a person's sexuality.

Some cultures have very strict cultural norms regarding sexual practices, while others are more flexible. Some cultures confer a distinctive identity on people who practice a particular form of sexuality, while others allow a person to engage in an array of sexual practices without adopting a distinctive identity associated with those practices (Nanda 2000). ***Sexual orientation*** refers to sociocultural identities associated with specific forms of sexuality. For instance, in American culture, sex between a woman and a man is conventionalized into the normative identity of **heterosexual**. If you are a person who practices that kind of sex (and *only* that kind), then most Americans would consider you to be a heterosexual person. If you are a person who engages in sex with someone of the same sex/gender category, then in American culture, you would be considered a gay person (if you identify as male) or a lesbian (if you identify as female). So anxious are Americans about these categorical identities that many young people who have erotic dreams or passing erotic thoughts about a same-sex friend may worry that they are "really" not heterosexual. As American norms have changed over the past several decades, some people who have romantic, emotional, or erotic feelings toward people of their own gender and another gender have adopted the identity of **bisexual**. People who may have erotic desires about and relations with others without regard to their biological sex, gender identity, or sexual orientation may consider themselves to be **pansexual**. Even more recently, some people who do not engage in sexual thoughts, desires, or practices of any kind have embraced the identity of **asexual**. While there are many aspects and manifestations of sexual orientation, sexual orientation is considered to be a central and durable aspect of a person's sociocultural identity.

In some cultures, heterosexuality was previously thought to be the most "natural" form of sexuality, a notion called **heteronormativity**. This notion has been challenged by research and the growth of the global LGBTQIA+ movement. In many other cultures, people are allowed or even expected to engage in more than one form of sexuality without necessarily adopting any specific sexual identity. This is not to say that these other cultures are consistently more liberal and tolerant of sexual diversity. In many societies, it is acceptable for people to engage in same-sex practices in certain contexts, but they are still expected to marry someone of the opposite sex and have children.

Scholars who have studied sexuality in many cultures have also pointed out that a person's gender identity, sexual orientation, and sexuality tend to change significantly over the life span, responding to different contexts and relationships. The term ***queer***, originally a pejorative term in American culture for a person who did not conform to the rigid norms of heterosexuality, has been appropriated by people who do not abide by those norms, particularly people who take a more situational and fluid approach to the expression of gender and sexuality. Rather than a set of fixed and durable identities, queer gender and sexuality are more fluid, constantly emerging, and contingent on multiple factors.

As complex as sex, gender, and sexuality can be, it is helpful to have a diagram illustrating the possible relationships among these factors. Activist Sam Killermann has developed a useful diagram known as "The Genderbread Person (https://openstax.org/r/the-binary-gender)," depicting the various aspects of identity, attraction, expression, and physical characteristics that combine in the gender/sexuality of whole persons.

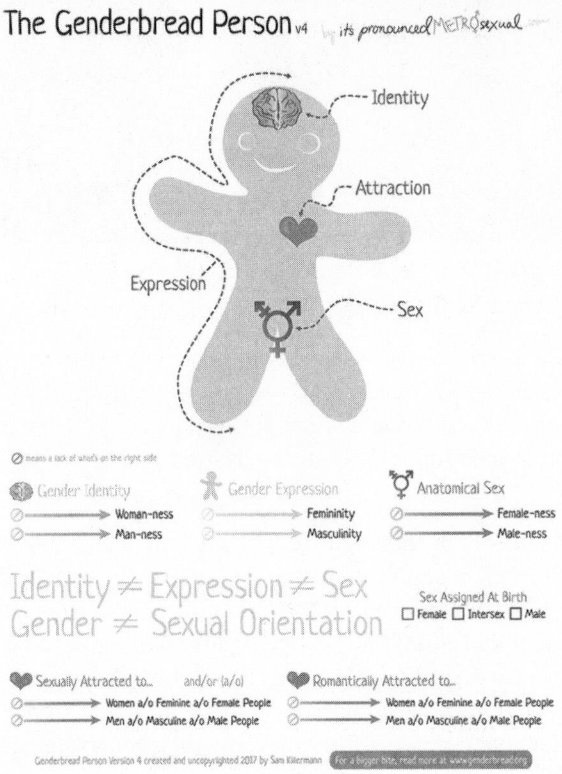

FIGURE 12.3 Sam Killermann's "Genderbread Person" illustrates how identity, attraction, expression, and physical characteristics all contribute to gender and sexuality. (credit: "Genderbread Person v4" by Sam Killermann/ Wikimedia Commons, Public Domain)

Evidence from Biological Anthropology

Given humans' close biological relationship to primates, one might expect to see similar dynamics of sex and gender between human and nonhuman primate social groups. Biologists and primatologists have examined sex differences in the biology and behavior of both nonhuman and human primates, looking for commonalities that might suggest a common biological genesis for sex/gender categories.

Primate Sex Differences: Biology and Behavior

In the 1950s, a time when American men were supposed to be breadwinners and American women were urged to be housewives and mothers, most primatologists believed that males were the public actors in primate social life, while females were passive, marginal figures. Primatologists of the time believed that males constantly competed against one another for dominance in a rigid group hierarchy, while females were more narrowly interested in raising young (Fedigan and Fedigan 1989). In fact, primatologists described the total social organization of primates in terms of male competition. This view went along with Charles Darwin's notion that males are forced to compete for the opportunity to mate with females and so, therefore, must be assertive and dominant. Females, in Darwin's theory, were shaped by evolution to choose the strongest male to mate with and then concern themselves exclusively with nurturing their offspring to adulthood.

By the 1980s, however, a number of strong studies were showing some very surprising things about primate social organization. First, most primate groups are essentially composed of related females, with males as temporary members who often move between groups. The heart of primate society, then, is not a set of competitive males but a set of closely bonded mothers and their young. Females are not marginal figures but central actors in most social life. The glue that holds most primate groups together is not male competition but female kinship and solidarity.

Second, social organization in primates turned out to be incredibly complex, with both males and females actively strategizing for desirable resources, roles, and relationships. Research on a number of primate species has demonstrated that females are often sexually assertive and highly competitive. Female primates actively exercise their preference to mate with certain male "friends" rather than aggressive or dominant males. For males, friendliness with females may be a much better reproductive strategy than fighting with other males. Moreover, many primatologists have begun to identify cooperation rather than competition as the central feature of primate social life while still recognizing competition for resources by both males and females in their pursuit of survival and reproduction (Fedigan and Fedigan 1989).

What this means, in a nutshell, is that (1) both females and males are competitive, (2) both females and males are cooperative, and (3) both females and males are central actors in primate social life.

While evidence suggests that in primate groups males and females are equally important to social life, this still leaves open the question of biological differences and their link to behavioral differences. The anatomy of primate males and females differs in two main respects. First, of course, adult females can and often do experience pregnancy and bear offspring. The females of most primate species are often pregnant or nursing for most of their adult lives and devote more time and resources to care of young than males do (although there are some notable exceptions, such as certain species of New World monkeys). And some researchers have noted the tendency of juvenile females to pay more attention to primate babies in the group than do juvenile males.

Second, male primates tend to be slightly bigger than females, although this difference itself is quite variable. The size difference between males and females of any species is referred to as **sexual dimorphism**. Male and female gibbons are nearly the same size, while male gorillas are nearly twice the size of females. Female chimpanzees are about 75 percent the size of males. Human females are about 90 percent the size of males, making human sexual dimorphism closer to gibbons than chimpanzees.

Some researchers suggest that a high level of sexual dimorphism is associated with strong male dominance, rigid hierarchy, and male competition for mating with females. Certainly these features reinforce one another in gorilla society. A low level of sexual dimorphism may be associated with long-term monogamy, as with gibbons. However, anthropologist Adrienne Zihlman cautions against making any firm judgments about the relationship between biological features such as size and behavioral features such as sexual relations. She remarks, "There is no simple correlation between anatomy and behavioral expression, within or between species" (1997, 100). Reviewing research on sex differences in gibbons, chimpanzees, gorillas, and orangutans, she concludes that each species features a unique "mosaic" of sex differences involving anatomy and behavior, with no clear commonality that might predict what is "natural" for humans.

FIGURE 12.4 Bonobo group hug. Bonobos, which share 99% of their DNA with humans, live in female-dominant groups that are mostly egalitarian and peaceful. (credit: "JaxZoo_1-5-17-7140" by Rob Bixby/flickr, CC BY 2.0)

Humans' closest primate relatives are chimpanzees and bonobos, both sharing 99 percent of their DNA with humans, and yet each species exhibits very different gender-related behaviors. Bonobos are female-dominant, while chimpanzees are male-dominant. Bonobo groups are mostly egalitarian and peaceful, while chimpanzee groups are intensely hierarchical, with frequent male aggression between groups. Sexual behavior among bonobos is remarkably frequent and extraordinarily variable, with a wide range of same-sex and opposite-sex pairings involving various forms of genital contact. Some researchers believe that sexual contact helps build social bonds and ease conflicts in bonobo groups. Bonobos have been called the "make love, not war" primate. Sexual behavior among chimpanzees is also variable but much more limited to opposite-sex pairings. A female in estrus may mate with several males, a pattern called opportunistic mating. Short-term exclusive relationships may form, in which a male guards a female to prevent other males from mating with her. Consortships also happen, in which a female and a male leave the group for a week or more.

With such variability between humanity's two closest DNA relatives, it is impossible to use nonhuman primate behavior to make assumptions about what is "natural" for human males and females. In fact, with regard to gender, the lessons of primatology may be that apes (like humans) are biologically quite flexible and capable of many social expressions of gender and sexuality.

Human Sex Differences: Biology and Behavior

Just as with primate research, research on human biological sex/gender differences has been considerably slanted by the gender bias of the (often male) researchers. Within the Euro-American intellectual tradition, scholars in the past have argued that women's biological constitution makes them unfit to vote, go to college, compete in the job market, or hold political office. More recently, beliefs about the different cognitive abilities of men and women have become widespread. Males are supposedly better at math and spatial relationships, while females are better at language skills. Hormonal activities supposedly make males more aggressive and females more emotional.

In her book *Myths of Gender*, biologist Anne Fausto-Sterling (1992) conducts a massive review of research on cognitive and behavioral sex/gender differences in humans. Looking very closely at the data, she finds that the vast number of studies show no statistically significant difference whatsoever between the cognitive abilities of boys and girls. A minority of studies found very small differences. For instance, among four studies of abstract reasoning abilities, one study indicated that females were superior in this skill, one study indicated that males were superior, and two studies showed no difference at all. Overall, when differences are found in verbal abilities, girls usually come out ahead, but the difference is so small as to be irrelevant to questions of education and employment. Likewise, more than half of all studies on spatial abilities find no difference between girls and boys. When differences are found, boys come out ahead, but the difference is again very small. Looking at the overall variation of skill levels in this area, only about 5 percent of it can be attributed to gender. This means that 95 percent of the differences are due to other factors, such as educational opportunities.

FIGURE 12.5 A girl solving math problems in school. Research has found no statistically significant difference between the cognitive abilities of boys and girls. (credit: "Uganda_13" by mattlucht/flickr, CC BY 2.0)

Even these tiny differences that may exist in the cognitive talents of different genders are not necessarily rooted in biological sex differences. Several studies of spatial abilities have shown that boys may initially perform better on spatial ability tests, but when given time to practice, girls increase their skill levels to become equal to boys, while boys remain the same. Some researchers reason that styles of play such as sports, often encouraged more by parents of boys, may build children's spatial skills. Parenting styles, forms of play, and gender roles—all elements of culture—may shape the data more than biology. Cross-cultural studies also indicate that culture plays an important role in shaping abilities. A study of the Inuit found no differences at all in the spatial abilities of boys and girls, while in a study of the Temne of Sierra Leone, boys outperformed the girls. Inuit girls are generally allowed more freedom and autonomy, while Temne girls are more restricted in their activities.

FIGURE 12.6 The relative freedom of Inuit girls may enhance their spatial abilities. (credit: "Children in Greenland" by Greenland Travel/flickr, CC BY 2.0)

Similar complexities emerge in the analysis of studies on aggression. Fausto-Sterling found that most studies revealed no clear relationship between testosterone levels and levels of aggression in males. Moreover, testosterone aggression studies have been riddled with problems such as poor methodology, questionable definitions of aggression, and an inability to prove whether testosterone provokes aggression or the other way around. Where differences in aggression between girls and boys are documented, some researchers have concluded that cultural factors may play a strong role in producing those differences. Anthropologist Carol Ember studied levels of aggression among boys and girls in a village in Kenya. Overall, the boys exhibited more aggressive behavior, but there were exceptions. In families lacking girl children, boys were made to perform more "feminine" work such as childcare, housework, and fetching water. Boys who regularly performed those tasks exhibited less aggression than other boys—up to 60 percent less for boys who performed a lot of this work.

As with the primate research on sex differences, research on the brains, bodies, and behaviors of male and female humans does not seem to suggest that significant behavioral differences are biologically hardwired. While researchers have discovered differences in the cognitive talents and social behaviors of males and females, those differences are very small and could very well be due to social and cultural factors rather than biology. As with bonobos and chimpanzees, humans are biologically quite flexible, allowing for a diverse array of forms of gender and sexuality.

Evidence from Archaeology

Seeking to understand the origins of human sociocultural formations of gender and sexuality, some researchers have turned to the archaeological record. Archaeologists use temporal sequencing, fossil evidence, comparison with living communities, and knowledge of the evolutionary process to piece together an understanding of the development of gendered and sexual behaviors in the context of human evolution.

Early theories of gender in human evolutionary history were shaped by the "man the hunter" hypothesis. In the 1950s and '60s, many anthropologists believed that hunting constituted the primary means of subsistence throughout humans' evolutionary past, up until the domestication of plants and animals around 10,000 years ago. As hunting was mainly done by men in contemporary gathering-hunting societies, researchers assumed that hunting was naturally and exclusively a male activity throughout prehistory. Women could not hunt, it was thought, due to the burdens of pregnancy, nursing, and childcare. It seemed likely that adult women stayed together with their children at the home base while men went out in small groups in search of game. In this view, tools were invented for hunting and processing meat and were mostly made by men. Dependence on meat gave men power and prestige, leading to male dominance over females. Hunting also spurred the development of language because communication was necessary to coordinate hunting expeditions. Tools and language, in turn, stimulated the development of larger brains. Hunting by men was therefore thought to be the central driving force in the evolution of humans' hominid ancestors.

FIGURE 12.7 A Kali'na man and woman in the Venezuelan savanna on a gathering and hunting trip. The gathering typically done by women contributes far more to the diets of contemporary gathering-hunting societies than the hunting typically done by men does. In most contemporary gathering-hunting societies, men and women are fairly

equal. (credit: Pierre Barrère/Wikimedia Commons, Public Domain)

In the 1970s, researchers from the emerging field of sociobiology drew from the "man the hunter" hypothesis to claim that certain gender roles and sexual relations evolved to be natural among humans. **Sociobiology** is a subfield of biology that attempts to explain human behavior by considering evolutionary processes. In regard to gender roles, for instance, sociobiologists sought to understand how evolution may have shaped men and women differently, encouraging gender-specific strategies for survival and reproduction. Many sociobiologists have argued that men, as hunters, evolved to be strong and aggressive, able to strategize in groups but in fierce competition to achieve the status of dominant male; in contrast, women were primarily engaged in childcare and food preparation and therefore evolved to be more nurturing and submissive, focused on attracting the attentions of men. Dependent on men to supply meat for themselves and their children, women would have been motivated to ensnare men in long-term monogamous relationships to ensure a constant food supply as well as protection from other aggressive males. Largely free from the responsibilities of childcare, men would have been motivated to mate with as many females as possible to ensure the greatest number of descendants. This view of the natural order of gender relations became very popular and widespread in American society.

Less well-known in American society is the thorough critique of the "man the hunter" hypothesis within archaeology and throughout the other subfields of anthropology. Around the same time that sociobiologists were elaborating on their theories of gender, many anthropologists were pushing back against the notion that hunting was the primary subsistence activity of gathering-hunting societies. As you'll recall from the discussion of such societies in, Work, Life, and Value: Economic Anthropology, gathering contributes far more to the diets of contemporary gathering-hunting societies than hunting does. Rather than staying at the home base, women and children go out gathering in groups several times a week, largely meeting their own nutritional needs as well as sharing with others. Pregnancy and nursing do not significantly limit the subsistence activities of women, as they remain active throughout pregnancy and carry infants in slings or on their hips until the children are able to keep up. While meat is highly valued, it does not make women dependent on men, and the ability to hunt does not make men dominant over women. In most contemporary gathering-hunting societies, men and women are fairly equal.

In archaeology, some feminist researchers have countered the "man the hunter" hypothesis with a "woman the gatherer" hypothesis. These researchers point to fossil evidence suggesting that women's activities were equally important to survival and development in humans' evolutionary past. These archaeologists note that the teeth of early hominids indicate that they were omnivorous, eating a wide variety of foods. The very large, well-worn molars of early hominid skulls indicate an adaptation to a diet of gritty foods such as nuts, seeds, and fruits with tough peels. Given the centrality of plant foods to the diets of contemporary gathering-hunting peoples, it seems likely that gathering was also the primary means of food-getting for humans' ancestors (though, of course, one must be cautious in making such generalizations). If gathering was so crucial, then quite possibly the ingenuity of early hominids might have been focused not only on making hunting gear but also on developing tools for gathering, such as digging sticks and stones for breaking open hard shells. As hominid babies lacked the grasping toes of other apes, it would have been more difficult for them to grasp hold of their mothers as they were carried out on gathering expeditions. Perhaps, then, an important invention might have been a baby sling made of animal skins, an object known as a *kaross* among the San peoples of the Kalahari in southern Africa. Unfortunately, as digging sticks and baby slings would have been made of organic materials, the fossil record contains no trace of them. While the stone tools used in hunting are prevalent in the fossil record, the organic tools used in gathering would have decomposed long ago.

If gathering was the crucial food-getting strategy of hominins or was at least equal in importance to hunting, then women likely enjoyed considerable social power alongside men. If women were gathering, they probably contributed to the development of the tools associated with gathering. On the move throughout the local environment, women likely knew where to find high-quality foods and when such foods were in season. If women could provide for themselves, they would have been free to become involved in romantic and sexual relationships on their own terms and to leave such relationships when they wanted. What is known about gathering in gathering-hunting societies completely overturns assumptions of male dominance embedded in the "man the hunter" hypothesis.

Beyond "man the hunter" and "woman the gatherer" hypotheses, cultural anthropologists who study gathering-hunting groups point out that the gendered division of labor in gathering-hunting societies is more flexible than these essentialist theories might suggest. In such societies, men also gather plant foods, and women sometimes hunt for honey or kill small game such as lizards and insects. As mentioned in the introduction to this textbook, a team of archaeologists led by Randy Haas recently discovered the 9,000-year-old bones of a woman buried with projectile points and other hunting implements in the Andes of South America (Gibbons 2020). Having reexamined archaeological reports on the burials of 10 other women buried with hunting tools, Haas and his team believe they may also have been female hunters.

FIGURE 12.8 A statue of Diana, Roman goddess of the hunt. Recent archaeological finds of females buried with hunting tools suggest that in early human societies, hunting was not an activity solely performed by males. (credit: "Diana of the Tower" by ego technique./flickr, CC BY 2.0)

As with evidence from primates and human biology, the archaeological evidence for the origins of human gender roles and sexual relations is not definitive. Rather, the main lesson seems to be that humans are biologically flexible and culturally variable in their expressions of gender and sexuality.

12.2 Performing Gender Categories

LEARNING OUTCOMES

By the end of this section, you will be able to:

- Explain how essentialism triggers circular thinking about gender.
- Describe the performative aspects of gender.
- Distinguish between public and private social realms and identify the consequences of this distinction for gender categories.
- Give an example of the sociocultural construction of masculinity.
- Define the concept of intersex.
- Give a detailed example of a culture with multiple genders.

So if gender is not a "natural" expression of sex differences, then what is it? Cultural anthropologists explore how people's ideas of gender are formed in their minds, bodies, social institutions, and everyday practices.

Nature, Culture, and the Performance of Gender

FIGURE 12.9 The "natural history" of gender, according to this English nursery rhyme, is based on little boys being composed of "frogs and snails and puppy dog's tails," while little girls consist of "sugar and spice and all that's nice." (credit: Walter Crane/Wikimedia Commons, Public Domain)

Gender not only influences how people *think* about themselves and others; it also influences how they *feel* about themselves and others—and how others make them feel. Romantic or sexual passion draws from gendered identities and reinforces them. In the words sung by Aretha Franklin, "You make me feel like a natural woman." There is something about gendered identity that can feel deep and real. The sense that some trait is so profoundly deep and consequential that it creates a common identity for everyone who has that trait is called **essentialism**. Gender essentialism is the basis of a lot of circular thinking. When a boy kicks a ball through the neighbor's window and someone says, "Boys will be boys!"—that's essentialist. You may be familiar with this little essentialist ditty from Euro-American culture:

> Sugar and spice and everything nice,
> that's what little girls are made of.
> Snips and snails and puppy dog tails,
> that's what little boys are made of.

In this view, gender is what you're "made of"—that is, your biological essence.

And yet, biology and archaeology have shown that gender differences are complicated and illusory. What *is* a natural woman . . . or a natural man? Cultural anthropologists find that some cultures consider men and women to be quite similar, while other cultures emphasize differences between genders. All cultures promote a distinctive set of ideal norms, values, and behaviors, considering those ideals to be natural and good. In cultures that consider men and women to be similar, those ideals apply equally to all people. In cultures that consider men and women to be quite different, one set of ideals applies to men and another set applies to women. In all cases, the content of those ideals varies enormously across cultures.

Cultural anthropologist Margaret Mead conducted research on gender in several societies in New Guinea. She confessed that she had initially assumed that gendered behaviors were grounded in biological differences and would vary only slightly across cultures. In her 1935 book, *Sex and Temperament*, she describes her surprise at discovering three cultural groups with vastly different interpretations of gender. Among the Arapesh and Mundugumor, men and women were considered temperamentally quite similar, with little acknowledgment of emotional or behavioral differences between them. The Arapesh valued cooperation and gentleness, expecting everyone to show tolerance and support for younger and weaker members of the group. In contrast, among the Mundugumor, both men and women were expected to be competitive, aggressive, and violent. Among the Tchambuli (or Chambri), however, men and women were assumed to be temperamentally different: men were seen to be neurotic and superficial, while women were thought of as relaxed, happy, and powerful. While Mead's dramatic findings have been subject to criticism, subsequent analysis and fieldwork by other anthropologists have largely substantiated her main conclusions (Lipset 2003).

Like race, gender involves the cultural interpretation of biological differences. To make things even more complicated, the very process of cultural interpretation alters the way those biological differences are perceived and experienced. In other words, gender is based on a complex dynamic of culture and nature. Gender identities feel more natural than, say, class or religious identities because they involve direct reference to one's body. Most people's bodies feel "natural" to them even with the knowledge that culture shapes the way individuals experience their bodies. In this way, gender is not so much natural as it is *naturalized*, or made to seem natural.

In the past three decades, many gender scholars have argued that gender is not so much a set of naturalized categories to which people are assigned as it is a set of cultural identities that people perform in their daily lives. In her influential book *Gender Trouble* (1990), philosopher Judith Butler describes gender as a kind of relation between categorical norms and individual performances of those norms. In childhood, people are presented with the idealized categories of male and female and taught how to enact the category to which they have been assigned. For Butler, gender is "an impersonation" because "becoming gendered involves impersonating an ideal that nobody actually inhabits" (1992).

If gender involves both established categories and everyday performances, then it's necessary to pay close attention to the idealized norms of gender constructed in a particular cultural context and the various ways in which people enact those norms in practice. In *Gender and Sexuality in Muslim Cultures* (Ozyegin 2015), researchers studying Muslim communities in Turkey, Egypt, Pakistan, Syria, and Iran examine the ideals of Muslim masculinity and femininity in those contexts, as well as how those ideals are enacted and resisted in everyday life. Salih Can Açıksôz describes how the Turkish government provides disabled veterans with access to assisted reproductive technologies so that they can father children. The aim of this program is to make them feel like "real men" again, renormalizing their masculinity in the context of heterosexual family life. Maria Frederika Malmstroöm shows how Muslim women in Cairo strive to achieve the purity and cleanliness associated with femininity through such practices as cooking, skin care, and becoming circumcised. The idea is that gender is not at all "natural"; you have to work at it every day and make sure you're doing it right. If you cannot seem to approximate your gender norm for some reason, then your family members, friends, and even the government may step in to help you perform it.

Women and Feminist Theories of Gender

Inspired by the women's movement of the 1960s, many female anthropologists in the early 1970s began taking a critical look at mainstream American anthropology, noticing how the discipline focused almost exclusively on the activities of men—both as researchers and objects of study. In most early and mid-20th-century ethnographies, men were represented as the major social actors, and men's activities were assumed to be the most important ones. Where were the women, and what were they doing? Calling for an "anthropology of women," many feminist anthropologists set out to correct the ethnographic record by focusing more on the voices, perspectives, and practices of women in cultures all over the world.

Examining the roles of women in many cultures, feminist anthropologists began to see some patterns. In contexts where women made strong and direct contributions to subsistence, they seemed to enjoy greater social status and equality with men. Among gatherer-hunters, for instance, where women's gathering activities provided the majority of calories in the overall diet, women held positions of equality. In contexts where women were relegated to the home as housekeepers and mothers, they were more subordinate to men and were not considered equal actors in sociocultural activities. Agricultural and industrial societies both created "public" spheres of work separate from the "private" sphere of the household. Women in these societies were more often assigned to work in the private sphere and sometimes even prohibited from entering public areas.

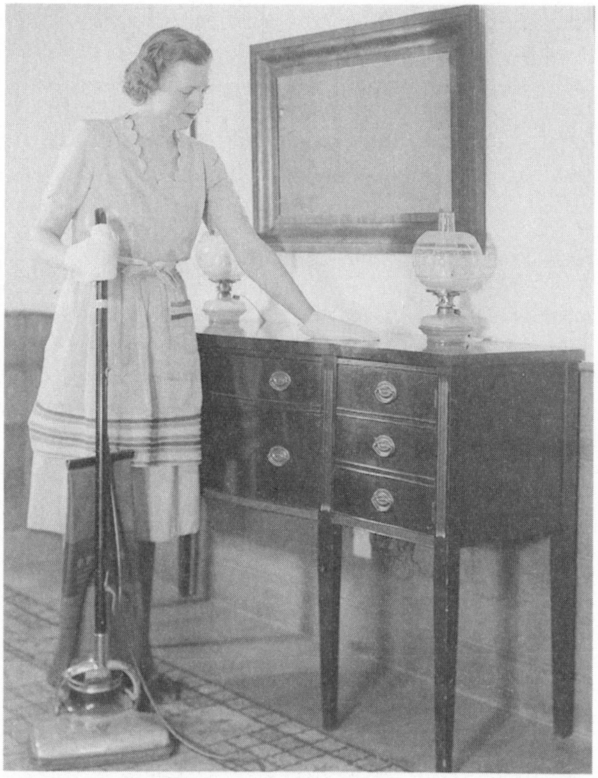

FIGURE 12.10 In the mid-20th century, a cult of domesticity assigned American women to uncompensated work in the home. (credit: US National Archives and Records Administration/Wikimedia Commons, Public Domain)

In capitalist market systems, the domestic work of housewives is uncompensated and virtually invisible. Cultural anthropologist Michelle Rosaldo (1974) argued that the division of sociocultural life into public and private spheres resulted in the marginalization of women.

While this early wave of feminist anthropology focused on women, more recently researchers have questioned the essentialism of this approach. Is gender always the most important factor in determining the status of women in all cultures? Gender intersects with race, class, ethnicity, age, sexuality, and physical ability to make the experiences of women diverse and complex, a position called **intersectionality**. Due to economic necessity, women of color in American society have more often been forced to work outside the home. In fact, many privileged White women have been able to hire domestic workers to relieve them of their household chores—and often those domestic workers have been women of color. For cooks, nannies, and housekeepers, the private domestic sphere of privileged women constitutes their own public sphere of work, supervised by the woman of the house. The experiences of people of color complicate the idea that women are subordinated through their confinement to the private domestic sphere.

Men and Masculinities

While men had been the primary focus of anthropological research up to the 1970s, they had always been studied as general representatives of their cultures. The establishment of gender studies in anthropology prompted both male and female anthropologists to view all persons in a culture through the lens of gender. That is, men began to be seen as not just "people" but people who are socialized and culturally constructed as men in their societies (Gutmann 1997). In the 1990s, a wave of scholarship emerged probing the identities of men and the features of masculinity across cultures.

Cultural anthropologist Stanley Brandes (1980) studied how men in Monteros, an Andalusian town in southern Spain, used folklore to express their ambivalent feelings of desire and hostility toward women. Through their jokes, pranks, riddles, wordplay, nicknames, and dramas, men in Monteros built camaraderie and constructed a male-centered ideology of dominance. A good part of each man's day in Monteros was devoted to telling jokes and playing pranks among other men. Many jokes expressed fears about the sexual power of women, in particular the ability of women to seduce and destroy their male victims. Brandes provides a revealing example of one such symbolic joke:

> A woman was walking along the streets of Madrid holding a dog in her arms so that it wouldn't get run over. She was beautiful, the woman, and a man walking alongside her said, "If only I were that dog, there in your arms!" Responded the woman, "I'm taking him to have him castrated. Want to come along?" (1980, 105)

Research on masculinity demonstrates that "male" is not a stand-alone category but is always held in opposition to "female," even when women are not present.

Other studies of masculinity have focused on the construction of masculinity through initiation rites, friendships, marriage, and fatherhood. Studying fatherhood among the Aka of central Africa, Barry Hewlett (1991) discovered that fathers in these communities are remarkably affectionate, attentive, and involved in the care of their children. Among families with young children, fathers spend 47 percent of their day within arm's length of their children and frequently hold and care for them, especially in the evenings. Ethnographic research suggests that men are not "naturally" awkward or inept at childcare, nor are they less able to forge intimate and emotional bonds with their children. Rather, men are socialized to perform specific versions of fatherhood as proof of their masculine identities.

FIGURE 12.11 A child expresses appreciation for his fathers at the National Equality March in 2009. For many men, devoted fatherhood plays an important role in shaping masculinity. (credit: "IMG_0789" by MYD Photos/flickr, CC BY 2.0)

With the inclusion of masculinity, the anthropological study of gender came to be dominated by the opposed categories of male and female. Many studies take it as given that people are assigned at birth to one of these two categories and remain in their assigned category for a lifetime. A significant number of people in every culture, however, are not obviously male or female at birth, and some people do change their gender identities from one category to another—or even to an entirely different gender category that is neither male nor female.

Intersex and the Ambiguities of Identity

A friend tells you, "My sister just had a baby last night!" You respond, "Is it a boy or a girl?" Your friend replies,

"Well, they don't know. Maybe neither, maybe both."

Based on a detailed analysis of extensive data, Anne Fausto-Sterling (2000) concluded that in about 1.7 percent of births, a baby's sex cannot be completely determined just by glancing at the baby's genitalia. (Note that due to different or changing considerations of sex determination, you may see different percentages or other differences in information; this text is using the most widely accepted and adopted research.) ***Intersex*** is an umbrella term for people who have one or more of a range of variations in sex characteristics or chromosomal patterns that do not fit the typical conceptions of male or female; the prefix *inter-* means "between" and refers here to an apparent biological state "between" male and female. There are many causal factors that can make a person intersex. Genetically, the baby may have a different number of sex chromosomes. Rather than two X chromosomes (associated with females) or one X and one Y chromosome (associated with males), babies are sometimes born with an alternative number of sex chromosomes, such as XO (only one chromosome) or XXY (three chromosomes). In other cases, hormonal activity or even chance occurrences in the womb can affect the baby's anatomy.

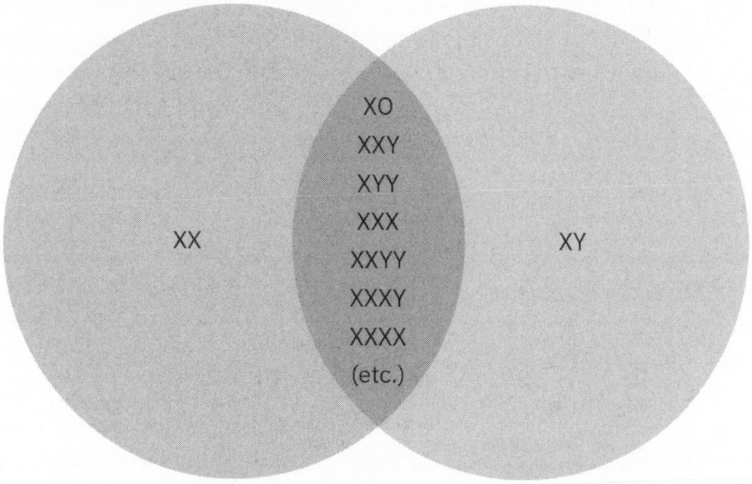

FIGURE 12.12 Chromosomal compositions associated with sex categories. On the far left, the combination of two X chromosomes is associated with female sex. On the far right, the combination of one X and one Y chromosome is associated with male sex. In the center, the most common intersex chromosomal combinations are listed. An embryo lacking an X chromosome is not viable. (attribution: Copyright Rice University, OpenStax, under CC BY 4.0 license)

While it is true that the majority of humans display biological characteristics associated with either one sex or another, 1.7 percent is not insignificant. If that percentage were applied to the global total of about 140 million babies born every year, it would mean that that more than two million of these babies could be intersex. On a more local level, if that percentage were applied to any town of 300,000 people, there could be more than 5,000 intersex people.

Beyond biology, the category of intersex reveals a great deal about the cultural mechanisms of gender. Intersexuality can be recognized at any point in a person's life, from infancy to well into adulthood. Parents often discover their child is intersex in a medical context, such as at birth or during a subsequent visit to the pediatrician. When a doctor explains that a child is intersex, parents may be confused and concerned. Some doctors who are uncomfortable with biological sex ambiguity may order tests to determine the child's chromosomal count and hormone levels and take measurements of the child's genitals. They may urge parents to assign a specific gender to the baby and commit to plans for hormonal treatments and surgical interventions to affix that assigned gender to the growing child. Doctors are often taught to present the chosen gender as the "real" underlying sex of the baby, making medical treatment a process of allowing the baby's "natural" (meaning unambiguous) sex to emerge. This conceptualization of intersex babies as "really" either male or female contradicts the complex mix of male and female traits presented by most intersex bodies (Fausto-Sterling 2000).

Fausto-Sterling disagrees with the practice of immediately affixing a sex to intersex babies through medical interventions. She argues that gender identity emerges in a complex interplay between biology and culture that cannot be assigned or controlled by doctors or parents. In an interview with the *New York Times*, she explained her position:

> The doctors often guess wrong. They might say, "We think this infant should be a female because the sexual organ it has is small." Then, they go and remove the penis and the testes. Years later, the kid says, "I'm a boy, and that's what I want to be, and I don't want to take estrogen, and by the way, give me back my penis."
>
> I feel we should let the kids tell us what they think is right once they are old enough to know. Till then, parents can talk to the kids in a way that gives them permission to be different, they can give the child a gender-neutral name, they can do a provisional gender assignment. (Fausto-Sterling 2001)

Many intersex people support a ban on what they call intersex genital mutilation, or IGM. In an article for *HuffPost* (https://openstax.org/r/an-article-for-huffpost), Latinx intersex author and activist Hida Viloria (2017) calls attention to the hundreds of intersex people who have come forward to say that IGM has harmed them. The underlying goal of sexual assignment surgery, Viloria points out, is to create bodies capable of heterosexual sex. Medical ethicist Kevin Behrens (2020) argues that surgical interventions should only be carried out when surgery serves the best medical interests of the child and, in most cases, medical intervention should be delayed until the intersex person is old enough to give informed consent. Behrens also emphasizes that parents and children have the right to know the truth about an intersex child's diagnosis and the possible consequences of any suggested treatment.

Intersex ambiguity and the rush to hide or eliminate it reveal important lessons about biology and culture. The process of determining what an intersex person was "meant to be" often involves a large set of biological variables, many of them subject to change over time. Those factors vary not only for intersex people but for everyone. Chromosomes alone do not make females and males. Rather, the interactions of genetic factors with hormones and environmental forces produce a complex continuum of gender. Instead of a binary of male and female separated by a hard boundary, many gender scholars recognize gender as a multidimensional spectrum of differences. There is far more biological variation within the cultural categories of male and female than between the two. This is not to deny the existence of biological differences but rather to complicate the concepts of sex and gender, allowing for the normalcy of ambiguity and the tolerance of variation.

Multiple Gender and Variant Gender

Many societies construct additional categories between male and female to accommodate people who do not fit into a binary gender system. The term ***multiple gender*** indicates a gender system that goes beyond male and female, adding one or more categories of **variant gender** to accommodate more sex/gender diversity. A variant gender is an added version of male or female that accommodates those who were not assigned to that category at birth but adopt that identity during the course of their lives. A person whose biology, identity, or sexual orientation contradicts their assigned sex/gender role can adopt a variant-gender identity. For instance, a person might be considered female at birth but later transition to a masculine version of female—what anthropologists term *female variant*.

Cultural anthropologist Serena Nanda (2000) has studied variant-gender categories in many societies, including Native North American societies and peoples in Brazil, India, Polynesia, Thailand, and the Philippines. The widespread practice of multiple gender indicates a common cultural need to accommodate the complexities of human sex/gender and sexuality. In contrast, European and Euro-American societies have inherited a rigid two-gender system that stigmatizes people who do not conform to the gender identity assigned to them at birth. Activists pressing for more gender flexibility can be inspired by examples of alternative gender in many non-European cultures.

When Spanish explorers first came to North America, they were astonished to find men in Native American societies who dressed as women, did the work of women, and had sexual relationships with men. Later, anthropologists who studied Native American groups discovered that some groups, including the Crow and the Navajo, had categories of **variant male** (assigned a male identity at birth but adopting a feminine identity later on) and **variant female** (assigned female at birth but adopting a masculine identity later on). Note that people in variant categories did not fully transition to the opposite gender but rather took on a masculine or feminine variant of the sex assigned at birth. Ignoring the Native American terms for variant gender, early European explorers referred to variant males as *berdache*, a Portuguese term that indicated a male prostitute—though that is not what they were at all. In 1990, as Native American LGBTQ people sought to resurrect their heritage of variant gender, they coined the pan-Indian term *two-spirit people*, meaning people with both male and female spirits.

Two-spirit people were highly valued and esteemed in Native cultures. Rather than facing stigma or rejection, their alternate gender identity was thought to give them special talents and spiritual powers. In many Native American societies, two-spirit people often became healers and spiritual leaders. They were typically very successful at performing the work of the opposite gender. Male-variant people were known for their excellent cooking and needlework, and many female-variant people were great hunters and warriors. Two-spirit people were also called upon to act as intermediaries between genders, such as in marriage arrangements.

Like gender-nonconforming people in many societies, two-spirit people began to realize their variant identities in childhood, rejecting the activities associated with their assigned gender. A boy might want to cook or weave, or a girl might prefer to hunt and play with the boys. If there were not enough boys to hunt, a family might even encourage a girl to develop a variant identity so that she could help provide meat to the family. Sometimes, children would experience visions or dreams guiding them to the tools associated with the opposite gender.

Generally speaking, people of variant gender had sexual relationships with people of the gender opposite their lived identity. So if a person took on the clothing and work of a woman, they would be expected to have intimate relationships with men, and people who lived as men would have relationships with women. Neither two-spirit people nor their opposite-gender partners were considered lesbian or gay.

With European colonization of North America came a much more restrictive system of gender categories and sexualities. As Euro-Americans expanded into Native American territories, Native Americans were pressured to assimilate to Euro-American norms. From 1860 to 1978, children were removed from their families and sent to assimilationist schools, where they were taught that Native cultures were backward and variant genders were sinful and deviant. By the 1930s, variant-gender practices had largely disappeared. However, with the rise of the American LGBTQ movement, many Native Americans have rediscovered the more flexible and tolerant gender system of their ancestors.

12.3 The Power of Gender: Patriarchy and Matriarchy

LEARNING OUTCOMES

By the end of this section, you will be able to:

- Explain the concept of gender ideology and identify two such ideologies.
- Discuss how patriarchy is embedded in practices and institutions.
- Suggest reasons for the absence of matriarchy.
- Give two examples that complicate views of patriarchal dominance.

In cultural constructions of gender, two or more genders are defined in an overall system that assigns various forms of behavior and activity to different categories or gendered realms of society. Some of those activities are considered more important than others, and some of those behaviors are more authoritative and dominant. Gender is not only a system of differences between the realms of female and male but also a system of power between those two realms.

Patriarchy: Ideology and Practice

The author of this chapter, Jennifer Hasty, reflects on what she learned about gender ideology while working as wedding videographer:

> *As a side gig to my anthropology job, I ran my own business as a wedding videographer in the Philadelphia metropolitan area from 2010 to 2017. While the whole venture was driven by economic necessity (I was teaching part-time), the wedding industry turned out to be a fascinating vantage point*

from which to view gender relations in American society. Most weddings were meticulously planned by the bride, with the groom deferring to her wishes or staying out of the whole process. Brides who were attracted to my artsy, minimalist film aesthetic tended to be middle-class professionals, college graduates heading into careers in education, finance, law, or medicine. Many of these weddings were grand potlatches of middle-class style and markers of identity.

Though my brides were well-educated women with professional jobs, when it came to planning their "special day," nearly all of them reverted to traditions infused with old-fashioned gender roles. Nearly all of them wore a long, white wedding dress, a symbol of virginal purity, although many of them had been cohabiting with their grooms (and some already had children with them).

FIGURE 12.13 A bride being escorted by her father to her wedding ceremony. Weddings reveal a lot about a culture's gender ideology. (credit: "Father of the Bride" by stevebrownd50/flickr, CC BY 2.0)

Nearly all of them insisted on being "given away" by their fathers, even when those fathers had been largely absent for some part of their childhood due to divorce. This notion of being a gift, given away to the groom, was so powerful that one bride, whose father was not there, declared in her personal vows, "I give myself in marriage to you." Grooms and their families did not use this language of human gift giving.

The notion that a woman is passed from the paternalistic domain of her father into the care and supervision of her groom reflects a larger **gender ideology** about the relations between men and women in family life. A gender ideology is a coordinated set of ideas about gender categories, relations, behaviors, norms, and ideals. These ideas are embedded in the institutions of the family, the economy, politics, religion, and other sociocultural spheres. As with racial and class ideologies, people often challenge the explicit terms of a gender ideology while actively participating in the institutionalized forms associated with it. Though women have made great strides in American public life in past decades, in their weddings, they still enact a gender ideology that positions them as dependent objects passed between men in the transaction of marriage. The power of gender ideology is that it most frequently operates below the level of consciousness. As you will recall from previous discussions of the term, an ideology that becomes naturalized as "common sense" becomes hegemonic.

Patriarchy is a widespread gender ideology that positions men as rulers of private and public life. Within the household, the eldest male is recognized as head of the family, organizing the activities of dependent women and children and governing their behavior. Family resources such as money and land are controlled by senior men. Men make decisions; women acquiesce. Beyond the family, men are accorded positions of leadership throughout society, and women are summoned to play a supportive and enabling role as marginalized subordinates.

Contemporary forms of patriarchy in American and European contexts are linked to the European development of capitalism in the 1600s. As economic activities moved out of households and into factories and offices, the household came to be defined as a private sphere, while the world of economic and political activities came to be called the public sphere. Women were assigned to the private sphere of family life, where they were expected to carry out nurturing roles as wives and mothers. Men not only governed the private sphere but also participated in the competitive and sometimes dangerous public sphere.

Different forms of patriarchy have emerged throughout the world. In India, the development of agriculture and the rise of the state resulted in the increasing subordination of women in patriarchal social institutions (Bonvillain 1995). Patriarchal ideology and social structure date back to the Vedic period (1500–800 BCE). In the Vedic communities of ancient India, men dominated economic and political life, and women were mostly excluded from these spheres. However, women could exercise some forms of authority as mothers in their households. Girl children, though not preferred, were generally treated well. Girls and boys both were educated and participated in religious activities. Female chastity and fidelity were highly valued, but women could engage in premarital sex without being shunned, and wives could divorce their husbands. Legally, however, daughters and wives were dependent on the men in their lives, who could make decisions on their behalf. A woman was not permitted to inherit property unless she was the only child. In the post-Vedic period, patriarchy was strengthened with the systematic codification of Hindu law. Patriarchy grew even more domineering, with the cultural spread of child marriage, wife-beating, female infanticide, and the disfigurement and ritual death of widows. When India came under Muslim rule in the 12th century, Islamic customs for veiling and secluding women further marginalized women in Hindu and Muslim communities alike.

Though contemporary India is a country of ethnic and religious diversity, patriarchy has become a dominant organizational force throughout Indian society. In rural areas, people often live in large extended family households structured by patrilineal descent. These families consist of a married couple, their sons and sons' families, and their unmarried daughters. Men are recognized as heads of their households, exercising authority over their wives and children. The division of labor assigns men to work as farmers and traders, providing food to the family. Women mainly work in the home but sometimes also help out with agricultural chores such as weeding and harvesting.

In the 19th century, a reform movement called for the elimination of many patriarchal customs such as child marriage and sati (the ritual death of widows). Reformers, most of them elite men and women, encouraged the education of girl children and the legalization of inheritance for women. In response, sati became outlawed, widows were allowed to remarry, the marriage age was fixed at 12, and women were permitted to divorce, inherit, and own property. In the latter part of the 20th century, the Indian state passed laws to enhance women's equality in many areas, including education, inheritance, and employment. Urban women in middle- and upper-class families have benefited from these reforms. However, in rural areas, many of the patriarchal customs outlawed by the state continue to be practiced.

Matriarchy: Ideology and (Not) Practice

As the term suggests, **matriarchy** means rule by senior women. In a matriarchal society, women would exercise authority throughout social life and control power and wealth. Like patriarchy, matriarchy is a gender ideology. Unlike patriarchy, however, matriarchy is not embedded in structures and institutions in any culture in the contemporary world. That is to say, it's *just* an ideology—not a dominant one, and certainly not hegemonic.

While societies with patrilineal kinship systems are strongly patriarchal, societies with matrilineal kinship systems are not matriarchal. This is a common source of confusion. In matrilineal kinship systems, children primarily belong to their mother's kin group, and inheritance passes through the maternal line. However, even in matrilineal societies, leadership is exercised by the senior men of the family. Instead of a woman's husband, it is her brother or mother's brother (her maternal uncle) who makes decisions about family resources and disciplines the behavior of family members. Scholars who theorize the existence of ancient matriarchies suggest that those societies were not only matrilineal but also dominated by the leadership of women as well as the values of fertility and motherhood.

Nineteenth-century social evolutionists such as Friedrich Engels and J.J. Bachofen postulated that matriarchy was the original form of human social organization, later replaced by patriarchy in societies all over the world. This notion was revived by feminist scholars in the 1970s, such as archaeologist Marija Gimbutas (1991), who postulated that the original matriarchal societies of the European Neolithic were overthrown in the Bronze Age by patriarchal invaders on horseback. Gimbutas argued that the Neolithic communities of Europe were peaceful, egalitarian, and **gynocentric**, or woman-centered. They worshipped a mother goddess associated with the fertility of women and the earth. High priestesses of this fertility cult were the primary leaders, supported by their brothers and a council of women. Warfare was unknown. Then, waves of Indo-European pastoralists swept across Europe on horseback, conquering the original matriarchal Europeans and establishing their violent, patriarchal order with its worship of male gods and veneration of warfare.

FIGURE 12.14 The Venus of Willendorf statue, found in southern Austria, is presumed to be about 25,000 years old. Some archaeologists speculate that this statue and the many others like it from Paleolithic Europe are symbols of a fertility cult or mother goddess. (credit: "A Female Paleolithic Figurine, Venus of Willendorf" by Wellcome Collection, CC BY 4.0)

Many archaeologists disagree with Gimbutas's interpretations of the archaeological record and her refusal to consider alternative and more mainstream interpretations of the same evidence by other archaeologists. Feminist archaeologist Ruth Tringham remarked that Gimbutas had "mystified the process of interpretation and presented her own conclusions as objective fact" (1993, 197). While Gimbutas's work on European matriarchy is criticized by scholarly archaeology, her ideas have been embraced and popularized by New Age feminists.

Where are the matriarchies? Why is patriarchy so prevalent while matriarchy is nonexistent? Nobody really knows the answers to these questions. Some anthropologists think that pregnancy and childcare marginalized women, while men were freer to participate in cultural practices, technologies, and institutions. Others suggest that women's reproductive power posed a threat to men. Patriarchy may have been developed as a system of subordination and control over the acknowledged power of women.

In the search for matriarchy, it could be that feminists are looking for the wrong thing. While anthropologists have not found societies in which women dominate and control men, there are plenty of cultural examples in which women and men enjoy relative equality and freedom from sexual oppression and control.

Gender and Power in Everyday Life

Contemporary anthropologists who study gender pay little attention to hypothetical debates about the origins of patriarchy or the possible existence of ancient matriarchy. Rather, cultural anthropologists are interested in how people interact with the cultural norms and systematized practices of gender in their societies. Gender is diffused throughout culture, embedded in systems of kinship, modes of subsistence, political leadership and participation, law, religion, and medicine. Anthropologists study how people move through these gendered realms in their everyday lives. They explore how identities and possibilities are shaped by the structures of gender as well as how people struggle against and sometimes transform gendered expectations.

Cultural anthropologists who study women in patriarchal cultures highlight the diversity of women's experiences and their various techniques of asserting their interests in difficult circumstances. In her study of the problem of fistula among women in Niger, Allison Heller (2019) explores how women navigate gendered realms as they cope with a debilitating reproductive problem. Obstetric fistula is a complication of childbirth in which tissues separating the bladder from the vagina are ruptured, often resulting in chronic incontinence (uncontrolled urination). Often the result of prolonged or obstructed labor, fistula disproportionately affects women in rural and poor communities, who frequently give birth without professional medical assistance. The incontinence, pain, and reproductive complications of fistula stigmatize many of the women who have this condition. A host of global aid and relief agencies depict such women as victims of fistula, rejected by their husbands and ostracized by their communities.

Heller's ethnography complicates this simplistic picture. In her interviews with women affected by fistula, Heller discovered that family structures and relationships profoundly shape women's experiences of fistula and the treatments available to them. In social and medical crisis, these women turn to their mothers for support and advocacy. Mothers may insist that their daughters be brought to the hospital in cases of complicated labor, thereby preventing or mitigating the severity of fistula. Mothers may also act as intermediaries between women and their relatives and neighbors, working to reduce the stigma of fistula and promote sympathy and acceptance.

Heller also found that marriage conditioned a woman's experience of fistula. Whether her marriage was arranged or a marriage "for love," a woman whose family supported her marriage was more likely to receive extended family support. Women who had strong relationships with their husbands were far less likely to be rejected by them after developing fistula.

Heller also followed women into the specialized clinics devoted to fistula care and surgical remediation. In what seems like a very unfair process, women with mild fistula are often the first to receive surgery, due to the increased likelihood of positive outcomes. Women with severe fistula may wait for months for their first surgery and then undergo several often-unsuccessful surgeries. The longer the women waited, the more likely their support networks were to wear thin or break down.

Contemporary anthropologists of gender study women's experiences of migration, genocide, religious practice, and media, among many other topics. As mentioned earlier, a growing number of studies also focus on the social construction of masculinity, exploring how men interact with the gendered expectations of their sociocultural contexts.

It is tempting to assume that men uniformly benefit from systems of male privilege, with particular benefits accruing to elite men. Researchers who study masculinity in cross-cultural settings have complicated this view. Cultural anthropologist Daniel Jordan Smith studied the challenges of enacting masculinity in Igbo communities of southeast Nigeria. In his book, provocatively titled *To Be a Man Is Not a One-Day Job* (2017), Smith demonstrates how gender is not simply ascribed at birth but presented as a lifelong project that men must constantly work to achieve. The struggle for masculine identity begins in childhood and intensifies in secondary school as boys learn "to love women and money" (2017, 30). As rural boys are often sent to towns and cities for schooling, the transition from boyhood to manhood frequently involves mastering strategies of urban survival, such as finding ways of making money to pay for consumer items that boost their prestige among peers and enable their romantic relationships. After schooling, a young man is expected to marry and become a father as well as fulfill his role in larger extended family structures. In his senior years, a man is expected to bury his own father with a spectacular funeral. Men learn these roles largely through their relationships with other men who counsel them as friends and mentors.

Central to the achievement of Nigerian manhood is money. The central markers of adult manhood all require substantial resources. Without money, a man cannot pay bride wealth to marry or provide for his children. In adulthood, men are expected to accumulate wealth through successful careers and business activities and then use their resources to support their families as well as expanding networks of dependents. Elite men who achieve these milestones later struggle to build and maintain impressive family houses, send their dependents to expensive schools, clothe their wives in fine fashions, and sponsor lavish weddings and funerals.

As these examples illustrate, the cultural anthropology of gender considers the situations people face as gendered persons and how they draw from available resources and relationships to fulfill their roles and sometimes challenge gendered expectations.

12.4 Sexuality and Queer Anthropology

LEARNING OUTCOMES

By the end of this section, you will be able to:

- Explain how sexuality is threaded through the life cycle and various realms of culture.
- Describe the prevalence of same-sex relationships in heteronormative societies.
- Define the concept and practices related to ritualized sexuality.
- Give two examples of transgender roles in heteronormative contexts.

Intersecting with gender, the anthropological study of sexuality explores the diversity of meanings, practices, relationships, and experiences associated with erotic interactions. Since the 1980s, the study of sexuality in anthropology has burgeoned into the dynamic subfield of **queer anthropology**. Anthropologists working in this subfield focus on areas of sociocultural activity distinguished from the presumed norms of heterosexuality and binary gender identities (Howe 2015).

Early Anthropological Studies of Sexuality

Cultural anthropologists have long been fascinated with sexuality. In his ethnography of sexual practices among the Trobrianders, Bronislaw Malinowski (1929) identifies sexuality as a central concern threaded throughout the sociocultural realms of everyday life. Of central importance to marriage, kinship, and gender relations, sexuality also pervades art, religion, medicine, economics, and even politics in Trobriand culture. Malinowski charts the sexual life stages of Trobrianders, starting with sexualized games in childhood and continuing with adolescent crushes and expeditions by groups of teenage boys or girls to nearby villages in search of amorous adventures. He describes the selection of marriage partners and the frequency of extramarital sexual relations among men. Throughout his analysis, Malinowski emphasizes that all societies must regulate the primal sexual impulse. In this functional view, sexual norms and rules function to maintain order and protect the institutions of marriage and kinship.

Like Malinowski (and writing in the same time period), Margaret Mead plots the sexual life stages of women and men in Samoan culture in her most famous book, *Coming of Age in Samoa* (1928). Unlike Malinowski, however, she emphasizes differences between the processes of sexual socialization in Samoa and the United States. Focusing on girls and women, Mead argues that Samoan culture had a more relaxed and open attitude toward sexuality. Throughout childhood, girls often witnessed the bodily realities of childbirth, menstruation, copulation, and death. In adolescence, both boys and girls were expected to experiment with romantic and sexual relationships. Free from the repression and strict sexual discipline of Euro-American culture, Samoans experienced adolescence as not a time of crisis but rather a golden era of freedom and adventure.

FIGURE 12.15 Three young Samoan women, circa 1890. In her most famous book, *Coming of Age in Samoa*, Margaret Mead explored the sexual life stages of women and men in Samoan culture. She found that adolescence was experienced as a golden age of romantic and sexual freedom. (credit: "My Trip to Samoa (1911) - 3 Samoan Girls Making Ava 1909" by Bartlett Tripp/Wikimedia Commons, Public Domain)

Shaped by the feminist movement, more contemporary approaches to gender roles and sexuality highlight structures of power in erotic relations between women and men. Over the past few decades, many Americans have become increasingly concerned about the prevalence of sexual assault on college campuses. Forms of sexual intimidation and violence can happen in many campus contexts, including offices and classrooms as well as student events and parties. An online survey conducted by researchers at the University of Oregon found that students in Greek life (fraternities and sororities) experience nonconsensual sexual contact more than three times as often as other students (Barnes et al. 2021). Anthropologist Peggy Reeves Sanday (1990) conducted ethnographic research on fraternity culture, focusing on how some young men in American fraternities engage in violent assault and criminal coercion against young women. Sanday describes how fraternity men used their privileged access to alcohol and party venues to lure insecure young women to parties where they were plied with alcohol, sometimes drugged, and then sexually assaulted by one or more fraternity members. Sanday argues that fraternity culture is often permeated with forms of verbal and physical aggression against women. Not confined to fraternities, the problem of sexual assault on campuses across the United States has prompted many universities to develop consent awareness training sessions, sexual assault response teams, and survivor support programs.

Same-Sex and Queer Studies

Though they may be provocative and enlightening, anthropological studies of heterosexuality are still focused on mainstream gender categories and norms. Even more challenging to traditional Western sensibilities are studies, first emerging in the 1970s and 1980s, that demonstrate the prevalence of same-sex erotic interactions in cultures all over the world.

A contemporary of Malinowski and Mead, renowned British anthropologist E. E. Evans-Pritchard spent his early career studying social organization and witchcraft among two different African groups, the Azande and the Nuer. Later in his career, Evans-Pritchard began thinking about the many stories he had heard in the course of his years studying African societies, particularly stories describing the prevalence of same-sex erotic practices in Zande society in precolonial times. In an article on the topic, he describes how unmarried adult warrior men, unable to marry due to the scarcity of marriageable women and forbidden to engage in adultery with other men's wives, often took younger men as sexual partners or "wives" (1970). The warrior paid bride wealth to the parents of the younger man and performed services to the young man's family just as he would have to the natal family of a female wife. The partners took on the roles of husband and wife, and the younger men referred to themselves as women. As the Azande did not approve of anal sex, male partners had sex "between the thighs"—that is, the older man penetrating between the thigh gap of the younger one.

Like the men, Zande women also commonly engaged in same-sex practices and relationships. In Zande culture, men were permitted to have more than one wife (a form of marriage called polygyny, as you will recall from Forming Family through Kinship). A husband took turns sleeping with each of his wives. In a family of several wives, then, a woman would wind up sleeping alone many nights. If she had married a royal husband with several hundred wives, she might have sex with her husband only a few times in her entire married life. Zande men and women told Evans-Pritchard that lonely wives would often get together at night, cut a sweet potato or manioc root into the shape of a penis, and tie it around the waist of one of the women. With this vegetable phallus, they took turns penetrating each other. Women could also formalize a "love-friend" relationship in public, widely considered by Zande men to be a cover for same-sex relations. Unlike male-male relationships, however, women's same-sex erotic practices were discouraged.

Sexual practices between senior and junior men have been found in many cultures, sparking controversies over questions of consent and child abuse. Studying a New Guinea group he called the "Sambia" (a pseudonym), anthropologist Gilbert Herdt (1984) described initiation rituals in which teenage boys were expected to fellate older male mentors in order to absorb the male essence that would make them into fully socialized men. Herdt termed this practice "*ritualized homosexuality*," though some have argued with the application of Western categories of sexuality to describe such symbolically complex ritual practices.

While some same-sex practices are ritualized, others are more informal and less public. Some cultures construct same-sex practices as a phase associated with adolescent experimentation and tutelage. As in many parts of contemporary Africa, girls in boarding schools in Ghana are known to experiment with same-sex relationships. In Ghana, it's called *supi* (possibly short for *supervisor* or *superintendent*). In boarding high schools, a senior girl might take a junior girl as a special friend (Dankwa 2009; Gyasi-Gyamera and Søgaard 2020). Some of these bonds are fairly casual. The junior girl runs errands for the senior girl, such as fetching water or food. The senior girl provides protection and help to the junior girl (such schools could be full of difficulties, including supply shortages and bullying). Some *supi* relationships can become emotionally and physically intense. The two girls often exchange gifts, write each other love letters, and fondle and caress one another. They might shower together or share a bed. *Supi* is not limited to a special category of girls (i.e., identified lesbians) but has been widespread among schoolgirls, nearly all of whom eventually marry men and fulfill their conventional roles as wives and mothers.

In the past two decades, evangelical Christianity in Ghana has branded same-sex relationships as evils to be rooted out through ceremonies resembling exorcism. While *supi* is an ambiguous practice, sometimes involving sexuality and sometimes not, it has been stigmatized by evangelicals in Ghana. Christian journalists have written stories about wealthy women who snatch away young wives, referring to lesbian relationships as *supi-supi*. Lurid popular films such as *Women in Love* (1996) and *Supi: The Real Woman to Woman* (1996) both sensationalize and condemn women's same-sex practices, associating them with a secret cult of mermaid worship called Mami Wata.

Many anthropological studies describe same-sex practices in societies that otherwise strongly value heterosexual marriage and fertility. In such contexts, sexuality is not so much an identity as it is a ritual, life stage, coping technique, or form of pleasure. Though sometimes shielded from public view, same-sex relations are seen as complementary to heterosexual relations in some cultural contexts, fully compatible with conventional demands for heterosexual marriage and family life. In his research on gender and sexuality in Nicaragua, for instance, Roger Lancaster (1992) found that conventionally masculine men could maintain their essentially heterosexual identities if they took the "active," penetrative role in same-sex encounters.

With the progress of the LGBTQIA+ movement originating in the United States and western Europe, people around the world who engage in same-sex and transgender practices have formed public identities and communities, calling for the acceptance and legal recognition of their relationships. Rather than indulging in same-sex pleasures as a substitute for "the real thing" or as something done "on the side," American gay and lesbian communities recast their own practices as "the real thing," a set of practices and relationships central to their whole way of life. This assertion has profound implications for notions of family and community. If heterosexual marriage and reproduction form the foundation of kinship systems based on the idea of biological descent, then same-sex relationships suggest new forms of kinship based on networks and shared values. In *Families We Choose* (1991), anthropologist Kath Weston explores how lesbian and gay families in the

San Francisco Bay Area constructed family networks that both reflected and challenged mainstream notions of family.

FIGURE 12.16 Boston Pride Parade, 2007. LGBTQIA+ people around the world have publicly advocated for the acceptance and legal recognition of their relationships. (credit: "Children in Wagon (Part 2)" by greenmelinda/flickr, CC BY 2.0)

PROFILES IN ANTHROPOLOGY

Esther Newton, 1940–

Personal History: Esther Newton (https://openstax.org/r/esther-newton) was born the child of an unmarried Protestant mother and an absent Jewish father. After she was born, she and her mother were ostracized from her mother's genteel upper-class family. Her mother later remarried. Growing up in the gender-rigid, heteronormative 1940s and 1950s, Esther flouted gender norms at an early age, becoming "an anti-girl, a girl refusenik" (Newton 2018, 60). She was bullied for her unconventional dress and behavior. As a young woman, she wore men's clothes, smoked Lucky Strike cigarettes, and dated hyperfeminine lesbian women. Thus, before she even came out as a lesbian, Newton self-consciously constructed her "butch" identity—"the first identity that had ever made sense out of my body's situation, the first rendition of gender that ever rang true, the first look I could ever pull together" (92).

For her undergraduate studies, Newton attended the University of Michigan, where she earned her BA with distinction in history. In *Margaret Mead Made Me Gay* (2000), Newton describes her reaction to reading the work of anthropologist Margaret Mead as a college student. Mead's relativistic portrayal of the flexibility of gender categories gave Newton consolation and ignited her interest in anthropology. She went to the University of Chicago to study anthropology at the graduate level with kinship scholar David Schneider.

Area of Anthropology: For her dissertation, Newton conducted fieldwork among men who dressed as women in the American Midwest. Entitled "The 'Drag Queens': A Study in Urban Anthropology" (1968), this pathbreaking work described the experiences, challenges, and culture of gender-nonconforming American men in a variety of theatrical and everyday settings. Her research on this topic was later published in her book *Mother Camp: Female Impersonators in America* (1972), the first major anthropological study of a gay or lesbian community in the United States. In spite of its initially lukewarm reception, the book has since become a classic in LGBTQIA+ studies.

Accomplishments in the Field: Hired in 1971, Newton was a founding faculty member of the State University of New York at Purchase, also known as Purchase College. She helped establish the disciplines of anthropology, women's studies, and gay/lesbian studies there. Newton taught at Purchase until 2006 and is now a professor emerita.

Importance of Her Work: In her memoir, My Butch Career (https://openstax.org/r/my-butch-career) (2018), Newton tells the story of the first half of her life, highlighting the challenges facing her generation of middle-class lesbians. She describes the difficulties of pursuing higher education and building a professional career, including the impossibility of coming out even as she studied and wrote about lesbian, gay, and gender-nonconforming communities in American society in the 1960s.

Esther Newton's work has been translated into French, Spanish, Hebrew, Polish, and Slovak. She is the subject of the documentary film *Esther Newton Made Me Gay*, currently in production, which has a trailer available to view (https://openstax.org/r/esther-newton-trailer). In an interview, Newton commented, "It's been fun being a film star" (2019).

Transgender Studies

Evans-Pritchard's research on male-male marriage among the precolonial Azande provided an example of young men who were socially constructed as women through their wifely role in these marriages. Across the continent, in West Africa, women in precolonial Igbo society could be ritually transformed into men and then engage in female-female marriages as husbands. In *Male Daughters and Female Husbands* (1987), Ifi Amadiume describes how a father with no sons could make his eldest daughter into an honorary "son" who could inherit and carry on the patrilineage. This woman became a "male daughter." If she were married, she would return to her natal compound to undergo a ceremony that transferred her into the social category of male. She would then wear men's clothes, live in the male section of the compound, perform men's work rather than women's, and participate in community life as a man. She could marry women who then became her wives (thus becoming a "female husband"). Those wives would have discreet liaisons with men in the area in order to bear children, who would belong to the lineage of the female husband.

It was also possible for Igbo women who became wealthy and powerful in their communities to take a title through ritual means that allowed them to take wives of their own, just as male daughters could. Even if she were married herself, a powerful woman could have wives to do most or all of her domestic work. Did these powerful women have sexual relations with their wives? Anthropologists just don't know. Amadiume describes women joking about sex between women in such marriages, but nobody knows how common it might have been.

Building on this earlier research, a fresh area of inquiry has developed in anthropology centered on the experiences, identities, and practices of transgender and gender-nonbinary persons and communities. *Transgender* describes a person who transitions from a gender category ascribed at birth to a chosen gender identity. ***Gender nonbinary*** describes a person who rejects strict male and female gender categories in favor of a more flexible and contextual expression of gender. Cultural anthropologists have described a great diversity in the expression of trans identities, pointing to the prevalence of transgender practices the world over.

Taking an innovative approach, anthropologist Marcia Ochoa (2014) devised a research project on "spectacular femininity" in Venezuela by examining two communities: female beauty pageant contestants and transgender sex workers who also hold beauty pageants. Ochoa traces the emergence of the beauty pageant in Venezuela and identifies this ritual competition as a carrier of notions of modernity and nationhood. She explores the competition of young women, or *misses*, in the Miss Venezuela pageant as well as the local and regional beauty pageants for *transformistas*, gay Venezuelans who identify as women. The stylized performances of *transformistas* carry over into their displays on Avenida Libertador in central Caracas, the neighborhood where they conduct their trade as sex workers. In order to compete in these realms of spectacular femininity, both *misses* and *transformistas* undergo painful surgical procedures to make their bodies conform to an exaggerated ideal of Eurocentric femininity.

FIGURE 12.17 Hellen Madok, a.k.a. Pamela Soares, Miss Brasil Transex winner, 2007 (left); transgender women at Trans Pride 2007 in Washington, DC (right). A fresh area of anthropological inquiry explores the experiences, identities, and practices of transgender and gender-nonbinary persons and communities. (credit: left, Silvio Tanaka/ Wikimedia Commons, CC BY 2.0; right, "DC Transgender Pride 2007" by FightHIVinDC/flickr, CC BY 2.0)

Ochoa's work is pathbreaking in its ability to bring together concepts often explored separately or held in opposition: heterosexuality and non-heterosexuality, gender and sexuality, and cis and trans identities (*cisgender* describes gender identity constructed on the sex assigned at birth). By juxtaposing *misses* and *transformistas*, she shows how these seemingly disparate concepts are threaded together in the complex web of Venezuelan culture.

The End of Gender?

In cultures that are strongly heteronormative with rigid two-gender systems, some people feel restricted in their gender identities and sexual practices. In many countries, efforts to create more flexibility in the expression of gender and sexuality have focused on gaining equal rights for and combating discrimination against women and LGBTQIA+ persons. In the past 50 years, this social movement has achieved great strides at national and global levels. In 2011, the United Nations Human Rights Council passed a resolution recognizing LGBTQIA+ rights. The United Nations subsequently urged all countries to pass laws to protect LGBTQIA+ persons from discrimination, hate crimes, and the criminalization of non-heterosexuality. Same-sex marriage has now been legalized in 29 countries, including the United States, Canada, Mexico, Taiwan, and most of western Europe. In many countries, however, same-sex acts and gender nonconformity are still criminalized, sometimes punishable by death.

Where progress has been made on human rights for LGBTQIA+ persons, these changes have made life much easier for many people, allowing them to feel secure in their families, their jobs, and their public lives. Some activists are concerned that such legal reforms do not go far enough, however. Gender and sexuality are not just legal issues; they are cultural issues as well. The strict heterosexual two-gender scheme common to European and American cultures is a system infused with patriarchal values, expressed in patriarchal practices and institutions. That is to say, inequality is built into the heteronormative system of gender. In order to achieve true freedom and full equality, is it necessary to get rid of categories of gender and sexuality altogether? Are gender categories inherently oppressive?

Some people think so, arguing that society should transition to more gender-blind forms of language and social relations. In the United States, a movement is underway to neutralize gender in everyday language. Whereas masculine pronouns (he/him) were previously the default way of referring to hypothetical persons or situations where gender is not specified, followed by a movement toward specifying both masculine and feminine pronouns (he or she/him or her), new conventions call for the use of third-person plural forms (they/ them) as singular pronouns instead, particularly to include people who identify as neither man nor woman.

For example, instead of saying, "Every person should wash *his* hands" or "Every person should wash *his or her* hands," one might say, "Every person should wash *their* hands." (Notably, this is already an accepted feature of everyday English that people commonly use without thinking about; if a housemate tells you, "Someone left a message for you," you're more likely to respond with "What did *they* want?" than with "What did *he* want?" or "What did *he or she* want?") Moreover, a convention is evolving that allows people to specify the pronouns they would prefer, either gendered (she/her, he/him) or neutral (they/them, other).

Will changes in pronoun usage bring about greater freedom and equality in patriarchal societies? Maybe. Many languages have gender-free pronouns, such as Twi, a West African language of the Akan peoples in central Ghana. However, though matrilineal, the Akans are also patriarchal. And gender is a very fundamental aspect of identity in Akan societies, structuring norms of dress, language, behavior, and relationships throughout a person's life. In other words, pronouns do not bear much relationship to the organization of gender in culture and social institutions. In the United States, the English language pronoun system might change to be gender neutral, but women and LGBTQIA+ people will still inhabit those cultural categories. Those categories will not just disappear.

Previous discussions of racial categories have addressed the fact that race is not a set of biological categories objectively found in nature. Rather, race, like gender, is socioculturally constructed. Even so, it is naive to pretend that race does not exist as a social reality that structures inequality in many societies. As discussed in, Social Inequalities, when people try to be "color blind," they ignore the sociocultural reality of race and make it more difficult to recognize and remediate racial inequalities. Similarly, the fact that gender is a social construct does not mean that people can easily transition to a gender-blind society. Scholars of gender and sexuality argue that American society still grants forms of authority and privilege to heterosexual men through the cultural norms pervading public and private life. Asserting a "gender blind" perspective may obscure forms of inequality and violence that operate through gender and sexuality. Race and gender are both powerful sociocultural categories embedded in social practices and institutions. Anthropology encourages recognition of the diversity and complexity of those constructed categories alongside acknowledgment of the real histories of marginalization and struggle. Perhaps changes in pronoun use are just the beginning of more far-reaching changes to come.

MINI-FIELDWORK ACTIVITY

Self-Reflection

Consider your own body. What do you do to your body on a daily or weekly basis? Why? For two nonconsecutive days, make careful note of all of the routine practices devoted to your body (including hygiene, dress, exercise, etc.). Are these practices shaped by notions of gender? Of sex or sexuality? Do these practices shape the way you think of your body as gendered? Do they influence the way you present yourself in social situations? Do you think they influence the way others interact with you? Consider how other people respond to and interact with your body (or refuse to interact with it). How are these interactions shaped by cultural notions of gender and sexuality? Are there notions of power embedded in these bodily practices? Patriarchy? Feminism? Heteronormativity?

Suggested Readings

di Leonardo, Micaela, ed. 1991. *Gender at the Crossroads of Knowledge: Feminist Anthropology in the Postmodern Era*. Berkeley: University of California Press.

Newton, Esther. 2000. *Margaret Mead Made Me Gay: Personal Essays, Public Ideas*. Durham, NC: Duke University Press.

Stryker, Susan, and Stephen Whittle, ed. 2006. *The Transgender Studies Reader*. New York: Routledge.

Key Terms

asexual not engaging in sexual thoughts or activities.

bisexual engaging in sexual thoughts or activities involving persons of one's own sex/gender category as well as a different sex/gender category (or multiple other such categories).

essentialism a sense that some trait is so profoundly deep and consequential that it creates a common identity for everyone who has that trait.

gay people whose enduring physical, romantic, and/ or emotional attractions are to people of the same sex or gender; usually refers to men who are attracted to other men, but may include women who are attracted to other women.

gender a set of cultural identities, expressions and roles that are assigned to people, often based upon the interpretation of their bodies, and in some cases, their sexual and reproductive anatomy.

gender ideology a coordinated set of ideas about gender categories, relations, behaviors, norms, and ideals.

gender nonbinary rejecting strict male and female gender categories in favor of a more flexible and contextual expression of gender.

gynocentric woman-centered.

heteronormativity the notion that heterosexuality is the most natural and normal form of sexuality.

heterosexual engaging in sexual thoughts or activities involving persons of a different sex/ gender category.

intersectionality the recognition that gender, race, class, ethnicity, age, sexuality, and physical ability all intersect to make the experiences of a person in any category diverse and complex

intersex born with differences in sex characteristics or chromosomes that do not fall within typical conceptions of male or female.

lesbian a woman whose enduring physical, romantic, and/or emotional attraction is to other women.

matriarchy a hypothetical gender ideology that positions women as rulers of private and public life.

multiple gender a gender system that goes beyond male and female, adding one or more other categories.

pansexual engaging in sexual thoughts or activities with others without regard to biological sex, gender identity, or sexual orientation. Pansexual people may refer to themselves as gender-blind, meaning that sex and gender are not determining factors in their erotic relations.

patriarchy a widespread gender ideology that positions men as rulers of private and public life.

queer originally a pejorative term in American culture for people who did not conform to the rigid norms of heterosexuality; now used as a term of pride among many members of the LGBTQIA+ community to highlight the fluid, constantly changing, and contextual nature of gender and sexuality.

queer anthropology a subfield of anthropology that focuses on areas of sociocultural activity distinguished from the presumed norms of heterosexuality and gender identities.

sex biological categories of male, female, and intersex.

sexual dimorphism a size difference between males and females of a species.

sexual orientation sociocultural identities associated with specific forms of sexuality.

sexuality erotic thoughts, desires, and practices and the sociocultural identities associated with them.

sociobiology a subfield of biology that attempts to explain human behavior by considering evolutionary processes.

variant female a category of persons who are ascribed female at birth but adopt a masculine identity later on.

variant gender a category of gender other than male or female.

variant male a category of persons who are ascribed male at birth but adopt a feminine identity later on.

Summary

Gender and sexuality are complex and highly variable aspects of culture. Examining evidence from primates and humans as well as the archaeological record, anthropologists have concluded that humans are highly variable, capable of many expressions of gender and sexuality. Cultural anthropologists describe how notions of femininity and masculinity are embedded in institutions and performed by people in their everyday practices. A growing area of research considers the experiences of intersex persons as well as efforts by parents and doctors to assign gender in ambiguous situations. Many cultures allow for greater flexibility beyond the dichotomy of male and female, providing alternative forms of masculinity and femininity for people who wish to transition out of their assigned categories. The study of gender and sexuality also shows how power operates among the categories of gender, particularly through forms of gender ideology such as patriarchy. Like gender, human sexuality is a highly flexible aspect of culture, expressed in a broad range of practices and institutions. Anthropologists have discovered that same-sex practices are quite common even in heteronormative contexts. Recent anthropological research illustrates how gender ideologies shape the identities and experiences of people in communities practicing different forms of sexuality.

Critical Thinking Questions

1. How would your life be different if you had been ascribed a different gender category at birth? Would your parents, siblings, and other relatives have treated you differently? Would your experiences in school have been different? Would you be the same person?
2. How did you learn to perform your assigned gender role? What lessons were explicitly taught, and what did you learn through observation and experience? Who taught you? Have you ever felt as though you were failing to successfully perform your gender role?
3. What would life be like in a matriarchal society? How might family life be different? How would government and religion be different? What values might be emphasized? Why do you think so?
4. Do all men benefit from patriarchy? How might men be limited or harmed by patriarchal beliefs and practices? Do some women benefit from patriarchy? How so?
5. Do you live in a heteronormative culture? How can you tell? Are things changing? What same-sex practices and relationships might have existed in the past in your culture?
6. What does the prevalence of transgender practices in many cultures tell us about human gender and sexuality? Do you think that your gender identity and sexual orientation are fixed, or might they change throughout your lifetime?
7. In your society, do men and women live in different subcultures? In what contexts are women and men segregated, either formally or informally? What forms of social interaction and bonding occur in those situations? What might be the function of the gendered subcultures found in many societies?
8. Would it be possible to entirely eliminate the concept of gender in your society? What might be the advantages and disadvantages of a gender-free society? How would the ideologies and practices of sexuality be transformed by such a change?

Bibliography

Amadiume, Ifi. 1987. *Male Daughters, Female Husbands: Gender and Sex in an African Society*. London: Zed Books.

Barnes, Melissa L., Alexis Adams-Clark, Marina N. Rosenthal, and Carly P. Smith. 2021. “Pledged into Harm: Sorority and Fraternity Members Face Increased Risk of Sexual Assault and Sexual Violence.” *Dignity: A Journal of Analysis of Exploitation and Violence* 6 (1). https://doi.org/10.23860/dignity.2021.06.01.09.

Behrens, Kevin G. 2020. “A Principled Ethical Approach to Intersex Paediatric Surgeries.” BMC Medical Ethics 21:108. https://doi.org/10.1186/s12910-020-00550-x.

Bonvillain, Nancy. 1995. *Women and Men: Cultural Constructs of Gender*. Englewood Cliffs, NJ: Prentice Hall.

Brandes, Stanley. 1980. *Metaphors of Masculinity: Sex and Status in Andalusian Folklore*. Philadelphia: University of Pennsylvania Press.

Butler, Judith. 1992. “The Body You Want: An Interview with Judith Butler.” By Liz Kotz. *Artforum*, November 1992. https://www.artforum.com/print/199209/the-body-you-want-an-inteview-with-judith-butler-33505.

Dankwa, Serena Owusua. 2009. “‘It’s a Silent Trade’: Female Same-Sex Intimacies in Post-Colonial Ghana.”

NORA: Nordic Journal of Feminist and Gender Research 17 (3): 192–205. https://doi.org/10.1080/08038740903117208.

Evans-Pritchard, E. E. 1970. "Sexual Inversion among the Azande." *American Anthropologist* 72 (6): 1428–1434. https://doi.org/10.1525/aa.1970.72.6.02a00170.

Fausto-Sterling, Anne. 1992. *Myths of Gender: Biological Theories about Women and Men.* 2nd ed. New York: Basic Books.

Fausto-Sterling, Anne. 2000. *Sexing the Body: Gender Politics and the Construction of Sexuality.* New York: Basic Books.

Fausto-Sterling, Anne. 2001. "A Conversation with Anne Fausto-Sterling: Exploring What Makes Us Male or Female." Interview by Claudia Dreifus. *New York Times*, January 2, 2001. https://www.nytimes.com/2001/01/02/science/a-conversation-with-anne-fausto-sterling-exploring-what-makes-us-male-or-female.html.

Fedigan, Linda Marie, and Laurence Fedigan. 1989. "Gender and the Study of Primates." In *Gender and Anthropology: Critical Reviews for Research and Teaching*, edited by Sandra Morgen, 41–64. Arlington, VA: American Anthropological Association.

Gibbons, Ann. 2012. "Bonobos Join Chimps as Closest Human Relatives." *Science*, June 13, 2012. https://www.sciencemag.org/news/2012/06/bonobos-join-chimps-closest-human-relatives.

Gibbons, Ann. 2020. "Woman the Hunter: Ancient Andean Remains Challenge Old Ideas of Who Speared Big Game." *Science*, November 4, 2020. https://www.sciencemag.org/news/2020/11/woman-hunter-ancient-andean-remains-challenge-old-ideas-who-speared-big-game.

Gimbutas, Marija. 1991. *The Civilization of the Goddess: The World of Old Europe.* Edited by Joan Marler. San Francisco: HarperSanFrancisco.

Gutmann, Matthew C. 1997. "Trafficking in Men: The Anthropology of Masculinity." *Annual Review of Anthropology* 26:385–409.

Gyasi-Gyamerah, Angela Anarfi, and Mathias Søgaard. 2020. "Caught between Worlds: Ghanaian Youth's Views of Hybrid Sexuality." In *Routledge Handbook of Queer African Studies*, edited by S. N. Nyeck, 254–265. New York: Routledge.

Heller, Alison. 2019. *Fistula Politics: Birthing Injuries and the Quest for Continence in Niger.* New Brunswick, NJ: Rutgers University Press.

Herdt, Gilbert H., ed. 1984. *Ritualized Homosexuality in Melanesia.* Berkeley: University of California Press.

Hewlett, Barry S. 1991. *Intimate Fathers: The Nature and Context of Aka Pygmy Paternal Infant Care.* Ann Arbor: University of Michigan Press.

Howe, Cymene. 2015. "Queer Anthropology." In *International Encyclopedia of the Social and Behavioral Sciences*, edited by James D. Wright, 2nd ed., 752–758. New York: Elsevier. https://doi.org/10.1016/B978-0-08-097086-8.12219-6.

Lancaster, Roger N. 1992. *Life Is Hard: Machismo, Danger, and the Intimacy of Power in Nicaragua.* Berkeley: University of California Press.

Lipset, David. 2003. "Rereading Sex and Temperament: Margaret Mead's Sepik Triptych and Its Ethnographic Critics." *Anthropological Quarterly* 76 (4): 693–713.

Malinowski, Bronislaw. 1929. *The Sexual Life of Savages in North-Western Melanesia: An Ethnographic Account of Courtship, Marriage, and Family Life among the Natives of the Trobriand Islands, British New Guinea.* London: George Routledge & Sons.

Mascia-Lees, Frances E., and Nancy Johnson Black. 2000. *Gender and Anthropology.* Prospect Heights, IL: Waveland Press.

Mead, Margaret. 1928. *Coming of Age in Samoa: A Psychological Study of Primitive Youth for Western*

Civilisation. New York: W. Morrow.

Mead, Margaret. 1935. *Sex and Temperament in Three Primitive Societies*. New York: W. Morrow.

Nanda, Serena. 2000. *Gender Diversity: Crosscultural Variations*. Prospect Heights, IL: Waveland Press.

Newton, Esther. 1972. *Mother Camp: Female Impersonators in America*. Englewood Cliffs, NJ: Prentice-Hall.

Newton, Esther. 2000. *Margaret Mead Made Me Gay: Personal Essays, Public Ideas*. Durham, NC: Duke University Press.

Newton, Esther. 2018. *My Butch Career: A Memoir*. Durham, NC: Duke University Press.

Newton, Esther. 2019. "Esther Newton Talks *My Butch Career: A Memoir*." October 3, 2019, in *Outtake Voices*, hosted by Charlotte Robinson. Podcast. https://voices.outtakeonline.com/2019/10/esther-newton-talks-my-butch-career.html.

Ochoa, Marcia. 2014. *Queen for a Day: Transformistas, Beauty Queens, and the Performance of Femininity in Venezuela*. Durham, NC: Duke University Press.

Ozyegin, Gul, ed. 2015. *Gender and Sexuality in Muslim Cultures*. Burlington, VT: Ashgate.

Rosaldo, Michelle Zimbalist. 1974. "Woman, Culture, and Society: A Theoretical Overview." In *Woman, Culture, and Society*, edited by Michelle Zimbalist Rosaldo and Louise Lamphere, 17–42. Stanford, CA: Stanford University Press.

Sanday, Peggy Reeves. 1990. *Fraternity Gang Rape: Sex, Brotherhood, and Privilege on Campus*. New York: New York University Press.

Smith, Daniel Jordan. 2017. *To Be a Man Is Not a One-Day Job: Masculinity, Money, and Intimacy in Nigeria*. Chicago: University of Chicago Press.

Tringham, Ruth. 1993. Review of *The Civilization of the Goddess: The World of Old Europe*, by Marija Gimbutas, edited by Joan Marler. *American Anthropologist* 95 (1): 196–197.

Viloria, Hida. 2017. "Doctors Resort to Nonsensical Reasoning to Justify Surgeries on Intersex Children." *HuffPost*, July 29, 2017. https://www.huffpost.com/entry/doctors-resort-to-nonsensical-arguments-to-justify_b_597b9b19e4b09982b7376474.

Weston, Kath. 1991. *Families We Choose: Lesbians, Gays, Kinship*. New York: Columbia University Press.

Zihlman, Adrienne L. 1997. "Natural History of Apes: Life-History Features in Females and Males." In *The Evolving Female: A Life History Perspective*, edited by Mary Ellen Morbeck, Alison Galloway, and Adrienne L. Zihlman, 86–104. Princeton, NJ: Princeton University Press.

CHAPTER 13
Religion and Culture

Figure 13.1 A man carries a Tibetan Buddhist prayer wheel, rotating it as a way of sending out prayers as blessings. (credit: "Person in face mask holding Tibetan Buddhist Prayer Wheel" by Grisha Grishkoff/Pexels, CC0)

CHAPTER OUTLINE

INTRODUCTION Religion is one of the most complex and pervasive of all sociocultural institutions. It is also universal. All cultures and societies across time have had beliefs and worldviews that can be classified as religious in nature, even within political institutions that are areligious or avow atheism. Innovative research also indicates that primates, most especially the human species, have evolved physically, socially, and emotionally toward a sense of spirituality and religiosity (see King 2007).

13.1 What Is Religion?

LEARNING OUTCOMES

By the end of this section, you will be able to:

- Distinguish between religion, spirituality, and worldview.
- Describe the connections between witchcraft, sorcery, and magic.
- Identify differences between deities and spirits.
- Identify shamanism.
- Describe the institutionalization of religion in state societies.

Defining Religion, Spirituality, and Worldview

An anthropological inquiry into religion can easily become muddled and hazy because religion encompasses intangible things such as values, ideas, beliefs, and norms. It can be helpful to establish some shared signposts. Two researchers whose work has focused on religion offer definitions that point to diverse poles of thought about the subject. Frequently, anthropologists bookend their understanding of religion by citing these well-known definitions.

French sociologist Émile Durkheim (1858–1917) utilized an anthropological approach to religion in his study of totemism among Indigenous Australian peoples in the early 20th century. In his work *The Elementary Forms of the Religious Life* (1915), he argues that social scientists should begin with what he calls "simple religions" in their attempts to understand the structure and function of belief systems in general. His definition of religion takes an empirical approach and identifies key elements of a religion: "A religion is a unified system of beliefs and practices relative to sacred things, that is to say, things set apart and forbidden—beliefs and practices which unite into one single moral community called a Church, all those who adhere to them" (47). This definition breaks down religion into the components of beliefs, practices, and a social organization—what a shared group of people believe and do.

FIGURE 13.2 An outdoor Christian worship service timed to coincide with the sunrise on Easter morning. Religion includes a great variety of human constructs and experiences. (credit: "Easter Sunrise Service 2017" by James S. Laughlin/Presidio of Monterey Public Affairs/flickr, Public Domain)

The other signpost used within anthropology to make sense of religion was crafted by American anthropologist Clifford Geertz (1926–2006) in his work *The Interpretation of Cultures* (1973). Geertz's definition takes a very different approach: "A *religion* is: (1) a system of symbols which acts to (2) establish powerful, pervasive, and long-lasting moods and motivations in men by (3) formulating conceptions of a general order of existence and (4) clothing these conceptions with such an aura of factuality that (5) the moods and motivations seem uniquely realistic" (90). Geertz's definition, which is complex and holistic and addresses intangibles such as emotions and feelings, presents religion as a different *paradigm*, or overall model, for how we see systems of belief. Geertz views religion as an impetus to view and act upon the world in a certain manner. While still acknowledging that religion is a shared endeavor, Geertz focuses on religion's role as a potent cultural symbol. Elusive, ambiguous, and hard to define, religion in Geertz's conception is primarily a feeling that motivates and unites groups of people with shared beliefs. In the next section, we will examine the meanings of symbols and how they function within cultures, which will deepen your understanding of Geertz's definition. For Geertz, religion is intensely symbolic.

When anthropologists study religion, it can be helpful to consider both of these definitions because religion includes such varied human constructs and experiences as social structures, sets of beliefs, a feeling of awe, and an aura of mystery. While different religious groups and practices sometimes extend beyond what can be covered by a simple definition, we can broadly define **religion** as a shared system of beliefs and practices regarding the interaction of natural and supernatural phenomena. And yet as soon as we ascribe a meaning to religion, we must distinguish some related concepts, such as spirituality and worldview.

Over the last few years, a growing number of Americans have been choosing to define themselves as *spiritual* rather than religious. A 2017 Pew Research Center study found that 27 percent of Americans identify as "spiritual but not religious," which is 8 percentage points higher than it was in 2012 (Lipka and Gecewicz 2017). There are different factors that can distinguish religion and spirituality, and individuals will define and use these terms in specific ways; however, in general, while religion usually refers to shared affiliation with a particular structure or organization, **spirituality** normally refers to loosely structured beliefs and feelings about relationships between the natural and supernatural worlds. Spirituality can be very adaptable to changing circumstances and is often built upon an individual's perception of the surrounding environment.

Many Americans with religious affiliation also use the term *spirituality* and distinguish it from their religion. Pew found in 2017 that 48 percent of respondents said they were both religious *and* spiritual. Pew also found that 27 percent of people say religion is very important to them (Lipka and Gecewicz 2017).

Another trend pertaining to religion in the United States is the growth of those defining themselves as **nones**, or people with no religious affiliation. In a 2014 survey of 35,000 Americans from 50 states, Pew found that nearly a quarter of Americans assigned themselves to this category (Pew Research Center 2015). The percentage of adults assigning themselves to the "none" category had grown substantially, from 16 percent in 2007 to 23 percent in 2014; among millennials, the percentage of nones was even higher, at 35 percent (Lipka 2015). In a follow-up survey, participants were asked to identity their major reasons for choosing to be nonaffiliated; the most common responses pointed to the growing politicization of American churches and a more critical and questioning stance toward the institutional structure of all religions (Pew Research Center 2018). It is important, however, to point out that nones are not the same as agnostics or atheists. Nones may hold traditional and/or nontraditional religious beliefs outside of membership in a religious institution. **Agnosticism** is the belief that God or the divine is unknowable and therefore skepticism of belief is appropriate, and **atheism** is a stance that denies the existence of a god or collection of gods. Nones, agnostics, and atheists can hold spiritual beliefs, however. When anthropologists study religion, it is very important for them to define the terms they are using because these terms can have different meanings when used outside of academic studies. In addition, the meaning of terms may change. As the social and political landscape in a society changes, it affects all social institutions, including religion.

Religious Affiliation	Percentage
Christian	70.6%
Jewish	1.9%
Muslim	0.9%
Buddhist	0.7%

Religious Affiliation	Percentage
Hindu	0.7%
*Unaffiliated/Nones	22.8%

TABLE 13.1 American religious affiliations and "nones," based on the Pew Research Center's Religious Landscape Study, 2014.

Even those who consider themselves neither spiritual nor religious hold secular, or nonreligious, beliefs that structure how they view themselves and the world they live in. The term **worldview** refers to a person's outlook or orientation; it is a learned perspective, which has both individual and collective components, on the nature of life itself. Individuals frequently conflate and intermingle their religious and spiritual beliefs and their worldviews as they experience change within their lives. When studying religion, anthropologists need to remain aware of these various dimensions of belief. The word *religion* is not always adequate to identify an individual's belief systems.

Like all social institutions, religion evolves within and across time and cultures—even across early human species! Adapting to changes in population size and the reality of people's daily lives, religions and religious/ spiritual practices reflect life *on the ground*. Interestingly, though, while some institutions (such as economics) tend to change radically from one era to another, often because of technological changes, religion tends to be more *viscous*, meaning it tends to change at a much slower pace and mix together various beliefs and practices. While religion can be a factor in promoting rapid social change, it more commonly changes slowly and retains older features while adding new ones. In effect, religion contains within it many of its earlier iterations and can thus be quite complex.

Witchcraft, Sorcery, and Magic

People in Western cultures too often think of religion as a belief system associated with a church, temple, or mosque, but religion is much more diverse. In the 1960s, anthropologists typically used an evolutionary model for religion that associated less structured religious systems with simple societies and more complex forms of religion with more complex political systems. Anthropologists noticed that as populations grew, all forms of organization—political, economic, social, and religious—became more complex as well. For example, with the emergence of tribal societies, religion expanded to become not only a system of healing and connection with both animate and inanimate things in the environment but also a mechanism for addressing desire and conflict. Witchcraft and sorcery, both forms of magic, are more visible in larger-scale, more complex societies.

The terms *witchcraft* and *sorcery* are variously defined across disciplines and from one researcher to another, yet there is some agreement about common elements associated with each. **Witchcraft** involves the use of intangible (not material) means to cause a change in circumstances to another person. It is normally associated with practices such as incantations, spells, blessings, and other types of formulaic language that, when pronounced, causes a transformation. **Sorcery** is similar to witchcraft but involves the use of material elements to cause a change in circumstances to another person. It is normally associated with such practices as magical bundles, love potions, and any specific action that uses another person's personal leavings (such as their hair, nails, or even excreta). While some scholars argue that witchcraft and sorcery are "dark," negative, antisocial actions that seek to punish others, ethnographic research is filled with examples of more ambiguous or even positive uses as well. Cultural anthropologist Alma Gottlieb, who did fieldwork among the Beng people of Côte d'Ivoire in Africa, describes how the king that the Beng choose as their leader must always be a witch himself, not because of his ability to harm others but because his mystical powers allow him to protect the Beng people that he rules (2008). His knowledge and abilities allow him to be a capable ruler.

Some scholars argue that witchcraft and sorcery may be later developments in religion and not part of the earliest rituals because they can be used to express social conflict. What is the relationship between conflict, religion, and political organization? Consider what you learned in Social Inequality. As a society's population rises, individuals within that society have less familiarity and personal experience with each other and must instead rely on family reputation or rank as the basis for establishing trust. Also, as social diversity increases, people find themselves interacting with those who have different behaviors and beliefs from their own. Frequently, we trust those who are most like ourselves, and diversity can create a sense of mistrust. This sense of not knowing or understanding the people one lives, works, and trades with creates social stress and forces people to put themselves into what can feel like risky situations when interacting with one another. In such a setting, witchcraft and sorcery provide a feeling of security and control over other people. Historically, as populations increased and sociocultural institutions became larger and more complex, religion evolved to provide mechanisms such as witchcraft and sorcery that helped individuals establish a sense of social control over their lives.

Magic is essential to both witchcraft and sorcery, and the principles of magic are part of every religion. The anthropological study of magic is considered to have begun in the late 19th century with the 1890 publication of *The Golden Bough*, by Scottish social anthropologist Sir James G. Frazer. This work, published in several volumes, details the rituals and beliefs of a diverse range of societies, all collected by Frazer from the accounts of missionaries and travelers. Frazer was an armchair anthropologist, meaning that he did not practice fieldwork. In his work, he provided one of the earliest definitions of magic, describing it as "a spurious system of natural law as well as a fallacious guide of conduct" (Frazer [1922] 1925, 11). A more precise and neutral definition depicts magic as a supposed system of natural law whose practice causes a transformation to occur. In the natural world—the world of our senses and the things we hear, see, smell, taste, and touch—we operate with evidence of observable cause and effect. Magic is a system in which the actions or causes are not always empirical. Speaking a spell or other magical formula does not provide observable (empirical) effects. For practitioners of magic, however, this abstract cause and effect is just as consequential and just as true.

Frazer refers to magic as "sympathetic magic" because it is based on the idea of sympathy, or common feeling, and he argued that there are two principles of sympathetic magic: the law of similarity and the law of contagion. The **law of similarity** is the belief that a magician can create a desired change by imitating that change. This is associated with actions or charms that mimic or look like the effects one desires, such as the use of an effigy that looks like another person or even the Venus figurine associated with the Upper Paleolithic period, whose voluptuous female body parts may have been used as part of a fertility ritual. By taking actions on the stand-in figure, the magician is able to cause an effect on the person believed to be represented by this figure. The **law of contagion** is the belief that things that have once been in contact with each other remain connected always, such as a piece of jewelry owned by someone you love, a locket of hair or baby tooth kept as a keepsake, or personal leavings to be used in acts of sorcery.

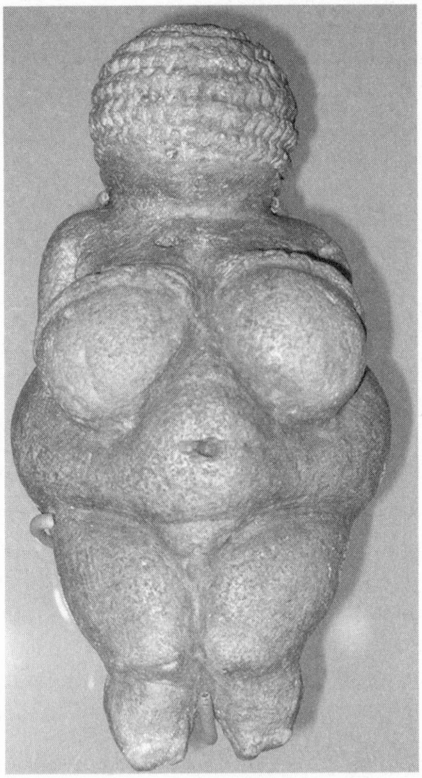

FIGURE 13.3 The Venus figurine was a genre of art most frequently associated with the late Upper Paleolithic period, 25,000–12,000 BCE. It is considered a form of magic because the exaggerated female body parts are believed to be related to ideas of female fertility and reproduction. (credit: “Venus von Willendorf” by Anagoria/ Wikimedia Commons, CC BY 3.0)

This classification of magic broadens our understanding of how magic can be used and how common it is across *all* religions. Prayers and special mortuary artifacts (grave goods) indicate that the concept of magic is an innately human practice and not associated solely with tribal societies. In most cultures and across religious traditions, people bury or cremate loved ones with meaningful clothing, jewelry, or even a photo. These practices and sentimental acts are magical bonds and connections among acts, artifacts, and people. Even prayers and shamanic journeying (a form of metaphysical travel) to spirits and deities, practiced in almost all religious traditions, are magical contracts within people's belief systems that strengthen practitioners' faith. Instead of seeing magic as something outside of religion that diminishes seriousness, anthropologists see magic as a profound human act of faith.

Supernatural Forces and Beings

As stated earlier, religion typically regards the interaction of natural and supernatural phenomena. Put simply, a supernatural force is a figure or energy that does not follow natural law. In other words, it is nonempirical and cannot be measured or observed by normal means. Religious practices rely on contact and interaction with a wide range of supernatural forces of varying degrees of complexity and specificity.

In many religious traditions, there are both supernatural deities, or gods who are named and have the ability to change human fortunes, and spirits, who are less powerful and not always identified by name. Spirit or spirits can be diffuse and perceived as a field of energy or an unnamed force.

Practitioners of witchcraft and sorcery manipulate a supposed supernatural force that is often referred to by the term **mana**, first identified in Polynesia among the Maori of New Zealand (*mana* is a Maori word). Anthropologists see a similar supposed sacred energy field in many different religious traditions and now use this word to refer to that energy force. Mana is an impersonal (unnamed and unidentified) force that can adhere for varying periods of time to people or animate and inanimate objects to make them sacred. One example is in the biblical story that appears in Mark 5:25–30, in which a woman suffering an illness simply touches Jesus's cloak and is healed. Jesus asks, "Who touched my clothes?" because he recognizes that some of this force has passed from him to the woman who was ill in order to heal her. Many Christians see the person of Jesus as sacred and holy from the time of his baptism by the Holy Spirit. Christian baptism in many traditions is meant as a duplication or repetition of Christ's baptism.

There are also named and known supernatural deities. A **deity** is a god or goddess. Most often conceived as humanlike, **gods** (male) and **goddesses** (female) are typically named beings with individual personalities and interests. **Monotheistic religions** focus on a single named god or goddess, and **polytheistic religions** are built around a pantheon, or group, of gods and/or goddesses, each usually specializing in a specific sort of behavior or action. And there are **spirits**, which tend to be associated with very specific (and narrower) activities, such as earth spirits or guardian spirits (or angels). Some spirits emanate from or are connected directly to humans, such as ghosts and ancestor spirits, which may be attached to specific individuals, families, or places. In some patrilineal societies, ancestor spirits require a great deal of sacrifice from the living. This veneration of the dead can consume large quantities of resources. In the Philippines, the practice of venerating the ancestor spirits involves elaborate house shrines, altars, and food offerings. In central Madagascar, the Merino people practice a regular "turning of the bones," called *famidihana*. Every five to seven years, a family will disinter some of their deceased family members and replace their burial clothing with new, expensive silk garments as a form of remembrance and to honor all of their ancestors. In both of these cases, ancestor spirits are believed to continue to have an effect on their living relatives, and failure to carry out these rituals is believed to put the living at risk of harm from the dead.

Religious Specialists

Religious groups typically have some type of leadership, whether formal or informal. Some religious leaders occupy a specific role or status within a larger organization, representing the rules and regulations of the institution, including norms of behavior. In anthropology, these individuals are called **priests**, even though they may have other titles within their religious groups. Anthropology defines priests as full-time practitioners, meaning they occupy a religious rank at all times, whether or not they are officiating at rituals or ceremonies, and they have leadership over groups of people. They serve as mediators or guides between individuals or groups of people and the deity or deities. In religion-specific terms, anthropological priests may be called by various names, including titles such as priest, pastor, preacher, teacher, imam (Islam), and rabbi (Judaism).

Another category of specialists is **prophets**. These individuals are associated with religious change and transformation, calling for a renewal of beliefs or a restructuring of the status quo. Their leadership is usually temporary or indirect, and sometimes the prophet is on the margins of a larger religious organization. German sociologist Max Weber (1947) identified prophets as having charisma, a personality trait that conveys authority:

> Charisma is a certain quality of an individual personality by virtue of which he is set apart from ordinary men and treated as endowed with supernatural, superhuman, or at least specifically exceptional powers or qualities. These as such are not accessible to the ordinary person, but are regarded as of divine origin or as exemplary, and on the basis of them the individual concerned is treated as a leader. (358–359)

A third type of specialist is **shamans**. Shamans are part-time religious specialists who work with clients to address very specific and individual needs by making direct contact with deities or supernatural forces. While priests will officiate at recurring ritual events, a shaman, much like a medical psychologist, addresses each individual need. One exception to this is the shaman's role in subsistence, usually hunting. In societies where the shaman is responsible for "calling up the animals" so that hunters will have success, the ritual may be calendrical, or occurring on a cyclical basis. While shamans are medical and religious specialists within shamanic societies, there are other religions that practice forms of shamanism as part of their own belief systems. Sometimes, these shamanic practitioners will be known by terms such as *pastor* or *preacher*, or even *layperson*. And some religious specialists serve as both part-time priests and part-time shamans, occupying more than one role as needed within a group of practitioners. You will read more about shamanism in the next section.

Shamanism

One early form of religion is **shamanism**, a practice of divination and healing that involves soul travel, also called shamanic journeying, to connect natural and supernatural realms in nonlinear time. Associated initially with small-scale societies, shamanic practices are now known to be embedded in many of the world's religions. In some cultures, shamans are part-time specialists, usually drawn into the practice by a "calling" and trained in the necessary skills and rituals though an apprenticeship. In other cultures, all individuals are believed to be capable of shamanic journeying if properly trained. By journeying—an act frequently initiated by dance, trance, drumbeat, song, or hallucinogenic substances—the shaman is able to consult with a spiritual world populated by supernatural figures and deceased ancestors. The term itself, *šamán*, meaning "one who knows," is an Evenki word, originating among the Evenk people of northern Siberia. Shamanism, found all over the world, was first studied by anthropologists in Siberia.

While shamanism is a healing practice, it conforms to the anthropological definition of religion as a shared set of beliefs and practices pertaining to the natural and supernatural. Cultures and societies that publicly affirm shamanism as a predominant and generally accepted practice often are referred to as *shamanic cultures*. Shamanism and shamanic activity, however, are found within most religions. The world's two dominant mainstream religions both contain a type of shamanistic practice: the laying on of hands in Christianity, in which a mystical healing and blessing is passed from one person to another, and the mystical Islamic practice of Sufism, in which the practitioner, called a dervish, dances by whirling faster and faster in order to reach a trance state of communing with the divine. There are numerous other shared religious beliefs and practices among different religions besides shamanism. Given the physical and social evolution of our species, it is likely that we all share aspects of a fundamental religious orientation and that religious changes are added on to, rather than used to replace, earlier practices such as shamanism.

FIGURE 13.4 Whirling dervishes enter a trance state during a ceremony in Turkey by practicing a rhythmic, spinning dance. In this state, they are able to commune with the deity. (credit: "Whirling Dervishes 2" by Richard Ha/flickr, CC BY 2.0)

Indigenous shamanism continues to be a significant force for healing and prophecy today and is the predominant religious mode in small-scale, subsistence-based societies, such as bands of gatherers and hunters. Shamanism is valued by hunters as an intuitive way to locate wild animals, often depicted as "getting into the mind of the animal." Shamanism is also valued as a means of healing, allowing individuals to discern and address sources of physical and social illness that may be affecting their health. One of the best-studied shamanic healing practices is that of the !Kung San in Central Africa. When individuals in that society suffer physical or socioemotional distress, they practice *n/um tchai*, a medicine dance, to draw up spiritual forces within themselves that can be used for shamanic self-healing (Marshall [1969] 2009).

FIGURE 13.5 Shamanism is an early form of religion. It is based on perceived contact between natural and supernatural realms. Here, a Kwakiutl shaman from the Pacific Northwest coast of the United States makes contact with supernatural forces. (credit: "Hamatsa emerging from the woods—Koskimo" by Edward S. Curtis/Library of Congress Prints & Photographs Online Catalog, Public Domain)

Shamanistic practices remain an important part of the culture of modern Inuit people in the Canadian Arctic, particularly their practices pertaining to whale hunting. Although these traditional hunts were prohibited for a time, Inuit people were able to legally resume them in 1994. In a recent study of Inuit whaling communities in the Canadian territory of Nunavut, cultural anthropologists Frédéric Laugrand and Jarich Oosten (2013) found that although hunting technology has changed—whaling spears now include a grenade that, when aimed properly, allows for a quick and more humane death—many shamanistic beliefs and social practices pertaining to the hunt endure. The sharing of *maktak* or *muktuk* (whale skin and blubber) with elders is believed to lift their spirits and prolong their lives by connecting them to their ancestors and memories of their youth, the communal sharing of whale meat connects families to each other, and the relationship between hunter and hunted mystically sustains the populations of both. Inuit hunters believe that the whale "gives itself" to the hunter in order to establish this relationship, and when the hunter and community gratefully and humbly consume the catch, this ties the whales to the people and preserves them both. While Laugrand and Oosten found that most Inuit communities practice modern-day Christianity, the shamanistic values of their ancestors continue to play a major role in their understanding of both the whale hunt and what it means to be Inuit today. Their practice and understanding of religion incorporate both the church and their ancestral beliefs.

FIGURE 13.6 Contemporary Inuit still use shamanistic practices when they hunt and fish. Here, an Inuit fisherman in Greenland goes out seeking fish. (credit: Renate Haase/Pixabay, CC0)

Above all, shamanism reflects the principles and practice of mutuality and balance, the belief that all living things are connected to each other and can have an effect on each other. This is a value that reverberates through almost all other religious systems as well. Concepts such as stewardship (caring for and nurturing resources), charity (providing for the needs of others), and justice (concern and respect for others and their rights) are all valued in shamanism.

The Institutionalization of Religion

Shamanism is classified as **animism**, a worldview in which spiritual agency is assigned to all things, including natural elements such as rocks and trees. Sometimes associated with the idea of dual souls—a day soul and a night soul, the latter of which can wander in dreams—and sometimes with unnamed and disembodied spirits believed to be associated with living and nonliving things, animism was at first understood by anthropologists as a primitive step toward more complex religions. In his work *Primitive Culture* (1871), British anthropologist Sir Edward Tylor, considered the first academic anthropologist, identified animism as a proto-religion, an evolutionary beginning point for all religions. As population densities increased and societies developed more complex forms of social organization, religion mirrored many of these changes.

With the advent of state societies, religion became institutionalized. As population densities increased and urban areas emerged, the structure and function of religion shifted into a bureaucracy, known as a **state religion**. State religions are formal institutions with full-time administrators (e.g., priests, pastors, rabbis, imams), a set doctrine of beliefs and regulations, and a policy of growth by seeking new practitioners through conversion. While state religions continued to exhibit characteristics of earlier forms, they were now structured as organizations with a hierarchy, including functionaries at different levels with different specializations. Religion was now *administered* as well as practiced. Similar to the use of mercenaries as paid soldiers in a state army, bureaucratic religions include paid positions that may not require subscribing to the belief system itself. Examples of early state religions include the pantheons of Egypt and Greece. Today, the most common state religions are Christianity, Islam, Buddhism, and Hinduism.

Rather than part-time shamans, tribal and state religions are often headed by full-time religious leaders who administer higher levels within the religious bureaucracy. With institutionalization, religion began to develop formalized **doctrines**, or sets of specific and usually rigid principles or teachings, that would be applied through the codification of a formal system of laws. And, unlike earlier religious forms, state religions are usually defined not by birthright but by conversion. Using **proselytization**, a recruitment practice in which members actively seek converts to the group, state religions are powerful institutions in society. They bring diverse groups of people together and establish common value systems.

There are two common arrangements between political states and state religions. In some instances, such as contemporary Iran, the religious institution and the state are one, and religious leaders head the political structure. In other societies, there is an explicit separation between religion and state. The separation has been handled differently across nation-states. In some states, the political government supports a state religion (or several) as the official religion(s). In some of these cases, the religious institution will play a role in political decision-making from local to national levels. In other state societies with a separation between religion and state, religious institutions will receive favors, such as subsidies, from state governments. This may include tax or military exemptions and privileged access to resources. It is this latter arrangement that we see in the United States, where institutions such as the Department of Defense and the IRS keep lists of officially recognized religions with political and tax-exempt status.

Among the approximately 200 sovereign nation-states worldwide, there are many variations in the relationship between state and religion, including societies that have political religions, where the state or state rulers are considered divine and holy. In North Korea today, people practice an official policy of *juche*, which means self-reliance and independence. A highly nationalist policy, it has religious overtones, including reverence and obeisance to the state leader (Kim Jong Un) and unquestioning allegiance to the North Korean state. An extreme form of nationalism, *juche* functions as a political religion with the government and leader seen as deity and divine. Unlike in a theocracy, where the religious structure has political power, in North Korea, the political structure is the practiced religion.

Historically, relationships between religious institution and state have been extremely complex, with power arrangements shifting and changing over time. Today, Christian fundamentalism is playing an increasingly political role in U.S. society. Since its bureaucratization, religion has had a political role in almost every nation-state. In many state societies, religious institutions serve as charity organizations to meet the basic needs of many citizens, as educational institutions offering both mainstream and alternative pedagogies, and as community organizations to help mobilize groups of people for specific actions. Although some states—such as Cuba, China, Cambodia, North Korea, and the former Soviet Union—have declared atheism as their official policy during certain historical periods, religion has never fully disappeared in any of them. Religious groups, however, may face varying levels of oppression within state societies. The Uighurs are a mostly Muslim ethnic group of some 10 million people in northwestern China. Since 2017, when Chinese president Xi Jinping issued an order that all religions in China should be Chinese in their orientation, the Uighurs have faced mounting levels of oppression, including discrimination in state services. There have been recent accusations of mass sterilizations and genocide by the Chinese government against this ethnic minority (see BBC News 2021). During periods of state oppression, religion tends to break up into smaller units practiced at a local or even household level.

13.2 Symbolic and Sacred Space

LEARNING OUTCOMES

By the end of this section, you will be able to:

- Distinguish between a symbol and sign.
- Explain the architectural dimensions of sacred space.
- Understand the meaning of sacred place.

Symbolism in Religion

Symbolism plays a vital role in religion. A **symbol** stands for something else, is arbitrary, and has no natural connection to its reference. There are two main types of symbols. A symbol can be a **metaphor**, meaning that it is completely disconnected from what it represents, such as the Islamic symbol of the crescent and star, which represents enlightenment brought about through God. Or a symbol might be a **metonym**, in which the part stands for the whole, such as the cross, which is an artifact of a specific portion of Christian history that is now used to stand for Christianity as a whole. Symbols are **multivocal** by nature, which means they can have more than one meaning. Their meaning derives from both how the symbol is used and how the audience views it. The more common and widespread a symbol, the more conflicting references and meanings may coexist. As an example, think of the U.S. flag; when draped over a veteran's casket, the flag has a different meaning from when it is waved at a rally or burned in protest. One symbol, multiple meanings.

FIGURE 13.7 (left) In the first image, fog represents the collision of warm and cold air over San Francisco Bay; it is a natural effect. (right) In the second image, the fog/smoke is artificially created onstage at a Rolling Stones concert to establish a particular mood and association. It is symbolic. (credit: (left) "Above the fog" by CucombreLibre/flickr, CC BY 2.0, credit : (right) "StonesLondon220518-82" by Raph_PH/Wikimedia Commons, CC BY 2.0)

The prevalence of symbolism in religion indicates that religions are learned and shared systems of belief. While there are empirical aspects to religion, especially in regard to religious practices such as dance, trance, and prayer, the meaning behind the practices is entirely learned. Symbolism is attached not only to supernatural deities and spirits but also to religious places, myths, and rituals. In the Ethnographic Sketch at the end of the chapter, you will read more about symbols and religion.

FIGURE 13.8 The tools used for working magic displayed on this traditional Wiccan altar include an athame, a ritual knife that is used in many rituals, among them the ritual of casting a circle (creating a sacred place). Also shown are a boline, sword, wand, pentacle, chalice, and censer. (credit: "Wiccan Altar" by Fer Doirich/Wikimedia Commons, CC0)

Religious Places

Anthropologists distinguish between **space**, an unmarked physical field on which imagination or action can occur, and **place**, a location that has sociocultural meaning(s) attached. Many religions and religious practices are defined by sacred places that serve as settings for **hierophany**, the manifestation of the sacred or divine.

Commonly, the sense of the sacred derives from the prior history and the use of a place. In most religions, sacred places are marked by other symbols. A Jewish home is identified as a special religious place. One way of marking this sacred place is by attaching mezuzahs, small casings containing a tiny parchment with a verse from the Torah to external and internal doorposts. Placings these mezuzahs at the points of entry mark the place inside as holy, sacred, and set apart. Like most religious places, the Jewish home is a densely symbolic place.

Religious places are part of the built environment, or places that people create as representations of their beliefs. Religious scholar Mircea Eliade focuses on religious places in his work *The Sacred and Profane* (1959), arguing that one "becomes aware of the sacred because it manifests itself, shows itself, as something wholly different from the profane" (11). He identifies three characteristics associated with sacred places:

- *Every sacred place is marked by a threshold*, which separates the two spaces, the sacred inside and the profane outside. It marks a passageway and a new mode of being: "The threshold is the limit, the boundary, the frontier." It is guarded in various ways and it is an "object of great importance" (25).
- *Every sacred place memorializes a hierophany*, or sacred event, by including an area within the sacred place that is most holy—usually where something sacred has occurred in the past. This is like an umbilical cord (Eliade calls it an axis mundi) that connects practitioner with deity and/or spirit, memorializing the occurrence of something special that happened (or happens) here. In many religious places, there will be an altar or some sort of commemoration in this spot.
- *Every sacred place represents an imago mundi*, an image or microcosm of the world as seen from the religious perspective. In some religious traditions, sacred places will be decorated with reminders of what is most valued by that tradition, using various types of artworks. In Catholic churches, for example, paintings of the events associated with the crucifixion of Christ, known as the stations of the cross, remind believers of Christ's sacrifice.

Eliade's characteristics of sacred places can be useful tools for beginning to understand the role of a place in a religion or a religious practice that is unfamiliar to us. They prompt us to look at the place through a believer's eyes: What happens here? What are the meanings associated with the different parts of this place? What are the proper ways to enter and exit and show respect? Because religion is heavily symbolic, we must strive to understand these places from inside the religious belief system. The practice of casting the Wiccan circle is a good example of creating religious place.

Wicca is a relatively new religious movement based on ancient pagan beliefs and rituals. It is sometimes referred to as a neo-pagan movement because it is a modern polytheistic movement focused on belief in nature spirits. Although it has historical roots, the movement itself began in the mid-1900s in England. Wicca is focused on the dual energies of the male and the female and typically involves the worship of a goddess and a god (sometimes along with other deities), celebrating the natural world and the idea that this dual spirit resides in nature. The pentagram, a five-pointed star, is the primary Wiccan symbol, representing the five classical elements: air, water, fire, earth, and aether (spirit). When Wiccans—also called witches, regardless of gender—gather to worship, they establish a religious place outdoors. This is done through a ritual called casting a circle. Using a ritual knife or sword that represents fire, the witch casting the circle will symbolically "cut" the circle in three dimensions by walking out the circumference on the ground to symbolically mark the boundaries and establish the threshold. Then the caster will call on the guardians of the watchtowers of the four directions—north, south, east, and west—and above to mark the spherical shape as the caster marks the space using salt water (earth and water) and incense (fire and air). Once the guardians are invoked, the circle is cast and the practitioners can enter for the sacred ritual. When the ritual ends, the circle is dismantled by reversing each of these actions and returning the ground to its profane (not holy) status.

The circle is sacred as soon as it is cast and remains sacred until the meeting ends and it is ritually deactivated. The circle is fluid, portable, and only cast for a single use each time. It serves as the entrance to the sacred portal in which the practitioners will encounter and interact with the spirits. Knowing how to properly cast the circle is critical, so a skilled witch is always in charge of this phase.

FIGURE 13.9 Notre-Dame Cathedral in Paris is a sacred place marked by numerous symbols. Note that elaborate stained glass, Gothic arches, candles, and incredibly high ceiling. It is shown here before a 2019 fire that caused considerable damage. (credit: "Inside Notre Dame" by Kosala Bandara/Wikimedia Commons, CC BY 2.0)

While Eliade's approach to sacred architecture remains useful, anthropology increasingly uses a phenomenological, or experience-based, approach when studying place. The phenomenological approach is based on the belief that the meaning of a place emerges as it is used. Within this approach, a church building is understood to *become* sacred when practitioners bring their beliefs and meanings regarding the sacred with them into the sanctuary. It is the meaning assigned to the place by the people entering it that establishes its sacredness. The phenomenological approach argues that the nature of a place emerges from its use and denomination as a sacred place. This a new perspective in anthropology that opens up exciting new fields in the study of religious place.

13.3 Myth and Religious Doctrine

LEARNING OUTCOMES

By the end of this section, you will be able to:

- Define myth.
- Explain the social importance of myth.
- Analyze mythic meaning using a structural approach.
- Explain the importance of oral tradition in religion.

The Role of Myth in Religion

Sometimes, our everyday usage of a word is the same as its scholarly use; when it comes to the word *myth*, however, this is not the case. *Myth* is used often in popular culture to mean something that is false or deceptive, a made-up story that is not true, as in the TV series *MythBusters*. In anthropology, however, **myth** is defined as a well-known story that explains primary principles, beliefs, and values outside of chronological time. Pieces of a myth may or may not be true. Its veracity is not what matters; it is most important for what it teaches. Many times, the characters within myths are culture heroes, semidivine persons whose experiences and lives serve as a teaching tool, allowing those within the culture to identify with them and learn from their challenges. Myths shape a society's worldview, explain its origins, and also teach and affirm social norms (Moro 2012).

There are various types of myths, including creation/origin myths, culture hero myths, and animal myths. The study of myth overlaps with many different scholarly disciplines, including anthropology, folklore, mythology studies, and psychology. Anthropology approaches the study of myth by examining each story for its primary messages about the society and culture it comes from.

Creation/origin myths are among the best-known and most universal myths. Among these, a common type of creation story is the earth-diver myth, famously studied by folklorist and anthropologist Alan Dundes (1962).

In **earth-diver myths**, a creator deity sends an agent, usually an animal, into deep waters to find a bit of mud that the deity will use to create dry land and, later, humans. Through this single act, the deity begins a creative cycle that will eventually result in life as it is known today. Although there are cultural differences in the way this myth is told, Dundes argues that the key elements of the myth are universal: a creator deity, an intermediary agent, and humans created from earth elements.

A Brief Structural Analysis of a Myth

FIGURE 13.10 Anthropologist Claude Lévi-Strauss (1908–2009) collected and analyzed myths as a way of studying culture. (credit: Michel Ravassard, UNESCO/Wikimedia Commons, CC BY 3.0)

Anthropologist Claude Lévi-Strauss saw myths as containing both universal messages about shared human experiences and concerns and particular messages about the cultures with which they are associated. His approach to understanding myth is part of the theory of **structuralism**, and it separates myth into its component parts in order to understand the underlying form—the structure. Lévi-Strauss believed that mythic structure was the same across all cultures. He argued that the concerns of all cultures, expressed within their myths, are very similar. Structural analysis can be very complicated. At each step, as the myth is gradually "stripped down," the information it reveals is more enlightening. There are approaches to structuralism that can be applied more quickly, however, allowing a more penetrating look at the "real story" within the myth.

A brief version of a structural analysis will have at least three major components: **binary oppositions**, which are two contrasting concepts; **mythemes**, which are the stripped-down minimal units, or story components, that form the structure of the myth; and the **primary messages** of the myth, which are universal. Let's look at a version of structuralism in action by analyzing a myth from the Tsimshian people of the Pacific Northwest coast of North America, collected by Franz Boas in 1916.

The Myth

"The Bear Who Married a Woman," collected by anthropologist Franz Boas (1916, 192):

1. Once upon a time there lived a widow of the tribe of the G·i-spa-x-lâ'ᵒts. Many men tried to marry her daughter, but she declined them all. The mother said, "When a man comes to marry you, feel of the palms of his hands. If they are soft, decline him; if they are rough, accept him." She meant that she wanted to have for a son-in-law a man skillful in building canoes.
2. Her daughter obeyed her commands, and refused the wooings of all young men. One night a youth came to her bed. The palms of his hands were very rough, and therefore she accepted his suit. Early in the morning, however, he had suddenly disappeared, even before she had seen him.
3. When her mother arose early in the morning and went out, she found a halibut on the beach in front of the house, although it was midwinter. The following evening the young man came back, but disappeared again before the dawn of the day. In the morning the widow found a seal in front of the house. Thus they lived for some time. The young woman never saw the face of her husband; but every morning she found an animal on the beach, every day a larger one. Thus the widow came to be very rich.

4. She was anxious to see her son-in-law, and one day she waited until he arrived. Suddenly she saw a red bear . . . emerge from the water. He carried a whale on each side, and put them down on the beach. As soon as he noticed that he was observed, he was transformed into a rock, which may be seen up to this day. He was a supernatural being of the sea.

The Binary Oppositions

In order to find binary oppositions, one must identity the important points within the myth—what exactly is asserted in the story. The opposite of each of these points, which may or may not be openly expressed in the myth, is the primary term's opposition. The oppositions form the structure of the myth because they identify what is important. Below are the binary oppositions in the first paragraph of the myth (1). Note that the specific words are not always critical, and sometimes there is more than one version of the quality that can be expressed.

> *Once upon a time there lived a widow of the tribe of the G·i-spa-x-lâ'ts.* (then vs. now, live vs. die, male vs. female, married vs. widowed, together vs. alone, member of the tribe v. nonmember *or* belong vs. not belong)
>
> *Many men tried to marry her daughter, but she declined them all.* (many vs. few, men vs. women, marry vs. not marry, daughter vs. son, child vs. childless, accept vs. decline, all vs. none)
>
> *The mother said, "When a man comes to marry you, feel the palms of his hands."* (female vs. male, mother vs. father, say vs. not say, man vs. woman, come vs. not come, marry vs. not marry, feel vs. not feel *or* test vs. not test *or* do vs. not do, palms of his hands vs. another body part)
>
> *"If they are soft, decline him; if they are rough, accept him."* (soft vs. rough, decline vs. accept, rough vs. soft, accept vs. decline)
>
> *She meant that she wanted to have for a son-in-law a man skillful in building canoes.* (female vs. male, want vs. not want, have a son-in-law vs. not have a son-in-law, man vs. woman, skillful vs. inept)

Even this cursory analysis reveals certain qualities that come up again and again: male versus female, married versus unmarried, belonging versus not belonging (expressed also as accepted versus declined). The emphases seem to be on sex, family, and legitimacy.

The Mythemes

In the "light" version of structuralism, the mythemes are best revealed by retelling the story in shorter and shorter versions, each time with fewer particular details. Using the first paragraph, again:

> (original) Once upon a time there lived a widow of the tribe of the G·i-spa-x-lâ'°ts. Many men tried to marry her daughter, but she declined them all. The mother said, "When a man comes to marry you, feel of the palms of his hands. If they are soft, decline him; if they are rough, accept him." She meant that she wanted to have for a son-in-law a man skillful in building canoes.
>
> (first retelling) Once upon a time there was a widow. Many men tried to marry her daughter, but she declined them all. The mother said, "Feel the palms of his hands, and if they are rough, accept him." She wanted a son-in-law who was skillful in building canoes.
>
> (second retelling) A widowed mother told her daughter to get a husband with rough hands. She wanted a hardworking son-in-law.

Note how the second version of the story has only mythemes of action and consequence. The information left in the mythemes is the critical information, the major points, of the myth. Lévi-Strauss argued that mythemes reveal universal cross-cultural concerns. All specific "local" information is removed. Considering the myth as a whole, the tribe and the characteristics to avoid can be omitted.

The Primary Messages

In this version of structuralism, the specific ways in which the messages are written are less important than what they are generally saying. The general messages are extracted from the emphasis within the binary oppositions. How much emphasis is put on something such as kinship? Sharing? There are several possible ways to say each of the following, but the central messages in this myth seem to be the following:

- Be careful what you wish for. (There may be unforeseen consequences to what you think you want.)
- Don't look a gift horse in the mouth. (Don't find fault with things that are good.)
- Family matters. (Kinship is important.)

Oral and Written Religious Traditions

Religion scholars often separate religions into oral traditions, or local or indigenous religions passed down across generations through storytelling, and written traditions, or world religions that are primarily associated with sacred, written texts. While each may use components of the other tradition—oral storytelling is still occasionally used in a religion that is primarily a written tradition, for example—the emphasis on either oral or written worship affects the nature of the religious system in various ways.

Religions that remain primarily oral, such as most tribal and non-state religions, rely on religious performance as a way of bringing history to life instead of storing this cultural knowledge in written form. Most oral traditions have a cyclical connection to time, interpreting the past as repeating in cycles over and over, and see themselves and their ancestors as connected by enduring relationships over time. One of the clearest contemporary examples of this is a concept in the belief systems of various Indigenous Australian peoples commonly known as Dreamtime. In her study of women's rituals and song lines among the Warlpiri people, Diane Bell (1993) became very interested in the *yawulyu* tradition, the women's Dreamtime rituals. Through rituals of song, dance, and ceremony, Warlpiri women bring their ancestors to life. In one specific ritual, they walk paths near their communities where various historic and mythic events are believed to have occurred. These ritualized walks are called storylines because the women believe they are actually reliving the events that occurred in those locations and bringing their ancestors to life by remembering what happened in these meaningful and sacred places. Men have their own storylines and Dreamtime. Among indigenous Australian peoples, as among many small-scale societies, religion is not separate from everyday life. Instead, it infuses what they do and how they think about themselves. Theirs are oral and performative traditions in which they walk alongside their ancestors as they walk the same trails that their ancestors walked and remember them by remembering their stories. In this way, they turn myth into ritual itself, one intermingling with the other. Myths, for the Warlpiri, are alive and relived when they are performed. Dreamtime connects the Warlpiri people to their ancestors and their history and strengthens their cultural identity.

Even in religious faiths that rely primarily on doctrine, storytelling remains critical. The phrase "people of the book," an Islamic reference to the Abrahamic religions—Islam, Christianity, and Judaism—is used to describe religious traditions that primarily, although not exclusively, rely on text and textual study. Each of these traditions has a primary sacred book used as the foundation of the religion—the Bible in Christianity, the Qur'an in Islam, and the Torah in Judaism. Yet while these traditions are based on scripture (writings), there are also significant oral components in the practice of these faiths. Many of the writings are based on earlier oral traditions and retain characteristics of oral performance, such as repetition for emphasis and to encourage remembering and story units that are self-contained and can be moved around. And each tradition utilizes oral performance in worship, reading aloud from their sacred texts during religious services.

PROFILES IN ANTHROPOLOGY

Manuel Zapata Olivella
1920–2004

Personal History: Zapata Olivella was born in Lorica, Colombia, in 1920 and studied medicine in the capital at the Universidad de Bogotá, eventually working as a physician and psychiatrist. He traveled throughout Latin America, Europe, and the United States, lecturing in the United States at Howard University and the University of Kansas. When introducing himself at the Library of Congress, he stated, "Soy Manuel Zapata Olivella, colombiano, novelista, médico, y antropólogo" (I am Manuel Zapata Olivella, Colombian, novelist, medical doctor, and anthropologist). His work— academic, literary, and medical—extends across all areas of what it means to be human.

Area of Anthropology: Born into a family of mixed ethnic and racial heritage—his father was of European and African ancestry, and his mother was of Indigenous and Spanish descent—Zapata Olivella was interested in identity and cultural diversity in Colombia. While traveling in the United States in the 1940s, he witnessed segregation and racial discrimination against Black Americans; he returned to Colombia and dedicated himself to studying the culture of *afrocolombianos* (Colombians of African descent), even as he continued his medical practice.

Accomplishments in the Field: For his ethnographic-literary works, Zapata Olivella received many awards throughout the Americas and Europe. Afro-Hispanic and Americanist scholars today value Zapata Olivella's work for its cultural detail and focus on an understudied and too often overlooked population.

Importance of His Work: His ethnographic work provided the material for him to write a series of historical novels, the best known of which is *Changó, el gran putas* (Changó, the badass, 1983), an epic novel tracing the African diaspora from its origins in the slave trade across generations. His work incorporated many of the syncretic religious and mythic elements of contemporary *afrocolombianos*. Speaking at a national literary event on the importance of studying Afro-Colombian identity and culture today, he said, "For young countries such as ours, to assert our traditions, our evolutionary reality, our creative force is to take possession of ourselves, to come of age" (Zapata Olivella 2010, 185). On the *afrocolombiano* experience in the Americas, Zapata Olivella published more than a dozen novels and numerous short stories and essays (Selected Correspondence).

13.4 Rituals of Transition and Conformity

LEARNING OUTCOMES

By the end of this section, you will be able to:

- Identify the characteristics of ritual.
- Describe how ritual reinforces social solidarity.
- Distinguish between the different types of ritual.
- Explain the social forces of liminality and communitas.
- Identify the stages of rites of passage.

The Varieties of Ritual Experience in Religion

Rituals, also called *rites*, are performative acts by which we carry out our religious beliefs, public and private. As sociologist Émile Durkheim noted, they follow a formal order or sequence, called a liturgical order; are performed in a place that is set apart and sacred during the time of the performance; and are inherently social. Unlike idiosyncratic behaviors that an individual may practice on their own, rituals are learned and shared. They foster social solidarity and identity within a community of believers (this a focus of Durkheim's). Even when performing a religious ritual alone, such as walking a labyrinth during meditation, the ritual itself, because it is learned as part of a larger body of religious practices, connects the individual to the larger community.

FIGURE 13.11 Walking a labyrinth, such as this one in Grace Cathedral in San Francisco, California, is experienced by many people as a meditative or prayerful ritual. (credit: “Grace Cathedral Labyrinth” by Jay Galvin/flickr, CC BY 2.0)

Rituals tend to have a common structure even though ritual and ritual performance can be quite variable. In his work *Ritual* (1993), West African writer and ritual scholar Malidoma Somé ([1993] 1997, 68) outlines the major stages of most ritual acts:

1. **Opening:** “setting the stage” by designating the purpose of the ritual and gathering the human participants
2. **Invocation:** calling upon the spirit world to join the group
3. **Dialogue:** establishing an open connection/communication between participants and the spirit world
4. **Repetition:** fixed sequences, prayers, and/or acts that are required to legitimize the ritual’s purpose
5. **Closure:** a blessing or other form of official dismissal for both human and spirit participants

Even when rituals are scripted and parts are carefully read and followed, individual participation and collaboration will subtly change a ritual each time it is enacted or performed. Rituals are never exactly duplicated, and not all rituals serve the same purpose. Some are primarily performed to affirm, strengthen, and maintain solidarity within the group; some are social markers of life transformations for individuals, families, or groups; and others address healing and the need for renewal. There are many categories of ritual: commemoration feasts or rituals (e.g., Christmas or Hannukah), which are usually held over a calendrical cycle, usually a year; divinatory rites to find the causes of illness, ask for healing, or prophesy about the future, which usually occur on an as-needed basis; and rites of rebellion, in which social rules and norms may be inverted to emphasize their value within a society. Incwala, a ritual found among the Swazi, a group in southern Africa, is a national holiday during which many social rules are suspended or inverted, allowing women to take on men’s public roles and men to take on women’s household duties in a public farce. Among the Swazi, this ritual is understood to illustrate the value of different gender roles in society as well as the importance of social norms in reducing social disorder. In the United States, Halloween is also a rite of rebellion, one in which children go out at night to beg for candy from neighbors. Among the most common broad types of *religious* ritual, though, are rites of intensification, rites of passage, and rites of affliction.

Rites of Intensification

Called by various names, such as rites of affirmation and calendrical rites, **rites of intensification** are performed to affirm, strengthen, and maintain bonds of solidarity. Most of the repetitive religious services that are offered through churches, synagogues, and mosques are rites of intensification. These rituals tend to have a rather stable and repetitive structure that allows practitioners to follow along easily. If you attend or participant in any kind of repetitive daily, weekly, or monthly religious ritual, it is likely a rite of intensification. These rites define and indoctrinate individuals so that they identify as a religious community, even though there may be other ritual acts accompanying it. It is not unusual in state religions for these rites to create unity among believers across cultures and nation-states. A good example is the daily practice of Islamic prayer, or *salat*. *Salat* involves praying in the direction of the holy city of Mecca at dawn, noon, midafternoon, sunset, and evening every day, regardless of where the believer is located or even what they are doing. *Salat* establishes a direct relationship between the believer and God and affirms one's membership in a global community of Muslims.

FIGURE 13.12 An Islamic congregation practices a rite of intensification called *salat*, or ritual prayer. (credit: "Istanbul" by FaceMePLS/Wikimedia Commons, CC BY 2.0)

Rites of Passage

First identified by anthropologist Arnold van Gennep in 1909, **rites of passage** mark social transformations in people's lives and establish a change in social status within their communities. Associated most commonly with birth, puberty, marriage, and death, these rituals can be prolonged ceremonies during which the individual receives instruction and preparation for this change in their lives. Gennep noted that there are three stages in a rite of passage—separation, transition, and incorporation—and that during the transition stage, the individual must traverse a threshold (*limen* in Latin) from their old social position or status to a new one.

1. ***Separation* (pre-limen).** The separation phase is marked by detachment from one's previous status. While the person or people involved may be physically separated and held in a special place, the separation normally occurs within daily life over a period of time and is always marked symbolically. Some examples of separation are the formal engagement of a couple with rings and a period of preparation for the upcoming marriage; the process of catechesis, or formal religious instruction, for young people planning to be baptized or confirmed in a Christian church; and wearing special clothing or colors while mourning the death of a family member.
2. ***Transition* (liminality).** The transition phase is marked by an ambiguity of status and associated with instruction and teaching. This phase is usually restricted to the period in which an active and public ritual transformation is taking place. The person or people involved, already separated from their previous status and identity, are now transformed into a new status. This is the most active phase of a rite of passage. It is highly scripted and almost always involves teachers, guides, or mentors who usher the individuals through the proper steps to a new social status. Some examples of transition are the marriage

ceremony itself, the actual baptism or confirmation ritual in the church, and the funeral service for a loved one.

3. ***Incorporation* (post-limen).** The incorporation phase is marked by a formal public presentation of the person or people who have gone through the ritual. During incorporation, different symbols are used to express a new social status and identity. In this last stage, those going through the transformation begin to assume the rights, privileges, and responsibilities of their new social status. This might include changing their names, moving to a new location, or wearing different clothing. In many rites of passage, this is an extended period that can last from months to years.

Anthropologist Victor Turner (1969) discusses in detail the significance of **liminality** in rites of passage. During liminality, an individual is what Turner calls "betwixt and between" (95), without social status or standing, outside of the structure, and in transition from one social stage to another. It is a form of social death. Often, the individual will be dressed in uniform, unmarked clothing and follow behaviors associated with humility and anonymity in their culture. There is also an expectation of total obedience during the change of status, as the individual depends on ritual leaders (gatekeepers) to teach, coach, and mentor them through the passage. If there is a cohort of individuals participating in the rite of passage, such as an age grade going through puberty rites, the participants will share a strong sense of equality and social bonding among themselves, referred to as **communitas**. Through Turner's research on the Ndembu of Zambia, anthropologists were better able to understand these common mechanisms of social change.

One example of a rite of passage among the Navajo of the southwestern United States is the Kinaaldá. The Kinaaldá is a traditional coming-of-age ceremony (a puberty rite) for young Navajo women that occurs shortly after a girl's first menstrual cycle and involves her extended family and community (Carey 2010; Meza 2019). Typically, the ceremony lasts four days and occurs both inside a traditional Navajo house, called a hogan, and in the surrounding area, where the girl will periodically run to ensure that she has a strong and healthy life. At the beginning of the ceremony, as separation begins, the girl lies down and her family straightens her limbs and helps dress her and prepare her for the transition. During the days of seclusion, there are many different tasks as the girl is initiated into womanhood. On the third day, she and her mother will bake a corn cake called an *alkaan*, and then, led by a Navajo medicine man or woman, they will sing prayer songs all night until the sunrise. During the final stage of the Kinaaldá, in the morning of the fourth day, the mother washes her daughter's hair and dries it with cornmeal (corn is a Navajo deity). The young woman will then take her last run toward the east, now followed by many young children, so that she might eventually become a loving mother whom her children will always follow. After the ceremony, she is reintroduced to her community as a woman and not a child; she is now considered a young adult.

Not all rites of passage are religious. There are also secular rites of passage, such as graduation or quinceañera, a celebratory birthday for 15-year-old girls in many Latin American communities. And sometimes the religious and the secular are intermingled, as in a marriage ceremony that is both civil and religious. Societies use both secular and religious rites of passage to mark changes in the life cycle of their members.

Rites of Affliction

Unlike rites of intensification and many rites of passage, **rites of affliction** are usually non-calendrical and unplanned. Normally classified as healing rituals or petitions for supernatural intervention, these rites seek remedy or compensation for the affliction. Whether directly through a shamanic journey or through the mediation of a religious leader, communities petition the spirits or deity for healing or a blessing. While illness and health in most Western societies are understood to be biomedical phenomena based on empirical evidence, in non-Western societies and in localized religious traditions across cultures, well-being is viewed as a relationship between body and soul and thus is believed to have a religious component.

While nonbelievers might refer to rites of affliction as **superstition**, a belief or practice that has no credible evidence for its efficacy, for believers, these religious rites allow them to plead for help and sometimes control the outcome of threatening life events. Rites of affliction, first described by vary greatly depending on the need. People may perform witchcraft and sorcery to determine the source of affliction, **exorcism** to remove the presence of an adverse spirit, or divination to identify the source of harm. **Divination** is a practice or test intended to gain understanding, guidance, or advice about an event or situation. There are literally hundreds of different methods of divination. Some examples include scapulimancy (burning the shoulder blade of a cow or antelope and reading a message in the burn pattern), tasseomancy (reading tea leaves at the bottom of a cup), oomancy (rubbing an egg over an area of illness or pain and then breaking it open to read a pattern), bibliomancy (randomly opening the Bible or another book and seeking a message in whatever passage is on that page), reading tarot cards, and checking astrological signs.

One common rite of affliction in the Christian tradition is the laying on of hands. This ritual appears in the Bible, used both as a means of conveying the Holy Spirit (Num. 27:15-23; Acts 8:14–19) and as an act of healing by Christ (Luke 4:40). Today, in many Pentecostal and Evangelical churches, congregations practice the ritual of laying on of hands. Believers place their hands on the shoulders or head of the congregant who seeks healing—whether from social, mental, or physical distress—in the belief that with fervent prayer and physical contact, the Holy Spirit can move from one individual to another to strengthen, heal, and anoint them with God's grace. Sometimes the "helpers" stand face-to-face or bend over the individual seeking help. Sometimes believers walk behind the individual in need, who sits in a chair, and then lay hands on their shoulders and pray, either silently or aloud so that the afflicted individual can hear the prayer being offered. In these acts, the religious community pools its spiritual and social resources and encourages the afflicted member—a powerful antidote to illness no matter the faith tradition.

Although they are not exclusively associated with rites of affliction and are sometimes performed as acts of obedience, celebration, spiritual merit, enlightenment, or even penance, **pilgrimage** is often practiced as a rite to seek redress and healing. A sacred journey to a shrine or holy place, pilgrimage is practiced in many religions. Some of the most famous pilgrimages are the hajj, an Islamic pilgrimage to Saudi Arabia; the Christian pilgrimage to the Sanctuary of Our Lady of Lourdes, a site in France where Mary is believed to have appeared; and the Hindu pilgrimage to the River Ganges in India.

FIGURE 13.13 The hajj is a Muslim pilgrimage to Mecca, pictured here, which is the birthplace of the prophet Mohammed. At the center of the photo, note the Ka'aba, the symbolic dwelling place of Allah. (credit: "Holy Ka'ba" by Camera Eye/flickr, CC BY 2.0)

The hajj is one of the five pillars, or primary tenets, of Islam. For believers with the physical ability and financial means, completing the hajj to Mecca, Saudi Arabia, is essential to their faith. While the pilgrimage itself may occur at any time during the last three months of the Islamic calendar, the last five to six days of the 12th month are those on which the most significant rituals occur. Based on the lunar calendar, the hajj is a movable feast, meaning it is a celebration whose dates vary each year and will occur in different seasons over a cycle of years. Because the Islamic calendar is a lunar calendar, it does not coincide annually with the Gregorian calendar followed by most of the Western world today.

Historically, pilgrims arrived by walking, using the travel time and its accompanying struggles to focus on growing in their faith. Some individuals continue this traditional means of completing the hajj, but other devotees arrive by boat, bus, or plane, dedicating themselves to contemplation once they arrive. Mecca is an important symbolic place for Muslims because it was the birthplace of the Prophet Muhammad. During the hajj ritual, the pilgrims will perform many faith acts, including circling the Ka'aba, a building at the center of the mosque representing the most sacred place, seven times clockwise to open the ritual; praying; running between the nearby hills of Safa and Marwah; clipping their hair; going east of Mecca to confess their sins and seek atonement; gathering pebbles to perform a symbolic stoning of the devil; buying sacrifice vouchers so that an animal will be sacrificed on their behalf; and then again circling the Ka'aba seven times, this time counterclockwise, to close the hajj.

13.5 Other Forms of Religious Practice

LEARNING OUTCOMES

By the end of this section, you will be able to:

- Identify utopian religious communities.
- Explain the historical and social importance of the Shakers.
- Identify secular religion.
- Give an example of secular religion.

Utopian Religious Communities

While the most typical form of religious community today is a group of people who share a common faith and set of beliefs and meet periodically to worship, there are other ways of creating religious community. One example, widespread in the United States during the 19th century, is utopian religious communities. A utopian community is a community intentionally established by a group of people seeking to live out their ideas of an ideal society. Utopian communities may be secular or religious. The utopian communities that are most successful share certain characteristics: they are physically separate from the larger society; establish a degree of economic self-sufficiency, through either agriculture or industry; and have a clear authority structure and ideology, or shared set of beliefs.

There have been dozens of utopian religious communities in American history. In the 19th century, many people in Europe viewed the United States as a blank slate, a country unburdened by history or tradition. The forced removal of Indigenous peoples opened up vast areas of land and natural resources to White settlers and new religious groups seeking autonomy. While many of these societies were short-lived, impractical, and troubled by discord, they were home to thousands of Americans during the 19th and 20th centuries. Today, we still find small utopian communities throughout the United States, some based primarily on religion (such as the Bruderhof) and others on sustainable economics (e.g., Serenbe in Fulton County, Georgia).

Religious utopian communities make particular religious beliefs the center of the community. Some such communities separate themselves completely from secular society, while others establish an enclave, a so-called heaven on Earth within the larger society, that members hope will spread outward and attract more converts. Although utopian religious communities are relatively rare today, they do exist. The Amish, found throughout the United States but primarily in Pennsylvania, Ohio, and Indiana, live in small, self-contained farming communities built around very traditional Swiss German and Protestant roots. The Amish have what they call a plain lifestyle based on simple technology, and they tend to separate themselves from the non-Amish communities around them. The Hutterites, now located primarily in Canada, are also from German Protestant roots and are much like the Amish, except they typically are more interactive with their non-Hutterite neighbors and do not prohibit more modern technology. The Bruderhof are more recent utopian religious communities, originating in the 1920s, also with German Protestant roots but now found in many different places, including South America, Africa, Europe, Australia, and the United States. The Bruderhof have a communal lifestyle based on biblical ideals, though they interact with communities around them. While they do have Bruderhof industries, such as a furniture industry for special-needs children, they also work and study in secular society.

Among the most successful of the 19th-century American religious utopian communities was the United

Society of Believers in Christ's Second Appearing, commonly known as the Shakers. Although they first formed near the city of Manchester in England in the mid-1700s, the group did not become a self-sustaining utopian community until after members immigrated to the United States in 1774. Their first settlement was established at Watervliet, New York, in 1776 under the leadership of an Englishwoman, Ann Lee. Mother Ann, as Shakers called her, and her original eight English followers traveled throughout New England seeking converts to join the community at Watervliet. Following Mother Ann's death in 1784, caused by beatings she received during her period of itinerant evangelism, the Shaker society began to develop a more formal structure that codified beliefs, social expectations, and a strict work ethic. By 1790, new members were required to sign covenants in which they pledged to consecrate all of their property to the society, work for the communal good of the group, follow a celibate life (with those who were already married ending their marriages prior to formally becoming a Shaker), and adhere to Shaker principles and beliefs. From a single, small settlement at Watervliet, Shaker societies grew and spread over 10 U.S. states—New York, Connecticut, Maine, Massachusetts, New Hampshire, Ohio, Indiana, Kentucky, Florida, and Georgia—with a membership at its height in excess of 6,000 individuals. Today, the Shakers survive as a single remaining society at Sabbathday Lake, Maine. There are now two remaining covenanted Shakers.

The Shakers are a millennialist Christian faith, meaning that they believe that Christ has already returned and is present now on Earth as the Holy Spirit within believers. With Christ within them, Shakers believe that it is their duty to establish a heaven on Earth. The Shaker principles of faith historically encompass a range of social and religious tenets. They believe that God is dual, both male and female, and they practice gender equality, vesting leadership in both men and women since their beginnings in the late 18th century. They also embrace a commitment to racial equality. Even during the 19th century, as the Civil War raged throughout the United States, this included the practice of housing Black people and White people within the same community with equal access to resources. Shakers are dedicated pacifists, refusing to engage in warfare, and they commit to hard physical labor and self-improvement, taking as their motto a phrase attributed to Mother Ann: "Hands to work and hearts to God."

The Shakers contributed a great deal to the material culture of the United States. Examples of products developed and successfully marketed by the group include paper seed packets (now used throughout the seed industry worldwide), their simple and graceful furniture, an improved washing machine, waterproof clothing, the circular saw, and medicinal herbs. Their artifacts, architecture, and music continue to be widely recognized and highly regarded. The Shaker song "Simple Gifts" (1848), borrowed and used by Aaron Copland in his ballet score *Appalachian Spring* (1944), has been performed at three U.S. presidential inaugurations.

While there are few Shakers left today, they remind us of the importance of religion as an enduring institution, the power of religion to bind people together into common cause, and the rich diversities embedded in the heart of faith traditions.

FIGURE 13.14 Shaker Ricardo Beldin, seated in a workshop at the Hancock Shaker Village in Massachetts, makes oval wooden boxes to sell in 1935. The Shakers, who took as their motto "Hands to work and hearts to God," earned a reputation for producing elegant and well-made objects for everyday use. (credit: "Brother Ricardo Belden, box maker" by Samuel Kravitt/Library of Congress Prints & Photographs Online Catalog, Public Domain)

Secular Religion

Secular religion is a system of beliefs held by a society that elevates social ideas, qualities, or commodities to a metaphysical, semidivine status. Often, the group sees itself in terms of a divine image, creating a situation in which, as Émile Durkheim famously said, "society = God." Various types and degrees of nationalism are a form of secular religion in which a group shows honor, respect, and allegiance to the nation itself as a sacred entity. For large and diverse societies, secular religion can create a powerful and enduring bond among otherwise very different groups of people. Often, philosophical ideas and materialism itself have been at the center of secular religion.

One of the most prominent examples of secular religion is nationalism, the belief that the nation-state and its interests are more important than those of local groups. U.S. sociologist Robert Bellah (1967) studied secular religion in the United States and documented the many ways that American society uses religious practices, such as myth, ritual, and sacred space, to elevate the idea of the nation-state. During occasions such as presidential inaugurations and the convocation of Congress, for example, it is routine to use sacred language and prayer, elevating the nation-state to a privileged, sacred status, blessed, ordained, and legitimized by religious imagery. Rituals such as raising the national flag while saying a pledge to the nation-state, flying flags at full versus half-mast, and draping flags over the coffins of deceased service members are practices of secular religion. Burials at nation-state cemeteries such as Arlington National Cemetery may be filled with imagery of secular religion, including a caisson, a bugler, a drummer, and gun salutes.

ETHNOGRAPHIC SKETCHES

Día de los Muertos

Experience of Marjorie Snipes, chapter author

In the Andean highlands of Argentina, most communities celebrate All Souls' Day, or Día de los Muertos (Day of the Dead), on November 1 and 2 every year. While this Catholic ritual commemorates the recently departed, usually those who have died in the past three years, it also includes elements of Indigenous religious practices and beliefs centered on Pachamama (Mother Earth). This integration of beliefs from more than one religious system is common across cultures and is called **syncretism**.

The practice of Día de los Muertos is a solemn occasion. Families prepare a favorite meal or food items that they associate with the recently departed and set a place setting for their soul (*alma*). Candles and flowers adorn the elaborately decorated family table. The meal remains available for the soul of the departed from the evening of November 1 until the evening of November 2. During that time, family members meet periodically around the table to offer prayers and to share remembrances of the deceased, and souls are invited to eat and prepare themselves for the journey to the spirit world. Souls of the departed are believed to remain strongly attached to their families and unwilling to leave the living world for three years following death. They must be coaxed by surviving family members to make a peaceful transition to the spirit world, where they can rest. In the southern Andes, many people believe that moths are visual symbols of the soul's presence. With candles lit throughout the night of November 1, families in rural Andean households often encounter moths. This serves as ritual affirmation.

On the evening of November 2, after a last prayer of departure, Andean families in El Angosto will gather the favorite foods of their departed and offer them to Pachamama by piling or burying the food into an altar of rocks. Each household has a family altar near their house, called a *mojon*, dedicated to Pachamama. It is a cairn predominantly consisting of white rocks, each believed to symbolize the goddess. The rocks may be naturally white, consisting of milky quartz, a common rock in the area, or they may be calcified or even painted white. During fieldwork, I asked people about the importance of the color white, but their answers were similar to the types of answers many of us would give to questions about our traditions: "This is her special color," "It's just this way," or "This is our custom." These truthful responses represent enculturation. As a scientist, though, I seek connections between the color white, stones, and Pachamama. I suspect there are several reasons that this color first began to be associated with Mother Earth: milky quartz is a common rock in the region and readily available; since the earth is considered to be Pachamama's body, the white rocks mimic the color of bone; and perhaps most significantly, the color white is associated with breast milk, a characteristic associated specifically with mothers. Understanding symbolism is important because it gives anthropologists a window into what matters most to those we are studying.

FIGURE 13.15 A cairn, or stack of rocks, built alongside the road to Mount Misti in Peru. These stacks of rocks are similar to those created as family altars by Andean families in El Angosto. (credit: "Mount Misti," by RichardJames1990/flickr, CC-BY-2.0)

MINI-FIELDWORK ACTIVITY

Participant Observation: Analysis of a Religious Service

Do fieldwork and an analysis of a religious service of your choice. With permission from the religious leader(s), attend the service and practice participant observation. Using what you have learned about sacred place and ritual, analyze the physical environment where the service is occurring. Where is/are the threshold(s)? Where is the axis mundi? How does the built environment contribute to the practice of religion and spiritual exercises? In the service itself, what are the primary themes, and how do different participant constituencies respond to these? Does the service conform to any of the rituals that you studied in this chapter? If so, how? After analyzing the service, reflect on your experience of doing this mini-fieldwork activity.

Key Terms

agnosticism the belief that God or the divine is unknowable and therefore skepticism is appropriate.

animism a worldview in which there is believed to be spiritual agency in all things, including natural elements such as rocks and trees.

atheism the lack of belief in a god or gods.

binary opposition two opposing concepts, commonly found in institutions such as kinship and in myth.

communitas a cohort of individuals participating in a rite of passage who share a strong sense of equality and social bonding among themselves.

deity a god, usually named, with individual personalities and interests.

divination a practice or test to discern knowledge about a certain event or situation.

doctrine a set of formal and usually rigid principles or teachings of a religious organization.

earth-diver myths creation myths in which a creator deity sends an agent, usually an animal, into deep waters to find mud that the deity will use to create dry land and humans.

exorcism the removal of an adverse supernatural spirit from a person.

goddesses female deities.

gods deities; often, specifically male deities.

hierophany the manifestation of the sacred or divine.

law of contagion the belief that things that have once been in contact with each other remain connected always; a theory of magic.

law of similarity the belief that things that are alike exert a force on each other; a theory of magic.

liminality a state in which an individual is viewed as being in a transition from one social stage to another.

magic a supposed system of natural law, the practice of which causes a transformation to occur.

mana an impersonal force that can adhere to people or animate and inanimate objects to make them sacred.

metaphor a symbol that is not naturally connected to what it represents.

metonym a symbol in which a part stands for the whole.

monotheistic religion a religion that centers on a single named god or goddess.

multivocal describes symbols that have more than one meaning.

myth a well-known story that teaches primary principles, beliefs, and values outside of chronological time.

mythemes the stripped-down minimal and portable units that form the structure of a myth.

none a person with no religious affiliation.

pilgrimage a sacred journey to a shrine or other holy place.

place a location that has sociocultural meaning attached to it.

polytheistic religion a religion that centers on a group of gods and/or goddesses, each devoted to a specific action or behavior.

priests full-time religious leaders who manage and administer at a high level within the religious bureaucracy.

primary messages the meaning of a myth, which can be applied universally.

prophet an individual associated with religious change who calls for a renewal of beliefs or a restructuring of the status quo. A prophet's leadership is usually temporary or indirect.

proselytization a recruitment practice in which members actively seek converts to the group.

religion a shared system of beliefs and practices that are highly regarded in society. Most often, religion is focused on the interaction of natural and supernatural phenomena.

rite of affliction a ritual invoked to seek some sort of redress, remedy, or compensation for an individual by means of supernatural intervention.

rite of intensification a ritual performed by a religious group to affirm, strengthen, and maintain bonds of solidarity.

rite of passage a ritual in which an individual or group marks a social transformation.

rituals performative acts by which people carry out religious beliefs, both public and private; also called rites.

secular religion a system of beliefs held by a society that elevates social ideas, qualities, or commodities to a metaphysical, semidivine status.

shaman a part-time religious figure who works to connect with deities on behalf of others.

shamanism a practice of healing and divination that involves soul travel to connect natural and supernatural realms in nonlinear time.

sorcery a practice involving the use of material elements to cause a change in circumstances to another person.

space an unmarked physical field; a place with no specific cultural meaning.

spirit supernatural being associated with specific activities, such as an earth spirit or guardian spirit (or angel).

spirituality a loose structure of beliefs and feelings about relationships between the natural and supernatural worlds.

state religion a formal religious institution with full-time administrators, a set doctrine of beliefs and regulations, and a policy of seeking growth by conversion of new practitioners.

structuralism a theory and method focused on identifying patterns in culture; also includes mythic analysis.

superstition a belief or practice that is believed to have no credible evidence for its efficacy.

symbol something that stands arbitrarily for something else and has no natural connection to its referent.

syncretism an integration or use of more than one religious system.

witchcraft a practice involving the use of intangible means to cause a change in circumstances to another person.

worldview a specific outlook or orientation that an individual or group of individuals holds on the nature of the world.

Summary

Religion is found across all cultures, and yet it can be difficult to define. French sociologist Émile Durkheim used an empirical definition, identifying religion as an institution related to "sacred things," with beliefs, practices, and a social organization. This definition provides a checklist for studying religion. Anthropologist Clifford Geertz, on the other hand, defines it as a system of symbols connected to moods, motivations, and a "general order of existence." While more abstract, this definition addresses the meaning and sense of identity that religion conveys to practitioners. In the United States today, people identify themselves religiously in a number of ways, including as "nones," people with no religious affiliation. Nones, agnostics, and atheists do have worldviews particular to their cultures, and they sometimes also have spiritual beliefs.

Religion has several common characteristics. Witchcraft and sorcery became part of religion as it evolved to adapt to world populations. In these cases, religion expresses social conflict within the society. Magic is also part of every religion, as religious belief systems are based on cause and effect, and anthropologists see magic as a profound human act of faith. Most religions also involve supernatural forces, such as gods and goddesses. Monotheistic religions focus on a single named god, while polytheistic religions involve a group of deities. Most religions have some type of leadership, either priests or shamans.

Shamanism is an early form of religion, found throughout human history, and possibly the explanation for mortuary artifacts and even cave painting. While shamanism is a healing practice, it is also a set of beliefs and practices regarding a supernatural world. As populations became larger, some shamanic cults developed into more organized and institutional forms of religion, leading to large state religions such as Christianity, Islam, and Buddhism. Shamanic practices can still be found within these larger religions.

Symbolism is common to all religions, regardless of whether they are small indigenous cults or state religious systems. Geographical space marked by symbolism can become a sacred place with specific meaning to religious practitioners. Religious myths, the stories behind the beliefs, are heavily marked with symbolic meaning. Religions can convey their beliefs through both oral and written traditions, with certain groups focused specifically on one or the other. Religious practice is known as ritual, and there are a variety of types of ritual, including rites of intensification, rites of passage, and rites of affliction.

Historically, there has been a great diversity in religious groups, including utopian religious communities that live separate from secular society and focus almost entirely on living a religious life. The Shakers are an example of this type of religious society. There are also examples of secular religion, in which the state or society itself is elevated as if it had a divine status.

Critical Thinking Questions

1. What is religion, and why do you think it is universal across cultures?
2. What is the role of religion in your life and the life of your family? Consider differences in gender, age, and generation. Has your own relationship with religion changed over your life?
3. Compare and contrast shamanism with more institutionalized religions, identifying elements they have in common and the ways in which they are different.
4. What is the significance of symbolism in religion?
5. Describe the attributes or characteristics of a religious place.
6. How do anthropologists approach the study of religious myths?
7. How do religious rituals strengthen a society?
8. What differences would you expect to find between communities in which there are diverse religious traditions and utopian religious communities?
9. What examples of secular religion do you encounter every day?

Bibliography

Bado-Fralick, Nikki. 2002. “Mapping the Wiccan Ritual Landscape: Circles of Transformation.” *Folklore Forum* 33 (1/2): 45–65. http://hdl.handle.net/2022/2424.

BBC News. 2021. “Who Are the Uyghurs and Why Is China Being Accused of Genocide?” June 21, 2021. https://www.bbc.com/news/world-asia-china-22278037.

Beauchamp, Zack. 2018. “Juche, the State Ideology That Makes North Korea Revere Kim Jong Un, Explained.” Vox. June 18, 2018. https://www.vox.com/world/2018/6/18/17441296/north-korea-propaganda-ideology-juche.

Bell, Diane. 1993. *Daughters of the Dreaming.* Minneapolis: University of Minnesota Press.

Bellah, Robert N. 1967. “Civil Religion in America.” *Daedalus* 96 (1): 1–21.

Boas, Franz. 1916. *Tsimshian Mythology.* Washington, D.C.: GPO. https://archive.org/details/tsimshianmytholo00boas/.

Carey, Harold, Jr. 2010. “Kinaalda: Celebrating Maturity of Girls among the Navajo.” Navajo People. December 16, 2010. http://navajopeople.org/blog/kinaalda-celebrating-maturity-of-girls-among-the-navajo/.

Clark, Christopher. 1995. “Thinking about American Utopian Communities: The Origins of a Discourse.” *Irish Journal of American Studies* 4:1–22.

Dubois, Thomas A. 2009. *An Introduction to Shamanism.* Cambridge: Cambridge University Press.

Dundes, Alan. 1962. “Earth-Diver: Creation of the Mythopoeic Male.” *American Anthropologist* 64 (5): 1032–1051.

Durkheim, Émile. 1915. *The Elementary Forms of the Religious Life.* Translated by Joseph Ward Swain. London: George Allen & Unwin.

Eliade, Mircea. 1959. *The Sacred and the Profane: The Nature of Religion.* Translated by Willard R. Trask. New York: Harcourt, Brace.

Frazer, James George. (1922) 1925. *The Golden Bough: A Study in Magic and Religion.* Abridged ed. New York: MacMillan. https://archive.org/stream/cu31924021569128/.

Geertz, Clifford. 1973. *The Interpretation of Cultures: Selected Essays.* New York: Basic Books.

Gennep, Arnold van. 1960. *The Rites of Passage: A Classic Study of Cultural Celebrations.* Translated by Monika B. Vizedom and Gabrielle L. Caffee. Chicago: University of Chicago Press.

Gottlieb, Alma. 2008. “How Are Anthropological Studies of Witchcraft Relevant Today?” Interview by Diana Yates. News Bureau. October 27, 2008. https://news.illinois.edu/view/6367/198785.

Harner, Michael. 1980. *The Way of the Shaman: A Guide to Power and Healing.* San Francisco: Harper & Row.

Harvey, Graham, ed. 2003. *Shamanism: A Reader.* New York: Routledge.

Ingold, Tim. 2018. *Anthropology: Why It Matters.* Medford, MA: Polity Press.

Ingold, Tim. 2019. "169: Tim Ingold." *Cultures of Energy: The Energy Humanities Podcast.* Hosted by Dominic Boyer and Cymene Howe. March 21, 2019. Podcast, 1:05:42. http://culturesofenergy.com/169-tim-ingold/.

Istomin, Kirill Vladimirovich, and Mark James Dwyer. 2010. "Dynamic Mutual Adaptation: Human-Animal Interaction in Reindeer Herding Pastoralism." *Human Ecology* 38 (5): 613–623.

Kanter, Rosabeth Moss. 1968. "Commitment and Social Organization: A Study of Commitment Mechanisms in Utopian Communities." *American Sociological Review* 33 (4): 499–517.

King, Barbara J. 2007. *Evolving God: A Provocative View of the Origins of Religion.* New York: Doubleday.

Kroeber, Karl. 1996. "Unaesthetic Imaginings: Native American Myth as Speech Genre." *Boundary 2* 23 (2): 171–197. https://doi.org/10.2307/303811.

Laugrand, Frédéric B., and Jarich G. Oosten. 2013. "'We're Back with Our Ancestors': Inuit Bowhead Whaling in the Canadian Eastern Arctic." *Anthropos* 108 (2): 431–443.

Lévi-Strauss, Claude. 1964–1971. *Mythologiques.* 4 vols. Paris: Plon.

Lipka, Michael. 2015. "A Closer Look at America's Rapidly Growing Religious 'Nones.'" Pew Research Center. May 13, 2015. https://www.pewresearch.org/fact-tank/2015/05/13/a-closer-look-at-americas-rapidly-growing-religious-nones/.

Lipka, Michael, and Claire Gecewicz. 2017. "More Americans Now Say They're Spiritual but Not Religious." Pew Research Center. September 6, 2017. https://www.pewresearch.org/fact-tank/2017/09/06/more-americans-now-say-theyre-spiritual-but-not-religious/.

Marshall, John. (1969) 2009. *N/um Tchai: The Ceremonial Dance of the !Kung Bushmen.* Disc 1. *!Kung Short Films.* DVD. Watertown, MA: Documentary Educational Resources.

Meza, Vivian. 2019. "Kinaaldá: A Navajo Girl Comes of Age in Traditional Ceremony." *Navajo-Hopi Observer.* June 4, 2019. https://www.nhonews.com/news/2019/jun/04/kinaalda-navajo-girl-comes-age-traditional-ceremon/.

Moro, Pamela A., ed. 2012. *Magic, Witchcraft, and Religion: A Reader in the Anthropology of Religion.* 9th ed. Dubuque, IA: McGraw-Hill.

Ong, Walter. 2012. *Orality and Literacy.* 3rd ed. With additional chapters by John Hartley. New York: Routledge.

Pallasmaa, Juhani. 2012. *The Eyes of the Skin: Architecture and the Senses.* 3rd ed. Hoboken, NJ: John Wiley & Sons.

Pew Research Center. 2015. "Religious Landscape Study." May 11, 2015. https://www.pewforum.org/religious-landscape-study/.

Pew Research Center. 2018. "Why America's 'Nones' Don't Identify with a Religion." August 8, 2018. https://www.pewresearch.org/fact-tank/2018/08/08/why-americas-nones-dont-identify-with-a-religion/.

Shermer, Michael. 2018. "The Number of Americans with No Religious Affiliation Is Rising." *Scientific American.* April 1, 2018. https://www.scientificamerican.com/article/the-number-of-americans-with-no-religious-affiliation-is-rising/.

Somé, Malidoma Patrice. (1993) 1997. *Ritual: Power, Healing, and Community.* New York: Penguin/Arkana.

Stein, Stephen J. 1992. *The Shaker Experience in America: A History of the United Society of Believers.* New Haven: Yale University Press.

Stephan, Karen H., and G. Edward Stephan. 1973. "Religion and the Survival of Utopian Communities." *Journal for the Scientific Study of Religion* 12 (1): 89–100.

Turner, Victor W. 1967. *The Forest of Symbols: Aspects of Ndembu Ritual.* Ithaca, NY: Cornell University Press.

Turner, Victor W. 1968. *The Drums of Affliction: A Study of Religious Processes among the Ndembu of Zambia.* Oxford: Clarendon Press.

Turner, Victor W. 1969. *The Ritual Process: Structure and Anti-structure.* Ithaca, NY: Cornell University Press.

Tylor, Edward Burnett. 1871. *Primitive Culture.* 2 vols. New York: G. P. Putnam's Sons.

Vansina, Jan. 1985. *Oral Tradition as History.* Madison: University of Wisconsin Press.

Weber, Max. 1947. *The Theory of Social and Economic Organization.* Translated by A. M. Henderson and Talcott Parsons. Glencoe, IL: Free Press.

Zapata Olivella, Manuel. 1983. *Changó, el gran putas.* Bogotá: Editorial Oveja Negra.

Zapata Olivella, Manuel. 2010. *Por los senderos de sus ancestros: Textos escogidos, 1940–2000*, compiled and presented by Alfonso Múnera. Bogotá: Ministerio de Cultura.

Zapata Olivella, Manuel. Selected Correspondence. Jean and Alexander Heard Library, Vanderbilt University. https://mzo.library.vanderbilt.edu/correspondence/index.php.

CHAPTER 14
Anthropology of Food

Figure 14.1 A fruit and vegetable vendor in Saigon, Vietnam. How many of these foods do you recognize? (credit: "Vietnam Sept 2012 3432 Market, Sa Dec, Viet Nam" by Lynda/flickr, CC BY 2.0)

CHAPTER OUTLINE

INTRODUCTION The study of food has a long history in anthropology and weaves together various subfields of the discipline. Among other things, food connects to nutrition and health, rituals and behaviors regarding production and consumption, and worldwide trade networks and the related diffusion of plants, animals, and artifacts. Distinguishing between what is and what is not food is a major concern within and across most human cultures. Food varies not only from one society to another but also across genders, classes, family groups, and seasons. As both a source of sustenance for the body and a means of establishing or advertising one's social status, **food** plays a major role in personal and cultural identity. In globalized Western culture, people regularly eat foods that originated in other cultures—such as sushi, gyros, tacos, spaghetti, and crepes, to name just a few—but practices such as avoiding certain foods (food prohibitions) and even eating one's family members or enemies (forms of cannibalism) are cross-cultural food traditions that are likely less familiar.

Culturally appropriate preparation and consumption of food requires a vast array of knowledge, artifacts, and rituals. In Figure 14.2, an Indigenous woman in Mexico is making tortillas, using a grinder and grindstone to transform corn into flour, which she then mixes with water to create a batter. Preparing flour in this traditional manner typically requires the cook to navigate various stages of food preparation, including choosing the best dried grains, nuts, spices, or herbs; assessing when a flour has reached the desired consistency; and physically being able to use the grindstone. The food utensils that the woman is using are not only tools but also symbols associated with the women who own and use them. Within families, these utensils may be passed down through generations. In some cultures, it is common for Indigenous women to inherit the grindstones of their mothers and grandmothers.

FIGURE 14.2 A woman in Puerto Vallarta, Mexico, makes tortillas. In the foreground are the *metate* (the large, flat stone) and the *mano* (the smaller, oblong stone) she used to grind dried corn into flour to create the batter for this traditional food. (credit: "Grinding Corn for Tortillas" by Terri Bateman/flickr, CC BY 2.0)

14.1 Food as a Material Artifact

LEARNING OUTCOMES

By the end of this section, you will be able to:

- Describe archaeological evidence of food.
- Identify some of the earliest stone tools associated with food preparation.
- Explain ways that archaeologists identify early human foods.
- Explain the relationship between archaeology and foodways research.
- Discuss the relationship between food and cultural heritage.

Food Artifacts

The study of early human diets is important in understanding the evolution of the human species. The size and shape of our skulls and teeth are directly linked with culture and diet. As foods became softer over time (primarily due to the use of fire and cooking) and meat became more common in the human diet, the size of human dentition decreased. Along with this reduction in the size of teeth, cooked foods, especially meats, made increased calories and nutrition available and also prompted brain growth. The most direct evidence of meat eating among early humans is butcher marks found on bone, estimated to be from as early as 3.4–2.6 million years ago (Wild 2019; Pobiner 2013). The earliest evidence of humans cooking a carbohydrate source is charred tubers recently identified by archaeologist Cynthia Larbey (Wild 2019) at Blombos Cave, in the Klasies River site in South Africa, and dated to 120,000 BP. Excavations at the archaeological site Shubayqa 1 in Jordan have uncovered the earliest evidence of charred breadcrumbs, indicating that humans were baking bread as early as 14,500 BP (Richter and Arranz-Otaegui 2018). From meat to potatoes to bread, humans and their diets have adapted to changing ways of life.

In the archaeological record, food evidence takes many forms. It may be a hearth or pottery container with food or drink residue, butchered animal bones, coprolites (fossilized fecal material), tools used in food processing, baskets or pottery used for storing food, or even garbage dumps or **shell middens** (large collections of discarded shells.) In historical sites, there may even be preserved food remains, such as corn kernels or alcoholic beverages still enclosed in containers. Studying food helps anthropologists better understand many aspects of human existence and culture, including the rhythms and activities of daily life, food exchange and preparation, feasting, ritual activities, population density, length of settlement at a site, division of labor, seasonal activities, diet and health, cultural traditions and preferences, and even social status within a group. Food is connected with almost all human activities.

Early Archaeological Sites and Food Utensils

By the emergence of *Homo habilis* around 2.6 million years ago, early human settlements were typically littered with the debris of stone tools that were most likely used in food production. There is evidence of tools that were used for hunting, skinning, crushing, slicing, and grinding. These earliest tools were chipped and flaked from pieces of stone to create objects that had both an edge and a point. As tools evolved and became more specialized, they became increasingly focused on specific aspects of food procurement and production.

Unfortunately, relatively little study has been done on tool production and its relationship to food preparation. Historically, utensils and food preparation have received little attention in scholarly research, likely because daily food preparation is part of domestic work, frequently associated with women, and often occurring as a private household activity. As archaeologists have somewhat recently turned their attention to the evolution of food production tools, they have begun to note interesting regional cultural patterns. Recent studies of grinding tools in the Near East, where cereal production first emerged, have called attention to "untapped potential in the understanding of food production" (Ebeling and Rowan 2004, 115).

Archaeologist Jennie Ebeling and her colleague Yorke Rowan have studied the evolution of grinding stones in the Near East from the Upper Paleolithic period (38,000–8000 BCE) into the Iron Age (1200–1000 BCE). Using a diverse collection of evidence, including excavated artifacts and archaeological sites, tomb paintings, written sources, and even ethnographic studies, they have formed a better understanding of the role of stone grinding tools in ancient Near Eastern food production. The earliest stone grinding tools were of two basic types: an earlier form consisting of mortars, deep concave bowl-like surfaces, paired with pestles, small oblong-shaped hand grinders (see Figure 14.3); and a later form that featured hand stones and grinding slabs (see Figure 14.4). Using **residue studies**, the chemical analysis of small amounts of materials left intact on surfaces, Ebeling and Rowan'determined that both types of grinding tools were used for not only nuts and cereals but also meat, bark, minerals, salt, and herbs. In some cases, they have been able to determine the origins of the grinding materials, which include locally sourced stone and much-sought-after **basalt**, a rugged igneous rock that resists the type of degradation that would leave small flakes of debris in the meal.

Ebeling and Rowan's study of grinding tools revealed a great deal about life in the Near East. By the emergence of the Neolithic Period around 10,000 BCE, some stone tools were beginning to be decorated with distinct geometric patterns and fashioned with pedestaled feet, developments in art and adornment that likely indicate emerging differences in social status between families. Dental and skeletal studies shed further light on the use of these tools. Dental decay accelerated during the Neolithic Period, suggesting increased consumption of carbohydrates such as cereal grains, which convert to sugar during the digestive process. Additionally, skeletal wear patterns (specifically compressed toes, which distort the alignment of the foot) are evident on the remains of women and young girls, most likely indicating that females were doing extensive daily work grinding cereals.

FIGURE 14.3 Mortars and pestles were some of the earliest stone grinding tools. (credit: Bugil/Wikimedia Commons, Public Domain)

Ancient Foodways and Food Reconstructions

Anthropologists are interested in **foodways**, a term used to describe a society's collection, production, and consumption of food. There is a particular interest in understanding how culinary traditions shape identity. It is not uncommon for archaeologists and cultural anthropologists to attempt to reconstruct food practices of the cultures they are studying, utilizing different types of clues. While written accounts, artwork, and visible food remnants help tell the story of a culture's foodways, anthropologists also use residue studies of traces of food and drink in pottery, baskets, and gourds and stable isotope analysis of human bones and teeth, in which they measure isotopes (radioactive elements found naturally in food) to determine the diet of an individual and the environment in which they lived. These clues to ancient foodways can reveal a great deal about daily life.

Archaeologist Lisa Duffy has studied ancient Maya cuisine using residue from pottery and grinding stones. Residues include many kinds of trace materials left behind on the artifacts, such as charred remains on the sides of a cooking pot or microscopic plant or animal remains on the surface of a vessel. So far, residues have been successfully recovered from seven ancient Maya sites across Guatemala and Belize, some dating from as early as 600 BCE. Some of the chemicals that have been identified indicate use of chili pepper, cacao, chocolate, and tobacco, among other herbs and spices. While chocolate compounds have been found on culinary artifacts from many different social strata, most other residues are specifically associated with certain social classes. Through studies such as this, foodways help scientists better understand the social differences and lifestyles of early cultures.

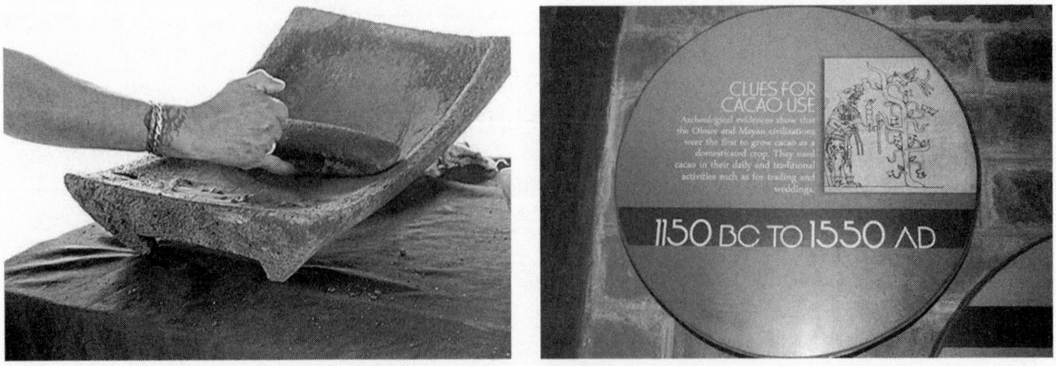

FIGURE 14.4 The Maya used chocolate as an important ingredient in their diets and grew cacao as a domesticated

crop. To make chocolate, seeds from cacao trees are fermented, dried, roasted, and ground into a paste. The grinding slab pictured here was traditionally used for the grinding stage in chocolate production. (credit: (left) "Making Chocolate Mayan Style Ixcacao Maya Belizean Chocolate Farm San Felipe Belize 2653" by bobistraveling/ flickr, CC BY 2.0; (right) "History of Chocolate, 1150 BC to 1550 AD, Olmec & Maya" by Gary Lee Todd/flickr, CC BY 2.0)

Foodways can also be explored by reconstituting foods in order to better understand their chemical and sensual characteristics. In one experiment, physicist Seamus Blackley and his colleagues, archaeologist Serena Love and microbiologist Richard Bowman, developed a technique to extract hibernating yeast microbes left behind on porous Egyptian ceramics. These yeast microbes were dated to 4,500 years ago. The first step in their experiment was to sequence the yeast's genome (i.e., map each of its genetic markers), through which they determined that it was not genetically the same as modern yeast and that it was as old as they had originally thought. The researchers then fed the yeast einkorn flour, made from a kind of wheat that would have existed at the time the yeast was originally active. As Blackley reported, "The yeast woke up right away.... It was kind of remarkable" (Blackley, Love, and Bowman 2019). The resulting bread was fine grained and well risen, with a pungent odor of brown sugar. Using experimental techniques such as these, archaeologists are able to tap into smells, tastes, and textures that were part of ancient foodways and may no longer exist in our cuisine today.

Food as Cultural Heritage

Sometimes, anthropologists find it useful to distinguish between the terms *culture*—which, as discussed in Chapter 3, The Concept of Culture, can be defined as beliefs, behaviors, and artifacts that a group uses to adapt to its environment—and **cultural heritage**, which comprises traditions passed down for generations and used as a way of identifying a group of people. In state societies peopled by diverse cultural groups, it is common for food to be used to distinguish one group from another. "Those people" eat "those things," and "my people" eat "these things." Later in this chapter, we will examine how national identities are shaped by food, but ethnic groups also define themselves by differences in food choices and food preparation. Within American culture, there are a number of familiar connections between certain groups and certain foods: the Pacific Northwest Coast Indigenous peoples and salmon; Jewish residents of New York City and bagels; people of German ancestry in Milwaukee, Wisconsin, and brats; residents of San Francisco's Chinatown and steamed pork buns—to name just a few.

While archaeologists are at work using various techniques to better understand the foodways of ancient cultures, some contemporary peoples are focused on reviving their own culinary heritages. Reviving and restoring seeds, recipes, and even early cooking techniques are part of learning more about earlier populations, diverse foodways, and traditional and perhaps once-lost flavors. For some people, this rediscovery is also a way of asserting or reclaiming their cultural identity.

Cherokee Ramps

Early studies of the foodways of the Eastern Band of Cherokee mention the prevalence of ramps, wild leeks that are similar to wild onions and grow in the Appalachian region of the United States. Ramps (*Allium tricoccum*) are eaten from the time they begin to sprout in March almost until they bloom in April or May. The bulb is eaten raw or is chopped up and fried with eggs. Some parboil the entire plant, and in recent years, ramps have been canned or deep-frozen by some Cherokee families. (White 1975, 324–325)

Used as a supplementary food by the Cherokee for generations and eventually adopted by European settlers in the Appalachians, ramps today continue to serve as a link to cultural identity. In his ethnographic research on the Eastern Band of the Cherokee Nation, anthropologist Max White (1975) explained that the Cherokee view plants as having *agency*, the ability to make choices about where to grow and whether to intervene to help people. The Cherokee cultivate relationships of respect with the native flora around them as part of an enduring relationship with their environment.

FIGURE 14.5 Ramps, wild leeks that are similar to wild onions, have long been an important part of Cherokee foodways. They are now increasingly in demand for urban cuisine as well. (credit: “Patch of Ramps” by Wendell Smith/flickr, CC BY 2.0)

Ramps, long valued as one of the first edible green plants to ripen in the spring, are prized by many people for their flavor and reported medicinal value for treating common colds, earaches, and circulatory disease (Rivers, Oliver, and Resler 2014, 7). Cherokee citizen and anthropologist Courtney Lewis (2012) has studied the recent legal and ethical issues surrounding the collection of ramps in the Qualla Boundary, U.S.-designated Cherokee land in North Carolina. Because the Great Smoky Mountains National Park (GSMNP) borders the western part of the Qualla Boundary, there had been a long-standing informal agreement allowing Cherokee citizens to collect traditional foods within the park as long as their collection did not endanger any species. Up until 2009, the relationship between the National Park Service (NPS) and the Eastern Band of Cherokee had been primarily amicable. However, in 2007, the NPS had decided to prohibit all harvesting of ramps within the GSMNP, based on an earlier study by an NPS botanist that warned that unregulated foraging could endanger some plant species. They began issuing citations in 2009, and on March 22 of that year, the NPS arrested a Cherokee family that was harvesting ramps, supposedly within park boundaries.

During the trial, there were many inconsistencies in the testimony and misunderstandings between the various parties, with the court often privileging Western scientific knowledge over Indigenous knowledge (Lewis 2012, 110). Cherokee scholars and elders pointed out that ramp production is cyclical, consisting of high production years followed by recovery cycles; that Indigenous harvesting techniques, which take just the stems and leaves instead of the roots, are different from those of non-Indigenous harvesters and allow for sustainable growth; and that many of the less productive ramp areas were not within traditional Cherokee foraging zones. Many of the zones in which ramps were deemed most threatened were outside of the traditional foraging areas and were most likely being harvested by non-Indigenous people meeting the demand for ramps in nearby upscale restaurants. In addition, given the increasing levels of air pollution and ongoing climate change, many wild plants in the Great Smoky Mountains are facing threats from sources other than local foraging. Although the trial ended with the Cherokee family charged for trespassing on federal lands, the legalities of ramp collection continue to be debated today.

While the controversies surrounding ramp collection have not completely subsided, there is increasing recognition of the importance of Indigenous foodways and cultural identity. Today, around 50 percent of U.S. national parks, including the Great Smoky Mountains National Park, allow some form of foraging within their boundaries (Linnekin 2019), regulated by all sorts of rules, guidelines, and informal agreements with local and Indigenous populations. The Eastern Band of the Cherokee Nation monitors ramps as part of its natural resource management in the Qualla Boundary and continues to negotiate for foraging rights on ancestral lands that the Cherokee deem to have belonged to them for thousands of years, now cut off by the national park. For many Cherokee families, foraging sites and trails are family secrets that have been passed down for many generations. In 2019, the GSMNP entered into a new agreement with the Eastern Band of Cherokee to allow its citizens to gather *sochan*, a kale-like plant located within park boundaries (Chávez 2019). Today, Cherokee still gather ramps within park boundaries in designated areas, but those gathering for non-subsistence needs are required to have a gathering permit issued by the GSMNP.

There are many examples of foods and dishes that are considered important to preserving ancestral identities. In 2006, UNESCO, the educational and cultural group of the United Nations, convened a working group to establish lists of intangible cultural heritage and a register of good safeguarding practices (https://openstax.org/r/ich.unesco) as a way to recognize and preserve the cultural traditions of humanity. Several special foods and cooking traditions are included on the lists as examples of endangered cultural heritage, such as flattened sourdough bread from Malta, *oshi palav* (a pilaf made with vegetables, rice, and meat) from Tajikistan, and the cultivation of the date palm in Bahrain, Jordan, Kuwait, and other areas of the Middle East.

It is not uncommon for a family to have special recipes and meals that they serve on holiday occasions as a way of remembering their past and of passing on traditions to new generations. Does your family follow any food traditions as a way of remembering your ancestors? Take a moment to consider the different roles that food plays in your own family.

14.2 A Biocultural Approach to Food

LEARNING OUTCOMES

By the end of this section, you will be able to:

- Identify a biocultural approach.
- Describe Three Sisters cropping as an Indigenous adaptation.
- Identify the various types of evidence that anthropologists use to reconstruct ancient foodways.
- Describe how contemporary dietary approaches connect with ancient foodways.

Food and the Biocultural Approach

Many anthropologists take a **biocultural approach** to their study of food, looking at how food plays both a cultural and a biological role in human lives. Food provides physical nourishment of our bodies and also a means of understanding who we are. How people procure and prepare foods and which foods are deemed appropriate for which occasions are important parts of cultural identity. Food is thus an area that weaves together the biological and cognitive aspects of our lives—an observation captured by the familiar phrase "you are what you eat." Although the biocultural approach continues to focus on food and identity, it also includes an emphasis on the nutritional science of food.

The biocultural approach can be applied to the study of food in many ways, from research into subsistence practices and traditional ways of raising crops to analysis of how groups assign meaning to the food of other cultures. As popular cultural artifacts, food-related knowledge and practices are shared from culture to culture as groups seek additional health benefits and food variety.

Subsistence and Biocultural Adaptation

Cereals (including corn, wheat, barley, and rice) and legumes (various types of beans) are the most common crops grown by subsistence farmers because they are versatile and economical and have a wide range of health benefits. In addition to carbohydrates, protein, vitamins, minerals, and fiber, they provide a substantial number of calories. In other words, cereals are a good investment of labor and have long-term health benefits. Indigenous peoples around the world have long been aware of the potential in these foods.

By the time Europeans arrived in the Americas, Indigenous peoples of North and Central America had been selectively breeding domesticated plants for thousands of years. Over many generations, the Indigenous peoples of the Americas had developed a detailed understanding of the health benefits and the risks associated with certain plants and the ways in which plants could be grown together to sustain higher yields. The "Three Sisters" is one traditional cropping system that grows specific plants near one another—usually some combination of corn, beans, and squash—so that each aids and supports the others' growth. This approach of placing plants of different types together in such a way as to benefit the growth of each is known as **intercropping**. While variations on the Three Sisters are found throughout Indigenous groups in North and Central America, the Haudenosaunee's use of the practice has been particularly well studied.

The Haudenosaunee people (also known as the Iroquois or Six Nations) of what is now the northern part of New York State practiced Three Sisters cultivation with maize, beans, and pumpkins, which are a form of squash. Seeds from each of these crops were planted together in small mounds in an unplowed field. Each mound contained several maize seeds in the middle, with bean and pumpkin seeds placed around the perimeter. (Note the difference from the row-based agriculture practiced on conventional American farms today.) Each of the plants in the mound offers a benefit to the others. The vigorous pumpkin vines, with their large leaves, quickly form a canopy that shades out weeds, preserves moisture in the soil, and prevents erosion. The bean plants, with the help of bacteria, are able to fix nitrogen in the soil, making it available as a fertilizer to the plants growing around them. And the fast-growing maize plants, which require lots of nitrogen for healthy growth, provide trellises for the climbing beans (Gish Hill 2020). In a 1910 study of Haudenosaunee culture, Arthur Parker, archaeologist and Iroquois historian, noted that these crops were planted together in part because the Haudenosaunee people believed they were "guarded by three inseparable spirits and would not thrive apart" (quoted in Mt. Pleasant 2016, 88). In the Haudenosaunee belief system, these three crops were believed to have been given to the people as gifts from the deities. The physical and spiritual sustenance provided by each food reminded the people of their cultural heritage each time they were consumed (Carnegie Museum of Natural History 2018). Although these foods were foundational to their diets, the Haudenosaunee added to the diversity of their cuisine through seasonal foraging of wild plants and animals.

Jane Mt. Pleasant (2016), a horticulturist and specialist in Indigenous cropping systems, has studied the caloric yield (the total calories provided by the harvest) of crops planted using the Three Sisters technique. She has found that when planted together, the three crops yield as much as two to four times the amount of total calories and protein than they would if the plants were cultivated alone. Corn plants in particular show a significant increase in protein when combined with the other sisters (92).

FIGURE 14.6 A Three Sisters garden usually includes corn, beans, and squash planted together in a small mound. The plants nourish and protect each other as they grow. Here, gardeners display a bountiful harvest from their Three Sisters garden. (credit: "IMG_4326" by Sterling College/flickr, CC BY 2.0)

Today, sustainable farming techniques are increasingly valued by people concerned about the ecological costs of conventional farming. Sustainable farming techniques, many of them grounded in traditional practices, offer ways to produce higher food yields, reduce fertilizer costs, build healthier soils, and avoid **genetically modified plants**, which have had their DNA deliberately altered in a laboratory setting. Iowa State University currently sponsors a Three Sisters gardening project (https://openstax.org/r/threesistersproject), which works collaboratively with Native American communities to raise awareness of the techniques, nutritional benefits, and cultural values of traditional intercropping methods. The project makes a point of working with **heirloom**

seed varieties, which are seeds that are not genetically modified, are open pollinated (meaning that the seeds can be saved for generations and will continue to breed true), and have been in existence for at least 50 years. One of their goals is to return the seeds to their home communities (Gish Hill 2020). There are many benefits to using heirloom seeds, including better flavors, better adaptation to local environmental conditions, the ability to save seeds to be grown in subsequent years, and increased genetic diversity, which contributes to long-term sustainability.

Increasingly, there is increased interest in new foods and cuisine worldwide. Many of these *re*discovered foods originate in the histories of Indigenous cultures. Using oral tradition, historical documents, and even genetic analyses, both Western and non-Western peoples are increasingly seeking to revive culinary heritage:

> Many Indigenous people are now on a path of rediscovery, preservation, and reinvention of these staple foods. The Three Sisters are experiencing a culinary resurgence after decades of lost knowledge due to forced relocation, cultural oppression, and genocide. Numerous tribes have found renewed health and spiritual bonds through efforts to sustain, cultivate, and cook with the Three Sisters. (Murphy 2018)

Food, Fads, Diets, and Health

In the fifth century BCE, the Greek historian Herodotus wrote about the Macrobians, a cultural group living in what is now southern Ethiopia who were supposed to have found a mythical "fountain of youth" in which people could bathe and become young again. Herodotus had heard that the Macrobians lived to be 120 years old and consumed only boiled fish and milk. Trying to explain the myths he had heard, he surmised that diet and special waters must have been the cause of their longevity. While this was not likely the first time that someone claimed a secret elixir or remedy for physical aging and illness, it is one of the earliest recorded dietary myths. Many more would follow. In 1558, Venetian patron of the arts Alvise Cornaro authored a best seller titled *Discorsi della vita sobria*, variously translated into English as *Sure and Certain Methods of Attaining a Long and Healthful Life* and *Discourses on a Sober and Temperate Life*, among other titles. In this text, he makes the following claims about human health:

> This sobriety is reduced to two things, quality, and quantity. The first, namely quality, consists in nothing, but not eating food, or drinking wines, prejudicial to the stomach. The second, which is quantity, consists in not eating or drinking more than the stomach can easily digest; which quantity and quality every man should be a perfect judge of by the time he is forty, or fifty, or sixty; and, whoever observes these two rules, may be said to live a regular and sober life. This is of so much virtue and efficacy, that the humours of such a man's body become most homogeneous, harmonious, and perfect; and, when thus improved, are no longer liable to be corrupted or disturbed by any other disorders whatsoever. (Cornaro 1779, under "A Compendium of a Sober Life")

History offers a long line of pseudoscientists, tonic peddlers, tinkerers, and even some thoughtful people hawking medicinal potions and diets reputed to solve every imaginable health problem. Many contained ingredients that are now widely recognized as harmful. In the late 19th century, a concerned consumer could try Mrs. Winslow's Soothing Syrup for teething children, which contained morphine and alcohol; Cocaine Toothache Drops; or a cocaine-infused wine called Vin Mariani, which was used in Europe for depression, malaria, and loss of appetite (Mitchell 2019).

New religious or philosophical movements were often associated with new diets intended to improve both physical and moral health. In the United States, the Graham diet enjoyed a period of popularity in the 19th century. The diet revolved around the consumption of *graham*, a flour made of the whole-wheat berry, including the bran covering. It was developed in the 1830s by Sylvester Graham, an evangelical minister touted by Ralph Waldo Emerson as the "prophet of bran bread" (Lobel 2012). Advertised as a remedy for sexual desire and gluttony, Graham's diet included various elements that constitute sound dietary advice even today: eat only two meals a day, and eat in moderation; use no spices, meat, alcohol, or tobacco; and consume lots of fruits, vegetables, and whole grains, including *lots of graham*. This diet became wildly popular in the mid-1800s, with religious groups such as the Shakers, the Christian Scientists, and the Seventh Day Adventists supporting aspects of this diet. Today, Sylvester Graham's contribution to the American diet is still evident in the graham cracker.

When the World Health Organization (WHO) was established in 1948, it fundamentally changed the way people think about health and diet. Compiling comparative data on health and lifestyle from around the world, the WHO engendered a greater awareness of health disparities between populations and a rising interest in the link between health and lifestyle. Noting that both chronic disease rates and average life spans varied greatly among cultural and national groups, people began to make connections between diet and health. Perhaps there was something to be learned from societies in which people enjoyed longer lives and had lower rates of chronic illnesses such as heart disease and diabetes. And so began a proliferation of healthy diets. Two of the most noteworthy today are the Mediterranean diet and the paleo diet.

FIGURE 14.7 The Mediterranean diet relies on fruits, vegetables, and olive oil, with very limited amounts of meat or saturated fats. This "Mediterranean Salad" is light and nutritious. (credit: "Mediterranean Salad / Ensalada Valenciana" by Lablascovegmenu/Wikimedia Commons, CC BY 2.0)

The Mediterranean diet is based on long-held dietary traditions in countries bordering the Mediterranean Sea. It was first presented formally as a healthier way of eating by U.S. physiologist and nutritionist Ancel Keys at a WHO meeting in Geneva, Switzerland, in 1955. Keys described the particular culinary practices found in the Mediterranean region and noted their related health benefits. These practices include high consumption of fruits, vegetables, and olive oil and low consumption of meats and saturated fats. Today, the Mediterranean diet is still recommended for improving cardiovascular health and blood cholesterol levels. In a recent study of 26,000 women (Ahmad et al. 2018), data showed that the risk of developing cardiovascular disease was 25 percent lower over 12 years among those following the Mediterranean diet (The Nutrition Source 2018).

Near Eastern archaeologist Oded Borowski (2004) has researched the origins and history of the Mediterranean diet. Textual sources, especially biblical texts, and an array of archaeological artifacts from across the region describe traditional foodways in the Middle East very similar to those still prevalent today—a diet consisting primarily of cereal grains, herbs, fruit, bread, oil, and fish, with occasional meat. Archaeological artifacts also point to a great deal of dietary continuity in this part of the world. Food processing and subsistence tools such as grinding stones, churns, nets, fishhooks, and sinkers; storage jars with food residues of substances such as grain, yeast, and wine; middens with preserved food remains in ancient garbage; and animal fossils of a variety of freshwater and saltwater fish all indicate the long historical trajectory of and cultural preference for these foods. This culinary tradition continues today throughout the Mediterranean area, including the Middle East, North Africa, and southern Europe (notably Italy and Greece).

FIGURE 14.8 The paleo diet is based on contemporary ideas of how our hunting and gathering ancestors might have eaten. It includes lean meats, fruits, vegetables, and nuts. Here, the meat kabobs are lying on a bed of vegetables. (credit: "IMG_0308.JPG" by Michael Arrington/flickr, CC BY 2.0)

Another very popular diet today, based partially on cultural and nutritional studies, is the paleo diet, sometimes called the Paleolithic diet, the caveman diet, or the Stone Age diet. This diet was first developed in the 1970s by gastroenterologist Walter Voegtlin, who argued that our bodies (and our digestive systems) have been evolutionarily designed for a hunting-and-gathering way of life. The paleo diet is made up of foods that are traditionally associated with this hunting-and-gathering lifestyle—fruits, vegetables, lean meats, fish, nuts, and seeds. The Mayo Clinic, one of the best-known US medical research centers, describes the paleo diet in this way:

> The aim of a paleo diet is to return to a way of eating that's more like what early humans ate. The diet's reasoning is that the human body is genetically mismatched to the modern diet that emerged with farming practices—an idea known as the discordance hypothesis. (Mayo Clinic Staff 2020, under "Purpose")

Biological anthropologists have done significant research on the foodways of Paleolithic-era people across different geographical areas. A great deal can be determined about what these early people likely ate using various means. Among these means are zooarchaeology (the study of the fossilized remains of animals), human anatomy and physiological studies, ethnographic studies of contemporary hunters and gatherers, and analysis of artifacts, coprolites (fossilized feces), and human skeletal and dental remains. Although there seems to have been a great deal of difference in the specific types of vegetables, fruits, meats, and fish that were eaten in various cultures, in general, Paleolithic diets and lifestyles were marked by low levels of fat consumption; high levels of food diversity, including some raw foods; and high levels of physical activity. Not all the paleo diets in circulation today follow these same guidelines. While anthropological research indicates that the actual Paleolithic diet likely consisted of 65 percent plant-based foods and 35 percent animal-based foods, many contemporary paleo recipes and prescriptions do not follow this formula strictly (Chang and Nowell 2016). In their research on the paleo diet, biological anthropologist Melanie Chang and Paleolithic archaeologist April Nowell encourage anthropologists to become more involved in current conversations about Paleolithic lifestyles and what they might suggest about a healthy human diet. There is, perhaps, still more we can learn about the *real* paleo diet.

Regardless of our contemporary diet practices, we can learn a lot from our ancestors. Their foodways, lifestyles, and traditional knowledge offer windows into both the evolution of our bodies and ways of eating that promote health and longevity. The information offered by anthropology's study of different cultures and historical periods can supplement our own knowledge base as we seek ways to improve our lives today.

PROFILES IN ANTHROPOLOGY

George Armelagos
1936-2014

Personal History: Born in Detroit, Michigan, George Armelagos (https://openstax.org/r/armelagos-george) earned his BA in anthropology from the University of Michigan and his MA and PhD from the University of Colorado Boulder. During his career, he taught at the University of Utah, the University of Massachusetts, the University of Florida, and finally at Emory University, where he was a distinguished professor of anthropology.

Area of Anthropology: Armelagos took a biocultural approach to understanding ancient human diseases, examining skeletal remains to reconstruct how human behavior intersected with disease and nutrition in early populations. His areas of focus were wide ranging and included nutritional anthropology, disease in human evolution, race and racism, skeletal biology, and medical anthropology. He was a pioneer of paleopathology, the study of ancient human disease. His research also extended into contemporary foodways and nutrition. His book *Consuming Passions: The Anthropology of Eating* (1980), which he coauthored with Peter Farb, was one of the first anthropology texts devoted wholly to the study of food. Armelagos also had an abiding interest in cooking and was a master chef who loved entertaining his friends.

Accomplishments in the Field and Importance of His Work: Armelagos's contributions to anthropology bridge the subfields of biological, archaeological, and cultural anthropology. He was also an accomplished professor who taught and mentored students throughout his career and even after retirement. He received numerous awards for research and service, including the Viking Fund Medal for distinguished research in physical anthropology, awarded by the Wenner-Gren Foundation for Anthropological Research in 2005. In 2008, he was awarded the Franz Boas Award for Exemplary Service to Anthropology by the American Anthropological Association. This annual award recognizes extraordinary achievements that have served the anthropological profession and the community beyond by applying anthropological knowledge to improve lives. In 2009, Armelagos was awarded the Charles R. Darwin Lifetime Achievement Award in the subfield of biological anthropology. His research and mentorship advanced the biological and cultural study of our species.

14.3 Food and Cultural Identity

LEARNING OUTCOMES

By the end of this section, you will be able to:

- Describe the relationship between food and cultural identity.
- Contrast food prescriptions with food proscriptions.
- Illustrate the connection between food and gender.

Food and Cultural Identity

Food travels across cultures perhaps more often and with more ease than any other tradition. Sometimes food carries with it related culinary practices (such as the use of chopsticks), and sometimes foods mix with existing culinary traditions to form new syncretic cuisines (such as Tex-Mex food, which evolved from a combination of Mexican and US Southwest food traditions). Like culture itself, foods are shared within and move between communities, adapting to changing circumstances and settings. Although it is adaptable, food is also tightly linked to people's **cultural identities**, or the ways they define and distinguish themselves from other groups of people. As part of these cultural identities, the term **cuisine** is used to refer to specific cultural traditions of cooking, preparing, and consuming food. While urban areas tend to shift and adapt cuisine more frequently than rural areas, those aspects of cuisine most tightly linked to identity tend to change slowly in all settings.

FIGURE 14.9 Japanese short-grain rice plays an important role in Japanese identity. Here, short-grain rice is served with a beef curry. (credit: Ocdp/Wikimedia Commons, Public Domain)

In her research on Japanese food and identity, cultural anthropologist, and Japanese scholar Emiko Ohnuki-Tierney (1993, 1995) explores the sociocultural construction of rice as a dominant metaphor for the Japanese people. Using evidence from official decrees, taxation documents, myths, rituals, woodblock prints, and poetry, Ohnuki-Tierney traces the long history of rice cultivation in Japan. Introduced from China, rice agriculture began during the Yamato period (250–710 CE). While the Chinese preferred long-grain rice, the Japanese cultivated short-grain rice, which they considered the only pure form of rice. During this period, a series of myths connecting short-grain rice to Japanese deities emerged in folktales and historical documents—evidence of Japanese efforts to distinguish themselves from the Chinese, who also relied on rice as an important source of calories. Over the years, rice developed into a staple crop that Japanese landowners used as a form of tax payment, indicating strong connections between Japanese land, Japanese short-grain rice, and the Japanese landowning elite. By the early modern period (1603–1868), as Japan became increasingly urban and eventually industrialized, agricultural life declined. People moved off the land and into cities, and rice began to take on new meanings. Symptomatic of a cultural identity strongly rooted in national history, rice became an increasingly sacred symbol of Japanese identity—a cultural memory with a long history that consistently tied being Japanese to eating domestic Japanese rice. As Japan opened to interactions with Western nations, the Japanese continued to use rice as a metaphor for national identity: while the Japanese referred to themselves as "rice-eaters," they referred to Western peoples as "meat-eaters."

For years, Japan has had a ban on importing any foreign-grown rice, even California export rice, which is primarily the Japanese short-grain variety and available at a significantly lower price. In 1993, Japan suffered a growing season that was colder and wetter than normal and had a low-producing rice harvest. US rice exporters were able to negotiate a trade deal allowing some limited rice exports to Japan. Yet most of this rice remained in warehouses, untouched. Japanese people complained that it was full of impurities and did not taste good. Today, on average, Japanese people consume only about 160 grams of rice daily, half of what they consumed 40 years ago (Coleman 2017). Yet their cultural and symbolic connection with domestic Japanese rice remains strong. Japanese short-grain rice is still referred to as *shushoku*, "the main dish" (Ohnuki-Tierney 1993, 16)—the symbolic centerpiece, even though it is now more frequently a small side dish in a more diverse cuisine. Ohnuki-Tierney notes that rice plays a particularly important role in the Japanese sense of community:

> Not only during ritual occasions, but also in the day-to-day lives of the Japanese, rice and rice products play a crucial role in commensal activities. Cooked white rice is offered daily to the family ancestral alcove. Also, rice is the only food shared at meals, served by the female head of the household, while other dishes are placed in individual containers. Rice stands for "we," i.e., whatever social group one belongs to, as in a common expression, "to eat from the same rice-cooking pan," which connotes a strong sense of fellowship arising from sharing meals. (1995, 229)

Although the meaning of rice has shifted during different historical periods—from a comparison between short-grain Japanese and long-grain Chinese rice to a way to distinguish rice-eating Japanese from meat-eating Westerners, then to a measure of the quality of what is grown in Japanese versus less desirable imported rice—the Japanese continue to hold a cultural identity closely connected with rice. Being Japanese means eating Japanese rice still today.

The relationship between food and cultural identity is readily apparent in Western societies. Most grocery stores have aisles containing goods labeled as "international foods" or "ethnic foods," and large urban areas often include neighborhoods featuring a conglomeration of restaurants serving diverse cuisines. In Washington, DC, the neighborhood of Adams Morgan is famous for its ethnic restaurants. Walking down the street, one might smell the mouthwatering aroma of *injera*, a sour, fermented flatbread from Ethiopia, or *bún bò hu?*, spicy lemongrass beef soup from Vietnam. Think about your own town and nearby urban areas. Where do you go to try new foods and dishes from other cultures?

Food Prescriptions and Proscriptions

As with all cultural institutions, there are various rules and customs surrounding food and eating. Many of these can be classified as either **food prescriptions**, foods that one should eat and are considered culturally appropriate, or **food proscriptions**, foods that are prohibited and not considered proper. These food regulations are social norms that connect production and consumption with the maintenance of cultural identity through food.

In the previous section, you read about the importance of Japanese short-grain rice as a symbol of Japanese identity. For many Japanese people, short-grain rice is a food prescription, something that they feel they should eat. Food prescriptions are common across cultures and nation-states, especially in regard to special holidays. There are many examples: turkey on Thanksgiving in the United States, corned beef on St. Patrick's Day in Ireland, special breads, and candy figurines on Día de los Muertos in Mexico, saffron bread and ginger biscuits on St. Lucia Day in Sweden, or mutton curry and rice on Eid al-Fitr in Muslim countries. Food prescriptions are also common in the celebration of commemorative events, such as the cakes eaten at birthday parties and weddings, or the enchiladas and tamales prepared for a *quinceañera* celebrating a young Latin American woman's 15th birthday. Most of these occasions involve **feasts**, which are elaborate meals shared among a large group of people and featuring symbolically meaningful foods.

One interesting example is the food eaten to mark the Dragon Boat Festival (Dragon Boat Festival, also called Duanwu), held in China on the fifth day of the fifth month of the Chinese lunar year. There are various origin stories for the Dragon Boat Festival. In one of them, the festival commemorates a beloved Chinese poet and government minister named Qu Yuan (ca. 340–206 BCE), who fell out of imperial favor and died by suicide, drowning himself. According to the story, people threw sticky rice dumplings into the river where he had drowned himself in order to distract the fish so that they could retrieve his body and give him a proper burial. The most important Dragon Boat food is *zongzi*, a sticky rice dumpling with different fillings, but the feast also traditionally includes eel, sticky rice cakes, boiled eggs, *jiandui* (a wheat ball covered in sesame seeds), pancakes with fillings, and wine.

FIGURE 14.10 *Zongzi*, a sticky rice dumpling, wrapped in bamboo leaves, prepared for the Dragon Boat Festival. Festival foods are typically associated with specific ritual events. (credit: "Dragon Boat Festival Zongzi" by Evan Wood/flickr, CC BY 2.0)

Food proscriptions, also called food taboos, are also common across cultures and contribute to establishing and maintaining a group's identity. Often, these rules and regulations about what not to eat originate in religious beliefs. Two examples are the vegetarianism practiced by many Hindus, which is grounded in the spiritual principle of *ahimsa* (nonviolence in relation to all living things), and *kashrut*, a Jewish principle that forbids mixing meat and dairy foods or eating pork or shellfish. Sometimes food proscriptions are active for limited periods of time. For many Christians, especially Catholics, the 40 days of Lent, a period of religious reflection commemorating the 40 days Jesus spent fasting in the desert, are a time when people give up certain foods or drinks to make a symbolic sacrifice. For many Catholics, this means fasting (withholding a measure of food) throughout the period and/or totally abstaining from meat on the special days of Ash Wednesday and Good Friday:

> For members of the Latin Catholic Church, the norms on fasting are obligatory from age 18 until age 59. When fasting, a person is permitted to eat one full meal, as well as two smaller meals that together are not equal to a full meal. The norms concerning abstinence from meat are binding upon members of the Latin Catholic Church from age 14 onwards. (United States Conference of Catholic Bishops n.d.)

Muslims observe Ramadan, a month-long commemoration of the prophet Muhammad receiving the revelations of the Quran, by fasting every day from sunup to sundown. The Islamic fast entails a prohibition on food and drink, including water. Every evening after sundown, Muslims eat a large meal that include fruits, vegetables, and dates to rehydrate for the next day's fast.

Some food prohibitions are customary and tied more to ancient cultural traditions than religion. Many food prohibitions pertain to meat. Among several East African groups, there is a prohibition against eating fish of any kind. This is called the *Cushitic fish taboo* because the prohibitions are found among many, but not all, cultural groups whose languages are part of the Cushite family, such as the Somali, Masaai, and Bantu peoples. Horsemeat was historically consumed infrequently in the United States until it was outlawed in 2005, primarily because of toxins in the meat related to the butchering process. Even before then, horsemeat in mainstream US society was a food prohibition. However, it is consumed throughout Europe, where there are butchers solely devoted to handling horsemeat.

FIGURE 14.11 A horse butcher shop in Italy. In many European countries, horsemeat is processed separately from other meats and sold at specialized butcher shops. (credit: Schellack at English Wikipedia/Wikimedia Commons, CC BY 3.0)

An interesting case of food rules and regulations across cultures is **cannibalism**, the act of eating an individual of one's own species. Although we do not usually think of human flesh as a menu item, in some cultures it is considered a kind of food, typically eaten as symbolic nutrition and identity. U.S. cultural and medical anthropologist Beth Conklin (1995) and Brazilian cultural anthropologist Aparecida Vilaça (2002) conducted research among the Wari' of western Amazonia in Brazil and found that prior to evangelization by Christian missionaries in the 1960s, the Wari' practiced two different types of cannibalism: *endocannibalism*, or eating members of one's own cultural group, and *exocannibalism*, or eating those who are "foreign" or outside of one's cultural group. Each form of cannibalism was associated with its own beliefs, practices, and symbolism.

The Wari' belief system is based on the principle that only the Wari' are real people. All non-Wari' others, people and animals alike, are not humans and thus can be considered meat (Vilaça 2002, 358). When speaking of the practice recognized by anthropologists as exocannibalism, the Wari' did not consider themselves to be practicing cannibalism at all; they saw non-Wari' people as not fully human and classified them as a type of prey. Endocannibalism was understood differently. Endocannibalism among the Wari' was practiced as part of the mourning process and understood as a way of honoring a Wari' person who had died. Following a death, the immediate family of the deceased arranged for non-kin and relatives by marriage to dress and prepare the body by dismembering, roasting, and eating virtually all of it. Consuming the flesh of the deceased was considered the ultimate act of respect, as the remains were not buried in the ground but in the living bodies of other Wari'. Once eaten by non-family Wari', the deceased could transform from humans into spirits and eventually return as prey animals to provide food for the living. For Conklin, this practice indicates *mutualism*, or the relationship between people and animals through the medium of food and eating:

> For Wari', ... the magic of existence lies in the commonality of human and animal identities, in the movements between the human and nonhuman worlds embodied in the recognition through cannibalism of human participation in both poles of the dynamic of eating and being eaten. (Conklin 1995, 95)

Cannibalism has been associated with many cultures, sometimes accompanying warfare or imperial expansion, as in the case of the Aztecs (Isaac 2002), and sometimes as a means of showing respect for and establishing kinship with the deceased (see Lindenbaum 1979 for an example in Papua New Guinea). Although there have been scholarly arguments around the nature and frequency of cannibalism (Arens 1979), there is increasing evidence that this was a practiced norm in many human societies. Some religions also incorporate symbolic cannibalism as a way of identifying with the deity.

Food can be deeply symbolic and plays an important role in every culture. Whether foods are prescribed or prohibited, each culture constructs meanings around what they define as food and the emotional attachments they have to what they eat. Consider your own plate when you next sit down to eat. What meanings are attached to the different foods that you choose? What memories do different foods evoke?

Food and Gender

While food itself is a material substance, humans classify and categorize foods differently based on cultural differences and family traditions. In many cultures, food is gendered, meaning some foods or dishes are associated with one gender more than with the other. Think about your own culture. If you were cooking a meal for only women or only men, would that influence the foods you chose to prepare? Although gender-specific food choices are stereotypes of male and female dietary preferences and every person has their own individual preferences, many social institutions and entertainment venues cater to gendered diets.

- When the television show *Man v. Food*, a show devoted to "big food" and eating challenges, premiered on the Travel Channel in 2008, it had some of the highest ratings of any show on that channel. Many of the foods showcased are those stereotypically associated with men (burgers, potatoes, ribs, fried chicken), and the host participates in local food-eating competitions, highlighting regional cuisines around the United States. In this show, food functions as a sporting activity under extreme conditions.
- Food delivery business GrubHub did a study of male and female ordering preferences in 2013–2014 at some 30,000 different restaurants in more than 700 US cities to "better understand takeout and delivery" (GrubHub 2018). In their results, they noted some significant differences between men's and women's ordering habits. Pizza was the most popular item for both men and women, but among other selections, women tended to order more healthy options, such as salads, sushi, and vegetable dishes, and men ordered more meat and chicken, with the most popular choices being General Tso's chicken, chicken parmesan, and bacon.

Food historian Paul Freedman traced the emergence of gendered foods and gendered food stereotypes in the United States back to the 1870s, when "shifting social norms—like the entry of women into the workplace—gave women more opportunities to dine without men" (2019b). Freedman notes that there was a rapid development of restaurants meant to appeal to women. Many of these featured lighter fare, such as sandwiches and salads, and some were referred to as "ice cream saloons," playing on a distinction between them and the more traditional type of saloon primarily associated with men (Freedman 2015). There was also growth in the recipe industry to provide women with home cooking options that allowed for quicker meal preparation.

Gendering foods, a practice often associated with specific life stages and rituals, is found across cultures and across time. In his study of marriage customs in the chiefdom of Batié in Cameroon, social anthropologist Emile Tsékénis notes that the marriage is formalized by an exchange of gendered foods between the couple's polygamous families:

> The groom offers raw "male" products (palm oil, plantain, and raffia wine) to the co-wives of the girl's mother, while the co-wives hand over the palm oil to the girl's father, and the girl's side offers "female" products (yams, potatoes, and/or taro) to the husband's side. (2017, 134)

This exchange of gendered foods between families mirrors the marriage ceremony and symbolically binds the couple's families together.

Gendered foods are also common during puberty rituals in many cultures, especially for young women, as female puberty is marked by the beginning of menstruation, an obvious and observable bodily change. In the Kinaaldá, the Navajo puberty ceremony for young girls that takes place shortly after the first menstruation, the girl and female members of her family together cook a corn cake in a special underground oven. The corn cake, called an *alkaan*, is understood as a re-creation of the first corn cake baked by the Navajo deity Changing Woman. After baking this first corn cake, Changing Woman offered a piece of it to the sun in gratitude for food and life. By reenacting this ritual, the young girl marks her own journey toward the creation of life, as she is now capable of becoming a mother.

FIGURE 14.12 Ashes smolder in a firepit in preparation for baking the corn cake that is used to celebrate a Navajo girl's Kinaaldá (puberty) ceremony. (credit: "Campfire 1" by Jaroslav A. Polák/flickr, Public Domain)

As we saw in Chapter 12, Gender & Sexuality, cultures may also celebrate foods that enhance sexuality. In some regions of Vietnam, there are restaurants that serve dog to male customers only, as dog meat is believed to enhance masculinity (Avieli 2011). Food contains and conveys many cultural beliefs. This can be compared to the joys attributed to chocolate in the United States, especially during the celebration of Valentine's Day. Do you have similar beliefs about food and sexuality?

14.4 The Globalization of Food

LEARNING OUTCOMES

By the end of this section, you will be able to:

- Describe the impacts of globalization on food and food diversity.
- Define food deserts and food oases.

Globalization of Food

Most people, when they think about food, consider it a local, individual choice based on personal preferences and economic possibilities. But food is a global commodity marketed by transnational corporations, health institutes, advertising campaigns, and subtle and not-so-subtle cultural messaging through global media such as movies, television, and online video. Most often, what people choose to eat is based on underlying structures that determine availability and cost. While there are now hothouse businesses growing year-round fruits and vegetables, affordability often prohibits everyone from having access to fresh, ripe foods. Instead, mainstream grocery stores most often stock foods imported across long distances. Most fruits and vegetables sold in the grocery store were harvested unripe (and often tasteless) so that they would last the days and weeks between harvesting and purchase.

FIGURE 14.13 Pallets of fruit being loaded on deck for shipment overseas. Most commercial fruits are harvested before they are ripe so that they will not spoil before arriving at a supermarket, often far from where they were picked. (credit: Dr. Karl-Heinz Hochhaus/Wikimedia Commons, CC BY 3.0)

In her work on food and globalization, anthropologist and food studies specialist Lynne Phillips points out the "crooked pathways" (2006, 38) that food takes to become a global commodity. Increasingly affected by transnational corporations, food today is marketed for endlessly higher profits. Food no longer goes simply from producer to consumer. There are many turns along the way.

Food globalization has numerous effects on our daily lives:

- The food chains from producers to consumers are increasingly fragile as a small number of transnational corporations provide the basic foods that we eat daily. Failures in this food chain might come from contamination during production or breaks in the supply chain due to climate crises, tariffs, or trade negotiations between countries. Our dependence on global food chains makes the food supply to our communities more vulnerable to disruption and scarcity.
- Our food cultures are less diverse and tend to revolve around a limited number of mass-produced meats or grains. With the loss of diversity, there is an accompanying loss not only of food knowledge but also of nutrition.
- As foods become more globalized, we are increasingly dependent on food additives to enhance the appearance and taste of foods and to ensure their preservation during the long journey from factory farm to table. We are also increasingly exposed to steroids, antibiotics, and other medicines in the meat we eat. This exposure poses health risks to large numbers of people.
- As plants and animals are subjected to ever more sophisticated forms of genetic engineering, there is an increasing monopoly on basic food items, allowing transnational companies to affect regulatory controls on food safety. As corporate laboratories develop patented seeds (such as the Monsanto Corporation's genetically engineered corn) that are super-producers and able to withstand challenges such as harsh climate conditions and disease, growers become dependent on the seed sold by these corporations. No longer able to save seed from year to year, growers have little choice but to pay whatever price these corporations choose to charge for their genetic material.
- Factory farming of all types, but especially large-scale animal farms, are major contributors to global warming. Not only do they produce large amounts of water and air pollution and contribute to worldwide deforestation, but as more and more forest is turned into pasture, the sheer number of livestock contributes significant levels of greenhouse gases that lead to global warming. Worldwide, livestock account for around 14.5 percent of global greenhouse gas emissions (Quinton 2019).

Food has long been an international commodity, even during the 17th and 18th centuries, when traders sought spice and trade routes connecting Europe and Asia. Today, however, food has become transnational, with production sometimes spanning many different countries and fresh and processed foods moving long distances from their original harvest or production. Because these migrating foods must be harvested early or packaged with preservatives that we may not know or even be able to pronounce, there has been a parallel development in local food movements, organic food movements, and farm-to-table establishments as people see the dangers of food globalization. In the very popular *The Omnivore's Dilemma: A Natural History of Four Meals* (2006), American author and food journalist Michael Pollan advocates that people should know the identity of the foods they eat and should make every effort to eat locally sourced products. Shortly after the book's publication, chef and author Jessica Prentice coined the term **locavore** to refer to those who eat locally and know the origins of their foods. In 2007, *locavore* was chosen as the New Oxford American Dictionary word of the year.

Food Deserts and Oases

Worldwide, access to nutritious and affordable foods is growing increasingly unequal. Areas with inadequate or unreliable access to nutritious foods are sometimes called **food deserts**. Food deserts present serious challenges to health and wellness in multiple ways and have been linked to eating disorders, obesity, and malnutrition. In Western nations, food deserts frequently correspond to other areas of social inequality, such as low-income and minority communities. Reduced availability of healthy and economical food often exacerbates many of the challenges these communities face.

FIGURE 14.14 Food deserts are common in Western countries, especially in and around urban areas. This chart shows areas in the United States where significant percentages of people both have no car and no grocery store within a mile of their home, which is about a twenty minute walk for a healthy adult. (credit: United States Department of Agriculture and Centers for Disease Control/Wikimedia Commons, Public Domain)

As the world population continues to grow (currently at around 7.9 billion people (https://openstax.org/r/world-population)), climate change accelerates, and food production becomes more and more concentrated in the hands of a few corporations, access to food will become increasingly critical to our survival. The story of progress embraced by Western society tells us that globalization and agricultural developments have stabilized and secured our food chains, but anthropological studies of foragers suggest otherwise. Agricultural production is tied to access to arable land, clean water, stable climate, and a reliable workforce. Periodically, crops (and animals) fail due to disease, drought, and even disruption from warfare and extreme weather, leading to scarcity and famine in many parts of the world. In addition, as families and communities produce less and less of their own food and become more and more dependent on intermediaries to gain access to food, their vulnerabilities increase. While there are many differences between state societies and foragers, there are valuable lessons we can learn from them. Foragers, facing the same unstable conditions that we all face worldwide, have a more varied and flexible diet and are able to adjust their needs seasonally based on local availability. They eat locally, and they adjust their needs to what is available.

There are also **food oases**, areas that have high access to supermarkets and fresh foods, and these are growing in number. Some are in urban or suburban areas, and some are in rural areas where sustainable farming supports a local community or restaurant. In Harrodsburg, Kentucky, the Trustees' Table serves food from the nearby Pleasant Hill Shaker gardens. Visitors to the Shaker site, a historic cloistered religious community, learn about the Shaker seed industry, plant varieties, and sustainable gardening techniques at Shaker Farm, then walk down to the Trustees' Table to have a farm-to-table meal. The seasonal menu features local Kentucky dishes that would have been common fare during the period of Shaker occupation (1805–1910), such as garlic potatoes, warm or cold salads, vegetable pot pies, and apple pie. By utilizing the foods raised in the nearby gardens, the Trustees' Table serves as a legacy restaurant that helps preserve and sustain Shaker research and farming on-site.

In Richmond, Virginia, an organization called Real Local RVA (https://openstax.org/r/reallocalrva) was founded in 2014 as a grassroots local food movement to support businesses and residential areas in the downtown area of the city. It expresses its core value as "collaboration over competition." The group sponsors monthly meetings, local farm tours, and community events highlighting businesses and prominent figures in the local food movement. The participants are all farmers, independent grocers, or local restaurants that source local ingredients and products as part of their mission. Besides advocating for small farms and independent businesses, Real Local RVA also sponsors workshops and education on sustainable farming, does joint marketing and "storytelling" about its partnership and the values of local food networks, and provide a recognizable brand to identify participating members for the wider urban community.

Although local food movements are increasingly popular, most still primarily operate in more affluent areas. As we develop more of these healthy initiatives, we also must expand the zones in which they operate, especially in cities, to include all of our neighbors and neighborhoods. Food and sociality go hand in hand. As Michael Pollan writes, "The shared meal elevates eating from a mechanical process of fueling the body to a ritual of family and community, from mere animal biology to an act of culture" (2008, 192).

The study of food in anthropology is important for many reasons. Food reveals cultural identities and physical vulnerabilities, and it helps build social networks and mark important life events. How often eating is prescribed, what foods are considered appropriate, who cooks, who serves whom, and what foods are most and least valued all vary across cultures. As anthropologists seek to understand human cultures, food is often a centerpiece ingredient in knowing who we are.

MINI-FIELDWORK ACTIVITY

Food Memories

Food plays an important role in long-term memory, as it is linked to smell, taste, and texture and often is a central feature of social functions, whether they be family dinners or holiday feasts. In this project, you will interview two individuals who are likely to have different food memories than you; they may be older, they may be living in a different part of the country (or world), or they may have lived part of their lives in a specific environment (rural or urban) that is different from yours. Ask each person to share with you stories about special holiday meals prepared and served as part of their family life, whether as a child or an adult. What foods do they most identify with specific holidays? How did they prepare and consume those foods? Were there specific gender roles during the preparation and holiday meals? After collecting and writing up what you have learned, what conclusions can you make about the role of food in human social and cultural life?

Key Terms

basalt an igneous rock frequently used for early grinding tools in the Near East.

biocultural approach a perspective that looks at both the cultural and biological roles that food plays in human lives.

cannibalism the act of eating an individual of one's own species.

cuisine the cultural traditions of cooking and preparing food.

cultural heritage traditions passed down through generations that serve as primary characteristics of how a group defines and identifies itself to other cultural groups.

cultural identity the ways in which people define and distinguish themselves culturally from other groups.

feasts elaborate meals of symbolically meaningful foods shared among large groups of people.

food a substance eaten for the purpose of nutrition and/or social status.

food deserts areas that lack access to nutritious and affordable foods.

food oases areas that have high access to supermarkets and fresh foods.

food prescriptions foods that one should eat and are considered culturally appropriate.

food proscriptions foods that are prohibited and are not considered proper as food; also called food taboos.

foodways the collection, production, and consumption of food; how culinary traditions shape cultural identity.

genetically modified plants plants whose DNA has been altered through human intervention.

heirloom seeds seeds that are not genetically modified, are open pollinated, and have been in existence for at least 50 years.

intercropping planting different seeds mixed together instead of in separate rows.

locavore a person who eats locally produced foods and knows their origins.

residue studies chemical analyses of small amounts of material left intact on surfaces in order to identify the substance.

shell midden a large collection of discarded shells, either food remains or waste piles from other activities.

Summary

Food is a ubiquitous artifact. Found everywhere during all periods of history, it is diverse and symbolic. The study of early human diets is important for understanding the evolution of humans, and archaeologists use various kinds of evidence to determine early foodways, from material artifacts such as food utensils to food residues and even coprolites. The study of ancient foods provides valuable information about health, economics, politics, and religion of early humans and the ways humans adapted to changing environments. Today, Indigenous groups such as the Cherokee are incorporating traditional foodways in cultural revitalization efforts, negotiating with the government to protect their ability to harvest wild foods on ancestral lands.

Many anthropologists take a biocultural approach to the study of food, examining the biological/nutritional role of food and its connection to identity. Agricultural practices such as the Three Sisters practice of the Haudenosaunee are good examples of ways in which human cultures have used their knowledge about food to develop sustainable and healthy farming techniques. Sustainable farming techniques, many of them grounded in traditional practices, typically produce higher food yields, reduce fertilizer costs, build healthier soils, and avoid genetically modified plants. There is also growing interest today in cultural foodways that may increase health and wellness, such as the Mediterranean diet, based on fruits, vegetables, and olive oil, and the paleo diet, which is based on our perspective of early human diets and includes lean meats, fruits, vegetables, and nuts.

Food plays a central role in cultural identity. Cultures practice food prescriptions, or specific foods considered critical to maintaining cultural identity, such as short-grain rice for the Japanese, and food proscriptions, which are food taboos, such as horsemeat in the United States. Feast foods are another way in which cultures use food to mark and symbolize special occasions. In short, what we eat as human societies defines who we are. Some societies, such as the Wari' in Brazil and many others, have also practiced forms of cannibalism as ways of defining kinship and humanity. Gender and religion are other areas in which food plays a major role in creating boundaries and identities.

Today, many foods are global commodities. Grocery

store foods, produced and distributed by transnational corporations, may be shipped many thousands of miles from their points of origin. Access to fresh food is a global challenge, especially in urban environments with concentrated populations. In food deserts, multiple forms of social inequality affect the health and wellness of the whole society. There are also growing numbers of food oases, where local movements offer farm-to-table meat and produce. Food plays an important role in our biological and cultural lives. Given the ongoing challenges of climate change, food insecurity is increasing worldwide as dependable food networks are shifting.

Critical Thinking Questions

1. What are the various ways in which food can be defined as an artifact?
2. What is the relationship between heritage foods and cultural identity?
3. How do archaeologists study early human diets? What evidence can they use to determine eating habits?
4. How does food serve as both physical and cultural nourishment?
5. Describe various food prescriptions and food prohibitions that are common in your own cultural practices.
6. What is the relationship between food and gender? How might food habits reinforce gender stereotypes? Give some examples from your own cultural practices.
7. How has globalization affected the cultural diversity and value of food?
8. Why should food deserts concern everyone in a society?

Bibliography

Ahmad, Shafqat, M. Vinayaga Moorthy, Olga V. Demler, Frank B. Hu, Paul M. Ridker, Daniel I. Chasman, and Samia Mora. 2018. "Assessment of Risk Factors and Biomarkers Associated with Risk of Cardiovascular Disease among Women Consuming a Mediterranean Diet." *JAMA Network Open* 1 (8). https://doi.org/10.1001/jamanetworkopen.2018.5708.

Arens, William. 1979. *The Man-Eating Myth: Anthropology and Anthropophagy*. New York: Oxford University Press.

Avieli, Nir. 2011. "Dog Meat Politics in a Vietnamese Town." *Ethnology* 50 (1): 59–78. http://ethnology.pitt.edu/ojs/index.php/Ethnology/article/viewArticle/6092.

Blackley, Seamus, Serena Love, and Richard Bowman. 2019. "A Conversation with the Team That Made Bread with Ancient Egyptian Yeast." Interview by Jenny G. Zhang. Eater. August 8, 2019. https://www.eater.com/2019/8/8/20792134/interview-seamus-blackley-serena-love-richard-bowman-baked-bread-ancient-egyptian-yeast.

Borowski, Oded. 2004. "Eat, Drink, and Be Merry: The Mediterranean Diet." *Near Eastern Archaeology* 67 (2): 96–107.

Braun, Adee. 2014. "Looking to Quell Sexual Urges? Consider the Graham Cracker." *Atlantic*, January 15, 2014. https://www.theatlantic.com/health/archive/2014/01/looking-to-quell-sexual-urges-consider-the-graham-cracker/282769/.

Carnegie Museum of Natural History. 2018. "The Three Sisters: Sustainers of Life." North South East West: American Indians and the Natural World. https://nsew.carnegiemnh.org/iroquois-confederacy-of-the-northeast/three_sisters/.

Chang, Melanie L., and April Nowell. 2016. "How to Make Stone Soup: Is the 'Paleo Diet' a Missed Opportunity for Anthropologists?" *Evolutionary Anthropology* 25 (5): 228–231.

Chávez, Karen. 2019. "Great Smokies Approves Historic Sochan Collecting Agreement with Eastern Band of Cherokee." *Citizen-Times*, updated March 27, 2019. https://www.citizen-times.com/story/news/local/2019/03/25/great-smoky-mountains-national-park-allow-cherokee-gather-sochan/3267860002/.

Coleman, Rei Kataoka. 2017. "Where Did Japan's Imported Rice Go?" Tokyo Review. July 7, 2017. https://www.tokyoreview.net/2017/07/where-did-japans-imported-rice-go/.

Conklin, Beth A. 1995. "'Thus Are Our Bodies, Thus Was Our Custom': Mortuary Cannibalism in an Amazonian Society." *American Ethnologist* 22 (1): 75–101.

Cornaro, Lewis [Alvise]. 1779. *Discourses on a Sober and Temperate Life*. London: Benjamin White. http://www.gutenberg.org/ebooks/30660.

Duffy, Lisa. 2020. "Ancient Maya Cuisine and Residue Analysis." Florida Museum of Natural History. Updated June 29, 2020. https://www.floridamuseum.ufl.edu/envarch/research/maya/residue-analysis/.

Ebeling, Jennie R., and Yorke M. Rowan. 2004. "The Archaeology of the Daily Grind: Ground Stone Tools and Food Production in the Southern Levant." *Near Eastern Archaeology* 67 (2): 108–117.

Farb, Peter, and George Armelagos. 1980. *Consuming Passions: The Anthropology of Eating*. Boston: Houghton Mifflin.

Freedman, Paul. 2015. "Women and Restaurants in the 19th-Century United States." *OUPblog*, Oxford University Press. March 30, 2015. https://blog.oup.com/2015/03/women-restaurants-united-states-history/.

Freedman, Paul. 2019a. *American Cuisine: And How It Got This Way*. New York: Liveright.

Freedman, Paul. 2019b. "How Steak Became Manly and Salads Became Feminine." The Conversation. October 24, 2019. https://theconversation.com/how-steak-became-manly-and-salads-became-feminine-124147.

Gish Hill, Christina. 2020. "Returning Corn, Beans, and Squash to Native American Farms." *JSTOR Daily*, JSTOR. November 24, 2020. https://daily.jstor.org/partner-post-indigenous-agriculture/.

Graff, Sarah R. 2020. "Archaeology of Cuisine and Cooking." *Annual Review of Anthropology* 49:337–354.

GrubHub. 2018. *Men vs. Women Eating Preferences: Online Ordering Data Reveals Gender Differences in Takeout Dining*. https://media.grubhub.com/files/doc_downloads/GrubHub-Inc-Men-vs-Women-Eating-Preferences-White-Paper_v001_b3cw14.pdf.

Isaac, Barry L. 2002. "Cannibalism among Aztecs and Their Neighbors: Analysis of the 1577–1586 'Relaciones Geográficas' for Nueva España and Nueva Galicia Provinces." *Journal of Anthropological Research* 58 (2): 203–224.

Lewis, Courtney. 2012. "The Case of the Wild Onions: The Impact of Ramps on Cherokee Rights." *Southern Cultures* 18 (2): 104–117.

Lindenbaum, Shirley. 1979. *Kuru Sorcery: Disease and Danger in the New Guinea Highlands*. Palo Alto, CA: Mayfield.

Linnekin, Baylen. 2019. "Complicated Rules for Foraging Aren't Helping Our National Parks." *Reason*, April 6, 2019. https://reason.com/2019/04/06/complicated-rules-for-foraging-arent-hel/.

Lobel, Cindy. 2012. "Sylvester Graham and Antebellum Diet Reform." The Gilder Lehrman Institute of American History AP US History Study Guide. July 31, 2012. http://ap.gilderlehrman.org/history-by-era/first-age-reform/essays/sylvester-graham-and-antebellum-diet-reform.

Mayo Clinic Staff. "Paleo Diet: What Is It and Why Is It So Popular?" Mayo Clinic. August 25, 2020. https://www.mayoclinic.org/healthy-lifestyle/nutrition-and-healthy-eating/in-depth/paleo-diet/art-20111182.

Mitchell, Dawn. 2019. "The Cure for What Ails You: Elixirs, Tonics and Snake Oil." *Indy Star*, updated January 4, 2019. https://www.indystar.com/story/news/history/retroindy/2019/01/03/cure-what-ails-you-elixirs-tonics-and-snake-oil/2288353002/.

Mt. Pleasant, Jane. 2016. "Food Yields and Nutrient Analyses of the Three Sisters: A Haudenosaunee Cropping System." *Ethnobiology Letters* 7 (1): 87–98. https://doi.org/10.14237/ebl.7.1.2016.721.

Murphy, Andi. 2018. "Meet the Three Sisters Who Sustain Native America." *Native Voices*, PBS. November 16, 2018. https://www.pbs.org/native-america/blogs/native-voices/meet-the-three-sisters-who-sustain-native-america/.

The Nutrition Source. 2018. "Diet Review: Mediterranean Diet." Harvard T. H. Chan School of Public Health. Updated December 2018. https://www.hsph.harvard.edu/nutritionsource/healthy-weight/diet-reviews/mediterranean-diet/.

Ohnuki-Tierney, Emiko. 1993. *Rice as Self: Japanese Identities through Time*. Princeton, NJ: Princeton University Press.

Ohnuki-Tierney, Emiko. 1995. "Structure, Event and Historical Metaphor: Rice and Identities in Japanese History." *Journal of the Royal Anthropological Institute* 1 (2): 227–253.

Phillips, Lynne. 2006. "Food and Globalization." *Annual Review of Anthropology* 35:37–57.

Pobiner, Briana. 2013. "Evidence for Meat-Eating by Early Humans." *Nature Education Knowledge* 4 (6): 1. https://www.nature.com/scitable/knowledge/library/evidence-for-meat-eating-by-early-humans-103874273/.

Pollan, Michael. 2006. *The Omnivore's Dilemma: A Natural History of Four Meals*. New York: Penguin Press.

Pollan, Michael. 2008. *In Defense of Food: An Eater's Manifesto*. New York: Penguin Press.

Quinton, Amy. 2019. "Cows and Climate Change: Making Cattle More Sustainable." Feeding a Growing Population, UC Davis. June 27, 2019. https://www.ucdavis.edu/food/news/making-cattle-more-sustainable.

Richter, Tobias, and Amaia Arranz-Otaegui. 2018. "Following a New Trail of Crumbs to Agriculture's Origins." *Sapiens*, July 16, 2018. https://www.sapiens.org/archaeology/oldest-known-bread-crumbs-discovered/.

Rivers, Bridgette, Robert Oliver, and Lynn Resler. 2014. "Pungent Provisions: The Ramp and Appalachian Identity." *Material Culture* 46 (1): 1–24.

Robb, Alice. 2014. "Will Overpopulation and Resource Scarcity Drive Cannibalism?" *New Republic*, June 19, 2014. https://newrepublic.com/article/118252/cannibalism-and-overpopulation-how-amazon-tribe-ate-their-dead.

Tsékénis, Emile. 2017. "Personhood, Collectives, and the Human-Animal Distinction: The Cases of the Cameroon Grassfields and Madagascar." *Anthropologica* 59 (1): 130–144.

United States Conference of Catholic Bishops. n.d. "Fast and Abstinence." Accessed September 30, 2021. https://www.usccb.org/prayer-and-worship/liturgical-year-and-calendar/lent/catholic-information-on-lenten-fast-and-abstinence.

Vilaça, Aparecida. 2002. "Making Kin out of Others in Amazonia." *Journal of the Royal Anthropological Institute* 8 (2): 347–365.

Waldstein, Anna. 2017. "Food, Anthropology Of." In *The International Encyclopedia of Anthropology*, edited by Hilary Callan. John Wiley & Sons. https://doi.org/10.1002/9781118924396.wbiea1605.

White, Max E. 1975. "Contemporary Usage of Native Plant Foods by the Eastern Cherokees." *Appalachian Journal* 2 (4): 323–326.

Wild, Sarah. 2019. "Scientists Find First Evidence of Humans Cooking Starches." *Sapiens*, June 21, 2019. https://www.sapiens.org/news/starches-first-evidence-humans-cooking/.

CHAPTER 15
Anthropology of Media

Figure 15.1 Anas Aremeyaw Anas, an investigative journalist from Ghana, participating in the Global Conference for Media Freedom in London, 2019. He keeps his face hidden during all public appearances in order to protect himself from retaliation. (credit: Foreign, Commonwealth & Development Office/flickr, CC BY 2.0)

CHAPTER OUTLINE

INTRODUCTION "I am sorry I cannot show you my face. Because if I do, the bad guys will come for me." Who is that masked man? That man is Anas Aremeyaw Anas, the famous investigative journalist from Ghana who gave a TED Talk (https://openstax.org/r/gaveaTEDTalk) about how he "names, shames, and jails" those "bad guys" (Anas 2013). Using controversial undercover methods, Anas has posed as a street hawker, a priest, a patient in a mental facility, a janitor in a brothel, and a boulder. His investigations have revealed widespread corruption in the Ghanaian judiciary, police service, electric company, Ministry of Youth and Sports, and passport office as well as a Ghanaian orphanage. He has exposed cocoa smuggling, rebel invasions, human trafficking, child slavery, torture of Africans in Thai prisons, unsanitary food production, forced prostitution, and abuse of people with mental illness in a hospital.

Anas has become a kind of anti-corruption superhero in Ghana, combining anonymity and celebrity to force social change. While his undercover research is mostly in person, he publishes the reports of his investigations as videos, many of which are available for viewing on his website (https://openstax.org/r/anasaremeyawanas). He has become famous worldwide through the spread of these videos and the accumulation of interviews and commentary on his work that can be found on the Internet. His intriguing persona illustrates the complexities of identity in the digital era. Though many have attempted to unmask him, his "real" identity remains a mystery.

As previous chapters have demonstrated, anthropologists are keenly interested in questions of identity and social action. The holistic approach leads anthropologists to consider how certain social, cultural, economic, and political conditions give rise to public figures such as Anas. Clearly, the phenomenon of Anas cannot be fully understood without attention to the functions of media at local, national, and global levels. At the local level, investigative journalism functions as a tool of anti-corruption, while global digital media function as a tool of celebrity. Are these two functions compatible or contradictory?

A new field of media anthropology has emerged in the past few decades to address such pressing issues. This chapter explores the anthropology of mass media, including how media functions at local, national, and global levels. It also addresses how social conditions and cultural forces shape a variety of media genres, including news media, photography, radio, television, and the Internet. Just as anthropologists bring their unique approach to other fields, the distinctive methods and concepts of anthropology contribute complex, holistic insights to the study of media.

15.1 Putting the Mass into Media

LEARNING OUTCOMES

By the end of this section, you will be able to:

- Define the basic function of media.
- Distinguish basic media from mass media.
- Describe the social phenomenon of technophilia.
- Explain why culture is important to the study of media.

FIGURE 15.2 Technophiles of the world. Modern communication technologies are widely used in most cultures of the contemporary world. (credit: top left, "Sinaw, Bedouin Woman with Mobile Phone" by Arian Zwegers/flickr, CC BY 2.0; top right, "Kiwanja_Burma_Calling_17" by Ken Banks, kiwanja.net/flickr, CC BY 2.0; bottom, "©UNICEF/ECU/2020/Arcos" by UNICEF Ecuador/flickr, CC BY 2.0)

People today live in an era of **technophilia**—that is, an age when people embrace technologies and incorporate them into every part of their lives, particularly their social lives. In contrast to the inert functionality of old-school cameras, watches, radios, and televisions, the new "smart" gadgets interact with their users, learn from them, make suggestions, and contact their friends and family members. Insofar as they facilitate users' interactions with other people and the world around them, these smart technologies become part of their users, akin to an extra organ for sensation and communication. Insofar as they communicate with users, nudging and prodding them, they become like a friend or family member themselves.

Part of what makes these smart technologies so attractive (and addictive) is that they function as means of connecting people to one another, carrying messages and data to other individuals and groups. As instruments of communication, all of these technologies are forms of **media**. At the most basic level, media are tools for storing and sharing information.

In this basic sense, media have always been essential to the development and durability of human culture. Early forms of symbolic communication, such as cave paintings and ancient writing systems, can be considered media, as they provided people with ways of fixing meaning in material objects that could be shared with people in other places and other times. The scope of these early forms of media was limited, however, by their singularity. People could visit a cave painting, but they could not send a copy of it to their friends. A scholar could inscribe a story on a cuneiform tablet, but that tablet could not be reproduced for a wider audience without the painstaking work of inscribing copies one by one. Up until 1000 CE, scholars in many parts of the world specialized in manually copying books and pamphlets, sometimes using wooden block prints carved out by hand. These methods were so expensive that only the very wealthy could afford to buy written forms of media.

All of this changed with the invention of the printing press, first in China and then in Germany (Frost 2021). Around 1000 CE, the Chinese artisan Bi Sheng created a set of blocks out of baked clay, each one manually inscribed with a Chinese character. To publish a page of text, he arranged the character blocks on an iron frame that could be pressed against an iron plate to create a print. Around 1440, the German entrepreneur Johannes Gutenberg independently invented a similar system of movable-type printing. Gutenberg also created a set of blocks, each one containing a letter, but his were made of metal. He used his invention to print calendars, pamphlets, and 180 now-famous copies of the Bible. Within decades, the printing press had spread from Germany to France, Italy, Spain, England, and the rest of western Europe.

VIDEO

To see how Gutenberg's printing press worked, watch this video of a demonstration (https://openstax.org/r/YouTubeDLctAw4JZXE) of the world's most complete working replica at Crandall Historical Printing Museum in Provo, Utah.

If manual writing systems are basic forms of media, then mechanically reproduced forms of communication are forms of **mass media**. Whereas forms of basic media operate between one sender and a small number of receivers, forms of mass media operate through a sender, a machine, and a potentially very large number of receivers. Originating in books and pamphlets produced using the movable-type printing press, the category of mass media has expanded over time with the development of new technologies, including photography, radio, television, and the Internet. Mass media are forms of communication facilitated by technology, allowing for broad distribution and reception by large numbers of people.

When considered from this angle, it may seem that technology is the most defining element of mass media. As machines, communication technologies might seem to function much the same in any context. When European printing presses were brought to Africa in the 19th century, they were used to publish newspapers that bore a family resemblance to European ones. If someone enables their mobile phone to function in another country while on vacation, they can use it to call their hotel or hail an Uber in much the same way they would use their phone at home.

Because communication technologies seem to function in uniform ways across contexts, people often assume that mass media are pretty much the same everywhere. Some provide news on current events. Some provide diversion and entertainment. Some allow users to communicate with individuals and groups. In this case, the differences one might see in mass media forms across cultures would be differences in technological sophistication or *penetration*, the word media scholars use to describe how widespread a communication technology is in a certain context.

Have you ever seen a Ghanaian video film? These are low-budget Ghanaian movies shot on video camera, usually completed within a few weeks and aimed at local audiences. They deal with social themes such as witchcraft and corruption, often combined with Christian redemption. Such video films are frequently criticized (by locals and foreigners alike) for their rudimentary editing and poor production values. When compared to Hollywood blockbuster movies, with their multimillion-dollar budgets and complex technological production processes, African video films may seem like a poor replica of the American form.

VIDEO

Watch *Darkness of Sorrow* (https://openstax.org/r/DarknessofSorrow) to see an example of a Ghanaian movie.

But that is not how West Africans view locally made video films. While many Ghanaians enjoy watching American films from time to time, the themes and issues explored in foreign films fail to resonate with their own experiences and concerns. In contrast, local video films engage with the desires and fears of Ghanaians, reinforcing forms of social identity and echoing familiar norms and values. Even as many Ghanaians criticize the rustic editing and uneven sound levels, local video films remain enormously popular among West African audiences.

Anthropologist Tejaswini Ganti (2012) conducted ethnographic research on the film industry in India. She describes how Indian films developed from rustic, homegrown forms of local entertainment to technologically sophisticated spectacles, forming the globalized industry of Bollywood. Ganti situates this transformation in the larger economic shifts of the 1990s and the accompanying neoliberal emphasis on global trade and middle-class consumerism in India. While earlier films focus on themes involving working-class and marginalized peoples, later films more often dramatize the lives of the professional, highly educated, and affluent classes. Thus, Ganti links the themes, technologies, and economic contexts of these films.

While technology may seem to be the defining feature of mass media, it is the immersion of communication technologies in local cultures that produces the total experience of mass media. At heart, mass media are not just technologies but forms of communication—technological vehicles for conveying forms of cultural meaning from senders to receivers. The language, images, symbols, and sounds used to convey meaning are all elements of culture. The thematic content of mass media is also profoundly cultural, shaped by local contexts of production and reception. Ways of consuming and interacting with mass media are also heavily determined by local social norms.

15.2 Putting Culture into Media Studies

LEARNING OUTCOMES

By the end of this section, you will be able to:

- Describe how an anthropologist might use participant observation to study media.
- Explain the relationship between modernity and media.
- Give an example illustrating the complex relationship between media and culture.
- Define the concept of cosmopolitanism.

In this section, the author of this chapter, Jennifer Hasty, describes her own experience using participant observation.

> *In the early 1990s, I went to the West African county of Ghana to study media and politics. I was specifically interested in the role of newspapers in the great wave of democratization across many African countries in that decade (Hasty 2005). Because I had some undergraduate training in journalism, I decided to volunteer as an intern at several newspapers and learn how news is produced in Ghana. I wound up working as a journalist for five different news organizations in the Ghanaian capital city of Accra over a period of several years. Through these experiences, I learned a great deal about how culture and history shape local news production, texts, and reception.*
>
> *When people outside of anthropology ask me about my fieldwork, I tell them (maybe too much) about working as a journalist in Ghana. They often respond with a perplexed look, saying, "Wait, I thought you said you were an anthropologist." When most people think about anthropological fieldwork, they think of quaint villages and rural locations, seemingly disconnected from the rest of the world. When they think of the topics anthropologists typically pursue, they think of religious rituals, political pageantry, complex kinship systems, and folk arts. That is, they think of the realm of "tradition."*
>
> *In fact, the contexts in which anthropologists work are not cut off from the rest of the world at all—and they never have been. People all over the world, in both rural and urban communities, are hooked up to global flows of information, images, ideas, commodities, and people. Newspapers, photography, radio, television, and the Internet are woven into daily life nearly everywhere one might go in the world.*
>
> *Recall the discussions of modernity in previous chapters. Historically speaking, modernity is the whole way of life associated with industrial and postindustrial societies—that is to say, the institutions and features of modernity emerged alongside industrialization and mass production. However, the features of modernity have spread across the globe to societies that are not primarily industrial or postindustrial. Features of modernity such as mass media, wage labor, and the nation-state shape the everyday lives of people in primarily agrarian, pastoral societies and gatherer-hunter societies. Anthropologists have abandoned the idea that some people live traditional lifestyles while others live modern ones. Rather, all people are modern in distinctive ways, shaped by local historical and cultural*

forces.

Since the early 1990s, anthropologists have been increasingly interested in the various forms of modernity that have emerged in non-European and non-American contexts. As a key tool of modernity, mass media have become the object of growing fascination in anthropology over the last three decades. My own first fieldwork was part of an early wave of media studies in anthropology, culminating in the establishment of an entire subdiscipline, media anthropology (Spitulnik 1993; Askew and Wilk 2002; Ginsburg, Abu-Lughod, and Larkin 2002).

By examining the use of media in contemporary sociocultural life, media anthropologists have learned that nearly all forms of culture are shaped by various genres of media. People take photographs and videos to commemorate cultural events and share their memories with others. They report on cultural topics in print media, radio, and television and discuss those issues on talk shows and social media. In fact, it's fair to say that mass media have become primary tools for defining, reinforcing, and reproducing local cultures. Rather than being opposed to tradition, mass media are key instruments for preserving and transmitting traditional cultures as well as modernity.

A few months ago, a Ghanaian journalist friend of mine, George Sydney Abugri, emailed me to ask if I could help him self-publish several books on Kindle Direct Publishing (KDP). Now retired, Abugri wanted to share his essays, poetry, and memoirs with Ghanaians, journalists, and scholars all over the world. In order to publish on KDP, you need a bank account from the United States or another "approved" country, and Ghana was not on that list. After a bit of textual wrangling, I was able to set up an account for him and get his books online so that he could find his global audience.

Anthropologists have a term for the kind of worldly orientation evident in Abugri's desire to speak to a global audience about global issues: ***cosmopolitanism****. Cosmopolitanism refers to a type of worldly knowledge and sophistication. Contemporary anthropologists, working in rural, village, and urban contexts, find that people in all settings have remarkable awareness of current world issues such as climate change, the Arab Spring, and the Me Too movement. One of Abugri's poems describes an incident on the German airline Lufthansa in which a White flight attendant claimed she could not understand Abugri's request for a glass of water. Cosmopolitan writers such as Abugri link their personal experiences to global issues such as race, environmentalism, and gender equality. Global issues and modern media forms are tightly integrated in the lives of both rural and urban peoples in cultures all over the world.*

15.3 Visual Anthropology and Ethnographic Film

LEARNING OUTCOMES

By the end of this section, you will be able to:

- Give examples of the early use of visual media in ethnographic fieldwork.
- Define the field of visual anthropology.
- Describe two examples of ethnographic film.
- Explain the ethical challenges associated with ethnographic film.

Although the subfield of media anthropology is relatively new, anthropologists have been incorporating media technologies into their methods of research and ethnographic representation since the early 20th century. An early pioneer of visual methods, Margaret Mead took some 200 photographs as part of her first fieldwork project in Samoa (Tiffany 2005). In the 1930s, Mead and Gregory Bateson used both photography and film in their joint fieldwork in Bali and New Guinea. Mead and Bateson embraced visual media as an innovative means of learning about social life and used photos and film to study childhood, public ceremonies, and dance. Together, they took about 33,000 photographs and recorded about 32,600 feet of film as part of their joint research (Jacknis 2020). Focusing on child development and dance, they used these visual materials to produce two photographic ethnographies and seven short films.

Visual anthropology is either the use of visual media as a research method or its study as a research topic. Whether they consider themselves visual anthropologists or not, most anthropologists take photos of the people and places they encounter in their fieldwork. Visual anthropologists go further, using photography and film to document important events for fine-grained future analysis. As moments frozen in time, photographs allow for analytical contemplation and shared consideration. Film can be slowed down or sped up to focus on certain aspects of individual action or group dynamics that might otherwise go unnoticed. Images may be magnified to reveal minute details. Both film and photography allow for images to be placed side by side for comparison.

Visual anthropologists are also interested in how people in the cultures they study produce their own visual representations in the form of art, photography, and film. Visual anthropologists are interested in popular paintings, billboards, and graffiti as well as forms of photography and film.

FIGURE 15.3 An image from Margaret Mead's film *Trance and Dance in Bali*. Margaret Mead was an early pioneer in the use of visual media in anthropology. (credit: Gregory Bateson and Margaret Mead/Wikimedia Commons, Public Domain)

Early on, cultural anthropologists recognized that visual media made it possible to share the experiences encountered during anthropological research with their colleagues and students, and the general public. One example of many is the film *Trance and Dance in Bali* (1951), written and narrated by Mead, which features a Balinese dance called the kris. The kris dance dramatizes the story of a witch whose daughter is rejected as a bride to the king. In retaliation, the witch plots to spread chaos and pestilence in the land. When the king sends an emissary with a convoy of servants to stop the nefarious plan, the witch turns the emissary into a dragon. She then causes the followers of the dragon to fall into trance. When the dragon-emissary revives his followers, they emerge in a somnambulant state, stabbing themselves with daggers but inflicting no harm. After dancing the kris dance, the dancers are brought out of their trance with incense and holy water. Included in the US Library of Congress, this stunning early use of film in anthropology can be viewed at the Library of Congress website (https://openstax.org/r/LibraryofCongresswebsite) or on YouTube (https://openstax.org/r/YouTubeZ8YC0dnj4Jw).

Ethnographic film is the use of film in ethnographic representation as either a method, a record, or a means of reporting on anthropological fieldwork. Like documentary films, ethnographic films are nonfiction films in which live-action shots are edited and shaped into a central narrative drama. While the line between documentary and ethnographic film is blurry, ethnographic film is associated with the work of professional anthropologists and tends to focus explicitly on depictions of sociocultural processes.

Before Mead and Bateson's professional use of film, several filmmakers had made amateur ethnographic films depicting aspects of non-Western cultures. The very popular film *Nanook of the North* (1922), made by explorer Robert Flaherty and based on 16 months of living with the Inuit, follows an Inuit family in the Canadian Arctic. The film focuses on the heroism of husband Nanook and wife Nyla as they struggle against the harsh elements to meet their needs and raise their children. The film documents Inuit lifeways such as traveling by dogsled and kayak, hunting walrus, and building an igloo out of glacier ice. In one controversial scene, the family visits a Canadian trading fort, where they express astonishment at instruments of modernity such as a phonograph. Though the film has been praised for its representation of Indigenous peoples as courageous and hardworking, others have criticized Flaherty for staging some of the events and even having his own common-law wife play the role of Nanook's wife in the film. Like Mead and Bateson's film, *Nanook of the North* is now held by the Library of Congress as one of the most significant examples of early documentary filmmaking. While some consider *Nanook* to be a precursor to ethnographic film, anthropologist Franz Boas dismissed it as completely irrelevant to anthropology due to Flaherty's use of artifice and staging (Schäuble 2018). The film can be viewed at the Internet Archive (https://openstax.org/r/nanookOfTheNorth1922) or on YouTube (https://openstax.org/r/nanooknorthvideo).

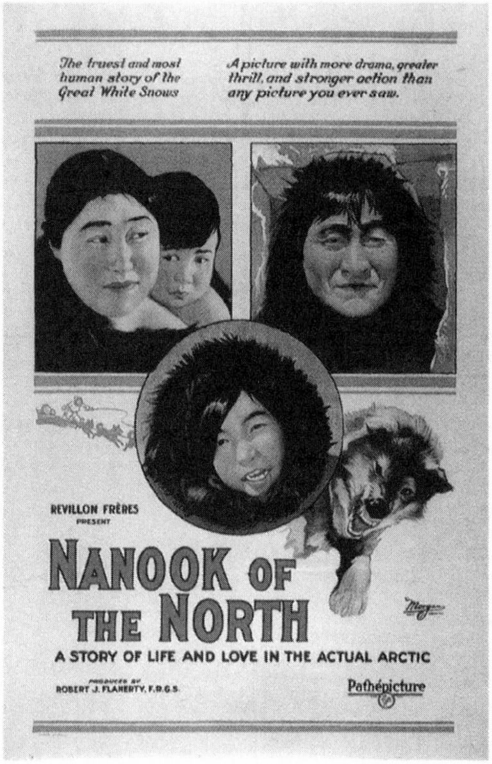

FIGURE 15.4 Promotional poster for *Nanook of the North*, considered by some to be one of the most significant examples of early documentary filmmaking. While based on field experience, a number of events in the film were staged. (credit: Robert J. Flaherty/Pathe Pictures/Wikimedia Commons, Public Domain)

From its roots in both amateur and professional filmmaking, ethnographic film became an increasingly important tool for teaching and popularizing anthropological research throughout the 20th century. In the 1950s, John Marshall and Timothy Asch pioneered a more objective, naturalist style of ethnographic film, attempting to avoid Western narratives and exoticization. With the development of the ability to simultaneously record sound in the 1960s, the commentary and conversations of people represented in ethnographic films became audible (even if translations still appeared in subtitles). Subjects could now address the camera directly. Around the same time, anthropologists began considering the power dynamics embedded in the production of ethnographic film—in particular, the ethical issues involved in White Western researchers controlling the representation of non-Western peoples.

Responding to these ethical challenges, many ethnographic filmmakers have turned away from the heavily crafted narrative methods of films such as *Nanook* toward a more purist style that represents unfolding action with little editing. New methods of representation have emerged, revealing the very act of filming itself and highlighting the relationship between filmmakers and those being filmed. Rather than using film as a means of teaching anthropology to students and the public, some experimental filmmakers conceptualize film as the creation of an entirely new sociocultural experience. The experimental ethnographic film *Manakamana*, for instance, directed by Stephanie Spray and Pacho Velez and released in 2013, comprises 11 long shots of Nepalese pilgrims taking cable car rides to a mountaintop temple in Nepal. Rather than teaching the viewer about an anthropological topic, *Manakamana* provides live-action portraits of people and their relationships against the backdrop of the rugged landscape passing below them. Spray and Velez are collaborators in Harvard University's Sensory Ethnography Lab, a project dedicated to the experimental use of multisensory methods to create ethnographic media. You can view a trailer for the film on YouTube (https://openstax.org/r/manakamanatrailer).

15.4 Photography, Representation, and Memory

LEARNING OUTCOMES

By the end of this section, you will be able to:

- Define the gaze and list important features of this concept.
- Give an example of the imperial gaze in popular photographic media.
- Describe the use of photography in colonial contexts.
- Discuss local techniques of self-representation through popular photography.

In addition to creating their own visual media, visual anthropologists conduct research on how the people they study produce visual media to represent themselves as well as cultural others.

Have you ever browsed through a copy of the magazine *National Geographic*? In the latter half of the 20th century, many American schools and middle-class households subscribed to this magazine as an educational resource for school-age children. Founded in 1888, the magazine has developed a reputation for its colorfully illustrated coverage of science, geography, history, and world cultures. Now owned in part by the Walt Disney Company, the magazine is published in 40 languages and has a global circulation of over six million.

What strikes many young people about *National Geographic* is not so much the informative textual content but rather the alluring images of non-Western peoples. Cultural anthropologist Catherine Lutz and sociologist Jane Collins (1993) set out to study how *National Geographic* depicted people in contexts outside the United States and western Europe. In their holistic approach, they conducted research into the production process at *National Geographic*, then subjected the photographs to rigorous content analysis, and finally interviewed people about how they made sense of the images.

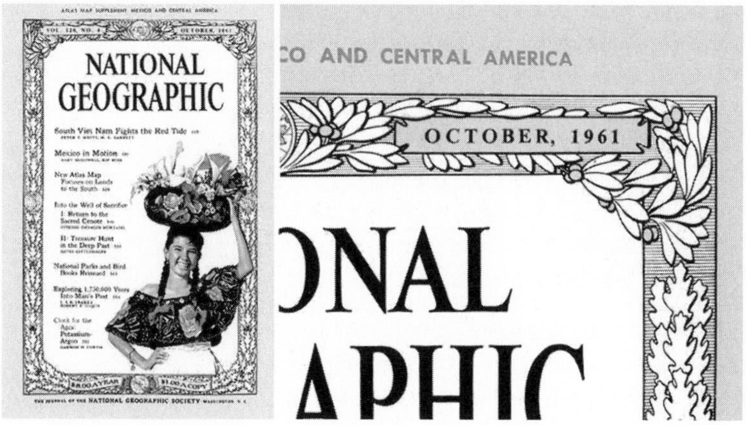

FIGURE 15.5 *National Geographic* cover from 1961 featuring the "exotic other." Researchers have noted that during the latter half of the twentieth century the magazine commonly portrayed non-Western people as exotic and close to nature. (credit: "NATIONAL GEOGRAPHIC Magazine - October 1961 - South Vietnam Fights the Red Tide - Nam Việt Nam chiến đấu chống thủy triều đỏ" by manhhai/flickr, CC BY 2.0)

Based on analysis of 600 *National Geographic* photos depicting non-Western peoples from 1950 to 1986, Lutz and Collins noted that the magazine portrayed non-Western peoples as exotic, idealized, and close to nature. Very rarely did photographs in the magazine reveal any traces of the complex colonial and postcolonial histories of their subjects or their entanglements in national and global processes. Instead, *National Geographic* photographs tended to depict happy people immersed in purely traditional lifeways. Without historical or political context, the apparent difference between "us" (the viewer) and "them" (the people depicted in the photographs) would seem to be developmental or evolutionary. In other words, the people depicted in the images were made to seem simpler or more backward than those viewing the images. Perhaps, the images seem to suggest, "they" have not yet achieved modernity. While emphasizing a theme of common humanity, the magazine nonetheless reproduced primitivist and orientalist stereotypes about non-Western peoples while obscuring the historical and political processes that have shaped their equally complex lifeways.

The Gaze of Photography

In the 1970s, film scholars developed the concept of **the gaze** to refer both to specific ways that viewers look at images of other people in visual media and to the gazes of those depicted within the images. Gaze theory attempts to understand what it means to view people and events through mass media.

Two key features of the gaze are important to this goal. First, the object being gazed at (the person or people in the image) is not aware of the viewer. This makes the gaze **voyeuristic**, like an anonymous peeping Tom looking through a window into a house. The gazer knows what is going, on but the people in the house (or the image) do not know they're being watched. Second, and because of the first point, the gaze implies a psychological relationship of power; the watching person has the power to scrutinize, analyze, and judge the watched people. The watcher can manipulate the perspective and conditions of watching. The watcher reserves the power to make sense of the image and to use the image however they please—for knowledge, pleasure, or criticism.

British film theorist Laura Mulvey (1975) used the concept of the gaze to develop a feminist approach to film studies. The **male gaze** describes how men look at women through any visual medium and even in everyday life. Beauty culture in western Europe and the United States positions women as objects to be gazed upon by men (and other women). Media scholars argue that women come to view themselves through the gaze of others, particularly men, who evaluate the attractiveness and desirability of their bodies. Thus, rather than experiencing her selfhood directly, a woman's self-image is routed through the male gaze.

The concept of the gaze is also used to think about other sociocultural power relations, particularly the historical processes of imperialism and colonialism. In the colonial period, the desire for conquest motivated strategic ways of gazing at cultural others. Through forms of media and image making developed in the 19th and early 20th centuries, Europeans developed an **imperial gaze**, positioning themselves as viewers of non-Western peoples. In the visual practices of empire, such as surveys and documentary photography, the lands and peoples were scrutinized, subjected to the domineering eye of European colonizers. The depictions of non-Western peoples in *National Geographic* are current manifestations of the imperial gaze.

Photography and the Colonial Gaze

Photography was invented in the early 19th century and became widespread in the period when European countries were beginning to establish formal colonial rule over African, Middle Eastern, and Asian territories. In colonial contexts, the imperial gaze framed how Europeans photographed colonial landscapes and colonized peoples, positioning them in strategic ways to justify colonial rule.

As the head of the Basel Mission Society's large archive of colonial photographs, historian Paul Jenkins (1993) has studied pictures taken by Swiss and German missionaries in Africa. The Basel Mission Society (BMS) was a Christian missionary group that participated in the larger trend of Christian missionizing in Africa in the late 19th and early 20th centuries. Jenkins's inquiry sought to understand what the BMS photos reveal about the people in the photographs, the people who took the photos, and the wider conditions in which the photos were taken.

Jenkins's analysis focuses on one particular missionary, Christian Hornberger, who worked in southeastern Ghana in the late 19th century. In 1863, the BMS asked Hornberger to take photographs depicting missionary activities in Ghana to be sold to European Christians who donated to the African missionary effort. Hornberger took many pictures of African children, the mission station, the local landscape, and scenes from Indigenous life. Jenkins points out that the earliest photographs taken by Hornberger emphasize the strangeness of African peoples and environments, while the later ones seem to emphasize the kind of common humanity found in later *National Geographic* photos. In Hornberger's later photographs, Africans are depicted in ways that would have been familiar to many Europeans: families are shown eating dinner together, women are depicted grinding corn, and local craftspeople are shown creating pottery.

A set of photographs of children dressed in European clothing caught Jenkins's eye. Who were these children, and why were there so many photos of them? Where were their parents? Digging deeper, Jenkins discovered that these were local "slave children" (1993, 100) bought into freedom by missionaries and taken to live on the mission compound. In West Africa at the time, people who fell into debt could "pawn" their children to work as servants in lieu of paying the debt. Sometimes, children were given to the priests of local shrines as payment for wrongdoing or gratitude for good fortune. As early Christian missionaries did not initially have much luck converting local peoples to Christianity, some BMS missionaries saw this practice as a way to both accumulate converts and drum up European support. BMS missionaries began offering European supporters the opportunity to "purchase" the freedom of a particular child, give the child a Christian name, and provide for the child's food, clothing, and other needs. Most of the African children in BMS photos of the time are subjects of this child-sponsorship program.

FIGURE 15.6 Hornberger's photograph of "emancipated" children. These children, who had been sold into servitude by their parents, were purchased by White missionaries and brought to live with them. Many were unhappy in this unfamiliar setting and ran way to reunite with their families. (credit: "L R and 2 Native Children, Congo, ca. 1900–1915" by Unknown/Wikimedia Commons, Public Domain)

While this may have seemed like a win-win scheme all around, the "liberation" of African slave children was apparently experienced by the many of the children as a new form of enslavement. Most were unhappy living on the mission compound, divorced from their home cultures, forced to wear uncomfortable clothing and speak a strange language. Many of them ran away, back to the families they had been serving before the missionaries intervened. By 1868, the BMS was forced to abandon the whole scheme. The backstory of Hornberger's photographs of these children vividly illustrates the strategic artifice of the imperial gaze—how missionaries used photography to position themselves as saviors while local people often saw them as agents of colonial domination. The entire collection of photographs from the Basel Mission Society is archived at the BM Archives website (https://openstax.org/r/bmarchives).

The Modernity of Postcolonial Photography

Focusing on more contemporary contexts, many media anthropologists analyze the images produced by postcolonial subjects themselves, along with the producers of those images and the production process. Rather than scrutinizing the imperial or ethnographic gaze, these scholars are interested in local forms of gazing at the self and others in photographs.

Anthropologist Liam Buckley (2000) has conducted research on studio photography in the West African country of Gambia. Through interviews with photographers and their subjects, Buckley traced the development of photographic strategies from the more realist style of the 1950s to the more fanciful and imaginative style common from the 1970s to the early 2000s.

In the 1950s, photographs were valued for faithfully depicting the character, mood, and personality of the subject, what people referred to as *jikko*. More recently, people began to prefer being photographed against elaborate studio backdrops depicting scenes of modern leisure and cosmopolitan travels. A staging popular with young people in particular features the subject relaxing amid an array of appliances, such as radio, television, and an open refrigerator full of cold beverages and tasty foods. Some backdrops depict subjects climbing the stairs to board an airplane or visiting a foreign tourist destination. Gambians use the term *juuntuwaay* to describe the props and imported goods included in these scenes, which might include bicycles, pens, and sunglasses. Young people use these objects to "'complete' themselves" (Buckley, 2000), thus using the photograph as a form of aspirational identity formation. The goal of this form of portraiture is not to depict personal *jikko* but rather to represent *jamano*, a sense of fashionable novelty and change.

15.5 News Media, the Public Sphere, and Nationalism

LEARNING OUTCOMES

By the end of this section, you will be able to:

- Describe the worldview presented in news media.
- Define the concept of the public sphere.
- Explain the importance of the public sphere to the study of news media.
- Distinguish from independent media.

While photography arrests attention with images, the various genres of news media draw people in with narratives about what's going on in their local communities and the larger world. A person who reads or views the news learns not only about current events but also about *what counts* as a current event—and, implicitly, what doesn't count as news (and thus doesn't matter to other people and shouldn't really matter to them). People learn to view the world in a certain way and to position their communities and themselves within that worldview. The top stories in national newspapers typically highlight the actions of political and economic leaders as the most important stories of the day. Political news is presented as an unfolding drama within or among nation-states—the United States establishes sanctions against Myanmar, for instance, or China takes action against Hong Kong protesters. Economic news is dominated by the gyrations of capitalist markets, both global and national, emphasizing the perspectives of the investors and business owners who make (or lose) money in those markets. Like the discipline of economics, news media take a market-centered approach to covering the economy, rather than a people-centered approach that might highlight labor conditions or environmental effects.

Some of the first news media were handwritten weekly newssheets that circulated in Venice in the 16th century, relaying information about European politics and wars. In the early 17th century, German and Dutch publishers began using the printing press to mass-produce newspapers for the growing population of literate readers in Europe, mainly merchants and lower-level government officials. Early newspapers reflected forms of discussion and debate emerging from the coffeehouses and salons of Europe, dominated by the concerns of the rising merchant classes that participated in those public arenas of discourse. German scholar Jurgen Habermas (1989) links this process to the emergence of the **public sphere**. Ideally, the public sphere is a domain of social life where people represent, learn about, and discuss the important issues of the day. It is distinct from both the private economic sphere and the sphere of public authority, including government, the military, and the police. The public sphere provides an important stage for the expression of a wide range of popular opinions with the goal of reaching consensus and influencing government policy. According to Habermas, newspapers were essential to the construction of the public sphere in western Europe and therefore were fundamental tools in the emergence of democratic forms of rule. A summary of Habermas's foundational argument about the rise and eventual corruption of the public sphere can be viewed on YouTube (https://openstax.org/r/habermasstructural).

Moreover, newspapers were key to processes of language standardization, uniting audiences from regional communities speaking various, sometimes mutually unintelligible dialects. As mentioned in a previous chapter, newspapers thus laid the foundation for the "imagined community" of the nation-state.

A glance at any national newspaper, whether in print or online, demonstrates how news media continue to serve as tools in the construction of public spheres and imagined communities today. With the invention of new genres of media, news discourse has expanded into radio, television, and the Internet, providing an even stronger force for the consolidation of national identities. Conducting research in Malaysia, media anthropologist John Postill (2006) describes how the Malaysian government strategically used state-sponsored media to consolidate a unified nation-state out of an ethnically diverse collection of former colonies. In one community, that of the Iban people on the island of Borneo, the state replaced local-language media with Malaysian-language media in an effort to bind the Iban more tightly to the state. Rather than completely erasing cultural differences within the nation-state, however, the Malaysian state media promoted a certain version of Iban "cultural heritage" while simultaneously undermining Iban political and cultural autonomy.

State media are media that are entirely or partially owned by the government. In many countries, including most African ones, the state has its own media apparatus, including a news agency, newspapers, and radio and television stations. **Independent media** are media that are privately owned. But wait, one might ask, isn't all news media supposed to be independent from government? If a state had its own news media, wouldn't that just be propaganda? In the United States, news media have traditionally emphasized journalistic independence and even critical opposition to the government. News media are thought to be the "watchdogs of the people," maintaining critical pressure on government leaders and institutions in order to maintain accountability and prevent corruption and abuse of power. This notion that journalists should be critical of government is a near-universal tenet of professional journalism in capitalist democracies. However, even in the United States, the government is heavily involved in shaping news texts and organizations. Through briefings and press releases, the White House press secretary and other public relations officials exert considerable control over the representation of the positions and activities of government officials. The American government funds the global media organization Voice of America, producing radio, television, and digital content in more than 47 languages all over the world. However, the most prominent American news organizations are independently owned and produced.

But are privately owned news media in capitalist countries completely independent? Rather than being dominated by the government, privately owned media are subject to the forces of the market as well as the demands of owners and investors. That is, their commitment to the truth may be challenged by their desire to sell their media to the largest audiences. If sensationalized conflict and conspiracy theories attract audiences, news media may become dominated by misleading half-truths and divisive fantasies. Another strong force threatening the independence of private media is the desire to sell lucrative advertising space to powerful business interests. If the people who pay for advertising favor a market-centered approach to economic issues, then stories about working conditions and environmentalism are likely to be marginalized by market news.

How do journalists handle the conflict between the pressures of government and commercial interests and their role as watchdogs for the public interest? For a firsthand example, read this account by chapter author, Jennifer Hasty,

> *When I first came to Ghana, I wanted to understand the role of newspapers in the wave of democratization sweeping across the African continent in the 1990s. In my first few days in Ghana, I bought as many newspapers as I could find and read them studiously, marking stories with marginal comments and comparing front pages side by side. The state-sponsored newspapers highlighted the benevolent actions of government in promoting economic development and social stability. Frequently, the front pages of such publications featured an enthusiastic headline about a government*

project to build a new road or market complex, illustrated with a color photograph of President Jerry Rawlings wielding a pickax or operating a bulldozer to officially launch the project. Most stories foregrounded the official speeches of government officials, emphasizing themes of national cohesion and responsible citizenship. In contrast, the front pages of the private newspapers shouted out bold allegations of corruption among government officials with stories often based on anonymous sources and rumor. In these papers, Rawlings was often depicted wearing mirrored sunglasses and army fatigues, portrayed as a barely reformed military coup leader with no interest in real democracy.

These two versions of the national political reality were completely at odds with one another. And yet, in my initial interviews, both state and private journalists maintained that they were the true forces of democracy in Ghana, protecting the interests of the people. Both maintained strong commitments to journalistic neutrality and objectivity. How could they produce such wildly different optics on the political sphere? How could state journalists fervently believe that they were promoting democracy when, in daily practice, they were echoing the public pronouncements of government officials and providing strategically flattering coverage of the actions of the state? How could private journalists claim to be responsible purveyors of truth when their sensational stories were so often based on rumor and stirred up political and regional conflicts?

Anthropologists frequently discover such contradictions between what people say they're doing and what they're actually doing. This is one of the advantages of long-term fieldwork; it gives anthropologists time to get behind the official story presented in texts and interviews by conducting extended periods of participant observation.

Working at the premier state newspaper, the Daily Graphic, I discovered that the whole working life of a state journalist is structured in such a way that the state does indeed seem to be a benevolent patron and the words uttered by state officials do seem to be the superior and responsible version of national reality. Every working day, state journalists were invited to state ministries to cover official events. They didn't have to scramble around trying to gain access to government officials, as private journalists did, and they never faced rejection or exclusion when they showed up at state functions. Instead, they were politely ushered into the realm of the state to witness some important (or not) announcement or action. After the event, state journalists were given copies of the speeches they'd just heard and provided with snacks and a beverage—and an envelope with a small sum of cash. This small gift was referred to as **soli***, short for solidarity, and it symbolized the implicit reciprocity between state officials and state journalists. When they got back to the newsroom, state journalists sat down, printed speeches in hand, and wrote stories depicting the state in the way they themselves had just experienced the state: a kind and thoughtful patron supporting the welfare and development of the people.*

At the three privately owned newspapers I worked for during my fieldwork, the working day was much more stressful and antagonistic. Considered divisive and irresponsible by the state, the private press had been banned by Rawlings's military government in the 1980s. In the 1990s, the private press was just reemerging as part of the overall process of democratization, but the government still considered private journalists to be political enemies. Rawlings issued angry public diatribes against the private press, threatening criminal libel suits with long prison terms. Not only were private journalists not invited to daily government events, but they were not even allowed to attend. Many government officials dodged the phone calls of private journalists, and some refused to speak to them at all. Ordinary Ghanaians, still spooked by the government repression of the previous decade, often demanded anonymity as a condition of speaking to private journalists. Excluded from official channels of public discourse, the private press was forced to rely on unnamed sources and rumors. From their point of view, the antagonistic representation of the state as corrupt and repressive was the truth as they experienced it every day.

Taken together, the state and private news media created a highly contentious public sphere with competing ideologies—versions of political reality associated with particular groups. While the government used the state press to build national unity, the private press challenged the legitimacy of the state and its commitment to democracy. Visit the news website Graphic Online (https://openstax.org/r/graphiconline), *the online news platform of the Daily Graphic.*

PROFILES IN ANTHROPOLOGY

Elizabeth Bird

Personal History: Elizabeth Bird (https://openstax.org/r/facebook1674658669247949) was born and raised in Newcastle upon Tyne in northeast England. As a child, she was an avid reader, especially drawn to historical and fantasy literature. Reading about various societies in different time periods, Bird developed an early interest in other cultures and the past. As a self-described "shy and rather unsociable" child (personal communication), she developed a more analytical view toward social groups. She remarks, "I have heard that many anthropologists grew up feeling they don't quite fit in—that would be me!"

Bird studied anthropology at Durham University and folklife studies at the University of Leeds, both in England. She then earned an interdisciplinary PhD from the University of Strathclyde in Scotland. A few years later, she moved to the United States, where she earned an MA in journalism from the University of Iowa. She then became a professor of anthropology at the University of South Florida.

Area of Anthropology: Bird pioneered the anthropology of news media. At Iowa, she wrote about the connection between folklore/myth and journalistic narratives, especially in tabloid newspapers.

Accomplishments in the Field: Anthropologists in the 1980s generally dismissed media as a topic for research, but Bird considered this view shortsighted given the ubiquity of media in societies all over the world and the centrality of media to contemporary culture. In her first book, *For Enquiring Minds: A Cultural Study of Supermarket Tabloids* (1992), Bird argues that tabloid newspapers such as the *National Enquirer* build on and feed larger cultural narratives in the general folklore of American life. In interviews with readers of the tabloid press, she discovers that they are attracted to tabloids for a variety of reasons and deploy a diverse set of strategies for finding meaning in these texts. Prescient of the conspiracy theories and "fake news" controversies of the early 21st century, Bird's work on tabloids the 1980s and 1990s found that many readers are alienated from mainstream American culture.

In this part of her career, Bird's main focus was on the audiences of media, using ethnographic and qualitative research to understand how people in a culture read and use media in their everyday lives. This research came together in her book *The Audience in Everyday Life: Living in a Media World* (2003). In this book, Bird explores how people pick and choose different elements of media as they construct their class and ethnic identities, participate in religious or political communities, and contemplate the meaning of scandals and other publicized cultural narratives. While much mass communication research has focused on "the audience" as a monolithic, unified entity, Bird shows how an ethnographic approach reveals "the audience" to be a highly differentiated assemblage of people using a wide variety of techniques to comprehend and use mass media as a cultural reservoir.

Importance of Their Work: Elizabeth Bird was among the first anthropologists to take media seriously as an object of serious academic study. While many mass communication scholars were analyzing the texts of news media, Bird used interviews and participant observation to explore how people actually make sense of these texts and weave them into their thoughts and practices.

Around 2009–2010, Bird moved away from media as an exclusive object of study, returning to earlier research on social history, heritage, and memory in a Nigerian community. Incorporating media analysis and oral histories, she now conducts research on a traumatic massacre that took place in that community in 1967. She documents how print and broadcast media have erased popular memory of the event and how social media has revived and activated personal memories of it. Bird has described the Asaba Memorial Project (https://openstax.org/r/asabamemorial) as "the highlight of [her] career."

15.6 Community, Development, and Broadcast Media

LEARNING OUTCOMES

By the end of this section, you will be able to:

- Explain how radio is associated with different themes and audiences than print media.
- Define the concept of community radio.
- Explain how community radio gives expression to local forms of identity and social action.
- Define the notion of Indigenous media.

The media scholar Marshall McLuhan is famous for his aphorism "**the medium is the message**" (1964, 23). What he meant by this is that each genre of media has its own set of features that suggest certain uses and kinds of content. In contrast to print media, radio allows for real-time talk and discussion as well as music. Radio reaches beyond the limited audience of avid readers who have time to focus on text to wider audiences of listeners who may be too busy to read or have not had access to formal education. As an oral medium, radio lends itself more readily to linguistic diversity. In places where many languages are spoken, often the language of state is the only one that circulates in written form, while the rest function as spoken languages only. Print media may therefore be limited to dominant languages, while the oral genre of radio can provide content in alternative and even multiple languages. Finally, while reading print media is largely a solitary and silent experience, radio provides a shared and noisy experience. A personal experience shared by Jennifer Hasty illustrates this.

> *In Ghana, I could nearly always hear a radio blasting from someone's compound or kiosk or car. Radio was woven into daily life, a sort of auditory backdrop to everyday work and leisure. News headlines were read out each day on the morning talk shows, generating discussions in households and buses as people made their way to work. On the popular radio talk shows, Ghanaians from all walks of life called in to broadcast their perspectives on the issues of the day. Even during the music shows, listeners participated with heartfelt requests dedicated to friends, lovers, and family members.*

Because of its distinctive features, the genre of radio is not as narrowly focused as print media on themes of political economy such as nationalism and democracy. While including attention to current events, radio typically provides listeners with a wider variety of content, including music, talk shows, drama, and quiz shows. In an effort to provide relevant content to the broadest spectrum of listeners in an area, local radio stations design their programming to reflect the tastes and issues of particular communities. Certainly, print media does this to some degree, but the audience for print media constitutes a narrower segment of the community. Radio attempts to address the community as a whole.

Commercial and state radio are dominant forces in the media landscapes of most countries, but an alternative form, **community radio**, has been growing rapidly in recent decades. *Community radio* refers to radio stations that are community owned and operated, staffed by groups of professionals and volunteers. The involvement of local volunteers allows for community participation in programming, production, and on-air performance. Community radio stations often focus on local current events, educational programs, and development initiatives. Typically, they are low wattage with minimal range and thus are nonprofit.

In places where people want to start up a community radio station but lack the capital and technological know-how, nongovernmental organizations (NGOs) and development organizations have provided support in partnership with community organizations. Such collaborations between community groups and foreign NGOs have made possible the start-up of community radio stations in many countries, including Nepal, Sri Lanka, and the Philippines. Throughout Africa, community radio stations sponsored by government and/or NGOs have been used to educate rural peoples about farming methods and spread public interest health messages. In Thailand, the global leader in community radio, more than 7,000 independent radio stations have been started since 2001.

Established in 1997, the Nepalese station Radio Sagarmatha was the first independent community radio station in South Asia. The station was started by the Nepal Forum of Environmental Journalists in an effort to break the government monopoly on radio and provide better coverage of community issues. Regulated by government, Radio Sagarmatha is not allowed to address political or economic issues. Focusing instead on community development, the station features daily discussion programs addressing such issues as public health, education, women's empowerment, and workers' concerns. Though not explicitly political, the station identifies itself as the defender of democracy and free speech in Nepal, giving voice to the people. In 2005, the army raided the studio, seizing equipment and arresting staff for rebroadcasting a BBC interview with a politician. The station reemerged after the incident and remains on air today. With 2.5 million regular listeners, Radio Sagarmatha is one of the largest and most successful community radio stations in the world.

Community radio stations in Brazil have faced similar forms of government regulation and harassment. Anthropologist Derek Pardue (2011) describes the expansion of community radio in the wake of political liberalization in the 1980s. As of 2013, there were 4,700 community radio stations operating in Brazil, an increase of 70 percent since 2002. Moreover, approximately 5,000 such stations have been shut down by government, their equipment confiscated and management prosecuted as felons. Associated with free speech and political activism, community radio attracts involvement by counterculture artists and performers such as the hip-hop communities of impoverished favela neighborhoods in São Paulo. Through community radio, local hip-hop artists narrate their stories of hardship and heroism, defining their spatially marginal neighborhoods as economically and politically marginalized *periferias* (peripheries). Pardue describes how community radio gives hip-hop artists and other community members a platform for demonstrating their awareness of social issues and command of information. Using slang that signals racial and class identities, they publicize otherwise unreported events and perspectives such as police violence and gang activities, providing a much more inclusive public sphere than commercial media.

In Australia, more than 400 independent radio stations broadcast in 70 different community languages. Many of these community radio stations have been started by Indigenous Australian communities as a means of cultural survival and language preservation. **Indigenous media** refers to the use of media by Indigenous communities for community identity, cultural representation, and activism. In the 1990s, some Indigenous broadcasters developed the ability to link community radio stations together in regional and national networks. As many Indigenous community stations featured call-in request programs, the linking of stations allowed a person in one community to publicly greet a relative in a faraway community with a song dedication. Anthropologist Daniel Fisher (2009) describes how radio has become a way for Indigenous Australian people to celebrate kinship connections in the context of kin dispersal due to government policy, travel, work, and incarceration. Throughout the 20th century, Indigenous children were seized from their families and sent to state institutions and foster homes in order to assimilate them into White Australian settler culture. In the present, Indigenous family ties are further troubled by the disproportionate numbers of young men incarcerated in Australian prisons. In this context, call-in request shows have become wildly popular on Indigenous radio networks, as relatives phone in to dedicate emotionally charged songs about love, separation, and loss to relatives in distant places.

Inspired by a wide variety of social issues, community radio is catching hold in the United States as well. In response to the domination of American radio by large media corporations, the US Congress passed the Local Community Radio Act in 2010, authorizing the Federal Communications Commission (FCC) to provide licenses to low-powered community radio stations. A group of community organizers in Madrid, New Mexico, just outside of Albuquerque, was awarded a license and began broadcasting KMRD 96.9 in 2015. As an alternative to commercial radio programming, KMRD, like many community stations, features more diverse and locally relevant content. Local DJs host call-in and talk programs about community issues and spin a wide variety of music, including alternative, pop, techno, garage, folk, and western. Local bands get frequent airplay, stimulating the local music scene. On Monday nights, you can hear a program devoted to African music, hosted by the author of this chapter. Those not within range of the station can listen to KRMD online (https://openstax.org/r/kmrdlisten). Over a thousand new community radio stations have emerged as a result of the Local Community Radio Act.

15.7 Broadcasting Modernity and National Identity

LEARNING OUTCOMES

By the end of this section, you will be able to:

- Identify ways in which governments and development organizations use broadcast media.
- Detail forms of modernity conveyed by broadcast media in non-Western contexts.
- Explain the cultural significance of soap opera.
- Describe the relationship between broadcast media and religious identities and experiences.

Broadcast media are, of course, not always grassroots tools of community expression and development. Even outside of the commercial domain, forms of radio and television are produced by development organizations and state governments to address specific development goals, a more top-down model of community broadcasting. Throughout the 1980s, a radio project for delivering basic education was carried out in the Dominican Republic by the US Agency for International Development. The project was designed to reach schoolchildren living in mountainous and isolated regions of the country. Gathering around radios in community centers, children listened to lessons on reading, math, science, and history. Students were given worksheets and books to supplement the radio lectures. Eighty-two community learning centers were established by 1982. Over time, local community groups and the Dominican government contributed funding to keep the project going. Similar programs to use radio for basic education have been established in other countries, including Mexico and Kenya.

As with radio, the potentially broad reach of television beyond literate audiences has made it useful as a medium of education, particularly for students lacking access to conventional brick-and-mortar schools. In most countries outside of western Europe and the United States, broadcast media were initially developed by the state because local elites often lacked the capital to start radio and television stations. In the 1960s, the newly independent African states used their newly formed state broadcasting corporations to consolidate diverse and distant populations as a united audience for national messages and initiatives.

In her research, communication scholar Carla Heath (1996) shows how Ghanaian children's television programs serve as a means of cultivating a distinctively modern national culture that embraces innovation and change while remaining grounded in Ghanaian cultural values. For one program, *By the Fireside*, Ghanaian schoolchildren were recruited to act out Ghanaian folktales, discussing how their moral messages could be applied to contemporary Ghanaian life. Against a background depicting a rural village, children in simple smocks and African-print clothing opened the show with songs and dances, then engaged in greetings, jokes, and riddles with the two adult storytellers. As a storyteller narrated a tale, the children acted out certain scenes and commented on the themes of the story in musical interludes. After the story, children were called upon to recite the moral lessons they had learned. In this way, traditional stories were summoned to discuss such contemporary issues as corruption, political conflicts, and juvenile delinquency. Heath argues that such programs promote a distinctive form of modern citizenship rooted in local morality and wisdom.

Anthropologist Lila Abu-Lughod (2002) similarly demonstrates how elites have used television dramas to cultivate the ideal of the virtuous modern citizen among women, youth, and rural people in Egypt. One serial drama, *Hilmiyya Nights*, focused on the lives of a group of characters from the traditional neighborhood of Hilmiyya in Cairo. The show dramatizes their fortunes and relationships from the 1940s, when Egypt was ruled by King Farouk and the British, all the way up to the Egyptian reaction to the US-led Gulf War of 1990. Rather than focusing solely on personal desires, trysts, and betrayals, as American soap operas do, the social lives of the *Hilmiyya Nights* characters were embedded in historical and political events, making the show a powerful form of commentary on Egyptian national life. Driven by its project of upliftment, the overall theme of the show was one of national unity. Characters from all classes were led astray by the temptations of sex, money, and power, but they inevitably came to see the errors of their ways, putting love of country above all personal desires. Interviewing women who watched *Hilmiyya Nights*, Abu-Lughod discovered that their love for the show had little to do with the uplifting messages about Egyptian citizenship. In fact, some identified strongly with the most problematic female characters, who schemed and connived in pursuit of sex and money.

Soap opera is a popular format targeted to female audiences in many parts of the world. In India, anthropologist Purnima Mankekar (1999) examined a number of television serials produced by the state television station, Doordarshan, in the 1980s and 1990s. In a well-rounded holistic analysis, Mankekar examines production, text, and reception, the latter an aspect often neglected in media studies. Mankekar interviewed the writers, directors, and producers of these programs and subjected the programs themselves to a fine-grained textual analysis. Her focus, however, was audience reception. Among the questions she asked were how Indian middle-class women viewed these programs, what sense they made of the content, and how they discussed the themes and issues and applied them to their own lives. Indian state television has always worked to cultivate an idealized notion of Indian womanhood, implicitly defined as Hindu, middle-class, north Indian, and upper caste. Mankekar's analysis focuses on two Hindu epic dramas, *The Mahabharat* (1989–1990) and *The Ramayan* (1987–1988). Through these dramas, state television constructed those ideals for the intended audience of Indian women. These epics feature two ideals of womanhood: Sita, who is demure, compliant, and self-sacrificing, contrasted with the enraged Draupaudi, whose reckless husband's political gamble results in her public humiliation. In interviews with Mankekar, women viewers discussed how they identified with each character in different ways and in relation to different contexts of their own lives. As the programs aired in the midst of rising Hindu nationalism in India, they became a means of asserting Hindu forms of heritage and morality as well as gendered identities.

While in the West, modernity is typically associated with rationality and secularism, many media anthropologists have studied how radio and television enable distinctly modern expressions of religious beliefs and experiences. Media anthropologist Katrien Pype (2015) has conducted research on television dramas in the Democratic Republic of the Congo, with a focus on the importance of religious themes and emotional forms of engagement. In one drama, *The Heart of Man*, two sophisticated urban women become witches in order to harm their romantic rivals. As a result of their occult rituals, one of the women goes blind, leading her to confess her sins to an evangelical pastor. The pastor grants her forgiveness and exorcises the demons from her body. So powerful were the depictions of witchcraft that some viewers reported feeling as if they had become bewitched themselves just by watching the show. Viewers interpreted their emotional responses as signs of the deeper meanings of the program. Not merely entertainment, Congolese television dramas structured by such tales of evangelical redemption are experienced as episodes in an ongoing spiritual war between the Holy Spirit and the devil. Though fictional, such television programs connect with the worldviews of evangelical Christians through the conduit of emotional and bodily response.

15.8 Digital Media, New Socialities

LEARNING OUTCOMES

By the end of this section, you will be able to:

- Define the concept of sociality.
- Explain how digital media enable new forms of sociality.
- Identify how digital media shape friendships and romantic relationships.
- Define the concept of media ideology.
- Provide a detailed example of the illicit use of digital media.

As much of this textbook demonstrates, anthropologists most often conduct research on topics involving face-to-face sociocultural interaction such as public ceremonies, religious rituals, work, political activities, and forms of economic exchange. Over the past 30 years, however, anthropologists have begun to conduct research on forms of culture in which face-to-face interaction has been replaced with screens and keyboards. In the Internet era, media anthropologists explore how people connect with others digitally, forming collective identities based on characteristics such as common interests, gender, race, ethnicity, and religion. Some anthropologists are interested in the entirely new modes of social interaction made possible by the Internet, such as hacking, blogging, and creating and sharing memes. Digital media also reshape other domains of sociocultural practice, such as shopping, financial transactions, transportation, religious worship, and kin relations. Encompassing the whole realm of social interaction, cultural anthropologists use the term **sociality** to describe how people construct and maintain their personal and group relations. Anthropologists are curious about how new forms of digital media function as tools of sociality.

Digital Socialities: Personal and Political

How do you talk to your friends on a day-to-day basis? How do you arrange to meet up as a group? If you're an American, it's very likely that texts and social media are involved in your communication and coordination with your friends. Studying American teens from 2004 to 2007, scholar Danah Boyd found that social networking sites such as Facebook were key to the formation of new friendships and the consolidation of friend groups, while texting deepened one-on-one relationships (Ito et al. 2010). In fact, friendship was the primary reason given by teens for engaging in digital forms of media (rather than, say, looking up information for school projects or texting their parents about where they are at midnight on a Friday night). Of course, the social preoccupation of American teens is not new, nor is it surprising. But digital media provide new modes of engagement, such as the "always on" texting of best friends or social media "friends" who are not really friends at all but strangers or even enemies. Social media also provide new tools for authoring self-identity as well as the ability to search out information about others that may undermine their own professed identities.

While American teens generally embrace social media and texting as ways of building friendships, they are considerably more troubled by the role of digital media in the other side of social relationships: breaking up. In an undergraduate class one day, anthropologist Ilana Gershon asked her students, "What counts as a bad breakup?" (2010). Expecting stories of lying and infidelity, Gershon was surprised to hear so many students complain about breakups via text or Facebook. Anyone who has ever signed into a social media site to discover that their sweetie's relationship status has changed to "single" knows the kind of confusion and heartache caused by using digital media in this way.

FIGURE 15.7 Perhaps not the best use of texting—on both sides. In societies all over the world, digital media have become essential elements of social interaction. (attribution: Copyright Rice University, OpenStax, under CC BY 4.0 license)

Intrigued by the ambiguities of digital etiquette in the realm of romance, Gershon wrote a book exploring how Americans use digital media to manage and even terminate ambiguous or troubled relationships. At the heart of the matter, according to Gershon, are **media ideologies**—that is, sets of ideas about the functionality of digital media and their relationship to other forms of communication, such as the telephone and face-to-face conversation. For some Americans, using digital messaging to break up is an ideal way of avoiding an intense emotional scene. This notion relies on a media ideology in which different forms of communication can usually be substituted for one another in the interests of efficiency and ease of use. For others, however, the text breakup is unfair, disrespectful, and cowardly, as the breaking-up process is made into a unilateral speech act rather than a consensual act based on dialogue. Digital media allow the breaker-upper to avoid witnessing the consequences of their action. In this media ideology, different forms of communication are appropriate to different forms of social action and cannot be substituted for one another without careful consideration of the emotional consequences.

In societies all over the world, digital media have become essential elements of social interaction, from the most personal and romantic relationships to larger, more public collectivities. Both media anthropologists and communication scholars have contributed to an effort to de-westernize media studies by exploring the use of digital media in contexts outside of the United States and western Europe. In societies with repressive governments, traditional media and face-to-face political action are often tightly controlled, making digital media important tools of social interaction and political resistance. Media scholars Annaelle Sreberny and Gholam Khiabany (2010) highlight the crucial role of blogging in popular expression and political activism in Iran over the past several decades. There are more than 700,000 blogs in Iran, many of them authored by women. Suppressed in the public arena, Iranian intellectuals have embraced blogging as a way to express their ideas. Though many Iranian blogs are devoted to personal reflections or commentary on entertainment or sports, Sreberny and Khiabany show how bloggers often convey subtle political messages in their seemingly personal writing. Like Egyptian and Indian soap operas, Iranian blogs are always embedded in sociopolitical contexts, whether they are explicitly political or not. Some blogs are, in fact, stridently political, and many political bloggers have been jailed by the government as dissidents.

Similarly, bloggers in Central and South America form activist communities working for social justice and equality (Arriaga and Villar 2021). Afro-Cuban activist Sandra Abd'Allah-Alvarez Ramírez blogs on issues of race and gender in Cuba. Journalist Silvana Bahia operates an organization in Brazil that works to spread the tools of digital technology to diverse communities, in particular Afro-Brazilian women. She has been involved in efforts to teach programming to women, showing them how to apply digital skills to further social projects. She envisions a more inclusive digital sphere that brings in the perspectives of Black, LGBTQ+, low-income, and disadvantaged groups.

Digital Shadowlands: Illicit Media

Digital media enable and enhance social interaction, deepening relationships and activating imagined communities for social change. However, these new forms of media have a darker side. Digital media are also a tool for piracy, smuggling, scams, human trafficking, and illegal forms of pornography. Frequently, these illicit forms operate across the gulf of global inequality separating wealthy societies from poorer ones. Human trafficking, for instance, often involves abducting youth from impoverished rural communities and smuggling them into urban and wealthier communities to be forced into prostitution. Piracy, on the other hand, often involves making illegal copies of music and movies produced in wealthier countries available to people in poorer communities who may not otherwise be able to afford them.

The digital shadowlands provide opportunities for those left out of legal, mainstream opportunities in the digital economy. Sakawa is a troubling example of this. Around 2010 in Ghana, a new social group emerged. People began to notice that some young men in their twenties were enjoying a very luxurious lifestyle: driving expensive cars such as Lexuses and Range Rovers, wearing designer clothing and shoes, drinking champagne, and living in enormous mansions. How were they becoming so wealthy? During this time, Ghana was experiencing an oil boom, but that wealth was concentrated among older elites. The vast population of poor and working-class people have not benefited all that much from oil wealth. Commonly, young men with little education are unemployed, with very little chance of ever escaping poverty. This new class of conspicuously rich young men were not particularly educated or well-connected, but they had discovered a new way to make money. Combining digital media with spiritual techniques, they had invented a new moneymaking scheme called **sakawa**.

A Hausa term meaning "putting inside," *sakawa* refers to magically enhanced Internet fraud, mainly targeting foreigners. Before they become sakawa practitioners, these young men are often unemployed, sleeping on the streets, not knowing where their next meal is coming from. Often, they report noticing very stylish and well-fed young people apparently making lots of money by doing something in Internet cafés. Sometimes the scammers actively recruit such targets, teaching them Internet skills to carry out the elaborate schemes. The typical con is pretending to be a woman romantically interested in men from Europe, the United States, or Asia. Another, less common scheme involves using fake documents to persuade foreigners to invest in gold, timber, or oil concessions. Even more important than technological skills are the sophisticated social skills involved in creating strategic online personalities, cultivating trust with foreign White men in faraway places, and knowing just how and when to make requests for money.

Many scammers report practicing these techniques for several weeks or months with only modest success, then learning about the "spiritual side" of sakawa. In order to become magnificently wealthy, sakawa practitioners believe it is necessary to become apprenticed to a spiritual leader who can guarantee great success in exchange for performing certain rituals on a regular basis. New apprentices are often instructed to sleep in coffins and anoint their bodies with special medicines. Some are required to have sex with several women each day and deliver their undergarments to the spiritual leader. Some must chew live cockroaches, lizards, or maggots. Ghanaians are horrified by rumors of incest and human sacrifice as scammers are said to perform more and more difficult forms of spiritual service to their masters. Though many refuse to reveal the exact nature of these rituals, numerous sakawa boys report that their efforts to extract money from foreigners suddenly became much more successful after performing them. With sudden windfalls from scamming, sakawa boys often throw epic parties and buy expensive gifts for their friends. In his documentary film *Sakawa*, Ghanaian filmmaker Ben Asamoah depicts the practices and communities of sakawa in Ghana.

VIDEO

A trailer to the documentary film *Sakawa* by Ben Asamoah can be watched on YouTube (https://openstax.org/r/sakawatrailer).

After a time, the thrill of this lifestyle wears off, and sakawa boys come to feel enslaved by the constant ritual demands of their spiritual leaders. If a sakawa boy refuses to perform assigned chores, however, he may break out in a rash, suffer paralysis, or become deaf or mute. Some report that friends have died when attempting to quit sakawa.

Sakawa is widely condemned in Ghanaian society. Government officials, journalists, and religious leaders have all spoken out against it, and the police have even arrested and prosecuted some sakawa scammers. Many Ghanaians lament the unbridled celebration of wealth as a marker of social status, arguing that children should be instilled with traditional values of hard work, honesty, and modest living.

Sakawa may seem like a shocking and unusual combination of digital media with supernatural beliefs and practices, but at the root of this phenomenon is a set of contradictory beliefs about wealth and power found in many cultures and historical periods. Consider the German legend of Faust, based on a 16th-century German alchemist. According to the legend, Faust, a bored and depressed scholar, makes a pact with the devil through the devil's emissary, Mephistopheles. The deal is that Mephistopheles will help Faust gain access to all worldly pleasures, including sex, power, and knowledge. In return, Faust will be required to turn his soul over to the devil after several years.

Forms of this **Faustian bargain** have emerged in many other parts of the world, particularly as societies are drawn into new forms of wealth and inequality in the global economy. For instance, anthropologist Michael Taussig (1980) conducted research on beliefs about the devil among people working in the sugar plantations of Colombia and the tin mines of Bolivia. Some wage laborers on sugar plantations were said to enter into contracts with the devil to increase their productivity, helping them make fast money. Most often, they bought flashy clothes and liquor with their newfound wealth but could not establish enduring prosperity. Taussig describes how workers in the Bolivian tin mines created a shrine to the devil to ensure their safety and help them find rich tin deposits. Taussig argues that people in peasant farming societies feel a sense of unease about capitalist forms of work, wealth, and inequality. To agrarian peoples steeped in communal values, it seems unfair that some laborers become wealthy while others work just as hard and fail. And yet, young people are drawn in by the compelling allure of money and commodities associated with labor in the globalized capitalist economy. According to Taussig, this conflicted feeling of unease gives rise to widespread beliefs about serving the devil for temporary gains.

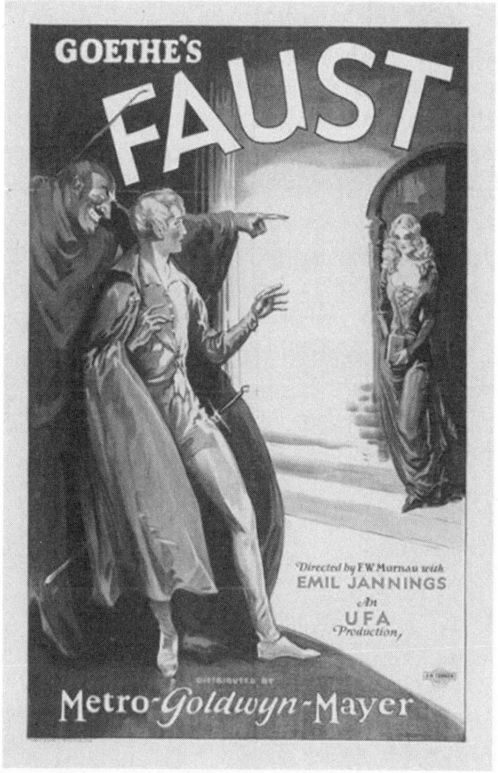

FIGURE 15.8 Poster for the 1926 film *Faust*, directed by F. W. Murnau and based on German writer Johann Wolfgang von Goethe's telling of a German folktale. According to the legend, Faust makes a pact with the devil to gain access to worldly pleasures in return for his soul. As globalization spreads access to wealth and material goods around the world, scholars have observed the spread of stories about people serving the devil for temporary gains. (credit: Metro-Goldwyn-Mayer, UFA/Wikimedia Commons, Public Domain)

For some young people around the world, digital media have provided paths to astonishing success and wealth, often through global relations and transactions. While new forms of digital trade and technological innovation may provide some well-educated and well-connected elites with a means of getting rich, the vast majority of young people in both wealthy and poorer countries are largely left out of the opportunities of the digital economy. Sakawa may seem like a disturbing form of digital delinquency to many Ghanaians and foreigners alike, but it dramatizes the widespread sense of unfairness and inequality in Ghanaian society as a whole. The phenomenon of sakawa suggests that disadvantaged groups must combine supernatural forms of power with their computer and social skills in order to get ahead. Hard work alone is never enough. The unfairness of this situation is symbolized by the ultimate doom faced by many sakawa scammers: unable or unwilling to keep up with the demands of their supernatural masters, they fall ill and die.

Exploring how forms of media intersect with economic, political, and religious realms as well as gender, ethnicity, and identity, anthropologists take a holistic approach to mass media. Studying photography, news media, broadcasting, and digital media, anthropologists discover the cultural contexts of media production and reception as well as new forms of sociality and transaction. As media technologies become more deeply embedded in people's lives and instrumental to social relationships and communities, the holistic lens of anthropology is key to understanding the profound sociocultural changes brought about by media innovations.

MINI-FIELDWORK ACTIVITY

Make a Photographic Documentary

Create a photographic documentary of a social event, such as a party, meeting, class, or other community gathering. Before the event, make a list of shots necessary to show what's really going on at the event. What people should you photograph? What actions should be depicted? What is socially significant about the event, and how can you convey that meaning through photos? As you prepare your final product, consider how the photos should be presented. Should they be altered or edited in any way after you take them? How should they be organized? Should they be presented in the order you took them or in some other order?

Suggested Readings

Askew, Kelly, and Richard R. Wilk, eds. 2002. *The Anthropology of Media: A Reader.* Malden, MA: Blackwell.

Ginsberg, Faye D., Lila Abu-Lughod, and Brian Larkin, eds. 2002. *Media Worlds: Anthropology on New Terrain.* Berkeley: University of California Press.

Key Terms

"the medium is the message" the notion that each genre of media has its own set of features that suggest certain uses and types of content.

community radio radio stations that are community owned and operated, staffed by groups of professionals and volunteers.

cosmopolitanism worldly knowledge and sophistication, often associated with involvement in global forms of media.

ethnographic film the use of film in ethnographic research, either as a method, a record, or a means of reporting on anthropological fieldwork.

Faustian bargain the idea that a person can engage in evil supernatural activities in order to gain access to worldly desires such as wealth, sex, and/or knowledge.

imperial gaze a set of conventions for how people in imperial or colonizing societies view the people and landscapes of subjugated territories.

independent media forms of print and broadcast media that are privately owned.

Indigenous media the use of media by Indigenous peoples for community identity, cultural representation, and activism.

male gaze a set of conventions for how men look at women.

mass media mechanically reproduced forms of communication targeting large audiences.

media tools for storing and sharing information.

media ideologies sets of ideas about the uses and functions of a particular genre of media.

public sphere a domain of social life in which people represent, learn about, and discuss the important issues of the day.

sakawa magically enhanced Internet fraud, mainly targeting foreigners.

sociality participation in social relations; how people construct and maintain their personal and group relationships.

soli short for *solidarity*; a small sum of money given by news sources to journalists at the end of an assignment in Ghana.

state media forms of print and broadcast media that are financially supported by the state and subject to government control.

technophilia the love of technology; characteristic of societies and eras of increasing technological innovation and its incorporation into everyday life.

the gaze a specific mode of looking at images shaped by the identities of viewer and viewed.

visual anthropology the use of visual media as a method of research or its study as a topic of research.

voyeuristic describes a gaze aimed at people who do not know they are being viewed.

Summary

Anthropologists use long-term ethnographic fieldwork and holistic perspectives to study media genres such as photography, film, radio, television, and digital media. In visual anthropology, gaze theory is used to think about the relationship between viewers and the people depicted in photographs, particularly in terms of gender, power, and cultural identity. Anthropologists studying news media focus on the construction of national public spheres of official ideology and political contest. Radio is often used by communities for more participatory and community-based forms of communication. Many anthropologists study how soap operas and other television programs promote forms of ethnicity, gender, and nationalism. Digital media construct entirely new forms of sociality, including illicit shadow forms of impersonation and scamming such as sakawa.

Critical Thinking Questions

1. Can you think of any genres of mass media not covered in this chapter? How could an anthropologist conduct research on those topics? What might be the focus of the research? What might be the challenges?
2. Do you take photographs to document your day-to-day life? If so, who constitutes the audience for these photos? What messages are you conveying by sharing images with others or viewing your own images? How does taking a photo influence the way you remember an experience?
3. Select a news story from the front page of a newspaper or the website of a national news organization. Why is this story on the front page? What techniques make the story appear to be true? What perspectives or facts are left out of the story? Does that make the story false? Are there different versions of truth?
4. What is your favorite television program? What notions of identity and sociality are depicted in

the show? Consider gender, race, ethnicity, class, sexuality, and nationalism. How might the show affect the way you view yourself and your community?

5. What social relationships in your life are made possible and/or enhanced by the use of digital media? Would you have the same sorts of friends and/or romantic relationships without digital interaction? How would your relationships be different without digital media?

Bibliography

Abu-Lughod, Lila. 2002. "The Objects of Soap Opera: Egyptian Television and the Cultural Politics of Modernity." In *The Anthropology of Media: A Reader*, edited by Kelly Askew and Richard R. Wilk, 376–391. Malden, MA: Blackwell.

Anas, Anas Aremeyaw. 2013. "How I Named, Shamed and Jailed." Filmed February 2013 in Long Beach, CA. TED video, 12:34. https://www.ted.com/talks/anas_aremeyaw_anas_how_i_named_shamed_and_jailed.

Arriaga, Eduard, and Andrés Villar, eds. 2021. *Afro-Latinx Digital Connections*. Gainesville: University of Florida Press.

Askew, Kelly, and Richard R. Wilk, eds. 2002 *The Anthropology of Media: A Reader*. Malden, MA: Blackwell.

Buckley, Liam. 2000. "Self and Accessory in Gambian Studio Photography." *Visual Anthropology Review* 16 (2): 71–91. https://doi.org/10.1525/var.2000.16.2.71.

Fisher, Daniel. 2009. "Mediating Kinship: Country, Family, and Radio in Northern Australia." *Cultural Anthropology* 24 (2): 280–312. https://doi.org/10.1111/j.1548-1360.2009.01132.x.

Flaherty, Robert, dir. 1922. *Nanook of the North*. Video, 77:57. https://archive.org/details/nanookOfTheNorth1922.

Frost, Randall. 2021. "Printing." In *The Gale Encyclopedia of Science*, edited by Katherine H. Nemeh and Jacqueline L. Longe, 6th ed., vol. 6, 3583–3587. Farmington Hills, MI: Gale.

Ganti, Tejaswini. 2012. *Producing Bollywood: Inside the Contemporary Hindi Film Industry*. Durham, NC: Duke University Press.

Gershon, Ilana. 2010. *The Breakup 2.0: Disconnecting over New Media*. Ithaca, NY: Cornell University Press.

Ginsburg, Faye D., Lila Abu-Lughod, and Brian Larkin, eds. 2002. *Media Worlds: Anthropology on New Terrain*. Berkeley: University of California Press.

Habermas, Jurgen. 1989. *The Structural Transformation of the Public Sphere: An Inquiry into a Category of Bourgeois Society*. Translated by Thomas Burger and Frederick Lawrence. Cambridge, MA.: MIT Press.

Hasty, Jennifer. 2005. *The Press and Political Culture in Ghana*. Bloomington: Indiana University Press.

Heath, Carla W. 1996. "Children's Television in Ghana: A Discourse about Modernity." *African Affairs* 96 (383): 261–275. https://www.jstor.org/stable/723861.

Ito, Mizuko, Sonja Baumer, Matteo Bittanti, Danah Boyd, Rachel Cody, Becky Herr Stephenson, Heather A. Horst et al. 2010. *Hanging Out, Messing Around, and Geeking Out: Kids Living and Learning with New Media*. Cambridge, MA: MIT Press.

Jacknis, Ira. 2020. "Margaret Mead, Gregory Bateson, and Visual Anthropology." Oxford Bibliographies. Oxford University Press, last modified July 29, 2020. https://doi.org/10.1093/obo/9780199766567-0250.

Jenkins, Paul. 1993. "The Earliest Generation of Missionary Photographers in West Africa and the Portrayal of Indigenous People and Culture." *History in Africa* 20:89–118. https://www.jstor.org/stable/3171967.

Lutz, Catherine A., and Jane L. Collins. 1993. *Reading National Geographic*. Chicago: University of Chicago Press.

Mankekar, Purnima. 1999. *Screening Culture, Viewing Politics: An Ethnography of Television, Womanhood, and Nation in Postcolonial India*. Durham, NC: Duke University Press.

McLuhan, Marshall. 1964. *Understanding Media: The Extensions of Man*. New York: McGraw-Hill.

Mead, Margaret, and Gregory Bateson, dir. 1951. *Trance and Dance in Bali*. Video, 21:40. https://www.loc.gov/item/mbrs02425201/.

Mulvey, Laura. 1975. "Visual Pleasure and Narrative Cinema." *Screen* 16 (3): 6–18. https://doi.org/10.1093/screen/16.3.6.

Pardue, Derek. 2011. "Place Markers: Tracking Spatiality in Brazilian Hip-Hop and Community Radio." *American Ethnologist* 38 (1): 102–113. https://www.jstor.org/stable/41241503.

Postill, John. 2006. *Media and Nation Building: How the Iban Became Malaysian*. New York: Berghahn Books.

Pype, Katrien. 2015. "The Heart of Man: Pentecostal Emotive Style in and beyond Kinshasa's Media World." In *New Media and Religious Transformations in Africa*, edited by Rosalind I. J. Hackett and Benjamin F. Soares, 116–136. Bloomington: Indiana University Press.

Schäuble, Michaela. 2018. "Visual Anthropology." In *The International Encyclopedia of Anthropology*, edited by Hilary Callan. Hoboken, NJ: John Wiley & Sons. https://doi.org/10.1002/9781118924396.wbiea1969.

Spitulnik, Debra. 1993. "Anthropology and Mass Media." *Annual Review of Anthropology* 22:293–315. https://www.jstor.org/stable/2155850.

Spray, Stephanie, and Pacho Velez, dir. 2013. *Manakamana*. Cambridge, MA: Sensory Ethnography Lab, Harvard University. Video, 118 min.

Sreberny, Annabelle, and Gholam Khiabany. 2010. *Blogistan: The Internet and Politics in Iran*. London: I. B. Tauris.

Taussig, Michael T. 1980. *The Devil and Commodity Fetishism in South America*. Chapel Hill: University of North Carolina Press.

Tiffany, Sharon W. 2005. "Contesting the Erotic Zone: Margaret Mead's Fieldwork Photographs of Samoa." *Pacific Studies* 28 (3–4): 19–45. http://ojs-dev.byuh.edu/index.php/pacific/article/view/2120.

CHAPTER 16
Art, Music, and Sport

Figure 16.1 The Colosseum in Rome played a role similar to a professional football stadium today. Here, tens of thousands of Romans gathered to view competitions that not only entertained but also contributed to a sense of belonging and identity. (credit: “Colosseum” by Rennett Stowe/flickr, CC BY 2.0)

CHAPTER OUTLINE

INTRODUCTION Think about the last concert or sporting event that you attended, observed on television, or watched on social media. What was the last piece of art that you saw in person, online, or on social media? Did you consider that your experience was likely a culmination of tens of thousands of years of human evolution? Would you consider graffiti on the sides of train cars to be art? Is a pickup game of football in the neighborhood sport? Figure 16.1 depicts a famous structure connected to sport that is now more often viewed as an art object—the Colosseum of Rome. The Colosseum served a role in ancient Roman society similar to an NFL (National Football League) stadium in contemporary American culture. Here gladiators battled animals such as lions and bears for the entertainment of a crowd of tens of thousands made up of all levels of Roman society.

As you read about the sociocultural diversity in art, music, and sports highlighted in this chapter, remember the central narrative of anthropology: *Human beings have developed flexible biological and social features that have worked together in a wide variety of environmental and historical conditions to produce a diversity of cultures.* Art, music, and sports have been and continue to be important elements of every culture on earth, helping to create a sense of collective identity and helping societies to hold together. Art, music, and sports both reflect the sociocultural diversity found around the world and have played roles in effecting cultural change. Art, music, and sports have shaped the evolution of societies, and the evolution of a societies has influenced art, music, and sports in turn. As you read this chapter, consider your own experiences with art, music, and sport. Consider what you are familiar with and what you appreciate. Reflect also on the art, music, and sport in your society that are not particularly interested in or moved by. Where do these preferences come from? To what degree are they individual and to what degree do they reflect connections to your culture and to the subcultures within it?

16.1 Anthropology of the Arts

LEARNING OUTCOMES

By the end of this section, you will be able to:

- Describe the anthropological approach to understanding art.
- Provide three examples of material artifacts of art.
- Identify forms of prehistoric art and describe how anthropologists have interpreted those forms.
- Provide two examples of purposes that art serves in a society.
- Define visual anthropology and describe its role in understanding culture.
- Describe the relationship between visual representation and cultural expression and memory.
- Provide three examples of body art and describe the cultural meaning of each.

The anthropology of the arts can include various approaches to interpreting art forms, including analyses of the symbolic meanings represented, the mediums through which art is disseminated, and even how the art is manufactured. Art is strongly anchored in the human experience.

How Do Anthropologists Approach Art?

You might be asking yourself, How does art reflect or guide the study of anthropology? The simple answer is that **art** is created by humans. While definitions of art vary and have historically been narrowly construed to fit within a Western understanding of the term (Morphy and Perkins 2006), a constant element has been the intentional application of imagination, creativity, and skill. Art is created with intent.

Art is a representation of the human experience, and anthropologists approach the study of art the same way they do any other aspect of human existence. Anthropologists take a holistic approach to any given topic, situating that topic among the broader context of a culture—its "language, environment, economy, religion, family life, governance and so on" (Plattner 2003, 15). All of these details are implicitly and inextricably embedded in the products of a culture, which cannot be fully understood and appreciated without some awareness of them. This is particularly important in regard to the arts, which rely so heavily on a shared cultural vocabulary. As Stuart Plattner (2003) asserts:

> Anthropologists think that artistic production . . . should be looked upon, not simply as applied aesthetics, but as an activity embedded in an *art world*, a complex set of social relationships. . . . It is wrong to focus on the unique art object, and ignore the complex set of human relationships which contributed to its creation. (15)

Anthropology lends itself to examining both the *how* and the *why* of the arts. Art is studied by anthropologists through methods such as observation, interviews, focus groups, and site assessments. Anthropological study of art includes ethnographic studies as well as inquiries in physical anthropology and archaeology (e.g., Upper Paleolithic cave paintings, Aboriginal rock paintings, etc.). Consider the work that is required to analyze an artistic creation or sporting event through these anthropological techniques. Such work could include unearthing and evaluating artifacts of ancient societies, interviewing theatrical performers, or attending a game or match. The study of art, music, and sports requires the same holistic, wide-ranging approach as do all other anthropological studies.

What is art? Who defines it? What is the difference, if any, between a cultural practice and a piece of artwork? These are all valid questions to consider when exploring the arts with the goal of better understanding human cultures. The modern understanding of art began in the 18th century, when the word *art* shifted from referring to any specialized skill (e.g., art of gardening) to referencing the *fine arts* (Kristeller 1990). Anthropologists consider that art has historical, economic, and aesthetic dimensions. Consider painters in ancient Roman times, who often had patrons of their work who supported their livelihoods. It could be said that such painters were people of lesser means; however, with a patron's support, they could earn a wage for expressing their talents. And in aesthetic terms, art provides a representation of what is considered beautiful within a certain cultural context.

The subfield of anthropological archaeology has approached the study of arts from its own specific perspectives. Archaeologists cannot observe how an art object was created or used and are unable to ask its creators or consumers the types of ethnographic questions that other cultural anthropologists may rely on. Archaeologists possess specialized knowledge pertaining to the sociohistorical and cultural contexts of early art. Their research on these art pieces provides other anthropologists with a starting point for analyzing older art. It also provides them with a more well-rounded understanding of the functionality and purposes of early art.

Material artifacts of art can include many of the things people interact with at home, work, or school. These include artifacts that are the results of various people's representations of the world, such as the architecture of the building one lives in or a favorite coffee shop. They can also be relics from ancient times, such as weapons, tools, and cave drawings. These relics can be found in the research and reports that art historians, anthropologists and archaeologists use to analyze the symbolic and cultural meaning of art. **Iconographic study** is the study of the visual images, symbols, or modes of representation collectively associated with a person, cult, or movement. Art is an expressive behavior that encompasses and expresses cultural worldviews, social status and hierarchy, myth, and cosmology.

FIGURE 16.2 These baskets, created by the Yokuts people of Central California and photographed by Edward Curtis, are one of many types of material artifacts of art that anthropologists rely upon when attempting to understand culture. (credit: "Baskets in the Painted Cave—Yokuts" by Edward S. Curtis/Library of Congress, Public Domain)

Studying Prehistoric Art

Much of what anthropologists consider prehistoric art consists of artifacts and materials used to facilitate the work necessary to sustain life. It also includes cave paintings created tens of thousands of years ago. Examples of such cave paintings are the Upper Paleolithic cave art dated to 40,000 to 64,000 years ago, which features stenciled figures of animals and artifacts, though not usually humans.

FIGURE 16.3 These prehistoric cave drawings are located in the Magura cave in Bulgaria. While cave drawings typically focus on large animals such as cave bears, horses, and bison, the drawings in the Magura cave include both humans and animals, and provide information about the solar calendar, religious festivals and other customs. (credit: "Prehistoric drawings in the Magura cave, Bulgaria" by Nk/Wikimedia Commons, Public Domain)

This rock art, often called cave art, served as a medium to archive the human experience, tell a story, and depict how prehistoric peoples saw the world around them. Figure 16.3 above demonstrates how someone saw animals that were being hunted—and, unusually for this type of art, the people doing the hunting. These drawings served as a communication tool, historical archive, and artistic representation of a period of time and the human experience of the people who were there.

Interpreting Art

Visual art can be viewed as important evidence in attempting to understand a culture. Throughout time, visual art has been used to convey the human experiences of a vast range of cultures. This art provides modern anthropologists with valuable perspectives on other cultures and other times that could be hard to gain access to through other means. The image of the Kangxi emperor in Figure 16.4 conveys pride, wealth, and strength, characteristics that this artist connects to the China's Qing dynasty, depicting the emperor as its representative. This image articulates the successes of this culture at that particular point in history. Detailed analysis of works of art can contribute to the sophistication with which anthropologists understand both individual cultures and the shifting nature of human cultures in general.

FIGURE 16.4 This painting of a Kangxi emperor is an expression of the wealth and strength of the Qing dynasty. (credit: "Armoured Kangxi Emperor" by Author of Qing Dynasty/Originally from sina.com/Wikimedia Commons, Public Domain)

Spiritual Art

Other forms of visual art are significant to spiritual and sociocultural practices and beliefs. One example is the mandala, a symbolic diagram consisting of various geometric patterns that represents the universe. Mandalas are a cultural practice in Tibet, India, Nepal, China, Japan, and Indonesia (Tucci [1961] 2001) and can be traced back to the fourth century CE. Typically square or circular in shape, they are used in Hinduism and Buddhism to focus attention during meditation.

One significant variation on the mandala is the sand mandala, a beautiful arrangement of colored sand that originated in India and is now a Tibetan Buddhist tradition. Specially trained Buddhist monks create elaborate patterns with the sand, beginning in the middle of the diagram and using concentric circles to work their way to the edge. Once constructed, the sand mandalas are then ritualistically destroyed in recognition of the Buddhist doctrine of impermanence and the transitory nature of existence.

Visual Anthropology

Visual anthropology is a subfield of anthropology and itself a form of anthropological inquiry. It includes the study of art as represented in photography and film. The field largely arose with the invention of the camera, as anthropologists started to document Indigenous groups of the time on film. Some of the best-known figures in the field of visual anthropology are Edward Curtis, whose images of Native Americans are discussed in detail in Chapter 19: Indigenous Anthropology, and Robert Flaherty, whose 1922 film *Nanook of the North* is frequently shown in introductory anthropology courses as an early example of documentary filmmaking.

While visual anthropology is often confused with ethnographic film, tfilm representations are only a small part of what the subfield encompasses. Visual anthropology is the study of all visual representations produced by human cultures, including dances, plays, and collections of art, from the beginning of time. In recent times, it has become a standard practice to use visual arts to articulate one's feelings, thoughts, and interpretations of things seen, heard, and witnessed. Many cultures practice visual arts and use them in a variety of scenarios. They may be used to capture a certain mood, a cultural trend, or a historical event.

As mentioned above, film and photography played a major role in the development of visual anthropology as a field. Film can be used to capture images of art, such as cave paintings, sculptures from Roman times, or modern-day theater. Further, film itself has become an important form of art. Film provides an artistic representation of the human experience as seen by its directors, performers, editors, and all who contributed to its development.

The field of visual anthropology has had a significant impact on how anthropologists look at art. It also has become a driving force in how anthropologists view **sociodemographic** evolution, or the evolution of human societies with respect to combinations of social (https://openstax.org/r/dictionarysocial) and demographic factors. The visual anthropology of art transcends generations, centuries, cultures, and other delineating categorical definitions. Consider Figure 16.5, which depicts tourists in the French Louvre, crowding around and photographing Leonardo da Vinci's famous painting the *Mona Lisa*. This photograph portrays the dimensions and complexity of the anthropology of art. It transcends the time of the *Mona Lisa* and is itself an expression of the human experience in a more recent time, including how humans relate to visual artifacts from an older time in history.

Because of its age, the *Mona Lisa* image is in the public domain and can be copied and reproduced anywhere. The painting has become the subject of many parodies or memes. A **meme** is an image, video, piece of text, etc., typically humorous in nature, that is copied and spread rapidly by internet users, often with slight variations. The prolific production of memes of the *Mona Lisa* has kept the image relevant in society over a long period of time. Read more on the memes that have been created of the *Mona Lisa* here. Have We Over-Hyped the Mona Lisa? (https://openstax.org/r/overhyped-monalisa)

FIGURE 16.5 The *Mona Lisa* is five centuries old and still captures the imagination. (credit: "Mona Lisa" by Bradley Eldridge/Wikimedia Commons, CC BY 2.0)

The Appreciation of Art

Neuropsychologist Dahlia Zaidel has proposed that people's appreciation of aesthetics stems from their cognitive and affective processes. This simply means that people are attracted to art on the basis of preexisting conditions and that their interest in art evolves through time as they have new experiences, develop appreciation for new things, and otherwise mature as humans.

Appreciation of art is a biological and neurological response. People's individual perspectives are innately grounded in biology and nature and neurology and nurturing. Think about someone you find attractive and the attributes of theirs that you find beauty in, or consider the last piece of clothing you bought because you liked how it fit, how it looked, or how others appreciated it. Attraction is a response based on a myriad of biological attributes that each individual person possesses and has since birth. These are anchored in laws of attraction. Humanity's attraction to art is as biologically founded as attraction to other things (Zaidel et al. 2013). Perhaps this is why some people like various types of art from different time periods that depict the human experience.

Pottery

Traced back to the Neolithic period, pottery is considered one of the oldest inventions of humankind. Pottery is an art form created by many cultures for both aesthetic and functional purposes, including storing and cooking foods, carbonization (the formation of carbon from organic matter), and ritualistic practices. It has long been an important artifact type in archaeology. Pottery is an example of a practical object that also contains features of artistic beauty. One example is the Acoma pottery created by the Pueblo culture. Acoma pottery is functional and was not created purely as what we would now consider to be works of art. However, the pottery itself is a material art. Much can be learned about a culture by analyzing both the functionality of a particular piece or style of pottery and the imagery or stories depicted within its details and designs. Pottery, such as the 20,000-year-old pottery pieces found in ancient China depicted in Figure 16.6, has been crucial to understanding cultural history. The creation of pottery merges human knowledge and experiences, including artistic resources, emerging technological processes, and the needs of a population at a given time (P. M. Rice 2015).

FIGURE 16.6 These pottery fragments were found in a cave in southern China and have been dated to 20,000 years ago. Pottery is viewed by anthropologists as both functional object and artistic expression. (credit: "Ancient Pottery" by Gary Todd/flickr, Public Domain)

Though it serves a functional purpose, pottery throughout history has often been adorned with decoration, color, and other aesthetically attractive features. Decorated pottery is assigned a high value in many cultures, with people paying large sums of money for especially decorative pieces.

Body Art

Various forms of body art are a foundational form of expression in cultures all over the world. All cultures decorate and modify the human body in some way, whether temporarily or permanently. Anthropological frameworks can be used to understand body art as both a form of visual art and a cultural tradition.

Tattooing is a form of body art that has been practiced for thousands of years. *Tattoo* is a Polynesian term. Polynesian tribes and people used tattoos to establish identity, personality, and status. The Maori, an Indigenous Polynesian people of New Zealand, have traditionally used tattoos as an expression of identity and cultural affiliation. Examples of this can also be found in the Tonga and Samoa warrior cultures, in which specific tattoo designs and placement on the body were used to demonstrate a warrior's affiliation with a particular group of elite warriors. In the mid-20th century, American sailors used tattoos to represent personal interests, aspects of their identity, and group affiliation. Such tattoos might include representations of a unit mascot, places individuals have visited, or things they found beauty in.

FIGURE 16.7 One American sailor tattoos another aboard a ship during World War II. Tattooing is widely practiced by cultures around the world to express both personal and group identity. (credit: "Two sailors aboard the American battleship USS New Jersey in 1944" by Fenno Jacobs. Department of Defense. Department of the Navy. Naval Photographic Center/National Archives and Records Administration/Wikimedia Commons, Public Domain)

There is clear evidence of the practice of modifying the body with markings dating as far back as 5,300 to 3,000 years ago (Deter-Wolf et al. 2016; Shishlina, Belkevich, and Usachuk 2013). Such markings are still practiced by some of these same cultures today, such as the Maori people. Ötzi, a naturally mummified man found in the Ötzal Alps whose death has been dated to around 3250 BCE, is the first known tattooed human. His tattoos were of lines and crosses across his body. They are believed to have been made by creating incisions in the skin and rubbing charcoal into the incisions.

Tattooing can be a way for individuals to express membership in a larger community. Not only are communities formed around having body art, but some may obtain tattoos as a mark of belonging to a certain community (e.g., tattoos of a cross as a symbol of the Christian faith). Tattoos in recent decades have come to serve many purposes, including memorializing loved ones, expressing aesthetic tastes, depicting personal histories, expressing emotions or feelings, and symbolizing rebellion (Dey and Das 2017).

A modified approach to the classic tattoo can be found in the art of scarification. **Scarification** is the branding, burning, or etching of designs into the skin. Scarification marks often identify someone as being affiliated with subcultures or other groups. The practice is also used to represent individual growth or the growth and development of a group or subset of a society.

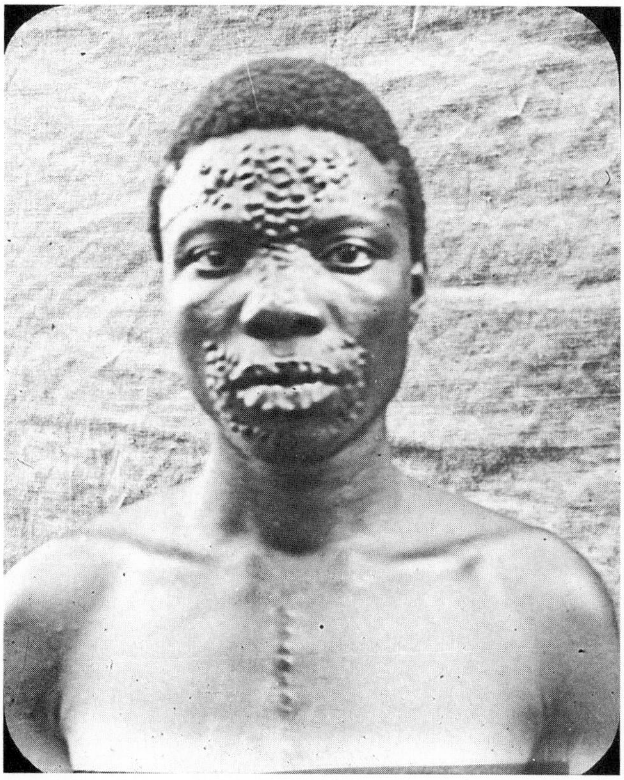

FIGURE 16.8 The patterned scarification visible on the face of this man was formed through the intentional creation and controlled healing of wounds. This image was taken in what was then the Belgian Congo by Christian missionaries in the early twentieth century. Scarification has been used by many cultures to mark group identity. (credit: "Man with Scarification Patterns, Congo, ca. 1900-1915" by Unknown/USC Digital Library/Wikimedia Commons, Public Domain)

Makeup has been an expression of visual art since prehistoric times. It is used to enhance beauty, cover up flaws, and represent cultural ideals of what beauty is and should be. It is often a sociocultural delineation of wealth and success. Piercings are used for many of the same reasons and have been found in the earliest of ancient African mummies. They may be seen as an expression of individuality or of identity and affiliation.

Another example of body art is **body painting**. In some cultures, body painting is limited to the face, while others cover their entire bodies. The painting of the whole body is a common practice among Indigenous Australian peoples (Figure 16.9). The purposes of this type of body art include, but are not limited to, subcultural identification and announcements of social status and accomplishments. The painting can be temporary or semipermanent, achieved through various types of paints and stains. Body painting follows uniform patterns and styles in some cultures and is independently driven in others. The specific designs might reveal an individual's position within their family, membership in a group, social position, tribal identity, and even precise ancestral history (Layton 1989).

FIGURE 16.9 These Aboriginal Australians have adorned their torsos with traditional body paint utilizing various conventions and motifs. (credit: "Aborigines on Palm Island, Qld - 1930s Perhaps" by Aussie~mobs/flickr, Public Domain)

Henna art is another example of body painting. Henna paint is derived from crushed, milled, and sifted henna leaves. It is applied directly on the skin in intricate designs that leave a red or orange stain once the paint is removed. Henna body art is used in various cultures of North Africa, Somalia, Southeast Asia, and the Indian subcontinent to adorn the hands and sometimes the feet of young women on special occasions, such as weddings and religious celebrations such as Eid al-Fitr (Chairunnisa and Solihat 2019). During weddings, women use henna to articulate cultural, familial, and religious affiliations. It is also used to accentuate the beauty of the bride and as a testament to the status of the family she is coming from and of the one she is marrying into.

FIGURE 16.10 The elaborate patterns on these women's arms are created using henna paste. After giving the paste time to stain the skin, it is washed away. The arm on the left shows the paste before washing, the arm of the woman on the right shows the color once the paste is removed. (credit: "Henna" by Rovich/500px/Wikimedia Commons, CC BY 3.0)

The grooming of hair is also a culturally significant practice in societies throughout the world. The way one styles or displays their hair can symbolize many things, including membership in a religious sect, racial affiliation, and alignment with pop cultural trends. Hair also has been seen as an indicator of social status. From an evolutionary perspective, the quality and amount of hair one has indicates robustness and has contributed to mate selection and group identification. Hairstyles, hair volume, and hair coverings all have contributed to cultural identity and have been viewed as artistic representations of the lived experiences of people in myriad cultures and times. In some traditional Muslim cultures, hair is concealed by headscarves called hijabs. This representation of modesty has become an icon of Middle Eastern tradition and culture.

Hairstyles are especially significant in African and African diasporic cultures. Hair played a significant role in ancient African civilizations, used to symbolize familial background, social status, tribal belonging, marital status, and spirituality. Hair-grooming practices, particularly time-intensive practices such as getting one's hair braided, are often social activities.

16.2 Anthropology of Music

LEARNING OUTCOMES

By the end of this section, you will be able to:

- Define ethnomusicology.
- Describe evidence of musical instruments in prehistory.
- Articulate the importance of sociocultural context to the understanding of music.
- Describe how music can form the basis of subculture and community.
- Evaluate the potential of music to impact processes of social change.
- Describe how cultural appropriation of music is related to social inequality and power.

Music

Music is found in wide-ranging settings and format, including chants, musicals, live performances, recorded performances, and spiritual rituals. In prehistoric times, music was used to communicate, to tell the stories of people and express important elements of cultures. Music articulates the human experience, focusing on what people want to remember about their history and what they desire for the future. It has been used to heal, to demonstrate power, and to archive the experiences of people. Present-day music is an extension and an evolution of the music that has come before. It is a medium that represents the depths of time, culture, and history. Prehistoric musical instruments, called *music artifacts* in anthropology, include woodwinds and percussion instruments of ancient nomadic tribes. These instruments began as rudimentary music artifacts and evolved into more sophisticated technological equipment invented and formed for the exclusive purpose of creating music.

Ethnomusicology

Someone who studies music from a global perspective, as a social practice, and through ethnographic field work is called an ethnomusicologist. The Society for Ethnomusicology defines ethnomusicology as "the study of music in its social and cultural contexts" (n.d.). Ethnomusicology is complex, requiring the work of many scientific disciplines. It requires study of many geographic areas, with a focus on the social practice of music and the human experience. Ethnomusicology is interdisciplinary, with a close relation to cultural anthropology. It is sometimes described as a historical research approach to understanding the cultures of people through their music. One well-known ethnomusicologist was Frances Densmore, who focused on the study of Native American music and culture.

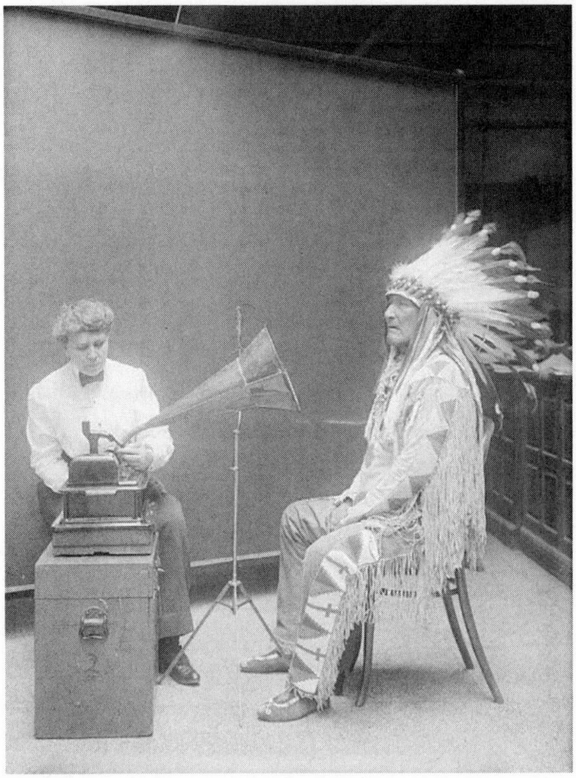

FIGURE 16.11 Frances Densmore was an American anthropologist and ethnographer. This image from 1916 shows her with Blackfoot chief, Mountain Chief. During this session, Mountain Chief listened to a song Densmore had recorded and interpreted it for her in Plains Indian Sign Language. (credit: “Piegan Indian, Mountain Chief, Listening to Recording with Ethnologist Frances Densmore” by National Photo Company/Library of Congress, Public Domain)

Musical Instruments in Prehistory

The field of ethnomusicology focuses on all aspects of music, including its genre, its message, the artist(s) who created it, and the instruments they used to do so. Have you ever considered why a particular musical instrument was created? Who made it? Why did they make it? What did they want it to do? How was it used? How did they dream up the design? Emily Brown (2005), formerly of the US National Park Service, studied the development of musical instruments in Ancestral Puebloan sites. Her study yielded insights into the types of instruments created. These included percussion and woodwind flutes that were used to create music culturally centric to the Puebloan people. Her study also yielded great insight into the structural hierarchy of those entrusted to manufacture music-making instruments. Not too dissimilar to today’s trade apprenticeships and master programs found in construction, Ancestral Puebloan people established a system of passing down the construction techniques central to creating musical instruments, ensuring that the knowledge would be carried on by future generations. Brown’s study connected music instruments to politics, music, social status, and social experiences.

The Structure and Function of Music in Different Societies

Music is grounded in the human experience. It is a theatrical expression of its creator’s thoughts and perceptions. The structure of music has evolved along with the experiences of the humans who created it. Examples of this can be found in the early 1800s hymns of Choctaw tribes. These hymns provide an artistic expression of traumatic experiences, referring to a time when the Choctaw people were removed from their homelands and relocated to reservation lands by the US government. They speak of both individual and collective experiences as these peoples made the arduous journey to their new locations. The songs speak about broken promises, the journey, and the fate of their people.

FIGURE 16.12 This trading card, published by the National Parks Service, commemorates the forced journey of the Choctaw people to reservation lands, commonly known as the Trail of Tears. The Choctaw people have commemorated this same journey in hymns. (credit: "Trail of Tears for the Creek People" by TradingCardsNPS/flickr, CC BY 2.0)

For enslaved people, music was a mechanism of emotional escape from difficult situations as well as a means of communicating with those speaking different languages during the Middle Passage, the journey from Africa to locations of forced labor. One of the most iconic spirituals, or songs for survival, is "Go Down Moses." Harriet Tubman, the legendary Underground Railroad conductor, said that she used this spiritual as a way to signal to those who were enslaved in the area who she wanted to help escape to freedom (Bradford [1886] 1995). The song ostensibly speaks about the experience of the Israelites enslaved by the Egyptians in ancient times. For enslaved Black people in America, the song spoke directly to their own longing for freedom. The chorus of "Go Down Moses" is as follows:

> Go down, Moses,
> Way down in Egypt's land.
> Tell ol' Pharaoh,
> Let my people go.
> Thus saith the Lord, bold Moses said,
> Let my people go,
> If not, I'll smite your firstborn dead,
> Let my people go.

Listen to this song on the Library of Congress website (https://openstax.org/r/locgovjukebox).

Numerous populations have utilized music as a means of resistance. During the civil rights movement of the 20th century, Black artists such as Nina Simone, Aretha Franklin, and Sam Cooke used their music as a way to challenge structural inequity. Aretha Franklin, a Black singer, songwriter, and pianist, wrote and performed music anchored in the Black church that came to represent Black American culture. She achieved national and international fame for her rich voice and heartfelt performances, and she was able to use her artistic talents to bring a message of both hope and resistance to her audience. Her songs spoke to both where people were and where they wanted to be.

Sam Cooke was an American singer who was given the nickname "King of Soul" by his fans and those in the music industry. Like many, he started out singing in church, but eventually his music and passion evolved to secular music. He is credited with having significant influence on the civil rights movement, and his music often explored themes of oppression and fighting for a cause. The music of his first band, Soul Stirrers, focused on stirring the listener's soul to engage in the movement for racial equality.

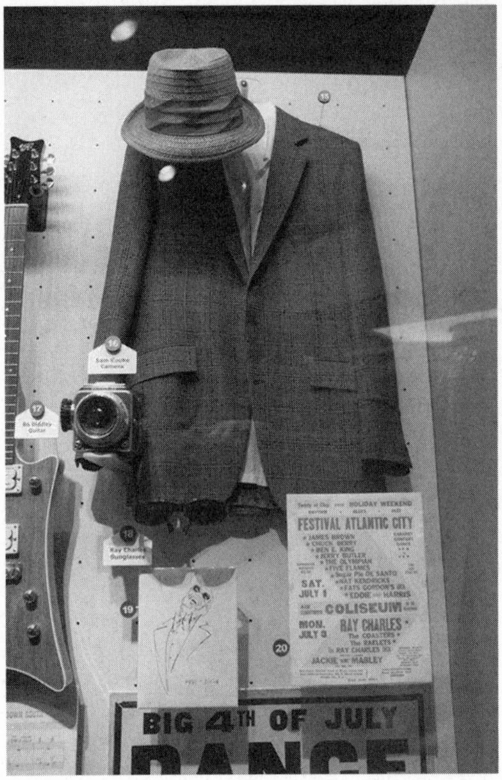

FIGURE 16.13 Sam Cooke's performance outfit and instruments are on display in the Rock and Roll Hall of Fame in Cleveland, Ohio. The music of Sam Cooke had considerable influence on the Civil Rights movement. (credit: "Sam Cooke's Outfit" by Steven Miller/flickr, CC BY 2.0)

Perhaps no artist in recent times is better known for using music as a catalyst for social change than Bob Dylan. Dylan was a 1960s-era musical artist who spoke to many cultures and generations about injustice and the need for inclusion and change. His 1964 song "The Times They Are a-Changin'" urged politicians and voters to support the civil rights movement. He was also well known for his opposition to the Vietnam War. His music may have very well changed the course of history, given his influence on his fans' thoughts, perspectives, and attitudes toward inclusion (Ray 2017).

FIGURE 16.14 American musician and songwriter Bob Dylan popularized many protest songs, including 1964's "The Times They Are a-Changin'." (credit: "Bob Dylan" by F. Antolín Hernández/flickr, CC BY 2.0)

PROFILES IN ANTHROPOLOGY

Zora Neale Hurston
1861–1960

FIGURE 16.15 In this image, Zora Neale Hurston exuberantly plays a traditional drum. (credit: "Zora Hurston, Half-Length Portrait, Standing, Facing Slightly Left, Beating the Hountar, or Mama Drum" by New York World-Telegram & Sun staff photographer/Library of Congress, Public Domain)

Personal History: Zora Neale Hurston was a Black American anthropologist, author, and filmmaker. She was born in Notasulga, Alabama, to a sharecropper turned carpenter and a former schoolteacher. All of her grandparents were born enslaved. Hurston moved to Eatonville, Florida, an all-Black town, in 1892, at the age of two. She often referenced Eatonville as her home, as she had no recollection of her time in Alabama. She lived in Eatonville until 1904, when her mother passed. At the time, Eatonville was a well-established Black community with a booming economy. According to multiple accounts, Hurston was never indoctrinated into feeling racial inferiority. While she was a resident, her father was elected mayor of the town. All the shop owners and government officials were also Black American elites. In adulthood, Huston often used Eatonville as the setting of her stories.

Huston left Eatonville due to a poor relationship with her stepmother. She enrolled in classes at Morgan College in Maryland, lying about her age of 26 to be eligible for a free high school education. She graduated in 1918 and attended Howard University, a historically Black university in Washington, DC, before transferring to Barnard College at Columbia University. At Barnard, Hurston studied under Franz Boas as an undergraduate and graduate student. She also worked with other foundational anthropologists, including Ruth Benedict and Margaret Mead.

Area of Anthropology: In addition to her time in academia, Hurston was a central figure in the Harlem Renaissance as a literary artist, working closely with Langston Hughes, among other writers. She was a pivotal literary artist whose work directly reflected the trials, tribulations, and successes of Black American communities and subsocieties that were often overlooked or exoticized (Jones 2009).

Hurston was a cultural anthropologist who was passionate about southern American and Caribbean cultural practices. She spent significant time in these geographical areas, immersing herself in the diverse cultures of Black people in the American South and the Caribbean.

Accomplishments in the Field: One of Hurston's most notable anthropological works is *Mules and Men* (1935), based on ethnographic research she conducted in lumber camps in north Florida. One focus of this work was the power dynamics between the White men who were in charge and the Black women laborers, some of whom the men took as concubines. In addition to this work, Hurston studied Black American song traditions and their relationship to the music of enslavement and to the musical traditions of pre–Middle Passage Africans.

Importance of Her Work: Hurston not only studied human society and culture as an anthropologist but was also an active participant in the arts. She was a central figure in the Harlem Renaissance, which was a flowering of Black culture centered in the Harlem neighborhood of New York City. Her most popular novel is *Their Eyes Were Watching God* (1937; Carby 2008). Her specific anthropological and ethnographic research focus areas were Black American and Caribbean folklore. She also worked for the Federal Writer's Project, part of the Works Progress Administration, as a writer and folklorist. Hurston is now an iconic figure for the Association of Black Anthropologists and several Black anthropological studies journals.

The Importance of Sociocultural Context in Understanding Music

Ethnomusicologist Patricia Campbell (2011) proposes that children's perspectives on musical interests are derived from their family, community, and environment. How did you learn about music you liked? What did your parents listen to, and what do you listen to? While you may have learned about and grown to like other music as you aged, your appreciation for music is founded in the sociocultural environment that you were raised in. Imagine growing up in a family that only listened to Bansuri bamboo flute music. Would you even know, for example, what rap music is?

Music as a Basis for Subculture and Community

The affiliation of music with identity became a common topic of inquiry in ethnomusicology in the 1980s, perhaps prompted by the music subcultures of the 1970s that arose among groups of people who did not identify with mainstream norms, values, or ideals. Among the music subcultures that emerged during that time was the punk subculture (Moran 2010). Though it was often seen as no more than youthful rebellion, the punk subculture formed its own community, values, and ideals founded in a do-it-yourself, or DIY, ethos. This can be found in the lyrics, music, and performances of punk groups such as the Ramones and the Clash, as well as more recent pop-influenced groups such as Green Day and Blink-182. The lyrics tell stories of needing to break from common ideals and values in order to think and do for oneself.

FIGURE 16.16 The rock band Green Day is one of many musical groups connected to specific subcultures in contemporary culture. (credit: “Green Day Concert Stage (Montreal) - Green Day Is Ever Green” by Anirudh Koul/ flickr, CC BY 2.0)

Cultural Appropriation

Cultural practices important to communities are often integrated into the fabric of each person’s identity. **Cultural appropriation** is defined as the improper or disrespectful use of a meaningful element of a culture or identity outside of its intended cultural context by someone who is not a part of that culture or identity (Young 2008). The act of cultural appropriation by dominant cultures threatens to erase remaining parts of a culture that may already be jeopardized. Cultural appropriation is tied to social inequity in that it involves a socially dominant group using the culture of a marginalized group for exploitative or capitalist gain. The cultural significance of the appropriated elements is lost. While the act of cultural appropriation is centuries old, there has been a renewed call from marginalized communities in recent years to understand how and why this practice is harmful.

Wesley Morris (2019) wrote an article for the *New York Times*’ 1619 Project regarding the mass appropriation of Black music. Morris noted instances of appropriation by artists such as Steely Dan, Eminem, and Amy Winehouse, all White American or British music superstars. Musical appropriation is the use of one genre’s musical contributions in other music that is not of the same genre, style, or culture. The power of Black music to articulate the history, struggles, and marginalization of Black people has appealed to other social groups as well, many of them drawn to the ability of this music to communicate its message with clarity and boldness. Morris also discusses how, more recently, the appropriation of Black lyrics, songs, and musical presentation styles has become a method of addressing the need for integration and integrated culture. This can be seen in Black artist Lil Nas X’s 2019 remix of his hit song “Old Town Road,” for which he teamed up with White country musician Billy Ray Cyrus to perform a duet. The song itself is a blending of cultures, musical and racial, and offers a social contribution to evolving efforts at inclusion.

16.3 An Anthropological View of Sport throughout Time

LEARNING OUTCOMES

By the end of this section, you will be able to:

- Describe the anthropology of sports.
- Explain how sports are a form of performance.
- Identify the role that sports can play for young people.

Sports are also deeply intertwined with the human experience. The anthropology of sports is a rapidly developing field that includes specialties such as physiological anthropology and human growth and development. Sports can be quite diverse; picture a Roman gladiator, a modern-day European football (soccer) player, and an ancient or recent Olympic competitor. Another example of a sport is Trobriand cricket, a bat-

and-ball game played by Trobriand Islanders that had evolved considerably since its introduction by Christian missionaries at the turn of the 20th century. Sports are expressions of passions and reflections of the human experience. They have been practiced by many cultures throughout time and across the globe. This section will specifically focus on how sports have impacted human culture and how human culture has impacted sports in turn. It will consider the historical foundation of the culture of sports and briefly analyze the way people interact with sports today, examining how human culture and societal practices are influenced by not only individual athletes but also social structures.

The Anthropology of Sports

Anthropologists understand sports as a cultural performance. The term **performance** can describe a plethora of actions, including any that are artful, active, or competitive—and sometimes some combination of all of these. Anthropologist Ajeet Jaiswal (2019) describes the anthropology of sports as the study of human growth and development. If one conceives of sports as a sort of performance, one also sees that each performance is unique to the performer. Each athlete, even the most impressive and seemingly unique, is a part of a larger performance. Consider your favorite sport or athletic competition. How long has it been in existence? Does it have roots in ancient times? Often, athletes and sports personalities—from Roman gladiators to more recent English footballers, American basketball players, and Olympic athletes—are considered singularly talented at their respective sports; however, without the broader cultural context that has cultivated gymnastics, tennis, soccer, and basketball, these talents would have no stage on which to perform.

Anthropologists who study sports do so within a larger context of sports and society. Interests of anthropologists researching sports might include archaeological research related to sports tools, cultural anthropological research pertaining to how humans interact with sports, or even biological/physical anthropological research on biological maturation or physical growth (Damo, Oliven, and Guedes 2008).

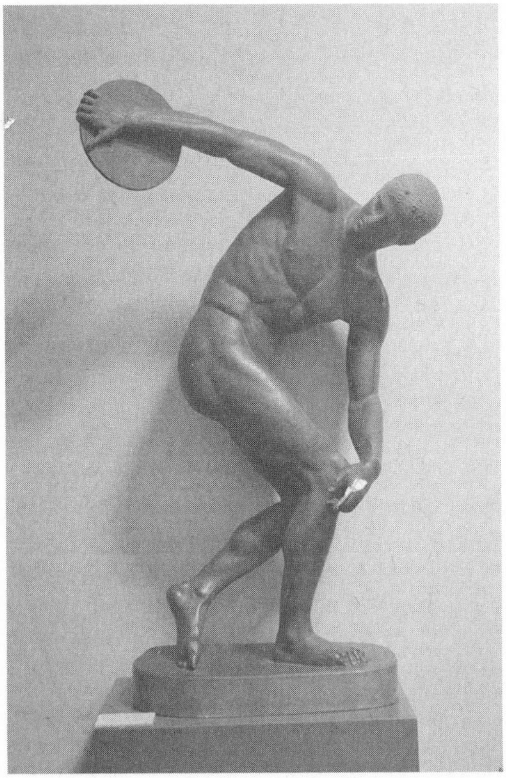

FIGURE 16.17 A Roman bronze reproduction of *Discobolus*, by the ancient Greek sculptor Myron. Throwing the discus, still an event in contemporary track and field meets, has been traced back to the original Olympic Games in Ancient Greece. (credit: "Myron (fl c 460-440 BC) - Diskobolus (Discus Thrower), Plaster Replica with Broken Left Hand, Right, Ashmolean Museum, Oxford, May 2013" by ketrin1407/flickr, CC BY 2.0)

Sports artifacts such as the weapons of gladiators and tools used in old and recent Olympic sports have offered significant contributions to the anthropology of material art. Picture your favorite sport. It likely involves a specific tool that is a representation of that sport. Notable examples of such tools and artifacts include the lacrosse sticks of the Iroquois, hammers from the oldest Olympic hammer-throw competitions, and the modern-day American football uniform, which is designed for safety and decorated to represent affiliation, professionalism, and individual athletes.

Sports have also offered theatrical performances since ancient times. Picture the gladiators of ancient Rome entertaining the wealthy who could afford the best seats or wealthy English footballers entertaining those who are likely less wealthy. The status reversal of sports entertainers and audiences in modern-day sports represents the dichotomous nature of social status and is just one of many examples of cultural change throughout time.

The Evolution of Sports

For most of documented human history, sports have been a significant part of the human experience for both audience and participants. Archaeological artifacts pertaining to sports, including colosseums, weapons, and artistic representations of competition, have been traced back to as early as 2000 BCE in China. These ancient sports featured competitions that tested the strength, stamina, and techniques of performers, such as footraces and physical fights. Today, many nations around the world participate in a version of the Olympic Games that were popular in the ancient Greek village of Olympia. Early events included a marathon run and wrestling. The Olympics were revived in the late 19th century, with the first modern games occurring in 1896 in Athens, Greece. Though rules and regulation may have been less stringent and defined in the sports of previous centuries, competition as entertainment has existed for millennia.

FIGURE 16.18 These professional lacrosse players are take part in a game that originated with the Indigenous people of what is now Canada. (credit: "Tailgate Bayhawks Game Navy Marine Corps Memorial Stadium" by Maryland GovPics/flickr, CC BY 2.0)

Sports can provide much more than mere entertainment to people and societies. Today, when thinking about modern sports, a person may think of professional athletes such as National Basketball Association (NBA) star Kobe Bryant or National Football League (NFL) great Walter Payton. In early competitions, the wealthy attended sporting events in which the athletes were typically not wealthy or privileged. In modern times, the commercialization of sports has largely reversed this trend, with "common" people attending sporting events to watch wealthy athletes compete. The business of sports has created opportunities for financial and cultural success for people with exceptional athletic abilities. The success of athletes such as Kobe Bryant created opportunities for other athletes, paving the way for the success of people who may not have otherwise thought it possible to experience the fame, notoriety, and financial success of a modern athlete (Chacko 2020).

FIGURE 16.19 Ed Smith was a running back in college and the NFL in the 1930s. As homage to his skill, he was asked to model for the Heisman Trophy, which has immortalized the now iconic "stiff arm" pose he took. (credit: "A Quick Stop to See the First Ever Heisman Trophy Statue @UChicago" by Cole Camplese/flickr, CC BY 2.0)

Youth Sports

Recreational sports for youth are common in various cultures. This can be especially important in marginalized communities, where youth sports are often viewed as deterrents from (or alternatives to) potentially dangerous activities or preventive structures that support youth development and community by focusing on positive actions that reduce adverse social behaviors. Youth sports programs are often community-building initiatives. One such initiative is the NFL's Play 60 program, which challenges NFL football players to engage in activities with underrepresented communities, encouraging kids of all skill levels to come together to play sports.

Among Indigenous Americans, an aggressive style of basketball called reservation ball, or **rezball** for short, is prominent in reservation communities. Rezball is different from traditional basketball, as the techniques used encourage relentlessly aggressive play and quick shooting. For youth on reservations, this may be one of a limited number of recreation opportunities. Rezball is documented in the Netflix docuseries *Basketball or Nothing* and a 2009 ESPN story about the role of rezball in the culture of Native American children.

16.4 Anthropology, Representation, and Performance

LEARNING OUTCOMES

By the end of this section, you will be able to:

- Identify how cultural identities, norms, values, and social structures are represented in art, music, and sports.
- Describe how art, music, and sports can function as means of resistance to dominant sociocultural forms and processes.

Art, music, and sports all articulate the experiences of people. One of these experiences might be resistance or rebellion. Whether it is a piece of art depicting a revolution, a rap song challenging the establishment, or a protest at a sporting event on a global stage, expression of the need for change are common in contemporary culture. This section will explore cultural identities; the use of art, music, and sports as resistance; and the representations created by each specialization.

Cultural Identities

Think about sporting team uniforms or a clothing style worn by members of a musical group. Each outfit on its own may not be distinct or significant, but when worn by a group of athletes or musicians and their fans, they become a source of identity. Since prehistoric times, art, music, and sports have been a source of cultural identity. Arts and sports have been intertwined with several human rights movements and the push for diversity, equity, and inclusion. Music has been a means of coded language for escape. Sports have long been a platform for cultural identity and has presented opportunities for cultural evolution and resistance. The Olympics are just one example of a sporting event that is linked deeply with national identity and nation pride.

FIGURE 16.20 The opening ceremonies of the Olympic games are celebrations of national identity and nation pride. (credit: "The team of Chile at the opening ceremony of the 1912 Summer Olympics" by photographer of IOC/Official Olympic Report/Wikimedia Commons, Public Domain)

Art as Resistance

Art is often used as an act of resistance. Graffiti and hip-hop are two forms of artistic expression that have been viewed as acts of resistance in modern times. The practice of **graffiti** as it is known today is reminiscent of ancient cave painting, as both are drawings, depictions, and writings on a wall. Ancient graffiti can help archaeologists understand general levels of literacy among a population of people or provide linguistic anthropologists with insight into the development of language through time.

While writings on walls is an ancient practice, graffiti became a popular form of cultural expression in Western countries in the 1960s. Modern graffiti is often performed in public view, as it is intended to make a statement. Today, during most political uprisings, researchers are able to easily find graffiti expressing views that inform and shape the political movement. Although many appreciate the communicative and artistic qualities of graffiti, others view it as visual pollution, and graffiti continues to be met with opposition.

One of the most iconic modern graffiti artists is Banksy, whose art is depicted in Figure 16.24. Banksy is the pseudonym of an English street artist who has been active for more than three decades (Ellsworth-Jones 2013). His identity remains unconfirmed. His work began to appear in the early 1990s in Bristol, England, and can now be found in cities around the world, including London, New York, and Paris. Based on reports from those who have secured interviews with him, Banksy views his art as an act of rebellion. He was often in trouble as a teenager, which is when he first began exploring art. His art typically responds to social or cultural issues. One example is his series in New Orleans, Louisiana, which critiqued the government response to Hurricane Katrina in 2005.

FIGURE 16.21 This mural by graffiti artist Banksy references both the Grim Reaper and the yellow "smiley face." (credit: "Banksy - Grin Reaper With Tag" by Szater/Wikimedia Commons, Public Domain)

Music as Resistance

Hip-hop is a form of music that has consistently served as a means of protesting injustice toward people of color. From its inception in the 1970s at neighborhood block parties, hip-hop has rapidly spread worldwide to influence various cultures, transitioning from the margins of American culture to a central element of global pop culture. The culture of hip-hop offers possibilities for rich anthropological exploration, including linguistics factors, performance, music, and lyricism. The messages expressed by hip-hop often include complex social commentaries.

With increased representation has come increased acceptance of hip-hop as a respected art form. In 2018, rap artist Kendrick Lamar was awarded a Pulitzer Prize for his album *DAMN.* and lauded by former president Barack Obama (Hubbard 2019). His fourth album release, *DAMN.* demonstrated why some call him one of the most influential rappers of his time. Perhaps better known is Public Enemy, the mid-1980s rap group created by Chuck D and Flavor Flav. The group's lyrics often cite their political beliefs and deep-seated opinions about American racism and the American media.

The evolution of hip-hop can be observed in many countries and societies. In the 1980s, it first began appearing in Japan and the Middle East. In Japan, it is thought to have begun with Hiroshi Fujiwara, who had an appreciation for old-school hip-hop and began to play it publicly. In the Middle East, some call it Arab rap or Arabic hip-hop. Heavily influenced by Western culture, these artistic representations demonstrate the vast and culturally diverse adoption of hip-hop as art and expression. Klash, the Muslim rapper shown in Figure 16.25, is well known in Middle Eastern cultures for telling the story of Muslim people through his artistry. Rap is not a subculture but a media and method for telling a story and at times expressing the resistance of a group of people.

FIGURE 16.22 Muslim rapper Klash with fellow rap artist Loon. From its origins in American inner cities, rap has spread around the globe. (credit: "klash with loon in jeddah city" by Ahmed550055/Wikimedia Commons, Public Domain)

Even more recently, Native American hip-hop has been a medium for Native Americans to tell their story and preserve the history of their peoples. Founded in American rap and hip-hop culture, this new form of expression has been embraced by rappers throughout Native American communities. It has been used to tell stories, explain history, and even encourage political activism on social issues.

Sports as Resistance

Throughout time, sports have been a global focal point for resistance. The Olympics have repeatedly been a site of global resistance and a setting for challenging societal norms and expectations. In Figure 16.26, Black American athletes Tommie Smith and John Carlos, gold and bronze medalists respectively, are depicted raising black-gloved fists during their medal ceremony as the US national anthem plays (Smith 2011). This gesture became known as the 1968 Olympics Black Power salute. Smith later described his raised, black-gloved fist as a symbol of support for all those who are and have been oppressed. Smith and Carlos made their demonstration in response to human rights violations perpetuated in the United States. Another example of resistance was seen four years later, when Jackie Robinson, the first Black player in Major League Baseball, wrote in his autobiography, recalling the opening game of his first World Series championship: "As I write this twenty years later, I cannot stand and sing the anthem. I cannot salute the flag; I know that I am a black man in a white world" (Robinson [1972] 1995, xxiv).

FIGURE 16.23 When Tommie Smith and John Carlos raised black-gloved fists at their Olympic medal ceremonies in 1968, they publicly expressed support for oppressed people and resistance to a culture viewed as perpetuating that oppression. (credit: "IMGP7613-olympics-mural" by Rae Allen/flickr, CC BY 2.0)

For many, a more familiar act of protest is likely NFL player Colin Kaepernick's kneeling during the singing of the nation anthem in 2016 following the shooting deaths of Black men Michael Brown, Alton Sterling, and Philando Castille at the hands of police officers (Lief 2019). In 2016, approximately 68 percent of all NFL players were Black (Gertz 2017). Kaepernick continued to kneel during the anthem for the remainder of the season. His gesture was a symbol of support for the Black Lives Matter movement, which seeks to end police brutality against Black people and other forms of racially motivated violence in the United States. Initially, feedback regarding Kaepernick's gesture within the sports world was negative. However, following the death of George Floyd in 2020, there has been an increased interest in understanding systemic oppression. This had led to initiatives by organizations such as the NFL, Black Lives Matter, and others to support inclusion and open dialogues about racism. Throughout the seasons following Kaepernick's initial act of kneeling, it became common practice in the world of professional sports for athletes to kneel in solidarity. This included Black players and some White players.

The 2016 Olympics in Rio de Janeiro were a demonstration of social stratification. Media coverage of the 2016 Rio Olympics reported on the less-than-acceptable environmental, safety, and health conditions. Athletes from more developed nations openly criticized the unsanitary and inhospitable conditions of the housing and training facilities, which included unpotable water sources, trash in commons areas, and dirty and unsanitary dormitories. While some protested silently, others used their global notoriety to publicly protest the conditions. The images and stories provided from Rio by journalists and mainstream media sources showed garbage-ridden streets, unsanitary rooms and facilities, and irreparably damaged buildings. For Rio, the Olympics were supposed to be a pinnacle of national pride and a positive contribution to the global stage. For many who attended, the event proved to be far less than the Olympic image depicted in popular imagination.

Integral Features

Art, music, and sports can themselves be forms of resistance and at the same time can display evidence of historical resistance. A protest, a cultural statement, the overthrow of a regime—all can be found in, and at times have even been started by, works of art, music, and sports. From the ancient Romans to professional American football players, people have used these mediums to fight for their causes and to ensure that the histories of their plights are recorded in the archives of time.

Art, music, and sports have told the stories of people since prehistoric times. Ingrained in the human experience, these mediums have been used to establish cultural and national identity. The images in art, the words of song, and the traditions of sport have had significant impacts on established norms and senses of personal and group identity. These aspects of the human condition are so foundational that each has been used as a form of resistance. Art, music, and sports have each contributed to the development of people and societies in important ways, and can each reveal important aspects of both past and current cultures.

MINI-FIELDWORK ACTIVITY

A Study of Ethnomusicology

Music is one of the most expressive and diverse forms of art. For this activity, do the following:

1. Review ethnomusicological study techniques.
2. Conduct your own ethnomusicological fieldwork. This can be done by interacting with musicians, attending a music event virtually or in person, or interviewing audience members at a musical performance. Interview both musicians and audience members about the meaning of the music. What did they hear? How did it make them feel? What did it make them want to do? Record the results of your interviews.
3. Additionally, record your own response to the music. What did you hear? How did it make you feel? What does it make you want to do?
4. Collect the information and write a 3–5-page comparative reflection paper on what you learned from your interviews and how they compare and contrast to your own experience and discoveries.

All music-making activities are appropriate, whether a formal or informal concert, a street performance, or gospel singing in church. You should maintain a field journal to record data, observations, and analysis.

Research and Literature Review Activity

1. Pick two (2) different examples of visual art, from the same time period but different socioeconomic microcultures, to compare and contrast.
2. Write a 3–5-page summary paper in which you do the following:
    - Identify people and/or studies that have reported on anthropological finds relevant to the images you selected.
    - Describe the evolution of the art form you are analyzing from an early time.
    - Explain how the anthropological studies you cite compare with other anthropological study approaches.
    - Address how the art studied is an evolutionary example of the human experience.
    - Evaluate what you perceive to be the future of the art as it continues to develop and evolve in future generations.

Resources

Basketball or Nothing. 2019. Philadelphia: WorkShop Content Studios. Netflix, 6 episodes.

Rice, Timothy. 2014. *Ethnomusicology: A Very Short Introduction.* New York: Oxford University Press.

Stone, Ruth M. *Theory for Ethnomusicology.* 2008. Upper Saddle River, NJ: Pearson.

Key Terms

art the application of human creative skill and imagination to produce works intended to be appreciated primarily for their beauty or emotional power, typically but not exclusively in a visual form such as a painting or sculpture.

body painting application of paint to the body

cultural appropriation the adoption, usually without acknowledgment, of cultural identity markers from subcultures or minority communities into mainstream culture by people with a relatively privileged status.

graffiti drawings, depictions, and writings on a wall typically without permission and meant for the public to see

iconographic study the study of visual images, symbols, or modes of representation collectively associated with a person, cult, or movement.

meme an image, video, piece of text, etc., typically humorous in nature, that is copied and spread rapidly by internet users, often with slight variations.

performance a musical, dramatic, or other form of entertainment presented before an audience.

rezball short for reservation ball, a style of basketball played in Native American reservation communities.

scarification the branding, burning, or etching of designs into the skin.

sociodemographic of, relating to, or involving a combination of social and demographic factors.

tattooing a form of body art where a mark, symbol, picture or design is placed on the skin. Tattooing has been practiced for thousands of years.

Summary

Art, music, and sports are deeply intertwined with the human experience. Anthropology offers the space to examine art, music, and sports through a cultural lens in order to study the ways in which they exist within sociocultural frameworks.

The anthropology of the arts is a subfield of cultural anthropology that explores the arts in a broader context within and between different cultural settings. Anthropologists study art differently than other social scientist, relying on data collection through direct, personal, in-depth observations of lived experiences and interactions. Art is expressed through a variety of formats, including music, visual art, literary art, and body art.

Anthropology explores the various cultural manifestations of humanity. All cultures decorate and modify the human body in some way, whether temporarily or permanently. Body art can be spiritual, cultural, or aesthetic. This includes tattooing, body paint, and hairstyling.

Ethnomusicology is a subfield of cultural anthropology that examines the music of different cultures and the people who make it, as well as the intended audience of the music. The interdisciplinary nature of ethnomusicology speaks to diverse approaches to studying the anthropology of music. Music as an art form expresses a wide array of perspectives and experiences.

Sports are a form of performance, and each participant performs within a broader cultural context. Anthropologists of sport are interested in studying sports within the context of society. Sports culture has resulted in cultural phenomena based on the popularity of athletes. Sports also serve as an escape for many populations with limited choices in recreational activities.

Critical Thinking Questions

1. How do people learn to create art and music in modern Western societies? Describe your own experiences becoming enculturated in the American style of creating art and music.
2. Pick a favorite image, one that was created specifically as an art object. This might be a painting, a photograph, a depiction of a sculpture, or something similar. Analyze it in an anthropological fashion. Who created it? Why was it created? Who was the audience or market for this object? What message(s) do you perceive when looking at it?
3. How far back can you trace the history of your favorite style of music? In your analysis, include instrumentation, rhythms, vocalizations (if any), and sites of performance.
4. What role(s) do sports play in your own culture? Address both informal sports (e.g., pickup games between friends) and professional/national teams.
5. How would global and racial inclusion in the United States differ without the contributions of

art, music, and sports professionals?

Bibliography

Boyd, Valerie. 2003. *Wrapped in Rainbows: The Life of Zora Neale Hurston*. New York: Scribner.

Bradford, Sarah H. (1886) 1995. *Harriet, the Moses of Her People*. Chapel Hill: University of North Carolina at Chapel Hill. https://docsouth.unc.edu/neh/harriet/harriet.html.

Brown, Emily J. 2005. "Instruments of Power: Musical Performance in Rituals of the Ancestral Puebloans of the American Southwest." PhD diss., Columbia University. ProQuest (AAT 3159726).

Calhoun, Craig, ed. 2002. *Dictionary of the Social Sciences*. S.v. "salvage ethnography." New York: Oxford University Press.

Campbell, Patricia Shehan. 2011. "Musical Enculturation: Sociocultural Influences and Meanings of Children's Experiences in and through Music." In *A Cultural Psychology of Music Education*, edited by Margaret S. Barrett, 61–81. New York: Oxford University Press.

Carby, Hazel V. 2008. "The Politics of Fiction, Anthropology, and the Folk: Zora Neale Hurston." In *Zora Neale Hurston's* Their Eyes were Watching God, edited by Harold Bloom, new ed., 23–40. New York: Infobase Publishing.

Cardona, Nina. 2015. "Bob Dylan Was a Catalyst, but the Nashville Cats Were the Ones Who Changed Music Row." WPLN News. Nashville Public Radio, June 19, 2015. https://wpln.org/post/bob-dylan-was-a-catalyst-but-the-nashville-cats-were-the-ones-who-changed-music-row/.

Chacko, Diya. 2020. "The Legacy of 'Kobe!' Jump Shots Lives On through Fans." *Los Angeles Times*, January 27, 2020. https://www.latimes.com/sports/lakers/story/2020-01-27/kobe-bryant-jump-shots-legacy.

Chairunnisa, Baiq Clara Dita, and Ade Solihat. 2019. "Henna Art in Global Era: From Traditional to Popular Culture." In *Joint Proceedings of the International Conference on Social Science and Character Educations (ICoSSCE 2018) and International Conference on Social Studies, Moral, and Character Education (ICSMC 2018)*, edited by Amika Wardana, Aman, and Alifi Nur Prasetia Nugroho, 220–225. Amsterdam: Atlantis Press. https://www.atlantis-press.com/article/125910003.

Damo, Arlei Sander, Ruben George Oliven, and Simoni Lahud Guedes. 2008. "Sports: An Anthropological Perspective." Translated by Letícia Maria Costa da Nóbrega Cesarino. *Horizontes Antropológicos* 4 (Selected Edition). http://socialsciences.scielo.org/scielo.php?script=sci_arttext&pid=S0104-71832008000100002.

Deter-Wolf, Aaron, Benoît Robitaille, Lars Krutak, and Sébastien Galliot. 2016. "The World's Oldest Tattoos." *Journal of Archaeological Science: Reports* 5:19–24. https://doi.org/10.1016/j.jasrep.2015.11.007.

Dey, Archita, and Kaustav Das. 2017. "Why We Tattoo? Exploring the Motivation and Meaning." *Anthropology* 5 (1). https://www.longdom.org/abstract/why-we-tattoo-exploring-the-motivation-and-meaning-36072.html.

Ellsworth-Jones, Will. 2013. "The Story behind Banksy." *Smithsonian*, February 2013. https://www.smithsonianmag.com/arts-culture/the-story-behind-banksy-4310304/.

Flax, Peter. 2019. "How Rez Ball Is Transforming the Health and Fitness of a Whole Community." *Men's Health*, October 31, 2019. https://www.menshealth.com/fitness/a29614983/rezball-indian-reservation-basketball/.

Gertz, Michael. 2017. "NFL Census 2016." ProFootballLogic. April 19, 2017. http://www.profootballlogic.com/articles/nfl-census-2016/.

Hoover, Joanne Sheehy. 2020. "Making Prehistoric Music: Musical Instruments from Ancestral Puebloan Sites." NPS.gov. National Park Service, last updated April 9, 2020. https://www.nps.gov/articles/musical-instruments-from-ancestral-puebloan-sites.htm.

Hubbard, Henry. 2019. "'Pulitzer Kenny' and the Culture of Classical Music: A Study of Cultural Prizes, Controversy, and a Capital-Based Alternative to Musical Value." PhD diss., Johns Hopkins University.

Jaiswal, Ajeet. 2019. "Anthropology and Sports." *International Journal of Research in Sociology and Anthropology* 5 (3): 29–30. https://doi.org/10.20431/2454-8677.0503004.

Jones, Sharon L. 2009. *Critical Companion to Zora Neale Hurston: A Literary Reference to Her Life and Work.* New York: Facts on File.

Johnson, Guy B. 1931. "The Negro Spiritual: A Problem in Anthropology." *American Anthropologist* 33 (2): 157–171. https://doi.org/10.1525/aa.1931.33.2.02a00020.

Kristeller, Paul Oskar. 1990. *Renaissance Thought and the Arts: Collected Essays.* Expanded ed. Princeton, NJ: Princeton University Press.

Large, David Clay. 2007. *Nazi Games: The Olympics of 1936.* New York: W. W. Norton.

Layton, Robert. 1989. "The Political Use of Australian Aboriginal Body Painting and Its Archaeological Implications." In *The Meanings of Things: Material Culture and Symbolic Expression*, edited by Ian Hodder, 1–11. Boston: Unwin Hyman.

Lief, Brian. 2019. "Athletes Engaging in Activism: Jackie Robinson, Muhammad Ali, Tommie Smith, and John Carlos and Their Influence on Colin Kaepernick." Sr. independent study thesis, College of Wooster. https://openworks.wooster.edu/independentstudy/8522/.

Moran, Ian P. 2010. "Punk: The Do-It-Yourself Subculture." *Social Sciences Journal* 2010:58–65. https://westcollections.wcsu.edu/handle/20.500.12945/2257.

Morphy, Howard, and Morgan Perkins. 2006. "The Anthropology of Art: A Reflection on Its History and Contemporary Practice." In *The Anthropology of Art: A Reader*, edited by Howard Morphy and Morgan Perkins, 1–32. Malden, MA: Blackwell.

Morris, Wesley. 2019. "Why Is Everyone Always Stealing Black Music?" *New York Times Magazine*, August 14, 2019. https://www.nytimes.com/interactive/2019/08/14/magazine/music-black-culture-appropriation.html.

Nettl, Bruno. 2005. *The Study of Ethnomusicology: Thirty-One Issues and Concepts.* New ed. Urbana: University of Illinois Press.

Plattner, Stuart. 2003. "Anthropology of Art." In *A Handbook of Cultural Economics*, edited by Ruth Towse, 15–19. Northampton, MA: Edward Elgar.

Ray, Sanjana. 2017. "How Bob Dylan Changed the Course of History through His Music." YourStory. May 24, 2017. https://yourstory.com/2017/05/music-of-bob-dylan/.

Rice, Prudence M. 2015. *Pottery Analysis: A Sourcebook.* 2nd ed. Chicago: University of Chicago Press.

Rice, Timothy. 2017. "Reflections on Music and Identity in *Ethnomusicology*." In *Modeling Ethnomusicology*, 139–160. New York: Oxford University Press.

Robinson, Jackie. (1972) 1995. *I Never Had It Made: An Autobiography of Jackie Robinson.* As told to Alfred Duckett. Hopewell, NJ: Ecco Press.

Shishlina, Natalia I., E. V. Belkevich, and A. N. Usachuk. 2013. "Bronze Age Tattoos: Sympathetic Magic or Decoration?" In *Tattoos and Body Modifications in Antiquity: Proceedings of the Sessions at the EAA Annual Meetings in The Hague and Oslo, 2010/11*, edited by Philippe Della Casa and Constanze Witt, 67–74. Zurich: Chronos.

Smith, Maureen Margaret. 2011. "The 'Revolt of the Black Athlete': Tommie Smith and John Carlos's 1968 Black Power Salute Reconsidered." In *Myths and Milestones in the History of Sport*, edited by Stephen Wagg, 159–184. New York: Palgrave Macmillan.

Society for Ethnomusicology. n.d. "About Ethnomusicology." Accessed September 1, 2021. https://www.ethnomusicology.org/page/AboutEthnomusicol.

Tucci, Giuseppe. (1961) 2001. *The Theory and Practice of the Mandala: With Special Reference to the Modern*

Psychology of the Subconscious. Translated by Alan Houghton Brodrick. Mineola, NY: Dover.

United Nations Educational, Scientific and Cultural Organization. (2021). "What Is Intangible Cultural Heritage?" Intangible Heritage. Accessed September 6, 2021. https://ich.unesco.org/en/what-is-intangible-heritage-00003.

Young, James O. 2008. *Cultural Appropriation and the Arts*. Malden, MA: Blackwell.

Zablan, Audriana. 2010. "Primitive Art." *Expressions of Time: New York City Arts* (blog). Macaulay Honors College, CUNY, November 1, 2010. https://eportfolios.macaulay.cuny.edu/weinroth10/2010/11/01/primitive-art/.

Zaidel, Dahlia W., Marcos Nadal, Albert Flexas, and Enric Munar. 2013. "An Evolutionary Approach to Art and Aesthetic Experience." *Psychology of Aesthetics, Creativity, and the Arts* 7 (1): 100–109. https://doi.org/10.1037/a0028797.

CHAPTER 17
Medical Anthropology

Figure 17.1 The US Army Corp of Engineers opened this community health clinic in the country of Benin in West Africa in 2013. The clinic has waiting, consultation, observation and treatment rooms, and a drug store. (credit: "Pehunco Health Clinic opens" by US Army Corps of Engineers/Wale Adelakun/flickr, Public Domain)

CHAPTER OUTLINE

INTRODUCTION Health and a preoccupation with maintaining it permeates all aspects of human culture. Health is a concern to humans everywhere. There is no end to the variety of ways cultures across history have treated health, healing, and medicine. Human health and well-being sit at the intersection of biology and culture. Both physical and social environments shape well-being and health outcomes. Medical anthropology is a holistic specialty that draws on all four fields of anthropology but primarily builds on cultural anthropology and biological anthropology to understand the health implications of a culture's impact on human physiology and well-being.

- How do you define health?
- How do you maintain your health?
- What factors do you think contribute to health and illness?

17.1 What Is Medical Anthropology?

LEARNING OUTCOMES

By the end of this section, you will be able to do the following:

- Define health, illness, sickness, and the sick role.
- Describe early research and methods in medical anthropology.
- Explain Franz Boas's influence in establishing the foundations of medical anthropology.
- Describe how medical anthropology has developed since World War II.

Social Construction of Health

The World Health Organization defines **health** as "a state of complete physical, mental and social well-being and not merely the absence of disease or infirmity" (World Health Organization 2020). Health is affected by multiple social, biological, and environmental factors. **Disease** is strictly biological—an abnormality that affects an individual's physical structure, chemistry, or function. Going back to the time of the ancient Greek physician Hippocrates, doctors have regarded disease as the result of both a person's lifestyle habits and the social environment in which they live. **Illness**, by comparison, is the individual's *sociocultural experience* of a disruption to their physical or mental well-being. An individual's perception of their own illness is shaped by how that illness is viewed, discussed, and explained by the society they live in. The social perception of another person's **sickness** affects that person's social well-being and how they are viewed and treated by others. **Sick roles** are the social expectations for a sick person's behaviors based on their particular sickness—how they should act, how they should treat the sickness, and how others should treat them. **Malady** is the term anthropologists use to encompass disease, illness, and sickness.

- *Health* is your state of well-being.
- *Disease* is a biological abnormality.
- *Illness* is your sociocultural experience of health.
- *Sickness* is a social perception of ill health.
- *Malady* is a broad term for everything above.

Term	Definition	Example
Health	State of well-being	Wellness prior to infection
Disease	A biological abnormality	Viral infection
Illness	A patient's sociocultural experience of disrupted health	Fever, sore throat, cough, worry about missing class, disappointment of missing an outing with friends
Sickness	A social perception of ill health	Expectations such as: stay home and rest if you have a fever; do not attend class or go out with friends; see a doctor if it lasts longer than 48 hours
Malady	A broad term for everything above	Disruption of health caused by a viral infection with fever, sore throat, cough; worry about missing work/class; and the social expectation you will stay home and rest

TABLE 17.1 Key Terms Used in Medical Anthropology

Foundational to medical anthropology is an understanding of health and malady that includes social experiences and cultural definitions. Medical anthropology studies how societies construct understandings of health and illness, including medical treatments for all types of maladies. Culture affects how we perceive everything, including health. Culture shapes how people think and believe and the values they hold. It shapes everything people have and do. Many cultures approach health and illness in completely different ways from one another, often informed by a number of societal factors. Medical anthropology provides a framework for common study and comparison between cultures, highlighting systems and illustrating how culture determines how health is perceived.

History of Medical Anthropology

While medical anthropology is a relatively new subfield, it has deep roots within four-field American anthropology, with a strong connection to early European anthropologists' study of religion. The holistic approach of Franz Boas was also key to the development of medical anthropology. One focus of Boas's research was analysis of the "race theory" common in the 19th and early 20th centuries in the United States. According to this theory, one's assigned racial category and ethnic background determined certain physical features as well as behavioral characteristics. Boas challenged this assumption through studies of the health and physiology of immigrant families in New York City in 1912. Boas found that there was a great deal of flexibility in human biological characteristics within an ethnic group, with social factors such as nutrition and child-rearing practices playing a key role in determining human development and health. He noted that cultural changes to nutrition and child-rearing practices, changes that are commonly a part of the immigrant experience, were linked to generational changes in biology. Boas provided empirical data from his own primary sources that refuted theories of biological inheritance as the source of social behaviors and revealed the impact of local environments (natural, modified, and social) in structuring cultural and physical outcomes. This foundation was starkly opposed to the inherent racism of social evolutionism, which was the dominant anthropological theory of his time.

Boas's students, such as Ruth Benedict, Margaret Mead, and Edward Sapir, all continued aspects of his work, taking their research in unique directions that affect medical anthropology to this day. Benedict's cultural personality studies, Mead's work on child-rearing practices and adolescence, and Sapir's work on psychology and language laid the foundations of psychological anthropology. Their foray into psychological anthropology was preceded by the work of British psychiatrist and anthropologist W. H. R. Rivers (1901), who studied the inheritance of sensory capabilities and disabilities among Melanesian populations while participating in the Torres Strait island expedition in 1898. He developed a great respect for his Melanesian research participants and utilized his research findings to denounce the "noble savage" fallacy. By demonstrating that a shared biological mechanism of inheritance and environmental influences shaped the Melanesian senses in the same way as it did the British, he illustrated that their mental capacity was the same as Europeans.

FIGURE 17.2 Franz Boas's study on immigrants to the United States showed that health is influenced by a number of factors, including many determined by one's social and physical environment. (credit: US National Archives and Records Administration/Wikimedia Commons, Public Domain)

Medical anthropology also has roots in the anthropology of religion, a subfield of anthropology that shines a lens on many aspects of health. The anthropology of religion looks at how humans develop and enact spiritual beliefs in their daily lives and at how these beliefs are utilized as a form of social control. A number of commonly studied key frameworks of the anthropology of religion—rituals of healing, taboos of health, shamanic healing, health beliefs, cultural symbolism, and stigma, among them—focus on health and health outcomes. A number of notable early religious anthropologists, including E. E. Evans-Pritchard, Victor and Edith Turner, and Mary Douglas, did work on subjects such as healing rituals, misfortune and harm, pollution, and taboo. Evans-Pritchard's work among the Azande people of North Central Africa continues to be foundational to medical anthropology. Especially important is the chapter "The Notion of Witchcraft Explains Unfortunate Events" from the book *Witchcraft, Oracles and Magic among the Azande*, which introduces the domain of causation and its many cross-cultural forms. This chapter directly impacted the concept of explanatory models, which we will cover in depth later in this chapter. The work of Victor and Edith Turner focused on ritual healing, pilgrimage, and socially enforced morality. Mary Douglas's *Purity and Danger* ([1966] 2002) examined the concepts of pollution and taboo as well as rituals designed to restore purity. Her work continues to be influential, particularly for medical anthropologists focused on sickness-related stigma and its impact on patients' illness experiences.

World War II brought about a profound change in the way anthropologists did their work. A number of Boas's students helped the British and United States governments during the war, a trend that continued after the war. Focusing on both public and private health initiatives, anthropologists increasingly worked to help people improve their health outcomes in the post-war era. These public health efforts were directly connected with the founding of the United Nations and the World Health Organization (WHO). In this period, well-being and health care were included in the declaration of human rights, and biomedical thinking became focused on "conquering" infectious disease.

The formal founding of the discipline of medical anthropology can be traced to the late 1970s. One landmark is the publication of George Foster and Barbara Anderson's (1978) medical anthropology textbook. However, many applied anthropologists and researchers in allied health fields, such as social epidemiology and public health, had been conducting cross-cultural health studies since the conclusion of World War II. These include Edward Wellin, Benjamin Paul, Erwin Ackerknecht, and John Cassell. Many of these early figures were themselves medical doctors who saw the limitations of a strictly biomechanical approach to health and disease.

PROFILES IN ANTHROPOLOGY

Paul Farmer, 1959–present, Jim Yong Kim, 1959–present

FIGURE 17.3 (left) Paul Farmer speaking at the University of Chicago in 2017. (credit: "Paul Farmer giving MacLeanPrize Lecture in 2017" by MacLean Center/Wikimedia Commons, CC-BY-3.0); (right) Jim Yong Kim speaking in New York City in 2018. (credit: "20th Anniversary Schwab Foundation GalaDinner" by Ben Hider/World Economic Forum/flickr, CC BY 2.0)

Personal Histories: Paul Farmer is a medical anthropologist and physician who first visited Haiti in 1983 as a volunteer. Inspired by this experience, Farmer set out to find a way to bring necessary treatments to parts of the world seemingly forgotten by modern medicine. When Harvard Medical School began offering a dual PhD/MD program, Farmer was among the first enrolled, and he soon founded Partners in Health (PIH) with his colleagues. Since then, he has championed affordable health care around the world. He is currently a professor of medicine and chief of the Division of Global Health Equity at Brigham and Women's Hospital, while still being actively involved in Partners in Health. Farmer has written extensively on the AIDS epidemic, infectious diseases, and health equity. In 2003, Farmer was the subject of Tracy Kidder's book *Mountains Beyond Mountains: The Quest of Dr. Paul Farmer, A Man Who Would Cure the World,* which is an accessible account of Farmer's work with Partners in Health. Farmer is married to Didi Bertrand Farmer, a Haitian medical anthropologist. They have three children.

Like Farmer, Jim Yong Kim was one of the first to enroll in Harvard Medical's dual medical anthropology PhD/MD program. He was a cofounder of Partners in Health while still in medical school, at a time when he was spending his summers in Haiti treating patients with limited access to health care. He championed the initial expansion of PIH into other countries, beginning with Peru. In 2003 Kim left Partners in Health to join the World Health Organization, becoming director of HIV/AIDs treatments and research in 2004. Under Kim, the WHO has fast-tracked a number of new treatments to help those affected by AIDS in Africa. Kim was the president of Dartmouth College from 2009 until 2012, when he became president of the World Bank. He held this position until 2019, when he left to join Global Infrastructure Partners.

Area of Anthropology: medical anthropology, applied anthropology

Accomplishments in the Field: Partners in Health was founded in 1987 by a group including Farmer and Kim, with the goal of setting up a clinic in Haiti to combat the devastation of the AIDS epidemic. Made up of volunteers, philanthropists, and medical students trained in anthropological methodology, the organization sought to combat the AIDS epidemic at a time when governments refused to adequately fund efforts to combat what was then perceived as a "gay disease." By the mid-1990s, PIH was offering patients in Haiti treatments that cost hundreds of dollars, as opposed to the tens of thousands of dollars they would have cost in the United States. They have since duplicated this work in other settings, and their methods have been used by countless nonprofits around the world to offer life-saving treatments to impoverished communities.

Importance of Their Work: Partners in Health works today in 11 countries, with a staff of over 18,000 spread across the globe. They build hospitals, health clinics, and research labs aimed at improving medical treatment and creating a more equitable global health care system. Their model has been replicated by countless organizations around the world to bring down the cost of health care and increase the quality of the care given.

Since the 1980s, medical anthropologists have diversified the field through interdisciplinary applications of anthropology and the applied use of medical anthropology in health care and government policy. The role of the anthropologist in this work often varies but is typically focused on translating cultural nuance and biomedical knowledge into policy and human-centered care. Today, the field of medical anthropology includes applied anthropologists working in medical settings, nonprofits, and government entities such as the Centers for Disease Control and Prevention (CDC), the National Institutes of Health (NIH), and the WHO. Academic medical anthropologists are problem-oriented researchers who study the complex relationship between human culture and health. As can be seen in the lives and careers of the medical anthropologists highlighted in this chapter's profiles, medical anthropologists frequently occupy both academic and applied roles throughout their career as they seek to apply insights from their research to effect positive change in the lives of those they study.

FIGURE 17.4 During the COVID-19 pandemic, medical recommendations informed emerging cultural taboos, highlighting the link between medicine and culture. (credit: "Covid-19" by Daniel Lobo/Daquellamanera.org/flickr, Public Domain)

17.2 Ethnomedicine

LEARNING OUTCOMES

By the end of this section, you will be able to do the following:

- Define ethnomedicine, traditional environmental knowledge, and biomedicine.
- Provide examples of cultural and societal systems that use religion and faith to heal.
- Define medical pluralism.

Ethnomedicine is a society's cultural knowledge about the management of health and treatments for illness, sickness, and disease. This includes the culturally appropriate process for seeking health care and the culturally defined signs and symptoms of illness that raise a health concern. Ethnomedical systems are frequently closely related to belief systems and religious practices. Healing can include rituals and natural treatments drawn from the local environment. Healing specialists in an ethnomedical system are knowledgeable individuals who undergo training or apprenticeship. Some examples of ethnomedical healers are midwives, doulas, herbalists, bonesetters, surgeons, and shamans, whose ethnomedicine existed in cultural traditions around the world prior to biomedicine. Anthropologists frequently note that ethnomedicinal healers possess knowledge of both how to heal and how to inflict harm by physical and sometimes metaphysical means. Ethnomedicine does not focus on "traditional" medicine, but instead allows for cross-cultural comparison of medical systems.

FIGURE 17.5 A Peruvian shaman prepares herbal medicine for an upcoming ritual. (credit: "Shaman" by Alan Kotok/flickr, CC BY 2.0)

Some forms of healing rely upon spiritual knowledge as a form of medicine. Within shamanism, people deliberately enter the spirit world to treat ailments, with the culture's shaman acting as an emissary. The goal may be to eliminate the illness or to at least identify its source. Similarly, faith healing relies upon a shared understanding of faith and local beliefs, with spirituality pervading the healing process. Exorcising individuals of possession by negative spirits is a common form of faith healing that occurs within Christian, Islamic, Buddhist, and shamanic frameworks. In many cases, cultures that utilize biomedicine also utilize some forms of faith healing.

Ethnopharmacology utilizes herbs, foods, and other natural substances to treat or heal illness. Traditional ethnopharmacological treatments are currently of great interest to pharmaceutical companies looking for new biomedical cures. Many common medicines have roots in ethnopharmacological traditions. Used in Chinese medicine, indigenous American healing, and traditional European medicine, willow bark is a widespread cure for headaches. In 1897, the chemist Dr. Felix Hoffmann, working for the Bayer corporation, isolated acetylsalicylic acid as the active pain-reducing ingredient in willow bark, giving the world Bayer aspirin.

The concept of **traditional ecological knowledge**, or TEK, refers to medical knowledge of different herbs, animals, and resources in an environment that provides a basis for ethnomedicine. Many cultures have been able to translate detailed awareness of their environments, such as where water is and where and when certain herbs grow, into complex and effective ethnomedical systems (Houde 2007). In 2006, Victoria Reyes-Garcia, working with others, conducted a comprehensive study of Amazonian TEK. Victoria and her colleagues collected information regarding plants useful for food and medicine from 650 research participants from villages along the Maniqui River in the Amazon River basin.

China's traditional medicine system is another excellent example of an ethnomedical system that relies heavily on TEK and ethnopharmacology. While many in China do rely upon biomedicine to treat specific health problems, they also keep themselves in balance using traditional Chinese medicine. The decision of which health system to consult is often left to the patient, but at times doctors will suggest a patient visit a traditional apothecary and vice versa, creating a complementary medical system that makes use of both approaches. While bound by geography prior to the 19th century, in today's globalized world a traditional Chinese doctor can use resources from anywhere around the world, whether it is dried body parts of a tiger or herbs found in another part of China. Chinese traditional medicine, as an ethnomedical system, is heaviiy influenced by culture and context. It focuses on balancing the body, utilizing a number of forces from the natural world. Traditional Chinese medicine makes use of substances as diverse as cicada shells, tiger livers, dinosaur bones, and ginseng to create medicine. Healers in this system are often in a role similar to Western pharmacists, concocting medicine in a variety of forms such as pills, tonics, and balms. The differences between a traditional Chinese medication healer and biomedical pharmacist include both the tools and ingredients used and the foundational assumptions about the cause of and treatments for various ailments. Around the world, traditional environmental knowledge is used both in place of biomedicine and alongside it.

Biomedicine is an ethnomedical system deeply shaped by European and North American history and rooted in the cultural system of Western science. It draws heavily from biology and biochemistry. Biomedicine treats disease and injuries with scientifically tested cures. Biomedical health care professionals base their assessment of the validity of a treatment on the results of clinical trials, conducted following the principles of the scientific method. It should be noted that as each health care professional is not conducting their own research, but instead relying on the work of others, this assessment still requires faith. Biomedicine places its faith in the scientific method, where other ethnomedical systems place their faith in a deity, the healer's power, or time-tested treatments passed down in traditional ecological knowledge. Biomedicine is not free from culture; it is an ethnomedical system shaped by Western cultural values and history. Biomedicine falls short of its ideal of scientific objectivity. Medical anthropologists have extensively documented the way systemic prejudices such as racism, classism, and sexism permeate biomedicine, impacting its effectiveness and perpetuating health inequalities. Still, in the Western world, biomedicine is often utilized as a point of comparison for other ethnomedical systems.

Biomedicine has been critiqued by medical anthropologists for assuming predominance over other forms of healing and cultural knowledge. In many contexts, biomedicine is presumed to be superior because it is clinical and based on scientific knowledge. Yet this presumed superiority requires that a patient trusts and believes in science and the biomedical system. If a person mistrusts biomedicine, whether because of a bad experience with the biomedical model or a preference for another ethnomedical approach, their health outcomes will suffer if they are forced to rely on the biomedical system. Biomedicine can also disrupt and threaten culturally established treatments and cures. For example, in a culture that treats schizophrenia by granting a person spiritual power and treating them as part of the community, labeling that individual as mentally ill according to biomedical terms takes away their power and removes their agency. In most cases, a hybrid model, in which biomedicine does not assume supremacy but instead works alongside and supports ethnomedicine, is the most effective approach. A hybrid model accords the ill the ability to choose those treatments that they think will best help.

FIGURE 17.6 An apothecary in a Nanjing hospital in China prepares a treatment grounded in traditional Chinese medicine. Contemporary medical facilities sometimes offer biomedical practice and ethnomedicine together in one setting. (credit: "Apothecary mixing traditional chinese medicine at Jiangsu Chinese Medical Hospital in Nanjing, China" by Kristoffer Trolle/flickr, CC BY 2.0)

Medical pluralism occurs when competing ethnomedical traditions coexist and form distinct health subcultures with unique beliefs, practices, and organizations. In many contemporary societies, ethnomedical systems coexist with and frequently incorporate biomedicine. Biomedicine is privileged as the dominant health care system in the United States, but in many metropolitan areas, people can also consult practitioners of Chinese medicine, Ayurvedic medicine, homeopathic medicine, chiropractic medicine, and other ethnomedicinal systems from around the world. Examples of medical pluralism are fairly common in contemporary Western society: yoga as a treatment for stress and as a form of physical and mental therapy, essential oils derived from traditional medicine to enhance health, and countless others. Contemporary cultures often fuse biomedicine and ethnomedicine rather than just choosing one or the other. However, the privilege and medical authority of biomedicine does not always afford people the right to choose, or may give them only a limited capacity to do so. Anne Fadiman's (1998) *The Spirit Catches You and You Fall Down*, which explores the conflicts between a small hospital in California and the parents of a Hmong child with epilepsy over the child's care, is a classic example of the cultural conflicts that can occur in medically pluralistic societies.

In many parts of the world, biomedicine has accompanied colonialization, and indigenous health practices have been suppressed in favor of biomedicine. Juliet McMullin's (2010) *Healthy Ancestor: Embodied Inequality and the Revitalization of Native Hawaiian Health* discusses the suppression of Hawaii's indigenous ethnomedical system as a long-lasting legacy of its colonial history. The book includes the efforts of contemporary Hawaiians to regain the healthy lifestyle of their precolonial ancestors. McMullin concludes that while contemporary biomedical health care professionals are more open to Hawaii's ethnomedical practices than their predecessors were, there is still work to be done.

17.3 Theories and Methods

LEARNING OUTCOMES

By the end of this section, you will be able to do the following:

- Discuss the importance of cross-cultural comparison and cultural relativism in study of human health.
- Explain why both objectivity and subjectivity are needed in the study of health.
- Discuss ethnographic research methods and their specific applications to the study of human health.
- Summarize the theoretical frameworks that guide medical anthropologists.

The Importance of Cultural Context

Culture is at the center of all human perspectives and shapes all that humans do. Cultural relativism is crucial to medical anthropology. There is a great degree of variety in the symptoms and conditions that cultures note as significant indicators of diminished health. How the sick are treated varies between cultures as well, including the types of treatments prescribed for a particular sickness. Cultural context matters, and health outcomes determined by culture are informed by that culture's many parts. The United States, for example, relies heavily on biomedicine, treating symptoms of mental and physical illness with medication. This prevalence is not merely an economic, social, or scientific consideration, but all three. A cultural group's political-economic context and its cultural beliefs, traditions, and values all create the broader context in which a health system exists and all impact individuals on a psychosocial level. Behaviors such as dietary choices and preferences, substance use, and activity level—frequently labeled as lifestyle risk factors—are all heavily influenced by culture and political-economic forces.

While Western cultures rely upon biomedicine, others favor ethnopharmacology and/or ritual healing. Medical anthropologists must attempt to observe and evaluate ethnomedical systems without a bias toward biomedicine. Medical anthropologists must be cautious of tendencies toward ethnocentrism. Ethnocentrism in medical anthropology takes the form of using the health system of one's own culture as a point of comparison, giving it preference when analyzing and evaluating other systems. An American anthropologist who studies ethnomedicine in the Amazon River basin must be careful to limit their bias toward a biomedical approach as much as they can. That is not to say that subjective experience and opinion need be discarded entirely, merely that bias should be acknowledged and where necessary limited. Admitting bias is the first step in combating it. Being aware of one's own ethnocentrism allows an anthropologist to analyze culture and medicine more truthfully.

Methods of Medical Anthropology

Medical anthropology is a highly intersectional subfield of anthropology. The field addresses both the biological and social dimensions of maladies and their treatments. Medical anthropologists must thus become comfortable with a wide-ranging tool kit, as diverse as health itself. Like all anthropologists, medical anthropologists rely on qualitative methods, such as ethnographic fieldwork, but they also must be able to appropriately use quantitative methods such as biometrics (including blood pressure, glucose levels, nutritional deficiencies, hormone levels, etc.) and medical statistics (such as rates of comorbidities, birth rates, mortality rates, and hospital readmission rates). Medical anthropologists can be found working in a myriad of endeavors: aiding public health initiatives, working in clinical settings, influencing health care policy, tracking the spread of a disease, or working for companies that develop medical technologies. The theories and methods of medical anthropology are invaluable to such endeavors.

Qualitative Methods

Within medical anthropology, a number of qualitative research methods are invaluable tools. Qualitative methods are hands-on, first-person approaches to research. An anthropologist in the room or on the ground writing down field notes based on what they see and recording events as they happen creates valuable data for themselves and for others.

Participant observation is a methodology in which the anthropologist makes first-person observations while participating in a culture. In medical anthropology, participant observation can take many forms. Anthropologists observe and participate in clinical interactions, shamanic rituals, public health initiatives, and faith healing. A form of participant observation, **clinical observations** allow the anthropologist to see a culture's healing practices at work. Whether a doctor is treating COVID-19 or a shaman is treating a case of soul loss, the anthropologist observes the dynamics of the treatment and in some cases actually participates as a patient or healer's apprentice. This extremely hands-on method gives the anthropologist in-depth firsthand experience with a culture's health system but also poses a risk of inviting personal bias.

Anthropologists observe a myriad of topics, from clinical interactions to shamanic rituals, public health initiatives to faith healing. They carry these firsthand observations with them into their interviews, where they inform the questions they ask. In medical anthropology, interviews can take many forms, from informal chats to highly structured conversations. An example of a highly structured interview is an illness narrative interview. **Illness narrative interviews** are discussions of a person's illness that are recorded by anthropologists. These interviews can be remarkably diverse: they can involve formal interviews or informal questioning and can be recorded, written down, or take place electronically via telephone or video conference call. The social construction of sickness and its impact on an individual's illness experience is deeply personal. Illness narratives almost always focus on the person who is ill but can at times involve their caregivers, family, and immediate network as well.

Another method commonly used in medical anthropology, **health decision-making analysis**, looks at the choices and considerations that go into deciding how to treat health issues. The anthropologist interviews the decision makers and creates a treatment decision tree, allowing for analysis of the decisions that determine what actions to take. These decisions can come from both the patient and the person providing the treatment. What religious or spiritual choices might make a person opt out of a procedure? What economic issues might they face at different parts of their illness or sickness? Health decision-making analysis is a useful tool for looking at how cultures treat sickness and health, and it highlights a culture's economic hierarchies, spiritual beliefs, material realities, and social considerations such as caste and gender.

Quantitative Methods

Quantitative methods produce numeric data that can be counted, correlated, and evaluated for statistical significance. Anthropologists utilize census data, medical research data, and social statistics. They conduct quantitative surveys, social network analysis that quantifies social relationships, and analysis of biomarkers. Analysis of census data is an easy way for medical anthropologists to understand the demographics of the population they are studying, including birth and death rates. Census data can be broken down to analyze culturally specific demographics, such as ethnicity, religion, and other qualifiers as recorded by the census takers. At times, an anthropologist may have to record this data themselves if the available data is absent or insufficient. This type of analysis is often done as a kind of background research on the group being studying, creating a broader context for more specific analysis to follow.

Also important to medical anthropologists are analyses of **medical statistics**. The study of medical records helps researchers understand who is getting treated for what sickness, determine the efficacy of specific treatments, and observe complications that arise with statistical significance, among other considerations. Analysis of census data combined with medical statistics allows doctors and other health providers, as well as medical anthropologists, to study a population and apply that data toward policy solutions. Famous examples include the World Health Organization's work on health crises such as HIV/AIDS, Ebola, and COVID-19.

Questionnaires are more personal to the anthropologist, allowing them to ask pointed questions pertinent to their particular research. Surveys make it possible for anthropologists to gather a large quantity of data that can then be used to inform the questions they ask using qualitative methods. Distribution methods for surveys vary and including means such as personally asking the questions, releasing the survey through a health care provider, or offering online surveys that participants choose to answer.

These are the most common methods used by medical anthropologists. Different theories are influential in determining which of the methods a particular research might favor. These theories inform how an anthropologist might interpret their data, how they might compose a study from beginning to end, and how they interact with the people they study. Combined with more general anthropological theory, each anthropologist must craft a composite of theory and method to create their own personalized study of the world of human health.

Theoretical Approaches to Medical Anthropology

Social Health

Biomedicine, the science-based ethnomedical system practiced in the United States, recognizes the impact physical health and mental health have on one another: when one falters, the other does as well. There is an increasing awareness in biomedicine of a third type of health, **social health**, which has long been recognized by many ethnomedical systems around the world. Each of the theoretical approaches to medical anthropology demonstrates that to develop a holistic understanding of human well-being, it is necessary to include mental, physical, and social health. Social health is driven by a complex set of sociocultural factors that impact an individual or community's wellness. At a macro level, it includes the cultural and political-economic forces shaping the health of individuals and communities. An individual's social health also includes the support a person receives from their extended social network, as well as the social pressures or stigma a person may face and the meaning that they ascribe to their experiences. Just as mental and physical health strongly influence one another, when a person's social health falters, their physical and/or mental health declines as well.

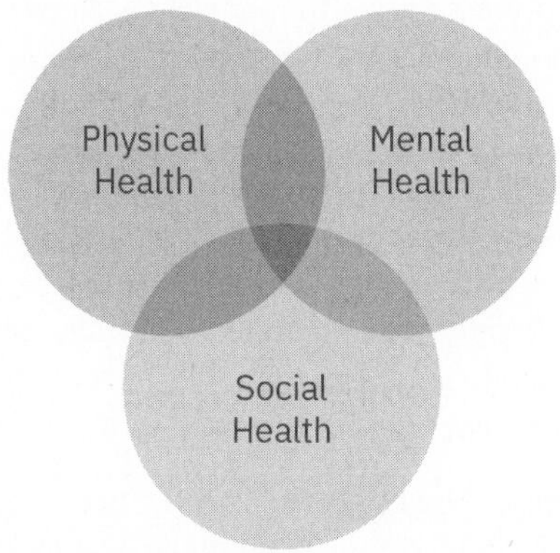

FIGURE 17.7 A person's overall health is informed by their physical health, their mental health, and their social health. When one falters, the others are affected. (credit: Copyright Rice University, OpenStax, under CC BY 4.0 license)

Physical environments—whether they are natural, constructed, or modified environments—shape cultural adaptations and behaviors. People living on islands and people living in deserts inhabit very different environments that inform their cultures and affect their biology. On the other hand, culture often affects how humans interact with their environments. People who work in offices in Los Angeles and hunter-gatherers in the Amazon River basin interact with their environments differently, relying upon very different subsistence patterns and sets of material culture. Culture also informs human biology. Eating a lot of spicy foods changes a person's biophysiology and health outcomes, as do dietary taboos such as refusing to eat pork. These dietary choices inform biology over generations as well as within a single lifetime.

The Biocultural Approach

The **biocultural approach** to anthropology acknowledges the links between culture and biology. Biology has informed human development and evolution, including the adaptations that have made culture, language, and social living possible. Culture, in turn, informs choices that can affect our biology. The biocultural approach analyzes the interaction between culture, biology, and health. It focuses on how the environment affects us, and the connections between biological adaptations and sociocultural ones. The biocultural approach draws on biometric and ethnographic data to understand how culture impacts health. The effects of environment on biology and culture are apparent in the treatment of survivors of the Fukushima Daiichi nuclear accident that occurred in 2011 in Japan. Studies regarding the genetic health of survivors focus on the combination of environmental damage and social stigma in Japan due to their potential exposure to radiation.

Symbolic Approach

Other theoretical approaches ask different types of questions. What does it mean to be a patient? What are the social expectations for the behaviors of a person diagnosed as suffering from a particular sickness? Why is it symbolically meaningful for a treatment to be prescribed by a medical doctor? These are questions typically asked by those utilizing a **symbolic approach** to medical anthropology. The symbolic approach focuses on the symbolic thinking and beliefs of a culture and how those beliefs affect social and especially health outcomes.

A person's beliefs affect how they perceive treatments and how they experience illness. The most obvious example of the symbolic approach at work is the **placebo effect**. If a person believes that a treatment will be effective, this belief will affect their health outcome. Often in medical trials, people who believe they are receiving a treatment but are in fact receiving a placebo, such as a sugar pill, will demonstrate physiological responses similar to those receiving an active substance. Accounting for the placebo effect is an important consideration for all medical studies. The opposite of the placebo effect, the nocebo effect, occurs when a person believes they are not receiving an effective medicine or that a treatment is harmful. Common to both phenomena is the importance of meaning-centered responses to health outcomes. One of the most potent examples of this is **voodoo death**, when psychosomatic effects—that is, physical effects created by social, cultural, and behavioral factors—such as fear brought on by culture and environment cause sudden death. Related to the symbolic approach of medical anthropology is the **symbolic interaction approach** to health utilized by medical sociologists. Both approaches recognize that health and illness are socially constructed concepts. The symbolic interaction approach to health focuses on the roles of the patient, caregiver, and health care provider and the interactions that take place between people occupying these roles.

Medical Ecology

Another major medical anthropology theory is **medical ecology**. Pioneered by Paul Baker and based on his work in the Andes and American Samoa in the 1960s and 1970s, medical ecology is a multidisciplinary approach that studies the effects of environment on health outcomes. Examples of these environmental influences include food sources, environmental disasters and damage, and how environmentally informed lifestyles affect health. Whereas the biocultural approach looks at the intersection of biology and culture, medical ecology focuses instead on how environment informs both health and the culture surrounding it.

A popular example of these connections can be observed in what are termed **Blue Zones**, certain locations around the world where a significant number of people regularly live exceptionally long lives, many over a century. These communities can be found in the United States, Japan, Columbia, Italy, and Greece. Common links between people who live in these places include a high-vegetable, low-animal-product diet (eggs and fish are the exception), a lively social life and regular activity, and a strong sense of cultural identity.

A negative example of the links between environment and health can be viewed in the Flint, Michigan, water crisis. In this case, pollution of the city water system negatively affected health outcomes due to high exposure to lead and Legionnaires' disease. Studies, including a long-term study by the National Institutes of Health, confirm that the water, central to the larger environment of Flint, negatively affected citizens of all ages, with particular harm caused to children and the elderly.

FIGURE 17.8 Okinawa is classified as a Blue Zone, indicating that there is a high concentration of people near or over 100 years old living there. The long lives of Okinawans demonstrate the contributions of diet and lifestyle to health. (Credit: "Sata angagi" by Hajime NAKANO/flickr, CC BY 2.0)

Cultural Systems Model

Culture is a chief consideration in another theory, the **cultural systems model**. Cross-cultural comparison is a core methodology for anthropology at large, and the cultural systems model is ideal for cross-cultural comparison of health systems and health outcomes. Cultures are made of various systems, which are informed by sociocultural, political-economic, and historical considerations. These systems can include health care systems, religious institutions and spiritual entities, economic organizations, and political and cultural groupings, among many others. Different cultures prioritize different systems and place greater or less value on different aspects of their culture and society. The cultural systems model analyzes the ways in which different cultures give preference to certain types of medical knowledge over others. And, using the cultural systems model, different cultures can be compared to one another.

An example of the cultural systems model at work is Tsipy Ivry's *Embodying Culture: Pregnancy in Japan and Israel* (2009), which examines pregnancy and birth in Israel and Japan. A particular focus is how state-controlled regulation of pregnancy and cultural attitudes about pregnancy affect women differently in each society. Despite both societies having socialized medicine, each prioritizes the treatment of pregnant women and the infant differently.

In the Israeli cultural model for pregnancy, life begins at a child's first breath, which is when a woman becomes a mother. Ivry describes a cultural model that is deeply impacted by anxiety regarding fetal medical conditions that are deemed outside the mother's and doctor's control. As every pregnancy is treated as high risk, personhood and attachment are delayed until birth. The state of Israel is concerned with creating a safe and healthy gene pool and seeks to eliminate genes that may be harmful to offspring; thus, the national health care system pressures women to undergo extensive diagnostic testing and terminate pregnancies that pass on genes that are linked to disorders like Tay-Sachs disease.

Japan, facing decreasing birthrates, pressures women to maximize health outcomes and forgo their own desires for the sake of the national birth rate. The cultural model for pregnancy in Japan emphasizes the importance of the mother's body as a fetal environment. From conception, it is a mother's responsibility to create a perfect environment for her child to grow. Mothers closely monitor their bodies, food intake, weight gain, and stressful interactions. In Japan, working during pregnancy is strongly discouraged. Ivry noted that many women even quit work in preparation for becoming pregnant, whereas in Israel mothers work right up to delivery.

The cultural systems model also allows medical anthropologists to study how medical systems evolve when they come into contact with different cultures. An examination of the treatment of mental illness is a good way of highlighting this. While in the United States mental illness is treated with clinical therapy and pharmaceutical drugs, other countries treat mental illness differently. In Thailand, schizophrenia and gender dysmorphia are understood in the framework of culture. Instead of stigmatizing these conditions as illnesses, they are understood as gifts that serve much-needed roles in society. Conversely, in Japan, where psychological diagnoses have become mainstream in the last few decades and pharmaceutical treatment is more prominent than it once was, psychological treatment is stigmatized. Junko Kitanaka's work on depression in Japan highlights how people with depression are expected to suffer privately and in silence. She links this socially enforced silence to Japan's high stress rates and high suicide rates (2015). The cultural systems model offers an effective way to evaluate these three approaches toward mental illness, giving a basis of comparison between the United States, Thailand, and Japan. Assigning ethnomedicine the same value as biomedicine rather than giving one primacy over the other, this important comparative model is central to the theoretical outlook of many medical anthropologists.

FIGURE 17.9 A sign outside of Aokigahara Forest asks people to reconsider taking their own lives. This public health initiative targets the cultural tradition of people dying by suicide in the Aokigahara Forest. (Credit: "Aokigahara (suicide forest) + very tired Liz" by Liz Mc/flickr, CC BY 2.0)

The cultural systems model encompasses a myriad of cross-disciplinary techniques and theories. In many cultures, certain phrases, actions, or displays, such as clothing or amulets, are recognized as communicating a level of distress to the larger community. Examples include the practices of hanging "the evil eye" in Greece and tying a yellow ribbon around an oak tree during World War II in the United States. These practices are termed **idioms of distress**, indirect ways of expressing distress within a certain cultural context. A more psychologically driven consideration is the cause of people's behaviors, known as **causal attributions**. Causal attributions focus on both personal and situational causes of unexpected behaviors. A causal attribution for unusual behavior such as wandering the streets haplessly could be spirit possession within the context of Haitian Vodou, while in the United States behaviors such as sneezing and blowing one's nose might be attributed to someone not taking care of themselves.

Causal attributions can be important to one's own illness. Anthropologist and psychiatrist Arthur Kleinman has concluded that if doctors and caregivers were to ask their patients what *they* think is wrong with them, these explanations might provide valuable information on treatment decisions. One patient might think that their epilepsy is caused by a spirit possession. Another might suggest that their developing diabetes in inevitable because of their culture and diet. These beliefs and explanations can guide a doctor to develop effective and appropriate treatments. The approach recommended by Kleinman is known as the explanatory model. The explanatory model encourages health care providers to ask probing questions of the patient to better understand their culture, their worldview, and their understanding of their own health.

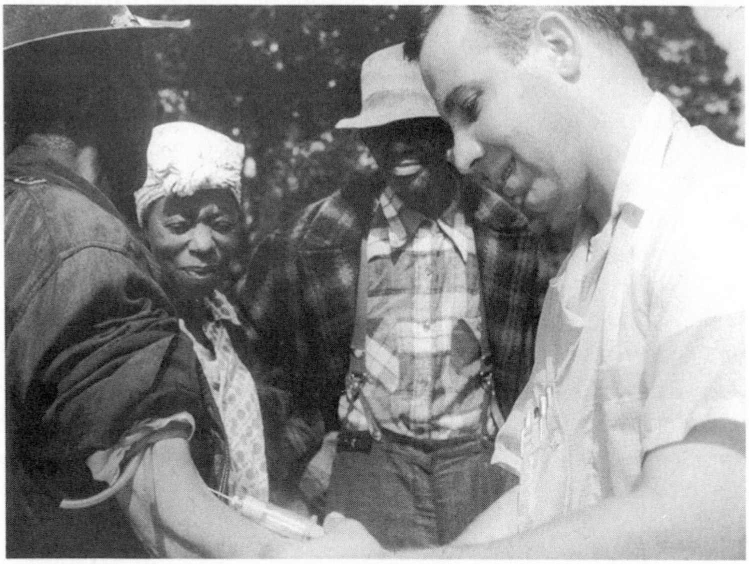

FIGURE 17.10 The Tuskegee syphilis experiment ran for 40 years, studying untreated syphilis in Black men who believed they were receiving treatment for other illnesses. (credit: National Archives Atlanta, GA (US government)/Wikimedia Commons, Public Domain)

Political Economic Medical Anthropology

Another medical anthropology approach is **critical medical anthropology (CMA)**, which is sometimes referred to as **political economic medical anthropology (PEMA)**. Critical medical anthropology has a specific interest in the inequalities of health outcomes caused by political and economic hierarchies. Critical medical anthropology advocates for community involvement and health care advocacy as ethical obligations. Defining biomedicine as capitalist medicine, this approach is critical of the social conditions that cause disease and health inequalities and of biomedicine's role in perpetuating these systemic inequalities. CMA is also interested in the medicalization of social distress, a process that has led to a wide range of social problems and life circumstances being treated as medical problems under the purview of biomedicine.

Systemic racism and **structural violence** create many negative health outcomes. Structural violence refers to the way in which social institutions, intentionally or otherwise, harm members of some groups within the larger society. Structural violence can affect things such as life expectancy, disability, or pregnancy outcomes and can lead to distrust of medical systems. The Tuskegee syphilis study, a decades-long "experiment" that studied the long-term effects of syphilis in Black men under the guise of medical treatment, is a prime example of structural violence at work within the United States medical system. Black men involved in the study were not told they had syphilis and were denied medical treatment for decades, with most dying of the disease. The government's internal mechanisms for halting unethical studies failed to stop this experiment. It was only when public awareness of what was happening resulted in an outcry against the study that the experiments were stopped.

Another area of interest to medical anthropologists working with a CMA approach is how medical systems might be inherently biased toward or against certain segments of society. The research of anthropologist Leith Mullings demonstrated a lifelong focus on structures of inequality and resistance. Her work in Ghana examined traditional medicine and religious practice through a postcolonial lens, which was critical of the colonial legacy of structural inequality she observed. Her work in the United States also focused on health inequalities, with a special interest in the intersection of race, class, and gender for Black women in urban areas. It has been documented that some doctors in the United States regularly ignore the pain of women, and this is especially true in cases where the doctor displays racial bias. This tendency has been cited in several studies, including a study in *The New England Journal of Medicine* that found that women are more likely to be misdiagnosed for coronary heart disease based on the symptoms they give and pain levels reported (Nubel 2000). Another study in the *Journal of Pain* found that women on average reported pain 20 percent more of the time than men and at a higher intensity (Ruau et al. 2012). Another example of research that takes a CMA approach is Khiara Bridges's 2011 *Reproducing Race*, which brings a critical lens to pregnancy as a site of racialization through her ethnography of a large New York City hospital. This medical racism contributes to the higher rates of African American infant and maternal mortality.

Merrill Singer has done work on the role of social inequalities in drug addiction and in cycles of violence. This work has led to his development of the concept of **sydnemics**, the social intersection of health **comorbidities**, or two health conditions that often occur together. For example, Japan's *hibakusha*, or atomic bomb survivors of Hiroshima and Nagasaki, do not live as long as Japan's normally long-lived population and are more likely to develop multiple types of cancer and other diseases tied to their exposure to nuclear radiation. In addition to these health risks, they face heavy discrimination from the larger Japanese population due to misinformation regarding nuclear radiation and radiation contamination. This discrimination carries over to the descendants of *hibakusha*, who have a higher rate of cancer than the average Japanese population despite having no detectable genetic damage from the atomic bombings. Studies are ongoing as to the cultural, economic, and genetic causes of this cancer. Syndemics is highlighted in the near-century-long struggle for numerous conditions caused by the atomic bombings to be recognized as related to the atomic bombings and thus treated by the Japanese government.

Critical theories of health are an applied method, analyzing medical systems and applying critical theory, often with the goal of improving the system or improving policy. Recommendations for improvements often come out of research but may also be the starting point of a research project, as part of a data-finding mission to highlight disparity in health outcomes. Whether it is systemic racism in biomedical treatment or power discrepancies in ethnomedical rituals, critical theories of health are a key part of exploring medicine in action and understanding real medical consequences. From birth to the grave, social inequalities shape health outcomes, life expectancy, and unnecessary human suffering. Critical medical anthropology scholarship demonstrates the social forces shaping disease and health, from drug addiction to the impacts of climate change. This work becomes a self-evident call of action. It is medical anthropology in action.

PROFILES IN ANTHROPOLOGY

Angela Garcia
1971-

Personal History: Angela Garcia (https://openstax.org/r/stanford.edu) comes from a small town along the Mexican border with New Mexico. She credits her background and upbringing with inspiring much of her later work in anthropology. Her early experiences have led her to focus on places where political and cultural spheres combine, resulting in inequality and violence. Within this framework, she has focused on medicine, postcolonial theory, and feminism. She first attended the University of California, Berkeley, and then earned a PhD from Harvard University in 2007, shortly thereafter publishing her first book, *The Pastoral Clinic: Addiction and Dispossession along the Rio Grande.*

Area of Anthropology: medical anthropology, feminist anthropology

Accomplishments in the Field: *The Pastoral Clinic* analyzes heroin addiction among Hispanic populations in New Mexico's Rio Grande region. Garcia's work focuses on the political and social realities that contribute to addiction and treatment, with dispossession as a central theme. The degradation of the surrounding environment and the economic decline of the Great Recession have been important factors in determining people's life choices. Also influential has been a political reality that denies many participation or power. Garcia describes addiction as a recurring reality in the lives of many, leading them in and out of rehab in an endless cycle. Garcia also describes the damaging effects of addiction on relationships within families and communities.

Garcia joined the Department of Anthropology at Stanford University in 2016. Her work has shifted to Mexico City, where she studies coercive rehabilitation centers run by the poor. She is particularly interested in political and criminal violence and in how informal centers like these exemplify the political and social climate within the larger Mexican nation. As much as these centers embody these realities, they also try to shift power away from pathways that lead to and encourage violence. In addition to this work, Garcia has also started examining addiction and mental illness in both Mexico and the United States Latinx (Latina/o) population.

Importance of Their Work: Garcia publishes and presents frequently in preparation for books she is currently writing. Her work is crucial to understanding dispossession and power dynamics within the United States and Mexico, including how immigration and migration affect access to health care and shape identity.

17.4 Applied Medical Anthropology

LEARNING OUTCOMES

By the end of this section, you will be able to do the following:

- Briefly explain how the biological processes of evolution and genetics impact human health and wellness.
- Describe how human migration, social behavior, and cultural values impact gene flow, genetic drift, sexual selection, and human reproduction.
- Define neuroanthropology.
- Provide two examples of culture-bound syndromes.
- Describe various ways in which political and economic forces impact health outcomes.
- Explain how globalization has increased the flow of pathogens and introduced new diseases and viruses.

FIGURE 17.11 Members of the Breathe Project, including anthropologist Ruth Fauman-Fichman (behind the speaker), protest the pollution caused by a decrepit steel mill near Pittsburgh, Pennsylvania. (credit: "US-Steel-Air-Pollution-1100712" Mark Dixon/flickr, CC BY 2.0)

Anthropology is an adaptable field of study. Its principles, theories, and methods can easily be applied to real-world problem-solving in diverse settings. Medical anthropology is designed to be applied to the critical study and improved practice of medicine. Medical anthropology has been employed in corporate settings, has been used by doctors who want to reduce ethnocentrism or apply a holistic approach to medical research and medical education, and has informed the work of academics who want to effect policy changes. The following are but a few examples of applied medical anthropologists working to create change in the real world.

Evolutionary Medicine and Health

A final theoretical approach to medical anthropology, emerging from biological anthropology, is **evolutionary medicine**. Evolutionary medicine sits at the intersection of evolutionary biology and human health, using the framework of evolution and evolutionary theory to understand human health. Evolutionary medicine asks why human health evolved the way it did, how environments affect health, and how we continue to affect our health through a number of factors including migration, nutrition, and epigenetics.

The story of human evolution is the story of gene flow and human migration. Each individual human carries specific gene combinations, and each human population carries with it a common set of genes. When people migrate, they bring those genes with them. If they have children, they pass those genes on in new combinations. Culture impacts population genetics in two ways: migration patterns and culturally defined rules of sexual selection impact the frequency of gene alleles, and thus genetic variation, in a human population. These genes often affect health outcomes, such as the likelihood of developing certain types of cancer or immunity to specific pathogens through exposure. The more frequently a human population interacts with other populations through migration, trade, and other forms of cultural exchange, the more likely it is that genetic material from one population will be introduced to the other. The current level of globalization makes it possible for genes to flow from one corner of the globe to another.

Moving into a new culture, whether forced or voluntary, requires adaptation. Adapting one's culture to new rules, new norms, and new expectations, as well as adapting one's identity to being a minority or facing oppression or prejudice, can affect the health of the migration population. An obvious example of this is the effects of slavery on Africans brought to the Americas. This impact is shown not just on their genetics, discussed elsewhere in this chapter, but also in their cultures. Syncretized religions like Haitian Vodou, Candomblé, and other African-inspired religions show the ways in which African populations adapted their beliefs to survive contact with oppression and cruelty, evolving and sanitizing certain elements while embracing others.

Populations that are physically isolated for long periods of time might experience negative effects from genetic drift as the frequency of rare alleles increases over time. Similarly, cultural groups that practice strict endogamy can experience negative effects from genetic drift. In isolation, populations can sometimes see a rise in the frequency of maladaptive gene variants, as in the case of Tay-Sachs disease found in ethnic minority populations that practice endogamy, such as Ashkenazi Jews or French Canadians. Among these populations, which have been relatively isolated from the populations around them, the genes that cause Tay-Sachs have become more common than in other populations. This suggests that isolation and segregation can result in unhealthy changes in a population's gene pool.

Another example of evolutionary medicine is the study of the effects of the development of agriculture and the growth of urbanization on human health. The development of agriculture caused human health to change in many ways. Food became more regularly available, but diet became less varied and the amount of work required to procure the food increased. The regular movement associated with a gathering and hunting lifestyle resulted in robust overall fitness, but people were also at a greater danger of succumbing to a fatal accident before reaching the age at which they successfully reproduced. Our current lifestyle, in which many sit behind a desk for eight hours a day, five days a week, damages our spines and overall health. While food availability in Western nations is second to none, people living in those societies struggle with health problems related to being overweight and underactive. Each lifestyle has its trade-offs, and evolution has, over the past ten thousand years, affected both modern and neolithic humans differently. Through evolutionary health, we can track these changes and their adaptations.

With human migration and the concentration of human populations in urban areas, disease has grown exponentially. Pathogens can now spread like wildfire across the world. In the past, disease has had a devastating effect on human populations. As just one example, the Black Death killed over a third of Europe's population, spreading via Silk Road merchants and the conquests of the Mongol Empire. Today we see yearly flare-ups of influenza and Ebola and are still dealing with the devastating effects of the COVID-19 pandemic that caused nations to close borders and people within nations to limit social contact with one another. Globalization not only makes it possible for pathogens and pandemics to spread, but also allows nations to cooperatively distribute vaccines and coordinate methods to contain viruses. Nations can now share medical data to help develop treatments and help one another in efforts to isolate and quarantine the sick and infected. On the other hand, international cooperation can hamper local response and prevent cities, provinces, states, and nations from acting in their own best interest.

FIGURE 17.12 World Health Organization (WHO) workers gear up to enter an Ebola ward in Lagos during the 2013–2016 Ebola pandemic. (Credit: Bryan Christensen/CDC Global/Wikimedia Commons, CC BY 2.0)

At the heart of each of these areas of study is **epigenetics**, or the change of the expression of a gene during a single human lifetime. Often prompted by environmental exposure and mutations over a lifetime, epigenetic shifts are heritable changes in a person's DNA that are phenotypical, meaning that they are linked to outwardly expressed traits. For example, studies show that people exposed to smoking in childhood tend to be shorter in adulthood. Similarly, trauma can stunt growth or increase the likelihood of developing specific maladaptations. The development of sickle cell anemia in the African American community has been linked to epigenetic adaptation to slavery in the United States, according to a 2016 study by Juliana Lindenau et al. This and other studies suggest that trauma can be inherited and can last generations. Epigenetics show evolution at work in real time, affecting both individuals and future generations.

Culture and the Brain

The human brain is a fascinating research topic, both medically and culturally. Different cultures conceptualize the brain, its functions, and its health differently. Biomedicine and ethnomedicine systems view human physiology in distinct ways, and these two systems typically have very different explanatory models for understanding the brain and its role in psychology and neurology. Anthropologists are interested in both of these explanatory models and the ways they influence treatment. Some topics of particular interest to medical anthropologists include how psychology affects biology and health, the stigma of mental health across cultures, addiction, culture-bound syndromes, and experiences and illnesses related to stress. Daniel Lende and Greg Downey brought together these topics under the heading of neuroanthropology (https://openstax.org/r/neuroanthropology), an emerging specialty that examines the relationship between culture and the brain.

As highlighted during the discussion of the cultural systems model, the acceptance of psychology is highly variable by culture. Societies that rely upon biomedicine are more apt to embrace psychological approaches to mental health problems. Encouraging other cultures to apply psychology and psychiatry sometimes requires an anthropologist's touch. One challenge for a medical anthropologist is convincing people who do not believe in mental health challenges that acknowledging and treating mental health issues is a better approach than ignoring them. India's slow but eventual acceptance of psychology is described by Rebecca Clay in a 2002 article. In this case, psychology was gradually normalized and accepted through a combination of Indian medical theory and psychological treatments and diagnoses. This culturally based path toward normalization indicates the need for cultural understanding and a nuanced approach by medical anthropologists.

Culturally specific nuance is especially important in understanding what anthropologists call culture-bound syndromes. Culture-bound syndromes refer to unique ways in which a particular culture conceptualizes the manifestations of mental illness, whether as physical and/or social symptoms. The condition is a "cultural syndrome" in that it is not a biologically based disease identified among other populations.

A prominent example is **susto**, a syndrome in Latino societies of the Americas. First documented by Rubel, O'Nell, and Collado-Ardon (1991), susto is stress, panic, or fear caused by bearing witness to traumatic experiences happening to other people around you. Originating with Indigenous groups in the Americas, this panic attack–like illness was seen as a spiritual attack on people and has a number of symptoms ranging from nervousness and depression to anorexia and fever. Cultural syndromes are not limited to non-Western societies, however. According to anthropologist Caroline Giles Banks (1992), **anorexia nervosa**, an eating disorder where the person does not eat in order to stay thin in accordance with the beauty standards in the United States and Europe, is a prime example of a culture-bound syndrome. Only in these cultures, with specific pressures on weight and beauty applied to women and men, does anorexia nervosa appear. But as these beauty standards spread with globalization and the spread of media from these cultures, so does the disease. Cultural syndromes are not restricted to cultures that prefer biomedicine or ethnomedicine: they are as diverse as human culture itself.

A related concept gaining ground in psychology is known as **cultural concepts of distress**, or CCD. These concepts, according to the Diagnostic and Statistical Manual of Mental Disorders (DSM) 5, "refer to ways that cultural groups experience, understand, and communicate suffering, behavioral problems, or troubling thoughts and emotions" (American Psychiatric Association 2013). In sum, CCD is used to describe how a culture explains and conceptualizes the unique manifestation of mental illness as physical and/or social symptoms.

The **psychobiological dynamic of health**—the measurable effect of human psychology on physical health—is a primary tool used by medical anthropologists to study health. The psychobiological dynamic of health helps anthropologists evaluate the efficacy of health-related treatments that may not accord with those used in their home culture. For example, ritual healing has real measurable effects on people, both the patient and those in attendance during the ritual, as long as they believe that the ritual has healing power. Similarly, for those who share a cultural belief in the power of such practices, being prayed over by a priest or blessed with holy water can offer effective healing power. Psychological belief grants healing efficacy. The same principle applies to biomedicine, as illustrated by the placebo/nocebo effect. Of course, belief alone cannot entirely negate the harmful or helpful effects of medicine or any other substance.

Another area in which psychology and health intersect is the experience and effects of stress, a human universal. Indeed, it is well established that mental stress can make someone physically sick. The work of anthropologist Robert Sapolsky (2004) analyzes the evolution of the human body to adapt to, use, and heal from stress. His analysis suggests that stress pushes humans to both physical and mental limits, that these limits differ in different humans, and that being pushed up against limits due to stress can result in growth. The human ability to adapt to stress is a difference from other primate species, and it likely developed over millions of years of evolution. While human bodies have evolved with stress and have sometimes grown as a result of stress, we were not evolved to withstand chronic stress over extended periods of time. Chronic stress induces a high rate of stress-related diseases, such as heart disease, indicating the limits of even evolution to adapt to long-term stressors.

Addiction is another area in which medical anthropologists have done significant work, analyzing how culture and biology contribute to addiction. Addiction comes in many forms and affects multiple measures of health. Medical anthropologist Angela Garcia tackles addiction in her book *The Pastoral Clinic: Addiction and Dispossession along the Rio Grande* (2010), which explores the intersection of race, class, immigration status, and dispossession with drug addiction and the ability to treat it. Focusing on a small town on the Rio Grande and specifically a clinic within that town meant to treat addiction, she tracks the trajectory of a number of patients and the factors that contributed to their addiction. Her analysis highlights the status of these patient as immigrants, minorities, and outsiders, which prevent reentry into society for many. Similarly, João Biehl's work *Vita: Life in a Zone of Social Abandonment* (2103) analyzes the effects of dispossession and homelessness on social health, looking specifically at the role of drugs in the highlighted zone. His exploration of *vita*, a place where people are "left to die" when their addiction or mental illness becomes too much of a burden, shows the cultural effects of mental health and addiction on Brazilian society and the struggles of the individuals abandoned there. In both works, the role of drugs is highlighted, exploring how cultures symbolically characterize problematic drug use and addiction and attach a stigma to admitting a problem and seeking treatment. The works also explore how drugs are justified and understood, illustrating both how drugs change the biochemistry of the brain and how the human mind characterizes the drugs, each shaping one another.

Reproduction

Reproductive health is another area in which medical anthropologists have made significant contributions by applying their knowledge and methods to real medical practices. Medical anthropologists have studied reproduction in many cultures, analyzing the practices, beliefs, and treatment of those who are pregnant, their children, and their supporting network. Another area of interest has been the ritualization of pregnancy. Robbie Davis Floyd (2004) has done work on birth as a rite of passage and the role of the midwife in modern birth practices around the world, with a focus on medicalized birth in the United States. Her work highlights ways in which the experience of birth is made more complicated by policy. Midwives are shown to decrease the chances of complications in births, yet in many places they are denied a role in the birthing process. Regardless of patient preference and the documented success of midwives, in most settings in the United States doctors and medical professionals are given preference over midwives. Floyd argues that this preference sometimes puts the patient at risk. In the Western biomedical system, doctors are preferred and imbued with **authoritative knowledge**, which is a sense of legitimacy or perceived authenticity.

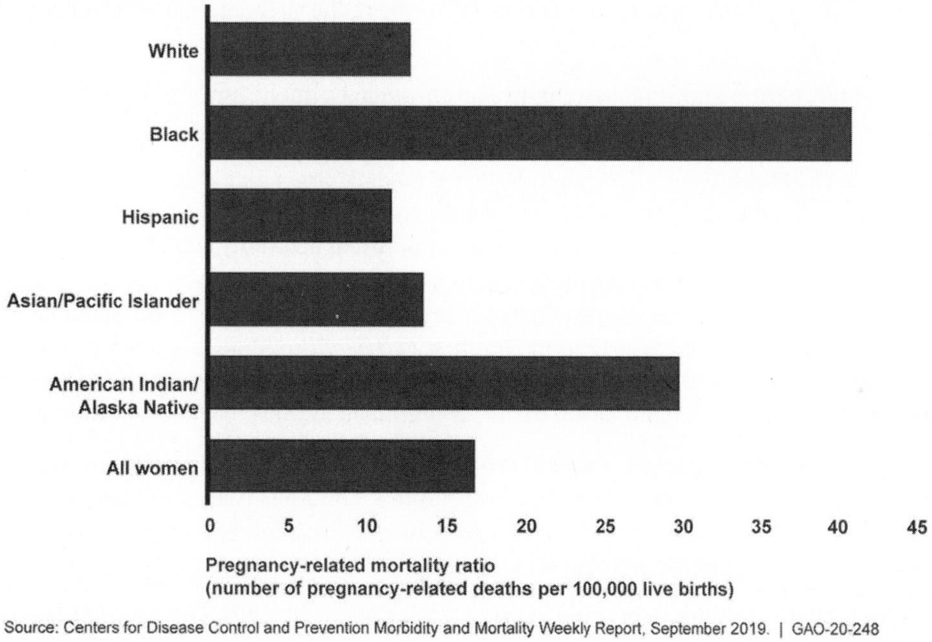

FIGURE 17.13 Women of color are much more likely to die in childbirth, according to a 2019 study by the CDC. This disparity is a central focus of the research of Dána-Ain Davis. (credit: "Figure 1: Pregnancy-Related Deaths per 100,000 Live Births by Racial/Ethnic Group, 2007-2016" by US Government Accountability Office (GAO)/flickr, Public Domain)

The work of Dána-Ain Davis (2019) on medical racism and inequalities in the health care system shows structural violence at work. Based on analysis of statistics and vivid ethnographic examples, Davis found that women of color experienced significantly higher rates of complications, including higher death rates for both mothers and infants, than White mothers and babies. Davis concludes that cultural bias and systemic racism are woven into the US health care system. These are often unacknowledged biases, unrecognized by those perpetrating them in the medical profession. Davis advocates for better policy to address these inequalities and help mothers maintain control over their bodies and the birthing process.

PROFILES IN ANTHROPOLOGY

Dána-Ain Davis
1958-

Personal History: Born in New York City, Dána-Ain Davis (https://openstax.org/r/danaaindavis) earned her PhD from City University of New York. Her work focuses on poverty, policy, and feminism, with a specific interest in urban areas of the United States. She is currently a professor of anthropology at Queens College (part of the City University of New York system). In addition to her teaching, she promotes change in policy and society through activism and her work in numerous political communities.

Before enrolling in college, Davis worked widely in publishing, broadcasting, and nonprofit work. She has worked for the *Village Voice* newspaper, the YWCA, the Village Center for Women, and Bronx AIDS Service. This work grounded her deeply in her community and the issues facing women, and in particular Black women in urban communities such as hers. These skills would aid her as she earned her PhD and began publishing her academic work.

She is the editor of *Feminist Anthropology*, a new journal focused on feminist anthropological work; sits on the editorial boards for *Cultural Anthropology* and *Women's' Studies Quarterly*; and in the fall of 2021 became the chair of her department.

Area of Anthropology: cultural anthropology, medical anthropology, public anthropology, feminist anthropology, urban anthropology

Accomplishments in the Field: Davis's first book, *Battered Black Women and Welfare Reform: Between a Rock and a Hard Place*, was published in 2006 and focuses on the intersection of gender, race, and economic realities. The book also features her work with the theory of **political economy**, which looks at how economic conditions, law, and policy affect wealth distribution across groups, in this case how economic conditions disadvantage Black women. Davis then worked on two edited volumes focused on feminism and gender, entitled *Black Genders and Sexualities* (2012) and *Feminist Activist Ethnography: Counterpoints to Neoliberalism in North America* (2013), before publishing *Feminist Ethnography: Thinking through Methodologies, Challenges, and Possibilities* (2016) about feminism anthropology and ethnographic work.

Davis's next work, *Reproductive Injustice: Racism, Pregnancy, and Premature Birth* (2019) fits more squarely into the realm of medical anthropology. This work examines the numerous issues that face women of color in regard to pregnancy and birth. Like her previous work, her latest book intersects with activism, aiming to improve medical and social justice for mothers and children.

Importance of Their Work: Activism sits at the heart of Davis's work, which has won numerous awards for promoting justice and change. Her academic and activist work has helped inform new policy changes at the local, state, and national levels. Her work informs continuing work in urban studies, feminist theory and practice, reproductive health for women of color, and welfare reform.

The Inequalities of Health

Attempting to address the inequalities of health care is a primary application of the work of critical medical anthropologists. Inequalities are apparent in relation to COVID-19, the global pandemic that has left no corner of the world untouched. A number of agencies in the United States, including the National Institutes of Health and the American Civil Liberties Union, have determined that Black and Latinx populations have been most negatively affected by the virus, both in health outcomes and overall deaths per capita relative to their portion of the population. Several states have emphasized the need to ignore personal safety for the sake of economic "health," essentially stating a willingness to sacrifice workers so their economic prospects do not falter. Meanwhile, people working on the front lines faced what is tantamount to class violence, as they could not afford to stay safely at home and social distance; indeed, it can be argued that later this class violence still applied, as the divide between remote working and those forced to work on-site created a stark contrast. The health of "essential workers" is put at risk. Aside from health care professionals, the category frequently falls along class lines, with the majority of "essential workers" employed in the service industry, in factories, or making deliveries. Economic inequalities and lack of access to health care providers both play a role in these trends. Similarly, the World Health Organization has highlighted how poorer countries have had their access to the many forms of COVID-19 treatment and prevention restricted by the demands of richer countries like the United States and Australia.

Another area in which medical anthropologists have documented health-related inequalities in the United States is access to nutritious foods. It has been well established that poor access to foods, particularly highly nutritious, diverse foods, can negatively affect health. People who live in food deserts, which are areas lacking access to good food, are more likely to develop debilitating illnesses and suffer from a basic lack of nutrition in several major fields. Amplifying the effect of food deserts is that these same areas often also lack access to health care services.

AIDS has provided a multigenerational study of the inequalities of health. At the beginning of the AIDS pandemic in the 1980s, the poorly understood disease was stated to be a "gay man's virus" because it seemed to only affect gay and bisexual men. Medical anthropologists began studying the AIDS virus as early as 1983, with Norman Spencer notably studying cases in San Francisco. As the virus spread to other populations, research became more common and well-funded, receiving state support in some cases. Yet between poor and late funding and the spread of misinformation that took decades to reverse, AIDS devastated populations around the world. Medical anthropologist Brodie Ramin (2007) has applied anthropological knowledge and methods to AIDS treatment in Africa, utilizing cultural understanding to develop more effective methods of medical treatment and enhance public trust in these treatment methods.

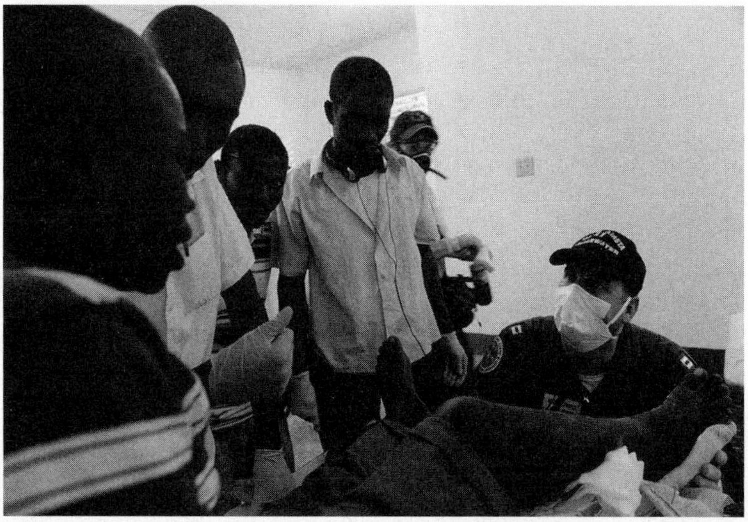

FIGURE 17.14 Partners in Health began treating HIV in Haiti at a time when world governments largely ignored it. Here, they offer help during the 2010 Haitian earthquake. (credit: "CG Officer works with Interpreter to Help Haitians" by Petty Officer 2nd Class Etta Smith/USCG Press/flickr, CC BY 2.0)

Even today, AIDS is highly stigmatized and poorly treated in many places in the world. For over two decades now, Paul Farmer and Jim Yong Kim, both anthropologists and medical doctors, have worked with their organization, Partners in Health, to provide better health outcomes and access to poor, remote parts of the world. Their work has been instrumental in helping treat AIDS and other diseases in places such as Haiti. Jim Yong Kim used his role in the World Bank Group to help create better outcomes as well. Medical anthropology has the power to shape policy at the highest level of global health institutions, but it has much to overcome. Medical anthropologists are well aware of the severity of the problems of structural violence, systemic racism, and massive health inequalities around the world.

The COVID-19 pandemic changed many aspects of many cultures, affecting people's professional, educational, and personal lives. Medical anthropologists Vincanne Adams and Alex Nading have already begun to analyze the social impact of COVID-19: "The pandemic continues to precipitate simultaneous dread over what is to come and loss over what appears to be gone forever, including loved ones, ways of life, and conceptual and literal safety nets" (2020). The COVID-19 pandemic has illustrated how deeply intertwined health and culture can be. Elisa J. Sobo's work on the anti-vaccine movement in 2016 is now freshly relevant, as some people fear and mistrust both the COVID vaccine and the health measures to slow or prevent the spread of the virus proposed by nonprofits and governments. Adams and Nading build upon Sobo's research, exploring the central role of belief and culture in the development of policy at the local, state, national, and international levels during the COVID-19 pandemic.

The COVID-19 pandemic has illustrated how deeply intertwined health and culture can be. Medical anthropology has a lot to offer public health and health care professionals. Incorporating medical anthropology and cultural competence into the training of health care professionals is a proactive step to begin addressing medical racism and the inequalities of health documented by medical anthropologists. It also gives health care professionals insight into the relationship between social health and physical and mental health priorities. The work of medical anthropologists on nutrition, reproduction, and infectious disease has significant implications for health care and public policy. Finally, understanding the wealth of cultural traditions and ethnomedical systems provides a greater appreciation for the diverse ways of understanding health and managing maladies. As the COVID-19 pandemic has demonstrated, health and health care are a complex social issue with global ramifications for billions of people.

MINI-FIELDWORK ACTIVITY

Health Perspectives Project: Interviews

Part 1: Develop Interview Questions

Select a health-related topic and develop ethnographic interview questions related to it. Keep it short: three to five questions relating to the anthropological topic you wish to study. Ideally, your interview questions will be open-ended rather than yes/no questions or questions that generate one word replies.

Part 2: Interview

Select appropriate people to interview, and set up a convenient time and place to interview them. Remember your safety is a top concern; do not meet with anyone in a place where you do not feel comfortable. Ideally, if you do not know the person well, you will want a public location that still affords a degree of privacy, such as the library or a coffee shop.

Interview Field Notes

Your notes should include the following:

- When and where the interview was conducted
- Your relationship to the interviewee (if any)
- The interviewee's
    - Age
    - Gender
    - Occupation
    - Native language
    - Nationality/country of origin
- Any other details that are relevant to your interview (Example: religion, sexuality, race/ethnicity, role in family, etc. Only ask these if it seems to be relevant to your topic and questions.)

Take notes not only on what the person said, but how they said it and what you think it might mean in a broader context. Reflect on body language, emotion, tone, and emphasis whenever possible.

Include significant quotes and your reflection on the quotes' significance in the context of the interview.

Explain why and how you selected the person that you interviewed. Do you think that you had the necessary rapport to receive full and honest answers? Was your interviewee knowledgeable about the topic of your interview? What additional questions might you want to ask in the future?

Reflect on your experience and what you might do differently next time.

Resources: Explore Medical Anthropology

- Culturally Connected (https://openstax.org/r/culturallyconnected) is an excellent educational resource for health care professionals that draws heavily on medical anthropology.
- Neuroanthropology (https://openstax.org/r/neuroanthropology) is a collaborative weblog created to encourage an interdisciplinary exchange.
- Somatosphere (https://openstax.org/r/somatosphere) is an online forum for debate and discussion in medical anthropology.
- Anthrolactology (https://openstax.org/r/anthrolactology) is a podcast series on anthropology, breastfeeding, science, and society.

Key Terms

anorexia nervosa a culture-bound syndrome present in North American and European cultures, characterized by a person not eating to meet beauty standards.

authoritative knowledge authority derived from perceived legitimacy, dependent on culture.

biocultural approach the assumption that culture is informed by physical and sociocultural elements.

biomedicine health care systems rooted in European and North American scientific knowledge.

Blue Zones communities around the world with a high concentration of people near or over the age of 100.

causal attributions a psychological concept used to study regular cultural behavior and how deviation from that behavior might be explained.

clinical observations an ethnographic method resulting in a straightforward, clinical study of a medical situation.

comorbidities two or more health conditions that often occur together.

critical medical anthropology (CMA) a theory that highlights a culture's inequalities, including inequalities in health care.

critical theories of health an applied theory aimed at pointing out issues within health care systems and changing them for the better.

cultural concepts of distress (CCD) a psychological term used to describe the way a culture experiences and expresses distress.

cultural systems model a theory that that analyzes how systems within a particular culture, including health care systems, affect one's worldview and actions.

disease a biological agent that negatively affects health.

epigenetics the changes in gene expression that take place during a person's lifetime, often through environmental exposure.

ethnomedicine a culture's traditional knowledge and treatments for the management of health and illness.

evolutionary medicine a method that uses evolutionary biology and culture to better understand human health.

health a state of complete well-being.

health decision-making analysis a study of the decisions that go into a person's health choices.

idioms of distress indirect ways that members of a culture show distress.

illness a person's experience of ill health, as defined by their culture.

illness narrative interviews an ethnographic method used to collect information about an informant's illness experience in their own words.

malady a term encompassing disease, illness, and sickness.

medical ecology a multidisciplinary theory studying the effects of environment on lifestyle and health.

medical pluralism the use of both ethnomedicine and biomedicine.

medical statistics statistics regarding treatments for medical illnesses that inform an anthropologist's study, as well as medical policy and health choices.

participant observation a methodology in which the anthropologist makes first-person observations while participating in a culture.

placebo effect the effect in which belief in a treatment's efficacy creates a positive health outcome.

political economic medical anthropology (PEMA) a theory that highlights a culture's inequalities, including inequality in health care.

political economy the connection of economics and politics and how they affect wealth and inequality.

psychobiological dynamic of health the measurable effect of human psychology on human biology.

sick roles the social expectation of a person suffering from a sickness.

sickness the cause of a person's ill health that signifies to others how to treat that person socially.

social health an acknowledgement that one's social interactions and standing are an important aspect of overall health.

structural violence violence caused by political and social systems that prevent groups from taking care of themselves in multiple ways.

susto a cultural response to stress and trauma in Latinx communities.

symbolic approach a theory focusing on how a culture's symbols affect social and health outcomes.

symbolic interaction approach to health and approach that focuses on the interaction between patient and caregiver(s).

syndemics the social intersection of comorbidities

in health outcomes.

traditional ecological knowledge (TEK) traditional knowledge of one's environment applied to the treatment of maladies.

voodoo death death brought on by psychosomatic belief in cultural and environmental effects.

Summary

Medical anthropology is the application of anthropological practice and methods to medicine. It considers how culture affects medicine and health. Medical anthropologists thus try to study medicine and health within the context of the culture it comes from, which is known as ethnomedicine. The history of medical anthropology stems from numerous other branches of anthropology, including religious anthropology and the study of rituals and health. Since World War II, anthropologists have often been involved in health initiatives around the world, with numerous health practitioners using anthropological methods to increase their efficacy.

Medical anthropological theory and practice is rooted in the work of Franz Boas. Medical anthropologists utilize various methods to gather data and study a culture's dimensions of health. In participant observation, an anthropologist takes part in the culture they are studying. Ethnographic interviews ask questions of cultural informants regarding their understanding of their culture's medical practices. Similarly, in illness narrative interviews, a person who has been ill is asked to describe their experience, both of being sick and how others treated them. Another method is to examine the choices people make when seeking medical treatment, a process called a health decision-making analysis. Anthropologists also use a number of quantitative methods, focusing on medical statistics, questionnaires, and surveys.

Medical anthropology embraces a number of theories. The biocultural approach analyzes the links between culture and biology, using aspects such as environment to understand how medicine and the culture around it develops. The symbolic approach to medical anthropology looks at the world of symbols that surrounding health and medicine in a particular culture, including the placebo effect and specific cultural phenomena such as "voodoo death." Medical ecology suggests that environment affects the development of culture and thus of medicine. The cultural systems model is a theory used for cross-cultural analysis, creating a frame of reference for comparison and looking at why certain cultures prefer certain types of knowledge. Critical medical anthropology (CMA) analyzes how social inequalities in a culture affect health outcomes. Critical theories of health apply medical anthropology theory and method to medical practice with the aim of changing medical policy at multiple levels.

Medical anthropology, perhaps more than any other type of anthropology, is easily applied to other fields. Medical practitioners apply anthropological theory and methods to better understand their patients and improve their health outcomes. Evolutionary medicine studies how humans have evolved with the goal of better treating illness. This requires a fusion of biological anthropology, genetics, and globalization. Medical anthropologists also work within neuroanthropology, combining psychology, neurology, and human biology to understand and improve human physical and mental health outcomes. Reproductive health is improved with an understanding of medical anthropology, as culture is highly important to birth and childcare.

Inequalities of health are a particularly important place for the application of the work of medical anthropologists. From food deserts to the AIDS epidemic, medical anthropologists have applied their work to solving real-world problems and innovated novel solutions that could later be applied to other problems, such as the COVID-19 pandemic.

Critical Thinking Questions

1. How do anthropologists navigate cultural definitions of health, sickness, and illness?
2. How was the development of medical anthropology aided by the anthropology of religion?
3. In what ways does understanding culture help caregivers determine the best treatment for their patients?
4. Why must medical anthropologists balance objective and subjective understandings of health with regard to culture?
5. How do social inequalities influence the spread of disease and impact health outcomes?
6. How have physical isolation and cultural

traditions of endogamy impacted the frequency of inheritable diseases?
7. In what ways do human migrations affect the development of human health, historically and currently?
8. How do political and economic forces affect health outcomes around the world?

Bibliography

Adams, Vincanne, and Alex Nading. 2020. "Medical Anthropology in the Time of COVID-19." *Medical Anthropology Quarterly* 34 (4). https://anthrosource.onlinelibrary.wiley.com/doi/full/10.1111/maq.12624.

American Psychiatric Association. 2013. *Diagnostic and Statistical Manual of Mental Disorders*, 5th ed. Washington, DC: American Psychiatric Association.

Baker, Paul T., ed. 1978. *The Biology of High-Altitude Peoples*. Cambridge, UK: Cambridge University Press.

Baker, Paul T., 1986. *The Changing Samoans: Behavior and Health in Transition*. Edited by Paul T. Baker, Joel M. Hanna, and Thelma S. Baker. Oxford, UK: Oxford University Press.

Banks, Caroline Giles. 1992. "'Culture' in Culture-Bound Syndromes: The Case of Anorexia Nervosa." *Social Science and Medicine* 34 (8): 867–84.

Biehl, João. 2013. *Vita: Life in a Zone of Social Abandonment*. Berkeley, CA: University of California Press.

Boas, Franz. 1912. "Changes in the Bodily Form of Descendants of Immigrants." *American Anthropologist* 14 (3).

Bridges, Khiara. 2011. *Reproducing Race: An Ethnography of Pregnancy as a Site of Racialization*. Berkeley, CA: University of California Press.

Clay, Rebecca C. 2002. "Psychology around the World." *Monitor on Psychology* 33 (5). https://www.apa.org/monitor/may02/india.html.

Davis, Dána-Ain. 2019. *Reproductive Injustice: Racism, Pregnancy, and Premature Birth*. New York: NYU Press.

Davis-Floyd, Robbie. 2004. *Birth as an American Rite of Passage*. Berkeley, CA: University of California Press.

Douglas, Mary. (1966) 2002. *Purity and Danger: An Analysis of Concepts of Pollution and Taboo*. London and New York: Routledge & Kegan Paul.

Evan-Pritchard, E. E. 1976. *Witchcraft, Oracles, and Magic among the Azande*. Oxford, UK: Oxford University Press.

Fadiman, Anne. 1998. *The Spirit Catches You and You Fall Down*. New York: Farrar, Straus and Giroux.

Foster, George M., and Barbara Gallatin Anderson. 1978. *Medical Anthropology*. Hoboken, NJ: John Wiley & Sons.

Garcia, Angela. 2010. *The Pastoral Clinic: Addiction and Dispossession along the Rio Grande*. Berkeley, CA: University of California Press.

Hahn, Robert A., and Arthur Kleinman. 1983. "Belief as Pathogen, Belief as Medicine: 'Voodoo Death' and the 'Placebo Phenomenon' in Anthropological Perspective." *Medical Anthropology Quarterly* 14 (4): 3–19.

Houde, Nicholas. 2007. "The Six Faces of Traditional Ecological Knowledge: Challenges and Opportunities for Canadian Co-Management Arrangements." *Ecology and Society* 12 (2): 34. http://dlc.dlib.indiana.edu/dlc/bitstream/handle/10535/2639/ES-2007-2270.pdf?sequence=1&isAllowed=y.

Ivry, Tsipy. 2009. *Embodying Culture: Pregnancy in Japan and Israel*. New Brunswick, NJ: Rutgers University Press.

Jones, James H. 1993. *Bad Blood: The Tuskegee Syphilis Experiment*. New York: The Free Press.

Kidder, Tracy. 2003. *Mountains Beyond Mountains: The Quest of Dr. Paul Farmer, A Man Who Would Cure the World*. New York: Random House.

Kitanaka, Junko. 2015. "The Rebirth of Secrets and the New Care of the Self in Depressed Japan." *Current Anthropology* 56 (S12).

Kleinman, Arthur, Leon Eisenberg, and Byron Good. 1978. "Culture, Illness, and Care: Clinical Lessons from Anthropologic and Cross-Cultural Research." *Annals of Internal Medicine* 88 (2): 251–58.

Lindenau, Juliana D., Sandrine C. Wagner, Simone M. de Castro, and Mara H. Hutz. 2016. "The Effects of Old and Recent Migration Waves in the Distribution of HBB*S Globin Gene Haplotypes." *Genetics and Molecular Biology* 39 (4): 515–23.

Louis-Jean, James, Kenney Cenat, Chidinma V. Njoku, James Angelo, and Debbie Sanon. 2020. "Coronavirus (COVID-19) and Racial Disparities: a Perspective Analysis." *Journal of Racial Ethnic Health Disparities* 7 (6): 1039–45.

McMullin, Juliet. 2010. *Healthy Ancestor: Embodied Inequality and the Revitalization of Native Hawaiian Health*. Walnut Creek, CA: Left Coast Press.

Moore, ReNika. 2020. "If COVID-19 Doesn't Discriminate, Then Why Are Black People Dying at Higher Rates?" American Civil Liberties Union. April 8, 2020. https://www.aclu.org/news/racial-justice/if-covid-19-doesnt-discriminate-then-why-are-black-people-dying-at-higher-rates/.

Nubel, Elizabeth G. 2000. "Coronary Heart Disease in Women—An Ounce of Prevention." *New England Journal of Medicine* 343 (8): 572–74.

Parsons, C. D. 1984.s "Idioms of Distress: Kinship and Sickness among the People of the Kingdom of Tonga." *Cultural Medical Psychiatry* 8 (1): 71–93.

Ramin, Brodie. 2007. "Anthropology Speaks to Medicine: The Case HIV/AIDS in Africa." *McGill Journal of Medicine* 10 (2): 127–32. https://www.ncbi.nlm.nih.gov/pmc/articles/PMC2323482/.

Rivers, W. H. R. 1901. "On the Function of the Maternal Uncle in Torres Straits." *Man* 1: 171–172.

Ruau, David, Linda Y. Liu, J. David Clark, Martin S. Angst, and Atul J. Butte. 2012. "Sex Differences in Reported Pain Across 11,000 Patients Captured in Electronic Medical Records." *Journal of Pain* 13 (3): 228–34.

Rubel, Arthur J., Carl W. O'Neil, and Rolando Collada-Ardon. 1991. *Susto: A Folk Illness*. Berkeley, CA: University of California Press.

Ruckart, Perri Zeitz, Adrienne S. Ettinger, Mona Hanna-Attisha, Nicole Jones, Stephanie I. Davis, and Patrick N. Breysse. 2019. "The Flint Water Crisis: A Coordinated Public Health Emergency Response and Recovery Initiative." *Journal of Public Health Management & Practice* 25 (Suppl 1): S84–S90.

Sakata-Yanagimoto, Mamiko, Yasuhisa Yokoyama, Hideharu Muto, Naoshi Obara, Naoki Kurita, Takayasu Kato, Yuichi Hasegawa, Yasushi Miyazaki, Mineo Kurokawa, and Shigeru Chiba. 2016. "A Nationwide Survey of Co-occurrence of Malignant Lymphomas and Myelodysplastic Syndromes/Myeloproliferative Neoplasms." *Annals of Hematology* 95:829–30.

Sapolsky, Robert M. 2004. *Why Zebras Don't Get Ulcers: The Acclaimed Guide to Stress, Stress-Related Diseases, and Coping*, 3rd ed. New York: W. H. Freeman.

Sarma, Amardeo, and Anna Veronika Wendland. 2021. "Ten Years of Fukushima Disinformation." *Skeptical Inquirer* 45 (4).

Singer, Merrill, Nicola Bulled, Bayla Ostrach, and Emily Mendenhall. 2017. "Syndemics and the Biosocial Conception of Health." *The Lancet* 389 (10072): 941–50.

Sobo, Elisa J. "Theorizing (Vaccine) Refusal: Through the Looking Glass." 2016. *Cultural Anthropology* 31 (3): 342–50.

Turner, Edith, and Victor Turner. 1978. *Image and Pilgrimage in Christian Culture*. New York: Columbia University Press.

Turner, Victor. 1967. *The Forest of Symbols: Aspects of Ndembu Ritual*. Ithaca, NY: Cornell University Press.

Turner, Victor. (1969) 2017. *The Ritual Process: Structure and Anti-Structure*. London and New York: Routledge.

World Health Organization. 2020. "Constitution of the World Health Organization." *Basic Documents*, 49th ed., 1–20. https://apps.who.int/gb/bd/pdf_files/BD_49th-en.pdf#page=6.

CHAPTER 18
Human-Animal Relationship

Figure 18.1 The relationships between humans and animals form a core part of all human cultures. Here, a man in Delhi sits beside his calf on a city street. (credit: “Mahimsyat sarva bhutani (veda)” by Abdel Sinoctou/Wikimedia Commons, Public Domain)

CHAPTER OUTLINE

18.1 Humans and Animals
18.2 Animals and Subsistence
18.3 Symbolism and Meaning of Animals
18.4 Pet-Keeping
18.5 Animal Industries and the Animal Trade

INTRODUCTION Take a moment to consider your relationships with animals. Where do you interact with animals? Do you encounter them on your plate, in your home, on your walks or visits to zoos and aquariums, in your vaccines and medical procedures, in your body lotion, or in the clothing or shoes you wear? Or do you encounter them mostly in books, movies, and poems?

Human-animal scholarship is a relatively new *interdisciplinary* specialty. Interdisciplinary specialties cross individual disciplinary boundaries, drawing on perspectives and theories from multiple academic areas, most commonly anthropology, sociology, psychology, biology, philosophy/ethics, and even economics. When we consider the multiple roles that animals play in human lives, it is easy to see how this topic intersects with so many disciplines: the breeding and care of animals is associated with biology; the use of therapy dogs in human populations, such as with prisoners or those suffering from post-traumatic stress disorder (PTSD), is associated with psychology; and the ways in which different cultural groups think about and use animals is an anthropological concern. As a result, human-animal scholars take an interdisciplinary approach to preparing for and conducting their research to better understand the relationships among humans, animals, and culture.

18.1 Humans and Animals

LEARNING OUTCOMES

By the end of this section, you will be able to:

- Restate the scientific meaning of *animal*.
- Describe the human-animal continuum.
- Define multispecies ethnography.
- Identify highlights in the domestication of dogs.

The Human-Animal Continuum

Nonhuman animals are part of many facets of our lives. Many people rely on animals as part of food and subsistence systems, particularly in the areas of hunting, herding, and agriculture. Some people worship deities who are all or part animal. Many people recognize animals as symbols of clans or sports teams. For example, did your school have an animal as the mascot for its sports or debate teams? Across cultures, people love animals as pets and companions, and, as recognized by evolutionary theory, humans are connected to animals as ancestors and relatives. Animals are integral parts of the lives of humans around the world, in which they play a variety of roles. Defining an animal, however, can be complicated.

With some exceptions, an **animal** is defined in science as a multicellular organism, either vertebrate or invertebrate, that can breathe, move, ingest and excrete food and food products, and reproduce sexually. This clearly also includes the human species. Western philosophical tradition supports this inclusion. The Greek philosopher Aristotle (384–322 BCE) grouped animals as being *blooded* (e.g., humans, mammals, birds, fish), *non-blooded* (e.g., shelled animals, insects, soft-skinned sea animals), or what he called *dualizers*, with mixed characteristics (e.g., whales, who live in the sea but have live births; bats, who have four legs but fly). Aristotle classified humans as animals with the intellectual ability to reason. In 1735, Swedish botanist Carolus Linnaeus introduced his *binomial classification*, which used two terms to identify every living organism: a genus and a species designation. In his work *Systema Naturae* (1735), Linnaeus divided the living world into two large kingdoms, the *Regnum Animale* (animal kingdom) and the *Regnum Vegetabile* (plant kingdom). Like Aristotle before him, Linnaeus classified humans as animals. Today, the scientific approach to the study of the animal kingdom accepts that there is a continuum between all living animal species with grades of difference between species. However, even though humans are animals, people across cultures define themselves as separate from animals.

French anthropologist Claude Lévi-Strauss (1908–2009) argued that cultures universally define themselves in opposition to what they view as **nature**, a domain they define as outside or on the margins of human culture. Humans and human culture are typically seen as everything that is *not* nature or animal. This makes animals and nature very important concepts to human societies, because they shed light on how people think of themselves as human beings in the world. Lévi-Strauss famously said of animals that they are "good to think" (1963, 89), meaning that animals provide good ways for humans to think about *themselves*. Animals are used as symbols in all cultures, a sign of the human tendency to identify similarities and differences between ourselves and (other) animals.

In all societies, culture plays an important role in shaping how people define animals. Cultures assign various meanings to animals; they are ancestral spirits or deities, companions, work animals, wild and dangerous creatures, and even objects on display in zoos or raised in factory farms for food. Think of American culture, which both loves and dotes on dogs as members of the family and raises pigs as a food commodity. In other cultures, dogs are considered a food species. Among the North American Lakota people, dog meat is considered a medicinal food (see Meyers and Weston 2020), and in Vietnam, specially designated restaurants serve dog meat as a male aphrodisiac (Avieli 2011). To further illustrate the blurring of boundaries between categories of animals, some species of pigs, such as the potbellied pig, are kept as family pets in the United States. How do cultures designate species as being one thing and not another?

FIGURE 18.2 Potbellied pigs are kept as pets in some countries. Here, a pet pig is ready for a walk in her neighborhood. (credit: "Potbellied Pig!" by Eric Chan/flickr, CC BY 2.0)

The study of group identity is central to anthropology. Different cultures distinguish what is animal from what is human by comparing "the other" with themselves. Sometimes called *us versus them*, *we versus they*, or even *the Other*, capitalized, this binary (two-component) comparison is a human tendency observed across cultures.

It is common for cultural groups to distinguish between humans and nonhuman species and also to designate some humans as "other" and not as fully human—comparable to animals or even isolated parts of animals. In the Andes, indigenous Quechua and Aymara speakers refer to themselves as *runa*, meaning "people" or "humans." Those who do not speak their languages and do not live in the Andes are, by extension, nonhuman and are typically referred to as *q'ara*, meaning literally "naked and bare," referring to their lack of social ties and community (Zorn 1995). This distinction between those within the group and those without is common among Indigenous groups all over the world as well as within Western societies. Although the origin of the word *frogs* as an epithet (nickname) for the French is contested, it appears to have begun within France itself as a way of referring to people who lived in Paris and ate frog legs. By the late 18th century, however, *frogs* had begun to show up in English newspapers and other written sources as a pejorative, insulting term for all French people (Tidwell 1948). Not to be outdone, the French have traditionally referred to the English as *rosbifs* (roast beefs), a food common in English cuisine.

Although these examples are relatively lighthearted, there is a dark side to human-animal imagery. In a recent book, German freelance journalist Jan Mohnhaupt (2020) examines the distorted relationships that some Nazi leaders had with animals. After coming to power in Germany in 1937, the Nazi state enacted many laws against the Jewish people, among them a 1942 law that made it illegal for Jewish people to own pets, while Nazi leader Adolf Hitler doted on his dog and military commander Hermann Göring kept lions as pets. Preventing them from having companion animals was yet another way in which the Nazis sought to dehumanize Jewish people. Human-animal relationships are important to our sense of selfhood.

In this chapter, we will explore various cultures' approaches to and understandings of nonhuman animals, including both living and symbolic animals, and the diverse ways in which humans interact with and think about these "other" beings.

Multispecies Ethnography

In his essay "Why Look at Animals?," English art critic and poet John Berger writes, "To suppose that animals first entered the human imagination as meat or leather or horn is to project a 19th century attitude backwards across the millennia. Animals first entered the imagination as messengers and promises" ([1980] 1991, 4). Recent trends in anthropological scholarship attempt to interact with these messengers and understand the relationship that humans and animals share. The term **polyspecific** refers to the interactions of multiple species. The relationships shared between humans and other species began with our ancestors millions of years ago.

The specialty of human-animal studies within anthropology suggests new forms of scholarship that deliberately move away from **anthropocentrism**, which focuses on humans as if they are the only species that matters. Human-animal studies opens a window into different ways of thinking about what it means to be human. One approach within the specialty, called **multispecies ethnography**, pays careful attention to the interactions of humans and other species within their shared environment—whether those other species be plant, animal, fungal, or microbial. Multispecies ethnographies are especially focused on the study of **symbiosis**, which is a mutually beneficial relationship between species.

Researchers conducting multispecies ethnographies utilize a broad, holistic approach that takes into account questions such as where and how interactions between humans and animals occur. This approach is more complex than traditional ethnography because it requires that the researcher acknowledge both the perspectives of nonhuman actors and their roles in how we see and understand ourselves.

Cultural anthropologists and ecologists Kirill Istomin and Mark James Dwyer (2010) conducted multispecies ethnographies between two different herding populations in Russia: the Izhma Komi, who live in northeast European Russia, and the Nenets in western Siberia. The two groups live in environments that are comparable in terms of geography, average temperatures, and precipitation, and they herd the same subspecies of reindeer year-round. Yet their herding styles are completely different. The Izhma Komi divide their reindeer into two large groups: a family group consisting of non-castrated males, females, and calves, called a *kör*, and a group of castrated males used for transportation and hauling, called a *byk*. Herders accompany the two groups to two separate grazing grounds during the day and direct them back to camp at night. While foraging for food, the reindeer stay within their particular groups and do not wander away. In contrast, the Nenets allow their reindeer to freely disperse and wander during the day, only occasionally observing their general whereabouts and well-being. Unlike the Izhma Komi herds, which stay in their two large groups, the Nenets animals forage in smaller groups and reunite at night as a single herd when they return on their own to camp for protection. Unlike wild reindeer, who do not routinely live in and around human encampments, these groups have a *symbiotic relationship* with their herders. The humans get meat, some limited milk, and leather for clothing, shoes, and trade products from the reindeer, and the reindeer get protection and supplemental foods at the campsite from the herders.

Istomin and Dwyer's research notes behaviors that the reindeer have learned from their human herders, but it also addresses social learning *within* the herds. In their interviews with the researchers, both Izhma Komi and Nenets herders told stories about the difficulties they faced when introducing new, so-called unmanageable animals into the herds. These new animals had not yet learned the herding routines of the group they were joining. Some wandered off and were lost before they could adapt to the particular herd culture. Istomin and Dwyer conclude that the animals *themselves* pass along behavioral knowledge to each other across generations as offspring follow and learn from their mothers and other adult reindeer. This conclusion challenges the notion that animal behavior is solely genetic and instinctual. Expanding ethnographies to include an understanding of what animals are doing and thinking is a primary objective of multispecies ethnography.

Despite its recent emergence in anthropology as a separate specialty, the multispecies perspective has a long history. Nineteenth-century amateur anthropologist Lewis Henry Morgan's research on the North American beaver (1868), which includes material on beavers' adaptation to and interaction with humans, remains one of the most insightful and perceptive works on the species. And the research conducted in the 1930s by British anthropologist Edward Evans-Pritchard on the relationship between the Nuer people of Africa and their cattle resulted in an ethnographic account of their interdependence, both socially and economically.

More recently, cultural anthropologist Darrell Posey used a multispecies ethnographic approach in his work "Wasps, Warriors, and Fearless Men" (1981). In this case, the relationships of interest are between humans and insects. Posey's work utilizes a lens of *ethnoentomology*, exploring the relationships that the Kayapó people of central Brazil have with local insects and how these relationships shape their perception of themselves as human. Posey documents how Kayapó warriors deliberately provoke a local species of wasp to sting them, using the "secret" of the venom to become more powerful:

The warriors dance at the foot of the scaffolding and sing of the secret strength they received from the wasps to defeat the giant beetle. The women wail ceremonially in high-pitched, emotional gasps as the warriors, two-by-two, ascend the platform to strike with their bare hands the massive hive. Over and over again they strike the hive to receive the stings of the wasps until they are semi-conscious from the venomous pain.

This ceremony is one of the most important to the Kayapo: it is a re-affirmation of their humanity, a statement of their place in the universe, and a communion with the past. (172)

FIGURE 18.3 Kayapó tribespeople continue to practice their cultural traditions while fighting to protect their ancestral lands from Western encroachment. One of these traditions involves deliberately provoking wasps to sting them in order to enter a sacred state. (credit: "VI Aldeia Multiétnica no XV Encontro de Culturas Tradicionais da Chapada dos Veadeiros" by Oliver Kornblihtt/Special Secretariat of Culture of the Ministry of Citizenship/flickr, CC BY 2.0)

A Case Study: Domestication of Dogs

Humans interact with and relate to animal species that live in the wild as well as those that depend on them for their survival. Animals that are dependent on human beings are typically the result of **domestication**. Evidence suggests that early humans quickly developed a clear understanding of how selective breeding works, encouraging animals that shared preferred characteristics to mate and produce offspring. These desired traits included a calm temperament; the ability to get along with **conspecifics**, or members of one's own species; usually a smaller body so that the animal could be gathered or herded in larger numbers; and an attachment to or tolerance of humans.

FIGURE 18.4 Dogs were among the earliest domesticated animals. Here, Siberian huskies race in a dogsledding event. Across cultures, dogs have been used for pulling and hauling loads. (credit: "Frauenwald,

Hundeschlittenrennen, 6” by Rainer Lippert, edited by Ritchyblack/Wikimedia Commons, Public Domain)

The dog (*Canis lupus familiaris*) is believed to have been among the earliest animal domesticates, possibly the first. The origins of the domesticated dog are controversial. Most scientists agree that dogs originated from wolves, particularly from the subspecies *Canis lupus pallipes* (Indian wolf) and *Canis lupus lupus* (Eurasian wolf). The wide variety among dog breeds indicates that other wolf subspecies were also involved in selective breeding, making today’s dogs animal hybrids.

Wolves have various natural instincts that make them excellent candidates for domestication. They are highly social scavengers who could easily have become accustomed to human settlements and food handouts at a young age, and they have a hierarchical social structure that includes status and submission within the pack, traits that would predispose them to conforming to human direction and domination. Dogs today vary genetically by only about 0.2 percent from some of their ancestral wolf subspecies.

Historically and cross-culturally, humans benefit in many ways from their relationships with dogs:

- *Guarding and protection.* Dogs are naturally territorial and highly social; they are both biologically and behaviorally prone to be keenly aware of their physical surroundings and their group (or pack). The impulse to guard and protect is a genetic trait that was easily manipulated in the species as humans selectively bred animals that were particularly loyal to their families and attentive to their property. As part of the domestication process, humans selected for dogs who exhibited a *bark-howl* response when alerted, with the result that domesticated dogs bark when concerned or excited. Among wolves, the bark is only used as an initial alert (Yin 2002). Wolves do not call attention to themselves as dogs do.
- *Hunting.* Descended as it is from a wild predator, the domestic dog can be an excellent hunter and retriever. A trained dog offers considerable benefits to humans in the hunting of prey. Some Indigenous groups, such as the Chono of Tierra del Fuego, Argentina, trained their dogs to dive and to fish for seals. The Tahltan people of Canada used dogs on bear hunts. In czarist Russia, borzoi dogs were used to hunt for wolves.
- *Herding.* Dogs were key to the development of pastoralism, a subsistence system based on herding animals. Many pastoral societies utilized dogs as shepherds for domesticated herds of sheep, goats, cattle, and even fowl. Once trained to identify and protect its herd, a dog can be a fierce defender of and guide for animals foraging away from human settlements. Trained herding dogs can shepherd their flocks on a consistent trail without constant human surveillance. Selective breeding moderated a natural instinct in dogs referred to as *eye-stalk-chase-bite*, a sequence of steps utilized by dogs to focus on another animal when hunting. This moderated instinct enables dogs to guide and protect another species by keeping the animals rounded up and moving away from danger. While not utilized by every pastoral society, dogs are considered vital to most pastoral societies, even today (see the Ethnographic Sketch at the end of the chapter).
- *Transportation.* Historically, dogs served as beasts of burden, especially in cultures that had no larger domesticated animals such as the horse, donkey, or cow. Many Indigenous peoples used dogs to carry young children or possessions. Among North American Indigenous cultures such as the Assiniboine, Apache, and Inuit, dogs were traditionally used for transportation. Some of these groups developed specialized technology, such as the travois and the sledge, that allowed them to harness a dog to a platform loaded with items to be moved.

FIGURE 18.5 Kainai women use dog travois, constructed of two shafts lashed to a platform, to carry their possessions. This photo was taken around 1910 in what is now southern Alberta, Canada. (credit: "Kainai Women and Dog Travois" by Provincial Archives of Alberta/Wikimedia Commons, Public Domain)

- *Meat.* In some cultures, domesticated dogs offer a dependable source of meat. Some of the earliest evidence of dog eating was found at a prehistoric rock shelter site located at Hinds Cave, Texas. At the Hinds Cave site, geneticist Raul Tito and his team identified domesticated dog remains in human coprolites (fossilized feces) dating to 9260 BP. From the Preclassic through the late Postclassic period (2000 BCE–1519 CE) in what is now Mexico, various Indigenous cultures, including the Olmec, Zapotec, Aztec, and Maya, raised and consumed dogs as a source of protein (Thompson 2008), eventually developing a hairless breed of dog known today as the Xoloitzcuintli. This breed existed when the Spanish arrived in Mexico in the 16th century.

FIGURE 18.6 The Xoloitzcuintli is a hairless dog first bred in Mexico. (credit: "MX MM XOLOITZCUINTLE" Milton Martínez/Secretariat of Culture of Mexico City/flickr, CC BY 2.0)

Although dogs are primarily pets in contemporary societies, they continue to play other important roles in a wide range of human activities. As just a few examples, dogs are used as drug detectives at airports, therapy animals for a wide range of human needs, and guides and helpers for those living with physical challenges. Dogs also continue to be used as shepherds, hunting companions, and guards.

18.2 Animals and Subsistence

LEARNING OUTCOMES

By the end of this section, you will be able to:

- Describe the role empathy plays in human-animal relations.
- Identify some characteristics of the ways that Indigenous hunter-gatherers and nomadic pastoralists relate to animals.
- Discuss the relationship between Rock Cree hunters and animals.

Human-Animal Empathy in Subsistence

One of the most important relationships between humans and animals is that centered on subsistence, the means by which a group of individuals makes a living. In hunting-and-gathering and **pastoral societies**, the relationships between humans and animals are critical to human survival. Serving as meat, tools for hunting and for herding other animal species, and sources of commodities such as wool and leather, these societies' animals are central to human lives. In such societies, human relationships with animals are typically characterized by **animal empathy**, or the sense of being attuned to the feelings or experiences of other beings—in this case, animals. Elaborate beliefs and rituals surrounding human-animal interdependence are common among hunter-gatherers and pastoralists.

The research of anthropologist Pat Shipman ([2015] 2017) suggests that human empathy and alliances with animals, especially dogs, gave humans an evolutionary advantage over animals. Relying on animals for survival prompted humans to develop not only improved hunting and meat-processing tools but also a deep understanding of their prey. Humans needed to be able to discern and predict animal behaviors, including migratory patterns. By the emergence of our species, *Homo sapiens*, some 300,000 years ago, humans had evolved to have a sophisticated empathic understanding of and relationship with animals. By the Upper Paleolithic (50,000–12,000 BP), humans were leaving testimonials to their empathic relationships with animals in cave paintings.

One of the most outstanding early examples of animal art is the paintings found in the Lascaux cave in southwestern France, depicting the animals and plants that humans encountered some 17,000 years ago. These paintings were likely created over a range of years by several generations of hunters. Of the more than 6,000 images of humans, animals, and abstract signs, some 900 are animals. Animals that appear in these paintings include horses, deer, aurochs (wild cattle), bison, felines, a bird, a bear, and a rhinoceros. One black bull measures 5.6 meters (approximately 17 feet) in length. The animal is painted as if its legs are in motion. One of the felines appears to be urinating to mark its territory.

FIGURE 18.7 Paintings of various animal species appear on the walls of the Lascaux cave in southwestern France. The paintings have been dated to ca. 15,000–17,000 BCE. (credit: "6 i Lascaux_painting" by Paul Smith/flickr, CC BY 2.0)

Lascaux (https://openstax.org/r/archeologie.culture) closed to tourists in 1963 to protect the extraordinary artwork inside. Today, it has been named a UNESCO World Heritage Site by the United Nations. This means that it is legally protected by international agreement with the goal of ensuring permanent conservation and protection. Lascaux is of inestimable value for understanding our common human history.

Animal Relationships among Indigenous Hunters

Many cultures continue to rely on wild animals for subsistence today. This dependence requires the mastery of various cognitive skills, including knowledge and understanding of animal behaviors. In all cultures, much of the socialization of children is connected to skills required for subsistence. In societies that rely on hunting for survival, children learn to be especially attentive to their environments. It is also common in such societies for children to keep pets, often the young of wild animals that have been hunted, such as birds and small mammals. Many wild animals are capable of being tamed by human handling when they are young. An animal is considered **tamed** when it has learned to tolerate human proximity and interaction for considerable periods of time.

FIGURE 18.8 Young lowland Amazonian children with a pet sloth in Peru. (credit: “Bad Hair Day in the Amazon” by Kevin Rheese/flickr, CC BY 2.0)

Indigenous hunter-gatherers subsist on what their environment freely provides. They do not produce food but rather collect it. Indigenous hunters typically view animals as fellow sentient and spiritual beings with whom they must maintain a relationship of mutual respect. Commonly, they practice elaborate rituals associated with hunting, both to show respect for their prey and to increase the likelihood of success in the hunt.

In his study of Yukaghir elk and reindeer hunters in Siberia, Danish anthropologist Rane Willerslev (2004) recorded many ritualistic hunting behaviors. These included taking a sauna bath several days before the hunt to diminish the hunters’ scent; using special language (code words) to talk about the hunt, never mentioning death or hunting directly, in order to deceive or confuse the animal spirits; and “feeding” a fire with alcohol and tobacco the night before the hunt to perfume the air and *seduce* the animal spirit to desire the hunter. Even so, the hunters are never overconfident about the hunt, as they believe they risk their own identities as human beings when trying to lure an animal and its spirit. The bond between hunter and hunted in Indigenous societies is often viewed as tenuous, a relationship between equals in which the balance of power could shift in either direction. During the hunt itself, Yukaghir hunters wear wooden skis covered in elk leather so that their movements sound like the movements of an animal in snow, and they practice thinking like the elk or reindeer to lower the animals' inhibitions so that they will allow the hunters to get near. The hunters even imagine themselves speaking to the animal, trying to diminish its fears. For the Yukaghir people, the hunt can be a dangerous interaction, and so respect is necessary at all times, even after the body of the animal has been taken.

A Case Study: Rock Cree Hunters

The Asinskâwôiniwak, or Rock Cree, are an Indigenous society of hunter-gatherers living in northwestern Manitoba, Canada. In his ethnography *Grateful Prey* (1993), cultural anthropologist Robert Brightman examines the various ways in which the Rock Cree think about and interact with animals. Once a foraging society subsisting on big game hunting, fishing, and fur trapping, today the Rock Cree are primarily settled on government lands and no longer nomadic. Their relationship with animals continues to be central to their cultural identity, however, and today they hunt and trap as part of a mixed subsistence system that includes both foraging and wage labor. The Rock Cree's hunting is informed by both Indigenous principles that place high value on big game animals such as bear, moose, and caribou and the current market price for animal products such as pelts.

During his research, Brightman observed a fascinating tension between humans and animals at the core of Rock Cree hunting culture. Because animals are believed to be both spirit and body and capable of regenerating (reincarnating), killing an animal has repercussions for the hunter. If the hunter does not treat the animal's body with respect after the kill, the animal spirit will not return to the hunter:

> The animals are endlessly regenerated, and yet they are finite. I am more powerful than the animal because I kill and eat it. The animal is more powerful than I because it can elude me and cause me to starve. The animal is my benefactor and friend. The animal is my victim and adversary. The animal is different from me, and yet it is like me. (Brightman 1993, 36)

Rock Cree hunters, who may be male or female, are frequently influenced by an animal spirit called a *pawakan* that appears in their dreams. Sometimes referred to as the "master of animals" in other Indigenous societies where it is also found, the *pawakan* is the head spirit of an animal species or type. Individual animals have a different and lesser spirit. The relationship that hunters have with the *pawakan* is complex and variable and depends on the hunter's behaviors and circumstances. The *pawakan* may provide the hunter with useful information about where a prey animal can be found and can persuade a specific animal to either go near the hunter or elude them. A sorcerer can even send a *pawakan* to frighten dangerous animals away from a potential human victim.

The Rock Cree believe that an animal can be successfully hunted only if it *voluntarily* offers itself to the hunter. Through offerings of prayers, songs, and bits of food and tobacco burned in a stove or outside fire, the Rock Cree symbolically interact with their prey prior to the hunt. Once the animal is slain, the hunter makes sure that no parts of its body are wasted. To waste any part of an animal would be disrespectful and would imperil the hunter's future success. The Rock Cree have detailed procedures for butchering, cooking, and eating animals and for disposing of the bones by hanging them in trees where they cannot be violated by other predators. They believe that once the people have finished with the animal and left its bones hanging, the animal will recover its bones and regenerate back into the environment. Sometimes, hunters or trappers say they recognize an animal and that it is the "same one" that was killed before (Brightman 1993, 119).

This study of the Rock Cree illustrates the intense and complex relationships that can exist between humans and wild animals. Many of these same kinds of relationships between hunters and animals also exist among the Netsilik people and other hunting populations. Indigenous hunter-gatherers have a fundamentally different view of their relationships with animals and of their own place in the world than do pastoralists or people living in industrial societies. This traditional wisdom and interconnected way of being in the environment is a valuable part of our shared human cultural heritage.

Animal Relationships among Nomadic and Transhumant Pastoralists

Like hunter-gatherers, pastoralists also have empathic relationships with animals, but the nature of those relationships is different. Pastoralism, which is subsistence based on herding animals, can be either nomadic or transhumant. **Nomadic pastoralism** is herding based on the availability of resources and involves unpredictable movements, as herders decide from day to day where they will go next. **Transhumant pastoralists** have patterned movements from one location to another.

The Izhma Komi and Nenets herders in Russia, discussed earlier in the chapter in the section on multispecies ethnography, practice nomadic pastoralism. While the relationship between nomadic pastoralists and their animals is based on respect and empathy, just as with hunter-gatherers, nomadic pastoralists are more involved in the daily lives of the animals they rely on. Typically, the animals are herded into human campsites each night, and often their movements are monitored during the day. The animals are not physically dependent on humans, but the two groups are involved with each other, as herders offer supplemental food to the reindeer to reinforce their connection to the human campsites for the night. Both hunter-gatherers and nomadic pastoralists rely on their animals for meat and leather, but nomadic pastoralists might also harvest milk and use the animals as transport, two practices that require the animals to be more accustomed to human handling. The pastoral herd is more dependable as a food source than the wild animals of hunter-gatherers, but it is also more labor intensive and time consuming, requiring humans to manage the animals according to a daily routine.

FIGURE 18.9 A Sami reindeer herder in Sweden. Pastoralists such as the Sami rely on their animals for meat and leather, as well as sometimes making use of their milk and using them to transport heavy materials. (credit: "A Day at Work" by Mats Andersson/Wikimedia Commons, CC BY 2.0)

Nomadic pastoralism is not as widely practiced as transhumant pastoralism, which evolved around the time of the rise of agriculture in Europe, Asia, and Africa. Transhumant pastoralists do not typically raise crops or forage for wild plants, and they are dependent on trade with agricultural societies for vegetable products. Interestingly, while there are cultures that practice strict vegetarianism and do not consume any meat products, such as the Hindu and Jain cultures in India, humans cannot live solely on meat. Arctic hunters who had no access to vegetation in the winter ate the stomach contents of grazing animals, such as caribou, to access vegetable matter. Transhumant pastoralists typically have a tenuous and competitive relationship with agriculturalist societies, as agriculturalists may not always have sufficient surplus for trade in years when there have been droughts or warfare, for example. At times, the relationships between sedentary agriculturalists and more mobile and dependent pastoralists break down into conflict involving threats, destruction of property, and even warfare.

Transhumant pastoralism is usually built around a seasonal migration between a family's two households in different geographical areas. It normally takes days or weeks to move people and herds between the households, so pastoralists often have mobile residences, such as yurts or tents, to use during travel. As we find in nomadic pastoral societies, transhumant pastoralists rely on their animals for various trade commodities such as meat, leather, wool and wool goods (e.g., ropes and blankets), and juvenile offspring. The most common domestic herd animals of transhumant pastoralists are cattle, sheep, goats, camelids (llamas and alpacas), and yaks.

18.3 Symbolism and Meaning of Animals

LEARNING OUTCOMES

By the end of this section, you will be able to:

- Identify totemism.
- Identify the roles of animals in the oral traditions of many human cultures.
- Describe the various ways animals are used in religious practices.

When we think of animals, we usually picture them as pets, food, or wildlife, but animals play a central role in the symbolism of human lives as well. Humans relate to animals not only as tangible beings but also as images and symbols that carry personal meaning and communicate cultural norms. While we can find animal symbols almost everywhere in human cultures, they play a particularly significant role in group identity.

Totemism

Totemism is a belief system in which a subcultural group acknowledges kinship with a spirit being, typically a plant or animal, that serves as the group's emblem or herald. Relationships with their totems mirror the social relationships they have with each other as subgroups within their society. Totemic groups, often referred to as clans, view themselves as descendants of nonhuman ancestors and maintain special relationships of respect with other species in the natural world. Totemism is an example of a *metaphorical relationship* between humans and the natural world, one that links humans, animals, plants, landforms, and even weather events into a unified web of life. Many Indigenous groups practice totemism and have ancestral alliances with certain animals and plants, demonstrated by the ways in which they talk about them in their myths and depict them in their artwork. Totemic cultures frequently practice shamanism as a way to communicate with animal and plant species.

FIGURE 18.10 The totem pole, a cultural practice of some North American Indigenous groups, exhibits the clan's

identity, with a focus on the connections that the clan has with ancestors, animals, and plants. This reproduction of a First Nations totem pole is on display in Stanley Park, Vancouver, Canada. (credit: "2014 06 27 Cher and Downtown Vancouver 065" by Blake Handley/flickr, CC BY 2.0)

The **totem**, an animal or plant believed to be spiritually connected to a group of people, is a symbol of identity for the subgroup. The Anishinaabe, a North American Indigenous tribe located along the midwestern border between Canada and the United States, was historically divided into various *doodeman* (clans), most of which had local animals as their totems. Examples of their totem animals include a loon, a crane, a fish, a bird, a bear, a marten, and a deer. All members of the same totemic clan identified with one another as descendants and relatives. The totemic identification that children received at birth (from their fathers' affiliations) connected individuals not otherwise linked by close social or biological relationships, creating a spiritual kinship within the clan through the common totem. Clans were often associated with specific occupations and work assignments within the larger tribe. Clans also determined marriage rules; members of the same clan could not marry one another, as it was considered to be incest. While the Anishinaabe today have fewer clans, and thus fewer animal totems, than when their population was higher, and the importance of clans and totems has lessened, they continue to value the identities that their ancestors constructed through the natural world.

The *totem pole* is a form of monumental architecture displaying the significant totems and historical events in a clan or family's ancestral history. It functions as a signpost that identifies the occupants of an area to those passing through and proclaims the pride that a people have in their ancestry. Extended families are grouped together in a clan. The totem pole serves to proclaim the clan membership that an extended family has had throughout its history. The story of the first creation of the Indigenous group and the major events that occurred in the life of that family, its clan, and its tribe are all depicted on the totem pole. Many, though not all, Indigenous groups in North America make totem poles. These poles are historical landmarks of cultural identity.

Although Western societies do not construct physical totem poles, they do utilize some of the same symbolism in sports mascots and family heraldry. Sports teams use different types of symbolism, but animal symbols are common. Often, teams choose animals that are local to their immediate environment or that connect with certain characteristics and behaviors with which the group wishes to identify. Some well-known teams with animal mascots are the Detroit Lions, the Tampa Bay Rays, and the Boston Bruins. What animal mascots do you know?

Animals in Oral Tradition

Animals play an important role in nearly all oral traditions and religions. Across cultures, including Western cultures in Europe and the United States, animals appear as protagonists in myths and stories. The animal characters in nursery rhymes, fairy tales, fables, and folktales teach adults and children lessons and morals and model personal characteristics, some peculiar to a specific culture and others more universal. For example, the story of Chicken Little, also known in the UK as Henny Penny, is one that many US children learn at an early age. It was collected in print in the early 19th century, but it has older roots as a European folktale. In this tale, Chicken Little goes out for a walk on a windy day, and an acorn falls on her head. She panics—the sky must be falling! She runs around the farm warning all the animals about the calamity that she believes is happening: "The sky is falling! The sky is falling!" The moral of the story is to have courage and not believe everything you hear.

"The Queen Bee" is an interesting European reflection on animals, recorded from oral tradition by the Grimm brothers in 1812 . In this story, three princes, all brothers, leave their castle home to seek their fortunes and travel around the world. Two of the brothers move about haphazardly, paying no attention to the animals around them, but the youngest son, with the insulting name of Simpleton, is more considerate to the animals they encounter. When the older brothers try to destroy an anthill, kill ducks, and chase bees out of their hive, Simpleton intervenes to protect the animals and stop his brothers from causing harm. Eventually, the three princes arrive at another castle, in which everything living has been turned to stone except for one very old man. The old man tells the princes that if they can perform three tasks, all of which depend on the help of animals, they will be able to wake up the castle and earn the hand of a princess. The animals, remembering how they were treated, agree to help only young Simpleton, who thereby gains the keys of the kingdom. The moral is that even the smallest animals serve a mighty purpose.

Many of the animal stories that are still told in Western societies were either collected by the Grimm brothers in the early 1800s (1812–1857) or taken from Aesop's Fables, a collection of stories supposedly told by Aesop, an enslaved Greek storyteller, around 500 BCE. These stories have made their way into children's storybooks and animated movies—including an animated version of Chicken Little.

Indigenous societies across cultures have their own sets of animal stories that provide instruction and wisdom. Some of the most common animal symbols among Native American cultures are the coyote, the raven, the bear, and the spider. Coyote and Raven often appear in stories as **tricksters**, animal spirits or deities who are lively and clever and get into trouble through thoughtless or unconventional actions. In the story of Coyote and Bluebird from the Pima people of the southeastern United States, Coyote envies Bluebird's plumage and asks for the secret to the beautiful blue color of the bird's feathers. Bluebird tells Coyote that these pretty blue feathers came from bathing in blue water. Coyote does the same and comes out with a fine blue coat. In his vanity, he tries to outrun his shadow so that he can see his beautiful blue body in the light, and he crashes into a stump head-on, landing in the dirt, which coats his blue fur and paints him a "dirty" color that he still has today. The moral of this tale is that vanity does not serve an individual well.

In West Africa, many myths focus on a supernatural figure named Anansi, the spider. Anansi is a **culture hero** who teaches lessons of bravery and morality. Culture heroes are typically associated with supernatural feats and are particular to each cultural group, exhibiting specific traits, actions, and discoveries that are significant in that culture. In one Anansi story cycle brought by enslaved Africans to the Caribbean area during the time of the Atlantic slave trade, Anansi goes fishing and fills his basket with many different sizes of fish. On his way home, he crosses paths with Tiger, who demands to know what Anansi is carrying in the basket. Scared, Anansi lies and says he has nothing. Tiger takes the basket and sees the fish. In a series of back-and-forth interactions, Anansi succeeds in outsmarting Tiger by agreeing to clean his fur. Tiger shakes down his long hair, and then Anansi uses it to tie Tiger to the trunk of a tree, picks up his basket of fish, and continues home. The moral of the story? *Use your wit to protect yourself and your possessions.* Or, perhaps, *Don't let a bully get the best of you.*

Animals in Religion

Animals play a role in most religions. Common functions include as objects of ritual sacrifice and as tokens symbolizing gifts, payments, or even messages between the human world and the divine. As just one example, think of the use of a dove in the Noah and the ark myth (Genesis 8:6–12). The dove is the first animal to bring back a piece of greenery, evidence that the flood had receded. With this promise, Noah begins preparations to leave the ark and start over. This use of animals as messengers and forms of sacred communication is seen across cultures.

In prehistoric Peru, wild guinea pigs were sacrificed and buried either alone or with humans. They appear in archaeological deposits in Peru as early as 9000 BP (Sandweiss and Wing 1997), and they continue to appear as sacrifices after their domestication around 4500 BP and through the Inca period that ended in the 16th century. Some of the sacrificed animals are whole and intact, mummified and desiccated, while others have been burned and their charred bones stored as ritual offerings inside elaborate ceramic jars. Guinea pigs were and still are a dependable source of meat in the Andes, where they traditionally live inside kitchens, nesting around the warmth of the cooking area. They are also used medicinally, their fat rubbed on areas of sickness to draw out pain and infection, and employed as divination tools. During divination rituals today, some Andean healers will rub a living guinea pig on a patient's body to draw out some of the illness and then cut the animal open to "read" it, looking for a sign of some type of abnormality in the guinea pig's organs that would mirror the location of the illness in the human patient. At Lo Demás, an ancient Inca fishing site south of Lima, Peru (ca. 1480–1540 CE), archaeologists have excavated multiple guinea pig sacrifices, some of which show characteristic signs of having been used for divination and healing prior to burial.

In India, where Hinduism is the predominant religion, it is common to see cows walking along city streets, undisturbed and roaming freely. Many Hindus practice vegetarianism, but even those who eat meat do not usually eat beef. Cattle are sacred in Hinduism. In the Vedas, the Hindu sacred texts, the cow is associated with Aditi, the mother of all gods. In a very famous study, "The Cultural Ecology of India's Sacred Cattle" (1966), cultural anthropologist Marvin Harris explores the economic rationale associated with revering cattle, arguing that cattle are considered sacred because they are more useful when allowed to live out their natural lifespans than when slaughtered at a young age for meat alone. In India, cattle provide dung that can be dried and used as fuel, traction for plowing fields, some limited milk production, and reproductive capacity. When cattle die of old age, beef and leather are then harvested by those in the lowest socioeconomic class. Keeping cattle alive as long as possible thus provides for a greater range of material assets than raising them for food. This economic rationale, however true it may be, does not negate the cultural and religious importance of cattle to Indian people. Understanding animals' symbolic roles is critical to understanding human belief systems.

FIGURE 18.11 A white elephant enjoys the rain in an elephant sanctuary in Phuket, Thailand. In Buddhism, the elephant symbolizes mental strength and endurance (Diamond 2011). Buddhists in Burma, Cambodia, and Thailand believe that the white elephant represents one of the reincarnations of the Buddha. (credit: "Elephant in the Rain" by Marc Dalmulder/flickr, CC BY 2.0)

Buddhism is a religion that reveres all life and sees humans and animals as intertwined, each capable of being **reincarnated** into the other, reborn into a new cycle of life inhabiting a new body of the same or another species. Because Buddhists believe in **karma**, a spiritual principle of cause and effect in which an individual's words, actions, and deeds in one life affect their conditions in the next life cycle, the relationship between humans and other animals should ideally be based on respect and sympathy. All forms of life are working toward enlightenment, a state of awakening and having a complete knowledge of the life process.

Animals are important in human belief systems. English art critic and poet John Berger ([1980] 1991) writes about the gaze between humans and other animals, saying that animals remind humans that we are not here on Earth alone, that we are all companion species. Many religious systems reflect the awareness that life is not the exclusive domain of the human species and that our world is a shared community. For more on animals and belief systems, see the Ethnographic Sketch at the end of the chapter.

18.4 Pet-Keeping

LEARNING OUTCOMES

By the end of this section, you will be able to:

- Define the pet as a cultural artifact.
- Trace the historical development of pets in Western societies.
- Provide examples of pets in Indigenous societies.
- Identify major behavioral and morphological characteristics of pets.
- Describe the economic impact of pet keeping in Western societies.

One of the most familiar and intimate roles that animals play in the lives of contemporary Western people is that of pets. **Pets** are animals that are either domesticated or tamed with whom humans have developed a long-term social bond. Pets are part of many human cultures.

Pets as Cultural Artifacts

Although specific pets are actual beings (many of us can think of the face of one or more pets we live or have lived with), pets in general can be understood as a cultural artifact. This means that the ways in which pets are treated and what is expected of them vary a great deal from one culture to another. Most pets live in or around human households, are considered the possessions of their human owners, and have limited ability to make freewill decisions. Chinese geographer and early scholar in human-animal studies Yi-Fu Tuan (1984) has studied the ways in which humans have dominated the living environment and their pets, with approaches varying between extremes of dominance and affection, love and abuse, cruelty and kindness. He argues that pets in Western societies are defined by emotion and nostalgia, an approach likely related to increasing distance between people and the natural world. Even within a culture that treats certain animals in a sentimental way, relationships with other animals can still be characterized by cruelty and dominance. Tuan writes, “Animals are slaughtered for food and clothing without a twinge of conscience. A few specimens and species, however, catch the fancy of people in a playful mood and are made into pampered pets or fervently supported causes” (1984, 162).

What we would recognize as *modern* pet keeping in the Western world—an approach characterized by keeping animals for no other purpose than to be companions for humans—emerged during the late 18th and early 19th centuries. Prior to that time, animals cared for by humans had functions or tasks within the household. As communities and towns became increasingly urban and people lost interaction with wild animals, the relationship between people and animals shifted in various ways. Many families were smaller and had more time to care for a pet. Animals had fewer assigned duties and responsibilities and were more available as companions. Improvements in medical and veterinary sciences lowered the risk of **zoonoses**, or diseases transmitted between animals and humans, although zoonotic infections continue to threaten human populations (consider COVID-19, for example). Lastly, a growing middle class with more affluence could afford the luxury of keeping pets. Modern pet keeping is marked by a relationship of demonstrative affection between people and their animals as well as by the economic development of pet industries, such as pet food companies, veterinary services, and even cremation and burial services.

Pet Keeping in Indigenous Societies

There is extensive evidence of pet keeping in Indigenous societies. In many hunter-gatherer societies, children keep numerous pets, most often birds, small rodents, and monkeys. These animals, often taken directly from the forest or wilderness area when they are still young, are considered valuable companions for children. Caring for the animals is thought to teach children to understand animals’ movements and personalities and help them develop a sense of stewardship for the natural world.

Animal ethicist James Serpell (1988) has found wide-ranging pet keeping throughout Indigenous societies in North and South America. The Waraõ in the Orinoco region of Venezuela keep birds, monkeys, sloths, rodents, ducks, dogs, and chickens as pets. The Kalapalo of central Brazil have a particular affection for birds and treat them as members of the family. The Barasana of eastern Colombia keep pet rodents, birds (especially parrots and macaws), peccaries (piglike mammals), and even young jaguars. And North American Indigenous groups are known to have tamed raccoons, moose, bison, wolves, bears, and especially dogs.

FIGURE 18.12 A Guaraní family with their dog in Mato Grosso do Sul, Brazil, in 2004. Pets are part of many human cultures. (credit: "Agrotoxico Ti Guarani Kaiova_Foto_Ana Mendes (23)" by Ana Mendes/Amazônia Real/flickr, CC BY 2.0)

While many Native Americans are very affectionate with their dogs, their style of "keeping" these dogs as pets differs a great deal from what most American are familiar with. In a 2020 article titled "What Rez Dogs Mean to the Lakota," Lakota tribal members Richard Meyers and Ernest Weston Jr. explain:

> In our culture, people traditionally don't own animals the way other cultures have pets; the animals are left wild, and may choose to go to a home to offer protection, companionship, or even to become a part of a community. People feed the dogs and care for them, but the dogs remain living outside and are free to be their own beings. This relationship differs from one where the human is the master or owner of an animal who is considered property. Instead, the dog and people provide service to one another in a mutual relationship of reciprocity and respect.

The roles of pets in human societies are very complex and depend on specific cultural traditions and ways of relating to animals, both wild and domesticated. It is important to note that pets play different roles across different cultures and cannot be easily defined.

The Making of Pets

In Western societies, domesticated animals have increasingly been subjected to extreme genetic manipulation in order to manufacture ever more novel and attractive pet animals. In Europe, the earliest kennel clubs, designed to develop and maintain breeds and record pedigrees, began as dog show societies in England in 1859 and were later established as governing bodies and official institutions, starting in 1873. Although dog breeds now come from all over the world and continue to be developed—a recent addition to the list of breeds recognized by the American Kennel Club (AKC) is the Biewer terrier, first recognized in January 2021—the majority of modern pet breeds were first developed in Victorian England, where pet keeping flourished and was adopted by all social classes.

Sometimes, this selective breeding of pets is detrimental to the health of the animal breed. In the English bulldog, for example, 86 percent of litters must be delivered by cesarian section because the pups' large heads and mothers' narrow pelvises have made live, natural births very challenging (Evans and Adams 2010). In addition, as dog breeders create more and more specialized pets, the gene pool becomes narrowed and less diverse, producing animals that are more prone to conditions such as cancer, hip dysplasia, deafness, hereditary epilepsy, and allergies. In pedigreed cats, which are subject to the same selective pressures in breeding, there are both heart and kidney problems that are thought to be accelerated by selective breeding.

One of the most commonly sought set of characteristics by people selectively breeding animals for pets is the appearance of a permanent juvenile state. **Neotony**, the tendency for an animal to maintain both physical and behavioral juvenile characteristics into adulthood, has been highly sought after in many domesticated animals. Some of the most commonly desired juvenile physical traits are larger and wider-set eyes, a smaller snout (or nose), a more globular (or rounded) skull, and fewer and smaller teeth (which leaves many dogs with crowded teeth and dental problems). Social neotony involves a cluster of traits relating to a strong and submissive attachment to humans and increased attentiveness to human behavior.

The overall size of animals is also a consideration when breeding pets. Consider the range of miniature animals we have selected for today: miniature horses, mules, and pigs; pygmy goats and hedgehogs; and others. Of all animals kept as pets, dogs have been the most manipulated in size. Today, there is a proliferation of "teacup" breeds that can be carried in the owner's pocket or purse. Small dogs offer many advantages to humans living in urban environments and small apartments, but there are few advantages for the dogs themselves. Most teacup versions are created by breeding the smallest animals in a litter. There are many health risks that accompany this process of extreme miniaturization, such as collapsing tracheas, digestive problems, heart defects, liver shunts, slipping kneecaps, and a host of dental challenges.

Pet keeping has deep roots in human societies and has changed over time. Interestingly, it has also been documented among some animals. Nonhuman animals have been known to form cross-species friendships and alliances and to take care of each other both in the wild and in captivity. One interesting example is the gorilla Hanabiko, called "Koko," who was trained to understand spoken English and communicate using a form of American Sign Language that her keeper called Gorilla Sign Language. Koko became interested in cats and signed that she wanted a kitten for Christmas in 1983. Her keepers at first provided her with a stuffed cat, but Koko insisted that she wanted a living one. On her birthday the following July, her keepers allowed her to choose a rescue kitten, which she named "All Ball" because he had no tail and was very fluffy. The relationship between Koko and her kitten, documented in many articles and videos, was a nurturing one in which Koko treated All Ball like her baby and her pet. Pet keeping says a great deal about the human need to reach across species for companionship, dominance, and affection. Perhaps, though, this is not solely a human need.

18.5 Animal Industries and the Animal Trade

LEARNING OUTCOMES

By the end of this section, you will be able to:

- Describe the evolution of zoos.
- Recognize the benefits of ecotourism.
- Define the use value of animals in biomedical research today.

In the past two centuries, Western societies have increasingly taken the approach of treating animals as a *commodity*—a raw material or resource for human use, a thing instead of a being. When we consider the relationships that many Indigenous societies have with animals, we can better realize how different the Western idea of animals is. Approaching the world and nature primarily as consumers rather than coequals, Western cultures face increasing environmental, socio-emotional, and resource-related challenges in all areas of life.

Zoos

Zoos have long been part of human societies. The earliest evidence of a zoo has been found in Hierakonpolis, the capital of Upper Egypt during the Predynastic period, today called Nekhen. Here, archaeologists have unearthed the mummified remains of a collection of wild and domesticated animals from about 5,000 years ago that included baboons, hippos, gazelles, crocodiles, a leopard, and cats and dogs. Some of the animals had injuries likely caused by being tied or enclosed in some way. Many of them were buried in the same way that humans were buried, and some were found inside human burials (Boissoneault 2015). Another famous historical zoo was that of the Aztec king Montezuma. When the Spaniards arrived in the Aztec capital of Tenochtitlán in 1519, they were surprised by the vast collection of animals housed in enclosures and rooms within the king's palace complex, including jaguars, bears, eagles, deer, fowl, ocelots, and little dogs. According to the Spanish chroniclers, the zoo had some 300 keepers to care for the animals. Similar to early pet keeping, zoos were typically associated with wealth and status.

Modern zoos emerged in the late 18th century during the period known as the Enlightenment, characterized by the development of science and the expansion of colonial empires. European zoos were filled with wildlife from new colonies and "foreign" lands and were considered places to see strange and exotic animals. The first modern zoos opened in Paris in 1793, London in 1828, and Philadelphia in 1874. These were all very popular public institutions that exhibited animals for entertainment and observation. The zoos were laid out like public parks, with small animal enclosures that allowed people to get up close to see.

There have been many changes in zoos over the last 50 years. With the signing of the Convention on International Trade in Endangered Species of Wild Flora and Fauna (CITES) in 1973 and the passage of the Endangered Species Act in the United States the same year, wild animal imports to US zoos declined sharply. This coincided with the development of breeding and conservation programs at zoos, some of which involve breeding rare and endangered species to be released back into the wild as part of a sustainable population. One species for which breeding efforts are currently underway is the giant panda. Animals are commonly moved from one zoo site to another and shared for breeding purposes in an effort to fortify the breed. Animals that are endangered may be part of a zoo preservation program. In some cases, critically endangered animals are cared for by zoos when they are young and vulnerable to predators and then reintroduced into the wild. The website of the Association of Zoos and Aquariums (AZA) features a long list of animals whose populations have been preserved through the efforts of zoos, including the black-footed ferret, the California condor, the Ohio River basin freshwater mussel, the golden lion tamarin, and the Oregon spotted frog. Zoos also sponsor research programs with goals such as creating sustainable populations in the wild, conserving wildlife habitats, improving animal health, or even collecting endangered species' genetic material (DNA) (DeMello 2012, 106).

What should be the role of zoos in contemporary Western societies? Should the zoo be closer to a theme park or a museum? Should the goal of a zoo be animal conservation or human recreation? These questions guide us as we continue to rethink the mission of zoos today.

PROFILES IN ANTHROPOLOGY

Barbara J. King
1956–

FIGURE 18.13 Anthropologist Barbara King with Cynthia Goat at the Farm Sanctuary in Watkins Glen, New York (credit: Charles Hogg)

Personal History: Born in New Jersey, King earned her BA from Douglass College (Rutgers University) and her MA and PhD from the University of Oklahoma, where she specialized in biological anthropology. Her doctoral field research in Amboseli National Park, Kenya, focused on foraging and social behaviors among yellow baboons. From 1988 to 2015, she served as professor of anthropology at the College of William & Mary in Williamsburg, Virginia, where she received numerous awards for outstanding teaching and mentorship. She is now a professor emerita, although she continues to have an active role in academia, research, publishing, and mentorship.

Area of Anthropology: King's research and contributions to the field are notable for their broad-ranging relevance across anthropological subfields and disciplines, among them linguistic and communication systems in primates, social relationships between species, the primate origins of religious thought, and the social and emotional lives of various animal species, including those being factory farmed. Her anthropological focus is often on the continuities between humans and other animals and the ethics of human-animal relationships. She has published seven books and numerous scholarly articles.

Accomplishments in the Field: Given the four-field scope of much of King's research, she has had considerable impact on many areas of academia. In 2002, King was awarded a Guggenheim Fellowship for "exceptional capacity for productive scholarship" and creativity. Two of her works, *Evolving God: A Provocative View on the Origins of Religion* (2007, Doubleday) and *How Animals Grieve* (2013, University of Chicago Press), have received prizes and awards as outstanding contributions to the field.

King is also an active public anthropologist, bridging gaps between academic research and the public. A contributor to the National Public Radio blog *Cosmos and Culture* from 2011 to 2018 and a full-time science writer since her retirement in 2015, King, through interviews, articles, and blogs, communicates the importance of science for public good and social change. Her research on animal grief, *How Animals Grieve*, was highlighted in her 2019 TED Talk, "Grief and Love in the Animal Kingdom (https://openstax.org/r/barbara_j_king)." King also regularly reviews books for various media outlets, including NPR, the *Washington Post*, and the *Times Literary Supplement*, and publishes in *Sapiens*, an online anthropology magazine devoted to public outreach. She is a self-described Twitter addict (@bjkingape).

Importance of Their Work

In her public role, King seeks to educate and incentivize people to make positive change for human and animal lives. In her newest book, *Animals' Best Friends: Putting Compassion to Work for Animals in Captivity and in the Wild* (University of Chicago Press, 2021), King issues a call to cultivate compassionate action toward all the animals sharing their lives with us. She challenges us to widen our lens on the world around us and become animals' best friends, whether they are in our homes, in the wild, in a lab, in a zoo, or destined to be thought of as food. "When we still ourselves and genuinely see the more-than-human-world, possibilities for helping animals bloom all around us—we may rescue rather than squish a spider in our home; resist an urge to crowd wild animals in order to snap selfies; advocate for non-animal models in laboratory science; refuse to support roadside zoos or swim-with-dolphin programs; and increase our plant-based eating" (Snipes, personal communication, 2021). For more on King's recent work, see her interview with nature writer Brandon Keim (https://openstax.org/r/youtube_kno1wWevRVg) on Earth Day 2021.

Ecotourism

Another way in which contemporary Western societies are attempting to address the damage caused by a commodified view of the natural world, including the animals living in it, is through **ecotourism**. This is tourism designed to be sustainable and to help preserve the flora and fauna of endangered natural environments. Often, the focus is on visiting threatened environments and observing wildlife in its natural habitat. Such tourism can earn money to aid in the conservation of these areas, provide employment for local residents, and raise awareness of the importance of biological, as well as cultural, diversity. Ideally, care is taken to ensure that tourists visiting natural areas do not disturb or damage the environment; however, there are no global standards for ecotourism, and some sites are more successful at protecting sensitive environments than others. The term *greenwashing* is sometimes applied to sites that promote the natural environment as an attraction while engaging in exploitative and environmentally destructive behavior.

FIGURE 18.14 The Galapagos giant tortoise is found only in the Galapagos Islands. It is being preserved today through ecotourism and conservation efforts. (credit: "Pinta Island Giant Galapagos Tortoise" by Arturo de Frias Marques/flickr, Public Domain)

An example of effective and increasingly responsible ecotourism is provided by the Galápagos Islands. The

Galápagos island chain was made famous by English naturalist Charles Darwin, who used his observations of the diversity of the ecosystem's animals to develop the theory of natural selection. Located 563 miles west of the coast of Ecuador, the Galápagos were listed by UNESCO as a World Heritage Site in 1978. Prior to that, the islands were only partially protected. Some of the Galápagos Islands were designated as wildlife sanctuaries in 1934, and the island archipelago became an Ecuadorian national park in 1959. Around that time, a few wealthy tourists began to travel to the islands to view their extraordinary biodiversity. By the 1990s, tourism had become very popular and a tourist industry had developed, with hotels, restaurants, and transportation. Today, the Galápagos National Park Service, which manages 97 percent of the island lands (the other 3 percent are contained settlements where local people live), has strict policies limiting the daily number of visitors. Local people serve as employees in the park and teach the value of conservation to tourists. It is the hope of the Galápagos National Park Service and the local people that this island ecosystem and its living inhabitants—such as the Galápagos giant tortoise, the Galápagos penguin, the blue-footed booby, the flightless cormorant, and the waved albatross—will be preserved for future generations.

Animals and the Medical Industry

In 2015, there were estimated to be some 192 million animals being used in biomedical laboratories across 179 countries worldwide (Taylor and Alvarez 2019). These animals are used for medical experiments, drug testing, product testing, and psychological research. The most commonly used animals in US labs are mice, rats, and birds, though a range of other animals—including rabbits, guinea pigs, hamsters, farm animals such as pigs and sheep, cats, dogs, and nonhuman primates—are used as well (Humane Society of the United States 2021). These animals come from various sources, including breeding programs within the biomedical labs themselves.

Although biologists, chemists, animal behaviorists, psychiatrists, and psychologists tend to be more frequently involved in medical research with animals, anthropologists—especially primatologists and linguistic anthropologists—also have a history of working with animals in laboratory settings. Primatologist Sue Savage-Rumbaugh carried out long-term cognitive studies of two bonobos, Kanzi and Panbanisha, from birth. Savage-Rumbaugh was interested in understanding how bonobos, which are closely related to humans, learn communication. She developed a computer-based language program using lexigrams, or symbols representing words, printed on a keyboard. Although lacking the vocal apparatus of a human, Kanzi and Panbanisha demonstrated advanced cognitive linguistic skills by responding to human speech and generating language by pressing lexigrams. In one study comparing Kanzi's language competence with that of a two-year-old human child, Kanzi scored significantly higher: 74 percent accuracy, compared to 65 percent accuracy for the two-year-old human (Savage-Rumbaugh et al. 1993). Studies such as this one shed light not only on animals' abilities but also on the continuities that exist between humans and animals.

There are two primary regulations in the United States that pertain to biomedical research animals: the Animal Welfare Act (AWA) and the Public Health Service Policy on Humane Care and Use of Laboratory Animals (PHS Policy). The AWA is a law passed by Congress in 1966 that originally covered the transport, sale, and handling of some animals and advocated for more humane animal practices in laboratories. The act has been amended several times (1970, 1976, 1985, 1990, 1991, 2002, 2007, 2008, 2014), including to add a requirement that researchers register their use of animals and also consider a database of alternatives if the procedure can cause any distress or pain. The act cover animals such as dogs, cats, rabbits, and nonhuman primates, but it does not cover those animals most commonly used in laboratory experiments: rats, mice, and birds. The PHS Policy applies to all research facilities that perform animal research and receive any type of federal funding; though not itself a law, its creation was mandated by the Health Research Extension Act, passed by Congress in 1985. This policy states that each institution conducting such research must have an institutional animal care and use committee (IACUC) that reviews all proposed animal research experiments. This committee must include at least five members, one of whom must be a veterinarian and another a person not affiliated with the institution. When reviewing research proposals, the IACUC is expected to evaluate whether (1) basic standards are met, (2) the use of animals is justified, (3) the research is not duplicated, and (4) pain and discomfort for the animals are minimized. The United Kingdom and the European Union have similar measures to regulate and oversee animal laboratory research.

Animal research has been critical to many advances in medicine, including the development of the first human vaccine to successfully eradicate smallpox, the polio vaccine, and treatments for HIV/AIDS, Alzheimer's disease, hepatitis, and malaria. Animals have played a crucial role in the development of many new drugs and therapies, and a significant amount of research conducted on animals also benefits veterinary medicine and other animals as well. However, the use of living animals for experiments and testing raises many ethical issues and has inspired a great deal of conflict and controversy.

Animals in Our Lives

Humans share their lives with animals in many ways, and how we think about ourselves as human beings rests primarily on the distinctions we see between ourselves and other species. English art critic and poet John Berger writes, "With their parallel lives, animals offer man a companionship which is different from any offered by human exchange. Different because it is a companionship offered to the loneliness of man as a species" ([1980] 1991, 6). Across cultures and across time, humans have looked toward animals as fellow participants in their lives. They actively participate in the ways we define ourselves. They feed us and accompany us. They work for us and protect us. They also serve as symbols and messengers that help us better understand our world. Our lives are intertwined in multiple ways.

What is an animal? What is the value of nonhuman animals in our lives? How do our attitudes about animals define who we are as human beings? Anthropologists and other researchers increasingly see the value of bringing animals into their research because animals are critical to understanding what it means to be human.

ETHNOGRAPHIC SKETCHES

Animal Familiarity

Experience of Marjorie Snipes, chapter author

FIGURE 18.15 A young female goat and her kid. (credit: "Nursing Kid" by swallowsan/flickr, CC BY 2.0)

During fieldwork in northwestern Argentina, I lived with a community of herders who tended goats and sheep, interviewing every day and taking copious notes. After six months of research, I took a two-week break from the field to return to the United States to welcome my new niece. When I returned to the field site, I had an accidental breakthrough.

However, let me back up. In this Andean community, herders believe that their flocks are gifts from Pachamama (Mother Earth), and women are the primary caretakers and shepherds for the animals. After I had lived in the community for about six weeks, one of the families gave me a small kid, or young goat, which I named Maisie. I suspected that this gift was a test to see if I was planning to be part of the community. I took care of Maisie every day, even though she remained a functioning member of another family's herd.

Goats normally reproduce toward the end of their first year, and Maisie was pregnant when I left for my two-week absence from the field. While I was gone, she gave birth to a male that the family named Vicente Beda, after a Catholic saint. When I arrived back at the household where I was staying, late in the day, Doña Florentina was eager for me to meet the newest member of my herd. We entered the corral, and the young kid came running up to me with no fear. When I commented about the familiarity, as young animals tend to be skittish around new people, Florentina responded, "But he knows you, Margo." And so I learned about the *librito* (little book) that they believe is located in the stomach area of each of their herd animals.

The *librito* contains information about an animal's life: who loves it, where it belongs, and when it will die. It is the shepherd's duty to discern the contents of the book through the animal's behavior, as she cannot openly read it. Animals who get lost frequently or have trouble bonding with the herd will be traded, as families believe such animals do not belong to them. And when it is time to select an animal for slaughter, the shepherd chooses an animal whose behavior indicates that the time is appropriate. While the signs vary according to the animal's disposition, it is normally a change of demeanor that the shepherd interprets as acquiescence. During slaughter, a woman typically holds the animal while a man cuts the throat. In all slaughters that I attended, the goat or sheep was killed peacefully, and butchering occurred quickly afterward—except one. The animal was a large ewe, and she was initially compliant with being handled, but at the moment that her throat was cut, her back feet scrambled and she tried to rise up. Everyone around me became very still and began to lower their voices, saying that it was not the right time for the ewe, that there had been a mistake. The shepherd had "made a mistake."

The ewe was not butchered. She lay there for about an hour while the family discussed where to take her for burial. She was buried far away from the corral and household.

MINI-FIELDWORK ACTIVITY

Multispecies Animal Observation

Ethnography increasingly utilizes methods aimed at incorporating a multitude of diverse voices. The purpose of this is not diversity for diversity's sake but to more accurately reflect and understand the various interactions that may occur within any field encounter. In this fieldwork activity, you will experiment with multispecies ethnography. Choose a wild animal (e.g., pigeon, duck, squirrel, insect, etc.), and observe it (with no interaction) for at least 15 minutes. During the observation, make consistent notes every 30 seconds to one minute, writing down the animal's behavior incrementally and how it interacts with its environment. Note also whether the animal seems to notice your presence or interact with you. Following the observation session, write up a multispecies ethnographic account, using the data you have collected to inform you of the possible intentions and thoughts of the animal as well as your own thoughts and reactions. Your write-up should be 500 to 750 words and should end with a paragraph reflecting on the experience of trying to write from an animal's perspective (based on human observation). Turn in the original timed notes along with the final paper.

Suggested Films

Cave of Forgotten Dreams. 2010. Directed by Werner Herzog. Creative Differences.

Eduardo the Healer. 1978. Directed by Richard Cowan. Serious Business Company.

People of the Seal. 2009. Directed by Kate Raisz. NOAA Ocean Media Center.

Key Terms

animal a multicellular organism, either vertebrate or invertebrate, that can breathe, move, ingest, excrete, and sexually reproduce.

animal empathy a human sense of understanding and sensing the feelings of other animals.

anthropocentrism the belief that the human perspective is the most important one; also called human exceptionalism.

conspecifics members of the same species.

culture hero an idealized animal or human figure associated with supernatural feats. A culture hero is particular to their cultural group, exhibiting specific traits, actions, and discoveries that are significant to that group of people

domestication the selective breeding of a species by humans to create animals better suited to human life.

ecotourism an international conservation movement to preserve the flora and fauna of endangered natural environments through conscientious tourism.

karma a Buddhist spiritual principle of cause and effect in which an individual's words, actions, and deeds in one life affect their conditions in the next life cycle

multispecies ethnography the study of the interactions between humans and other species within their shared environment.

nature a domain defined by cultures as outside or on the margins of human culture.

neotony a tendency for an animal to maintain both physical and social juvenile characteristics into adulthood.

nomadic pastoralism herding that is based on the availability of environmental resources; involves unpredictable movements, as herders decide from day to day where they will go next.

pastoral societies societies in which primary subsistence is based on herding groups of animals.

pets animals, whether domesticated or tamed, with whom humans have a social bond.

polyspecific interaction involving multiple species.

reincarnation rebirth into a new cycle of life, inhabiting a new body of the same or another species.

symbiosis a mutually beneficial relationship between species.

tame a behavioral condition in which humans encourage wild animals to tolerate human proximity and interaction.

totem an animal or plant believed to be spiritually connected to a group of people.

totemism a belief and classification system in which a group of humans claims a spiritual kinship with a plant or animal that serves as the group's emblem.

transhumant pastoralism herding in a regular, patterned movement from one location to another.

trickster an animal spirit deity who is very lively and clever and gets into trouble through thoughtless or unconventional actions.

zoonoses plural form of *zoonosis*, singular; diseases transmitted from animals to humans, usually involving a wild animal host. Many zoonoses mutate and become more virulent in their human hosts (e.g., COVID-19, measles, HIV, influenza).

Summary

Animals play essential roles in many areas of human life. While it may be difficult to define an animal, and sometimes controversial to speak the scientific truth that human are animals, too, the continuum between *us* and *them* is incontrovertible. In describing animals, anthropologist Claude Lévi-Strauss said that they are "good to think" of (1963, 89) because they show up prolifically in our cultures. Human-animal scholars often use a research approach known as multispecies ethnography as a way of understanding the symbiosis between humans and animals.

Of all animal species, the dog has played the most transformative role in human cultures historically. An early domesticate, dogs have served as guards, hunters, herders, transport, food, and (most commonly) companions in many different societies. Many human subsistence systems depend on animals; hunting, herding, fishing, and factory farming are the primary ways in which humans access meat. Indigenous hunters practice empathy and appreciation as ways of connecting as predators to prey, and many pastoralists have a symbiotic relationship with their herd animals, migrating periodically to provide pasture for their herds. Animals are also symbols. In totemic societies, animal species and relationships are used as ways of ordering human society; human groups have relationships of respect with their totemic emblem and identify with some of the qualities of the animal. Animals also play important roles in oral tradition and religious systems as teachers, messengers, and sacrificial tokens. Many religious systems reflect the awareness that life is not the exclusive domain of the human species and that our world is a shared community.

Animals are also pets and cultural artifacts. Domesticated animals have been genetically reconfigured to meet the needs of human societies. This includes selectively breeding for *neotony*, a tendency for an animal to maintain both physical and behavioral juvenile characteristics. While many Indigenous societies practice pet keeping as companionship and sometimes also as a way to teach young children about animal behaviors, in modern Western societies, pet keeping has become an industry.

There are also animal trades in Western societies, from zoos, aquariums, and circuses to wild animal reserves where ecotourism generates funds to preserve wild animal habitats. Often, these industries have both negative and positive attributes. In the medical industry, animals have long served as human stand-ins for research. Increasingly today, there are laws and regulations to improve the plight of animals in medical labs, but this continues to be a challenge, and the improvements are rarely adequate. Still, the contributions that animals have made to human health and welfare have been substantial, whether in labs, on farms, in forests, or in our homes. Animals have always mattered to human beings.

Critical Thinking Questions

1. What various roles do animals play in human lives?
2. What specific roles have dogs had in human societies across time?
3. How does the relationship between people and animals vary across subsistence practices?
4. What types of relationships do Indigenous hunters have with wild animal prey?
5. How do different cultures use animal symbolism?
6. In what ways are pets a cultural artifact?
7. How do modern societies participate in the animal trade?
8. Some Western societies have made advances in protecting animals used in the medical industry. Do you believe these advances are sufficient, or should societies continue to push for reform?

Bibliography

Almagor, Uri. 1985. "The Bee Connection: The Symbolism of a Cyclical Order in an East African Age System." *Journal of Anthropological Research* 41 (1): 1–17.

Avieli, Nur. 2011. "Dog Meat Politics in a Vietnamese Town." *Ethnology* 50 (1): 59–78. https://ethnology.pitt.edu/ojs/index.php/Ethnology/article/viewArticle/6092.

Berger, John. (1980) 1991. "Why Look at Animals?" In *About Looking*, 3–28. New York: Vintage Books.

Boissoneault, Lorraine. 2015. "Leopards, Hippos, and Cats, Oh My! The World's First Zoo." JSTOR Daily. November 12, 2015. https://daily.jstor.org/leopards-hippos-cats-oh-worlds-first-zoo/.

Boylan, Michael. n.d. "Aristotle: Biology." Internet Encyclopedia of Philosophy. https://iep.utm.edu/aris-bio/.

Brightman, Robert. 1993. *Grateful Prey: Rock Cree Human-Animal Relationships*. Berkeley: University of California Press.

Crocker, Jon Christopher. 1985. *Vital Souls: Bororo Cosmology, Natural Symbolism, and Shamanism*. Tucson: University of Arizona Press.

DeMello, Margo. 2012. *Animals and Society: An Introduction to Human-Animal Studies*. New York: Columbia University Press.

Diamond, Wendy. 2011. "Thailand: Buddha's Animal Kingdom." *HuffPost*, September 19, 2011. https://www.huffpost.com/entry/thailand-buddhas-animal-k_b_969662.

Evans, Katy M., and Vicki J. Adams. 2010. "Proportion of Litters of Purebred Dogs Born by Caesarean Section."

Journal of Small Animal Practice 51 (2): 113–118.

Gadsby, Patricia, and Leon Steele. 2004. "The Inuit Paradox." *Discover*, January 19, 2004. https://www.discovermagazine.com/health/the-inuit-paradox.

Harris, Marvin. 1966. "The Cultural Ecology of India's Sacred Cattle." *Current Anthropology* 7 (1): 51–66.

Humane Society of the United States. 2021. "Animals Used in Experiments FAQ." https://www.humanesociety.org/resources/animals-used-experiments-faq.

Hurn, Samantha. 2012. *Humans and Other Animals: Cross-Cultural Perspectives on Human-Animal Interactions*. London: Pluto Press.

Ingold, Tim, ed. 1994. *What Is an Animal?* Rev. ed. New York: Routledge.

Ingold, Tim. 2000. "Hunting and Gathering as Ways of Perceiving the Environment." In *The Perception of the Environment: Essays on Livelihood, Dwelling and Skill*, 40–60. New York: Routledge.

Istomin, Kirill Vladimirovich, and Mark James Dwyer. 2010. "Dynamic Mutual Adaptation: Human-Animal Interaction in Reindeer Herding Pastoralism." *Human Ecology* 38 (5): 613–623.

Kirksey, S. Eben, and Stefan Helmreich. 2010. "The Emergence of Multispecies Ethnography." In "Multispecies Ethnography," special issue, *Cultural Anthropology* 25 (4): 545–576.

Lévi-Strauss, Claude. 1963. *Totemism*. Translated by Rodney Needham. Boston: Beacon Press.

McKie, Robin. 2011. "Love of Animals Led to Language and Man's Domination of Earth." *Guardian*, October 1, 2011. https://www.theguardian.com/science/2011/oct/02/anthropology-pat-shipman-animals-language.

Meyers, Richard, and Ernest Weston Jr. 2020. "What Rez Dogs Mean to the Lakota." *Sapiens*, December 2, 2020. https://www.sapiens.org/culture/rez-dogs/.

Mohnhaupt, Jan. 2020. *Tiere im Nationalsozialismus*. Munich: Carl Hanser.

Morgan, Lewis Henry. 1868. *The American Beaver and His Works*. Philadelphia: J. B. Lippincott.

Ostrander, Elaine A., and Robert K. Wayne. 2005. "The Canine Genome." *Genome Research* 15 (12): 1706–1716. https://doi.org/10.1101/gr.3736605.

Peterson, Anna Lisa. 2001. *Being Human: Ethics, Environment, and Our Place in the World*. Berkeley: University of California Press.

Posey, Darrell A. 1981. "Wasps, Warriors and Fearless Men: Ethnoentomology of the Kayapó Indians of Central Brazil." *Journal of Ethnobiology* 1 (1): 165–174. https://ethnobiology.org/sites/default/files/pdfs/JoE/1-1/Posey1981.pdf.

Pringle, Heather. 2011. "Earliest American Dogs May Have Been Dinner." *Science*, May 6, 2011. https://www.science.org/content/article/earliest-american-dogs-may-have-been-dinner-rev2.

Ritvo, Harriet. 1988. "The Emergence of Modern Pet-Keeping." In *Animals and People Sharing the World*, edited by Andrew N. Rowen, 13–31. Hanover, NH: University Press of New England.

Sandweiss, Daniel H., and Elizabeth S. Wing. 1997. "Ritual Rodents: The Guinea Pigs of Chincha, Peru." *Journal of Field Archaeology* 24 (1): 47–58.

Savage-Rumbaugh, E. Sue, Jeannine Murphy, Rose A. Sevcik, Karen E. Brakke, Shelly L. Williams, and Duane M. Rumbaugh. 1993. "Language Comprehension in Ape and Child." *Monographs of the Society for Research in Child Development* 58 (3–4): i–252.

Serpell, James A. 1988. "Pet-Keeping in Non-Western Societies: Some Popular Misconceptions." In *Animals and People Sharing the World*, edited by Andrew N. Rowen, 33–51. Hanover, NH: University Press of New England.

Shipman, Pat. (2015) 2017. *The Invaders: How Humans and Their Dogs Drove Neanderthals to Extinction*.

Cambridge, MA: Belknap Press of Harvard University Press.

Snipes, Marjorie M. 1996. "When the Other Speaks: Animals and Place as Social Space in the Argentine Andes." PhD diss., University of Wisconsin–Madison. ProQuest (AAT 9636601).

Spröer, Susanne. 2020. "Hitler's Dogs, Göring's Lions: How the Nazis Used and Abused Animals." DW. June 8, 2020. https://p.dw.com/p/3dJUC.

Taylor, Katy, and Laura Rego Alvarez. 2019. "An Estimate of the Number of Animals Used for Scientific Purposes Worldwide in 2015." *Alternatives to Laboratory Animals* 47 (5–6): 196–213. https://doi.org/10.1177/0261192919899853.

Thompson, Marc. 2008. "Itzcuintle: Ancient Mexican Dog Food." In "Dogs in the Southwest," special issue, *Archaeology Southwest* 22 (3): 9.

Tidwell, James N. 1948. "Frogs and Frog-Eaters." *American Speech* 23 (3–4): 214–216.

Tuan, Yi-Fu. 1984. *Dominance and Affection: The Making of Pets.* New Haven, CT: Yale University Press.

Willerslev, Rane. 2004. "Not Animal, Not *Not*-Animal: Hunting, Imitation and Empathetic Knowledge among the Siberian Yukaghirs." *Journal of the Royal Anthropological Institute* 10 (3): 629–652.

Yon, Sophia. 2002. A New Perspective on Barking in Dogs (*Canis familiaris*). *Journal of Comparative Psychology* 116(2):189-93.

Zorn, Elayne. 1995. "(Re-)Fashioning Identity: Late Twentieth-Century Transformations in Dress and Society in Bolivia." In *Contact, Crossover, Continuity: Proceedings of the Fourth Biennial Symposium of the Textile Society of America, September 22–24, 1994,* 343–354. Los Angeles: Textile Society of America. https://digitalcommons.unl.edu/tsaconf/1057/.

CHAPTER 19
Indigenous Anthropology

Figure 19.1 David Lewis, the author of this chapter, with a Kalapuya canoe donated to Grand Ronde Tribe by the Willamette Heritage Center. The canoe was found preserved in the clay of the Calapooia River in Oregon. (credit: Dean Rhode, Public Domain)

CHAPTER OUTLINE

INTRODUCTION The author if this chapter, David Lewis, explains his deep connection to the material:

I, David Lewis, am the author of this chapter and a Native scholar—a member of the Confederated Tribes of the Grand Ronde Community of Oregon. I am a descendant of the original Santiam Kalapuya, Takelma, and Chinook tribes of western Oregon. I connect the real-world problems facing Indigenous peoples to the overwhelming lack of knowledge about Native peoples held by most non-Native people in American society. I have experience researching Indigenous peoples throughout the Pacific Rim, but in my PhD work, I have focused on the Native peoples of Oregon.

Scholars of Indigenous peoples will normally focus on one or a few Indigenous cultures in their work, but in any region, a cross section can be found of the sociopolitical themes present in a global context. Because of my research focus, this chapter contains mainly examples from Oregon and the Northwest Coast, with the inclusion of a few other case studies and examples from other regions. This chapter privileges North American subjects over global Indigenous subjects. Regardless of this focus, be aware that most of the topics discussed here exist in some form in all global Indigenous cultures, especially those that have undergone colonization and a struggle for sovereignty and rights, which include nearly all Indigenous peoples today.

19.1 Indigenous Peoples

LEARNING OUTCOMES

By the end of this section, you will be able to:

- Name different terms used for Indigenous peoples and describe the history and current connotations of each.
- Explain what is meant by the statement that Indigenous peoples have become minorities in their own lands.
- Define blood quantum and explain its current application.
- Explain what is meant by the phrases "urban Indian" and "reservation Indian" and describe social and cultural characteristics associated with each.
- Provide two examples of 20th-century challenges experienced by Native peoples in the United States.
- Explain the need for Native perspectives in studies about Native peoples, using the debate over oral histories as an example.

Indigenous peoples are those peoples who are the original human populations of a land. They are also referred to as Native peoples, tribal peoples, tribes, First Nations peoples, and Aboriginal peoples. In the United States, they are often referred to as American Indians or Native Americans. The terms used to refer to Indigenous peoples are contextualized by the nation or territory they are a part of. For instance, in the United States as a whole, the more general term is currently Native Americans, but in the southwest portion of the United States, American Indians is quite common, while in Alaska and Canada these peoples refer to themselves as First Nations. Hawaiian Indigenous peoples prefer the term Hawaiian. In Mexico, Indigenous peoples are called *la gente indígena de México*. In Australia, the commonly accepted terms are Aboriginal peoples and Torres Strait Islander peoples, referring to two broad but distinct cultural groups, and Indigenous Australians, referring collectively to both.

Terms used for Indigenous peoples often reflect political, social, and economic systems. **Indians** is a term that was once very commonly used in the United States to describe the nation's original inhabitants. The word is a significant part of the legal and political history of these peoples, appearing in hundreds of treaties and thousands of federal documents pertaining to legal rights. But many "Indian" people do not like the word because it was first imposed by Christopher Columbus, who mistakenly thought that his journey across the Atlantic Ocean had landed him in India. Pointing out that the term *Indian* is a case of mistaken identity, many Indigenous peoples prefer to be labeled by their specific tribal names. There is not one mind about which terms to use for Indigenous peoples. There are scholars who refuse to use words such as *Indian* and scholars who embrace the word. Some scholars advocate changing the use of the term *Indian* in history books and historical documents. However, changing historic texts alters the original expression and the meanings associated with it. To change terms in this context would literally change history and mislead students of this history.

There has been another tendency in American culture to misuse the term *Native American* to refer to a single monoculture. The majority of Americans have never spent time with Native individuals or engaged in any studies of Native peoples and thus do not have any true knowledge of actual Indigenous cultures. Until recently, Native cultures and Native history have not been accurately covered in educational institutions. Only in the past decade has there been significant movement toward offering accurate characterizations of Native peoples in public schools in the United States. While this is a positive development, stereotyping of and even racism toward Native peoples remain. The most accepted and appropriate way to refer to any Indigenous person is to use their actual tribal association, if known, rather than a general term such as Native American.

The scholarly debate over these words is somewhat separate from the way the terms are used in Native communities. Many Indigenous communities have no issue with the word *Indian* and think the whole debate over word choice is a distraction from the real-world problems that affect their communities, such as poverty, substance use issues, poor health care, and inadequate education.

Minorities in Their Own Lands

Indigenous peoples are thought of as minorities in most countries. Many colonizing peoples sought to eliminate Indigenous peoples and practiced various strategies to reduce their power to control land and natural resources and even to maintain their cultures and identities. Historically, adult Indigenous people, and even some young people, were forced to work for colonizers, often doing hard labor or other menial tasks, without any opportunities to accumulate wealth or claim a position of higher class. Christianity in various forms was forced on Indigenous peoples through government policies. Children were either not offered any education at all or forced into **boarding schools** where they were required to adopt the colonial culture. In this manner, many Indigenous people lost touch with their cultural heritage, and most Indigenous groups dwindled in number, some disappearing altogether. This trend was particularly pronounced in Latin American countries. Most people living in these countries today have some Indigenous ancestry, but as Indigenous identities have been so discouraged, few openly identify with this portion of their heritage, choosing to focus on their White and/or Spanish identities. It is evident that **assimilation** pressures, the process of changing the culture of a person or group of people to some other culture, through socialization or education, have largely succeeded when remaining peoples who identify as Indigenous become minorities within their own native territories.

FIGURE 19.2 Chemawa Indian Training School in Salem, Oregon (left) and members of the Chemawa Indian School battalion in 1914. (right) This boarding school was created in 1885 and is still operating today. Education policy before the 1970s focused on assimilating Native peoples. Current policies are more supportive of Native culture. (credit: left, "Chemawa Indian School, Winowa Hall, 5495 Chugach Street Northeast, Salem, Marion, OR" by Steve Viale/Library of Congress/Wikimedia Commons, Public Domain; right, *The Chemawa American*/Wikimedia Commons, Public Domain)

Many Native Americans, along with members of other Indigenous groups such as the **Maori** of New Zealand, do not like to be categorized as minority groups in their own homelands. Native Americans in the United States and the Maori tribes of New Zealand have treaties and sovereign rights that accord them access to and ownership of resources that other immigrant minority groups do not have. Some federal funding for programs is allotted to "minority groups" as a whole, including Native peoples. The Native peoples meant to benefit from this funding have commented that this approach does not recognize the special relationships the treaty-bound Indigenous peoples have with the state. The Maori especially have asked not to be considered a minority group. Instead, they wish to claim rights granted them by the Treaty of Waitangi to the services and resources of the federal New Zealand government.

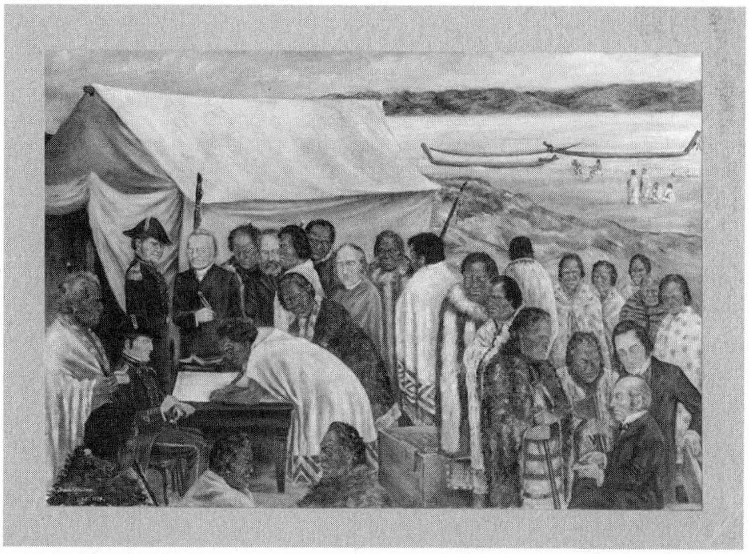

FIGURE 19.3 This illustration, done by Maori artist Ōriwa Tahupōtiki Haddon, depicts Maori chiefs signing the Treaty of Waitangi with representatives of the British Crown in 1840. This treaty is recognized as granting the Maori people rights to the services and resources of the federal New Zealand government. (credit: "The Signing of the Treaty of Waitangi" by Ōriwa Haddon/Archives New Zealand/flickr, CC BY 2.0)

Membership in a Tribal Community

Tribal relations among mixed-race Indigenous people in the United States are governed according to a series of rights first created through federal laws and policies, then later adopted by individual tribal nations. Tribal nations now have the right to manage their own membership laws and policies, with each tribe setting its own **blood quantum** rules for membership. *Blood quantum* refers to a genealogical relationship to one's original tribal people. Full-blooded Native people issue from parents who are both full-blooded members of a tribe, while half-blooded Native people have parents or grandparents who have at least 50 percent Native blood. A person can even be a full-blooded Native, with parents from two tribes, but be considered half-blooded by the tribe they are enrolled in because the tribe only acknowledges the Indigenous blood from the enrollment tribe (Ellinghaus 2017). Some of the terms for people of mixed heritage in the Americas are **mestizo** (common in Latin America) and **Métis** (common in Canada). Some nations, such as Canada, assign different rights to people of mixed Indigenous heritage; Métis communities are accorded different rights from First Nations communities.

Although Indigenous heritage is preferred in most Native communities, the rate of outmarriage is such that pure Indigenous bloodlines are becoming rare. In the United States, most Native people have mixed heritage. An exception is the Navajo Nation, which has a significant number of full-blooded Navajo members due to its large population of more than 300,000 members.

Normally, individuals have to prove they have a blood quantum of a certain percentage to enroll in a tribe. Some tribal policies require a strict accounting of only the bloodlines that originate within that tribe. Other tribes allow for any Indigenous blood as counting toward membership requirements. The latter policy is closer to the cultural practices followed by many Native peoples before they became wards of the federal government. It was common for many tribes to adopt people who moved into their area and took up their culture. In addition, marriage customs of all tribes, which disallowed marriage between individuals too closely related, encouraged members to marry outside of their village or tribe. Spouses brought into a village would be adopted without discrimination. In tribes in Oregon, women would more commonly go to their husbands' villages. In other cultures, such as that of the Seneca of the Northeast, men would move to their wives' villages.

Some scholars view blood quantum as a means for the United States government to prevent people from claiming tribal heritage, ultimately causing tribes to self-terminate. This view is not shared by all tribal peoples. Blood quantum was written into most tribal constitutions in the 1930s as a means of determining tribal citizenships. This policy has caused numerous problems in contemporary communities, where tribal members sometimes attempt to marry their cousins in order to "marshal" their blood—that is, raise or maintain the percentage of blood quantum in their offspring (Nenemay 2005). Scholars have noted that most tribes will continue to lose members due to outmarriage unless membership requirements are changed, even though most blood quantum requirements are currently well below one-half. Many tribal communities are shifting policies so that individuals can claim tribal membership by establishing descent from an enrolled tribal member (Thornton 1997).

Membership in the Grand Ronde tribe of Oregon requires a 1/16 blood quantum of Grand Ronde blood and an ancestor or parent who was on a tribal roll or record in the past. The tribe counts only genealogical connection to original tribal residents of the reservation. Unfortunately, many people have moved on and off the reservation over the years, and records have not been accurately maintained. Proving past residence on the reservation is difficult. In addition, more restrictive changes to the membership requirements since 1999 have reduced the number of members. One controversial change made in 1999 requires that the parent of a potential new member must have been enrolled in the tribe at the time of the prospective member's birth. This change denies membership to the children of those who became members after having children and the children of those born during the period between 1956 and 1983, when tribal rolls were not maintained. One result has been split families, in which younger children born when their parents were on the tribal roll are deemed members, while their older siblings are not eligible for enrollment.

The issue has become politicized at the reservation, with some enrolled members fearing that a flood of new enrollments would impact services and funds and others wanting to expand enrollment to allow more descendants into the tribe. These questions of identity, both political and social, will likely continue to excite debate in the coming decades, as many tribes acknowledge that unless they change membership requirements, they may cease to exist in the future.

Tribal Groups and Communities

Most Indigenous communities are extremely poor and face a number of challenges resulting from centuries of colonization, settlement, and exploitation. In the United States, Canada, and Australia, Indigenous peoples were forcibly relocated to **reservations**, often marginal lands "set aside" for Native peoples after European settlers and colonists claimed their original homelands. Many North American reservation communities have been, and continue to be, kept in a state of perpetual poverty. Reservations typically have few employment opportunities, high substance addiction and alcoholism rates, and high morbidity rates caused by long-term persistent poverty. Some tribes have been successful in making good education available to young people through successes in casino development and effective management of federal education grants, but there is a significant disparity of completion rates at all levels of education. A 2011 report by the Higher Education Research Institute found that among those enrolled in four-year degree programs, approximately 17 percent of Native students completed the degree within four years, compared to 45 percent of Asian students, 43 percent of White students, 26 percent of Latinx/Latina/Latino students, and 21 percent of Black students (DeAngelo et al. 2011, 10; see also Al-Asfour and Abraham 2016).

In the United States, tribal reservations were historically prevented from developing their own industries by the Nonintercourse Act sections of the **Trade and Intercourse Acts**. This legislation made it illegal to sell products beyond the borders of a reservation, which were viewed in the same way as state borders. Tribes can petition Congress to approve a reservation-based industry, but the petition can take decades to be approved. Many reservations have languished for two centuries with few or no jobs or opportunities for Native peoples (Miller 2012). Those who leave reservations for jobs rarely return as full-time residents. Still, Indigenous people on reservations in the United States enjoy the comfort of living within their own cultures and face less discrimination in their communities than they would in White-dominated communities.

People of mixed Indigenous heritage who can "pass" as White have often done so, thus abandoning their Indigenous ancestry. Many took advantage of opportunities to move to cities and get jobs as "White" people, enjoying the pay and social benefits that went along with those jobs and social identities. This path was followed by many Native people in the United States beginning in the later 19th century. The exodus to the cities reached a peak in the 1950s and 1960s following the United States' **termination** of the status of 109 tribes. Termination refers to a US federal policy adopted in 1953 that voided the treaty agreements between the federal government and Native peoples. The US government then repossessed and sold reservation property in a process called liquidation. Terminated tribal peoples were released from reservation lifeways with no money or resources. They were no longer federally recognized Native peoples and had no rights to ask for federal services or assistance. Most of the tribes that underwent termination were restored beginning in the 1970s.

Many of those who underwent termination moved to urban environments in search of work, resulting on populations of " **urban Indian**" communities. During World War II, the Keiser Shipyards in Portland employed a number of Native people, many of them women (https://openstax.org/r/oregonhistoryproject), who left regional reservations for work. The twentieth century trend of Native peoples moving to cities creating has resulted in significant populations of "urban Indians."

Today, the majority of Native people in the United States live in urban environments. This movement has created tensions within Indigenous communities. The phrase "urban Indian" has taken on negative connotations within some Indigenous contexts. Some "reservation Indians" accuse urban Natives of willingly giving up their status, land, and culture. While some urban Natives struggle with feeling disconnected from their tribal identities, many maintain a connection with reservation communities by visiting on weekends and holidays and participating in special events such as tribal government meetings.

Urban Native communities typically include groups to benefit Native people, such as educational and culture-based organizations and civic-minded business associations. Many of these groups include people from various tribes who work together to plan community spiritual activities such as powwows, support urban Indigenous food systems, or serve on culture-based committees. Tribal nations often have offices in urban communities that offer services to their citizens and serve as a site of sovereign activities of the tribe. Indigenous-language learning groups are now quite common in urban centers, especially at universities and tribal offices. Universities in many ways form cultural centers for urban Indigenous people, offering Native centers, employing Indigenous scholars, and funding cultural activities and events.

There are several tribal offices in Portland, Oregon, which has one of the largest concentrations of off-reservation Native people in the United States, with an estimated 40,000 people of Native descent. On the west side of town is the Portland-area office of the Confederated Tribes of the Grand Ronde. This office hosts weekly cultural education programs called Lifeways, which are free to tribal community members, along with classes in wood carving, drawing, storytelling, and the Chinuk Wawa language. Other services offered to tribal members living in the Portland metro area include jobs programs, food distributions, and a large boardroom equipped for hosting formal meetings. Also in Portland are the offices of the Confederated Tribes of Siletz Indians (https://openstax.org/r/ConfederatedTribesofSiletzIndians), the Native American Youth and Family Center education organization, the Oregon Native American Chamber of Commerce (https://openstax.org/r/AmericanChamber), and the Columbia River Intertribal Fish Commission (https://openstax.org/r/ColumbiaRiver). Portland is the site of community organizations such as the Bow and Arrow Culture Club, which hosts annual cultural gatherings and the large intertribal Delta Park Powwow. The radio station KBOO (90.7) consistently features Native programming.

The Native population of Portland is a broad mixture of enrolled tribal people and unenrolled descendant people from throughout the United States. There are also large numbers of Indigenous peoples from other countries, with concentrations of Latina/Latino and Pacific Islander peoples. In addition, the Hawaiian community has deep roots in the region due to the inclusion of Hawaiian labor in the 19th-century fur trade of the Pacific Northwest.

20th-Century Challenges

In the 20th century, some tribes grew self-sufficient or even wealthy by harvesting or extracting the natural resources on their reservations. The land of the Osage Nation of Oklahoma was found to contain vast reserves of underground oil. Members of the nation who had oil under their allotments became wealthy, so much so that some were among the wealthiest people on the planet during the height of the oil boom. But soon after acquiring this wealth, White neighbors began marrying into the tribe. Tribal members began being murdered, and authorities were slow to launch any investigations. Eventually, White relatives ended up owning much of the Osage lands. The story of the Osage murders is documented in several books, including *Killers of the*

Flower Moon by David Grann, which was made into a motion picture directed by Martin Scorsese.

FIGURE 19.4 An oil field in the town of Denoya, on the Osage Reservation. Although the discovery of oil on their lands initially brought some members of the Osage Nation considerable wealth, it also made them the target of unscrupulous White neighbors. Many Osage were murdered, with their White relatives coming into possession of their land and the petroleum beneath it. (credit: Oklahoma Historical Society/Wikimedia Commons, Public Domain)

In a similar story, the Klamath tribe of Oregon established a very successful logging operation on their reservation in the early 20th century. The reservation included a million acres of ponderosa pine. The Klamath people established sawmills and sold the timber off the reservation, becoming quite wealthy. They even built an airfield on the reservation. But their prosperity did not last. The federal government had been serving as the bank administrator of the Klamath money and managing their profits. It became apparent that some money had gone missing and that the land was being poorly managed by federal agents. The tribe successfully sued the government for mismanagement, but they only received a percentage of the money they were owed.

In the 1940s, tribal liquidation/termination began to be discussed with the Klamath people. Some Klamath people initially liked the idea of termination because it would free them from control by the federal government. They were initially told they would receive their reservation land, but the government later told them the land would be sold. Termination began in 1954. In 1961, the remaining unsold reservation lands were turned into the Winema National Forest. Klamath members were forced to leave their homelands and find employment in regional cities. The result of termination was that the Klamath lost their land and many rights as Native people. Their population was dispersed, making it difficult to keep the culture alive. By the 1960s, most of the tribal languages were extinct, and many people had lost connections with their tribal past. In the 1970s, some of the tribal elders, many who had remained in the vicinity of the original reservation, began activating for restoration. The tribe was restored in 1983 (Lewis 2009).

An extreme example of the disenfranchisement of Native people is the movement of Indigenous peoples who were part of the Okie migration of the 1930s. The Okie migration was to the movement of people out of Oklahoma during the Dust Bowl crisis, in which agriculture yields collapsed due to drought and poor land management practices. Topsoil blew away in large clouds, and thousands lost their land and their jobs. These thousands included a large percentage of mixed-blood Native people. Those who could no longer earn a living farming the degraded land moved west in search of work in Arizona, California, Oregon, and other western states. These migrants led difficult lives, working at low-paying jobs and moving constantly in search of seasonal work. One result of this movement westward was a shift of Native populations to the West and a related collapse of tribal populations in Oklahoma. Among the artifacts of the Okie migration are photographs taken by federal workers who visited the migrant encampments. Likely the most famous of these images is the one now known as *Migrant Mother*, taken in 1936 by photographer Dorothea Lange. The subject of Lange's photo has been identified as Florence Thompson, a Cherokee woman.

FIGURE 19.5 *Migrant Mother*, one of the most famous photographs taken by Dorothea Lange, features a Cherokee woman, Florence Thompson. Like many people during this period, she and her family moved from place to place following farm work during the Dust Bowl crisis of the 1930s. (credit: "Destitute Pea Pickers in California. Mother of Seven Children. Age Thirty-Two. Nipomo, California" by Dorothea Lange/Library of Congress, Public Domain)

By the 1970s, most Indigenous people in the United States were still very poor. In this period, a number of laws were passed to help Native people. These laws gave tribes the rights to control their cultures, educate their people, and administer their own foster care. These rights were difficult to act on, however, without financial resources. In the 1980s, tribes began seeking new ways of making money to take care of their citizens. In 1988, Congress passed the Indian Gaming Regulatory Act. This law allowed Native peoples to establish casinos on their reservations. The caveat is that tribes must "compact" with the state they reside in to secure the right to operate a casino. Many Indigenous people have criticized this stipulation, stating that needing to ask permission places them at a lower level of sovereignty than the states. According to the federal government's own laws, tribal reservations are federal trust lands with sovereignty on par of that of the states. Still, most tribes have compacted with the states they reside within, agreeing as part of the compact to cede a percentage of casino profits to the state to aid with funding for services such as education and road maintenance. Tribal casino profits have made it possible for many tribes to establish fully operational governments that offer services and programs for their members in areas such as health care, housing, education, and jobs.

There have been challenges to tribes' rights to establish casinos, the most notable occurring in California during Arnold Schwarzenegger's tenure as governor. Governor Schwarzenegger refused for years to meet with Native representatives to discuss a statewide casino compact, even after voters overwhelmingly approved tribal casinos twice. The tribes felt that Nevada casino operators, who could lose significant revenue from the competition, were influencing the California government. The tribes won a lawsuit in 1999, and many tribes subsequently signed compacts with the state. There have been continued lawsuits against California stating that the compacts require too large a portion of casino profits. Still, tribes in California now have the right to establish casinos, and the income is greatly improving services to tribal members.

FIGURE 19.6 Morongo Casino Resort and Spa in Cabazon, California, operated by the Morongo Band of Cahuilla Mission Indians, is one of hundreds of tribal casinos across the United States. Many have incorporated cultural elements into their design, such as Morongo's woven net design. (credit: "Morongo Casino Resort & Spa Is an Indian Gaming Casino, of the Morongo Band of Cahuilla Mission Indians, Located in Cabazon, California" by Carol M. Highsmith/Library of Congress, Public Domain)

Perspectives

Indigenous peoples have undergone some five centuries of colonization. During this time, the societal structures of the colonial states have emphasized the perspectives of non-Indigenous peoples, broadly identified as White people. Histories have been written to benefit White people, to support their colonizing cultures and to legitimize their takeover of vast territories from Indigenous peoples. Minority perspectives, including Indigenous perspectives, have not been emphasized and have even been sometimes intentionally repressed. Indigenous peoples have struggled with disempowerment in their sovereign relations with state systems and in legal proceedings over their sovereign rights. Many Indigenous peoples still struggle to prove that they are part of a legitimate nation. State-sponsored erasure of Native culture and history has caused losses of and changes to tribal cultures and languages.

Beginning the later 20th century, both Indigenous and non-Indigenous scholars have noted that history has long been presented in a way that is biased toward a White perspective. This bias has been critiqued as a form of systemic racism. In most academic institutions, until relatively recently, most if not all professors were White. There were few opportunities for Indigenous people to establish positions of influence over the presentation and study of Indigenous history and culture. **Native studies** programs began to be developed at various universities in the United States in the 1970s, a movement that coincided with greater opportunities for Indigenous scholars to conduct research on their own peoples. Indigenous people are now actively working to write their own histories and describe their cultures and philosophies from Indigenous perspectives. Indigenous scholarship has made great strides, but there is still a hesitancy in academia to allow Indigenous people to establish positions of authority or introduce Indigenous ways of thinking. Among the academic disciplines, anthropology in particular has made strong progress in recognizing the value and validity of Indigenous perspectives.

An interesting example of recent changes in approaches to Indigenous perspectives is the ongoing debate over **oral histories**. For much of the 19th and 20th centuries, Indigenous "myth texts" were collected from tribes and studied by anthropologists, linguists, and folklorists. Studies of this material typically utilized a linguistic or philosophical framework. The texts were understood, much like Greek mythology, as supernatural stories with a special focus on the godlike animals appearing in them, such as Coyote, Raven, and Blue Jay. Also of interest to early scholars of such texts were their performative aspects and the metaphorical commentary they offered about human existence. A debate emerged between some scholars such as Dell Hymes, who noted that the texts were most valuable as "original texts" or direct ethnographic translations, and others such as Claude Levi-Strauss, who concluded that there was no original text and every version was plagiarized from a previous storyteller. In this authenticity debate, the texts were treated as literature, with little recognition of the historical events appearing in many of the stories (Hegeman 1989). This inability to see the historical value of these texts reflects a bias toward written material and against knowledge presented via **oral tradition**.

Read about how translations of oral histories are analyzed and updated in the online journal *Quartux* (https://openstax.org/r/onlinejournal).

VIDEO

David Lewis, the author of this chapter, discusses the loss of many native languages and reads translations of "A Kalapuya Prophecy (https://openstax.org/r/davidlewisexpanding)".

Many of these assumptions about myth texts have changed in the past 70 years. One study of Crater Lake in Oregon, conducted by geologists in the 1940s, determined that the lake was on the site of what once had been a large volcano, Mount Mazama, known as Moy Yaina by the Indigenous people of the area. When the volcano exploded, the top of the mountain fell inside the cone and formed a caldera, which in time filled with water, resulting in Crater Lake. This event happened some 7,000 years ago. This established geological event is reflected in Indigenous oral traditions. A Klamath tribal oral history tells the story of two mountains, Moy Yaina and Mlaiksi (Mount Shasta in California), having a fight. The Klamath oral history clearly delineates a double volcanic event, with Moy Yaina and Mlaiksi erupting at the same time, but Moy Yaina erupted with a larger explosion and therefore lost the fight. Geological evidence of the explosion spoken of in this myth indicates that Klamath oral history does indeed reflect actual history. Similar oral histories of thousands of Indigenous peoples are now acknowledged to reflect many natural events, especially those that significantly changed the earth in some manner. Oral histories of tsunamis, Ice Age floods, volcanic eruptions, catastrophic fires, and other events are now acknowledged in the stories of many peoples. New understandings of the legitimacy of Indigenous oral histories are leading to increased research into numerous areas of Indigenous knowledge systems.

FIGURE 19.7 Crater Lake, Oregon, and the remains of Mount Mazama. Wizard Island in the center is the original top of Mazama, having fallen into the volcanic cone some 7,000 years ago. A record of these geological events is evident in the oral traditions of Indigenous peoples native to this area. (credit: "Crater Lake National Park, United States" by Amy Hanley/Unsplash, Public Domain)

ETHNOGRAPHIC SKETCHES

Kalapuyan Traditional Ecological Knowledge

Written by David Lewis.

The Kalapuya of the Willamette Valley were native to the interior lands of western Oregon. The Willamette

River and its tributaries drained the Willamette Valley and joined with the Columbia River in the vicinity of present-day Portland. The river served as a highway of trade and travel about the valley and to the trading center at Willamette Falls. The Kalapuya had salmon runs, but not the concentration of salmon fishery sites seen on the Columbia River. They did have expansive prairies and oak savannas that supported a vegetable-rich lifeway. Hunting of deer and elk was always a part of their lives, but they followed a lifestyle of camping at root-digging sites through the summers. Root camps would be established in midsummer near a camas field. They would dig camas for a week, then cook the camas in pit ovens while in the camp. The camas bulbs would cook for three to four days in the underground ovens, changing to a brown color. The cooked bulbs became sweet and were highly desired by the Kalapuya. Cooked camas would be stored in cool underground storage spaces or hung in plank houses for wintertime use. The Kalapuya would store many types of roots and grains in this manner and would also prepare dried salmon and meat for winter storage. In the fall, acorns and hazelnuts could be gathered, and in marshy lakes or the Willamette slough, wapato could be gathered in great quantities. Wapato, or Indian potato, would be stored or traded to other peoples for other foods and trade items. The Tualatin Kalapuya, a northern Willamette Valley tribe of Kalapuya, especially had much wapato at Wapato Lake as well as large amounts of oak savanna on the Tualatin plains. Almost all foods were gathered and prepared in the encampments and then brought back to the villages later. Acorns would be gathered, shelled, and left to rest in cool creeks to let the tannins leach out, then dried and ground into a meal. From this, the Kalapuya would create a mush cooked in woven baskets. Hazelnuts would be shelled and dried on hot rocks in the sun, then eaten on the spot or saved for later. Hazel switches would be harvested from the bushes to make strong baskets. At other times of the year, some Kalapuya would travel into the mountains to pick berries or gather weaving materials for making baskets. Baskets, hats, and large woven mats made from tules and cattails for sitting or lying on would be used by the maker or traded for other items. Most weaving materials would have to be dried for a year before being rehydrated and woven into a useful basket.

The Kalapuya were very community oriented. If other Kalapuya or neighboring tribal peoples were starving, they would help them and feed them. Trade could happen at any time of the year, but in the winters, Kalapuya might approach neighboring tribes to trade for additional food or wealth items they desired. Dried and smoked salmon could be acquired from the Clackamas and Multnomah, who would prepare plenty when the salmon ran. From the Coos, they acquired seashells. The Klickitat had exceptionally good baskets, and the Chinook had canoes and prepared salmon as well as items from throughout the trading sphere of the Columbia River. The Kalapuya specialized in camas and root digging and were dependent on other tribes for quantities of other products.

19.2 Colonization and Anthropology

LEARNING OUTCOMES

By the end of this section, you will be able to:

- Articulate the contributions of Vine Deloria Jr. to the critique of anthropology and the growth of Native studies and Native scholarship.
- Define the practice of “othering” and explain how it has affected and continues to affect Indigenous people in the United States.
- Evaluate the historic issues related to anthropologists serving as cultural experts.
- Relate how anthropology has aided colonialism and propose some ways these practices may be reversed.

Anthropology has been criticized by numerous anthropologists and other scholars as participating in the colonization of Indigenous societies. While settlers took land and resources from tribes and forced them to relocate to reservations, anthropologists gathered knowledge from Indigenous peoples for their own purposes. Another critique has focused on the right claimed by some anthropologists to speak for Indigenous peoples. Books written by early anthropologists have been viewed as disempowering Native peoples, claiming a place of greater legitimacy than the perspectives of Native people themselves. Some anthropologists in the late 19th and early 20th centuries collected images of Indigenous people posed and dressed to fit a stereotypical conception of “Indians.” Edward S. Curtis was one such anthropologist and photographer. Although his photos are rendered beautifully, they reflect his own conceptions rather than the realities of life for Native peoples at the time the photographs were taken. Curtis and many of his contemporaries are now critiqued for privileging their personal perspectives over the stark realities of Native peoples impoverished on reservations.

FIGURE 19.8 This photograph of three Sioux chiefs, taken by Edward S. Curtis circa 1905, does not reflect actual cultural practices. At this time, these men were living on a Sioux reservation and would have dressed much like other Americans. Curtis posed these men on horses and in traditional regalia to please an American audience eager to see stereotypical images. (Credit: "Sioux Chiefs" by Edward S. Curtis/Library of Congress, public domain)

Deloria's Critique

These criticisms of anthropology gained strength in the 1960s, with several Native scholars questioning in particular the higher value assigned to academic scholarship than to the voices of Native peoples. These critiques caused many scholars to reassess the nature of anthropological research.

Vine Deloria Jr. was a Sioux scholar who gained fame in the 1960s. Deloria openly challenged the legitimacy of anthropology as a discipline, criticizing anthropologists for benefiting from their research projects, whether through selling books or achieving tenure at their universities, while those they studied rarely received any benefits. Deloria developed his evaluation over a long career consisting of five decades of scholarship. One focus of his scholarship was the biased nature of supposedly "objective" scientific research, which he called "an entrenched state religion" (1997, 211). He also accused Western academics of relying on notions of Native peoples that were biased by stereotypes and assumptions.

In many ways, Deloria inspired the growth of Native studies programs. His critical arguments resonated with tribal communities and were, and still are, an inspiration to generations of Indigenous scholars. His critiques have resonated with the discipline as a whole as well, resulting in adjustments and changes to anthropological methods and practices. There are now many more Indigenous and minority scholars in anthropology than ever before, in part aided by Deloria's critique. Maori scholar Linda T. Smith describes the mission of these scholars in this way: "Telling our stories from the past, reclaiming the past, giving testimony to the injustices of the past are all strategies which are commonly employed by Indigenous peoples struggling for justice. . . . The need to tell our stories remains the powerful imperative of a powerful form of resistance" (2021, 38). Indigenous specialties have been developed in most areas of anthropology, including Indigenous anthropology and Indigenous archaeology. Deloria's criticisms have also been influential in the creation of the fields of public anthropology, public archaeology, and applied anthropology, all of which seek to establish a closer relationship with research subjects and apply research findings to address current problems.

The Othering of Indigenous Peoples

Othering, discussed earlier in this text, refers to viewing those from different cultures or backgrounds as "other," or inherently and importantly different from oneself or one's own "type" of people. Indigenous peoples have been particularly affected by a tendency to be viewed as other by White society. As Linda Smith writes, "A critical aspect of the struggle for self-determination has involved questions relating to our history as Indigenous peoples and a critique of how we, as the Other, have been represented or excluded from various accounts" (2021, 31). The "otherness" that Smith refers to reflects tendencies both to not think about Indigenous peoples at all and to deliberately deny Indigenous cultures an equal share of the history of their land. Indigenous histories and contexts are viewed as something "other" than White histories and contexts and are largely ignored. Othering happens in every conceivable context and affects almost all aspects of social existence, including social mobility, civil rights, getting a job, and applying for grants and funding. Othering figures strongly into sometimes subconscious determinations as to whether a person is the right type of person for a specific position or role. Othering is a form of discrimination and racism. Othering has played a large role in recent discussions of policing in the United States. Othering is influential in the ongoing issue of missing and murdered Indigenous women. Many police agencies are not investigating missing Indigenous women because they are the other—Indigenous—and the women are singled out by predators because they are clearly Indigenous.

Cultural Experts and Authority

Anthropologists have noted the value of tribal cultural experts to their research projects. A cultural expert is immersed in the culture of their Indigenous community and has insight into the intricacies of their community. Cultural experts have been used by anthropologists since the beginnings of anthropology. However, when reporting information provided by cultural experts, anthropologists have too often taken a position of authority that somewhat disempowers these same cultural experts. Those learning about an Indigenous society will typically turn to the published ethnographic literature on the subject. This literature will most likely present an outsider's understanding of that society, frozen in a specific time frame and based on a single research project. This gives the readers a warped understanding of the culture they are interested in, only completely valid within the time frame of the study.

Cultural experts, on the other hand, adapt and modify their insights and knowledge as they age. It is now common for researchers to seek out cultural experts to provide contemporary understandings of a culture and society. In addition, many researchers will now form collaborations with cultural experts that assign ownership and authorship to the cultural expert or the culture they are researching. Within this approach, the anthropologist becomes the compiler or editor of any publications, or perhaps the lead author of a team of authors. Many Indigenous scholars now conduct their own research, taking the roles of lead authors and editors of studies. Tribes are also taking control of research projects, contracting with anthropologists who agree to conduct the work with significant tribal input and review.

Indigenous Societies as Colonial Societies

Indigenous societies are in many ways colonial societies. Most Indigenous people are of mixed heritage, and Indigenous cultures have changed in ways that make them more similar to the surrounding White communities. As just one example, many Indigenous peoples have adopted Christianity as their primary religion. But in most Indigenous communities, there is space for Indigenous traditions and spirituality as well. Sometimes, White and Indigenous cultures exist parallel to one another. Such hybrid societies are often criticized by Indigenous and non-Indigenous people as no longer being Native or Indigenous, but this criticism reflects an understanding of what it means to be Indigenous that is frozen in time. Many people envision Native cultures as they existed in the 19th century as being the "true" cultures, while the cultures of Native people living in urban suburbs with automobiles and ranch-style houses are viewed as tainted or inauthentic. Culture is not a static thing; it is dynamic, constantly changing to fit the context of the present. Native peoples continue to maintain a cultural core that is Indigenous while they adopt the technology and trappings of contemporary society.

Decolonizing Anthropology

In the 1970s, a movement began to "decolonize anthropology." This movement seeks to address anthropology's role in collecting and taking ownership of Native knowledge and culture and to speak out against anthropological analyses and products that support colonialism. One aspect of anthropological practice that has been particularly criticized is a tendency to treat Native people purely as research subjects, without acknowledging their agency or their rights, such as the right to protect their buried ancestors or control their knowledge, stories, and even place names. As part of the "decolonizing" movement, scholars began developing research protocols to address these criticisms. The Indigenous perspective has begun to be recognized as valuable, and people from diverse backgrounds have been welcomed into the discipline.

In the 1990s, the Southwest Oregon Research Project (SWORP) was established to collect and return to those to whom it pertained knowledge collected by anthropologists and other researchers. The SWORP project began under the leadership of George Wasson of the Coquille Indian Tribe of Oregon. Wasson worked with Smithsonian Institution and University of Oregon administrations to copy and collect documents pertaining to some 60 western Oregon tribes and return the resultant collection to the university archives. The project eventually hosted three trips to Washington, DC, to collect more than 200,000 pages of anthropological and federal documents from the National Anthropological Archives and the National Archives and Records Administration. The collections were then organized and hosted in the University of Oregon Special Collections. In 1995 and 2001, copies of these documents were given to some 17 tribes in Oregon and the surrounding region. This project served in a very real sense to decolonize the anthropology of the past by returning Indigenous knowledge to tribal peoples.

Peoples receiving the SWORP collections have been free to access the knowledge collected from their ancestors over a 100-year time period, from the 1850s to 1950, and build on this knowledge with further projects to restore tribal culture. In one instance of a successful restoration, techniques for creating the traditional canoes of the Clackamas Chinook were studied in an effort to restore both the production and use of these canoes in the Northwest region. Scholars made use of a SWORP collection of files created by anthropologist Philip Drucker, which described traditional methods of construction and traditional designs. Since the 1990s, there has been a marked resurgence in traditional canoe construction on the Northwest Coast. Tribal nations along the Northwest Coast now undertake an annual canoe journey that involves hundreds of communities and thousands of tribal members. These developments have been aided by the preservation and return of cultural knowledge.

FIGURE 19.9 A Chinook canoe built using traditional construction techniques, circa 1825. The surface of these canoes was typically charred to prevent decay.(credit: "Image from Page 286 of 'The American Museum Journal' (c1900-[1918])" by American Museum of Natural History/Internet Archive Book Images/flickr, Public Domain)

FIGURE 19.10 A crew from the Grande Ronde Tribe launch a Chinook canoe from the beach at the Swinomish Tribal Community Center. In recent decades, there has been a revival in traditional canoe construction on the Northwest Coast. (credit: "Canoe Crew Preparing for Launch" by John Clemens, US Geological Survey/flickr, Public Domain)

Some tribal scholars have raised concerns that many ethnographic and anthropological field notes are untrustworthy sources because they are the products of biased research practices and may reflect anthropologists' efforts to confirm previously conceived ideas about tribal peoples. The critics rightly note that some anthropologists may have altered their findings to fit stereotypical notions. Tribal peoples have thus been wary of relying solely on field notes to reconstruct cultural practices, taking care to compare the field notes of anthropologists with elder knowledge to devise valid restoration projects for culture and language.

The existence of field notes themselves is somewhat controversial among Native communities. Some Indigenous people have criticized the act of writing down Indigenous stories, which were normally oral literatures. This same criticism calls into question the legitimacy of all field notes collected from peoples who rely on oral histories. Some Indigenous scholars thus refuse to use any ethnographic notes, viewing them as biased documents. However, another perspective is that many of these field notes were collected from tribal cultural experts who willingly participated in the collection of their stories and knowledge. Many of these cultural experts were elders in their communities who wanted to save their culture and language, not passive participants unaware of the outcomes of their work with anthropologists. From this perspective, these elders knew what they were doing and were aware that they may hold the last remaining knowledge of certain cultural practices or languages; therefore, their work and contributions need to be respected by all scholars today.

PROFILES IN ANTHROPOLOGY

Beatrice Medicine (Sihasapa and Minneconjou Lakota)
1923–2005

Personal History: David Lewis recollects: *I had an opportunity to meet Dr. Beatrice Medicine (https://openstax.org/r/appliedanthro) when she visited the University of Oregon in the early 2000s. Medicine gave numerous presentations about her work. The most impactful presentation was her study of Scandinavian revivalists who were recreating Native American traditions in Europe and Russia. She told stories of how the Lakota community met with these revivalists and decided to help them practice the culture correctly. What they had been practicing emulated Native cultures as stereotyped in Hollywood films, including a US cavalry* *charge and a tom-tom drumbeat. This was clearly inaccurate, and the Lakota decided that if the revivalists really wanted to represent Lakota culture, they should help them do it correctly. Medicine and other Lakota culture bearers then took on the responsibility of going to Europe to meet some of these groups and teach them the correct culture.*

Additionally, Medicine told stories of how anthropologists who came to reservations in the 19th century were sometimes fooled by Native collaborators. She noted that some of the stories collected were made up on the spot by men who realized that they would be paid for more stories. So, they created stories of history and events for the anthropologists, earned a few extra dollars, and later made fun of the anthropologists for not really knowing the culture. Some of these stories were published in anthropologists' language texts and are now part of the legacy of the discipline. Much of the legacy of oral histories involves tribal mistrust of the products of anthropologists, considered to be inaccurate and biased—a feeling supported in part by this story. But Medicine's discerning of the reason behind the creation of new stories provides additional contexts that then partly refute the distrust of anthropologists once the intentions of the Native collaborators are known. The stories themselves are not worthless to tribal people who study them today, and they teach scholars about tribal peoples' ingenuity and humor.

Medicine's storytelling was very powerful. She did not follow the typical narrative that presented anthropology as a handmaiden of colonialism, instead showing how she, as an anthropologist, could help people understand others and apply anthropology to work out problems in the world. Medicine's series of talks at the University of Oregon was inspiring to Native scholars and provided examples of how we could use anthropology to help our peoples when we returned to our Native communities, as many will.

Area of Anthropology: Dr. Beatrice Medicine was a scholar, anthropologist, and educator known for her work in the fields of Indigenous languages and cultures, applied anthropology, gender studies, and Native history. She was born on the Standing Rock Reservation in North Dakota and spent years teaching, traveling, and working in anthropology throughout the world before returning to Standing Rock to retire. In her final years she helped build an elementary school at the reservation.

Accomplishments in the Field: Medicine was able to shift seamlessly and effectively between her roles as a Native person and an anthropologist. She had a lot of faith that anthropology could understand and recover from the effects of our colonial histories. Medicine worked to promote applied anthropology as a way for the discipline to contribute in positive ways to Native societies. She inspired many young Native scholars and anthropologists to use anthropology to help Native peoples. As one of the few Native and women anthropologists of her time, she faced and overcame many challenges posed by the paternalistic White men in the discipline.

Importance of Her Work: For her work, Medicine earned numerous awards, including a Distinguished Service Award from the American Anthropological Association (1991), the Bronislaw Malinowski Award from the Society for Applied Anthropology (1996), and the George and Louise Spindler Award for education in anthropology from the American Anthropological Association (2005). The Applied Anthropology Association established a travel award in her name, and her life's work was featured in a 2015 panel at the American Anthropological Association's annual meeting.

Medicine's most influential book is *Learning to Be an Anthropologist and Remaining "Native"*, published by the University of Illinois Press in 2001.

For more information, see the Indigenous Goddess Gang's Matriarch Monday post honoring Dr. Beatrice Medicine (https://openstax.org/r/MatriarchMonday).

19.3 Indigenous Agency and Rights

LEARNING OUTCOMES

By the end of this section, you will be able to:

- Explain the significance of Indigenous peoples being declared "domestic dependent nations" in the United States.
- Discuss Indigenous rights to natural resources and the degree to which Native nations have been successful in asserting these rights.
- Describe some traditional techniques used by Indigenous peoples to create cultural objects as well as efforts to restore this knowledge.
- Articulate two features of Indigenous philosophies and worldviews and explain how researchers access Indigenous philosophies and worldviews.
- Describe political responses to federal government policies pertaining to Indigenous peoples in the United States.
- Articulate Indigenous critiques of the use of Indigenous names and images as mascots for sports teams.

Treaties and Removal

In the mid-19th century, the United States federal government shifted its approach toward purchasing tribal lands rather than conquering Indigenous nations. Many Native societies had already suffered greatly due to White settlement and were ready to sign **treaties** that would guarantee them protection on **federal Indian reservations**. Population loss caused by epidemic disease also played a role in many tribes' decisions to sign treaties with the federal government. Those who signed treaties received payment for lands, money for schools, and support in establishing Western farming practices in addition to land allotments on a reservation where federal authorities were to guarantee their safety.

As White settlement expanded into the western United States, Indigenous peoples both on and off federal reservations were subject to waves of removal from their lands. Areas set aside for reservations that had once seemed undesirably remote for White settlement became increasingly desirable as the White population grew. In the 1830s, tribal peoples living on reservations east of the Mississippi River were forced to move to what is now Oklahoma, then called Indian Territory. The tribes were promised that they would be able to keep their new reservation lands in perpetuity. However, when political currents changed, largely due to the pressures of European immigrants moving westward who desired land for settlement, the land formerly designated Indian Territory was opened to White settlement, and reservations diminished.

The most famous Native removal was the Cherokee Trail of Tears in 1838. After President Andrew Jackson signed the Indian Removal Act in 1830, the US Army forced an estimated 16,000 Cherokee then living in the southeast United States to walk to Indian Territory. An estimated 5,000 of these people died on the trail. The Cherokee Trail of Tears was not the only removal. Each time the United States expanded its borders into Indian Territory, tribes were forced to move to smaller reservations with less desirable, resource-poor lands. The Choctaw were removed from Florida to Oklahoma in 1831, and the Creek were removed in 1836, leading to an estimated 3,500 of their 15,000 people dying. Twenty years later, the United States assumed sole title to the lands of the Oregon Territory and removed 4,000 Native people from some 60 different tribes onto two reservations, the Coast and Grand Ronde Reservations. During the western Oregon "Trails of Tears," members of tribes then living on the temporary Table Rock and Umpqua Reservations were forced to walk more than 300 miles in the dead of winter to the Coast and Grand Ronde Reservations, with many dying from exposure. Once at the Coast and Grand Ronde Reservations, the tribes were made to live with many other tribes from five different language families and to join as one tribe on the reservations.

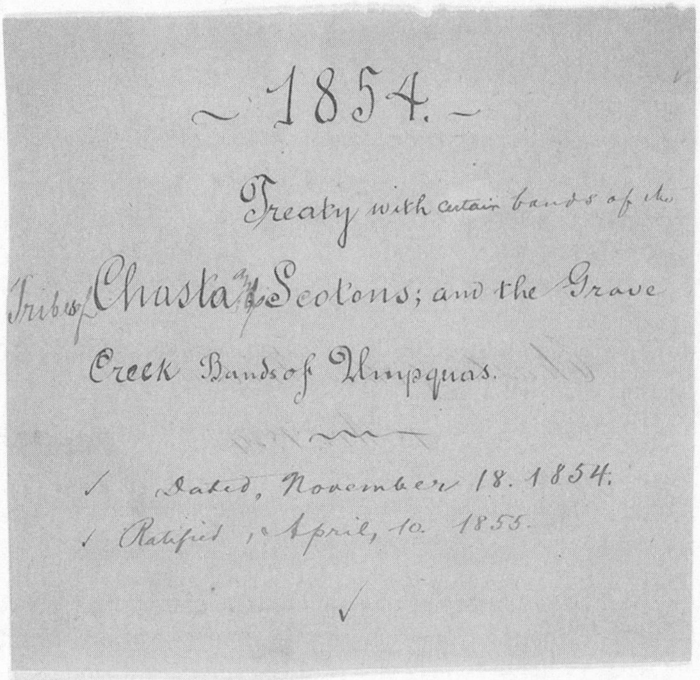

~ 1854. ~

Treaty with certain bands of the Tribes of Chasta & Scotons; and the Grave Creek Bands of Umpquas.

✓ Dated, November 18. 1854.
✓ Ratified, April, 10. 1855.

✓

FIGURE 19.11 The cover page of a treaty with certain bands of the Chasta (Chastacosta) and Scoton tribes and the Grave Creek band of the Umpqua tribe, negotiated in 1854 and ratified in 1855. (credit: “Small Brown Cover Sheet: ‘1854. Treaty with Certain Bands of the Tribes of Chasta and Scotons; and the Grave Creek Bands of Umpquas. Dated, November 18, 1854. Ratified, April 10, 1855’” by US Government/US National Archives and Records Administration, Public Domain)

In all parts of the United States, life on the reservations was very challenging. Native peoples had to build their own houses and establish means of producing food and other necessities with limited resources. Federal aid, although guaranteed in the treaties, was slow to arrive and sometimes lost in transit or simply missing. For the first 20 years of the Grand Ronde Reservation, residents lived in poverty with inconsistent food and health care and poorly planned schools. On Oregon reservations, the tribal peoples did not receive their treaty rights of individual plots of farmland until at least 1873. While the government had guaranteed food, by 1860, it was clear that federal officials could not be counted on for regular food shipments. Thousands of Native people died at early ages in the first two decades due to malnutrition and newly introduced diseases. Similar stories can be told for all tribes in the United States. Problems were also caused by untrained, unqualified, and corrupt government officials who stole food, money, and supplies.

Domestic Dependent Nations

The legal status of Native nations was greatly influenced by several paternalistic rulings by the US Supreme Court in the 1830s. Three rulings known as the **Marshall court trilogy** (*Johnson v. M’Intosh*, 1823; *Cherokee Nation v. Georgia*, 1831; *Worcester v. Georgia*, 1832) determined that tribal peoples were domestic sovereign nations within the United States and dependent on the federal government to guarantee their sovereignty. These rulings meant that all reservations were “federal lands,” not part of the states, with the federal government as the administrator. Native rights, therefore, must be given through federal authorities or named in treaties with the federal government.

This state of dependency has caused much consternation among Native peoples ever since. As “domestic dependent nations,” many aspects of tribal societies—including management of money, land, education, health care, and other programs—have been administered by the federal government. Beyond the question of the appropriateness of this arrangement, there have been innumerable documented cases of Native peoples not receiving the services or funds they were promised. Between 1910 and the 1980s, Native peoples filed hundreds of civil cases against the federal government for mismanagement of service, land, and money. By the

1940s, there were so many cases that the federal government established a special jurisdictional court, the Indian Claims Commission, to deal with the volume of lawsuits. Under the Indian Claims Commission, many cases were consolidated to make the process more efficient. Originally planned to exist for 10 years, the court was extended into the 1970s, as hundreds of cases had been filed and it was taking decades to decide many of them. The Klamath tribe, for example, filed seven **Indian Claims** lawsuits for mismanagement of the money they earned through logging operations. The Klamath cases were combined and decided in the 1950s, with some payouts from their lawsuits extending into the 1960s. The Indian Claims Commission ended in 1978, having cleared 546 dockets and named 342 awards totaling $818,172,606.64.

One example of a successful Indian Claims case (number K-344) involved California tribal members of groups called the Mission Indians and other tribes from Northern California. These tribes had signed 18 treaties with the federal government in 1851. The treaties were never ratified, and as such, the tribes were never paid for their lands. After the treaties were found hidden in the vast record collections of the National Archives in 1905, the California tribes began working on a case for payment for the lands, for which they filed suit in 1928. The first case was not decided until 1942, with the court declaring that "the Indians of California consist of wandering bands, tribes, and small groups, who had been roving over the same territory during the period under the Spanish and Mexican ownership, before the [1848] treaty between Mexico and the United States whereby California was acquired by the United States" (Indians of California ex rel. U. S. Webb v. United States, 98 Ct. Cl. 583, 1942) This decision meant that the tribes were determined not to have a case for the return of lands and could only ask for cash payments. A second case was decided in 1964. Payments from both cases did not come until 1969, when the court gave the tribes 47 cents per acre for the 64 million acres of California lands they had once occupied, a total of $29.1 million. Court awards were subject to political maneuvering and arbitration within the House of Representatives over how much the tribes would actually receive. In the case of K-344, the award amount was based on the value of the lands in 1851, which had skyrocketed in value over the more than a century that had passed. Many tribal members were very upset by the paltry sum awarded for the wealthy lands of California.

Water, Fishing, and Agency

FIGURE 19.12 A Hupa person fishing in Trinity River in Northern California in the early 1900s. Fishing rights became a particular source of conflict between Indigenous and White people in the northwestern United States in the 1960s. (credit: "Fish-Weir across Trinity River—Hupa" by Edward S. Curtis, Smithsonian Institution/flickr, Public Domain)

From the 1960s to the 1980s, an issue of particular concern to the tribes of the northwestern part of the United States was fishing rights. The "fishing wars" were a series of political and legal battles over whether Indigenous peoples had the right to fish in their usual and accustomed places, as promised in numerous treaties.

Following the Belloni (*Sohappy v. Smith/United States v. Oregon*, 1969) and Boldt (*United States v. Washington*, 1974) court decisions, the tribes of Washington State, including those that had been terminated and not yet restored, maintained their rights to fish in their usual and accustomed ways—and their right to half the catch in the state of Washington.

These decisions affirmed tribal sovereignty rights promised in ratified treaties but had the negative consequence of causing delays in the restoration of other tribes from termination. Many sport fishermen's organizations feared that an increase in restored tribes would impact fishing for non-Natives. Both the Siletz and Grand Ronde tribes experienced delays related to fears about fishing in their federal restorations in the 1970s and 1980s. Ultimately, both tribes were forced to give up fishing and hunting rights to become federally restored. Ironically, neither the Grand Ronde nor the Siletz have fishing or hunting rights in their ratified treaties. Both tribes concluded that restoration of the tribal governments was more important than holding out for fishing and hunting rights.

FIGURE 19.13 Two Native men dip-net fishing at Celilo Falls on the Columbia River, circa 1950. Some tribes were forced to give up the right to fish in their traditional locations in return for the restoration of their tribal status. (credit: "Men Fishing at Celilo Falls on the Columbia River" by Gerald W. Williams/OSU Special Collections & Archives/flickr, Public Domain)

The Klamath tribe of Oregon was terminated in the 1950s, along with tribes in California, including the Karuk and Yurok, all of whom traditionally relied on fish from the Klamath River. In the 1970s and 1980s, these tribes were restored by the US federal government with their rights intact. The Klamath tribe of Oregon is the only tribe on the river with a ratified treaty that guaranteed fishing rights. During the termination period, the federal government had built numerous dams and water reclamation projects on the river and given away water resources to farmers and ranchers in the area. Dams such as the Shasta Dam had destroyed many salmon runs, and the water giveaways had taken much-needed in-stream flows out of the river, making the river warmer and less environmentally friendly to fish. When local tribes were restored, they began demanding rights to fish the river again. These rights were decided in a series of court decisions determining that the Klamath tribe's water rights preceded those of farmers and municipalities, meaning that their rights to in-stream flows needed to be upheld. Numerous projects are underway to eliminate the dams on the Klamath River and return it to its original state.

FIGURE 19.14 A Klamath woman in a traditional Klamath canoe harvesting wokas, the seeds of the yellow pond lily, circa 1923. (credit: "The Wokas Season—Klamath" by Edward S. Curtis/Library of Congress, Public Domain)

Tribes with fishing rights in their treaties are now encroaching on the territories of tribes without such rights, leading to legal and political maneuvering between tribes. In Oregon, the Grand Ronde tribe was forced to purchase land at a key fishing location, Willamette Falls, and had to sidestep federal permissions, working with the state to gain "ceremonial" rights. Ultimately, the intertribal conflicts are caused by tribal adherence to federal bureaucratic processes that rely on legal or political channels to resolve problem rather than traditional tribal methods that bring people to the table to form agreements under traditional protocols.

Culture and Language

Native languages are the most threatened part of the cultures of Native peoples. Many tribes now have only a handful of people who fluently speak the tribe's language. Of the estimated 10,000 languages once spoken worldwide, at least half have now gone extinct with no speakers, and there are 3,018 Indigenous languages spoken worldwide that are today endangered. One assessment of the 115 Indigenous languages currently spoken in the United State rates two as healthy, 34 as in danger, and 79 likely to go extinct within a generation (Nagle 2019). The rate and severity of language loss is connected to the remaining population of the tribe, whether the tribe has a functioning cultural center, and whether the language continues to be spoken in the households of tribal members. In large part, tribal people of the United States are becoming English-only speakers (Crawford 1995).

Language recovery and revitalization have become a focus of many Indigenous peoples. Many tribal members consider knowledge of their language to be the true determinant of tribal identity. Complex understandings of philosophies and lifeways are embedded in language. In addition, tribes believe that their ancestors' spirits visit members of the tribe to speak with and advise them, and if a person does not know the language, they will not be able to understand them. Tribes are now working to restore, preserve, stabilize, and teach their languages to the next generations to preserve their knowledge and cultural identities. The University of California, Berkeley, developed a master-apprentice program that is helping many Indigenous groups develop more language speakers by partnering fluent speakers with young tribal members. Even with this type of training, it can take years to learn to fluently speak the language. Another approach is the language immersion program, inspired by Hawaiian and Maori educational models. The immersion model places students in immersive classrooms for a period of several years, in which only the Native language is spoken. Evening classes are also offered for adult learners.

In addition to efforts to restore Native languages, many tribes and urban tribal organizations offer cultural education classes to teach traditional skills. Art and craft classes are quite popular. Classes offered by Native instructors teach traditional techniques for making bows and arrows, weaving baskets, drawing in traditional styles, beading, and making moccasins, among others. History is another area that is receiving some attention. As just one example, the Cherokee Nation has instituted a history program for tribal members and tribal government staff so that all people working with and for the tribe have a shared understanding of history. Finally, Native events and celebrations typically draw substantial crowds. Many tribes and organizations host events such as powwows and tribal dances annually. These events are free to attend and present many different styles of dance and drum music, along with the opportunity to shop for Native arts and crafts. Powwows are usually multi-tribal events, in part reflecting the origin of these events in intertribal boarding schools.

Tribal cultures and languages are a deep part of Native identity. There was a time in the United States when Native people were heavily exposed to assimilation pressures. During this time, many Native people stopped identifying as Native and did not teach their language or culture to their children or grandchildren. Acceptance of Native peoples has now shifted in most regions of the United States, and Indigenous peoples do not experience as much overt racism as they have in the past, although there are still some areas in the United States—many on the borders of tribal reservations—where overt racism against Indigenous peoples persists (Ashley 2015). Many of the descendants of once reservation-bound tribes are now actively seeking to reassociate themselves with their tribal cultures, recognizing this part of their heritage as a central part of their identity.

Traditional Material Culture

The traditional material cultures of Indigenous peoples showcase an impressive array of styles and skills. Native art was heavily collected by individuals and museums in the 19th century, when there were fears that Indigenous cultures were disappearing. Native art remains popular today. While many Indigenous artists continue to work in traditional styles, some are also incorporating contemporary styles and techniques. Native material cultures embed much cultural philosophy. As anthropologist and museum director Nancy Parezo says, “To anthropologists, Native American/First Nation arts are windows to understanding other cultures and societies. They can be specimens used to support evolutionary theories or explain the maker’s cultural concepts of beauty—to show universal concepts and cultural differences, shared meanings, and modes of communication” (1990, 12).

FIGURE 19.15 Klickitat baskets. Traditional techniques and stylistic motifs in Native material culture reveal a great deal about a people’s cultural beliefs. (credit: “Image from Page 123 of ‘How to Make Indian and Other Baskets’ (1903)” by George Wharton James/Internet Archive Book Images/flickr, Public Domain)

Artistic styles such as **petroglyphs**, in which images are carved into stone, and **pictographs**, or drawings, can be appreciated as both historic and spiritual statements. The petroglyph site in Cascadia Cave, near Sweet Home, Oregon, has hundreds of carvings. The most easily recognizable are the bear paws on the wall of the cave. There are also numerous lines, zigzags, and holes carved out of the cave wall. Willamette Forest Service archaeologist Tony Farque noted that people had long thought that the place was used to gain "bear power" for Native shamans. However, when one steps back, it is apparent that the decorated area of the wall is bordered by a large relief of a salmon, with one hole as its eye and the carved lines creating gills. The cave is now understood as a site where Indigenous peoples—Kalapuya, Molala, and other tribes in the region—sought to gain power when fishing in the nearby South Fork Santiam River, where salmon were known to spawn.

Cultural sites such as Cascadia Cave are in danger of being destroyed by too much attention from archaeologists and the public. For more than a century, Cascadia Cave has been visited by thousands of tourists who have touched the walls, dug in the ground in search of artifacts, taken rubbings of the carvings, and sometimes even carved their initials or painted over petroglyphs to make them stand out more. All these activities degrade the site. Early archaeologists did much the same, digging into the ground and moving many yards of dirt, which has caused rainfall to pool at the walls of the cave. The pooling moisture accelerates the growth of mosses and other plants, which also degrade the walls of the cave. Digging also destroys the archaeological context of the site. It is important to note that in many countries, including the United States, it is illegal to dig up and remove archaeological materials. Those who continue to dig up materials for private collection or for sale are conducting illegal activities. Many of the sites illegally dug are cemetery sites, containing the remains of people and cultural artifacts that are related to descendant tribal populations today.

FIGURE 19.16 Cascadia Cave petroglyphs. Note that the bear paws have been painted to make them more distinct, but this partially destroys the context of the petroglyphs. Additional petroglyphs are all over this portion of the wall. (credit: 46percent/Wikimedia Commons, Public Domain)

Weaving arts are another significant aspect of material culture for many Indigenous peoples. **Basketry** techniques were and still are used to construct vessels used for regular household and resource-gathering activities. Indigenous groups developed various techniques for weaving, such as right twist, left twist, overlay, and false embroidery. These techniques result in decorative styles unique to individual tribes. Weaving techniques make use of many natural materials. Large objects such as mats were typically made with cattail and tule, while baskets could be made from a wide variety of materials, including juncus, hazel branches, cedar bark, bear grass, spruce roots, willow, and maidenhair fern. Some materials were chosen for their stability and durability, others for their flexibility, and still others for their color and luster. Dyeing weaving materials created complex color variations. Baskets were even used for cooking. The technique for boiling water in a basket is similar across many cultures: the basket would be tightly woven, normally with a double weave, and then filled with water. The fibers of the basket and the tight weave created a watertight exterior; additionally, some traditions coated the fibers with grease or pitch. Hot rocks, heated in a fire, would be placed in the basket to make the contained liquid boil. In this manner, food could be cooked without destroying the basket.

FIGURE 19.17 (left) A Papago/Tohono basket maker working in 1916. (right) Classes teaching traditional basket weaving help to keep the art alive. (credit: left, "Papago Basketmaker at Work, Arizona" by H. T. Cory/National Archives and Records Administration/Wikimedia Commons, Public Domain; right, Jim Heaphy/Wikimedia Commons, Public Domain)

Many tribes now offer classes to teach people the basic techniques and styles particular to their tribal heritage. The Confederated Tribes of Grand Ronde offer classes in carving, weaving arts, beading, regalia making, drum making, and other arts associated with the 27 tribes that make up the confederation. Arts and crafts are intermixed with education about Native philosophy, spirituality, and language. Some people attend classes for years to master the art style they enjoy, and tribal members may apprentice with master artisans to learn more advanced techniques. Many artisans are creating works of art that are inspired by deep feelings of Native identity, using their art to define themselves and their people within the contexts of both the present and the past. Several artists have become professionals and are producing work for galleries, exhibits, exterior monuments, and contracted sales. The artists employ traditional arts as well as contemporary sculptures and artistic traditions such as painting, drawing, and illustration. Many traditional three-dimensional artworks, such as cedar statues, are now rendered in metal, stone, or even glass so that they are more durable and can survive the rigors of contemporary tourism.

Indigenous Philosophy and Worldviews

A shared element of Indigenous philosophy across various cultures is the conception of humans existing in relationship to the world around them. Native peoples believe they are deeply connected to the natural world; animals are viewed as relatives, and plants, rocks, and mountains are all understood to have **animistic** spirits. Rivers, lakes, and even the seasons themselves are also understood as having spirits. Many Native American peoples believe that animals were once their brothers and sisters. It is believed that from the actions of some of the godlike animals, such as Coyote, Beaver, and Raven, much of the world was made. Many Native peoples gain shamanic powers by forming close relationships with certain animals. These powers might include the ability to heal, to poison, to call salmon, to call weather, to fish, or to communicate with animals. Typically, these abilities are gained through ceremonies designed to familiarize people with their spirit helpers at a young age. Ceremonies differ, but a common format involves a youth going off by themselves into a special natural area—such as a forest, hilltop, or mountain cave—and fasting and meditating until they hear their helper spirit. In this manner, many Native peoples are connected to spiritual powers; the most powerful may become a shaman or spiritual leader of their tribe. Details of these types of ceremonies are kept secret within each tribe. One reason for this secrecy is a concern that non-Native people might attempt the same ceremonies without guidance and perhaps hurt themselves or the world around them in the process.

Native philosophy is understood to be embodied in the elders of the tribes. By living a full life within their particular cultural context, tribal elders gain wisdom about their people and culture. Many maintain tribal languages, too. Elders are honored and supported by younger members of their societies, who in turn learn about tribal traditions and philosophies from the elders. Elders come to their position partly through age, but normally they are recognized by their tribes when they exhibit great wisdom. Certain elders may have greater status than others depending on how well versed they are in their traditions and how respected they are by the community.

Native philosophy can also be gleaned through the study of oral histories. Many oral histories relate to subjects such as how the world was formed, how humans relate to animals, and how to acquire food, offering moral and ethical lessons. Oral histories may also be records of historic events, such as when the tribe was removed to a reservation, when many people died from disease, when a tsunami forced the people to escape to a mountain, when the land was changed by geological activity, or when there was a war. Oral histories are often full of metaphors and symbols of powerful spiritual forces that caused the event. One example is the story told by the Wasco people of when Coyote and Wishpoosh (Beaver) fought on the Columbia River and created the Columbia Gorge. This oral history reflects Native explanations of a series of flood events that occurred when rushing floodwaters carved out the Columbia Gorge in Oregon. The Missoula floods occurred from 18,000 to 15,000 years ago during the large Ice Age. The floods, perhaps as many as 90 of them, are noted by geologists to have been caused by the breaking of glacial ice dams behind which was Lake Missoula. During fluctuations in the warming period, the ice dams burst, and millions of hectares of water from the glacial lake flooded down the Columbia to carve out the Columbia River Gorge. The dams would refreeze and burst again, perhaps hundreds of times, to scour the lands east of the Columbia of topsoil and carve out the gorge. The topsoil would be deposited in the Willamette Valley (Allen, Burns, and Burns 2009). It is remarkable that Native peoples maintained oral histories documenting this event for at least 15,000 years. The Wasco oral history of Wishpoosh and Coyote is only one such story of this event. All tribes in the region have a story that mentions a flood of this magnitude.

FIGURE 19.18 Columbia River Gorge. A story told by the Wasco people relates how the gorge was created when Coyote and Wishpoosh (Beaver) fought on the Columbia River. (credit: Hux/Wikimedia Commons, Public Domain)

Indigenous worldviews are embedded in ceremonies as well. The Tolowa Nation of Northern California practices Nee-dash, their world renewal ceremony, also called the Feather Dance, on the winter and summer solstices. This ceremony lasts as long as 10 days and is meant to showcase the wealth of the tribe. Dancers, both men and women, wear regalia and dance continuously for the 10 days of the ceremony. Each day, they increase the number of necklaces they wear and the wealth displayed in their regalia. When the dancers become "wealthier," it is a metaphor for the growth of food, understood as the wealth of the land, that begins in the spring of each year. Dancers move in a semicircle, men on one side and women on the other, as a leader sings Native ceremonial songs and stamps out a beat on the hard-packed earthen floor with a tall stamper stick. Dancers take turns "coming out" and dancing, individually or in twos, threes, or larger groups, understood to be displaying their ceremonial power in hunting, fishing, or gathering. An audience of tribal people is normally situated around the benches of the dance house, men on one side and women on the other. The dances are meant to renew the earth to ensure strong returns of seasonal fish runs, good hunting opportunities, and rich yields of acorns or berries. The ceremony honors the land, the animals, and the plants that sustain the people. This ceremony establishes a spiritual relationship in which people are not separate from nature but a part of it, with the responsibility to act as stewards of its great wealth.

FIGURE 19.19 Tolowa Dee'ni Feather Dancers perform during a ceremony at the University of Oregon in 2001. The Feather Dance is understood to affirm a spiritual relationship between people and nature, with humans acknowledging the responsibility to act as stewards of its great wealth. (credit: David G. Lewis, Public Domain)

Most Indigenous cultures have ceremonies similar to this, centered on events such as the first salmon catch, the first hunt, or the first gathering of any important food. First salmon ceremonies for the Takelma peoples of the Rogue River Valley in Oregon involve a young man taking the bones of the first salmon caught that year down to the bottom of the Rogue River. These ceremonies are an important way for Native peoples to acknowledge and recommit themselves to a responsibility to steward the natural world in order to sustain its health and vibrancy so that the people who rely on it may thrive into the future.

Indigenous Critique: Rights, Activism, Appropriation, and Stereotypes

In the contemporary era, the publications of academics have had a great deal of influence on how tribes have been treated by the federal government and other groups. A 1997 essay, titled "Anthropology and the Making of Chumash Tradition," included the authors' opinion that the Coast Chumash tribe were descendants of Mexican people, and not Native people of North America at all (Haley and Wilcoxon 1997). The essay relied in part on rumors that were later refuted as unproven by archaeologist Jon Erlandson (1998). These claims, even disproven, aided other Native peoples in accusing the Coast Chumash of not being Native, resulting in many social and political problems for the community. Scholarly publications such as these can affect the ability of tribal nations in the United States to gain federal recognition status because all applicants for federal recognition must establish continuous culture and governance. Public and scholarly opinions can have a huge effect on whether tribes get recognized and are able to restore their culture and sovereignty after centuries of colonization.

Responses to the disempowering effects of colonialism have sometimes been overtly political. In the 1960s, the **American Indian Movement** (AIM) took actions to bolster tribal sovereignty throughout the United States. AIM was involved with several highly public activities, including an occupation at Mount Rushmore in 1971 in protest over the illegal taking of Sioux lands and the carving of presidents' faces in a mountain sacred to the Sioux. AIM also participated in the occupation of Wounded Knee in 1973, the site of a historic battleground, in protest over the failure to impeach Oglala Sioux president Richard Wilson; the resulting standoff with federal law enforcement lasted 71 days. Public awareness of the federal government's oppression of Native peoples grew when a large military force was deployed during a second occupation of Wounded Knee, an event called Wounded Knee 2. AIM's work was part of a larger civil rights movement that involved Black, Latina/Latino, and women activists as well as the growing anti–Vietnam War movement. This larger movement created political shifts in the United States that benefited Native communities (Johansen 2013).

FIGURE 19.20 The Trail of Broken Treaties Protest of 1972, part of the American Indian Movement for greater political rights and tribal sovereignty. (credit: "TrailBroken.AIM.WDC.12oct02" by Elvert Barnes Protest Photography/flickr, CC BY 2.0)

Beginning in the 1970s, several laws were passed by Congress to empower tribes. These included policies pertaining to education (Indian Education Act, 1972), child foster care (Indian Child Welfare Act, 1978), college education (Tribally Controlled Colleges and Universities Assistance Act, 1978), freedom of religion (American Indian Religious Freedom Act, 1978), and rights to archaeological sites and remains (Archaeological Resources Protection Act, 1979, and Native American Graves and Repatriation Act, 1990). This period also saw the end of the national policy of termination and a turn toward allowing tribes that had been terminated to be restored, with self-determination becoming standard federal policy.

Stereotypes

Native peoples have also become vocal in confronting stereotypes about them. The first Western stereotypes of Native peoples in North American depicted them in primitivist terms as **noble savages**, living in harmony with nature, with no notions of laws, time, or money. Implicit in this view was the idea that Indigenous peoples were not fully civilized and did not deserve the same rights as White, Christian people. Their land could thus be taken away. This stereotype has been described by writer Albert Memmi "as a series of negations: they were not fully human, they were not civilized enough to have systems, they were not literate, their languages and modes of thought were inadequate" (Smith 2021, 31). Throughout the history of the United States, these stereotypes have been used to progressively take more and more away from Native peoples. When reservations were first established, they were said to be permanent homes, but as White settlers began to see these lands as attractive places, the notion was again raised that Native peoples were not using the land appropriately.

FIGURE 19.21 Chief Joseph of the Nez Percé tribe (Niimiipuu), pictured with a stoic "noble savage" look. The stereotype of Indigenous people as "noble savages" has been used as justification for taking their land away from them. (credit: "Joseph—Nez Percé" by Edward S. Curtis/Library of Congress, Public Domain)

Additional stereotypes originated with early anthropological research. Notions that Native peoples could not digest alcohol, were lazy and would not work, were not intelligent enough to become civilized, or were dying off as a population because they did not have a civilized culture have all been perpetuated by scholars who embraced social evolutionary theories about human societies. The idea that societies and civilizations existed in competition with one another, and that Native peoples were not competitive because they were savages or barbarians, was inspired by Lewis Henry Morgan's proposal of a hierarchy of civilizations. These ideas have been heavily refuted, but the stereotypes persist and continue to affect Native peoples in prejudicial ways.

Recently, the issue of **Indian mascots** has received a lot of attention. In the early 20th century, private and professional sports teams and franchises begin to name their athletic teams after Native groups or some characteristic words referring to Native peoples. Common names include the Warriors, Chiefs, Indians, Reds, Redskins, and Braves. Some of these names may have been chosen to honor the strength and resilience of people who had survived centuries of war with colonizing peoples. Regardless of the original intention, as time went on, fans of many of these teams developed practices that disparaged Indigenous peoples. Many mascots were cartoonish or savage caricatures. These mascots may have been the only exposure many American people had to Native peoples, at a time when there was no valid education about Native peoples offered in public schools.

The first significant challenge to the use of such mascots was led by Charlene Teters, a student at the University of Illinois, against the university's mascot, Chief Illiniwek, in the 1980s. Teters criticized various aspects of the chief's presentation, including the headdress, regalia, and dance style, the latter of which was the invention of students who took the role of mascot each year. The campaign against this mascot continued for some 20 years, with many fans and alumni of the university countering that the mascot was meant to honor the Illiniwek people. The mascot was finally dropped by the university in 2007.

Much opposition to mascots is connected not to the use of the figure itself but to the behavior of fans. Practices such as dressing in red paint, wearing outfits of fake feathers and fake headdresses, and using arm motions such as the "tomahawk chop" to show team spirit have offended Native groups. Names might also carry meanings not fully understood by fans. Controversy around the Washington Redskins' name and mascot lasted for some 30 years. Many fans weren't aware that the term *redskins* was used in states such as California and Oregon to refer to Native scalps collected by White American militia members. These scalps, or redskins, could be returned to the state government for a bounty. At certain periods in U.S. history, hundreds of Native people were killed, and whole villages sometimes destroyed, by militia seeking redskins to collect these bounties. In 2020, the Washington Redskins dropped the name, becoming known as the Washington Football Team until a replacement name was chosen. Similarly, in 2019, the Cleveland Indians dopped its "Chief Wahoo" mascot, and in 2021, the team changed its name to the Cleveland Guardians.

In some cases, tribal nations have collaborated with universities to develop more respectful mascot images. The University of Utah has collaborated with the Ute tribe in designing its mascot image featuring a feather, and Florida State University has worked with the Seminole tribe to develop its Appaloosa horse rider and spear imagery. There remains a political divide in the debate about mascots, with some Native activists believing there should be no Indian mascots, while others think that sovereign tribal nations, as sovereign governments, should be able to decide how their people are characterized by organized athletic organizations.

19.4 Applied and Public Anthropology and Indigenous Peoples

LEARNING OUTCOMES

By the end of this section, you will be able to:

- Explain how tribal cultures are using anthropology to secure rights to sites of cultural significance.
- Describe how anthropologists and Native scholars aid Indigenous peoples using anthropology.
- Discuss how Indigenous peoples create networks to help one another.

Applied anthropology, which applies anthropological research and methods to contemporary problems, addresses much of the critique of anthropology offered by Vine Deloria Jr. and others. Many Indigenous peoples have become active participants in applied anthropological research, both seeking out and collaborating with anthropologists to work on projects that they themselves have defined. Many tribes now take a directive approach with researchers, offering contracts and funding for anthropologists who will work on issues that the tribes think are important. As tribes develop their reservation infrastructure, many have established archaeology programs to protect their rights to sites of importance. Many have asked scientists to create GIS (geographic information system) products, which feature layers depicting various resources and characteristics on a map, to manage their lands and help them effectively consult with states, the federal government, and private agencies. The layering of information in the GIS can create deeply immersive maps and models that include information about types of vegetation, the environmental history of lands, changes to lands, and any other information than can be captured and mapped. Layered information can be activated or removed from a map to meet specific aims. Tribes can now reference both the information available through scholarly studies and information about their lands and peoples from their own internal studies, which they do not typically share outside of the tribe. In many ways, tribes are now more knowledgeable about the archaeology of their territory than most institutions and are making plans to protect and preserve cultural sites and resources.

Public anthropologists aim to engage with communities and involve the general public in their work as much as possible. In doing so, they empower communities to address their own problems. Many public anthropologists publish their research in readily accessible formats, such as newspapers and popular magazines. The Internet offers many ways for public anthropologists to reach a broader audience. Blogs and digital journals make it possible for anthropologists to make information broadly available in order to benefit the greatest number of people.

The author of this chapter, David Lewis, describes his own efforts to make anthropological research more readily available:

I produce a blog, the Quartux Journal (https://openstax.org/r/QuartuxJournal), which I began in 2014. At that time, I was engaged in a decade-long series of studies of the tribal peoples of western Oregon. Years of research had given me much to write about. The blog offered a means of releasing that information quickly and without charge to a broad group of colleagues and the public who desired information about Native peoples. Many of my readers are educators seeking content for high school or college classes they are teaching about Native peoples. This blog began at a time when Native groups and the state of Oregon were developing Native curricula for public schools, and it has become an essential curriculum tool for educators in the region. Educators have written back about the lack of resources and the great aid the blog has offered in filling their need for facts about the tribes of Oregon. The blog has now grown to more than 450 essays about tribal peoples throughout western Oregon and beyond. Its essays are easily read in about 10 minutes and are not jargon laden. There are currently more than 1,000 subscribers to this blog. The essays have inspired additional research on Native peoples' history and has lent Native contextual details to local studies of the histories of Oregon.

MINI-FIELDWORK ACTIVITY

Research Activity: Native American Peoples

Conduct research into Edward S. Curtis's photographs of Native North American peoples. The majority of his images are online in the Library of Congress Edward S. Curtis Collection (https://openstax.org/r/LibraryofCongress).

After picking at least one image, research the circumstances under which Curtis took the photograph. Curtis himself offers clues to his subject and location, sometimes even identifying his subjects by name. Then, research the tribe the subject(s) was or were a part of, including where the tribe was living at the time the photo was taken and their socioeconomic situation. Expect to conduct research to locate the correct historic sources. Finally, compare the culture portrayed in the photo and noted by Curtis's information with your research findings. Note differences and ways in which Curtis may have altered the context.

One reference for research is the video *Edward Curtis: Photographing the North American Indian* (https://openstax.org/r/EdwardCurtis), available from the Smithsonian Institution.

Present your research in a formal report of 3–5 pages, including full references and the image being researched.

Suggested Readings

Biolsi, Thomas, and Larry J. Zimmerman, eds. 1997. *Indians and Anthropologists: Vine Deloria, Jr., and the Critique of Anthropology.* Tucson: University of Arizona Press.

Deloria, Vine, Jr. (1969) 1988. *Custer Died for Your Sins: An Indian Manifesto.* Norman: University of Oklahoma Press.

Deloria, Vine, Jr. (1970) 2007. *We Talk, You Listen: New Tribes, New Turf.* Lincoln: University of Nebraska Press.

Deloria, Vine, Jr. (1995) 1997. *Red Earth, White Lies: Native Americans and the Myth of Scientific Fact.* Golden, CO: Fulcrum.

Deloria, Vine, Jr. 1999. *Spirit & Reason: The Vine Deloria, Jr., Reader.* Edited by Barbara Deloria, Kristen Foehner, and Sam Scinta. Golden, CO: Fulcrum.

Deloria, Vine, Jr. 2003. *God Is Red: A Native View of Religion.* 3rd ed. Golden, CO: Fulcrum.

Harrison, Faye V., ed. 2011. *Decolonizing Anthropology: Moving Further toward an Anthropology for Liberation.* 3rd ed. Arlington, VA: American Anthropological Association.

Ngũgĩ wa Thiong'o. 1986. *Decolonising the Mind: The Politics of Language in African Literature.* Portsmouth, NH: Heinemann.

Said, Edward W. 1978. *Orientalism.* New York: Pantheon Books.

Smith, Linda Tuhiwai. 2021. *Decolonizing Methodologies: Research and Indigenous Peoples.* 3rd ed. London: Zed Books.

Key Terms

American Indian Movement a social and political organization with many local chapters around the United States of activist Native people focused on confronting the federal and state governments over racist policies and actions. AIM was most active in the 1970s and 1980s.

animistic of or relating to a spiritual belief that everything in the world has its own living spirit.

assimilation the process of changing the culture of a person or group of people to some other culture, through socialization or education.

basketry an art form of many Indigenous peoples, created from woven plant matter. Each tribe has its own traditions and styles, with some tribes using many styles.

blood quantum a term first applied by the US federal government to determine which people had rights to services and land at reservations. The term has become a characteristic to define who is eligible for citizenship in a tribe, with membership open only to those who have a minimum blood quantum of Indigenous genealogical ancestry.

boarding schools educational institutions established by federal authorities to efficiently educate and assimilate Indigenous children through an immersive environment.

Indian Claims a series of more than 700 lawsuits brought by tribal nations in the 20th century against the US federal government to demand repayment for failures in the administration of a variety of responsibilities.

Indian mascots characterizations of a Native person or group used to represent athletic teams, often portraying savage or cartoonish stereotypes. The practice is considered highly racist toward Native peoples.

Indians a commonly used term for Native Americans first applied by Christopher Columbus, who mistakenly thought the Indigenous peoples he encountered were people of India.

Indigenous peoples the original populations of a land and those who carry culture and experiences from an Indigenous culture. Indigenous peoples may also be referred to as Native peoples, tribal peoples, tribes, First Nations peoples, Aboriginal peoples, or American Indians or Native Americans.

Maori the Indigenous peoples of New Zealand.

Marshall court trilogy three Supreme Court decisions—*Johnson v. M'Intosh* (1823), *Cherokee Nation v. Georgia* (1831), and *Worcester v. Georgia* (1832)—that determined that tribal nations are domestic sovereign nations within the United States and dependent on the federal government to guarantee their sovereignty.

mestizo Latin American term for a person of mixed heritage, normally Indigenous and Spanish or Indigenous and another White ethnicity.

Métis Canadian term for a person of partial Indigenous heritage. A Métis person has different rights from a First Nations person.

Native studies an educational discipline that originated from the critiques of studies of tribal communities by non-Native scholars. Native studies programs seek to center Indigenous knowledge and experience in studies of Indigenous peoples and societies.

noble savages a romanticist term used to suggest that Native peoples were uncivilized and primitive, living in harmony with nature.

oral histories spoken, rather than written, narratives of past events.

oral tradition cultural knowledge that is passed on through oral, rather than written, form.

petroglyphs images carved into stone and sometimes painted.

pictographs drawings on the wall of a cave or rock shelter or on animal hide.

public anthropologists anthropologists who work to make their research, analysis, and products available to the public through publication and presentation of their work in public, easily accessible places.

reservations lands given to Indigenous tribes as supposedly permanent places for their communities to live and practice their culture, usually through treaty or executive order.

termination a US federal policy adopted in 1953 that involved voiding the treaty agreements between the federal government and Native peoples, enabling the government to repossess and sell property that had been part of reservations in a process called liquidation. Terminated tribal peoples are no longer federally recognized Native peoples and have no rights to ask for federal services or assistance. Between 1954 and the 1970s, 109 tribes underwent termination. Most were federally restored between the 1970s and the 1990s.

Trade and Intercourse Acts federal laws that administer trade between states and across federal borders. The law affects the ability of

Native nations to establish industries and sell products or services beyond their borders.

treaties agreements between sovereign entities, in this context Native nations and the United States.

urban Indian a Native person who lives in an urban environment; sometimes a negative title used by those living on reservations to refer to Native people who are assumed to have willingly given up their culture, land, and Native identities.

Summary

This chapter addresses many issues involving Native peoples that are a result of the colonization of Indigenous peoples, the effects of a long history of governmental administration, and the manipulation of Native history and cultures in public spheres. Indigenous peoples in the United States today have lived through a long period of cultural collapse and are subject to extreme competition for land, rights, and resources. This chapter focuses primarily on the Indigenous peoples of Oregon within the United States. The issues faced by these people are similar to those faced by Indigenous peoples around the world, including a history of colonization, removal from traditional lands to reservations, signing away land and rights in treaties, and forced education in boarding schools. Disempowerment of tribal sovereignty, disenfranchisement from lands and resources, and forced assimilation have significantly affected Native peoples.

In addition, Indigenous peoples of the United States face significant problems adjusting to contemporary society. The general lack of education about Indigenous peoples has caused a lack of knowledge about Native history and culture in society. Within this culture, mascots and stereotypes are challenging to Native peoples, who face racism in society. Contemporary tribal nations struggle to restore cultures and governance systems. Native peoples must adjust to the cross-culturalism of modern society while they seek to maintain tribal identities and memberships in tribal nations. Scholarly studies of Native peoples are also addressed, as the studies and perceptions of anthropologists have significantly affected how tribes are perceived today.

Critical Thinking Questions

1. How would you characterize the impact of colonialism on Indigenous peoples?
2. Considering this chapter and overlapping subjects in previous chapters, what changes have been made within the discipline of anthropology in the 20th and 21st centuries?
3. What role have casinos played in tribal economic development?
4. How have Indigenous critiques and Indigenous perspectives changed and developed anthropology?
5. Should Native American human remains and funerary objects be collected for scientific research or returned to tribes? Explain your answer.
6. Why are language recovery and language reclamation important to maintain Indigenous cultures? Explain your answer using details from the text.
7. Address Indian mascots or stereotypes you have encountered in your experience. In what ways might they be viewed as dishonoring Native peoples?
8. What roles are tribal communities taking with regard to applied anthropology?

Bibliography

Al-Asfour, Ahmed, and Marry Abraham. 2016. “Strategies for Retention, Persistence and Completion Rate for Native American Students in Higher Education.” *Tribal College and University Research Journal* 1 (1): 46–56. https://issuu.com/collegefund/docs/tcurj_v1_1_full_journal_high-resolu.

Albers, Patricia, and Beatrice Medicine. 1983. *The Hidden Half: Studies of Plains Indian Women*. Washington, DC: University Press of America.

Allen, John Eliot, Marjorie Burns, and Scott Burns. 2009. *Cataclysms on the Columbia: The Great Missoula Floods*. Rev. 2nd ed. Portland, OR: Ooligan Press.

Ashley, Jeremy. 2015. “Native American and Multi-ethnic Experiences with Racial Discrimination in Indian

Reservation Border Towns." PhD diss., Northern Arizona University.

Brayboy, Bryan McKinley Jones, K. Tsianina Lomawaima, and Malia Villegas. 2007. "The Lives and Work of Beatrice Medicine and Vine Deloria Jr." *Anthropology & Education Quarterly* 38 (3): 231–238. https://www.jstor.org/stable/25166623.

Crawford, James. 1995. "Endangered Native American Languages: What Is to Be Done, and Why?" *Bilingual Research Journal* 19 (1): 17–38.

DeAngelo, Linda, Ray Franke, Sylvia Hurtado, John H. Pryor, and Serge Tran. 2011. *Completing College: Assessing Graduation Rates at Four-Year Institutions.* Los Angeles: Higher Education Research Institute, University of California, Los Angeles. https://heri.ucla.edu/DARCU/CompletingCollege2011.pdf.

Deloria, Vine, Jr. (1969) 1988. *Custer Died for Your Sins: An Indian Manifesto.* Norman: University of Oklahoma Press.

Deloria, Vine, Jr. (1995) 1997. *Red Earth, White Lies: Native Americans and the Myth of Scientific Fact.* Golden, CO: Fulcrum.

Deloria, Vine, Jr. 1997. "Anthros, Indians, and Planetary Reality." In *Indians and Anthropologists: Vine Deloria, Jr., and the Critique of Anthropology,* edited by Thomas Biolsi and Larry J. Zimmerman, 209–221. Tucson: University of Arizona Press.

Ellinghaus, Katherine. 2017. *Blood Will Tell: Native Americans and Assimilation Policy.* Lincoln: University of Nebraska Press.

Erlandson, Jon McVey. 1998. "The Making of Chumash Tradition: Replies to Haley and Wilcoxon." *Current Anthropology* 39 (4): 477–510. https://doi.org/10.1086/204760.

Haley, Brian D., and Larry R. Wilcoxon. 1997. "Anthropology and the Making of Chumash Tradition." *Current Anthropology* 38 (5): 761–794. https://doi.org/10.1086/204667.

Hegeman, Susan. 1989. "Native American 'Texts' and the Problem of Authenticity." *American Quarterly* 41 (2): 265–283. https://www.jstor.org/stable/2713025.

Hinton, Leanne. (2001) 2013. "The Master-Apprentice Language Learning Program." In *The Green Book of Language Revitalization in Practice,* edited by Leanne Hinton and Ken Hale, 217–226. Leiden: Brill.

Johansen, Bruce E. 2013. *Encyclopedia of the American Indian Movement.* Santa Barbara, CA: Greenwood.

Lewis, David Gene. 2002. "Native Experience and Perspectives from Correspondence in the SWORP Archive." In *Changing Landscapes: "Sustaining Traditions"; Proceedings of the 5th and 6th Annual Coquille Cultural Preservation Conferences,* edited by Donald B. Ivy and R. Scott Byram, 25–39. North Bend, OR: Coquille Indian Tribe.

Lewis, David Gene. 2009. "Termination of the Confederated Tribes of the Grand Ronde Community of Oregon: Politics, Community, Identity." PhD diss., University of Oregon. http://hdl.handle.net/1794/10067.

McNickle, D'Arcy. 1968. "The Sociocultural Setting of Indian Life." *American Journal of Psychiatry* 125 (2): 219–223.

Medicine, Beatrice. 2007. *Drinking and Sobriety among the Lakota Sioux.* Lanham, MD: AltaMira Press.

Memmi, Albert. (2003) 2010. *The Colonizer and the Colonized.* Translated by Howard Greenfield, with an introduction by Nadine Gordimer. New York: Earthscan.

Miller, Robert J. 2012. *Reservation "Capitalism" Economic Development in Indian Country.* Santa Barbara,CA: Praeger.

Nagle, Rebecca. 2019. "The US Has Spent More Money Erasing Native Languages Than Saving Them." *High Country News,* November 5, 2019. https://www.hcn.org/issues/51.21-22/indigenous-affairs-the-u-s-has-spent-more-money-erasing-native-languages-than-saving-them.

Nenemay, Kimberly Alice. 2005. "An Exploratory Study of Tribal Enrollment, Blood Quantum and Identity among the Confederated Salish and Kootenai Tribe of Western Montana." PhD diss., Rutgers University. ProQuest (AAT 3180991).

Parezo, Nancy J. 1990. "The Challenge of Native American Art and Material Culture." *Museum Anthropology* 14 (4): 12–29. https://doi.org/10.1525/mua.1990.14.4.12.

Smith, Linda Tuhiwai. 2005. "Imperialism, History, Writing, and Theory." In *Postcolonialisms: An Anthology of Cultural Theory and Criticism*, edited by Gaurav Desai and Supriya Nair, 94–115. New Brunswick, NJ: Rutgers University Press.

Smith, Linda Tuhiwai. 2021. *Decolonizing Methodologies: Research and Indigenous Peoples*. 3rd ed. London: Zed Books.

Thornton, Russell. 1997. "Tribal Membership Requirements and the Demography of 'Old' and 'New' Native Americans." *Population Research and Policy Review* 16 (1–2): 33–42. https://doi.org/10.1023/A:1005776628534.

CHAPTER 20
Anthropology on the Ground

Figure 20.1 The Museum of Anthropology at the University of British Columbia in Vancouver, Canada, showcases anthropological artifacts and culturally diverse histories. (credit: "UBC Museum of Anthropology" by Wpcpey/Wikimedia Commons, CC BY 4.0)

CHAPTER OUTLINE

20.1 Our Challenging World Today
20.2 Why Anthropology Matters
20.3 What Anthropologists Can Do

INTRODUCTION In "Waddling In," a provocative essay published in 1985, interpretive anthropologist Clifford Geertz proposed that among the various academic disciplines, anthropology was uniquely capable of leading into the future. He pointed out the fundamental changes anthropology faced as it headed into the 21st century—changes in its traditional subject focus, its traditional field sites, and its wide, holistic perspective, which Geertz referred to as "walking barefoot through the Whole of Culture" (1985, 623):

> Pulled in opposed directions by technical advances in allied disciplines, divided within itself along accidental ill-drawn lines, besieged from one side by resurgent scientism and from the other by an advanced form of hand-wringing, and progressively deprived of its original subject matter, its research isolation, and its master-of-all-I-survey authority, [anthropology] seems not only to stay reasonably intact but . . . to extend the sway of the cast of mind that defines it over wider and wider areas of contemporary thought. We have turned out to be rather good at waddling in. In our confusion is our strength. (624)

In our confusion is our strength. For Geertz, this *confusion* reflects anthropology's flexibility as a science and a humanity and its acknowledgment that we do not yet know everything about who we are as a species. Our ongoing mission is to be open to what comes next, open to the potential of what it means to be human. This is especially important at this moment in history when global challenges remind us of how much remains to be done for every person to have a life of dignity. Instead of predicting the end of anthropology, "Waddling In" challenges anthropologists to discover an ever-widening relevance and importance for the discipline, in a world of ongoing cultural change.

Anthropology is both an academic and an applied discipline. What anthropology reveals about human culture and human biology can be used to improve lives today. Anthropology is deeply relevant to contemporary lives in many ways. Museums are a common way in which anthropological knowledge is presented to the public, interpreting cultural and biological diversity and inspiring new generations of scholars and a broader public. The Museum of Anthropology at the University of British Columbia, shown in Figure 20.1, is an example of one way anthropologists share their knowledge in a public space. But there are many other ways in which anthropologists interact with and influence our global community.

20.1 Our Challenging World Today

LEARNING OUTCOMES

By the end of this section, you will be able to:

- Identify some of the most critical global challenges.
- Define ethnosphere.
- Analyze the importance of the ethnosphere today.

Critical Global Challenges

Today humanity faces a growing number of global problems, most of them linked to one another and to long-standing historical inequities and injustice. Many of the problems people experience in their daily lives derive from major global issues, which intersect with and affect cultural traditions and contemporary social behaviors. In other words, our global problems are deeply connected to the ways we live locally. Local and global problems connect and reinforce each other.

FIGURE 20.2 The United Nations headquarters in Geneva, Switzerland. In 2021, the United Nations identified 22 critical global issues humanity currently faces. (credit: "Palais des Nations Unies, à Genève" by Groov3/Wikimedia Commons, CC0)

In 2021, the United Nations (UN) identified 22 critical global issues, several worsened by the COVID-19 pandemic. These are challenges that "transcend national boundaries and cannot be resolved by any one country acting alone" (United Nations 2021). Many of these challenges, which affect all nations, are particularly harmful to those facing discrimination, environmental and social racism, and economic poverty. As you read through these "global issues," notice how many of these challenges are linked together (e.g., Africa, decolonization, democracy, poverty, global health, etc.). Go through this list and note which of these impact you and which might have affected your ancestors. Consider such things as cost of goods and services, possible effects on health and welfare, and even the political instability that might result from these issues, creating global ripple effects. Also, consider how populations suffering various injustices might experience greater impacts than those in otherwise stable communities.

- *Africa*: promoting democratic institutions, supporting economic and social development, and protecting human rights.
- *Aging*: responding to the growth of aging populations (ages 60 and over) worldwide.
- *AIDS*: continuing to reduce infection and death rates in the global fight against AIDS.
- *Atomic energy*: promoting the safe, secure, and peaceful operation of more than 440 nuclear reactors generating electricity worldwide.
- *Big data for sustainable development*: monitoring inclusiveness and fairness in the application of new data sources, technologies, and analyses.
- *Children*: protecting the rights of every child to health, education, and protection and expanding children's opportunities.
- *Climate change*: responding to the unprecedented challenges of shifting weather patterns that threaten food production and create climate emergencies.
- *Decolonization*: continuing to monitor and encourage self-determination among former colonies, which the UN refers to as a "sacred trust." When the UN was founded in 1945, approximately 750 million people were living in colonies and dependencies; today, fewer than two million live under colonial rule.
- *Democracy*: strengthening democracy, "a universally recognized ideal" and a core value of the UN, as a way of strengthening human rights.
- *Ending poverty*: reducing global poverty rates, which could increase by as much as 8 percent of the world's population during the COVID-19 pandemic.
- *Food*: working toward food security and increasing nutrition for the most vulnerable population groups, especially during COVID-19.
- *Gender equality*: promoting gender equality as both a fundamental human right and a critical factor in achieving peaceful and sustainable societies.
- *Health*: monitoring, promoting, and protecting health concerns worldwide. Much of the leadership in this area is provided by the World Health Organization (WHO).
- *Human rights*: continuing the ongoing effort to guarantee human rights around the globe. This is a central focus of the UN's work, as set out in the UN Charter (https://openstax.org/r/un-charter) and the Universal Declaration of Human Rights (https://openstax.org/r/universal-declaration-of-human-rights).
- *International law and justice*: continuing to promote international law and justice across the three pillars of international peace and security, socioeconomic development and progress, and respect for fundamental human rights and freedoms.
- *Migration*: ensuring the orderly and humane management of migration, finding practical solutions to migration problems, and providing humanitarian assistance to refugees and internally displaced persons.
- *Oceans and the law of the sea*: ensuring peaceful, cooperative usage of the oceans and seas to the common benefit for humanity and combating the rising threat of pollution and waste from transport vessels and oil tankers.
- *Peace and security*: helping restore peace and preventing disputes from escalating into war.
- *Population*: promoting sexual and reproductive health and individuals' ability to manage the size of their families.
- *Refugees*: providing aid and safe haven to the millions of people forcibly displaced worldwide. In 2019, an estimated 79.5 million people were refugees, 26 million of them under the age of 18.
- *Water*: managing the competition between individual and commercial needs for access to water, which is critical for all human populations.
- *Youth*: providing for a more just, equitable, and progressive future for persons between the ages of 15 and 24, including ensuring access to health, education, and employment and working toward gender equality.

Private philanthropists have been working on some of these same problems as well. In 2020, the Bill and Melinda Gates Foundation, founded in 2000 to work collaboratively with governments to solve critical global health issues, expanded their focus by naming three major action areas for their multibillion-dollar foundation, in addition to ongoing educational priorities:

- *Climate change*: increasing clean energy, providing zero-emissions energy to low-income countries, and developing innovative approaches to food production.
- *Gender inequality and gender-based violence*: expanding access to education to improve women's lives and increasing women's leadership positions in government, finance, and health.
- *Global health*: sponsoring initiatives to deliver vaccinations and otherwise combat major global diseases, such as AIDS and malaria. (Bass and Bloomberg 2020)

These lists represent only the beginning of the challenges that face us as human beings living on one shared planet. Underpinning these challenges are many others, none more important than the loss of diversities. We face devastating losses in three major areas of diversity: *biological diversity*, as species are increasingly endangered or become extinct; *cultural diversity*, as Indigenous peoples, minorities, and smaller populations in more isolated areas, such as rural areas, face encroachments on their lands and their lives, including their right to exist as diverse cultures; and *linguistic diversity*, with thousands of languages already extinct and many more facing imminent extinction. As diversity declines, our species has fewer options and less flexibility. When we consider that most innovation builds on preexisting forms—whether of biology, culture, or language—the loss of anything that once existed is also a loss of potential, of *what could have been*.

But all is not doom and gloom. Hope is offered by disciplines, such as anthropology, that work to value and preserve diversities. Anthropology has taken a lead role in bringing positive change to our global world. Projects in which anthropological knowledge and insight is applied to current challenges include language reclamation and revitalization, primate conservation and habitat enrichment, revitalization of traditional foodways and technologies, and other projects to revive, restore, and encourage cultural, biological, and linguistic diversity.

The Ethnosphere

When considering the many challenges facing us as a global community, we must also acknowledge our **assets**—the tools and conditions we can harness to increase value and effect positive change. We do not enter our future empty-handed. To some extent, our challenges and assets have evolved together, hand in hand. As we face concerns about another possible global health pandemic, for example, we bring with us a depth of scientific knowledge based on earlier experiences, having learned and retooled our responses to be better prepared for those things we have experienced before. As we begin to combat overwhelming climate crises after decades of abusing our environment, we have knowledge and tools to make positive changes while continuing to educate people about our physical world, pollution, and global warming. We understand the causes of most of our challenges, and we have the ability to harness large groups of people globally to work together to address them, with an impressive array of technology at our fingertips. We are not a helpless species. We are not necessarily smarter or wiser than our ancestors were, but we do have one great treasure—we have what our ancestors left to us. We have the accumulation of all their cultural wisdom, ingenuity, and humanity.

In 2001, Canadian cultural anthropologist Wade Davis coined the term **ethnosphere** to refer to the sum total of all of human knowledge across time:

> You might think of the ethnosphere as being the sum total of all thoughts and dreams, myths, intuitions and inspirations brought into being by the human imagination since the dawn of consciousness. The ethnosphere is humanity's great legacy. It is the product of our dreams, the embodiment of our hopes, the symbol of all that we are and all that we have created as a wildly inquisitive and astonishingly adaptive species. (Davis 2003)

FIGURE 20.3 Anthropologist Wade Davis coined the term *ethnosphere* to describe the totality of the human cultural legacy across time and cultures. (credit: "Wade Davis" by Cpt. Muji/Wikimedia Commons, CC0)

The diverse ways in which humans have solved or managed the challenges of our lives, many of them challenges that we have inflicted on ourselves because of greed and ignorance, is a rich storehouse for our future. Too often, contemporary people feel there is little to learn from those who are different from us or who came before us, but the solutions to our current problems are founded upon this legacy.

Humans have faced grave environmental challenges more than once in our species' history. Our ancestors also faced global climate challenges. The last glacial period occurred between 120,000 and 11,500 years ago. During that time, alternating periods of global cooling and warming displaced human populations and forced them to adapt to new plants and animals as they migrated and ultimately peopled the globe. One of the notable consequences of the last years of the glacial period was the extinction of some 177 species of megafauna (large mammals), including woolly mammoths, giant deer, and saber-toothed cats. There have been two primary theories about these extinctions, which occurred worldwide (in Europe, Africa, Asia, and North and South America). Did the animals go extinct due to climate change and habitat loss or to overkilling by human big-game hunters? Recently, researchers at Aarhus University in Denmark studied the extinction of megafauna species through global mapping techniques that compared timelines of human occupation and of animal extinction (Sandom et al. 2014). In about one-third of the animal extinctions, the correlation of the dates of the earliest arrival of human hunters and the extinction of the animals was clear and consistent. While the majority of cases were not consistent, they did not present contrary evidence to the theory of human overkill and environmental exploitation. It appears that humans were involved in mass extinctions and environmental changes even in these early periods.

FIGURE 20.4 The skeleton of a woolly mammoth, a large mammal that was most likely hunted to extinction by early humans. (credit: "Siegsdorfer Mammut" by Lou Gruber/Wikimedia Commons, Public Domain)

And yet people have also been involved in animal reintroductions and species conservation. Today, U.S. National Parks have reported a variety of species reintroduction success stories. In several national parks across the United States, native animal species have been reintroduced to better manage habitats, conserve endangered species, and support a healthy ecosystem. Among the most successful reintroduced species are California condors, Pacific fishers, black-footed ferrets, gray wolves, bald eagles, desert pupfish, bighorn sheep, elk, and nēnē, a species of goose native to Hawaii (Errick 2015).

Entomologist Edward O. Wilson has devoted his life to studying and working to protect **biodiversity**, the astounding variety of plants and animals on our planet that together form a healthy ecosystem. As part of the biological web of life, humans are important actors. Within the ethnosphere lies the wisdom of generations of human interactions with other species for food, medicines, clothing, shelter, protection, companionship, and economic exploitation. Many of the tools related to this valuable knowledge are found within Indigenous cultures, too many of them also endangered or extinct today. By preserving and valuing the ethnosphere and its diversity, we preserve ourselves, our children's futures, and the hopes we have for our planet.

Anthropology plays a major role in preserving, valuing, and teaching about the ethnosphere. In this critical role, anthropology makes an important difference in how well we encounter the future—whether we will adapt and thrive or face ever-increasing threats to our survival. Whether you are a practicing anthropologist, a student of anthropology, or someone who enjoys learning about our diverse world, including its diverse peoples and cultures, you have a role to play in bringing about a more hopeful future.

20.2 Why Anthropology Matters

LEARNING OUTCOMES

By the end of this section, you will be able to:

- Explain the characteristics of anthropology that make it uniquely relevant today.
- Describe and give an example of anthropological values.
- Analyze the importance of anthropological skills.

A Uniquely Relevant Discipline

As you learned in What is Anthropology?, anthropology is a unique discipline. Not only does it study all aspects of what it means to be human across time, with a focus on evolution and how changes occur in our bodies and cultures, but it also examines the ways in which we adapt to different social and physical environments. This process of adaptation is a primary source of cultural and biological diversity. Anthropology is also holistic, examining the context of and interconnections between many parts of our lives and weaving together our biology, our traditions, and the diverse social and physical environments in which we live. The anthropological approach views humans as part of a wider system of meaning, as actors and change-makers within a dynamic environment populated by others. Across cultures, those others can include other species (plant and animal) and spirits as well as other human beings. It is the human ability to imagine and construct the universe in which we live that most interests anthropologists.

In most four-field introductory classes, students are surprised at the breadth of anthropology, but this wide lens is the cornerstone of the discipline. Today, anthropologists increasingly approach the study of humans as a dynamic construct. We see humans as agents in motion, undergoing change as a normal state of being, rather than as objects in a petri dish, preserved and inert. This means that anthropological studies are by necessity messy and in flux, as our subject matter makes change. Because holism, adaptation, and adjustment are critical to anthropological studies, we bring an especially powerful lens to attempts to understand complex, large-scale global problems.

Few of our challenges today are simple. Solving the climate crisis requires changes not just to our use of fossil fuels but also to the ways in which we produce food, bathe, heat and cool our houses, and travel. Each culture and each community must be aware of its power and potential to enact positive change. Both a scientific and a humanistic approach are needed to solve our current global challenges.

Anthropological Values

The anthropological perspective is grounded by principles and standards of behavior considered important to understanding other people and their ways of life. These include the value of all cultures; the value of diversities, biological and cultural; the importance of change over time; and the importance of cultural relativism and acknowledging of the dignity of all human beings. These anthropological **values** undergird our discipline.

The study of culture intersects with each of the four subfields and highlights the importance of diversity. From the beginning, humans have used ingenuity to tackle problems and provide solutions to challenging circumstances. Anthropologists study and value this extraordinary process of human creativity, documenting it in living and past cultures, in our languages and symbol systems, and even in our bones, through cultural procedures such as elongating women's necks (as is practiced by the Kayan people of Myanmar) or flattening/elongating people's heads (practiced by the Chinookan peoples of North America). Even our diets, which are cultural artifacts of adaptation, are written on our bones. The consumption of corn, for example, is measurable as carbon isotopes in human bone. Anthropology celebrates this human uniqueness and diversity, understanding that different ways of being are humanity's greatest legacy—a foundation embodied in the concept of the ethnosphere.

FIGURE 20.5 Kayan women use neck rings from an early age to make their necks appear longer. The rings actually push down the clavicle and compress the rib cage. This is a sign of beauty among the Kayan. (credit: "IMG_0547" by Brian Jeffery Beggerly/flickr, CC BY 2.0)

Anthropological studies produce documentation of immeasurable worth. Through anthropological research, we collect, preserve, and share the stories of living humans as well as human artifacts, sites, and bodies. Together, these documents form a valuable database. Field notes and artifacts from the earliest anthropologists document diversity that has since disappeared. Franz Boas taught his students how to make life masks of the people they were studying to document the physical diversity of different groups of people (A. Singer 1986). This vast collection of some 2,000 life masks is now preserved at the Smithsonian Institution as an archival resource for understanding environment, culture, and biological adaptations. Many masks document ethnic groups that are now extinct. Anthropology collections (https://openstax.org/r/naturalhistory) are of inestimable value for future research.

The Council for the Preservation of Anthropological Records, or CoPAR (https://openstax.org/r/copar.umd), works with anthropologists, librarians, and archivists to obtain and preserve anthropological records and make them available both for the study of human diversity and as a record of the history of the discipline. The organization has two primary goals. The first is to educate anthropologists on the value and urgency of saving documents. The second is to help train archivists and information specialists in best practices for handling the sometimes very sensitive information within these documents while also facilitating them in making sure that the information is available to scholars anywhere (Silverman and Parezo 1995).

Diversity is a product of adaptation and change over time. As cultural groups encountered different challenges in their environments, they used ingenuity and innovation to address these challenges, sometimes borrowing other cultures' solutions when applicable. In the high Andes of South America, the steep mountainous inclines mean that there is little flat ground for growing food. In response to this challenge, Inca farmers used terrace farming, building steplike terraces into the hillside to create areas of flatter surfaces for growing crops (see Figure 20.6). Forms of terrace farming are found all over Asia and in parts of Africa, with cultures in each area adapting the use of terraces to meet specific climatic conditions and crop requirements (e.g., paddy rice cultivation requires small earthwork borders to allow for flooding). In short, there is no one way to do something; every solution is calibrated to particular needs. Today, with increasing urgency to minimize our carbon footprints, architects are designing homes to meet clients' demands for net-positive houses—that is, houses that produce more energy than they consume through solar power and lower-energy appliances (Stamp 2020). As we work toward reducing our dependence on fossil fuels, the architectural and construction industries are beginning to adapt to these changing needs and demands.

FIGURE 20.6 Adaptations: (left) By cutting these steplike terraces into the mountain, Andean farmers created more arable land for farming. (right) In this net-positive house in Australia, the solar panels, increased insulation, and lower-energy appliances all contribute to a "net zero" energy design. (credit: (left) "Peru Terrace Farming" by J. Thompson/Wikimedia Commons, Public Domain; (right) "The Zero-Emission House" by Keirissa Lawson, CSIRO/ Wikimedia Commons, CC BY 3.0)

Besides culture and diversity, anthropology is also about the human power to change. Through adaption, evolution, and even acclimatization (short-term adaptation to environmental change), the human body has evolved alongside human cultures to make us a species uniquely capable of adapting to almost any environmental or social conditions. Humans can survive even in such inhospitable environments as outer space (thanks to the human-designed technology that makes up the International Space Station) and the polar regions (where human-built structures and protective gear make habitation possible at McMurdo Station in Antarctica). And humans have survived health crises such as the COVID-19 pandemic and historical tragedies such as slavery and warfare. The ability to change, redirect, reassess, reimagine, and innovate has sustained our species across time.

Diversity matters more today than ever. Where diversity is valued, there is greater potential for innovation and collaboration. A central value of anthropology, evident in both research and applied work across communities, is anthropologists' focus not only on understanding other cultures and different ways of living but also on *translating* them—that is, communicating what is learned across cultures in order to share it more broadly.

The most important anthropological value, however, is cultural relativism, or suspending judgment about other cultures until one gains a clear understanding of the meaning and significance of what those cultures do and believe. Cultural relativism requires us to understand the rationale, purpose, and meaning of cultural traditions and knowledge before we decide on their validity. And it provides significant advantages in better understanding others:

- It allows us to see the worth, dignity, and respect of all persons, allowing for initial exchange and collaboration between "us" and "them."
- It reminds us to approach the study of other cultures without automatically judging them as inferior, thus minimizing ethnocentrism.
- It helps us keep an open mind about the potentials and possibilities inherent in our species.

First formally introduced by Franz Boas, cultural relativism laid the groundwork for the discipline of anthropology, a science that would study what it means to be human in all its diverse forms. Boas and his students worked to apply cultural relativism across racial, ethnic, linguistic, and socioeconomic boundaries, documenting the rich cultural traditions of Indigenous peoples, minority communities, and immigrants. The concept, though, has undergone a great deal of debate since the 1948 Universal Declaration of Human Rights by the United Nations. Is anything okay if a culture decides it is? Are there any boundaries to cultural relativism? Do we have to accept everything that a group does, or can an anthropologist ultimately judge that a practice is damaging, harmful, and not deserving of being respected and upheld?

While these debates remain, anthropologists still value cultural relativism (and the worthiness of other peoples and cultures), although perhaps in a modified form that anthropologist Michael Brown calls *cultural relativism 2.0*. As Brown states, cultural relativism 2.0 is "a call to pause before judging, to listen before speaking, and to widen one's views before narrowing them" (2008, 380). In other words, *first give people a chance*.

Anthropology is important today, perhaps even more than when it formally began some 150 years ago. As French anthropologist Maurice Godelier says:

> Anthropology—together with history—is one of the social science disciplines best able to help us understand the complexity of our now globalized world and the nature of the conflicts and crisis we are experiencing. In such a world, it would be irresponsible and indecent for anthropologists [to] stop trying to understand others. (2016, 75–76)

20.3 What Anthropologists Can Do

LEARNING OUTCOMES

By the end of this section, you will be able to:

- Describe the primary areas where the anthropological approach is relevant.
- Identify the ways that anthropologists are specifically trained for today's challenges.
- Explain how anthropological skills can help address contemporary problems.

What Anthropologists Do Today

Anthropologists are at work now to make a difference in our lives. There are various ways in which anthropologists and those utilizing an anthropological lens or framework contribute critically needed skills and resources in the 21st century.

- *Research*. Sometimes referred to as *pure* or *theoretical* research, fieldwork is conducted in all kinds of settings in order to answer practical and theoretical questions that form the basis of anthropology. How do cultures change? How do artifacts and technology evolve within a culture? How do trade and exchange affect the development of cultures?

  Many of the chapters in this text feature stories about anthropological research and its importance in understanding what it means to be human. Each of the subfields engages in distinct types of field research as ways to test theories and advance our knowledge of human beings. Theoretical research is the backbone of academic anthropology.

- *Research and development*. Research and development are associated with practical applications, such as creating or redesigning products or services for governments or corporations. Anthropologists who work in research and development contribute what they know about human behavior and the world around us to projects that serve the interests of human organizations and the human community.

  Cultural anthropologist Genevieve Bell worked for 18 years in research and development for Intel Corporation, the world's largest semiconductor chip manufacturer. Her focus at Intel was on user experience, researching how people use technology and apply it in their lives with the goal of designing more relevant and user-friendly products. Intel valued the way Bell's deep knowledge of human behavior and human culture helped the company better anticipate their clients' needs. Bell's insights helped make Intel a more competitive corporation. She has described her job as "mak[ing] sense of what makes people tick, what delights and frustrates them, and . . . us[ing] those insights to help shape next generation technology innovations. I sit happily at the intersection of cultural practices and technology adoption" (*City Eye* 2017).

FIGURE 20.7 Anthropologist Genevieve Bell works with tech and engineering industries, applying anthropological concepts to make technology more user-friendly and better adapted to our everyday lives. (credit: "Genevieve Bell" by Kevin Krejci/flickr, CC BY 2.0)

In a TED Salon talk titled "6 Big Ethical Questions about the Future of AI (https://openstax.org/r/genevieve_bell_6)," Bell explains that the technological revolution of artificial intelligence is already in progress, affecting many aspects of our lives. She says that the challenge now is to use artificial intelligence "safely, sustainably, and responsibly." Bell advocates for human-scale technology. Using skills and knowledge gained through her training as an anthropologist, she looks at the ways in which technology, culture, and environment interact. In her work today, she continues to use an anthropological approach: "It's about thinking differently, asking different kinds of questions, looking holistically at the world and the systems" (Bell 2020).

Bell left Intel in 2017 to serve as a distinguished professor at the Australian National University College of Engineering and Computer Science, where she serves as the director of the School of Cybernetics and continues to research the interface between culture and technology.

- *Public policy*. Anthropologists are involved in public policy making all over the world. Anthropological skills and outlooks are increasingly valuable to the development of principles and regulatory measures that increase public safety and resolve real-world problems. Applying a holistic approach to these issues allows government and nongovernment organizations to avoid some problems and better anticipate future challenges.

  The American Anthropological Association (AAA) (https://openstax.org/r/ParticipateAndAdvocate) has identified five public policy areas that would greatly benefit from an anthropological approach. In each of these areas, the AAA hopes to involve more anthropologists in public policy in the 21st century and to work collectively to message international, national, and local agencies about the importance of anthropological knowledge and involvement:

  - *Social and cultural aspects of health*: identifying ways in which categories of race, ethnicity, gender, socioeconomic status, and age hinder medical delivery.
  - *Culture and diversity in education*: understanding the diversities that affect educational delivery and

the gaps that exist in current educational policies due to such things as changing demographics and new information technologies.
- *An interdisciplinary approach to the environment*: focusing on the ways in which anthropological knowledge contributes to understanding the human dimensions of the environment and interfacing with federal agencies actively seeking to support this type of environmental research.
- *Economic, social, and cultural aspects of the information revolution*: examining the human dimensions of the information revolution and the impact that it is having on our work and personal lives.
- *Globalization and its impact on public policy*: specifically, focusing on issues of conflict and war and the effects of globalization on transnational communities.

One of the challenges that anthropologists face is better educating governments and corporations about the skills they can bring to understanding and addressing contemporary problems. Working collaboratively within and beyond the discipline is important for advancing an awareness of the possibilities that anthropologists offer as public policy advocates.

PROFILES IN ANTHROPOLOGY

Gillian Tett
1967-

FIGURE 20.8 British cultural anthropologist Gillian Tett is a journalist and the U.S. managing editor of the *Financial Times*. (credit: "Gillian Tett FT Autumn Party 2014 Crop" by Financial Times/Wikimedia Commons, CC BY 2.0)

Personal History: Gillian Tett is a British author and journalist who trained in anthropology. She studied at Clare College, Cambridge University, where she earned her PhD in social anthropology after conducting doctoral research in Tajikistan, in what was then the Soviet Union. Tett intentionally chose to turn her anthropological gaze outside of the university setting, where she believed her training would have greater impact.

Area of Anthropology and Importance of Her Work: Though is trained as a social anthropologist, Gillian Tett works for the *Financial Times*, a global daily newspaper, as chair of the editorial board and editor at large in addition to her role as a journalist. Her articles on finance, business, and political economy appear in the *Financial Times* and in various leading newspapers and media outlets. She forecast early warnings about the 2008 economic downturn, applying her anthropological knowledge and skills to understand emerging global economic patterns, and she participates frequently in conferences on finance and global economics. Tett also contributes to new directions in anthropology; at the joint 2019 American Anthropological Association and Canadian Anthropology Society/La société canadienne d'anthropologie Annual Meeting, she served as a discussant in a presidential session on the topic of breaking down silos in anthropology,

Accomplishments in the Field: Tett has earned various commendations and awards in and outside of the field of anthropology, including the British Press Award for Business and Finance Journalist of the Year in both 2008 and 2009. She was awarded the President's Medal of the British Academy in 2011, given in recognition of "academic-related service activity" beyond the academy. Her book *Fool's Gold: How Unrestrained Greed Corrupted a Dream, Shattered Global Markets, and Unleashed a Catastrophe* (2009), which takes a cultural anthropological approach to analyzing the global economy and financial system, was a *New York Times* best seller and was chosen as the 2009 Financial Book of the Year by *Spear's* magazine. In 2014, Tett received the Royal Anthropological Institute's Marsh Award for Anthropology in the World, which "recognises an outstanding individual based outside academia, one who has shown how to apply anthropology or anthropological ideas to the better understanding of the world's problems" (Royal Anthropological Institute 2021). Her latest book is *Anthro-Vision: A New Way to See in Business and Life* (2021), published by Simon & Schuster.

- *Applied or practicing anthropology*. Anthropologists are engaged in wide-ranging work on the ground in real-life situations, helping address numerous current and emerging needs in communities around the world. Many work within nongovernmental agencies. Some anthropologists are already engaged in efforts pertaining to the COVID-19 pandemic, gathering preliminary data and working to streamline access to treatment and preventative measures.

  In 2014, the WHO reached out to sociocultural anthropologists to help address an outbreak of the Ebola virus in Mali. They sought the help of these anthropologists as liaisons to connect with the local people and lessen their anxieties about the disease, help those recovering cope with the stigma of having had Ebola, and build a bridge between the community and the health system. They also sought anthropological direction on how best to interact with local people while respecting their culture and traditions. The WHO described some of the roles of the anthropologists who aided in this project:

  > The social anthropologists have also helped train teams searching for Ebola patients and monitoring Ebola contacts, teaching them to make allowances for local culture and the rules of hospitality and politeness when visiting families. These factors are key to getting the message across and being heard by members of the community. (World Health Organization 2015)

The global emergency of COVID-19 mobilized a number of anthropologists, especially those in the applied field of medical anthropology. Medical anthropologist Mark Nichter (2020), who has studied emerging diseases and global health for much of his career, was returning from fieldwork in India and Indonesia when COVID-19 cases started being diagnosed in the United States. He traveled from Asian countries, where people were wearing masks and showing a high level of concern for the disease, into Europe and then the United States, where there seemed to be little concern. These different attitudes prompted him to think about other pandemics he had experienced as a medical anthropologist and about how complex these global events can be. Deeply aware of issues of social inequality, he worried about the poor infrastructure conditions in so many countries and the dense populations in refugee camps. What would happen in water-insecure areas where accessing any kind of water, especially clean water for handwashing, was difficult? He wondered just how bad this was going to be as a global event.

During lockdown in the United States, Nichter used his training as a medical anthropologist to create positive change within his community. He first developed a COVID-19 primer, explaining health concepts about COVID-19 and methods of slowing and preventing transmission in everyday terms to help professors and teachers educate themselves and their students. The primer quickly began circulating on campuses in the

United States and around the world. Nichter also worked with fellow anthropologists in a special working group supported by the American Anthropological Association to identify research areas of critical need. Many of these research areas concerned structural threats and areas where mortality data were revealing disparities, indicating that certain populations were more vulnerable than others. Third, Nichter began advocating and working for COVID-19 testing resources, the development of contact tracing, and symptom monitoring to better contain outbreaks within communities. Lastly, he helped develop a health care worker support network with both online and grassroots resources, knowing that frontline workers would be those most taxed by the pandemic. Nichter advocates for what he calls *anticipatory anthropology*. In the context of medical anthropology, anticipatory anthropology acts to shore up the fault lines that have emerged in the global health system, working toward creating stronger resistance to the next health care emergency. "COVID-19 provides an opportunity to build alliances and momentum for significant health care reform" (Nichter 2020).

Anthropological skills are increasingly vital to developing and communicating culturally relevant messages. While global health initiatives are very prominent within the field of applied and practicing anthropology, the range of interventions is wide. Applied anthropology projects might involve improved farming techniques and heirloom seed banks, better educational services, and even work on the front lines with persons displaced by war, migration, or climate emergencies.

Anthropological Skills and Resources

Anthropologists are trained to look at the larger context and understand how smaller, local environments fit into overarching forces. They aim to hold a multicultural perspective that represents various constituencies and to interact with people around them with the goal of better understanding where they are coming from and what things *mean* to them. Anthropologists gather and analyze data that reflects real life *on the ground and in the streets*. The central anthropological specialty is an unfettered interest in human beings.

In 2020, career research and employment website Zippia interviewed a group of teaching and practicing anthropologists about the anthropological skills they believe are most valuable in today's job market. The two quotes below illustrate the breadth of career preparation that anthropology provides:

> Organizations are looking for people who can articulate the value of their experiences. Anthropology provides a broad array of skills. Some [are] more general, such as critical thinking and written and oral communication and teamwork. Some skills are more specific, such as survey and excavation for archaeology positions, research design, data analysis skills (qualitative and quantitative), and familiarity with research ethics. —*John Ziker*

> Young graduates need to think quickly and with skepticism, read situations from multiple angles, and have openness to variable solutions. This means that they need skills in understanding pluralistic vantage points, judging where information comes from and who it benefits and who it hurts, and being gifted at recognizing and acknowledging their own biases. Anthropology teaches these skills as it prepares graduates for work in a wide array of fields. —*Suzanne Morrissey* (Stark et al. 2020)

Anthropologists and anthropology students, undergraduate and graduate, fit into a wide array of careers and contribute valuable skills and resources to their communities everywhere. As people specialists, anthropologists understand how to approach diverse peoples, elicit information about and from them, and work with that information to understand broader situations. Some of the broadly applicable skills that different anthropologists have include interviewing; excavating; mapping; analyzing data using various types of methodologies, including mixed methods (combining qualitative and quantitative methods); applying ethics in difficult, emerging situations; and engaging with new technologies in the sciences. All of these are 21st-century skills and resources. However, the most advantageous of an anthropologist's skills is an attitude of respect and dignity toward diverse peoples everywhere. In our global world, this may be the most important asset of all. As anthropologist Tim Ingold says, anthropologists "study ... *with* people" and "learn *from* them, not just *about* them" (2018, 32).

How Anthropology Can Lead in the Future

Career and employment trends today align with what anthropologists do, whether or not one is a full-time practicing anthropologist. Students heading into any fields that address the human condition, past or present, will benefit from studies in anthropology. Within colleges and universities across the world, there is a reemergence of transdisciplinary approaches that utilize methods and perspectives from multiple disciplines to study and propose solutions to complex problems. This educational model, sometimes called the *matrix model* (National Academy of Sciences, National Academy of Engineers, and Institute of Medicine 2005), has resulted in the development of new interdisciplinary degree programs such as the biomedical informatics program at Stanford University; the Indigenous food, energy, and water systems program at the University of Arizona; and the science, medicine, and technology in culture program at Union College. Training in anthropological holism is the ideal foundation for working in teams with multiple interests and a shared focus on the larger context. Specifically, the four-field approach in anthropology prepares researchers to apply a keen perception of the ways in which biology and culture interact and influence each other.

With the increasing prominence of social media and grassroots communication across cultures, it is important that emerging leaders have the ability to interview people, elicit relevant information from them, and analyze what they think, do, and desire. Anthropologists are trained to interact with others, seek connections and patterns in what they observe, and analyze the symbolic significance of what they find.

Anthropologists are also trained to work in the field, *wherever and whatever the field may be*, taking their offices and research labs into the communities in which they work and live. Accustomed to being flexible and adaptable to the needs of the situation and letting the field dictate how best to accomplish their work, anthropologists have the skills, technology, and experience to work well in a global community.

In the 20th century, academia sought to become ever more specialized, constructing departments, specialties, and subspecialties to home in on very particular subjects such as a disease, a genre of literature, or a type of religion. This approach was an advance over the more generalist approach that was common in the 19th century, in which academics were trained in very broad fields such as medicine, ancient history, or culture. Now, in the 21st century, the shift is toward a more complex and multifaceted understanding of how we live and the challenges we face. Many anthropology programs today provide vocational skills and workplace training. There is a growing awareness that we need to develop the ability to think both generally and systematically (such as in an ecosystemic approach) while also seeking to understand the particularities of specific challenges. Anthropology, with its holistic approach, mixed methodology analyses, and deep, abiding appreciation of diversity and the dignity of all people, is situated at the crossroads of what comes next. This is how anthropology can guide us as we move into the future.

As Geertz said, "We have turned out to be rather good at waddling in" (1985, 624). Anthropological skills are based on flexibility and adaptation to a changing world, open-mindedness and openness to new ideas, and a willingness to engage with complex issues in order to find solutions to problems facing our world today. The anthropological skillset is critical in the 21st century.

You can read more about the important work of anthropologists today in the Profile features in each chapter. Through research and work such as the examples featured there, anthropologists are changing the world.

MINI-FIELDWORK ACTIVITY

Global Challenges

Choose three global challenges, and research more about them. Consider how these three global challenges are linked to one another and to long-standing historical inequities. Collect information on the current state of each problem in the United States and worldwide, what measures are being taken to mitigate the problem, and whether there are any local initiatives in your own community. Consider both campus and community organizations. Using what you have learned about anthropology, propose three anthropological skills that you could employ to help address each of these challenges.

Key Terms

asset a tool or condition that can be harnessed to increase value and effect positive change.

biodiversity the variety of plants and animals that exist on Earth and form a living ecosystem.

ethnosphere the sum total of all of human knowledge across time.

values principles and standards of behavior that are considered important.

Summary

As a discipline, anthropology includes academic and applied aspects that focus on, respectively, developing new theories and solving practical problems. Today, we face a growing number of global problems, most of them linked to one another and to long-standing historical inequities and injustice. Many of the problems we experience in our local lives derive from these major issues, and every one of them intersects with and affects cultural traditions and contemporary social behaviors. In 2021, the United Nations identified 22 critical global issues that transcend national boundaries and affect people everywhere, with those who suffer various forms of injustice typically experiencing greater effects from these challenges than those living in more stable communities. Three of the challenges are major actions areas for philanthropic organizations such as the Bill and Melinda Gates Foundation: climate change, gender inequality and gender-based violence, and global health. Intersecting with these global issues are the devastating losses we face in terms of biological, cultural, and linguistic diversity.

The term *ethnosphere*, first coined by Canadian cultural anthropologist Wade Davis, refers to the sum total of all human knowledge across time—the human cultural legacy. The diverse ways in which we humans have solved or managed the challenges of our lives are a rich storehouse for our future. Too often, contemporary people feel we have little to learn from those who are different from us or who came before us, but the solutions to our current problems are founded upon this legacy. As globalization proceeds, conjoining our lives in myriad ways, it is important to remember that diversity is a storehouse of critical knowledge from the generations before us and the cultures around us, many of which are fighting today to survive. By preserving and valuing the ethnosphere's diversity, we preserve ourselves, our children's futures, and the hopes we have for our planet.

The anthropological approach views humans as part of a wider system of meaning, as actors and change-makers within a dynamic environment populated by others. Across cultures, those others can include other species, plant and animal, and spirits as well as other human beings. It is the human ability to imagine and construct the universe in which we live that most interests anthropologists. The anthropological perspective is grounded by principles and standards of behavior considered important to understanding other people and their ways of life. These include the value of all cultures; the value of diversities, biological and cultural; the importance of change over time; the importance of cultural relativism; and an acknowledgment of the dignity of all human beings. These anthropological values undergird our discipline.

Anthropological studies produce documentation of immeasurable worth. Through anthropological research, we collect, preserve, and share the stories of living humans as well as human artifacts, sites, and bodies. Today, anthropologists and those using an anthropological lens contribute to the 21st century in various ways, including through research, research and development, public policy, and applied or practicing anthropology. Career and employment trends today align with what anthropologists do, whether or not one is a full-time practicing anthropologist. Students heading into any field that addresses the human condition, past or present, will benefit from studies in anthropology.

Critical Thinking Questions

1. What do you consider to be the three most critical global issues? Why?
2. In what ways is the ethnosphere valuable to our lives today?
3. Do you have any traditional forms of knowledge? If so, how do you use them? Think about practices such as cooking.
4. What anthropological skills can best address the problems our global community faces today?
5. What are the most valuable anthropological skills

in today's professions?
6. Why does anthropology matter?
7. Consider your own academic major or career goals. How can anthropological skills be applied to your professional aspirations?
8. How can anthropology lead in the future?

Bibliography

Bass, Dina, and Bloomberg. 2020. "Bill and Melinda Gates Add Climate Change and Gender Equality to Their Foundation's Focus." *Fortune*, February 10, 2020. https://fortune.com/2020/02/10/bill-melinda-gates-foundation-climate-change-gender-equality-focus/.

Bell, Genevieve. 2020. "6 Big Ethical Questions about the Future of AI." Filmed October 2020. TED video, 14:39. https://www.ted.com/talks/genevieve_bell_6_big_ethical_questions_about_the_future_of_ai.

Boss, Shira J. 2001. "Anthropologists on the Job." *Christian Science Monitor*, January 2, 2001. https://www.csmonitor.com/2001/0102/p9s1.html.

Brown, Michael F. 2008. "Cultural Relativism 2.0." *Current Anthropology* 49 (3): 363–383.

City Eye. 2017. "Genevieve Bell: A Cultural Anthropologist Studying Technological Innovations." WeAreTheCity. September 22, 2017. https://wearethecity.com/genevieve-bell-anthropologist-technology/.

Davis, Wade. 2001. *Light at the Edge of the World: A Journey through the Realm of Vanishing Cultures*. Vancouver, BC: Douglas & McIntyre.

Davis, Wade. 2003. "An Interview with Anthropologist Wade Davis." By Alex Chadwick. NPR. May 27, 2003. https://legacy.npr.org/programs/re/archivesdate/2003/may/mali/davisinterview.html.

Errick, Jennifer. 2015. "9 Wildlife Success Stories." *Park Advocate*, National Parks Conservation Association. November 2, 2015. https://www.npca.org/articles/880-9-wildlife-success-stories.

Geertz, Clifford. 1985. "Waddling In." *Times Literary Supplement*, June 7, 1985, 623–624.

Godelier, Maurice. 2016. "In Today's World, Anthropology Is More Important Than Ever." *AIBR: Revista de Antropologia Iberoamericana* 11 (1): 59–76. https://doi.org/10.11156/aibr.110104e.

Harrell-Bond, B. E., and E. Voutira. 1992. "Anthropology and the Study of Refugees." *Anthropology Today* 8 (4): 6–10.

Henig, David. 2020. "Anthropology Has a Village Problem." *Etnofoor* 32 (1): 139–144.

Ingold, Tim. 2018. "Why Anthropology Matters." *British Academy Review*, no. 32, 30–32. https://www.thebritishacademy.ac.uk/publishing/review/32/why-anthropology-matters/.

National Academy of Sciences, National Academy of Engineers, and Institute of Medicine. 2005. *Facilitating Interdisciplinary Research*. Washington, DC: The National Academies Press. https://www.nap.edu/catalog/11153/facilitating-interdisciplinary-research.

Nichter, Mark. 2020. "Engaging the Pandemic." *Anthropology News*, June 19, 2020. https://anthropology-news.org/articles/engaging-the-pandemic/.

Redding, Terry, and Elizabeth K. Briody. 2020. "Breaking Down Silos in Anthropology." *Anthropology News*, September 16, 2020. https://www.anthropology-news.org/articles/breaking-down-silos-in-anthropology/.

Sandom, Christopher, Søren Faurby, Brody Sandel, and Jens-Christian Svenning. 2014. "Global Late Quaternary Megafauna Extinctions Linked to Humans, Not Climate Change." *Proceedings of the Royal Society B* 281 (1787). https://doi.org/10.1098/rspb.2013.3254.

Silverman, Sydel and Nancy J. Parezo. 1995. Preserving the Anthropological Record. 2nd ed. Wenner-Gren Foundation for Anthropological Research, Inc.

Singer, Andre, dir. 1986. *The Shackles of Tradition: Franz Boas (1858–1942)*. Video. London: Royal Anthropological Institute.

Singer, Natasha. 2014. "Intel's Sharp-Eyed Social Scientist." *New York Times*, February 15, 2014. https://www.nytimes.com/2014/02/16/technology/intels-sharp-eyed-social-scientist.html.

Stamp, Elizabeth. 2020. "How the Architecture Industry Is Reacting to Climate Change." *Architectural Digest*, March 2, 2020. https://www.architecturaldigest.com/story/climate-change-design-architecture.

Sillitoe, Paul. 2007. "Anthropologists Only Need Apply: Challenges of Applied Anthropology." *Journal of the Royal Anthropological Institute* 13 (1): 147–165.

Stark, Miriam, Brian Bates, John Ziker, Suzanne Morrissey, Amber VanDerwarker, Jeremy Spoon, Douglas Wilson, et al. 2020. "Experts Weigh In on Current Job Market Trends." Zippia. December 13, 2020. https://www.zippia.com/anthropologist-jobs/trends/.

United Nations. 2021. "Global Issues." https://www.un.org/en/global-issues/.

World Health Organization. 2015. "Anthropologists Work with Ebola-Affected Communities in Mali." January 2015. https://web.archive.org/web/20210121202145/https://www.who.int/features/2015/anthropologists-ebola-mali/en/.

INDEX

C

D

E

F

T

U

V

W

X

Y

Z